THE ENCYCLOPEDIA OF
AMERICAN
RELIGIONS

VOLUME I

THE ENCYCLOPEDIA OF
AMERICAN RELIGIONS

VOLUME I

J. GORDON MELTON, EDITOR

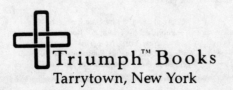
Triumph™ Books
Tarrytown, New York

TRIUMPH® BOOKS Edition 1991
Published in arrangement with Gale Research

J. Gordon Melton

Library of Congress Cataloging-in-Publication Data

Encyclopedia of American religions : a comprehensive study of the major
religious groups in the United States / J. Gordon Melton, editor. —
Triumph Books ed.
    p.   cm.
   Reprint. Originally published: 3rd ed. Detroit, Mich. : Gale
Research, © 1989.
   Includes bibliographical references and indexes.
   ISBN 0-8007-3025-9 (v. 1). — ISBN 0-8007-3026-7 (v. 2). — ISBN
0-8007-3027-5 (v. 3)
   1. Sects—United States.   2. Cults—United States.   3. Sects—
United States—Directories.   4. Cults—United States—Directories.
5. United States—Religion.   I. Melton, J. Gordon.
[BL2525.M449   1991]
291'.0973—dc20   91-11412
                                      CIP

Copyright © 1989 by Gale Research
Published by Triumph® Books
New York, New York
An Imprint of Gleneida Publishing Group
Printed in the United States of America

Contents

Indexes

Introduction

The Encyclopedia of American Religions (EAR) continues the effort begun more than a decade ago to provide a comprehensive survey of religious and spiritual groups in America. The first edition, published in 1979, was the first such attempt made since the 1936 *Census of Religious Bodies.* The second edition of the *Encyclopedia* significantly expanded that coverage and provided additional descriptive details and up-to-date statistical information on the organizations listed. This third edition takes another significant step toward the goal of providing current and detailed data on American religious organizations. While continuing the new features introduced in the second edition (such as the arrangement of material into historical essays and descriptive directory listings, and the extensive and comprehensive indexes), this edition also increases the *Encyclopedia*'s coverage with some 250 new entries including, for the first time, coverage of the religious bodies of Canada. It also revises, updates, and expands the information contained in most of the entries listed in the second edition. With the addition of the Canadian churches and religious groups, the *Encyclopedia* can now be said to have become an *Encyclopedia of (North) American Religions.*

New Features in this Edition

1) New Introductory Essays. Two new introductory essays, entitled ''An Interpretive View of the Development of American Religion'' and ''A Historical Survey of Religion in Canada, 1500 to the Present,'' provide an overview of American and Canadian religion. Together these essays provide a comprehensive picture of the evolution of North American religion and project some trends for the immediate future. These introductory essays also place the essays covering each denominational family history, comprising Part 1 of the *Encyclopedia,* into a larger context.

2) Some 250 New Entries. This edition provides coverage of some 250 groups not profiled in the second edition. Many of these are newly formed groups; others are groups about which information was not received in time to include in earlier editions, or of which the author has only recently become aware. New entries in this edition are by no means limited to small, obscure churches, but include recently formed bodies such as the four-million member Evangelical Lutheran Church in America created on January 1, 1988, and the larger Canadian-based churches.

3) Coverage of Canadian Religious Groups. The full inclusion of Canadian churches in this *Encyclopedia* seemed the proper manner to document the complex, intertwined story of Canadian and United States religious bodies. As work on the *Encyclopedia* progressed, it became evident that a large percentage of the churches and religions operating in the United States had members in Canada. In addition, many of the larger churches whose membership did not cross the Canadian-American border had strong sisterly relationships that grew directly out of present-day doctrinal agreement and were most often rooted in older historic organizational ties. Also, many present-day Canadian churches began as units of a church headquartered in the United States and have become autonomous in recent decades. It is expected that coverage of Canadian churches will increase in future editions.

Contents and Arrangement

The Encyclopedia of American Religions consists of three sections: the general introductory essays; the essays containing historical information on individual religious families; and the current descriptive directory listings.

The two introductory essays survey the general movement of American and Canadian religious history and provide an integrated view of the growth and development of the various religious perspectives now found in North America.

This three-volume edition of the *Encyclopedia* follows the same format, with the Essay Chapters (Part 1) and the Directory Listings (Part 2) divided across the volumes. The Indexes are included in their entirety in each of the three volumes, with entries keyed to the appropriate volume.

Part 1 of the *Encyclopedia,* the ''Essay Chapters,'' contains 22 general essays that trace historically the rise of the 19 major religious families and traditions, into which most U.S. and Canadian bodies can be classified. A select list of bibliographic source materials appears at the end of each chapter. These source lists are representative of the comprehensive files on each group maintained at the Institute for the Study of American Religion at the University of California—Santa Barbara.

Part 2 of the *Encyclopedia,* the "Directory Listings Section," is organized into 24 sections. The first 22 sections correspond to the essay chapters in Part 1 of the *Encyclopedia,* and they contain current directory and descriptive information about the individual churches, religious bodies, and spiritual groups that constitute each major religious family. They also contain information on churches for which no current address could be obtained and defunct churches. The final two directory listings sections—Unclassified Christian Churches and Unclassified Religious Groups—are new to this edition and include some 50 groups which cannot be classified within any of the distinct religious families.

Typical directory entries include the following details:

> *Sequential Entry Number* (used in indexes to refer to an entry)
>
> *Religious Organization Name* (including address)
>
> *Description of Organization's History, Beliefs, and Organization*
>
> *Membership* (most recent statistics as reported by the group)
>
> *Educational Facilities* (lists post-secondary educational institutions sponsored and/or supported by the group)
>
> *Periodicals* (periodicals and newsletters issued by the group)
>
> *Remarks* (includes additional information not applicable to the basic headings listed above)
>
> *Sources* (lists selected source materials used to develop the entry as well as sources for further readings)

Compilation Methods

The information contained in the entries has been assembled from material obtained directly from the religious bodies listed, and from files at the Institute for the Study of American Religion which contain basic materials on each of the groups discussed in this edition. Each group was asked to return a questionnaire containing updated information on their organization and the majority of groups graciously complied. In some cases, follow-up telephone conversations were held to obtain additional data.

Indexes

Six indexes are included to assist the user in locating information in the introductory essays, essay chapters, and directory sections. Because of the differences in format between the essay chapters and directory sections, citations in the indexes refer to both ***page numbers*** (for items appearing in the introductory essays and essay chapters) and ***entry numbers*** (for items appearing in the directory sections).

EDUCATIONAL INSTITUTIONS INDEX. An alphabetical listing of post-secondary educational institutions sponsored and/or supported by religious organizations described in this edition.

PERIODICALS INDEX. An alphabetical list of periodicals and newsletters regularly issued by the religious groups listed in the directory sections. (This index does not cover source materials listed at the end of each essay chapter nor publications listed under the heading "Sources" within each directory entry.)

GEOGRAPHIC INDEX. The United States appears first, with entries arranged alphabetically by state and subarranged by city. Canadian entries are listed next, with entries arranged alphabetically by province and subarranged by city. The remaining non-U.S. entries follow alphabetically by country, with entries subarranged by city. Entries include organization name and address, followed by the entry number in parentheses.

PERSONAL NAME INDEX. An alphabetical listing of persons mentioned in the essay chapters and the directory sections.

SUBJECT INDEX. Provides access to the material in the essay chapters and the directory sections through a selected list of subject terms.

RELIGIOUS ORGANIZATIONS AND INSTITUTIONS INDEX. An alphabetical listing of religious groups and other organizations mentioned in both the essay chapters and the directory sections.

Supplement Adds to Coverage

A supplement, covering newly identified and newly formed religious groups, is published between editions of the *Encyclopedia*. The supplement also supplies updated information on groups described in the latest edition.

Companion Volume Covers Religious Creeds

American Religious Creeds, published in 1987, provides a comprehensive compilation of 464 religious creeds, confessions, statements of faith, summaries of belief, and articles of religion currently acknowledged by many of the churches or religious groups described in this edition of the *Encyclopedia*. It also includes extensive notes on the history and textual variations of creeds, reflecting changing social, political, and doctrinal climates throughout the centuries. The material is arranged by major religious families, following, with minor variations, the approach used in the *Encyclopedia*.

Institute for the Study of American Religion

The Institute for the Study of American Religion was founded in 1969 for the purpose of researching and disseminating information about the numerous religious groups in the United States. More recently, the Institute's scope has been expanded to include religious groups in Canada, making it the only research facility of its kind to cover so broad a range of activity. After being located for many years in Evanston, Illinois, the Institute moved to Santa Barbara, California, in 1985. At that time, its collection of more than 25,000 books and its extensive files were donated to the Special Collections department of the library of the University of California—Santa Barbara. *The Encyclopedia of American Religions* has been compiled in part from the Institute's collection of more than 25,000 volumes and its thousands of files covering individual religious groups.

Users with particular questions about a religious group, suggested changes in the *Encyclopedia,* or information about any group not listed are invited to write to the Institute in care of its director:

> Dr. J. Gordon Melton
> Institute for the Study of American Religion
> Box 90709
> Santa Barbara, CA 93190-0709

Selections from the Introduction
to the First Edition

The Encyclopedia of American Religions explores the broad sweep of American religions and describes over 1,200 [now 1,588] churches. Some churches in the *Encyclopedia,* such as certain Hindu and Jewish bodies, follow a tradition several thousand years old. Others were born yesterday, like Garner Ted Armstrong's Church of God International, formed in the summer of 1978. With few exceptions, if a church existed in the United States in 1976 [now 1989], it is discussed in the *Encyclopedia.*

In my years of study of American religion I discovered three kinds of religious institutions: primary religious bodies (i.e., churches), secondary organizations which serve the primary bodies, and tertiary organizations which strive to change the primary bodies. The *Encyclopedia* treats only the primary religious bodies, but it does refer to the two other kinds of institutions, so some comment on all three types is necessary here.

In defining primary religious bodies (a church, denomination, sect, or cult), I established certain criteria. First, a church seeks the chief religious loyalty of its members. Second, it meets requirements of size. If it is organized into congregations, it has at least two congregations, or it has one congregation of more than 2,000 members who make a measurable impact on the country through the mass media. If a church is not organized into congregations, it meets the size requirement when its members come from more than one state and from beyond a single metropolitan area. The third criterion concerns faith: a primary religious body tends to promote its particular views. For instance, it may encourage belief or disbelief in the Trinity. Or it may try to discourage the wearing of neckties; some holiness churches consider wearing neckties ostentatious.

I waived the size requirement for primary religious bodies whose beliefs are at odds with those of most people in our culture. For example, some Satanic groups are discussed in the *Encyclopedia* although they do not have enough members to meet my size criterion for primary religious bodies. The vast majority of churches in the *Encyclopedia* do, however, meet my three criteria.

Most primary religious bodies share other traits. Their leaders "marry and bury," as the saying goes. The churches usually hope to expand: they plan to make converts and form additional congregations. Finally, a number of primary religious bodies, though under-represented in America, have large foreign branches.

Much of the money and time given to religious enterprises in the United States is channeled not into the primary religious bodies, but into secondary and tertiary religious institutions. Secondary religious organizations, service agencies, perform tasks for one or more primary body. The tasks include missionary work, the education of seminarians, the publication of church materials, the sale of religious articles, and care for orphans and the aged.

Tertiary organizations try to change a number of primary religious bodies by promoting one special issue. For example, ecumenical organizations seek the unity of churches. However, few churches supporting the ecumenical organizations have specific plans to merge with other churches; so ecumenists try to change the attitudes of the churches. Among the country's ecumenical groups are several which draw members from various religious families (e.g., the National Council of Churches and the National Association of Evangelicals) and many more whose members are limited to one family (e.g., the Christian Holiness Association, the Pentecostal Fellowship of North America, the World Baptist Alliance, the International New Thought Alliance, the American Council of Witches, the Midwest Pagan Council, and the Buddhist Council of Hawaii).

Tertiary organizations have been formed to promote peace (the Fellowship of Reconciliation), a belief in creation instead of evolution (the Bible Science Association, Inc.), the psychic (the Spiritual

Frontiers Fellowship), spiritual healing (the International Order of St. Luke, the Physician), Pentecostalism (the Full Gospel Businessmen's Fellowship, International), and Sabbatarianism (the Bible Sabbath Association).

Because the country is virtually flooded with secondary and tertiary organizations the primary religious bodies form only a small percentage of American religious institutions. It is to the primary bodies, though, that the secondary and tertiary organizations look for members and support.

In describing American's 1,200 [1,588] primary religious bodies, I am departing from the church-sect-cult categories of Ernst Troeltsch. He pioneered in describing various Christian bodies, not in doctrinal, but in social terms, treating churches as far more than defenders of certain beliefs. In the latter part of his work, *The Social Teachings of the Christian Churches* (New York: Macmillan, 1931), Troeltsch examined the Christian churches of post-Reformation Europe. He discovered three types of groups: the dominant state churches, the sect groups (schismatic groups that broke away from the state churches), and the mystical groups (the latter came to be called cults). Unfortunately, American sociologists applied Troeltsch's categories to American religions. With time, the popular media attached pejorative connotations to the words "sect" and "cult," connotations Troeltsch never intended. To understand Troeltsch properly, one must remember that he described only Christian religions. Furthermore, he studied countries with Christian state churches, to which all citizens were expected to belong. The United States has no state church and has far more non-Christian churches than Europe had before 1800, the terminal point of Troeltsch's study.

American religions do not yield to so simplistic a set of categories as the church-sect-cult triad. Instead of using those three classifications, I examined religions family by family, and have found 17 [now 19] distinct families. This approach, I hope, does justice to the amazing variety within the American religious experience. Ten of the 17 [19] religious families in the United States basically follow Christian beliefs and practices; seven do not.

Within the 17 [19] families of American religions, the member bodies of each family share a common heritage, thought world (theology in its broadest sense), and lifestyle. These three features define each individual religious body and illuminate its relationship to other churches in the family.

It has become fashionable to use other characteristics in classifying religious bodies, characteristics such as ethnicity, class, racial composition, type of leadership (priest? guru? pastor?), and the degree of acceptance of or hostility to the world. While these characteristics provide useful information, they are entirely inadequate in explaining the formation, development, relationships, and continuing life of the broad spectrum of America's religious bodies. Elements of ethnicity are, for example, most helpful in identifying sub-groups within the older European church traditions brought to America in the eighteenth and nineteenth centuries. Lutheran, Reformed, and Pietist churches split along ethnic lines, each sub-group using its own language. But as language barriers disappeared, the ethnic orientation of the churches diminished. Thus Swedish Baptists in America are more likely to develop joint programs, to merge, or to share missionary concerns with German or English or even black Baptists than with Swedish Lutherans or Swedish Pentecostals. The strength of family relationships overrides ethnic considerations.

In order to understand any family or its members, it is necessary to understand the family's heritage, thought world, and lifestyle. In many families, one of the three features—heritage, thought world, and lifestyle—is dominant. For the Lutheran family and those churches within the liturgical family, heritage is the feature setting them apart from other churches. Lifestyle is the key feature for four families in particular: the Communal, Holiness, Pentecostal, and Psychic families. Group ownership of property and certain self-imposed disciplines put communes into a class of their own. A day-to-day striving for perfect love dominates holiness preaching and teaching, with worldly activities prohibited. Pentecostals seek certain gifts of the Spirit, such as speaking in tongues, prophesying, and healing, so Pentecostals have a distinctive lifestyle in both their worship and their daily lives. Finally, the psychics are set apart from other religious groups because of their interest in extrasensory perception, psychokinesis, and communication with spirits through seances and visions.

If heritage and lifestyles distinguish certain families so does the thought world for other families. For fundamentalists and for the Protestant churches, especially those which follow John Calvin's

Reformed theology, the features distinguishing them from each other is their thought world. They hold divergent views on these topics in particular: sacrament, ecclesiology, the sovereignty of God, perfection, and the nature of the end time. But even where there is agreement, sharing a thought world does not necessarily mean holding identical views. Rather, it means sharing some beliefs which set the context for constant debate over specifics. Adventists, for example, expect Christ to return soon, but violently argue among themselves about the nature of his return, the possibility of pinpointing the date of his return, and the significance of certain world events as signs of his return.

Of particular interest to me are the families of "hidden religions" outside the country's religious mainstream. The spiritualists who hold seances are within the hidden families; so are the Buddhists, the Sufis, and the witches in their covens. Such groups are invisible to many Americans, but often they have large national followings. Several congregations that belong to these sizable but hidden families meet within a few blocks of my home in Evanston, Illinois. But had I not searched hard for these congregations, I would never have found them.

Many years of searching have gone into my study of America's religions. I might be better qualified to study the country's religions if I were a detective instead of a Methodist minister. I have examined endless printed material and interviewed countless church founders and leaders—all with the aim of understanding the heritage, lifestyle, and thought world of the religions. To say the least, the task has had its challenges. Some churches exaggerate or deny aspects of their lifestyle or history. Many Pentecostals say their church was founded at Pentecost, in 33 A.D., and hide their recent origins. Other churches try to gloss over the career their founder led before establishing their church. Among such founders, David Berg (of the Children of God), L. Ron Hubbard (of the Church of Scientology), A. A. Allen (of the Miracle Revival Fellowship), and Sun Myung Moon (of the Unification Church), have followed or still follow vocations quite different from that of a spiritual leader. For example, Hubbard was an undercover agent for the Los Angeles Police Department, a fiction writer, and an explorer before founding his church.

Some religious bodies function as such but deny their religious nature. One such is the World Plan Executive Council, popularly called Transcendental Meditation. Other dislike denominational labels and refuse to list themselves in a phone book or give brochures to non-members. The Cooneyites, also called the Two-by-Two's, have developed the shunning of publicity into a fine art.

To paint a picture of America's religious bodies in 1978 is not to describe them as they will be in 1988 [or 1998]. Families dwindle and expand. The major church in a family (one that claims more than half the family's members) may divide in half in a decade, torn by schism. Smaller churches in a family may consolidate—e.g., through merging all-black and all-white churches. Lutherans, once divided according to European ethnic origins and language, have consolidated in this century and then redivided over doctrinal issues. The Eastern religious bodies in this country—originally composed of Hindu and Buddhist immigrants—have attracted young American devotees, thereby blending the West with the East. Despite changes within families, however, the identity of the families remains the same. An intense conservatism governs religious bodies; they would rather lose dissident members than change. Further, churches rarely jump from one family to another. Theological and organizational patterns tend to perpetuate themselves. True, institutions adjust to the changing society, but only begrudgingly. The division of religions into families (denominationalism) is fundamental to religious life in the United States. We do not live in a post-denominational age. The ideals of ecumenism have swept through American Christianity, firing imaginations, creating cooperation structures, and breaking down walls of intolerance and hostility between religions. But if ecumenism has illustrated anything, it has been this: the religious family is strong. It will endure.

J. Gordon Melton

Introductory Essay 1
An Interpretive View of the
Development of American Religion

The United States is currently home to more than 1500 different primary religious organizations—churches, sects, cults, temples, societies, missions—each seeking to be the place of expression of the primary religious allegiances and sentiments of its members and adherents. The majority of these organizations are Christian churches, and the overwhelming majority of Americans who engage in any outward religious activity are members of one of the more than 900 Christian denominations. Prior to the 1880s, the Christian churches had little competition, except for the Native American religions, which they saw at best as dying faiths soon to be replaced by Christianity. The churches enjoyed the favor of the influential elite of society. They had the support of the government, the approbation of the press, and the control of education at all levels. However, at the same time, the churches also faced a public, the majority of which treated religion with attitudes that varied from indifference to open hositility. However, naively expressed, the church existed as an instrument of the state, another element in the overall system of social control.

In the United States, that situation began to change dramatically at the time of the American Revolution. With the exception of several New England states, formal ties between church and state were cut, and each succeeding decade brought an end to more and more of the numerous informal ones. For many congregations, the Revolution included the loss either temporarily or completely of their buildings. The Anglican church lost the most, and its situation was made all the more severe by the sudden departure of the majority of its ministers to England and the loss of its legal status.

After the war, groups which had assumed the controlling positions in American religious life began to take second place to groups which had played little or no prior role in the nation's life. The changes became evident during the Second Great Awakening, the popular term usually applied to the period of the rise of the Methodists, Baptists, Disciples of Christ, and Cumberland Presbyterians, and the evangelistic endeavor which led to their churching of the then western frontier. From the beginning of the nineteenth century, the church moved from a position of disestablishment in the midst of an indifferent public to the creation of what amounts to a powerful new religious establishment through its ownership of ever-increasing sums of real estate and stock, and its steady penetration of the indifferent public, the majority of which it has finally won to its membership. The last two centuries have seen Christian church membership increase in both number and percentage of the population every decade. Since 1900, while the nation's population increased three and a half times, church membership increased sevenfold. At the same time, the church has step-by-step relinquished control of education, lost its favored status in the press, and must fight for its right to criticize the government or lobby for what it considers just laws. The church has also been rent with schism (from 20 denominations in 1800 to more than 900 in 1988), while at the same time having to face competition from the literally hundreds of different varieties of the great world religions and an imposing assortment of new innovative American faiths, including a revived and assertive Native American spirituality.

This *Encyclopedia* covers the story of American religion from the entrance in the sixteenth century of the Europeans determined to convert the Native Americans through the pluralistic religious situation of the late twentieth century. It is a story of religious conquests and losses, the search for simply a place to be alone, the rise and fall of utopian dreams, and the attempts by different religions to find ways to exist in close proximity with constant war and rumor of war.

The Native Americans in 1500: The First Settlers

10,000 years ago, 40,000 years ago, or even more than 100,000 years ago, depending upon which source is consulted, the first human settlers arrived in what today is called North America. They may have walked, or they may have built a crude boat, but they crossed the Bering Strait (periodically a land bridge in the past) and moved across the continent to establish their residences, learn the arts of survival and culture, and generally claim the land for their people. Over the years they differentiated themselves as separate peoples (tribes, nations, ?), emphasizing hunting, agriculture, trading and/or fishing in their conquests of the very different environments, climates, and resources the land provided. They also developed religion which took at least as many forms as there were tribes.

Possibly 30 million Indians inhabited North America in 1500. They were divided into groups which spoke more than 200 languages. They also showed such immense variation in religion as to make it improper to speak of an Indian *religion*, rather a number of Indian *religions*.

However, the white people who began their conquest of North America in the sixteenth century paid little attention to the Native Americans' religions. Beyond writing up accounts of them with varying levels of sophistication, the program of the European was to totally replace Indian religions with the observance of Christianity. For this reason, the religions of the Indians and the faiths of European origins, until recently, rarely interacted. Once the Europeans took control, Indian religions were offered no role in the conquering culture and to a large extent were eradicated, either by the deaths of their adherents or their conversion to some form of Christianity.

Major Themes in the Development of American Religion

In the movement from the religious situation in 1500 to that of the late nineteenth century, four factors arise as dominant elements in the shaping of American religious patterns: *immigration, religious freedom, proselytism, and denominationalism.* Of the more than 1,500 religious groups presently existing in the United States, the overwhelming majority originated by the direct immigration of their members/practitioners to the United States and their establishing centers for worship and for the recruitment of new members among the general population. The largest number of the remaining groups are schisms of those immigrant groups. The actual number of new religions that have developed in America, apart from Native American faiths, is relatively small, and such indigenous American religions are all the more noteworthy for that fact: Adventism (which includes both Seventh-Day Adventism and the Jehovah's Witnesses), Christian Science, New Thought, Theosophy, Pentecostalism, and Scientology.

Understanding *immigration* as the first of the four factors shaping American religious life also underscores the role of ethnic-national settlements in setting the initial patterns of American religious life during the colonial period. Spanish Catholics came to Florida, New Mexico, and California. French Catholics settled the Gulf Coast from Mobile to New Orleans and the Mississippi River Valley north to St. Louis and St. Paul. The British settled New England and the southern colonies. The Dutch came into New York (formerly New Netherlands), the Swedes colonized Delaware, and the Germans made up a substantial portion of William Penn's colony. In the nineteenth century, the patterns of immigration would again change the face of American religion as, for example, Germans and Scandinavians moved into the area north and west of Chicago to create the still dominant Lutheran belt from Milwaukee to Butte. The influx of Italians and Irish would take control of New England from British Congregationalists and place it in the hands of Roman Catholics. The influx of Hispanics into the area north of the Rio Grande River would return that area lost to Protestants at the time of the gold rush to Roman Catholic hegemony.

The overall consideration of immigration must not neglect the role of immigration laws, especially after 1882, in shaping religious patterns in America. For example, the normal growth of Asian religions, which were being established among immigrants in the last half of the nineteenth century, was thwarted by the imposition of a series of laws from 1882 to 1924. But the 1924 law, which all but stopped immigration from Asia, also stopped the flow from Southern and Eastern Europe. Thus while the law slowed the growth of Eastern religions, it also strongly affected Judaism, Eastern Orthodoxy, and Islam. In like measure, the lifting of the 1924 restrictions in 1965 contributed directly to the massive expansion of these religions during the last two decades and is even now completely altering the overall shape and structure of the American religious community.

Religious freedom, both in concept and practice, has expanded in America. Credit for the first accomplishments in that direction must go to the early colonists in New York, Rhode Island, Pennsylvania, and Maryland. An early symbol of that expanded freedom was the colonists' reception of Jewish settlers.

Generations before most Europeans were thinking about religious toleration, the Dutch had become the most religiously tolerant nation on the continent. In their American colonies that tolerance was demonstrated by the welcome given to fleeing Brazilian Jews who established the first synagogue in North America in New York. Rhode Island, which had been founded by Roger Williams fleeing the intolerance of the Massachusetts Puritans, welcomed the second congregation of Jews. It is not surprising to find one of the other colonial congregations in Philadelphia.

Religious liberty was, of course, immensely forwarded by the American Revolution and the Bill of Rights to the Constitution. That the constitutional convention refused to grant any group, in this case any Christian church, the power, prestige, and privilege of being the nation's established religious body was both an important experiment and a significant act of infidelity. As an experiment, it tested a major axiom of European thought, that a nation needed one religious body (i.e., a state church) as a necessary force in uniting the nation and assisting in social control. In America's post-Revolutionary success, the experiment proved the untruth of the assumption. At the same time, the experiment would not have been possible had not the convention also recognized both that no religious group served more than a small fraction of the population, and that the great majority of the public did not support any religious organization. This twofold observation was amply verified in the decades after the Revolution when, in total, the churches could claim on their roles less than 20 percent of the now free people.

The freedom guaranteed by the First Amendment has been steadily broadened during the last 200 years. Within a few decades all of the states dropped the last remnants of their formal religious establishments. The implications of the First Amendment for unpopular religions have gained increasing attention and clarity. And society itself tolerates an ever-increasing variety of religious belief and practice. The heightened toleration experienced during this century has been disseminated from the large impersonal urban complexes which both permit divergent religious groups to develop apart from the watchful and critical eyes of small-town society and provide a concentrated pool of the potential recruits needed by any new religion in its critical first years of existence.

The freedom to practice a new religion includes the freedom to *proselytize*. From 1800 to the present, no activity apart from immigration has so altered the pattern of American religion as the evangelical efforts of religious groups. Following the American Revolution, the older colonial churches dominated the religious life. However, they were prepared neither in theology nor organization to respond to the irreligious public that confronted them at the end of the eighteenth century. The Methodists and Baptists, both of whom were evangelically oriented, were prepared, and by the middle of the nineteenth century, they replaced the Congregationalists, Presbyterians, and Episcopalians as the large dominant church bodies, a position they have never relinquished.

At the same time, in the religiously free situation, innovative religious movements, movements which would have been suppressed by the government under a state-church regime, were permitted to grow and proselytize as well. Thus early in the nineteenth century, new Christian churches such as the Cumberland Presbyterian Church and the Disciples of Christ broke from older bodies, and completely new ways of doing religion appeared, from Swedenborgians to Latter-Day Saints (Mormons), from Spiritualists to Transcendentalists. The number of new religious gestalts multiplied decade by decade. Soon after each new religious movement organized, it further divided thus producing an array of similar organizations and eventually new religious denominational families. Throughout the nineteenth century, almost all of the major new divergent religious thrusts were Christian. However, during the last two decades of the nineteenth century, Hinduism, Buddhism, and Islam were introduced into American life and looked for converts among a public only 35 percent of whom had joined a church.

During the twentieth century, the role of proselytizing activity has been spectacular. As the nation's population multiplied three and a half times (from 75 million to 250 million), Christian church membership multiplied seven times, and the percentage of church members doubled from slightly more than 30 percent to more than 65 percent. Religious affiliation climbed even higher as the Jewish, Muslim, Buddhist, Hindu, and occult-metaphysical communities, minuscule at the turn of the century, each developed constituencies numbering in the millions.

The dual effect of freedom of religion and proselytizing activity leads directly to the consideration of *denominationalism*. In a religiously free society, denominations, voluntary religious associations of like-minded (and like-spirited) people, are the basic form of the religious life. In spite of the various predictions of the fading of denominations (through the ecumenical movement) or the decline of their importance (through increasing individualized religion), they remain, and for the foreseeable future will remain, the bedrock of American religion. Denominations are the stable primary religious associations formed in those societies which do not impose a single dominant religious structure. In a state-church society, for example, there is one "religion" and may be a number of dissenting "sects." In a free society there are a number of more or less competing religious organizations, no one of which has a majority of the population in its membership. Some, because of such factors as their many years in existence, their inherent appeal, and/or their aggressive programs for conversion, have many members. Others, primarily because they are new, lack substantial appeal, and/or limit proselytizing efforts, remain small.

Denominations, whatever their size, provide the primary religious identification for most religious people. They offer regular times and facilities for the affirmation of beliefs in group activity, worship, study, and service. Often associated with and supported by the denominations are a variety of what might be termed secondary or paradenominational religious organizations. These organizations usually specialize in one limited task in relation to one or a small group of similar primary religious organizations. Included among the paradenominational organizations are independent publishers, religious leadership training schools (seminaries, Bible colleges, etc.), missionary organizations, evangelical ministries, and social service agencies. On occasion a secondary or paradenominational structure (especially evangelical ministries engaged in the conversion of individuals) will transform into a new primary group and enlarge its services to include all of those normally provided by a primary religious group. Within an evangelical group, such a transformation can be noted when the group stops sending its recruits to the supporting denominational structures and begins forming congregations of its converts. Such a transformation occurred in the 1970s among some Jewish-Christian evangelical groups which began to form ethnic Jewish-Christian synagogues.

Within the pluralistic environment of the late twentieth century, the formation of so many new competing religious groups has eroded the exclusive and dominant positions of some of the older and more established religious organizations. This erosion of position has been most evident in the major defeats suffered by conservative Christian groups on such issues as abortion legislation, prayer in public schools, the display of religious symbols in government-owned facilities, and the elimination of the Christian facade that had been placed over many facets of public and social life. Interpreted by many as signs of secularization, the defeats are more adequately understood when seen as manifestations of (1) the growing seriousness with which dissenting religious positions are treated and (2) an increasing sensitivity toward religious concerns that has developed within the public sphere. Coupled with this new sensitivity is the loss of ability by even the most powerful religious bodies to enforce their own ideas on the populace at large, especially at the national level. What power that remains is largely a veto power.

With these forces in mind, we can now turn to a brief consideration of the movement of religion from the arrival of the Spanish conquistadors and padres to the complex pluralistic religious environment of today. That development will be considered in six overlapping periods. The Native American period begins in pre-history and extends to the nineteenth century. The Catholic Era began around 1500 and continued in part of the country until the nineteenth century. The period of Western European (primarily British) conquest begins around 1600, with the arrival of the settlers in Virginia. The Revolutionary Era begins with the disruptions of the 1770s and carries through the transitions into the new religious environment established by the Constitution. The period of the churching of the nation can be said to begin in 1801 and to continue to this day. The period of transition from Christian dominance into a pluralistic society of shared religious hegemony began in the 1880s and has also continued to this day.

The Native Americans to 1800

The first settlers came into North America in the prehistoric past and moved across the continent eventually settling almost every niche. By the time of the coming of the Europeans, the differing peoples manifested a wide variety of governmental structures, economic systems, and family forms. The structure of their religious life was equally varied, and there are few threads that run through all the Indian religions. As is true of most religion prior to the segregation of life into the modern distinction between secular and sacred, Indian religions tended to be at one with the whole life of the people among whom they existed. Religion was intimately tied to the problems of tribal survival, the self-identity of individuals as tribal members, and the organization of tribal routine.

Just as the religious aspect of life was integrated into other aspects of tribal life, so tribal life was integrated into the natural environment chosen by the tribe for its home, including the climate, terrain, and the animal and plant life. Indians took the land seriously and lived by its seasonal changes. Survival demanded an intense and intimate relationship with nature, and that nature was seen to be permeated with life power, sometimes viewed as one force, but often differentiated into many particular powers.

Some Europeans thought of the Indians as being without religion, an opinion that highlights some essential truths about Native American spirituality. There was, for example, no word or term in any Indian language that could be translated "religion." There was also, generally speaking, a lack of what might be considered worship, since in most Indian religions, ceremonies and actions were not a matter of supplication of a deity so much as the development of a working relationship with the sacred realm. Ceremonies and action created a matrix within which life moved, and that movement tended to be circular, following the coming, going, and return of the seasons. The sacred realm was the realm of the pervasive powers.

Living with the powers that existed in and sustained the world led many tribes to develop forms of magic, the art and practice of manipulating the spirit powers. Most tribes had functionaries who practiced the arts of magic and used them for good or ill. These "religious" leaders were among those most threatened by the arrival of Christianity and its priests.

The particular life and beliefs of the different tribes were articulated in a variety of *myths* that described in story format the underlying structure of reality. These verbal expressions of life, which ranged from the sacred to the mundane, embodied the Indians' rather sophisticated understandings of both the immediate environment and the larger world, gave a rationale for the accepted behavioral standards for the tribe, and supplied the answers to the basic religious questions.

The coming of the Europeans had little immediate impact for the great majority of Indian tribes who encountered white people only with the push to settle the interior of the continent in the nineteenth century. However, those tribes located on the lands first colonized frequently faced disastrous results. Not an insignificant amount of damage was done by the spread of new diseases in defense of which the Native American had no weapons of immunity nor medicine. Measles and small pox were especially deadly. At the very least, those Indians residing in close proximity to the new settlements became the targets of missionary efforts. Almost every church group, soon after its arrival in the New World and its establishment of a stable presence among the white settlers, turned its attention to missionary activity among the Indians. The most extensive missions were established by Roman Catholics in the St. Lawrence River Valley, Florida, the Gulf Coast, and across the Southwest from Texas to California. John Eliot is remembered as the primary missionary supported by the New England Puritans. The desire to support his work inspired the formation in England in 1649 of one of the first of the voluntary missionary societies soon to become so popular in evangelical circles. Anglican missions to the Indians were promoted by one of these societies, the Society for the Propagation of the Gospel in Foreign Parts (S.P.G.).

Despite the dedication of the missionaries, their efforts often fell victim to seemingly unrelated forces that tended not only to destroy the missions but the Native American's entire culture. For example, King Philip's War (1675-76) led to the destruction of the towns of the "Praying Indians" established so successfully by Eliot's converts. Other missions were destroyed when the land upon which they were established changed hands from one nation to another, usually after a war. In such a manner many of the Catholic missions were lost to the British.

However, the missions themselves tended to intrude in most destructive ways into the Indians' culture. Typical of the disruption of Indian life caused by the Europeans was the Spanish movement into the land of the Chumash Indians who inhabited the California coast from present-day Malibu to San Luis Obispo. The Spanish found the Chumash organized into numerous villages each ruled by a chief, termed a *wot*, who provided moral authority and general guidance. The wots was assisted by a *paha*, who presided at the principal festsivals and ceremonies. The Chumash had established a hunting-fishing-gathering-trading economy which had in turn produced an artistic culture of high standards. When the Spanish first arrived in

1769, the Chumash welcomed the new settlers and provided them needed items from their abundant supply.

The missionaries who accompanied the Spanish explorers discovered that the Chumash lived in a larger universe permeated with power that had been scattered through the world at the point of creation. Individuals were allowed to use the power, if they possessed the proper knowledge. They could also gain access to the powers through a dream helper, a personified form of a natural reality, such as a bear, an eagle, or even a plant such as *datura.* Important to Chumash "religion" was the balancing of all the powers that existed. Special people, *antaps,* knew the secret knowledge to keep the powers balanced.

However, with the arrival of the Spanish, the village organization, the economy, and the religious tradition were attacked at the core. The Indians were invited to convert to the Roman Catholic faith and to abandon the villages for the mission. At the mission an alternative economy was established that included candle making, agriculture, iron working, and masonry. The missions and pueblos provided a new economy which soon involved enough Indians that it undercut the older economy still maintained by those who refused to accept mission life. But those Indians who did move to the pueblo were often blocked in their participation in the new economy. They were trapped between the long-term goals of the missionaries and the immediate objectives of the colonial government. In the 60-plus years of their existence, the missions completely obliterated the old village life of the Chumash. The mission period ended in 1833 with secularization, the removal of the missions from the control of the Franciscans and the redistribution of their lands to Mexican settlers. The Chumash were thus left with neither the villages of their ancestors nor the new life forced upon them by the missions. Those who survived retained but a remnant of their original beliefs and practices.

Other Indian tribes in those lands first invaded by Europeans in the seventeenth century reacted in a variety of ways toward their new neighbors. Most at first accepted the Europeans and allowed Christian priests to move among them. Others, some following an initial acceptance, found themselves at war with both the white settlers and their ministers. The settlers increasingly wanted the Indians' territory and resources, and the ministers wanted to change their religious perspective. As the Indians fought the encroachments of Christianity, the churches counted the victims of such fighting as martyrs.

In the end, however, the Indians were forced to seek some means of accommodating to the reality of a permanent European presence. Some accepted the settlers, even to the point of taking sides in the periodic wars, while at the same time resisting the missionaries' pressure to change their thoughts and ways. They signed treaties and gave concessions. But the trends were against them, and gradually they were forced into designated parcels of lands and targeted for conversion by the various churches. As the dust of the American Revolution settled, there was still hope that the Indian's life and religions could survive to some extent, but the new nation on the East Coast of the continent had caught a vision of the West and eagerly rushed to claim it as its own. In the process it was quite willing to push the Indian out of the way.

The Catholic Era: The Coming of the Spanish

The largest religious body in the United States today and throughout the twentieth century has been the Roman Catholic Church. Its members were also the first to arrive, conquer, and colonize parts of the land now making up the United States. Shortly after the discovery of the New World by Christopher Columbus, the rulers of Spain appealed to Pope Alexander VI to settle the dispute between Spain and Portugal over their claims to the new lands. In 1493, the pope drew a line in the middle of the Atlantic east of which Portugal would have hegemony and west of which Spain would operate. The line would have left Portugal with Africa and the islands off the Atlantic coast, but without any access to the new world. In 1494 the line was moved farther west and as a result Portugal received Brazil. From Cuba and then Mexico, Spain began a program of conquest and settlement that included North America. The governmental drive to develop the Spanish empire and the church's desire to convert and Christianize the native populations often came into conflict. While the church won many smaller victories in its attempts to champion the cause of humane treatment, in the end, the government usually dominated the situation.

The actual movement of Spain into what is now the United States was occasioned by the settlement in Florida of a group of French Huguenots (Protestants) along the St. Johns River (near present-day Jacksonville) in 1564. Having previously claimed Florida as its own, the offended Spanish established a settlement at St. Augustine and quickly moved to destroy the St. Johns River colony. From there, Spanish missionaries established missions that at one point reached as far north as South Carolina and briefly the Chesapeake Bay area. The missions in Florida, in spite of their ups and downs, were most successful through several generations.

The second movement of Spain into what is now the United States was from Mexico in the Southwest. In 1540 Francisco Vasquez de Coronado began his famous trek which took him from New Mexico to central Kansas. In his easternmost exploration, he came upon the village of Quivera. Returning to his advance base in New Mexico, Coronado ordered his expedition members home. The Franciscans, however, decided to stay. Two of their number, Brother John of the Cross and Brother Luis Descalona, settled in the Bernalillo-Pecos area of New Mexico. Father Juan de Padilla journeyed back to Quivera. Brother John and Brother Luis were successful to the point of angering the Indians own religious functionaries. They eventually disappeared, believed to have been killed. Father de Padilla was successful at Quivera, but was killed when he tried to extend his work to other tribes.

Further movement into the southwest was to wait a generation. In 1598, an expedition headed by Juan de Onate moved into New Mexico and established a settlement along the Rio Grande River. The church built at this settlement, called San Juan and later San Gabriel, was the second oldest church in America. The site now is in ruins, for in 1609 a new capital for the territory was established at Santa Fe, and San Gabriel abandoned. Missionary work led to the founding of some 11 missions by 1617 and 43 by 1625. The work of the missions was not without its problems. There was much resistance by many of the New Mexico tribes to the missionary efforts and a number of priests were killed. The Indians' resentment of both the efforts to destroy their culture and the cruelty of the Spanish rulers boiled over in 1680. Led by a medicine man, Pope, the Indians revolted and drove the Spanish south of El Paso. It was 12 years later before the Spanish moved back into New Mexico and established a permanent presence. About this same time, a Jesuit priest, Father Eusebio Kino (d. 1711), was traveling through northern Mexico and Arizona. In 1697 he founded San Xavier del Bac, the beginning of a small but continuous Roman Catholic presence in the territory.

The Spanish government and the Franciscan missionaries moved into Texas in 1691 but abandoned the work in 1693, after an Indian revolt. A permanent presence was established in 1703 at a mission along the Rio Grande. In 1715, following the development of a plan to both conquer the land and convert the Indians, the original missions were again occupied, and under the capable leadership of Father Antonio Margil de Jesus, the missionary work extended throughout the territory.

The Arrival of the French

While Spain and Spanish Roman Catholicism were occupying Florida and establishing their hegemony from Texas to California in the Southwest, France was moving from its original settlements in the St. Lawrence River Valley of Canada to claim territory along the Atlantic coast, in the Great Lakes region, through the Mississippi Valley, and along the Gulf Coast west of Florida. Actually, the first Roman Catholic chapel in the New World was erected on an island off the coast of Maine in 1604, though the colony on the island soon failed. The French initiated their more permanent settlement in 1608 at Quebec which they used as a base for Jesuit missionaries who fanned out to work among the tribes, primarily the Mohawk, Iroquois, Algonquin, and Huron, in the land along what is now the Canada-United States border. The Indian mission became famous more for the martyrs it produced than the numbers it converted. In the 1640s, a number of priests including Isaac Joques and Jean de Brebeuf were tortured and killed. The work was lost in the 1700s as the British took over the territory from the French.

In 1669, a Jesuit priest, Jacques Marquette (1637-1675), began the French push into the Great Lakes region. His initial exploratory trip was followed by a career working among the Indians of Illinois and Wisconsin, the first mission being established in 1684. He was followed by others. The work initiated by Marquette was balanced by exploration and settlement along the Gulf Coast as early as 1685 when Robert LaSalle, who had followed Marquette's explorations by some some of his own in the Great Lakes in 1678 and in the Mississippi Valley in 1682, sailed into the Gulf in 1685 and founded Fort St. Louis on the coast of what is now Texas. His actions also established Spain and France as competitors in east Texas. Following LaSalle's short lived experiment, others established Biloxi (1697), Mobile (1702), and New Orleans (1718). New Orleans would become the major dissemination point for Catholicism northward along the Mississippi River. In New Orleans, the first religious institute for women, the Ursuline Convent, was built, and from there the missionary work among the southern Indians was launched.

The progress of the Roman Catholic work in North America, indeed of religion in general, was greatly altered in 1769 by events on the other side of the world. The Seven Years War, which involved the three major powers in North America, was concluded and on February 10 the Treaty of Paris signed. Britain received most of the territory claimed by France, including Canada and all its American territory east of the Mississippi River (except New Orleans). From Spain, Britain received Florida in partial exchange for Cuba. Except for Quebec, Catholic influence was radically curtailed for several generations in the colonies ceded to Britain. The ceding of Louisiana to Spain in 1769 did little to assist the spread of Catholicism there, which continued with a predominantly French constituency.

Spanish Catholicism was expanding in only one place—California. While the first Spanish expedition led by Jaun Rodriguez Cabrillo had sailed along the California coast in 1542, it was not until 1769, the year of the Treaty of Paris, that settlement and the opening of a mission in California began at San Diego. Following the establishment of Spanish towns, Father Junipero Serra (1713-1784) founded nine missions along the coast of California, the first of 21 such missions opened as far north as Sonoma. Unfortunately, the push into California came just as Spain was weakening at home, hence it was unable to properly exploit the new colony.

The Catholic work west of the Mississippi grew slowly through the arrival of new settlers and the conversion of the Indians, but was increasingly thwarted by the westward push of the new American nation. First, in 1800 France again took control of Louisiana, but sold it to the United States three years later. Further westward expansion of the United States climaxed in the Treaty of Guadalupe Hildago in which Mexico ceded Texas, New Mexico, most of Arizona, and California to the United States. With quick and massive movement of predominantly non-Catholic settlers into the formerly Catholic southwest after the Treaty, the Catholic era can be said to have come to an end.

The British Era: Anglicans and Congregationalists

The movement of Western and Northern Europeans and their religions into the North American continent, apart from the Viking explorations, began in the late fifteenth century with the arrival of John Cabot. On his first voyage (1497) he probably reached as far south as Maine and on his second (1499-1501) he seems to have sailed along the coast from Maine to Maryland. However, it would not be until 1584 that exploitation of the American coast began with the attempted settlement of a colony on Roanoke Island, and the more important and subsequently successful colony at Jamestown in 1606. With the establishment of Jamestown, the Church of England came to North America in fact (though previously services had been held by chaplains assigned to the explorers' ships). To a largely unknown priest of the Church of England, Robert Hunt, goes the honor of having been the first non-Catholic Christian minister to reside and pastor in North America. He came to Jamestown in the spring of 1607. His career was short and the date of his death never recorded. He died along with the majority of the early Jamestown settlers. The more substantial career of Alexander Whitaker (1585-1616), who arrived in 1611 to serve the church at the new settlement of Henrico, is more illustrative of the progress of the Church of England. Whitaker served the colony for many years and actively promoted increased migration by Britons.

Virginia became the first of the British settlements along the Atlantic coast. In 1620, a group of Puritan Separatists popularly called the Pilgrims, landed at Plymouth, Massachusetts. They were followed a decade later by a second group, this time non-Separatist Puritans popularly called simply the Puritans, who founded the Massachusetts Bay Colony and began to spread out across Massachusetts, Connecticut, and most of New England. The range of opinion represented by the Pilgrims, the Puritans, and the Church of England is the product of a whole era of post-Reformation church life in Great Britain.

England had gone through the Protestant Reformation of the sixteenth century in a much different manner from most of the countries on the continental mainland. It had emerged during the reign of Elizabeth I with a church that drew major components from both Roman Catholicism and Protestantism. The Church of England, Anglicanism, was the inheritor of Elizabeth's *via media*. However, there were Protestants who were not content with anything less than a fully Protestant church. Their cause was strengthened by the union of Scotland and England in 1607 with the advent of James I to the throne. Scotland had gone through a reformation and established Presbyterianism.

Puritanism is the name given to the movements whose goal was to purge the Church of England of its unwanted Romanish elements. The different Puritan sects disagreed as to the priorities for a purification of the church. One group looked for some minor changes, mostly of a pietistic and worshipful nature within the Church of England, but sought no basic changes in its government. Others looked to the Presbyterians of Scotland for their model. They sought the establishment of Presbyterianism as the state church of England. The most radical of all, the Separatists, wished to separate from any state church, and call only committed disciples of Christ into a visible and voluntary fellowship. Alexander Whitaker was a mild Puritan, loyal to the established church, but with definite Presbyterian tendencies. The Pilgrims of Plymouth were Separatists. The Puritans of Massachusetts and Connecticut were neither Presbyterians nor Separatists. In their new setting they developed a new form of Puritanism, Congregationalism. Like the Separatists, these Puritans wanted a congregation of converted believers and wanted to place authority for the governance of the church in the local congregation. Unlike the Separatists, however, they wished to remain in close association with the state, to be the established church for their colonies, to identify as much as possible church membership with membership in the political community. Only church members could vote or hold government office. They sought to possess all of the prerogatives of the Church of England since they were but its purified branch, not a separate schismatic body. And the Puritans in at least one important aspect copied the church of the homeland, in that they were as little tolerant of those who deviated from the Puritan path as the Elizabethan bishops in England had been of the Puritans.

The Other Colonies

While Anglicanism was spreading from its base in Virginia and Congregationalism was spreading through New England, other colonies were being formed with quite different religious bases. Early in the seventeenth century the Dutch had begun to explore the coast of America. In 1609 Henry Hudson sailed up the river that now bears his name as far as the present city of Albany, New York, and staked a Dutch claim for the area. The Dutch established the colony of New Netherlands in 1624 and two years later founded New Amsterdam on Manhattan Island. As tolerant as the Dutch were, they still retained a state church which, since the overthrow of the Spanish, had been reformed. Thus, at the beginning of the colony's life, two lay officers, called in the Dutch Reformed structure comforters of the sick, were among the earliest settlers. Peter Minuit (1580-1658), director general of the colony, famous for his purchase of Manhattan, was a French Reformed lay elder who led services until 1628 when Jonas Michaelius (1577-?), the first ordained Reformed minister, arrived in the New World to begin a three year pastorate. He immediately organized a congregation, still in existence today and known as the Marble Collegiate Church, the oldest continuously existing Protestant church in North America. The term "collegiate" referred to the collegial relationship which developed among the early Reformed congregations formed in New Netherlands. Reformed congregations spread on Long Island and northward along the Hudson River. In 1642, the church at Fort Orange (now Albany) was organized by Johannes Megapolensis (1603-1670).

The colony enjoyed its most prosperous period during the governorship of Peter Stuyvesant (1646-64). Stuyvesant administered the company's religious policies which included both discouraging the establishment of competing worship centers and encouraging very diverse groups to migrate to the colony. Thus, Stuyvesant recognized the chaos created by the adherents of so many different churches in his colony, but continually refused to let them organize. For example, in 1649, when a group of Lutherans called a minister from Holland, Stuyvesant forbade him to preach and eventually forced him to return to Europe. Interestingly, the company took a quite different perspective on Jews, who, over Stuyvesant's protests, were welcomed as refugees in 1654 from the former Dutch colonies in Brazil. In New Netherlands, they organized the first Jewish congregation and built the first synagogue.

In 1638, Swedes founded Ft. Christiana (now Wilmington, Delaware), and the following year Reorus Torkillus, the first Lutheran minister in America, arrived to establish true and befitting worship in the Lutheran mode. Lutheranism spread among the Swedish and Finnish settlers until 1655 when the Dutch overran the colony and took control. They permitted one Lutheran pastor to remain and Lutheran worship to continue.

Conditions changed considerably in 1664 when the British took New Netherlands and changed it to New York. While opening an Anglican chapel, the government was forced to adopt a policy of liberal toleration of a variety of worship among its new predominantly non-Anglican subjects. A generation later the government imposed an Anglican establishment on the colony, although the Dutch were allowed to continue their distinctive worship and survive today as the Reformed Church in America.

A new life for Roman Catholicism began in Maryland. Two Jesuits arrived in 1634 with the first colonists that included both Catholics and Protestants. Struggling with the problems of continued actions against the Catholic community (the Jesuits were expelled in the early 1640s), the colony passed a Toleration Act in 1649 which granted freedom of worship to all Christian sects. That act stayed in effect until 1692 when the Church of England was officially established. However, by that time the presence of so many dissenters kept the establishment weak and allowed the strong Catholic presence to remain largely unmolested.

Rhode Island originated in the dissenting views of Roger Williams, a teacher in the Congregational Church in Massachusetts. Unhappy with Williams' Separatist tendencies, in 1635 the authorities banished him from the colony. Finding temporary shelter among the Pilgrims at Plymouth, he moved on in 1636 to found Rhode Island. Drawing upon his experience with Puritan intolerance and his Separatist opinions, he established a colony and society far ahead of its time. Government and religion were separated and the persecuted sects such as the Quakers welcomed. Like many who adopted a Separatists perspective, Williams became a Baptist and is generally credited with founding the first Baptist congregation in America, though he soon withdrew from the Baptists and thereafter labeled himself a mere "Seeker."

As important as Williams is to Rhode Island and Baptist history, his real import is in the development of the sectarian tradition of church-state relations. Williams is the ultimate source and Rhode Island the ultimate example for the perspective on religious freedom that would eventually come to the fore in America. In 1644, he authored one of the great classics of religious liberty, *The Bloody Tenant of Persecution,* that would voice in full the ideals of religious freedom, far earlier than those Puritan voices in the next century who would begin to grapple with the breakdown of Congregationalist authority among New Englanders. In 1663 his ideals would be written into the Rhode Island charter.

Following the example of Williams, William Penn created Pennsylvania as a haven for Quakers and other religious minorities. The first settlers into Penn's colony were Welshmen who arrived in 1682, but they were soon followed by the Quakers and representatives of numerous German groups, Penn having recruited heavily among Germany's persecuted sects. As a result Pennsylvania not only became the originating point for groups such as the Mennonites, Amish, German Rosicrucians, and the Church of the Brethren, but also for the German Lutheran and Reformed churches.

Thus by the last decades of the seventeenth century, the southern and middle colonies (except for Pennsylvania) had an Anglican establishment, and the New England colonies (except for Rhode Island) were still dominated by Congregationalism. Throughout the 1600s, the Congregational establishment remained strong enough to deal with (banish, imprison, or execute) most dissidents. To the contrary, the Church of England's establishment was weak in most areas, there being no bishop in the colonies and many parishes lacking priests. This weakness was due primarily to the presence in significant numbers of both the irreligious and the dissenting sects, especially the Presbyterians and the Baptists, and in Maryland, the Roman Catholics, none of which had anything to gain from a strong Church of England presence.

The Eighteenth Century

Toward the end of the seventeenth century, however, changes in England were causing people to look more positively at the church in what was emerging as the British Empire and to promote means to strengthen it. Initial efforts were made to extend the church into areas where it had little or no presence. King's Chapel was forced upon Boston in 1692. The next year, New York passed an establishment act even though there had been no call for Anglican worship. The minuscule Anglican community of Philadelphia organized Christ Church in 1694.

The most important step in the revival and extension of the Church of England in the colonies followed the appointment of Thomas Bray (1656-1730) as commissary for Maryland in 1696. Bray, unable to travel to America immediately, devoted his time to the organizing of the Society for the Promotion of Christian Knowledge, which began sending libraries to the New World. After a brief sojourn in the colonies in 1699, Bray returned to England and organized the Society for the Propagation of the Gospel (SPG) in 1701. With backing at the highest levels of the church, the society recruited priests for America and sent more than 300 men to staff the churches during the next three quarters of a century. The SPG put the Church of England in a position to compete with the other churches, but much of its gains were countered by the growth of Presbyterians, and Baptists, and later in the century, the influx of Pietism.

Presbyterians had been coming into the colonies throughout the seventeenth century but had been overwhelmed and in many cases, especially in New England, absorbed by the Congregationalists. Scattered Presbyterian churches were formed in New Jersey as early as 1667, but it was not until the arrival of Francis Makemie (1658-1708) in 1683 that the church began to assume a significant presence. Makemie traveled through the middle colonies organizing churches among the Scottish, Irish, and British settlers. The first presbytery was organized in Philadelphia in 1706 and included churches in Virginia, Maryland, and Delaware. It soon reached out to congregations in New York and New Jersey, and by 1716 was able to divide into four presbyteries and form a synod. The continued immigration from Scotland and Ireland promoted the rapid increase of the church's membership during the first half of the century and its spread throughout the colonies.

The development of Presbyterianism in the American colonies coincided with the emergence of a new movement in Germany. Philip J. Spener (1635-1705), a Lutheran minister at Frankfurt, began to appeal for a deeper Christian life through prayer, Bible study, loving service, and the informal gatherings of Christians. These issues were addressed in his 1675 dissertation, *Pia Desideria,* out of which the Pietist Movement was born. Forced out of Frankfurt he found his way to Berlin where he received the support in 1694 to found the University at Halle, which became the institutional center of the movement. The movement received a considerable boost in the early 1700s when Moravian refugees, Czechoslovakian Protestants, settled on the estate of Count Zinzendorf, which they renamed Herrnhut.

Pietism was spread to America primarily by the correspondence of American ministers with the Pietist leaders and became visible through the development of an evangelistic thrust among Presbyterians. The beginnings of this "revival" party is usually attributed to German-born Theodore J. Frelinghuysen, (c. 1691-1748), who came to America as a Dutch Reformed minister, and William Tennent (1673-1746), founder of the "log cabin" college in Bucks County, near Philadelphia. Among his most capable students were his three sons, Gilbert, John, and William Jr. The development of the Presbyterian revivalists began to split the Presbyterians over the acceptance and rejection of the new emphases.

Moravian Pietism was brought to the United States in 1735 by a group under the direction of Bishop August G. Spangenberg (1704-1792). On the voyage across the Atlantic, Spangenberg had a most important encounter with a young Anglican minister, John Wesley. The event led Wesley to worship with the Moravians upon his return to London and became integral to the series of events leading to his spiritual awakening in 1738. Wesley would go on to lead the most important phase of the Pietist Movement in England, Methodism. Among Wesley's close friends and associates from college days was George Whitefield (1714-1770). In 1739, Whitefield called Wesley to Bristol, England, to take charge of his ministry among the miners. The move was, for Wesley, an important step in the development of Methodism. Whitefield's trip to America became a major event in the development of American religion.

George Whitefield began his evangelistic tour of the American colonies in Georgia. As he moved northward he rallied his support and each stop involved more people in what became a national revival of religion. It would later be called the Great Awakening. By the time he reached New England in the fall of 1740, the revival had drawn many unconverted into the churches; it sparked the Presbyterian and Baptist membership which soared at a spectacular rate between 1740 and 1780. But the Awakening would also lead directly to major splits among the Presbyterians, Congregationalists, and even the Baptists, many of whom rejected what they saw as the emotional excesses of the meetings led by Whitefield and his imitators. People would often react in seemingly uncontrolled fits in the process of responding to the preacher's call to turn from sin. There is every evidence that rejection of the revivalism was strongest among the wealthier and educated classes in the cities and most acceptance found among the poorer and less educated peoples in the countryside.

In 1741 the Presbyterians divided into New School (accepting of revivalism) and Old School. The Congregationalists of New England experienced measurable losses as a new wave of Separatist congregations were formed by those persons most affected by the revival. The Separatists insisted upon a converted regenerate membership and tended to accept adult baptism as a sign of the regeneration. While some would eventually return to the Congregationalist fold, most of these congregations would become Baptist. Meanwhile, the Regular Baptists also split, as new Separate Baptists demanded that church members give a clear evidence of a conversion experience. In their enthusiasm for the revival, they developed what seemed to the older Baptists to be an informal and noisy worship style, led by preachers who spoke in a distinctive, shrill, sing-song manner.

As the revival progressed among the English-speaking colonists, at least one new group which was to take on some importance in the next century appeared. German Lutherans began to filter into New Jersey, Pennsylvania, and New York in the first half of the century. The first congregation was organized at Hackensack, New Jersey, around 1704. By 1750, there was a string of congregations along the Hudson River through New Jersey into southeast Pennsylvania.

Attempts to organize were stifled in New York by the Dutch regime (which favored the Reformed church) and slowed in New Jersey and Pennsylvania where German settlers were slow to adapt to a government which would supply tax money for neither the building of churches nor the support of the ministry. The most prominent minister among the Lutherans was Henry Muhlenberg (1711-1787). Muhlenberg arrived in 1742 from the Pietist center at Halle, and brought some of that spirit with him. In 1748 he organized the Evangelical Lutheran Ministerium of Pennsylvania, regarded as the first Lutheran synodical organization in America. The second synod, the New York Ministerium, was not created until after the war, in 1786.

All churches were assisted by the attention given religion by the Great Awakening, and those who most readily adopted the revivalistic techniques began a generation of growth. By the beginning of the American Revolution, though almost totally confined to New England, the Congregationalists retained their status as the largest church in the colonies, with approximately 675 congregations. They were followed by the Presbyterians with 450, the Anglicans and Baptists with approximately 400, and lesser numbers of Lutherans (more than 200), Quakers (190), Reformed (180), and Roman Catholic (50). Had it not been for the American Revolution, there is every reason to believe that the churches in the American colonies might have developed much as they did in Canada. Because of the Revolution, a different course would be taken.

And because of the Revolution, it is important to make note of Methodism, the main organization in the British phase of the eighteenth century Evangelical Awakening. In the 1750s Methodism spread through England and reached Wales, Ireland, and Scotland. At about the same time, Methodists began to migrate to the American colonies, and by 1766 the first Methodist chapel was established by Robert Strawbridge (d. 1781) at Leesburg, Virginia. In 1769 Methodist founder John Wesley sent the first two preachers to oversee and promote the work in America. While centers were being established in the cities and at a few plantations along the coast, Methodism had barely begun when its work was interrupted by the Revolution. No one was aware of the difference in American religion it was to make once peace returned.

Revolution and Transition

The churches in the colonies had gone through wars before. After each they had merely resumed their work and returned to normal. But the Revolution was different. It was not just another war. It destroyed a whole way of life and produced a new society. Religiously considered, the new nation that arose out of the success of the Revolution provided a distinct way of structuring religion, voluntary associations cut off both from official state support and public revenues. Each church would have to adjust to the new ways, and as might be expected, some would do it with far greater acumen than others. Necessary to the coming of this new world was a new religious-philosophical element which began to intrude upon the thinking of America's social and literary elites in the decades prior to the fight with the British homeland.

The Development of Deism

Nurtured within the bosom of Anglicanism as the Revolution approached was a new philosophy which denied the major affirmations of orthodox Christianity and set itself against the churches' leadership role. The new perspective was called Deism, and its importance lay not so much in the number of its adherents (which seems to have been quite small), but in 1) its acceptance by many of the men who were to provide the theoretical framework for the Revolution and the Constitution of the new nation, 2) the compatibility of its major affirmations with the irreligious elements of the American public, and 3) the role it played in further diluting the strength of the Church of England.

Such leading figures as Thomas Jefferson, Benjamin Franklin, George Washington, and James Madison, while retaining their formal affiliation with the established church, had left it in their hearts and begun to speak against it. Striking at the heart of Anglican control in the colonies, they opposed the designation of the Church of England (or any church) as the established church in the new nation.

Deists undergirded their attack on established religion with a general attack upon traditional Christianity. They derided theologians for creating complicated and speculative cosmologies beyond the comprehension of the people. They focused especially upon the concept of particular revelation, that God revealed certain truths to one person and not everyone, and the dogmas (such as the Trinity) which were derived from those claims of revelation. They argued that real religion was centered upon issues of reason and morality. They elevated reason above all religious speculation and demanded a rational Christianity.

The passing of the First Amendment with its clauses on religious freedom, though hammered through by the Deists, represents the coming together of the sectarian Protestant arguments for religious liberty which had developed out of persecution, and the Deist arguments which had developed out of their theological speculations and general anticlericalism. While Roger Williams had argued for freedom from persecution and the creation of a free environment for proselytization of unbelievers, the Deists bemoaned the evils of speculative systems imposed by clerics on an unwilling public. They had despaired of finding theological truth around which to unify amid the variety of opinions everywhere espoused. Such religious speculation was of little consequence. All religions agreed upon the need for moral behavior, and a rational moral code included most everything that was important religiously. Given the Deist stance, no reason remained for persecuting people or even for demanding conformity on matters of mere religious opinion and speculation.

The Effect of Disestablishment

The Revolution, or more directly, the resulting Constitution of the new nation, served to free religion within the republic. While apologists for state established religion have argued for its role in promoting religion in general and have cited disestablishment as a sign of societal secularization, religious establishments have done as much to suppress religious expression as they have to support it. Established religions, such as colonial Congregationalism in New England, were organized in accord with the wishes of the social elite. Through the state religion, the government controlled, regulated, and limited religious expression. It discouraged the formation and expression of religion, especially among those most alienated from the ruling class. It thus kept and/or drove many otherwise potentially religious people into a state of irreligion by limiting their choice to a religion in which they do not believe or no religion at all.

In situations dominated by a state religion, only the most committed (in New England's case, the Quakers) persist in their religious alternative as the state attempts to bring them into conformity. The volumes on religious persecution are filled with accounts of those who did resist, and American colonial history has its chapters in such volumes.

In freeing those formerly persecuted for their religious impulses, the First Amendment also created a situation in which new innovative religious gestalts could emerge. And as new varieties of religion became available, greater numbers became involved with the religious life. In the United States, the long term result of religious freedom has been the steady growth of the percentage of the population who claim membership in a religious group (beginning with little more than 15 percent in 1790) and, in the last half of the twentieth century, the voluntary movement of the overwhelming majority of the American public into religious organizations (currently above 75 percent). The destruction of government-backed religious controls has produced the most religious nation on earth.

Aftermath of the Revolution

The American Revolution, significant battles of which occurred in every part of the colonies, thoroughly disrupted the entire country. For the churches, it meant disruption of services, confiscation and even destruction of church buildings, and loss of members. Congregations were divided by conflicting loyalties, though interestingly enough, no new church bodies appeared as a result of the war.

In one sense the Congregationalists were least affected by the war. A number of ministers were identified with the Patriots' cause, and in spite of the church's identification with the state prior to the Revolution, its conflicts with the British government (such as its resistance to the planting of a Church of England congregation in Boston) left it in good standing when peace returned. Congregationalism did not, however, remain unscathed. First, it suffered an immediate loss of membership and a membership drain through the remainder of the century as British Loyalists left New England to resettle in Canada. Also, even though Congregationalism was the country's largest church body and had its membership concentrated in New England, it had to recognize that the majority of New Englanders were not church members. Out of that recognition, Connecticut passed a Toleration Act in 1784, a prelude to complete disestablishment in 1818. Massachusetts, the last to separate church and state, disestablished the church in 1833.

In the long run, Congregationalism suffered more severely from the spread of the deistic religious spirit in New England. Harvard had already become infected with anti-Trinitarian thought, and by the time Massachusetts disestablished, the church was in the midst of the Unitarian controversy which would result in the loss of many of its most prominent parishes. In spite of the losses to Canada and to the Unitarians, Congregationalism continued to grow at a very slow pace, but it steadily fell in the ranking of Protestant churches. It continued to exert a significant influence for another century primarily through its educational leadership and the allegiance of New England's elite to its ranks.

As the war closed, there was some doubt as to whether Anglicanism could ever find a place in American life. Identified as the church of the enemy, it existed in an extremely hostile atmosphere. The SPG missionaries deserted it. Of the few who remained, many were not allowed to serve their parishes because of their Loyalist sympathies. The rector at Boston's King's Chapel defected to the Unitarian cause and took the church with him.

Disestablishment also came swiftly and harshly to the Church of England in the colonies. The church had been so intricately tied into secular structures, disestablishment destroyed both its financial base and legal status. Formerly somewhat dependent on the leadership of bishops, of which it now had none, it lost almost a decade in the search for episcopal authority. The need for a bishop led the Connecticut parishes to reorganize and select one of their number, Samuel Seabury (1729-1796), as their bishop-elect. He was able to obtain apostolic orders from the nonjuring Scottish bishops (bishops whose church rejected the established Presbyterian church of Scotland), but the ministers and parishes in the southern and middle colonies did not want Scottish orders. They reorganized and elected William White (1748-1836), Samuel Provoost (1742-1815), William Smith, and David Griffith as their bishops-elect and waited for an opening in England. White and Provoost were finally able to obtain orders in London in 1787. They proceeded to organize the Protestant Episcopal Church in the U.S.A. and rebuild its work among the still loyal members located primarily in southeastern Pennsylvania, Delaware, Maryland, and Virginia. They also were able to bring the work under Seabury in New York and Connecticut into the larger fellowship. Like the Congregationalists, the new church was able to keep the allegiance of many of the new nation's more wealthy citizens.

Entering the country in the 1760s, the Methodists were almost too small to count as the Revolution began. However, they were solidly identified with the Church of England, having constituted themselves as a religious society within that church. Because of Wesley's political tracts, they were also identified with the Tory cause. Like the Anglican priests, the Methodist preachers, except for Francis Asbury (1745-1816), returned to England as a result of the Revolution. Methodism was largely shut down and Asbury forced to live in retirement during the war years. After the war, the Methodists were the first to greet Washington with protestations of loyalty, and then quickly turned to the task of reorganizing in the light of the changed situation. In 1784 the American preachers met at Barrett's Chapel in rural Maryland to organize the Methodist Episcopal Church. They elected Asbury their first bishop and began to develop their life now free of the Church of England. They were, along with the Baptists, to receive the greatest benefits from the changes which occurred.

Presbyterians, primarily identified with the Revolution, lost little, considering that their churches, concentrated in New Jersey, Pennsylvania, and Delaware, were in close proximity to much of the fighting. They benefited greatly from the continued influx of Scottish and Scottish-Irish immigrants, and membership grew substantially from 1770 through the end of the century.

Few groups so benefited from the Revolution as did the Baptists. They had been the most vocal of the two major dissident churches in colonial America, especially upon the issues of religious freedom and disestablishment, and had become as a whole strong supporters of the Revolution. After the war, they led the fight in New England for disestablishment and when it occurred were quick to claim the spoils.

Like the Baptists, the Quakers held their own during the war years. As a group the pacifist Friends did not participate, a perennial source of community hostility during wartime, but the war did not seem to stop their growth. They began the nineteenth century as one of the larger colonial bodies.

The Dutch Reformed and the German groups (Lutheran, Reformed, Mennonite, etc.) of Pennsylvania were basically dependent upon immigration for growth. The war seemed but a momentary pause in the slow growth of the Dutch and the rapid growth of the German groups, with the Reformed and Lutherans receiving the most increase. The German Lutherans had begun to arrive in the colonies early in the eighteenth century. They came from all sections of the still divided nation-to-be and were only beginning to be organized as the war began. Leading spokespersons represented a wide spectrum of opinion on the Revolution, from those opposed to the colonists' cause to those who defended the German king who sat on the British throne. When the war ended the Lutherans resumed their very basic task of learning to build churches, print religious literature, and provide pastoral leadership in a land which refused to support their church in ways which they had been taught to expect.

The Churching of the West: Change through Immigration and Proselytism

By the turn of the century, all of the churches had recovered from the war and reorganized for work in the new United States. The new country presented them with a monumental task. Within the first generation the geographical area of the United States greatly expanded, first to the Mississippi River and then by the Louisiana Purchase to the Rockies and beyond. Along with the geographical expansion, the population exploded due to immigration. Beginning with almost four million in 1790 (when the first census was taken), the population tripled by 1830 and almost doubled again by the time of the Civil War. After the war, the numbers increased even more dramatically, with more than 12 million coming in each of the last two decades of the century.

Throughout the century, no religious group was able to adequately cope with the massive population growth. Few, other than the Roman Catholics, could cross the language barrier from English majority to the German minority (the only significant minority through the early nineteenth century). In the attempts, however, religious groups could essentially adopt one of three programs: First, some religious groups sought out those immigrants who shared their Old World country of origin and defined their basic task as providing them with the American version of the same familiar church that they had left at home. Many groups, mostly the non-English speaking ones such as the Lutherans, received most of their growth in this manner, the Roman Catholic church being most successful.

Second, many immigrant groups, both English-speaking and not, brought their religion with them and established a new branch of the church of their homeland in America. Thus the number of new denominations increased steadily as most of the European sects were transplanted to America. In the establishment and growth of the predominantly immigrant/ethnic churches and religions lies half the story of American religion in the next century.

Third, the majority of the population had left behind a situation in which church membership and citizenship were largely synonymous, and in their new free situation they chose to support no religion, profess no religious affiliation, and/or join no church. Churches could begin massive efforts to bring the population into the religious life they offered. Most churches engaged in evangelism, some limited to one language or ethnic group. In the relative success of their evangelistic endeavors lies the other half of the story of the next phase in American religion.

The Second Great Awakening

Symbolic of the changes which were to occur in the new nation was a conference of Methodist ministers in Lexington, Kentucky, April 15-16, 1790. Though still establishing itself along the eastern seaboard, Methodism was already reaching out to the new settlers on the other side of the mountains. Under Bishop

Asbury's direction, 12 preachers departed the conference to ride their circuits throughout Kentucky and into Tennessee. Six years later the church had recruited enough members and preachers to justify formally designating the area as a new conference, and in so doing, the general conference further enlarged the new conference to include all of the as yet unchurched territory to the west and north.

While Methodists were directing their circuit riders into the newly settled land, the lay-oriented Baptists were migrating in large numbers, setting up worship in private homes, and establishing chapels led by part-time farmer preachers. By 1800 they had no less than 10 associations (of congregations) west of the mountains.

No less than the Methodists and the Baptists, the Presbyterians and Congregationalists felt the responsibility to plant Christian churches in the West. To some extent they had been influenced by the revivalistic fervor which had been present throughout the eighteenth century. Very soon after the war they began to form missionary societies and recruit ministers to pastor among their members who had migrated westward, to gather new converts, and to establish missions among the Indians. At least theoretically realizing the scope of the daily growing task, in 1801 the two theologically similar groups laid aside their organizational difference to unite efforts to convert the West. Missionaries were recruited and sent west to establish congregations, build colleges, and civilize the wilderness.

In the expanding frontier, measures as dramatic as the expanding country were needed. Some means of attracting the attention of the scattered and irreligious populous was needed. The program of the Plan of Union led to the establishment of some churches among groups of transplanted Easterners. These new congregations called the available seminary-trained pastors, and developed the familiar forms of parish life. Following such a plan, both Congregational and Presbyterian churches began to appear in the new population centers in the West. Because of their more efficient organizational structure, the Presbyterians were better equipped to plant congregations systematically, and soon turned the earlier situation around and received many of the scattered Congregational churches into their membership.

The program of the Presbyterians and the Congregationalists was simply inadequate for the West. They could not train ministers fast enough to serve the growing population. They could not move fast enough to keep up with the expanding frontier. Most importantly, they could not adapt fast enough to the new society being created in the West. The two churches, especially the Congregationalists, began to be left behind.

To the contrary, the Methodists and the Baptists seemed perfectly suited to the new land. They were extremely mobile. Since they emphasized their preachers' willingness and ability to preach far above any educational demands, they could train and deploy new circuit riders with great speed. They gave revivalistic and evangelistic activity their highest priority. They stood ready to exploit any means to winning the unsaved.

The first new means for churching the frontier was the camp meeting. The idea grew out of a sacramental conference among Presbyterian churches under the leadership of James McGready (1758?-1817) in the Red River area of Kentucky. McGready was a graduate of the "Log Cabin" college and an enthusiastic preacher. At a four-day sacramental meeting held for the Red River church he served in 1800, emotions flowed freely and many were converted, especially by the unplanned exhortations of a visiting Methodist, John McGee. McGready, noting the excitement, publicized the next meeting and news of the events at Red River spread across the region. The next summer, more than 10,000, including preachers of a variety of denominations, attended the gathering at Cane Ridge, Kentucky. The event became a turning point. The camp meeting combined entertainment, a break in the loneliness of farm life, and religion.

The Methodists and Baptists, and those Presbyterians associated with McGready, lost no time in integrating the camp meeting into their regular program. In 1811 alone, the Methodists organized more than 400 of them. But the Presbyterians in the East were not as enthusiastic. They condemned its excesses in 1805 and rejected McGready's work in the newly formed Cumberland Presbytery. In no small part, the church simply could not supply ministers fast enough to keep up with the new churches created out of the evangelistic efforts of McGready. Unable to reconcile his differences with the church, McGready and his colleagues formed the Cumberland Presbyterian Church.

The Cane Ridge meeting also changed the thinking of Presbyterian minister Barton Stone (1772-1844) who came away not only with a revivalistic mission but a conviction that the different churches who gathered at

Cane Ridge should put away their differences and unite in the task of converting the frontier. Stone and his followers left the Presbyterian church and assumed the simple designation of Christian. In a similar action Thomas and Alexander Campbell withdrew from the Baptists in western Pennsylvania and took the name Disciples of Christ. Finally discovering each other, the two groups united in 1832.

Thus present on the frontier were four groups ready to evangelize the land, and evangelize they did. The Baptists, already among the larger church bodies due to their revivalistic efforts in the previous century, quickly moved to become the largest church body in America during the decades immediately after the Revolution. However, the Methodists moved even quicker. From a few thousand members in 1784, they jumped ahead of the Baptists in the 1820s and during the rest of the century never looked back. The Cumberland Presbyterians were able to keep pace for most of the time, and after the 1832 merger of the Stone and Campbell movements, the Disciples of Christ enjoyed spectacular growth.

About the same time that Methodist membership surpassed the other churches, a new phase of revivalism began with the introduction of the "new measures." Developed by Congregationalist evangelist Charles G. Finney (1792-1875), the new measures were designed to create a climate for revival and promote the crisis of decision, and in the hands of Finney and those who learned his techniques they brought literally millions into the churches. The techniques included the use of protracted meetings, community-wide evangelistic campaigns with no announced ending date; testimony meetings in which people told of their conversion experience (even females talked); the anxious bench, a place designated for those wrestling with decision; and cottage prayer meetings. The new measures, rejected by Finney's church, but adopted with great success by Baptists and Methodists, institutionalized revivalism.

Immigration in the Nineteenth Century

While the evangelistic endeavors of the Methodists and Baptists were altering the shape of the religious community, immigration was having an equal effect. Of the millions that immigrated prior to the Civil War, the single largest group was Irish, followed by the Germans. The Irish were predominantly Roman Catholic and while most Germans were Lutheran, many were also Roman Catholic. In addition, with the purchase of Louisiana, the French Roman Catholics of the territory were brought into the American Church. By mid-century, Roman Catholic membership rivaled that of the Methodists and Baptists. By the end of the century, with additional immigration from Poland and Italy, the church had jumped out ahead of both and emerged as the largest religious group in America.

The growth of the church is easily traced through the development of its hierarchy. Following the Revolution, John Carroll (1735-1815) was first appointed superior of the American mission in 1784 and in 1790 consecrated as the first bishop for the United States with his see in Baltimore. In 1808 Baltimore was made an archdiocese and New York City, Philadelphia, Boston, and Bardstown, Kentucky, received bishops. In 1846, 1847, and 1853 respectively, archdioceses were named in Oregon City (later Portland) for the American Northwest, St. Louis, and San Francisco. During the second half of the century, the sites of the early bishops on the East Coast would be elevated to metropolitan (archdiocese) status, as would Chicago, Dubuque, St. Paul, and Milwaukee.

Second only to Roman Catholicism in receiving positive results from immigration were the Lutherans. First from massive German immigration in the first half of the century and then from Scandinavian immigration in the last half, the Lutherans grew in spite of their overall rejection of revivalism. The impact of Lutheranism on the country was, however, severely limited by the splintered condition of the church. As groups of Lutherans flocked into the country and settled in the frontier, they retained their linguistic and national boundaries, tended to organize separate synods in each region of the country, and were further split by internal doctrinal discord. Of major concern for the German community were issues of Pan-Germanism (i.e., union with the German Reformed Church) and the confessional-doctrinal emphasis championed by Charles P. Krauth (1823-1882) opposed to the pietist-experiential emphasis championed by Samuel S. Schmucker (1799-1873). By mid century, the Lutherans were divided into more than 100 separate autonomous bodies. Since the end of the Civil War, they have pursued a process of union which has seen that number reduced to fewer than 20, with the overwhelming majority now in one denomination, The Evangelical Lutheran Church in America (1988).

The Presbyterians, apart from the Cumberlands, were able to hold their own in the growing nation because of significant immigration from Scotland and Northern Ireland. Like the Lutherans, the Scots brought with them the problems of the homeland, and in America the Presbyterians split into a number of bodies reflective of the Scottish divisions.

During the nineteenth century, the Quakers received no significant immigrant support, faced a major schism just as the western movement grew in significance, and abandoned growth in the South over the slavery issue. Most importantly, Quakers quickly discovered that aggressive revivalism conflicted with their emphasis upon the inner light. Early in the century, they simply ceased to grow in significant numbers. They remain as a small body whose significance lies in its idealistic dissent on a number of issues such as peace and social justice, which has placed it outside the mainstream of American life but given it a remarkable role as a change agent in that society.

Slavery and the Development of the Black Churches

In the nineteenth century, one issue seriously split the American religious community: slavery and its accompanying racial attitudes. The slavery issue, considered in its broadest aspect, had two overarching influences on the development of religious life in America. First, it split several of the older predominantly white denominations so deeply that the divisions have yet to be healed. Second, it led to the development of a number of separate predominantly black denominations.

As the division between the white people of the North and South divided over the institution of slavery, the churches which included those people felt the same tension as the nation. The largest of the Protestant groups, the Methodist Episcopal Church divided first. It had originally tried to keep the peace in the family by pushing the abolitionists out into the Wesleyan Methodist Church in 1843. But the next year it opened the general conference with the scandal of a bishop from Georgia who had inherited some slaves. Bishop Andrew refused to move from his home state, was unable by Georgia law to free his slaves, and planned to continue as an active, traveling bishop. The church, unable to resolve the issue, voted to divide itself into two jurisdictions. The outcome was a division of the church into the Methodist Episcopal Church and the Methodist Episcopal Church, South.

The Baptists faced a similar problem precipitated by the refusal of the American Baptist Foreign Missionary Convention to accept slaveholders for positions as missionaries. In 1844 the Alabama and Georgia state conventions had forced the issue. After their rebuff, in 1845 the Southerners formed the Southern Baptist Convention. The Presbyterians waited until the war began, but in 1861, they too split into two bodies.

The issues raised by the slavery debates in the middle of the nineteenth century had been argued by the Methodists in the northern states soon after the formation of the Methodist Episcopal Church. Staunchly abolitionist at its beginning, it stepped back from its position as it grew in the South. Northern congregations which had been integrated began to institute segregationist policies. Blacks were relegated to balconies, were the last to be served communion, and were generally treated as second class citizens. Some walked out and formed all black congregations. Finally, in the early nineteenth century, the majority of free black people in the North left the Methodist Episcopal Church to found three black denominations: the African Methodist Episcopal Church, the African Methodist Episcopal Zion Church, and the Union Church of Africans. The first black Baptist churches in the North were organized in Boston (1804), New York (1808), and Philadelphia (1809). It was not until the 1830s that the first associations were formed, the Providence Baptist Association in Ohio and the Wood River Association in Illinois. Missionary work by blacks led to the formation of the most substantial organizations. The American Baptist Missionary Convention formed by blacks in 1840 not only sent foreign missionaries, but directed the organization of Baptist freedman after the Civil War.

In the South, black Baptists appeared as the church spread among slave owners. The first congregations of black Baptists were not organized until just before the American Revolution, however, as most slave owners were reluctant to allow independent organizations, including religious ones, among the slaves. Methodist slaves were known from almost the time of Methodism's arrival in the colonies in the 1760s. Quite early they were organized into classes and at least two black local preachers, Harry Hoosier and Richard Allen, traveled and preached with Francis Asbury.

After the Civil War, the black Baptist and Methodist churches enjoyed a period of growth as they expanded their work among the freedmen. Churches such as the African Methodist Episcopal Church, under the control of northern freed blacks, had not been allowed to recruit in the South, and quickly made up for lost time. The Methodists also added a new major organization, the Colored (now Christian) Methodist Episcopal Church, originally composed of the former slave members of the Methodist Episcopal Church, South, segregated during the Reconstruction era. Black Baptists formed a number of regional and national organizations which merged in the 1890s to become the National Baptist Convention. Most black people in the United States are Baptists, approximately 60 percent if we can believe the figures. The several million Methodists form the second greatest block.

In lesser numbers, black people have been proselytized by and have responded to most religious traditions found in America, and have formed religious organization representative of those different religious families. After the Civil War, most of the larger denominations established missions among the freedman. Unfortunately, apart from slavery, Northerners showed the same racial attitudes concerning blacks which were prevalent in the South. Even so, some blacks became (Northern) Methodists, Presbyterians, Congregationalists, Episcopalians, and Roman Catholics. While welcoming black members as a whole, these churches instituted a pattern of racial segregation at the congregational and regional levels.

On the other hand, in joining the predominantly white denominations, black church members brought into the black community all of the diverse religious commitments, theological tensions, and variation in worship of white society. As in the white community, the black denominational structures became the stable organizational units which shaped the larger religious community and set the pattern of belief and action at the congregational level. The varying response to issues facing the black community—the ethiopianism of the 1930s, the Civil Rights movement in the 1960s (which split the Baptists), and the attempt to identify a common black religious experience in the 1970s—has largely followed denominational biases.

The Indian Response to the Western Spread of Christianity

Early Indian policy of the newly formed United States focused upon the "civilization" of the Indian and envisioned the Christian churches as the main agent in that process. In 1819 the government passed a measure creating a "Civilization Fund" through which it subsidized church missions aimed not only at conversion but Americanization of the Native Americans. Even prior to the 1819 action, pressures were mounting for the removal of the Indians to the far west. A major step in that program followed the discovery of gold in Georgia, and the subsequent passing of the Removal Act of 1830 that pushed most of the members of the Five Tribes out of the Southeast.

Following the Civil War, as serious settlement west of Independence, Missouri, expanded, the settlers' demands for Indian lands led to a series of Indian wars and the confinement of the Indians to designated reservations. The pressures on the Indians in the face of the overrun of the land by whites and the development of the dependency of the Indians on the government and the churches, had two significant religious consequences. First, many Indians responded to the evangelical efforts of the hundreds of missions established by Christian churches and converted to Christianity.

Almost all of the larger church bodies have Indian members, the result of missions established in the nineteenth or early twentieth century. In recent years, the majority of the older Christian churches have also moved to remove the Native American congregations from any stigma as a mission and to integrate them into the total life of the denomination. However, many smaller churches and independent missionary agencies continue to support "missions" on or near the reservations and have since World War II developed additional missions in the urban centers where many Indians migrated.

As the Indian life was disrupted by the westward rush of white society, some Indians who did not accept Christianity developed alternatives which attempted to go beyond the tradition of any particular tribe and reach all Native Americans with a combination of religious fervor and political protest. Of the several movements which developed, the Ghost Dance movement was by far the most important. Born among the Paiute in the 1870s, the movement found its great prophet in Wovoka (1858-1932), a Paiute who lived most of his life in Nevada. Near his 30 birthday, he had a revelation during a solar eclipse. To those who practiced the distinctive circular dance already a part of the movement, the revelation promised a return of the Indian dead, the eradication of sickness, and a time of prosperity. A date during 1891 was set for the change. In the meantime, he urged followers to drop any overt hostility to the whites and become "civilized." The prophecy found immediate support among the Plains tribes, especially among the Oglala Sioux. They introduced the holy shirt, the design of which had been received in a vision, which would protect the wearer from any harm, even the bullets of the U. S. Army.

The Ghost Dance movement climaxed at Wounded Knee (1890) where 300 Ghost Dance participants were killed, a clear demonstration of the inability of the shirts to provide the promised protection. While the dance survived into the middle of the twentieth century, it had lost its mass appeal and left a vacuum soon to be replaced with another movement developed in Mexico. The peyote religion spread as the Ghost Dance receded, and offered a mystical alternative to the earlier apocalytic movement. Drawing upon both Christian and Native American themes, it added the strong psychological impact of the peyote's ability to alter consciousness. While preaching many of the values which the white culture wished to spread among the Indians, it, in addition, offered a note of defiance in its use of the peyote. After the formal incorporation of the movement as the Native American Church in 1918, it spread among numerous Indian tribes and became a powerful force in building the Native Americans' identity as one people. It also enjoyed an interesting history in the courts as it established its right to use the sacred cactus.

The Post-War Schism of American Protestants

In the last half of the nineteenth century, the major North American Protestant groups were rent with controversy. Tensions became evident as a new set of issues which demanded a response confronted the churches. The challenges of the new issues were qualitatively different from those at the beginning of the century that had demanded an increase in activity and endeavor. These issues appeared as new ideas that carried the force of scientific and academic backing. They also demanded acceptance of a totally new world view.

From Germany came a new way of looking at the Bible. Critical scholars had begun to question the accuracy of the biblical texts in several ways. Some challenged the legitimacy of the miracle stories in the name of science. What could not happen within the boundaries of the known laws of the universe, probably did not happen. Others challenged the integrity of the texts, especially the first five books of the Bible. They denied the Mosaic authorship and suggested that these books were a complex edited narrative created by combining into a single text several older texts which had been written by different people in different circumstances. The new scholarship was seen by many as defying the authority of the Bible, which most Christians understood rather literally.

For many the challenge to biblical authority by the German critics seemed to resonate with the new claims in the sciences of geology and biology. Geologists studying the nature of various earth-building processes such as volcanos concluded that the Earth was not a few thousand years old, but hundreds of thousands, even millions of years old. Charles Darwin and his colleagues concluded that not only had life forms evolved from one species to another but that even humanity was a product of evolution from other primates. The new sciences presented a complete alternative to the literal biblical account of God creating the species and separately creating the first man and woman.

Also, as the overseas mission programs of the churches expanded, interest in and information about religions in foreign lands grew. To some, it became evident that Buddhism, Hinduism, Islam, and the other great world religions offered a sophisticated spirituality and would not simply capitulate in the face of the presentation of the Christian message. Some voices arose to suggest that Eastern religions could possibly teach the West something vital and important. The impact of the other religions was brought home at the 1893 World's Parliament of Religions where Hindu Swmai Vivekananda, theosophist Annie Besant, and Buddhist Anagarika Dharmapala drew huge audiences.

While new ideas challenged church leaders' thoughts, immigration was producing unprecedented growth in American urban centers ill equipped to deal with sudden heavy population increases. Industrialists looking for cheap labor exploited the new urbanites. Slums appeared as they were crowded into inadequate housing. Drunkenness was common. Churches could not (or would not) expand fast enough to serve the immigrants (many of whom spoke no English and/or came from Roman Catholic countries). Scholars and activists began to suggest that older solutions to social problems, usually directed towards reforming individuals through hygiene, education, and hard work, were inadequate. What America needed was a change in the system which allowed slums and exploited workers to exist. Answers were suggested by the new science of sociology, which suggested that social problems could be solved by human manipulation of social structures. Among the most popular solutions was some form of socialism.

Church leaders responded to these intellectual and social challenges in basically two ways. A growing number of them suggested a positive response to the new ideas and began to seek ways of reconciling Christianity to biblical criticism, evolution, the existence of sophisticated world religions, and the crises in the cities. Those who took such a positive stance, yielding to the demands of the modern age, came to be called Modernists. Other church leaders saw in the Modernist revisions of the faith not just adapting to a new situation but the destruction of Christianity and its replacement by a different gospel. They responded by calling their ministerial colleagues and the churches of the land to once again affirm the nonnegotiable fundamentals of the faith, and in so doing they became known as Fundamentalists.

Modernism, the progenitor of contemporary liberal Protestantism, came to be identified with a variety of specific opinions. Modernists accepted biblical criticism and redefined the nature of biblical authority. In the process they discarded the literal interpretation of the early chapters of Genesis and the biblical miracle stories and emphasized instead the eternal lessons to be drawn from them. They accepted the opinions of geologists and biologists about the age of the universe and the evolutionary origin of humanity. However, they suggested that evolution was not a process without obvious purpose; that is it did not follow natural selection, but derived from the constant action of God, drawing life and humanity to higher levels of attainment. This perspective was called theistic evolution.

In their encounter with world religions, Modernists such as James Freeman Clarke, a Unitarian professor teaching at the University of Chicago, attempted to make the case for the superiority of Christianity, not as true religion over against the falsehood of all other religions, but as the most true religion in a world of religions of partial truths. Each religion contains elements recognized as good and noble, but only Christianity contains goodness and truth in their fullness. As a major expression of this approach, the League of Liberal Clergymen in Chicago organized the World's Parliament of Religions in 1893.

In their response to the cities, Modernists borrowed well known biblical symbols which they identified with the socialist program of radical changes in late nineteenth century society. They spoke of building the kingdom of God and ushering in a millennium of peace and justice through the reorganization of social patterns. They called their message the social gospel.

Modernist theology was optimistic in the extreme and based upon a positive view of human nature. Humanity, in its opinion, had evolved beyond its animal nature over many thousands of years. The human condition was not so much due to sin and human depravity. It was an effect of the continued presence of the animal past. Humans had evolved out of the animal world, and they could now evolve mentally and spiritually; they inevitably must evolve into the life of the kingdom of God. Progress became the watchword of Modernism, and a utopian hope for humanity's future undergirded every action.

Fundamentalists claimed that Modernism undercut biblical authority in the name of science and replaced Christian commitments with a different religion, hardly recognizable as Christian. As the nineteenth century moved to its close, they began to see seminary professors spreading Modernism in their class rooms and ministers voicing it from prominent pulpits. The most visible erosion appeared in the Baptist, Presbyterian, and Congregationalist churches, those older churches with a strong Calvinist confessional heritage. In the first stage of the battle, the conservatives charged individuals with deviating from confessional standards. Beginning in the 1870s, the public was treated to a series of heresy trials, the most famous being the Presbyterian actions against David Swing, Charles Briggs, and Henry Perserved Smith. A variety of denominations took official action (from censoring to dismissal) against instructors in their schools who voiced Modernist opinions.

At first, the conservatives showed their strength, but by the turn of the century sentiment turned against them. The denominations became reluctant to condemn Modernists who were filling more and more denominational posts. Sensing a loss of control, the conservative began to organize. Interdenominational conferences, the most famous being the annual gatherings at Niagara Falls, provided places for conservatives to find strength, strategize, and organize. Out of the Niagara conferences came a series of statements of faith affirming "fundamental" beliefs. The conservatives also began to establish independent schools where fundamental doctrines would be upheld and taught. Among the first were Moody Bible Institute in Chicago and the Philadelphia College of the Bible.

The conservative cause received a significant boost in the first decade of the twentieth century when Presbyterian California oilman Lyman Stewart began to divert money to the conservative cause. In 1906 he helped establish the Bible Institute of Los Angeles, which became the nexus for West Coast Fundamentalists. He brought R. A. Torrey from Moody to be the dean of the college. Withdrawing from Immanuel Presbyterian Church, he gave the initial endowment for the independent Church of the Open Door, the pulpit of which Torrey also assumed. He gave money toward the production of the Scofield Reference Bible (published in 1909), whose notes, written by lawyer turned pastor C. I. Scofield, systematically presented the Fundamentalist position. In 1909 he gave the money to produce a series of booklets, *The Fundamentals,* which were mailed to pastors across the country. These booklets, which gave the conservatives their name, launched a new assertive phase of the conservative movement. That new phase took organizational form immediately after World War I, with the formation of the World Christian Fundamental Association.

Fundamentalism and Modernism represent two distinctly different ways of viewing the world and Christianity. The battles of the nineteenth century set the issues and created two camps within each of the affected denominations. In the decades between the World Wars the growing hostility between the camps would lead to showdown battles that finally divided the Presbyterians and Baptists, and left the Modernists firmly in control of the older denominations. The Fundamentalists were pushed out into new denominations, the formation of which permanently institutionalized the Fundamentalist-Modernist controversy and has kept it alive to this day. The cleavage within the Protestant camp in North America between conservative evangelical Protestants and liberal Protestants shows no sign of being resolved, as both sides have strong support from large denominational bodies.

Methodists Divide

While Presbyterians and Baptists launched their fights over doctrinal issues, the Methodists had little time for the debate. They believed that heartfelt religion and the living of the Christian life were more important than doctrinal purity. When the early Niagara conferences began to produce doctrinal statements, the Methodists had little sympathy for the emphasis placed upon the depravity of man. They championed the possibility of human perfection and the need for sanctified holy living.

After the Civil War the church had been swept by a revival as evangelists promised the born again Methodists the possiblity of a second encounter with the Holy Spirit as dramatic and almost as important as the first born again experience. This encounter, this second blessing, as it was termed, would go beyond justifying the sinner and guaranteeing a place in heaven; it would actually make the Christian blessed in perfect love. This theme of holiness and perfection had been present, with varying emphases, throughout Methodist history. But as it reached a new peak in its acceptance, numerous holiness camp meeting associations were established throughout the several Methodist denominations.

In the 1880s, Methodists began to back away from the holiness emphasis. Prominent leaders championed the cause of gradual growth in grace over against a single critical event such as the second blessing. Critics also charged that the associations were placing too much emphasis upon the minutiae of the personal habits of Christians. District superintendents struggled to control the otherwise independent holiness associations. The tension reached a climax in Illinois where holiness leaders began to call for members to "come out" of the indifferent and often hostile Methodist church and form independent holiness congregations. While never leaving in large enough numbers to slow the steadily climbing Methodist membership figures, many holiness people did separate to found congregations which would soon band together in small regional holiness denominations. A few of these remain today, but most merged into the older schismatic Methodist churches which had retained a holiness emphasis (the Wesleyans and the Free Methodist Church) or combined with other regional bodies to form national denominations, such as the Church of the Nazarene.

Even before the independent holiness groups had consolidated their gains, the movement was swept with a new teaching which originated in a holiness Bible school in Topeka, Kansas, under the leadership of Charles Fox Parham. The teaching promised that not only was there a second blessing available to Christians, there was a third: the baptism of the Holy Spirit. While the second blessing cleansed the heart, the third filled the believer with power. Accompanying Spirit baptism and confirming its truth, proponents asserted, were supernatural manifestations, the gifts of the Spirit, the first and most important being the individual's miraculously speaking in a foreign language which, under normal circumstances, he or she did not understand. They saw speaking in tongues as a new revival of the events of Pentecost described in the biblical Book of Acts.

Pentecostalism was taken from Topeka to Houston by Parham and from Houston to Los Angeles by Parham's student, William J. Seymour, a black holiness preacher. In Los Angeles pentecostal manifestations created a sensation, and for more than three years Seymour led daily meetings held in the building on Azusa Street to which visitors flocked from around the continent. Within those three years the pentecostal movement spawned congregations across North America.

The holiness and pentecostal movements attracted the most conservative Methodists just as Fundamentalism would later attract the most conservative Baptists and Presbyterians. By the time of the major schisms in the 1920s, Methodism had already lost many of those who would possibly have aligned themselves with the Fundamentalists, especially in their affirmations of biblical authority and creation. Methodism passed through the heat of the Fundamentalist battles with only minor skirmishes. But just as Fundamentalism created a major schism in Protestantism, so too did the holiness and pentecostal movements, both now claiming millions of adherents in America and still growing.

Homegrown Religion

In the midst of the expansion of religion as the nation was being churched in the nineteenth century, new religious impulses appeared among the New Englanders who were being subjected to the efforts of the revivalists. Though often beginning with issues raised by the older religious groups, they provided new solutions and in the process created genuinely new gestalts of the religious life. Among the first was the Latter-Day Saints, popularly called the Mormons. Sharing many common roots with the equally indigenous Disciples of Christ, the church sought a unity of religions of the frontier, and found that unity in a new revelation given to Joseph Smith Jr. Spiritualism grew up in reaction to scientific critiques of religious hopes for an afterlife. Accepting the critique, it then utilized scientific models to claim that spiritualist phenomena provided "proof" that life after death is real. New England Transcendentalism, which centered upon the community at Brook Farm was among the first American religion to draw upon Asian wisdom themes.

While Mormonism and Spiritualism emerged in the countryside, the important late nineteenth century groups Theosophy, Christian Science, and New Thought started their work in the cities—New York, Boston, and Chicago. Over the years each movement produced numerous splinter groups (more than 100 can, for example, be traced to Theosophy) that would result in the formation of a new family of religions. Each would also build its own agenda without particular reference to the continuing life of the Christian churches and the ideas deemed important in their centers of learning.

The same impulse that produced the nineteenth century sectarian movements were similar to impulses that had sought expression in previous centuries. Only in the nineteenth century, the promise of religious freedom allowed these groups to emerge, proselytize, and to a relative degree prosper. In previous centuries, their founders would possibly have been outlawed and the groups hounded out of existence. In this century they had only to withstand the press of popular opinion.

Immigration 1880-1924

By 1880 the population of the United States had reached above 50 million. During the next 25 years, before the brakes were applied to immigration, it would double. People of many nationalities, previously represented by only scattered individuals, now came in large numbers. In colonial times, immigration had brought those religious groups which still dominate the patterns of American religious life. After the American Revolution and through most of the nineteenth century, immigration would continually add members to the older groups and steadily bring new ones, most of which were variations of the older groups. The spurt of immigration between 1880 and 1924 would substantially alter America's religious landscape (already bulging with the indigenous innovative religions) by markedly increasing the variety of religious expression. Greeks, Romanians, Bulgarians, and Serbians brought all the variations of Eastern Orthodoxy. Russian and Polish Jews overwhelmed and recreated the small German Jewish community. The Japanese added their expressions of Buddhism to the Chinese forms. Indians brought Sikhism and Hinduism.

Eastern Orthodoxy had been introduced into California in the early nineteenth century and into Alaska even earlier. However, it remained small and the few parishes of the Russian Orthodox Church housed believers of every national-ethnic group. In the late nineteenth century, immigration brought people from predominantly Orthodox lands in such numbers that each was in turn able to organize separate parishes and eventually form separate dioceses. Some groups, such as the Ukrainians, were able to create autonomous jurisdictions for the first time in the free climate of North America. After the Russian Revolution, and again after World War II, the Orthodox churches would further divide along political lines creating even more new church groups.

Jews had come to America in three waves. In the seventeenth century, a small number of Sephardic Jews (Jews with a Spanish background) emigrated to the colonies. The first synagogue, Congregational Shearith Israel was organized in New York in 1728. The second synagogue, in Newport, Rhode Island, still stands, but its members were driven out by the British capture of the city during the Revolution. There were approximately 3,000 Jews in America as the colonial era ended.

During the nineteenth century enough German Jews came into the United States to overwhelm the small colonial community. By 1840 there were approximately 15,000 Jews. Most importantly, the new immigrants were heirs of a liberalizing influence that had grown among German synagogues. They wanted revision of the traditional forms of Jewish life and worship, stripping away nonessential items which tended to alienate the non-Jewish community. By the middle of the century, in religiously free America, they created a new way of practicing Judaism, Reform Judaism. In response the more traditional Jews organized to defend their old ways. They became known as Orthodox Jews.

The wave of Eastern European Jews which began in the 1880s overwhelmed the German Jewish community as completely as it had overwhelmed the colonial community. More than three million came, and both Orthodox and Reform communities vied for the immigrants' allegiance. In the midst of this tension, a new form of Judaism, which attempted to mediate between the two camps, appeared. Conservative Jews respected the tradition, but made some mild reforms of what were considered less essential items. Over several decades, each group attained approximately the same number of adherents, and each organized both rabbinical and congregational associations on a national level.

Religiously, the Jewish community is built around the three ways of practicing Judaism: Reform, Conservative, and Orthodox. Equally important, standing outside of these three groups were the large number of Jews who adhered to none of the three. As with the settled Gentile community, approximately one-half of the Jewish immigrants acknowledged no religious affiliation. Over the years, in the pluralistic climate of the United States, many of those unattached Jews found their way into the wide variety of non-Jewish religions, especially non-Christian forms, and some became prominent leaders. Other created Jewish versions of non-Jewish religions such as Christian Science and Humanism.

No groups were so affected by the immigration laws as were the Asians. In the 1850s Chinese began to arrive in America in large numbers. While many were Christians, a large number followed the several Chinese faiths, especially Buddhism. Anti-Chinese feeling led to the passage of an exclusion act in 1882. Japanese and Filipinos began to move into the West Coast to replace the Chinese as cheap labor. They brought their Buddhism and Catholicism respectively. However, public opinion began to turn against the Japanese and in 1908 a "gentleman's agreement" was reached with Japan to limit further immigration. During the first decade of the twentieth century, East Indians, mostly Punjabi, also came into Washington, Oregon, and California. As with the Japanese, they found themselves the object of public hostility. In 1917 Congress passed an Asian Exclusion Act which stopped immigration from all of Asia, except Japan. Prior to the 1917 act, several forms of both Hinduism and Buddhism had been introduced into America and had attracted non-Asian converts. After the 1917 act, that growth, now slowed considerably, continued through the development of non-Asian Hindu and Buddhist groups, most of which were small, with membership limited to a single urban center. They often existed quietly for years, relatively unknown even by their immediate neighbors.

However, in 1924 an omnibus immigration quota act, which assigned strict limits to the number of immigrants from each country that could enter the United States, stopped significant immigration not only from Asia, including Japan, but also from Southern and Eastern Europe. Thus not only was the spread of Buddhism and Hinduism stifled, but the growth of the Eastern Orthodox and Jewish communities measurably slowed. Since each of these communities possessed strong ethnic bondings that prevented evangelism outside of the ethnic group, further growth depended upon the community's birth rate.

Twentieth Century Pluralism: New Pattern for the Twentieth Century

At the beginning of the twentieth century, between 30 and 40 percent of the American populous were affiliated with a church or religious group. The majority of America remained unchurched, but a tremendous growth had been experienced by religion in general and the Christian churches in particular. They had doubled the percentage of the population in the churches. While the population had grown by 20 times, church membership had more than doubled that rate. In the process the number of different religious organizations had grown even more. There were fewer than 40 denominations in 1800. By the beginning of the twentieth century, some 200 different religious bodies representing 16 different denominational families could be found.

Most religious people were in the major Christian bodies, the largest of which had become the Roman Catholic church. Over against Catholicism, the major Protestant churches found some unity and saw themselves collectively as the majority party in the land. In 1908 they gave expression to that unity by creating the Federal Council of Churches. The creation of the Federal Council occurred as the churches were facing the great conservative-liberal splits between Fundamentalists and Modernists and between Methodism and the holiness churches. The council became the forum of liberal Protestantism. Among its first acts was the adoption of a slightly altered version of the Methodist Social Creed, an early statement of social concerns which incorporated important elements of the social gospel.

The council became the first successful expression of the ecumenical movement. Drawing upon the ideal of the unity of Christianity which stood in stark contrast to the numerous divisions of the church, especially in America, ecumenists expressed the desire for the organic unity of Protestantism. The movement generated periodic waves of enthusiasm throughout the twentieth century, and can claim major accomplishments in the uniting of churches within the several Protestant families highlighted by the formation of the Evangelical Lutheran Church in America from mergers in 1918, 1930, 1960, and 1988; the United Methodist Church from mergers in 1939 and 1968; the Presbyterian Church (USA) from mergers in 1906, 1958, and 1983; and the United Church of Christ from mergers in 1931 and 1948.

Rejection of the council and the ecumenical movement became an additional affirmation for the Fundamentalists as they pulled out of the larger denominations. In its place they organized two councils, the American Council of Christian Churches (1941) and the National Association of Evangelicals (1942), the former being the more conservative of the two. They limited their ecumenical activity to those with whom they were in essential doctrinal agreement. Pentecostals gave outward expression both to their growth and their distinctive presence in the American community by the organization of the Pentecostal Fellowship of North America. Years earlier, at the beginning of the holiness revival, a National Holiness Campmeeting Association had been created. During the twentieth century it went through a process of reorganization to emerge as a council of holiness churches, and in 1970 took the name Christian Holiness Association.

The first half of the twentieth century continued the pattern of growth for the various religious groups, in the midst of which liberal Protestants extended the ecumenical ideal to open contacts and build bridges of understanding with the Roman Catholic and Jewish communities. Those contacts were fruitful enough in the public sphere that by the middle of the century, sociologist Will Herberg could rightfully speak of America's three faiths—Protestant, Catholic, and Jew.

But other groups were also growing. The nineteenth century foreign language groups went through a process of Americanization and were ready to interact with the larger community. The Eastern Orthodox leaders formed the Standing Council of Orthodox bishops in 1960. The International New Thought Alliance formed earlier in the century had grown up with the metaphysical churches.

Since 1965

The gradual restructuring which had been occurring throughout the twentieth century was given a new impetus in 1965. That year Congress rescinded the Asian Exclusion Act and redistributed immigration quotas allowing Asian, Eastern European, and Middle Eastern countries to send immigrants as never before. In the decades since its passing, *this single act has done more to readjust the religious community in America than any other force*. This action once again allowed the flow of immigrants from those countries which had been excluded in 1917 and 1924. The result as been twofold.

First, those communities which have their roots in Eastern and Southern Europe have been strengthened. Second, immigration from Islamic countries has for the first time occurred in significant numbers, with believers from throughout the diverse Muslim world settling in America. Eastern religions have extended their presence in America through both first-generation immigrant organizations and the unexpected conversion of thousands of young adult Americans to both Buddhism and guru-led Hindu religions. More than 100 different Hindu denominations have been planted in America since 1965 and more than 75 forms of Buddhism currently exist. Each community now claims from three to five million adherents. Their rate of growth continues to be among the highest in the country.

During the twentieth century, the New Thought metaphysical churches (Religious Science, Divine Science, and the Unity School of Christianity) have become a familiar sight on American street corners. Now numbering adherents in the hundreds of thousands, their influence has permeated the mainstream of American culture through the spread of their literature. Unity material, especially its devotional monthly *Daily Unity,* now enters millions of homes. Even more noticeable is the spread of metaphysical thought through the extensive ministry of ministers such as Norman Vincent Peale, Robert Schuller, and Oral Roberts, all of whom have been influenced by New Thought ideas.

Occult religions, among the least understood religious options, have broken out of the small esoteric groupings that were so typical at the beginning of the twentieth century. Spiritualism, often thought of as merely a nineteenth century fad, passed through periods of revival after every war, and perpetuated itself in all of the major urban complexes. Theosophy, based upon teachings delivered to Helena P. Blavatsky by what she claimed were ascended masters of wisdom, while never claiming more than a few tens of thousands of members, has spawned more than 100 like organizations. Thus, while occultism has yet to claim the number of, for example, Buddhism or Hinduism, it can truthfully claim this century as the time of an occult revival. Astrology reaches a steadily growing segment of the public. One needs no better indicator of the penetration of public consciousness by occult (as well as related Eastern) ideas than the recent surveys which revealed that almost one-fourth of Americans believe in the concept of reincarnation, the idea that human souls inhabit a series of physical bodies over several lifetimes.

While the number of people attracted to metaphysics and the occult has increased with each generation, the distrust of organization that permeates both movements prevents the growth of metaphysical groups to the extent that the spread of metaphysical ideas would seem to warrant. To perpetuate itself, the community must rely upon periods of the revival of its major concerns within the larger secular community, as it has yet to develop structures which can pass its teachings to the next generation through more traditional family structures. The New Age Movement of the 1980s has been the latest period of revival. It has raised public awareness of metaphysical and occult ideas and brought thousands into the previously established occult-metaphysical fellowships and led to the formation of many new ones.

American Religious Groups in the 1980s

As of the 1980s, American religion can be seen as divided into 10 recognizable groups of denominations, each of which claims a substantial number of adherents through the membership of its member denominations. Each group is united by some common beliefs and commitments and separated from other groups by adherence to a distinct way of practicing religion. Six of these groups are Christian and together can claim both a majority of American citizens and the bulk of America's religious adherents. The Christian community is divided into Roman Catholic, Eastern Orthodox, Liberal Protestant, Conservative Evangelical, Holiness, and Pentecostal-Charismatic.

There are more than 50 million Roman Catholics in America making it three times larger than its closest competitor, the Southern Baptist Convention. It exists both as a single organization, and as a very inclusive mixture of ethnic parishes, religious orders, and diverse theologies. The church assumed an important role in the nineteenth century. It grew to become the nation's largest religious body and in many cities claimed the allegiance of the majority of citizens. Its earlier attempts to integrate its life into the American fabric and become an active participant in shaping social policy were thwarted by strong anti-Catholic sentiments, one of the few concerns around which competing Protestant sects could unite. Also, at the end of the nineteenth century, some prominent Catholic leaders proposed a program for realigning the church in America with some important American values. They also called the church to emphasize its likenesses with Protestantism rather than the differences. Unfortunately, this program, which became known in Europe as "Americanism," was denounced in a papal encyclical in 1899, and the American church entered a period of being turned in upon itself. Only since World War II, with the generation of new leadership, the changes wrought at Vatican II, and the election of John F. Kennedy as president, has the church created a more positive image and been accepted as a stable and legitimate part of the American religious landscape. Its new and acknowledged role in American society is manifest in the thoughtful attention now given the regular pronouncements on public policy made by the National Conference of Catholic Bishops.

Similar, but in may ways essentially distinct from Roman Catholicism, is Eastern Orthodoxy. Emerging in America in the early twentieth century, the Orthodox groups have been committed to the preservation of both the Orthodox faith and the ethnic heritage of their constituencies. They have been united by the problems resulting from the expansion of governments hostile to religion in many of their ethnic homelands. In the wake of World War II they have emerged as vocal participants, as well as a force with which to be reckoned, in the wider debates and ecumenical discussions. Many of the Orthodox groups, besides uniting in the Standing Conference of Orthodox Bishops, have extended their influence through affiliation with the National Council of Churches.

In the late nineteenth and early twentieth century, Protestantism split into a least four major camps, each distinct enough from the other and united enough to be considered a separate religous grouping. Aligned within the National Council of Churches (which superseded the Federal Council of Churches) are the major liberal Protestant denominations. They include the Protestant Episcopal Church, The Evangelical Lutheran Church in America, the Presbyterian Church (U.S.A.), the United Church of Christ, the United Methodist Church, the American Baptist Churches in the U.S.A., and the six major black Protestant groups (three Methodist churches and three Baptist conventions). As a whole, these are the older and larger Protestant bodies, the most socially oriented, the most accepting of contemporary scholarship (both secular and sacred), the most visible religious bodies in America.

One measure of the relative prominence of religious groups in a society is the role given particular religious groups in public settings. During most of American history, Protestantism's leadership in shaping America was religiously unchallenged. Liberal Protestantism, as it took control of the older, larger church organizations assumed possession of that leadership position. Through the National Council and its constitutive bodies, liberal Protestantism continues that tradition of leadership and guidance to the nation on the important national and international social issues. Slowly it has acknowledged that it now shares that leadership position with at least the Roman Catholic Church and the Jewish community. But as the twentieth century draws to a close, that primal leadershp role is actively challenged at every turn, especially by the three conservative dissenting Protestant groups: the evangelical conservatives (whose most conservative element is Fundamentalism), the holiness churches, and the pentecostals (or charismatics). These groups have rejected the leadership of the older Protestant groups. Counting the 16-million member Southern Baptist Convention as a part of the evangelical conservative grouping (as its most liberal wing), it has claimed a constituency of some 40 million, equal in size to the combined membership of the affiliates of the National Council of Churches. Based upon that assessment of support, evangelical conservatives emerged in the public sphere in the 1980s as a group claiming the Protestant heritage of leadership over against that of the National Council of Churches and its member organizations. They have claimed additional support from the membership of the liberal Protestant churches which repeatedly has been shown to be out of step with their churches' public pronouncements. Liberal Protestantism has also been unique in its steady loss of members since the 1960s. Evangelicals claim, with some justification, that those members have been lost to evangelical churches, which in fact adhere more closely to the American Protestant tradition.

The holiness and pentecostal churches have been identified with the conservative evangelical camp on some basic issues such as the mutual affirmation of the authority of the Bible, and on important public positions such as opposition to abortion, support of prayer and the teaching of creationism in the public schools, and support for the state of Israel. They have remained distinct bodies within the evangelical consensus due to intense doctrinal differences, such as their support for a female ministry. Both holiness and pentecostal groups have grown throughout the twentieth century, but during the last two decades pentecostalism has made spectacular strides. It has, for example, come to dominate the air time given religion on radio and television. The Church of God in Christ with more than three million members has led pentecostalism in overtaking Methodism in the number of black adherents. The Assemblies of God now claims more than two million and both the United Pentecostal Church and the Church of God (Cleveland, Tennessee) have more than a half million.

The various major groups of Christians follow what are described below in the various chapters of this *Encyclopedia* as denominational families. But among Anglicans, Lutherans, Presbyterians, Congregationalists, Methodists, and Baptists the split between liberal and conservative groupings seems to rival the denominational families structures in importance. That split between conservatives and liberals, however, relates to a limited (though important) number of theological and social issues, which together constitute only a small percentage of the churches' religious life. Conservative and liberal Lutherans, for example, still agree on the majority of issues that make them Lutheran. The same could be said for the other denominational families. And while they align themselves on certain issues along liberal and conservative lines, they also participate in family traditions which have both national and international organizational expression. In that regard, liberals and conservatives will join together to support fellowship groups such as the Lambeth Conference of Bishops of the Anglican Communion, the Lutheran World Federation, the World Alliance of Reformed Churches (Presbyterian and Congregational), The World Methodist Council, and the Baptist World Fellowship.

The larger denominational communities still have responsibility for congregational life, worship, the production of educational materials, pastoral care, and continuing the family traditions. Those family traditions remain very much alive, and attempts to unite groups across those family lines in either liberal or conservative Protestant churches have failed time and again because of strongly-held denominational differences. The Consultation on Church Union, so promoted in the 1970s, is merely the most recent prominent example of such failure. The commitments to denominational distinctives provides stability amid shifting perspectives on various social issues and ephermeral ecumenical enthusiasms.

The American Jewish community is the most prominent religious community in America apart from the several Christian groups and the only one with a continuous presence since the colonial period. In the public sphere, George Washington acknowledged their presence after the Revolution, Jewish chaplains served on both sides during the Civil War, and during the twentieth century, Jewish rabbis have been invited to preside equally with Protestant and Catholic leaders in public religious celebrations, such as Thanksgiving.

New openness toward the Jewish community has come in the wake of the Holocaust (a reference to the six million Jews killed during the Nazi regime), the establishment of the state of Israel, and the new position toward the Jewish community articulated by the Roman Catholic Church during the Second Vatican Council. The Vatican statement, promulgated in 1965, refuted a once popular Christian position that blames the Jews for Christ's death and has created a new basis for Jewish-Christian dialogue. That dialogue has tended to focus upon two issues: the Middle East and the evangelization of Jews by Christians. In the last generation, Roman Catholics and liberal Protestants have largely withdrawn support for missionary activities toward the Jewish community, but have been most supportive of Palestinians in the Middle East. Evangelical Christians, on the other hand, have continued to increase support for Jewish missionary endeavors while at the same time supporting the complete backing for Israel by the American government.

In the new dialogue, the major spokespersons for the Jewish community are the American Jewish Committee and the Synagogue Council of America. The former provides a meeting ground for both secular and religious Jews, and the latter represents the different Jewish congregational and rabbinical associations in a manner similar to the National Council of Churches.

Arising to challenge the Jewish position in America, the Islamic community has, since World War II, paralleled the spectacular growth of Methodism after the American Revolution. It now virtually equals the Jewish community in size and has emerged as a potent political force balancing the Jewish-allied support for Israel in the public debates on the Middle East. Awareness of the size of the Islamic community was quite low until recently because of public images that identified it solely with the Arab world. In fact, the Islamic world stretches from Indonesia through China and India, through the Arab world, and across the African continent. In America it has received the additional support of a significant number of black people. Only in the 1970s did impressive mosques (the Islamic houses for prayer and worship) become visible in most American cities.

The Islamic community will not in the foreseeable future challenge in size any of the Christian families. But with pluralism growing, as the largest non-Christian religious group, its agenda will have to be taken with inceasing seriousness and will, in all likelihood, undergird the most significant shifts in public positions taken by the Christian community.

The presence of Buddhists and Hindus in significant numbers in America is leading to the second most important shift in American religion. Accommodation to the presence of Jews in an otherwise Christian-dominated society, was made by reference to a common Judeo-Christian heritage. Islam is also a product of that same heritage. Hinduism and Buddhism provide the most complete alternative on the most basic issues to Christianity. Dismissed for many decades as cults, Hindu and Buddhist groups have begun to rise above that negative label through alignment with the large immigrant communities that have brought millions of Asians to America and are now forcing the encounter of Asians and non-Asian Americans at every level of society.

The Buddhist community matured the quickest. Two visible signs of that maturity appeared in 1987 with the naming of the first Buddhist chaplain in the armed forces and the formation of the American Buddhist Congress. The congress will serve as a vehicle for building a more adequate understanding of Buddhists and Buddhism in American society and a voice for the Buddhist community's opinions on matters of public policy. Less organized nationally, Hindus are represented by the Hindu Vishwa Parishad, a national ecumenical agency.

Not to be forgotten in the massive pluralism so evident in contemporary American life is the continuance and the revival of Native American religions and religious traditions. While most Native Americans are now members of Christian churches, the traditional religions were never totally stamped out, and in many tribes a core of people who practiced the old religions remained a continuous presence. Then in the 1970s, along with the spread of numerous young-adult-oriented new religions, a variety of new Native American religions drawing heavily on traditional themes and traditionalist movements within particular tribes appeared. These new movements have a double importance. Not only have they given new life to traditional faiths, they have produced the first visible influx of traditional Native American religion into the white culture. During the 1980s, non-Native Americans who identify with environmental concerns, the occult, and/or transpersonal psychology have found parallel concerns in Native American themes of oneness with the sacred land, shamanism, and the transformative power of Indian rituals.

Besides the large families of religious groups described above, America is the home to a number of other diverse religious groups from the three million member Church of Jesus Christ of Latter-Day Saints to the very small witchcraft covens of 10 to 15 members. There is a small but vocal atheist-humanist community, the relgiously irreligious, so to speak, important far beyond its size because of its support within the academic world. While the relative sizes of the individual communities vary, America, and to a lesser extent Canada, have become a microcosm of world religion. Every major world religious community is now present in strength. While a majority of Americans have become Christian (and the community as a whole shows no evidence of declining), the climate of mutual respect and honor demanded by pluralism in a free religious society has given the world religions and interfaith issues the highest priority on the agenda of the older Christian bodies, which had until a generation ago largely limited interfaith contact to Jewish-Christian dialogue. The results of this new pluralism are only beginning to be discerned.

Selected General Sources in American Religious History
[Further listing related to each religious family group are given at the end of each chapter.]

Ahlstrom, Sydney E. *A Religious History of the American People.* Garden City, NY: Doubleday and Co., 1975. 2 Vols.

Albanese, Catherine L. *America: Religions and Religion.* Belmont, CA: Wadworth Publishing Company, 1981. 389 pp.

Gaustad, Edwin Scott. *Dissent in American Religion.* Chicago: University of Chicago Press, 1973. 184 pp.

_____. *A Documentary History of Religion in America.* Grand Rapids, MI: William B. Eerdmans Publishing House, 1982. 2 Vols.

_____. *Historical Atlas of Religion in America*. New York: Harper & Row, 1976. 189 pp.

_____. *A Religious History of America*. New York: Harper & Row, 1966. 421 pp.

Handy, Robert T. *A Christian America*. New York: Oxford University Press, 1981. 269 pp.

Hudson, Winthrop S. *Religion in America*. New York: Charles Scribner's Sons, 1981. 486 pp.

Hutchison, William R. *The Modernist Impulse in American Protestantism*. Oxford: Oxford University Press, 1976. 347 pp.

Johnson, Douglas W., Paul R. Picard, and Bernard Quinn. *Churches and Church Membership in the United States, 1971*. Washington, DC: Glenmary Research Center, 1971. 237 pp.

Marsden, George M. *Fundamentalism and American Culture*. Oxford: Oxford University Press, 1980. 307 pp.

Marty, Martin E., ed. *Out Faiths*. Royal Oak, MI: Cathedral Publishers, 1975. 236 pp.

_____. *Pilgrims in Their Own Land*. Boston, MA: Little, Brown and Company, 1984. 500 pp.

_____. *Protestantism in the United States*. New York: Charles Scribner's Sons, 1986. 290 pp.

Mead, Sidney E. *The Lively Experiment*. New York: Harper & Row, 1963. 220 pp.

_____. *The Nation with the Soul of a Church*. New York: Harper & Row, 1975. 158 pp.

Melton, J. Gordon. *Biographical Dictionary of Cult and Sect Leaders*. New York: Garland Publishing Company, 1986. 354 pp.

_____. *A Directory of Religious Bodies in the United States*. New York: Garland Publishing Company, 1977. 305 pp.

Morris, Richard R. *Encyclopedia of American History*. New York: Harper & Brothers, 1953. 776 pp.

Moyer, Elgin S. with Earle Cairns. *The Wycliffe Biographical Dictionary of the Church*. Chicago: Moody Press, 1982. 449 pp.

Myers, Gustavus. *History of Bigotry in the United States*. New York: Capricorn, 1960. 474 pp.

Noll, Mark, et al, eds. *Eerdman's Handbook to Christianity in America*. Grand Rapids, MI: William B. Eerdmans Publishing Company, 1983. 507 pp.

Piepkorn, Arthur C. *Profiles in Belief*. New York: Harper & Row, 1977-79. 3 Vols.

Quinn, Bernard, et al. *Churches and Church Membership in the United States, 1980*. Atlanta, GA: Glenmary Research Center, 1980. 321 pp.

Smith, H. Shelton, Robert T. Handy, and Lefferts A. Loetscher. *American Christianity*. New York: Charles Scribner's Sons, 1960. 2 Vols.

Sweet, William Warren. *Religion in Colonial America*. New York: Charles Scribner's Sons, 1951. 367 pp.

_____. *The Story of Religion in America*. New York: Harper & Brothers, 1939. 656 pp.

Introductory Essay 2
A Historical Survey of Religion in Canada,
1500 to the Present

The Initial Conquest of Canada: Native Americans in Canada

During the centuries before the invasion and conquest of what is today known as Canada, as with the United States, the vast territory was inhabited by the many tribes of Indians or Native Americans. The density of population was not great, there being an estimated 220,000 persons in 1500. Most affected by the first settlements were tribes such as the Hurons which inhabited the shores of the St. Lawrence River, but eventually almost every tribe felt the impact of the spreading out of European culture and governmental rule. The establishment of the dominance of the whites effectively did away with the self sufficient cultures of the Indians and eventually made them dependent upon the larger resources developed by the new arrivals.

While much of the religious life of the tribes was either destroyed or transformed as tribal members responded to Christian missionary efforts, the story of North American Indian religion, especially as it continues in its contemporary forms, is integral to the story of Canadian religion.

As with the Indian tribes in what is now the United States, the Indians of Canada had a significant variation of religious belief and practice from the Huron and Algonquin in the east, to the Blackfoot of the plains, to the Eskimo of the Arctic reaches, to the Kwakiutl and the other tribes of British Columbia known so widely for their totem poles. They also shared with the American Indians the characteristic of integrating religion into their tribal self identity and survival. Because of the harsher climate, the religion of the Canadian Indians reflected their tie to the land and the needs of survival even more than was the case with the tribes further south.

The initial settlement of the Europeans in the 1600s had its impact primarily upon the tribes of the St. Lawrence Valley. Both the Hurons and the Iroquois became entangled in the wars of the British and French for control of Canada and the subject of various missionary activities. The first Jesuits arrived in 1611, and it is among the Hurons and Iroquois that many of them worked. It is also among these tribes, quite apart from the missionaries, that the most destructive influence of the European intrusion became manifest. The Jesuits became trapped in the war which developed between the two tribes over the supply of beaver fur that was being rapidly exhausted through the early decades of the seventeenth century. The Indians had become dependent upon the European goods which they purchased with fur. In the resultant hostilites the Hurons were annihilated.

With the exception of the few traders that began to penetrate the interior, the majority of Canadian Indians did not have to deal with the whites until the nineteenth or even the twentieth century. The British initiated the penetration of the west through fur trading companies which established settlements along the coast of Hudson Bay. During the 1700s, the traders began the serious push inland that led to the company's control of the western half of Canada that persisted until it gave way to the new Dominion of Canada in the last half of the nineteenth century.

After the French era, as Canadians moved into Indian lands and gradually took possession of most of them, the level of hostilities proved to be far lower than in the United States. Canada established a pattern of making treaties with the Indians that included land grants and, with few exceptions, honoring those treaties. It also pursued a policy of punishing violations of the treaties by non-Indians.

The relatively peaceful nature of the long-term relationship between the Canadian government and the Indian tribes has allowed for the development of Christian missions and the conversion of the majority of Indians to Christianity. Roman Catholics, the Anglican Church, and the churches now composing the United Church of Canada all developed strong missions, especially in western Canada. On the other hand, traditional Indian religions have been able to survive and may be found among tribes in all sections of the country.

Especially notable among the surviving tribal religions of Canada are the Eskimo religions which had been dominated by the shamans, the ubiquitous leaders in Eskimo religious matters. The shamans, much like a modern medium, entered a trance state during which they allowed various spirits to take possession of their consciousness and use their body to speak and dance. Integral to the shaman's work, and almost definitive of shamanism as opposed to common mediumship, was "soul flight," in which the shaman was believed to send his/her soul to the spirit realm on some errand such as the obtaining of advice on an important question that had arisen in the tribe.

The practice of shamanism was also seen as integral to the survival of Eskimo tribes in which starvation was frequently an immediate problem. They would predict (and even try to control) the weather and the supply of game. They would send their soul to placate a goddess such as Sedna believed to control the sea mammals, or to locate the caribou and entice its appearance for the hunters. It was their job to spot violations of taboos that were believed to inhibit the luck of the hunt. They also attempted to improve fertility in the tribe using their special powers to aid barren females. The extent of the practice of shamanism has been significantly limited by the inroads of not only Christianity but of secular education and the modern technological world in general. Its future is unclear, given the current rebirth of shamanism in other areas of the culture.

The Arrival of Europeans in Canada

It is currently assumed that the first sighting of North America by a European occurred around the year 986 C. E. when Bjarni Herjulfson and his crew of Norse sailors were blown off course while sailing in the waters off Greenland. Some 15 years later, Leif Ericson explored the coast of North America, though scholars disagree as to the exact area described in the early accounts of his trips. Several other trips followed, however, the full extent of Norse exploration has been greatly hindered by the production of a number of fraudulent artifacts purporting to be relics of the Norse explorers.

For the purposes of later history, however, the exploration of Canada really began with the arrival of John Cabot off Newfoundland in the summer of 1497. Cabot's voyage was followed by other explorers looking for the Northwest Passage as well as French ships which began exploitation of the fishing grounds off Newfoundland. Both the British and French established their early claim to Canadian territory. Then in 1534 Jacques Cartier arrived at the mouth of the St. Lawrence River to confirm the claim on New France made by Giovanni de Verranzano in 1523. Further British claims to present day Canada would be delayed until the 1570s and the three voyages of Martin Frobisher followed by John Davis, George Weymouth, and John Knight.

During the sixteenth century, the economic pursuits of the explorers and their financial backers overrode any religious goals which might have been expressed for the new world that was being discovered. The first settlers were not particularly religious people. Nevertheless, both Roman Catholicism and Anglicanism were introduced, though no permanent structures were created. Cartier included among his crew a priest who celebrated the first mass in Canada when the ship docked at Gaspe Peninsula. Anglican services were first held by a Master Wolfall, chaplain on Frobisher's third voyage. The first communion service according to the rite of the Church of England was held in 1578 in Baffinland. During the century, French efforts were concentrated upon the St. Lawrence Valley, to be joined by British settlement of Newfoundland after Frobisher's voyages.

In the late 1500s the French settled and began seriously to develop the trading business in the St. Lawrence Valley. Though the companies were responsible for supplying and supporting Roman Catholic priests in their Canadian centers, they did little to further the cause of religion during the remaining years of the sixteenth century. One must look to England for the emergence of the religious impulse in any public manner. In 1583, Sir Humphrey Gilbert was sent to claim Newfoundland for England, and in the establishment of the colony he proclaimed that worship according to the Church of England should prevail. However, he was lost at sea on his return voyage home, and the colony soon dissolved.

Finally, early in the seventeenth century, a permanent religious structure was created with the founding first of Arcadie (1603-1613) in Nova Scotia and subsequently of Quebec (1608) by Samuel de Champlain (ca.1570-1635). Champlain not only introduced Roman Catholic worship into his settlements, but seems to have been the first to articulate forcefully the desire to convert the indigenous residents of the surrounding lands. To that end, in 1615 he introduced the Roman Catholic Order of Recollects (one of several Franciscan orders), and when they proved ineffective, in 1625 he invited the Jesuits to begin work. Arriving with the first wave of Jesuits was Father Jean Brebeuf, who authored a number of reports which provide some of the best observations on French Canada during the 15 years between the first report and 1649, the year of Brebeuf's death by torture at the hands of those he was attempting to convert. During Brebeuf's Canadian career, the French territory expanded, new towns such as Montreal (1642) were founded, and more priests arrived (the Sulpicians joined the first two orders in the 1640s).

The success of the Catholic missionaries was demonstrated clearly in 1659 when Francois de Montmorency Laval (1623-1708) was appointed vicar apostolic for Canada. That appointment was not disconnected from the increased interest in New France by the king, who designated it an official colony by a royal decree just four years later. Further growth of the church led to Laval being named the first bishop of Quebec in 1674.

The unfruitful Protestant efforts to colonize Canada continued in the 1600s, when a group of Danish Lutherans established a short lived settlement on Hudson Bay. Their minister was among the first to die of scurvy, which ravaged the colony shortly after it began. Meanwhile, under James I the British renewed their interest in Canada. In 1610 he issued a charter for a colony in Newfoundland. John Gay of Bristol responded by establishing a "plantation" on Conception Bay and in 1612 brought Erasmus Stourton, an Anglican priest, to the colony. Stourton thus became the first resident non-Roman Catholic clergyman to reside in Canada. Stourton remained in Canada for 15 years during which time a charter for a Scottish (Presbyterian) settlement was issued by James I (1622) on the lands formerly settled by the ill-fated colony in Arcadie. The new colony, however, was no sooner established on a permanent basis than war broke out between France and England. In the treaty settling the conflict in 1632, Nova Scotia was returned to France and the settlers moved to Newfoundland. In 1633 Charles I chartered the colony of Newfoundland and decreed in the document that the worship according to the prayer book of the Church of England should be conducted (by ship's officers in the absence of clergymen) each Sunday.

The British Era in Canada: The End of French Dominance

During the rest of the century, both British and French colonization of Canada continued, though the French expansion into the upper reaches of the St. Lawrence and Great Lakes region far outstripped any British efforts. As colonization proceeded, British and French Canadians also found themselves in ongoing conflict as the worldwide interests of their home countries continually overlapped. The intermittent hostile actions periodically disrupted their lives and altered the development of Canada. During the seventeenth century the French were able to continue their expansion in spite of the conflict, but after 1698 the trend of world events began to favor the British in Canada. In that year the Anglican Society for the Promotion of Christian Knowledge began to actively support the Reverend John Jackson, the minister resident in St. John's, Newfoundland (and the only Church of England priest in the territory). Three years later they turned their commitment over to the newly created missionary organization, the Society for the Propagation of the Gospel (SPG), which began to send missionaries into Canada. The British position and that of the Church of England was greatly improved in 1713 when the Treaty of Utrecht ended French-British hostilities for a generation. The British moved to build and consolidate their strength in Canada.

The beginning of the end of French power can be more clearly seen with the reopening of war in 1744. Their successful action against the French stronghold of Louisburg in Nova Scotia, and its subsequent return with the peace treaty signed in 1748, forced the British to further strengthen their position in Nova Scotia. In 1749, they founded the city of Halifax as a military stronghold to counter Louisburg. The establishment of Halifax became a signal event in Canadian religious history, for it was here that the religious patterns that have dominated subsequent Canadian history initially became visible. Immediately after the founding of the community, non-Roman Catholic Christianity in all of its variety appeared in Eastern Canada.

Responding to government action, the SPG promised six ministers and six school masters to the new city, and shortly after their arrival on June 13, 1750, the foundation stone of St. Paul's Church was laid. (Today's St. Paul's congregation worships in the oldest church building in Canada.) And, since King George of

England was also king of Hanover, he encouraged his German subjects to emigrate. German Lutherans became a significant percentage of the early population of the new town and moved to erect St. George's Lutheran Church the following year. A German Reformed congregation also appeared, and St. Matthew's Church (which served both Congregationalists and Presbyterians and was filled by British subjects from Ireland, Scotland, and New England) rounded out the religious life of the community.

The stabilization of life in Halifax was accomplished just as war returned. In 1755 the British moved against Arcadie and removed the French settlers (later to be immortalized in Longfellow's poem "Evangeline"). In 1758 Louisburg fell and the following year Quebec fell. With the capture of Quebec, the British effectively ended French control of Canada, though further action continued into the next year. Following the fall of Quebec, the first Anglican service in the city was conducted in the chapel of the Ursuline Convent by a former Roman Catholic priest, Michel Houdin, chaplain for the British forces.

Under British Rule

The Treaty of Paris of 1763, which made official the accomplishments of the war, also necessitated the altering of relations between the French Canadians and the now hostile government. While guaranteed religious freedom by the treaty, the British government moved to replace the Roman bishop with an Anglican one and to subvert the stability of the Catholic community by sending all the children to Anglican schools. When a new bishop was selected, the government refused to permit his consecration. The property of the Recollects and the Jesuits was confiscated, and both orders, as well as the Sulpicians, were forbidden to receive new members from abroad. This trend was reversed in 1774 when the Act of Quebec granted a high degree of tolerance. The local suspicion toward the Catholic community was appreciably lessened when the French not only refused to support the Americans' attempt to gain them as allies in the American Revolution but actively joined efforts to turn back the attempted invasion by the rebels.

Meanwhile, as soon as the war had ended, additional Protestant groups made their way to Canada. They came not so much to the newly conquered territory but to the Maritime Provinces, where so many Protestant firsts occurred. The first truly Presbyterian church in Canada was founded at Londonderry, Nova Scotia, in 1761 by a group of Irish Presbyterian immigrants. The growth of both Congregationalism and Presbyterianism throughout the decade led in 1770 to a somewhat unique occurrence brought about by the inability of the German Reformed congregation in Halifax to obtain a minister from Pennsylvania. They decided to have one of their own members, Bruin Romcas, ordained. In response to their situation, two Congregationalist ministers joined with two Presbyterian ministers to constitute a presbytery for purposes of the ordination.

Around 1760 the first Baptists arrived to take possession of the land abandoned by the Arcadians. The arrival of the small Baptist community in Nova Scotia coincided with the expansion of the Congregationalists, both groups migrating from New England. Many of the Congregationalists were partial to the New Light position which accepted the theology and practices of the Great Awakening. Many New Lights found themselves more at home with the Baptists than with their more staid Old Light Congregationalists. The issue was forcefully raised by one Henry Alline, a talented New Light preacher who forced a division of the Congregationalists. Alline's followers soon drifted into the Baptist camp and provided the initial substance out of which a significant Canadian Baptist church would emerge.

Finally, around 1775, as Alline's influence was reaching its peak, there appeared from among a group of Cornish immigrants in Nova Scotia the first Methodists. William Black Jr. emerged as their leader and traveled the communities of the province both establishing Methodism and opposing Alline. After the American Revolution, Black looked to the Methodists in the United States for assistance. He traveled to Maryland in 1784 to attend the organizational session of the Methodist Episcopal Church. For a number of years he attached himself to the American church, by which he was eventually ordained, and from which he was assigned assistants to extend his missionary endeavors. Eventually, however, the Canadians grew to resent American leadership and Black turned to the Wesleyan Methodists in England who accepted responsibility for the now growing work.

Of more than passing interest was the development in Nova Scotia of both Methodist and Baptist work among blacks. During the American Revolution, many blacks, most former slaves, were promised freedom and a stake if they remained loyal to Britain. After losing the war, the British transported many of these black people to Nova Scotia, particularly to some towns along the southeastern coast. Among them were both Baptist and Methodist preachers, who led the congregations formed in the several black communities. William Black regularly visited the Methodists. Over the next few years the blacks waited on the British government which never gave the promised stake. Finally, the British abolitionists raised the money to transport them to Freetown, Sierra Leone, where they became the seed from which the Baptist and Methodist churches of that country were to grow.

In the generation after the founding of the city of Halifax, the major religious pattern to be developed in the next centuries of Canadian history was established. The Church of England (or Anglican church) and those Protestant churches introduced into Nova Scotia during the 1750s and 1760s joined the Roman Catholic Church in creating a dominant consensus in Canadian religious life and thus initiated the major factor in the emerging Canadian religious story. *Any account of Canadian religion must center upon the movement of the Roman Catholics, Anglicans, Presbyterians, Congregationalists, Methodists, Lutherans, and Baptists in their efforts to church the sprawling nation, their successes and failures in relating to one another, and their ability to adjust to the growing ethnic and religious pluralism of twentieth century Canadian life.* The focus upon these groups certainly does not deny or diminish the important contributions of the hundreds of other Canadian religious groups. It merely recognizes that due to the simple appeal of these groups to the masses of Canadian citizens, they set the pace to which the others must relate.

At least two other groups found their way into Canada during this initial period and opened their own niches in the religious community. For example, as early as 1762, American Quakers arrived in Nova Scotia from Nantucket, Rhode Island. Though their original effort to settle did not last many years, it heralded a more permanent Quaker thrust into Canadian life a few years later. Second, the missionary-minded Moravian Church, directing its attention farther north, arrived in 1771 when missionary Jens Haven established work at Nain, Labrador. The Moravians pioneered both Christian missionary and educational work among the Eskimo population. While never large, it was the forerunner of other like efforts.

The Settlement of Lower and Upper Canada (Quebec and Ontario)

Even as the settlement and development of the church in Nova Scotia and the Maritime Provinces proceeded, the new British administration had to deal with the 70,000 French-speaking residents living in Canada proper, over which they now had governmental control. The British showed every intent of replacing Roman Catholic authority with the complete establishment of the Church of England. They confiscated the properties of the Jesuits and Recollects and forbade all orders to accept novices. They initiated plans to educate all Catholic children in Anglican schools. Loyal Catholics in both Canada and France registered their opposition in every way possible. Assisted by the unrest in the colonies to the south, a decade of protest met with measurable success. Not needing a second revolt on their hands, the British moved to pacify the French by passing the Quebec Act of 1774. Although it returned some measure of religious toleration to the Catholic community, antagonism continued for many years while the Church of England continued to pursue other means of cutting into Catholic support. However, the Roman Catholic community continued to grow and by 1784 numbered 130,000, aided substantially by the immigration of Catholics from the Highlands of Scotland during this period.

Though the British took control of eastern Canada and the St. Lawrence River Valley in 1763, growth of the Church of England was slow, at least for several decades. Primarily the colonies to the south attracted more immigrants from Europe to their warmer climate. Thus a population favorable to Anglicanism did not arrive in great numbers until after the American Revolution sent waves of Loyalists north to escape rebel rule. Most of these were Loyalist Protestants and many were Anglicans. The growth provided by the Loyalists justified the establishment of the first see for British North America, and Charles Inglis (1734-1816) was consecrated as the first bishop in 1787 with his seat in Halifax, Nova Scotia. Six years later Jacob Mountain (1749-1825) was concentrated as the first bishop of Canada with his seat in Quebec City.

Faced with the continued resistance of the French Canadians to proselytizing actions and to ensure that they remained peaceful and loyal British subjects, the Parliament in England passed the Constitutional Act of 1791. It divided Canada by setting off Lower Canada (Quebec), where most of the French lived, from Upper Canada (Ontario), where most of the British lived. Ontario was just beginning to receive the first waves of Loyalists. Each province had a separate parliament but were administratively under a single governor-in-chief. Important for the churches, the act also set aside land for the support of the clergy of the Church of England and made specific provision for the support of Anglican clergy and the erection of rectories. The provisions of the 1791 act greatly assisted the Anglican church in its spread and development across Canada. Parishes were established, churches and schools erected, and new ministries initiated. While not leading to success in Quebec, the expansion of the church in Ontario was demonstrated by the necessity of placing a bishop in Toronto in 1839. Government support undoubtedly gave the Anglicans immense advantage for several decades, but also seriously hindered the church's long-term development. The bishop's attempt to administer the Canadian church's affairs from England discouraged local development of active lay commitment. Thus when the government withdrew financial support several generations later, the church had to quickly create a new ecclesiastical structure equipped to mobilize member loyalty and voluntary financial support.

Upper Canada, now known as Ontario, was soon to become the most densely populated section of Canada, and religiously the most diverse. The Loyalists brought with them the great variety of religions previously established in the American colonies. And, as Upper Canada was opened, new settlers directly from the British Isles brought with them the profusion of sects that arose as Protestant dissenters proliferated both in number and in number of factions.

Presbyterians were among the most numerous of the new settlers. As early as 1791 Presbyterian congregations started by American ministers appeared on the Niagara Peninsula and by 1833 founded the Niagara Presbytery. Growth was assisted by the movement into the church of many former Congregational-ists. They were soon joined by immigrants directly from Scotland, who established congregational outposts of the Church of Scotland, and the several dissenting groups which had been created through protests over the taking of a loyalty oath and complaints about the church's patronage system. Each group established its own synod, leaving the Presbyterians with the task of reconciling their differences, most of which were nondoctrinal and irrelevant to the Canadian environment.

Methodism, having gotten its Canadian start in Nova Scotia, found a second unrelated beginning in Upper Canada in the settlements of the war veterans in the 1780s. In 1791, Methodist Bishop Francis Asbury directed the Reverend William Losee from New York into Upper Canada where he oversaw the construction of the first Methodist chapel in the region which was built on Paul Huff's farm near the Bay of Quinte. Most influential in the development of the church were the Ryersons, originally an Anglican family who settled near Lake Erie in 1799. The sons all became Methodists, and Egerton Ryerson (1803-1882), in particular, manifested a marked ability as an educator and apologist for the family's new faith, which was a frequent target of Anglican critics. Originally trained for the legal profession, Ryerson joined the ministry in the 1820s and rose to prominence as the first editor of the Methodist periodical *The Christian Guardian.* Among his many accomplishments, he fought to break the hold of the Anglicans on university education, and eventually became the first principal of Victoria College.

The original work of the Methodists in Upper Canada was under the care of the Methodist Episcopal Church which had been organized in the United States in 1784. During the early nineteenth century, Methodists from the several factions in England—the Wesleyans, the Primitive Methodists, the Bible Christians—established competitive work and taunted those who were still attached to the disloyal former colonies. The War of 1812 clearly demonstrated the problem of any church organization attempting to hold a membership across the American-Canadian border. After the war, Canadian Methodists initiated a staged break with their American comrades and merged with the British Wesleyan Connection in 1833.

Because of the very visible support of prominent Congregationalist ministers in the American Revolution, the equally important existence of many Congregationalist Loyalists is frequently overlooked. While most of these Loyalists left the United States by the short and easy sea route from New England to Nova Scotia, by the first decade of the 1800s Congregationalist congregations appeared in Quebec among settlers who simply stepped across the border from Vermont. The period of the greatest Congregationalist expansion was during the ministry of Henry Wilkes, for more than 50 years pastor of a church in Montreal. He established Canadian ties with British Congregationalists and received funds from the London Missionary Society for the establishment of congregations in both Canadas. Wilkes did much to change the negative image of Congregationalists, whose identification with the Revolution had caused many of their number to become Presbyterians.

Lutherans led a migration of people of German background into the Canadas in the late eighteenth century. They were accompanied in their migrations by members of other German groups, with whom they had to compete to gain and even hold members. While many of these settlers were dedicated to keeping the German language alive, the inevitable process of Americanization took its toll. They also lost members to the English-speaking Anglicans and the evangelistically oriented Methodists. The first wave of Lutherans, war veterans, received grants of land in Dundas, Lennox, and Addington counties in the 1780s. A decade later, responding to an invitation for Germans to settle in Ontario, a group of unhappy New York residents managed to receive a grant of 64,000 acres upon which the town of Markham was built.

In spite of the early and continued establishment of new congregations throughout the first half of the nineteenth century, the Lutherans suffered from a dire lack of clergy leadership and a resultant isolation of one organization from another. Only in the middle of the century, as Lutherans in the Synod of Pittsburgh learned of the state of the Ontario Lutherans, were qualified ministers sent to their aid. A Canadian Conference was finally created in 1853.

Baptists entered Upper and Lower Canada in three waves, the first coming into the Niagara area just as the Revolution commenced. Baptists filtered into Quebec in the 1790s and were joined in 1815 by a group migrating from Scotland. Once settled, the Baptists spread quickly. An association formed in 1816 became the precursor of many more. However, the Baptists were very hesitant to unite in larger efforts above the associational level. Inherently independent, they were further divided over the question of the admission of non-Baptists to communion. Only in 1851, when the issue of the disposal of the government's clergy reserves (in which the Baptists by principle never participated) became a significant issue, did the Baptists finally form the Regular Baptist Missionary Convention of Canada West.

Further New Churches

During the period of the initial settlement of Upper Canada, a number of new church groups were introduced into the country. The encouragement of German immigration, for example, brought not only Lutherans but Mennonites and United Brethren as well. The first Mennonites came into the Niagara Peninsula in 1786 and during the next three decades approximately 2,000 migrated into Ontario. Many were a part of the predominantly Lutheran settlement at Markham. Others founded Ebytown, now the city of Kitchener. In 1824 the first congregation of Amish settled in Waterloo County.

Early in the nineteenth century, Germans from two groups heavily influenced by the Methodists—the United Brethren in Christ and the Evangelical Association—began to preach and build churches among the German-speaking settlements. In 1816 John Dreisbach of the Evangelical Association traveled in Ontario, but did not establish any congregations. However, four years earlier, United Brethren had been among German immigrants who moved from Pennsylvania into the Waterloo area. By 1825 a circuit had been established, and the Ontario Conference was created in 1856. Permanent Evangelical Association work had an unusual beginning. Several Waterloo families who had returned to the United States encountered association members in Ohio. Informed of the Canadian situation, ministers began to travel to Chippawa and the Waterloo area, and subsequently the other German-speaking communities. The first German-language Sunday school in Canada was founded by the Evangelical Association ministers at what is now Kitchener.

Before diverting attention from German-speaking groups, it should be noted that among the migrants into Upper Canada after the Revolution were members of the Church of the Brethren, a pacifist group. Their church did not assume any permanent presence, however, as some of the families soon returned to the United States.

The great movement to church the western United States (then the area from the Appalachians to the Mississippi River), usually termed the Second Great Awakening, spawned several new denominations, among them the Christian Church (Disciples of Christ). Very soon after its formation, this highly evangelical group, loosely organized and, except for its few peculiar emphases, doctrinally close to the Baptists, moved into Canada almost immediately. In 1807 Thomas Campbell formed the first rudimentary organization, the Christian Association, and by 1810 work had spread to the Maritime Provinces. A few years later centers could be found at Poplar Hill and Norval in Upper Canada.

During the first half of the nineteenth century, Ontario also became the home of a number of groups which had broken from the mainstream of the Western Christian tradition. Most of these groups were imported from the United States where they had originally emerged. As early as 1832 Unitarians under the leadership of Benjamin Workman began to gather in Montreal. His efforts would become the basis for a strong congregation, but not before he had moved on to Toronto, where in 1845 he formed the first Unitarian congregation in Canada. While the Church of Jesus Christ of Latter-day Saints did not move into Canada in a substantial fashion until late in the century, it did make an important incursion in 1842. Missionaries in Toronto that year converted John Taylor. Taylor left Toronto for Nauvoo, Illinois, and became a close associate of Mormon leader Joseph Smith, Jr. He was one of the two men to survive the attack in which Smith was murdered; he eventually became president of the church. He is remembered today as one of the last leaders of the church to vigorously defend the practice of polygamy.

Jewish Presence in Canada to 1850

Though an occasional Jew will make a brief appearance at odd moments in Canadian history, the French ban on Jewish presence in New France served to keep them out of Canada until the middle of the eighteenth century. In 1749 some Sephardic Jews (of Spanish-Portuguese origin) organized in Halifax and bought a cemetery. However, the small, short-lived community soon disappeared. A decade later the first of a number of prominent Jewish merchants in Upper and Lower Canada appeared in the person of Samuel Jacobs who settled near Montreal. He was joined the next year by Samuel Hart who established his headquarters in Three Rivers. As other Jews arrived, several of whom prospered in their businesses, Congregation Shearith Israel, modeled on the congregation of the same name in New York City, was formed. Though most of the members were of English background (and thus would seem to favor the Ashkenazic worship forms), they adopted the Sephardic ritual of their New York brethren. In 1777 they erected a building. Congregation Shearith Israel seems to be one of two Canadian synagogues in existence for the next several generations. Records also speak of the "Hart synagogue" in Three Rivers. By 1825 there were still fewer than 100 Jews in Canada. This lack of numbers did not keep them from petitioning in 1828 for full recognition as a religious community (which would alow them to keep their own records of births, marriages, and deaths), which was granted the next year. Then in 1832 Canadian Jews were granted their equal rights as British subjects (which removed any barriers to their holding public office or serving as officers in the military), a privilege not granted British Jews until 1858.

Though still small in comparison to the total population, the Jewish population in Upper Canada grew perceptively during the middle nineteenth century. A Jewish community emerged in Toronto in the 1840s. Following a general pattern in new Jewish communities, first, in 1849 a cemetery was purchased, and then a congregation, the Sons of Israel, was organized in 1856. In 1859 a second congregation, following the Ashkenazic ritual, was opened in Montreal. By 1860 there were approximately 1,200 Jews in Canada.

The Canadian Era Begins: Mid-Century Changes

During the middle of the nineteenth century, the major issue affecting all of the Christian churches in Canada was the changing relationship between the Canadian government and the Anglican church. By the action of the British government in the decades after the fall of Quebec, the Church of England in Canada became the established church of Canada. By law and with the backing of public funds, the worship and education of the people in the tradition of the Church of England was to be developed, encouraged, and maintained. Ministers were directly responsible to the Lord Bishop of London. In 1787 the Crown appointed the first bishop for British North America, and the governors of Nova Scotia and Quebec were given specific orders to assist him in the exercise of his jurisdictional duties. The church, in spite of local episcopal authority, remained in a missionary situation and developed no synodical structures.

In 1791, integral to the action which separated the two Canadas (Upper and Lower), the government set aside lands specifically for the support of the clergy and the church. As the church expanded, the government provided revenue to create new dioceses and appoint bishops. Decade by decade, however, forces grew in favor of unifying the separated Canadian provinces into a single governmental entity under a form of home rule which would be largely autonomous of England without breaking completely with the Empire. The growing autonomy in the Canadian government forced significant shifts in the relations between the Anglican church in Canada, the Church of England, and the governments. The crux of the changes centered upon the disposition of the clergy reserves.

Vocal opposition to the 1791 provisions for clergy land grants had arisen from the beginning. Secular interests demanded the use of the revenues from the lands (which consisted of some 2.5 million acres) for other purposes, such as nonsectarian public education. The churches joined the battle from their varying perspectives. Some opposed the unfair advantage given the Anglicans (especially the Presbyterians who wanted their share in light of their establishment in Scotland), while some, such as the Canadian branch of the Free Church of Scotland, opposed government support of churches on principle. The Anglicans were heavily dependent on these lands, which directly supplemented the financial support from the church in England and the Society for the Propagation of the Gospel, the foreign missionary structure of the Church of England. The loss to the church would be significant. By mid-century, however, it was a foregone conclusion that the loss would occur, and in 1853 all of the clergy land reserves were secularized. The drawn-out battle over the clergy reserves had also created an unwanted side effect for the Anglicans. By focusing the shared opposition to the Anglican's favored-child status, the issue united the Protestant churches against the Church of England in Canada.

The financial concerns thrust a second issue upon the Canadian Anglicans: the development of self-government. Because of its status as a missionary arm of the Church of England, it had not been free to develop internally. Each diocese worked as a separate unit directly responsible to authorities in England. In 1851, as the land reserves issue was reaching a climax, five of the seven Canadian bishops met and called for the creation of a province of Canada under a metropolitan (archbishop) and the creation of diocesan synods that would include lay participation. These new structures would facilitate the transformation of the church into a voluntary association which relied upon its own membership for its major financial support. The first synod, that of the Diocese of Toronto, met in 1857. Four years later the bishop of Montreal was appointed metropolitan of the Canadian province and an initial provincial synod for what was to be termed the Church of England in Canada held. The province did not include Manitoba and the territories to the west, which developed as a separate province, as did British Columbia. Eventually, in 1893 the several provinces were united into an autonomous General Synod under a primate of all Canada. Thus by the end of the century the Anglicans in Canada had emerged as another independent member of the developing worldwide Anglican communion.

Religion Moves into the Canadian West: Where is Rupert's Land?

Chartered in 1670, the Hudson Bay Company had been given exclusive rights to the land north and west of Ontario. During the last half of the nineteenth century their monopoly collided with the needs of Canada for expanded territory. Land was becoming scarce, immigration was increasing, and population was exploding. At the same time a new sense of Canadian nationalism emerged with some degree of support from the British homeland. The completion of the transcontinental railroad across the United States (1869) merely highlighted the advantages of such a railroad across Canada.

Thus in 1867, when the four Canadian provinces (Ontario, Quebec, Newfoundland, and the Maritime) united in a confederation, they immediately looked west. In 1870 the confederation took in Rupert's land, today known as Manitoba, and in 1871, on the condition that a transcontinental railroad be built, it added British Columbia. Railroad construction began soon afterward, and the line to Winnipeg was finished in 1881. It took only four more years to complete the track to the Pacific Coast. Though Alberta and Saskatchewan would not become provinces until 1905, the completion of the railroad effectively opened them to massive immigration. The older churches, which had already established initial centers, quickly moved in with the new immigrants, and just as importantly, numerous new religious groups found a home in the newly opened territory.

In 1812 Thomas Douglas, the fifth Earl of Selkirk (1771-1820), with the cooperation of the Hudson Bay Company, founded Kildonan, a community of Scottish immigrants, on the Red River near present-day Winnipeg. In order to protect the settlers from the rival North West Company, he hired some German mercenaries. Concerned for the religious life of the soldiers, many of whom were Roman Catholic, he requested a priest, and in 1818 the Diocese of Quebec sent Father Joseph Norbert Abbe Provencher. Besides serving the immediate community, he began to expand work to neighboring sites and to Indian and Eskimo missions. He soon received the aid of the Oblates of Mary, who took special responsibility for the missionary work. The growth of the work initiated by Provencher led in 1844 to his being named Vicar Apostolic, and in 1847 he became the first bishop of St. Boniface (Manitoba). During the first half of the nineteenth century,

Provencher provided the foundation for Roman Catholic expansion in western Canada through the conversion of the native population, the immigration of Catholics from around the world, and the recruitment of members from among the new (but previously non-Catholic) settlers.

Anglican work in the West was initiated by the Reverend John West, who served at Kildonan in the absence of a Presbyterian minister which the colonists really wanted. With Anglican funds he built two schools, one for the colonists' children and one for the Indians. His missionary endeavors produced one priest, Henry Budd, from the Indian parishioners. His efforts were bolstered in 1822 when the Church Missionary Society decided to take responsiblity for Indian missions and began to send clergymen from England. By 1849, two years after the naming of a Roman Catholic bishop, David Anderson was consecrated the first Anglican bishop of Rupert's Land. In 1865 Robert Machray became bishop of Rupert's Land, a post he held for the rest of the century. During this period, operating independently of the province (limited to the dioceses to the east until the creation of the General Synod in 1893), he developed Rupert's Land into a separate province that included nine dioceses between Manitoba and the Rocky Mountains.

The Other Churches Come to Manitoba

The Methodists' movement into the Northwest followed a series of unusual events in England. The Canadian Methodist preacher Egerton Ryerson had an Indian friend, Peter Jones, who traveled to England. His speeches before a variety of Methodist audiences excited them over the possibilities of missionary work among the Indians of Upper Canada. Learning of Jones' work, Hudson Bay company officials, possibly looking for a way to gain some social control (through religion) over the Indians, invited the Methodists into their territory. To the company, Jones seemed a living demonstration that the Methodists could deal with the native population. Within a few years the Wesleyan Methodist Connection, by-passing the Canadian Methodists, sent James Evans, Thomas Hurlburt, and Peter Jacobs to establish work on Manitoulin Island. Evans soon broke with the Hudson Bay Company and established Norway House in northern Manitoba. Among his major contributions was the development of a syllabic system for printing the Cree Indian language, a system that was easliy adapted to other languages. Evans career overlapped that of Robert Rundel, who moved among the tribes farther west from his base in Edmonton, Alberta.

The Wesleyans supported the missions around Norway House and Edmonton for several decades but in 1853 turned the work over to the Canadian Methodists. The following year John Ryerson made a trip through the territory and in his report made note that he uncovered 18 Protestant missionaries of which 13 were Anglican, four Methodist, and one Presbyterian.

That one Presbyterian was John Black, a recent graduate of Knox College (Toronto), who had settled in Kildonan to serve the Scots who had waited 20 years for a Presbyterian minister. Black stayed in Kildonan for more than 30 years. The Presbyterian work expanded in the 1860s through James Nisbet, who went out from Kildonan to found the town of Prince Albert, Saskatchewan, and initiate Presbyterian work in that future province.

By mid-century settlers began to trickle into western Canada in increasing numbers, and the other churches came soon to provide their spiritual nurture. In 1873 the first Baptist missionary arrived in Winnipeg, and throughout the decade churches were started in Saskatchewan and Alberta. The Baptists turned their attention to the various non-English-speaking immigrants who began to pour into the area and soon raised up a number of ethnic churches. Early churches tended to be located along the railroad route which brought the immigrants to their new homes.

Across the Rockies: Even Farther West

British Columbia developed somewhat independently of the steady western movement of Canadian life. In like measure, the stream of both Roman Catholic and Anglican development flowed along an independent course only to be merged at the end of the nineteenth century. In British Columbia two paths to the farthest reaches of Canada converged. Many of the earliest settlers trekked northward from California along the Pacific Coast. Then in 1792 Alexander MacKenzie made it over the mountains to the coast and initiated the rich fur trade which was started by the North West Company in 1806. The West Coast remained company territory (the North West Company and then after 1821 Hudson Bay Company) until British Columbia joined the confederation in 1871. Also, during much of this time (until the settlement of the boundary between Canada and the United States in 1846), the entire Pacific Coast north of California was disputed territory. As a result, the progress of the Roman Catholic missionary work begun in 1838 in the area was delayed almost a decade when the bishop of Quebec, who had initiated work in the Oregon Territory, questioned his prerogative in sponsoring the mission. The territory seemed to also belong to the bishop of St. Louis, in the United States.

That Oregon Mission included not only Oregon and Washington, but Fort Vancouver and all of British Columbia. Soon after their arrival, the first priests, Francis Norbet Blanchet and Modeste Demers, began to envision the possibilities of bringing the Indian population into the church. They saw a bright future if only a bishop, with authority to recruit a cadre of priests and religious workers, could be sent to the Northwest. Within a year they began to request a bishop. In 1843 Rome responded by appointing Blanchet as vicar apostolic for the territory. Blanchet, somewhat overwhelmed, requested that the vast territory under his authority be further divided. Then, immediately after the border between the United States and Canada was established by treaty in 1846, the holy see named Blanchet bishop of Oregon and the same day (July 24) appointed him archbishop of a new province of Oregon City. Four day later his brother, Augustine Magloire Blanchet, was named bishop of Walla Walla (Washington), and the next year Modeste Demers became bishop of Vancouver, part of the Oregon City province.

From 1847 the work prospered for several years, only to be ravaged by the California gold rush. By 1855 only seven priests were left in the province, the rest having followed their flocks south. Three years later, the diocese's fortunes reversed with the discovery of gold on the Fraser River in British Columbia, and the town of New Westminster emerged quickly as a new population center. With the completion of the railroad in the 1880s the number of residents of British Columbia steadily increased and the work of the church stabilized into a pattern of growth that has followed the population trends.

The Church of England in Canada was much slower to respond to the needs on the Canadian Pacific Coast than was the Roman Catholic Church. In part it was distracted by its mid-century problems of building a new financial base and redefining itself independently of the bishops in England. Also, being a national church, the settlement of the boundary dispute with the United States had much more severe implications for the extension of the ministry.

Following the 1846 treaty, the Hudson Bay Company abandoned its major post on the Columbia River and in 1849 founded Fort Victoria on Vancouver Island. An Anglican priest, R. J. Staines, was appointed priest and schoolmaster of the new settlement. He worked alone for a decade, there finally being the addition of a lay teacher in 1857 and a missionary to the Indians in 1858. Then in the wake of the discovery of gold and the influx of thousands into the area, an urgent request for assistance in British Columbia fell into the hands of a wealthy and devout heiress in London. She endowed a bishopric for British Coumbia, and in 1859 the Reverend George Hills was consecrated for the new diocese. Hills recruited men and raised funds before his arrival in Victoria in 1860. With this initial financial backing from the Church of England, he was able to organize the work without financial support from the Canadian government, and he put it on a firm and stable foundation from the beginning. The new Dioceses of New Westminster (at the mouth of the Fraser River) and Caledonia (centered on the headwaters of the Fraser) created in 1879, become the backbone of the province of British Columbia in the next century.

The initiation of Congregationalist work in British Columbia grew out of concern in Great Britain for slaves who had escaped their life in the United States and found their way to the Vancouver area. In 1859 the Colonial Missionary Society sent a minister to Victoria both to create a church and serve the black residents. His interracial efforts met strong opposition from the larger community of white residents and the work collapsed when the Society withdrew the missionary. A decade later a second missionary was sent, and he organized two congregations, one each in 1879 and 1881. But little progress could be cited for Congregationalism in western Canada as a whole. It had trouble competing with the more aggressive Presbyterians and Methodists.

The other Protestant churches lagged behind in their movement to the coast. A Presbyterian minister arrived at Fort Camosun on Vancouver Island in 1861. Beginning in the courthouse, he established what was the only

Presbyterian congregation west of Kildonan. A Baptist, John Morton, arrived in 1862 to homestead some 600 acres of what is now downtown Vancouver. A generation later, enough Baptist churches had been formed to justify the formation of the Baptist Convention of British Columbia in 1897.

With the formation of the Roman Catholic and Anglican dioceses in western Canada and the movement of the older churches into the territory especially after the completion of the railroad, the initial churching of Canada could be said to have been completed. All of the churches were to continue to grow and spread as the population grew, but that growth consisted of the spreading of the already dominant structure. In the process of that further growth, a number of issues were to come to the fore to which the churches would have to give their time and energy. As their sister churches south of the border, all of the Canadian churches were forced to respond to those same new ideas and realities that emerged so forcefully as factors of late nineteenth century life—biblical criticism, the biological and geological sciences, urbanization, and historical conscious-ness—out of which was to grow an embittered phase of the Fundamentalist-Modernist controversy. By the end of the century, the Protestants were focused upon the possibilities of building a united church from the multitude of sectarian and regional church bodies.

Other Groups in Western Canada

Dating largely from the opening of the West by the railroad, Canada became home to a wide variety of ethnic groups and an even wider variety of new (at least for Canada) religions. Among the first new groups to arrive in the West, Mennonites from Russia settled along the Red River south of Winnipeg in 1874. A second wave after World War II settled on farms in Alberta, Saskatchewan, and Manitoba. In America these Mennonites split into several factions, the largest being the General Conference Mennonite Church.

After the Mennonites, other churches also representative of the European Free Church tradition have found western Canada a suitable place for settlement. Possibly the most controversial of these groups is the Doukhobors, which began to arrive in 1899. Controversy followed their attempts to keep their religious practices intact in the face of Canadian laws (such as those dictating educational standards). One group has been accused of violent (at least against property) protest, and some fame has come to the groups for the practice of shedding their clothes in public situations as a means of additional protest.

Following their inability to reach a suitable accord with the United States government after its entry into the war, the pacifist, communally organized Hutterite Brethren systematically sold their American farms and relocated in western Canada. Though many later returned to the United States, the Hutterites retain a strong Canadian presence.

Eastern Europeans also began to move into the West prior to the turn of the century and continued after immigration restrictions were lifted in the United States in 1924. For example, more than 8,000 Romanians, mostly farmers, came to Alberta, Saskatchewan, and Manitoba prior to World War I. The first church, St. Nicholas, was built in Regina, Saskatchewan, in 1902. Canadian Ukrainians, now headquartered in Winnipeg, were present in numbers when the struggle for Ukrainian independence led them to organize separately from the Russian Orthodox Church. The first congregation was formed in Saskatoon, Saskatchewan.

Scandinavian ministers came into Manitoba as early as the 1870s to begin work among the Swedes. An Evangelical Covenant Church was organized at Winnipeg in 1904, about which time ministers of the Evangelical Free Church arrived to initiate work among the Norwegians and Danes. The first Evangelical Free Church was organized in 1913.

Mormons, members of the Church of Jesus Christ of Latter-day Saints, also made their entry into Canada during this period. In 1887 a group of 41 led by Charles Ora Card migrated north from Salt Lake City to what is today the province of Alberta. At that time Canada had no laws against polygamy. They founded the town of Cardston, about 40 miles from Lethbridge, where a temple was built and from which the church has spread throughout Canada. At a later date, members of the Reorganized Church of Jesus Christ of Latter-day Saints would also begin to colonize Canada.

As with the United States, Asian immigration into Canada commenced on the West Coast following the gold rush. Of the Chinese who flocked to the gold fields, many stayed to introduce Buddhism to Canada. By the end of the nineteenth century, Indians, primarily Punjabis, migrated to British Columbia and brought their Sikh faith with them. The construction of the first house of worship, a *Gurdwara,* was initiated in 1906 in Vancouver.

These churches mentioned represent only a few of the many ethnic church groups which were established in western Canada, only to be joined by new indigenous churches which split from the older church bodies. Together they have given western Canada the same pluralistic flavor so evident in the large urban centers in the eastern half of the nation.

A New Consciousness for a New Century: The Growth of Modernism and Fundamentalism

Modernism, a theological perspective which accepted and even celebrated the changing world of the late nineteenth and early twentieth century, blossomed in Canada as it did throughout the West. Responding to the scholarly community, the Modernists embraced the new "scientific" approach to history (as exemplified in critical methodologies) and society (through the new discipline of sociology), and the radical new assertions of biology and geology. British scholars exposed Canadian churchmen to the historical-critical methods of Bible study as early as 1860 through the publication of the book *Essays and Reviews,* which attempted to inform the British public about the new German scientific critique of Scripture. In Canada the book initiated a continuing debate over the authority of the Bible, the integrity of the biblical text, and the nature of miracles, that led to the adoption of both historical and textual criticism in Bible classes in most Canadian seminaries. In like measure, Charles Darwin's *Origin of the Species* (1859) and *The Descent of Man* (1871) provoked extended and heated debate over the supernatural origins of humanity, a debate which still divides. The issues raised by Darwin were given added weight by the new discoveries in geological sciences which called for pushing back the age of the Earth by hundreds of thousands of years. Modernists accepted the new discoveries and developed a theology which placed humanity within the unfolding process of evolution.

Canadians also responded to the social displacements of urbanization, especially as Toronto and Montreal grew with the late nineteenth century influx. By the 1890s Canadian voices had arisen to address the social implications of Christianity and build new urban ministries. In 1890, for example, Presbyterian D. J. McDonnell opened mission houses near the slums in Toronto and began night classes for the education of working women. Closely tied to the social gospel was a new belief in the goodness and perfectiblity of humans that saw the race progressing into the kingdom of God. Given a new view of their long history on Earth, thinkers began to project a future in almost utopian terms.

Among the leading Canadian Modernists was Presbyterian George Monro Grant (1835-1902), author of the best selling book *Ocean to Ocean,* an optimistic look at the Canadian future first published in 1873. First at Dalhousie University and then at Queen's Theological College he championed the Modernist cause, demanding that all religious teaching become intellectually respectable. He was joined by Professors John Watson and George Paxton Young.

The progress of Modernist thought was not always smooth. Methodist George Workman was forced to resign his post at Victoria University in 1899 after his public denial of the "dictation theory" of biblical inspiration, a frequent step in the acceptance of biblical critical methodology. Finding a post at another school, he was again forced out in 1907. D. J. McDonnell, pastor of St. Andrew's Church in Toronto, though acquitted, was forced to stand trial by the General Assembly of the Canadian Presbyterian Church for a comment denying the doctrine of everlasting hell.

Possibly the most disturbed by the growth of the new theological perspectives were the Baptists. Shortly after the turn of the century charges were leveled at McMaster University, the Baptist's university in Toronto, with the primary target being one professor, H. T. Matthews. Matthews was accused of attacking the integrity of the Book of Genesis. Arising to lead the attack on McMaster was Thomas T. Shields, the pastor of Jarvis Avenue Baptist Church in Toronto, soon to become an internationally known spokesperson for Fundamentalism, the conservative theological perspective which based its perspective on a defense of the unique Divine authority of the Bible and the traditional Christian affirmations (the fundamentals). Fundamentalists vigorously fought the growing acceptance of critical methods of Bible study, the social gospel, and evolution. After an examination, the Baptist Convention of Ontario and Quebec exonerated

Matthews, which led Shields and his supporters to break with the conventions. Several new Baptist groups emerged from that break.

By World War II the issues raised by the controversy had been settled in the Modernists favor, and the majority of the churches had gone on to other matters. In Canada, Fundamentalism remained strong only in a few smaller conservative churches.

The Move to Unify

At the same time that Modernism grew within the larger churches, a drive to unite the scattered sects of Protestantism gathered strength. While there had been no schisms among Canadian Protestants such as those that rented the churches in the United States at the time of the Civil War, the churches in the late nineteenth century existed in a disunited state because of sectional divisions over the vast Canadian territory, as well as the establishment of many similar but organizationally separate churches by each new wave of immigrants. Efforts to unify led to the formation of the United Church of Canada in 1925 and the Canadian Council of Churches in 1944.

The work of uniting the churches began as individual denominations found similar groups of like mind and began a process of denominational family cooperation. For example, in the early nineteenth century the Methodists searched out means to bring together the nonepiscopal British Wesleyans with those who were episcopally led. The process of merger culminated in 1864 when the Canadian branches of all the various British Methodists merged into a single Methodist body for the country. The even larger number of Presbyterian bodies followed a similar pattern between 1817 and 1879. The Congregationalists had two major unions in 1906 and 1907.

While the Methodists, Presbyterians, and Congregationalists were merging their denominational families, as early as the 1860s serious proposals for unions across denominational lines were entertained by Methodists and Presbyterians. Similar proposals were considered in the 1870s by Congregationalists and Presbyterians, and a decade later by Anglicans with all three. However, nothing came of these discussions prior to the turn of the century.

Then in 1902, an idea originally suggested by George M. Grant in 1874 of a united "Church of Canada," began to bear fruit. That year the Methodist general conference issued an overture to its sister denominations to appoint committees to plan for union. The overture was received favorably by the Presbyterians and Congregationalists at their gatherings during the next two years, and the three initiated work on a "basis of union" document in December 1904. After four years an agreement was reached and passed on to the three churches. Main topics of discussion included doctrine (which led the Baptists to decline participation) and polity (over which the Anglicans ultimately withdrew). A variety of names were proposed and discussed. Once submitted to the denominations, a lengthy struggle to gain commitment to the plan and the proper enabling legislation to have the plan adopted and implemented ensued. Finally, in 1925 the Methodist, Presbyterian, and Congregationalist churches merged to form the United Church of Canada, which immediately assumed its place as the third major church body in the country.

By the time of the formation of the United Church of Canada, the spirit of Christian cooperation and unity, at least on the councilor level, was growing. In the United States the Federal Council of Christian Churches was fruitfully functioning. On the international level the conferences which were to lead to the formation of the World Council of Churches were underway. The idea of a council to facilitate communication, prevent duplication of efforts, coordinate ministries, and provide fellowship seemed both useful and a practical step toward unity. Thus in 1944 12 denominations came together to form the Canadian Council of Churches. It included both Protestant and Eastern Orthodox bodies. Over the years the Lutherans, one of the few major Christian bodies not among the charter members, joined, while the Baptist Federation of Canada withdrew (even though its major component, the Baptist Convention of Ontario and Quebec, immediately joined). In more recent years the Canadian Conference of (Roman) Catholic Bishops has become an associate member. The council now includes the overwhelming majority of Canadian Christians in its member organizations.

Judaism from 1850 to the Present

Though always a small minority, the Jewish community of Canada spread as the country grew. They were among the first settlers in the west. A synagogue appeared in Victoria, British Columbia, in the 1860s. The first informal congregational service was held in Winnipeg in 1882 and Congregation Beth El organized two years later. A congregation is noted in Regina, Saskatchewan, in 1913.

Beginning in the late nineteenth century, Jews migrated to Canada in large numbers. More than 80,000 arrived between 1900 and the beginning of World War I. Most of the new arrivals were Orthodox, and even though Reform Judaism had appeared among Canadians quite early, it never gained the support it had in the United States. During the period between the wars, the religious segment of the community did align itself with the three main Jewish groups, Conservative, Reform, and Orthodox, with both Sephardic and Ashkenazic Orthodox congregations in existence. Most of the congregations also aligned with the one of the several congregational associations headquartered in New York City.

Immediately after World War II, Canadian Jewry experienced a second major wave of immigration, as survivors of the war and the Holocaust poured into the country. During the last generation, the community has grown from 200,000 to approximately 300,000. Again, the new arrivals tended to be Orthodox, and included members of several Hassidic groups (such as the Lubavitchers) and have kept the community predominantly Orthodox, though the growth of Conservative congregations has been noticeable and a few Reconstruction synagogues have appeared.

The Other Religions

Throughout Canada since the middle of the nineteenth century, the larger church bodies have been faced with the organizational splintering of Christendom. While finding some unity in the formation of the United Church of Canada and the Canadian Council of Churches described above, their efforts have always been countered by the schisms in Canadian church bodies. For example, a large minority of the Presbyterian Church refused to join the United Church of Canada, and remains today as a separate organization though a member of the Canadian Council of Churches. Added to the schisms are the arrival of new churches from Europe and, most importantly, the constant importation of the hundreds of sectarian bodies which have formed in the United States and see Canada as a mission field.

During the 1850s, for example, Spiritualism, which had started in New York, had spread across Canada from Ontario to the Maritimes, and letters attesting to the power of the spiritualistic phenomena regularly filled the pages of the early spiritualist periodicals. During the twentieth century, Canadians formed several national associations.

The holiness movement came to Canada in the 1800s, and in Canada it produced some new churches, the most prominent being that led by Ralph Cecil Horner (1854-1921), a former Methodist. He organized and led the Holiness Movement Church, but when asked to retire as its bishop in 1919, he left to found the Standard Church of America.

Pentecostalism spread to Canada quickly from the 1906 revival on Azusa Street in Los Angeles. Canadians then were to initiate two of the important teachings in Pentecostalism which were to lead to the development of two new subgroupings producing a score of new denominational organizations. Possibly the first Canadian Pentecostal was R. E. McAleister. At a camp meeting in Los Angeles in 1913, he preached on water baptism in the name of "Jesus only," thus initiating what was to become the Apostolic or non-Trinitarian Pentecostalism. Then in 1948 in western Canada, at an independent Bible school, the Sharon Orphanage and School at North Battleford, Saskatchewan, a pentecostal revival began and swept across North America. The Latter Rain Revival brought a new emphasis on prophecy and the laying-on-of-hands to Pentecostalism and, though considering itself a nondenominational movement, it produced more than 20 new denominations in North America.

The Church of Christ, Scientist came to Canada during the life of its founder, Mary Baker Eddy, and in 1906-1907 became the location of two important court cases involving Christian Scientists. In both cases, parents who had used Christian Science treatment in the place of standard medical assistance were convicted of manslaughter in the deaths of their children.

While a growing number of Christian sects found their way to Canada prior to World War II, in more recent decades, Canada has faced the same rapid proliferation of new and diverse groups, especially in its major cities. Many of these have also been imported from the United States, but many have also come directly from Asia and the Middle East (usually by way of Europe or Australia). For example, the Baha'i Faith was brought to Canada in 1903 when Canadian architect William Sutherland Maxwell married an American. However, it was not until 1949 that the work grew to a point that it could be set apart under its own National Spiritual Assembly. Included among the recently arrived are not only teachers seeking to convert Canadians, but also a new wave of Asian immigrants who are building Buddhist and Hindu temples. Besides the more well known, such as the Unification Church and the International Society for Krishna Consciousness, Canada is the headquarters of the Zen Lotus Society, Yasodhara Ashram Society, the Sivananda Vedanta Yoga Centers, and the Kabalarian Philosophy.

Thus Canada is currently at one with the whole of Western society. While showing no sign of giving up Christianity, which shows every sign of continuing as the faith of the majority of Canadians in the foreseeable future, Canada is now home to an ever-increasing number of the world's faiths which are arising to take their place in building the future of the nation.

Sources of Material on Canadian Religious History

Carrington, Philip. *The Anglican Church in Canada*. Toronto: Collins, 1963. 320 pp.

Centennial of Canadian Methodism. Toronto: William Briggs, 1891. 339 pp.

Cronmiller, Carl R. *A History of the Lutheran Church in Canada*. Toronto: Evangelical Lutheran Synod of Canada, 1961. 288 pp.

Epp, Frank H. *Mennonites in Canada, 1920-1940*. Toronto: Macmillan of Canada, 1982. 640 pp.

Grant, John Webster. *The Canadian Experience of Church Union*. Richmond, VA: John Knox Press, 1967. 106 pp.
_____. *The Church in the Canadian Era*. Toronto: Mc-Graw-Hill Ryerson, 1972. 241 pp.

Guenter, Jacob G. *Men of Steel*. Saskatoon, SK: The Author, 1981. 261 pp.

Kilbourn, William. *Religion in Canada*. Toronto: McClelland and Stewart, 1868. 128 pp.

Masters, Donald C. *A Short History of Canada*. Princeton, NJ: Van Nostrand Company, 1958. 191 pp.

McInnis, Edgar. *Canada, A Political and Social History*. Toronto: Rinehart & Company, 1959. 619 pp.

Moir, John S. *The Church in the British Era*. Toronto: McGraw-Hill Ryerson, 1972. 230 pp.

Quiring, Walter, and Helen Bartel. *Mennonites in Canada, a Pictorial Review*. Altona, MB: D. W. Friesen & Sons, 1961. 208 pp.

Rosenberg, Stuart E. *The Jewish Community in Canada*. Toronto: McClelland and Stewart, 1970. 231 pp.

Sanderson, J. E. *The First Century of Methodism in Canada*. Toronto: William Briggs, 1908-10. 2 Vols.

Silcox, Claris Edwin. *Church Union in Canada*. New York: Institute of Social and Religious Research, 1933. 493 pp.

Walker, J. U. *History of Wesleyan Methodism in Halifax*. Halifax: Hartley and Walker, 1834. 279 pp.

Wilson, Douglas J. *The Church Grows in Canada*. Toronto: Canadian Council of Churches, 1966. 224 pp.

Part 1

Essay Chapters

Chapter 1

Western Liturgical Family

Directory listings for the groups belonging to the Western Liturgical Family
may be found in the section beginning on page 61.

A strong liturgical life is the distinguishing feature of the oldest Christian churches that have continued to our day. These churches have other distinguishing characteristics, true—creeds, orders, sacraments, language, and culture. Liturgy, however, is the place where these other characteristics find their expression. So it seems appropriate to group these churches together as the liturgical family.

In this family are the many church bodies of four major traditions: the Eastern Orthodox tradition, the non-Chalcedonian Orthodox tradition, the Western Roman tradition, and the Anglican tradition.

Most of the liturgical churches celebrate seven sacraments: baptism, the eucharist, holy orders, unction, marriage, confirmation, and penance. Few topics exist among Christians on which there is such a variety of thinking as on the sacraments. Some nonliturgical groups, such as the Methodists, celebrate only two sacraments—baptism and holy communion—while other nonliturgical groups, such as the Baptists, have no sacraments. Some churches consider baptism and holy communion not sacraments but ordinances, and add a third ordinance, footwashing. A fully developed sacramental system, however, characterizes the members of the liturgical family.

Other characteristics of the liturgical churches are allegiance to creeds and belief in Apostolic succession. Each creed, a statement of doctrines, originated in the early centuries of the church or is a variation on an early creed. Each church professes that it inherits an unbroken line of authority from the Apostles who founded the Christian church at Pentecost.

Speaking of this unbroken line, Bishop Sion Manoogian says of the Armenian church, "The Armenian Church was founded by two of the Apostles of Our Lord, St. Thaddeus and St. Bartholomew, in the first century. This is the reason for its sometimes being called the Armenian Apostolic Church" (Sion Manoogian, *The Armenian Church* n.p., n.d. 2, 15). Dean Timothy Andrews says of the Greek Orthodox Church, "It is the church founded by Christ, received its mission on Pentecost, propagated throughout the world by the Holy Apostles" (Timothy Andrews, *What Is the Orthodox Church?* [pamphlet, 1964], 7). The Church of the East traces its conversion, establishment, and Apostolic

succession to the 70 disciples (Luke 10:1) and the 12 Apostles, but more particularly to Mar Shimun Koopa (St. Simon Peter), Mar Tooma (St. Thomas), Mar Addai (St. Thaddeus), Mar Mari (St. Mari, one of the 70 disciples), and Mar Bar Thulmay (St. Bartholomew). The Roman Catholic Church traces its origins to St. Peter, the first bishop of Rome.

People hold conflicting views concerning the relationship of the four traditions of the liturgical family to the Apostles and to the first century church. Most agree, however, that the peculiar traits of the traditions evolved as Christianity spread to various cultures and as church councils formulated doctrines. The Conciliar Era, a time of debate and discussion, lasted from 325 A.D. to 787 A.D. Seven councils were held during that time.

The First Ecumenical Council was called in 325 A.D. at Nicea, near Constantinople. Its focus was the teaching of Arius about the nature of Christ. Arius said the Son is not of the same substance as the Father but was created as an agent for creating the world. The council condemned Arius and declared his teaching heretical. This action caused an immediate defection in the church in Egypt. In various places Arian Christians remained in some force for a number of years, especially during a continuing Arian controversy in the fourth century. The barbarians who sacked Rome in 401 A.D. were Arians, and since the sixth century a beautiful Arian baptistry has stood near the Orthodox one in Ravenna, Italy.

The Second Council met at Constantinople in 381 A.D. and continued the development of the doctrine of the Trinity. It said the Father, Son, and Holy Spirit are coeternal and consubstantial.

The Third Council met at Ephesus in 431 A.D. This council met to discuss the opinions of Nestorius, who had been made patriarch of Constantinople in 428 A.D. Nestorius believed that Christ was not the Son of God, but that God was living in Christ. The two natures, said Nestorius, were separable. The debate centered upon the use of the phrase "Theotokos" ("Mother of God"). The Nestorians rejected the term, saying that Mary bore Christ, not God. The council ruled against Nestorius and deposed him as patriarch. A Nestorian

1

Council was organized a few days later and deposed its opposition. Although Nestorius was imprisoned and eventually banished to Egypt, his followers formed a strong church in Syria and Persia. Later missionary activity pushed the Nestorian church into India and China. It is represented today by the Church of the East, part of the non-Chalcedonian Orthodox tradition.

The Fourth Council met at Chalcedon in 451 A.D. It drafted what came to be known as the Chalcedonian Creed:

"Therefore, following the holy Fathers we all with one accord teach men to acknowledge one and the same Son, our Lord Jesus Christ, at once complete in Godhead and complete in manhood, truly God and truly man, consisting also of a reasonable soul and body; of one substance with the Father as regards his Godhead, and at the same time of one substance with us as regards his manhood; like us in all respects, apart from sin; as regards his Godhead, begotten of the Father before the ages, but yet as regards his manhood begotten, for us men and for our salvation, of Mary the Virgin, the God-bearer; one and the same Christ, Son, Lord, Only-begotten, recognized IN TWO NATURES, WITHOUT CONFUSION, WITHOUT CHANGE, WITHOUT DIVISION, WITHOUT SEPARATION; the distinction of natures being in no way annulled by the union, but rather the characteristics of each nature being preserved and coming together to form one person and subsistence, not as parted or separated into two persons, but one and the same Son and Only-begotten God the Word, Lord Jesus Christ; even as the prophets from earliest times spoke of him, and our Lord Jesus Christ himself taught us, and the creed of the Fathers has handed down to us."

This creed is considered the "orthodox" solution to the Christological problems of the early church by the Roman Catholic, Greek Orthodox, and most Protestant churches. However, some Eastern and Egyptian Christians rejected the creed's emphasis on the two natures of Christ. The non-Chalcedonian Orthodox tradition is one of the four main traditions of the liturgical family. Many non-Chalcedonians were called Monophysites because they felt the human and divine in Christ constituted only one nature. Today the Armenian church and the Coptic church represent part of the non-Chalcedonian Orthodox tradition.

The first four councils—at Nicea, Constantinople, Ephesus, and Chalcedon—served to isolate the non-Chalcedonian Orthodox tradition from the Eastern Orthodox and Western Roman traditions. The Eastern Orthodox tradition developed centers of authority in Antioch, Alexandria, and Constantinople. The Western branch's center of authority was in Rome. This East-West division was more a cultural than a doctrinal separation. The churches allowed culture and politics to lead them toward an eventual break. When the official division came in 1054 with mutual excommunications, the churches were declaring to the world what had already been a reality for some time. This explanation is not to say that there are no important differences of doctrine, rites, or ecclesiastical practices between the two churches, or to deny that these differences have grown stronger since 1054. It is merely to show how even these pale into insignificance when set against the

glaring differences caused by rival cultures, conflicting empires, and 800 years of lack of meaningful communication.

Of the three oldest traditions of the liturgical family—the Eastern Orthodox tradition, the non-Chalcedonian Orthodox tradition, and the Western Roman tradition—only the third failed to remain fairly stable down through the nineteenth century. In the first tradition, the Eastern Orthodox Church split jurisdictions along national and cultural lines. It was able to preserve unity by granting local autonomy to the various national groups. In the non-Chalcedonian Orthodox tradition, the Coptic Church and the Armenian Church fell under the rule of rising Islam after the sixth century. The force of an overpowering enemy served to keep them both small and united. In the Western Roman tradition, however, the Roman Catholic Church attempted an imperial stance, trying to provide a religious blanket to cover all of Western culture. Consequently, it was to suffer when secular power deserted it. Not only did the various Protestant and post-Protestant groups break off from it, but the fourth major liturgical tradition emerged from it: the Anglican.

The church in England had been at odds with the see of Rome as early as Thomas A'Becket, the twelfth-century Archbishop of Canterbury. In the sixteenth century, the marriage problems of Henry VIII caused the break with Rome. With few immediate changes in the church beyond confiscation of church property by Henry, the Church of England had to wait for the Protestantizing of Edward and the mediating of Elizabeth for a genuinely new orientation. The development and spread of the Elizabethan prayerbook alone is reason to look upon the Anglicans as a separate liturgical tradition.

Each of the four major liturgical traditions was brought to the United States by immigration of its Old World disciples, with the exception of the Old Catholics. The traditions came as structures to preserve the Old World customs and cultures in the secular environment of the United States. Churches were founded wherever a significant group of immigrants or their descendants resided. These churches remained under the supervision of ancient sees and kept much closer contact with the sees than with neighboring American churches. There was little attempt to evangelize beyond the boundaries of the immigrants' particular ethnic groups. Schism would wait until the twentieth century for most groups, when Americanization and the desire for native American bishops would become major issues.

THE OLD CATHOLIC MOVEMENT. The Western Roman liturgical tradition suffered other divisions beside that of the Anglicans. The most conspicuous of these developed during the seventeenth century in Port Royal, France, when Jansenists—members of a mystical movement that carried on the work of Dutch theologian Cornelius Jansen (1585-1638)— found themselves in opposition to the Jesuits, priests of a religious order obedient to the pope. Jansenists believed that the human will was not free and that redemption was limited to only some of humankind. Thus Jansenists were condemned by the pope and opposed by the Jesuits. The Jesuits accused the Jansenists of being Protestants, hence heretics; the Jansenists accused the Jesuits of despotism and laxity in doctrine and discipline. In alliance with the French monarchy, the Jesuits began a persecution that eventually broke the power of the Jansenists, many of whom fled to Holland in the territory of the see of Utrecht.

As the Jansenists moved into Holland from Port Royal, Utrecht's newly consecrated bishop, Peter Codde, entered into relations with them. When the pope demanded that Codde subscribe to the condemnation of the Jansenists, he refused and was accused of Jansenism. Rival parties developed—one behind Codde and another behind Theodore de Cock. De Cock, for various reasons, was banished from Holland by the government. Codde was deposed by the pope and ceased exercising his functions.

Without episcopal functionaries, the see soon began to wither, as no ordinations or confirmations could occur. This problem was somewhat alleviated by the unexpected stop in Amsterdam of Dominique Marie Varlet, newly consecrated bishop of Babylon, on his way to Persia in 1719. In Amsterdam, he confirmed more than 600 children, the first confirmed in 17 years. For this act he was suspended from office. He returned to Europe and settled in Amsterdam. In 1724 Varlet consented to consecrate a new archbishop of Utrecht, Cornelius van Steenoven. When van Steenoven died shortly thereafter, Varlet consecrated Cornelius Wuytiers. Several other consecrations for neighboring dioceses such as Haarlem and Deventer followed, insuring that the apostolic succession would not be lost. For approximately 150 years the Church of Utrecht, commonly called the Old Catholic Church, continued with only episcopal supervision as the dividing line between it and Rome.

Though the Old Catholic movement traces its history back to the see of Utrecht in Holland in 1702, it dates officially from the 1870s and the reaction to the declaration of papal infallibility at the First Vatican Council. In 1870 the First Vatican Council declared the pope infallible when speaking on matters of faith and morals, prompting large numbers of Roman Catholics to leave their church and seek communion with the Church of Utrecht. Even before the council, opposition in anticipation of the declaration arose, particularly in Germany. In 1871 in Munich a congress of opponents, led by Von Schulte, a professor of canon law, was held. Three hundred delegates, including representatives from the churches of Utrecht and England, came. These representatives organized the Old Catholic Church along national lines. In 1873 Joseph Hubert Reinkens, a professor of church history at Breslau, was elected bishop and was consecrated by the bishop of the church at Deventer. A constitution was adopted in 1874 that recognized national autonomy and established an international Synod of Bishops. The archbishop of Utrecht now presides over the episcopal conference.

The Old Catholic Church retained most of the doctrines of Rome but rejected ecclesiastical unity under the pope. In 1874 the Old Catholic Church dropped the compulsory fasting and auricular confession of the Roman Catholic Church, and feast days were reduced. By 1880 vernacular mass began to replace the Latin. The seven sacraments were continued, but baptism and the eucharist were elevated to prime importance. The Roman Catholic Church has recognized the validity of Old Catholic (Utrecht) orders though the exercise of the episcopal powers is illegal.

Because the Church of England (the Anglican Church) was so similar to the Old Catholic Church on the Continent, no attempt was made to introduce the later church into England. However, during the nineteenth century there arose men who wished to function as bishops outside of either the Roman or Anglican communions. In some cases these were former priests in older communions. Some were representatives of ethnic communities expressing nationalistic enthusiasms. The Old Catholic movement developed an anti-authoritarian character. Most of its bishops have been self-appointed and have small followings. They have pressed for recognition of orders while keeping independence of jurisdiction. As an attempt at legitimization, they have sought recognition or reconsecration by bishops of the Eastern Orthodox Church (often after rebuff by the archbishop of Utrecht, the head of the Old Catholic Church). What began as a specific protest against the pope's authority turned into a drive by independent bishops to set up schismatic dioceses.

With the growth of independent dioceses and recognition by various Eastern and Western churches, the variation in ritual and doctrine has increased tremendously.

As the Old Catholic movement developed in America, a chaotic episcopal scene emerged. Many bishops claim dioceses which exist only on paper and ordinations by bishops whose existence cannot be verified. A few churches seem to be oriented to serve the homosexual community. A few have been confidence schemes.

In the United States, most of the Old Catholic churches derive their orders through two lines of succession, that of Joseph Rene Vilatte or Arnold Harris Mathew. A third faction traces its lineage to miscellaneous Eastern and Western orders through Hugh George de Willmott Newman. Neither Vilatte's nor Mathew's churches remained in communion with the European Old Catholic churches, which entered into full communion with the Church of England in 1932 and with most of the churches of the Anglican communion by 1936.

Arnold Harris Mathew. Arnold Harris Mathew (1852-1919) began his professional career as a Roman Catholic priest. After serving several parishes, he became a Unitarian. He flirted with the Church of England for a while, changed his name, and married. Eventually he made peace with Rome and settled down as a layman and author. He penned a number of items, including collaboration in editing the third edition of H. C. Lea's *History of Sacerdotal Celibacy in the Christian Church* early in this century. Then in September 1907 he began corresponding with Bishop Eduard Herzog, an Old Catholic bishop in Switzerland. In these letters, and later ones to Bishop J. J. Van Theil of Haarlem, he suggested the formation of an Old Catholic church in England.

Mathew had in the years previous to his correspondence become associated with a group of disgruntled ex-Catholics, led by Father Richard O'Halloran. Under O'Halloran's guidance, Mathew was elected bishop of the Old Catholics in England. The problem was to get valid orders. The church at

Utrecht, the central see of the Old Catholic Church, was very hesitant, but finally on April 22, 1908, Mathew was consecrated in Utrecht by the archbishop, under protest from the Anglicans.

Mathew returned to England to find that O'Halloran had lied to him and there was no following waiting to accept him as their bishop. Mathew immediately wrote the archbishop of Utrecht informing him of the deceit and offering to resign. When his resignation was refused, Mathew accepted his circumstances as a mission. The Reverend W. Noel Lambert turned over his independent chapel to become St. Willibrord's Procathedral and Mathew's headquarters.

In 1910 Mathew secretly consecrated two ex-Roman Catholic priests as bishops without informing Utrecht and without the assistance of other validly consecrated bishops. Mathew declared his independence from Utrecht and succeeded in building a small church. He died in lonely poverty, but before his death, Mathew set the stage for Old Catholicism in America.

Among Bishop Mathew's significant consecrations were those of Prince de Landas Berghes et de Rache, Duc de St. Winock, who established Mathew's succession in the United States, and Frederick Samuel Willoughby, who founded the Liberal Catholic Church. Mathew's consecrations also included that of John Kowalski of the Polish Mariavite Church.

The Duc de Landas Berghes was an Austrian nobleman consecrated by Bishop Mathew of the Old Catholic Church on June 28, 1913, probably with the idea of setting up an independent church in Austria. De Landas Berghes was prevented from returning to Austria from England because of World War I, however, and fled to the United States to escape arrest as an enemy alien. During his short career, before his submission to Rome in 1919, he consecrated as bishops Fathers W.H. Francis Brothers and Henry Carfora, the direct sources of most Old Catholic bodies in America to date because of the many men that they consecrated as bishops.

Joseph Rene Vilatte. The man who first brought the Old Catholic Church to America was Joseph Rene Vilatte. French-born, Vilatte appeared in Wisconsin in the 1880s preaching Old Roman Catholic doctrines among French and Belgian immigrants. He had had a checkered religious education under an ex-Roman Catholic priest, Father Charles Chiniquy, and had come to believe both Roman Catholic and Protestant positions invalid. After marked success in Wisconsin, Vilatte went to Berne and obtained ordination from Bishop Herzog, but a protest from the Anglicans prevented his obtaining consecration from Utrecht, the central see of the Old Catholic Church. He finally, after a long search, obtained consecration as archbishop of the archdiocese of America on May 29, 1892, from Archbishop Alvarez of Ceylon, who had received his orders from the Syro-Jacobite Church of Malabar.

Vilatte briefly returned to Roman Catholicism in 1899-1900, but soon became frustrated, resumed his independent work and for the next 20 years operated as an archbishop for the American Catholic Church. Given his Roman background

and his Orthodox orders, it is not surprising that both Old Catholic and independent Eastern Orthodox jurisdictions sprang from his activity. Also, because the Syro-Jacobite Church of Malabar refused to recognize the various consecrations he performed, even for leaders in his own church, he became further removed from the mainstream of American church life. Finally, in 1925, he again returned to the Roman Catholic Church, and renouncing his separatist and independent course of action, died in the arms of *Mater Ecclesia*. His own American Catholic Church, after the death of Archbishop Frederick E. J. Lloyd, Vilatte's successor, was taken over by bishops with Theosophical leanings and moved totally into the Liberal Catholic Church community.

Hugh George de Willmott Newman. Among the most colorful bishops in the independent Catholic community, Hugh George de Willmott Newman (1905-) can be credited with introducing an increasingly common practice among the autonomous bishops, that of seeking numerous reconsecrations in order to legitimize an otherwise miniscule ecclesiastical jurisdiction by having its bishop embody a wide variety of lines of apostolic succession, both East and West. Such jurisdictions would symbolize the ecumenical church.

Newman was originally consecrated in 1944 by Dr. William Bernard Crow, whose orders derived from Luis Mariano Soares (Mar Basilius) of the small Syro-Chaldean church in India, Ceylon, Socotra, and Messina. However, within the next decade Newman received no less than nine additional consecrations, usually in ceremonies in which he in turn reconsecrated the other bishop (thus passing along the apostolic lineages he had already received). Of the several consecrations swapped by Newman, that with W. D. de Ortega Maxey of the Apostolic Episcopal Church was most important for the American scene, as Maxey not only established an American branch of Newman's Catholicate of the West, but became the prime source for American bishops to receive Newman's lineages.

Episcopally led churches have traditionally based their legitimacy on their ability to trace their line of succession from the original 12 Apostles. That is, for a bishop to be validly consecrated, and thus able to validly ordain priests, that bishop must himself be consecrated by a validly consecrated bishop. Thus, the story of the independent Old Catholic jurisdictions in America is the story of the search for legitimacy through ever more valid consecrations. It has become common for independent bishops to receive multiple consecrations, especially after changing allegiance to a different jurisdiction.

The importing of Eastern orders for a Western church, and the intermingling of Eastern and Western lineages in bishops such as Newman, also initiated a complex mixing of liturgies. The independent jurisdictions have felt free to adopt, regardless of the practices of the body from which they received their apostolic succession, any number of liturgies— Roman, Anglican, Eastern, or even Theosophical, while some have written their own. Since many of the American jurisdictions are quite small, with an unpaid clergy and congregationally owned property, one of the few real decisions the bishop can make is in regard to the liturgies that the congregations may use.

Adopting the practice introduced by Bishop Mathew of having an unpaid clergy, the Old Catholic (and independent Orthodox) church has splintered into more than 100 jurisdictions. Priests and bishops, since they have no financial tie to any given jurisdiction, can leave at will, and frequently do. The constant flux within the jurisdictions has made the problem of straightening out the line of succession extremely complex; however, the work begun in this area by H. R. T. Brandweth, Peter Anson, and Arthur C. Piepkorn has been expanded in recent years by Karl Pruter, Bertil Persson, and Alan Bain (without whose assistance this chapter could not have been completed).

Since the Roman Catholic Church's Second Vatican Council and the adoption of the new liturgy for the mass, a new set of independent Catholic jurisdictions has appeared that has an allegiance to the Latin liturgy and several practices largely abandoned in the post-Vatican church. Some of these traditionalist jurisdictions have sought and received Old Catholic orders for their episcopal leadership, while others (such as the followers of Swiss Archbishop Lefebvre) have waited for some kind of recognition from Rome. That recognition having never come, the aging Archbishop Lefebvre broke with Rome in 1988 and consecrated four bishops to carry on his work. Previously, Vietnamese Archbishop Ngo-Dinh-Thuc had already consecrated bishops for an equally conservative Latin Rite Catholic Church. Possibilities of reconciliation seem remote.

THE ANGLICAN TRADITION. The Church of England, also called the Anglican church, developed in the sixteenth century when King Henry VIII came into conflict with papal authority. Henry had no doctrinal problems with Rome. In fact, because of his early theological writing, he had been given the title "defender of the faith" by the pope. But two issues led to his break with Rome: his desire for a male heir and his financial needs. Rome granted him an annulment for one marriage, but would not later grant him a divorce for another marriage. So he determined to separate the English church from papal jurisdiction. Besides, he knew the wealthy monasteries would be a good source of revenue for running his kingdom and waging war. This made the break from Rome doubly beneficial to him. The Church of England kept its already existing structure, with bishops, clergy, church buildings, and congregations continuing under the archbishop of Canterbury instead of under the pope. The church was still Roman in doctrine, liturgy, and organization.

Not until Edward VII, Elizabeth I, and Oliver Cromwell was the present character of the Anglican church molded. The pendulum of the church swung from Protestant under Edward to Catholic under Mary, called Bloody Mary for the persecutions accompanying the enforced return to Catholicism. Elizabeth took the throne aware that both Edward and Mary had found strong support for their choice of religions. So Elizabeth adopted a *via media* (middle way), blending both Roman and Protestant elements. During her reign the Thirty-nine Articles of Religion were promulgated, with some articles condemning Roman beliefs and practices, some articles preserving Roman elements. Purgatory, indulgences, venerating saints' relics, and celebrating the liturgy in any tongue other than the vernacular were among the Roman elements condemned. However, Elizabeth retained the traditional episcopal structure even though it had been under attack during her time and Edward's, and though many English Puritans objected to ordained priests.

The Book of Common Prayer, the Anglican liturgical book which replaced the Roman missal, has gone through several editions. The edition published during Elizabeth's reign is crucial: it makes concrete the distinctive character of Anglicanism that has continued to this day. That edition includes the Thirty-nine Articles of Religion, creeds, church calendar, and liturgical services. Material on the sacraments in that edition is intentionally vague, to allow various interpretations of the eucharist. Anglicans recognize only two sacraments—baptism and the Lord's Supper. Anglican doctrine on the church shifted from the Roman emphasis on the bishop to the Calvinist emphasis on the congregation. *The Book of Common Prayer* says the church exists where the Word of God is preached, the sacraments are duly administered, and the faithful are gathered.

A certain Anglophilia aligns the church with British tradition. When Rome commissioned St. Augustine to be a missionary in England in 597 A.D., he found Christians already in England, so many Anglicans insist their church was not formed by Rome and that the Anglican Church in England predates the arrival of the Roman Catholic Church in England. Anglicanism is thus a tradition separated from Roman Catholicism by its liturgical differences, its condemnation of some Roman beliefs and practices, and its alignment with British tradition. With the expansion of England in the seventeenth century, the Anglican tradition spread throughout the world.

The Anglican tradition entered North America with the coming of the British explorers in the sixteenth century. Worship according to the Church of England was established at St. John's, Newfoundland, in 1583, where the Reverend Erasmus Stourton became the first Anglican minister to reside in North America. Anglican services were held for the first time in what is now the United States on August 13, 1587, at the ill-fated Roanoke colony in Virginia. They were permanently established in 1607 in Jamestown. The first minister at Jamestown was Robert Hunt, who, unfortunately, died soon after his arrival in America. His efforts were followed by the more substantive career of Alexander Whitaker, who served the colony as pastor of Henrico, the second church in Virginia for many years.

Throughout the 1600s, the Church of England spread through British North America, finally entering even Puritan Boston in 1692. It was given a significant boost in 1701 by the establishment of the Society for the Propagation of the Gospel, a foreign missionary arm of the Church of England, and by the arrival of society founder Thomas Bray. Appointed commissioner, with some of the powers of a bishop, Bray settled in Maryland and directed the missionary endeavor. The work in Canada expanded immensely in the late eighteenth century, following a series of events beginning with the British seizure of Quebec (1759) and the subsequent Treaty of Paris in 1763, which gave Canada to the British. The American Revolution then sent large numbers of British loyalists northward. The growth is no better symbolized than by the placing of Charles Inglis, a former parish priest from New York, in Halifax as the first bishop of the Church of England for Canada in 1787.

While aiding church growth in Canada, the American Revolution almost destroyed Anglicanism in the American colonies. Identified as antipatriotic by the public, the Church of England in America also lost its legal status, most of its priests (who returned to England), and its financial base. The church was virtually cut off from the homeland because the bishops in England initially refused to pass along episcopal orders. Samuel Seabury, elected bishop by the remaining priests in Connecticut, was consecrated by Scottish bishops in 1784. It was not until 1787, the same year a bishop was placed in Nova Scotia, that William White and Samuel Provoost were consecrated in London and a working accord was reached between the new Protestant Episcopal Church in the United States and the Church of England.

While the church in America grew as an independent body, the church in Canada prospered as a missionary branch of the Church of England and was officially designated as the Church of England in Canada; it changed its name to the Anglican Church in Canada in 1955.

The Protestant Episcopal Church, the Anglican Church in Canada, the Reformed Episcopal Church (nineteenth-century splinter group), and a few congregations of the Philippine Independent Church provided the main substance of the Anglican tradition for North America until the mid-1960s. At that time, North American Anglicanism was split by members protesting changes in the church, primarily related to a shifting moral code (manifest in new attitudes toward sexuality), revisions of the Prayer Book, and the acceptance of females into the priesthood. Schisms began in 1964 with the formation of the Anglican Orthodox Church, but accelerated in 1976 after females had been ordained in both Canada and the United States. The Anglican Catholic Church and the Anglican Catholic Church in Canada are the two largest bodies of the 10 or more churches formed among dissenting Anglicans. In their formative stages, these churches turned to the Philippine Independent Church for episcopal orders. Bishop Francisco Pagtakhan, the missionary bishop whose jurisdiction covered North America, performed the consecrations. As a result of these and other actions, Pagtakhan had severe disagreements with the church in the Philippines in the mid-1980s, and left to form the Philippine Independent Catholic Church, which has now established parishes in North America.

SOURCES—WESTERN LITURGICAL FAMILY

THE WESTERN LITURGICAL TRADITION

Alan, Kurt. *A History of Christianity*. Philadelphia: Fortress Press, 1985. 474 pp.

Algermissen, Konrad. *Christian Denominations*. St. Louis: B. Herder Book Co., 1946. 1051 pp.

Frankforter, A. Daniel. *A History of the Christian Movement*. Chicago: Nelson-Hall, 1978. 317 pp.

Johnson, Paul. *A History of Christianity*. London: Weidenfeld and Nicolson, 1976. 556 pp.

Mirgeler, Albert. *Mutations of Western Christianity*. New York: Herder and Herder, 1965. 158 pp.

Sheldon, Henry C. *Sacerdotalism in the Nineteenth Century*. New York: Abingdon, 1909. 461 pp.

Thompson, Baird. *Liturgies of the Western Church*. Cleveland: The World Publishing Company, 1962. 434 pp.

ROMAN CATHOLICISM

Bokenkotter, Thomas. *A Concise History of the Catholic Church*. Garden City, NY: Doubleday, 1977. 431 pp.

Brantl, George, ed. *Catholicism*. New York: Washington Square Press, 1962. 277 pp.

Foy, Felician A. *Catholic Almanac*. Huntington, IN: Our Sunday Visitor, issued annually.

———. *A Concise Guide to the Catholic Church*. Huntington, IN: Our Sunday Visitor, 1984. 158 pp.

Frederic, Catherine. *The Handbook of Catholic Practices*. New York: Hawthorn Books, 1964. 320 pp.

McKenzie, John L. *The Roman Catholic Church*. New York: Holt, Rinehart and Winston, 1969. 288 pp.

THE ROMAN CATHOLIC CHURCH IN NORTH AMERICA

Catholicism in America. New York: Harcourt, Brace and Company, 1954. 242 pp.

Ellis, John Tracy. *American Catholicism*. Garden City, NY: Doubleday, 1965. 196 pp.

———. *Documents of American Catholic History*. Chicago: Henry Regnery Company, 1967. 2 Vols.

Hennesey, James. *American Catholics*. Oxford: Oxford University Press, 1981. 397 pp.

Kelly, George A. *The Battle for the American Church*. Garden City, NY: Doubleday, 1979. 513 pp.

Maynard, Theodore. *The Story of American Catholicism*. Garden City, NY: Doubleday, 1960. 694 pp.

ROMAN CATHOLIC THOUGHT

Abbott, Water, ed. *The Documents of Vatican II*. New York: Guild Press, 1966. 793 pp.

Abell, Aaron I. *American Catholic Thought on Social Questions*. Indianapolis: Bobbs-Merrill, 1968. 571 pp.

Berkouwer, G. C. *Recent Developments in Roman Catholic Thought*. Grand Rapids, MI: Wm. B. Eerdmans Publishing Company, 1958. 81 pp.

Bokenkotter, Thomas. *Essential Catholicism*. Garden City, NY: Doubleday, 1985. 437 pp.

Burghardt, Walter J., and William F. Lynch. *The Idea of Catholicism*. New York: Meridian Books, 1960. 479 pp.

A Catholic Catechism. New York: Herder and Herder, 1958. 448 pp.

Fremantle, Anne. *The Papal Encyclicals*. New York: New American Library, 1956. 317 pp.

O'Brien, John A. *Understanding the Catholic Faith*. Notre Dame, IN: Ave Maria Press, 1955. 281 pp.

Trese, Leo J. *The Creed—Summary of the Faith*. Notre Dame, IN: Fides Publishers, 1963. 155 pp.

ROMAN CATHOLIC LITURGY

Lefebvre, Gaspar. *The Spirit of Worship*. New York: Hawthorn Books, 1959. 127 pp.

Segundo, Juan Luis. *The Sacraments Today*. New York: Maryknoll, 1974. 154 pp.

The Treasures of the Mass. Clyde, MO: Benedictine Convent of Perpetual Adoration, 1957. 128 pp.

ROMAN CATHOLIC POLITY

McKnight, John P. *The Papacy.* London: McGraw-Hill Publishing Company, 1953. 400 pp.

Scharp, Heinrich. *How the Catholic Church Is Governed.* New York: Paulist Press, 1960. 128 pp.

Tillard, J. M. R. *The Bishop of Rome.* Wilmington, DE: Michael Glazier, 1983. 242 pp.

EASTERN RITE ROMAN CATHOLICISM

Attwater, Donald. *The Christian Churches of the East.* Milwaukee: Bruce Publishing Company, 1961. 232 pp.

———. *Eastern Catholic Worship.* New York: Devin-Adair Company, 1945. 224 pp.

Liesel, N. *The Eastern Catholic Liturgies.* Westminster, MD: Newman Press, 1960. 168 pp.

ANTI-CATHOLICISM

Billington, Ray Allen. *The Protestant Crusade.* New York: Macmillan, 1938. 514 pp.

Chiniquy, Charles. *Fifty Years in the Church of Rome.* Grand Rapids, MI: Baker Book House, 1960. 597 pp.

de la Bedoyere, Michael. *Objections to Roman Catholicism.* Philadelphia: J. B. Lippencott Company, 1965. 185 pp.

McLoughlin, Emmett. *Famous Ex-Priests.* New York: Lyle Stuart, 1968. 224 pp.

OLD CATHOLICISM

Anson, Peter F. *Bishops at Large.* London: Faber and Faber, 1964. 593 pp.

Bain, Alan. *"Bishops Irregular."* Bristol, Eng.: The Author, 1985. 256 pp.

Brandreth, H. R. T. *Episcopi Vagantes and the Anglican Church.* London: S.P.C.K., 1961. 140 pp.

Conger, Yves. *Challenge to the Church.* Huntington, IN: Our Sunday Visitor. 1976. 96 pp.

Davies, Michael. *Pope Paul's New Mass.* Dickinson, TX: Angelus Press, 1980. 673 pp.

Groman, E. Owen, and Jonathan E. Trela. *Three Studies in Old Catholicism.* Scranton, PA: Savonarola Theological Seminary Alumni Association, 1978. 37 pp.

Huelin, Gordon, ed. *Old Catholics and Anglicans, 1931-1981.* Oxford: Oxford University Press, 1983. 177 pp.

Moss, C. B. *The Old Catholic Movement.* Eureka Springs, AK: Episcopal Book Club, 1977. 368 pp.

Piepkorn, Arthur Carl. *Profiles in Belief.* Vol. I. New York: Harper & Row, 1977. pp. 29-56, 73-80.

Pruter, Karl, ed. *A Directory of Autocephalous Anglican, Catholic and Orthodox Bishops.* Highlandsville, MO: St. Willibrord Press, 1987.

Pruter, Karl, and J. Gordon Melton. *The Old Catholic Sourcebook.* New York: Garland, 1983. 254 pp.

CHURCH OF ENGLAND AND THE WORLDWIDE ANGLICAN COMMUNION

Dart, J. L. C. *The Old Religion.* London: S.P.C.K., 1956. 210 pp.

Flindall, R. P., ed. *The Church of England, 1815-1948.* London: S.P.C.K., 1972. 497 pp.

Hardy, E. R., Jr., ed. *Orthodox Statements on Anglican Orders.* New York: Morehouse-Gorham Co., 1946. 72 pp.

Neill, Stephen. *Anglicanism.* London: A. R. Mowbrays, 1977. 421 pp.

Wand, J. W. C. *What the Church of England Stands For.* London: A. R. Mowbray, 1951. 131 pp.

ANGLICANISM IN NORTH AMERICA

Addison, James Thayer. *The Episcopal Church in the United States, 1789-1931.* New York: Charles Scribner's Sons, 1951. 400 pp.

DeMille, George E. *The Episcopal Church Since 1900.* New York: Morehouse-Gorham Company, 1955. 223 pp.

Herklots, H. G. G. *The Church of England and the American Episcopal Church.* London: A. R. Mowbray & Co., 1966. 183 pp.

Konolige, Kit and Frederica Konolige. *The Power of Their Glory.* N.p.: Wyden Books, 1978. 408 pp.

Manross, William W. *A History of the American Episcopal Church.* New York: Morehouse-Gorham Co., 1950. 415 pp.

Sydnor, William. *Looking at the Episcopal Church.* Wilton, CT: Morehouse-Barlow Co., 1980. 142 pp.

Woolverton, John Frederick. *Colonial Anglicanism in North America.* Detroit: Wayne State University Press, 1984. 331 pp.

THE NEW ANGLICANS

Armentrout, Donald S. *Episcopal Splinter Groups.* Sawanee, TN: The School of Theology, The University of the South, 1985.

Dibbert, Roderic B. *The Roots of Traditional Anglicanism.* Akron, OH: DeKoven Foundation of Ohio, 1984. 13 pp.

A Directory of Churches of the Continuing Anglican Tradition. Eureka Springs, AK: Fellowship of Concerned Churchmen, 1983-84.

Joseph, Murray, *"Priests Forever."* Valley Forge, PA: The Brotherhood of the Servants of the Lord, 1975. 16 pp.

Opening Addresses of the Church Congress at St. Louis, Missouri, 14-16 September 1977. Amherst, VA: Fellowship of Concerned Churchmen, 1977.

A Retired Priest. *The Broken Body.* N.p.: The Author, 1980. 38 pp.

Chapter 2

Eastern Liturgical Family

Directory listings for the groups belonging to the Eastern Liturgical Family
may be found in the section beginning on page 109.

THE EASTERN ORTHODOX TRADITION. The Eastern church and the Western Roman church coexisted as two branches of the same church for centuries. However, cultural differences, politics, and doctrinal disagreements finally led to official division and mutual excommunication in 1054. The Eastern church dominated the eastern Mediterranean basin, spreading through Greece, Egypt, Asia Minor, the Arab countries, and the Slavic nations. In the early Middle Ages, this dominance was weakened by the loss of the "heretical" churches (the non-Chalcedonian Orthodox churches) and then by the Moslem conquests.

In each area, the Eastern church developed an episcopal structure of national autonomous sees. Certain sees were more prominent and had been designated patriarchates. They included Alexandria, Antioch, Jerusalem, and Constantinople. In more recent years, patriarchates have been designated in Bulgaria, Serbia (Yugoslavia), Russia, and Romania. Autocephalous churches, headed by a bishop but without a patriarchate, exist in the Ukraine, Cypress, Albania, Greece, Poland, and Georgia (U.S.S.R.). Autonomous churches, headed by a bishop, self-governing on internal matters, but dependent on a patriarchate for the appointment of its primate (head bishop) and relations with other churches, exist in Finland, Estonia, Czechoslovakia, Latvia, and Lithuania, and at Mt. Sinai.

The patriarchs are represented by the "ecumenical" patriarch of Constantinople, though his position of primacy is one of honor, not power. All of the patriarchs are of equal authority and none has the right to interfere with the work in another's territory. They are, however, "in communion" with each other and in the United States the bishops of the churches who directly relate to the ecumenical patriarch work together as the Standing Conference of Canonical Orthodox Bishops in the Americas. Most Orthodox Christians in America are members of these churches.

To most Americans, familiar with only the Roman and Anglican traditions, the Eastern Orthodox tradition presents several distinctive features. The celibate priesthood of the Roman Catholic Church is not demanded. In the East priests marry (though they must do so before ordination). Monks do not. Bishops are drawn from the ranks of the monks. Priests who are not monks are not eligible for the episcopacy. The Eastern church does not recognize the authority of the bishop of Rome over the various patriarchs of the Eastern church. The Eastern churches recognize only the seven ecumenical councils held between 325 A.D. and 787 A.D. because no further councils occurred at which the bishops of Rome and the Eastern patriarchs worked together.

The Eastern church rejects the *filioque* doctrine of the Roman Catholic Church. *Filioque* is the Latin word for "and the Son," added to the creed to assert that the Holy Spirit proceeds from the Father and the Son. Some theologians of the Eastern church insisted the Holy Spirit proceeds from the Father through the Son. The Eastern church rejected the *filioque* doctrine partly because John 15:26 makes no mention of the Son and instead speaks of "the Spirit of truth who proceeds from the Father."

The Greek *Liturgy of St. Chrysostom* is used throughout the Eastern church. The various national bodies have translated it into their native tongues, and in America English is being increasingly used.

Those areas where Orthodoxy exists only as a small minority religion, geographically removed from the ancient centers, are designated Orthodoxy in Diaspora. The largest diaspora community is the more than three million Orthodox Christians in the United States.

Orthodoxy entered the United States in the eighteenth century following the discovery of Alaska by Russians in 1741. In 1743 an Aleutian by the name of Andreu Islands was baptized. The Russian Orthodox Church was firmly established in 1794 when seven monks came to Paul's Harbor and consecrated the first church. By 1841 a seminary was in operation in the Aleutian Islands. The first diocese, created after Alaska was purchased by the United States, was moved to San Francisco in 1872.

Spotty movement of Orthodox Christians into North America began in the first part of the nineteenth century, but did not become significant until the 1890s. Prior to 1891, the only parishes were those in Alaska and the single church in San Francisco. At this time, The Russian Orthodox church included members from all ethnic backgrounds and had all of

North America under its hegemony. Then, the movement of people from the Middle East and from Eastern and Southern Europe increased significantly because of growing tension in Russia, Turkish and Russian expansion, and the general suffering occasioned by Work War I, until it was all but stopped by the immigration quota limitations imposed in 1924. Immigrants settled in the northern and eastern urban centers but found their way to the prairies of western Canada and the farmland of California. As significant numbers of each national group arrived, they began efforts to form their own unique parishes and then to organize separate dioceses. By the early twentieth century, the Russian church began to lose its ethnic parishes and the various ethnic branches of the Orthodox church formed.

As these new branches were formed, one by one, most were severely tested by two outside forces. First, the inevitable process of Americanization—the demands of conformity, especially in language—divided the generations, and on occasion led to schism. Of more concern, however, was the Russian Revolution and the spread of atheist regimes in predominantly Orthodox countries. As the Orthodox churches have tended to be aligned with the state, the loss of state support was devastating. The actual hostility of a government that appeared ready to either destroy or subvert the church to its own purposes called into question the relationship of American and Canadian churches to the patriarchal headquarters caught in the revolutionary situations. Some Americans demanded loyalty to the patriarchs and accommodation to the new regimes, while others with equal strength demanded autonomy from the homeland. Beginning in the 1920s with the Russians and accelerating after World War II, schism rent almost every branch of Eastern Orthodoxy in North America.

The structure of American Orthodoxy was dramatically changed in 1970 with the creation of the Orthodox Church in America by the merger of several of the Russian churches. Russian Orthodoxy, by reason of its early arrival date, has always had a primacy in America. Many of the currently existing independent Orthodox bodies were formed under its care. In recent years, the growth of the Greek Orthodox Church in America has led to challenges to Russian primacy, challenges based on the claims of the ecumenical patriarch in Istanbul as the first among equals in world Orthodoxy. The argument was somewhat academic since each American church was directly related to a different overseas see. The Orthodox Church in America, unattached to a foreign see, was authorized by Patriarch Alexis in Moscow, whose right to grant such status has been questioned by the Greek Orthodox.

The new body, the Orthodox Church in America, aims at uniting Orthodox of all ethnic groups into a single American Orthodox body. This is the natural result of a growing demand for American autonomy. Archbishop Philip of the Antiochean church has been among the new church's most vocal advocates. The new body is the only Orthodox church which has all of the structures necessary to continue without outside help. These structures include seminaries, monasteries, and charitable institutions.

THE EMERGENCE OF INDEPENDENT ORTHODOXY IN THE TWENTIETH CENTURY. During the nineteenth century, Orthodox believers from many of the European national churches migrated to America. A few, such as the Greeks, remained autonomous and eventually formed their own ethnic church. Others, such as the Syrians, began as an ethnic group under the care of the Russian church, which, because it was the first Orthodox church to establish work, had a special hegemony within the United States. Once in the United States with its multiethnic atmosphere, geographically removed from its homeland, the Orthodox church became subject to a variety of forces that split its community into a number of ecclesiastical factions. The first major splinter began as a movement to unite American Orthodoxy.

Aftimios Ofiesh (1890-1971) came to America in 1905 to work among Syrians, then a part of the Russian Orthodox Church. In 1917 he was consecrated bishop for the Syrian work, succeeding Bishop Raphael Hawaweeny. On February 2, 1927, the Russian bishops gave him the duty of caring for the American-born Orthodox, especially the English-speaking parishes, not otherwise being given proper care. By their action they created a new jurisdiction, the American Orthodox Church, as an autonomous body with filial relationship to the Russian Church.

The project met immediate opposition. The non-Russian bishops were not supportive of a united American Orthodoxy as proposed and the ecumenical patriarch, the nominal head of all Orthodox churches, denounced the project as schismatic. The Greeks were angered by Ofiesh's publication of a magazine, *Orthodox Catholic Reporter*. Especially offended were the Episcopalians, who considered themselves the American form of Orthodoxy and who were providing the Russians with large amounts of financial support. They applied pressure on Metropolitan Platon to abandon Ofiesh. Even though soon abandoned by the Russians, Ofiesh continued in his project and, beginning with Emmanuel Ato-Hotab (1927) and Sophonius Bashira (1928), he consecrated four bishops to head his independent work.

The problem with Ofiesh was not the only trouble to disturb the Russian church during the 1920s. As a result of the Russian Revolution and the coming to power of an antireligious regime, the close allegiance of the church to the Russian government was called into question, especially after the imprisonment of the patriarch of Moscow in 1922. Soviet supporters within the Russian church in 1924 organized a sobor (convention) of what came to be called the Living Church faction. They voiced support of the Soviet government and elected the only American at the Sobor, John Kedrowsky, bishop of America. He came to America and with his sons, Nicholas (later his successor as bishop of America) and John, and through court action took control of St. Nicholas Cathedral in New York City. However, he was rejected by a synod of the American Russian church in 1924 which declared its autonomy in administrative matters from the church in Russia.

While the Russians were splintering into several factions, the Greeks, never under Russian control, were having their own problems. In 1908, the Greek parishes in America were transferred from the direct authority of the ecumenical patriarch to the holy synod of the church in Greece. That arrangement did not provide the necessary leadership for the burgeoning American church, so in 1918, the ecumenical patriarch began the process of establishing the American church as an archdiocese, a task finally accomplished in 1922. However, that arrangement also did not resolve the leadership question, and in 1930 the ecumenical patriarch reasserted his hegemony in America by appointing a representative to come to the United States and take over leadership of the archdiocese.

Meanwhile, as organizational trouble plagued the church, it was further divided by internal problems in Greece. A faction of the American membership opposed the transfer of the allegiance of the American church from the church in Greece to the ecumenical patriarch. In the 1930s they removed themselves from the archdiocese and sought consecration of a new bishop by the church in Greece. Thus in 1934, Christopher Contogeorge, with the blessing of the church in Greece, was consecrated the archbishop of Philadelphia by Albanian Bishop Fan Stylin Noli, assisted by Bishop Sophonius Bashira. Archbishop Christopher was the consecrator of Bishop John Kedrowsky's successor, Nicholas Kedrowsky.

By the mid-1930s Archbishop Christopher and Bishops Sophonius, Nicholas (Kedrowsky), and Fan constituted a group of independent Orthodox bishops both organizationally and emotionally separated from the larger body of Orthodox bishops and faithful. These four participated in a number of consecrations of new bishops, both in their several jurisdictions and in other independent Orthodox churches. From their lineage came Bishops Joseph Klimowicz, Walter A. Propheta, and Peter A. Zurawetzky, who in turn consecrated most of the men who head the presently existing independent Orthodox churches.

There is one strain of independent Orthodoxy that has a history independent of the bishops discussed above, those which derive from Archbishop Joseph Rene Vilatte of the American Catholic church (discussed in the previous chapter as one of the founders of Old Catholicism in America). Vilatte's episcopal orders came from a small Orthodox body in India and during the later years of his life he consecrated individuals who adopted an Orthodox stance, most notably George A. McGuire, founder of the African Orthodox Church. Also, at least one person from the Vilatte lineage participated in the consecration of Propheta.

Finally, it should be noted that just as both Orthodox and Catholic jurisdictions derived from the work of Vilatte, so too have they both derived from the independent Orthodox bishops. Most notably, Christ Catholic Church derived as an Old Catholic body from the previous jurisdiction of Peter Zurawetzky.

THE NON-CHALCEDONIAN ORTHODOX CHURCHES. Separating during the years of the great Ecumenical Councils, the Christian churches of Egypt, Armenia, and the Middle East, for a variety of reasons, refused to ratify one or more of the creeds, primarily the Chalcedonian Creed of 451 A.D., which most of the Eastern Orthodox world accepted as a standard of orthodox Christian

faith. Both the Roman Catholic Church and the Eastern Orthodox churches have branded these churches as heretical in faith, though the Armenian church has vigorously protested such labeling as a misunderstanding of its position both theologically and relationally to the Council of Chalcedon.

The Nestorians. The monk Nestorius, who became patriarch of Constantinople in 428 A.D., believed that Christ was not the Son of God, but that God was living in Christ. The two natures of Christ—divine and human—were separable, said Nestorius. Further, he said Mary bore the human Christ, not God. Thus she was not "Theotokos," the God-bearer. And it was not God who suffered and died. Nestorius preached his doctrines throughout the Eastern church. In 431 A.D., the Third Council of the early church met at Ephesus to treat the teachings of Nestorius. The council ruled that Mary was "Theotokos," and that the human and divine natures are inseparably bound together in the one person of Christ. The council condemned Nestorius, declared his teachings heretical, and deposed him as patriarch of Constantinople. These actions began a four-year battle of ecclesiastical and imperial politics. The result was Nestorius' banishment and the burning of his books.

The Nestorians continued to spread Nestorius' beliefs. They conducted missionary work in Persia, India, and China, and won followers in Arabia and Egypt. Under the Mohammedans they were essentially free from persecution until the modern era. They survive to this day as the Church of the East. Their largest losses have been to proselytizing efforts by Roman Catholics, Jacobites (to whom they lost much of the church in India), and more recently Protestants.

The Church of the East belongs to the non-Chalcedonian Orthodox tradition in the sense that it opposes the statement of the Council at Chalcedon, 451 A.D., that Christ was "begotten...of Mary the Virgin, the God bearer."

When the Nestorians were rediscovered in the 1830s by Protestant missionaries, their preservation of an old Aramaic dialect also became news. They have since made this dialect the language of their Scripture translation. The seven sacraments they observe are baptism, ordination, the holy eucharist, anointing, remission of sins, holy leaven, and the sign of the cross. The holy leaven refers to the belief that a portion of the bread used at the Last Supper was brought to the East by the Apostle Thaddeus and every eucharist in the Church of the East is made from bread continuous with that meal. The sign of the cross is considered a sacrament and a very specific formula is prescribed for its rubric.

As with all of the Eastern churches, relation with a particular Apostle is assumed. The Church of the East claims a special relationship with the Apostle Thaddeus, who visited the kingdom of Oshroene soon after Pentecost, and with Mari (one of the 70 disciples). Supposedly there was correspondence between Abgar, the ruler of Oshroene, and Christ, in which the former invited Jesus to settle at Edessa, the capital city.

The liturgy of the Church of the East is that of the "Holy Apostles Addai and Mari" (Saints Thaddeus and Mari), who brought it from Jerusalem. The leadership of the church is found in the patriarchate, which has since 1350 been hereditary in the family of Mar Shimun. Since the patriarch is celibate, the office passes from uncle to nephew. Under the patriarch are the metropolitans and bishops. The priests are allowed to marry at any time, even after their ordination.

The Monophysites. The Monophysite churches, like the Eastern Orthodox and Roman Catholic, emphasize liturgy in their church life; they believe strongly in an Apostolic succession, and they derive their doctrinal position from the ancient creeds. Their distinctiveness comes from the content of their creed, which differs more from both Constantinople and Rome than the latter two differ from each other. The Monophysite churches are united on doctrine, but have lines of succession and liturgy with a national flavor.

The distinct Monophysite doctrines derive from the fifth century discussions on the nature of Christ. It was the Monophysite position that Christ was one person of one (mono) nature (physis), the divine nature absorbing the human nature. In the context of the debate, Monophysitism was opposed to Nestorianism, which said that Christ had two natures but that they were separable.

Monophysitism was condemned by the Fourth Council of the early church, held at Chalcedon in 451 A.D. The council formulated what came to be called the Chalcedonian Creed, which says Christ is "of one substance with the Father as regards his Godhead, and at the same time of one substance with us as regards his manhood." Rejecting this creed, most of the Armenian, northern Egyptian, and Syrian churches broke away from the main body of the Christian church. In general, the Monophysite churches accept only the first three councils of the early Christian church (those at Nicea, Constantinople, and Ephesus) as valid and binding.

Theologians continue to debate Monophysite Christology. Some writers contend that the Monophysite churches are Eutychean; i.e., that they follow the teaching of Archimandrite Eutyches, a monk of Constantinople, who asserted the unity of nature in Christ in such a way that the human nature was completely fused and absorbed in the divine. Others, however, assert that the Monophysite churches (at least some of them) are not Eutychean, but Orthodox with a very "undeveloped terminology." The Armenian, Syrian, and Coptic churches represent the Monophysite tradition, but they deny the label "Monophysite" and deny that they teach any submergence of Christ's human nature.

The Armenian Churches. According to tradition, Christianity was brought to Armenia by Thaddeus and Bartholomew, two of the original 12 apostles. By 260 A.D., a bishopric had been established in Armenia and was referred to in Eusebius's *Ecclesiastical History.* In 301 A.D. Tiridates II, the King of Armenia, became the first Christian monarch. St. Gregory the Illuminator, who converted Tiridates, worked with the King's blessing to organize the Armenian church. Through the church a written language was developed and a literate Armenian culture emerged. As is common with Monophysite churches, the Armenian church accepted only the first three ecumenical councils (those at Nicea, Constantinople, and Ephesus), and uses the Nicene Creed.

Members of the Armenian church did not attend the Council of Chalcedon in 451 A.D. and rejected its decisions.

Ecclesiastical authority in the Armenian church was invested in the catholikos who originally resided at Vagharshabat in central Armenia. There, close to the palace, Gregory built Etchmiadzin, the great cathedral. Because of changing political fortunes, the catholikos was frequently forced to move, first to Dovin (484), then among other places to Argina (944), Tauplour (1054), Domnplov (1065), and finally to Sis, in the Kingdom of Lesser Armenia or Cilicia (1293). In 1441 an assembly was held at Etchmiadzin and a catholikos was installed. The catholikos at Sis at that time took the title catholikos of Cilicia. Both sees—Etchmiadzin and Cilicia—have functioned until the present.

There are several minor peculiarities in the Armenian church's sacraments, distinguishing it from other churches in the liturgical family. Holy communion is customarily celebrated only on Sunday and on special occasions and cannot be celebrated twice in the same day. Pure wine (without water) and unleavened bread are used and the laity receive the eucharist by intinction. The eucharist is served to infants immediately after baptism by touching the lips with the elements.

Armenians in America. During the last 1500 years Armenia has suffered foreign domination and persecution by Moslems and Russians. The most terrible of these persecutions were the ones begun by the Turks in 1890 and carried on intermittently for the next 30 years. The effect was practically to destroy and scatter the Armenian nation. The arrival of Armenians in America really dates from the immigration begun as a result of the massacres. The anti-religious persecution by the Russians after World War I followed the Turkish onslaughts.

Armenians in America began to form churches in the early twentieth century. The first was organized in 1891 in Worcester, Massachusetts. After 1921 American Armenians began to divide politically into two factions. One group remained intense nationalists, loyal to an independent Armenia and its symbols. The other group, often described as Pro-Soviet, accommodated themselves to and then supported the inevitable Russian dominance of Armenia. The political division was deeply felt throughout the entire American Armenian community, including the church.

Though practically autonomous, the Armenian church in America recognized the authority of the catholikos of Etchmiadzin. Archbishop Levon Tourian was designated by the see of Etchmiadzin as the supreme prelate of the Armenian Apostolic Church in America. Shortly after his arrival he managed to offend both political parties in contradictory statements concerning the nationalist flag. The continued polarization of the two factions led in 1933 to a split in the church itself.

The split occurred during the annual meeting of the national church council. Pro-Soviet lay delegates began to hold rump sessions and from their meeting a second church was, in effect, begun. While there was little doubt of the legal continuance through the church council, Archbishop Tourian recognized the Pro-Soviet group and declared some of the nationalist priests "unfrocked." A few months later Bishop Tourian was assassinated during High Mass in New York City. So deep was the split in the Armenian community that as one writer observed, "Armenians have come to hate one another with a passion that has exceeded at times even a hatred for the Turks" (Sarkis Atamian, *The Armenian Community* [New York: Philosophical Library, 1955], 358).

The Syrian Churches. Antioch, an ancient city of Syria, is the place where the followers of Jesus were first called Christians (Acts 11:26). In the early centuries, Antioch was the center of a large Christian movement rent by the Monophysite controversy concerning whether Christ had two natures, human and divine, or one (mono) nature (physis). Jacob Baradeus, a resident of Antioch though bishop of Edessa, was both a favorite of Empress Theodora and a fervent Monophysite. After his consecration in 542 A.D., he toured all of the area from Turkey to Egypt organizing churches. Those churches under his authority were to take his name in later years.

The evangelical zeal of the Jacobites was hindered and much of their gains destroyed in the conquests of Islam. In 1665 the Jacobites gained strength in India and Ceylon when the Nestorian Malabar Christians came under the Antiochean patriarch. This action more than doubled the size of the church and today makes up more than 60 percent of its worldwide membership of 100,000.

The Jacobites have several distinctive practices. Baptism is by triune infusion (pouring). Auricular confession to the priest is not used. During the eucharist the priest waves his hand over the elements to symbolize the operation of the Holy Spirit. The action is also used in ordination ceremonies.

The Coptic Churches of Egypt and Ethiopia. At one time the church in Egypt, the Coptic church, was among the largest in Christendom. But in 451 A.D., Dioscurus, the patriarch of Alexandria, was deposed by the Council of Chalcedon, the fourth of the general councils in the early centuries of Christianity. There began an era of persecution of the Copts, first by their fellow Christians and then after 640 A.D. by the Arab conquerors. Beginning with heavy taxes, the persecutions became bloody toward the end of the first millennium A.D. By the end of the Middle Ages, the Coptic church had shrunk from six million to 15,000 members. Growth since that time has been slow, but religious toleration in the nineteenth century helped, and by the middle of the twentieth cetntury, there were three to five million members.

The Coptic church developed its own traditions. Its members are proud of Egypt as the childhood home of Jesus and the location of the ministry of St. Mark, who traditionally is credited with Egypt's initial evangelization. Several liturgies are used, but the most popular is the Liturgy of St. Basil, written by St. Basil the Great (b. 330 A.D.). There is particular veneration of the Virgin, manifest in the 32 feasts in her honor during the ecclesiastical year. In 1971 she is said to have appeared over the Coptic Cathedral in Cairo.

The head of the Coptic church is the patriarch of Alexandria with his see at Cairo. In 1971 this office was assumed by Pope Shenouda III. On May 6, 1973, Pope Shenouda greeted Pope Paul VI with a kiss of peace on a visit to St. Peter's Basilica in Rome.

Ethiopia accepted Christianity in the fourth century and the first bishop, Frumentius, was consecrated by Athanasius, who was the patriarch of Alexandria. The Ethiopian church came under the jurisdiction of the Coptic church in Egypt and followed its theological lead. Isolated by its mountains, Ethiopia withstood the advances of Islam but was cut off from the rest of Christendom. It reached its heights of glory in the thirteenth century under King Lalibela, who gave his name to a city of churches, 10 of which were hewn from solid rock. Modern history for this church began when Catholic missionaries sought to bring the Abyssinians under the Roman pontiff. They almost succeeded in the seventeenth century when for a few years Roman Catholicism was accepted by the ruler.

The Ethiopian church differs from the Coptic church in that it has absorbed strong Jewish traits. It accepts the Apocrypha as scripture, venerates the Sabbath along with Sunday, recognizes Old Testament figures as saints, and observes many Old Testament regulations on food and purification.

SOURCES—EASTERN ORTHODOX FAMILY

EASTERN ORTHODOXY

Adeney, Walter F. *The Greek and Eastern Churches*. New York: Charles Scribner's Sons, 1908. 634 pp.

Attwater, Donald. *The Dissident Eastern Churches*. Milwaukee: The Bruce Publishing Company, 1937. 349 pp.

Benz, Ernst. *The Eastern Orthodox Church*. Garden City, NY: Doubleday, 1963. 230 pp.

Bulgakov, Sergius. *The Orthodox Church*. London: Centenary Press, 1935. 224 pp.

Handbook of American Orthodoxy. Cincinnati: Forward Movement Publications, 1972. 191 pp.

Kuzmission, Joe. *Eastern Orthodox World Directory*. Boston: Braden Press, 1968. 305 pp.

Lau, Emhardt Burgess. *The Eastern Church in the Western World*. Milwaukee: Morehead Publishing Co., 1928. 149 pp.

Le Guillou, M. J. *The Spirit of Eastern Orthodoxy*. Glen Rock, NJ: Paulist Press, 1964. 121 pp.

Orthodoxy, A Faith and Order Dialogue. Geneva: World Council of Churches, 1960. 80 pp.

Parishes and Clergy of the Orthodox, and Other Eastern Churches in North and South America. New York: Joint Commission on Cooperation with the Eastern and Old Catholic Churches of the General Convention of the Protestant Episcopal Church, 1964-65. 187 pp. Rev. ed., 1967-68. 184 pp. Rev. ed., 1970-71. 208 pp.

Schmemann, Alexander. *The Historic Road of Eastern Orthodoxy*. New York: Holt, Rinehart and Winston, 1963. 343 pp.

Zernov, Nicolas. *The Church of Eastern Christians*. London: Society for Promoting Christian Knowledge, 1942. 114 pp.

ORTHODOX LITURGY

Dalmais, Irenee-Henri. *Eastern Liturgies*. New York: Hawthorn Books, 1960. 144 pp.

The Orthodox Liturgy. London: Society for Promoting Christian Knowledge, 1964. 110 pp.

Sokolof, D., comp. *A Manual of the Orthodox Church's Divine Service*. Jordanville, NY: Holy Trinity Russian Orthodox Monastery, 1968. 166 pp.

ORTHODOX THEOLOGY

Allen, Joseph J. *Orthodox Synthesis*. Crestwood, NY: St. Vladimir's Seminary Press, 1981. 231 pp.

Lossky, Vladimir. *The Mystical Theology of the Eastern Church*. London: James Clarke & Co., 1957. 252 pp.

Maloney, George A. *A History of Orthodox Theology Since 1453*. Belmont, MA: Nordland Publishing Company, 1976. 388 pp.

Platon, Metropolitan. *The Orthodox Doctrine of the Apostolic Eastern Church*. London, 1857. Reprint. New York: AMS Press, 1969. 239 pp.

INDEPENDENT ORTHODOXY

Anson, Peter F. *Bishops at Large*. London: Faber and Faber, 1964. 593 pp.

Bain, Alan. *"Bishops Irregular."* Bristol, England: The Author, 1985. 256 pp.

Brandreth, H. R. T. *Episcopi Vagantes and the Anglican Church*. London: S.P.C.K., 1961. 140 pp.

Morris, John W. "The Episcopate of Aftimios Ofeish." *The Word* Part One: 25, 2 (February 1981) 5-9; Part Two: 25, 3 (March 1981) 5-9.

Pruter, Karl, and J. Gordon Melton. *The Old Catholic Sourcebook*. New York: Garland Publishing, Inc., 1983. 254 pp.

Tillett, Gregory. *Joseph Rene Vilatte: A Bibliography*. Sydney, Australia: The Vilatte Guild, 1980. 23 pp.

NON-CHALCEDONEAN ORTHODOXY

Butler, Alfred J. *The Ancient Coptic Churches of Egypt*. Oxford: Claredon Press, 1884. 2 Vols.

Elmhardt, William Chauncey, and George M. Lamsa. *The Oldest Christian People*. New York: AMS Press, 1970. 141 pp.

Fortescue, Adrian. *The Lesser Eastern Churches*. London: Catholic Truth Society, 1913. 468 pp.

Issac, Ephraim. *The Ethiopian Church*. Boston: Henry N. Sawyer Company, 1968. 59 pp.

McCullough, W. Stewart. *A Short History of Syriac Christianity to the Rise of Islam*. Chico, CA: Scholars Press, 1982. 197 pp.

Meinardus, Otto, F. A. *Christian Egypt Faith and Life*. Cairo: The American University in Cairo Press, 1970. 513 pp.

Ramban, Kadavil Paul. *The Orthodox Syrian Church, Its Religion and Philosophy*. Puthencruz, Syria: K. V. Pathrose, 1973. 167 pp.

St. Mark and the Coptic Church. Cairo: Coptic Orthodox Patriarchate, 1968. 164 pp.

Sarkissian, Karekin. *The Council of Chalcedon and the Armenian Church*. New York: The Armenian Church Prelacy, 1965. 264 pp.

———. *The Witness of the Oriental Orthodox Churches*. Artelias, Lebanon: The Author, 1970. 91 pp.

Chapter 3

Lutheran Family

Directory listings for the groups belonging to the Lutheran Family
may be found in the section beginning on page 147.

Lutheranism represents the first widely successful western breach of the authority of the Roman Catholic church. The teachings of Martin Luther, coupled with the power of the German princes who supported him, precipitated a dramatic break with Roman Catholicism throughout Europe in the early sixteenth century. Lutheranism embraces the two basic precepts of Luther's writings: first, that salvation is by grace through faith alone; and second, that the Bible is the sole rule of faith and the sole authority for doctrine. Lutheranism is distinct from other Reformation churches because of its continued emphasis on a sacramental liturgy and because of Luther's understanding of the eucharist.

LUTHERAN DOCTRINE. Word and sacrament are the keystones of Lutheran church life. "Word" refers to the appeal to the Bible instead of to both the Bible and tradition. "Sacrament" refers to the high regard Lutherans have for the two sacraments they observe—baptism and the eucharist—and Luther's theology of the eucharist. Luther's belief that salvation is by grace through faith alone finds expression in Lutherans' interpretation of the Bible and reliance on it, and in their celebration of the sacraments.

A discussion of the importance of the Word to Lutherans must start with Luther's background. He was a Bible scholar and a professor at the University of Wittenburg in what has become East Germany. He translated the Bible into German and based his theology on the Bible. Before he broke with the Roman Catholic Church, he was an Augustinian monk who strove to merit salvation through ascetic practices. In studying the Bible, however, he found that salvation does not come by man's action but only by God's free gift. Thus comes the emphasis on man's sinfulness in Lutheranism: a person who breaks one law is as guilty as a person whose whole life is the breaking of laws. Luther saw that the whole point of Christ's coming was to bring salvation; human beings could not earn it by themselves.

It remains for each person to welcome grace by faith in Christ. This emphasis contrasts with the traditional Roman Catholic emphasis on both faith and good works. Further, this emphasis contradicts a practice popular in Luther's time—the selling of indulgences (by which people paid to cancel the punishment they would receive in purgatory for their sins). Proceeds from the sale of indulgences in Germany were being used to finance the building of St. Peter's Basilica in Rome.

Luther's discovery that the righteousness (goodness) of God is man's only reason for hope came during the winter of 1513-14, in what is called his "tower experience," so named because it occurred while he was in the monastery tower. Among biblical passages supporting his doctrines are Romans 1:17: "For in it (the gospel of Jesus) the righteousness of God is revealed through faith, for faith. He who through faith is righteous shall live," and Ephesians 2:8: "For by grace you have been saved through faith. This is not your own doing, but the gift of God, not because of works, lest anyone should boast."

Because of Gutenberg's invention of the printing press in the fifteenth century, Luther's translation of the Bible could be made widely available. His translation of the New Testament was published in 1522, and the Old Testament in 1534, and they quickly became best-sellers in Germany. Lutherans then and now have used the Bible as their only standard for faith and doctrine. Further, Luther used it to counter a range of traditional Catholic elements. First, Luther found that only two sacraments, baptism and the eucharist, had a biblical basis. Hence Lutherans do not consider the following to be sacraments: penance, confession, holy orders, unction, and marriage. Second, Luther argued against a number of practices that Roman Catholics consider sanctioned by tradition if not by the Bible. For example, he argued that the celibate priesthood has no biblical basis, and he soon left the Augustinian priesthood and married a former nun. Among pious practices Lutherans abandoned were monastic life, the veneration of relics, radical fasting, pilgrimages, hair-shirts, scourges, and the rosary. Lutheran piety instead developed around hearing the Word in the liturgy, receiving the eucharist, and reading the Bible. Third, Luther cited the Bible to counter the authority of the pope, and claimed the Bible as the source of his own authority to reform the church.

To discuss the importance of "sacrament" for Lutherans involves treating both Luther's understanding of the

15

eucharist, and other elements discussed in the next section that make Lutheran liturgy distinctive.

Luther's doctrine of the eucharist is called consubstantiation, a departure from the Roman Catholic doctrine called transubstantiation. Consubstantiation means Christ is present everywhere, but his presence is especially focused in the eucharist. The bread and wine still exist, but under the guise of bread and wine is Christ, who is received by the believer physically. This reception occurs, said Luther, because of Christ's promise at the Last Supper that it would occur. Transubstantiation, on the other hand, means that the essence of bread and wine are replaced by the essence of Christ, who becomes present physically.

The doctrine of consubstantiation allowed Lutherans to preserve their liturgical worship instead of denying the sacraments altogether. So Lutheran liturgy is distinct from that of the Anabaptists, who do not have any sacraments, although they do observe a memorial meal. The consubstantiation doctrine also kept Lutherans from following the Reformed tradition, which replaces belief in Christ's physical presence in the sacramental elements with belief only in his spiritual presence in the eucharist.

LUTHERAN LITURGY. Lutheranism vies with the historic Catholic and Orthodox traditions for its emphasis on liturgy. In the early 1520s Luther began revising the Sunday service and found himself in conflict with those reformers, such as Andreas von Carlstadt, who looked for radical changes in the worship. Luther developed a form of worship in Wittenburg which followed the form of the Roman liturgy but which emphasized the use of the vernacular in preaching, in the liturgy, and in hymns. Vestments, candles, and pictures became optional. The church calendar remained in use.

Luther did change the format of the service by bringing the sermon into the worship, and on days when the eucharist was not served, a sermon substituted for it. Gregorian music was continued but gradually was replaced. The medieval outline that was standard for each liturgical service continued and remains basic in Lutheran liturgy. This outline is reflected in the *Agenda*, forms of worship adopted by the Lutheran churches in the United States in 1958.

No discussion of Lutheran liturgy would be complete without mention of Lutheran hymnology. All Protestants are familiar with Luther's "A Mighty Fortress Is Our God," which became the battle hymn of the Reformation. In 1524 Luther published his first hymn book and a second was published before the year was out. The popular hymns not only spread Luther's ideas on man's sinfulness and God's righteousness, but became integral to the worship and distinguish Lutheran liturgy from most other liturgical services.

POLITY. Polity is largely a low-priority subject among Lutherans. Bishops, though rare, have not been entirely unknown. The tendency generally, however, is for churches to operate somewhere between a congregational polity and a form of presbyterianism in which power is vested in the synod or body of ministers.

Luther advocated cooperation between church and state. He said a Christian ruler, acting in a Christian manner, should govern the secular sphere, and the church should govern the religious sphere. Thus the Christian ruler and the church, each in their respective spheres, would oversee the activities of all the people in the state.

THE "CONFESSING" CHURCH. Luther's doctrinal insights and his criticisms of Roman Catholicism were first publicly presented in the Ninety-five Theses he nailed to the church door in Wittenburg in 1517, and then in the three treatises of 1521. His position did not find confessional status until 1530, with the Augsburg Confession. Princes who were following Luther and breaking the unity of the Roman Catholic Church had to account for that to the Holy Roman Emperor. So they presented the Augsburg Confession to him to explain their position. As written by Melanchthon, a professor of Greek and a New Testament scholar at Wittenburg, it has remained the central statement of Lutheran essentials. It includes traditional Christian beliefs such as belief in the Trinity and the resurrection of the body. But it goes further to elaborate on statements concerning humanity, specifically, on man's sinfulness, forgiveness of sin, and justification by grace through faith alone. Lutherans rallied around the Augsburg Confession, and Roman Catholics united against it. It became the standard under which Lutherans later entered the Thirty Years' War.

The Augsburg Confession began the practice of the "confessing" church. Typically, when pressed by a contemporary situation, Lutheran (and Reformed) churches will summarize a stance in the form of a "confession of faith" which says to the world, "Here we stand; we can do no other." In the twentieth century such statements were issued to counter Nazism.

To the Augsburg Confession were added other confessions and documents which further clarified a Lutheran position as opposed to other religions. These documents include the Larger and Small Catechism (1529), written by Luther, the Smalcald Articles (1537), and the Formula of Concord (1577). These, along with the three ecumenical creeds (the Apostles' Creed, the Nicene Creed, and the Chalcedonian Creed), were collected in 1580 into the *Book of Concord*. This is the basic collection of Lutheran doctrinal writings, a clear statement of the truths Lutherans feel are taught in Scripture and the starting point for other theological endeavors.

ORIGINS. At least three dates vie with each other for the beginning of Lutheranism. The most widely accepted date is October 31, 1517, the day Luther nailed his Ninety-five Theses for debate to the door of the Castle Church in Wittenburg. Outside the scholarly circles of Lutheran seminaries, this date goes virtually unrivaled as the beginning date not only of Lutheranism but also of the entire Reformation. Lutheran scholars have pointed out, however, that other dates are worthy of consideration. Some cite Luther's discovery of the meaning of the righteousness of God during the winter of 1513-14. This was the so-called "tower experience," which supplied the theological insights inherent in the Ninety-five Theses.

The third and most valid year for the origin of Lutheranism is 1530. The years 1514 and 1517 cannot really qualify as dates of origin because no Lutheran church existed then. The year 1530 brought the publishing of the Augsburg Confession. What had been an almost chaotic movement had a document around which to rally. The congregations which wished to identify with Luther could be said to have become a public entity. So 1530 might best be considered the first year of the Lutheran church.

LUTHERANS IN AMERICA. After 1530, Lutheranism spread in Germany, Sweden, Denmark, Finland, and Norway. An independent church was established in each country. But when the Lutherans came to the U.S., they entered a vast country as compared to the smaller European states. So Lutherans from any one European country were scattered throughout America, seeking good farm land especially in the Midwest and along the Southern seaboard. Everywhere they spread, each linguistic group established a synod, an autonomous Lutheran church. Each group was independent of the churches of other linguistic groups, and typically was independent of the churches in other American states. The rapid immigration in the nineteenth century led to the creation by 1850 of more than 150 Lutheran church bodies. The history of American Lutheranism is thus the history of the merger of these 150 synods into 21 Lutheran churches today.

For no other family of American religions does national origin make such a difference. For example, the Roman Catholics, who came to the U.S. from all over Europe, remained one ecclesiastical entity when they arrived here. Roman Catholic immigrants from various national and linguistic groups did not create diverse denominational bodies. To give another example, most Methodists came to the U.S. from the British Isles and thus did not create churches divergent from the European Methodist churches (with two minor exceptions). For neither Catholics nor Methodists did national origin matter as much as for Lutherans.

Lutheranism did not enter North America by the establishment of the usual center on the Atlantic coast. It made its appearance, if briefly, in Manitoba, on Hudson's Bay. In 1619, the year before the Puritans landed in Massachusetts, Jens Munck, a Danish explorer, founded a colony at what is today known as Fort Churchill. Among the colonists was Rasmus Jensen (1579-1620), a Lutheran pastor. The colony prospered for several months until in the dead of winter scurvy began to kill its residents. Only three men remained to sail back to Denmark in the spring. It would be more than 100 years before a second group of Lutherans would arrive in what today is Canada, this time to a more hospitable climate in Nova Scotia.

During the 1740s Lutherans descended upon Nova Scotia from two directions. The first group arrived from Maine where a German colony had been created in 1740 by Samuel Waldo. They were part of an expedition to capture Louisburg from the French. After the battle, a few of the Germans remained and settled in the new English city of Halifax. There they were joined in 1749 by some Germans who came with the original 4,000 settlers and in 1750 by a group of about 300 German colonists. A church, St. George's, was organized and a building erected. The congregation, however, was continually beset by pastors who converted to Anglicanism. Eventually the church was lost, but not before a permanent Lutheran congregation was established at Lunenburg, a congregation still in place when the loyalist German subjects of King George who had been in America began to arrive in Canada after the American Revolution.

Lutheranism was first brought to the United States by Swedes who established a colony, Fort Christina, on the Delaware River in 1638. The Reverend Reorus Torkillus, the first Lutheran pastor in the New World, accompanied them. The Swedes were bolstered by the arrival of German Lutherans who began to settle in Pennsylvania in the last half of the century. By the middle of the eighteenth century, they were firmly entrenched in Pennsylvania and the surrounding territory. In March 1734, the Salzburgers created a third Lutheran center in Georgia.

In 1742 Henry Melchior Muhlenberg came to the colonies, and from his work and ministry, organized Lutheranism in the U.S. is dated. Installed as pastor of three congregations in Pennsylvania, he began to reach out to other parishes and to write Germany for continued help. In 1748 he led in the organization of the Ministerium of Pennsylvania, the first Lutheran synod in the colonies. He also opened his home to ministerial candidates. In 1792 a new constitution was adopted. Lay persons were first allowed to come to meetings of ministers in 1796, and the organizational tie to Germany was effected in that year.

The decades following the war were ones of expansion and the addition of new synods—New York (1786), North Carolina (1803), Ohio (1818), Maryland (1820), and Tennessee (1820). The General Synod (1820) was a cooperating body for the various state synods. Accompanying the growth was the emergence of tension over the issue of Americanization. Theologian Samuel S. Schmucker became a leading "liberal" who advocated the use of English in worship and a strong "pietistic" emphasis (a stress on piety and religious experience instead of on rigid doctrinal conformity). Schmucker was opposed by the newly arriving immigrants, who came in great numbers in the second quarter of the century. They were orthodox and conservative.

Emerging as the leader of the "conservatives" was Carl Ferdinand Wilhelm Walther, who had migrated from Saxony in 1839. He began to publish *Der Lutheraner* to argue for his position and was influential in setting the form of Lutheranism for such synods as Missouri (1846), Buffalo (1845), and Iowa (1854).

During the middle of the century, the Scandinavian Lutherans began to arrive in great numbers and to form their own synods. The first Norwegian Synod was formed in 1846. The Swedes in the General Synod joined with recent immigrants to form the Augustana Synod in 1860. Lars Paul Esbjorn led the Swedish schism. Other synods were formed by the Finns (1890), Danes (1872), Slovaks (1902), and Icelanders (1885).

The great strength of Lutheranism shifted away from the East Coast in the nineteenth century and became dominant in the states north and west of Chicago. Centers were established along the Mississippi River at St. Louis, Rock Island, and Minneapolis.

The large influx of immigrants who took control away from the older, liberal eastern leaders like Schmucker delayed but could not avoid the problems created by Americanization. The use of English and adaptation to "American" mores increasingly plagued the church and reached its culmination during World War I. There is little doubt that English-speaking churches were able to fan the flames of prohibition by attacking their German brethren who supported the German brewers (Schlitz, Anheuser-Busch).

From the last quarter of the nineteenth century until the present time, the major thrust in the Lutheran family has been intrafamily ecumenism. Although Lutherans have entered ecumenical discussions with those of other faiths, these discussions have never reached the stage of definite plans for a merger. Within Lutheranism, however, there has been a century of merger by the multitude of independent synodical bodies established in the nineteenth century. Merger was usually preceded by the formation of cooperative councils. The more conservative Lutheran churches formed the Lutheran Synodical Conference in 1872. The conference included such synods as the Missouri Synod, the Synod of Evangelical Lutheran Churches, the Evangelical Lutheran Synod, and, until 1892, the three synods of Wisconsin, Michigan, and Minnesota. Only the Missouri Synod and the Synod of Evangelical Lutheran Churches remain in the Lutheran Synodical Conference. For all practical purposes, the conference has fallen apart, due to the Missouri Synod's negotiations with more liberal Lutheran bodies. The National Lutheran Council (1918-66) and the American Lutheran Conference became the arena for the largest number of mergers by various linguistic traditions as they became Americanized. Major mergers in the 1960s made these obsolete and they were replaced by the Lutheran Council in the U.S.A., in which the three larger churches participated: the Lutheran Church in America, the American Lutheran Church, and the Missouri Synod. In 1977, after many years of debate, the Missouri Synod withdrew from the council.

The withdrawal of the Missouri Synod from the Lutheran Council in the U.S.A. was in the midst of an internal controversy which was to bring conservative forces to the forefront of the synod's life. It also led to the withdrawal of more liberal elements, those generally associated with Concordia Theological Seminary. Those who left the synod in 1976 formed the Association of Evangelical Lutheran Churches. They almost immediately entered into merger talks with the two larger Lutheran bodies, the Lutheran Church in America and the American Lutheran Church. That three-way merger was completed in 1987 and the new church, the Evangelical Lutheran Church in America (1988) was officially inaugurated on January 1, 1988. The new church currently counts over half of all Lutherans in the United States in its membership, though more than 2.5 million remain in the Missouri Synod.

THE APOSTOLIC LUTHERANS. One group, the Finnish Apostolic Lutherans, has developed outside of the main thrust of Lutheran history in America. The product of an intense pietistic movement originating in a geographically isolated part of northern Scandinavia, and centered in a relatively isolated part of the United States, the Apostolics

have moved along a distinct pathway, though still very Lutheran in faith and life. Their small numbers have, due to their splintering, accounted for a relatively large number of Lutheran church bodies.

In the 1840s, in northern Sweden in the area generally called Lapland, a young pastor, Lars Levi Laestadius, led a revival in the state church, the Swedish Lutheran church. The movement was based on Laestadius' powerful preaching of repentance. The revival spread from Kaaresuvanto to all of northern Scandinavia. Characteristic of the revival were deep sorrow for sin, public confession of sin before the whole congregation, and the experience of deliverance. Among the leaders of the emerging revival was Juhani Raattamaa, a lay preacher. Raattamaa discovered the Power of the Keys or the practice of absolution by which a representative of the church laid hands on the penitent and pronounced forgiveness. The penitent was to believe these words as if Christ had pronounced them. The Laestadians believed that God sent times of visitation on all peoples and that there were Christians in all churches, but they laid emphasis on the need to follow the Bible to attain salvation.

Finns (Laplanders) and other Scandinavians from near the Arctic area began to migrate to America in the 1860s due to economic problems in Scandinavia. They settled in Minnesota and the Upper Peninsula of Michigan. Antti Vitikka began to preach among the Finns and in 1870 gathered a Laestadian group at Calumet, Michigan. The congregation called Solomon Korteniemi as their pastor and in 1872-73 organized the Solomon Korteniemi Lutheran Society. Korteniemi proved a poor leader and was succeeded by John Takkinen, sent from Sweden. Under his leadership in 1879 the name "Apostolic" Lutheran was chosen.

The Apostolic Lutherans grew and prospered in their American home but quickly became rent with controversy, which splintered them into five separate churches. Each faction goes under the name of Apostolic Lutheran and is distinguished by its nickname and its doctrine and practice. Only one group has organized formally as a church body.

The first schism in the Apostolic Lutheran movement occurred in the Calumet congregation in 1888. Members opposed to the "harsh rule" of Takkinen elected John Roanpaa and seized the church property. In 1890 Arthur Leopold Heideman arrived from Lapland to serve this new congregation.

In Europe in 1897, the Laestadians split into the Church of the First Born and the Old Laestadians. In America, the Takkinen congregation aligned with the Church of the First Born and the followers of Arthur Heideman aligned with the Old Laestadians.

Another schism occurred in Europe when a Pietist party, called the New Awakening, left its Pietist church in Finland. In 1910 the New Awakening sent Mikko Saarenpaa and Juho Pyorre to America.

These three prime groups, the Old Laestadians, the Church of the First Born, and the New Awakening, share the common Laestadian Lutheran doctrinal heritage as transmitted through Raattamaa. Raattamaa had taught that justification and conversion came by hearing the Gospel preached by the church of Christ. The New Awakening, however, believed that conversion could occur without hearing the Word. The New Awakening accused the Laestadians of moral laxity and emphasized a strict moral life. The New Awakening also departed from the other Laestadians on their belief in the "third use of the law," i.e., that the Ten Commandments were in force for Christians. For the Old Laestadians the only law was the law of Christ, the commandments of love. The Old Laestadians tended to believe that the church must be outwardly one. Hence they tended to be ultra-exclusivist.

A fourth schism occurred among the Old Laestadians when an emphasis on evangelism—redemption, forgiveness, and the righteousness of Christ—was opposed to an emphasis on Christian life and conduct and the repentance from sin. The evangelicals were inspired by the fervent preaching of Heideman and felt that the preaching of free grace would produce good fruit of itself.

The Apostolic Lutherans have always had a congregational government, in part a reaction to Scandinavian Lutheran episcopacy. Like other extreme congregationalists, they have resisted organization but can be distinguished by doctrinal position, periodicals, and foreign alignments.

SOURCES—THE LUTHERAN FAMILY

Martin Luther

Bainton, Roland. *Here I Stand*. New York: Abingdon-Cokesbury, 1950.

Booth, Edwin. *Martin Luther, Oak of Saxony*. Nashville: Abingdon-Press, 1966. 271 pp.

Luther, Martin. *Three Treatises*. Philadelphia: Fortress Press, 1960.

———. *Works*. Edited by Jaroslav Pelikan and Helmut T. Lehman. 55 Vols. St. Louis: Concordia Publishing House and Philadelphia: Fortress Press, 1958-67.

Ritter, Gerhard. *Luther, His Life and Works*. New York: Harper & Row, 1963. 256 pp.

What Luther Says, An Anthology. St. Louis: Concordia Publishing House, 1959.

The Lutheran Church Worldwide

Bergendoff, Conrad. *The Church of the Lutheran Reformation*. St. Louis: Concordia Publishing House, 1967. 339 pp.

Bodensieck, Julius, ed. *The Encyclopedia of the Lutheran Church*. Minneapolis: Augsburg Publishing House, 1965. 3 Vols.

Lucker, Edwin L., ed. *Lutheran Cyclopedia*. St. Louis: Concordia Publishing House, 1975. 845 pp.

Lutheran Churches of the World. Minneapolis: Augsburg Publishing House, 1972. 333 pp.

Nelson, E. Clifford. *The Rise of World Lutheranism*. Philadelphia: Fortress Press, 1982. 421 pp.

Vajta, Vilmos, ed. *The Lutheran Church, Past and Present*. Minneapolis: Augsburg Publishing House, 1977. 392 pp.

Lutherans in North America: Historical

Cronmiller, Carl R. *A History of the Lutheran Church in Canada*. Toronto: Evangelical Lutheran Synod of Canada, 1961. 288 pp.

Nelson, E. Clifford, ed. *The Lutherans in North America*. Philadelphia: Fortress Press, 1980. 564 pp.

Nichol, Todd W. *All These Lutherans*. Minneapolis, MN: Augsburg Publishing House, 1986. 126 pp.

Thorkelson, Wilmar. *Lutherans in the U.S.A*. Minneapolis: Augsburg Publishing House, 1969.

Wallace, Paul A. W. *The Muhlenbergs of Pennsylvania*. Philadelphia: University of Pennsylvania, 1950. 358 pp.

Weideraenders, Robert C., and Walter G. Tillmanns. *The Synods of American Lutheranism*. N.p.: Lutheran Historical Conference, 1968. 209 pp.

Wentz, Abdel Ross. *A Basic History of Lutheranism in America*. Philadelphia: Muhlenburg Press, 1964. 439 pp.

Wolf, R. C. *Documents of Lutheran Unity in America*. Philadelphia: Fortress Press, 1966. 672 pp.

Doctrinal

Allbeck, Willard Dow. *Studies in the Lutheran Confessions*. Philadelphia: Fortress Press, 1968. 306 pp.

Arnold, Duane W. H. and C. George Fry. *The Way, the Truth, and the Life*. Grand Rapids, MI: Baker Book House, 1982. 300 pp.

Gritsch, Eric W., and Robert W. Jenson. *Lutheranism*. Philadelphia: Fortress Press, 1976. 214 pp.

Hamsher, Paul O. *This I Believe, My Lutheran Handbook*. Lima, OH: The C.S.S. Publishing Co., n.d. 86 pp.

Schink, Edmund. *Theology of Lutheran Confessions*. Philadelphia: Muhlenberg Press, 1961.

Schramm, W. E. *What Lutherans Believe*. Columbus, OH: Wartburg Press, 1946. 156 pp.

Liturgy

Reed, Luther D. *The Lutheran Liturgy*. Philadelphia: Muhlenberg Press, 1947. 824 pp.

Stauffer, S. Anita, Gilbert A. Doan, and Michael B. Aune. *Lutherans at Worship*. Minneapolis: Augsburg Publishing House, 1978. 96 pp.

Polity

Asheim, Ivar, and Victor R. Gold, eds. *Episcopacy in the Lutheran Church*. Philadelphia: Fortress Press, 1970. 261 pp.

Chapter 4

Reformed-Presbyterian Family

Directory listings for the groups belonging to the Reformed-Presbyterian Family
may be found in the section beginning on page 157.

The Reformed-Presbyterian tradition is based on the work of John Calvin, who established the Reformed church in Geneva, Switzerland, in the 1540s. The various churches that trace their origins to Calvin are set apart from other Christian churches by their theology (Reformed) and church government (Presbyterian).

Calvin's theological system was shaped by his belief in God's sovereignty in creation and salvation. The other major theological tenets of Calvinism—predestination and limited atonement—are built on this belief in God's sovereignty. Strictly interpreted, predestination means that the number and identity of "the elect" (those who are saved) were ordained by the sovereign God before the beginning of the world. Christ's atonement for sin was thus limited to the elect; salvation is not possible for all humanity, but only for those predestined to be saved. The issue of a strict or lenient interpretation of predestination has divided both European and American Calvinists.

Churches in the Reformed-Presbyterian tradition have a presbyterial form of church government. The presbytery is a legislative and/or judicial body composed of clergy and laity in equal numbers from the churches of a given region. The laity are elected by the members of the church. The word "presbytery" is also sometimes used to refer to the ruling body of the local church, but the name "Presbyterian" derives from the regional governing body.

Thus the name of this tradition is "Reformed" for Calvin's theology (an attempt to reform the Roman Catholic church) and "Presbyterian" for the form of church government based on the presbytery. The name for this tradition also reflects history. On the continent, Calvinists established Reformed churches. In the British Isles, predominantly in Scotland, Calvinists established Presbyterian churches. In America, the Reformed churches and the Presbyterian churches all belong to the Reformed-Presbyterian tradition, along with the Congregational churches. In this chapter, the word "Reformed" applies to Calvinist theology, worship, and churches using Calvinist theology. The word "Reformed" is not used to refer to the whole Reformation, a movement much broader than Calvinism, although Calvin played a major role in that movement.

Reformed theology involves many beliefs in addition to the distinguishing tenets mentioned above—beliefs in God's sovereignty, in predestination, and in limited atonement. Reformed theology affirms the commitments associated with the creeds of the early centuries of Christianity: beliefs in God, Christ, the Holy Spirit, and the Trinity.

Beyond these beliefs come those shared by Reformed theology with other Protestant theologies: the belief in salvation by grace through faith, and the reliance on the Bible as the sole authority for faith and doctrine. With the followers of Martin Luther and Ulrich Zwingli, Calvinists were Protestants in that they protested various doctrines and practices of the Roman Catholic Church during the sixteenth century movement called the Reformation. The Protestant emphasis on salvation by grace through faith stands opposed to the Roman Catholic understanding of salvation through faith and good works. Further, when Protestants claim the Bible as their sole authority for faith and doctrine, they negate the Roman Catholic reliance on both the Bible and tradition. Reformed churchmen were generally hostile toward practices sanctioned by tradition unless the practices could be substantiated by Scripture.

Within Reformed theology, the definition of the church makes no reference to bishops or apostolic succession (the line of succession by ordination from the Apostles to modern times), two elements that are crucial to churches in the liturgical tradition. Instead, Reformed theology defines the church as the place where the "pure doctrine of the gospel is preached" and the "pure administration of the sacraments" is maintained. By the "pure doctrine of the gospel" is meant the gospel preached by ordained ministers according to Calvinist emphases (e.g., predestination). By the "pure administration of the sacraments" is meant the administration only of baptism and the Lord's Supper as sacraments. This practice contrasts with Roman Catholicism's celebration of seven sacraments and some churches' rejection of all sacraments. (The Zwinglians and the Anabaptists serve as two examples of those rejecting all the sacraments. Zwinglians considered the eucharist a memorial meal, not a sacrament. The Anabaptists had no sacraments but did have ordinances, including foot washing and adult baptism.)

Though not without some differences, Lutherans and Roman Catholics accepted the doctrine of the real physical presence of Christ in the sacraments. The followers of Calvin supplanted this idea with the belief in the spiritual presence apprehended by faith. The effect is to change the sacrament as a special focus of Christ's presence in the world and to move away from the sacramental world of the liturgical churches. The Reformed world is a secular world. God is present and can be apprehended by faith in all activities.

Worship in a Reformed church is centered on the preaching of the sermon, which ideally combines the exposition of Scripture with the ordered presentation of a great truth of the faith. While having been influenced by the emotive appeal of the Methodists in modern times, the Reformed sermon still serves primarily a teaching function. Prayers and hymns rehearse the basic tenets of the Reformed faith—confession, forgiveness, and the acknowledgement of the sovereignty of God. Hymns for many years were limited to the Psalms set to music, and the church produced many editions of Psalters. Most now use hymn books, though the Psalms remain important.

As spelled out in the Second Helvetic Confession (1566), the characteristics of Reformed worship are the Word of God properly preached to the people, decent meeting spaces purged of anything offensive to the church, and services conducted in order, modesty, discipline, and in the language of the people. Gone are the aesthetic/theological/sacramental appeals of worship. Gone are "offensive" elements such as statues, vestments, saints' festivals, indulgences, pilgrimages, and relics. Reformed worship is directed on a cognitive level—preaching, worship understandable to the layman, logical thoughts and ordered behavior, and a disciplined atmosphere.

The Reformed theological position was codified in confessions in the sixteenth and seventeenth centuries. The main Reformed confessions are the First Helvetic Confession (1536), the Belgic Confession (1561), the Second Helvetic Confession (1566), the Canons of the Synod of Dort (1619), and the Westminster Confession of Faith (1647). Also necessary to understanding the Reformed faith is the Heidelberg Catechism (1693). The above description of Reformed theology aligns with these confessions, all of which make the same basic doctrinal statements and in addition address whatever current crisis and/or local debate prompted the confessions. Along with other documents written by the Westminster Assembly of Divines in the 1640s, the Westminster Confession is the confession that has had the greatest impact on U.S. churches in the Reformed-Presbyterian tradition. Baptist documents are also derived from the Westminster documents.

Calvin developed the doctrine of two spheres of action, the secular and religious. Although his Reformed church in Geneva was a state church, he ended any interference of the state in church affairs such as the celebration of church festivals or the appointment of church officials. Calvin set up a theocracy, a form of government designed to have God as its head. The church defined the magistrates' authority as coming from God and the church had power over the magistrates in that magistrates were church members. Thus religion had considerable power over all social activities; Calvin was the most powerful man in Geneva. The theocracy was patterned on Calvin's *Institutes of the Christian Religion*.

The presbyterial system is a state church system and was designed for intimate communion with the secular authority. It was based on a parish system in which the country would be divided into geographic areas with one church to a parish. All people who had been baptized would be members. The church and state together, each in its proper area, would keep order. The most notable example of the interworking of church and state in Geneva concerned a heretic, Servetus. Among other objections to orthodox Christian doctrines, Servetus had likened the Trinity to the three-headed hound of hell. Calvin condemned Servetus as a heretic, but the secular authorities in Geneva tried and executed him.

Within the presbyterial system of the Reformed-Presbyterian tradition, clergy and lay people together rule the church. The preaching elders (ministers) are the pastors and teachers. The ruling elders, lay people, are to assist the teaching elders in discipline and in the governance of the church. Deacons collect the offering and see to its distribution. In the local congregation, the ministers and elders together make up the consistory or session, occasionally called the presbytery. In some cases the deacons also belong to the consistory. All ministers and elders are called and elected by the other elders.

The ministers and elders form a series of judicial and legislative bodies. The local consistories or sessions are grouped into a presbytery or classis or coetus. From this body of all the ministers in a given region, plus an equal number of elected elders, comes the name for the presbyterial form of government. The presbyters, those in the presbytery, have the power within the church. Several presbyters (usually a minimum of three) may come together to form a synod (or classis) and synods may form an even larger body such as the General Assembly of the United Presbyterian Church. Each body has specific functions and usually a protest of a decision at one level can be appealed to a higher level. (In actual practice among some Presbyterian churches, a congregational form of government prevails and the presbytery functions as an advisory forum and facilitates cooperative endeavor.)

Both Luther and Calvin established state churches, as did Ulrich Zwingli. Zwingli died in 1531; his church in Zurich, Switzerland, was soon absorbed into Calvin's Reformed church. The Anabaptists (discussed in Chapter Eight) opposed all state churches, whether Lutheran, Calvinist, or Roman Catholic, and they were persecuted by the state churches. The Reformation brought its share of bloodshed.

Calvin's doctrine, more than the doctrine of any other religion, moved with the rising mercantile society and justified secular activity in the world. By contrast, Anabaptism was a world-denying view that sheltered the elect against a hostile, sinful, secular society. The Anabaptist tradition continues in the Mennonites, the Amish, the Quakers, and the Church of the Brethren. Lutheranism retained a more sacred character than Calvinism; Lutheranism spread by refurbishing Catholic forms.

Calvinism, however, rose on the emerging middle class of Western Europe.

Calvin, who lived from 1509 to 1564, wrote the single most influential Protestant theological text, the *Institutes of the Christian Religion*, and was the first Protestant systematic theologian. He gained a reputation for intellectual brilliance while a student in Paris. After a 1533 sermon in which he pleaded for the reform of the Roman Catholic Church, he was forced to leave Paris. In Geneva, he introduced reforms, but in 1538 he was forced to leave Geneva because of the severity of the reforms. (Later his church would be characterized by stern morality, austerity, and insistence on attending church.) A noted preacher, Calvin went to Strassburg for several years and from there he maintained communication with those in Geneva. In 1541 the people of Geneva recalled him. From then on Geneva was the headquarters for Calvin and the Reformed Church.

There the future leaders of Calvin's reform found a haven from non-Calvinist magistrates of other areas. William Tyndale, Miles Cloverdale, and John Knox exported Calvin's ideas from Geneva to the British Isles. By 1600 representatives of the Reformed faith were making themselves heard throughout all of Central Europe.

THE SPREAD OF CALVINISM. As early as 1555 a Protestant congregation was organized in France by a disciple of Calvin. In 1559 the first synod of the French Reformed Church met. The next centuries for the French Reformed Church, or the Huguenots as they were popularly called, were years of persecution. In 1598, Henry IV issued the Edict of Nantes and began a brief period of toleration. But Louis XIV revoked the edict in 1685, and periods of persecution followed until the Constitution of 1795 granted religious freedom.

Reformed church advocates entered the Netherlands very soon after Calvin's reign in Geneva began. The religious wars which followed led to revolution by the Protestants and the formation of two countries, predominantly Reformed Holland and predominantly Catholic Belgium. This separation was completed in 1579 under the Protestant leader, William of Orange. In Holland in 1618 a major controversy which had troubled Calvinism for several decades reached a climax with the Synod of Dort. The synod was called to refute what was considered the theological heresies of Jacob Arminius (1560-1609), former professor of theology at the University of Leyden. In 1610, the year after Arminius' death, his followers summarized his theories in a five point remonstrance, which led to his followers becoming known as the Remonstrants.

Arminius' revision of Calvin's thought affirmed: (1) a general atonement, i.e., that Christ died for every person; (2) that God's foreknowledge of who would accept Christ's saving grace came before his predestination and election of them; (3) that God's grace could be resisted; (4) that humans were fallen and in need of God's grace, but were capable of responding to it; (5) that while with God's grace victory over sin was possible, it was also possible for individuals to fall away from grace. The Synod of Dort responded by affirming that: (1) Christ died only for those elected to salvation; (2)

predestination and election to salvation constituted an act of God's sovereign will (rather than being the natural result of his foreknowledge); (3) God's grace given to an individual is irresistible; (4) humans were so depraved that they could do nothing for their own salvation; (5) God's elect will persevere to the end.

The canons of the Synod of Dort became the official doctrine of the Dutch church and of many Reformed church bodies. Arminian ideas found their way to England and became the hallmark of John Wesley and the Methodists. Among those in attendance at Dort were several of the British Separatists then residing in Holland who later to come to America as the Pilgrims.

No other centers of Reformed faith on the continent grew as did Switzerland, France, and Holland. However, the faith did seep into the surrounding countries, and synods were formed in Czechoslovakia and Hungary. Also, in Italy the Reformed faith began to dominate the Waldensians. Because of its affinity with Lutheranism, the Reformed church moved north into Germany and, while never challenging Lutherans for control, became a large minority religion. It is from this body that the 1693 Heidelberg Catechism emerged; its teaching was to have a profound influence on the interpretation of Calvin in Reformed history.

The leading center of Reformed faith in the British Isles was Scotland. A devout follower of Calvin, John Knox returned to Scotland in 1559 after a year and a half on a French galley and 12 years' exile in Europe. He found the country ripe for Protestantism. He quickly became the leader of the cause which in another year saw the Scottish parliament abolish Catholicism and begin to set up Presbyterianism, the name given the Reformed Church in Scotland. Despite recurrent battles with then Episcopal England, Presbyterianism was firmly settled in Scotland and became the seedbed from which the Reformed movement could spread to Ireland and England.

In 1603 James I of England invited the Scots to settle the rebels' land in Ulster (Northern Ireland) which had been forfeited to the crown. So many came to Ireland that soon Ulster was dominantly Protestant and, in spite of James' Catholic preferences, he reasoned that Presbyterians were better than people with no religion at all. Irish Catholics were not so quick to give in to the Protestant intruders and religious wars ensued. By 1642 things had quieted to a point that the first presbytery in Ireland could be formed, but a stable accord has never been reached between Irish Catholics and Presbyterians.

In England, Reformed-Presbyterian thinking was labeled Puritanism. This name came as a result of the different Reformed thinkers' uniting around the issue of "further purifying the church," as the latter stages of the Reformation brought Elizabeth I to the throne in 1558 with her *via media* solution to religious strife. (For a discussion of Elizabeth's blending of both Roman Catholic and Protestant elements, see the section in Chapter One on the Anglican tradition.) The two major groups within Puritanism were the Independents and the Presbyterians. Most Puritans were Reformed in their thinking, but beyond that they varied from those who merely wished to simplify church vestments and worship to the Independents who wished to set up a congregationally-organized church, one in which the highest authority lay within the local church instead of in a regional or national governing body. The years 1558 to 1649 were years of struggle, persecutions, war, and on-again, off-again toleration among proponents of the various churches in England. In 1649, Puritan Oliver Cromwell succeeded in his revolt against the monarchy and established the Puritan Commonwealth. Although Cromwell was an Independent, the Presbyterians were dominant in Parliament, so when Cromwell's reign began, Presbyterianism became the dominant church in England. Up to that time the Presbyterians and Independents had sustained a united front against the Episcopalian state church of the monarchy. However, once Puritanism gained the position of state church, the factions within Puritanism—Presbyterians and Independents—no longer needed to be united against Episcopalianism and their differences with each other intensified. The Congregationalists, a group within the Independents, began to press for a state church based on a congregational system instead of on a presbyterial system. The Congregationalists wanted to remain attached to the Church of England in the sense that the Congregationalists would preach the doctrines of the Church of England but they would choose their own ministers, own their own property, and would not come under the authority of the bishops of the Church of England. The Congregationalists were opposed by another party within the Independents, the Separatists. This latter party wished to become separate from any episcopal entanglements.

In 1660 Presbyterianism lost its state church position because the monarchy was restored to power, and the Anglican Church returned as the state church. Presbyterians became another small English sect among other sects. The Restoration therefore meant the end of Presbyterian power, but Reformed theology remained dominant in England's Protestant circles, including Presbyterians, Congregationalists, and Separatists.

Years before Cromwell came to power, Parliament paved the way for the establishment of Presbyterianism by abolishing the system of bishops in 1642-43. Parliament also convoked the Westminster Assembly of Divines to reorder the Church of England. This assembly, meeting for a number of years, produced the three most important works in Reformed history (apart from Calvin's *Institutes* from which they derived): The Larger and Shorter Catechisms, the Westminster Confession of Faith, and the Directory of Public Worship. Even though only four Scots were in the Westminster Assembly, the Church of Scotland quickly adopted the Westminster documents. These documents remain to this day the basic works in doctrine and standards for most Presbyterian churches around the world.

With time, the Separatists, a group within the Independents, divided into Brownists and Baptists. Robert Browne was among the first to move toward the idea of a "sect" church of pure Christians as opposed to a universal or state church of all baptized citizens. The Baptists were even more radical than the Brownists. The Baptists were anti-liturgical, not having any sacraments. For them baptism is an ordinance and is reserved for adults instead of being available also to children.

The various groups mentioned above existed as parties within the Puritan movement in England from the late 1500s until the 1689 Act of Toleration, which allowed them freedom to develop fully as distinct sects. The Brownists, however, did not exist for long.

IN NORTH AMERICA. Among the very first European Christians in the New World were members of the Reformed church. As early as 1564, Huguenots (French Protestants), fleeing persecution, settled along the St. John's River near present-day Jacksonville, Florida. The colony was destroyed the next year by the Spanish who had already claimed the territory. During the last half of the century, others began to flee to the towns of New France along the St. Lawrence River. They continued to arrive until forbidden to migrate by Cardinal Richelieu in 1628. Huguenots did not prosper, but a few did survive in Canada until the fall of Quebec in 1749. They were soon absorbed into other Protestant churches.

With the establishment of Halifax in 1749, German and Dutch members of the Reformed church, as well as Congregationalists and Presbyterians (primarily from Scotland), became residents of the new city. At first they shared the same building. As years passed they spread through Nova Scotia founding churches. Growth of the Reformed faith was greatly augmented by the arrival of the Loyalists, many from New England, after the American Revolution. The first synods were formed in 1795 and 1796 by two factions of the Scottish Presbyterians.

Dissension, already high among the Scots, was made even higher by the New Englanders, among whom was Henry Alline, a fervent disciple of Newlightism, the revival-oriented separatist Congregationalism which had been inaugurated by the First Great Awakening, prior to the American Revolution. Alline drew away many Congregationalists into independent congregations which eventually became the birthing place of the Baptists of the province.

The story of the Reformed-Presbyterian tradition in colonial America is the story of the establishment of American branches of the various European Reformed churches. As early as 1611 the Reverend Alexander Whitaker arrived in Virginia with his Presbyterian views. The Pilgrims and Puritans arrived in the 1620s to establish American Congregationalism. Dutch Calvinists were in New York as early as 1623. French Huguenots settled along the coast of the colonies. Quickly Americanized, they joined the Presbyterian Church. The backbone of American Presbyterianism was the vast migration of the Scottish-Irish Ulsterites. Between 1705 and 1775 more than 500,000 Ulsterites reached America and settled in its middle section, particularly the Carolinas. Germans began to arrive in the late 1600s and settled in Pennsylvania. The Calvinists among them organized the Reformed church.

Francis Makemie, recognized as the father of American Presbyterianism, landed in the colonies in 1683 to begin organizing the scattered Presbyterians. About 1705 (the date is not clear), he organized the first presbytery (of

Philadelphia). Makemie died in 1708 as the great Scottish-Irish immigration was beginning. In 1717 the Synod of Philadelphia was organized with 19 ministers, 40 churches, and 3,000 members.

The Reformed traditions have displayed several interesting patterns of growth in America. The churches of the Reformed tradition (with the possible exception of Presbyterianism) are regional churches. Largely continental in their background, they are concentrated in those areas in the Northeast and Midwest where large-scale German migration occurred. The Congregationalists were located largely in the Northeast but gained strength in the Midwest through mergers in 1931 and 1958.

Significant in the spread of the Reformed churches were the anti-evangelical, anti-revivalistic policies of church leaders in the eighteenth and nineteenth centuries. The Reformed churches gained new members largely through groups of laymen who migrated West, formed congregations, and called a pastor.

Education has been a major contribution of the Reformed tradition to Protestantism. The churches always insisted on a college-trained clergy, and they created numerous colleges for that purpose. They have based their program on a theologically sound-teaching ministry. A large number of the outstanding theologians in American history were out of this tradition—Cotton Mather, Jonathan Edwards, John Williamson Nevin, Horace Bushnell, Benjamin Warfield, and Reinhold and H. Richard Niebuhr.

The Plan of Union of 1801 was an agreement between Presbyterians and Congregationalists concerning their frontier congregations. The Plan of Union provided that where there were small groups of Presbyterians and Congregationalists, the groups would unite and be served by a minister from either church. Because more Presbyterian ministers went to the frontier than Congregationalist ministers, most of those united churches became Presbyterian. The "frontier" of the early 1800s was the area west of the Allegheny Mountains.

Splintered into a number of separate denominational bodies in the nineteenth century, Presbyterians made significant strides in bringing members together into one organization during the twentieth century. The most important step in the merging process was accomplished in 1983 when the two largest Presbyterian bodies, split since before the Civil War, merged to form the Presbyterian Church (U.S.A.). The story of this church and its antecedents constitutes the majority of Presbyterian history in the United States.

CONGREGATIONALISM—A VARIATION OF THE REFORMED TRADITION. Congregationalism, a form of Puritanism that lies between Presbyterianism and Separatism, was developed in America within the Massachusetts Bay Colony by the Puritan leadership. In distinction from the Presbyterians, who looked for the development of a state church modeled on the theocracy which Calvin established in Geneva and headed by a synod of elders (presbyters), the Congregationalists looked for a state church which was congregationally oriented. While agreeing with the Separatists on the issue of the local church, Congregationalists disagreed

with them in that they wished to keep their supportive ties to the state. In colonial America, Separatism was first represented by the Pilgrims at Plymouth, Massachusetts. All three groups were Reformed in their theology and acknowledged the Westminster documents, but differed fundamentally on their desires for church organization and its relation to the state. Eventually, Congregationalism would absorb the Separatists of Plymouth, but a new separatists movement would emerge in the 1700s and survive as Baptists.

Congregational organization had four distinctive features. First, the church was built on the covenant of people together. A church was not formed until the people constituted it. Second, the church was tied to a place. It was the covenanted people in a specific location. Ideally, the whole countryside would be divided into parishes, geographic areas each with one congregation. The importance of place is reflected in the fact that the Mayflower Compact (a civil version of the church covenant) was not drawn up until the Pilgrims reached the New World. Third, the church was to be an established church. In New England it had intimate ties with the government, and ministers drew their salaries from the civil authority. Finally, the church was to be the sacred institute for the society. The clergy spoke directly to issues of public morals, expected to be consulted on matters of importance to public life, and often represented the colony as political figures.

The early Congregationalists have often been confused with those Independents who desired a church totally cut off from state affiliation, control, and finance. While it is true that Congregationalism later became independent of state authority, it is well to keep in mind the movement's original aim to be a state church.

Meeting at Cambridge, Massachusetts, in 1648, representatives of the four Puritan colonies issued what came to be called *The Cambridge Platform*. It became the basic document of Congregational policy in New England. As stated in the Platform, "The Government of the Church is a mixed Government . in respect of Christ the Head and King of the Church, and the sovereign power residing in Him, it is a Monarchy; in respect of the Body of Brotherhood of the Church, and Power from Christ granted unto them, it resembles a Democracy; in respect of the Presbytery, and Power committed unto them, it is an Aristocracy." The basic unit was the visible congregation united into one body by a covenant. The care of the church was left to elders (pastors, teachers, and ruling elders) and deacons, all elected by the congregation.

Churches, though equal, were to maintain communion with one another by means of synods. Synods, though not of the essence of the church, were deemed necessary to the times, to establish truth and peace. Composed of elders and other messengers, synods were to "debate and determine controversies of Faith and Cases of Conscience; to clear from the Word holy directions for the Holy Worship of God, and good Government of the Church; to hear witness against maladministration and corruption of manners in any particular church; and to give Directions for the Reformation thereof." Churches were enjoined not to remove themselves from the communion of the other churches. In its developed form, Congregationalism was very close to Presbyterianism rather than to the independent congregational policy which later became typical of the Baptists. Developed Congregationalism was also far removed from the free church structure of the Plymouth Brethren.

A key element in Congregationalism was the power granted by the church to the secular magistrate. The magistry was encouraged to restrain and punish idolatry, blasphemy, heresy, schism, and like actions. When the power of the magistry was removed from Congregationalism by the American Revolution, the churches adopted an independent congregationalism, but always with a tendency to presbyterial forms.

It has often been asserted that Congregationalism was a noncreedal church. However, when asked to prepare a creed, the same body that drew up the Cambridge Platform adopted the Westminster Confession of Faith, which placed Congregationalism doctrinally within British Calvinism (Puritanism).

The first branch of the Reformed tradition in America was Congregationalism, the church of the Puritans. They landed in 1620 and 1630 and established their theocracy. Their church operated as a state church until disestablished after the American Revolution. It adopted the Westminster Confession shortly after promulgation by the English divines. It was the church of the New England patriots, Harvard and Yale universities, and of famous ministers, Jonathan Edwards, Timothy Dwight, Cotton Mather, Thomas Hooker, and Charles Chauncy. It also became the seedbed upon which Unitariansim, Universalism, and Christian Science were to grow. Only in the twentieth century, as it became a major force in Reformed family ecumenism, did it produce schismatic churches.

SOURCES—REFORMED-PRESBYTERIAN FAMILY

HISTORY, EUROPEAN

Grimm, Harold J. *The Reformation Era*. New York: Macmillan, 1954. 675 pp.

Leith, John H. *An Introduction to the Reformed Tradition*. Atlanta: John Knox Press, 1977. 253 pp.

McNeill, John T. *The History and Character of Calvinism*. New York: Oxford University Press, 1954. 466 pp.

Reaman, G. Elmore. *The Trail of the Huguenots*. London: Frederick Muller, 1964. 318 pp.

Reed, R. C. *History of the Presbyterian Churches of the World*. Philadelphia: Westminster Press, 1912. 408 pp.

Thompson, Ernest Trice, and Elton M. Eenigenburg. *Through the Ages*. Richmond, VA: The CLC Press, 1965. 480 pp.

HISTORY, NORTH AMERICAN

Armstrong, Maurice, Lefferts A. Loetscher, and Charles A. Anderson. *The Presbyterian Enterprise*. Philadelphia: The Westminster Press, 1956. 336 pp.

Bratt, James D. *Dutch Calvinism in Modern America*. Grand Rapids, MI. William B. Eerdmans Publishing Company, 1984. 329 pp.

Jamison, Wallace N. *The United Presbyterian Story*. Pittsburgh: The Geneva Press, 1958. 253 pp.

Lingle, Walter L. *Presbyterians, Their History and Beliefs*. Richmond, VA: John Knox Press, 1944. 127 pp.

Slosser, Gaius Jackson, ed. *They Seek a Country*. New York: Macmillan, 1955. 330 pp.

Trinterud, Leonard J. *The Forming of an American Tradition*. Philadelphia: Westminister Press, 1949. 352 pp.

Watts, George B. *The Waldenses in the New World*. Durham, NC: Duke University Press, 1941. 309 pp.

THEOLOGY

Beardslee, John W., III, ed. *Reformed Dogmatics*. New York: Oxford University Press, 1965. 471 pp.

Bratt, John H., ed. *The Heritage of John Calvin*. Grand Rapids, MI: William B. Eerdmans Publishing Company, 1973. 222 pp.

Calvin, John. *The Institutes of the Christian Religion*. 2 Vols. Philadelphia: Westminster Press, 1960.

Cochrane, Arthur C., ed. *The Reformed Confessions of the Sixteenth Century*. Philadelphia: Westminister Press, 1966. 336 pp.

Geer, Felix B. *Basic Beliefs of the Reformed Faith*. Richmond, VA: John Knox Press, 1960. 80 pp.

Gettys, Joseph M. *What Presbyterians Believe*. Clinton, SC: The Author, 1953. 128 pp.

Osterhaven, M. Eugene. *The Spirit of the Reformed Tradition*. Grand Rapids, MI: William B. Eerdmans Publishing Company, 1971. 190 pp.

Schaff, Philip. *Creed Revision in the Presbyterian Churches*. New York: Charles Scribner's Sons, 1890. 67 pp.

LIFE AND WORSHIP

Mackay, John A. *The Presbyterian Way of Life*. Englewood Cliffs, NJ: Prentice-Hall, 1960. 238 pp.

Melton, Julius. *Presbyterian Worship in America*. Richmond, VA: John Knox Press, 1967. 173 pp.

Nichols, James Hastings. *Corporate Worship in the Reformed Tradition*. Philadelphia: Westminister Press, 1968. 190 pp.

CONGREGATIONALISM

Hiemert, Alan, and Andrew Delbanco, eds. *The Puritans in America*. Cambridge: Harvard University Press, 1985. 438 pp.

Jenkins, Daniel. *Congregationalism: A Restatement*. London: Faber and Faber, 1954. 152 pp.

Starkey, Marion L. *The Congregational Way*. Garden City, NY: Doubleday, 1966. 342 pp.

Walker, Williston. *The Creed and Platforms of Congregationalism*. Philadelphia: Pilgrim Press, 1960. 604 pp.

Wells, Donald F. *Reformed Theology in America*. Grand Rapids, MI: William F. Eerdmans Publishing Company, 1985.

Chapter 5

Pietist-Methodist Family

Directory listings for the groups belonging to the Pietist-Methodist Family
may be found in the section beginning on page 181.

The movement called Pietism gave rise to three groups of churches—the Moravian churches, the Swedish Evangelical churches, and the Methodist (Wesleyan) churches—all of which will be treated in this chapter. First, however, Pietism itself must be considered.

Pietism was an evangelical reaction to trends within Protestantism in the late seventeenth century. The regular church life of the Protestant churches, mainly the Lutheran and Calvinist churches, had taken on a certain rigidity, and their creeds reflected the systematic theology of the second generation Lutheran and Calvinist scholastics. Pietism countered both the rigidity and the sectarian scholasticism. Without abandoning doctrine, Pietism sought to change the emphasis of those churches from divisive formulations to spiritual experience. The dominant characteristics of the movement were (1) a Bible-centered faith, (2) the experienced Christian life (guilt, forgiveness, conversion, holiness, and love within community), and (3) free expression of faith in hymns, testimony, and evangelical zeal. The earliest representatives of the movement include Philipp Jacob Spener (1635-1705) and August Hermann Francke (1663-1727).

Spener is credited with originating a basic form taken by Pietists—the *collegia pietatis* (association of piety). In despair over the impossibility of reforming Lutheranism, he began to organize small groups which met in homes for Bible study, prayer, and discussions, leading to a deeper spiritual life. These groups spread throughout Europe and were known in England as religious societies.

Francke was Spener's most famous disciple. Forced out of the University of Leipzig and later dismissed from the University of Erfurt, he became a teacher at the newly formed University of Halle and turned it into a Pietist center. (Leipzig, Erfurt, and Halle are in East Germany.) During the three decades Francke taught there, Halle graduated more than 200 ministers a year. Besides the deeply experienced faith taught at Halle, Francke encouraged missionary endeavors. He began an orphan house in 1698. Knowledge of his work brought financial help and allowed the work to include a pauper school, a Bible institute, a Latin school, and other facilities to aid destitute children. Most early missionaries came from among Halle's graduates.

From Halle, Pietism spread throughout the world. Correspondence between Francke and Cotton Mather led to the establishment of religious societies in the Boston churches, and Pietistic literature lay directly behind the American revival movement of the 1730s and 1740s called the Great Awakening. In Germany, Pietism renewed the Moravian Church, which then began to spread its own version of Pietism. The Moravian Church carried the Pietist faith to England where Pietism became a strong influence on John Wesley, the founder of the Methodist movement. Moravians working in Sweden helped establish the Swedish Evangelical Church. Thus three groups of churches emerged from the Pietist movement: the Moravian churches, the Swedish Evangelical churches, and the Methodist churches.

However, most of Pietism's influence was absorbed by the Lutheran Church and the Calvinist groups (the Reformed Church, the Presbyterian Church, and the Congregational Church). Although Pietism did lead to schism in the American churches, most of the schismatic churches reunited with their parent bodies.

A note of contrast: the Pietist churches are very different from the European free churches. The latter, discussed in Chapter Eight, include the Mennonites, the Amish, the Quakers, and the Brethren. The Pietists were distinct from the European free churches because the Pietists were open to traditional Christian practices and beliefs, and lacked hostility to their parent bodies. Instead of rejecting the forms of the past, as the European free churches did, the Pietists worked with the forms of the past and sought the life of the spirit within them. In general, the free churches of the past and the present have opposed infant baptism, opposed traditional ideas of church and sacrament, and opposed many liturgical practices. In contrast, Pietists have accepted Reformation ideas of church and sacrament, have baptized infants, and have used simplified versions of liturgical forms. Whereas the European free churches sprang up as a protest to state churches (whether those were Roman Catholic, Anglican, Lutheran, or Calvinist), Pietist groups began as societies within Protestant state churches and only later removed themselves from their parent churches and became independent entities.

THE MORAVIANS. The Moravian churches of today exist only because the Pietist movement gave life to an almost extinguished Moravian Church. Thus the Moravians are distinct among Pietists: the Moravians represent not so much a new church created by Pietism as a renewed church recreated by Pietism. That recreation occurred in 1727. The story of the Moravian churches, however, starts in the ninth century with the founding of the early Moravian Church.

Cyril and Methodius, missionaries of the Greek Orthodox Church, arrived in the ninth century in Moravia, an area in what is now called Czechoslovakia. There they established a Greek-based Slavic church. At first the Moravians were encouraged by the Roman Catholic Church, but later Rome forced a Latin rite upon them. The Moravians considered this a repressive move. They became discontented with being Catholic, and their discontent was heightened by a young priest named John Hus (1369-1415). From his pulpit in Prague, he began to throw challenges in the face of the Roman Catholic Church. He questioned the practice of selling indulgences, which were promises of the remission of punishment due for sins. Hus also questioned the denial of the cup to the laity in holy communion, and the moral corruption of the papacy. Hus's career coincided with the time when three men were claiming to be the pope, each having a segment of Europe behind him. In 1414, at the Council of Constance called to determine the one true pope, Hus was invited (with a safe conduct promise) to state his case. He was arrested and burned at the stake. The Hussite Wars followed and eventually Hus's followers, concluding that Hus's ideas would never positively effect the Roman church, formed their own church—the Unitas Fratrum or "Unity of the Brethren." The church existed for its early years as a Reformed Roman church, turning to Bishop Stephen of the Waldensian Church for apostolic ordination. It published the Bible in the Czech vernacular—the Kralitz Bible, which affected Czechoslovakia as strongly as Luther's Bible affected Germany.

The religious wars of the late sixteenth and early seventeenth centuries all but destroyed the once prosperous Unitas Fratrum. On June 21, 1621, 15 Brethren leaders were beheaded in Prague. The persecutions brought an end to all visible manifestation of the Unitas Fratrum.

In 1722 a few families from the former Unitas Fratrum fled from Moravia to Saxony, a region in East Germany. Soon more than 300 exiles had settled in Saxony on Count Zinzendorf's estate, called Herrnhut. The exiles held conferences and drew up a "Brotherly Agreement." Their bickering, though, led Zinzendorf to invite as many as would come to a communion service at his manor church on August 13, 1727. This date is considered to be the birth of the Renewed Unitas Fratrum (or Moravian Church) as there occurred an amazing "outpouring of the power of God," which Moravians compared to Pentecost. The wranglings and strife were over. Zinzendorf received a copy of the "discipline" of the old Unitas Fratrum and began to set the church in order. Ordination in the apostolic succession was secured from Daniel Ernest Jablonsky. Jablonsky, a court preacher in Berlin, was one of the ordained bishops in the line of the old Unitas Fratrum. Jablonsky ordained David Nitschman as the first bishop of the restored church.

The arrival of the Moravians on the estate of Zinzendorf largely determined the Moravian future. Zinzendorf was a Pietist and he led the Moravians into placing great stress upon religious experience and the relation of the individual with God. Numerous forms were developed to foster this deep faith. Among them was the love feast, an informal service centering on holy communion but also including a light meal, singing, and a talk by the officiating minister. The litany, a lengthy prayer form for corporate and private devotions, was added to the Herrnhut services in 1731. Its present form is a modified Lutheran litany. The idea of small groups of dedicated Christians meeting together regularly for worship and exhortation and service was taken from the German Pietists and used extensively, especially in the mission field. Moravian meetings were the model of early Methodist societies developed by John Wesley.

The *Daily Texts* was a book which grew from a need of the early Herrnhut settlers, the need for a "watchword" from the Scripture for daily use. They at first copied scriptural passages by hand on bits of paper to be drawn from a container each day. This practice evolved into an annual volume of texts. For each day there was a text from both the Old and New Testaments and a hymn stanza to amplify the text. This book, printed annually, has had an influence far beyond the membership of the church, as it circulates widely to nonmembers.

The most characteristic aspect of Moravian piety was its mission program. Zinzendorf, early in his life, became convinced that he was destined to do something about the neglected peoples of the world. In 1731 he traveled to Copenhagen, where he met Anthony Ulrich, a black man and slave from the Danish West Indies. Ulrich told Zinzendorf of his people's plight. Back at Herrnhut, Zinzendorf told Anthony Ulrich's story, preparing the way for the slave to arrive and tell it himself. The response was immediate, and David Nitschmann and Leonhard Dober were chosen as the first missionaries to the oldest Moravian mission—St. Thomas. The Moravians then proceeded to establish missions all over Europe. Zinzendorf, a Lutheran himself, gave strict orders for the Moravians not to encroach upon state church prerogatives. They became merely preachers of the Word and were welcomed in many Protestant lands. In England they moved into an established church structure and set up "religious societies" for Bible study and prayer, never encouraging anyone to leave his state church. John Wesley was a member of one of these societies for a while.

In 1872 re-entrance into Czechoslovakia was permitted with the Edict of Toleration, and the first congregation in Bohemia was established in 1872. Other mission work included British Guiana, Surinam, Southern Africa, Java, Nicaragua, Jordan, Alaska, and Labrador, all established before 1900. In 1735 the Moravians came to the American colonies.

Moravians in America. The settling of Moravians in America in 1735 had a two-fold purpose: the securing of a settlement in the New World in case Germany again became intolerant, and a mission to the Indians. The first group of settlers in the New World was led by Bishop August Gottlieb Spangenberg. He traveled to Georgia on the same ship that brought John Wesley, the founder of Methodism, to the colony of George Oglethorpe in Georgia. Wesley was impressed with Spangenberg and the Moravians and records a number of conversations with Spangenberg. Soon after settling in Savannah, the Moravians opened an Indian school. The Moravians were, however, caught in the war between the British (Georgia) and the Spanish (Florida). Their refusal to bear arms led to their being looked down upon. By 1740 the Moravians left Georgia for Pennsylvania. They established the town of Nazareth and the following year Bishop David Nitschmann arrived and began to settle Bethlehem. In December of 1741, Zinzendorf arrived, and on Christmas day he organized the Moravian Congregation in Bethlehem, the first in America.

Under Spangenberg's leadership a semi-communal arrangement was worked out in Bethlehem which soon made it a self-sufficient settlement, able to bear its own mission program to the Indians. Churches were soon organized at Nazareth and Lilitz in Pennsylvania, and Hope, New Jersey.

In 1749 the British Parliament acknowledged the Moravian Church as "an Ancient Protestant Episcopal Church," thus in effect giving an invitation to settle in other British colonies. The Moravians took advantage of Parliament's recognition of their church and settled in North Carolina on property owned by Lord Granville. Rising persecution in Germany encouraged the Moravians to come to America.

Spangenberg and five others went to North Carolina in 1752 and had surveyors lay out what is now Forsyth County. The first settlers, 15 in all, arrived in 1753 and settled in Bethabara. In 1766 the permanent settlement of Salem was laid out. From this beginning other churches and settlements developed.

Moravian settlements in Canada originated as an extension of their continued missions to convert the Indians. After an unsuccessful attempt in 1752 to establish a mission to the Indians along the Labrador coast, Moravian missionaries were able to find work in 1771 in Nain. By the early nineteenth century four stations were activated along the rugged terrain across the Labrador Basin from New Herrnhut, the Moravian settlement in Greenland. A second thrust into Canada occurred in 1792 when, in an effort to escape a possible Indian war, missionaries moved into Canada along the Thames River and established Fairfield, Ontario. Though destroyed in the war of 1812, the center was rebuilt and became a stop along the underground railroad for slaves fleeing to Canada. A third field in Canada opened in 1894 when some German families who had moved to Alberta from Russia contacted the church headquarters in Pennsylvania and asked for affiliation. By encouraging the development of this colony and adding members who moved into the area from the eastern United States, the church grew and now has its own Canadian District to serve the congregations of Western Canada.

METHODISM. Among Methodist historians there is a wide disagreement about when Methodism began; however,

organizational continuity in the Wesleyan movement dates to late 1739 when the first society was formed by John Wesley and 18 other persons "desiring to flee from the wrath to come . and be saved from their sins." The number of societies grew and in 1744 the first Methodist conference was held as Wesley called his lay ministers together to confer with him. Wesley made all the decisions and assigned the preachers to their tasks.

Methodism's founder, John Wesley (1703-91), the son of an Anglican clergyman, attended Oxford to study for the ministry. While at Oxford he formed a religious society called the Holy Club by other students. To this group was first applied the derisive title "Methodists" party because of their strict daily schedules.

Wesley left Oxford and became a missionary to the Indians in Georgia. This adventure ended in failure. However, while on the voyage to America he encountered the Moravians and was very impressed with their simple piety and their leader Bishop August Gottlieb Spangenberg. In Georgia, he also encountered the writings of Scottish Pietist Thomas Halyburton, whose personal religious experience closely paralleled his own. Arriving back in London, Wesley affiliated with the Moravians and in particular with Peter Bohler, who would soon be on his way to America as a missionary to the slaves. Activity with Bohler led Wesley to his own crisis experience which occurred at the religious society at Aldersgate on May 24, 1738. Wesley described what happened in his *Journal*:

"In the evening, I went very unwillingly to a Society in Aldersgate Street, where one was reading Luther's Preface to the Epistle to the Romans. About a quarter before nine, while he was describing the change which God works in the heart through faith in Christ, I felt my heart strangely warmed. I felt I did trust in Christ; Christ alone, for salvation; and an assurance was given me, that he had taken away my sins, even mine, and saved me from the law of sin and death."

This experience became the turning point in Wesley's life. During the next year he visited Germany (seeing the Moravians), broke with the Moravians over several points of practice, and began the United Societies. Innovations by Wesley included field preaching, the use of lay preachers (Wesley's assistants), and the discipline of the societies.

The United Societies were a group of dedicated Christians within the state church, Anglicanism. As with continental Pietism, doctrine was not at issue as much as the application of doctrine to life. Some doctrinal innovations did occur concerning the Christian life—Wesley's emphasis on the witness of the Spirit and Christian perfection. These doctrines often led to excesses and accusations of "enthusiasm," the eighteenth century euphemism for "fanaticism."

Those who experienced this evangelical awakening were organized into societies, the basic document of which was the General Rules. Those in the society were expected to evidence their desire for salvation:

First: by doing no harm, avoiding evil of every kind, especially that which is most generally practiced.

Second: by doing good of every possible sort, and as far as possible to all men.

Third: by attending upon the ordinances of God.

Wesley wrote that following the third rule involved the public worship of God, the ministry of the Word (either read or expounded), the Supper of the Lord, family and private prayer, searching the Scriptures, and fasting and abstinence.

The society was to be thought of as a gathering of people, not as a place. Wherever the society met was where it held its regular worship services and most importantly the quarterly meeting. Once each quarter Wesley visited each society. He inquired into the lives of the members relative to the General Rules and issued quarterly tickets. The tickets admitted members to the society for the next three months. Wesley served communion and usually a love feast was held, an informal service centering on holy communion but also including a light meal, singing, and a talk.

Wesley lived almost the entire century and the issue of doctrinal standards for Methodism came to the fore late in his life. Early doctrinal concerns had been set in the *Minutes of the Conference* but additional doctrinal questions were raised in 1777 by the predestinarian Calvinists and in the 1780s by the establishment of the Methodist Episcopal Church in America. The Calvinist controversy set Methodism firmly against predestinarian doctrines. Wesley opposed the Calvinist idea of irresistible grace: if grace comes, you cannot refuse it; if it does not come, you cannot obtain it. Wesley said grace is freely given to each person and each person can freely respond to the gospel. The formation of American Methodism caused Wesley to set doctrinal standards in his letter to the preachers in America: "Let all of you be determined to abide by the Methodist doctrine and discipline published in the four volumes of *Sermons* and the *Notes on the New Testament*, together with the *Large Minutes of the Conference*."

To Wesley's *Sermons*, the *Notes on the New Testament*, and the *Large Minutes of the Conference*, the Twenty-five Articles of Religion are added as a fourth source for determining the Methodist perspective on doctrine. The articles were derived from the Thirty-nine Articles of Religion of the Church of England, of which they are an abridgment. Wesley specifically excluded the Anglican articles on hell, creeds, predestination, bishops, excommunication, and the authority of the church, and he shortened others.

The remaining articles cover the major affirmation of traditional Christianity—the Trinity, Christ (including His virgin birth and physical resurrection), the sufficiency of the Bible, sin, and the salvation of humanity. The church is viewed as the place where the Word of God is preached and the sacraments duly administered. There are two sacraments—baptism (usually by sprinkling) and the Lord's Supper.

A number of the items specifically refute Roman Catholic doctrines concerning the existence of voluntary works above and beyond the commandments of God, purgatory, other sacraments, mass as a sacrifical ceremony, celibate priests, and the uniformity of worship services. Methodists receive both elements (bread and wine) in the Lord's Supper rather than just the bread.

Methodists are set apart from the free church position of the Mennonites by their acknowledgment of the legitimacy of taking oaths in legal situations.

The articles of religion grounded Methodism in traditional Christian doctrines and the *Sermons, Notes*, and *Minutes* stated Methodist opinion on current issues. The articles are themselves derivative of continental Reformed confessions and, with the exception of predestination, place Methodism in a Reformed theological tradition. The Reformed tradition, based on the work of John Calvin, shows up most clearly in articles v, ix, xii, xiii, xvi, and in the anti-Roman Catholic articles x, xi, xiv, xv, xix, xx, and xxii. Methodists have always identified with Reformed theologian Jacob Arminius, whom they interpreted as rejecting the Calvinist emphasis on predestination. Wesley named the first Methodist periodical *The Arminian Magazine*. The Twenty-five Articles of Religion are a common core of doctrinal agreement for all Methodists and are included in doctrinal statements by almost all Methodist bodies.

In England, Methodism remained as a society within the Anglican church and as such, was spread throughout the British Commonwealth by the missionary vision and activity of the Reverend Thomas Coke. The British Wesleyans became independent of the Anglican church in 1795.

Wesleyanism in America. Methodist history in the colonies began in the 1760s with the migration of Methodist laypeople and preachers. The first society on record was in Leesburg, Virginia, in 1766, and the second in New York City. Methodism spread in the middle colonies and developed early centers in Baltimore, Philadelphia, and Wilmington.

The first crisis for American Methodists was the Revolutionary War. Because of their attachment to the Church of England and Wesley's antirevolutionary traits, their loyalty was suspect. After the war, because of the independence of the colonies from England, Wesley decided to allow the American Methodists to set up an independent church. In September 1784, he ordained Thomas Coke as a superintendent and sent him to America with instructions to set up the church and to ordain Francis Asbury. This organization was accomplished at the Christmas Conference held at Lovely Lane Chapel in Baltimore.

Francis Asbury (1745-1816) was second only to Wesley in molding American Methodism. He came to America in 1771 and during his first 13 years of service emerged as the unquestioned leader of the American brethren. He was ordained bishop in December 1784 (the American preachers preferred the term bishop to superintendent) and formed the Methodist Episcopal Church. His appointments of ministers to their congregations covered the United States, Nova Scotia, and Antigua.

As the Methodists grew in number, their organization became more sophisticated, but several features important for understanding Methodists and their schisms have remained constant. These features are the conference and itinerary. The basic structure of Methodism is the conference, a name derived from Wesley's practice of having regular meetings with his preachers to confer with them before deciding on issues. The local church charge conference, district conference, annual conference, and general conference form a hierarchy of authority. The local church charge conference is the annual business meeting of the local congregation. There the congregation elects officers and sets the budget. The district conference is primarily a funnel; it lets local congregations know the messages of bishops and annual conferences. The annual conference is a regional conference chaired by the bishop, whose duty it is to assign ministers to their churches (charges) each year, and to publish those assignments at the annual conference. The general conference is made up of representatives of all the annual conferences in the country. The general conference meets quadrennially, is the church's highest legislative body, and writes the Discipline, the book of church order.

The phrase "annual conference" has a meaning in addition to that described above. For a minister to belong to an annual conference means that he or she has contractual relationships with the church in that area. The minister agrees to be available for assignment, and the church guarantees that he or she will receive an appointment to a congregation and also receive a salary. The phrase "annual conference" thus connotes an association of ministers, a fellowship, a sense of belonging.

Itineracy is the second important structural feature of Methodism. Ministers itinerate; that is, they travel to various congregations within their own region (usually part of a state) as they are assigned by the bishop of that region. The assignments were traditionally for one year, but the length of the minister's stay is expanding. In addition to itinerant ministers, Methodists have both ordained and unordained local preachers who do not travel but belong to only one congregation. They are licensed by the church and they preach, assist the minister, and occasionally act as interim pastors.

During the nineteenth century the itinerant, the circuit rider of folklore, would often be assigned to a charge with 20 or 30 preaching points on it. The circuit rider would travel his circuit every two, three, or four weeks. The effect of this type of organization was to cover the land, but it also put the ministers in many places on weekdays—not on Sundays. This became an issue in the nineteenth century as Methodism grew and stable congregations emerged which wanted to meet on Sundays instead of on weekdays.

GERMAN METHODISTS. During the first generation, Methodism in America spread among German-speaking people in the middle Colonies, and German congregations and leaders emerged. Attempts to merge the English-speaking and German-speaking Methodist and Pietist groups in the early 1800s failed. A major factor in the failure was Asbury's belief that there should be no perpetuation of German work since English would quickly be the only language in America. Asbury was essentially correct, but he failed to foresee the large German migrations of the 1800s. Eventually the Methodist Episcopal Church had to organize its own German-speaking mission to cope with the demand for ministry.

Two separate Wesleyan churches developed among America's German-speaking population: the United Brethren in Christ, and the Evangelical Association. These two churches merged with each other and then with the United Methodist Church. Prior to these mergers, various schismatic churches formed from the two German-speaking churches.

One of the most interesting schismatic churches is now defunct: the Republican United Brethren church. It was formed by members of the White River Conference of the United Brethren in Christ during the Mexican War. The church's origin can be traced to an informal meeting of ministers and members of the White River Conference at Dowell Meeting House, Franklin Circuit, Indiana, on March 12, 1848. At the meeting, a resolution was passed protesting conference action concerning the Reverend P. C. Parker. (Parker had been expelled from the ministry for "immorality" because of his participation in the war.) This resolution was refused publication; therefore, an appeal was made to the general conference. The 1853 general conference, however, sustained Parker's expulsion and passed a strong anti-war resolution. The convention also acted in support of a belief in "the doctrine of the natural, hereditary, and total depravity of man." That doctrine refers to the sinfulness of man after the fall, by which sinfulness the will is in bondage and is unable to turn to God. The protest of the three actions of the general conference became the formal basis for withdrawal. At a meeting at Union Chapel, Decatur County, Indiana, on September 8-12, 1853, the new church was organized. The church was small (the first conference listed only two charges) and existed for only a short time. In the 1860s, the church became part of the Christian Union.

BLACK METHODISM. Of the religiously affiliated black people in America, the second largest number belong to Methodist churches. (The largest number belong to Baptist churches.) Blacks were a part of Methodism almost from the beginning; first mentioned by John Wesley, the founder of Methodism, in his *Journal* were servants of Nathaniel Gilbert, the pioneer of Methodism in the West Indies. In America they were members of the earliest societies, a few being named in the records. At least two, Richard Allen and Harry Hoosier, were present at the Christmas Conference in Baltimore in 1784, when the American Methodist Church was established as a separate church from English Methodism. Harry Hoosier traveled often with Bishop Francis Asbury, the first Methodist bishop, and Richard Allen emerged as the leader of the Philadelphia black Methodist group. By 1800 a large free black constituency was present in Baltimore, New York, Wilmington, North Carolina, and Philadelphia, quite apart from the large membership among the slaves.

Forms in keeping with the master-slave relationship were adopted as more and more blacks became church members. These included segregated services, church galleries, and later separate congregations. Dislike of practices derogatory of black people became apparent first among the free black members in the Northern urban centers. Only after the Civil War was significant dissent vocalized.

NON-EPISCOPAL METHODISM. No concern—except for the race issue—has led to the number of schisms within

Methodism as has the protest against the episcopal polity of the Methodist Episcopal Church. The first group to depart over polity questions and to subsequently form a nonepiscopal church was the Republican Methodists led by James O'Kelley. His small church eventually became a part of the Christian Church (a constituent part of the present-day United Church of Christ). More significant, however, was the Methodist Protestant schism in the 1920s. This created the first major alternative to the Methodist Episcopal Church and finally merged with the two large episcopal branches in 1939. The merger of the Methodist Protestant Church left many of its pastors and members dissatisfied and led to no less than six schisms. Members refused to move from the relatively small denomination into the 10 million-member Methodist Church (1939-1968), now the United Methodist Church. They also rejected the episcopal system and, in the South, feared the possibility of racial integration, which did occur in the 1960s. Such churches as the Methodist Protestant Church (1939-), headquartered in Mississippi, and the Bible Protestant Church, now known as the Fellowship of Fundamental Bible Churches, centered in New Jersey, originated from the merger of the Methodist Protestant Church in 1939.

Besides the schisms growing out of the Methodist Protestant Church, there have been other protests that included rejection of episcopal authority and led to the formation of new church bodies. Most notable was the Congregational Methodist movement in Georgia in the 1880s. More recently the Southern Methodists and the Evangelical Methodists have followed that pattern. One could also see the holiness movement (generally regarded as the only doctrinal schism in Methodism) as a polity schism caused by the inability of the bishops and district superintendents to control the numerous holiness associations that had emerged to focus holiness doctrinal concerns. In fact, most holiness churches adopted a nonepiscopal form of government.

Methodism in British America: Methodism developed in Canada and the West Indies quite apart from its development in the United States. The first Methodist work in Canada began in 1765 under the direction of Lawrence Coughlan, an Irishman. However Coughlan was ordained as an Anglican priest in 1867 and took his work into the Church of England in Canada with him. A more permanent Methodist presence occurred in 1772 when a group of settlers from Yorkshire in Southwest Great Britain found their way to Nova Scotia. Among them were some Methodists, and among the Methodists was William Black (1760-1834). Converted in 1779, he began almost immediately to preach in the scattered settlements, especially spurred by the anti-Methodist remarks of Newlight (later Baptist) preacher, Henry Alline. He sought assistance from England and Methodist founder John Wesley placed him in contact with the Methodists in the American colonies.

As the arrival of numerous Loyalists in Nova Scotia swelled Black's responsibilities, in 1783 he finally journeyed to the United States to seek help from the Methodist Episcopal Church. The work developed quickly, and as it grew he was appointed presiding elder for the Nova Scotia District. The relationship with the American church continued until 1800 when it was shifted to the British Wesleyan Conference, by which time it had spread through the Maritime Provinces.

As the work was spreading through the Maritimes, a second thrust into Canada developed when William Losee (1757-1832) was sent by Bishop Francis Asbury to check upon the Methodists among the Loyalists who had settled in the neighborhood of Kingston, Ontario. The new mission was initially placed under the care of the New York Conference, but the need for separating it from American control became evident, especially following the War of 1812. Unfortunately, a misunderstanding occurred in early negotiations with the British Wesleyans which prevented their being allowed to assume responsibility for the Ontario congregations as they had in Nova Scotia. Thus in 1824 the Canadian work was set apart as the independent Methodist Episcopal Church in Canada.

Still a third beginning for Methodism in Canada followed the beginning of a Wesleyan Methodist mission in Western Canada in 1840 when James Evans (1801-1846) was appointed as a missionary in Rupert's Land (Manitoba). From his settlement at Norway House, north of present-day Winnipeg, he began a mission to the Indians, which led to his development of a new script for use with the Indian languages. His accomplishments opened the west to a vital Methodist presence.

During the nineteenth century, a variety of forms of Methodism, representatives of the different British splinter groups, entered Canada. Prior to 1884, the Canadian Methodists went through a process of merger which brought almost all of them into a single body, the Methodist Church, Canada. That body merged into the United Church of Canada in 1925 and now continues as a constituent part of that church.

Methodism in the West Indies started with the return of Nathaniel Greene to his plantation on Antigua in 1760. During his just completed trip to England, he had encountered John Wesley, founder of Methodism, and been converted. He organized a class of more than 200, mostly blacks who lived on the plantation, and it is from this class that Methodism spread throughout the islands. Work in the islands was given a significant boost by the visits of Thomas Coke, Wesley's assistant, beginning in the winter of 1786-87, and picked up by the Wesleyan Methodist Missionary Society (in England) after Coke's death in 1814. The work became independent as the autonomous Methodist Church in the Caribbean and the Americas in 1967.

At the beginning of the twentieth century, West Indian Methodists migrated to the United States. Rather than affiliate with any of the Methodist churches they found, all of which had an episcopal polity, they organized to carry on the work much as they had been used to in the island. Thus the United Wesleyan Methodist Church of America came into existence. In more recent years, the United Methodist Church has developed a close working relationship with the West Indian Methodist Conference and has accepted some oversight of the United Wesleyans in the United States.

SOURCES—PIETIST METHODIST FAMILY

PIETISM

Gerdes, Egon W. "Pietism Classical and Modern." *Concordia Theological Journal*, April 1968, pp. 257-68.

Stoeffler, F. Ernest. *German Pietism During the Eighteenth Century*. Leiden: E. J. Brill, 1973. 282 pp.

SCANDINAVIAN PIETISTS

Covenant Memories, 1885-1935. Chicago: Covenant Book Concern, 1935. 495 pp.

Norton, H. Wilbert, et al. *The Diamond Jubilee Story of the Evangelical Free Church of America*. Minneapolis: Free Church Publications, 1959. 335 pp.

Olsson, Karl A. *By One Spirit*. Chicago: Covenant Press, 1962. 811 pp.

——. *A Family of Faith*. Chicago: Covenant Press, 1975. 157 pp.

MORAVIANS

Hamilton, J. Taylor and Kenneth G. Hamilton. *History of the Moravian Church*. Bethlehem, PA: Interprovincial Board of Christian Education, Moravian Church in America, 1983. 723 pp.

Schattschneider, Allen W. *Through Five Hundred Years*. Bethlehem, PA: Comenius Press, 1956. 148 pp.

Weinlick, John Rudolf. *Count Zinzendorf*. New York: Abingdon Press, 1956. 240 pp.

THE WESLEYAN TRADITION

Bishop, John. *Methodist Worship*. London: Epworth Press, 1950. 165 pp.

Bucke, Emory Stevens, ed. *The History of American Methodism*. 3 vols. New York: Abingdon, 1965.

Davies, Rupert, and Gordon Rupp, eds. *A History of the Methodist Church in Great Britain*. 3 vols. London: Epworth Press, 1965-83.

Green, Vivian H. H. *John Wesley*. London: Nelson, 1964. 168 pp.

Nagler, Arthur Wilford. *Pietism and Methodist*. Nashville: Publishing House of the M. E. Church, South, 1918. 200 pp.

Schmidt, Martin. *John Wesley, A Theological Biography*. 2 vols. New York: Abingdon, 1963-73.

UNITED METHODISM

Albright, Raymond W. *A History of the Evangelical Church*. Harrisburg, PA: The Evangelical Press, 1956. 501 pp.

Andersen, Arlow W. *The Salt of the Earth*. Nashville; Norwegian-Danish Methodist Historical Society, 1962. 338 pp.

Davis, Lyman E. *Democratic Methodism in America*. New York: Fleming H. Revell, 1921. 267 pp.

Douglas, Paul F. *The Story of German Methodism*. New York: The Methodist Book Concern, 1939. 361 pp.

Eller, Paul Himmel. *These Evangelical United Brethren*. Dayton, OH: The Otterbein Press, 1950. 128 pp.

Godbold, Albea, ed. *Forever Beginning, 1766-1966*. Lake Junaluska, NC: Association of Methodist Historical Societies, 1967. 254 pp.

Graham, J. H. *Black United Methodists*. New York: Vantage Press, 1979. 162 pp.

Harmon, Nolan B. *Encyclopedia of World Methodism*.

——. *Understanding the United Methodist Church*. Nashville: Abingdon, 1977. 176 pp.

Norwood, Frederick A. *Sourcebook of American Methodism*. Nashville: Abingdon, 1982. 683 pp.

——. *The Story of American Methodism*. Nashville: Abingdon, 1974. 448 pp.

Stokes, Mack B. *Major United Methodist Beliefs*. Nashville: Abingdon, 1971. 128 pp.

Tuell, Jack M. *The Organization of the United Methodist Church*. Nashville: Abingdon, 1977. 174 pp.

Wallenius, C. G., and E. D. Olson. *A Short Story of the Swedish Methodism in America*. Chicago, 1931. 55 pp.

Wunderlich, Friedrich. *Methodist Linking Two Continents*. Nashville: The Methodist Publishing House, 1960. 143 pp.

OTHER METHODISTS

Richardson, Harry V. *Dark Salvation*. Garden City, NY: Doubleday, 1976. 324 pp.

Chapter 6

Holiness Family

Directory listings for the groups belonging to the Holiness Family
may be found in the section beginning on page 203.

The desire to follow Christ's call, "Be ye perfect as my father in heaven is perfect" (Matt. 5:48), has resulted in holiness churches. These churches take the drive for perfection or holiness as their primary focus and are distinguished from most other Christian churches by the unique doctrinal framework within which holiness or sanctification is understood. The corollary to this drive has been separation from Christians who did not in their opinion reach high enough toward the goal of perfection. Thus holiness churches are also distinct from other churches because of the focus on perfection and the resultant separatist practices.

John Wesley, the founder of Methodism, gave impetus to the formation of holiness churches. Though the Wesleyan movement of the eighteenth century was only in part a perfectionist movement, Wesley did encourage the ethical life and a goal of perfection, and numerous churches now strive for what they call Wesleyan holiness.

Wesley's understanding of perfection developed through two phases: first, an emphasis on sinlessness, and second, on love. While at Oxford as a college student, Wesley formed the holy club, a group of students in search of the holy life. In his early sermon, "Christian Perfection," Wesley defined perfection as holiness, saying Christians are perfect in that they are free from outward sin. Wesley felt mature Christians are free from evil tempers and thoughts, and such perfection is possible in this life.

Wesley was immediately challenged for his doctrine of perfection. In answers to his accusors he had to emphasize that perfection did not apply to mistakes, infirmity, knowledge or freedom from temptation. Also, he said there was no perfection that did not admit of further progress. Wesley himself began to see the harmful consequences of defining perfection as absence of sin, and he redefined perfectionism in terms of love. His ideas on perfection are gathered together in his *Plain Account of Christian Perfection*. The line between the Pietist-Methodist family and the holiness family is difficult to draw. There have always been individual Methodists who stressed holiness and sanctification. Further, many holiness churches are schismatic bodies that broke away from various Methodist churches, and some holiness churches use the word Methodist in their titles. However, the holiness churches place greater stress than Methodist churches on the second blessing and on a lifestyle reflecting sanctification.

THE UNDERSTANDING OF HOLINESS. The distinctive elements of the holiness way of being Christian focus upon their teachings concerning sanctification and perfection and the lifestyle which they believe should naturally flow from such teachings. The sanctification experience, also called the second blessing or second work of grace in the life of the believer, culminates a process of becoming holy that begins when the believer accepts Jesus Christ as his/her personal Savior. The first step in the process, justification, the first work of grace, is also called the born again experience. That event is followed by a period of growth in grace, in becoming actually holy in one's life. Both justification and the growing process are seen as involving the activity of the Holy Spirit with the individual. The process leads to the second work of grace in which the Holy Spirit cleanses the heart from sin and imparts His indwelling presence which gives power for living the Christian life. A consensus opinion on sanctification is found in the statement of the Wesleyan Church.

"Inward sanctification begins the moment one is justified. From that moment until a believer is entirely sanctified, he grows daily in grace and gradually dies to sin. Entire sanctification is effected by the baptism of the Holy Spirit, which cleanses the heart of the child of God from all inbred sin through faith in Jesus Christ. It is subsequent to regeneration and is wrought instantaneously when the believer presents himself a living sacrifice, holy and acceptable to God, and is thus enabled through His grace to love God with all the heart and to walk in all His holy commandments blameless. The crisis of cleansing is preceded and followed by growth in grace and the knowledge of our Lord and Savior, Jesus Christ. When man is fully cleansed from all sin, he is endued with the power of the Holy Spirit for the accomplishment of all to which he is called. The ensuing life of holiness is maintained by a continuing faith in the sanctifying blood of Christ, and is evidenced by an obedient life."

35

In John Wesley's thought, the process of sanctification was to be seen as the goal toward which the Christian's life led. The arrival at the state of sanctification in which one was freed from sin and made perfect in life generally occurred only at the end of one's days on earth. However, in the mid-nineteenth century, deriving in large part from the ministry of Phoebe Palmer, coeditor of *The Path of Holiness*, a prominent Methodist and holiness magazine, a subtle but important divergence with Wesley crept into holiness though. In her writing and speaking, Palmer began to picture sanctification as more the beginning of the Christian life rather than the goal. As Charles Edward White has pointed out in his recent study, *The Beauty of Holiness*, Palmer advocated sanctification as the immediate possibility of any believer, and she encouraged all, no matter how new in the faith, to seek it as the instantaneous gift of the Holy Spirit. This subtle change of emphasis led both to a renewed concentration upon the search for holiness among Methodists, but also created a reaction from many Methodists who saw in Wesley's understanding of the gradual process of the development of the life of holiness a reason to reject the renewed emphasis upon sanctification.

In the last half of the nineteenth century personal holiness, symbolized by a rigid code of behavior, became the distinguishing theme in the holiness lifestyle. John Wesley, who wrote the *General Rules* for the Methodists, is the source of this trend. He disapproved of flashy clothes, costly apparel, and expensive jewelry, and in the early nineteenth century holiness schisms from Methodism, a consistent voice was one deploring the departure of the Methodists from the *General Rules*. The strictest personal codes came in the late nineteenth century. They were in part a reaction to the social gospel emphasis in the larger denominations. There is also strong evidence that such codes were and are tied to the frustrations of people left behind by urbanization, mechanization, and population growth. Without status in mass society, people reject it and find virtue in the necessity of their condition. Holiness was and is to be found in asceticism and rejection of worldliness.

The rejection of the worldliness theme has led to typical holiness intrafamily polemics over exactly what constitutes worldliness. Churches have split over the acceptance of television or the style of clothing, such as neckties. Other issues include the attitude toward divorced people, cosmetics, swimming with the opposite sex, dress in high school gym classes, and the cutting of females' hair (I Cor. 11: 1-16).

At one time the holiness movement concentrated much of its attention on social issues and public morality. The Wesleyan and Free Methodists both were abolitionist oriented and at different times the holiness movement was tied to the great crusades for temperance and women's rights. Beginning with the co-mingling of Wesleyan and Quaker ideas during the era of John Gurney, pacifism has had a strong hold on the holiness movement and is the major remnant of the social imperative. Many Pentecostal churches have inherited this pacifist emphasis.

Among the holiness groups, sacraments have not been an important part of church life. Some churches have two sacraments—baptism and the Lord's Supper—as the Wesleyan Church does. Some consider baptism and the Lord's Supper to be ordinances, not sacraments. Churches such as the General Eldership of the Churches of God add footwashing as a third ordinance. Finally, other churches, most notably the Salvation Army, have neither ordinances nor sacraments.

HOLINESS MOVEMENT IN AMERICA. The strain of perfectionism in Wesleyan teaching was not the most emphasized doctrine in early nineteenth century Methodism. On the heels of the great American revival of 1837-38, however, centers of interest in the Wesleyan doctrine of perfection or holiness, as it was termed, emerged. One phase of this interest came in 1839 with the sanctification experienced by Charles G. Finney. Sanctification, in this context, means holiness; it means becoming perfect in love. Finney, a Congregationalist and the most famous evangelist of his day, had learned of sanctification from the Methodists and from reading Wesley's *Plain Account of Christian Perfection*. At the same time, Finney became involved in a search for social holiness, making society perfect in love, justice being the social form of love. Finney defended women's rights, participated in the antislavery crusade, and as a pacifist protested the Mexican War (1846-1848). After experiencing sanctification in 1839, Finney began to write on it and preach it. In 1844 his colleague at Oberlin, Asa Mahan, published his book, *Scripture Doctrine of Christian Perfection*, which became the major statement of the Oberlin position. Because of his non-Methodist background, Finney had a great effect on other soon-to-be holiness greats—T.C. Upham, William Boardman, and A.B. Earle. Thus, the first wave of holiness in the United States began outside of Methodism, by Methodized Presbyterians, Baptists, and Congregationalists. Prior to 1855 only one Methodist gained any reputation for perfectionist thinking, Timothy Merritt, editor of the *Guide to Christian Perfection* (later called the *Guide to Holiness*), but Finney had raised an issue for the whole Methodist Episcopal Church, and Methodists could no longer ignore their heritage.

Without any weakening or demise of the Oberlin holiness crusade, the holiness movement began a new phase after the revival of 1857-58. The new center of interest was the "Tuesday Meeting for the Promotion of Holiness" led by Mrs. Phoebe Palmer, a member of Allen Street Methodist Church in New York City. Mrs. Palmer's efforts were aided by the publication of two books, *Christian Purity* by Randolph S. Foster and *The Central Idea of Christianity* by Jesse T. Peck. Both men were soon to be bishops. The revival which was spreading from Allen Street to the whole of Methodism was interrupted by the Civil War, but picked up momentum as soon as the hostilities ceased. During the war, the Palmers, Phoebe and her husband, Walter, bought Merritt's *Guide to Holiness* and in 1866 they toured the country, establishing centers of the sanctified wherever they preached.

It was not long until ministers rallied to the cause. The camp meeting proved to be the prime structure to carry on the work and in 1867 William Osborn of the South New Jersey Conference of Methodists and John S. Inskip of New York set up a national camp meeting at Vineland, New Jersey.

During this camp meeting the "National Camp Meeting Association for the Promotion of Holiness" was formed, and Inskip became its first president. Bishop Matthew Simpson personally aided the work which prospered under episcopal approval.

The holiness movement grew tremendously among Methodists in the first decade after the Civil War. In 1872 Jesse T. Peck, Randolph S. Foster, Stephen Merrill, and Gilbert Haven, all promoters of the holiness revival, were elected Methodist bishops; and, with their encouragement, the movement was given vocal support through the church press. In 1870 a second national press organ was begun by William McDonald of the New England Conference. *The Advocate of Holiness* became the organ of the Camp Meeting Association. The revival reached some of the most influential members of the church: Daniel Steele, first president of Syracuse University and then professor of systematic theology at Boston University; William Nast, father of German Methodism; Bishop William Taylor; wealthy layman, Washington C. DePauw; and women's rights leader, Frances Willard. A new generation of preachers came along ready to make their mark as ministers of the holiness gospel: Beverly Carradine, J. A. Wood, Alfred Cookman, John L. Brasher, and Milton L. Haney. The movement grew and developed; and, like the Finney revival, there was little or no fear of schism.

While this new work spread quickly among the Methodists, that begun by Finney did not die but continued to bear fruit. While the Oberlin position never really caught on with non-Methodists, leaders from the Quakers, Presbyterians, and Baptists preached the second blessing. William Boardman carried the message to England where, in conjunction with R. Pearsall Smith, a Presbyterian, he began the "Oxford Union Meeting for the Promotion of Scriptural Holiness." The Oxford meetings then formed the base for the Keswick Movement, which became the main carrier of the holiness movement in the Church of England. Smith's wife, Hannah, wrote one of the great classics of the Keswick era, *The Christian's Secret of a Happy Life*. The Keswick brand of holiness, which emphasized the giving of power instead of the cleansing from sin, gained its adherents in the United States: Dwight L. Moody, R.A. Torrey, Adroniram J. Gordon, A.B. Simpson, and evangelist Wilbur Chapman.

At the height of this wave of success something went wrong; schisms began to dominate the movement, and a third phase began: the establishment of independent holiness churches. The voice for schism began to be heard in the 1880s, became dominant in the 1890s and by 1910 had almost totally removed the holiness movement from the main denominations into independent holiness churches. The movement out of Methodism was a response to at least three forces antagonistic to the holiness movement. First, a theological critique began to be heard. Men such as J.M. Boland, author of *The Problem of Methodism*, attacked the second blessing doctrine and maintained that sanctification was accomplished at the moment of conversion. James Mudge in his *Growth in Holiness Toward Perfection or Progressive Sanctification* argued for progressive rather than instantaneous sanctification. Borden Parker Bowne, representing a growing army of German-trained theologians, simply dismissed the whole issue of sanctification as irrelevant.

The second force of growing concern to Methodist leaders was the mass of uncontrollable literature and organizations which the holiness movement was producing. By 1890 the number of books, tracts, pamphlets, and periodicals coming off the press to serve the holiness movement was enormous. Independent camp meeting associations covered the country and in many places competed with local churches for the allegiance of members. Since camp meetings were independent, bishops and district superintendents had only the power of moral suasion to control what happened at the meetings or what was read throughout the movement. For some, this state of affairs was felt as a direct threat to their power. Others were genuinely concerned with excesses, fanaticism, and heterodox teaching. In either case, the loss of control led to an anti-holiness polemic.

The third cause for the holiness schism is found in the genuine shift of power which occurred between 1870 and 1890 in the Methodist Episcopal Church and the holiness movement itself. By 1890 the bishops who promoted the holiness movement and gave it official sanction had been replaced largely by others who were cool to the holiness heat. Within the holiness movement itself were regional and national leaders who were unhappy under the yoke of an unsympathetic hierarchy which was moving further away from their position each day. Not wishing to be confined in their ministry, they bolted the church. Among the first to leave were Daniel S. Warner, who founded the Church of God at Anderson, Indiana, and John P. Brooks. Brooks, a leader in the Western Holiness Association, in 1887 published *The Divine Church*, which called for all true holiness Christians to come out of Methodism's church of mammon. *The Divine Church* became the theological guide to lead the way to the formation of independent churches.

The "come-out" movement created pressure on those who chose to stay in to justify their position. Thus, the 1890s saw loyalists publishing books against "come-outism," and calling for strengthening of the camp meetings. Beverly Carradine called for remaining in the church, but favored the establishment of independent holiness colleges. Asbury College, Wilmore, Kentucky, and Taylor University, Indiana, represent the partial success of Carradine's view. These efforts by the loyalists were significantly unsuccessful, however, and by 1910 only minor pockets of holiness teaching (such as the Brasher Campgrounds in Alabama) remained in the larger Methodist churches.

CONTEMPORARY DEVELOPMENTS. Possibly because of the intense controversy during the formative years of the older holiness churches, there is a strong sense of identity within the holiness family among the various members. This image is focused not only in the doctrinal unity and similarity of lifestyle, but in the several ecumenical structures. These structures are home to a wide range of groups, from those who still keep ties with the United Methodist Church (Wesleyans, Free Methodists), all the way over to groups like the Church of God of the Mountain Assembly, which has Baptist origins.

The oldest ecumenical structure is the Christian Holiness Association. This body, which includes most of the larger holiness churches in its membership, is a continuation of the National Holiness Camp Meeting Association, which guided the movement from the 1870s. After the establishment of the various denominational structures it remained as a meeting ground for these new organizations and those who remained in their original churches, primarily Methodists. Increasingly, it served the denominational bodies and in 1970 assumed its present name to recognize that fact.

One longstanding, if minor, theme in the holiness movement was that perpetuated by the Keswick Conventions. Growing up primarily among the holiness supporters of the Church of England, it supported the idea of suppression of the evil tendencies in man, as opposed to the eradication taught by the Wesleyans. Keswick ideas did not produce many new groups but did find a home among one large body, the Christian and Missionary Alliance.

THE GLENN GRIFFITH MOVEMENT. As the holiness movement has grown since World War II, and has become more accommodating to the world, some of its members have begun to protest this accommodation. They say they wish to preserve the "old-fashioned Scriptural holiness" in which they were raised. The leader of this movement was the Reverend Glenn Griffith, a former minister from the Church of the Nazarene. The revival services he held in 1955 between Nampa and Caldwell, Idaho, attracted many people to him. His movement spread, finding advocates in all of the larger holiness churches. Members left those churches to follow Griffith; this splintering from the holiness churches is still continuing.

Even before Griffith gave focus to the protest movement, the Rev. H.E. Schmul facilitated fellowship among conservative holiness churches and ministers. The structure used by Schmul to promote this fellowship was the Interdenominational Holiness Convention. It was begun by Schmul, a Wesleyan Methodist minister, in 1947. Its magazine, *Convention Herald*, served as a placement service for evangelists seeking appointments for revival meetings. Leaders of the various splinter movements within holiness churches had participated in the Interdenominational Holiness Convention. After the new churches were formed, these leaders moved into key positions in the Convention. The Interdenominational Holiness Convention continues to operate informally with membership open to individuals, congregations, and churches.

SOURCES—HOLINESS FAMILY

GENERAL SOURCES ON SANCTIFICATION AND HOLINESS

Dieter, Melvin E.,et al *Five Views of Sanctification*. Grand Rapids, MI: Academic Books, 1987. 254 pp.

Fenelon, Francois de Salignac de La Mothe. *Christian Perfection*. New York: Harper & Row, 1947. 208 pp.

Finney, Charles G. *An Autobiography*. Westwood, NJ: Fleming H. Revell, 1876. 477 pp.

———. *Sanctification*. Fort Washington, PA: Christian Literture Crusade, n.d. 105 pp.

Law, William. *A Serious Call to a Devout and Holy Life*. New York: E. P. Dutton, 1906. 355 pp.

Lindstrom, Harold. *Wesley and Sanctification*. New York: Abingdon, 1946. 228 pp.

THE HOLINESS MOVEMENT IN AMERICA

Bundy, David D. *Keswick: A Bibliographical Introduction to the Higher Life Movements*. Wilmore, KY: B. L. Fisher Library, Asbury Theological Seminary, 1975. 89 pp.

Dayton, Donald W. *The American Holiness Movement, A Bibliographic Introduction*. Wilmore, KY: B. L. Fisher Library, Asbury Theological Seminary, 1971. 59 pp.

Dieter, Melvin Easterday. *The Holiness Revival of the Nineteenth Century*. Metuchen, NJ: Scarecrow Press, 1980. 356 pp.

Jones, Charles Edwin. *A Guide to the Study of the Holiness Movement*. Metuchen, NJ: Scarecrow Press, 1974. 918 pp.

Lambert, D. W. *Heralds of Holiness*. Stoke-on-Trent: M.O.V.E. Press, 1975. 80 pp.

Miller, William Charles. *Holiness Works: A Bibliography*. Kansas City, MO: Nazarene Publishing House, 1986. 120 pp.

Nazarene Theological Seminary. *Master Bibliography of Holiness Works*. Kansas City, MO: Beacon Hill Press, 1965. 45 pp.

Peters, John Leland. *Christian Perfectionism and American Methodism*. New York: Abingdon, 1956. 252 pp.

Pollock, J. C. *The Keswick Story*. London: Hodder & Stoughton, 1964. 190 pp.

Smith, Timothy L. "The Holiness Crusade." In vol. II of *The History of American Methodism*. Ed. Emory Stevens Buck. Nashville: Abingdon, 1965, pp. 608-59.

———. *Revivalism and Social Reform*. Nashville: Abingdon, 1957. 253 pp.

White, Charles Edward. *The Beauty of Holiness*. Grand Rapids Francis Asbury Press, 1986. 330 pp.

HOLINESS THOUGHT

Arthur, William. *The Tongue of Fire*. Winona Lake, IN: Light and Life Press, n.d. 253 pp.

Boyd, Myron F., and Merne A. Harris, comps. *Projecting Our Heritage*. Kansas City: Beacon Hill Press of Kansas City, 1969. 157 pp.

Carradine, Beverly. *The Sanctified Life*. Cincinnati: The Revivalist, 1897. 286 pp.

Foster, Randolph S. *Christian Purity*. New York: Nelson & Phillips, 1869. 364 pp.

Kuhn, Harold B., ed. *The Doctrinal Distinctives of Asbury Theological Seminary*. Wilmore, KY: Asbury Theological Seminary, n.d. 100 pp.

Palmer, Phoebe. *Faith and Its Effects*. New York: Walter C. Palmer, 1854. 352 pp.

Rose, Delbert E. *A Theology of Christian Experience*. Minneapolis: Bethany Fellowship, 1965. 313 pp.

CRITICAL APPRAISALS

Boland, J. M. *The Problem of Methodism*. Nashville: The Author, 1889. 331 pp.

Ironside, Harold A. *Holiness, the False and the True*. New York: Loizeaux Brothers, 1947. 142 pp.

Mudge, James B. *Growth in Holiness Toward Perfection, or Progressive Sanctification*. New York: Hunt and Eaton, 1895.

Nevins, John W. *The Anxious Bench*. Chambersburg, PA: German Ref. Church, 1844. 149 pp.

Warfield, Benjamin B. *Perfectionism*. Philadelphia: The Presbyterian and Reformed Publishing Company, 1958. 464 pp.

Chapter 7

Pentecostal Family

Directory listings for the groups belonging to the Pentecostal Family
may be found in this section beginning on page 231.

The Pentecostal movement claims several million Americans and millions more overseas. As Pentecostals have taken their place in the world Christian community, they have emphasized their orthodoxy. They have had few doctrinal disagreements with the various churches from which they grew. In fact, the confessions of faith of the Pentecostal churches reflect their heritage, be that heritage Methodist or Baptist or holiness (rooted in the holiness movement and churches, discussed in the preceding chapter). The dividing line between Pentecostal churches and the mainline Protestant churches has been clear, though, from the beginning of modern Pentecostalism in 1901. What makes Pentecostals distinct?—their new form of religious experience highlighted by speaking in tongues.

The Pentecostal experience may be defined as seeking and receiving the gift of speaking in tongues as a sign of the baptism of the Holy Spirit. In turn, that baptism may be defined as the dwelling of the Holy Spirit in the individual believer. From the initial idea and experience of the baptism of the Holy Spirit and speaking in tongues, flows the belief in other gifts of the Holy Spirit manifested in the New Testament church (I Cor. 12:4-11). Those gifts include healing, prophecy, wisdom (knowledge unattainable by natural means), and discernment of spirits (seeing nonphysical beings such as angels and demons).

SPEAKING IN TONGUES. Glossolalia, speaking in tongues, was a part of the experience of Jesus' disciples at Pentecost (Acts 2) and reappeared at several important points in the growing church. In Paul's *Epistle to the Corinthians*, "tongues" are mentioned as one gift or "charisma" among others such as healing, working miracles, and prophecy. "Tongues" usually appear in connection with other "gifts of the Spirit" although, historically, the other gifts have often appeared without the accompanying verbal gift. The experience of "tongues," if not common, was well known in the ancient world. The phenomenon is manifest today in a number of tribal religions, as well as among Pentecostals.

What are "tongues"? To the outsider, hearing someone speak in "tongues" is like hearing so much gibberish. To the Pentecostal, it is speaking under the control of the Holy Spirit. Pentecostal lore is full of tales of people who have been able to speak in a foreign language at a moment of crisis, although they did not know the language. Believers regard such instances as supernatural occurrences.

Social scientists generally look to a different explanation. Linguist William Samarin would separate glossolalia from zenoglossia. Glossolalia, says Samarin, is not truly a language. It is a verbalized religious experience. Only a few vowels and consonants are used, not enough to make a language as we know it. Glossolalia is the common prayer speech heard at Pentecostal churches. Xenoglossia is the utterance of an existent foreign language by one who has no knowledge of it. A rare occurence, it nevertheless has been noted and recorded in the literature of psychical research. Both telepathy and spirit contact have been hypothesized as the source of the xenoglossia.

LIFESTYLE AND WORSHIP. Along with the new form of religious experience centered upon speaking in tongues comes the second distinguishing mark of the Pentecostal: a lifestyle reordered around that religious experience. The Pentecostal convert lets his or her religious experience dominate daily life. The Pentecostal encourages others to have the baptism of the Holy Spirit; Pentecostals talk about that experience often; when they pray, they pray in tongues; they see healings as signs of God's immediate presence; they pay attention to other gifts of the Holy Spirit; and finally, they tend to look down on those who do not speak in tongues.

Pentecostals are pejoratively called "holy rollers" for their free, loud, participatory style of worship and their constant attention to the gifts of the Spirit, especially tongues. In contrast to the more orderly services in the Methodist and Baptist churches, Pentecostals seem to have a very free, spontaneous service which includes hymns that emphasize rhythm, extemporaneous prayers, and frequent interruption of the service with "amen's" and "tongues." Those who visit Pentecostal services for the first time are startled by the seeming lack of order. The freedom and spontaneity are limited, however. Even the most free congregation falls into a narrow pattern, repeated week after week with little variation.

It is the worship and the lifestyle keyed to religious experience—the constant search for the experience and the endless talk about it—that really separate Pentecostalism from the older Protestant denominations. Such distinctions are more felt than rationalized and are rarely articulated.

When conservative Christians such as Baptists and the Reformed talk about the doctrinal differences between themselves and the Pentecostal movement, they discuss disagreements about the baptism of the Holy Spirit and the gifts of the Spirit. They say the gifts of the Spirit were given to the early church and disappeared after the Apostles died. Some charge the Pentecostals with demon possession. By contrast, the Pentecostals insist the end of time is near, and the words of the prophet Joel (Joel 3:1) are being fulfilled:

"It shall come to pass in the last days, says God, that I will pour out my Spirit on all mankind: Your sons and daughters shall prophesy, your young men shall see visions and your old men shall dream dreams."

According to Acts 2:17, Peter referred to this passage on Pentecost.

HEALING. If speaking in tongues makes Pentecostals controversial, so does healing. Objections to healing center not as much on the reality of healing as on the form that healing ministers have assumed. Mainline Christians are offended by the seeming overfamiliarity with God assumed in praying for God to heal, as well as the loud, demanding style of many evangelists. The critics also object to the emotional, crowd-psychology-oriented healing services which seem to manipulate those in attendance. The recent controversy centered on the child-evangelist, Marjoe Gortner, is typical of the polemics. Gortner conducted healing services as a child, but came to the decision that what he was doing was not valid. So he invited filmmakers to follow him in a year's work of Pentecostal healing, filming what he did. The resultant movie and book were exposés of Pentecostal healing.

However, the Pentecostals have raised an important issue for contemporary Christians: the question of healing as a sign of God's work among his people. Pentecostals join both Christian Scientists, who refrain from using medicine and doctors, and Episcopalians in raising this issue. An Episcopalian physician, Charles Cullis, held healing services at the turn of this century in his summer camp at Old Orchard, Maine. Many of the spiritual healing ministries in this country can be traced to an additional Episcopalian source: the Order of St. Luke, a spiritual healing group. Thus Pentecostals are not alone in their interest in healing as a gift of the Spirit.

"TONGUES" IN HISTORY. The first manifestation of "tongues" in the modern era occurred in the late seventeenth century in France. The times were a blend of persecution and miraculous events. After the revocation of the Edict of Nantes, state suppression of Protestants began in southern France, among other places. In the mountainous region of Languedoc in the 1680s more than 10,000 people were victims of the stake, galley, and wheel. Partially in reaction to this persecution, strange psychic phenomena began to occur. At Vivaris, in southern France, a man had a vision and heard a voice say, "Go and console my people." At Berne, people saw apparitions and heard voices. There arose prophets who were viewed as miraculous because, although young and untutored, they spoke fluently and with wisdom.

Among the French mountain villages was a poor unlettered girl, Isabella Vincent. The daughter of a weaver, Isabella left home after her father accepted a bribe to become a Catholic and after she witnessed a massacre of Huguenots (French Calvinists). She was a Huguenot, and she fled to her Huguenot godfather. On February 12, 1688, she had her first ecstatic experience. She entered a trance in which she spoke in tongues and prophesied. She called for repentance, especially from those who had forsaken their faith for gold. Her fame spread. People marveled at her perfect Parisian French and her ability to quote the mass *verbatim* and refute it. She was finally arrested, but others rose to take her place. In 1700, a movement began among the youth, and children as young as three entered ecstatic states and prophesied. Continued persecution was followed by war and eventual migration to other parts of Europe, where these people became known as the French Prophets.

A few manifestations of "tongues" were noted in the eighteenth century among the Quakers in England and the Methodists in America. In the 1830s, however, two groups emerged who spoke in tongues with some frequency: in England, the Catholic Apostolic Church, and in America, the Church of Jesus Christ of Latter-day Saints. Both accepted the experience as part of a gifted, charismatic church life. Then, after the Civil War "tongues" began to manifest themselves within the holiness churches and thus came into historical continuity with the present-day Pentecostal movement. In 1875, the Reverend R.B. Swan, a holiness minister, was one of five people in Providence, Rhode Island, who spoke in tongues. This group grew and soon became known as the "Gift People." Jethro Walthall reported speaking in tongues as early as 1879. This evangelist from Arkansas at first accepted tongues as part of a total experience of "being carried outside of himself," but later identified it with Pentecost and became a superintendent of the Assemblies of God, discussed in this chapter. In 1890, Daniel Awrey, an evangelist from Ohio, experienced "tongues." In the 1890s, members attending the meetings of R.G. Spurling in Tennessee and North Carolina, and W.F. Bryant of Camp Creek, North Carolina, spoke in tongues. The experience was later identified with Pentecost and these two men became leaders in the Church of God (Cleveland, Tennessee) discussed in this chapter. Besides these and other isolated incidents of "tongues," in the 1890s, there appeared a new movement in the holiness church which was to be a direct precursor of Pentecostalism as it exists today—the fire baptism.

As a movement, fire baptism was an "experience" preached by some holiness ministers looking for something more than their holiness experience had given them. The first such minister was the Reverend B.H. Irwin who had derived the experience from the writings of John Fletcher, an early Methodist. Fletcher, in his works, had spoken of a "baptism of burning love," but it is doubtful if he was implying any of what Irwin was seeking. Fire baptism, a personal religious experience of being filled with and empowered by the Holy Spirit, took its name from the Holy Spirit's descent upon the

Apostles in the form of tongues of flame—the first Pentecost. In 1895, the first fire-baptized congregation (the first church to seek and receive fire baptism) was organized at Olmitz, Iowa. From there fire baptism was spread by itinerant evangelists. Holiness leaders labeled this new experience, which they termed "The Fire," heresy and fanaticism. Opposition did not keep the teaching from spreading and, within three years, there were nine state associations organized and six more waiting to form, including two in Canada. Formal organization of the Fire-Baptized Holiness Association took place in 1898 at Anderson, South Carolina, and a periodical, *Live Coals of Fire*, was started in 1899. Later, the Fire-Baptized Holiness Association was to accept as a body the Pentecostal emphasis on speaking in tongues as a sure sign of the Spirit's presence within the believer. The early experience of tongues and the development of the Fire-Baptized Holiness Association set the nineteenth century stage for the twentieth century Pentecostal movement. Three years would be significant in its development—1901, 1906, and 1914.

1901—Topeka, Kansas. The beginnings of the modern Pentecostal movement centered on the Reverend Charles Parham. After leaving the Methodist Episcopal Church, Parham opened the Bethel Healing Home in 1898 in Topeka. He had been inspired by the healing ministry of John Alexander Dowie of Zion, Illinois. In 1900, he began an extended tour of holiness and healing ministries from Chicago to New York to Georgia. Returning to Topeka, Parham found his work undermined and usurped. Undaunted, he purchased a building just outside of town and began the Bethel Bible College in the fall of 1900. Over the Christmas holidays, before leaving to speak in Kansas City, he assigned his students the task of investigating the "baptism of the Spirit," sometimes called the Pentecostal blessing. Upon returning, Parham got a report: "To my astonishment, they all had the same story, that while different things occurred when the Pentecostal blessing fell, the indisputable proof on each occasion was that they spoke with other tongues" (Sarah E. Parham, *The Life of Charles F. Parham* [Joplin, MO: Press of the Hunter Printing Co., 1969], 52).

Immediately they turned to seek a baptism with an indication given by utterance in "tongues." On January 1, 1901, the Spirit fell, first on Agnes Ozman, and a few days later on many others, and then on Parham himself.

Thus Agnes Ozman became the first person in modern times to seek and receive the experience of speaking in tongues (glossolalia) as a sign of being "baptized with the Holy Spirit." At that moment was inaugurated the Pentecostal Movement.

This small beginning, of fewer than 40 people, did not portend the growth that was to come. Parham closed the school and with his students set out to spread the message of the new Pentecost. He traveled and preached through Missouri and Kansas, and climaxed his tour with a revival in Galena, Kansas, which lasted for four months in the winter of 1903-04. In 1905, he began work in Texas for the first time. He made Houston his headquarters and in December 1905 opened a Bible school. Parham at this point let the

mantle of leadership pass to William J. Seymour, who studied under Parham in Houston.

1906—Azusa Street, Los Angeles, California. The Pentecostal scene shifts to the West, to California, where in 1906 William J. Seymour, a black holiness minister, arrived to preach at a small Baptist church. The church refused to hear him after his first sermon, but he was invited to preach at a member's home on Bonnie Brae Street. After three days of his preaching, the Spirit fell and "tongues" were heard on the West Coast. The meeting quickly outgrew the small home and a former Methodist church building was rented on Azusa Street. From here was to develop the revival which was to send the Pentecostal experience around the world.

The Pentecostal outpouring in Los Angeles did not occur in a vacuum, but was the culmination of earlier events. From the spring of 1905, Frank Bartlemen and Joseph Smale had been giving wide publicity to the 1904 Wales revival under Evans Roberts. From Armenia, a number of Pentecostals who spoke in tongues had arrived to begin a new life in America. All quickly lent support to the Bonnie Brae phenomena.

After the initial speaking in tongues on April 9, the meeting grew and spread. Significant in this growth was the occurrence on April 18, just nine days after the initial experience, of the great San Francisco earthquake. More than 125,000 tracts relating the earthquake to the Azusa Street happenings and the "endtime" were promptly distributed. News of the revival was also widely circulated in holiness and other religious periodicals. Attracted by the excitement, people came to Los Angeles from across the country. As they received the baptism, they went home to spread the word. Pentecostal centers appeared in Illinois, New York, North Carolina, and as far away as Sweden, England, India, and Chile.

1914—Hot Springs, Arkansas. From 1901 until 1914, the Pentecostals existed primarily within the holiness movement. The holiness movement was oriented toward an experience that ratified the believer's sanctity, the experience of the "second blessing," after which the believer would be holy forever. As the Pentecostal movement spread, many holiness churches accepted speaking in tongues as a final guarantee of holiness, a more sure sign than the "second blessing," and they called the Pentecostal "baptism of the Holy Spirit" the third experience. (The first, preceding the second blessing, was justification—the discovery of Christ as the personal savior.)

The holiness movement thus had supplied the basic problem (sanctification, life in the Spirit) which had caused concern for the "baptism of the Holy Spirit." The early Pentecostal leaders and members came from holiness churches, and holiness periodicals spread the word of the revival. Most important, the holiness churches, like the synagogues for Paul, became the first centers for Pentecostal evangelism. However, growth of the movement caused many holiness churches to express disapproval of it. Resistance varied from the mild policy of the Christian and Missionary Alliance to radical rejection by the Pentecostal Nazarene Church, which dropped the word "Pentecostal" from its title to manifest its opposition.

Growing hostility, factionalism within the movement, and the need for coordination of activities led in December 1913 to a call for a 1914 meeting of all who desired fuller cooperation at the Grand Opera House, Hot Springs, Arkansas. Out of this meeting grew the Assemblies of God. More important, from this organization came the impetus for the eventual organization of additional independent churches. Pentecostal denominationalism had begun.

With time, three Pentecostal churches took a special place in the American Pentecostal movement: the Assemblies of God, the Church of God (Cleveland, Tennessee), and the Church of Our Lord Jesus Christ of the Apostolic Faith. Many other Pentecostal churches are offshoots of these three or are modeled on them and deviate from them on only a few points.

For practical purposes, a parenthetical subtitle is given to some churches in this encyclopedia. Thus the Church of God (Cleveland, Tennessee) calls itself simply the Church of God, but its headquarters are in Cleveland, Tennessee, so that is added to its title to distinguish it from the many other churches also called the Church of God.

As various Pentecostal churches came into existence, they adopted different forms of church government. Some are congregational, some connectional. The congregational churches share four characteristics: the local churches operate autonomously; they choose their own ministers; they own their property themselves; and they allow their regional and national church bodies to have only advisory authority over the local churches. In connectional churches, the regional and national church bodies have varying levels of power to legislate on doctrinal and organizational matters. Some Pentecostal churches with a connectional polity are close to a presbyterial system; some are close to an episcopal system with bishops.

CONTEMPORARY DEVELOPMENTS.
Among the second and third generation Pentecostal denominations, a marked tendency to lessen the overtly emotional, loud and spontaneous lifestyle is quite noticeable, particularly in urban centers. Symbolic is the regular use of printed weekly church bulletins that contain an order of worship for the Sunday morning service.

Also characteristic of modern Pentecostal bodies is the development of ecumenical structures and the development of neo-Pentecostalism as a movement within mainline Christian churches.

Ecumenical efforts within Pentecostalism began with the World Conference of Pentecostals held at Zurich, Switzerland in May 1947. This conference served as inspiration for the formation of the Pentecostal Fellowship of North America, constituted at Des Moines, Iowa, October 26-28, 1948. This body has among its members all the larger trinitarian Pentecostal denominations (17 Canadian and United States bodies representing more than one million members in 1970).

Meetings of Pentecostals around the world have continued (Paris, 1949; London, 1952; Stockholm, 1955; Toronto, 1958;

Jerusalem, 1961; Helsinki, 1964; Rio de Janeiro, 1967; Dallas, 1970 and 1974). Along with these conferences have been attempts, increasingly successful, to engage the older ecumenical bodies in dialogue. Emerging as the central figure in the effort has been David J. DuPlessis, a South African Assemblies of God minister (1905-87). DuPlessis was a key organizer of the early world Pentecostal conferences, worked on the staff of the Second Assembly of the World Council of Churches in Evanston, Illinois, in 1954, and generally served as Pentecostalism's roving ambassador to non-Pentecostal Christians.

SUBFAMILIES.
Doctrinal differences and racial discrimination led Pentecostals to divide into six subfamilies. Additional small groups may be discerned, such as the snake handlers, but the far-reaching divisions has resulted in only six subfamilies. In general, Pentecostals fall into three doctrinal groups, all of which split along racial lines with blacks forming large denominations, thus creating a total of six groups.

The earliest doctrinal disagreement occurred between those Pentecostals who came out of the holiness movement, primarily former Methodists, and those who came directly into the Pentecostal experience, primarily former Baptists. The holiness people saw the Pentecostal experience (receiving the baptism of the Holy Spirit and speaking in tongues) as a third experience following justification and sanctification. The Baptists insisted that any believer was capable of receiving the Pentecostal experience, without the intermediate "second blessing" assuring sanctification, the key experience of the holiness movement. Many Pentecostals split over the issue of two experiences (justification and the baptism of the Holy Spirit) or three experiences (justification, sanctification, and the baptism of the Holy Spirit).

No sooner had these two positions become evident than another serious theological issue arose. A group of ministers began to preach a "Jesus only" doctrine which amounted to a monotheism of the second person of the Trinity. This denial of the Trinity by what are generally termed "Apostolic" Pentecostals has been the most serious family split, and the "Jesus only" people generally do not participate in the family ecumenical structures. Blacks have formed especially large denominations of the "Jesus only" type.

This discussion of Pentecostal subfamilies would be incomplete without a mention of neo-Pentecostalism. That is the movement of the 1960s and 1970s to form Pentecostal fellowships within the mainline Christian denominations. Neo-Pentecostalism also goes by the name of charismatic renewal. Its leaders were never a part of the older Pentecostal bodies, and have formed charismatic fellowships within the Roman Catholic, Lutheran, United Methodist, Presbyterian, and Episcopal churches.

In the 1970s these fellowships have served two functions. First, they have kept many Pentecostals within their mainline Christian churches, making unnecessary their move to the older Pentecostal churches. Second, the fellowships have been places where new denominations, separate from both the older Pentecostal churches and the mainline Christian churches, could form. Thus the same fellowships have served two disparate functions, although they were established as organizations for Pentecostals *within* the mainline denominations.

THE APOSTOLIC, ONENESS, OR "JESUS ONLY" MOVEMENT. In 1913 at the Los Angeles Pentecostal camp meeting, the fledgling Pentecostal movement, barely beginning its second decade of existence, came face to face with a new issue. R.E. McAlister, a popular preacher, speaking before a baptismal service, shared his thoughts that, in the apostolic church, baptism was not done with a Trinitarian formula but in the name of Jesus Christ. While raising much opposition, McAlister's message found favor with Frank J. Ewart and John C. Scheppe. Scheppe's emotional acceptance of the "new" idea had a powerful impact on the camp. Ewart afterwards joined McAlister in a revival meeting in Los Angeles and began to note results whenever he called upon the name of Jesus.

The movement spread under the leadership of Ewart and evangelist Glenn A. Cook. They were able to bring in such key leaders as Garfield Thomas Haywood of Indianapolis, E.N. Bell, and H.A. Goss, all prominent leaders in the Assemblies of God. Ewart became editor of *Meat in Due Season*, the first oneness periodical.

The advocacy of oneness ideas, mostly by members of the Assemblies of God, came to a head in 1916 at the Assemblies of God General Council meeting in St. Louis. A strong Trinitarian stance was placed within the Statement of Beliefs. One hundred and sixty-six ministers were expelled by that act and many Assemblies were lost; the era of formation of "oneness" churches began.

The oneness Pentecostals deny the Trinity and uphold the oneness of God. Jesus is identified with God the Father (Isaiah 9:6, John 10:30), God the creator (John 1:1), the bodily presence of God. The Holy Spirit is not considered a third person within the Trinity but the spirit and power of God and Christ. Salvation is by repentance, and water baptism is considered an essential part of salvation. Baptism is by immersion in the name of Jesus only (Acts 2:38) rather than the common trinitarian formula (Matthew 28:19).

Apart from the Trinitarian and baptismal questions, oneness people are typical Pentecostals. The oneness message has had particular appeal among black people, and the largest bodies are primarily black in membership. Of the several Apostolic Churches, the United Pentecostal Church is the largest white church.

BLACK PENTECOSTAL CHURCHES. There has been vigorous discussion in both popular and scholarly literature of the tie-in between black religion and Pentecostalism. Much of this discussion has been plainly derogatory and borders on racism. Pentecostalism, distinguished by its emotionalism and escapism, has been seen as an example of primitive religious forms. Fortunately, the growth of neo-Pentecostalism has led to a complete re-evaluation of the authenticity of the Pentecostal forms. With the new appreciation comes the opportunity to see, with new perspective, the key role which black people played in the early development of Pentecostalism, and more importantly, the manner in which

they have taken the form far beyond its development by their white brothers and sisters.

Modern Pentecostalism began in the short-lived integrated Topeka Bible School founded by Charles Parham. Among those students who received the baptism of the Holy Spirit was a black woman, Sister Lucy Farrow. It was Sister Farrow who took Pentecostalism to Houston and opened the door for Parham to begin his Bible school there. Among his pupils was one W.J. Seymour, a black minister with the Church of God (Anderson, Indiana).

After Seymour received Parham's message, he traveled to Los Angeles where in 1906 he gathered a group of black believers into meetings that were eventually held at the Azusa Street Mission. As the gifts of the Spirit became manifest, whites began to attend the meetings and receive the baptism from the blacks who led the services.

Racism was overcome for only a short time; almost immediately white leaders began to develop their own movements. Although most Pentecostal churches remained integrated for one or two decades, eventually almost all of the groups split along racial lines. There is little doubt that the early splintering among Pentecostals throughout the country was because the black leadership at Azusa was unacceptable to whites.

The preaching of "Jesus only" by Garfield Thomas Haywood, a black minister in Indianapolis, forced the Assemblies of God to deal with the "oneness" doctrine that denied the Trinity. Haywood's congregation became the nucleus of the first "oneness" denomination, the Pentecostal Assemblies of the world.

Pentecostalism swept the black community and created some large, if hidden, denominations. They compiled impressive figures for foreign mission work in Africa and the West Indies, where Pentecostalism has become the major faith in places. The Church of God in Christ now claims upwards of three million members worldwide.

DELIVERANCE (HEALING) MOVEMENT. Almost from the beginning, healing has been a major emphasis of the Pentecostal movement. It represents the culmination of a healing movement begun in evangelical churches by Charles Cullis, an Episcopal physician in Boston who held healing services at the turn of this century at his summer camp at Old Orchard, Maine. Albert Benjamin Simpson was healed at this camp and later made healing part of his four-fold gospel that presented Christ as savior, sanctifier, healer, and coming king. In the early years of this century F.F. Bosworth, Paul Rader, John D. Lake, and Smith Wigglesworth were popular healing evangelists and, of course, Aimee Semple McPherson was the most popular of all. The years between the wars saw the emergence of numerous independent healing evangelists, popular targets of exposé writers.

After the Second World War a group consciousness developed among some of the Pentecostal evangelists. In 1946 the Reverend William Marrion Branham, then a Baptist minister, claimed a visit by an angel and was told to start a healing ministry. That visit was the beginning of a remarkable "supernatural" ministry of healings, prophecies, and other paranormal phenomena. Branham began to tour the country in revival meetings. In 1947, Gordon Lindsay began *The Voice of Healing Magazine*. Gradually, without giving up their independence, other evangelists became associated with Branham and their activities included in *The Voice of Healing*. Branham died in 1965. In the years since his passing, deliverance ministers have emerged as a significant force within Pentecostalism.

In many cases, the deliverance evangelists have remained independent and travel at the request of churches or groups such as the Full Gospel Businessman's Fellowship. Others are leaders of large evangelistic missionary organizations. Evelyn Wyatt, T.L. Osborn, and Morris Cerullo head such organizations. Others have become heads of church-forming bodies (both in the United States and abroad) which constitute new primary religious groups. These include W.V. Grant, Neal Frisby, the late William Branham, Gordon Lindsay, Kathryn Kuhlman, and A.A. Allen. For most of the above, evangelistic endeavors among members of Pentecostal and mainline Christian churches is still the primary activity, with their deliverance churches forming relatively small bases of operation.

SNAKE HANDLING. One group of Pentecostals are sharply distinguished from the rest by their peculiar practice of "preaching the signs." In the Gospel of Mark 16: 17-18, Jesus promised his followers that certain signs would follow them: speaking in tongues, the ability to heal the sick, and the casting out of demons. Most Pentecostals accept these three. Those who "preach the signs," however, go beyond these to accept Jesus's promise that they may take up venomous serpents and drink poisons without experiencing any harm. This promise has led to the practice popularly called snake handling. The original group that practiced the signs, that is, that handled snakes and drank poison (usually strychnine) in worship services, arose very soon after the Pentecostal movement spread to the Appalachian Mountain region.

In 1909 George Went Hensley, a preacher with the Church of God (Cleveland, Tennessee) in rural Grasshopper Valley, became convinced that the references in Mark 16: 17-19 to taking up poisonous snakes and drinking poison were, in fact, commands. He captured a rattlesnake and brought it to an open air revival meeting for participants to handle as a test of their faith. In 1914 Ambrose J. Tomlinson, head of the Church of God, asked Hensley to demonstrate snake handling to the church's annual assembly, so, with his tacit approval, the practice spread throughout the mountainous and rural South.

Those who engage in snake handling are Pentecostals who accept the basic theology by which people seek and receive the baptism of the Holy Spirit, evidenced by speaking in tongues. Snake handlers also accept the rigid ethical code of most holiness and Pentecostal bodies: dress is plain; the Bible is consulted on all questions in an attempt to discern worldly behavior; the kiss of peace is prominent. The snake handlers, however, go beyond the Pentecostals in their belief that holding venomous reptiles and drinking poison are signs of an individual's faith and possession of the Holy Spirit. The handling of snakes and drinking of poison are done while in

an ecstatic state, referred to by members as "being in the Spirit."

The first and crucial test of the practice of snake handling was the near-fatal bite received by Garland Defries, which led to much unfavorable publicity and caused many snake handlers, who thought themselves immune to bites, to reevaluate the practice. Snake handling came under considerable attack within the Church of God, whose leaders denounced it as fanaticism. In 1928 the church formally forbade its continuation, thus forcing the snake handlers into separate congregations and small churches, primarily in rural areas.

A second test of snake handling came in 1945 when Lewis Ford, a member of the Dolly Pond Church of God with Signs Following (Dolly Pond, Tennessee), was fatally bitten. His death brought the first widespread public attention to snake handling and led to Tennessee legislation against it. Despite this legislation the practice continues in clandestine meetings in Tennessee and throughout the South.

Periodically, a person will be bitten and die at a snake handling meeting. Such rare occurrences usually become the subject of media attention with accompanying outcries against the practice. However, given their infrequency, these deaths have usually led to little more than a few ephemeral attempts to regulate the behavior of church members. The churches soon resume their normal routine. In 1975, some meaningful action was taken following the death of two church members from drinking poison. The Tennessee Supreme Court moved to strengthen that state's prohibitions on both snake handling and the ingestion of poison at religious services.

Since Lewis Ford's death in 1945, the following are among those who have been reported killed as a result of snake bites: Columbia Gay, Jolo, West Virginia (1961); George Went Hensley, Atha, Florida (1965); Beulah Ray Bucklen, Fraziers Bottom, West Virginia (1973); Lonnie Richardson, East Lynn, West Virginia (1974); Richard Williams, Columbus, Ohio (1974); Aaron Long, Baxter, Kentucky (1978); John Lee Holbrook, Mullinsville, West Virginia (1982); Mack Ray Wolford, Long Bottom, West Virginia (1983); Richard Barrett, Cartersville, Georgia (1984); Charles H. Prince, Canton, North Carolina (1985); Shirley McLeary, Baxter, Kentucky (1986); and Marion Rowe, Harlan, Kentucky (1986).

THE LATTER RAIN MOVEMENT. During the mid-twentieth century, one new movement has deeply affected the development of Pentecostalism. Beginning in a small Bible college in western Canada in 1948, the Latter Rain Movement found enough initial support among leaders in the two largest Pentecostal groups in the United States and Canada respectively, the Assemblies of God and the Pentecostal Assemblies of Canada, that each moved quickly to suppress its influence among their ministers and churches.

The movement began as a revival at Sharon Orphanage and Schools in North Battleford, Saskatchewan, among students assembled by former Pentecostal Assemblies ministers George Hawtin and P.G. Hunt and Four-Square Gospel minister Herrick Holt. The revival was accompanied by a visible manifestation of the gifts of the Spirit, especially healing. As word of the events were spread, visitors came to North Battleford and invitations were issued for the leaders to come to different parts of the continent.

As it developed, the movement was characterized by an emphasis upon the gifts of healing and prophecy, the practice of the laying-on-of-hands to impart gifts to different people, and allegiance to the five-fold ministry of Ephesians 4:11. As the movement spread, it was accused of fanaticism and the leadership of the Assemblies of God moved against it. In 1949 the general council passed a six-part resolution, denouncing the movement because, among other practices, (1) it relied too heavily upon present-day apostles and prophets (i.e., a self-appointed charismatic leadership); (2) it practiced the confessing and pronouncing of forgiveness by one member upon another; (3) it advocated the practice of bestowing spiritual gifts by the laying-on-of-hands; and (4) it distorted Scripture so as to arrive at conclusions not generally accepted by members of the Assemblies.

Though neither experienced any major wholesale defections, both the Pentecostal Assemblies of Canada and the Assemblies of God began to lose pastors and their churches. Possibly the most prominent defection was Stanley Frodsham, longtime editor of the *Pentecostal Evangel*, who withdrew from the Assemblies of God after its 1949 resolution. Within a short time the movement was firmly entrenched in Vancouver, British Columbia; Portland, Oregon; Detroit, Michigan; Memphis, Tennessee; Los Angeles, California; and Philadelphia, Pennsylvania. During the 1950s, especially as the healing revival led by William Marrion Branham and Oral Roberts grew, the Latter Rain spread.

Many of the early centers grew into large congregations, and a few emerged as seeds for new denominations (or more precisely, congregational associations). Some of these were distinguished by the peculiar teachings and emphases of the founder/leader. Such groups as the Church of the Living Word, the Body of Christ Movement, and the International Evangelical Church and Missionary Association are prominent examples.

SOURCES—PENTECOSTAL FAMILY

GENERAL SOURCES

Hunter, Harold D. *Spirit Baptism, A Pentecostal Alternative.* Washington, DC: University Press of America, 1983. 310 pp.

Kelsey, Morton T. *Tongue Speaking.* Garden City, NY: Doubleday, 1968. 252 pp.

Kydd, Ronald A. N. *Charismatic Gifts in the Early Church.* Peabody, MA: Hendrickson Publishers, 1984. 100 pp.

Roebling, Karl. *Pentecostals Around the World.* Hicksville, NY: Exposition Press, 1978. 120 pp.

Sherrill, John L. *They Speak with Other Tongues.* Westwood, NJ: Fleming H. Revell Company, 1965. 143 pp.

Synan, Vinson. ed. *Aspects of Pentecostal-Charismatic Origins.* Plainfield, NJ: Logos International, 1975. 252 pp.

——. *The Holiness-Pentecostal Movement in the United States.* Grand Rapids: William B. Eerdmans Publishing Company, 1971. 248 pp.

BIBLIOGRAPHICAL SOURCES

Faupel, David W. *The American Pentecostal Movement, A Bibliographical Essay.* Wilmore, KY: B. L. Fisher Library, Asbury Theological Seminary, 1972. 56 pp.

Jones, Charles Edwin. *A Guide to the Study of the Pentecostal Movement.* 2 vols. Metuchen, NJ: Scarecrow Press, 1983.

Martin, Ira J. *Glossolalia, The Gift of Tongues, A Bibliography.* Cleveland, TN: Pathway Press, 1970. 72 pp.

HISTORICAL

Bartleman, Frank. *How Pentecost Came to Los Angeles.* Los Angeles: Privately Printed, 1928.

Davis, George T. B. *When the Fire Fell.* Philadelphia: The Million Testaments Campaign, 1945. 104 pp.

Dayton, Donald. *"From Christian Perfection to the Baptism of the Holy Ghost": A Study in the Origin of Pentecostalism.* Chicago: The Author, 1973. 16 pp.

Ewart, Frank J. *The Phenomenon of Pentecost.* Hazelwood, MO: World Aflame Press, 1975. 207 pp.

Frodsham, Stanley H. *With Signs Following.* Springfield, MO: Gospel Publishing House, 1946. 279 pp.

Gaver, Jessyca Russel. *Pentecostalism.* New York: Award Books, 1971. 286 pp.

Hollenweger, Walter J. *The Pentecostals: The Charismatic Movement in the Church.* Minneapolis: Augsburg, 1972. 522 pp.

Kendrick, Klaude. *The Promise Fulfilled.* Springfield, MO: Gospel Publishing House, 1961. 237 pp.

McClug, L. Grant, Jr. *Azusa Street and Beyond.* South Plainfield NJ; Bridge Publishing, 1986. 245 pp.

Nichols, Thomas R. *Azusa Street Outpouring.* Hanford, CT: Great Commission International, 1979. 35 pp.

Riss, Richard Michael. *The Latter Rain Movement of 1948 and the Mid-twentieth Century Evangelical Awakening.* Vancouver, BC: Regent College, 1979. 261 pp.

Strachey, Ray. *Group Movements of the Past.* London: Faber & Faber Ltd., 1934. 276 pp.

Valdez, A. C., and James F. Scheer. *Fire on Azusa Street.* Costa Mesa, CA: Gift Publications, 1980. 139 pp.

Wallace, Mary H. *Profiles of Pentecostal Preachers.* Hazelwood, MO: World Aflame Press, 1983. 281 pp.

Wagner, Wayne, ed. *Touched by the Fire.* Plainfield, NJ: Logos International, 1978. 163 pp.

Whittaker, Colin C. *Pentecostal Pioneers.* Springfield, MO: Gospel Publishing House, 1983.

GLOSSOLALIA AND THE SPIRITUAL GIFTS

Goodman, Felicitas D. *Speaking in Tongues, A Cross-Cultural Study of Glossolalia.* Chicago: University of Chicago Press, 1972. 175 pp.

Kildahl, John P. *The Psychology of Speaking in Tongues.* New York: Harper & Row, 1972. 110 pp.

Samarin, William. *Tongues of Men and Angels.* New York: Macmillan Company, 1972. 277 pp.

Sneck, William Joseph. *Charismatic Spiritual Gifts.* Washington, DC: University Press of America, 1981. 298 pp.

APOSTOLIC OR ONENESS PENTECOSTALS

Clanton, Arthur J. *United We Stand.* Hazelwood, MO: The Pentecostal Publishing House, 1970. 207 pp.

Foster, Fred J. *Their Story: Twentieth Century Pentecostals*. Hazelwood, NJ: World Aflame Press, 1981. 193 pp.

Richardson, James C., Jr. *With Water and Spirit*. Martinsville, VA: The Author, n.d. 151 pp.

BLACK PENTECOSTALS

Nelson, Douglas J. *For Such a Time as This, The Story of Bishop William J. Seymour and the Azusa Street Revival*. Birmingham, England: University of Birmingham, Ph.D. Dissertation, 1981. 346 pp.

Hollenweger, Walter J. *Black Pentecostal Concept*. Special issue of *Concept 30* (1970).

Tinney, James S. "William J. Seymour: Father of Modern Day Pentecostalism." In *Black Apostles*. Ed. Randall K. Burkett and Richard Newman. Boston: 1978. pp. 213-25.

DELIVERANCE MOVEMENT

Harrell, David Edwin, Jr. *All Things Are Possible*. Bloomington: Indiana University Press, 1975. 304 pp.

Melton, J. Gordon. *A Reader's Guide to the Church's Ministry of Healing*. Independence, MO: The Academy of Religion and Psychical Research, 1977. 102 pp.

SIGNS MOVEMENT

Carden, Karen W., and Robert W. Pelton. *The Persecuted Prophets*. New York: A. S. Barns & Co., 1976. 188 pp.

Holliday, Robert K. *Tests of Faith*. Oak Hill, WV: The Fayette Tribune, 1968. 120 pp.

La Barre, Weston. *They Shall Take Up Serpents*. New York: Schocken, 1969. 208 pp.

NEOCHARISMATIC MOVEMENT

Bradfield, Cecil David. *Neo-Pentecostalism, A Sociological Assessment*. Washington, DC: University Press of America, 1979. 75 pp.

A Charismatic Reader. New York: Evangelical Book Club, 1974. 741 pp.

Culpepper, Robert H. *Evaluating the Charismatic Movement*. Valley Forge, PA: Judson Press, 1977. 192 pp.

O'Connor, Edward D. *The Pentecostal Movement in the Catholic Church*. Notre Dame, IN: Ave Maria Press, 1971. 301 pp.

Quebedeaux, Richard. *The New Charismatics*. Garden City, NY: Doubleday, 1976. 252 pp.

Shakarian, Demos. *The Happiest People in the World*. Old Tappen, NJ: Chosen Books, 1975. 187 pp.

Synan, Vinson. *In the Latter Days*. Ann Arbor, MI: Servant Books, 1984, 168 pp.

NON-PENTECOSTAL EVALUATIONS OF PENTECOSTALISM

Bauman, Louis S. *The Tongues Movement*. Winona Lake, IN: Brethren Missionary Herald Co., 1963. 47 pp.

Charismatic Countdown. Washington, DC: Review and Herald Publishing Association, 1974. 80 pp.

Dollar, George W. *The New Testament and New Pentecostalsim*. Minneapolis: Central Baptist Theological Seminary, 1978. 141 pp.

Gustafson, Robert R. *Authors of Confusion*. Tampa, FL: Grace Publishing Company, 1971. 105 pp.

Kinghorn, Kenneth Cain. *Gifts of the Spirit*. Nashville, TN: Abingdon, 1976. 126 pp.

Noorbergen, Rene. *Charisma of the Spirit*. Mountian View, CA: Pacific Press Publishing Association, 1973. 191 pp.

Robinson, Wayne A. *I Once Spoke in Tongues*. Old Tappen, NJ: Spire Books, 1975. 128 pp.

Stolee, H. J. *Pentecostalism*. Minneapolis: Augsburg Publishing House, 1936. 142 pp.

THE LATTER RAIN MOVEMENT

HOEKSTRA, RAYMOND G. *THE LATTER RAIN*. PORTLAND, OR: WINGS OF HEALING, 1950.

RISS, RICHARD MICHAEL. *THE LATTER RAIN MOVEMENT OF 1948 AND THE MID-TWENTIETH CENTURY EVANGELICAL AWAKENING*. VANCOUVER, BC: REGENT COLLEGE M.A. THESIS, 1979.

Chapter 8

European Free-Church Family

Directory listings for groups belonging to the European Free-Church Family
may be found in the section beginning on page 303.

Until recently, histories of the Reformation have treated Luther and Calvin as superstars and have described the radical reformers as threats to the Reformation. The radicals, who protested Luther's and Calvin's continued tie to the state, have been considered by such historians to be utopian dreamers, revolutionaries, mystics, anarchists, and heretics. According to past historians, the radicals were rightfully the object of scorn for Catholic, Lutheran, and Calvinist alike.

Modern scholarship, however, has rediscovered the radicals, and history is being rewritten to give them their rightful place as makers of the Reformation. (The Reformation occurred in sixteenth-century Europe. It was the movement of protest and reform that began in the Roman Catholic Church and eventually was carried on largely outside of that church.)

One scholar goes so far as to say of the modern publication of radical Reformation documents, "They have the same significance for the interpretation of the whole of modern church history as the discoveries in the Dead Sea caves and in upper Egypt are having for New Testament studies and early church history" (George H. Williams, *The Radical Reformation* [Philadelphia: The Westminster Press, 1962], xix).

Who were the radical reformers? They were men who, like Luther and Calvin, were interested in the reform of the church but who, because of a variety of backgrounds, outlooks, and theologies, placed their emphases on much different points as the crux of needed reform. For most, faith, sacrament, and liturgy were not as significant as the doctrine of the church in its relation to the state. The radicals frowned upon involvement in secular activity, and were typically persecuted by the state. Most radicals came from the lower class, so they built upon the traditional adversary relationship between the lower class and the ruling class. The radicals took the ideas of the Reformation (ideas such as the priesthood of believers and the freedom of the Christian man) to such an extreme that Luther and Calvin were horrified.

Most of the radicals came to a bloody end in war or persecution, and many saw their movements entirely destroyed. Because of this destruction, men such as Thomas Müntzer, Hans Denck, and Michael Sattler did not leave a surviving remnant to carry on their work. Others, such as Caspar Schwenckfeld, Jacob Hutter, and Melchior Hofmann, were able to leave movements which survived and exist today. Among the churches that trace their roots to the radical reformers are the Mennonites, the Amish, the Brethren, the Quakers, and the Free Church Brethren. All of these churches belong to the free church family, meaning that they are not state churches but free associations of adult believers. The free churches emphasize free will, contrasting sharply with strict Calvinists who believe in predestination—that the number and identity of the elect was ordained before the beginning of the world.

The radical Reformation can be dated from Christmas Day 1521, more than four years after Luther's Ninety-five Theses were nailed to the church door in Wittenburg. On this day, Andreas Bodenstein of Carlstadt—a man called simply Carlstadt by historians—celebrated the first "Protestant" communion. (Protestant services today follow the trend set by that service.) He preached and without vestments read the "Mass," but omitted all references to sacrifice, did not elevate the host, and gave both bread and wine. Each act was a significant repudiation of the beliefs or practices of the Roman Catholic Church. Behind this communion service was the strong contention of the supremacy of spirit over letter, the supremacy of grace over works, and the common priesthood of all believers. From these events were to flow others initiated by men who were already thinking as Carlstadt.

The career of Thomas Müntzer (1490?-1525) was one of the results of the activity of Carlstadt. In 1520, Müntzer appeared at Zwickau, a town in Saxony, where, as minister to one of the churches, his radicalism began to emerge. He urged people to respond spontaneously and immediately to the leadings of the Holy Spirit. He defined the church as the Spirit-filled saints gathered together in a community. His definition avoided any mention of bishops or sacraments and thus was at odds with a traditional understanding of the church. He aroused the laity in support of him against his more conservative colleagues. After being removed from his pastorate, Müntzer spent several years as a wandering preacher, becoming more and more radical and embittered. In a famous sermon in 1524 before the German princes, he

49

called upon them to take up the sword to defeat the forces of anti-Christ (the pope) and bring in the kingdom.

A number of events, including an astrological conjunction, converged in 1524 and occasioned an uprising of the peasants of Germany. Not the least of these events was the preaching of Müntzer and his radical colleagues. As the Peasants' War began, Müntzer, having given up on the immovable princes, joined the peasants' forces at Mühlhausen. He was ready to wield his sword for the kingdom. He saw the Peasants' War as his instrument. When the revolt was put down, Müntzer was captured. His career ended on the executioner's block and his flock was scattered.

Contemporaneous with Müntzer's short career in the north, other radical reformists appeared in southern Germany and Austria. Their first spokesman was Hans Denck. While at Nuremberg as rector of a parish school, Denck had come under the influence of Carlstadt and Müntzer. Denck was expelled from Nuremberg by Lutherans who feared him as a competitor. In the fall of 1525, Denck became the spiritual leader of a group at Augsburg. In the spring of 1526 (under the influence of Swiss refugee Balthasar Hubmaier), he led in the reconstitution of his group as a truly reformed church by the adoption of the apostolic practice of believer's baptism. By that practice only adult believers in Christ were baptized, the procedure believed to have been used by the Apostles. Thus anabaptism, or rebaptism of those who were baptized as infants, emerged as a central factor in the radical reformation. Denck saw the church as an adult, self-disciplined fellowship. His criteria for understanding the church naturally excluded infants, thus *antipedobaptism* (literally against the baptism of infants) became a central teaching of the movement. From this belief and this practice was to come the fully developed Anabaptist understanding of the church as an association of adults (not children) acting freely.

Denck was forced out of several cities as his reputation caught up with him. In 1527, he arrived in Augsburg to participate in a synod of Anabaptist leaders. After the meeting, many were arrested and died martyrs' deaths, so the meeting is called the Martyrs' Synod.

The main item of concern for the synod was the eschatalogical program of John Hut, an Austrian Anabaptist leader who had been rebaptized by Denck. Hut repudiated the peasants for taking up arms and interpreted current events as symbols of the nearness of the end of time. God would do his work. The saints, while suffering at present, would live to see the new kingdom appear. Hut proceeded to build an underground movement throughout Bavaria and Austria.

When the synod met, three issues concerning the coming kingdom were under discussion: the manner and time of its approach, the role of Anabaptists to prepare for it, and the role of the magistry in the present time. No clear-cut decisions were reached on these points. After the synod, Hut was arrested and died in a fire in his cell. The inability of the synod to bring the radicals into one mind, the attacks of the Lutherans on some radical excesses in doctrine, and

disillusionment with his role in God's reformation led Denck to recant. He died of the plague a few years later.

Contemporaneous with the rise of South German and Austrian Anabaptists was the rise of Swiss Anabaptists, popularly known as the Swiss Brethren, under the leadership of Michael Sattler. Within the Swiss Brethren a mature, articulate Anabaptist stance would be formed, and from them would come the most important statement of the Anabaptist position.

Swiss Anabaptism arose in the 1520's to protest a state church. The church in question was that of Ulrich Zwingli (1484-1530), the leader of the Reformation in Switzerland. Zwingli took religious control of the canton of Zurich, with the power structures of Zurich establishing the Zwinglian Church for all in the area. The Swiss Brethren insisted that only the righteous should belong to the church; not every person who happened to reside in the territory controlled by the state. After the vote to establish the Zwinglian Church, the Swiss Brethren withdrew from Zurich.

They determined to continue their efforts to restore the true Church. Two leaders of the Swiss Anabaptists, Conrad Grebel and George Blaurock, became the center of controversy. On January 21, 1525, layman Grebel rebaptized Blaurock, a priest, and that action led to months of disputation. The Brethren grew, even though they were persecuted. Doctrinally, they had a double problem. First, they had to counter Zwingli's ideas, which were very popular. Second, they had to clarify for people their differences with Müntzer and Hut. Müntzer and Hut had poor reputations, and people mistakenly associated the Swiss Brethren with them. It was in the attempt to refute Müntzer and Hut that Michael Sattler came forward as a leader of refugees in Strassburg. Upon his return to Switzerland, Sattler found himself leader of the Schleitheim Synod. There the mature Anabaptist position was hammered out in a document originally called "The Brotherly Union of a Number of Children of God Concerning Seven Articles," now called the Schleitheim Confession.

Schleitheim Confession The Schleitheim Confession set the distinctives of the Anabaptist position. Rejecting the state church in which citizenship and church membership were almost the same, the Anabaptists were looking for a church of true believers. Hence they acknowledge baptism for converted adult believers only and limited the taking of communion to those who had been rightfully baptized. Having given up the disciplinary machinery of the state, they were left with the ban, a form of excommunication of fallen and as yet unrepentant members, as their only tool of discipline. They admonished Anabaptists to withdraw from the world and its wickedness. In that light, church members were to make no use of the sword, for either secular or sacred purpose. That position extended to an avoidance of serving as a magistrate. Finally, the Anabaptists refused to swear oaths. All of these positions were based upon their study of the Bible. (A complete copy of the Schleitheim Confession is to be found in the accompanying volume, *The Encyclopedia of American Religions: Religious Creeds*, pp. 417-420).

From the Schleitheim Confession emerges the distinctive doctrinal and ethical position of the Anabaptist churches. This stance would be accepted, with minor modifications, by the various bodies which survived the era of persecution. The church is composed of those united to Christ by believer's baptism and who have separated themselves from the evil world. The church is a minority group, pilgrims in a hostile world trying to isolate themselves from its influence and forces. Specifically, certain items—war, the use of violent force against one's neighbor, civic affairs, courts, oaths, worldly amusements, and serving as a magistrate—are to be studiously avoided as things of the world.

Pacifism, in particular, has arisen as the essential point in the avoidance ethic and these churches have been characterized as the historical peace churches. Christians obey the laws of the land, as is possible for pacifists (and any attempting to live withdrawn), but their essential authority is to be found in the church.

The church is the disciplined fellowship. It appoints its own leadership and accepts its authority as the leadership administers it. Its prime force is the ban, a practice based on Matthew 18:15-17, which is similar to excommunication. Menno Simons is credited with emphasizing a modified form of banning termed shunning, in which the church stops all dealing with an erring brother, including eating with him, with the intent of winning him back to the straight and narrow. This practice is based on I Corinthians 5:11.

The church was opposed to both popish and anti-popish works and church services. From this position comes a lay-oriented, non-liturgical, non-creedal, Bible-oriented church. Their opposition to the state church, a position that was articulated as well as manifested by their very existence, led to the appellation, "free church." Non-liturgical worship in its extreme form can be seen in the classic Quaker service.

The Bible is the prime document from which the Anabaptists derive their belief and practice. Their method of Biblical interpretation, which will not utilize tradition and philosophy, becomes literalistic. Sacraments become ordinances, symbolic acts: baptism is an initiatory ceremony and the Lord's Supper a memorial act. Foot washing, for which there is a more unequivocal command than either baptism or the Lord's Supper, is also practiced, especially in those churches of Swiss origin.

Though all the European free churches believe in adult baptism, they have a wide variety of modes. The Mennonites pour water on the person being baptized, while the Church of the Brethren has triune immersion, the practice of entering the water once for each person of the Trinity.

LATER HISTORY After the Schleitheim Confession, three events were to remold the Anabaptists—the fall of the town of Münster; the death of the martyrs; and the rise of Menno Simons.

The Radical Reformation had continually been punctuated by apocalyptic thinking, including a few instances of militancy. These tendencies came to a climax in the town of Münster. Radicalization there began with the pastor, Bernard Rothmann. His popular sermons led to the Protestantization of the community in 1531. Rothmann's Lutheran views became more and more radical, and he began to defend believer's baptism. Other Anabaptists heard of Rothmann and began to flock to Münster as the new Jerusalem. Among the immigrants were Jan Mathijs and his major supporter, Jan of Leiden. The immigrants adopted the apocalyptic theory that the end of time was imminent and would be caused by God's direct intervention in human affairs.

By the beginning of 1534, the radicalization of the city was complete and Mathijs was quickly rising to power. All Catholics and Lutherans were expelled, and the city armed itself for the siege that would follow that expulsion. Mathijs imposed his religious beliefs. The town adopted a communist lifestyle while it made military preparations for the siege. In the midst of these reforms Mathijs was killed. Jan of Leiden took over and began to set up a theocracy with himself as God's vicar. The strict discipline worked effectively during the siege. After a particularly heavy battle, Jan introduced polygamy.

The beleaguered city finally was betrayed and captured. Jan had imposed ruthless authority on the people. After his capture, he was tortured to death. With only a few minor exceptions, the Münster episode ended any apocalypticism in the Anabaptism movement.

That episode, however, did not bring to a close the killings of Anabaptists. *The Martyrs Mirror*, a book which functions for Anabaptists much as John Foxe's *Book of Martyrs* functions for English Protestants, records the trail of blood of Anabaptists killed for their faith. The book was first published in 1554. Persecution left a stamp upon the members of the free churches, who came to see themselves literally as wandering pilgrims in a hostile world.

Anabaptists flocked to Menno Simons in the Netherlands. Emerging in 1537 as a leader, Menno began a series of books which set down a moderate free church position and rallied the disintegrating Anabaptist forces. It is to Menno's credit that the forces were held together and survived until 1577 when toleration was granted in Holland. The followers of Menno became, with few exceptions, the surviving Anabaptist community.

In addition to the apocalyptic Anabaptism of Münster and the moderate Anabaptism of the Swiss Brethren was a third form of Anabaptism. It turned inward in what has been termed a spiritualist or mystical movement. Among the first to espouse the spiritualist perspective was Hans Denck. An early leader in the Anabaptist movement, Denck recanted in his despair at its divisions and began to turn inward. He had long been a student of the mystic John Tauler, and to Tauler he turned. He began to preach of the God who meets us as a Light, a Word, and a Presence. He was followed by others such as Sebastian Franck, Johann Bünderlin, and Christian Entfelder.

As a whole, the spiritual Anabaptists collected no following and left no following. One exception was Caspar Schwenckfeld, a Silesian courtier turned prophet. In successive steps, he became a disciple of Luther, a critic of the Reformation as outward and shallow, an Anabaptist theologian with some peculiar views on the sacraments and

Christ, and a mystic leader with a large following that still exists. But Schwenckfeld was the exception.

What the spiritual reformers did primarily was to create a literature with Anabaptist devotional and mystic leanings that became (1) the basis of a mystical movement within the free churches much like the one in medieval Catholicism and (2) the inspiration for later mystical, devotional movements, primarily Quakerism and to a certain extent Pietism. Each of these strains was to find a home in colonial Pennsylvania.

SWISS AND DUTCH MENNONITES. The central surviving Anabaptist tradition owes its name to one of its major leaders, Menno Simons (1496?-1561). Simons, a Dutchman, was born in Witmarsum in the Netherlands. While a Roman Catholic priest, Simons was led to believe that the bread and wine were *not* the real body and blood of Christ. A 1531 execution of an Anabaptist led him to investigate infant baptism. Continued investigation of Anabaptist views convinced him they were right. Finally, in 1536, a year after his own brother's death as an Anabaptist, Menno Simons left his Catholic heritage. Because of his abilities, he immediately became a leader in the Anabaptist community. His main tasks became keeping the community protected from authorities and free from militarism (which had led Anabaptists to take complete control of Münster and wage a long battle to defend it) and from heresies such as apocalyptic beliefs that the world would soon end through God's direct intervention. Some of Menno's followers found toleration in East Friesland in the Netherlands, under the Countess Anne. It was she, in recognizing the peaceful followers of Menno in contradistinction to the militarists and apocalyptics, who first dubbed them "Menists." The main part of Simon's active life was spent writing in defense of his new-found faith and hiding from the authorities, who had put a price on his head.

Menno's views were similar to those outlined by the Swiss Brethren at Schleitheim. It can be argued, and has been, that the Mennonites are the legitimate inheritors of the Swiss-German Anabaptist tradition, as most of the other Anabaptists have disappeared from the contemporary world. In essentials, the Mennonites certainly share the Swiss and German Anabaptists' views on rebaptism, pacifism, religious toleration, separation of church and state, opposition to capital punishment, opposition to holding office, and opposition to taking oaths. On two points only did Menno Simons differ—his use of the ban and his doctrine of incarnation.

Menno joined in the argument with the Brethren on the strict versus the liberal use of the ban. Menno advocated the strict use as the only means to keep the church free of corrupt sects. He also advocated "avoidance" or shunning all who were banned. Shunning was centered upon the idea of not eating with the person under the ban; this practice created a significant ingroup problem when one member of a family was under the ban. The practice of avoidance was liberalized over the years by the main body of Mennonites, but originally it was their distinguishing feature.

Menno has also been accused of compromising the humanity of Christ by minimizing the human properties said to have been received from Mary. This slight difference in Christology, which led many to accuse him of antitrinitarianism, has not been a major factor in recent Mennonite history.

The unique doctrinal position of the Mennonites was systematized in 1632 in the Dordrecht Confession, named for the town in the Netherlands at which it was written. It is consistent with the Schleitheim Confession, but deals more systematically with basic Christian affirmations. It affirms God as Father, Son, and Holy Ghost (the Trinity); the restoration of all humanity though Christ, who was foreordained to his saving work before the foundation of the world; and the incarnation of Christ as the Son of God. Those who are obedient through faith, and follow the precepts of the New Testament are considered Christ's children. Baptism is for repentant adult believers. The visible church consists of those who have been baptized and incorporated into the communion of saints on earth. Within that church, the Lord's Supper is observed as an ordinance, as is the washing of the feet.

The state is seen as the gift of God and Mennonites are admonished to pray for it and support it in all manners not directly opposed to the commandments of God. Two ways in which God's will and the state are seen to conflict are in the state's demand for oaths and in its drafting of young men for military service. The Mennonites generally refuse to swear oaths (for example, in a court of law) or to bear arms.

In one respect the Dordrecht Confession goes beyond the Schleitheim Confession. Not only does it advocate the use of the ban (excommunication) but also of shunning (avoidance of eating, drinking or socializing with a fallen and unrepentant church member). This practice, still used in some of the more conservative Mennonite bodies has been a source of considerable controversy especially when it has become an issue between a church member and a spouse who is being shunned. On such cases the church is not allowed to eat dinner with the spouse.

The Mennonite movement spread slowly, and the late 1500s was a period in which many names were added to the roll of martyrs. The movement spread into Germany and Switzerland, building on small groups of Anabaptists already there. Mennonites settled and migrated as rulers first allowed toleration and then rescinded the privilege. In 1763, Catherine the Great of Russia offered religious toleration to German settlers who would populate the southern Steppes. Moravians, Mennonites, and Hutterites flocked to Russia; the Mennonites, mostly Prussians, settled in Crimea and Taurie. The Mennonites developed in southern Russia a unique history because of the special status granted them by the Russian government. A self-governing Mennonite community arose, the government approaching that of a theocracy. The end of Russian paradise came in the 1870s when the Czar introduced universal military service as a policy among the German colonists. This policy was part of a general Russification program in face of the growing military power of Prussia. The Mennonites, pacifists, refused to join the military. So in 1874, a six-year mass immigration to the United States and Canada began. Those that remained in Russia prospered until 1917 when they became victims of the

Bolsheviks. They still survive, however, in small scattered communities.

Reference to Mennonites in America occurs as early as 1643 in the records of New Netherlands. In 1633, a communal experiment led by Cornelius Pieter Plockhoy appeared on Delaware Bay, then a part of New Netherlands. The first permanent Mennonite colony was established in 1683 at Germantown, Pennsylvania; this date is usually accepted by Mennonites as their date of origin in America. Several factors encouraged Mennonites to come to the U.S. First, religious persecution in Europe caused many to immigrate. Second, William Penn and George Fox were seeking German converts, and appealed to members of Mennonite communities to come to America. Finally, the German Quakers (former Anabaptists) already in America wrote their friends and relatives asking them to move to Pennsylvania.

This growing Mennonite element is credited with American history's first public protest against slavery and was very influential in the later Quaker antislavery position. The Mennonites were an agricultural people and began to spread north and west of Germantown. The group's size was bolstered by immigration from the Palatine in the early eighteenth century.

The Revolutionary War became the first major crisis in the American Mennonite community, leading to their first schism. The issue was support of the Continental Congress. The majority argued that they could not support the Congress because such support would involve them in the war.

One leader, Christian Funk, argued in favor of support, including the special war tax, drawing support from Jesus' words on taxation (Matt. 22:21). Funk was excommunicated and with his followers formed the Mennonite Church (Funkite), which existed until the mid-nineteenth century. It died as all the participants in the original dispute died.

Continued immigration and the natural expansion of the Mennonites, who are prone to have large families, forced them west looking for new land. The early nineteenth century found Mennonites making settlements in Ontario and the Old Northwest Territory, and after the Civil War, the prairie states. This growing migration and wide separation geographically set the stage for formation of schismatic churches that would reach major proportions in the 1880s.

While no distinct and sharp lines can be drawn, there are rough ethnological distinctions within the Mennonite community. Some of the American splintering of churches can be traced to the Swiss, Dutch, or German background of the colonies. The largest distinction among the Mennonites as a whole is between the Western European and Russian settlers. Most of the Western European Mennonites came in the initial wave of settlers into Pennsylvania in the eighteenth century and pushed west into Canada and Indiana. The Russian immigrants are those Mennonites who migrated in the nineteenth century and settled in the western United States, primarily Kansas, and Canada.

Mennonites have been proud of a heritage of biblical theology and avoidance of hairsplitting, unproductive attempts at philosophical sophistries. Nevertheless, they have a definite theological heritage in Swiss and Dutch Anabaptist ideas. Except for the distinctive themes illustrated in the Schleitheim Confession, Mennonites would have little problem with the major affirmations of mainline Christian churches. These have never been a point of conflict.

Crucial for Mennonites are ecclesiology and separation from the world. Mennonites share a doctrine of the church based on the concept of ecclesia, the called-out fellowship of believers in mission. The tendency is to emphasize the local congregation and to build wider fellowships based on a commonality of belief. Ministers (bishops) arise out of the fellowship as do deacons; the exact methods for choosing them varies. Casting lots was a favorite method. The Dordrecht Confession of 1632 was adopted by the American church and is still a doctrinal standard for most Mennonites. According to the Dordrecht confession, the Bible is the source of belief, and emphasis is placed upon the believer's direct encounter with the living Christ and the work of the Spirit within. The pietism, emphasis on the practical life in the Spirit, is worked out in the mutual, shared existence of the church. The church, not the state, is the basic society for the true Christian, according to the Dordrecht Confession.

THE AMISH. Among the more liberal Swiss Mennonites of the late seventeenth century, there arose a party led by one Jacob Amman, a minister in the Emmenthal congregation. Because his family records have not been found, little can be said of him except for the practices he promoted among both the Swiss Mennonites and the Swiss Brethren. Amman insisted upon a strict interpretation of discipline. For his practices he appealed to Menno Simons' writings and to the Dordrecht Confession of Faith of 1632, which has become the recognized statement of doctrine for both Amish and Old Mennonites in America.

In his preaching, Amman stressed the practice of avoidance. A member whose spouse was under the ban was neither to eat nor sleep with him or her until the ban was lifted. Amman also reintroduced foot washing. Non-religious customs of the period—hooks and eyes instead of buttons, shoestrings instead of buttons, bonnets and aprons, broad brimmed hats, and beards and long hair—became identifying characteristics of church members.

All of the Mennonites during Amman's time were in a loose federation and strove to remain of one mind. Amman's strict interpretation of the "avoidance" clause in the ban led to a division among the Mennonites, with some following Amman and separating themselves from the others. Amman placed under the ban all who disagreed with him. After a few years of separation, Amman and his associates tried to reconcile with the other Mennonites, but the reconciliation efforts failed. Since then, the Amish have been independent of the Mennonites.

In the early 1700s, the Amish began to appear in America, the earliest congregation on record being the one along North Kill Creek in Berks County, Pennsylvania. Colonies were later planted in eastern Pennsylvania, Ohio, Indiana, Illinois, and Iowa. Until recently, their strength had been in Lancaster County, Pennsylvania.

The Amish represent a reactionary faction in the Mennonite movement. They have gone far beyond a practice common to Western Christianity of seeking to actualize an apostolic church. The Amish have attempted to freeze a culture, that of the late seventeenth century. As time has passed and the surrounding culture has discarded more and more elements of Jacob Amman's time, greater and greater pressure has been placed on the Amish to conform with the modern world. Each generation has brought new issues to Amish leaders. Decisions must constantly be made on accommodating to the prevailing culture on different points. Public school laws, consolidated farming (and the shortage of available farm lands), automobile-oriented road systems, and tourists are just a few of the issues that have joined perennial Amish problems such as in-breeding. A lack of consensus on these issues has produced the several schisms they have experienced.

In order to deal with the various "liberal" trends and local schisms, a general conference was held in Wayne County, Ohio, in 1862, followed by others annually for several years. The conferences only accentuated the various trends. Before the conferences were discontinued, the more conservative "Old Order" Amish withdrew and organized separately. Others formed more liberal bodies which have moved toward the Mennonites in practice.

THE RUSSIAN MENNONITES. Some Anabaptist brethren, instead of coming to America, chose instead to go to Russia at the invitation of Catherine the Great in the 1760s. Catherine wanted colonists to develop newly acquired territory and promised religious freedom and local autonomy. Colonies were settled mainly in southern Russia and the Crimean area. Yet there arose in Russia a "pharaoh who knew not Joseph," Czar Alexander II.

In 1870, a program of Russification was begun by the Czar. Its thrust was directed at German colonists, including the Mennonites, whose presence seemed threatening to the rising Russian military power. Local autonomy was ended, the Russian language was to replace German, schools were to come under Russian tutelage, and exemption from universal military service was dropped. Immigration seemed the only recourse for the Mennonites. Among those who came to America, many belonged to the Mennonite Church, the first church described in this chapter. Other Russian immigrants belonged to churches which, in Russia, had broken off from the Mennonite church there. The settlers brought these previously formed schismatic churches to America: the Evangelical Mennonite Church (Kleine Gemeinde), the Evangelical Mennonite Brethren conference, the Mennonite Brethren Church, and the Crimean Brethren, whose members in this country joined the Mennonite Brethren church in 1960. These churches are described below, as is the General Conference Mennonite Church, which was formed in this country instead of in Russia.

The first immigrants to North America included Bernard Warkentin, Cornelius Jansen, and David Goerz, who were prominent in the resettlement program. New communities were established in open lands from Oklahoma to Manitoba, with the largest settlements in Kansas.

THE BRETHREN. Among those awakened by the Pietist movement of the late seventeenth century, a movement that stressed personal piety over rigid doctrinal conformity, was a group of citizens of the Palatinate, an area now in West Germany. Influenced by the Mennonites in the vicinity, they decided to separate themselves from the state church. Their leader, Alexander Mack, recorded the event:

"In the year 1708 eight persons agreed to establish a covenant of a good conscience with God, to accept all ordinances of Jesus Christ as an easy yoke, and thus to follow after their Lord Jesus—their good and loyal shepherd—as true sheep in joy or sorrow until the blessed end . . These eight persons united with one another as brethren and sisters in the covenant of the cross of Jesus Christ as a church of Christian believers" (Donald F. Durnbaugh, *European Origins of the Brethren* [Elgin, IL: The Brethren Press, 1958], 121). As a part of the act of forming the new church, they rebaptized themselves, thus placing themselves in the Anabaptist tradition, a tradition reinforced by their German language upon their arrival in America.

While the Palatinate had changed state churches after the religious wars, neither Catholics, Lutherans, nor Reformed were happy with separatists, those who wanted to separate from the state church. People like the Brethren were subject to persecution, and rather than give up their faith, the Brethren migrated, first to Wittgenstein and then the Netherlands. Toleration diminished even more as they began to receive members from the state church.

During this time, the Brethren became influenced by Gottfried Arnold, the historian. Arnold had written several books on the early life of the church which he believed normative for all Christians. He introduced through his writings the idea of triune immersion as the proper mode of baptism. The believer, on his knees in the water, is immersed three times in the name of the Father, Son, and Holy Spirit. The Brethren also continued a close contact with the Mennonites.

By 1719, little more than a decade after their formation, the Brethren began to think about the New World as a home. Having become familiar with William Penn's experiment in Pennsylvania from his continental visits and those of his Quaker followers, they began to migrate to Germantown. The migration was completed by 1735 and the few remaining Brethren in Europe became Mennonites.

The first Brethren Church in America was established in 1723 after the Brethren had corresponded with their European counterparts. They chose Peter Becker (1687-1758) as their pastor. He proceeded to baptize the first American converts and preside over the first love feast, a service which included foot washing, a group meal, and the Lord's Supper. This church is the mother congregation of the present-day Church of the Brethren.

THE FRIENDS (QUAKERS). The middle 1600s in England was a time in which the early stages of the Reformation were beginning to be felt in a practical way. Dissidents whose perspective reflected the religious ferment of the continent began to appear. One of the men whose perspective was in line with that of the continental radical reformers was

George Fox—mystic, psychic, social activist, and founder of the Quakers.

Fox (1624-1691) had begun to preach in 1647 after experiencing an inner illumination and hearing a voice which said, "There is One, even Christ Jesus, that can speak to thy condition." The experiences of the inner light came as a psychic-spiritual awakening, and Fox developed a reputation as "a young man with a diserning spirit." Fox was a powerful preacher and a charismatic personality. A wide variety of the gifts of the Spirit (I Cor. 12:4-11) appeared regularly throughout his ministry.

Fox was an intense activist on the social scene. He was an early prohibitionist and a preacher against holidays, entertainments, and sports, saying that such activities directed man's thoughts to vanity and looseness. During the wars waged when Oliver Cromwell ruled England, Fox emerged as a peace advocate, a position held by many radical reformers. Thrown into prison for his activities, he converted the jailer and became a pioneer prison reformer.

A group of followers soon gathered around Fox and, in 1667, they were organized into a system of monthly, quarterly, and yearly meetings. Their one doctrinal peculiarity was their belief in the inner light. The Quakers believed that God's revelation was not limited to the Bible but continued in a living daily contact between the believer and the divine Spirit. The light would lead to the road to perfection. Fox's followers, always on the edge of mere subjectivism, escaped it by constantly testing their light by the teachings and example of Jesus.

The Bible is the source book of the Quaker faith and from it Fox drew many ideas which became part of the peculiar ethos of Quaker life and an offense to non-Quakers. For example, Fox believed that much of the activity of the world was vanity. He exhorted Quakers to lead simple lives which were not wasted in frivolity. Dress was to be simple. No wigs were to be worn, nor were gold or vain decorations on clothing. A Quaker costume developed from these injunctions. The biblical use of the familiar tense (thy and thou) became standard for Quakers, although most have now deserted this practice.

The Quaker organization was built around "meetings" for friends in a certain area. These meetings—monthly, quarterly, and yearly—handled business on an increasingly geographical basis. For many years, the monthly and quarterly meetings handled organization and discipline. They developed as needs manifested themselves. As early as 1668, a "General Meeting of Ministers" was held. This meeting, repeated in 1672, evolved into the yearly meeting as a general organizational body. Thus the word "meeting" can mean "church."

Quaker worship also took on a particular form, in negative reaction to Anglican formality and liturgy and in positive reaction to the inner light doctrine. Without clergy, the Quakers would sit in silence and wait for the Spirit to move. Often, no word would be spoken, but as Francis Howgill noted: "The Lord of heaven and earth we found to be near at hand, and we waited on him in pure silence, our minds out of all things, His heavenly presence appeared in our assemblies, when there was no language, tongue or speech from any creature."

Through the years under the influence of other Protestants, particularly the holiness churches that take John Wesley as their founder, free church worship patterns began to replace the Quaker meeting. For example, the Quakers adopted such practices of the holiness churches as a more programmed worship service, with a minister who would preach. Contemporary Quakers can be divided into the unprogrammed, who follow the old Quaker meeting format, and the programmed, who have an ordered worship which includes hymns, vocal prayer, Bible reading, and a sermon.

Quakers in the United States. Quakers found their way to America within a decade of the beginning of George Fox's public ministry in England; individuals arrived as early as 1655. They found at first no more favorable home in the colonies than they had left in England. However, soon Rhode Island became their sanctuary and the first meeting was established there in 1661. George Fox's visit in 1671-73 spurred the growth of the infant group.

In the 1660s, the man destined to become the most important figure in the early life of the Quakers in the colonies— William Penn (1644-1718)—joined the British Friends. Penn was the son of a British admiral, and becoming a Quaker after meeting George Fox, he became deeply impressed by the problem of persecution which they faced. Heir to a small fortune from the king, Penn accepted a tract of land (the state of Pennsylvania) instead of the money. Here he established a Quaker colony and began the great experiment of trying to mold a colony on a biblical model. To the everlasting credit of Penn, religious freedom was the order of the day, even for Jews and Turks.

In the next century, American Quakers would begin to make social history. Believing as they did in social justice, especially as it expressed itself in the equality of man, Quakers would begin a campaign against slavery. One of their number, John Woolman, would be a widely traveled leader in early Christian anti-slavery efforts. A mission was begun among the Indians, in line with the same belief in the equality of man. Friends controlled the Pennsylvania government until 1756, when they gave up their seats rather than vote for war measures during the French and Indian War.

The first General Meeting of Friends was held in 1681 at Burlington, New Jersey, and for several years one was held each year at both Burlington and Philadelphia. In 1685, these two meetings assumed the name The General Yearly Meeting for Friends of Pennsylvania, East Jersey, and of the Adjacent Provinces. This became the Philadelphia Yearly Meeting, the oldest Quaker group still in existence in the United States.

Quakers, induced by the promise of freedom of conscience, migrated into tracts of land in the southern United States and established large settlements. Slavery soon became an issue and in the decades before and after 1800, most Quakers left the South as a protest and moved to Indiana and Ohio. To this day, Quaker strength lies across the Midwest and is virtually non-existent south of the Ohio River.

As Quakerism expanded westward, regionally based yearly meetings were formed as autonomous units but in harmony with eastern counterparts. As time passed and issues came and went, these yearly meetings became the bases for denominational units and late nineteenth century ecumenical endeavors.

The general unity of American Friends remained until the 1820s, when schism began to rend the Friends and produced the various denominational bodies which exist today. Philadelphia remains as a home of broadly based, if more conservative, Quakerism.

Quakers, while fitting clearly within the free church tradition and following the European spiritual Anabaptist faith, deviate from other groups at several points. The baptism issue, a matter of intense Anabaptist interest, was solved by dropping water baptism entirely. As a natural outgrowth of Schwenckfelder belief in the primacy of the spiritual, Quakers hold that the one baptism of Ephesians 4:4-5 is the inward baptism of the Holy Spirit. (See the article on the Schwenckfelder Church in America.) Women also have had an unusual status, their right to full participation having been accepted at an early date. They were accepted into the ministry earlier than in most other churches.

Doctrinally, Quakers have followed a Protestant lead and profess a belief in the fatherhood of God, Jesus Christ as Lord and Savior, the Holy Spirit, salvation by faith, and the priesthood of believers. Quakers do, however, take a free church anti-creedal stance, and while most Quaker bodies have a statement of belief, they usually preface it with a disclaimer against a static orthodoxy, and a wide range of beliefs are present. Evangelical practices became a dominant element in the nineteenth century and, as the century closed, Wesleyan holiness became a force. In the early twentieth century, a liberal-conservative split began to emerge, leading to several schisms. The conservative elements tended to identify with holiness ideals and withdrew from the larger Friends' Meetings to form most of the smaller bodies. The Evangelical Friends Alliance formed in 1847 serves as an ecumenical body for the conservatives.

While divided into several denominations, Quakers have been able to keep an intense social activism witness in some intra-family structures. The American Friends Service Committee founded during World War I emerged as an expression of national loyalty seeking to serve in war-alternative activities. It has gained wide respect for its refugee work. The Friends Committee for National Legislation is a non-partisan lobby group.

Other European Free Churches: Besides the churches in the four main free church traditions which have been discussed aboved, Europe has been the birthing place of numerous free church groups over the centuries. Some of these are the product of the particular ministry of one person, the church forming around his/her teachings. Some have followed the emergence of a revival movement in a given limited area. Still others represent a renewal of piety among a particular ethnic group within a larger society or the protest of what is felt to be a repressive action by a state church. In each case, however, they represent a new religious impulse separate

from a country's dominant religious establishment. The great majority of the European free churches have never been transplanted to North America.

Among the groups which have come, a number have arrived from Russia. Beginning with what was termed the Great Schism in the seventeenth century, the Russian Orthodox Church watched a number of dissenting sects disturb the unity of the religious landscape. In the 1650s, the somewhat natural division between the better educated urban hierarchy of the Russian church and the poorer and less educated clergy and laity in the scattered rural communities was accentuated by a controversy over ritual. The controversy centered around Nikon (1605-1681), a young monk who, having attained the favor of the czar, rose from obscurity to become the church's patriarch. Nikon tried to introduce a greater degree of uniformity into Orthodox worship, using the Greek church as his standard. He placed very high on his program the correcting of the numerous corrupt service books then in use. Most of his changes were received as simply new innovations. Gradually, as unrest with changes led to the burning of new ritual books, the Czar abandoned him, and Nikon was banished. However, at the same council of the church in 1666 at which Nikon was deposed, his reforms were adopted. Those who opposed the reforms, the Raskol, were excommunicated. The Raskol, or Old Believers, developed as a separate body after the council. They would later divide into two main groups, the *Popovtsy*, or priestists and the *Bezpopovtsy*, or priestless.

The immediate problem of the Popovtsy was the establishment of episcopal leadership, as no bishops chose to join with them. Bishops were most necessary for the ordination of priests. For almost two centuries, they gained their priests from among those who left the state church. It was not until the nineteenth century that they were able to develop a hierarchy. In 1844 some Old Believers residing in the territory controlled by the Austro-Hungarian Empire were able to persuade the government to designate an Old Believers' episcopal see at Bela Krynica (or Belokrinitsa). In 1846, Ambrose, the former bishop of Sarajevo, assumed the new position. Before the Russian government could react, Ambrose consecrated a number of bishops for the Popovtsy Old Believers. Bishops in this 'Belokrinitskaya' line of succession continue to the present with archbishops in Moscow and in Galati, Romania (where the see of Bela Krynica moved after being overrun by the Russians during World War II).

In 1918, in the wake of the Russian Revolution, Patriarch Tikhon consecrated a bishop for the 'Yedinovertsy,' a group of Old Believers which had made a partial peace with the established church at the beginning of the nineteenth century. The established church had agreed to ordain their priests and allow them to follow the old rites. Their first bishop was killed in 1921 by the Communists, and it is believed that his successor met a similar fate. A third line of Popovtsy, the *Beglopopovtsy*, or Wandering Priestists, gained their own episcopal authority in the Soviet Union following World War II. The archbishop resides at Kuibyshev (Samara).

The second group of Old Believers, the Bezpopovtsy, orginated as people began to argue against the legitimacy of an episcopally ordained priesthood who alone could dispense the sacraments. As the basic argument was accepted, disagreements as to its implications multiplied. Some argued that they possessed a presbyterial succession of priestly authority and that their priests, ordained by a presbytery (a group of priests rather than a bishop), were able to administer the sacraments. Others argued that the Russian Church had gone into apostasy and hence lost the sacramental office altogether. As differing opinions appeared, so did numerous divisions of the Bezpopovtsy. Without a hierarchy to provide a point of visible unity, differing parties turned into new sects with great ease. Eventually, most groups moved to limit their sacraments to those which laymen could administer--baptism and absolution. Communion was either dropped (some claiming that every meal eaten in the right spirit constituted a communion with Christ) or served with elements believed to have been consecrated in the days of true priests, that is, before Nikon.

Marriage became the most crucial problem for the Priestless, as such union can only be consecrated by a valid priest. Some tried celibacy, while others did away with marriage but allowed sexual relations as a concession to the flesh. Eventually, most adopted a form of marriage which was simply blessed by the community elder.

Somewhat different in their origin are the various groups which arose around new mystical impulses in the decades after the Great Schism. Leaders of these new groups emphasized the role of inner illumination, the place of morality over ritual, and the need for simple biblical faith uncorrupted by the teachings of the Greek fathers. Among the most important of these new groups were the Khlysty, the Doukhobors, and the Molokans.

The Khlysty originated in 1631 in Kostroma Province when a peasant, Daniel Filippov, proclaimed himself God Sabaoth, who had come to give new commandments to the people. He selected another peasant to be his main prophet whom he designated as the Christ. The mystical and ascetic doctrine of the Khlysty found many supporters throughout Russia, and a series of Christs appeared to lead the group from generation to generation. The periodic attempts by the government to suppress them usually spurred their further spread.

Among people in the Ukraine attracted to the Khlysty mystical emphases, but repulsed by some of their more radical notions, there arose a sect called the Doukhobors (literally, Spirit Wrestlers), originally a derisive name given to them by the Russian archbishop at Ekaterinoslav. During the leadership of Sabellius Kapustin over the group, they were deported to the Molochnye Valley. Kapustin took the opportunity to reorganize the Doukhobors into a communal society. Leadership continued in Kapustin's family after his death until 1886. At that time a split occurred and Peter Verigin emerged as the leader of the larger faction. It was he who arranged for most of his followers to leave Russia for Canada at the end of the nineteenth century. With the assistance of Leo Tolstoy, approximately 7,400 settled in western Canada beginning in 1899.

The Molokans were started by Simeon Uklein (b. 1733), the son-in-law of a Doukhobor leader in the late eighteenth century. He rejected his father-in-laws distain for the Bible and his claims to be "Christ.' Taking approximately 70 followers, he formed a rival group. He proclaimed the Bible the sole authority for the faithful and rejected the allegorical methods so favored by the more mystical sects. He emphasized moral content more than concerns for inner illumination. Among their moral precepts was pacifism.

The Molokans' problems in Russia began with the introduction of compulsory military service by the Czar, but became crucial after their refusal to bear arms in the Russo-Japanese War. Approximately 2,000 came to the United States between 1904 and the beginning of World War I.

Besides the Russsian groups, free churches from various parts of Europe such as Norway and Switzerland have been transplanted to America. In all likelihood, others, as yet operating quietly out of members' homes, have arrived, and more will come in the future.

SOURCES—EUROPEAN FREE CHURCH

GENERAL SOURCES

Durnbaugh, Donald F. *The Believer's Church*. New York: The Macmillan Company, 1968. 315 pp.

Grimm, Harold J. *The Reformation Era*. New York: Macmillan Company, 1973. 594 pp.

Jones, Rufus M. *Spiritual Reformers of the Sixteenth and Seventeenth Centuries*. Boston: Beacon Press, 1914. 362 pp.

Littell, Franklin H. *The Anabaptist View of the Church*. New York: The Macmillan Company, 1952. 231 pp.

Spotts, Charles D. *Denominations Originating in Lancaster County, Pennsylvania*. Lancaster, PA: Franklin and Marshall College Library, 1963. 41 pp.

Williams, George H. *The Radical Reformation*. Philadelphia: The Westminster Press, 1962. 924 pp.

THE MENNONITES

Bender, Harold S. *Two Centuries of American Mennonite Literature, 1727-1928*. Goshen, IN: The Mennonite Historical Society, 1929.

The Complete Writings of Menno Simons, 1491-1561. Scottsdale, PA: Herald Press, 1956. 1092 pp.

Epp, Frank H. *Mennonites in Canada, 1786-1920*. Toronto: Macmillan of Canada, 1974. 480 pp.

Mennonites of Canada, 1920-1940. Toronto: Macmillan of Canada, 1982. 640 pp.

Hostetler, Beulah Stauffer, *American Mennonites and Protestant Movements*. Scottdale, PA; Herald Press, 1987. 366 pp.

Hostetler, John A. *Mennonite Life*. Scottsdale, PA: Herald Press, 1959. 39 pp.

MacMaster, Richard K. *Land, Piety, Peoplehood*. Scottdale, PA: Herald Press, 1985. 340 pp.

The Mennonite Encyclopedia. 4 vols. Scottsdale, PA: Mennonite Publishing House, 1955-59.

Quiring, Walter and Helen Bartel, *Mennonites in Canada, A Pictorial Review*. Altona, MN: D. W. Friesen & Sons, 1961. 208 pp.

Smith, C. Henry. *The Mennonites*. Berne, IN: Mennonite Book Concern, 1920. 340 pp.

Smith, Elmer L. *Meet the Mennonites*. Witmer, PA: Allied Arts, 1961. 42 pp.

Springer, Nelson P., and A. J. Klassen. *Mennonite Bibliography, 1631-1961*. 2 vols. Scottsdale, PA: Herald Press, 1977.

Waltner, James H. *This We Believe*. Newton, KS: Faith and Life Press, 1968. 230 pp.

Wenger, John Christian. *The Doctrines of the Mennonites*. Scottsdale, PA: Mennonite Publishing House, 1950. 160 pp.

THE AMISH

Hostetler, John A. *Amish Life*. Scottsdale, PA: Herald Press, 1959. 39 pp.

————. *Amish Society*. Baltimore: The Johns Hopkins Press, 1963. Rev. ed. 1968. 369 pp.

————. *An Annotated Bibliography on the Amish*. Scottsdale, PA: Mennonite House, 1951. 100 pp.

Rice, Charles S., and Rollin C. Stinmetz. *The Amish Year*. New Brunswick, NJ: Rutgers University Press, 1956. 224 pp.

Schreiber, William. *Our Amish Neighbors*. Chicago: University of Chicago Press, 1962. 227 pp.

Smith, Elmer Lewis. *The Amish*. Witmer, PA: Applied Arts, 1966. 34 pp.

————. *The Amish People*. New York: Exposition Press, 1958. 258 pp.

THE RUSSIAN MENNONITES

Smith, C. Henry. *The Coming of the Russian Mennonites*. Berne, IN: Mennonite Book Concern, 1927. 296 pp.

Stucky, Harley J. *A Century of Russian Mennonite History in America*. North Newton, KS: Mennonite Press, Inc., 1974. 119 pp.

THE BRETHREN

The Brethren Encyclopedia. 2 Vols. Philadelphia, PA: The Brethren Encyclopedia, Inc., 1983.

Durnbaugh, Donald F. "A Brethren Bibliography, 1713-1963." *Brethren Life and Thought* 9, 1-2 (Winter and Summer, 1964): 3-177.

————. *The Brethren in Colonial America*. Elgin, IL: The Brethren Press, 1967. 659 pp.

————. *The European Origins of the Brethren*. Elgin, IL: Brethren Press, 1958. 463 pp.

————. "Guide to Research in Brethren History." Elgin, IL: Church of the Brethren General Board, 1977. 16 pp.

Holsinger, H. R. *History of the Tunkers and the Brethren Church*. Lathrop, CA: The Author, 1901. 827 pp.

Mallot, Floyd E. *Studies in Brethren History*. Elgin, IL: Brethren Publishing House, 1954. 382 pp.

Sappington, Roger E. *The Brethren in the New Nation*. Elgin, IL: Brethren Press, 1976. 496 pp.

Willoughby, William G. *Counting the Cost*. Elgin, IL: Brethren Press, 1979. 176 pp.

THE FRIENDS (QUAKERS)

Baltzell, E. Digby. *Puritan Boston and Quaker Philadelphia*. Boston: Beacon Press, 1979. 585 pp.

Barbour, Hugh, and Arthur O. Roberts. *Early Quaker Writings, 1650-1700*. Grand Rapids, MI: William B. Eerdmans Publishing Company, 1973. 622 pp.

Benjamin, Philip S. *The Philadelphia Quakers in the Industrial Age*. Philadelphia: Temple University Press, 1976. 301 pp.

Brinton, Howard H. *Children of Light*. New York: Macmillan Company, 1938. 416 pp.

Comfort, William Wistar. *The Quaker Way of Life*. Philadelphia: The Blakiston Company, 1945. 178 pp.

Elliott, Errol T. *Quakers on the American Frontier*. Richmond, IN: Friends United Press, 1969. 434 pp.

Evans, Thomas. *A Concise Account of the Religious Society of Friends*. Philadelphia: Friends Books Store, n.d. 161 pp.

Finding Friends around the World. London: Friends World Committee for Consultation, 1982. 128 pp.

Holder, Charles Frederick. *The Quakers in Great Britain and America*. Los Angeles: Neuner Company, 1913. 669 pp.

Jones, Rufus. *The Quakers in the American Colonies*. New York: W. W. Norton & Company, 1966. 606 pp.

Kenworthy, Leonard S. *Quakerism*. Durbin, IN: Prinit Press, 1981. 215 pp.

Van Etten, Henry. *George Fox and the Quakers*. New York: Harper, 1959. 191 pp.

Other European Free Church Traditions

Bolshakoff, Serge. *Russian Nonconformity*. Philadelphia: Westminster Press, 1921. 192 pp.

Conybeare, Frederick C. *Russian Dissenters*. Cambridge, MA: Harvard University Press, 1921. 370 pp.

Struve, Nikita. *Christians in Contemporary Russia*. New York: Charles Scribner's Sons, 1967. 464 pp.

Part 2
Directory Listings Sections

Section 1

Western Liturgical Family

An historical essay on this family is provided beginning on page 1.

Roman Catholic Church

★1★
ROMAN CATHOLIC CHURCH
National Conference of Catholic Bishops
1312 Massachusetts Ave., N.W.
Washington, DC 20005

[Introductory note: The Roman Catholic Church is by far the largest ecclesiastical community in the United States, more than three times as large as the Southern Baptist Convention, its closest rival. That fact, coupled with its position as the largest Christian body in the world and as such the bearer of much of the Christian tradition, gives it a special position in any survey of religious bodies. Overwhelmingly Western Christian churches can trace their origins to dissent from Roman Catholicism, on one or more points. Even within a predominantly Protestant country such as the United States, the Roman Catholic Church provides a measuring rod by which other Christian groups (approximately two-thirds of those treated in this *Encyclopedia*) can locate themselves. Understanding the lives of these groups presupposes some knowledge of their variation from Catholicism. The Roman Catholic Church was also one of the first churches to come to America, bringing with it the long history of Western Christianity. The matter of the origin of the Roman tradition and of the emergence of the See of Rome as the dominant body in the West is a matter of intense debate among ancient-church historians. Most agree, however, that by the fifth century Rome was the ecclesiastical power in the West, and Rome's bishop was the leading episcopal authority. Further, for the next millennium, the story of Christianity in the West is largely the story of Rome. The detailing of this story and the elaboration of this developing tradition is far beyond the scope of this volume. Interested readers are referred to the volumes cited at the end of this entry for a sample of books which treat those topics. This volume will merely provide a summary of basic material about the Church and its historical development in the West, the emergence of religious orders, its history in the United States, its basic beliefs and practices, and its organization. The long history of the Church and some of its sanctioned but less than universal practices (Eastern rite liturgies, localized forms of piety, etc.) will be treated primarily as background for understanding those groups that have dissented with the Church.]

History. The Roman Catholic Church is that Christian religious community whose members are "baptized and incorporated in Christ, profess the same faith, partake of the same sacraments and are in communion with and under the government of the successor of St. Peter, the pope, and the bishops in union with him." (quoted from *A Concise Guide to the Catholic Church* by Felician A. Foy). The rise of the Roman Catholic Church to a position of dominance within the Christian community can be traced through a series of steps beginning with the geographical spread of the Church throughout the Roman Empire and beyond and the emergence of an authority structure built around bishops (mentioned in the New Testament, but hardly the figures of authority as exist today). Then the conversion of the Emperor Constantine pulled the Church out of its role as just another religion competing in the Roman forum.

In 303 A.D. Diocletian initiated a plan designed to stabilize the vast empire he ruled. He divided it into Eastern and Western sections. Over each section he placed a senior emperor assisted by a junior emperor with the right of succession. Diocletian then voluntarily resigned and the four appointees took his place: the senior emperor Constantius Chlorus and his junior partner, Severus, in the West, and Galerius and his junior partner, Maximinus, in the East. However, upon the death of the emperor in the West, his son Constantine usurped the power and Severus, the rightful successor, was killed.

In the midst of his rise to power Constantine identified himself with (only much later was he baptized) what was at the time a very small Christian community. According to Christian historian Eusebius, he saw a vision over the Milvian bridge where he was to meet his rival. The vision was of a cross in the sky with words around it saying, "In this sign you will conquer." Constantine ordered this sign painted on the shields of his soldiers; defeated his rival, and emerged as sole ruling power in the West. One of his first acts was to give Christianity freedom by granting it an equal legal status with paganism. In the East, Galerius followed Constantine's lead. Under Constantine, the idea that Christianity best flourished under the protection of the empire began its ascendancy along with its corollary that the empire and the emperor were not only capable but were in fact divinely appointed to rule and to render that protection. Both the centuries of intimate union between the "Christian" state and the Christian Church and the church-state theory based upon that union were initiated at this time, even before the Church became the dominant religious power in the empire.

Then in 330 C. E., Constantine transferred his capital from Rome to Byzantium (now Istanbul) in the East. He renamed it Consantinople and over the next decades initiated a whole new thrust in culture. But in so doing, he abandoned Rome and created a severe power vacuum throughout the West. The Church and the bishop of Rome, the Pope, emerged as the organization with both the will and the ability to accomodate to the new situation. Christian bishops took up temporal authority and, given the emperors' acceptance of their role, became an elite ruling class. The bishops in the more important towns of the empire came to be known as archbishops and those in the major cities, such as Antioch, Alexandria, Constantinople, Rome, were known as patriarchs. the Roman patriarch assumed some preeminence both as successor to Peter, who died in Rome, and patriarch of the significant urban center in the West.

But while the bishop of Rome claimed a primacy of honor and privilege, the Eastern patriarchs, claimed a similiar prestige as well. The emperior resided in the East. The ecumenical councils were held there. Most Christians lived there, where Christinity had begun and had its longest history. However, the Western Church had an opportunity for growth and development that it would not miss.

Pope Gregory the Great, elected in 590, in a very real sense the founder of the modern papal structure, began the process of centralizing the entire Western Church, then loosely organized into a set of dioceses, upon Rome. He brought to the office a vision, discipline, missionary instinct, and sense of order and rule to the church. If the pope's power of jurisdiction and supremacy had been ill defined previously, it was Gregory who sharpened the definition. A high civil official before becoming a monk, he used his organizational ability to reorganize church finances, thus making it financially independent. He consolidated and expanded the Church's power. He exercised hegemony for the Church throughout the West and sent forth missionaries (usually monks) to claim lands for the faith. He took major steps to convert the Germanic tribes, end Arianism in Spain, and gain the loyalty of the Irish church. Gregory sent Augustine to England where he converted the king and established the

see at Cantebury. The papacy emerged as the international center of the Western Church in power as well as prestige. The church that emerged under Gregory's successors looked to Rome, not to the Emperor in Constantinople nor his representative at Revenna.

Two centuries after Gregory, the emperor Charlemagne (742- 814) consolidated secular political rule in almost all of Europe and reestablished an empire to match the spiritual realm delineated by the Church. A bond was forged, and the marriage between the Western Church and the Western empire took place. The Eastern emperor became a mere figurehead to the West.

The dissipation of Charlemagne's empire into the hands of numerous local monarchs set the stage for Pope Gregory VII, elected in 1073, the founder of the papal monarchy. By Gregory's time, Western Christendom had grown "larger" than the territory of any empire. Gregory, monarch of his own country, but more importantly, the representative of a religion that transcended the boundaries of both his country and the empire as it then existed, began to assume more universal powers, full political and spiritual supremacy. He encouraged remote territories such as Spain, Denmark, and Hungary to accept the protection of the Holy See, implying that he, the pope, was the real universal center of things rather than any emperor. He insisted that the pope could be judged by none; that the pope alone could depose, move and/or restore bishops. He took authority to depose rulers or to absolve subjects from their allegiance to their rulers. Under Gregory and his successor, the Papacy exercised its greatest temporal authority in the West. The extensive corruption of that power, felt throughout the church at every level, created the need for reform and set the stage for Martin Luther, John Calvin, and the Protestant and Radical Reformers.

The Reformation can best be seen as the convergence of numerous factors upon Northern and Western Europe in the sixteenth century. The Church was beset with internal problems and was also filled with voices calling for its reform and a new emphasis upon spirituality in place of its preoccupation with political involvement. Several centuries of reform efforts had also coincided with the rise of strong national states which further stripped the Holy Roman Emperor of real power to hold structures together in the West. Once Luther's cause gained support, other independent reform efforts proceeded, ranging from those of Calvin in Switzerland and Henry VIII in England to the more radical Swiss Brethren (Mennonites) and Unitarians. Once the political power supporting the Roman Catholic Church was broken, the establishment of various independent and locally controlled chruches became possible.

The Reformation divided the West among five Christian traditions (Roman, Lutheran, Reformed, Anglican, and Free Church) and fostered the further division of the non-Roman traditions into the many individual organizations with linguistic, political, nationalistic, and doctrinal divergences, leading, of course, to the numerous churches seen in this century (and described in various sections of the *Encyclopedia*). While Rome remained in control of the largest block of territory, it had to devise new ways of relating to religiously divided societies, especially in those countries which had both a Roman Catholic presence and a hostile Protestant ruler.

The Reformation also occurred at the same time as the discovery, exploration, and settlement of the Americas. Roman Catholicism settled in most of South and Central America and became the dominant religious force. In North America, with the early settlers, the Church found a much different situation, i.e., a predominantly Protestant society moving quickly toward a religious freedom and pluralism not hinted at since the days of the Roman Empire.

A note about religious orders: the forces of reform that disrupted the Church in the sixteenth century were not new to Western Christianity. Reform had been expressed and acted upon by numerous movements throughout its history. Some of these reformers became rival movements, largely remembered today as the great heretical movements (Gnosticism, Montanism, etc.). When the Church gained access to political power, it turned upon those movements and left a record of persecution that came back to haunt it in later centuries. However, with reformist, mystical, and enthusiastic movements not defined as heretical (but nevertheless potentially schismatic) the Church had a more creative solution in the formation of ordered religious communities. The schismatic tendencies of, for example, Protestantism and the Free Church families, constantly led to the formation of new sects. In Roman Catholicism, however (and to a lesser extent in Eastern Orthodoxy), these tendencies resulted in the various orders of monks, nuns, and lay brothers and sisters. Many such orders show all of the characteristics of sectarian bodies, including liturgical and theological peculiarities, distinctive dress, and special missional emphases. The only difference is that theses groups remain in allegiance to the bishop of Rome. Many orders operate effectively outside of local diocesan control and report directly to the orders' officials, who in turn report directly to the Pope or curia. Of course, by accepting new religious movements as ordered communities, the Church is able both to nurture geniune religious enthusiasms and control their excesses.

From the fifth to the twelfth centuries, there was practically only one religious order in the church: the Benedictines. Then, in the twelfth century, a variety of new types of religious communities appeared on the scene with many derivative branches. Not only was the Benedictine Order no longer held to be the only safe road to heaven but, by the twelfth century, a noticeable decline had set in. Some monasteries had become socially exclusive and had become fossilized into great symbols of stability from which no innovations could be expected. New orders were needed. First, there were the

Augustinians (Luther's order), an informal group compared to the structured Benedictines, dedicated to practical service to others (in contrast to self perfection of the former monks) and to survival in a world of change. The Cistercians, on the other hand, wanted to flee change, flux, and the world and return to pristine Benedictine rigor and purity. They moved into the some of the uninhabited lands of Europe, first growing rapidly, then like the Benedictines before them, succumbing to success.

The new town culture of the late Middle Ages brought into existence the two most influential orders of the time, the Franciscans and Dominicans. Founded by middle class men (Francis of Assisi was the son of a merchant) as an order of brothers (fratello in Italian) or friars, they were not, as older orders, to withdraw from the world but to penetrate it. They gave to the age the common spectacle of the traveling friar and itinerant preacher.

Roman Catholicism in America. The Roman Catholic Church came to America with the early Spanish and French explorers. Priests accompanied Hernando de Soto and Francisco Coronado, and some, like Jacques Marquette and Junipero Serra, became explorers in their own right. The first missions were begun in Florida after the founding of St. Augustine in 1565. Spanish priests and (after 1573) Franciscans developed the missions. The settlement of large segments of America by European Catholic countries largely determined the earliest religious development of America. Florida, the Gulf Coast of present-day Alabama and Mississippi, California, and the Southwest were Spanish territory. The French settled Canada, Louisiana, and the Mississippi Valley. The early Catholic hegemony is reflected in the many towns named for the saints they revered.

Under the leadership of an English Catholic convert, George Calvert (who became the first Baron of Baltimore) a small band of British Catholics settled on the East Coast and, in 1634, founded the colony of Maryland. In stark contrast to their neighbors in Pennsylvania, many of whom had come to America fleeing Roman Catholic persecution, these Catholics had come fleeing Protestant attacks. In 1649 Calvert issued the famous Act of Toleration offering the "free exercise" of religion to residents. Unfortunately, Catholic control of the colony was soon lost, and in 1654 the Act was repealed and Catholicism prohibited. Four Catholics were executed and the Jesuits driven out. Not until 1781 were Catholics allowed to participate in public life.

Catholicism existed in America for over two centuries without a bishop. There had been no confirmations and all clergy were ordained abroad. Since 1757, the colonies had been nominally under the bishop in London, but after the American Revolution a resident bishop was needed. The person chosen for the task was John Carroll, a member of the most prominent Catholic family in the colonies and a cousin to Charles Carroll, one of the signers of the Declaration of Independence. By the end of the century Carroll would have approximately 50,000 Catholics under his care.

During the nineteenth century, several factors shaped the life of the Church. First, the dominance of people of British and German ancestry, both with a strong anti-Catholic bias from the days of the Reformation, meant that Catholics would frequently have to exist in a hostile environment. (This reached its height in the mid-nineteenth century during the so-called Know Nothing era.) Secondly, the Church grew massively as literally millions of immigrants from predominantly Roman Catholic countries poured into the United States. At the same time, the Church became divided internally into many ethnic groupings, as Catholics from different countries and speaking different languages settled into homogeneous communities. They tended to locate in pockets in the cities and recreated (as much as possible) life in the old country. To this day many of the nation's leading cities retain a large Catholic element and many neighborhoods retain remants of these immigrant communities. The many ethnic groups also contrasted strongly with the predominantly Irish clergy and hierarchy. Attempts to play down ethnicity and "Americanize" parishes (in part by assigning priests from outside the predominant ethnic group in a parish) caused considerable friction. It was also the cause of the only major schism from within the Church in the United States, the Polish National Catholic Church. The parochial school system, mandated in 1884, was originally established to assist Catholic immigrants as they adjusted to life in non-Catholic America.

Growth of the Church during the nineteenth century (which lasted until immigration from mostly Catholic countries was curtailed in 1921) was spectacular. By 1822 Baltimore had been designated an archepiscopal see and bishops resided in Boston; New York; Philadelphia; Norfolk, Virginia; New Orleans; and Bardstown, Kentucky. By 1900 there were over 12,000,000 Catholics in the United States (eclipsing by far the largest Protestant church), and by 1930 there were over 20,000,000. During the next half-century, Church membership would more than double in size

Beliefs. The Roman Catholic Church bases its beliefs on the revelation of God as given through the Bible, and on tradition handed down from the Apostles through the Church. The essential beliefs have come to be summarized in several creedal statements, especially those developed by the early ecumenical councils: the Apostles Creed, Nicene Creed, and Athanasian Creed. Until recently, new converts to the Church were asked to sign a "Profession of Faith," which included a re jection of a number of false doctrines, a promise of obedience to the Church, and a statement of belief. Though no longer required, the statement of belief, printed below, remains an authoritative guide to the Church's essential belief:

"One only God, in three divine Persons, distinct from and equal to each other, that is to say, the Father, the Son, and the Holy Ghost; the Catholic doctrine of the Incarnation, Passion, Death, and Resurrection of our Lord Jesus Christ; the personal union of the two natures, the divine and the human; the divine maternity of the most holy Mary, together with her spotless virginity; the true real and substantial presence of the Body and Blood, together with the Soul in the Eucharist; the seven Sacraments instituted by Jesus Christ for the salvation of mankind, that is to say, Baptism, Confirmation, Eucharist, Penance, Extreme Unction, Orders, and Matrimony; Purgatory, the Resurrection of the Dead, Everlasting Life; the primacy, not only of honor, but also of jurisdiction, of the Roman Pontiff, successor of St. Peter, prince of the apostles, Vicar of Jesus Christ, the veneration of the saints and their images; the authority of the Apostolic and Ecclesiastical traditions, and of the Holy Scriptures, which we must interpret and understand, only in the sense which our holy mother, the Catholic Church, has held, and does hold; and everything else that has been defined, and declared by the Sacred Canons, and by the General Councils, and particularly by the holy Council of Trent and delivered, defined and declared by the General Council of the Vatican, especially concerning the primacy of the Roman Pontiff and his infallible teaching authority.

Defined by the first Vatican Council, the doctrine of papal infallibility remains the most controversial of Roman Catholic beliefs. It grows out of and is an expression of the Church's long held belief in its being kept from error by the power of the Holy Spirit. The Pope's words are considered infallible only when speaking *ex cathedra*, i.e., in his office as pastor and doctor of all Christians, and when defining doctrine on matters of faith or morals to be held by all Christians. More often than not, Papal statements do not fall into this category. However, Catholics are enjoined to give heed to Papal messages as part of their obedience to the Church's teaching authority.

Two relatively recent papal statements in which the Pope has been deemed to have spoken *ex cathedra* concerned what is possibly the second most controversial area of Roman Catholic doctrine (at least to most Protestant Christians), the understanding of the Virgin Mary. During the nineteenth century the veneration of the Virgin Mary took on a new importance within Roman Catholicism, and it found expression in numerous new pietistic forms and practices, many built around the several apparitions, such as those at Lourdes (France) and Fatima (Portugal). In the last century the doctrine of the Immaculate Conception (the sinless birth of Mary) was declared. In 1950 her bodily assumption into heaven was defined.

Supplementing the beliefs of the Church are the moral precepts which are considered binding upon each Church member. They are required to do the following: 1) participate in Mass on Sundays and specified holy days and to abstain from work and business concerns that impede worship; 2) fast and abstain on appointed days (primarily during the Lenten season); 3) confess their sins at least annually; 4) receive the Eucharist during the Easter season (for American Catholics between the first Sunday of Lent and Trinity Sunday); 5) contribute to the support of the Church; and 6) observe the laws of the Church concerning marriage.

Worship in the Catholic Church is centered upon the liturgy, the major components being the following: the Eucharist (the Mass) and the other six sacraments; sacramentals (sacramental-like signs such as holy water, rosaries, holy medals, etc.); sacred art; sacred music; the prayer cycle of the Liturgy of the Hours (the Divine Office); and the designation of the liturgical year and calendar.

Individuals are brought into the Church through baptism, through which original sin is washed away. The Mass, instituted by Christ at the Last Supper, is a real sacrifice of Christ using the elements of bread and wine. During the liturgy of the Mass, the Church teaches that the bread and wine change (the change is termed "transubstantiation") into the body and blood of Christ. The Eucharist is the major sacramental expression encountered by Church members on a regular basis. Confirmation, usually given to youth or adult converts immediately after finishing a period of instruction in the faith, is generally conferred by the bishop, and it empowers individuals with the force of the Holy Spirit. Penance is the means by which the faithful confess and receive forgiveness for present sin. Holy Orders sets aside Catholic males (unmarried and celibate) for specified priestly functions. The annointing of the sick (unction) is performed when the individual is in danger of death, in hope of an improvement in the state of health, as well as for forgiveness of sins at the time of death. Finally, matrimony binds two people together in God's eyes.

Over the years, supplementing the sacramental life, the Church has broadly defined the life and structure of faith through the liturgical calendar. The calendar focuses attention on the essentials of the faith and commemorates the life of the Virgin Mary and the saints. The liturgical year begins with Advent and includes as its high points Christmas, Lent, Easter, and Pentecost. Worship is further enhanced by the promotion of a variety of devotional practices, inluding prayers said using the rosary, novenas, and meditation on the stations of the cross (picturing Christ's passion and death).

Organization. The Roman Catholic Church derives its authority as the Church founded by Christ through the Apostles. The signs of Christ's Church are its oneness in doctrine, worship, and practice; its holiness by the indwelling of the Holy Spirit; its apostolic nature; and its catholicity or universal aspect. The Apostolic authority has been passed, generation by generation, through the bishops of the Church, especially the Pope, the successor to Peter, the first bishop of Rome. The Pope resides in Vatican City, a small sovereign state outside of Rome,

Italy. The curia is located there, where the college of cardinals meets.

The Pope, the Supreme Pastor of Christians, is elected by the College of Cardinals. The College, which evolved out of the synod of the clergy of the diocese of Rome, includes the principal advisors and assistants to the Pope, who help administer the affairs of the Church. It was officially constituted in 1150, and twenty-nine years later the selection of its members was left to the reigning Pope. Members of the College are of three types: cardinal bishops, the bishops of dioceses geographically neighboring the diocese of Rome; cardinal priests, bishops of dioceses away from Rome who have been assigned to a church in Rome; and cardinal deacons, bishops assigned to administrative offices in the Roman curia. Generally, the archbishops of the most important sees in the United States are appointed cardinal priests.

The offices of the Roman Catholic Church that administer its affairs worldwide are called the curia. It includes the Secretariat of State, the Council for the Public Affairs of the Church, and numerous other departments, congregations, tribunals, and secretariats. Worldwide, the Church is divided into a number of dioceses. The largest and most important are designated archdioceses, with an archbishop who generally has some supervisory rights over the neighboring dioceses. Dioceses are grouped into provinces, provinces into regions, and regions into conferences. In 1966, bishops in the United States were formed into the National Catholic Conference in the United States. The Church as a whole is governed according to canon law, the rules of the Church. A revised edition of that law, written during the Second Vatican Council, was issued in 1981. The 1,752 canons cover all aspects of Church life, from the nature and structure of the Church to the rights and obligations of the faithful.

In the years after the split between the Roman Catholic Church and the Eastern Orthodox Churches in the eleventh century, communities that had a history as Eastern Orthodox were converted to Catholicism, and they came under the jurisdiction of the Pope. In many cases these churches were allowed to keep their Eastern liturgical life. There are six patriarchs who preside over nongeographical dioceses of all of the faithful of their respective rite, wherever in the world they might be found. These churches retain a married priesthood. Eastern rite Catholics began to emigrate to the United States in the late 1700s, and parishes were founded in the nineteenth century. The presence of Eastern Catholic and Eastern Orthodox parishes so close together in the relatively free environment of the United States facilitated the movement of members (and sometimes even whole parishes) from one church to another.

Membership: In 1987 there were 52,893,217 members, 53,382 priests, and 19,596 parishes in the United States. In Canada there were 11,375,914 members, 11,794 priests, and 5,932 parishes. There are over 851 million Roman Catholics wordlwide.

Educational facilities: For a complete list of institutions of higher learning supported by the Roman Catholic Church see the latest edition of either *The Official Roman Catholic Directory* (New York: P. J. Kenedy & Sons) or *Catholic Almanac* (Huntington, IN: Our Sunday Visitor). Each is regularly revised and updated.

Periodicals: There are over 500 Church-related newspapers and 300 magazines published in the United States. For a complete list see the latest edition of either the *Catholic Almanac* or *The Official Roman Catholic Directory*.

Sources: Felician A. Foy, *A Concise Guide to the Catholic Church*. Huntington, IN: Our Sunday Visitor, 1984; Aloysius J. Burggraff, *Handbook for New Catholics*. Glen Rock, NJ: Paulist Press, 1960; Daughters of St. Paul, *Basic Catechism with Scripture Quotations*. Boston: St. Paul Editions, 1984; Sister M. Catherine Frederic, *The Handbook of Catholic Practices*. New York: Hawthorn Publishers, 1964; Matthew F. Kohmescher, *Catholicism Today*. New York: Paulist Press, 1980. John Tracy Ellis, *American Catholicism*. Garden City, NY: Doubleday, 1965; John Tracy Ellis, ed., *Documents of American Catholic History*. Chicago: Henry Regnery, 1967. 2 Vols.; James Hennesey, *American Catholics*. Oxford: Oxford University Press, 1981; Theodore Maynard, *The Story of American Catholicism*. Garden City, NY : Doubleday, 1960. Walter J. Burghardt and William F. Lynch, *The Idea of Catholicism*. New York: Meridian, 1960; John L. McKenzie, *The Roman Catholic Church*. New York: Holt, Rinehart and Winston, 1969; J. M. R. Tillard, *The Bishop of Rome*. Willmington, DE: Michael Glazier, 1983; Heinrich Scharp, *How the Catholic Church is Governed*. New York: Paulist Press, 1960.

Old Catholicism

★2★
AMERICAN CATHOLIC CHURCH (SYRO-ANTIOCHEAN)
Current address not obtained for this edition.

In the late 1930s, Archbishop Daniel C. Hinton, the third primate of the American Catholic Church, resigned in favor of Bishop Percy Wise Clarkson. Clarkson was the founder-pastor of the jurisdiction's most successful parishes in Laguna Beach, California. However, he had strong theosophical leanings, and strengthened the tendency to move the American Catholic Church into theological alignment with the Liberal Catholic Church. Among those who strongly opposed the direction in which Clarkson was leading was Ernest Leopold Peterson (d. 1959), a black man who had been consecrated in 1927 by the former primate, Archbishop Frederick E. J. Lloyd.

Peterson authored the liturgy used by the church prior to Clarkson's leadership.

Peterson withdrew from Clarkson's jurisdiction and formed the American Catholic Church (Syro-Antiochean), which continued in the faith and practice of the American Catholic Church. In 1950, Peterson consecrated Herbert F. Wilkie, who succeeded as primate in 1959.

Membership: The church reported 40 churches, 4,663 members, and 66 clergy in 1961, but as of the last report in 1979, three churches, 501 members, and eight clergy remained.

★3★
AMERICAN ORTHODOX CATHOLIC CHURCH, ARCHDIOCESE OF OHIO
(Defunct)

The American Orthodox Catholic Church, Archdiocese of Ohio was a short-lived religious organization established by the Most Rev. Charles T. Sutter. He had been pastor of St. Jude's parish, now a part of the Orthodox Catholic Church of North and South America, but was consecrated in 1979 by Archbishop Richard B. Morrill (Mar Apriam) of the Holy Orthodox Catholic Church, Eastern and Apostolic. Sutter established his see in Zanesville, Ohio, and by early 1982 had established parishes in Miami and Pompano Beach, Florida; a religious order in Coconut Creek, Florida (the Missionary Order of Saint Jude the Apostle); and a school in Rogers, Arkansas (the University of the Holy Transfiguration). However, in the summer of 1982, Sutter dissolved the corporation and retired from his priestly and episcopal offices. Information on the subsequent fate of the several parishes is not available.

★4★
AMERICAN ORTHODOX CATHOLIC CHURCH - WESTERN RITE MISSION, DIOCESE OF NEW YORK
% Most Rev. Joseph J. Raffaele
318 Expressway Dr., S.
Medford, NY 11763

Joseph J. Raffaele, a Roman Catholic layperson, founded St. Gregory's Church, an independent traditionalist Latin-rite parish, in Sayville, New York, on August 28, 1973. Three months later, he was ordained by Bishop Robert R. Zaborowski of the Archdiocese of the American Orthodox Catholic Church in the U.S. and Canada (now called the Mariavite Old Catholic Church). Raffaele developed a congregation among traditionalists who felt spiritually alienated from the post-Vatican II Roman Catholic Church. The parish grew slowly, and Raffaele and his assistants continued to work in secular jobs (the standard Old Catholic pattern), devoting evenings and weekends to the church. The parish moved from Sayville to Shirley to Ronkonkoma, New York. During the mid-1970s Bishop Zaborowski insisted upon the acceptance of Mariavite (i.e.

Polish) liturgical patterns by the congregations under his jurisdiction. Both St. Gregory's and Fr. Raffaele left the Mariavite Old Catholic Church. Shortly after, Archbishop Zaborowski issued an excommunication decree.

Raffaele joined the Mount Athos Synod under Bishop Charles C. McCarthy (a bishop in the American Orthodox Catholic Church under Archbishop Patrick J. Healy). On July 18, 1976, McCarthy consecrated Raffaele and raised his associate priest, Gerard J. Kessler, to the rank of monsignor. Six months later, in December 1976, St. Gregory's and Raffaele, due to some personal disagreements with McCarthy, left the Mt. Athos Synod and became an independent jurisdiction, the American Orthodox Catholic Church-Western Rite Mission, Diocese of New York.

The new jurisdiction continues as a traditionalist Latin Rite Catholic Church, though Eastern Rite usage is allowed. The jurisdiction accepts the Baltimore Catechism (minus the papal references) as a doctrinal authority and uses the 1917 Code of Canon Law (again minus the papal references). Clerical celibacy is not demanded, but female priesthood is rejected. No collection is taken on Sunday at worship services. Communion is open to all.

In 1978 St. Matthias Church, in Yonkers, New York, was begun as the first mission parish. In 1979 St. Gregory's moved into a newly purchased building in Medford, New York. That same year, Raffaele consecrated Elrick Gonyo as an independent Uniate bishop in Stuyvesant, New York. In 1979, Raffaele and Gonyo consecrated Kessler as the auxiliary bishop for the jurisdiction.

The Congregation of the Religious of the Society of St. Gregory the Great provides a structure for priests, brothers, and nuns who wish to live an ordered life. There is also a third order, a lay fraternal organization for women (deaconesses).

In 1986, the church reported a significant spiritual renewal within the jurisdiction that led to the production of a new contemporary liturgy. The new mass was first used at the parish at Medford on Pentecost Sunday 1986 and later mandated for use throughout the jurisdiction. The renewal also launched an exploration of new nonparochial forms of ministry to extend the missionary outreach, including an intercessory prayer circuit, a healing ministry, and the use of lay ministers. Glad Tidings Ministries, a multimedia spiritual outreach also arose out of the renewal.

Membership: In 1988 the church reported one congregation in Medford, New York, with statewide outreach serving approximately 200 members. There is Spanish-speaking work in Miami, and outreach centers were being established in New Jersey and Massachusetts. It had two bishops and five priests.

Periodicals: *Glad Tidings*, 318 Expressway Drive South, Medford, Long Island, New York 11763.

Sources: *"Milestones," American Orthodox Catholic Church*. Medford, N.Y.: St. Gregory's Church, 1983.

★5★
AMERICAN PRELATURE
℅ Most Rev. Derek Lang
2103 S. Portland St.
Los Angeles, CA 90007

History. The American Prelature continues the ministry begun by Archbishop Richard A. Marchenna (1932-1982) as the Old Roman Catholic Church. Marchenna's consecration to the bishopric in 1941 by Archbishop Carmel Henry Carfora (1916-1958) began a tumultuous career in Carfora's North American Old Roman Catholic Church culminated in his deposition and excommunicated in 1952. With several clergy and four parishes, he organized the Old Roman Catholic Church and entered into communion with Gerard George Shelley, originally consecrated by Marchenna. Shelley, while serving as bishop in England, had received the lineage of B. M. Williams, and claimed the direct succession of Archbishop Arnold Harris Mathew, who had founded the Old Catholic Church in England.

Following Carfora's death, Marchenna laid claim to Carfora's succession through Cyrus A. Starkey. Starkey, Carfora's coadjutor, who left the North American Old Roman Catholic Church after Carfora's death, had asked Marchenna to become the supreme primate of the Old Roman Catholic Church.

Marchenna slowly put together one of the larger of the Old Catholic jurisdictions. Then, in 1974, he consecrated an openly homosexual priest, Fr. Robert Clement, head of the Eucharistic Catholic Church. That action led to his break with Shelley and the loss of many of his priests. Following Marchenna's death, Derek Lang, formerly episcopal vicar for Nicaragua and regionary bishop for North America at the time of Marchenna's death, assumed the leadership of the now decimated jurisdiction. Among other offices, Marchenna had appointed Lang Titular Bishop of Middleburg (a sixteenth-century diocese that had ceased to reorganize it into the American Prelature, thus "replacing the less modest titles and structures used by his predecessors." He also moved the headquarters to the West Coast.

Beliefs. The American Prelature follows the belief and practices of pre-Vatican I Roman Catholicism and the North American Old Roman Catholic Church, differing only in matters of administration. It accepts the decrees promulgated by the Council of Trent (1565) but does not accept the infallibility of the pope or other documents related to the excessive powers inherent in the pope's teaching office.

Organization. The American Prelature is headed by its archbishop. He oversees work in Los Angeles, California; and a hospital, seminary, and mission in Nicaragua.

Membership: In 1988, the prelature reported approximately 2,000 members (and some 20,000 constituents), mostly in Nicaragua. There were two centers in Los Angeles.

Educational facilities: St. Martin's Seminary, La Esperanza, Zelaya, Nicaragua.

Sources: *Old Catholic Church (Utrecht Succession).* Chicago: Old Catholic Press of Chicago, [1980].

★6★
ANCIENT TRIDENTINE CATHOLIC CHURCH
Box 26414
San Francisco, CA 94126

The Ancient Tridentine Catholic Church was founded in 1983 by the Most Rev. Thadeus B. J. Alioto as a contemporary Catholic community adhering to those rites and the liturgies of the Roman Catholic Church in universal use prior to Vatican II. It uses both the Tridentine Latin Liturgy and the Dominican Rite Liturgy. It is at one in faith and practice with the Roman Catholic Church. It acknowledges the bishop of Rome (the Pope) as the Vicar of Christ. It subscribes to the Seven Ecumenical Councils and the essence of Vatican I and II.

The church traces its apostolic succession through His Beatitude Mar David I (Wallace de Ortega Maxey). Mar David I consecrated Alioto on Pentecost Sunday in May 1983. Mar David I was himself consecrated in 1927 by William Montgomery Brown (of the Old Catholic Church in America), assisted by Bishops George Augustus Newmark (of the American Old Catholic Church in Louisiana) and Edwin Wallace Hunter (of the North American Old Roman Catholic Church). At the invitation of Mar Georgius (Hugh George de Willmott Newman), leader of the Catholicate of the West, Mar David went to England in 1946 and exchanged orders with a number of prelates. In that conference, Mar Georgius named Mar David I as the Supreme Hierarch of the Catholicate of the Americas. Upon the consecration of Alioto, Mar David I entered a semiretired state. In 1985 he conferred the title of archbishop and the pallium (symbol of office) upon Alioto and assumed the title of archbishop emeritus of the Ancient Tridentine Catholic Church.

Integral to the church is the Order of the Holy Spirit headed by Mar Ignatius Mack, its bishop. Mar Ignatius was consecrated by Alioto in 1987. Previously Mar Ignatius had been consecrated archimandrite by Archbishop Herman Adrian Spruit of the Church of Antioch. In 1985, at the same time that Mar David elevated Alioto to the archbishopric, he laid hands on Mar Ignatius and passed the Eastern lineage of Ulric Vernon Herford received through Mar Georgius. The

Order of the Holy Spirit follows the ancient Syro-Chaldean liturgy in its rites and sacraments. The church holds intercommunion with the Tridentine Catholic Church and the Traditional Roman Catholic Church in the Americas.

Membership: In 1988 the church reported about 120 families in its seven active parishes in San Francisco, Daly City, Yuba City, and Monterey, California; Silver Cliff, Colorado; and Merida, Mexico. The church is served by nine priests.

Remarks: Mar David I's career has carried him through a variety of ecclesiastical organizations and positions. In 1951 he resigned his position with the Catholicate of the West and joined the Universalist Church. In 1970 (at a time when the Catholicate had no American parishes or priests in the United States) he resumed his episcopal role and consecrated Alan S. Stanford, with whom he founded the Catholic Christian Church. A few years later, however, he disassociated himself from Stanford.

★7★
APOSTOLIC EPISCOPAL CHURCH
℅ Mt. Rev. Paul Schultz
Box 6
Glendale, CA 91209

Alternate address: International headquarters: ℅ Archbishop Bertil Persson, P. O. Box 7048, S-17107 Solna, Sweden.

The Apostolic Episcopal Church grew out of a missionary movement by a group of American churchmen in the State of New York to provide spiritual ministrations for the scattered adherents of the Near Eastern churches. The movement began in 1922, but it was not until 1924 that a group succeeded in forming the Anglican Universal Church of Christ in the United States of America (Chaldean). Canonical authority for the new body came through the leadership of Mar Antoine Lefberne, who had been consecrated in 1917 by Maran Mar Yosif Emmanuel II Thomas, patriarch of the Chaldean Catholic Church. Serving with him were two other bishops also consecrated by the Chaldean patriarch, Mar James (Fernand Portal) and Mar Evodius (E. R. Smith).

In 1925, Mar Antoine, assisted by Mar James and Mar Evodius, consecrated Arthur Wolfort Brooks (1888-1948) who took the ecclesiastical name, Mar John Emmanuel. Brooks had left the Protestant Episcopal Church in 1926 and served in the Anglican Universal church for the next four years. In 1929, he was consecrated sub conditione by William Montgomery Brown of the Old Catholic Church in America. Then, in 1930, he left the Anglican Universal Church and formed his own jurisdiction, the Apostolic Episcopal Church (Holy Eastern Catholic and Apostolic Orthodox Church).

The new church spread by absorbing other independent missionary congregations such as the black congregation in Manhatten headed by the Rev. John Chrysostom More-Moreno. As the church grew, other bishops were added. In 1934, Brooks consecrated Harold F. A. Jarvis and Charles W. Keller. In 1946, he elevated W. D. de Ortega Maxey (Mar David I)to be his successor as archbishop-primate. Later that same year, he consecrated Herman P. Abbinga.

Mar David I succeeded Brooks in 1984, but three years later resigned and did not function as a bishop for a number of years. He was succeeded by Archbishop Jarvis, who was in turn succeeded by Percy Cedarholm, who had been consecrated by Abbinga in 1953. By the time of Cedarholm's primacy in the 1970s, the church had all but ceased to exist in the United States, and Cedarholm became the primate for Europe and Asia. He was succeeded by the present Archbishop Bertil Persson in 1977. Persson, known among Old Catholic bishops as one of the most learned and scholarly of the independent jurisdiction leaders, has attempted to rebuild the Apostolic Episcopal Church in part through coalitions with other independent groups. He serves as the missionary general for Europe for both the Philippine Independent Catholic Church and the Igreja Catolica Apostolica Brazileira; the superintendent of the Caribbean Episcopal Church of the British Isles; and the chaplain of Scandinavia for the Patriarchal Order of the Holy Cross of Jerusalem of the Melkite-Greek Catholic Church under Patriarch Maximos V. Hakim.

The Apostolic Episcopal Church describes itself as an evangelic-ecumenical-ecclesiatical movement created by assembling Christians of different creeds. Under Archbishop Persson, it has entered full communion with a number of independent jurisdictions.

In 1986, Mar David I, having resumed his episcopal functions, though outside of the Apostolic Episcopal Church, led in a service of enthronement of Persson as archbishop primate of the Apostolic Episcopal church. He was assisted by Bishop Paul Schultz, currently the head of the Apostolic Episcopal Church for the United States; Bishop Ronald R. Ramm of the Ancient Christian Fellowship; Emile F. Rodriguez-Fairfield of the Mexican National Catholic Church; and four other bishops.

Membership: Not reported.

Remarks: Almost immediately after his consecration, Abbinga returned to his native Holland and established the Apostolic Episcopal Church in that country. However, On October 28, 1946, little more than a month after his original consecration, he accepted consecration from Hugh George de Willmott Newman (Mar Georgius), who had consecrated Mar David I. Over the next six years, his tendencies toward theosophy and the Liberal Catholic Church (in which he had been a priest) reasserted themselves, and he gradually drifted from the Apostolic

Episcopal church. In 1952, following his excommunication by Mar Georgius, he founded an independent jurisdiction, the Oosters Apostolisch Episcopale Kerk.

Sources: *The Divine Liturgy, Holy Eucharist.* Queens, NY: Apostolic Episcopal Church, 1943; Bertil Persson, *A Collection of Documentation on the Apostolic Succession of Joseph Rene Vilatte with Brief Annotations.* Solna, Sweden: The author, 1974; Bertil Persson and Shmouel Warda, *Aramaic Idioms of Eshoo (Jesus) Explained.* Solna Sweden: St. Ephrem's Institute, 1978.

★8★
CATHOLIC CHARISMATIC CHURCH OF CANADA
La Cite de Marie
11,141 Rte. 148, R.R. 1
Ste. Scholastique
Mirabel, PQ, Canada J0N 1S0

The Catholic Charismatic Church of Canada was founded in 1957 by the Most Rev. Andre Barbeau, the church's archbishop, also known as Patriarch Andre the First, a former Roman Catholic priest in the Diocese of Montreal. In 1968, he was consecrated by Bishop Charles Breardly of the Old Holy Catholic Church, a small British Old Catholic jurisdiction. The purpose of founding the church was "to assist the Roman Catholic Church in its mission as a supplemental rite." Since his consecration, Patriarch Andre has responded to statements in the reports of Vatican II inviting new rites and the formation of new patriachates as they are needed. The Catholic Charismatic Church is conceived as such a new venture, "a new stem, spouting out of the Church, a progressive-conservative sort of Patriarchate." Immediately after its establishment, Archbishop Barbeau petitioned the pope concerning the status of the rite.

The church follows the teachings and practices of Roman Catholicism. It observes the seven sacraments and supports the papacy in all matters. It has offered the Roman Catholic Church its new rite, one written by the patriarch, which obligates itself only to the essentials of the Catholic faith. It seeks to preserve a proper freedom. Also, limiting itself to the essentials, the church sees itself as being a ready avenue for reconciling former Catholics to the church. The rite is also charismatic, meaning that it is a mystical liturgy.

The church is headed by its archbishop. There are other bishops and a number of priests. Though there are several parishes, such as the Holy Wisdom Community in San Diego, California, most priests are worker priests and are encouraged to create household sanctuaries. As mysticism and religious experience is emphasized over scholastic endeavors, priests are not required to have the seminary education usually expected of a Roman Catholic priest. Priests are not committed to celibacy, and may marry. Individuals not wishing to assume priestly duties are invited to become part of the permanent deaconate. While the church has not accepted women priests as yet, neither has it closed the door on the possibility. The church's headquarters, La Cite de Marie (the City of Mary), established in rural Quebec, was in part inspired by *The City of God*, a mystical classic written by Mary of Agreda.

Membership: Not reported.

Remarks: Over the years, for purposes of establishing ecumenical relations, Archbishop Barbeau has received a number of reconsecrations, a common practice among independent Catholic jurisdictions. In 1973, he was consecrated by G. R. Armstrong (of unknown affiliation). In 1976, he was consecrated by Robert S. Zeiger, then of the Apostolic Catholic Church of the Americas, assisted by Gordon I. DaCosta. That same year he was consecrated by German Bishop Joseph Maria Thiesen of L'Eglise Catholique Apostolique Primitive D'Antioche et le Tradition Syro-Byzantine. In 1980 he was consecrated by Patrick K. McReynolds of the American Orthodox Catholic Church, assisted by Andre Letellier and J. Letellier.

Sources: Archbishop Andre Barbeau, *Liturgie des Saints Mysteres*. Montreal, PQ: La Cite de Marie, 1971.

★9★

CATHOLIC CHRISTIAN CHURCH
Current address not obtained for this edition.

W. D. de Ortega Maxey began his episcopal career on January 2, 1927, when he was consecrated by William Montgomery Brown, a bishop in the Old Catholic Church in America, at that time headed by Archbishop W. H. Francis Brothers. Maxey functioned in various capacities during the next two decades, including a period as general secretary of the Temple of the People, an international theosophical body headquartered in Halcyon, California. During the 1940s he became associated with the Apostolic Episcopal Church founded by Arthur Wolfort Brooks. He traveled to England at the close of World War II and was consecrated again by Hugh George de Willmott Newman and named Supreme Hierarch of the Catholicate of the Americas. Upon Maxey's return to New York, Brooks, who had previously accepted the title of hierarch of the Catholicate of the United States, reconsecrated Maxey and placed him in charge of the Apostolic Episcopal Church on the West Coast. Maxey served the two intertwined bodies and, for a period following Brooks death in 1948, he headed them. However, in 1951, he resigned his episcopal positions and joined the Universalist Church.

In 1977 Archbishop Maxey again assumed authority as an archbishop and founded the Christian Catholic Church. With the assistance of Archbishop Joachim of the Western Orthodox Church in America, he consecrated Alan S. Stanford as his co-adjutor. Stanford now heads ministries in San Francisco, California, through the church's chapel, the Holy Order of the Society of St. Jude Thaddeus, and the National Catholic Street Ministry Project. In addition

to the work in San Francisco, the church reports three mission stations. There are two bishops and three priests.

Membership: Not reported.

★10★

CATHOLIC CHURCH OF THE APOSTLES OF THE LATTER TIMES
Monastery of the Apostles
Box 308
St. Jovite, PQ, Canada J0T 2H0

The Catholic Church of the Apostles of the Latter Day emerged out of the career of Michael Collin (d. 1974), a former French priest who claimed to be the true pope of the Roman Catholic Church. He had been ordained in 1933, but two years later claimed a mystical consecration which, in fact, made him a bishop. In 1935, Collin founded the Apostles of Infinite Love, an ordered community, which received formal ecclesiastical approval. In 1950 he had a second vision in which he claimed to have received full apostolic authority directly from Christ, in a manner like that received by St. Paul. He claimed universal jurisdiction, on the same level as the bishop of Rome. In 1951 it was widely reported that Collin had been defrocked by the church. His supporters claim, however, that the action never occurred. Collin worked quietly for a number of years, but in 1960 took a more public stance by claiming to be Pope Clement XV, the true holder of the papal office. He established headquarters for his papal court at a farmhouse in Clemery, Lorraine, France, which was called *Le Petit Vatican de Marie Coredemptrice*. In 1965 he quietly received a formal consecration from an independent French bishop with Old Catholic lines, and thus formally received the apostolic succession by the laying-on-of-hands. Clement's followers were frequently referred to as the Renovated Church of Christ.

The Order of the Mother of God was one of two North American groups to accept the authority of Clement XV. It began in 1958 after its founder, Fr. Jean de la Trinite, had been told by the Blessed Virgin to build a monastery from which would come the new apostles that would provide leadership in the age to come. He established the monastery at St. Jovite, Quebec. Because of Fr. Jean's own vision of the Virgin, great attention was paid to the several prominent apparitions of her experienced by others over the previous century, and Marian piety became a dominant part of their lifestyle. The rule given by the Virgin at the apparition at La Salette, France, was adopted by the group.

Soon after Clement XV's public announcement, a priest from the monastic community was sent to observe. He confirmed Clement's legitimacy to the Canadian group, and convinced Clement of Fr. Jean's divine mission. Over the next few years Fr. Jean was ordained and consecrated to the episcopacy by Clement. Along with the French followers, the Canadian group joined the traditionalist attack upon the changes being introduced by Vatican II in the 1960s. The Order announced to North America that Peter was no longer in Rome and that papal authority had passed to Clement.

A crisis came in 1967 when Father John was attacked by Canadian Roman Catholic priests because of his association with Clement. In the midst of the controversy, on May 9, 1969, Clement named Father John his successor under the name Gregory XVII. Following Clement's death in 1974, the Canadian group broke with the French followers, who did not recognize Gregory's authority.

In belief and practice, the order follows pre-Vatican II Catholicism. It is staunch in its practice of devotion to the Blessed Virgin Mary and has a different ecclesiology built around its papal leader. They advocate the existence of a mystical church consisting of people aligned to Gregory XVII.

Membership: Followers have been reported throughout North America, though most are concentrated in Quebec.

Periodicals: *Magnificat*, Monastery of the Apostles, Box 308, St. Jovite, PQ, Canada J0T 2H0.

Remarks: There is one other movement which derives from Clement XV, the Church of St. Joseph, in Cicero, Illinois, which is not connected to the church led by Pope Greogry XVII.

Sources: Fr. Jean-Gregory de la Trinite, *Escaping the Shipwreck.* St. Jovute, PQ: Editions Magnificat, 1976; Father Jean-Gregory de la Trinite, *When Bad Faith Hides Behind the Law.* St. Jovite, PQ: Editions Magnificat, 1968; *When Prophecy Comes True.* St. Jovite PQ: Editions Magnificat, 1972; *The Eclipse of the Church.* St. Jovite, PQ: Magnificat Editions, 1971; Gregory XVII. *Universal Encyclical for Christian Unity.* St. Jovite, PQ: Editions Magnificat, 1975.

★11★

CATHOLIC LIFE CHURCH
℅ Most Rev. A. L. Mark Harding
1955 Arapahoe St., Suite 1603
Denver, CO 80202

The Catholic Life Church was founded in 1971 by the Rev. A. L. Mark Harding and the Rev. Peter A. Tonella, a former Roman Catholic priest who had married in the 1950s. Tonella first joined the Protestant Episcopal Church but soon left it to become bishop of St. Petersburg, Florida, under Bishop Peter A. Zurawetzky of the Christ Orthodox Catholic Patriarchate. The church grew quickly, ministering to Latinos in Denver, Colorado, where the church had gathered several congregations. Mark Harding, who was consecrated bishop by Tonella and Walter X. Brown of the Archdiocese of the Old Catholic Church, supported the small denomination with

funds he earned as the owner and operator of four pornographic bookstores in Denver. The church virtually disappeared when Harding, who had become its patriarch, was arrested and sentenced to prison. After his confinement ended in the fall of 1981, Harding resumed his ministry as patriarch and presiding bishop.

Membership: Not reported.

★12★

CHRIST CATHOLIC CHURCH (PRUTER)
℅ Most Rev. Karl Pruter
Box 98
Highlandville, MO 65669

Christ Catholic Church was founded by the Rev. Karl Pruter, a Congregationalist minister deeply involved in the liturgically-oriented Free Catholic Movement, a fellowship among ministers and lay people of the Congregational and Christian Churches in the 1940s. The movement did not fair well after the merger of the Congregational-Christian Churches with the Evangelical and Reformed Church to form the United Church of Christ. The subsequent splintering found leaders of the movement in different denominations. Despairing of the situation, in 1965, Pruter made a pilgrimage to Europe, where he met with many Old Catholic leaders. He returned to the United States, settled in Boston, Massachusetts, and searched for a free Catholic Church and/or bishop. Finding neither, he turned to independent Orthodox Archbishop Peter A. Zurawetzky and under his authority began a church in Boston's Back Bay area. He emphasized the contemplative life, mysticism, and an experiential faith. The growing congregation soon opened a mission in Deering, New Hampshire.

In 1967 Archbishop Peter, assisted by Archbishop Uladyslav Ryzy-Ryski of the American World Patriarchs, consecrated Fr. Pruter to the episcopacy as bishop of the Diocese of Boston. The next year, he designated the diocese as an independent communion. The two jurisdictions met in synod, and accepted the Constitution and Canons given to the new body by Archbishop Peter.

Bishop Pruter has been a most aggressive publisher and distributor of literature for the several interests which have dominated his life. St. Willibrord's Press, founded by Bishop Pruter, has become the major publisher of Old Catholic literature, and Pruter has become a major author, having written many tracts and pamphlets as well as more substantive books such as *The Teachings of the Great Mystics* and *A History of the Old Catholic Church*. He also operates Tsali Bookstore which specializes in American Indian literature and Cathedral Books which specializes in peace material.

Christ Catholic Church is Old Catholic in faith. It adheres to the Holy Scriptures, the ecumenical creeds, the seven ecumenical councils, and the Confession of Utrecht. Both lay and clergy retain the right of private judgment on matters of doctrine, but a clergyman found to be heterodox by the presiding bishop may be deprived of clerical faculties. The church uses a venacular liturgy, *"The Christ Catholic Mass,"* which follows the Old Catholic pattern. Bishop Pruter has been an energetic advocate for peace, while equally opposed to abortion.

Headquarters of the church have moved from Boston to New Hampshire to Scottsdale, Arizona, to Chicago, Illinois, to its present location in Highlandsville, Missouri, where Bishop Pruter serves as pastor for the Cathedral Church of the Prince of Peace, a small chapel described as the smallest catherdal in the world.

Membership: In 1988 Christ Catholic Church reported 1,088 members in 10 parishes served by 12 priests in the United States. There was one parish in Canada with an additional 138 members.

Periodicals: *St Willibrord Journal*, Box 98, Highlandville, MO 65669.

Remarks: As this volume goes to press, word was received that on April 17, 1988, Bishop Pruter consecrated Frederick P. Dunleavy of the Ontario Old Roman Catholic Church to the episcopacy and that the two jurisdictions have been united.

Sources: Karl Pruter and J. Gordon Melton, *The Old Catholic Sourcebook*. New York: Garland, 1983; Karl Pruter, *The Story of Christ Catholic Church*. Chicago: St. Willibrord's Press, 1981; Karl Pruter, *The Teachings of the Great Mystics*. Goffstown, NH: St. Willibrord's Press, 1969; Karl Pruter, *A History of the Old Catholic Church*. Scottsdale, AZ: St. Willibrord's Press, 1973.

★13★
CHURCH OF SAINT JOSEPH
2307 S. Laramie
Cicero, IL 60650

The Church of Saint Joseph began as an independent traditionalist Catholic parish in the 1960s by Fr. Henry Lovett, a former associate of Fr. Gommar A. DePauw, head of the Catholic Traditionalist Movement. Lovett moved to Illinois from New Jersey with the intention of creating a parish to be aligned to DePauw's efforts, but disagreements with him led to the founding of St. Joseph's as a completely independent effort. Lovett looked at several other traditionalist groups (i.e., those opposed to the innovations of Vatican II), but rejected affiliation with any. In 1970 he met John Higgins, who had recently been consecrated as a bishop by Pope Clement XV, the traditionalist French priest who claimed to be the true pope. Higgins was consecrated soon after Bishop Jean de la Trinite, head of the Order of the Mother of God and Clement's major North American supporter, had broken away from Clement's jurisdiction. Lovett invited Higgins to come to Cicero as the episcopal leader for the parish.

Higgins first heard of Michael Collin, the French papal claimant, while studying in Rome. Higgins traveled to Clemery, Lorraine, where he concluded he had discovered the secret of Fatima. In 1917 at Fatima, Portugal, three children claimed to have seen the Blessed Virgin. Among the several messages she gave was one "secret," which was supposed to be revealed in 1960. As of 1986, that secret, written down by one of the three children who saw the Virgin, is the private possession of the Vatican and has never been revealed. Speculation on its content has been a major object of speculation by Marian devotees. Higgins believed that the content of the message was that beginning in 1960, "There shall be no more conclaves for the election of the Pope." Instead, each pope will choose his successor. Pope John XXIII, it is claimed, chose Clement XV.

Higgins saw Clement as the instrument by which the Roman Catholic Church could be returned to its pre-Vatican II state. However, following Clement's death in 1974, Higgins broke with the French followers and refused to accept any of the several claimants to his position. The parish follows pre-Vatican belief and practice, except for its belief in Clement's authority.

Membership: There is but a single congregation affiliated with Bishop Higgins, with several hundred members.

Sources: Norbet Blei, "Catholics Reborn," in *Chicago Sunday Sun-Times, Midwest Magazine* (November 30, 1975).

★14★
COMMUNITY OF CATHOLIC CHURCHES
℅ Most Rev. Thomas Sargent
3 Columbia St.
Hartford, CT 06106

The Community of Catholic Churches is a small jurisdiction formed in 1971 as a result of a group of Old Catholic priests and bishops deciding to abandon the traditional Catholic hierarchical structure. They removed the purely administrative functions from their ecclesiastical offices and formed a fellowship of clergy and parishes. Priests kept their sacradotal functions and provided priestly leadership for the parishes, most of which are house churches. The groups is led by Senior Bishop Thomas Sargent and Convenor, the Most Rev. Lorraine Morgenson.

The Community generally follows Catholic doctrine and practice, but sets no particular doctrinal standard for members. It also allows the option of dual membership in other churches. It differs from other Old Catholic groups in that it had been willing to ordain both females and homosexuals to the priesthood.

Membership: In 1984 the Community of Catholic Churches claimed five churches, nine clergy, and 60 confirmed members.

★15★

CONFRATERNITY OF CHRISTIAN DOCTRINE, SAINT PIUS X
℅ Most Rev. Msgr. Hector Gonzales
10 Stagg St.
Brooklyn, NY 11206

The Confraternity of Christian doctrine, Saint Pius X, can be traced to December 8, 1958, when Fr. Hector Gonzalez formed the Puerto Rican National Catholic Church as a Spanish-speaking Old Catholic body for the Commonwealth. The original intentions and hope were to affiliate with the Polish National Catholic Church, and the new church adhered strictly to the Declaration of Utrecht of September 24, 1889, one of the definitive documents of Old Catholicism. Gonzales opened negotiations with the primate of the Polish National Catholic Church in 1959.

The PNCC withdrew from the negotiations in 1960, in part due to the presence of the Protestant Episcopal Church (with whom, at that time, it was in full communion on the island. Gonzales then turned to Eastern Orthodoxy, and in 1961 was received into the Patriarchial Exarchate of the Russian Orthodox Church in the Americas. The next year his church was registered as La Santa Iglesia Catolica Apostolica Orthodoxa de Puerto Rico, Inc., i.e.. The Holy Catholic Apostolic Church of Puerto Rico. The church for a time kept its revised tridentine ritual, with a few necessary Orthodox alterations. However, within a short time, the Orthodox liturgy was translated into Spanish and introduced into the Puerto Rican parishes. Gradually, other changes were introduced, and some members began to feel that the church had lost its identity and was being totally absorbed into Russian Orthodoxy, as its Spanish Western Rite Vicariate.

Gonzales led the fight against the Russification of the vicariate, but after the replacement cement of Archbishop John Wendland as head of the Exarchate, he found that he had lost his major support within the jurisdiction. In 1968, with his followers, Gonzales withdrew and reestablished the Western Rite Vicariate. Parishes and missions were organized in the Dominican Republic, the United States, and Brazil. In 1977, for the sake of the future of the movement, the clergy and laity together decided to seek the episcopacy for Gonzalez. As a bishop, however, strict restrictions were imposed upon him. He is allowed to perform the minor episcopal functions, especially the rite of confirmation, and in some extreme cases the ordination of men to the diaconate and priesthood. However, he is not allowed to consecrate or assist in the consecration of anyone to the epicopal office.

Gonzales received epicopal consecration from the hands of the Portuguese bishop Dom Luis Silva y Vieria. Bishop Vieria's apostolic succession comes from a dissident Roman Catholic group in Brazil (the Apostolic Church in Brazil) formerly headed by Monsignor Salomao Ferraz.

Ferraz was received as a bishop in the Archdiocese of Rio de Janeiro by order of Pope Pius XII. Pope John XXIII appointed him Auxiliary of Rio de Janeiro. Later Pope Paul VI appointed him to one of the commissions working on Vatican II. Before his reception into the Roman Catholic Church, however, he had been consecrated a bishop by Dom Carlos Duarte Costa, leader of the Catholic Apostolic Church in Brazil. In 1979, in recognition of the geographical spread of the movement, its name changed to the United Old Catholic Episcopate. The term "Old Catholic" created enormous confusion for the movement. The term was chosen to indicate its adherence to pre-Vatican II doctrine and practice, and in no way implied the group's association with the Old Catholicism that had appeared in protest of papal infallibility after Vatican I. Therefore, Msgr. Gonzalez and the jurisdiction's clergy, with the approval of the laity, moved to change the offical name to more accurately reflect its position. The episcopate became the Confraternity of Christian Doctrine with the name of its patron saint, Pope Pius X, added as a means of honoring the virtues of the late pope, known as a true defender of the faith and a champion against modernism.

The confraternity continued to use the Roman Tridentine Rite Liturgy of Pope Pius V and the revised liturgy of Pope John XXIII. It accepts the seven traditional sacraments of the Roman Catholic Church, all the councils of the church with the exception of Vatican II. It recognizes the pope as the Vicar of Christ and bishop of Rome and acknowledges the See of Rome as the center of Catholic Christianity. Since the total separation from Eastern Orthodoxy, the church demands clerical celibacy. Many of the currently active clergy were ordained in the Roman Catholic Church in the years prior to Vatican II.

Membership: In 1987, the confraternity claimed 31,000 active members scattered throughout the western hemisphere. In the United States, there were 21 priests and members of religious orders, and 38 priests and members of religious orders overseeing missions in the Dominican Republic, Puerto Rico, Venezuela, Columbia, and Brazil.

★16★

ECUMENICAL CATHOLIC DIOCESE OF AMERICA
151 Regent Place
W. Hemstead, NY 11552

In 1984 a number of former priests of the Roman Catholic Church formulated a plan for responding to the unresolved problems of Vatican II. Growing out of a number of renewal groups, the priests sought a means to implement a practical ecumenism which would bring Christians together across denominational lines; equal rights for females; a more pastoral approach to divorce and remarriage; and a role for married priests. Many of the leaders of the new movement were themselves married. The priests called for an alternative church-like organization characterized by all of the features of institutionalized catholicism, but flexible enough to respond to the major unresolved problems. Such an organization would provide a place for those not served by the Roman Catholic Church, such as married priests, former nuns, and dissatisfied Catholics who were having difficulty forming their spiritual lives.

Plans for the new diocese were implemented at a gathering in Chicago in August 1984 by representatives of four Catholic renewal groups: The Federation of Christian Ministries, Women Church Speaks, CORPUS, and Maryknoll-in-Dispersion. Prior to the gathering, Fr. Peter Brennan of West Hempstead, New York, received Old Catholic episcopal orders and was chosen the diocese's first bishop. He is assisted by Patrick J. Callahan of Yorba Linda, California.

The Ecumenical Catholic Diocese of America considers itself a progressive Roman Catholic Church attempting to move the church in a forward, rather than conservative, direction. Except for those issues which brought it into existence, the Ecumenical Catholic Diocese of America is in basic agreement with the Roman Catholic Church. It considers itself under the wider pastoral care of the pope and views the papacy as the center of Christian unity. While respecting the pope, the Ecumenical Catholic Diocese of America is jurisdictionally independent.

Membership: Not reported.

★17★
ECUMENICAL ORTHODOX CATHOLIC CHURCH-AUTOCEPHALOUS
% Most Rev. Francis J. Ryan, Primate-Apostolos
  Western Rite
Box 637, Grand Central Station
New York, NY 10017

The Ecumenical Orthodox Catholic Church-Autocephalous was formed in the 1970s by its Archbishop Francis J. Ryan. Ryan had been consecrated by Archbishop Uladyslav Ryzy-Ryski of the American World Patriarchs in 1965. It is a small jurisdiction. During the 1970s, the Secular Brothers of the Poor, currently an independent Old Catholic apostolate in Paterson, New Jersey, was an integral part of the church.

Membership: Not reported.

★18★
EVANGELICAL CATHOLIC COMMUNION
% Most Rev. Marlin Paul Bausum Ballard
Box 8484
Baltimore, MD 21234

The Evangelical Catholic Communion was formed in 1960 by Michael A. Itkin and other members of the Eucharistic Catholic Church. The new organization took its name from the group formed by Ulric Vernon Herford in

England in 1902 following his consecration by Mar Basilius of the Syro-Chaldean Church in India, Ceylon, Socotra, and Messina, a small Orthodox Church headquartered in southern India. Itkin's second consecration by Christopher Maria Stanley carried the apostolic lineage from Herford through British Archbishop Hugh George de Willmott Newman. In 1968 the Itkin-led group split. Itkin founded the Community of the Love of Christ, while the remaining members reorganized under Marlin P. B. Ballard.

The communion describes itself as an independent body of believers, catholic in faith, standing for social justice, peace, and goodwill among men. It emphasizes the love of God and neighbor; the communion of man with man; the living of a sacramental life; and the uniting of humanity into one sacramental faith. It is governed by a Holy Synod.

The several bishops and their dioceses tend to follow an independent course. Most congregations are small and led by ordained worker/priests who earn their livelihood in secular pursuits. Occupations within the helping professions are preferred.

Membership: Not reported. As a policy, the Communion does not give out statistics of membership. The Universal Christian Church, directly under Bishop Ballard has centers in Baltimore, Maryland; South Newberry, Virginia; Hartford, Connecticut; Lake Worth, Florida; Houston, Texas; Delmarra, Delaware; and the Hamptons, Long Island, New York.

★19★
EVANGELICAL ORTHODOX (CATHOLIC) CHURCH IN AMERICA (NON-PAPAL CATHOLIC)
Current address not obtained for this edition.

The Evangelical Orthodox (Catholic) Church in America (Non-Papal Catholic) was originally founded as the Protestant Orthodox Western Church in 1938 by Bishop Wilhelm Waterstraat in Santa Monica, California. When he retired in 1940 he chose as his successor Father Frederick Littler Pyman. In 1943 Pyman was consecrated bishop by Archbishop Carmel Henry Carfora, of the North American Old Roman Catholic Church (Rogers). Under Bishop Pyman the Protestant Orthodox Western Church remained an integral part of Archbishop Carfora's jurisdiction until 1948, when Pyman withdrew and changed the name of the Church to The Evangelical Orthodox (Catholic) Church in America (Non-Papal Catholic).

Bishop Pyman had hoped to create a "bridge church," and he led his small denomination in adopting ing the Leipsic Interim of 1548, a document drawn up as part of a sixteenth-century process to create reconciliation of Protestant and Catholic differences. But the twentieth century promulgation under Bishop Wilhelm Waterstraat and Bishop Pyman drew no reaction from either Protestants or Catholics.

In most respects the church adheres closely to the Old Catholic position. The church recognizes the office and authority of the Supreme Pontiff, but only Christ is considered infallible. Clerical celibacy is optional. Oral confession is not required. Both the Latin and vernacular mass is said.

Upon Bishop Pyman's retirement in the 1970s, the leadership of the church passed to Archbishop Perry R. Sills, who had been enthroned as Bishop Pyman's successor and Second Regionary Bishop on June 30, 1974. On the previous day he had been consecrated by Archbishop Pyman, and Bishops Larry L. Shaver, William Elliot Littlewood and Basil. In 1984 Sills affiliated with the Patriarchial Synod of the Orthodox Catholic Church of America, an association of independent bishops.

Membership: In the early 1980s the church reported six parishes and 10 clergy, but gave no membership figures.

Sources: *The Evangelical Orthodox (Catholic) Church.* Santa Monica, CA: Committee on Education, Regionary Diocese of the West, 1949.

★20★
FOR MY GOD AND MY COUNTRY
Necedah, WI 54646

For My God and Country is an organization which developed as a result of the visions of the Blessed Virgin Mary by Mary Ann Van Hoff (d. 1984) and the subsequent establishment of the Queen of the Holy Rosary Mediatrix of Peace Shrine, an independent Catholic shrine at Necedah, Wisconsin. Van Hoof had her first apparition of the Virgin on November 12, 1949, one year after a reported apparition in Lipa City, Philippines. Then on April 7, 1950 (Good Friday), a series of apparitions were announced by the Virgin and as promised occurred on May 28 (Pentecost), May 29, May 30, June 4 (Trinity Sunday), June 16 (Feast of the Sacred Heart), and August 15 (Feast of the Assumption). As word of the apparitions spread, crowds gathered. More than 100,000 people attended the events of August 15, 1950.

On June 24, 1950, the chancery office of the Diocese of LaCrosse (Wisconsin) released information that a study of the apparitions had been initiated. In August, Bishop John Treacy announced that preliminary reports had questioned the validity of the apparitions, and he placed a temporary ban on special religious services at Necedah. He temporarily lifted the ban for the announced event on August 15. An estimated 30,000 people attended a final apparition on October 7, at which it was claimed that the sun whirled in the sky just as at the more famous site of Marian apparitions at Fatima, Portugal in 1917. On October 18, the group that had grown around Van Hoof

published an account of the visions and announced that a shrine was to be built and completed by May 28, 1951, the anniversary of the first public apparition.

In spite of the negative appraisal by Bishop Treacy and an editorial in the Vatican's newspaper in 1951 condemning the visions, the activity at Necedah continued, and people attended the public events at which Van Hoof claimed to be conversing with the Virgin Mary. Finally, in June, 1955, Treacy issued a public statement declaring the revelations at Necedah false and prohibiting all public and private worship at the shrine. Approximately 650 pilgrims attended the August 15, 1955 (Feast of the Assumption), apparition in defiance of Treacy's ban. In September, details of the exhaustive study of the shrine (by then operating under the corporate name For My God and My Country, Inc.) were released. The report attacked Van Hoof as a former spiritualist who had never been a practicing Roman Catholic. While the report of the diocese lessened support, worship at the shrine continued, and efforts were made to have a second study conducted. Finally, in 1969, Bishop F. W. Freking, Treacy's successor as bishop of LaCrosse, agreed to reexamine the case. For a time during the study, the shrine was closed to visitors. In 1970 the commission again produced a negative report, and in June 1972, Freking warned the corporation officers to cease activities or face church sanctions. Such sanctions were invoked in May 1975, when seven people were put under an interdict. In spite of the interdict, the work at the shrine has continued although there were several problems in the intervening years. In 1979, leaders of the shrine affiliated it with the small independent North American Old Catholic Church, Ultrajectine Tradition. In the wake of the resignation of the bishops and priests of that church, it dissolved (see Remarks). Then on May 18, 1984, Mary Ann Van Hoof died. In spite of these setbacks, the group that has developed around the shrine, many of whose members had moved immediate area, have continued to pursue the program initiated under the direction of the visions. In line with a strong anti-abortion polemic, the Seven Sorrows of Our Sorrowful Mother Infant's Home has been opened to assist unwed mothers and unwanted children. The construction of the St. Francis Home for Unfortunate Men has also continued.

Membership: As of 1988 there were more than 300 people affiliated with For My God and Country residing in the Necedah area, with several thousand supporters scattered around North America.

Periodicals: *Shrine Newsletter*, ℅ For My God and My Country, Necedah, WI 54646.

Remarks: For several years the shrine was affiliated with the now defunct North American Old Roman Catholic Church, Ultrajectine Tradition. That affiliation was formally acknowledged in May 1979, with the presentation to the shrine's supporters of Old Catholic Bishop Edward Michael Stehlik as archbishop and metropolitan of the church. On May 28, 1979, Stehlik dedicated the shrine, 29 years after the first public apparition. The church was at one in doctrine with the Roman Catholic Church, except in its rejection of the authority of the papal office. Stehlik has been consecrated by Bishop Julius Massey of Plainfield, Illinois, pastor of an independent Episcopal Church. Massey had been consecrated by Denver Scott Swain of the American Episcopal Church.

The North American Old Catholic Church, Ultrajectine Tradition faced one crisis after another. During 1980 Stehlik and the priests he brought around him came under heavy attack in the press for falsifying their credentials. Stehlik's assistant, Bishop David E. Shotts, formerly of the Independent Ecumenical Catholic Church, was arrested for violation of parole from an earlier conviction of child molestation. Then in January 1981, Stehlik quit the church, denounced the apparitions as a hoax, and returned to the Roman Catholic Church. He was succeeded by Francis diBenedetto, whom he had consecrated. However, on May 29, 1983, diBenedetto, in the midst of a service at the shrine, announced his resignation, further labeled the shrine a hoax, and returned to the Roman Catholic Church. In the wake of diBenedetto's leaving, a large number of adherents also quit and returned to communion with the Roman Catholic Church.

Sources: Henry H. Swan, *My Work at Necedah*. 4 Vols. Necedah, WI: For My God and My Country, 1959; Mary Ann Van Hoof, *The Passion and Death of Our Lord Jesus Christ*. Necedah, WI: For My God and My Country, 1975; Mary Ann Van Hoof, *Revelations and Messages*. 2 Vols. Necedah, WI: For My God and My Country, 1971, 1978.

★21★
HOLY PALMARIAN CHURCH
Current address not obtained for this edition.

The Holy Palmarian Church began when apparitions of the Blessed Virgin Mary were claimed to have been experienced by Clemente Dominguez Gomez (b. 1946) of Palmar de Troya, Spain. Gomez began seeing the Virgin and having accompanying prophetic visions in 1968. The content of these visions, which included predictions of a number of cataclismic events (schism in the Catholic Church following the death of Pope Paul VI and a Communist revolution in Spain after the death of General Francisco Franco), were circulated internationally soon after they began. In 1970 the Roman Catholic Archbishop of Seville denounced them as lacking any validity. During the 1970s, the messages were circulated in the United States and trips to America were sponsored by St. Paul's Guild in Orwell, Vermont, and the Mount Carmel Center in Santa Rosa, California, though neither center was ever given formal status in the Holy Palmarian Church.

Other claims of Marian apparitions contemporaneous to those at Palmar de Troya took a decided traditionalist stance against the innovations introduced by Vatican II. In the face of continued rebuff by the Catholic hierarchy, Gomez's followers formed the Carmelite Order of the Holy Face. Gomez came into contact with retired Vietnamese Archbishop Pierre Martin Ngo-Dinh-Thuc, formerly archbishop of Hue. Thuc was also a traditionalist, then living in Italy. On December 31, 1975, Thuc traveled to Spain and ordained Gomez and four of his associates. On January 11, 1976, he consecrated Gomez, one of the other recently ordained priests, and three additional priests from other dio ceses to the episcopacy. During 1976 Gomez and his associated bishops ordained and consecrated other priests and bishops. In September 1976, Thuc, Gomez, and all the affiliated priests and bishops were formally suspended from performing their priestly offices and excommunicated. Almost immediately Thuc repented his action, and the excommunication (though not the suspension) was lifted.

After the death of Pope Paul VI in 1978, Gomez was declared the new pope by his supporters and took the name Pope Gregory XVII. By this time the Palmarian Church had spread throughout the Roman Catholic world, particularly in the Spanish-speaking part.

Membership: Not reported.

★22★
INDEPENDENT ECUMENICAL CATHOLIC CHURCH (SHOTTS)
(Defunct)

The Independent Ecumenical Catholic Church was formed in 1976 by Rev. John Michael Becket, a former Universalist minister, and Bishop David E. Shotts. Fr. Becket was placed in charge of Saint Jude Abbey and the Brothers of the Sacred Rosary. However, the year after its founding, Fr. Becket left the church and placed himself under the Ecumenical Catholic Communion headed by M. P. B. Ballard.

The church followed the Tridentine Roman Catholic liturgy, but used the English translation of 1951. Its doctrine was Catholic, all seven sacraments were served. No excommunication was recognized. Flowing from its commitment to ecumenicity, members of a variety of Christian groups, including some Protestant churches, were allowed to take communion.

Membership: In 1977 the Church reported four churches, 200 members, and eight ordained clergy. However, in 1979 Shotts, who had been charged in a child molestation case, also abandoned the church and placed himself under Archbishop Edward Stelik of the North American Old Catholic Church, Ultrajectine Tradition, headquartered in Necedah, Wisconsin. The Independent Ecumenical Catholic Church is presumed to have dissolved.

INDEPENDENT OLD ROMAN CATHOLIC HUNGARIAN ORTHODOX CHURCH OF AMERICA

% Most Rev. Archbishop Edward C. Payne, Catholicos-Metropolitan
Box 261
Weatherfield, CT 06109

The Independent Old Roman Catholic Hungarian Orthodox Church of America was founded in 1970 as the Independent Catholic Church by Bishop Edward C. Payne. Payne was consecrated in 1969 by Archbishop Hubert A. Rogers of the North American Old Roman Catholic Church (Rogers). Originally, he rejected the liturgy used by the N.A.O.R.C.C. and decreed that the Anglican Rite be used by his congregations as it most nearly corresponded to the Scriptural norm of St. Paul's First Letter to the Corinthians.

Soon after the establishment of the Independent Catholic Church, Payne was attracted to Eastern Orthodoxy. He met Archbishop Peter A. Zurawetsky, who was in communion with Payne's consecrator, and through Zurawetsky he met Archbishop Uladslau Ryzy-Ryski, who had been constructing the American World Patriarchs. It was Ryzy-Ryski's goal to establish an international association of ethnic Orthodox jurisdictions by appointing archbishops over each national group. In 1972, he elevated Payne to be archbishop of New England, in a diocese affiliated with the American World Patriarchs. Three years later he elevated Payne to be metropolitan of Urgo-Finnic Peoples and patriarch of the Orthodox Catholic Autocephalous Church in Dispersion.

At that time, Payne, who was Hungarian by birth, had about 20 Hungarian families in his Connecticut congregation, and other families in his archdiocese in Pennsylvania and Florida. During the intervening years, Payne has asserted the Hungarian roots of the church, both through the orders that can be traced through the N. A. O. R. C. C. to the Austro-Hungarian Archbishop, the Duc de Landas Berghes, and the role assigned by Ryzy-Ryski. This heritage led to adoption of the jurisdiction's present name in 1984.

The church is Old Catholic in doctrine and practice and accepts the Declaration of Utrecht. It rejects papal infallibility as well as the universal pastorship of the pope. It also rejects the recent doctrinal statements on the Immaculate Conception and Bodily Assumption of the Virgin Mary. Open communion is practiced. No ordination of homosexuals is allowed.

Membership: In 1988 the Church reported eight congregations, 13 clergy and approximately 300 members in the United States and the congregations and more than 100 members in Canada.

Educational facilities: Independent Catholic Seminarium, Hartford, Connecticut.

Periodicals: *The Independent Catholic*, 171 Colby, Hartford, CT 06106.

LATIN-RITE CATHOLIC CHURCH

Box 16194
Rochester, NY 14616

The Latin-Rite Catholic Church is the American branch of the church aligned to Archbishop Pierre Martin Ngo-Dinh-Thuc, the traditionalist leader of an international Roman Catholic movement which rejects the authority of the current pope, John Paul II. Thuc was formerly archbishop of Hue, Viet Nam, who retired to Italy during the papacy of Pope Paul VI and the sessions of Vatican II. He was strongly opposed to the innovations introduced by the church council and in December 1975 ordained a group of men associated with the claimed apparitions of the Blessed Virgin Mary at Palmar de Troya. The following month he consecrated five priests to the episcopacy. Thuc, and all those whom he consecrated, were suspended from exercising their office and excommunicated by the papacy. Thuc repented, and his excommunication was lifted. However, Thuc's suspension from his bishop's office was not lifted. The other bishops and priests did not recant their actions but went on to form the Holy Palmarian Church.

Thuc remained in retirement until April 1981, when he again exercised his office of bishop by consecrating George J. Musey, head of the Servants of the Sacred Heart of Jesus and Mary, Friendwood, Texas. In October 1981, Thuc secretly consecrated two traditionalist priests from Mexico, Moises Carmona and Adolfo Zamora. Formerly supporters of traditionalist Archbishop Marcel Lefebvre, they rejected his leadership when reports surfaced of negotiations with the Vatican. After their consecration, Carmona and Zamora established the Union Catolica Trento (Tridentine Catholic Union), referring to the allegiance to the canons of the Council of Trent prior to Vatican II. In May 1982, he consecrated Fr. Gerard des Lauriers (s. 1988), a former supporter of Lefevre, who in turn consecrated Gunther Storch of Munich, Germany (1985); Robert McKenna of Connecticut (1986); and Franco Munari of Italy (1987).

Soon after the establishment of the church in Mexico, Thuc's lineage was further extended in the United States with the consecration of Louis Vezelis, head of the Order of St. Francis of Assisi in Rochester, New York. Vezelis was consecrated in 1982 by Carmona, assisted by Zamora and Musey. Soon after Vezelis' consecration, the Latin-Rite Church founded at Coeur d'Alene, Idaho, by Archbishop Francis K. Schuckardt had been consecrated in 1971 by traditionalist Bishop Daniel Q. Brown. Schuckardt believed and taught that Pope John XXIII was neither a true nor false pope, but an interim pope, but he believed John XXIII's successors (Paul VI, John Paul I, John Paul II) to be false popes. This position was based on an underlying premise that the Vatican had been taken over by Freemasons who had murdered Pius XII in order to complete their infiltration of the Curia. John Paul II was seen to be an instrument of the Freemasons. By introducing the New Mass and the false pope, the Roman Catholic church had moved into apostasy. Schuckhardt and seven people broke with the Roman Catholic church in 1968 and began a new organization promoting traditionalist life and values. Within a short time the Tridentine Latin-Rite Church had grown to more than 800 members, and by 1980 there were approximatly 3,000. Schuckhardt established the Congregation of the Mary Immaculate Queen, "and through it the Our Lady of Fatima Cell Movement," the prime structure through which it reached out to traditionalist Roman Catholics around the United States. In 1978 the congregation bought Mount Saint Michael, a former Jesuit center in Spokane, which became its main headquarters. The 350-acre tract now houses the congregation, a seminary, the cell movement, two parochial schools, and several related organizations. The movement encountered stiff opposition from the Roman Catholic church in the Northwest, which officially condemned the group. Former members accused it of cult-like practices and filed lawsuits, one of which resulted in a substantial judgment against the group. However, in 1984, Schuckhardt split with the remaining leadershp of the Tridentine Latin-Rite Catholic Church and he, with a small number of followers, left. The Tridentine Latin-Rite Church then came under the episcopal authority of Bishop Musey.

Meanwhile, the Orthodox Roman Catholic Church Movement, founded by Fr. Francis E. Fenton and led through the early 1980s by Fr. Robert McKenna, had developed some irreconcilable differences with McKenna who was moving into the influence of the movement developing around Thuc. After his consecration in 1986, the ORCM dissolved and McKenna took those who were willing into the Latin Rite Catholic church. In 1987, McKenna consecrated two other bishops, J. Vida Elmer of New York and Richard Bedingfeld, British-born leader of a traditionalist movement among the Zulus of South Africa. Musey consecrated Conrad Altenbach (d. 1986) of Milwaukee, Wisconsin, in 1984 and in 1987 consecrated a French priest, Michael Main, head of an Augustinian order in Thiviers, France.

Membership: Not reported. In 1986 centers were to be found in most states of the union, Canada, and New Zealand.

Educational facilities: Mount St. Michael Seminary, Spokane, Washington.

Periodicals: *The Seraph*, ℅ Order of St. Francis of Assisi, Box 16194, Rochester, NY 14616; *The Reign of Mary*, North 8500 St. Michael's Road, Spokane, WA 99207; *Salve Regina*, Box 40025, Spokane, WA 99202.

★25★
MARIAVITE OLD CATHOLIC CHURCH, PROVINCE OF NORTH AMERICA
℅ His Eminence, Most Rev. Robert R. J. M. Zaborowski
2803 10th St.
Wyandotte, MI 48192

The Mariavite Old Catholic Church was incorporated in 1972 as the American Orthodox Catholic Church (changed in 1973 to the Archdiocese of the Old Catholic Church in America and Canada). It assumed its present name in 1974. The founder of the church is the Robert R. J. M. Zaborowski who claims apostolic lineage from the Mariavite Old Catholic Church headquartered at Plock, Poland.

The Mariavite Movement can be traced to the mid-nineteenth century in Poland and the founding of a variety of new monastic communities within the Roman Catholic Church which stressed the inner life and spirituality. Among these was a sister house opened in 1883 at Plock, by Feliksa Magdalena Kozlowska (1862-1921), known more popularly by her religious name, Mother Maria Francis. The new community followed the second rule of the Franciscans (originally written for the Sisters of St. Clare) to which was added a particular devotion to the Most Blessed Sacrament exposed to view in the monstrance, a form of devotion attributed to the Virgin Mary during her life at Nazareth. The name Mariavite derives from the Latin words meaning "Mary's life."

Mother Maria Francis was also a visionary, and her visions received a considerable amount of publicity. As a result the community at Plock grew into a movement throughout Poland which included both men and women and attracted a number of priests. It's spread also attracted the attention of church authorities who began to attack both the visions of Mother Maria Francis and the appropriateness of such a movement being led by a female. The appointment of Fr. John Michael Kowalski to the position of Minister General of the Congregation of Mariavite Priests in 1903 did little to ease the tension. In 1904 the church demanded the disbanding of the Order which was followed in 1906 by the excommunication of Kowalski and Mother Maria Francis. While most of their former following disavowed their relationship with them, the pair decided to continue their movement. They formed the independent Mariavite Catholic Church. Kowalski traveled to Holland and in 1909 was consecrated to the episcopate by Archbishop Gerard Gul of the Old Catholic Church. The church was renamed the Mariavite Old Catholic Church. Following the death of Mother Maria Francis, Bishop Kowalski assumed full leadership of the church. During his reign a number of controversial practices were introduced including a married priesthood and the ordination of females to the priesthood. Also the Latin mass was rendered into Polish. The new practices were largely opposed by both the church's membership and leadership, and several schisms occurred. In 1923 one group led by four priests left the church and founded the Old Catholic Church in Poland. A few years later a second group founded the Old Catholic Church of Poland. Finally, in 1935, the several bishops under Kowalski separated themselves and took control of the Mariavite Old Catholic Church. (Kowalski then moved with his following to the town of Felicianow and reorganized as the Mariavite Catholic Church.)

As a former Roman Catholic who had affiliated with the Old Catholic movement, Zaborowski became acquainted with the Old Catholic Church of Poland and was ordained by one one of its episcopal leaders, Archbishop Joseph Anthony Mazur. At the time of his ordination he also became acquainted with Archbishop Francis Ignatius Boryszewski of the Polish Catholic Church, an independent jurisdiction headquartered in Jersey City, New Jersey. In 1972, assisted by some French bishops with Mariavite orders, Boryszewski (who also possessed Mariavite orders) consecrated Zaborowski. Upon the death of Archbishop Mazur later that year, Zaborowski succeeded to the role of archbishop and the following year changed the name of the jurisdiction to reflect its Mariavite heritage.

The Mariavite Old Catholic Church follows the orthodox theological heritage of the Mariavite Old Catholic Church of Plock. It accepts the early creeds of the undivided Catholic Church, but considers the statement of papal infallibility erroneous and the recent pronouncement of the dogmas of the Immaculate Conception and the Assumption of the Virgin Mary as invalid. It recognizes the seven sacraments. Auricular confession is optional. Special devotion is paid to the the Lord Jesus Christ as present in the Blessed Sacrament and members are obliged to render such devotion a minimum of one hour per week plus a hour per month in a congregational gathering. Special devotion to Mary as Our Lady of Perpetual Help is also practiced. The church is headed by its prime bishop (Archbishop Zaborowski) and the council. The council is selected by the General Chapter of the Church (composed of all bishops and clergy). All clergy belong to the Religious Order of St. Francis of Assisi. However, they do no live together in a monastery. Rather they serve as parish priests and missionaries. Clergy, who follow the first and third Rule of St. Francis, are assisted by lay brothers who adhere to only the third Rule and sisters who follow the Rule of St. Clare.

Membership: The Mariavite Old Catholic Church has reported a spectacular rate of growth. From its modest beginnings (it reported only 487 members, in eight centers and 32 clergy in 1972), it claimed, by 1980, to have 301,009 members in 117 churches served by 25 clergy in the United States. An additional 48,990 members were claimed for the 58 churches in Canada and several hundred members were claimed for churches in France and West Germany. By 1984, the church claimed 358,503 members, 48 clergy, and 157 parishes in the United States as well as an additional 29,350 members in two congregations in Paris, France and West Germany.

Educational facilities: The Mariavite Academy of Theological Studies, 2803 Tenth Street, Wyandotte, MI 48192-4994.

Periodicals: *The Mariavita Monthly*, 2803 Tenth Street, Wyandotte, Michigan 48192-4994.

Remarks: A number of factors have raised doubt about the accuracy of the facts and figures reported by the Mariavite Old Catholic Church. In spite of its reported growth from 1972 to 1975, observers have been unable to locate any of the congregations affiliated with the church except the small chapel in Archbishop Zaborowski's residence in Wyandotte, Michigan. Zaborowski has consistently refused to share with inquirers the names and address of any of the claimed parishes or their priests. Doubts have also been raised about Archbishop Zaborowski's ordination and consecration. During the early 1970s he circulated copies of his ordination (1968) and consecration (1972) certificates. They bore the names of Bishop Francis Mazur and Ambrose as prime officiants, and they were on forms bearing the title "Antiqua Ecclesia Romanae Catholicae" (i.e. "Old Roman Catholic Church"). It was supposed by observers (and claimed by Zaborowski) that he had been ordained by the same Bishop Francis Mazur who had been consecrated by Archbishop Carmel Henry Carfora of the North American Old Roman Catholic Church. More recently, Zaborowski has circulated a different set of certificates bearing the title of the Mariavite Old Catholic Church, Province of North America (a name not used until two years after his consecration) and bearing signatures of Archbishop (not bishop) Francis A. Mazur and Archbishop Francis Ignatius Boryszewski as prime officiants. The signatures on the two ordination certificates do not resemble each other in the least. (Archbishop Zaborowski had claimed that he himself had confused the Bishop Mazur consecrated by Carfora and Archbishop Mazur of the Old Catholic Church of Poland.) The earlier ordination certificate also carries no signatures of any other bishops who might have assisted in the ordination. In like measure, Zaborowski claims that Archbishop Boryszewski wished his role in the consecration service suppressed until his death, and hence it was not revealed until 1975. However, the signatures of those bishops whose names appear on both consecration certificates vary in great detail. It should also be noted that even a third ordination certificate exists which claims that Zaborowski was ordained in 1965 by a Roman Catholic bishop, the Most Rev. G. Krajenski (living in exile) and signed by the Most Rev. Cardinal Wojtyla, Ordinary of the Diocese of Kracow. Neither exist on any registry of Roman Catholic bishops.

Sources: Jerzy Peterkiewicz, *The Third Adam*. London: Oxford University Press, 1975; Robert R. R. Zaborowski, *What Is Mariavitism?* Wyandotte, MI: Ostensoria Publications, 1977; Robert R. Zaborowski, *Catechism*. Wyandotte, MI: Ostensia Publications, 1975; Robert R. Zaborowski, *The Sacred Liturgy*. Wyandotte, MI: Ostensoria Publications, 1975.

★26★
MEXICAN NATIONAL CATHOLIC CHURCH
% Rt. Rev. Emile F. Rodriguez-Fairfield
4011 E. Brooklyn Ave.
East Los Angeles, CA 90022

During the presidency of General Plutarco E. Callas (1924-28), Mexico put into effect provisions of the 1917 Constitution aimed at curbing the political power of the Roman Catholic Church. With Callas' tacit consent, a rival Mexican-controlled Catholic body free from any connection to foreign interests was formed. The leaders turned to Archbishop Carmel Henry Carfora of the North American Old Roman Catholic Church (Rogers) for episcopal orders. On October 17, 1926, Carfora consecrated successively Jose Joaquin Perez y Budar, Antonio Benicio Lopez Sierra, and Macario Lopez y Valdez. Perez y Budar became primate and patriarch.

Before returning to Mexico, Bishop Lopez y Valdez visited his family in Los Angeles, California, and contacted a Bishop Roberto T. Gonzalez, pastor of El Hogar de la Verdad, an independent spiritualist church operating within the Mexican community in East Los Angeles. Lopez developed a friendly relationship with Gonzalez. Gonzalez died in 1928, and two years later, Lopez consecrated Gonzalez's successor, Alberto Luis Rodriguez Y Durand. By this act the Mexican National Catholic church was able to extend its territory into Southern California. El Hogar de la Verdad gradually became known as the Old Catholic Orthodox Church of St. Augustine of the Mystical Body of Christ.

Over the next decades, as church-state relations improved in Mexico, the National Church, which by 1928 had claimed 120 priests and parishes in 14 Mexican states, began to dissolve. The largest remnant united with the Orthodox Church in America and became its Mexican Exarchate in 1972. Its bishop, Jose Cortes y Olmas was named exarch. The Los Angeles parish survived as the single American outpost of the church. In 1955, Bishop Rodriguez, being in poor health, consecrated Emelio Federico Rodriguez y Fairfield as his successor.

In 1962, Fairfield decided to affiliate with the Canonical Old Roman Catholic Church, the American branch of the Old Roman Catholic Church headed by British Archbiship Gerard George Shelley. Following Shelley's death, Fairfield joined Bishop John J. Humphreys in consecrating a new archbishop in 1982. When Shelley's successor, Michael Farrell, resigned a month after his consecration, Fairfield emerged as the senior bishop of the church. Then in 1983, with the death of Jose Cortes y Olmas, Fairfield became the sole possessor of episcopal orders from the Mexican National Catholic Church. On September 13, 1983, he was installed as archbishop-primate of the Iglesia Ortodoxa Catolica Apostolica Mexicana.

Membership: Only one parish, in East Los Angeles, California, of the Mexican National Catholic Church remains. It has less than 100 members.

Sources: Paul Schultz, *A History of the Apostolic Succession of Archbishop Emile F. Rodriguez-Fairfield from the Mexican National Catholic Church, Iglesia Ortodoxa Catolica Apostolica Mexicana*. Glendale, CA: The Author, 1983.

★27★
NORTH AMERICAN OLD ROMAN CATHOLIC CHURCH (ROGERS)
% Most Rev. Archbishop James H. Rogers
118-09 Farmers Blvd.
St. Albans, NY 11412

The North American Old Roman Catholic Church (Rogers) dates to October 4, 1916, when the Duc de Landas Berghes, in the United States to escape confinement in England during World War I, consecrated the Rev. Carmel Henry Carfora at Waukegan, Illinois. The Italian-born Carfora had come to the United States to do Roman Catholic mission work among the immigrants in West Virginia, but by 1911 had broken with Rome. In 1912 he sought consecration from Bishop Paulo Miragalia Gulotti, who had been consecrated by Archbishop Joseph Rene Vilatte, and proceeded to form several independent Old Catholic parishes. After his second consecration, he broke with Bishop W. H. Francis Brothers, also consecrated by Landes Berghes, settled in Chicago, Illinois, and began to organize his own jurisdiction, which he named the North American Old Roman Catholic Church. (Brothers organized the Old Catholic Church in America.) During his lengthy life, Carfora was able to build a substantial church which may have had as many as 50,000 members. He absorbed numerous independent parishes, many of an ethnic nature. He also consecrated numerous bishops (at least 30) most of whom left him to found their own jurisdictions, both in the United States and in foreign lands. In the mid 1920s a shortlived union with the American Catholic Church was attempted under the name The Holy Catholic Church in America.

Even before Carfora's death in 1958 the North American Old Roman Catholic Church began to collapse, and remnants of what was once a growing ecclesiastical unit now exist as several small jurisdictions. Most have simply disappeared. Splintering began with Samuel Durlin Benedict, who left Carfora a few years after his 1921 consecration to found the Evangelical Catholic Church of New York, a small group that did not survive his death in 1945. In 1924 Carfora consecrated Edwin Wallace Hunter, who in 1929 assumed the title of archbishop of the Holy Catholic Church of the Apostles in the Diocese of Louisiana. This church also died with its founder in 1942. In 1931 Carfora consecrated James Christian Crummey, who, with Carfora's blessing, founded the Universal Episcopal Communion, an ecumenical organization that attempted to unite various Christian bodies (with little success). Crummey broke relations in 1944 and died five years later. The Communion did not continue into the 1950s. This pattern continued throughout Carfora's lifetime. More then 20 jurisdictions trace their lineage to Carfora.

The pattern of Carfora's consecrating priests beyond any ecclesiastical substance to support them, followed by their leaving and taking their meager diocese to create an independent jurisdiction, continued throughout Carfora's life. The major loss of strength by Carfora's N.A.O.R.C.C., however, came in 1952 when 30 parishes under Bishop Michael Donahue, moved, with Carfora's blessing, into the Ukrainian Orthodox Church. Donohue was received as a mitered archpriest.

Carfora was succeeded as head of the North American Old Roman Catholic Church by Cyrus A. Starkey, his coadjutor, but before the year was out, the synod met and set aside Starkey's succession. It elected Hubert A. Rogers (1887-1976) who had served for five years as coadjutor but had been deposed by Carfora just a few months before his death. Rogers, while proving a most capable leader, was a West Indian. Most of the nonblack priests and members refused to accept his position and withdrew. This final splintering of the church left it predominantly black in membership, which it remains. H. A. Rogers was succeeded by his son James Hubert Rogers, the present archbishop.

The N. A. O. R. C. C. advocates a faith in complete agreement with pre-Vatican I Roman Catholicism: "The Old Roman Catholic Church has always used the same ritual and liturgy as the early Church practiced, abiding by the same doctrines and dogmas; following the exact teaching given by the Apostles of Christ, and continuing through valid historical succession down to the present time." In one point it follows Old Catholic rather than Roman Catholic practice: Carfora married, and a married priesthood is allowed at all levels in the N.A.O.R.C.C. The practice has been passed on to those churches that derived from it.

Membership: In 1965 the Church reported 30 parishes, 18,500 members, and 112 clergy. However, by 1985 it could report only four parishes, 470 members, and 16 priests.

Periodicals: *The Augustinian*, Box 1647, G.P.O., Brooklyn, NY 11202.

Sources: Jonathan Trela, *A History of the North American Old Roman Catholic Church.* Scranton, PA: The Author, 1979.

★28★
NORTH AMERICAN OLD ROMAN CATHOLIC CHURCH (SCHWEIKERT)
4200 N. Kedvale
Chicago, IL 60641

The North American Old Roman Catholic Church (Schweikert) is one of several Old Catholic jurisdictions which claims to the legitimate successor to the North American Old Roman Catholic Church formed by Archbishop Carmel Henry Carfora. Archbishop John E. Schweikert (d. 1988) based his claim upon his consecration by Bishop Sigismund Vipartes a Lithuanian bishop who had served in Westville, Illinois, under Bishop Carfora beginning in 1944.

Archbishop Carfora died in 1958 and was succeeded by Cyrus A. Starkey, his coadjutor. However, the synod of the N.A.O.R.C.C. put aside his succession in favor of Hubert A. Rogers, who had been coadjutor until a few months before Carfora passed away. Starkey left the N.A.O.R.C.C. in 1960, and Richard A. Marchenna claimed that Starkey named him as his successor (see Old Roman Catholic Church (Marchenna)). According to the records of the N.A.O.R.C.C., Schweikert was consecrated by Marchenna on June 8, 1958.

Following Starkey's death in 1965, Schweikert asserted a claim to be his successor against that of Marchenna. He also claimed that Vipartes, not Marchenna, consecrated him in 1958. Through Vipartes (consecrated by Carfora in 1944) and Starkey, Schweikert claimed to be Carfora's legitimate successor.

Headquarters for the church are in Chicago, Illinois, in a building complex that also houses a sisterhood of nuns: the Order of Our Most Blessed Lady, Queen of Peace. The sisters operate a school for retarded children. Belief and practice follow that of the North American Old Roman Catholic Church, though Bishop Schweikert discontinued the practice of an unpaid clergy and promoted a more democratic church structure. In 1962 Schweikert consecrated Robert Ritchie as bishop of the Old Catholic Church of Canada, founded in 1948 by the Rt. Rev. George Davis. The two jurisdictions remain in communion.

Membership: In 1982 the North American Old Roman Catholic Church (Schweikert) reported 130 parishes and missions, 62,383 members, and 150 clergy, figures that reflect the continuing increase in numbers reported during the last decade.

Remarks: It must be noted that during the past decade researchers have been unable to locate any parishes under Archbishop Schweikert's jurisdiction other than the single parish and affiliated mission, both in the Chicago area, over which he serves as pastor. Archbishop Schweikert consistently refused to reveal the names of any priests or the addresses of any parishes under his jurisdiction.

★29★
NORTH AMERICAN OLD ROMAN CATHOLIC CHURCH-UTRECHT SUCCESSION
% Rt. Rev. E. R. Verostek
3519 Roosevelt Ave.
Richmond, CA 94805

The North American Old Roman Catholic Church-Utrecht succession dates to 1936 when Bishop A. D. Bell, who had been consecrated in 1935 by Archbishop W. H. Francis Brothers of the Old Catholic Church in America, accepted reconsecration from Archbishop Carmel Henry Carfora of the North American Old Roman Catholic Church. In 1938 Bell consecrated E. R. Verostek who succeeded Bell. Then in 1943 Carfora commissioned Elsie Armstrong Smith (d. 1983) as Abbess of a new order, the Missionary Sister of St. Francis. As an independent order the sisters have conducted a ministry of visiting the sick, offering intercessory prayers and service to the Church--making vestments and publishing pamphlets and prayerbooks. Over the years the congregations under their leadership separated from the main body of the North American Old Roman Catholic Church, though it continues to follow its lead in theology and practice. The Missionary Sisters are headquartered in Mira Loma, California, where they maintain a chapel.

Membership: In the early 1980s, the church reported six parishes with less than 200 members.

★30★
OLD CATHOLIC CHURCH IN AMERICA (BROTHERS)
% Metropolitan Hilarion
1905 S. Third St.
Austin, TX 78704

The Old Catholic Church in America is one of the oldest independent Catholic bodies in the United States, founded in 1917 by W. H. Francis Brothers (1887-1979). Brothers, prior of a small abbey under the patronage of the Protestant Episcopal Church, began to move under the umbrella of several independent Catholic bishops. He was ordained in 1910 by Archbishop Joseph Rene Vilatte and the next year took the abbey into the Polish Old Catholic Church headed by Bishop J. F. Tichy. Tichy resigned due to ill health, and in 1914, Brothers became bishop-elect of a miniscule body that had lost most of its members to the Polish National Catholic Church. Then Brothers met the Duc de Landas Berghes, the Austrian Old Catholic bishop, spending the war years in the United States. He consecrated Brothers and then Carmel Henry Carfora (later to found the North American Old Roman Catholic Church) on two successive days in October 1916.

Brothers broke with both Landas Berghes and Carfora, renamed the Polish Old Catholic Church, and assumed the titles of archbishop and metropolitan. He began to build his jurisdiction by appointing bishops to work within ethnic communities. He consecrated Antonio

Rodriguez (Portuguese) and attracted Bishops Stanislaus Mickiewicz (Lithuanian) and Joseph Zielonka (Polish) into the church. Most important, former Episcopal Bishop William Montgomery Brown joined his college of bishops. The church grew and prospered, and in 1927, the Episcopal Synod of the Polish Mariavite Church gave Brothers oversight of the Mariavites in the United States. In 1936, the Church reported 24 parishes and 5,470 members.

By the 1950s, the once prosperous church began to suffer from the Americanization of its ethnic parishes and the defection of its bishops. In 1962, Brothers took the remnant of his jurisdiction into the Russian Orthodox Church and accepted the title of mitred archpriest. However, five years later he withdrew from the Russian Church, and reconstituted the Old Catholic Church in America. He consecrated Joseph MacCormick and his successor. Brothers retired in 1977, and MacCormack organized the synod which administers the affairs of the church. He also began the slow process of rebuilding the jurisdiction. An important step was the acceptance of the Old Catholic Church of Texas, Inc., an independent jurisdiction formerly associated with the Liberal Catholic Church International, and its leader Robert L. Williams, Metropolitan Hilarion, into the church in 1975.

Metropolitan Hilarion serves as resident leader of Holy Name of Mary Old Catholic Church and Saint Hilarion's Monastery in Austin, Texas. The monastery has three resident members and follows the rules of Saint Benedict. The liturgical use is that of Sarum, the restored and historically accurate text which has been published along with its Gregorian music, by the monastery. The Texas church stresses Western Orthodoxy, in remembrance of Archbishop Arnold Harris Mathew's union with Antioch in 1911 and in honor of Metropolitan Hilarion's visit with Elias IV, Patriarch of Antioch, in Oklahoma City in 1977.

The Old Catholic Church in America follows the Old Catholic tradition passed to it from Bishop Mathew. It is in agreement with roman Catholicism except in its denial of dogmatic status to the doctrines of the Immaculate Conception of the Blessed Virgin Mary (as well as other more recent papal pronouncements on Mary) and papal infallibility. The Julian calender is used and kept in publication by the monastery in Texas.

In 1984, Metroploitan Hilarion consecrated Ivan Divalakov as Archbishop of Belgrade (Yugoslavia).

Membership: In 1988 the church claimed four congregations, 500 members, and 12 clergy. Affiliated congregations in Yougoslavia have approximately 2,000 members.

Sources: William H. F. Brothers, *Concerning the Old Catholic Church in America*, 1925; William H. F. Brothers, *The Old Catholic Church in America and Anglican Orders*. 1925; John LoBue, "An Appreciation,

Archbishop William Henry Francis Brothers, 1887-1979."
The Good Shepherd, 1980.

★31★

OLD CATHOLIC CHURCH IN NORTH AMERICA (CATHOLICATE OF THE WEST)

℅ Rev. Dr. Charles V. Hearn
2210 Wilshire Blvd., Suite 582
Santa Monica, CA 90403

The Old Catholic Church in North America was established in 1950 by Grant Timothy Billet and several Old Catholic bishops. Billet had been consecrated by Earl Anglin James of Archbishop Carmel Henry Carfora's North American Old Roman Catholic Church. Billet established headquarters in York, Pennsylvania, and organized the interdenominational American Ministerial Association which attracted a wide variety of clergy under its umbrella. During the 1970s, he reported a membership of the church at approximately 6,000, a highly inflated figure. Billet died in 1981. He was succeeded by the present archbishop and patriarch, Charles V. Hearn, a psychotherapist and noted counselor on alcoholism. He reorganized the church and reincorporated both it and the American Ministerial Association in California. The church generally follows Roman Catholic doctrine and practice. However, celibacy is not a requirement for the priesthood.

Membership: In 1988 the Church reported 26 churches in the United States with affiliated work in seven countries. There were 43 clergy and 188 members.

Educational facilities: Trinity Hall College & Seminary, Louisville, Kentucky and Denver, Colorado.

★32★

OLD CATHOLIC CHURCH OF CANADA

216 Tragina Ave., N.
Hamilton, ON, Canada L8H 5E1

The Old Catholic Church of Canada was founded in 1948 by the Rt. Rev. George Davis. In 1962, Davis' successor, Robert Ritchie, was consecrated by Archbishop John E. Schweikert of the North American Old Roman Catholic Church, with which the Canadian body is in communion. The church follows Old Catholic doctrine, rejecting papal infallibility and such recent additions to the Roman Catholic Church dogma as the Immaculate Conception of the Virgin Mary. An English-language translation of the Latin Rite is used in worship. Celibacy is optional for all clergy.

Membership: Not reported.

★33★

OLD CATHOLIC CHURCH-UTRECHT SUCCESSION

℅ Most Rev. Roy G. Bauer
21 Aaron St.
Melrose, MA 02176

Archbishop Roy G. Bauer was consecrated in 1976 by Bishop Armand C. Whitehead of the United Old Catholic Church and Bishop Thomas Sargent of the Community of Catholic Churches, but served as a bishop under Archbishop Richard A. Marchenna of the Old Roman Catholic Church. In 1977, he, along with Bishops John Dominic Fesi, of the Traditional Roman Catholic Church in the Americas, and Andrew Lawrence Vanore, accused Marchenna of usurping authority, and resigned their positions in the church. Bauer together with Vanore went on to found the Old Roman Catholic Church-Utrecht Succession, following the faith and practice of the parent body. Bauer was elected presiding archbishop in 1979.

The church accepts the Baltimore Catechism and, in general, pre-Vatican II Roman Catholic theology with the exception of the dogmas of papal infallibility, the Immaculate Conception, and the Bodily Assumption of the Virgin Mary. The doctrines on the Virgin Mary are acceptable as pious belief. The church is headquartered in Boston, and parishes are located in Denver, Colorado; Orlando, Florida; Pennsylvania; California; Texas; and several locations in Massachusetts. In 1984 Bishop Bauer affiliated with the Patriarchial Synod of the Orthodox Catholic Church America, an association of independent Orthodox and Catholic bishops. Archbishop Bauer is assisted by two auxillaries: Bishop Andros (Andrew Lawrence Vanore) and Bishop Patrick Callahan.

Membership: In 1988, the church reported approximately 900 members in nine congregations. The archbishop is assisted by two bishops and 16 priests.

★34★

OLD ROMAN CATHOLIC CHURCH IN NORTH AMERICA

℅ Most Rev. Francis P. Facione
3827 Old Creek Rd.
Troy, MI 48084

The Old Roman Catholic Church in North America was formed in 1963 as the Old Roman Catholic Church (English Rite) by Bishop Robert Alfred Burns. Burns was ordained in 1948 by Archbishop Carmel Henry Carfora of the North American Old Roman Catholic Church. He left the N.A.O.R.C.C. and joined the Old Roman Catholic Church. On April 14, 1961 he was appointed metropolitan vicar general by the church's presiding Archbishop Richard A. Marchenna. A month later he was elected bishop-auxillary and consecrated on October 9, 1961. He left Marchenna's jurisdiction in 1963 and aligned himself with British Bishop W. A. Barrington-Evans, Primate of the Old Roman Catholic Church (English Rite), a small

British jurisdiction. Burns was appointed archbishop of Chicago. In 1973, the year before his death, Burns reported to the *Yearbook of American Churches* that there were 186 churches, 65,128 members and 201 clergy in his jurisdiction. In fact, he had only a few clergy, most of whom were bishops, and only one or two parishes.

After Archbishop Burns' death in 1974, a synod elected Bishop Andrew Johnston-Cantrell, whom Burns had consecrated in 1973, to succeed him. That same synod elected Dr. Francis C. Facione, a professor at Wayne State University, as Suffragan Bishop. Bishop Facione was consecrated several weeks later on St. Andrew's Day. Early in 1975, Johnston-Cantrell resigned, due to health reasons, and Bishop Facione was elected by the synod to a 10-year term as presiding bishop. He was also appointed ordinary of the newly created Diocese of Michigan and the Central States.

The tranquility of the Old Roman Catholic Church (English Rite) was disturbed in 1978 by publicity surrounding the activities of Chicago Bishop Richard A. Bernowski. Bernowski, who had been accorded canonical recognition for an independent ministry in 1977, was accused of a variety of immoral and illegal actions in the Chicago press. The council of bishops attempted a formal ecclesiastical inquiry into the allegations but were refused any cooperation by Bernowski. The council of bishops, accordingly, withdrew their recognition of him. Then in October 1978, Bernowski was shot to death in front of his home. As the investigation into his death proceeded, Bernowski was revealed to be the manager of a bar in suburban Chicago, head of a male prostitution ring, and the "front" for a crime syndicate. Operator of a state-funded program for youth, Bernowski had originally come under investigation because of a beating that had taken place at St. Martin's Center on Chicago's southside.

Membership: Not reported.

★35★
OLD ROMAN CATHOLIC CHURCH (HAMEL)
Current address not obtained for this edition.

The Old Roman Catholic Church (Hamel) was founded by Earl Anglin James who had been consecrated as bishop of Toronto by Archbishop Carmel Henry Carfora of the North American Old Roman Catholic Church in 1945. The following year, however, he associated himself with Hugh George de Willmott Newman (Mar Georgius) of the Catholicate of the West. During the summer of 1946, Mar Georgius had extended the territory of the Catholicate to the United States through W. D. de Ortega Maxey. In November, by proxy, he enthroned James as exarch of the Catholicate of the West in Canada. James was given the title Mar Laurentius and became archbishop and metropolitan of Acadia.

Mar Laurentius led a colorful career as an archbishop. He claimed a vast following, at times in the millions. He collected degrees, titles and awards, and as freely gave them out to those associated with him. He became affiliated with a wide variety of international associations. In 1965, he consecrated Guy F. Hamel and named him his coadjutor with right of succession. After James' retirement in 1966, Hamel was enthroned as the Universal Patriarch and assumed the title of H. H. Claudius I.

Guy F. Claude Hamel became one of the most controversial figures in Old Catholic circles. He was ordained in 1964 by Bishop William Pavlik of the Ontario Old Roman Catholic Church. However, before the year was over, Pavlik excommunicated him. Hamel then spent a short period under Michael Collin, a French prelate who had assumed the title of Pope Clement XV. He then went under Mar Laurentius.

After becoming head of the Old Roman Catholic Church, Hamel began to appoint an international hierarchy, a list of which was published in the April 1968 issue of *C. P. S. News*, the church's periodical. The list included not only most of the Old Catholic bishops in the United States and Canada (many of whom have taken pains to denounce Hamel) but also many people who were never associated with him--the Rev. Arthur C. Piepkorn (Lutheran theologian), Archbishop Irene (Orthodox Church in America), and Bishop Arthur Litchtenberger (Protestant Episcopal Church). The publication of this list, which enraged many whose names were listed and amused others who recognized the names of many long-dead prelates, was followed in 1970 by a conviction for fraud in an Ontario court. In the years since the conviction, Hamel has continued to lead the Old Roman Catholic Church, but lost most of the genuine support he had gained prior to 1970.

The Old Roman Catholic Church follows the creeds of the early Christian Church and the Pre-Vatican II rituals. All seven sacraments are administered, and devotion to the Virgin Mary, as well as the veneration of images and relics of the saints is espoused.

Membership: Not reported.

Periodicals: *C. S. P. World News*, Box 2608, Station D, Ottawa, Ontario, Canada K1P 5W7.

Remarks: His Holiness Claudius I has recently died, and the future of the jurisdiction is, at present, in question.

Sources: *Disciplinary Canons and Constitutions of the Old Roman Catholic Church (Orthodox Orders*. Havelock, Ont.: C.S.P.News, 1967; Guy F. Claude Hamel, *Broken Wings*. Cornwall, Ont.: Vesta Publications, 1980 Guy F. Claude Hamel, *The Lord Jesus and the True Mystic*. Toronto: Congregation of St. Paul, (1968).

★36★

OLD ROMAN CATHOLIC CHURCH (SHELLEY/ HUMPHREYS)

% Most Rev. John J. Humphreys
5501 62nd Ave.
Pinellas Park, FL 33565

The Old Roman Catholic Church (Shelly/Humphreys) emerged out of a dispute between Archbishop Gerad George Shelley (d. 1980), primate of the Old Roman Church in England and America, and Archbishop Richard A. Marchenna (d. 1984), head of the jurisdiction in the United States. In 1974, Marchenna consecrated Fr. Robert Clement as bishop of the Eucharistic Catholic Church, an openly homosexual jurisdiction. As a result, Shelley, acting as Marchenna's superior, excommunicated him and those who followed his leadership.

Both those who followed Shelley and those who stayed with Marchenna continued to use the name Old Roman Catholic Church. Following Shelley's death, Father Michael Farrell of San Jose, California, was chosen as the new primate. On June 13, 1981, he was consecrated by Bishop John J. Humphreys, formerly the church's vicar general in the United States, who had been consecrated by Shelley soon after the split with Marchenna. Farrell resigned after only a brief time in his office, and in 1984 Humphreys was elected the new primate.

The church follows the doctrine and practice of the Western Roman tradition as held by the Old Catholics.

Membership: In 1988 the church reported three parishes, all in Florida.

Remarks: In the 1960s Archbishop Humphreys had briefly worked with Fr. Anthony Girandola, one of the early married Roman Catholic priests. Girandola, who had become somewhat of a celebrity after his founding of an independent parish in St. Petersburg, Florida, interested Humphreys in sharing leadership of the parish so that he could respond to media appearances.

Sources: John J. Humphreys, ed., *Questions We Are Asked*. Chicago: Old Roman Catholic Information Center, 1972.

★37★

OLD ROMAN CATHOLIC CHURCH, ARCHDIOCESE OF CHICAGO (FRIS)

Current address not obtained for this edition.

In 1970 Archbishop Robert A. Burns, of the Old Roman Catholic Church (English Rite), now the Old Roman Catholic Church in North America, consecrated Howard Fris, giving him the right to succession. However, three years later he removed Fris and replaced him with Andrew Johnston-Cantrell. Fris proceeded to found his own church and took some of Burns' small following with him. After Burns' death, the corporation of the Old

Roman Catholic Church (English Rite) lapsed, as no one filed the annual reports during the bickering and infighting of that period. Fris revived the corporation and had it assigned to himself.

It is unknown if Burns knew of Fris' personal problems at the time of the consecration in 1970, but there is no doubt that they led to his deposition. They did not stop his continuing to function as the leader of his small flock. Though an alcoholic himself, in the late 1970s Fris opened St. Teresa's Manor, described as a home for alcoholics and wayward men. Because of Fris' ecclesiastical connections, social service agencies in the city began to refer men to the Manor. Then in 1979 Fris was arrested for contributing to the sexual delinquency of a child and the theft of credit cards. In the publicity accompanying his arrest and conviction, it was discovered that both of the priests working with him at the manor also had long records of arrest and conviction for felonies. Fris died in 1981, reportedly of cirrhosis of the liver.

Fris' conviction and the public scandal accompanying it did not destroy his jurisdiction, and he continued to lead his diocese. He performed at least one consecration, and after his death, his coadjutor John Kenelly, succeeded him. St. Teresa's Manor was closed, but Bishop Kenelly heads the Missionaries of St. Jude who minister to the residents of a private hotel for the mentally disturbed, alcoholics, and elderly, located on the north side of Chicago.

Membership: In 1979 the Archdiocese claimed 13 clergy and two parishes. It considers the residents of the hotel as lay members.

Sources: *Old Catholic Church (Utrecht Succession).* Chicago, Old Catholic Press of Chicago, (1980).

★38★

OLD ROMAN CATHOLIC CHURCH (ENGLISH RITE) AND THE ROMAN CATHOLIC CHURCH OF THE ULTRAJECTINE TRADITION

% Most Rev. Robert Lane
4416 N. Malden
Chicago, IL 60640

A single church body with two corporate names, the Old Roman Catholic Church (English Rite) and the Roman Catholic Church of the Ultrajectine Tradition is headed by Bishop Robert W. Lane. Lane, a priest in the Old Roman Catholic Church (English Rite) headed by Archbishop Robert A. Burns, was consecrated by Howard Fris on September 15, 1974. Both Burns and Lane perceived that Fris had failed to follow the correct form for the ceremony, and later that same day, Burns reconsecrated Lane.

Burns died two months later. Lane left Fris's jurisdiction and placed himself under Archbishop Richard A. Marchenna of the Old Roman Catholic Church.

Meanwhile, during the last year of his life, Burns had allowed the corporation papers of his jurisdiction to lapse. Lane learned of the situation and assumed control of the corporate title. He was at this time serving as pastor of St. Mary Magdelen Old Catholic Church in Chicago.

According to Lane, in 1978 Marchenna offered him the position of co-adjutor with right to succession. He had, however, developed some disagreements with Marchenna and both refused the position and left the Old Roman Catholic Church. He had previously incorporated his work for Marchenna in Chicago as the Roman Catholic Church of the Ultrajectine Tradition. Upon leaving the Old Roman Catholic Church, Lane formed an independent jurisdiction which continues both former corporations.

The Old Roman Catholic Church (English Rite) and the Roman Catholic Church of the Ultrajectine Tradition are thus two corporations designating one community of faith maintaining a Catholic way of life. It is like the Roman Catholic Church in most of its belief and practice. It retains the seven sacraments and describes itself as "One, Holy, Catholic, Apostolic, and Universal." It differs in that it uses both the Tridentine Latin mass (in both Latin and English translation) and the Ordo Novo. It has also dropped many of the regulations which govern Roman Catholic clergy, most prominently the provision prohibiting the marriage of clergy.

During the mid-1980s, Bishop Lane established six vicariates which function as proto-missionary dioceses. Within each vicariate are one or more quasi-parishes, i.e., communities of the faithful which have not as yet attained parish status. Vicariates are located in St. Louis, Missouri; Minneapolis, Minnesota; New Orleans, Louisiana; Seattle, Washington; and Fullerton and San Diego, California.

Membership: In 1987 Bishop Lane reported 20 congregations in the United States including one Polish-speaking mission in San Diego, California. These was one congregation in Hamburg, Germany.

Educational facilities: Seminary of St. Francis of Assisi, Chicago, Illinois (currently inactive).

★39★
OLD ROMAN CATHOLIC CHURCH IN THE U. S. (HOUGH)
(Defunct)

Joseph Damien Hough, while under the jurisdiction of Bishop Richard A. Marchenna of the Old Roman Catholic Church, formed a congregation of Oblates of St. Martin of Tours and was designated bishop-elect in 1964. However, following a dispute with Marchenna in 1966, Hough obtained Marchenna's permission to withdraw, and founded the Old Roman Catholic Church in the U.S. In early 1969 Hough was consecrated by Bishop Robert Raleigh of the American Catholic Church (Malabar

Succession) with right of succession. Following Raleigh's death, Hough, being the only ultrajectine bishop in California, gathered the faithful into his reorganized church, which combines both Marchenna's and Raleigh's traditions. The ultrajectine element predominates, and worship and belief follow the ultrajectine tradition. Headquarters were established in Venice, California, and all members of the church resided in the state. Both Roman and ultrajectine Catholics were admitted to the services and holy communion. Bishop Hough was in communion with the Old Catholic Church in England, then under Bishop Gerard George Shelley. Hough retired in the early 1980s, and the jurisdiction he headed dissolved.

★40★
OLD ROMAN CHURCH IN CANADA
℅ Most Rev. Fredricke P. Dunleavy
1065 Woodbine Ave.
Toronto, ON, Canada M4C 4C5

The Old Roman Church in Canada began in 1962 when Archbishop Richard A. Marchenna of the Old Roman Catholic Church consecrated William Pavlik (d. 1965) as bishop of Canada. Pavlik was to head the newly created diocese of Ontario. In 1963 Pavlik separated from Marchenna and formed the Ontario Old Catholic Church. The next year he consecrated Nelson D. Hillyer as his coadjutor. Hillyer became head of the church following Pavlik's death. In recent years it has assumed its present name.

Following Archbishop Hillyer's death, Frederick P. Dunleavy was elected by the synod to succeed him as bishop. He was consecrated on April 17, 1988, by Bishop Karl Pruter of Christ Catholic Church. In November 1987, Bishop Dunleavy began a period of service as general secretary of the Student Christian Movement of Canada.

The church follows the Nicene Creed, including the filioque clause, "Of the Son," which states that the Holy Spirit proceeds from both God the Father and God the Son. The *Knott Altar Missal*, published in English, is used for worship. The church does not accept papal infallibility, nor does it recognize changes introduced into the Roman Catholic Church by Vatican Council II.

Membership: There is only one parish, St. Andrew the Apostle in Toronto, in this small jurisdiction which in 1988 reported 55 families as members and 23 families as associates.

★41★
OUR LADY OF THE ROSES, MARY HELP OF MOTHERS SHRINE
Box 52
Bayside, NY 11361

Our Lady of the Roses, Mary Help of Mothers Shrine emerged from the visionary experiences of Veronica Lueken (b. July 12, 1923), a New York housewife, which began in 1968. Initial visitations from St. Therese of Lisieux (1873-1897) were followed on April 7, 1970, by a visit from the Blessed Virgin Mary. The Virgin announced that beginning April 7, 1970, nine years to the day after the initial apparitions of the Virgin to some children at Garabandal, Spain, she would begin regular visits to Lueken. As announced, she appeared to Lueken outside St. Robert Bellarmine Catholic Church in Bayside, Queens, New York. At the first apparition, the Virgin announced she would return on the eve of the major feast days of the church, especially those dedicated to her. She requested that a shrine and basilica be erected on the grounds occupied by St. Robert's. She revealed herself as "Our Lady of the Roses, Mary Help of Mothers," and designated Lueken as her voicebox to disseminate the future messages.

The messages have focused upon the denoucement of many modern trends, especially changes within the Roman Catholic Church. Prediction of an imminent chastisement of the world on the level of the destruction of Sodom and Gomorrah or the flood in Noah's time have added an urgency to the warnings against doctrinal and moral disintegration. Admonitions have been given against abortion, the occult, immodest dress, and freemasonry. Within the church, the messages have denounced the taking of communion in the hand instead of the mouth, the Catholic Pentecostal Movement, the use of recent Bible translations (which replaced the Douay-Rheims version), and religious textbooks which omit vital teachings of the Church.

As the apparitions continued, Lueken's following grew. The Roman Catholic Diocese of Brooklyn instituted an investigation and, in an official statement, the chancery office denied any miraculous or sacred qualities to the apparitions and messages. However, the crowds attending the frequent vigils grew beyond the lawn of St. Robert's and into neighboring yards. In April 1975 a restraining order against any outside vigils was obtained, and during the following month St. Robert's refused the use of the building for vigils. This crisis forced the moving of the site away from the location of the mandated shrine. Since that time, gatherings have been held at Flushing Meadows Park in Queens.

The break with the Roman Catholic Church was followed by continued polemics. The messages have become increasingly critical of the church. In the fall of 1975, the messages endorsed the idea, popular among some traditionalist Catholics, that an imposter had been substituted for Pope Paul VI. Periodic denounciations of the apparitions came from various Catholic bishops, especially those whose members continued to frequent the shrine. Renewed attempts to vindicate the miraculous nature of the apparitions have centered upon successful prophecies of events, such as the New York blackout and the death of Pope John Paul I and a set of unusual photographs which show what many people believe to be supernatural lights and manifestations. The Bayside apparitions have been widely publicized, and accounts of the events and reprints of the messages have appeared in numerous independent Marian publications. Support for the apparitions has come from the Center of Our Lady of the Smile in Lewiston, Maine; the Apostles of Our Lady in Lansing, Michigan; Faithful and True, a publishing center in Amherst, Massachusetts; and *Santa Maria*, an independent periodical published in Ottawa, Canada. For several years (1973-77), the Order of Saint Michael, a Catholic lay group in Quebec, Canada, supported Lueken in its quarterly publication *Michael*, but the group broke with her after a disagreement.

Lueken withdrew from her followers and the public during the mid-1970s. She speaks to no one except her closest followers, though she regularly appears at the site of the apparitions. At such times she is surrounded by a cadre of male followers distinguished by their white berets. Women followers wear blue berets.

Membership: Not reported. Depending upon the weather, as many as several thousand people attend the vigils in Bayside. Schedules are publicized around the United States and Canada. Literature is mailed to many thousands across North America, though the majority remain otherwise members of the Roman Catholic Church.

Sources: de Paul, Vincent, *The Abominations of Desolations: AntiChrist Is Here Now*. St. Louis, MO: The Author, 1975; Grant, Robert, "War of the Roses" in *Rolling Stones*, no. 113 (February 21, 1980), pp. 42-46; *Our Lady of the Roses, Mary Help of Mothers*. Lansing, MI: Apostles of Our Lady, 1980.

★42★
ORTHODOX ROMAN CATHOLIC MOVEMENT
(Defunct)

Among the first efforts to organize traditionalist members of the Roman Catholic Church was the Orthodox Roman Catholic Movement (ORCM), founded by Fr. Francis E. Fenton. Fenton began holding traditional Latin masses in a private home in Sandy Hook, Connecticut in 1970. In 1972 the group was large enough to purchase a chapel in Brewster, New York. Later they purchased another chapel in Monroe, Connecticut, which has been the headquarters of the movement ever since. Fr. Robert McKenna was installed as pastor of the Monroe church in 1973. Four additional priests joined the ORCM in the fall of 1975, and with the aggressive outreach of the movement, the church began to grow with congregations emerging in Florida, Colorado, and California, as well as in a number of locations in the Northeast.

The movement was controversial even among traditionalists who shared the opinion that the new mass was unsound. Fr. Fenton was a vocal member of the John Birch Society and was continually criticized for his affiliation. Leaders and members approved of his anti-Communism but not of his membership in a non-Catholic organization. Further conflict between Fr. Fenton and Fr. McKenna erupted when Fr. McKenna was added to ORCM's board. A two-year battle for control left McKenna in charge. Fenton left the movement to found the Traditional Catholics of America.

McKenna continued to lead the movement into the 1980s and by 1985 it had 15 associated chapels and missions. However, in 1986 McKenna was consecrated as a bishop by Gerard des Lauriers, a bishop in the lineage of Archbishop Pierre Martin Ngo-Dinh-Thuc, in the wake of which the Orthodox Roman Catholic Movement dissolved. Many disagreed with McKenna's decision to seek consecration in what had become a schismatic church.

Sources: Francis Aidan Gasquet, *Breaking with the Past*. Statford, CT: Orthodox Roman Catholic Movement, undated reprint of 1914 edition; *The Essential Roman Catholic Catechism*. Monroe, CT: Orthodox Roman Catholic Movement, 1973; Francis E. Fenton, *The Roman Catholic Church: Its Tragedy and Its Hope*. Stratford, CT: Orthodox Roman Catholic Movement, 1978.

★43★
POLISH CATHOLIC CHURCH
(Defunct)

The Polish Catholic Church existed throughout most of the twentieth century as one remnant of the organization begun by independent Polish Bishop Stephen Kaminski which did not join with the Polish National Catholic Church. Kaminiski died without designating a successor or consecrating a bishop for his jurisdiction. Several of his priests, however, continued to serve their parishes awaiting a new opportunity to reestablish Kaminski's diocese. One such priest was Francis Ignatius Boryszewski. During the 1920s, Boryszewski worked under Archbishop Carmel Henry Carfora of the North American Old Roman Catholic Church (Rogers) but in 1927 affiliated with the American Catholic Church, headed by Archbishop Frederick E. J. Lloyd. Like Kaminski, Lloyd had been consecrated by Archbishop Joseph Rene Vilatte. In 1928 Boryszewski began a new parish in New York City, St. Peter and St. Paul Polish Catholic Church. The following year Bishop Lloyd, assisted by Bishops Gregory Lines and Daniel C. Hinton, consecrated Boryszewski to head an independent Polish Catholic Church in communion with the American Catholic Church. (It appears that Polish Mariavite Bishop

J. M. P. Prochniewski consecrated Boryszewski a second time in a separate ceremony in 1930.)

The Polish Catholic Church followed Roman faith and practice but rejected the authority of the Roman Catholic Church. The small jurisdiction never grew very large, but Bishop Boryszewski continued to pastor the church in New York City until his death in the 1970s.

Sources: *Fifth Year Book*. New York: St. Peter and St. Paul Polish Catholic Church, 1933; *Church Directory and Year Book*. New York: St. Peter and St. Paul Polish Catholic Church, 1933.

★44★
POLISH NATIONAL CATHOLIC CHURCH
% Mt. Rev. John F. Swantek
1002 Pittston Ave.
Scranton, PA 18505

In the last decades of the nineteenth century, nationalistic enthusiasms engulfed the Polish communities in the U.S. Tension developed from the assignment of non-Polish priests to predominantly Polish parishes. Efforts directed toward autonomy developed in Chicago, Buffalo, and Scranton. In Chicago an independent Polish parish, All Saints Catholic Church, whose formation had been encouraged by Old Catholic Bishop Joseph Rene Vilatte, had developed under Father Anthony Kozlowski. In Buffalo an independent congregation was formed and called Father Stephen - Kaminski as its priest. Other independent parishes developed in Cleveland and Detroit.

All of these churches were placed under Vilatte. Kaminski was elected bishop and sought consecration from Vilatte. Kozlowski challenged Kaminski's claims and went to Europe where he sought consecration from Bishop Herzog of the Old Catholic Church. Vilatte consecrated Kaminski in 1898 and two factions, often bitter rivals, developed.

A third group of Polish nationals emerged in Scranton, Pennsylvania, where the issue was local control of church property. In consultation with Father Francis Hodur, their former priest, the Poles constructed an independent church and in 1897 Hodur accepted the pastorate. After unsuccessful attempts to remain within the Roman Catholic Church, the Poles organized a second church in nearby Dickson City.

Other independent congregations followed, and in 1904 a synod met in Scranton. At that time the Polish National Catholic Church of America was organized and Hodur was elected bishop. In 1907 he received orders from Utrecht, the central see of the Old Catholic Church. That same year Kozlowski died, and most of his followers were received into Hodur's diocese.

The Polish National Catholic Church of America differs little from the Roman Catholic Church as it was before the changes brought about by the Second Vatican Council of the 1960s. It has added some feast days of a nationalistic flavor and elevated the preaching of the gospel to the status of a sacrament. Bishop Hodur became known for his rejection of a doctrine of eternal hell. There is local control of property and the congregation does have a say in naming their priest. The liturgy, which for many years was said in Polish, has been translated into English and is being used in a higher percentage of the masses year by year.

In 1914 Hodur helped to start a Lithuanian National Catholic Church and in 1924 he consecrated Father John Britenas as its bishop. The body became independent but was eventually reabsorbed. The Polish National Catholic Church of America grew steadily through the first half of the twentieth century. It became the only substantial American Old Catholic jurisdiction and the only one in communion with the Old Catholic See of Utrecht. For many years it was in communion with the Protestant Episcopal Church but broke fellowship after the later decided to accept female priests. During the last two decades it has suffered greatly from Americanization, especially the abandonment of the Polish language by younger members, and the mobility of its members, many of whom have moved into areas not served by a PNCC parish. From a peak of 162 churches in 1960, the church has experienced a loss of almost one-third of its parishes.

The PNCC is organized into four American dioceses: Central (headquartered in Scranton); Eastern (headquartered in Manchester, New Hampshire); Western (headquartered in Chicago); and Buffalo-Pittsburgh (headquartered in Buffalo, New York). There is also a Canadian diocese headquartered in Toronto. A very active mission, begun after World War I, produced a growing National Church in Poland. A bishop was appointed in 1924. Cooperation has also been initiated between the Polish National Catholic Church of America and the Puerto Rican National Church. The PNCC is a member of both the World Council of Churches and National Council of Churches.

Membership: In 1980 the PNCC reported 110 churches and approximately 280,000 members.

Educational facilities: Savonrola Theological Seminary, Scranton, PA.

Periodicals: *Rola Boza* (God's Field), 529 E. Locust St., Scranton, PA 18505; *Polka*, 1002 Pittston Ave., Scranton, PA 18505; *PNCC Studies*, 1031 Cedar Ave., Scranton, PA 18505.

Sources: *A Catechism of the Polish National Catholic Church.* [Scranton, PA]: Mission Fund Polish National Catholic Church, 1962; Paul Fox, *The Polish National Catholic Church.* Scranton, PA: School of Christian Living, [1955]; Laurence Orzell, *Rome and the Validity of Orders in the Polish National Catholic Church.* Scranton, PA: Savonarola Theological Seminary Alumni

Association, 1977; Stephen Wlodarski, *The Origin and Growth of the Polish National Catholic Church.* Scranton, PA: Polish National Catholic Church, 1974; Robert William Janowski, *The Growth of a Church, A Historical Documentary.* Scranton, PA: The Author, 1965.

★45★

POLISH OLD CATHOLIC CHURCH IN AMERICA
(Defunct)

The Polish Old Catholic Church in America derived from the Polish Mariavite Church. The Mariavite movement dates from 1893 when Sister Felicia (Maria Franciska Kozlowska), a member of the Third Order of St. Francis, a Roman Catholic order, claimed to have had a vision of the Blessed Virgin. In the vision she was told to establish a mixed order of men and women dedicated to the Blessed Virgin. Thus Sister Felicia founded the Mariavites and the order spread, carried by its strong mystical element. Polish Roman Catholic bishops denounced the vision and labeled it hallucinatory. They ordered the disbanding of the Mariavites, but the members refused to obey. They were excommunicated in 1906. They found support from the Russian Church and were eventually able to obtain priestly orders from the Old Catholic Church at Utrecht. Denied a place in the Roman Catholic Church, the order transformed into a large denomination. Freed from Roman authority, they made several innovations on traditional Roman Catholic practices. They ordained females to the priesthood and episcopacy. They placed a great emphasis upon the veneration of the Virgin. It is estimated that over a half million Mariavites can be found in Poland.

During the first decades of the twentieth century, Mariavites began to migrate to the United States. Many joined the Polish Old Catholic Church of America, founded in 1913 by Joseph Zielonka, a former priest of the Polish National Catholic Church. Zielonka sought consecration from Paolo Miragalia Gulotti, an independent Italian bishop. In 1925 Zielonka brought his jurisdiction into the Old Catholic Church in America, headed by Archbishop W. H. Francis Brothers. After fifteen years with Brothers, Zielonka left the Old Catholic Church in America and established the Old Catholic Archdiocese for the Americas and Europe. In 1960 the church had 22 parishes and 7,200 members.

In 1961 Zielonka died and was succeeded by his suffragan Peter A. Zurawetzky, a Ukrainian by birth. His leadership was immediately questioned by Fr. Felix Starazewski, pastor of the parish in South River, New Jersey, who claimed to be Zielonka's true successor. Many of the Polish parishes, opposed to Zurawetzky's attempt to make the Church more inclusive followed Starazewski in founding the Polish Old Catholic Church in America.

In the decades since its founding, the church, consisting originally of a few parishes in the northeast (primarily New Jersey and Massachusetts), found it was unable to overcome the forces of Americanization and a mobile society, and the parishes declined in strength. No evidence of the Polish Old Catholic Church in America had been found during the 1980s, and it is presumed to have ceased to exist.

★46★
SERVANT CATHOLIC CHURCH
℅ Most Rev. Robert E. Burns
50 Coventry Lane
Central Islip, NY 11722

The Servant Catholic Church first convened on the Feast of All Saints in 1978 and finalized its polity in January 1980 with the election of its first Bishop-Primate, Robert E. Burns, SSD. Burns was consecrated on July 13, 1980, by Archbishop Herman Adrian Spruit of the Church of Antioch. A second bishop, Patricia duMont Ford, served the church from 1980 through 1986, when at which time she retired from active ministry to pursue feminist theological studies. Ivan MacKillop-Fritts, OCC, Abbot-General of the church-sponsored religious community, the Order of the Celtic Cross, was elevated to the episcopate on November 30, 1984, and serves now as bishop of the church's western diocese headquartered in Springfield, Oregon. The core teaching of the church, termed "eleutheric theology," is rooted in the perception that the essence of the Christian kerygma lies in the proclamation of freedom. All the church's ministries—liturgical, pastoral, sacramental, and social action—reflect this belief system. The church's two-year theological training curriculum centers upon the study of eleutherics. Resonances of this teaching are found in the church's liturgy and in its code of canon law. The church recognizes the sacraments of initiation (baptism), restoration (penance and healing), union (holy, euchartist), instruction (proclamation and teaching), and holy orders. Confirmation and matrimony are designated as sacramental rites.

Though receiving orders from Liberal Catholic sources, the College of Bishops of the Servant Catholic Church has rejected theosophy as "inauthentic teaching." The church is ecumenically linked by an intercommunion agreement with the Charismatic Catholic Apostolic Synod. EICAS sponsors ministering communities in three states. The Servant Catholic Church also reaches out ecumenically to other ecclesiastical bodies that share its commitment to peace, justice, effective pastoral ministry, sound theological education, and the admission of women to the three-fold, Catholic-ordained ministry.

Membership: In 1984 the church reported three congregations, five priests, and 118 members.

Educational facilities: The Whithorn Institute, Ronkonkoma, New York.

Periodicals: *The Newsletter*, 50 Coventry Ln., Central Islip, New York 11722.

Sources: *The Sacramentary and Daily Office of the Servant Catholic Church.* Central Islip, NY: Theotokos Press, 1981.

★47★
SLAVES OF THE IMMACULATE HEART OF MARY
Box 22
Still River, MA 01467

The Slaves of the Immaculate Heart of Mary emerged in the 1940s as one of the first groups protesting the growing accomodation of the Roman Catholic Church to liberal ideas, particularly the acceptance of the possibility of salvation outside of the Roman Catholic Church. Leader of the group was Fr. Leonard Feeney (d. 1978), a Jesuit priest who had become a popular Catholic writer in the 1930s. Feeney taught at Weston College in Cambridge, Massachusetts, but made his second headquarters the Thomas More Bookstore in Harvard Square. The store, opened in 1940 by Mrs. Catherine Goddard Clarke, become a center for Catholic students. With Feeney's help, it grew into a school in its own right, and from its programs new converts were brought into the church, members for religious orders recruited, and numerous lay people educated in Catholic thinking.

Trouble began in the late 1940s when Feeney began to attack the secularism at Harvard. He broadened his attack to include the liberalism of the church. Fenney charged that some were moving away from the traditional Catholic position which stated that outside the (Catholic) church there was no salvation. Welded together by Fenney's rhetoric and leadership, the core group of the bookstore school became a committed group of dedicated conservative Catholics. The church moved to quiet Feeney by urging him to take a position at the College of the Holy Cross, but he refused to leave the bookstore. Secretly, a group at the bookstore organized a new religious order, the Slaves of the Immaculate Heart of Mary, pledged to Feeney and his attempts to preserve the church in its purity.

Tension increased when four teachers associated with Feeney, who also taught at Boston College (a Jesuit institution), wrote a letter to the General of the Society of Jesus and accused some of their faculty colleagues of heresy. The college fired the four for promoting intolerance and bigotry. When Feeney defended them, Archbishop Cardinal Richard Cushing silenced him and then forbade Catholics to associate with the Cambridge center. The Slaves and Feeney interpreted Cushing's actions as another blow to traditional Catholic faith.

Following the silencing, Feeney was dismissed from the Society of Jesus and in 1953, excommunicated. His excommunication marks the establishment of the Slaves of the Immaculate Heart of Mary as a group independent of the Roman Catholic Church. They saw themselves as a small remnant still holding to the true faith. The group established a residence compound, purchasing several adjacent homes and erecting a high fence around the property. The school lost its accreditation, which led to its loss of funding from the post World War II G.I. Bill and its eventual closing. The Slaves made money by publishing a series of popular books on Catholic themes and selling them door-to-door in the Boston area. They generally spent their Sundays in Boston Commons defending their position within the heavily Catholic community.

In 1958 the Slaves moved from Cambridge to a farm near Still River. An ascetic lifestyle became predominant and eventually all of the adults accepted a vow of celibacy. Children, which made up half the community's membership, were raised collectively.

After a period of relative quiet, the community went through a series of changes that ended its life as a separated community. In 1974, Fenney led 29 men and women of the community back into communion with the Roman Catholic Church. Then in 1988, the 14 remaining sisters of the group were formally received back into communion and the order regularized. The Slaves of the Immaculate Heart of Mary began a new life as an order recognized by the Roman Catholic Church.

Sources: Leonard Feeney, *The Leonard Feeney Omnibus*. New York: Sheed & Ward, 1944; *Our Glorious Popes*. Still River, MA: Slaves of the Immaculate Heart of Mary, 1955; *The Communion of Saints*. Still River, MA: Slaves of the Immaculate Heart of Mary, 1967; *The Holy Family*. Still River, MA: Slaves of the Immaculate Heart of Mary, 1963; Robert Connor, *Walled In*. New York: New American Library, 1979.

★48★
SOCIETY OF ST. PIUS V
8 Pond Place
Oyster Bay Cove, NY 11771

Fr. Clarence Kelly was among the first American priests to graduate from the seminary established by traditionalist Archbishop Marcel Lefebvre at Econe, Switzerland. In 1973 Lefebvre ordained Kelly, who returned to America with four other priests to found the United States branch of the Society of St. Pius X. Kelly served as United States superior of the society, and as superior of the North-East District when the territory was divided in 1978. In the early 1980s, however, he and Fr. Donald J. Sanborn, superior of St. Thomas Aquinas Seminary in Ridgefield, Connecticut, became concerned about Lefebvre's contacts with Pope John Paul II and his attempts to accomodate the innovations introduced since Vatican II, innovations that had led to the formation of the seminary and the society.

In March 1983 nine society priests, including Sanborn and Kelly, sent a letter to Lefebvre, calling his attention to their objections on a number of issues: 1) the introduction of liturgical changes at St. Thomas Aquinas Seminary; 2)

the use of doubtfully ordained priests in missions in the Southwest; 3) the archbishop's desire to introduce the liturgical changes of Pope John XXIII throughout the society; 4) the improper dismissal of priests; 5) the society's usurpation of teaching authority; 6) the need to subordinate loyalty to the fraternity to loyalty to the church; and 7) the liberal acceptance of marriage annulments by Lefebvre. Lefebvre responded to the letter by dismissing Sanborn from his post at the seminary and dismissing all the priests from their place in the society.

Despite disagreements with Lefebvre, the society continued its activities as before, including publication of its two periocicals and services at its churches and missions. In 1984, four priests previously ordained by Lefebvre joined the society, resulting in further expansion. Also that year, Fr. Kelly founded a congregation of sisters in Round Top, New York, known as the Daughters of Mary, Mother of Our Savior. As of the beginning of 1988, the community had 22 members. The society also operates four elementary schools and two high schools.

The society operated under its founding name until the fall of 1987 when it adopted its present name.

Membership: In 1988 the Society reported approximately 50 missions and churches under its care.

Periodicals: *The Bulletin*, 8 Pond Place, Oyster Bay Cove, NY 11771; *The Roman Catholic*, Box 217, Oyster Bay, NY 11771.

Remarks: In July 1983 the Society of St. Pius X filed a lawsuit asking the court to award them the property of those churches which had been a part of the society before the schism, but which had aligned themselves with Roman Catholics of America. Parts of that suit have been resolved, the society winning property in Philadelphia and the Roman Catholics of America, property in Norfolk, Virginia. Other property disputes remain to be resolved.

★49★
SOCIETY OF ST. PIUS X
Box 1307
Dickinson, TX 77539

Of the several groups of traditionalist Roman Catholics, the Society of St. Pius X claims the largest number of adherents. Prior to the 1980s, the society was the only traditionalist group which had orders from, and the support of, a Roman Catholic bishop with undisputed episcopal orders--Archbishop Marcel Lefebvre.

Marcel Lefebvre (b. 1905) was raised in a pious Catholic family and spent much of his adult life in Africa as a missionary. After World War II he steadily rose in the African hierarchy as vicar-apostolic of Dakar (1947) and then apostolic delegate for French-speaking Africa (1948). In 1955 Pope Pius XII appointed him archbishop of Dakar. Pope John XXIII appointed Lefebvre to serve on the Central Preparatory Commission of Vatican II. The Council's rejection of all the work prepared by that commission, and the initiation of a number of changes and reforms, disturbed Lefebvre. In 1962, he was appointed by Pope John XXIII as bishop of Tulle (France) and shortly thereafter, was elected superior general of the Holy Ghost Fathers, the religious order of which he was a member. However, Lefebvre found the ruling elite of that order quite accepting of the liberal decisions of Vatican II, and in 1968 resigned his post and retired from public life.

Lefebvre's retirement was soon interrupted by several theological students who, knowing of the Archbishop's opposition to the decisions of Vatican II, sought his assistance. There was no seminary where they could receive traditional Catholic training in theology and spiritual formation. Reluctantly, Lefebvre responded to their overtures for help and in 1969 opened the Fraternite Sacerdotale de Saint Pius X, attached to the University of Fribourg. Fribourg was like other universities, and the Fraternite soon moved to Econe, Canton of Valais, Switzerland, to create a full seminary curriculum. In this venture Lefebvre had the full approval of local bishops. As word spread that a seminary built on pre-Vatican II patterns existed, enrollment increased and growth was rapid.

In 1974, the official attitude toward Econe changed; in November, the French bishops issued a joint statement against adherents of the Latin mass. Informally, the statement was tied to a policy of no longer accepting graduates from Econe into the French dioceses. On May 6, 1975, official approval for Econe was withdrawn by the bishop of Fribourg charging that the seminary opposed the teachings of Vatican II and the authority of Pope Paul VI.

In the wake of the new attitude toward his work, Lefebvre continued his efforts, frequently staying but one step from excommunication. The next major battle began in the spring of 1976 as Lefebvre prepared to ordain some graduates of his seminary. Paul VI publicly rebuked him, but Lefebvre persisted with his plans and ordained 13 seminarians in June. On July 22 Paul VI suspended him from exercising any further priestly functions. Lefebvre responded by traveling to Lille, France, on August 29, 1976, by and publicly celebrating mass and denouncing some of the "uncatholic" practices of the Roman Catholic church. His actions led to a personal meeting with Paul VI the following month, which lessened, but did not end, the tension between the two.

Shortly after the meeting with the pope, Lefebvre traveled to England for his first mass there, and the next year he went to the United States. His continued activity inspired the outstanding French theologian Yves Conger to write a book attacking Lefebvre and led Paul VI to threaten excommunication. Since Paul VI's death, Lefebvre has continued to promote the Society of St. Pius X and to negotiate with Pope John Paul II, viewed by many as a very conservative pope. Those negotiations, which produced concessions from Lefebvre, have led some to reject his leadership of the movement.

The Society of St. Pius X had its origin in the United States when several Americans traveled to Econe to study. Upon returning to America, they established centers in East Meadow, New York; Houston, Texas; and San Jose, California. They were soon joined by Fr. Anthony Ward, ordained at Econe in 1975, who founded St. Joseph's Seminary at Armada, Michigan. Fr. Clarence Kelly, one of five Americans ordained in 1973 by Lefebvre, began a periodical entitled *For You and For Many*. It tied together traditionalist supporters around the United States.

By the end of 1975, there were more than 50 congregations served by the priests of the society, and the search for permanent chapel sites was begun. In March 1978, Frs. Kelly, Donald J. Sanborn, and Hector Bolduc met with Lefebvre and decided to divide the work into two districts. Kelly remained superior of the Eastern and Northern Districts and Bolduc was appointed head of the new Western and Southern, headquartered in Houston, Texas. In the Houston suburb of Dickinson, Bolduc founded Angelus Press, which became the major source for literature about Lefebvre and the work of the society.

That same year the society was split by a bitter conflict over the relationship between Lefebvre and the pope. Since the beginning of the society, Lefebvre has continually acknowledged the pope to be the leader of the church, and has tried to obtain the freedom to keep the traditional liturgy and doctrine within the Roman Catholic Church. However, some of his followers in America, including nine priests led by Frs. Kelly and Sanborn, took a more conservative stance. They tended to reject all changes since Vatican II and even some liturgical adjustments made by Pope Pius XII. In 1983, they outlined their complaints in a seven-point letter that included a request for independence from Lefebvre, superior general of the order. In response, Lefebvre, who interpreted their action as evidence of constant disobedience, expelled them from the order. The following year, Fr. Boldec also left the society. A court suit ensued, in which the expelled priests tried to retain the property of the Northeast District of the society, over which they had previously had control, and bring it into their new organization, the Society of St. Pius V. In 1968 the court returned all the major property, including the seminary, to the society.

After the court suit, a reorganization of the Society of St. Pius X established new leadership in the Northeast District. Fr. Richard Williamson became superior of the seminary and Fr. Francois Laisney the new district superior. Also, a community of Camelite nuns was established in Phoenixville, Pennsylvania. Annual retreats for the clergy, to which traditionalist priests from outside the society are invited, have been initiated.

The society operates a number of elementary and secondary schools, Angelus Press, and two seminaries in the United States. There is also a Canadian district headquartered at Shawinigan, Quebec. Around the world, the society is represented in a number of national districts.

The society insists that in spite of its organizing separate parishes, schools, houses for the religious, and seminaries (analgous in part to the work of various religious orders), it remains a vital part of the Roman Catholic Church, not a separate denomination.

Membership: In 1988 there were approximately 120 churches, chapels, and missions with 25 priests, 11 nuns, and 15,000 faithful affiliated with the society in the United States. There were 20 congregations in Canada and approximately 250 priests and 150,000 faithful worldwide.

Educational facilities: St. Thomas Aquinas Seminary, Winona, Minnesota; Jesus and Mary Seminary, El Paso, Texas; St. Mary's College and Academy, St. Mary's, Kansas.

Periodicals: *The Angelus*, Box 1307, Dickinson, TX; *Crusade*, US 24, Postal Drawer 159, St. Mary's, KS 66536; *Verbum*, 209 Tackora Trail, Ridgefield, CT 06870.

Sources: Michael Treharna Davies, *Apologia Pro Marcel Lefebvre; Part I, 1905-1976.* Dickinson, TX: Angelus Press, 1979; Jose Hanu, *Vatican Encounter: Conversations with Archbishop Lefebvre.* Kansas City, KS: Sheel Andrews and McMeel, 1978; Yves Conger, *Challenge to the Church.* Huntington, IN: Our Sunday Visitor, 1976; Marcel Lefebvre, *Liberalism.* Dickinson, TX: Angelus Press, 1980; Michael Davies, *Pope Paul's New Mass.* Dickinson, TX: Angelus Press, 1980.

★50★

THEE ORTHODOX OLD ROMAN CATHOLIC CHURCH
Box 49314
Chicago, IL 60649

Thee Orthodox Old Roman Catholic Church is one of several bodies which claims to carry on the work of the Old Roman Catholic Church (English Rite) headed by the late Archbishop Robert Alfred Burns (d. 1974). It was founded by Peter Charles Caine Brown, generally known by his ecclesiastical title, Archbishop Simon Peter. Brown was originally ordained in 1972 by Bishop Anthony Vruyneel of the Orthodox Old Roman Catholic Church of Bellgarden, California. In 1973 he met Markus I (Leo Christopher Skelton) and was consecrated by him. On August 14, 1973, he was enthroned as archbishop. On December 18, 1974, he was appointed chancellor of the jurisdiction headed by Burns. He succeeded to the role metropolitan on December 31, 1974.

Membership: Not reported. In 1983 the church claimed 2,369 members, 19 congregations, and 36 priests.

★51★

TRADITIONAL CATHOLICS OF AMERICA
Box 6827
Colorado Springs, CO 80934

In the late 1970s, Fr. Francis E. Fenton encountered opposition from some of the leadership in the Orthodox Roman Catholic Movement, due in large part to his membership in, and vocal support of, the John Birch Society. While approving the anti-Communist attitude of Fr. Fenton, they disapproved of the manner in which he had chosen to express it. As the issue raged, Fenton moved to Colorado and began to reorganize those loyal to him, forming the Traditional Catholics of America. Their beliefs and practices are similar to those of the Orthodox Roman Catholic Movement.

Membership: In 1985 the Traditional Catholics reported eight chapels and missions.

Periodicals: *The Athanasian*, Box 6827, Colorado, CO 80934.

Sources: Francis E. Fenton, *The Roman Catholic Church: Its Tragedy and Its Hope.* Stratford, CT: Orthodox Roman Catholic Movement, 1978.

★52★

TRADITIONAL CHRISTIAN CATHOLIC CHURCH
Current address not obtained for this edition.

The Traditional Christian Catholic Church was founded by Archbishop Thomas Fehervary and is built around a group of immigrants from Austro-Hungarian stock who came to Quebec in 1965 following the failure of the Hungarian revolt. Fehervary had been consecrated in 1945 by Archbishop R. M. J. Prochniewski of the Polish Mariavite Church, and he had served an independent Hungarian church since 1939. The faith and practice accord with that of the Roman Catholic Church before the Second Vatican Council of the 1960s, and the church opposes the innovations of that Council. Priests are unsalaried, but (unusual among Old Catholics) they are university-trained.

Membership: In 1972 the Church reported one parish in Canada, three missions in the United States, three missions in Western Europe, two missions in Eastern Europe and one mission in Hong Kong. One mission in New York City became independent in 1976 as the Tridentine Catholic Church currently headed by Archbishop Leonard J. Curreri. No current statistics have been reported.

★53★

TRADITIONAL ROMAN CATHOLIC CHURCH IN THE AMERICAS

% Most Rev. John D. Fesi
Friary Press
Box 470
Chicago, IL 60690

History: The Traditional Roman Catholic Church in the Americas was formed in June 1978 by John D. Fesi, a bishop consecrated by Damian Hough, head of the Old Roman Catholic Church in the U.S. Fesi had begun his ecclesiastical career as a Franciscan friar in the Franciscan Provine of Christ the King, a community within the Archdiocese of the Old Catholic Church in America (now known as the Orthodox Catholic Church in America) under the leadership of Archbisop Walter X. Brown. In 1972, Brown created the Vicariate of Illinois and consecrated Msgr. Earl P. Gasquoine as its bishop. Gasquoine in turn appointed Fesi as Vicar of Religious with the title of reverend monsignor. As part of his duties, Fesi managed Friary Press, which printed a quarterly periodic al, *The Franciscan*, and pamphlets for the Archdiocese. The community dissolved shortly after Fesi's leaving the Archdiocese in 1973.

After his departure from Brown's jurisdiction, Fesi was approached by Damian Hough, with whom he became associated. On June 30, 1974, Hough, assisted by Bishops Joseph G. Sokolowski and John A. Skikiewicz, consecrated Fesi as a bishop. During this time, Fesi also worked at the Church of St. Mary Mystical Rose, an independent Polish Catholic parish in Chicago. It had originally been founded in 1937 in response to a vision of Maria Kroll, a young Polish immigrant. The parish was, in effect, an independent Catholic jurisdiction headed by Skikiewicz, who had pastored the church for many years. During the 1970s, as his health failed and he could no longer handle the parish work, Fesi was appointed his successor. Though once a strong congregation, support had dwindled and services were being held in the rectory basement hall. After Skikiewicz's death, support further dwindled until the church's board sold the property)which is today the site of a parish of the Polish National Catholic Church). Fesi founded the Traditional Roman Catholic Church a short time later.

Beliefs: The Traditional Roman Catholic Church follows the doctrine and liturgy of the pre-Vatican II Roman Catholic Church. The Tridentine Latin mass is celebrated, and the Baltimore Cathechism is used in teaching. The seven sacraments are kept, and baptism is considered essential for salvation. Veneration of the images and pictures of the saints is promoted. Abortion is condemned. *Organization:* The church is organized hierarchically. Under the bishop, there is an ecclesiastical structure consisting of priests, deacons, subdeacons, acolytes, exorcists, lectors, and doorkeepers. Priests are allowed to marry, unless they belong to a religious order. the priests are organized into a synod that meets annually.

Joseph G. Sokolowski, Hough consecrated Fesi on June 30, 1974. Fesi took his friars into the Old Roman Catholic Church headed by Marchenna. Though *The Franciscan* was discontinued, Friary Press became the church's major publishing arm.

During his years with Brown and Marchenna, Fesi and the Franciscans assisted at the Church of St. Mary Mystical Rose, an independent Old Catholic parish in Chicago. Bishop Skikiewicz pastored the congregation which had been founded in 1937 in response to a vision of Maria Kroll, a young Polish immigrant. The church was in effect an independent Old Catholic jurisdiction. Eventually, Fesi was appointed associate pastor. Marchenna appointed Fesi head of the Vicariate of Illinois and eventually the Church of St. Mary Mystical Rose became part of the vicariate. Though a strong congregation, after Skikiewicz's death the support dwindled and the building was sold.

The Traditional Roman Catholic Church in the Americas follows the Old Catholic tradition. It keeps the seven sacraments and teaches that baptism is essential for salvation. Veneration of images and pictures of the saints (who are present in a mystical manner in their image) and especially the Blessed Virgin Mary (whose intercession is essential to salvation) is promoted. Abortion is condemned. The church is organized hierarchically. Under the bishop is an ecclesiastical structure which includes priests, deacons, subdeacons, acolytes, exorcists, lectors, and doorkeepers. Priest are allowed to marry. A synod meets annually.

Membership: In 1987, the church reported 14 parishes, 26 priests and 981 members.

Educational facilities: Our Lady of Victory Seminary, Chicago, Illinois.

Periodicals: *The Larks of Umbria*, Friary Press, Box 470, Chicago, IL 60690.

Sources: John Dominic Fesi, *Apostolic Succession of the Old Catholic Church*. Chicago: Friary Press, [1975?]; John Dominic Fesi, *Canonical Standing of Religious in Regards to the Sacred Ministry*. Chicago: Friary Press, 1975; John Dominic Fesi, *Reasons for Divorce and Annulment in Church Law*. Chicago: Friary Press, 1975.

★54★

TRIDENTINE CATHOLIC CHURCH

% Archbishop Leonard J. Curreri, Primate
Sacred Heart of Jesus Chapel
1740 W. Seventh St.
Brooklyn, NY 11223

The Tridentine Catholic Church was formed in 1976 by Fr. Leonard J. Curreri, formerly a priest in the Traditional Christian Catholic Church headed by Archbishop Thomas Fehervary. In 1974 Fehervary moved to extend his Canadian-based jurisdiction to the United States by ordaining and commissioning Curreri and two other priests. However, the following year, on April 23, 1977, Curreri was consecrated a bishop by Francis J. Ryan of the Ecumenical Catholic Church of Christ. (He was subsequently reconsecrated subconditionally July 30, 1977 by Archbishop Andre Barbeau of the Catholic Charismatic Church of Canada.) Curreri then called a synod at which the Tridentine Catholic Church was organized as a separate jurisdiction.

The Tridentine Catholic Chur ch follows the doctrines and practices of the pre-Vatican II Roman Catholic Church. It rejects the Novus Ordo. It also rejects the doctine of papal infallibility, the ordination of women to the priesthood, and abortion under any circumstances. It leaves the matter of birth control to individual consciences.

Membership: In 1988 the church reported five congregations and three clergy in the United States.

Sources: Leonard J. Curreri, *De Sacramentis*. Brooklyn, NY: n.d.; Leonard J. Curreri, *More Questions and Answers on the Tridentine Catholic Church*. Brooklyn, NY: n.d.; Leonard J. Curreri, *Questions and Answers on the Tridentine Catholic Church*. Brooklyn, NY: n.d.; Leonard J. Curreri, *Seccessio Apostolica*. Brooklyn, NY: 1984.

★55★

TRIDENTINE OLD ROMAN COMMUNITY CATHOLIC CHURCH (JONES)
% Most Rev. Charles T. Sutter
1956 Gardena Ave..
Long Beach, CA 90813

The Tridentine Old Roman Community Catholic Church was organized in 1976 by Fr. Jack Alwin Jones, generally known by his church name Jacque A. Jones. Jones was consecrated as a bishop in 1980 by Bishops Lawrence E. Carter of the North American Old Roman Catholic Church-Utrecht Succession and Thomas Sargent of the Community of Catholic Churches. In the mid-1980s, however, Jones resigned his leadership of the single parish of the jurisdiction, St. John the Apostle Church in Bellflower, California, and turned the corporation over to Bishop Charles T. Sutter.

Sutter had recently moved to southern California from Ohio, where he had been the founder of the American Orthodox Catholic Church, Archdiocese of Ohio. He had founded the jurisdiction following his 1979 consecration by Mar Apriam I (Archbishop Richard Bruce Morrill), head of the Holy Orthodox Catholic Church, Eastern and Apostolic. During the early 1980s, Sutter's jurisdiction had parishes and a religious order in Florida and a school in Arkansas. However, inthe summer of 1982, the corporation was dissolved and Sutter later moved to the West Coast.

Membership: In 1988, there was one small parish in Long Beach, California.

★56★

UNITED OLD ROMAN CATHOLIC CHURCH (WHITEHEAD)
% Most Rev. Armand C. Whitehead
527 82nd St.
Brooklyn, NY 11209

The United Old Catholic Church resulted from the 1963 merger of three independent jurisdictions, the Catholic Episcopal Church and two other churches. The archbishop and head of the new merged body was Armand C. Whitehead, consecrated in 1960 by Michael A. Itkin, soon left Itkin's jurisdiction to found the Catholic Episcopal Church. Whitehead was consecrated a second time by James Edward Burns in 1970.

In general, doctrine and practice conform to the seven ecumenical councils held between 325 A.D. and 787 A.D., and the canons of the Roman Catholic Church prior to 1880. Distinctive features of the church include a vernacular liturgy, non-obligatory use of the sacrament of penance, and recognition of the primacy (though not the supremacy or infallibility) of the Pope. None of the newer doctrines of the Virgin Mary are accepted, such as her bodily assumption into heaven. Also, "individual bodily parts of our Blessed Lord" such as the "Sacred Heart" are not held in special veneration.

Membership: In 1967, the United Catholic Church reported 3 parishes and approximately 100 members. As of 1984, Archbishop Whitehead was living in semi-retirement and recent information on activities of the church have not been reported.

★57★

UNIVERSAL CHRISTIAN CATHOLIC CHURCH
Current address not obtained for this edition.

In 1947, the Universal Christian Apostolic Church was founded in Vancouver, British Columbia by William F. Wolsey. Wolsey received apostolic succession eight years later when he was consecrated by British Old Catholic bishops Hugh George de Willmott Newman (Mar Georgius) of the Catholicate of the West and Harold Percival Nicholson (Mar Joannes), who had left Mar Georgius to found the Ancient Catholic Church. Wolsey claimed a degree in Bio-Psychology from the Taylor School of Bio-Psychology, out of which he claimed to have developed a psychiatric method compatible with Christianity.

The Universal Christian Apostolic Church believes in the "usefulness" of the original Christian doctrine, but attempted to be nonsectarian in its interpretation. Unique to its perspective are beliefs in Christian doctrine as a living philosophy best manifested in the work of the Christian Ministry and in Jesus as a perfect manifestation of the "Christos," the Christ-Spirit. The Christ-Spirit is thought of as enthusiasm plus "that something more." Those who are annointed with it reveal the actual presence of Jesus, which gives life to worship and ritual.

Membership: Since Wolsey's death in the 1980s, there has been no sign of the church's continuance. It may be defunct.

Remarks: Remarks: Wolsey became known during his career as a collector of degrees and a member in a number of honorary societies and orders. These, along with a number of open membership organizations which he had joined, were duly noted on his lengthy curriculum vitae.

Sources: William Franklin Wolsey, *Vivesco*. North Burnaby, BC: Universal Life Foundation, 1957; Meernaidoo T. Somanah, *The Philosophy and Spiritual Teachings of the Modern Saint, Patriarch-Archbishop Dr. William F. Wolsey*. Port Louis, MR: Standard Printing Establishment, 1971; Meernaidoo T. Somanah, *Mahatma Gandhi and Other Dedicated Souls*. Port Louis, MR, 1968; Shyam Sundar Agarwal Sarad, *The World Jnana Sadhak Society and Its Founder*. Jalpaiguri, W. Bengal, IN: The Author, 1966.

★58★
UNIVERSAL EPISCOPAL COMMUNION
(Defunct)

The Universal Episcopal Communion was organized in 1930 by James Christian Crummey (d. 1949), a Chicago theosophist, with the hope of uniting the various small and divided Old Catholic jurisdictions of North America and eventually other continents. During the 1920s, Crummey became a priest under Archbishop Carmel Henry Carfora of the North American Old Roman Catholic Church. On March 19, 1931, Carfora consecrated him as a bishop. As a step toward uniting the Old Catholics, he conceived of an additional organization in which bishops could coordinate activity but which would not attempt to control them in their independent ministries. This second body, hardly indistinguishable from the first, was called the Universal Christian Communion. Crummey headed both bodies and kept them within Carfora's jurisdiction until 1944 when he withdrew. At that point, the Universal Episcopal Communion and the Universal Christian Communion became independent entities. Joining him in leaving Carfora were Bishops Mather W. Sherwood and Murray L. Bennett. The two communions lasted until Crummey's death but disolved soon afterwards, neither having attained any significant support from their targeted constituency.

Sources: Henry R. T. Brandreth, *Episcopi Vegantes and the Anglican Church*. London: Society for Promoting Christian Knowledge, 1947; Peter Anson, *Bishops at Large*. London: Faber and Faber, 1964.

Anglicanism

★59★
AMERICAN EPISCOPAL CHURCH
155 Riverbend Dr., #4
Charlottesville, VA 22901

The American Episcopal Church was formed in Alabama in 1968 by a group of former clergy and members of the Protestant Episcopal Church and the Anglican Orthodox Church. They sought a more loosely organized structure than that offered by the Anglican Orthodox Church and organized the new jurisdiction with a congregational polity. The church turned to James Charles Ryan, better known by his Indian name, K. C. Pillai, for episcopal orders.

An Indian nationalist and convert to Christianity, Pillai sought an alternative to the Anglican Church in India, which in the 1940s still resisted placing Indians in episcopal positions. Pillai journeyed to England and received episcopal orders from the Evangelical Church of England (an offshoot of the Reformed Episcopal Chur ch) and then met Hugh George de Willmott Newman. In 1945, he was consecrated *sub conditione* by Newman, who commissioned him to head an Indian Orthodox Church under Newman's leadership. In 1948, the year India became independent, Pillai came to the United States where he eventually settled.

The congregations that made up the infant American Episcopal Church turned to Pillai, and he responded by becoming their first primate. The Indian Orthodox and the American Episcopal Church merged. In December 1968, Pillai consecrated James H. George as "Bishop of Birmingham." Bishop George succeeded Pillai as primate when he died in 1970.

On February 11, 1970, George consecrated Anthony F. M. Clavier as suffragan bishop. Having found the very loose structure of the church unworkable, the pair spearheaded a reorganization plan that led to the adoption of a more centrally organized polity. To accomplish the reorganization, it proved necessary for all of the clergy to resign from the church and to reconstitute it anew. Then the new American Episcopal Church, meeting in a general convention in April 1970, ratified a constitution and canon more in keeping with Anglican tradition. After the reorganization, Bishop George resigned as primate and Clavier succeeded him. The following year, George resigned from the church altogether and joined in the formation of the Anglican Church in America (now a part of the Anglican Episcopal Church). Clavier served as primus until 1976 when Harold L. Trott succeeded him. In 1981, Trott resigned both as primus and as a member of the church, and Clavier once again resumed duties as primus.

About this same time, the bishops of the American Episcopal Church received conditional reconsecration from Bishop Francisco Pagtakhan, assisted by bishops Sergio Mondala and Lupe Rosete, all of the Philippine Independent Church. Also consecrated at this service were the bishops of the Holy Catholic Church, Anglican Rite Jurisdiction of the Americas (with whom, at the time, merger talks were underway).

During the 1980s, the church has continued to grow. In May 1982, two dioceses and a majority of the members of the Anglican Episcopal Church joined the American Episcopal Church after a majority had voted to merge the two churches. In 1986, churches in Mexico that had formed in the late 1970s were recognized as a diocese. The Rt. Rev. Roberto Martinez-Resendiz, formerly sufragan bishop of Central Mexico of the Protestant Episcopal Church, became the first bishop of the new diocese.

Beliefs: The American Episcopal Church is theologically conservative and follows the 1928 Book of Common Prayer in its liturgy and teachings. In 1984, it adopted a "Solemn Declaration" avowing its allegiance to the ancient creed, the teachings of the seven Ecumenical Councils, and the Chicago-Lambeth Quadrilateral of 1886-1888. The 1801 text of the Anglican Thirty-nine Articles of Religion are accepted.

Organization: The church is episcopal in that it is headed by bishops, but also democratic in that laity share in the decision making process at every level of church life. The church is governed by the General Synod consisting of the House of Bishops, the House of Clergy; and the House of Laity. The General Synod meets biennially in the fall. At present there are four dioceses in the United States and one in Mexico. In 1983, the Diocese of the Southwest, which had withdrawn from the Anglican Catholic Church, united with the American Episcopal Church. It joined the Diocese of the South, the Diocese of the Eastern States, and the Diocese of the West.

The church is in communion with the Church in India and the Anglican Diocese of Pakistan.

Membership: In 1988, the church reported 5,000 members in 90 parishes served by 120 priests. There were 13,200 members worldwide.

Educational facilities: Diocesan Training Center, Orlando, Florida; St. George's College, San Antonio, Texas; St. George's College, San Antonio, Texas; St. Alban's Center, Eureka Springs, Arkansas.

Periodicals: *Ecclesia*, 3206 Heritage Circle, Henderville, NC 28739.

Sources: Anthony F. M. Clavier, *The American Episcopal Church.* Valley Forge, PA: Brotherhood of the Servants of the Lord, 1975. (Revised ed.: Greenville, SC: American Episcopal Church, 1976); Anthony F. M. Clavier, *The*

Principles of Reformed Catholicism. Cincinati: Diocese of the Eastern States, American Episcopal Church, 1976.

★60★
ANGLICAN CATHOLIC CHURCH
% The Most Rev. Louis W. Falk
4807 Aspen Dr.
West Des Moines, IA 50265

While dissent over what many felt was theological and moral drift in the Protestant Episcopal Church led to the formation of several small protesting bodies, large-scale dissent occurred only after a series of events beginning in 1974 gave substantive focus to the conservative protest. In 1974 four Episcopal bishops (in defiance of their colleagues and the church) ordained eleven women to the priesthood. The following year, the Anglican Church of Canada approved a provision for the ordination of women. Then in 1976, with only a token censure of the bishops, the Protestant Episcopal Church regularized the ordinations of the eleven women. It also approved the revised *Book Of Common Prayer* which replaced the 1928 edition most Episcopalians had used for half a century.

The events of the mid 1970s led to the calling of a Congress of Episcopalians to consider alternatives to the Protestant Episcopal Church and to find a way to continue a traditional Anglican Church. In the months leading up to the congress, several congregations and priests withdrew from the Episcopal Church and formed the provisional Diocese of the Holy Trinity. They designated James O. Mote as their bishop elect. Eighteen hundred persons gathered in St. Louis in September 1977 and adopted a lengthy statement, the "Affirmation of St. Louis," which called for allegiance to the Anglican tradition of belief (as expressed in the ancient creeds and the teachings of the church fathers) and practice (as exemplified in the 1928 edition of the Book of Common Prayer). It specifically denounced the admission of women to the priesthood, the liberal attitudes to alternative sexual patterns (especially homosexuality), and both the World Council of Churches and the National Council of Churches. It affirmed the rights of congregations to manage their own financial affairs and expressed a desire to remain in communion with the See of Canterbury.

Throughout 1977 more congregations left the Protestant Episcopal Church, and others were formed by groups of people who had left as individual members. Following the September congress, three more provisional dioceses were established, and bishops elected. The Diocese of Christ the King elected Robert S. Morse; the Diocese of the Southwest elected Peter F. Watterson; and the Diocese of the Midwest elected C. Dale D. Doren. Bishops were sought who would consent to consecrate the new bishops-elect, and four finally agreed. Of the four Paul Boynton, retired suffragan of New York, was the first to withdraw from the consecration service, due to illness. Then Mark Pae of the Anglican Church of Korea, a close personal friend of Dale Doren, withdrew under pressure from his fellow bishops. But he did send a letter of consent to the consecration. On January 28, 1978, with Pae's letter to confirm the action, Albert Chambers, former bishop of Springfield, Illinois and Francisco Pagtakhan, of the Philippine Independent Church, consecrated Doren. Doren in turn joined Chambers and Pagtakhan in consecrating Morse, Watterson, and Mote.

Having established itself with proper episcopal leadership, the new church, unofficially called the Anglican Church of North America, turned its attention to the task of ordering its life. A national synod meeting was held in Dallas in 1978. Those present adopted a name, the Anglican Catholic Church, and approved a constitution which was sent to the several dioceses (by then seven in number) for ratification. In May 1979, the bishops announced that five of the seven dioceses had ratified the actions of the Dallas synod; thus, the Anglican Catholic Church had been officially constituted.

The early 1980s was a period of flux for the Anglican Catholic Church. It emerged as the single largest body of the St. Louis meeting, claiming more than half of the congregations and members. But along the way, it lost two of its original dioceses and three of its original bishops. The dioceses of Christ the King and the Southeast and their bishops (Morse and Watterson) refused to ratify the constitution. They instead continued under the name "Anglican Church of North America." The Diocese of the Southeast soon broke with the Diocese of Christ the King and became an independent jurisdiction. Then, in 1984, Watterson resigned as bishop and joined the Roman Catholic Church. His action effectively killed the diocese, and member churches were absorbed by the other Anglican bodies, primarily the Anglican Catholic Church.

While dealing with the loss of the dioceses of Christ the King and the Southeast, the church continued to grow as new and independent congregations joined; additions more than made up for losses. Bishop Doren resigned in 1980, but only two congregations followed him. In 1981 several priests and parishes left to form the Holy Catholic Church, Anglican Rite Jurisdiction of the Americas. The largest schism occurred in 1983 when the Diocese of the Southwest under Bishop Robert C. Harvey withdrew and took twenty-one congregations in Arkansas, Texas, Oklahoma, New Mexico, and Arizona. Later that year they joined the American Episcopal Church.

The Anglican Catholic Church describes itself as the continuation of the traditional Anglicanism as expressed in the Nicene and Apostles' Creeds, and it holds to the liturgy of the Book of Common Prayer, 1928 edition. It rejects women in the priesthood and holds to traditional standards of moral conduct, condemning specifically "easy" divorce and remarriage, abortion on demand, and homosexual activity.

At its national convention in 1983, Louis W. Falk, bishop of the Diocese of the Missouri Valley, was elected as the ACC's first archbishop. While serving as archbishop he continues as pastor of St. Aldan's parish in Des Moines, Iowa.

Internationally, the church is in communion with the equally conservative Anglican Catholic Church-Australia, which is under Canadian oversight. In what is termed its Original Province, the church has parishes in Puerto Rico, Columbia, and Guatemala. In 1984 a Province for India was created. It has five dioceses and 3,000 members and, as of 1988, Bishop Falk serves as metropolitan for the providence. The American church has also developed direct oversight of a new conservative Anglican movement developing in New Zealand.

Membership: In 1988 the church reported 12,000 members, 200 parishes, and 200 priests in the United States. Worldwide membership included an additional 8,000 members.

Educational facilities: Holyrood Seminary, Liberty, New York.

Periodicals: *The Trinitarian*, 3141 South Josephine, Denver, CO 80210.

Sources: *A Directory of Churches of the Continuing Anglican Tradition.* Eureka Springs, AK: Fellowship of Concerned Churchmen, 1983-4; Perry Laukhuff, *The Anglican Catholic Church.* Eureka Springs, AK: Fellowship of Concerned Churchmen, 1977; *Opening Addresses of the Church Congress at St. Louis, Missouri, 14-16 September 1977.* Amherst, VA: Fellowship of Concerned Churchmen, 1977.

★61★
ANGLICAN CHURCH OF NORTH AMERICA
℅ Rt. Rev. Robert T. Shepherd
Chapel of St. Augustine of Canterbury
1906 Forest Green Dr., N.E.
Atlanta, GA 30329

The Anglican Church of North America traces its origin to the Independent Anglican Church founded in Canada in the 1930s by William H. Daw. Later he led his jurisdiction into the Liberal Catholic Church headed by Bishop Edward M. Matthews and in 1955 was consecrated by Matthews. In 1964 Daw and Bishop James Pickford Roberts left Matthews to found the Liberal Catholic Church International. Daw assumed the role of primate, but withdrew in 1974 in favor of Joseph Edward Neth. He resumed the primacy in 1979, when Neth was forced to resign after consecrating a priest of another jurisdiction without church approval.

In 1981 Daw participated in the formation of the Independent Catholic Church International, which brought together a number of independent Old Catholic,

Anglican, and Liberal Catholic jurisdictions in both North America and Europe. Meanwhile, the Liberal Catholic Church International and Daw reasserted its Anglican roots in the wake of the formation of the Anglican Catholic Church in Canada and the consecration and untimely death of its first bishop, Carmino M. de Catanzaro. The Liberal Catholic Church International repudiated Theosophy and changed its name to the North American Episcopal Church. In 1983 P. W. Goodrich, primate of the ecumenical Independent Catholic Church International, resigned to become primate of the North American Episcopal Church. Goodrich had originally been consecrated by Daw as bishop for the small Independent Catholic Church of Canada.

Goodrich's leadership of the North American Episcopal Church was shortlived, however, and within a year he was forced out and Archbishop Daw again resumed the primacy. Two bishops, Rt. Rev Robert T. Shepherd and Rt. Rev. M. B. D. Crawford, have been consecrated to administer the work of the church in America and Canada respectively. The first American parish was established in Atlanta, Georgia, in 1983. In June 1984, the church's name was changed to Anglican Church of North America.

The Anglican Church of North America, as other continuing Anglican Bodies, accepts the 1977 affirmation of St. Louis and follows the practices of the Protestant Episcopal Church and the Anglican Church of Canada prior to the changes of the 1970s. It differs from other continuing Anglican bodies in that it believes that a single jurisdiction should be established for all of North America rather than several jurisdictions divided along national and regional lines. It also stresses the collegiality of all levels of the clergy and the laity.

Membership: In 1984 the Church reported 10 congregations, 8 priests and 250 members in the United States and Canada.

Educational facilities: St. Matthias' Cathedral Seminary, Hamilton, Ontario, a correspondance school.

Periodicals: *Our Anglican Heritage.* 43 Medina Sq. East, Keswick, Ontario, Canada L4P 1E1.

★62★
ANGLICAN EPISCOPAL CHURCH OF NORTH AMERICA
% Most Rev. Walter Hollis Adams
789 Allen Ct.
Palo Alto, CA 94303

The Anglican Episcopal Church of North America was founded in 1972 by Walter Hollis Adams, a veteran of the British Foreign Office who had retired in California. That same year, Adams was consecrated by William Elliott Littlewood of the Free Protestant Episcopal Church. Later that year he was consecrated *sub conditione* by Herman

Adrian Spruit of the Church of Antioch, and the next year by Frederick Littler Pyman of the Evangelical Orthodox (Catholic) Church in America (Non-Papal Catholic).

Adams spearheaded efforts in the 1970s to bring together a number of traditional Anglican groups which, by the end of the decade, had either disappeared or merged into the Anglican Episcopal Church. These included, among others, the Anglican Church of America, the Episcopal Church (Evangelical), and the United Episcopal Church. In 1981 intercommunion was established with the American Episcopal Church (since revoked) and the Holy Catholic Church, Anglican Rite Jurisdiction of the Americas. On September 26, 1981, Adams was the first of several bishops to e consecrated (in Adams case *sub conditione*) by Bishops Francisco Pagtakhan, Sergio Mondala, and Lupe Rosete of the Philippine Independent Church, an effort initiated by Pagtakhan to promote unity among Anglican traditionalists.

In May 1982, the Anglican Episcopal Church and the American Episcopal Church met in Seattle, Washington, to discuss steps towards unity. This effort failed for a variety of reasons (Adams was undergoing emergency surgery at the time of the meeting). However, Anglican Episcopal Church Bishops John M. Hamers and Frank H. Benning withdrew from the church and, taking some of their respective dioceses with them, joined the American Episcopal Church.

In 1983, the Anglican Catholic Church (ACC) initiated discussions with Adams looking toward the merger of the two jurisdictions. At separate synods in 1985, the two formally approved the merger in which the Anglican Episcopal Church would retain its identity as the non-geographical Diocese of St. Paul within the ACC. This union was shortlived, for on July 14, 1986, with the backing of the clergy and parishes, Adams announced the withdrawal of the diocese and the reconstitution of the Anglican Episcopal Church of North America. In a manifesto published two weeks later (July 29, 1986), he accused the ACC heirarchy of intending, contrary to their previous agreement, to eliminate the special status of the Diocese of St. Paul, its bishop, and its clergy.

The Anglican Episcopal Church is traditional Anglican, with roots deeply embedded in the Church of England. It uses the King James Version of the Bible and the 1928 Book of Common Prayer. It believes the Holy Bible to be the inspired Word of God. It accepts the Apostles, Nicene and Athasian Creeds, and the Thirty-nine Articles of Religion as found in the Book of Common Prayer. The church permits a broad spectrum of ceremonial (encompassing both high and low emphases). It has also taken the lead in supporting the recent efforts of the Bishop of London (Great Britain) and the Archbishop of Sydney (Australia) to establish a world-wide unity of faith among traditional Anglicans.

The church has two diocese, each headed by a bishop. Bishop Adams is the ordinary for the Diocese of St. Paul. In January 1987, Robert Henry Voight, a former priest of the Protestant Episcopal Church in the U.S.A., was consecrated bishop for the Diocese of the Southwest. In that service, Adams was joined by four bishops from the United Episcopal Church of North America and the Anglican Rite Jurisdiction of the Americas.

Membership: In 1988 the Anglican Episcopal Church reported 15 congregations, 1,000 members, and 15 clergy, all in the United States.

Educational facilities: Laud Hall Anglican Episcopal Seminary, Deming, New Mexico.

Periodicals: *Anglican Episcopal Tidings*, Box 1693, Deming, NM 88031.

Remarks: The Episcopal Church (Evangelical) was formed in 1977 by Rt. Rev. M. Dean Stephens and former members of the Protestant Episcopal Church who wished to continue to "teach the faith of Our Father as given to the Church in England and subsequently to the Episcopal Church in America" bt which had been abandoned by the Protestant Episcopal Church. Stephens, formerly associated with the American Episcopal Church, had edited their periodical *Ecclesia*. In 1982, Stephens left the Anglican Episcopal Church and was reconsecrated in the Holy Catholic Church, Anglican Rite Jurisdiction of the Americas.

The United Episcopal Church was founded in 1973 by former members of the Anglican Orthodox Church under the leadership of bishops Troy A. Kaichen, Thomas J. Kleppinger, and Russell G. Fry. Under Kleppinger's leadership the church joined the Anglican Episcopal Council and subsequently merged with the Anglican Episcopal Church. Kleppinger served as suffragan to Bishop Adams and continued to edit the periodical *Episcopal Tidings*, which he had begun several years before. (Most recently, Kleppinger has transferred to the Anglican Catholic Church.)

The Anglican Episcopal Church describes itself as traditional. It uses the King James Version of the Bible and the Book of Common Prayer, 1928 edition, and it holds to the Apostles' and Nicene Creeds and the Articles of Religion. The Church is Evengelical and can be said to have its roots in the low church party of the Protestant Episcopal Church. As can be seen in its history, it has aggressively reached out of various splinter groups that came out of the Episcopal Church during the 1970s.

ANGLICAN ORTHODOX CHURCH
℅ Most Rev. James Parker Dees
323 E. Walnut St.
Box 128
Statesville, NC 28677

Rev. James Parker Dees, a priest in the Protestant Episcopal Church, was the first of the modern spokespersons to call the members of that church who opposed the changes in liturgy and program to come out and separate themselves from apostasy. A low church Episcopalian, he had trouble with both liberalism, which he felt denied biblical authority, and sacerdotalism among high church members. He therefore left the Episcopal Church and in 1963 formed the Anglican Orthodox Church. The following year he received episcopal orders from autocephalous Ukrainian Bishop Wasyl Sawyna and Old Catholic Bishop Orlando J. Woodward (who later joined the United Episcopal Church of America). Formed in the southern United States in the early 1960s, the North Carolina-based group found its greatest response among Episcopalians who rejected the Protestant Episcopal Church's departure from scriptural teaching and sound biblical doctrine.

The Anglican Orthodox Church follows the low church in a very conservative manner. It adheres to the Thirty-Nine Articles and uses the 1928 edition of the Book of Common Prayer. The polity is episcopal, but local congregations are autonomous and own their own property. Much power has been placed in the hands of the presiding bishop in order to provide a strong center of leadership and reduce the opportunity for error.

The Anglican Orthodox Church was able to bring together many pockets of dissent, however, and has created a strong church. By 1972 it had 37 congregations, though some were lost to other Anglican splinters as the decade progressed. Dees established Cramner Seminary, which in 1977 had four full-time students. He also has brought the church into communion with like-minded churches in Pakistan, South India, Nigeria, the Fiji Islands, Rhodesia (Zimbabwe), Madagascar, Colombia, South Africa, the Philippines, and Liberia.

As other Anglican groups have formed, Dees was pressed to draw sharp lines of distinction. He has argued against the doctrinal "looseness" and high church tendencies in other groups of Anglicans. He has continued his campaign against the growing "apostasy" he sees within the Protestant Episcopal Church, and has concentrated his attention upon building the Anglican Orthodox Church as a viable and continuing denomination.

Membership: In 1988 the church reported congregations and members in most of the 50 states. Foreign work, both missionary and with other jurisdictions in communion with the church, has given it a worldwide constituency of over 300,000.

Educational facilities: Cramner Seminary, Statesville, North Carolina.

Periodicals: *The News*, Box 128, Statesville, NC 28677.

Sources: James P. Dees, *Reformation Anglicanism*. Statesville, NC: Anglican Orthodox Church, 1971.

★64★
CELTIC EVANGELICAL CHURCH
% Rt. Rev. Wayne W. Gau
1666 St. Louis Dr.
Honolulu, HI 96816

The Celtic Evangelical Church is a small Anglican body formed in 1981 by its presbyter-abbot, Wayne W. Gau, and others who had formerly been members of the Celtic Catholic Church. Without rejecting the authenticity of the episcopal credentials of that church's bishop, Dwain Houser, they had asked numerous questions that had remained unanswered.

At its first general synod in November 1981, the church adopted a nine-point doctrinal statement. It is evangelical in its approach and regards the teachings and liturgy of the original Celtic church as authoritative. There are seven sacraments: two major sacraments, baptism and the eucharist, necessary for all Christians; and five minor sacraments, confirmation, penance, holy orders, matrimony, and unction, warranted by scripture but not mandatory. It acknowledges the Real Presence of Christ in the bread and wine of the holy eucharist. The filioque clause in the Nicene Creed is rejected, following th practice of the Eastern Orthodox churches. Worship is conducted in Latin following the ancient Celtic rite.

The Church has nurtured one religious order for men, the Community of St. Columba. Members are engaged in research in the ancient liturgies of Christianity, with special emphasis upon Celtic and Gallican rites. The order's work is directed by Canon James H. Donalson. It accepts associate members from other denominations.

In 1983, the church signed a concordant of intercommunion with the Catholic Apostolic Church of America, a small Anglican jurisdiction with parishes in the southwestern United States. That concordant was terminated in 1985, when the Catholic Apostolic Church united with the Holy Catholic Church, Anglican Rite Jurisdiction of the America. However, in 1987, Msgr. James B. Gillespie left the Anglican Rite Jurisdiction and reorganized the Catholic Apostolic Church of America as an independent jurisdiction. The Celtic Evangelical Church reinstituted the concordant with the revived church.

Membership: In 1984, the Church had one congregation in Hawaii.

Periodicals: *The Celtic Evangelist*, 1666 St. Louis Drive, Honolulu, HI 96816

★65★
DIOCESE OF CHRIST THE KING
% Rt. Rev. Robert S. Morse
St. Peter's Pro-Cathedral
6013 Lawton
Oakland, CA 94618

The Diocese of Christ the King shares the history of that larger conservative movement which participated in the 1977 congress at St. Louis and approved the "Affirmation" adopted by the delegates. The diocese was one of the four original provisional dioceses that were formed. Its bishop-elect, Robert S. Morse, was consecrated along with the other new Anglican bishops in Denver, Colorado on January 28, 1978, by Bishops Albert Chambers, Francisco Pagtakhan, and C. Dale D. Doren. However, Bishop Morse and other members of his diocese were among those most opposed to the new constitution adopted by the synod at Dallas in 1978 by the group which took the name Anglican Catholic Church. Neither the Diocese of Christ the King nor the Diocese of the Southeast ratified the constitution, preferring instead to work without such a document. They called a synod meeting for Hot Springs, Arkansas, on October 16-18, 1978, two days immediately prior to the opening of the Anglican Catholic Church synod at Indianapolis, Indiana. Those gathered at Hot Springs decided to continue informally to use the name "Anglican of North America." They adopted canons (church laws) but no constitution.

The new jurisdiction immediately faced intense administrative pressures. In response to the "Anglican Church of North America" claiming many congregations in California and the South, the Anglican Catholic Church established a new structure, the patrimony, to facilitate the movement of existing congregations into the church and to assist the formation of new congregations in areas not covered by existing diocesan structures. Both Bishop Morse and Bishop Watterson viewed the patrimony as an attempt to steal the congregations under their jurisdiction.

The pressure from the Anglican Catholic Church did not keep the two dioceses in the "Anglican Church of North America" from facing crucial internal issues. Bishop Watterson argued for a strict division of the Anglican Church of North America into geographical dioceses with the understanding that neither bishop would attempt to establish congregations or missions in the other's diocese. The diocese of Christ the King rejected Watterson's suggestions, and the Diocese of the Southeast became a separate jurisdiction. The Diocese of Christ the King proceeded to initiate work in the South.

Once separated, the Diocese of the Southeast experienced continued internal problems. In 1980 nine congregations withdrew with the blessing of Bishop Francisco Pagtakhan (who was becoming increasingly dissatisfied with the Anglican Catholic Church) and formed the Associated Parishes, Traditional Anglo-Catholic. Pagtakhan named Fr. J. Bruce Medaris as archdeacon. This new jurisdiction dissolved very quickly and merged back into Anglican Catholic Church. Finally, in 1984, Bishop Watterson resigned his office and joined the Roman Catholic Church. His jurisdiction dissolved and the remaining congregations realigned themselves with the other Anglican bodies. The dissolution of the Diocese of the Southeast left the Diocese of Christ the King the only diocese in the "Anglican Church of North America."

The Diocese of Christ the King is at one in faith and practice with the other Anglican bodies, holding to the faith of the undivided primitive church to which Episcopalians have always belonged, as spelled out in the affirmation of St. Louis. It rejects both the National Council of Churches and the World Council of Churches. It differs from the Anglican Catholic Church only in matters of administration.

Membership: In 1983 the Diocese of Christ the King had 35 parishes with an estimated 3,000 to 5,000 members.

Educational facilities: Saint Joseph of Arimathea Anglican Theological College, Berkeley, California.

Sources: *A Directory of Churches in the Continuing Anglican Tradition 1983-84*. Eureka Springs, AK: Fellowship of Concerned Churchmen, 1983-84.

★66★
DIOCESE OF THE SOUTHWEST
(Defunct)

The shortlived Diocese of the Southwest was originally formed in 1978 as a constituent part of the Anglican Catholic Church. In 1982 it left the ACC and for several months existed as an independent jurisdiction. In December 1983 it merged into the American Episcopal Church. It no longer exists as a separate body.

★67★
FREE PROTESTANT EPISCOPAL CHURCH
Current address not obtained for this edition.

The Free Protestant Episcopal Church was established in 1897 by the union of three small British episcopates: the Ancient British Church (founded 1876/77); Nazarene Episcopal Ecclesia (founded in 1873); and Free Protestant Church of England (founded in 1889). Leon Checkemian, an Armenian, the first primate of the new church, was supposedly consecrated by Bishop A. S. Richardson of the Reformed Episcopal Church in 1890, though present claims indicate that he was consecrated in 1878 by an Archbishop Chorchorunian. In either case, no papers have been produced, and the validity of the consecration is questioned by many. In 1952, Charles D. Boltwood became the fifth person to hold the post of primate.

The faith of the Free Protestant Episcopal Church is the same as the Protestant Episcopal Church. The Thirty-nine Articles are accepted. There are, however, seven doctrines condemned as contrary to God's word: 1) that the church exists in only one order or form of polity; 2) that ministers are "priests" in any other sense than that in which all believers are a "royal priesthood;" 3) that the Lord's table is an altar on which the oblation of the body and blood of Christ is offered anew to the Father; 4) that Christ is present in the elements of bread and wine in the Lord's Supper; 5) that regeneration and baptism are inseparably connected; 6) that the law should punish Christians with death; and 7) that Christians may wear weapons and serve in war except in aiding the wounded or assisting in civil defense. In these seven objections, the sacramentalism of Anglo- Catholicism is explicitly denied and conscientious objection to carrying arms in war is elevated to dogma.

The Free Protestant Episcopal Church came to America in 1958 when Boltwood, on a trip to Los Angeles, consecrated Emmet Neil Enochs as archbishop of California and primate of the United States. On the same trip, John M. Stanley was consecrated bishop of Washington; subsequently four additional bishops were consecrated for the United States. The primate was directly responsible to the bishop primus in London. In 1967 the Free Protestant Episcopal Church reported 23 congregations plus a number of affiliated missions, and there were an estimated 2,000 members in the United States and Canada.

The Free Protestant Episcopal Church dissipated as various bishops passed orders to men who established other jurisdictions. These included such groups as the Autocephalous Syro-Chaldean Church of North America, which received orders from Bishop Stanley; the Anglican Episcopal Church, whose founder was consecrated by a Free PEC bishop, W. E. Littlewood; and the Apostolic Catholic Church of the Americas, formed by former Free Protestant Episcopal Bishop Gordon I. DaCosta. The last United States Primate Albert J. Fuge, retired without naming a successor.

★68★
HOLY CATHOLIC CHURCH, ANGLICAN RITE JURISDICTION OF THE AMERICAS
℅ Most. Rev. G. Wayne Craig, Archbishop
Box 14352
Columbus, OH 43214

In the several years following the 1977 St. Louis congress, the Anglican Movement grew to encompass more than 200 congregations. However, as it grew, it splintered into several factions due to administrative disagreements as well as the issue of the domination of the Anglican Catholic Church by the Anglo-Catholic (high-church) perspective. Some congregations remained outside of the various diocesan structures altogether. Bishop Francisco Pagtakhan of the Philippine Independent Church, who had participated in the original consecrations of the four Anglican bishops in 1978, became increasingly disturbed at the splintering and lack of unity in the Anglican Movement. In 1980, asserting his role as the ecumenical and missionary officer for the Philippine Independent Church, Pagt akhan decided to create an "umbrella" for those in the Anglican Movement who were searching for a home where they could "belong to a genuinely canonical part of the One, Holy, Catholic and Apostolic Church." Thus in March 1980, in Texas, he initiated the incorporation of the Holy Catholic Church, Anglican Rite Jurisdiction of the Americas.

On September 26, 1981 (with the permission of the supreme bishop of the Philippine Independent Church, the Most Rev. Macario V. Ga) Bishop Pagtakhan, assisted by retired bishops Sergio Mondala and Lupe Rosete, consecrated Robert Q. Kennaugh, F. Ogden Miller, and G. Wayne Craig, all former priests in the Anglican Catholic Church. Kennaugh became head of the Diocese of St. Luke, centered in Corsicana, Texas, and archbishop for the jurisdiction. Miller was named bishop of the Diocese of St. Matthew with headquarters in California. Craig became bishop of the Diocese of St. Mark with headquarters in Columbus, Ohio. In 1982 Herman F. Nelson was consecrated as bishop for the Diocese of St. John the Evangelist with headquarters in Venice, Florida. Shortly thereafter, Kennaugh retired as archbishop, and Craig was named to that post. In 1985 the Anglican Rite Jurisdiction received Bishop Harold L. Trott into the Church as the Bishop of the Missionary Diocese of Reconciliation. Trott had left the American Episcopal Church in 1979 and had formed the Pro-Diocese of Reconciliation (consisting of several congregations in California and New Mexico) while waiting for a larger body with which to affiliate.

In 1986 the jurisdiction accepted Rt. Rev. Lafond Lapointe, a Haitian-born bishop who had been exiled from his homeland for political reasons. In the intervening years he had worked in the Haitian-American community in Chicago, Illinois. After the fall of the dictatorship in Haiti he was able to return as the Bishop of the Anglican Diocese of Haiti. He reconstituted L'Iglise Orthodox Apostolique Haitienne, an independent church established in 1874 by Bishop James Theodore Holley with the approval and backing of the Protestant Episcopal Church. Holley died in 1911 and his church was absorbed into the Episcopal Missionary Diocese in 1913.

Also, in recent years, the Anglican Rite Jurisdiction of the Americas has established close ties to Los Hermanos Franciscanos de la Providencia, a Franciscan order in Puerto Rico. Retired Archbishop Robert Q. Kennaugh has become the bishop-protector of the order. The community works both in the rural area of the island and operates a medical clinic in Santo Domingo.

The Anglican Rite Jurisdiction of the Americas has no differences in doctrine and practice with the larger Anglican Movement and emphasizes its thorough commitment to "the unity of genuine continuing Anglicanism." The jurisdiction has moved to establish intercommunion with other Anglican bodies and to accept otherwise independent congregations under its umbrella.

Membership: In 1988 the jurisdiction had 19 clergy, 14 congregations, and 1,000 members in the United States. There was one mission with approximately 2,000 members in seven congregations and two native priests in Haiti.

Educational facilities: Anglican Theological Collegium, Columbus, OH.

Periodicals: *The Anglican Evangelist*, Box 785, Rincon, GA 31326.

Sources: Roderic B. Dibbert, *The Roots of Traditional Anglicanism*. Akron, OH: Dekoven Foundation, 1984; *The Prologue*. Akron, OH: DeKoven Foundation, 1984; *Official Directory of Bishops, Clergy, Parishes*. Akron, OH: Holy Catholic Church, Anglican Rite Jurisdiction of the America, Office of the Secretary of the ARJA Synod, 1985.

★69★
OLD EPISCOPAL CHURCH
% Rt. Rev. Jack C. Adam
Box 2424
Mesa, AZ 85204

The Old Episcopal Church is a small diocese in the Southwest headed by Rt. Rev. Jack C. Adam, Bishop of Arizona. A former Protestant Episcopal Church priest, he left the Episcopal Church and was consecrated by Archbishop Walter Propheta of the America Orthodox Catholic Church in 1972.

Membership: Not reported. There are several parishes in Arizona and New Mexico.

★70★
PHILIPPINE INDEPENDENT CHURCH
% St. Andrew's Episcopal Cathedral
Queen Emma Sq.
Honolulu, HI 96813

The Philippine Independent Church emerged from the political struggles of the nineteenth century which led to full independence of the Philippine Islands. Following the defeat of the Spanish in 1898, the United States took control of the Philippines, rather than grant it full governmental autonomy. A revolt, led by Emilio Aguinaldo, developed against American rule. In that area of the country briefly controlled by Aguinaldo, a military vicar general, Gregorio Aglipay (1860-1940), was appointed to head the Roman Catholic Church. In 1899 the Roman Catholic Archbishop of Manila excommunicated Aglipay, and the church under his control reorganized as the Iglesia Filipina Independiente.

As a guerrilla general, Aglipay became a hero to many, and was the last of the revolutionary leaders to surrender. He retained the loyalty of the members of the new church and spent the remainder of his life guiding it. The progress of the church was checked by a 1906 ruling of the country's supreme court, which awarded most of the church's property to the Roman Catholic Church. Early in the century Aglipay became influenced by Unitarian views (which deny the doctrine of the Trinity), and he led the church in their acceptance. The extent of the theological drift was clearly demonstrated by the 1939 appointment of Dr. Louis C. Cornish, president of the American Unitarian Association, as the honorary president of the church.

The dominance of Unitarian thought was ended after Aglipay's death by his successor as supreme bishop, Isabelo de los Reyes, Jr.. A Trinitarian, Reyes led the church to adopt a strong Trinitarian Declaration of Faith in 1947 which included acceptance of the Apostles' and Nicene Creeds. Concurrently, the Protestant Episcopal Church recognized the Philippine Independent Church. The following year the supreme bishop and two other bishops of the Philippine Independent Church were consecrated by the Protestant Episcopal Church, giving them the Anglican lineage of apostolic succession.

The Philippine Independent Church began work in the United States during the years of negotiation, which led to the establishment of full intercommunion with the Protestant Episcopal Church in 1961. With the blessing of the Episcopal bishop in Hawaii, a mission among Filipino-Americans was initiated in 1959. By the mid-1970s three parishes, meeting in Episcopal churches, had been established. Services were held in both the English and Ilocano languages. The church has subsequently established congregations in other states.

The Philippine Independent Church established communion with the Protestant Episcopal Church, the Philippine Episcopal Church, and other Anglican bodies through the terms of the Bonn agreement of 1931, which brought the Church of England and the Old Catholic Church into accord. As of 1985 it maintained communion with a number of Anglican bodies, the Old Catholic Churches in Europe, the Polish National Catholic Church, and the Lusitanian Catholic-Apostolic Evangelical Church. It is a member of the World Council of Churches.

Membership: As of 1985 there were a reported 4,500,000 members, 726 parishes, and 688 priests worldwide, most in the Philippines.

Periodicals: *Aglipayian Review*, Box 2484, Manila, PH.

Remarks: Since the late 1970s relations between the Protestant Episcopal Church and the Philippine Independent Church have been strained due to the participation of several Philippine bishops in the consecration of bishops for independent conservative Anglican jurisdictions established by former Episcopalians. In 1978 Francisco Pagtakhan, Bishop Secretary of Missions for the Philippine Independent Church, participated in the consecration of several bishops for what became the Anglican Catholic Church, the Diocese of Christ the King, and the United Episcopal Church of North America. Then in 1980, Pagtakhan led in the founding of the Holy Catholic Church, Anglican Rite Jurisdiction of the Americas, and with Bishops Sergio Mondala and Lupe Rosete, consecrated three bishops for the new church. In 1982 he broke relations with that jurisdiction and established rival work in a new Anglican Rite Diocese of Texas.

Sources: Richard L. Deats, *Nationalism and Christianity in the Philippines*. Dallas, TX: Southern Methodist University Press, 1967; Gerald H. Anderson, ed., *Studies in Philippine Church History*. Ithaca, NY: Cornell University Press, 1969.

★71★

PROTESTANT EPISCOPAL CHURCH IN THE U.S.A.
815 Second Ave.
New York, NY 10017

The Church of England came into the American colonies with the first British settlers. The first church was established at Jamestown in 1607, and in 1619 an act of the Virginia legislature formally declared Virginians to be members of the Church of England. By the time of the American Revolution, more than 400 Anglican parishes were spread along the coast from Georgia to New Hampshire.

The American Revolution created a crisis for the church in the new nation because, in spite of the large number of parishes, the church in the colonies had no bishop. War with England meant England would not be sending a bishop to America, so there was no way to ordain new priests or consecrate future bishops. Further, many priests (already in short supply) sided with England in the Revolution and returned to England. Thus the war left Anglican congregations highly disorganized. In 1783 the Connecticut churches sent Samuel Seabury to England to be consecrated. But, because he would not swear allegiance to the British Crown, he could not be consecrated. He was finally consecrated by the Non-juring Church of Scotland in 1784. Upon Seabury's return in 1785, the Connecticut priests held a convocation to organize their parishes.

Meanwhile, a second movement to reorganize the American parishes was undertaken in the Middle Colonies (mainly in Pennsylvania and Virginia) under the leadership of William White. A series of meetings over the next several years resulted in the adoption of the "Ecclesiastical Constitution of the Protestant Episcopal Church in the United States." William White and Samuel Provoost were chosen as bishops. They sailed for England and were consecrated by the archbishop of Canterbury in 1787, after Parliament had rescinded the requirement of an oath of loyalty to the Crown for any consecrated bishop from "foreign parts." In 1789 the new constitution was adopted by all the American churches (including Bishop Seabury's diocese). The Protestant Episcopal Church was born, the church that represents the Anglican tradition in the U.S.

The Protestant Episcopal Church, popularly called the Episcopal Church, grew and became a national body during the nineteenth century. Within its membership three informally organized but recognizable groups developed: the high church of the Anglo-Catholic group; the low church evangelicals; and the broad church party (the group between the high church and low church groups). The differences between these groups was largely based upon their approach to liturgy and the Eucharist. Episcopalians have followed the liturgy of the Prayer Book which is built upon a belief in the Real Presence of Christ in the Eucharist. The Church of England passed to American Episcopalians a repudiation of the particular explanation of that doctrine of the Real Presence called "transubstantiation." High Church Episcopalians have tended to emphasize the forms and ceremonies associated with the Roman tradition and have tended toward a Roman explanation of the Real Presence. In contrast, Low Church Episcopalians have emphasized the "Puritan" element introduced into the Anglican Church after the Reformation. They have opposed the emphasis on outward ceremony, centering their attention upon the reading and preaching of the Word.

During the 1840s the American Church began to receive the influence of the Oxford Movement, a high church revival in the Church of England. Among the personages identified with the movement was John Henry Newman, who later joined the Roman Catholic Church. In the wake of the revival, church architecture and sanctuary furnishings began to change. The Gothic church became common. The common arrangement of furniture in the sanctuary centered upon a table, and the pulpit was replaced with a center altar, the common arrangement today.

The broad church party, which reached into both high-church and low-church camps was identified mostly by its liberalism in matters of discipline, doctrine, and Biblical interpretation. Broad churchmen generally avoided too much emphasis upon ceremony and found their identification in their enclusive spirit. They were open to a variety of creedal interpretations and would often open their pulpit and altar to non-Episcopalians.

During the mid-twentieth century new issues began to become prominent in the church, and these led to new lines of division that cut across the older groupings. Dissent within the church appeared around the issues of laxity in church moral standards (especially an acceptance of sexual immorality), the ordination of women priests, the reported use of funds contributed to the National Council of Churches and World Council of Churches for "far-left" political causes, and the church's involvement in various social crusades (from civil rights and women's liberation to gay liberation). In addition, disagreements evolved over the introduction of extensive revisions of the 1928 edition of the *Book of Common Prayer*, made available in a revised prayer book. These issues came to a head in 1976 when the General Convention of the church approved the ordination of women and the revised *Book of Common Prayer*. Several thousand who disapproved of the changes left the church in the late 1970s. (Following the movement out of the Episcopal Church, the Anglicans, as the conservatives called themselves, tended to split along the older party lines).

Membership: In 1985 the church reported 2,739,422 members in 7,294 congregations served by 13,940 priests.

Educational facilities: Seminaries: Berkeley Divinity School at Yale, New Haven Connecticut; Church Divinity School of the Pacific, Berkeley, California; General Theological Seminary, New York City, New York; George Mercer Jr., Memorial School of Theology, Garden City New York; Nashotah House, Nashotah, Wisconsin; Protestant Episcopal Theological Seminary in Virginia, Alexandria, Virginia; Seabury-Western Theological Seminary, Evanston, Illinois; University of the South, School of Theology, Sewanee, Tennessee.

Colleges and universities: Bard College, Annandale-on-the-Hudson, New York; Hobart and William Smith College, Geneva, New York; Kenyon College, Gambier, Ohio; St. Augustine's College, Raleigh, North Carolina; St. Paul's College, Lawrenceville, Virginia; Trinity College, Hartford, Connecticut; University of the South, Sewanee, Tennessee; Voorhees College, Denmark, South Carolina.

Periodicals: *The Episcopalian*, 1930 Chestnut Street, Philadelphia, PA 19103; *The Living Church*, 407 E. Michigan Street, Milwaukee, WI 53202; *Historical Magazine*, Box 2247, Austin, TX 78705.

Remarks: In 1967 the General Convention adopted the designation "Episcopal Church" as an official alternative name.

Sources: William & Betty Gray, *The Episcopal Church Welcomes You*. New York: Seabury Press, 1974; William W. Manross, *A History of the American Episcopal Church*. New York: Morehouse-Gorham, 1950; Edward Lambe Parsons and Bayare Hale Jones, *The American Prayer Book*. New York: Charles Scribner's Sons, 1946; W. Norman Pittenger, *The Episcopalian Way of Life*.

Englewood Cliffs, NJ: Prentice-Hall, 1957: Massey H. Shepherd, Jr., *The Worship of the Church*. Greenwich, CT; Seabury Press, 1954; William Synder, *Looking at the Episcopal Church*. Wilton, CT: Morehouse-Barlow, 1980. Kit Konolige and Frederica Konolige, *The Power of Their Glory*. N.p: Wyden Books, 1978.

★72★
PROVISIONAL DIOCESE OF ST. AUGUSTINE OF CANTERBURY
(Defunct)

The Provisional Diocese of St. Augustine of Canterbury was formed in 1978 by Canon Albert J. duBois (1906-1980), former head of the American Church Union, and five former parishes of the Diocese of the Holy Trinity (of what is now the Anglican Catholic Church). It was the desire of the parishes to unite with The Roman Catholic Church, though they wished to retain their own liturgy, forms of piety, and their traditional lay involvement in the life of the Church. The group was led by its "senior priest," Canon duBois; the Rev. John Barker, head of the "Clericus," a priests' conference; and Dr. Theodore L. McEvoy, head of its "Laymen's League."

In 1980 Archbishop John R. Quinn, Roman Catholic Archbishop of San Francisco, announced a plan by which Anglicans could come into the Roman Catholic Church and keep their own priests, an approved Anglican liturgy, and a common identity. In 1981, James Parker became the first priest to move from the Protestant Episcopal Church to the Roman jurisdiction. By 1985, twenty-three married priests had been re-ordained as Roman priests. Five parishes had been received by the Vatican.

★73★
REFORMED EPISCOPAL CHURCH
4225 Chestnut St.
Philadelphia, PA 19104

History: The Reformed Episcopal Church was founded on December 2, 1873, in New York City at the call of the Rt. Rev. George David Cummins, formerly the assistant bishop of Kentucky in the Protestant Episcopal Church in the U. S. A. As an evangelical, Cummins viewed with alarm the influence of the Anglo-Catholic movement within the Episcopal church. He had come to believe that it had fatally compromised the Protestant character of Anglican doctrine and worship and that it had bred intolerance to evangelical preaching and worship.

Throughout the 1860s, factions within the Episcopal church had been clashing over ceremonial and doctrinal issues, especially concerning the meaning of critical passages of the *Book of Common Prayer*. These clashes reached a climax for Cummins in October 1873, when he was publicly attacked by his fellow bishops for participating in an ecumenical communion service under the aegis of the Evangelical Alliance in New York City. On November 10, 1873, he resigned his office of assistant

bishop and on November 15 issued the call to other evangelical Episcopalians to join him in organizing a new Episcopal church for the "purpose of restoring the old paths of the fathers..."

Beliefs: At the organization of the new church, a declaration of principles was adopted and the Rev. Charles E. Cheney was elected bishop to serve with Cummins (Cheney was consecrated by Cummins on December 14, 1873). In May 1874, the Second General Council approved a Constitution and Canons for the church and a slightly amended version of *The Book of Common Prayer*. In 1875, the Third General Council adopted a set of Thirty-nine Articles as an explanatory supplement to the Church of England's Thirty-nine Articles of Religion.

Organization: Although Cummins died in 1876, the church had grown to seven jurisdictions in the U.S. and Canada. Although substantial growth ceased after 1900, the Reformed Episcopal Church now comprises three synods (New York-Philadelphia, Chicago, and Charleston-Atlanta-Charlotte) and a Special Missionary Jurisdiction with churches in Arizona and California. It maintains a theological seminary in Philadelphia which offers a three-year curriculum and houses a library and archival resources.

The church is governed by a triennial general council, and elects a presiding bishop from among its serving bishops to be executive head of the church; however, most authority lies at the synodical and parish levels. It has maintained in its doctrine the principles of episcopacy (in historic succession from the apostles), Anglican liturgy, Reformed doctrine, and evangelical fellowship, and in its practice, it continues to recognize the validity of certain non-episcopal orders of evangelical ministry. The church was briefly a member of the Federal Council of Churches at its inception. It is currently a member of the National Association of Evangelicals. It has instituted dialogue in response to invitations from the Episcopal Church in 1920, 1931-41, and in 1987-88.

Membership: In 1988, the church reported between 7,000 and 10,000 members in 102 congregations and missions, and 94 ministers.

Educational facilities: The Theological Seminary of the Reformed Episcopal Church, 4225 Chestnut St., Philadelphia, PA 19104; Cummins Memorial Theological Seminary, 705 S. Main St., Summerville, SC 29483.

Periodicals: *The Episcopal Recorder*, 901 Church Rd., Oreland, PA 19075; *The Reformed Episcopalian*, South St. at Central Ave., New Providence, NJ 07974.

Sources: *The Book of Common Prayer*. Philadelphia: The Reformed Episcopal Publication Society, 1932; Charles Edward Cheney, *What Reformed Episcopalians Believe*. N.p. [Philadelphia?]: Christian Education Committee,

Reformed Episcopal Church, 1961; Allen C. Guelzo, *The First Thirty Years: A Historical Handbook for the Founding of the Reformed Episcopal Church, 1873-1903.* Philadelphia: Reformed Episcopal Publication Society, 1986; Paul A Carter, "The Reformed Episcopal Schism of 1873: An Ecumenical Perspective," in *Historical Magazine of the Protestant Episcopal Church*, 33, 3 (September 1964); Warren C. Platt, "The Reformed Episcopal Church: The Origins and Early Development of its Theological Perspective," in *Historical Magazine of the Protestant Episcopal Church*, 61 (1983).

★74★

SOUTHERN EPISCOPAL CHURCH
℅ Most Rev. B. H. Webster
2315 Valley Brook Rd.
Nashville, TN 37215

The Southern Episcopal Church was formed in 1953 by ten families of All Saints Episcopal Church in Nashville, Tennessee. Its constitution was ratified in 1965. The presiding bishop is the Rt. Rev. B. H. Webster. He is assisted by fellow bishops William Green, Jr., Henry L. Atwell, and Huron C. Manning, Jr. The church is governed by the National Convention composed of all bishops (House of Bishops) and the lay and clerical delegates. The 1928 *Book of Common Prayer* is standard for worship. The church sponsors an American Indian mission as well as foreign work in four countries, including a mission in India started in the mid-1980s. American parishes can be found in Tennessee, Alabama, Georgia, the Carolinas, Florida, Ohio, Indiana, Oklahoma, and New York.

Membership: In 1984 the Church reported 72,000 members in 14 congregations with 17 priests.

Educational facilities: Holy Trinity College, Nashville, Tennessee.

Periodicals: *The Southern Episcopalians*, 2315 Valley Brook Road, Nashville, TN 37215.

★75★

UNITED EPISCOPAL CHURCH (1945) ANGLICAN/ CELTIC
Office of the Chancery
526 North Maple
Murfreesboro, TN 37130

History. The United Episcopal Church (1945) Anglican/ Celtic (UEC) was formed in 1945 in Plainfield, Illinois, by Bishops Julius Massey, Albert Sorensen, and Hinton Pride. They envisioned a restored church of Anglican/ Celtic heritage. St. Paul's Cathedral was designed and built in Plainfield. During the process of its early growth, several previously founded churches affiliated with the UEC, including the Norwegian Seaman's Mission in Chicago. In the mid-1950s, Bishop James E. Burns, who had previously founded several Anglican churches,

brought his jurisdiction into the United Episcopal Church. Burns had originally been consecrated by William H. Schneider, who like Massey had been consecrated by Denver Scott Swain of the American Episcopal Church (1940s). Burns also persuaded the Rev. Orlando J. Woodward, pastor of the independent Bethany Presbyterian Church in Fort Orlethorpe, Georgia, to bring his congregation into the jurisdiction. Woodward had been ordained by Archbishop William Francis Brothers of the Old Catholic Church in America, but had introduced the congregation he served to the Episcopal Prayer Book and led it to adopt the Thirty-nine Articles of Religion of the Protestant Episcopal Church in the U.S.A. as its standard of doctrine.

After a period of growth, during which time Woodward served as presiding bishop (1961-1965), the church entered a period of decline. Woodward suffered a near-fatal illness, several of the priests retired, and bishops Massey and Sorensen died. It was during this time with the church nearly moribund that Bishop Burns consecrated Richard C. Acker, who founded the United Episcopal Church of America as a successor organization. However, in the 1980s, Woodward was able to resume his duties as presiding bishop and began reviving the UEC. New parishes were created and in 1988, with the assistance of Karl Pruter, head of Christ Catholic Church, Woodward consecrated Ted D. Kelly as the church's chancellor.

Beliefs. The UEC accepts the Thirty-nine Articles of Religion common to Anglicanism and uses the 1928 edition of the *Book of Common Prayer*. It considers the traditional teachings of the Anglican faith to be binding and not subject to alteration or debate. It also accepts as valid those practices and the liturgical worship as introduced intothe ancient British Isles by the Celtic and Gallic monks and missionaries, and which, when integrated into the traditions of St. Augustine of Canterbury, produced the Anglican tradition. The church recognizes two greater sacraments, baptism and the Holy Eucharist, and five lesser ones: confirmation, confession, holy orders, marriage, and unction. It retains the spectrum of high (more liturgical), low (less formal), and broad church emphases in the expression of worship.

Organization. The church follows an episcopal polity. The governance is invested in the National Convention consisting of the all the bishops (the College of Bishops) and all the priests and lay delegates from each parish (the House of Delegates). The presiding bishop presides at the convention meetings. In 1987 Bishop Woodward and Fr. (now Bishop) Kelly founded the Missionary Order of St. Jude, dedicated to the assistance of the poor and needy. The church is opposed to the admission of women to the priesthood.

Membership: In 1988 there were 18 congregations approximately 780 members, 12 priests, eight deacons, and 16 candidates for holy orders in the United States. There was one congregation in Canada and affiliated parishes in India, Puerto Rico, and Africa.

★76★

UNITED EPISCOPAL CHURCH OF AMERICA
% Rt. Rev. Charles E. Morley
Box 18223
Pensacola, FL 32523

The United Episcopal Church of America started in 1970 as an independent Anglican parish meeting in the home of Howard Love of Columbia, South Carolina. The congregation decided to affiliate with the American Episcopal Church (AEC) and called former Protestant Episcopal priest Richard C. Acker (d. 1985) to the pulpit. Acker was installed in 1971 by Archbishop Anthony F. Clavier, head of the American Episcopal Church. In 1973 the congregation withdrew from the AEC. Over the next few years Acker became acquainted with Bishop James E. Burns of the United Episcopal Church (1945) Anglican/ Celtic. Burns' consecration of Acker in 1976 led to the formation of the United Episcopal Church of America over which Acker served as archbishop. Acker was succeeded as head of the church by Charles Edward Morley, whom he consecrated in 1984.

The church uses the King James Version of the Bible, the 1928 edition of the *Book of Common Prayer*, and the 1940 hymnal of the Protestant Episcopal Church in the U.S.A.

Membership: Not reported.

★77★

UNITED EPISCOPAL CHURCH OF NORTH AMERICA
% Most Rev. C. Dale D. Doren
2293 Country Club Dr.
Upper St. Clair, PA 15241

In 1980 C. Dale David Doren, senior bishop of the Anglican Catholic Church and head of its mid-Atlantic diocese, resigned. He contended that the Anglican Catholic Church was becoming exclusively "high-church" or "Anglo-Catholic" in its stance. With only two congregations, he formed the United Episcopal Church of the U.S.A. (known since 1985 as the United Episcopal) and the United Episcopal Church of North America. It adheres to the traditional beliefs and practices of the Protestant Episcopal Church as exemplified in the 1928 *Book of Common Prayer* and the Thirty-nine Articles of Religion.

The UEC tends to the "low-church" end of the Anglican spectrum. Each parish is independent and holds title to properties and control over temporal affairs. The jurisdiction adopted the 1958 Protestant Episcopal Church Constitution and Canons (with specific changes in relation to church properties) as its own. The presiding bishop was given the title of archbishop, but the church invested little power in the office. In 1984 Archbishop Dorn consecrated Albion W. Knight as a missionary bishop to assist him in leadership of the jurisdiction's affairs.

Membership: Not reported. Parishes of the church are found in Pennsylvannia, Ohio, New York, Maryland, New Hampshire, and Florida. In 1984, membership was estimated to be less than 1,000.

Periodicals: *Glad Tidings*, Box 4538, Pensacola, Florida 32507.

Section 2

Eastern Liturgical Family

An historical essay on this family is provided beginning on page 9.

Orthodoxy

★78★

AFRICAN ORTHODOX CHURCH
℅ Rt. Rev. James A. Ford
137 Allston St.
Cambridge, MA 02139

The Protestant Episcopal Church, like all American denominations with both episcopal leadership and a significant black membership, faced the problems and pressures related to electing and elevating their first black member to the bishopric. Within the Episcopal Church the cries for a bishop drawn from among black members grew even louder after the Civil War. They were refused, the leadership arguing that, since the church did not recognize racial distinctions, it could not elevate a man to the bishopric just because he was black. A step toward the solution came in 1910 with the creation of black "suffragan" bishops, bishops without right to succession and without vote in the house of bishops.

Among those who complained that suffragans were not enough was Dr. George A. McGuire (1866-1934), an Episcopal priest who had emigrated from the West Indies. In 1921 he left the Protestant Episcopal Church and founded the Independent Episcopal Church. McGuire had had a distinguished career in the Episcopal Church, serving parishes in both the United States and Antigua, and he had been considered for the post of Suffragan Bishop of Arkansas. He declined in order to study medicine at Jefferson Medical College, where he graduated as a Doctor of Medicine in 1910. Upon graduation, he served at St. Bartholomew's Episcopal Church in Cambridge, Massachusetts. He was then called to be the Secretary of the Commission for Work among the Colored People under the Church's Board of Missions.

After several years as Secretary, he moved back to Antigua, where he remained for six years building the church where he was baptized, St. Paul's in Sweets. When fellow West Indian Marcus Garvey formed the United Negro Improvement Association, McGuire returned to the United States to support him. Working with Garvey only strengthened his dissatisfaction in serving a church where black people were systematically denied positions of leadership, and he became determined to pursue an independent course.

On September 2, 1921, in the Church of the Good Shepherd in New York City, a meeting of independent black clergy resolved itself into the first Synod of the African Orthodox Church, and designated McGuire as its bishop elect. The Synod then entered into negotiations with the Russian Orthodox Church in America in their search for episcopal orders for their newly elected bishop. The Russians indicated a willingness to consecrate McGuire, but only if they controlled the newly created jurisdiction. The idea of non-Black control had no appeal to either McGuire or his followers. They then turned to the American Catholic Church, headed by Archbishop Joseph Rene Vilatte. Vilatte was willing to confer orders and ask little or nothing in the way of control. On September 29, 1921, Bishop Vilatte, assisted by Carl A. Nybladh, consecrated Dr. McGuire in the Church of Our Lady of Good Death in Chicago.

The Church experienced slow but steady growth, although most of the individual congregations were small. The priests were seldom full-time clergy, although every church was encouraged to contribute something to their support. McGuire emphasized education and led in the organization of a seminary for the training of clergy. The first class numbered fourteen men. The school provided professional training for its students, while accommodating to the generally lower educational level of its applicants. It has not tried to become an accredited degree-granting institution.

Archbishop McGuire led the Church until his death in 1923, and it enjoyed peace and stability. After his death the leadership of the church fell into the hands of Archbishop W. E. J. Robertson. Shortly after his elevation to the archbishopric, dissatisfaction arose among the group of clergy, and a schism, the Holy African Church was created. The dissidents were led by Bishop R. G. Barrow, who had been McGuire's closest associate. In time, Barrow was succeeded by Bishop F. A. Toote and then Bishop Gladstone St. Claire Nurse. Bishop Nurse led the efforts to reunite the two factions. On February 22, 1964, the two bodies joined together under Robertson, who adopted the Patriarchal name of Peter IV. Just prior to the merger he consecrated several bishops, an obvious effort to insure his continued control of the Church. Nurse did not protest Robertson's action, and upon the death of the Patriarch was elected by the bishops to be the new primate of the Church. He quickly brought all the elements of the Church together and upon his death, leadership passed very easily to Archbishop William R. Miller, who served as the Church's Primate from 1976 until August of 1981. At the Annual Synod of the Church, he resigned and was succeeded by Archbishop Stafford J. Sweeting.

The denomination remains small in the United States, but it has affiliated parishes in the West Indies and Africa (Nigeria, Ghana, and Uganda). Recently, the Church lost one of its strongest parishes when Bishop G. Duncan Hinkson of Chicago left to found the African Orthodox Church of the West.

Membership: In 1983 the Church reported 17 parishes and 5,100 members in the United States.

Educational facilities: Endich Theological Seminary, New York, New York.

Periodicals: *The Trumpet*, %Rev. Fr. Harold Furblur, Box 1925, Boston, MA 02105.

Sources: Arthur C. Terry-Thompson, *History of the African Orthodox Church*. New York: The Author, 1956; *The Divine liturgy and Other Rites and Ceremonies of the Church*. Chicago: African Orthodox church, 1945; Randall K. Burkett, *Garveyism as a Religious Movement*. Metuchen, NJ: Scarecrow Press, 1978; Richard Newman, "The Origins of the African Orthodox Church" in *The Negro Churchman*. Millwood, NY: Kraus Publishing Co., 1977.

★79★
AFRICAN ORTHODOX CHURCH OF THE WEST
% Most Rev. G. Duncan Hinkson
St. Augustine's African Orthodox Church
5831 S. Indiana St.
Chicago, IL 60637

In 1984 Bishop G. Duncan Hinkson, a physician and pastor of St. Augustine's African Orthodox Church, on the southside of Chicago, left the African Orthodox Church and formed a new jurisdiction. While following the teachings and ritual of its parent body, it is administratively independent. Bishop Hinkson consecrated Bishop Franzo King to lead work in San Francisco.

Membership: In 1985, the Church had two parishes, one in Chicago and one in California with several hundred members.

Periodicals: *Expression*, % One Mind Temple, 351 Divisadero St., San Francisco, CA 94117.

★80★
ALBANIAN ORTHODOX ARCHDIOCESE IN AMERICA
270 Cabot St.
Newton, MA 02160

The Albanian Orthodox Archdiocese in America can be traced to 1908, when the first Albanian parish in the U.S. was established in Boston. In the same year, an Albanian-American immigrant, Fan Stylin Noli, was ordained to the priesthood by Metropolitan Platon of the Russian Orthodox Church. Father Noli returned to Albania in 1920 where he had a prominent political career, eventually becoming prime minister. He became a bishop in 1923, but in 1930 (due to Turkish domination of Albania), he returned to the United States and organized the American parishes into the Albanian Orthodox Archdiocese in America. The Archdiocese remained in communion with the Church in Albania until after World War II when a Communist government hostile to the Church took control of the country, and, in the eyes of the Archdiocese, subverted the leadership of the Church. While retaining orthodox belief and practice, the Archdiocese became independent. Noli was succeeded by Metropolitan Theodosius.

Membership: In 1978 the Archdiocese reported 16 parishes, 40,000 members and 25 priests.

Periodicals: *The Vineyard (Vreshta)*, 270 Cabot St., Newton, MA 02160.

★81★
ALBANIAN ORTHODOX DIOCESE OF AMERICA
% The Rev. Ik. Ilia Katra, Vicar General
54 Burroughs St.
Jamaica Plain, MA 02130

In 1949 His Grace Mark I. Lipa came to the United States with authority from the Ecumenical Patriarch in Constantinople to organize the Albanian faithful (which had become independent under Fan Noli of the Albanian Orthodox Archdiocese in America). The following year he formed the Albanian Orthodox Church in America, now known as the Albanian Orthodox Diocese of America. It is a member of the Standing Conference of Canonical Orthodox Bishops in America.

Membership: In 1982 the Diocese reported 10 parishes, 5,250 members and 3 clergy.

Periodicals: *The True Light*, 54 Burroughs Street, Jamaica Plain, MA 02130.

★82★
AMERICAN CARPATHO-RUSSIAN ORTHODOX GREEK CATHOLIC CHURCH

℅ Rt. Rev. Nicolas Smisko
312 Garfield St.
Johnstown, PA 15906

The American Carpatho-Russian Orthodox Greek Catholic Church was founded in the 1930s by a group of former members of the Roman Catholic Church who had migrated to the United States from Carpatho-Russia. Carpatho-Russia had been forcefully converted from Eastern Orthodoxy to the Roman Catholic Ruthenian Rite by a series of rulers who basically followed the Latin Rite. Once in the United States, a process of further Latinizing Ruthenian Rite parishes began. Among other issues, attempts were made to curtail the assignment of married priests to American parishes.

As early as 1891, a Carpatho-Russian Catholic parish sought to return to Eastern Orthodoxy. It was soon joined by others. Then in 1936, approximately forty parishes which had left Roman jurisdiction organized and selected Orestes P. Chornock as their leader. The next year they designated him their bishop-elect and turned to the ecumenical patriarch in Constantinople for recognition. In 1938 the patriarch consecrated Chornock and authorized the American Carpatho-Russian Orthodox Diocese as an independent body. In 1966 the patriarch elevated Chornock to the dignity of a metropolitan. The present ruling bishop is the Rt. Rev. Nicolas Smisko.

The American Carpatho-Russian Orthodox Greek Catholic Church is an independent autonomous body directly under the authority of the ecumenical patriarch. It has a working relationship with the Greek Orthodox Archdiocese of North and South America, whose archbishop is the exarch of the patriarch. The archbishop intercedes when the appointment of a new bishop is requested by the church and has the task of consecrating him. The Church is at one with Eastern Orthodox faith and practice, though its liturgy still retains a few minor peculiarities reflective of its Roman Catholic history. The Church is a member of the Standing Conference of Canonical Orthodox Bishops in the Americas.

Membership: In 1976 the Church reported 70 parishes, 100,000 members, and 68 priests.

Periodicals: *Cerkovny Vistnik–Church Messenger*, 419 S. Main St., Homer City, PA 15748.

★83★
AMERICAN EASTERN ORTHODOX CHURCH
Current address not obtained for this edition.

Since the second century, India has had Eastern Orthodox churches that call themselves Mar Thomas churches. They claim that St. Thomas the Apostle founded them. In the 1930s the Church of England was India's state church. When the Christian Missionary Society of the Church of England attempted to convert members of the Mar Thomas churches, a controversy arose. One of its results was that Bishop Anthony Devan left India and came to the U.S. to locate members of the Mar Thomas churches residing there. He succeeded in locating a few families, and he ordained four priests, thus establishing the American Eastern Orthodox Church. It continues the tradition of the Mar Thomas Christians. It is one in faith and practice with the Orthodox churches. St. Thomas is honored on the Sunday after the Resurrection (Easter), July 19 (his birthday), and October 19 (anniversary of his martyrdom). The Liturgy of St. Basil is used.

Membership: In 1973 there were 5 parishes, 5 mission stations and 1,240 members.

Sources: *Following Christ in the American Eastern Orthodox Church*. Las Vegas, NV: St. George Monastery, 1967.

★84★
AMERICAN HOLY ORTHODOX CATHOLIC EASTERN CHURCH
(Defunct)

The American Holy Orthodox Catholic Eastern Church was incorporated in 1933 under the leadership of Cyril John Clement Sherwood, popularly known by his ecclesiastical name, Clement I. His Holiness Clement I had previously belonged to the Benedictine community founded by Archbishop W. H. Francis Brothers of the Old Catholic Church in America. In 1927, however, he received priestly orders from Archbishop Frederick E. J. Lloyd of the American Catholic Church and three years later was consecrated by Bishop William F. Tyarks of the African Orthodox Church. He was then reconsecrated in 1932 by Bishop George A. McGuire of the African Orthodox Church, and throughout the rest of his life he considered this latter consecration as his true one.

The American Holy Orthodox Catholic Eastern Church followed Eastern Orthodox faith and practice, but it was established as a completely autocephalous jurisdiction, autonomous of all foreign bishops and church bodies. Headquarters of the church were established in Sts. Peter and Paul Church in New York City. For a while Clement issued a periodical, *The Voice of the Community*. Clement founded a coalition of various independent orthodox and catholic bishops, the Orthodox Catholic Patriarchate of America. Clement died in 1969. Following his death, leadership of the Patriarchate passed to Archbishop

George A. Hyde of the Orthodox Catholic Church of America. In succeeding years, the already weakened organization ceased to exist (though it has recently been re-established by Archbishop Alfred Louis Lankenau who succeeded Hyde as head of the Orthodox Church in America. At the same time, the American Holy Orthodox Catholic Apostolic Eastern Church was received into the Orthodox Catholic Church in America as its Eastern Rite Diocese, and it ceased to exist as a separate body.

★85★
AMERICAN INDEPENDENT ORTHODOX CHURCH (BRIDGES)
516 W. Caldwell
Compton, CA 90220

The American Independent Orthodox Church was founded in 1976 by Richard W. Bridges, whose episcopal orders were conferred in 1980 by Bishops Gregory Voris, C. Engel, and Hans B. Kroneberg. It adheres to the faith of the Seven Ecumenical Councils and the Three Ecumenical Creeds, and it is designed to use both Eastern and Western rites. While not open to ordaining females to the priesthood, it is open to receiving homosexuals into Holy Orders.

Membership: Not reported. In the early 1980s, the Church claimed 2 parishes, 3 priests and 75 members.

★86★
AMERICAN ORTHODOX CATHOLIC CHURCH (HEALY)
(Defunct)

One of the several jurisdictions formed by clergy who were with Archbishop Walter A. Propheta's American Orthodox Catholic Church, this jurisdiction of the same name was formed by Bishop Lawrence Pierre, formerly the Auxiliary Bishop for New York and the Eastern States. It continued the beliefs and practices as well as the name of Propheta's Church, being bi-ritualistic (i.e, it allowed both Eastern and Western liturgies be used in its parishs' worship services). Archbishop Pierre was succeeded by Archbishop Patrick J. Healy as primate. Upon the death of Healy in 1984, the jurisdiction dissolved.

★87★
AMERICAN ORTHODOX CATHOLIC CHURCH (IRENE)
% Most Rev. Milton A. Pritts
851 Leyden St.
Denver, CO 80220

The American Orthodox Catholic Church (Irene) was founded in 1962 and incorporated three years later. Its presiding head is a female-bishop known only as Archbishop Irene, consecrators unknown. Spokesperson of the Church is Bishop Emeritus Milton A. Pritts, who had

been consecrated by Archbishop WalterA. Propheta of the American Orthodox Catholic Church.

The Church is Orthodox in faith and practice, accepting the forms presented in the *Service Book* edited by Isabel Florence Hapgood, and the principles enuciated in such standard orthodox volumes as Fr. John Meyendorff's *The Orthodox Church*. The Revised Standard Version of the Bible is used. It differs in the following: 1) it would consider otherwise qualified women and homosexuals for the priesthood and 2) it believes that apostolic succession is not necessary to the establishment of a valid church or ministry. A resolution passed by the Grant Synod of the Church, January 6, 1979 stated, "We now hold with the Churches of England, Sweden, Congregational, Presbyterian, Lutheran, Methodist, Christian Scientists, and others who are determined to revive lay selection and authority of the congregation to avoid the further creation of hierarchies."

Although renouncing the necessity of apostolic succession and the idea of building further hierarchies, the church has claimed to have a ministry with valid apostolic episcopal orders and claims to have built an elaborate hierarchy. The jurisdiction, divided into 53 dioceses, is spread over all of North America. Apart from Bishop Pritts, the names of Church officers and bishops and the addresses of their diocesan headquarters have not been available for publication.

Membership: Not reported. There is some doubt as to the size of this Church in light of the unverifiable nature of its claims and the inability to locate any parishes associated with Bishop Pritts or Archbishop Irene.

★88★
AMERICAN ORTHODOX CATHOLIC CHURCH (PROPHETA)
% Mt. Rev. Dom Lorenzo, O.S.B.
Holy Trinity Monastery
Box 323
Shirley, NY 11967

History. The American Orthodox Catholic Church was incorporated in 1965 by Walter A. Propheta (1912-1972), a former Ukrainian Orthodox priest. In 1964 he was consecrated to the episcopacy by Archbishop Theodtus Stanislaus DeWitow of the Holy Orthodox Church in America and Archbishop Joachim Souris, an independent Greek bishop. The following year he was elevated to archbishop and began the task of building an independent and indigenous American Orthodoxy. Propheta saw himself in the lineage of and assuming the task of Archbishop Aftimios Ofiesh who in 1927 had tried to initiate an American Orthodox Church. As Archbishop and Patriarch Woldymyr I (as Propheta was ecclesiastically known), he built his jurisdiction by consecrating a number of men to the episcopacy. Many of these soon left him to found their own autonomous jurisdiction and others left as a result of the struggles for control of the church after Propheta's death. As a result, Propheta unwittingly gave birth to a number of new church organizations, some of which kept the name of his church with some minor variation.

At a synod held in 1972, John A. Christian (d. 1984) was elected to succeed Propheta as primate. He was succeeded by the present archbishop, Dom Lorenzo, elected in 1984. Lorenzo had been consecrated by Archbishop Uladyslau Ryzy-Ryski of the American World Patriarchs and Lawrence Pierre in 1977. Archbishop Christian, just before his retirement, elevated him to the office of metropolitan of New York in 1978. At the time of his election Lorenzo was serving as both metropolitan of New York and apostolic administrator of the church.

Beliefs. The American Orthodox Catholic Church is Orthodox in doctrine and follows the decrees of the seven Ecumenical Councils. It adheres to the Nicene Creed, and requires adherence only to the traditional Orthodox text. It allows the Western text to be used if the disputed filioque clause is understood in an Orthodox sense of a single procession. (Note: The filioque clause, "from the Son," was added to the Nicene Creed by the Roman Catholic Church and is generally not used in Eastern Orthodox Churches. It refers to a complicated theological argument concerning the relation of the Holy Spirit to the Trinity.)

The church does not require, but has no barriers to the faithful holding and propounding a variety of specifically Roman Catholic beliefs such as papal infallibility, transubstantiation, or the immaculate conception of the Blessed Virgin Mary. The church professes that charity, godliness, and truthfulness are more important than strict doctrinal definitions. A variety of rites are allowed, though the Eastern is most frequently used.

Organization. The church follows an episcopal polity and is governed by the primate and the Holy Synod. The practice of a celibate clergy is by and large maintained, but secular deacons and priests may be married before ordination. (Special dispensations for marriage after ordination may be granted by the Holy Synod.) On disciplinary issues, the church follows the canons of the Ecumenical Councils.

Membership: In 1987 the church reported five congregations and two monasteries in the United States. Membership is estimated to be several hundred.

Educational facilities: God's Benevolence Institute, 801 Levering #3, Los Angeles, CA 90024.

Remarks: Among the most active centers of the American Orthodox Catholic Church has been God's Benevolence Institute headed by Bishop Patrick McReynolds. The institute is an interdenominational association for ancient studies and practices with the goal of establishing a monastery of "canons regular and secular," the Community of God's Benevolence. McReynolds had originally started the community after being ordained for an independent ministry by Bishop Michael A. Itkin of the Community of the Love of Christ (Evangelical Catholic). In 1975 he was consecrated by Edward C. Payne and became suffragan bishop of the Independent Catholic Church. In 1981 he left Payne and subsequently became a bishop in the American Orthodox Catholic Church.

McReynolds is one of the most educated of the independent bishops, having received his master's degree from Fordam and as of 1988 being enrolled in a Ph.D. program at UCLA. Prior to his moving to Los Angeles, California, McReynolds built the institute's work in Spokane, Washington, where there is a small congregation, God's Benevolence Orthodox Catholic Church. In 1988, there were five fellows and 25 associate fellows in the institute in Spokane and a second chapter being built in Los Angeles.

Sources: *American Orthodox Catholic Church, Ecclesiatical History.* Los Angeles: Archdiocese of So. California and the Western Province, 1974; Walter M. Propheta, *Divine Liturgy for 20th Century Christians.* New York: American Orthodox Church, 1966.

★89★
AMERICAN ORTHODOX CHURCH
% Archbishop Aftimios Harold J. Donovan, Exarch
San Antonio, Los Vanos
Laguna 3732, Philippines

The American Orthodox Church was established in 1981 by Harold Donovan as the Orthodox American Catholic Church, Diocese of the Ozarks under a charter from the Orthodox Church of the Philippines. Donovan was originally consecrated by Bishops Howard Fris and John Kenelly of the Old Roman Catholic Church, Archdiocese of Chicago. However, in 1982, Donovan was reconsecrated by Archbishop John A. Christian of the American Orthodox Catholic Church (Propheta) in order to establish formal continuity with the original American Orthodox Church established by Archbishop Aftimios Ofiesh in the 1920s. Donovan took the religious name of the late archbishop and is currently known as Archbishop Aftimios Donovan. On January 1983, Archbishop Christian, in cooperation with the Orthodox Church in the Philippines, established an exarchate known as the North American Synod of the Holy Eastern Orthodox Catholic and Apostolic Church (shortened to its present name the following year).

The Church follows Eastern Orthodox belief and practice. The liturgy of St. Germain is used and sacraments are administered according to the American Rite of St. Germain, an abbreviated and modified formula based upon the Byzantine Rite.

The exarchate retains formal ties to both the Orthodox Church in the Philippines and the American Orthodox Catholic Church headed by Archbishop Christian. Its parish work includes two missions in Los Angeles, one to Oriental-Americans and one to Hispanic-Americans.

Membership: In 1984 the Church reported 3 parishes, 3 clergy, and less than 150 members.

Educational facilities: Seminary of the Orthodox Catholic Church in the Philippines, Manila, Philippines.

Periodicals: *The Orthodox Catholic*, Box 389, Ozark, MO 65721.

Sources: *The Liturgy*. Springfield, MO; American Orthodox Church, 1983.

★90★
AMERICAN WORLD PATRIARCHS
% Most Rev. Emigidius J. Ryzy
19 Aqueduct St.
Ossining, NY 10562

Uladyslau Ryzy-Ryski (1925-78), a Byelorussian priest, was consecrated in 1965 by Archbishop Walter A. Propheta of the American Orthodox Catholic Church as the Bishop of Laconia, New Hampshire and the New England States. During this period he also met Archbishop Peter A. Zurawetzky of the Old Orthodox Catholic Patriarchate of America, who on November 4, 1967, in the presence of a congregation of four, elevated him to the status of Archbishop. Without leaving Propheta's jurisdiction, Ryzy-Ryski began to create archbishops-patriarchs for each national/ethnic group and, quite apart from any laity demanding leadership, to build a hierarchy which he envisioned as international in scope. The World Patriarchate was very loosely structured, and established in large part by the elevation to patriarchial status of other independent bishops not otherwise required to recognize Ryzy-Ryski's authority or come under his jurisdiction. In 1972, as one of the last acts before his death, Propheta excommunicated Ryzy-Ryski from the American Orthodox Catholic Church, an action which merely spurred the growth of the American World Patriarchs, who established patriarchs for Canada, Hungary, West Germany, Puerto Rico, Colombia, Haiti, Santo Domingo, Brazil, Peru, Argentina, El Salvador, Nigeria, the West Indies, Norway, Sweden, Formosa, and the Ukraine. Only rarely were new congregations established as a result of a patriarch being named. Occasionally, the new patriarch could claim a small following.

In connection with the American World Patriarchs, Ryzy-Ryski organized a the Peoples University of the Americas. an educational center designed to meet the needs of various ethnic and immigrant groups in the Bronx, New York. A well-educated man, with a good academic background, he led a faculty which offered a wide variety of courses in the humanities, and especially in English as a second language. The school also provided the World Patriarchs with a seminary.

Since the death of Patriarch Uladyslau Ryzy-Ryski in 1980, the work has continued under his brother, Archbishop Emigidius J. Ryzy, who holds the title of Apostolic Administrator of All American World Patriarchates. He is assisted by Archbishop Adam Bilecky, Patriarch II of the American World Patriarchate and Archbishop Zurawetsky.

Membership: In 1988 the church reported 15,431 members, 15 congregations, and 53 priests in the United States. There were also one congregation and three priests in Canada. Affiliated work was to be found in 17 foreign countries.

Educational facilities: Peoples University of the Americas, American College and Seminary, Bronx, New York; Universidad de los Pueblos de las Americas, San Juan, Puerto Rico.

★91★
ANTIOCHIAN ORTHODOX CHRISTIAN ARCHDIOCESE OF NORTH AMERICA
% Metropolitan Philip, Primate
358 Mountain Rd.
Englewood, NJ 07631

In 1892 the Russian Orthodox Church began a Syrian Mission in the United States to provide spiritual guidance for Orthodox Christians from the Eastern Mediterranean basin. In 1904 the first Orthodox bishop ever consecrated in America, Archimandrite Raphael Hawaweeny, became the bishop of the Syrian Mission of the Russian Orthodox Church. Then in 1914 Metropolitan Germanos came to the United States and began organizing Syrian churches. These two efforts paralleled each other until 1925 when an independent church was created. In 1936, Archimandrite Antony Bashir was elected and consecrated bishop by the American Syrian churches. He became metropolitan of New York and all America in 1940 and provided leadership for almost 30 years.

In the 1936 election in which Anthony Bashir was elected to the bishopric, Archimandrite Samuel David of Toledo, Ohio, polled the second highest number of votes. On the same day that Archbishop Anthony Bashir was consecrated in New York, Russian bishops consecrated Samuel David as archbishop of Toledo. Archbishop Samuel David was condemned and excommunicated by Archbishop Antony Bashir in 1938 but then recognized the following year. The Antiochean Orthodox Archdiocese of Toledo, Ohio, and Dependencies that he led existed as a separate body until 1975.

In 1966 the Most Rev. Philip Saliba succeeded Bashir and became primate of the Antiochian Orthodox Christian Archdiocese of New York and all North America.

Archbishop Philip has been a leader in promoting the use of English in the liturgy. He has given priority to missions and has extended his work to Australia and the South Seas.

In 1958, Archbishop David died, and hope for reunion of the two Antiochian churches emerged. Archbishop Michael Shaheen succeeded Archbishop David and conducted talks toward union, which were finally consummated in 1975. The new Antiochian Orthodox Christian Archdiocese of North America selected Archbishop Philip as head of the church with the title of metropolitan.

Membership: In 1987 the Archdiocese reported 150 parishes, 300,000 members, and 200 priests.

Periodicals: *The Word*, 52 78th St., Brooklyn, NY 11209; *Again*, Box 106, Mt. Hermon, CA 95041.

Remarks: In February 1987, the former Evangelical Orthodox Church (EOC) was received as a body into the Antiochian Orthodox Christian Archdiocese of North America, thus ending for its members a pilgrimage that began almost two decades earlier. The Evangelical Orthodox church had its roots in the late 1960s, when a number of the staff of Campus Crusade for Christ left their positions. Some launched independent ministries; some affiliated with various independent evangelical churches. In the early 1970s seven of these leaders--Peter Gilquist, John Braun, Dick Ballew, Ken Berven, and Jack Sparks--banded together as the New Covenant Apostolic Order (NCAO).

The formation of the NCAO afforded a context for study which led to a concentrated reappraisal of a common view of Evangelical Protestant Christians that the first century church had become corrupted over the centuries until restored by Evangelicals in relatively modern times. Gathering in Chicago in 1979, the leaders of the movement announced the formation of the Evangelical Orthodox Church to supercede the NCAO and to call Evangelicals back to their historic roots. Special emphasis was placed upon ritual, a subject largely neglected in Evangelical circles. The new church immediately turned its attention to a search for valid Orthodox episcopal orders. Initial talks were held with the Orthodox Church in America. While a major obstacle was overcome when the leaders of the EOC professed their belief in the Blessed Virgin Mary as *theotokos*, the Mother of God, the talks eventually reached a stalemate. Finally, the EOC was able to work out an arrangement with the Antiochian Church by which the leaders dropped their designation as bishops and were reordained by Archbishop Philip.

Over the years the leaders of the EOC have written a number of books which received wide circulation within Evangelical circles. Most of these were published by Thomas Nelson, where Gilquist worked as an editor, and included Gilquist's *Why We Haven't Changed the World*

and *It Ain't Gonna Reign No More* by Jon Braun. Most notable among them was *The Mindbenders* by Jack Sparks, an anticult book that led to a lawsuit for libel by the Local Church, one of the groups treated in the volume, and its eventual withdrawal by the publishers.

Sources: *The Divine Liturgy of John Chrysostom*. Santa Barbara, CA: Evangelical Orthodox Church, Santa Barbara Diocese, n.d.; Jon E. Braun, *It Ain't Gonna Reign No More*. Nashville, TN: Thomas Nelson, 1978; Jack Sparks, *The Mindbenders*. Nashville, TN: Thomas Nelson, 1977.

★92★
APOSTOLIC CATHOLIC CHURCH OF THE AMERICAS
% Most Rev. Gordon I. DaCosta
408 S. 10th St.
Gas City, IN 46933

The Apostolic Catholic Church of the Americas dates to a 1976 merger of two jurisdictions headed by Bishops Robert S. Zeiger and Gordon I. DaCosta. Zeiger had been consecrated in 1961 by Archbishop Peter A. Zurawetzky of the Old Orthodox Catholic Patriarchate of America as an Orthodox bishop for Westerners. However, in 1962 Zieger left Zurawetzky's jurisdiction and formed the American Orthodox Catholic Church headquartered in Denver, Colorado. The church was conceived as American in its autonomy, Orthodox in its faith and practice, and Catholic in its universality.

Gordon I. DaCosta was a priest and bishop of the Free Protestant Episcopal Church. He left that jurisdiction in 1971 and formed the Anglican Church of the Americas, in Indiana. The Anglican Church of the Americas was designed to continue the work of, and update the structure of, the Free Protestant Episcopal Church (then in the process of losing any American presence) and to avoid any conflict over the similarity of name with the Protestant Episcopal Church. Over the first few years of its existence, the Anglican Church moved toward Orthodoxy in both faith and liturgy and in 1976 merged into the American Orthodox Catholic Church headed by Bishop Zeiger. At the time of the merger, the American Orthodox Catholic Church took on a second name, the Apostolic Catholic Church of the Americas. This second name became its most frequently used designation, though both names are officially correct.

Soon after the merger, Zieger resigned both his office and membership in the church and joined the Roman Catholic Church as a layman in a Uniate Ruthenian congregation. DaCosta was elected as his successor. (As of 1984 Zeiger remains connected to the church as its registered agent. The church is registered in Colorado while DaCosta resides in Indiana.)

The Apostolic Catholic Church of the Americas describes itself as Western Orthodox. It is Orthodox in that it accepts as authority the Sacred Scriptures, the Apostolic Tradition, the doctrinal decrees of the Seven Ecumenical Councils, and the writings of the church fathers. It follows Eastern practice in making clerical celibacy optional. It rejects females as candidates for the priesthood. The Church is Catholic, but not Roman; Evangelical but not Protestant; and Orthodox, but not Eastern.

As of 1985, the church is headed by two bishops: Gordon I. DaCosta and Herbert Robinson of Bellingham, Washington. A third bishop, C. F. Quinn, who headed a large congregation in Dallas, Texas, recently died. Church property is owned locally by the boards of individual congregations. Thus, church government is a complex mixture of episcopal and congregational polity.

Membership: In 1984 the church reported nine parishes, missions, and chaplaincies and had an estimated membership of less than 500.

Periodicals: *The Door*, 4201 Fairmount Street, Dallas, Texas 75219.

Sources: *The Order of Daily Prayer*. Dallas: Diocese of Texas, Apostolic Catholic Church, n.d.

★93★
ASSOCIATION OF OCCIDENTAL ORTHODOX PARISHES
% Father Stephen Empson
57 Saint Marks Place
New York, NY 10003

The use of the Western Rite in Orthodox Churches has experienced a revival during the twentieth century as Eastern Orthodoxy has flourished in the West. It has a long history, though little noticed due to the predominance of the Roman Rite. It was the opinion of some, verified by such examples as the Western Rite Vicariate within the Antiocean Orthodox Church, that Western Rite parishes do not remain Western within a predominantly Eastern Rite church body. The Orthodox Church of France is a totally Western Rite diocese founded in 1953 by Fr. Evgraph Kovalevsky and several other priests who withdrew from the Russian Orthodox Church. As priests in Lithuania they had followed a Western Rite, and Fr. Kovalevsky had pastored a Western Rite parish opened in 1944 in Paris. That parish became the source of several others.

After leaving the Russian Orthodox Church, the priests and their parishes affiliated with the Russian Orthodox Church Outside of Russia. Bishop John Maximovitch ordained several new Western Rite priests and saw to the publication of the liturgy, the old Gallican Rite according to Saint Germain, Bishop of Paris (555-576), not to be confused with the eighteenth-century occultist of the same name. The death of Bishop John led to a break with the Russian Church, and, as relations worsened, Kovalevsky,

who had been consecrated in 1964, led his followers in forming an autonomous diocese. But he died in 1970 without having a successor consecrated. Finally, in 1972, the Patriarch of Romania agreed to consecrate Pere Gilles Hardy as the new bishop of the Orthodox Catholic Church of France. He is known as Bishop Germain. The Western Rite was reintroduced to America by Father Stephen Empson who founded a parish in New York City. In 1981 he organized the Association of Occidental Orthodox Parishes to further promote Western Rite Orthodoxy.

Membership: In 1984 the Association had five parishes (New York City; Brooklyn, NY; Chicago; Dorchester, MA; and Fullerton, CA) and a monastery in Jacksonville, Florida. Internationally, the Western Orthodox Church had 60 parishes, most in France, but including two each in Switzerland and Spain and one each in Germany, Belgium, and Argentina.

Periodicals: *Axios*, 800 S. Euclid St., Fullerton, CA 92632 (unofficial publication).

★94★
AUTOCEPHOLOUS SLAVONIC ORTHODOX CATHOLIC CHURCH (IN EXILE)
2237 Hunter Ave.
New York, NY 10475

The Autocephalous Slavonic Orthodox Catholic Church (in Exile) dates its existence to the coming of Saint Cyril and Saint Methodius to Moravia in the ninth century. Worship was established according to the Greek Orthodox Church and in 1620 a jurisdiction of the Podcarpathian Church was founded. It was always a small jurisdiction in a predominantly Roman Catholic land. Following World War I, when Czechoslovakia declared its independence, Orthodox believers asked for their own independent church. Under the Serbian orthodox patriarch, the church was organized in 1921 and a bishop, Gorazd Pavlik, was consecrated. However, in early 1923, the ecumenical patriarch consecrated a rival archbishop named Sabbazd. Both churches existed side by side until the Nazi occupation and World War II, during which they both disappeared. In 1946 the church reappeared under the patriarch of the Russian Orthodox Church in Moscow who appointed an Exarch to head the small group.

Some perceived the action of the Russian patriarch to be a takeover of the Czechoslovakian church and in 1946 a group of priests and laity formed an underground church movement. In 1968, one of the leaders of this movement, Bishop Filotej, fled the country and settled in America, where he founded the Slavonic Orthodox Church. In 1969 he consecrated Bishop Andrew Prazsky as his coadjutor archbishop, and after Archbishop Filotej's death in 1970, Archbishop Andrew became the head of the church.

Archbishop Andrew soon established communion with the Ukrainian Autocephalous Orthodox Church in the United

States of America and in the early 1970s accepted provisional reconsecration from Archbishop Hryhorij Osijchuk (1898-1985) and Archbishop Hennadij. In 1980 the episcopal leadership of the two churches united their efforts into a single *sobor*, or synod, which now has oversight of both churches. Archbishop Andrew stepped aside at that time in favor of Archbishop Hryhorij. In 1970 Archbishop Andrew was elected Metropolitan Archbishop of the united sobor, and has led both churches since that time (except for two years when Archbishop Hryhorij served a second time).

The Slavonic Church is Orthodox in faith and practice. The church's strength is in the Bronx where it ministers to Slavic Americans of various national backgrounds, many first generation immigrants.

Membership: Not reported.

Sources: Boden Clarke, *Lords Temporal and Lords Spiritual*. San Bernardino, CA: Borgo Press, 1986.

★95★
AUTOCEPHALOUS SYRO-CHALDEAN CHURCH OF NORTH AMERICA

℅ Most Rev. Bertram S. Schlossberg (Mar Uzziah)
9 Ellington Ave.
Rockville, CT 06066

The Autocephalous Syro-Chaldean Church of North America traces its origins to Hugh George de Willmott Newman, popularly known by his ecclesiastical name Mar Georgius. Mar Georgius was the first of the independent bishops to have himself consecrated numerous times in order to embody the several episcopal lineages both East and West, which he in turn passed on to the many individuals he consecrated. Among the people to whom he passed these various lines of apostolic succession was Charles D. Boltwood, a bishop in the British-based Free Protestant Episcopal Church. In 1959, three years after his reconsecration by Newman, Boltwood became primate of the church. Among his first actions, Boltwood consecrated John M. Stanley (May 3, 1959) as bishop of the state of Washington.

During the 1960s, Stanley withdrew from the Free Protestant Episcopal Church and formed the Syro-Chaldean Archdiocese of North America. In so doing he claimed the lineage of the Church of the East received by Newman from W. S. M. Knight who had received the lineage from Ulric Vernon Herford (Mar Jacobus). Stanley, as archbishop of the new jurisdiction, took the ecclesiastical name Mar Yokhannan.

The series of events which led to the formation of the Autocephalous Syro-Chaldean Church of North America began at the meeting of the Holy Synod of the Syro-Chaldean Archdiocese, December 13-14, 1974. The synod designated Archpriest Bertram S. Schlossberg as bishop-elect with the task of organizing a Diocese of New York.

By that action Schlossberg came under the direct authority of Archbishop James A. Gaines who had authority from the archdiocese for the eastern half of the United States. Together, on April 16, 1976, they incorporated their new work as the Autocephalous Syro-Chaldean Archdiocese of the Eastern United States of America. On October 31, 1976, Gaines consecrated Schlossberg as bishop of the Northeast and in December erected the Diocese of the Northeast, over which Schlossberg was assigned.

The actions of Gaines and Schlossberg were followed by a split with Mar Yokhannan, who attempted to dissolve both the Autocephalous Eastern Archdiocese and the Diocese of the Northeast. Eventually, on April 2, 1977, Mar Yokhannan released Schlossberg and Gaines from "all canonical obedience" and then withdrew from the Syro-Chaldean Archdiocese and joined the Church of the East. Gaines (Mar Jacobus) and Schlossberg (Mar Uzziah) then reorganized all of the work formerly under Mar Yokhannan and in October 1977 incorporated the Autocephalous Syro-Chaldean Church of North America, with Mar Jacobus as metropolitan and Mar Uzziah as bishop of the Northeastern Diocese.

The Syro-Chaldean church follows the Orthodox theology of the Church of the East. It affirms the Bible as the Word of God and both the Apostles' and Nicene Creeds. It keeps seven sacraments: baptism, confirmation, holy communion, reconciliation, annointing for healing, holy matrimony, and holy orders. It uses the Liturgy of Mar Addai and Mar Mari as its official liturgy, but allows parishes great freedom in choosing other forms of worship. The church sees itself as evangelical—believing that all persons need to repent and be converted to Christ; catholic—stressing the historical doctrines, sacraments, and practices of Christianity; and charismatic—accepting the emphasis upon the ministry of the Holy Spirit as preached in the contemporary Charismatic movement. It is strongly opposed to the acceptance of homosexuality (which it considers a sin) and abortion. Women are ordained to the deaconate but not to the priesthood.

Membership: In 1988 the church reported 1000 members and 13 clergy in four parish churches and one mission. It sponsors a church in the Philippines.

Educational facilities: Christ the King Seminary and School of Discipleship, Rockville, Connecticut.

★96★
BULGARIAN EASTERN ORTHODOX CHURCH (DIOCESE OF NORTH AND SOUTH AMERICA AND AUSTRALIA)

Metropolitan Joseph
550 A, W. 50th St.
New York, NY 10019

Bulgarians arrived in the United States throughout the nineteenth century and by 1907 were numerous enough to begin establishing congregations independently of the Russian Orthodox Church parishes in which they had mainly worshipped. The first parish was formed in Madison, Illinois. Soon, the Holy Synod in Sophia established a mission to oversee their American members. Finally, in 1938, a diocese was created and Bishop Andrey Velichky came from Bulgaria as its head. Bishop Andrey returned to Bulgaria during World War II and worked on various projects among which was the handling of negotiations between the ecumenical patriarch in Istanbul and the Bulgarian patriarch which led to the healing of a seventy year-old broken relationship. During this period, the ecumenical patriarch elevated the diocese in America to a metropolia and gave it jurisdiction for Bulgarians in North and South America and Australia.

Soon after the war ended, Archbishop Andrey returned to America. In 1947 he incorporated the Bulgarian Eastern Orthodox Diocese of America, Canada and Australia. The constitutional assembly meeting in March of that year realigned its relationship to the Church in Bulgaria by declaring that while it saw itself as part of the whole of Bulgarian Orthodoxy, it could not accept orders from the church leaders in Sophia as long as a Communist regime ruled their homeland. They then proceeded to formally elect Andrey as their leader. The Holy Synod reacted by declaring the election null and void. The American diocese ignored the Synod and for the next fifteen years the diocese operated independently of the church leaders in Sophia. In 1962 the Church in Bulgaria recognized the Metropolia and reestablished a working relationship. In 1972 the Church was divided into two dioceses, and Bishop Joseph Znepolski succeeded Archbishop Andrey as Metropolitan.

The Bulgarian Eastern Orthodox Church follows standard Orthodox faith and practice. It is a member of the Standing Conference of Canonical Orthodox Bishops in the Americas.

Membership: In the mid-1970s (latest report available) the Church had 18 parishes and an estimated membership of 105,000.

★97★

BULGARIAN EASTERN ORTHODOX CHURCH, DIOCESE OF NORTH AND SOUTH AMERICA
519 Brynhaven Dr.
Oregon, OH

The reestablishment of relations between the Orthodox Church in Bulgaria and the Bulgarian Eastern Orthodox Church (Diocese of North and South America and Australia) and the resultant manifestation of that accord in the joint visitation of North American parishes in 1963 by Bishop Andrey (Velichky), metropolitan of the American church and Bishop Preiman, metropolitan of Nevrokop, Bulgaria, led to major protests throughout the Church. Bishop Andrey was accused of violating the declaration made in 1947 that the Bulgarian Church in

America would not accept any orders from the Church in Bulgaria. In March 1963, protesting leaders representing eighteen churches and missions met in Detroit, Michigan and reconstituted themselves as the Bulgarian Eastern Orthodox Church (Diocese of the United States of America and Canada) and elected Archimandrite Kyrill Yonchev as their bishop.

They turned to the Russian Orthodox Church Outside of Russia for support. The Russians, also cut off from their homeland by a hostile regime, gave the new Bulgarian jurisdiction their canonical protection and their bishops consecrated bishop-elect Yonchev in 1964 at their monastery in Jordanville, New York.

The Bulgarian Eastern Orthodox Church differs from its parent body only in matters of administration. It lays claim to all properties belonging to the undivided Church in America though it has not been able to take control of them. It is stanchly anti-Communist.

Membership: In the mid-1970s, the Church reported 21 parishes and missions.

★98★

BYELORUSSIAN AUTOCEPHALIC ORTHODOX CHURCH IN THE U.S.A.
% Archbishop Mikalay, Primate
Church of St. Cyril of Turau
524 St. Clarens Ave.
Toronto, ON, Canada

Byelorussia is that section of the U.S.S.R. directly north of the Ukraine and East of Poland. A national church had been organized there in 1291 under Greek jurisdiction. With time, it came under the control of the patriarch in Moscow, the head of the Russian Orthodox Church. In 1922 a split developed in the Byelorussian church when the Minsk Council of clergy and laity, under the leadership of Metropolitan Melchizedek, attempted to organize an autonomous Byelorussian church free of Moscow. Such action met the disapproval of both the government and the patriarch of the Russian Church. Within a short period of time, all the Byelorussian leaders had been arrested and sent to Siberia, and the church reverted to its dependent status. During the Nazi occupation of Byelorussia, the church attempted again to organize independently, but their efforts ended with the defeat of the German occupation forces.

The Byelorussian Autocephalic Orthodox Church in the U.S.A. is one of two Orthodox groups among Byelorussian immigrants. It emerged among refugee Byelorussians in Germany after the War. Their own bishops having returned to the Russian Church, clergy and laity turned to the Ukrainian Church. Metropolitan Polikarp not only blessed the reorganization of an autonomous church among the Byelorussians, but in 1948 granted permission for one of his bishops, Bishop Siarhej, to leave his jurisdiction and join the new church. In 1949, accompanied by his former Ukrainian colleagues, Siarhej consecrated a second bishop for the church, Bishop Vasil. As the church spread among immigrants around the world, two more bishops were consecrated in 1968.

Present Primate of the Church is Archbishop Mikalay, elected in 1984 at a convention at the church in Highland Park, New Jersey. He resides in Toronto, Canada. In the United States, parishes are located in Cleveland, Ohio; Detroit, Michigan; and Dorothy, New Jersey. The Church also oversees parishes in England (3), Belgium, and Australia.

★99★
BYELORUSSIAN ORTHODOX CHURCH
190 Turnpike Rd.
South River, NJ 08882

When refugees and immigrants from Byelorussia came to the West after World War II, some organized as the Byelorussian Autonomous Orthodox Church and elected their own bishops. Others formed independent congregations and sought the canonical blessings of other Orthodox bishops. The Byelorussian Orthodox Church consists of three congregations who placed themselves under the jurisdiction of Archbishop Iakovos, head of the Greek Orthodox Archdiocese of North and South America, in his role as Exarch in America for the ecumenical patriarch. Besides the congregation in South River, New Jersey, parishes are found in Chicago and Toronto.

Membership: Not reported.

★100★
BYZANTINE CATHOLIC CHURCH
% Most Rev. Mark I. Miller
Box 3682
Los Angeles, CA 90078

The Byzantine Catholic Church was formed in 1984 by a merger of the Byzantine Old Catholic Church and the Holy Orthodox Catholic Church, Eastern and Apostolic. The Byzantine Old Catholic Church was a jurisdiction in the Old Catholic tradition whose history is intimately tied to the career of its leader, Bishop Mark I. Miller.

As a child, Miller was adopted and, taking the name of his new parents, was raised as Oliver W. Skelton. He joined the American Orthodox Catholic Church. Upon ordination as a priest, he assumed the religious name Leo Christopher (Skelton), as he became known throughout the Old Catholic movement after his consecration as a bishop by Christopher J. Stanley in 1965. In 1966, Skelton left Stanley and the American Orthodox Catholic Church and became a cardinal in the Orthodox Old Catholic Church headed by Claude Hamel. Headquartered in Enid, Oklahoma, Skelton functioned under the name, Old Roman Catholic Church (Orthodox Orders), a corporation he had formed in 1964. Upon leaving Hamel, whom he

accused of exercising capricious and authoritarian leadership, Skelton changed the name of his organization to the Orthodox Old Roman Catholic Church II and assumed the ecclesiastical name Mark I. He established headquarters in Hollywood, California.

In the mid-1970s, Skelton reorganized the Orthodox Old Roman Catholic Church II and changed its name to the North American Orthodox Catholic Church. During this period, he was moving, both theologically and liturgically, away from Old Catholicism and toward Eastern Orthodoxy. In April 1975, he had his secular name changed legally to that of his natural parents and became Mark I. Miller.

Two further reorganizations of his jurisdiction in 1981 and 1983 transformed the North American Orthodox Catholic Church into the Byzantine Old Catholic Church. The major reorganization in 1981 resulted from clergy engaged in what were termed "unOrthodox actions." Miller promulgated a number of additions to the Disciplinary Canons, most notably new regulations prohibiting the ordination of females and the assumption of the bishopric by married clergy. The name was changed to the World Independent Orthodox Catholic Church (and Her Dependencies). Finally, in 1983, the World Independent Orthodox Catholic Church assumed the name that it took into the 1984 merger, the Byzantine Old Catholic Church.

After the new church was formed, His Beatitude Metropolitan Richard B. Morrill, head of the Holy Orthodox Catholic Church, became the president of the Sacred Synod of Bishops and administrator of the church. His Beatitude Mark (I. Miller) became vice president of the Sacred Synod of Bishops and ecclesiastical administrator and chief justice of the Spiritual Court of Bishops. However in 1984, only a few months after the merger, Morrill withdrew and reconstituted the jurisdiction he formerly headed. His Beatitude Mark I succeeded him as Primate of the church.

The Byzantine Catholic Church is Orthodox in faith and practice. It uses the several Eastern liturgies (most prominently St. John Chrysostom's, and St. Basil's).

Membership: In 1988 the Byzantine Catholic Church reported 400 members in two congregations in the United States. Affiliated parishes are also found in Italy, Nigeria, and Zaire, with 40,000 members reported.

Educational facilities: The International Theological Seminary, Van Nuys, California.

Periodicals: *Maranatha! The Lord Cometh.* Box 3682, Los Angeles, CA 90078.

★101★
CATHOLIC APOSTOLIC CHURCH IN AMERICA
% Mt. Rev. Jerome Joachim
600 Fell St., Suite 400
San Francisco, CA 94102

Though officially reconstituted in 1983, the Catholic Apostolic Church in America continues an unbroken existence from 1950 when Stephen Meyer Corradi-Scarella established an American outpost of the Catholic Apostolic Church in Brazil. The Catholic Apostolic Church in Brazil was formed in 1946 by Dom Carlos Duarte Costa, a former bishop of the Roman Catholic Church who had been excommunicated by Pope Pius XII because of his criticism of the church during World War II. Among those who Costa consecrated was Dom Luis F. Castillo-Mendez, who succeeded him as patriarch of the church in 1949. Corradi-Scarella was consecrated by Mendez in 1949 and established the church as an exarchate with headquarters in New Mexico. During the 1960s, following the death of Costa, Corradi-Scarella lost touch with the Brazilian group and began to associate with the various Old Catholics in the United States. By 1970 he called his jurisdiction the Diocese of the Old Catholic Church in America.

The church grew slowly until the 1970s. In 1973 Corradi-Scarella was joined by Francis Jerome Joachim, a priest ordained by Archbishop Bartholomew Cunningham of the Holy Orthodox Church, Diocese of New Mexico. Joachim brought an Eastern Orthodox perspective with him, in contrast to Corradi-Scarella's Catholic tradition, but soon became his chief associate. Corradi-Scarella arranged for Joachim's consecration by Archbishop David M. Johnson of the American Orthodox Church, Diocese of California, on September 28, 1974. Two months later, on December 1, 1974, Corradi-Scarella, then almost seventy years old, resigned in favor of Joachim.

Under Joachim the small jurisdiction grew, at one point having almost 100 clergy, but lost significant strength due to the defections of many to other independent jurisdictions. In 1980 Joachim renamed his jurisdiction the Western Orthodox Church in America (formerly the National Catholic Apostolic Church in America). At the request of Mendez, Joachim changed the name of the church back to the Catholic Apostolic Church of North America. In 1985, Joachim was name Primate of All North America and the church recognized as the Autocephalous Catholic Apostolic Church in Brazil in North America.

Membership: In 1988 the church reported 5,000 members in 20 parishes served by 25 priests in the United States. There were three parishes in Canada served by two priests, and mission parishes in Australia and Mexico.

Educational facilities: St. John Chrysostom Theological Seminary, San Francisco, California; St. Charles Academy of Theology, San Francisco, California.

Periodicals: *Journal Apostolica*, 600 Fell St., Suite 400, San Francisco, CA 94102.

★102★
EASTERN ORTHODOX CATHOLIC CHURCH IN AMERICA
% Most Rev. Dismas Markle
321 S. Magnolia Ave.
Sanford, FL 32771

Among the several bodies claiming to carry on the mission of Archbishop Aftimios Ofiesh, the Eastern Orthodox Catholic Church in America can make one of the strongest cases for being the real antecedent body of Aftimios' independent jurisdiction. The first bishop consecrated by Aftimios was Bishop Sophonius Bashira in 1931. Aftimios' retirement and Bishop Joseph Zuk's unexpected death just months after his consecration by Ofiesh, left Sophronius in charge. He turned to Metropolitan Benjamin Fedchenkov of the Moscow Exarch (now the Patriarchal Parishes of the Russian Orthodox Church in the United States and Canada), one of several warring Russian Orthodox factions, and with his blessing, consecrated John Chrysostom More-Moreno in 1933. Sophronius soon left the United States and More-Moreno took up the task of creating an American Orthodox church, in 1951, by forming the Eastern Orthodox Catholic Church in America.

The church follows the practice of Orthodoxy in both liturgy and theology. For many years it published the influential monthly periodical, the *American Review of Eastern Orthodoxy* (suspended in 1980).

Membership: In 1974 the Church reported 4 churches, 13 clergy, and 315 members.

★103★
ESTONIAN ORTHODOX CHURCH IN EXILE
% Rev. Sergius Samon
5332 Fountain Ave.
Los Angeles, CA 90029

In 1944 the Union of Soviet Socialist Republics gained political hegemony over Estonia. Primate of the Estonian Orthodox Church Archbishop Alexander fled to Sweden where he organized The Estonian Orthodox Church in Exile. The church is under the Greek Orthodox Church's ecumenical patriach in Constantinople and at one in faith and worship with the Greek Orthodox Church.

In 1949 the Very Reverend Sergius Samon established the first congregation of the Estonian Church in North America at Los Angeles. Large numbers of Estonians had come to the United States and Canada following World War II. Congregations were subsequently established in San Francisco, Chicago, and New York City. Canadian parishes were established in Vancouver, Toronto, and Montreal.

Membership: In the mid-1970s, the Church reported 1,700 members in North America.

★104★
FINNISH ORTHODOX CHURCH
Current address not obtained for this edition.

The first Orthodox missionaries reached Finland in the tenth century and founded Valamo Monastery. While the church has remained small, it has persisted. Finland gained independence from Russia in 1919 and a wave of nationalism swept the church. In 1923 the church was given autonomy under the Greek Orthodox Church's ecumenical patriarch in Constantinople. The following year a non-Russian bishop was named primate. The church is Orthodox in faith and practice and uses the Finnish and Russian languages. The selection of archbishops must be submitted to Constantinople for approval.

In 1955 the first attempts to call together Orthodox Finns residing in the United States found most already attached to Russian congregations, but a small mission chapel was established in the Upper Peninsula of Michigan. It was not able to minister to the 1,300 Orthodox Finns and ceased to exist in 1958. A new plan was implemented in 1962 by Father Denis Ericson of Lansing, Michigan. Using Lansing as a base, he travels to four worship stations. Services are in English, but Finnish hymns and customs are preserved.

Membership: Not reported.

★105★
FREE SERBIAN ORTHODOX CHURCH--DIOCESE FOR THE U.S.A. AND CANADA
% Metropolitan Iriney *Kovachevich*
Box 371
Grayslake, IL 60030

The Serbian Orthodox Church in Diaspora, formerly the Serbian Orthodox Free Diocese of the United States and Canada, like the Serbian Orthodox Church in the United States and Canada, claims the history of Serbian Orthodoxy in America since the 1890s. It remains, however, as that branch which remained loyal to Bishop Dionisiji *Milivojevich* after he was defrocked by the Belgrade Patriarch. That action began a lengthy series of court battles between Bishop Dionisiji's followers and the appointed representatives of the Belgrade church authorities. In 1978 the courts finally awarded the property at Libertyville, Illinois to the Belgrade representatives. Bishop Dionisiji died in 1979, a few months before his followers left the property.

The Free Serbian Church, as it was popularly called, purchased property at nearby Grayslake, Illinois, and began to build a new headquarters complex. The massive Gracanica Monastery was dedicated in 1984. Dionisiji was succeeded by Bishop Iriney. Under his leadership the

stanch anti-Communist and anti-Tito stance adopted by his predecessor has continued.

Membership: In 1988 the church reported 30,000 members, 53 parishes, and 49 priests.

Educational facilities: St. Sava Seminary, Lake Villa, Illinois.

Periodicals: *Diocesean Observer*, Box 371, Grayslake, IL 60030.

Sources: *A Time to Choose*. Third Lake, IL: Monastery of the Most Holy Mother of God, 1981; *Gracanica*. Grayslake, IL: Serbian Orthodox Free Diocese of the United States and Canada, 1984; Jovan Todorovich, *Serbian Patran Saint, Krsna Slava*. Merrilville, IN: The Author, 1978; Bishop Dionisije, *Patriarch Gherman's Violations of the Holy Canons, Rules and Regulations of the Serbian Orthodox Church in Tito's Yugoslavia*. Libertyville, IL: The Serbian Orthodox Diocese in the U.S.A. and Canada (Free Serbian Orthodox Church in Free World), 1965; *Divine Liturgy, Prayers, Catechism*. Libertyville, IL: St. Sava Seminary Fund, 1979; Nicholai D. Velimirovich, *The Life of St. Sava*. Libertyville, IL: Serbian Eastern Orthodox Diocese for the United States of America and Canada, 1951.

★106★
GREEK ARCHDIOCESE OF VASILOUPOLIS
44-02 48th Ave.
Sunnyside/Woodside, NY 11377

The Greek Archdiocese of Vasiloupolis was founded in 1970 when Archimandrite Pangratios Vrionis was consecrated by Romanian Bishop Theofil Ionescuand Albanian Archbishop Christoforus Rado to serve among the Greek-Americans who had migrated to Long Island from Albania, Romania, and parts of Russia. Vasiloupolis (royal city) refers to Queens, New York, where Bishop Pangratios was consecrated. The church grew out of a refugee program started by Fr. Alexander Tzuglevitch, pastor of St. Nicolas Russian Orthodox Church in New York City. At a "Synod of the Diaspora" Archimandrite was chosen to be the bishop over these people, who had declared their desire for a leader who was traditionalist with a multicultural background, an American citizen, and missionary-minded. In addition he would have to be approved by the exiled royal families of Greece and Romania.

Through the 1970s Pangratios moved to build the archdiocese which had grown primarily through the addition of conservative ethnic parishes. In 1973 he consecrated Archbishop Theodore (Sergius) Irtel as exarch of Mexico and Guatamala. Bishop Theodore was succeeded by Bishop Benedict who serves as both exarch for Mexico and bishop of the Missionary Diocese of the Western United States with his headquarters at New Sarov Monastery in Blanco, Texas.

Among Archbishop's Pangratios' consecrators had been Archbishop Christoforus Rado, who around 1958 had formed the Independent Albanian Orthodox Church of St. Paul. Archbishop Christoforus died in 1974. While some of his parishes joined the Orthodox Church of America, some came under Pangratios, who consecrated Bishop Stavros Skembi to lead them. Pangratios also inherited the following of Greek-Romanian Bishop Theofil. In 1981 Pangratios consecrated Stephen Degiovanni to minister to a group of Italo-Greek immigrants located on Long Island and in New Jersey.

Most recently the archdiocese has grown by the acceptance into it of the former Holy Order of MANS, an independent jurisdiction founded by Fr. Paul W. Blighton (d. 1974). The church is Orthodox in faith and takes a traditionalist stance. It is an Old Calendarist group, meaning its liturgical life follows the Julian rather than the Gregorian calendar. It opposes what it considers to be the modernist trends and attempts at liturgical reform represented in the churches which make up the Standing Conference of Orthodox Bishops in America.

Membership: Not reported.

Remarks: The Holy Order of MANS (Mysterion, Agape, Nous, Sophia) began in San Francisco, California, in the early 1960s, having grown out of a vision of Fr. Blighton, its founder. It emerged as an ordered community which accepted both men and women into full participation. During its years of separate existence, the order had a definite esoteric and mystical element in its teachings, which were summarized in a lengthy set of tenets. It also developed a significant social service program. Blighton was succeeded as director general of the order by the Rev. Andrew Rossi who led the church toward an acceptance of Eastern Orthodoxy.

Sources: *Book of the Master Jesus.* San Francisco, CA: Holy Order of MANS, 1974. 3 Vols. *The Golden Force.* San Francisco, CA: Holy Order of MANS, 1867. Paul Blighton, *Memoirs of a Mystic.* San Francisco, CA: Holy Order of MANS, 1974.

★107★
GREEK ORTHODOX ARCHDIOCESE OF NORTH
**   AND SOUTH AMERICA**
% His Eminence Archbishop Iakovos
8-10 E. 79th St.
New York, NY 10021

As early as 1767 Greek Orthodox Christians settled in New Smyrna, Florida. Greek merchants in New Orleans established Holy Trinity, the first Greek Orthodox Church in America, in 1864. Other parishes sprang up across the country. No attempt was made to organize the parishes until 1918 when the Greek Orthodox Archdiocese of North and South America was organized. Archbishop Alexandros headed the archdiocese from 1922. He began the extensive work of bringing the many Greek parishes

under his jurisdiction. The greatest progress in this direction was made by his successor, Metropolitan Athenagoras Spiru, who became the ecumenical patriarch in 1948.

The Greek Orthodox Archdiocese has over the years become the largest in the United States. It has seven districts, each headed by a bishop, and Archbishop Iakovos, as chairman of the Standing Conference of Canonical Orthodox Bishops and Exarch for the ecumenical patriarch, has been a recognized spokesman of the Greek Orthodox community to the outside world.

Currents of change which have flowed through the Orthodox world have made Archbishop Iakovos a subject of intense controversy. As criticism has been directed against the growing openness of Patriarch Athenagoras toward Rome and the World Council of Churches, Archbishop Iakovos has been criticized for approving this openness and initiating contact on his own in the United States with various Protestant and Catholic bodies. Ultra-traditionalists see such ecumenical activity as compromising Orthodox faith. Mt. Athos, the most famous Orthodox monastery, has become a center of traditionalism and has produced spokesmen critical of Archbishop Iakovos and of changes in the contemporary church.

Liturgy being the most important aspect of Orthodox church life, changes affecting liturgy are met with extreme resistance. The Greek Archdiocese follows the Eastern Rite and the Liturgy of St. John Chrysostom. However, traditionally the Orthodox liturgy has followed the Julian calendar, which twentieth century liturgists have largely replaced with the Gregorian. Many of those who have left the Greek Archdiocese reject his use of the Gregorian calendar.

Membership: In 1977 the Archdiocese reported 1,950,000 members, 535 churches and 655 priests.

Educational facilities: Holy Cross School of Theology, Brookline, Massachusetts; Hellenic College, Brookline, Massachusetts.

Periodicals: *Orthodox Observer*, 8-10 E. 79th Street, New York, NY 10021.

Sources: *The Divine Liturgy of St. John Chrysostom.* Brookline, MA: The Greek Orthodox Theological Institute Press, 1950; Demetrios J. Constantelos, *An Old Faith for Modern Man.* New York: Greek Orthodox Archdiocese, 1964; Demetrios J. Constantelos, *The Greek Orthodox Church.* New York: Seabury Press, 1967; George Poulos, *A Breath of God.* Brookline, MA: Holy Cross Orthodox Press, 1984; Fotios K. Litsas, *A Companion to the Greek Orthodox Church.* New York: Department of Communication, Greek Orthodox Archdiocese of North and South America, 1984.

★108★
GREEK ORTHODOX CHURCH OF AMERICA
Current address not obtained for this edition.

The Greek Orthodox Church of America was formed on December 1, 1971, at a meeting held in Miami, Florida, for the purpose of forming a federation of independent Greek Orthodox Churches. Many of these churches had grown out of local schisms and were headed by priests who had left the jurisdiction of Archbishop Iakovos. Members object to what they see as a movement "to Catholicize and Protestantize the church." They hope to preserve Greek faith, language, and traditions. They believe in local control of property, not archdiocesan ownership. As of 1974 the church was without episcopal supervision but was seeking it from various sources.

A moving force in the Greek Orthodox Church of America is Father Theodore Kyritsis. He was defrocked by Archbishop Iakovos and went under the jurisdiction of Bishop Petros of the Hellenic Orthodox Church in America. Bishop Photios of the Greek Orthodox Diocese of New York was installed as archbishop in Memphis in St. George's Greek Orthodox Church which Kyritsis pastored, and has since then been a vocal opponent of Archbishop Iakovos.

Membership: In the mid-1970s the Church had 10 parishes scattered around the United States from Miami to Rhode Island, Pennsylvania, Michigan, and Tennessee.

★109★
GREEK ORTHODOX DIOCESE OF NEW YORK
Current address not obtained for this edition.

The Greek Orthodox Diocese of New York was formed in 1964 at Philadelphia, Pennsylvania, by priests and laity formerly under the jurisdiction of Archbishop Iakovos of the Greek Orthodox Archdiocese pf North and South America. They objected to the administration of Archbishop Iakovos and are the only Orthodox body in the West which allows the laity the sole right to elect the bishops and to keep the monies of the church under the control of the members. Oxford-educated Bishop Photios was elected archbishop, and Theocletos of Salimis, auxiliary bishop. The installation of the archbishop took place in St. George's Greek Orthodox Church in Memphis, where Archbishop Photios resided for several years.

Archbishop Photios has gathered the largest group of Greek Orthodox followers not under Archbishop Iakovos. In 1965 jurisdiction was extended to Australia. Archbishop Photios was in communion with the late Bishop Dionisije of the Serbian Orthodox Free Diocese of the United States and Canada and Bishop Alexis of Adelaide, Australia, of the Byelorussian Autocephalic Church.

Membership: Not reported.

★110★
HELLENIC ORTHODOX CHURCH IN AMERICA
Current address not obtained for this edition.

In 1952 Archimandrite Petros, a monk from Mt. Athos, arrived in the United States and began to gather scattered groups of independent communities which follow the Julian calendar. In 1962 he was consecrated Bishop of Astoria (Long Island, New York) by two Russian bishops who use the Julian calendar, Archbishop Leontios of Chile and Bishop Serapim of Venezuela, and the Hellenic Orthodox Church came into existence. It is at one with Orthodoxy except on the calendar issue.

Bishop Petros began a monthly periodical, *The Voice of Orthodoxy*. By 1967 he directed five churches and missions and 9,000 members. In each parish he established a parochial school to teach the Orthodox faith and the Greek language. The New York headquarters produced a radio show which carries the same name as the periodical.

Membership: Not reported.

★111★
HOLY APOSTOLIC ORTHODOX CATHOLIC CHURCH
(Defunct)

The Holy Apostolic Orthodox Catholic Church was founded in the mid-1960s with headquarters in Fort Lauderdale, Florida. During the 1970s it claimed to have a seminary and an elaborate hierarchy, including two archbishops and one bishop in the United States, and additional archbishops in West Germany, the Canal Zone, Hong Kong, and Switzerland. During the 1980s, no manifestation of the church or its founder Archbishop Mark Cardinal Evans has been seen. The Church professed the Orthodox faith as based in the Nicene Creed without the filoque clause and used the Liturgy of St. John Chrysostom without alteration.

Sources: *Ecclesiatical Proclamation, Divine Liturgy.* N.p.: Home Missions Department of the Holy Apostolic Orthodox Catholic Church, 1965.

★112★
HOLY EASTERN ORTHODOX CHURCH, ITALIO-BYZANTINE
Current address not obtained for this edition.

Orthodoxy established itself in southern Italy and Sicily in the Greek communities which had established themselves in ancient times. Most of these Greek churches came under the authority of the Roman Catholic Church after the Synod at Bari in 1097 A.D. Only two bishops refused to submit and they led their Orthodox followers into what became an increasingly underground church. The church survived in spite of severe measures to convert its members to Catholicism. Cut-off from mainline Orthodoxy, however, it developed several peculiarities, including a married bishopric. It also has a mobile episcopacy, in part due to the persecution it felt, and began to designate their bishops as being "in" a See location rather than "of" a See City. Thus, their present Primate is Bishop Umile Natalino, Bishop in Venetio. The Church became fully autonomous in 1428.

The first Italian Orthodox priests came to America in 1904 and established parishes in Brooklyn, Newark and Philadelphia. Progress was slow until 1979 when two men, Emilio Rinauldi and Luciano Gaudio, were elcted Bishop in Newark (NJ) and Las Vegas (NM) respectively. They were consecrated by a deputation of bishops from Italy headed by the late Primate Constantino, Bishop in Catania.

The Church is Orthodox in theology. The two bishops have administrative responsibility for that section of the United States in which they reside. Bishop Gaudio announced plans to build a monastic complex New Mexico. The Church was affiliated with the Holy Orthodox Church, American Jurisdiction headed by Bishop James Francis Miller which merged into the Orthodox Catholic Church of America.

Membership: Not reported.

★113★
HOLY EASTERN ORTHODOX CHURCH OF THE UNITED STATES
% Most Rev. Trevor W. Moore
1611 Wallace St.
Philadelphia, PA 19130

The Holy Eastern Orthodox Church of the United States (Orthodox Catholic Archdiocese of Philadelphia, Metropolitan See) dates itself to 1927 and the establishment of the American Orthodox Church under Bishop Aftimios Ofiesh, as authorized by the American bishops of the Russian Orthodox Church. In 1971 Archbishop Trevor Wyatt Moore and the priests under his jurisdiction incorporated the Orthodox Catholic Archdiocese of Philadelphia. Moore had been consecrated in the Aftimios lineage, on July 11, 1971, by Archbishops Peter A. Zurawetsky and Uladyslau Ryzy-Ryski. A month later Ryzy-Ryski, head of the American World Patriarchs, in his plan to establish a hierarchy of patriarchs representing the various ethnic groups, elevated Moore to archbishop with jurisdiction for the English-speaking world. Then, in 1972, he designated Moore a metropolitan.

From the very beginning, the archdiocese was incorporated independently as a self-protective measure against any irregularities, heterodoxy, or heresy that might develop within the American World Patriarchs. Within a few years, Metropolitan Trevor saw a significant drift within the American World Patriarchs as evidenced by its following an unacceptable pan-ecumenism, developing anti-Russian attitudes, espousing the use of a self-created

Western liturgy, and most importantly, failing to perpetuate the necessary conditions set forth by the synod of Russian bishops in 1927 for the American Orthodox Church. Metropolitan Trevor had rigorously followed those conditions in theology, liturgy, and otherwise.

As a result of the irregularities, the archdiocese severed all connections with the American World Patriarchs in 1976; when the official name became the Holy Eastern Orthodox Church of the United States, an abridgment of the original name given to Aftimios' jurisdiction, the Holy Eastern Orthodox Catholic and Apostolic Church in North America.

Metropolitan Trevor asserts that his jurisdiction is the only remnant of the original jurisdiction headed by Archbishop Aftimios in that it is the only one which adheres to all of the conditions set forth in the original charter and constitution. It has remained truly Orthodox in all aspects of its life and, while independent, acknowledges the primacy of the Russian jurisdiction and preserves a filial relationship to the Orthodox Church of Russia by the Patriarchial Authority of Moscow and All Russia. [Note: In Orthodox practice, the first Orthodox Church to initiate work in a new couthry is generally acknowledged to have canonical primacy for that country. In the case of the United States, the Russian Orthodox Church was present for a century prior to any other Orthodox jurisdiction's establishment of a parish.]

Beliefs. The church is strictly Eastern Orthodox in faith and practice and adheres to the Byzantine rite. It holds to the Nicene Creed and follows its Eastern text.

Organization. The church is episcopal in polity. It is organized into the Metropolitan See of Philadelphia, the Orthodox-Greek Catholic Missionary Eparchy of Trenton and All New Jersey, and the Orthodox-Greek Catholic Diocese of Providence and All New England. Congregations can be found in Pennsylvania, New Jersey, Rhode Island, Massachusetts, Virginia, Florida, Illinois, and Nebraska. There is a mission church in Puerto Rico.

The church has been most attuned to the issues that have dominated the established churches in the United States, particularly in matters of social concern. It has spoken out forcefully on peace and nonviolence. It operates a social service center in Philadelphia, Pennsylvania, and through its affiliated Society of the Helpers of Saint Herman of Alaska, a mental health ministry in Florida. It has been active in civil rights and interracial and intercultural efforts, particularly in Spanish-speaking communities. Through it all Metropolitan Trevor has become one of only a few independent Orthodox leaders to gain some recognition from the larger Christian community, through his authorship of several books and service as an editor-at-large for the *Christian Century* magazine.

Membership: In 1988, the church reported 2,400 members in 13 parishes in the United States and one mission in Puerto Rico.

Periodicals: *Tserkobnost*, 1611 Wallace Street, Philadelphia, PA 19130.

★114★

HOLY ORTHODOX CATHOLIC CHURCH
% Most Rev. Paul G. Russell
5831 Tremont
Dallas, TX 75214

This body began in 1965 as the American Orthodox Church but changed its name in 1972 to the Holy Orthodox Catholic Church. It is headed by Bishop Paul G. Russell, who was consecrated on August 22, 1976 by Bishops David Baxter and William Henry. The group accepts the idea of female priests and would ordain a homosexual to Holy Orders, but in all other respects the Church holds to the Orthodox-Catholic faith. It is headquartered in Dallas, and claims six priests and three parishes. Membership is unknown.

Membership: In 1983 the Church reported 3 parishes and 6 priests.

★115★

HOLY ORTHODOX CHURCH, AMERICAN JURISDICTION
% Most Rev. W. Francis Forbes
Box 400
138 Overby Dr.
Antioch, TN 37013

Histoy: The Holy Orthodox Church, American Jurisdiction, though formed in 1974, has roots in the establishment in the 1920s of a Western Rite parish in the American Orthodox Church by Archbishop Aftimios Ofiesh. During his attempt to unify American Orthodoxy, Aftimios ordained former Episcopal priest William Albert Nichols to the Orthodox priesthood with the understanding that he would follow the ancient Western Gregorian Rite. The two also formed a nonmonastic order, the Society of the Clerks Secular of St. Basil, commonly known as the Basilian Fathers. It became the missionary arm of the Western Rite work, with Nichols as its superior-general.

This action occurred just as the Russian Orthodox Church withdrew its support of Aftimios. In 1932, among his last actions before turning his diocese over to the Syrian Orthodox Church, he consecrated Nichols (who assumed the ecclesiastical name Mar Ignatius) and made him archbishop of a new Western Rite archdiocese. Eventually, as Nichols' health failed, Alexander Tyler Turner was elected superior-general, was consecrated bishop (taking the name Mar Alexander) in 1939, and succeeded Nichols as head of the diocese.

In 1960, the former remaining Basilians entered the Antiochean Orthodox Christian Archdiocese of North America under Bishop Anthony Bashir, who had received permission from the patriarch of Antioch to establish a Western Rite Vicariate. After Alexander's death in 1971, only one of the Basilians, Fr. William Francis Forbes, remained to carry on the Western Rite work. He succeeded Turner as head of the Basilians in 1973. Seeing the efforts were producing little fruit in the Antiochean Church, in 1974 he withdrew and accepted consecration from two bishops in the Aftimios-Ignatius line of succession, Archbishop John M. Martin. He founded The American Orthodox Church, but soon changed it to its present name. He also sold the Basilian motherhouse property in New York and moved the headquarters of both the Basilians and the church to Antioch, a suburb of Nashville, Tennessee, where the Cathedral of St. Basil is located.

Beliefs: The church is thoroughly Orthodox in faith and sacramental practice. It accepts the Nicene Creed. The majority of parishes follow the Western Rite, though the Eastern Rite is allowed a few follow it.

Organization: The ecclesiastical order of the church is vested in its synod of bishops, which has six members. The synod has authority over its metropolitan-archdiocese of Nashville, and the dioceses of Boston (Bridgewater), Massachusetts; Philadelphia, Pennsylvania; and New Orleans, Louisiana; The Basilian group remains a part of the church. The church has no connection with other Orthodox bodies, especially those claiming to be American Orthodox and/or deriving authority from Archbishop Aftimios.

Membership: In 1988, the church reported more than 1,500 members, with one priest serving in Canada and one in England.

Periodicals: *The Communicator*, Box 400, Antioch, TN 37013.

★116★

HOLY ORTHODOX CHURCH, DIOCESE OF NEW MEXICO (CUNNINGHAM)
Current address not obtained for this edition.

The Holy Orthodox Church, Diocese of New Mexico was formed by Archbishop Bartholomew Cunningham a former priest of the Roman Catholic Church and seminary professor. Cunningham was consecrated by Bishops Colin James Guthrie and Robert S. Zeiger of the American Orthodox Catholic Church on June 23, 1968 and served under Guthrie until the present Holy Orthodox Church, Diocese of New Mexico, was established in 1970. The church is Orthodox in faith and practice. It is open to the ordination into the priesthood of otherwise qualified homosexuals but rejects females for holy orders.

Archbishop Batholemew died in 1984 and the future status of the Diocese is in question.

Membership: In the early 1980s, the Church reported 15 parishes and a few hundred members, primarily in New Mexico and Illinois.

★117★
HOLY ORTHODOX CHURCH IN AMERICA
10 E. Chestnut
Kingston, NY 12401

The Orthodox Church in America grew out of the early interest in Christian Mysticism of Rosicrucian George Winslow Plummer. Plummer had been one of the founders of the Societas Rosicruciana in America, covered in a separate item in this Encyclopedia, in 1907 and became its leader when Sylvester Gould died two years later. In the 1920s Plummer's particular interest in mysticism led him to found the Seminary of Biblical Research through which he issued lessons on Christian mysticism. About this same time he founded the Anglican Universal Church and sought consecration from a Puerto Rican bishop, Manual Ferrando.

In 1934 Plummer was reconsecrated by Bishop William Albert Nichols of the American Orthodox Church originally founded by Lebanese Orthodox bishop, Aftimios Ofiesh and took the religious name, Mar Georgius. Following his consecration, he reconsecrated three of his bishops of the Anglican Universal Church and incorporated as the Holy Orthodox Church in America. The Holy Orthodox Church in America (Eastern Catholic and Apostolic) accepted through Nichols the mandate of Bishop Ofiesh to develop an American Eastern Orthodoxy.

The Holy Orthodox Church, while endorsing the canons of the Seven Ecumenical Councils, has remained intimately connected to the Rosicrucian organization which Plummer headed. The original episcopal leadership was drawn from the S.R.I.A. and the original parishes were all located in cities with an S.R.I.A. group. The liturgy of the church is that of St. John Chrysostom, however, a special emphasis is placed upon spiritual healing and special services for that purpose are held weekly.

Plummer died in 1944 and was succeeded by Archbishop Theodotus Stanislaus DeWitow (formerly Witowski). From his death in 1973 to 1981 the church was without a bishop. The work was carried on by three deaconesses, two of whom, Mrs. G. E. S. DeWitow (a.k.a. Mother Serena), widow of the last archbishop, and Lucia Grosch were consecrated in 1981 by Archbishop Herman Adrian Spruit of the Church of Antioch. Mother Serena is the current presiding bishop.

Membership: In 1983 the Church reported that it had one church, and one chapel, and a membership of less that 100.

★118★
HOLY UKRAINIAN AUTOCEPHALIC ORTHODOX CHURCH IN EXILE
Current address not obtained for this edition.

The Holy Ukrainian Autocephalic Orthodox Church in Exile was organized in New York City in 1951 among immigrants who had left the Ukraine, primarily that part formerly controlled by Poland, as a result of the disruptions of World War II. A diocese was formed under the guidance of Archbishop Palladios Rudenko, former bishop of Krakiv, Lviv and Lemkenland, and Archbishop Ihor Huba, former bishop of Poltava and Kremenchuk, both refugees then living in the United States. The church was incorporated in 1960.

Membership: In 1972 the Church had only two parishes, one in West Babylon and one in Syracuse, New York.

★119★
MACEDONIAN ORTHODOX CHURCH
% Rev. Spiro Tanaskaki
51st & Virginia Sts.
Gary, IN 46409

Another schism in the Serbian Church occurred in 1947 when under pressure of the government a new church was created to serve the geographic area of Macedonia, now existing in Yugoslavia, Greece, and Bulgaria, though its strength was in South Serbia. In 1959 the patriarchate was "forced" to recognize it as autonomous but under the Belgrade patriarch, and Bishop Dositej was placed at its head. In 1967 Dositej proclaimed separation and independence, an act not recognized by the patriarch (or anyone but Marshall Tito) and thus became schismatic.

The Macedonian Church was begun in Gary, Indiana, in 1961 during a visit of Rev. Spiridon Tanaskovski. Other parishes were established in Syracuse, New York, and Columbus, Ohio. They are under the jurisdiction of Bishop Kiril who resides in Skoplje, Yugoslavia. In 1972 a schism developed in the Sts. Peter and Paul Macedonian Orthodox Church in Gary, Indiana. As a result of disputes, Rev. Tanaskovski left and founded a new church, St. Clement Ohridski, which he claims is loyal to the American flag and not to Tito.

Membership: Not reported.

★120★

OLD ORTHODOX CATHOLIC PATRIARCHATE OF AMERICA
66 N. Brookfield St.
Vineland, NJ 08360

Not all of the independent Polish Catholic Churches founded in the late-nineteenth and early-twentieth century joined with the Polish National Catholic Church. Some of these parishes had associated with independent Old Catholic bodies which had grown out of the work of Archbishop Joseph Rene Vilatte and his American Catholic Church, especially the Old Catholic Church in America headed by Archbishop W. H. Francis Brothers and the Polish Catholic Church of Bishop Stephen Kaminski. In 1937 some of these churches joined with several parishes of Slavic (Lithuanian) background and came together to form the Polish Old Catholic Church. They incorporated in New Jersey and elected Bishop Joseph Zielonka as their leader. Zielonka had been consecrated some years previously by Paolo Miraglia-Gulotti and had served as a bishop under Brothers.

Under Zielonka's capable leadership the church grew and by the time of his death in 1961 consisted of 22 parishes. Most were located in New Jersey with others in Pennsylvania and Massachusetts. The growth phase under Zielonka, however, was completely reversed under his successor, Peter A. Zurawetzky. Zurawetzky, Zielonka's suffragan, had been consecrated in Springfield, Massachusetts, in 1950. Patriarch Joseph Klimowicz of the Orthodox Catholic Patriarchate of America; Archbishop Konstatin Jaroshevich (a Byelorussian prelate who had been consecrated by Archbishop Fan Stylin Noli of the Albanian Orthodox Church); Archbishop Zielonka; Metropolitan Nicholas Bohatyretz of the Ukrainian Orthodox Church; and Old Catholic Bishop Peter M. Williamowicz participated in the consecration service.

Among his first acts, Zurawetzky changed the name of the Church to Christ Catholic Church of the Americas and Europe, an expression of a desire to move beyond ethnic and language barriers in his jurisdiction so that all nationalities might feel welcome. The future looked promising, but problems began to plague the newly named Church almost immediately. First some churches and clergy did not accept Archbishop Peter's leadership. They also did not like the name change. Second, Fr. Felix Starazewski asserted a claim to be the legitimate successor of the late Bishop Zielonka, and he and his church in South River, New Jersey, refused to honor the jurisdiction of Archbishop Peter. His defection led the way and other congregations departed for either the Polish National Catholic Church or one of the other independent Catholic or Orthodox bodies.

Third, and most importantly, Zurawetzky shifted his attention away from building his jurisdiction through expanding parishes and membership to growth by uniting with other independent Old Catholic and Eastern Orthodox bodies. He thus brought into his jurisdiction the divisiveness which had led to the splintering of these independent groups in the first place, and exacerbated the situation by assuming the title of Patriarch in America. Gradually all of his time and energy were poured into the actualization of a dominating vision, an American Patriarchate. At the same time his churches, consisting largely of Eastern European ethnic parishes, were being further reduced by the inevitable processes of Americanization.

By 1965, the Church having been reduced to a handful of communicants and clergy, a new possibility emerged. Rev. Karl Pruter, who had come from the Free Catholic Movement in the Congregational Church, was ordained by Archbishop Peter, and organized a nonethnic congregation in Boston, out of which a second congregation emerged. The Church of St. Paul was organized in Hobbs, New Mexico, by Fr. Daniel Smith. Then Zurawetzky moved to enlarge the Patriarchate. Assisted by Archbishop Uladyslau Ryzy-Ryski, he consecrated Pruter who consented to the consecration only on the condition that they be set aside as an independent jurisdiction to be called, Christ Catholic Church, Diocese of Boston, now known simply as Christ Catholic Church. Then, Smith was consecrated, but after a short while in Hobbs, he moved to Denver and withdrew from Archbishop Peter's jurisdiction altogether. Another briefly successful venture was the establishment of the Monastery of Our Lady of Reconciliation at Glorieta, New Mexico, in 1969. Fr. Christopher William Jones was a successful author and minister to many of the disenchanted youth of the late 60s and early 70s. However, shortly after Archbishop Peter consecrated him, he too left to form an independent, self-governing jurisdiction.

As of the mid-1980s, Archbishop Peter has no congregations in his jurisdiction, but maintains a chapel at Vineland, New Jersey, and a home in Chicago. He continues his efforts to build the Patriarchate.

Membership: As of 1985 there are no parishes in the Patriarchate, though several clergy remain affiliated.

Periodicals: *Our Missionary*, 5520 West Dakin, Chicago, IL 60641.

★121★

ORTHODOX CATHOLIC CHURCH IN AMERICA
% Most Rev. Walter X. Brown
2450 N. 50th St.
Milwaukee, WI 53210

The Orthodox Catholic Church in America, until recently known as the Archdiocese of the Old Catholic Church of America, began in 1941 when Bishop Francis Xavier Resch, who had been consecrated by Archbishop Carmel Henry Carfora of the North American Old Roman Catholic Church, broke with that jurisdiction and began the independent Diocese of Kankakee, centered upon his parish in Kankakee, Illinois. In a short time he had parishes in Illinois, Indiana, Michigan, and Wisconsin. However, these parishes, consisting primarily of first generation Eastern European immigrants, developed a more broadly based constituency as the second generation became Americanized. In 1963, Resch consecratd Fr. Walter X. Brown to the episcopacy. Brown moved the headquarters to Milwaukee, where the church developed a seminary, several programs for the treatment of alcoholism and drug abuse, and several new parishes.

During the 1980s, under Brown's leadership, the church has moved steadily from an Old Catholic to an Eastern Orthodox position. The church accepts both the Eastern and Western Orthodox tradition of the seven ecumenical councils and the unanimous opinion of the fathers of the Christian Church. The faith, practices, and discipline of the Eastern Orthodox churches has been adopted. The seven sacraments are practiced, and the Nicene Creed is followed in the church's own statement of faith. Individual parishes may use either the Western Gregorian or Eastern Byzantine rites.

The church supports two monastic communities, one Eastern and one Western, in Milwaukee. It became a charter participant in the recently organized Holy Orthodox Synod of America, a council of independent Orthodox jurisdictions in America which seek to facilitate cooperation within the larger American Orthodox community.

Membership: In 1988, the church reported 2,100 members, ten congregations, and 16 clergyin the United States. Churches are located in Dallas and Lubbock, Texas; Erie, Pennsylvania; Chicago, Illinois; Racine, Madison, Watertown, and Milwaukee, Wisconsin; Davenport, Iowa; St. Petersburg, Florida; Ludington, Michigan; Brooklyn, New York; and Ottawa, Ontario, Canada.

Educational facilities: Holy Cross Theological Seminary, Milwaukee, Wisconsin.

Periodicals: *The Messenger*, 2450 N. 50th St., Milwaukee, WI 53210.

Remarks: In 1986 the Orthodox Catholic Church in America entered into an agreement of intercommunion with the Orthodox Catholic Church of America, headed by Archbishop Alfred Louis Lankenau. The two jurisdictions jointly formed the Holy Orthodox Synod of America, a confederation of independent Orthodox bishops for the purposes of sharing and fellowship.

Sources: John Cyprian Holman, *The Old Catholic Church of America*. Milwaukee, WI: Port Royal Press, 1977; Francis X. Resch, *Compendium Philosophiae Universae*. Lake Village, IN: The Author, 1950.

★122★
ORTHODOX CATHOLIC CHURCH IN AMERICA (VERRA)
% Most Rev. Michael Edward Verra
238 Mott St.
New York, NY 10012

The Orthodox Catholic Church (Verra) (through the mid-1980s known as the American Catholic Church, Archdiocese of New York) was formed in 1927 by James F.A. Lashley. In 1932, Bishop William F. Tyarks (having been recently deposed from the African Orthodox Church by Archbishop George A. McGuire), consecrated Lashley. Lashley, a black man, built a substantive independent jurisdiction which in the mid-1960s reported 20 churches under its leadership. These included nine in the United States and 11 in the West Indies. Bishop Verra succeeded to leadership upon the death of Archbishop Lashley.

The Church takes as its standards of faith the Holy Bible, the first Seven Ecumenical Councils, the Synod of Jerusalem of 1692, and the accumulated teachings of the Church Fathers. Specifically rejected is the universal authority and infallibility of the Pope, purgatory and limbo, the docrtine of the Immaculate Conception of the Virgin Mary, transubstantiation, and the use of unleaven bread in the Eucharist. The church used a Western liturgy adjusted for its Orthodox beliefs concerning the procession of the Holy Spirit. Both icons and statues are used. Clergy may marry.

Membership: In 1988 the church reported two parishes and five priests in the United States. There were also two parishes in Trinidad.

★123★
ORTHODOX CATHOLIC CHURCH OF AMERICA
% Most Rev. Alfred Lankenau
Box 1222
Indianapolis, IN 45206

Several jurisdictions derive their orders from Archbishop Joseph Rene Vilatte, founder of the American Catholic Church through the orders given to the African Orthodox Church. In 1926 William F. Tyarks, a priest in the American Catholic Church who had been ordained by Vilatte's successor, Archbishop Frederick E. J. Lloyd in 1916, left Lloyd's jurisdiction and with other priests and members formed the American Catholic Orthodox Church. The group applied to the African Orthodox Church for orders and Archbishop George A. McGuire consecrated Tyarks in 1928.

In 1930 Tyarks consecrated one of the priests who had come from the American Catholic Church with him, Cyril John Clement Sherwood (1895-1969). Sherwood soon left Tyarks and was reconsecrated by McGuire in 1932. The next year he formed the American Holy Orthodox Catholic Apostolic Eastern Church. Sherwood's career overlapped that of Archbishop Aftimios Ofiesh's greatest activity, and Sherwood became acquainted with his vision of a united American Orthodoxy. He incorporated it in an ecumenical organization, the Orthodox Catholic Patriarchate of America.

Among Sherwood's bishops was George A. Hyde, whom the Patriarch consecrated in May 1957. Hyde had formed the Eucharistic Catholic Church in Atlanta, Georgia in 1946. This first exclusively gay ministry in America continued until 1959 when Hyde moved to Washington, D.C. and formed the Society of Domestic Missionaries of St. Basil the Great, an order of priests. The following year he left Sherwood and formed the Orthodox Catholic Church of America. He believed that Sherwood was too narrowly Eastern in his approach to liturgy and theology and wanted to restructure the church making it open to Western rite Orthodox practice. In spite of leaving Sherwood's jurisdiction, Hyde continued to participate in the ecumenical Orthodox Catholic Patriarchate of America.

In 1969 Sherwood died. At a meeting of the Synod the next year, Hyde was elected to succeed him as head of the Patriarchate, and the Holy Orthodox Catholic and Apostolic Eastern Church voted to become the Eastern Rite Diocese of the Orthodox Catholic Church of America. Thus Archbishop Hyde took control of all the work begun by Sherwood.

Doctrinally, the Orthodox Catholic Church of America follows the teachings of the Seven Ecumenical Councils and rejects the doctrinal innovations such as purgatory, papal infallibility, the immaculate conception, communion in one kind only, and an unmarried clergy. The Church uses both the Eastern and Western rites in its liturgy. Under Hyde's administration, the Church was active in promoting a ministry to homosexuals and is the ultimate source of the presently existing Eucharistic Catholic Church. After Hyde's retirement, this and other special ministries were discontinued in favor of work directed to all people.

In 1983 Hyde retired and Alfred Louis Lankenau, bishop of the Diocese of Indianapolis and Chicago, was elected to succeed him. Under the new Archbishop, the Orthodox Catholic Patriarchate of America, which had ceased to function during the 1970s, has been revived and several Catholic and Orthodox jurisdictions have affiliated. In 1983, the Holy Orthodox Church, American Jurisdiction, headed by Archbishop James Francis Miller, which had broken from the church of the same name headed by Archbishop William Francis Forbes, merged into the Church.

Membership: In 1984 the Church reported parishes located in Maine, New York, Rhode Island, Indiana, Illinois, Georgia, South Carolina, Florida, New Mexico, and the District of Columbia with mission parishes in Pennsylvania, Ohio, and California.

Remarks: In 1986 the Orthodox Catholic Church of America entered into an agreement of intercommunion with the Orthodox Catholic Church in America led by Archbishop Walter Xavier Brown and jointly formed the Holy Orthodox Synod of America. The synod is a confederation that independent Orthodox bishops may join.

Sources: George Augustine Hyde, ed., *The Genesis of the Orthodox Catholic Church of America*. Indianapolis: Orthodox Catholic Church of America, 1981; George Augustine Hyde, ed., *The Courage to Be Ourselves*. Anderson, SC, Ortho-Press, 1972; R. J. Bernard, *A Faith for Americans*. Anderson, SC: Ortho, 1974; *The Divine Liturgy*. Elberton, GA; Orthodox Catholic Church of America, 1966.

★124★
ORTHODOX CATHOLIC CHURCH OF NORTH AND SOUTH AMERICA
Box 1213
Akron, OH 44309

The Orthodox Catholic Church of North and South America was inspired by the ideal of the American Orthodox Church founded by Archbishop Aftimios Ofiesh under the guidance of Patriach Tikhon of the Russian Orthodox Church. A new attempt to bring this into reality began with Bishop Joseph W. Alisauskas, Jr. (d. 1980), who had been consecrated in 1968 by Archbishop William Henry Francis Brothers of the Old Catholic Church in America. Early in the 1960s, Brothers had taken his jurisdiction into the Russian Orthodox Church, but in 1967 he withdrew and reconstituted the Old Catholic Church in America. Alisauskas left Brothers's jurisdiction in 1969 and formed the Orthodox Catholic Diocese of Connecticut and New England, a name selected to designate accurately its geographic extent. In choosing the name, he was also drawing upon the impulse of Archbishop Joseph Rene Vilatte, who had originally ordained Brothers as a priest in 1910. The church adopted a new constitution in 1976, at which time it assumed its present name.

Associated with Alisauskas in Cleveland, Ohio, was the Holy Mother of God monastic community, founded in 1962 by Roman Bernard, a layman. Bernard was ordained by Alisauskas and in 1968 consecrated Bishop of Ohio City and Cleveland. He was elevated to the rank of metropolitan in 1978 and suceeded Alisauskas as Archbishop Roman in 1980.

The Orthodox Church of North and South America is Orthodox in faith and practice, but follows a variety of liturgical rites including the Orthodox-Byzantine, the Ambrosian-Milanese, a modified (de-protestantized) Anglican, the Gallican (but only in the van der Mensbrugghe translation, approved by the 1985 synod meeting), and the Roman Tridentine.

Membership: In 1988 the church had 12 parishes and missions, three mission stations (Philadelphia, Pennsylvania; Pennsboro, West Virginia; and Montreal, Quebec), and a semimonastic community in England. Holy Protection Monastary is currently located at Barberton, Ohio.

Periodicals: *The Orthodox Catholic Voice*, Box 1213, Akron, OH 44309; *The Image*, 594 Fifth Ave., N.E., Barberton, OH 44203; *The Shepherd*, 929 Lorain Ave., Zanesville, OH 43701; *The Western Orthodox Catholic*, Box 406, Willow Station, Cleveland, OH 44127.

Remarks: According to Archbishop Roman, Archbishop Brothers had always considered himself head of The Western Orthodox Catholic Church of America and had a large, oval, episcopal ring (used for sealing official documents) which bore that designation. Vilatte, consecrated by the Oriental Orthodox Patriarchate of Antioch, had been permitted to use the title: Exarch of the Old Catholic Church in America, a tacit admission of the Patriarchate's equation of "Old Catholic" and "Western Orthodox." Since that time the name "Old Catholic" has taken on a variety of meanings not envisioned by the Patriarchate in 1892.

★125★

ORTHODOX CHURCH IN AMERICA

% Most Blessed Theodosius, Archbishop of
   Washington, Metropolitan of All
   America and Canada
Very Rev. Daniel Hubiak, Chancellor
Box 675
Syosset, NY 11791

The Orthodox Church in America is the oldest continuously existing Eastern Orthodox body in North America in general and the United States in particular. As the first Orthodox church to arrive, it assumed a hegemony over what became in the nineteenth century a multi-ethnic Orthodox community, and many of the presently existing independent Orthodox churches in America began as parishes and/or a diocese within what is today known as the Orthodox Church in America.

The OCA began in Alaska with the arrival of missionaries of the Russian Orthodox Church. In 1794 eight monks and two novices arrived on Kodiak Island to follow up on the work of converting the Native Americans already begun by a generation of Russian lay people in the Aleutians. Among these ten was Father Herman, later canonized by the Church. In 1824 John Veniaminov, a married priest, was sent to the Aleutians. After the death of his wife, he was consecrated the first bishop of a missionary diocese. Bishop Innocent had an outstanding career in Alaska, building the first cathedral at Sitka, among other accomplishments. He was called in 1868 to be the Metropolitan of Moscow, the highest office in the Church and finally in 1977 canonized.

The sale of Alaska to the United States left the Missionary Diocese on its own. It moved its headquarters to San Francisco in 1872 and changed its name to the Russian Orthodox Church, Diocese of the Aleutian Islands and North America. The period during the episcopacy of Bishop Nicolas beginning in 1891 was a time of noted growth. The Alaskan Mission was expanded, and the work in Canada and the Eastern United States began.

In 1905 the diocese moved its headquarters from San Francisco to New York City. Its growth was recognized by its elevation to the rank of archdiocese. Under the archbishop was a bishop for Alaska and an Arabic-speaking bishop, Bishop Raphael Hawaweeny, who as Bishop of Brooklyn had oversight of Orthodox from the Middle East. Two additional bishops in Cleveland and Pittsburgh were soon added. The church progressed steadily until disrupted by events in Russia during World War I.

The Russian Revolution proved a disaster for the American Russian church. Russian Orthodox Christians had always carried a special loyalty for the royal family which had been executed by the new government in Moscow. Also, money from Russia which had always assisted in the support of the archdiocese was abruptly curtailed, to be almost immediately followed by a wave of immigration by refugees looking to the Church for spiritual guidance and support. The patriarch of Moscow was arrested and the American church split over loyalty to him versus acceptance of the new govenment. Representative of what was termed the "Living Church," those supportive of the Communist regime arrived in the United States in 1923. At a synod of the Russian Church in 1924 in Detroit the credentials of the Living Church were rejected and the Church asserted its administrative, judicial and legislative independence from Russia. It assumed a new name, the Russian Orthodox Greek Catholic Church of America and declared the imprisoned Archbishop Platon, "Metropolitan of All America and Canada," an action which led then to be popularly called the "Metropolia." Their major loss came in court. Before they were able to legally validate their separation from Moscow, the Living Church representatives were able to win the transfer of the title of St. Nicolas Cathedral in New York City into their hands.

In 1925 Archbishop Platon died. He was succeeded by Archbishop Sergius who in 1927 issued a Declaration calling for loyalty and cooperation with the new Russian government. Prior to this Declaration, the bishops of the Russian Orthodox Greek Catholic Church of America had cooperated with other Russian bishops around the world caught outside of Russia and also cut off by the Revolution. Following the Declaration, Metropolitan Platon declared his loyalty to Sergius but specifically denied him any power to make administrative decisions concerning the American church. In spite of the challenges of the several competing branches of Russian Orthodoxy, one stanchly opposed to any cooperation with the Church under Communist domination (Russian Orthodox Church Outside of Russia), and the other administratively tied to the Patriarch of Moscow (the American Exarchate of the Russian Orthodox Catholic Church), the Russian Orthodox Greek Catholic Church in America retained the support of most American believers.

During the years following the turmoil of the Russian Revolution, the Metropolia assumed the position that it would give recognition to the spiritual authority of the patriarch in Moscow, if he would recognize its administrative autonomy. However, the Church in Russia continued its support of those parishes in the Exarchate who recognized his complete authority. Finally, in 1970, the separation of the Metropolia from the Church in Russia was ended when the patriarch of Moscow, His Holiness Alexis, granted autonomous status to the Russian Orthodox Greek Catholic Church of America, renamed the Orthodox Church in America. The Exarchate was disolved and most of its parishes moved into the OCA.

For quite different reasons, the creation of the Orthodox Church in America created a controversy within the larger American Orthodox community. For many years there had been various attempts to move away from the ethnic divisions within American Orthodoxy. In creating the Orthodox Church in America, the Russian community asserted its status as the oldest Orthodox church in North America and as such the most fitting focus of Orthodox unity. Other Orthodox groups, particularly the Greek Archdiocese, saw the emergence of the OCA as a unilateral effort not deserving of recognition.

The OCA is headed by its archbishop, Metropolitan Theodosius, whose jurisdiction extends throughout the western hemisphere. There are nine dioceses in the United States, one in Canada and an exarchate in Mexico. Also under its canonical jurisdiction are the autonomous Albanian Orthodox Archdiocese and the Romanian Orthodox Episcopate of America. The latter places the OCA in a peculiar position, having a relationship with the Romanian Episcopate while holding membership in the Standing Conference of Canonical Orthodox Bishops which includes the rival Romanian Orthodox Church of America.

Membership: In 1978 the Church reported 440 parishes, 1,000,000 members and 531 priests.

Educational facilities: St. Tikhon's Orthodox Theological Seminary, South Canaan, Pennslyvania; St. Vladimir's Orthodox Theological Seminary, Tuckahoe, New York.

Periodicals: *The Russian Orthodox Messenger*, 59 East 2nd Street, New York, NY 10003; *The Orthodox Church*, Box 39, Pottstown, PA 19464.

Sources: Sophie Koulomzin, *The Orthodox Christian Church through the Ages*. New York: Russian Orthodox Greek Catholic Church of America, 1956; *The Orthodox*

Liturgy...according to the Use of the Church of Russia. London: Society for Promoting Christian Knowledge, 1964; Constance Tarasar, *Orthodox America, 1794-1976: Development of the Orthodox Church in America.* Syosset, NY: The Orthodox Church in America, Department of Archives and History, 1975.

★126★
ORTHODOX CHURCH OF AMERICA
% Most Rev. David Baxter
502 East Childress
Morrilton, AR 72110

The Orthodox Church of America was formed on June 29, 1970 by Bishop David M. Baxter. Bishop Baxter had been consecrated the previous year by Archbishop Walter A. Propheta of the American Orthodox Catholic Church, assisted by bishops John A. Christian, and Foster Gilead. The church uses the Western Rite, but places emphasis upon its Eastern orders and Eastern spirituality. Its basis of faith is the Nicene Creed, the Seven Sacraments, and the necessity of Orders in the Apostolic Succession.

Membership: In 1983 the Church reported 5 parishes, 14 priests, and 214 members.

Educational facilities: St. Herman Seminary, Morrilton, Arkansas, a correspondance school.

★127★
ROMANIAN ORTHODOX CHURCH IN AMERICA
% His Eminence The Most Rev. Archbishop Victorin (Ursache)
19959 Riopelle
Detroit, MI 48203

The Romanian Orthodox Church in America, officially known as the Romanian Orthodox Missionary Archdiocese in America and Canada, had its beginning in the formation of the first Romanian Orthodox parish in North America, formed at Regina, Saskatchewan, in 1902. It was followed two years later by a parish in Cleveland, Ohio, the first in the United States. These parishes and others to follow functioned under the hegemony of the Russian Orthodox Church. A diocese was created in 1929 and a bishop assigned in 1935. Bishop Policarp Morusca returned to Romania at the beginning of World War II and after the war was detained and finally in 1948 involuntarily retired by the new Romanian government. In 1950 a new bishop, consecrated and sent by the Church in Romania arrived. The appearance of Bishop Andrei Moldavan divided the American church which had a bylaw providing for the consecration of a bishop only after the election by a diocesan congress.

The majority of the American Romanian Orthodox reject Moldovan. The Romanian Orthodox Church of America began with the twelve parishes that accepted him. They organized as the Canonical Missionary Episcopate in the United States, Canada, and South America. The Church is fully Orthodox in faith and practice, a member of the Standing Conference of Canonical Orthodox Bishops in the United States, and differs from the larger Romanian Orthodox Episcopate of America in administration.

Membership: In 1980 the Church had 13 parishes and 12,835 members in the United States, with 19 additional parishes in Canada and one in Venezuela.

Periodicals: *Credinta—The Faith*, 19959 Riopelle, Detroit, MI 48203.

★128★
ROMANIAN ORTHODOX EPISCOPATE OF AMERICA
% Rt. Rev. Nathaniel, Bishop
2522 Grey Tower Rd.
Jackson, MI 49201

The first Romanian Christians came to America at the end of the nineteenth century. A parish of the Romanian Orthodox Church was organized in Regina, Saskatchewan, in 1902, and two years later St. Mary's Church was founded in Cleveland. Individual congregations cooperated with Russian bishops and were related directly to the hierarchy in Romania. After a quarter of a century, a church congress was held in Detroit and in 1929 the Romanian Orthodox Episcopate (diocese) of America was organized. In 1935 the first bishop, His Grace Polycarp Morusca, came to the United States and settled in Grass Lake, Michigan.

In 1939 Bishop Polycarp went to Romania but due to political events could not return. After World War II he was detained by the Romanian government and in 1948 placed in retirement. The Romanian patriarchate, without the knowledge or consent of the American diocese, consecrated a new bishop, the Reverend Andrei Moldovan, the parish priest in Akron, Ohio, who had gone to Romania to be consecrated, without the concurrence or support of the American parishes. His return to the United States created a major crisis as the status and bylaws of the diocese provided for ordination of bishops only after election by the diocesan congress. The majority party (48 parishes) declared themselves in full separation from the Romanian patriarchate. Later, in 1951, they elected Viorel (Valarian) D. Trifa, who had recently arrived in the United States, as their bishop. Through a fraternal tie, Trifa was able to bring the Episcopate under the canonical protection of the Russian Orthodox Greek Catholic Church of America (now the Orthodox Church in America), which recognized Trifa's church as a self-governing body.

The Episcopate faced a second major crisis in the 1970s when Bishop Trifa was charged with concealing an alleged role in Nazi atrocities in Romania. In 1980 he surrendered his United States citizenship, and in 1984 went into exile in Portugal. He died there in 1987 and

was succeeded by Bishop Nathaniel Popp, the present leader of the Episcopate.

Membership: In 1988 the episcopate reported 53 parishes, 55,000 members, and 83 clergy, including 12 parishes and 12 clergy in Canada.

Periodicals: *SOLIA, The Herald*, 146 W. Courtland St., Jackson, MI 49201-2208.

Sources: *Holy Liturgy for Orthodox Christians*. Jackson, MI: Romanian Orthodox Episcopate, n.d.; Valerian D. Trifa, *Holy Sacraments for Orthodox Christians*. Jackson, MI: Romanian Orthodox Episcopate, n.d.; *Beliefs of Orthodox Christians*. Jackson, MI: Romanian Orthodox Episcopate, n.d.

★129★
RUSSIAN ORTHODOX CHURCH IN THE U.S.A., PATRIARCHIAL PARISHES OF THE
St. Nicholas Patriarchal Cathedral
15 E. 97th St.
New York, NY 10029

Following the Russian Revolution, the members of the Russian Orthodox Church in both Russia and the United States were split over rejecting or acknowledging the new government which had risen to power. Within the United States, especially after the arrest of the Patriarch of Moscow, the sentiment was largely against any accommodation and the American archdiocese declared itself administratively autonomous of the homeland. Meanwhile, within the Soviet Union, a reorganization of the church by leaders of the so-called "Living Church," those who supported accommodation to the Communist government occurred. With government backing, they assumed control of the Church and elected John Kedrowsky as the new bishop for the West. Kedrovsky arrived in America in 1923 prepared to take up his leadership role. However, at the same synod meeting in 1924 at which the Church declared its autonomy, Kedrovsky's credentials were rejected. As the official representative of the Church in Russia, however, he did find some support, and in 1926 won possession of the headquarters cathedral in New York City.

Kedrovsky's situation was further complicated in 1933 by the arrival of Metropolitan Benjamin Fedchenkov. In the year that Bishop John had lived in the United States, the Church in Russia had regained some stability and the Living Church faction had died away. Metropolitan Benjamin represented a more acceptable accommodationist position and he gained some support. He established the American Exarchate of the Russian Orthodox Catholic Church. However, for another decade Bishop John, succeeded by his son Nicolas Kedrovsky, whom he had consecrated, kept possession of St. Nicholas Cathedral. Finally in 1945, after the death of both Bishop John and Nicolas, the Kedrovsky faction was left without either support of the Church in Russia or an episcopal leader. Rev. John Kedrovsky, Bishop John's other son signed the cathedral over to the Exarchate.

Negotiations continued sporadically in an attempt to work out differences between the church authorities and the larger autonomous Russian Orthodox Greek Catholic Church of America. These reached fruition in 1970. The Russian Orthodox Greek Catholic Church of America became the Orthodox Church in America and recognized the Patriarch of Moscow as its spiritual authority. The Patriarch, in turn, recognized its autonomous status. As part of the agreement, the Exarchate was disolved. At the time of the disolution of the Exarchate, it was agreed that any parishes which wished to remain under the direct administrative authority of the Moscow patriarchy could remain outside of the Orthodox Church in America. These several parishes reformed as the Patriarchal Parishes of the Russian Orthodox Church in the United States and Canada. A vicar bishop was placed in charge of the approximately 40 parishes. St. Nicholas remained with the Patriarchal Parishes and served as its headquarters. Over the years parishes have been allowed to transfer to the OCA. The church is also a member of the National Council of Churches.

Membership: In 1985, the church reported 9,780 members in 38 parishes served by 45 priests.

Periodicals: *One Church*, 727 Miller Avenue, Youngstown, OH 44502.

Sources: M. Pokrovshy, *St. Nicholas Cathedral of New York, History and Legend*. New York: St. Nicholas Cathedral Study Group, 1968.

★130★
RUSSIAN ORTHODOX CHURCH OUTSIDE OF RUSSIA
% His Eminence Vitaly, Metropolitan
75 E. 93rd St.
New York, NY 10028

Following the Russian Revolution and the cutting of lines of authority and communication between the Patriarch of Moscow and bishops serving Russian Orthodox communities outside of Soviet control, attempts were made to reorganize the church. In 1921 a conference of Russian Orthodox bishops in exile met at Sremski Karlovtsy, Yugoslavia. Among the participants was Metropolitan Platon, leader of the American archdiocese. Metropolitan Platon continued to work with the Council of Bishops Abroad until 1926 when he ran into conflict over the movement toward autocephalous status of the American church. Metropolitan Platon declared the Council of Bishops an uncanonical organization. The Council dismissed Platon and assigned Bishop Apollinary in his place.

Bishop Apollinary was elevated to archbishop in 1929 and, after a short period of leadership, he died in 1933.

He was succeeded by Bishop Vitaly. Efforts to heal the schism between the Church Abroad and the autonomous Russian Orthodox Greek Catholic Church of America (popularly called the Metropolia) led to a temporary reproachment in 1935 which continued through the period of World War II. In the mid-1940s, however, it became evident that the larger body wished some realignment with the Patriarch of Moscow and, in 1946, it broke completely with the Church Abroad. The American followers of the Church Abroad asserted their continuity with Russian Orthodoxy in America and declared the Metropolia schismatic. Since that time the Russian Orthodox Church Outside of Russia has been the major voice of the anti-Soviet faction of Russian Orthodoxy, and it has tried to continue the traditional practices of the Russian Church.

Membership: In 1988 the Church reported 135 parishes in the United States, 25 parishes in Canada, and 37 parishes in South America. There were approximately 100,000 members in the United States. There are affiliated congregations on every continent.

Educational facilities: Holy Trinity Orthodox Seminary, Jordanville, New York.

Periodicals: *Orthodox Life*, Holy Trinity Monastery, Jordanville, NY 13361; *Orthodox America*, Box 3132, Redding, CA 96099.

Sources: M. Rodzianko, *The Truth About the Russian Church Abroad*. N.p.: 1975; *A Cry of Despair from Moscow Churchmen*. New York: Russian Orthodox Church Outside of Russia, 1966; *Fiftieth Anniversary of the Russian Orthodox Church Outside of Russia*. Montreal: Monastery Press in Canada, 1971.

★131★
SACRED HEART CATHOLIC CHURCH (ARRENDALE)
Current address not obtained for this edition.

The Sacred Heart Catholic Church was founded in 1980 by Archbishop James Augustine Arrendale and other former members of Archbishop James Lashley's American Catholic Church, Archdiocese of New York. Arrendale was consecrated on August 10, 1981 by Bishop Pinachio, who was assisted by Bishops Donald Anthony and William Wren. The group adheres to the teachings of the Seven Ecumenical Councils and the three Ecumenical Creeds. Archbishop Arrendale died in 1985 and the future course of the Archdiocese is in doubt.

Membership: In 1983 the Church reported three parishes, two priests, and 50 members.

★132★
SERBIAN EASTERN ORTHODOX CHURCH FOR THE U.S.A. AND CANADA
% Rt. Rev. Bishop Firmilian
St. Sava Monastery
Box 519
Libertyville, IL 60048

Few churches have been so affected by the changes in modern Europe as the Serbian Church. Present maps (if they show it at all) reveal Serbia as a part of Yugoslavia, a country welded together out of a number of pre-World War II, pre-Tito states. An independent Serbian Orthodox Church had been established in 1219 under Archbishop St. Sava. A patriarchate was established in the fourteenth century. From 1389 to 1815 Serbia was under Turkish rule and the church suffered severe persecution, but a nineteenth century revival followed independence from Moslem control.

In 1765 Serbian autonomy was ended, and the church returned to the jurisdiction of the ecumenical patriarch in Constantinople, who began a Hellenization program. In 1832 the archbishop of Belgrade was given the title metropolitan, and in 1879, as a result of the Congress of Berlin, the Serbian Church regained autonomy. In 1920 it joined with the independent Serbian churches in Montenegro, Bosnia, Herzegovina, Dalmatia, and Croatia to form the Serbian patriarchate. The seat was established in Belgrade and its independence recognized by the ecumenical patriarch in 1922.

Immigrants from Serbia began to arrive in the U.S. in significant numbers in the 1890s. In 1892 Archimandrite Firmilian arrived and began to organize parishes. The first was in Jackson, California, but others soon followed by Chicago; Douglas, Alaska; and McKeesport, Steelton, and Pittsburgh, Pennsylvania. All of these early parishes were placed under the jurisdiction of the Russian Orthodox Church in America. The Serbian Church began to seek autonomous status as early as 1913. With Russian encouragement, Serbian Father Mardary was sent to the United States to organize an independent diocese in 1917. In 1919 the Russians elevated him to archimandrite. In 1921 the Serbs separated from the Russian Orthodox Church and Mardary became the administrator. In 1926 he was consecrated bishop for the American diocese. The Serbian Church grew slowly in this country until World War II, when a flood of refugees came into the United States. St. Sava Monastery at Libertyville, Illinois, was built soon after Bishop Mardary's consecration, and the church headquarters are currently established there. On November 14, 1970, King Peter, deposed monarch of Yugoslavia, died; he was buried in the Monastery.

The changes in political structure in Yugoslavia after World War II drastically altered the American diocese. In 1940 Bishop Dionisije Milivojevich was sent to the United States to assume authority for the church. Because Dionisije was a vocal anti-Tito spokesman and defender of the Serbian monarchy, Marshall Tito, the new ruler of Yugoslavia, encouraged the Belgrade patriarch to release Dionisije. At the same time, Tito moved against the church by confiscating all church property, thus placing the church under his financial control. The American Archdiocese was divided into three dioceses. Dionisije was left in charge of the Midwest. He rejected the actions of the patriarch in Belgrade, which he interpreted as coming from an atheist government bent on absolute control of the church. He was suspended from office and the following year excommunicated. He appealed the actions of the Belgrade patriarch to the clergy and laity of the American church and individual congregations, and priests began to take sides. Each side filed suit against the other, and two churches have evolved: the Serbian Orthodox Church in the United States and the Free Serbian Orthodox Church–Diocese for the U.S.A. and Canada.

The Serbian Orthodox Church in the United States of America and Canada is the canonical body loyal to the Mother Church with its Patriarchal See in Belgrade, Yugoslavia. In 1963 it was reorganized into three dioceses. Leading the church is Bishop Firmilian of the Midwestern American Diocese headquartered at Libertyville, Illinois. During the period of the 1960s and 1970s when the headquarters property of the church at St. Sava Monastery was being contested in the court and under the control of Bishop Dionisiji, the Midwestern Diocese erected a large church building in Chicago which served (until 1980) as its temporary headquarters. The Western American Diocese is headquartered in Alhambra, California, and the Eastern American Diocese in Edgeworth, Pennsylvania. In 1983 the Canadian parishes were separated from the Eastern Diocese and organized into a new Canadian Diocese. The Serbian Orthodox Church in the United States of America and Canada is a member of the Standing Conference of Canonical Orthodox Bishops. Through its ties to the church in Belgrade, it is also a member of the World Council of Churches.

Membership: In 1984 the Church reported 97,123 members, 78 parishes and missions and 73 priests.

Periodicals: *The Path of Orthodoxy*, Box 36, Leesdale, PA 15056.

Sources: Djoko Slijepchevich, *The Transgressions of Bishop Dionisije*. Chicago: The Author, 1963; Nicholai D. Velimirovich, *The Life of St. Sava*. Libertyville, IL: Serbian Eastern Orthodox Diocese, 1951; Nicholai D. Velimorovich, *The Faith of the Saints, Catechism of the Eastern Orthodox Church*. (Libertyville, IL): The Serbian Eastern Orthodox Diocese for the United States of America and Canada, 1961.

★133★
TURKISH ORTHODOX CHURCH
Current address not obtained for this edition.

The Turkish Orthodox Church was established in 1926 when excommunicated priest Paul Eftymios Karahissaridis claimed to have had his sentence of excommunication lifted by two members of the Holy Synod of the Greek Orthodox Church and that Bishops Cyril of Erdek and Agathangelos of Prinkipo consecrated him. Karahissaridis became popularly known as Papa Eftim. The new church grew out of a controversy begun by Papa Eftim's demanding a Turkish Church independent of the Greek Orthodox ecumenical patriarch in Constantinople. In 1933 Papa Eftin introduced a Turkish language version of the Divine Liturgy and ordained his son Socrates Ermis Karahissaridis and nephew Nicholas Doren to the priesthood. (Ermis became Eftim II.) The relations of the Turkish movement and the ecumenical patriarch have remained shaky and very much tied to Turkish-Greek relations. In 1962 Eftim II succeeded his ailing father as head of the church. Papa Eftim died in 1968.

On December 6, 1966, the Turkish Orthodox Church came to the United States with the appointnment of the Most Rev. Civet Kristof (a.k.a. Christopher M. Cragg) as metropolitan archbishop of New York and patriarchal exarch and primate of the Turkish Orthodox Church in America. Cragg, a well-educated black American of Ethiopian ancestry, had been consecrated by Archbishop Christopher Maria Stanley in 1965 and named Auxiliary Bishop of New York for the American Orthodox Catholic Church headed by Archbishop Walter A. Propheta. He edited the jurisdiction's periodical, the *Orthodox Catholic Herald*, which became the first periodical for the Turkish Orthodox Church. Kristof issued the first copies of *Orthodoks Mustakil*, the new periodical for the Turkish Orthodox Church, in 1969.

Membership: In 1969 the church reported 14 churches and 6 mission parishes.

Remarks: The Turkish Church continued to exist throughout the 1970s but during the early 1980s, Archbishop Cragg moved to Chicago and opened a health clinic. His stationary carried the title, American Orthodox Church, Diocese of Chicago and North America.

Sources: Most Reverend Metropolitan Kristof, *A Brief History of the Turkish Orthodox Church in America (Patriarchal Exarchate)*. New York: Turkish Orthodox Church in America, Exarchal Office, (1967?).

★134★
UKRAINIAN GREEK-ORTHODOX CHURCH OF CANADA
9 St. John's Ave.
Winnipeg, MB, Canada R2W 1G8

At the time of the Russian Revolution, the Ukrainian National Republic came into existence and Ukrainian Orthodox Christians began asserting their independence. Full separation from the Russian Orthodox Church and the proclamation establishing an autonomous national body came about in 1919. As news of the Revolution spread, immigrants to Canada acted quickly to found an independent jurisdiction. Approximately 150 delegates met in July 1918 at Saskatoon, Saskatchewan. Growth of the new jurisdiction was augmented by the movement of Eastern rite congregations of the Roman Catholic Church into Orthodoxy. At the time Rome was attempting to have the Eastern churches adopt the Latin rite.

In 1919 Metropolitan Germanos of the Antiochean Orthodox Church agreed to take the new work under his jurisdiction as a temporary measure. Rev. S. W. Sawchuk became the administrator. He traveled to Europe to attempt to secure a bishop, but was prevented entry to the Ukraine by Soviet officials. In 1924 John Theodorovich arrived in the United States to care for the Ukrainian Orthodox. The Canadians accepted him as their spiritual head, though Rev. Sawchuk continued to administer the work. In 1946 Archbishop Theodorovich asked to be relieved of his Canadian obligations. The Council of Bishops of the Ukrainian Autocephalous Orthodox Church in Exile suggested that Bishop Mstyslaw Skrypnyk lead the Canadian work which was growing into the largest segment of Ukrainian Orthodoxy outside of the Ukraine. He began his tenure in 1947 and retired in 1950. In 1951 Skrypnyk was succeeded by Metropolitan Ilarion Ohienko and an assistant, Archbishop Michael Horoshij. The jurisdiction is currently headed by Metropolitan Wasyly.

The church also operates St. Andrew's Theological College, adjacent to the University of Manitoba in Winnipeg. It is the only center for Ukrainian Orthodox theological education of its kind outside of the Soviet Union and is used by other Ukrainian jurisdictions of the United States, England, and Western Europe.

Membership: In 1987 there were 140,000 members in 250 congregations, and 85 priests.

Educational facilities: St. Andrew's Theological College, Winnipeg, Manitoba.

Periodicals: *Visnyk*, 9 St. John's Ave., Winnipeg, MB, Canada R2W 1G8.

Sources: Peter Bilon, *Ukrainians and Their Church*. Johnstown, PA: Western Penn. Branch of the U.O.L., 1953.

UKRAINIAN ORTHODOX CHURCH OF THE U.S.A.
Box 495
South Bound Brook, NJ 08880

History. Ukrainian Christians, primarily Roman Catholic followers of the Uniate Eastern Rite, arrived in the United States and organized parishes in the nineteenth century. However, they soon encountered efforts of the Roman Church in America to further Latinize the Uniate parishes. In response, some left and joined the Russian Orthodox Church, in spite of what many felt were imperial designs against Ukrainians. In 1915 a Ukrainian National Church was founded. It placed itself under independent Catholic bishop, Carmel Henry Carfora, head of the National Catholic Diocese in North America and later primate of the North American Old Roman Catholic Church, with an understanding that it would affiliate with the Ukrainian Orthodox Church when and if it was allowed to exist in the Ukraine. In 1917, as the Russian Revolution progressed, the Ukrainian National Republic came into existence and, in 1919, it proclaimed the Ukrainian Autocephalous Orthodox Church the official church of the land. Unable to find a bishop who could give them orders, the clergy and lay leaders assembled at a church council in 1921 and consecrated several candidates for bishop by the laying-on-of-hands of all present. In this manner Archpriests Wasyl Lypkiwsky and Nester Sharayiwsky were elevated to the office of bishop. Lypkiwsky was designated metropolitan.

The Ukrainian-Americans immediately began to establish an independent church. An initial All-Ukrainian Orthodox Council of the American Ukrainian Orthodox Church met in 1922. It petitioned for a bishop and two years later John Theodorovich, who had been consecrated by Metropolitan Lypkiwsky, arrived to head the new church. He established his see in Philadelphia in 1926.

The arrival of Bishop John (who had been consecrated in 1921 in the Ukraine by the Autocephalous Church) led other Uniate congregations to leave the Roman jurisdiction and become Orthodox. In response Rome appointed a bishop over its Ukrainian parishes. However, the new bishop soon came into conflict with many of the members. They broke with Rome and, not yet resolved to become Orthodox, formed the independent American-Ukrainian Greek-Catholic Church. During the 1920s, the parishes decided to become Orthodox and looked to Archbishop Aftimios Ofeish, head of the American Orthodox Church, for episcopal leadership. In 1932 he consecrated Joseph Zuk (d. 1934) as the bishop of the Ukrainian Orthodox Church of America. He was succeeded by Bishop Bohdan T. Shpilka.

The Ukrainian Orthodox Church of the U.S.A. and the Ukrainian Orthodox Church of America existed side-by-side for several decades as competitors. Several attempts at union failed. However, in 1948, the Ukrainian Orthodox Church of America elected Mystyslaw Skrypnyk, then head of the Ukrainians in Canada, as their new Archbishop and named Bishop Bohdan as the auxiliary. Resigning from his Candian post, Skrypnyk took the lead in seeking ways to unite the two churches. Through several gatherings in which members of both churches participated, the barriers to union were removed. As agreed to in the negotiations, Archbishop John was reconsecrated in order to silence any objections to the regularity of his original consecration.

Archbishop John was elected metropolitan of the new church, Archbishop Skrypnyk headed the consistory, and Archbishop Hennadij became the auxiliary bishop. Bishop Bohdan did not join the union, and with several parishes continued to exist separately as the Ukrainian Orthodox Church of America (Ecumenical Patriarch).

Archbishop Skrypnyk emerged as the most potent leader in the new church and eventually succeeded to the post of metropolitan, which he still retains. He developed the Saint Andrews the Firstcalled Memorial Center, the headquarters complex in South Bound Brook, New Jersey which now includes the seminary, St. Sophia Press (the publishing enterprise), a museum and archives, and the Home of Ukrainian Culture.

Beliefs. The church is at one in faith and practice with all of Orthodoxy. It accepts the Nicene Creed. It adheres closely to a rule against instrumental music and uses only vocal music in its worship.

Organization. The church is headed by its primate, Metropolitan Mstyslaw, archbishop of Philadelphia. He is assisted by archbishops in Chicago and New York. The archbishop is also designated the metropolitan of the church in diaspora. In this task he is assisted by archbishops in Paris, France and Australia. Eparchies have been established for Latin America, Great Britain, Western Europe, and Australia and New Zealand. A sobor of bishops meets every two years. In some countries, general sobors of synods of the church meet every three years to establish general and specific administrative policies. The church is also served by the United Ukrainian Orthodox Sisterhoods and the Ukrainian Orthodox League of the USA. The church is in communion with the Ukrainian Greek-Orthodox Church in Canada.

Membership: In 1988 the church reported 85,000 members, 92 congregations and 108 priests in the United States.

Educational facilities: St. Sophia Orthodox Theological Seminary, South Bound Brook, New Jersey.

Periodicals: *Ukrainian Orthodox Word* (Ukrainian and English editions), Box 495, South Bound Brook, NJ 08880; *Bipa (Faith)*, 201-63 27th St., Bayside, NY 11360;

UOL Bulletin, % St. Michael Ukrainian Orthodox Church, 7047 Columbia Ave. Hammond, IN 46324.

Sources: Peter Bilon, *Ukrainians and Their Church.* Johnstown, PA: Western Pa. Branch of the U.O.L., 1953.

★136★
UKRAINIAN ORTHODOX CHURCH IN AMERICA (ECUMENICAL PATRIARCHATE)
St. Andrew's Ukrainian Orthodox Diocese
90-34 139th St.
Jamaica, NY 11435

In 1950 the two branches of the Ukrainian Orthodox Church in America united. The initial attempts toward union had followed the replacement of Bishop Bohdan T. Shpilka as ruling bishop of one branch of the church by Mystyslaw Skrypnyk. At the time of the union, Bishop Bohdan declined to participate in the new church and withdrew with his following and reorganized as the Ukrainian Orthodox Church in America. Bishop Bohdan had led the Ukrainian Orthodox Church from 1934 to 1950 and had been consecrated in 1937 on orders of the ecumenical patriarchate. He retained that relationship after he broke with Bishop Skrypnyk.

Bohdan died in 1965. He was succeeded by Andrei Kuschak, but not before a document in which Bohdan aledgedly passed his succession to Demetius Sawka was declared invalid. The Church is identical in faith and practice to the Ukrainian Orthodox Church in the U.S.A. As of 1987, the office of primate and metropolitan was vacant.

Membership: In 1977 the Church reported 28 parishes, 25,000 members and 35 priests. A 1980 survey indicated 23 parishes 3,465 confirmed members and an additional 2,000 adherents.

Periodicals: *Ukrainian Orthodox Herald*, 90-34 139th Street, Jamaica, NY 11435.

★137★
UNIVERSAL SHRINE OF DIVINE GUIDANCE
% Most Rev. Mark A. G. Karras
30 Malta St.
Brooklyn, NY 11207

Father Mark Karras, the son of a Greek priest, was consecrated by Archbishops Peter A. Zurawetzky of the Old Catholic Patriarchate of America, assisted by independent Greek bishop, Joachim Souris, Archbishop of Byzantium, on July 18, 1955, and the following month founded the Universal Shrine of Divine Guidance. He was assisted in this enterprise by Veronica Perweiler, whom he consecrated as "abbess" the following year. The teachings of the Universal Shrine are based upon the idea that humanity has entered a third and final state of spiritual and moral evolution. Thus, the Universal Shrine is a continuation, with significantly new emphases, of the Pentecostal Church, and the Apostolic episcopacy. The first stage was the regulatory period of Judaism and the second the instructional stage of Christianity. In the third stage, a period of fulfillment through enlightenment and grace will ensue. Bishop Mark promulgates a pure philosophy of faith in God and spiritual values, a universal faith emphasizing moral achievement and merit. At the heart of the doctrine is the Christian teaching of love.

Membership: Not reported.

Sources: Mark Karras, *Christ Unto Byzantium*. Miami, FL: Apostolic Universal Center, 1968.

★138★
WESTERN ORTHODOX CHURCH IN AMERICA
% Most Rev. C. David Luther
1529 Pleasant Valley Blvd.
Altoona, PA 16602

The Western Orthodox Church grew out of the Catholic Apostolic Church of Brazil founded by former Roman Catholic Church bishop, Carlos Duarte Costa, which had been brought to the United States by Bishop Stephen Meyer Corradi-Scarella, an independent bishop in New Mexico. In 1973 Corradi-Scarella gave Fr. Charles David Luther, a priest he had ordained, directions to found the Community of the Good Shepherd as a fellowship of priests and priest in training. In 1977 the name was changed to Servants of the Good Shepherd. The Community accepts qualified men into the priesthood, trains them and assists them in starting mission churches, usually as worker-priests.

In 1977 Luther was consecrated by Bishop Charles R. McCarthy assisted by Jerome Joachim and W. D. de Ortega Maxey. In 1974 Joachim had succeeded Corradi-Scarella as head of the National Catholic Apostolic Church in America. In 1980 he renamed his jurisdiction the Western Orthodox Church in America. After his consecration Luther brought the Servants of the Good Shepherd into Joachim's jurisdiction. He became bishop of the Diocese of Altonna and was later (1981) made archbishop. In 1983, however, Joachim and Luther decided to become independent of each other. Joachim and his following became the Catholic Apostolic Church in America, while Luther retained the name, Western Orthodox Church in America.

The Western Orthodox church in America, while possessing Catholic orders, is Orthodox while following a Western Rite. In 1984, Luther consecrated Richard James Ingram as Bishop of Hobart (Indiana) and James Franklyn Mondok as Bishop of Euclid (Ohio). The Church is affiliated with the Ecumenical Church Federation, a fellowship of independent bishops and other Christian leaders organized by Bishop Alan Bain, Archbishop for the British Isles of the Apostolic Episcopal Church.

Membership: In 1981 there were 25 priests and over 100 seminarians studying for the priesthood affiliated with the Servants of the Good Shepherd.

Educational facilities: Duarte Costa University, Altoona, Pennsylvania; Duarte Costa School of Religion, Altoona, Pennsylvania.

Periodicals: *The Herald*, Box 2733, Des Plaines, IL 60017-2733.

Sources: *A Brief Description of the Servants of the Good Shepherd*. Altoona, PA: n.p., (1980?).

Non-Chalcedonian Orthodoxy

★139★
ARMENIAN APOSTOLIC CHURCH OF AMERICA
℅ Archbishop Mesrob Ashjian
138 E. 39th St.
New York, NY 10016

In 1933, the Armenian Church in America split along political lines as a result of the Soviet dominance of Armenia. The Armenian Apostolic Church of America continues the church that began to form in the 1890s among Armenian-Americans and whose members were most commited to a free and independent Armenia. This church existed without official sanction until 1957 when Zareh I, the newly elected catholicos of the See of Cilicia, took it under his jurisdiction. Located in Sis, the capital of Lesser Armenia since the fifteenth century, the See of Cilicia moved to Lebanon in the twentieth century.

In 1972, the Prelacy of the Armenian Apostolic Church of America was divided into the Eastern States and Canada, and the Western States. His Eminence, Archbishop Dater Saskissian, prelate of the Western Prelacy and His Eminence, Archbishop Mesrob Ashjian, of the Eastern. Archbishop Ashjian succeeded Archbishop Karekin Sarkissian in 1977.

Membership: In 1988, the church reported 350,000 members in 37 churches with 40 priests in the United States. There were four churches in Canada. Affiliated congregations were located in 12 countries with a reported worldwide membership of 900,000.

Educational facilities: Armenian Theological Seminary, Bikfaya, Lebanon.

Periodicals: *The Outreach*, 138 E. 39th St., New York, NY 10016.

Sources: Karekin Sarkissian, *The Council of Chalcedon and the Armenian Church*. New York: Armenian Church Prelacy, 1965; Karekin Sarkissian, "Armenian Church in Contemporary Times" in A. J. Arberry, ed., *The Church*

in the Middle East. Cambridge: Cambridge University Press, 1969; Karekin Sarkissian, *The Witness of the Oriental Orthodox Churches*. Antelias, Lebanon: The Author, 1970.

★140★
ARMENIAN CHURCH OF AMERICA
℅ His Eminence Torkom Manoogian, Primate
630 Second Ave.
New York, NY 10016

The Armenian Church of America is the continuing faction of the Armenian Church, which since 1933 has attempted to accomodate to the merger of Armenia into the Union of Soviet Socialist Republics. It is under the jurisdiction of the See of Etchmiadzin in Soviet Armenia. It is headed by Archbishop Torkom Manoogian, with a western diocese under the leadership of Bishop Elisha Simonian.

Membership: In 1979, the Church reported 66 churches, 61 clergy, and 450,000 members.

Periodicals: *Bema*, 630 Second Ave., New York, NY 10016; *The Mother Church*, 1201 N. Vine St., Hollywood, CA 90038.

Sources: *The Handbook on the Divine Liturgy of the Armenian Apostolic Holy Church*. Boston: Baikar, 1931; Sion Manoogian, *The Armenian Church and Her Teachings*. N.p.: The Author, n.d.; Papken Gulesserian, *The Armenian Church*. New York: Diocese of the Armenian Church in America, 1966; Hogop Gurlekian, *Christ's Religion in Every Branch of Life and the Armenians Really Alive*. Chicago: The Author, 1974.

★141★
APOSTOLIC CATHOLIC ASSYRIAN CHURCH OF THE EAST, NORTH AMERICAN DIOCESE
℅ His Grace, Mar Aprim Khamis, Bishop of the North American Diocese
744 N. Klidare
Skokie, IL 60076

Alternate address: His Holiness Mar Dinkha IV, Catholicos Patriarch, Box 3257, Sadoun, Baghdad, Iraq.

Victims of Turkish expansion, the Church of the East was dispursed in the late nineteenth century and its headquarters in northern Kurdistan was abandoned. Scattered members of the church began to arrive in America in the 1890s, but for many years were without organization. Early in this century, there were several visitations by the bishops. They found a flock served by an insufficient number of priests and deacons meeting whenever space was available. All of this changed in 1940 when Mar Eshai Shimun XXIII, the 119th patriarch of the church, moved his headquarters to Chicago. A church-reorganization program was initiated. Priests and deacons were ordained; churches were purchased and built; administration was put in efficient order; and a publishing program, including a new periodical, was begun. The progress of the Church has continued under the present patriarch, who has reestablished the international headquarters in Iraq.

Membership: In 1983, the Diocese reported 13 churches, 35,000 members, and 65 clergy.

Periodicals: *Voice from the East*, Box 25264, Chicago, IL 60626.

Sources: *The Liturgy of the Holy Apostles Adai and Mari*. London: Society for Promoting Christian Knowledge, 1893. Mar O'Dishoo, *The Book of Marganita (The Pearl) on the Truth of Christianity*. Kerala, India: Mar Themotheus Memorial Printing & Publishing House Ltd., 1965; Yulpana M'Shikhay D'eta Qaddishta Washlikhayta O'Qathuliqi D'Mathnkha, *Messianic Teachings*. Kerala, India: Mar Themotheus Memorial Printing & Publishing House Ltd., 1962; *Rules Collected from the Sunhados of the Church of the East & Patriarchial Decrees*. San Francisco: Holy Apostolic and Catholic Church of the East, 1960.

★142★

CATHOLIC APOSTOLIC CHURCH AT DAVIS
% Gates of Praise Center
921 W. 8th St.
Davis, CA 95616

The Catholic Orthodox Church at Davis was founded in 1972 by Albert Ronald Coady. Coady was ordained in May 1972 by Archbishop John Marion Stanley of the Orthodox Church of the East. In June 1972 Stanley consecrated Coady at a service in Trichur, India. That consecration was confirmed in July 1972 in a service of enthronement conducted by Archbishops Walter A. Propheta, John A. Christian, Laurence F. Pierre, and C. Clark, all of the American Orthodox Catholic Church (Propheta). Stanley also participated in that ceremony. Originally known as the Christian Orthodox Church, it became the Eastern Catholic Church Syro-Chaldean Rite before taking its present name in the mid-1980s.

The church is Eastern in its liturgy and accepts the Nicene Creed like the Orthodox Church of the East. It is also charismatic in that it accepts the current manifestation of the gifts of the Spirit (I Corinthians 12) in its worship life.

Membership: Not reported.

★143★

COPTIC ORTHODOX CHURCH
% Archpriest Fr. Gabriel Abdelsayed
427 West Side Ave.
Jersey City, NJ 07304

Since World War II, an increasing number of Copts have left Eqypt because of Moslem discrimination. Many of these have come to the United States. In 1962, the Coptic Association of America was formed to serve the Coptic Eqyptians in New York City and vicinity and to work for the establishment of regular pastoral care. The following year Bishop Samuel, bishop of public, ecumenical, and social services, was delegated to come to the United States by Pope Kyrillos VI to meet with the Coptic Association and implement pastoral care. In 1965 Father Marcos Abdel-Messiah was ordained in Cairo and sent as a priest to Toronto to establish the Diocese of North America. In 1967 Father Dr. Rafael Younan arrived in Montreal. By 1974 there were nine priests serving four churches in New York, plus other churches in Los Angeles, Houston, Detroit, Jersey City, St. Paul, Indianapolis, Milwaukee, Chicago, and several smaller centers. There are fewer than 2,000 adult Copts in North America. An English translation of *The Coptic Orthodox Mass and the Liturgy of St. Basil* has been produced and educational literature has been initiated by Father Marcus Beshai of Chicago.

Membership: In 1983, the Church reported 9 churches, 2,332 members, and 17 priests.

Sources: Fayek M. Ishak, *A Complete Translation of the Coptic Orthodox Mass and Liturgy of St. Basil*. Toronto: Coptic Orthodox Church, Diocese of North America, 1973; *St. Mark and the Coptic Church*. Cairo: Coptic Orhtodox Partriarchate, 1968; *The Agprya*. Brooklyn, Abdelsayed, "The Coptic-American: A Current African Cultural Contribution in the United States of America." *Migration Today* 19 (1975) 17-19.

★144★

ETHIOPIAN ORTHODOX CHURCH IN THE UNITED STATES OF AMERICA
% His Eminence Abuna Yeshaq, Archbishop
Holy Trinity Ethiopian Orthodox Church
140-142 W. 176th St.
Bronx, NY 10453

Alternate address: % His Holiness Abuna Tekle Haimanot, Box 1283, Addis Ababa, Ethiopia.

The beginning of the twentieth century saw a developing nationalism within the Ethiopian Church, at that time still under the Patriarch of Alexandria. Due in part to the diplomacy of Emperor Haile Selassie, in 1929, five native bishops were consecrated, though they were without dioceses and could not perform other consecrations. In 1944, the Emperor established the Theological College in Addis Ababa. Immediately after World War II, the Emperor negotiated an agreement with the Egyptians that led, in 1948, to the promulgation of the Statue of Independence of the Ethiopian Orthodox Church, thus freeing it from Alexandria and the Coptic Orthodox Church in Eqypt. That same year, it joined the World Council of Churches. Finally, in 1959 the bishop of Addis Ababa was raised to the rank of patriarch and chosen from among the Coptic monks. This action gave the church its actual autonomy.

Following the overthrow of Haile Selassie in 1974 and the establishment of a Marxist government in Addis Ababa, the Church came under severe attack. In 1976, His Holiness Abuna Theopolis, the Patriarch was removed from office, arrested, and has not been seen since. Whether he is still alive is unknown. Several other high ranking church leaders were exiled or remain under detention. In 1978, Archbishop Abba Matthias, head of the Ethiopian monastery in Jerusalem, defected to the United States and began a campaign to alert the Western world to the religious persecution in Ethiopia.

In 1959, the same year the Ethiopian Church attained full independence, Laike Mandefro, was one of several Ethiopian priests who came to the United States to study. Originally associated with Abuna Gabre Kristos Mikeal of the Ethiopian Coptic Orthodox Church of North and South America, who sponsored their entrance into the United States, they soon broke relations with him, and under the authority of His Grace Archbishop Theopolis, began to gather Ethiopian-Americans into a congregation in Brooklyn, later relocated to the Bronx. As his work grew, he was raised to the rank of archimadrite and placed in charge of the Ethiopian Church in the West. He moved to Jamaica in 1970, where by 1977, there were congregations in Kingston, Montego Bay, Ocho Rios, Linsted, and St. Ann, with missions throughout the Carribean. In 1974, the American branch became an "affiliated communion" with the National Council of Churches. The Jamaican branch is a full member of both the Jamaica Council of Churches and the Caribbean Conference of Churches. More recently Archimadrite Mandefro was consecrated a bishop and made Archbishop of the Western Hemisphere Diocese.

Membership: In 1984, the Church reported 34 parishes and missions, 5,000 members, and 15 clergy. There are approximately 10,000 members in 7 parishes and 3 missions in Jamaica.

Periodicals: *The Structure of the Church*, 140-142 West 176th St., Bronx, NY 10453.

Sources: Enrico S. Molnar, *The Ethiopian Orthodox Church*. Pasadena, CA: Bloy House Theological School, 1969; K. M. Simon, *The Ethiopian Orthodox Church*. Addis Ababa: n.p., (195-?); Lisa Bessil-Watson, comp., *Handbook of Churches in the Caribbean*. Bridgetown, Barbados: Cedar Press, 1982.

★145★
ETHIOPIAN ORTHODOX COPTIC CHURCH, DIOCESE OF NORTH AND SOUTH AMERICA
1255 Bedford Ave.
Brooklyn, NY 11216

The Ethiopian Orthodox Coptic Church, Diocese of North and South America, was formed by Most Rev. Abuna Gabre Kristos Mikael, an Ethiopian-American who established his jurisdiction under the authority of the Archbishop Walter A. Propheta of the American Orthodox Catholic Church. In 1959, he traveled to Ethiopia, was ordained, and then elevated to the rank of Chorepistopas by Abuna Basilios. late patriarch of Ethiopia. He then served as sponsor for a group of three priests and five deacons sent by Abuna Basilios to the United States for advanced study and to develop an American branch of the Ethiopian Orthodox Church. However, the priests, led by Fr. Laike Mandefro, broke relations with Mikael and centered their efforts on a parish in Brooklyn, New York, later relocated to the Bronx, which was directly under the authority of the Patriarch in Addis Ababa. The Ethiopian Orthodox Coptic Church remains in communion with the American Orthodox Catholic Church, from which some of the clergy were drawn.

In the few years of its existance it has established churches in Trinidad, Mexico, and Pennsylvania; in Brooklyn there are two churches, one with a Latin and one with a Coptic Ethiopian rite, the rite commonly followed by the church. The worship is in English. The priests are both celibate and married, and all bishops are celibate, the common Eastern church practice. Most of the members and clergy are black, but the church made news in 1972 by elevating a white man to the episcopate as bishop of Brooklyn.

Friction has developed between the two "Ethiopian" churches, each questioning the legitimacy of the other.

Membership: Not reported. It is estimated that several hundred members can be found in the three parishes in New York and Pennsylvania.

★146★
HOLY APOSTOLIC-CATHOLIC CHURCH OF THE EAST (CHALDEAN-SYRIAN)
% Metropolitan Mikhael
190 Palisades Dr.
Daly City, CA 94015

The Holy Apostolic-Catholic Church of the East (Chaldean-Syrian) is one of several jurisdictions which claim a derivation from the Church of the East. Their beginnings are traced to 1938 with the United States arrival of David Stanns (Mar David) as an independent bishop. Stanns passed his lineage to Richard Bruce Morrill, presently head of the Holy Orthodox Catholic Church, Eastern and Apostolic. Morrill consecrated

Joseph Russell Morse (Mar Joseph I), founder of the Western Orthodox Church. In June 1974, Morse consecrated M. H. Speierer-Ruess von Plauen-Brankovic (Michael Rice) to be his coajutor. Rice assumed the ecclesiatical title of Mar Mikhael of Eritrea. Toward the end of the decade, Mar Mikhael left Morse's jurisdiction and established the Holy Apostolic-Catholic Church of the East.

The belief and practice of the church is Orthodox. Like the Church of the East, it holds to the doctrines of the first two Ecumenical Councils, affirms the virgin birth of Jesus, His incarnation and sacrificial atonements, and the Holy Trinity. The Bible, consisting of the Old and New Testaments, is the authority for the church, which uses the Peshitta, the Bible translated directly from ancient Aramaic texts. The jurisdiction differs from some Eastern bodies in that it has entered into the Charismatic Renewal and continues to believe and teach that the gifts of the Holy Spirit (I Corinthians 12) are meant for today.

Membership: In 1983 the church reported 15 parishes and 3,500 members in the United States.

Remarks: The author's volume, *The Old Catholic Sourcebook* (Garland, 1983), co-authored with Karl Pruter, incorrectly identified Mar Mikhael with Michael A. Itkin, a bishop who also resides in the San Francisco Bay area, who also derives his orders from the Church of the East and who has taken the same ecclesiastical name. Itkin, however, heads a church which is openly identified with the homosexual community and which accepts homosexuals into the priesthood. In this regard, Itkin and the Community of the Love of Christ which he heads should be sharply distinguished from the Holy Apostolic-Catholic Church of the East.

★147★
HOLY APOSTOLIC CATHOLIC CHURCH, SYRO-CHALDEAN DIOCESE OF SANTA BARBARA AND CENTRAL CALIFORNIA
(Defunct)

The Holy Apostolic Catholic Church, Syro-Chaldean Diocese of Santa Barbara and Central California was founded by Michel Djorde Milan d'Obrenovic (d. 1986). In 1971, d'Obrenovic became the head of a small group in Cornville, Arizona, consisting of former Roman Catholics, Old Catholics, and Serbian Orthodox. Having been chosen the group's pastor, he sought ordination from Christ Catholic Church. The attempt was unsuccessful, and he was later ordained by Archbishop Gerret Munnik of the Liberal Catholic Church, Province of the United States. After a few years he left the Liberal Catholics and was consecrated by Bishops John Marion Stanley, of the Orthodox Church of the East, and Elijah Coady, of the Christian Orthodox Church (now the Catholic Apostolic Church in Davis) in 1977. The Holy Apostolic Catholic Church follows the practice and belief of the Church of the East, without the charismatic-pentecostal emphasis introduced by Stanley and accepted by Coady.

Quite apart from his ecclesiastical career, d'Obrenovic developed a second identity under his birth name, George Hunt Williamson. D'Obrenovic claimed to be a descendent of the Yugoslavian royal family of d'Obrenovic (the last member of which was supposed to have been assassinated in 1903) and he used the name Williamson because it was easier for Americans to pronounce. As George Hunt Williamson, he became one of the first people in the early 1950s to claim direct contact with the entities inhabiting flying saucers. He was present when George Adamski made his initial contact with the Venusian in the California Desert, and eventually as Brother Philip, founded the Brotherhood of the Seven Rays.

Membership: The church had only one parish located in Santa Barbara, California. No evidence of that parish has been found since d'Obrenovic's death in 1986.

Sources: George Hunt Williamson, *Other Tongues--Other Flesh.* Amherst, WI: Amherst Press, 1953; George Hunt Williamson, *Secret Places of the Lion.* London: Neville Spearman, 1959; George Hunt Williamson, *Road in the Sky.* London: Neville Spearman, 1959; George Hunt Williamson, *The Saucers Speak.* London: Neville Spearman, 1963; Brother Philip (George Hunt Williamson), *The Brotherhood of the Seven Rays.* Clarksburg, WV: Saucerian Books, 1961.

★148★
HOLY ORTHODOX CATHOLIC CHURCH, EASTERN AND APOSTOLIC
Current address not obtained for this edition.

The Holy Orthodox Catholic Church, Eastern and Apostolic is one of several jurisdictions which traces its beginnings to the arrival in the United States of David Stanns (Mar David) in 1938. Stanns passed his episcopal lineage, claimed to have been derived from a branch of the Church of the East in India, to Richard Bruce Morrill (Mar Apriam), who established the Holy Orthodox Catholic Church. In 1984 Morrill merged his jurisdiction with the Byzantine Old Catholic Church, headed by Bishop Mark I. Miller (Mark I), to form the Byzantine Catholic Church. After only a few months of association, Morrill left the Byzantine Catholic Church and reconstituted the Holy Orthodox Catholic Church.

The church's synod meets every three years. It is Orthodox in faith and practice.

Membership: In 1984 the church claimed seven parishes and missions in the United States. Foreign work was reported in Brazil, Chile, Liberia, Mexico, Nigeria, Trinidad, Zaire, and Zimbabwe. As of January 1983, there were 66 parishes, one school, one mission station, 70 priests, and 106,079 members worldwide.

Educational facilities: Orthodox Academy of Education, Tarzana, California.

Periodicals: *Maranatha*.

★149★
MALANKARA ORTHODOX (SYRIAN) CHURCH
% His Grace Dr. Thomas Makarios
Episcopal Diocesan House
1114 Delaware Ave.
Buffalo, NY 14209

The Malankara Orthodox (Syrian) Church dates itself to the arrival of St. Thomas, one of the disciples of Jesus, in India in 52 C.E. St. Thomas worked near southern India and was martyred on St. Thomas Mount, Madras. After existing independently for many centuries, the church developed a relationship with the Roman Catholic Church in 1599 at the synod of Daimper. That relationship ended in 1653 in what is frequently referred to as the "Coonan Cross incident." In a very dramatic action, church members grasping a rope which symbolically tied them to a cross erected at Mattancherry, Cochin, renounced the Roman Catholic faith and the authority of the pope both for themselves and succeeding generations.

The Malankara Church soon affiliated with the Syrian Church of Antioch. After separating from the Roman Church, it was left without a bishop. The Syrian Church refused to consecrate a bishop, but provided for the ordination of priests. In 1772 Thomas Palakomatta IV was consecrated as Dionysius I. A century later, the head of the Indian Church found himself engaged in a quarrel with another bishop claiming authority over the Indian Christians. He asked the Syrian patriarch, who had consecrated the rival, to assist him. In 1975 Mar Peter came to India, excommunicated the rival, and reorganized the Indian Church into seven dioceses, each headed by a bishop subject to him.

The following decades were spent asserting the independent position of the church from both the Syrian patriarch (who tried to assume title to church property) and the followers of the excommunicated rival. Two decisive events ended the controversy: first, in 1912, the Syrian Patriarch cooperated in the creation of the Catholicate of India by declaring the defunct Catholicate of Edessa (Syria) reestablished in India. Second, the last lawsuit was settled in 1958 when the Indian courts recognized the authority of the Indian Catholics in all matters of church administration.

The Malankara Orthodox Church was brought to the United States in the late 1960s by immigrants from southern India. A diocese was created in the 1970s, and in 1980 the first church building, St. George's Orthodox Church, Staten Island, New York, was purchased and dedicated.

The church is similar in faith and practice to the Syrian Orthodox Church of Antioch and the Syrian Orthodox Church of Malabar. The church was a charter member of the World Council of Churches. The present patriarch of the church is His Holiness Moran Mar Basilius Mar Thoma Mathews I, whose chair is located at the Catholicate Palace at Kottayam, Kerala.

Membership: In 1988 the church reported 5,000 families in 37 congregations in the United States and four in Canada. Included were two missions for non-Indians in Spokane, Washington, and Coeur d'Alene, Idaho.

Sources: Leslie Brown, *The Indian Christians of St. Thomas*. Cambridge: Cambridge University Press, 1956; Donald Attwater, *The Christian Churches of the East*. Milwaukee: Bruce Publishing Company, 1962; Kadavil Paul Pamban, *The Orthodox Syrian Church, Its Religion and Philosophy*. Vadayampady, Puthencruz, India: K.V. Pathrose, 1973.

★150★
ORTHODOX CATHOLIC SYNOD OF THE SYRO-CHALDEAN RITE
% Most Rev. Bashir Ahmed
100 Los Banos Ave.
Daly City, CA 94014

The Orthodox Catholic Synod of the Syro-Chaldean Rite was formed in 1970 by Bishop Bashif Ahmed and is one of several bodies to continue the tradition of Mar Jacobus (Ulric Vernon Herford), who brought the Syro-Caldean Church to the West in 1902. Raised a Unitarian, Herford journeyed to the Orient on a quest to find a means of uniting East and West. In 1902 he was consecrated by Mar Basilius Soares, Bishop of Trichur, and head of a small body of Indian Christians called the Mellusians. Mar Basilius had been ordained to the priesthood by Julius Alvarez (who had consecrated Joseph Rene Vilatte) and consecrated to the episcopacy by Mar Antonius Abd-Ishu of the Nestorian linage. Upon his return to England, Herford founded the Evangelical Catholic Communion.

The Orthodox Catholic Synod of the Syro-Chaldean Rite derives from a schism of the Evangelical Catholic Communion, an American church founded by Michael A. Itkin. Itkin had led his orgainzation to take a positive activist stance in support of homosexuals. Rejecting Itkin's leadership, Ahmed founded an independent jurisdiction within the same tradition.

Membership: Not reported.

★151★
ORTHODOX CHURCH OF THE EAST
% Archbishop John Marion Stanley
Rte. 4, Box 322
Vashon, WA 98070

History. The Orthodox Church of the East (also known as the Church of the East in America) was founded in 1959 by Bishop John Marion Stanley, and is one of several churches claiming affiliation with the ancient Church of the East through the lineage of its episcopal orders. Stanley was consecrated to the bishopric in 1959 by Charles D. Boltwood of the Free Protestant Episcopal Church as Bishop of Washington. Boltwood also granted Stanley a mandate for an autocephalous body under Boltwood's guidance. Boltwood was originally consecrated by Archbishop William Hall, whom he succeeded as head of the church, but was later consecrated *subconditione* by Hugh de Willmott Newman of the Catholicate of the West. Newman passed to Boltwood the lineage of Mar Basilius Soares, head of a small body of Indian Christians who have their orders from the Church of the East.

In 1963, Boltwood withdrew from the Catholicate of the West, but remained in communion with Stanley. During this period, Stanley was elevated to metropolitan of the United States by Newman, who gave him the ecclesiastical title of Mar Yokhannan (Aramaic for "Bishop John"). Stanley then experienced the pentacostal baptism of the Holy Spirit accompanied by speaking in tongues. He in turn led his jurisdiction into the acceptance of the pentacostal experience and the exercise of the gifts of the Holy Spirit as mentioned in I Corinthians 12. He also became a popular speaker at the interdenominational Full Gospel Businessmen's Fellowship International conferences.

Also in 1963, Stanley became concerned over the report on Newman in Peter Anson's study of independent bishops, *Bishops at Large*. Under the direction of Metropolitan Archbishop Howard of Portland and the Roman Catholic Archdiocese of Seattle, Stanley, as Mar Yokhannan entered into dialogue with Rome. For five years cathedrals throughout the world were opened to him to celebrate the Eastern rite.

In 1970, in the Catholic Church of the Holy Resurrection in New York City, Patriarch Woldymyr I (Walter A. Propheta (1912-1972), founder of the American Orthodox Catholic Church, performed an Economia so Stanley could serve as his apostolic delegate for foreign missions. In 1971, Propheta appointed Stanley as exarch plenepotentiary to carry full authority from the patriarch in dealing with problems in church leadership overseas. Stanley's church and clergy remained in his jurisdiction, and he continued in the Church of the East Rite.

Bishop Stanley remained with the American Orthodox Catholic Church until October 24, 1977, when Patriarch Mar Apriam I (Richard B. Morrill) of the Holy Orthodox Catholic Church, Eastern and Apostolic, gave his patriarchial blessing and letter to return the Orthodox Church of the East to an autonomous and autocephalous independent status. Some of the prelates and clergy in Stanley's jurisdiction had previously been under Mar Apriam I. Since that time, the Orthodox Church of the East has remained autonomous, though in dialogue, with the Church of the East in Iraq and the Church of the East in India. It also remains in open communion with the Free Protestant Episcopal Church.

Beliefs. The Orthodox Church of the East in America is Orthodox in faith and practice and accepts the Nicene Creed, using the Eastern text. It follows the Syro-Chaldean (Aramaic) liturgy of the Holy Apostolic Catholic Assyrian Church of the East, but uses an English text based upon the archbishop of Canterbury's committee's translation of Kirbana Kadisha (Holy Eurcharist), the shortened form approved by the Metropolitan of India in 1976 during his visit to Santa Barbara, California. It also follows the Church of the East's Hebraic standards of no statues or pictures in the sanctuary, but does not emphasize the *malka*, i.e., the tradition of dough kept since the Last Supper from which the eucharist is prepared. Members make room for praising in tongues (speaking-in-tongues) following the ancient liturgy's words, "We make new harps in our mouths, and speak a new tongue with lips of fire."

Organization. The Orthodox Church of the East follows an episcopal polity. It keeps the biblical practice of bishops being the husbands of one wife (which the patriarch of the Church of the East reinstated). Women are not admitted to the priesthood but many serve as deaconesses up to the rank of archdeaconess. There is no restriction as to their ministering in the gifts of the Spirit whenever it is appropriate and necessary.

Bishop Stanley also founded the Messianic Believer's Trust, a parachurch organization promoting charismatic (pentacostal) renewal. It cooperates with the Believers Charismatic Fellowship, a similar organization, in the publication of the *The Messianic Messenger*. Another organization under the church is the World Alliance for Peace, which promotes peace among the people of God, primarily by developing bridges among Christians, Muslims, and Jews. Recent efforts have included an Israeli Children's tennis match for peace before the 1988 Olympic Games in Seoul, Korea, and the preparation for a Pacific Peace Conference that will include representatives from Nicaragua and Costa Rica.

The church has a bible school and hospital under its direction in India. A mission work in Pakistan cooperates with other churches in relief programs for Afghan refugees and goodwill within the Muslim government. It is also working to develop an accredited graduate school in Pakistan.

Membership: In 1988, the church reported two congregations, one in Bremerton, Washington, and one in Malibu, California. Other congregations formerly in the jurisdiction have become autonomous. There is one congregation each in India nad Pakistan.

Educational facilities: Suviseshapuram Bible and Technical School, Kerala, India.

Periodicals: *The Messianic Messenger*, 3130 Jefferson St.-36, Napa, CA 94558.

★152★
SYRIAN ORTHODOX CHURCH OF ANTIOCH (ARCHDIOCESES OF THE UNITED STATES AND CANADA) (JACOBITE)
% Archbishop Mar Athanasius Y. Samuel, Primate
49 Kipp Ave.
Lodi, NJ 07644

The Syrian Orthodox Church of Antioch (Archdiocese of the United States and Canada) dates itself to the beginnings of Christianity in Antioch as recorded in the Acts of the Apostles in the New Testaments, but has been greatly affected by two events. In the fifth century, the church refused to accept the decisions of the Council of Chalcedon concerning the Person of Christ and as a result developed a doctrinal position similar to that of the Coptic and Armenian churches. In the following century the church experienced a marked revival of spiritual life under St. Jacob Baradaeus (500-578) and in recognition of his work has frequently been referred to as the Syrian Jacobite Church.

The church came to the United States through the migration of members in the late ninteenth century. In 1907 the first priest was ordained and sent to work in America. Archbishop Mar Athanasius Y. Samuel moved to America in 1949 and was soon appointed patriarchial vicar. The archdiocese was formally created in 1957. Archbishop Samuel received some fame in the 1950s as a result of his having purchased the first of what were to become known as the Dead Sea Scrolls.

The archdiocese adheres to the faith of the first three ecumenical councils. It accepts the Nicene Creed but not the Chalcedonian formula and its teaching on the two natures of Christ. There are seven sacraments: baptism, mooron (confirmation), the Eucharist, confession (and penitence), marriage, ordination to the priesthood, and the anointment of the sick.

The archdiocese is an integral part of the Syrian Orthodox Partiarchate of Antioch and All the East, the headquarters of which is located in Damascus, Syria. The patriarchate is a member of the National Council of Churches. There is an annual convention of the archdiocese.

Membership: In 1988 the archdiocese reported 30,000 members in North America divided between 20 parishes in the United States and five parishes in Canada. There were 28 priests.

Sources: Mar Ignatius Ephrem I, *The Syrian Church of Antioch, Its Name and History*. Hackensack, NJ: The Archdiocese of the Syrian Church of Antioch in the United States and Canada, n.d.; Mar Severius Ephrem Barsoun, *The Golden Key to Divine Worship*. West New York, NJ: 1951; Anaphora. Hackensack, NJ: Metropolitan Mar Athanasius Yeshue Samuel, 1967; Kadavil Paul Ramban, *The Orthodox Syrian Church, Its Religion and Philosophy*. Vadatampady, Puthencruz, India: K.V. Pathrose, 1973; Athanasius Yeshue Samuel, *Treasure of Oumran*. Philadelphia: Westminster Press, 1966.

★153★
SYRIAN ORTHODOX CHURCH OF MALABAR
% Dr. K. M. Simon
Union Theological Seminary
Broadway and 120th St.
New York, NY 10027

From the time of the ancient church, there has existed on the southwest Malabar coast of India a people who by legend were first evangelized by the Apostle Thomas. Relations with the Roman See were established in the Middle Ages. In the fifteenth century when the Protugeuse began to colonize the Malabar coast, they attempted to Latinize the church, and after a period of tension most of the church withdrew from papal jurisdiction in 1653. In 1665 the Syrian Jacobites sent their representative to the Malabar coast and eventually many of the Malaber Christians were brought under the Syrian patriarch of Antioch. A Malabar bishop was consecrated in 1772 and there are approximately 1,500,000 Christians in his jurisdiction today.

The Syrian Orthodox Church of Malabar has established a mission in New York directly under the patriarch of Antioch. There is only one congergation (as of 1967) which meets at Union Theological Seminary every Sunday and on holidays. Its approximate 150 members are drawn from students, diplomatic personnel, and permanent residents. Periodic services are also held in Philadelphia, Washington, DC. and Chicago. Dr. K. M. Simon is the vicar-in-charge.

Membership: Not reported.

Sources: *An English Translation of the Order of the Holy Ourbana of the Mar Thoma Syrian Church of Malabar*. Madras, Diocesan Press, 1947; Kadavil Paul Ramban, *The Orthodox Syrian Church, Its Religion and Philosophy*. Vadayampady, Puthencrez: K. V. Pathrose, 1973.

★154★
WESTERN ORTHODOX CHURCH
Current address not obtained for this edition.

The Western Orthodox Church is one of several small jurisdictions which grew out of the ministry of Most Rev. David Stanns (Mar David), an independent bishop who founded the American Coptic Orthodox Church. That church was continued by Archbishop Richard Bruce Morrill (Mar Apriam) of the Holy Orthodox Catholic Church, Eastern and Apostolic. Joseph Russell Morse established the Western Orthodox Church and its Diocese of the Pacific Coast in 1972. In 1973 he was consecrated bishop and elevated to archbishop in 1974.

The Western Orthodox Church is described as Western because it uses the English language in its worship. It is Coptic in that Archbishop Morrill, who succeeded Archbishop Stanns, gave permission for the establishment of the church with an English-speaking Coptic liturgy. It is charismatic in that the gifts of the spirit are recognized and used in the worship of the church. It is orthodox and acknowledges the Nicene Creed.

Membership: Not reported.

Section 3

Lutheran Family

An historical essay on this family is provided beginning on page 15.

Lutheranism

Sources: Uuras Saanivaara, *The History of the Laestadian of Apostolic-Lutheran Movement in America* Ironwood, MI: National Publishing Company, 1947; *Constitution and By-Laws*. n.p.: Finnish Apostolic Lutheran Church of America, 1929.

★155★

APOSTOLIC LUTHERAN CHURCH OF AMERICA
% Rev. George Wilson, President
New York Mills, MN 56567

The Apostolic Lutheran Church of America is the only branch of the Laestadian (Finnish Apostolic Lutheran) movement to organize formally. Since 1908 the Old Laestadians had held an annual "Big Meeting." It was primarily a time for theological discussions and for affirming consensus. In 1928 the Old Laestadians announced the intention of establishing a national church. In 1929 the constitution and by-laws were adopted, asserting the authority of the Bible and the Book of Concord. A congregational government and a mission program were established. The church body ordains ministers, establishes institutions, and helps found new congregations. The Old Laestadians practice the laying-on-of hands for absolution after the confession of fe!t sin to a confessor. They also believe in the three baptisms: of water (establishing the covenant between God and his children), of the Holy Spirit (the bond of love), and of blood (godly sorrow).

The Apostolic Lutheran Church is headed by a president and a central board. There are two districts. Congregations are located in Michigan, Minnesota, the Dakotas, Massachusetts, Washington, Oregon, and California.

Membership: In 1985 the church reported 49,972 members, 49 congregations, and 32 ministers.

Educational facilities: Apostolic Lutheran Seminary, Hancock, Michigan.

Periodicals: *Christian Monthly*, Apostolic Book Concern, Rte. 1, Box 150, New York Mills, Minnesota 56567.

★156★

APOSTOLIC LUTHERANS (CHURCH OF THE FIRST BORN)
Current address not obtained for this edition.

The branch of the Apostolic Lutherans, generally called the First Borns, are a continuation of the congregation headed by John Takkinen. They are aligned with the followers of Juhani Raattamaa headquarted at Gellivaara, Finland. They differ from the Old Laestadians (i.e., the Apostolic Lutheran Church) by their emphasis on the simplicity of the Christian life. They turn to the elders of Gellivaara for particular decisions on moral questions. They forbid neckties, pictures on walls, taking photographs, hats on women, Christmas trees, life insurance, and flowers at funerals.

The First Borns were among the first to introduce English in worship and to publish English books. They hold Big Meetings every summer. They print their church news in Valvoju, an unofficial publication circulated among Apostolic Lutherans. By latest count (made in the 1940's) there were approximately 2,000 members. Churches are located in Michigan; Wilmington, North Carolina; Wilmington, Deleware; Brush Prairie, Washington; and Gackle, North Dakota. Ther are approximately twenty-five congregations.

Membership: Not reported.

Sources: Uuras Saanivaara, *The History of the Laestadian or Apostolic-Lutheran Movement in America*. Ironwood, MI: National Publishing Company, 1947.

147

★157★
APOSTOLIC LUTHERANS (EVANGELICALS NO. 1)
Current address not obtained for this edition.

That branch of the Apostolic Lutheran Movement generally referred to as the Evangelicals No. 1 began under the inspiration and preaching of Arthur Leopold Heideman who emphasized positive evangelism. Among the Apostolic Lutherans, they lay the least emphasis on confession and sanctification. They use, but do not consider important, public confession. The Evangelicals No. 1 have experienced two splits. In 1921-22 a group led by Paul A. Heideman returned to the beliefs of the Old Laestadians. In 1940 a split occurred over the place of the commands and counsels of Christ and the Apostles and the use of confession. The Evangelicals No. 1 represent those who hold that the commands of Christ are necessary as a norm for Christian living. They believe themselves to be the one church of true believers.

Membership: Not reported.

Sources: Uuras Saavinaara, *The History of the Laestadian or Apostolic-Lutheran Movement in America.* Ironwood, MI: National Publishing Company, 1947.

★158★
APOSTOLIC LUTHERANS (EVANGELICALS NO. 2)
Current address not obtained for this edition.

Formed in 1940 and having broken from the Apostolic Lutherans (Evangelicals No. 1), that branch of the Apostolic Lutheran Movement generally called the Evangelicals No. 2 rejects the need of the commands and counsels of Christ because, they say, the grace of God works in believers to bring about a denial of unrighteousness and worldly lusts, and it works to instill godly and righteous behavior. They reject the confession of sins as a Roman Catholic institution, and they do not emphasize absolution. The law, they believe, should be preached to unbelievers, but only the gospel of free grace, to believers.

Like the Evangelicals No. 1, this group believes itself to be the one true church of Christ. Founders of the group include John Koskela, Victor Maki, John Taivalmaa, and Andrew Leskinen.

Membership: Not reported.

★159★
APOSTOLIC LUTHERANS (THE HEIDMANS)
Current address not obtained for this edition.

The Heidemans are the second largest group of Apostolic Lutherans. The group was formed in 1921-22 by members of the Apostolic Lutherans (Evangelicals No. 1) who

separated and returned to the Old Laestadian position. Thus they resemble the Old Laestadians group, but they remain outside of its organization. The leader of the group was Paul A. Heideman, son of A.L. Heideman , who was for many years the only ordained minister in the group. He was assisted by a number of preachers.

Membership: Not reported.

Periodicals: *Rauhan Tervehdys*; *Greetings of Peace*.

★160★
APOSTOLIC LUTHERANS (NEW AWAKENING)
Current address not obtained for this edition.

Possibly the smallest branch of the Laestadians or Apostolic Lutheran Movement is the New Awakening group. They teach the "third use of the law," i.e., that Christians must abide by the Ten Commandments in addition to Christ's two laws of love of God and love of neighbor. They also teach a second experience following conversion. The second experience is the "circumcision of the heart," in which one's heart is deeply broken but then experiences a fuller knowledge of Christ's redemptive work and of sanctification.

Membership: Not reported.

Sources: Uuras Saanivaara, *The History of the Laestadian or Apostolic-Lutheran Movement in America.* Ironwood, MI: National Publishing Company, 1947.

★161★
ASSOCIATION OF FREE LUTHERAN CONGREGATIONS
3110 E. Medicine Lake Blvd.
Minneapolis, MN 55441

History. The Association of Free Lutheran Congregations was formed in 1962 by congregations that refused to enter the merger of the Lutheran Free Church with the American Lutheran Church. Among the organizers was the Rev. John P. Strand, who became president at its founding. The dissenting congregations (about 40 in number) met at Thief River Falls, Minnesota, for the organization. They opposed the American Lutheran Church's membership in the World Council of Churches; the liberal theology reflected in new attitudes toward the Bible and the Roman Catholic Church; compromises of congregational polity; high-churchism; and the lack of emphasis on personal Christianity (including the condoning of social dancing and social drinking).

Beliefs. The association adheres to the traditional Lutheran confessional documents, especially the Unaltered Augsburg Confession and Luther's Small Catechism. The group believes the Bible is the Word of God, complete, infallible, and inerrant, and rejects all affiliations and associations that do not accept the Bible alone as definitive for life and practice. The association specifically rejects the liberal drift of Lutheran theology that accepts modern biblical criticism. It also has refused to make any move toward Roman Catholicism unless the Roman Catholic Church first accepts the Lutheran principles of justification by faith alone and the role of the Bible as the supreme authority for humanity.

The church is rather free in liturgical practice. A variety of biblical translations are used. Simplicity in worship is encouraged and centrality is given to preaching. Founding members cited the "High-church" tendencies in the American Lutheran Church as one cause of their staying out of the merger.

Organization. The association continues the congregational structure of the former Lutheran Free Church. Final human authority rests in local churches, under the Word of God and the Holy Spirit. Representatives of the congregations meet annually in conference. The conference oversees the seminary and bible school, mission work in Brazil and Mexico, and a home mission program.

Membership: In 1988, the association reported 25,250 members, 190 churches, and 139 ministers in the United States. There are four churches and four ministers in Canada.

Educational facilities: Association Free Lutheran Theological Seminary, Minneapolis, Minnesota; Association Free Lutheran Bible School, Minneapolis, Minnesota.

Periodicals: *The Lutheran Ambassador*, 3110 E. Medicine Lake Blvd., Minneapolis, MN 55441.

★162★
CHURCH OF THE LUTHERAN BRETHREN OF AMERICA
1007 Westside Dr.
Box 655
Fergus Falls, MN 56537

The Church of the Lutheran Brethren of America resulted from a revival in the 1890s among the Lutherans of the Midwest. Many people began to question certain practices in their parishes concerning church order. Most of their questions dealt with the "unconverted," those who had not had a personal conversion experience that infused them with an awareness of Christ as their savior. Some people, such as K.O. Lundelberg, said practices like the following had no basis in Scripture: the acceptance of the "unconverted" into church membership, requiring the oath in confirmation from "unconverted" youth, elaborate ritual worship, and admitting the "unconverted" to communion. Some independent congregations were begun and Rev. Lundelberg began to publish a Norwegian-language newspaper, *Broderbaandet*. In 1900, at a convention in Milwaukee, Wisconsin, the Church of the Lutheran Brethren was organized.

The Brethren differ from other Lutherans in that they accept only those who profess a personal experience of salvation. Confirmation has been discontinued; rather, children are instructed and wait until they have individual conversions before becoming members. Worship is simple and non-liturgical with free prayer and testimonies, and with lay participation. Communion elements are distributed by the elders to communicants in their pews. Otherwise, the church accepts basic Lutheran doctrine.

The policy is congregational. Together the congregations form the synod with a president and other officers. A board of foreign missions oversees work in Japan, Africa, and Formosa. The Lutheran Bible Schools begun in 1903 moved to Fergus Falls in 1935. In 1948, the name was changed to Lutheran Brethren Schools, which includes Hillcrest Lutheran Academy and the Lutheran Bible School and Seminary. Two homes for the aged, Sarepta Home and Broen Memorial Home, are supported by the church.

Membership: In 1985, the Lutheran Brethren reported 11,374 members in 108 congregations and a total of 148 ministers.

Educational facilities: Lutheran Bible School and Seminary, Fergus Falls, Minnesota.

Periodicals: *Faith and Fellowship*, 704 Vernon Avenue, W., Fergus Falls, Minnesota 56537.

Sources: A.A. Petersen, *Questions and Answers about the Church of the Lutheran Brethren of America*. Fergus Falls, MN: Lutheran Brethren Publishing Company, 1962. Joseph H. Levang, *The Church of the Lutheran Brethern, 1900-1975*. Fergus Falls, MN: Lutheran Brethern Publishing House, 1975.

★163★
CHURCH OF THE LUTHERAN CONFESSION
460 75th Ave., N.E.
Minneapolis, MN 55432

The Church of the Lutheran Confession began in 1957 when over thirty pastors and congregations of the Wisconsin Evangelical Lutheran Synod withdrew to form the Interim Conference. In 1960 they were joined by two pastors and congregations of the Evangelical Lutheran Synod to form the Church of the Lutheran Confession.

Membership: In 1986, The Church of the Lutheran Confession reported 8,852 members in 68 churches with 78 ministers.

Educational facilities: Immanuel Lutheran College, Eau Clair, Wisconsin.

Periodicals: *The Lutheran Spokesman*, 11315 E. Broadway, Spokane, WA 99206, *Journal of Theology*, Immanuel Lutheran College, Eau Claire, WI 54701.

Sources: Mark...Avoid...Origin of CLC. Eau Claire, WI CLC Bookhouse. 1983.

★164★
CONCORDIA LUTHERAN CONFERENCE
Central Ave. at 171st Place
Tingley Park, IL 60477

The Concordia Lutheran Conference was formed in 1956 by former members of the Lutheran Church-Missouri Synod who wished to "continue in the former doctrinal position of the Missouri Synod" in the face of what they saw as a deviation. They particularly emphasize the Bible as the inerrant word of God and as the only source and norm of Christian doctrine and life. Like their parent body, they accept the Book of Concord as the proper exposition of the Word of God. The church is nonseparatist in orientation and seeks unity with all other Lutherans and Christians on a basis of unity of faith.

Membership: In 1984, the Concordia Lutheran Conference reported a membership of seven congregations, 350 members, and eight ministers.

Educational facilities: Concordia Theological Seminary, Tingley Park, Illinois.

Periodicals: *The Concordia Lutheran*, Central Ave. at 171st St., Tingley Park, IL 60477.

Sources: H. David Mensing, *A Popular History of the Concordia Lutheran Conference.* n.p.: 1981.

★165★
EVANGELICAL LUTHERAN CHURCH IN AMERICA
% Truman Larson
Rte. 1
Jackson, MN 56143

Elling Eielsen was a young Norwegian immigrant who was ordained in America. He led the formation of the Evangelical Lutheran Church in America, the first Norwegian Lutheran synod in the New World, in 1846. Growth of the synod was slow partly due to the demand for proof of conversion prior to admission to membership. Controversy arose as some clergy demanded the admission of all who accepted the Christian faith and led a moral life. In 1876 a constitution revised along these lines was accepted and the name changed to Hauge's Norwegian Evangelical Lutheran Synod (which became part of the American Lutheran Church). At this time Eielsen and his supporters withdrew and formed the Evangelical Lutheran Church in America according to the Old Constitution.

Eielsen himself died in 1883 but the Synod has continued as a small body.

Doctrine is at one with other Lutheran bodies. Liturgy is simple. (Eielsen had also protested domination by university-trained clergy, clerical garb, and a too formal liturgy.)

Membership: In 1985, the Church reported on two congregations with a total membership of 50. There are no ordained ministers.

★166★
EVANGELICAL LUTHERAN CHURCH IN AMERICA (1988)
8765 W. Higgins Rd.
Chicago, IL 60631

The Evangelical Lutheran Church in America (1988) was formed January 1, 1988, by the merger of the Lutheran Church in America, the American Lutheran Church, and the Association of Evangelical Lutheran Churches. This merger created not only the largest Lutheran body in America, but the fifth largest denomination in America. Through the lineage of the Lutheran Church in America, the Evangelical Lutheran Church in America continues the work of the earliest Lutheran organizations in America: the Philadelphia Ministerium (1748) and the New York Ministerium (1786). It also culminates a process of merger of diverse American Lutheran churches and synods which had been attempting to unite Lutherans since the first half of the nineteenth century.

History: The Lutheran Church in America, the largest body merging into the new church, was formed in 1962 by the merger of four Lutheran bodies: The United Lutheran Church in America, the Finnish Evangelical Lutheran Church (Soumi Synod), the American Evangelical Lutheran Church, and the Augustana Evangelical Lutheran Church which for most of its life was known simply as the Augustana Synod. The 1962 merger was the culmination of no fewer than eight previous mergers, the most significant of which was the 1918 merger of the General Synod, the General Council, and the General Synod of the South to form the United Lutheran Church in America, the largest Lutheran body through most of the twentieth century. The General Synod had in turn been created by the 1820 merger of the older Lutheran associations: the Philadelphia Ministerium, part of the New York Ministerium, and the North Carolina Synod. The membership of the churches in the United Lutheran Church in America tradition was primarily German-American.

The Augustana Synod had originated in 1851 when the Synod of Illinois was established by Lutheran immigrants in the midwest. Around 1860 the Swedish and Norwegian elements in the Illinois Synod withdrew and formed the Scandinavian Augustana Synod. That synod joined with the remainder of the New York Ministerium in 1867 to form the very loosely associated General Council. In 1918, when the General Council merged into the United Lutheran Church in America, the Augustana Synod refused to join in the merger and remained an independent body until 1961.

The Finnish Evangelical Lutheran Church was formed in 1890 in Calumet, Michigan. It used the liturgy of the Church of Finland. The American Evangelical Lutheran Church dated to 1872 when Danish-American Lutherans formed the Kirklig Missions Forening. Through the merger of these Finnish and Danish synods into the larger German, Swedish, and Norwegian bodies, the Lutheran Church in America became the most complete amalgamation of Lutherans across ethnic boundaries and heralded the Americanization of Lutheran immigrant communities (a process through which all immigrant communities in America must eventually pass).

Another body entering into the 1988 merger, the American Lutheran Church, was formed in 1960 by the merger of three Lutheran bodies: The United Evangelical Lutheran Church, the Evangelical Lutheran Church, and the American Lutheran Church (1930-1960). The merged church retained the name of the group formed in 1930 by the merger of the Ohio (1818), Bufffalo (1845), Texas (1851) and Iowa (1845) Synods. All were of German background. The United Evangelical Lutheran Church was founded in 1896 by the union of two separate synods of Danish background. The Danish Evangelical Lutheran Association was formed in 1884 by pastors seceding from the Norwegian-Danish Conference of 1870. The Danish Evangelical Lutheran Church in North America was created in 1894 by a group which had withdrawn from the Danish Evangelical Lutheran Church of America (which eventually merged into the Lutheran Church in America). The Evangelical Lutheran Church was the result of a merger in 1917 of the different Norwegian Lutheran bodies established in America in the nineteenth century: the United Norwegian Church, the Norwegian Synod, and the Hague Synod. The American Lutheran Church was the first major merger of Lutheran groups across ethnic lines.

The Association of Evangelical Lutheran Churches, the newest and the smallest of the bodies to enter into the 1988 merger, was formed in 1976 by ministers and churches which withdrew from the Lutheran Church-Missouri Synod. The formation of the association followed many years of increased tensions within the Missouri Synod spurred by a series of complaints by conservative members about a perceived liberal drift within the church. Conservatives demanded the withdrawal of pulpit and altar fellowship from the liberal American Lutheran Church. (Pulpit fellowship refers to the practice of changing ministers between congregations for Sunday morning worship. Altar fellowship refers to the acceptance of members from other denominations during the practice of holy communion.) Further, conservatives asked for the end of cooperation with both the American Lutheran Church and the Lutheran Church in America in the

Lutheran Council in the U. S. A. Most importantly, they demanded an investigation of the Concordia Theological Seminary, whose faculty, they alleged, was teaching doctrine contrary to offical synod standards. Among the key items to which objection was raised was the teaching of modern biblical criticism which compromised the belief in the inerrancy of the Bible.

The question of the synod's ability to control teaching at the seminary came to a head in 1972. J. A. O. Preus, president of the Missouri Synod, issued a report accusing some of the teachers at the seminary of teaching false doctrines. Seminary president John Tietjen was singled out for particular criticism. This action increased the polarization of the two visible parties in the synod, and the conservative group increased its demands that the synod enforce doctrinal standards, particualrly a literal interpretation of the Bible. The liberals, whose strength centered upon the seminary, insisted upon greater freedom to interpret the Bible and teach theology. Following a defeat at the 1973 meeting of the synod, the liberals organized Evangelical Lutherans in Mission (ELIM). Early in 1974 Tietjen was suspended as president of Concordia. In reaction, 43 of the 47 professors went on strike and were supported by three-fourths of the student body who voted to boycott classes. Forced to leave Concordia, the faculty and students established Concordia Seminary in Exile (popularly known as Seminex). ELIM supported the new seminary and prepared itself to remain as a liberal dissenting group within the synod.

The next two years saw the process of polarization increasing as conservatives, then in total control of the synod, pressed for total conformity with traditional doctrinal standards and threatened removal of voices of dissent. The liberals fought a defensive action until 1976 when, feeling no longer able to remain in the fellowship, they left to join the Association of Evangelical Lutheran Churches. While retaining the formal doctrinal standards of the Missouri Synod, the new church emphasized openness, diversity, and ecumenism. It immediately established pulpit and altar fellowship with the American Lutheran Church, and the Lutheran Church in America, which it saw as merely a first step to the realization of complete union.

Lutheran work began in Canada in the 1740s, and for many decades the Canadian work was affiliated with the American synods and churches. Congregations affiliated with the American Lutheran Church became an independent body in 1967, and those affiliated with the Lutheran Church in America became an independent body in 1986. (The history of these congregations can be found under the entry for the Evangelical Lutheran Church in Canada).

Beliefs: The Evangelical Lutheran Church in America is the most liberal of Lutheran church bodies in North America. It has as its doctrinal standard the Bible and the Augsburg Confession. It considers the remaining books of the *Book of Concord* as valid interpretive documents to be used in understanding the Augsburg Confession.

Organization. The Evangelical Lutheran Church in America is headed by a presiding bishop. Elected as the new church's first presiding bishop was Herbert Chilstrom of the former Lutheran Church in America. The church is divided into synods, each headed by a bishop. During the final merger process, headquarters for the new church were established in Chicago. Adminstratively, the boards and agencies remain in flux as this volume goes to press. Fortress Press (Philadelphia) and Augsburg Press (Minneapolis) serve the new denomination. The church is a member of both the National Council of Churches and the World Council of Churches.

Membership: In 1985 the Lutheran Church in America reported 2,898,202 members in 5,817 churches, and the American Lutheran Church had 2,332,316 members in 4,940 churches. The Association of Evangelical Lutheran Churches brought 112,000 members and 276 churches to the merger. The new church has approximately 5,300,000 members.

Educational facilities: *Seminaries*: Lutheran School of Theology at Chicago, Chicago, Illinois; Lutheran Theological Seminary, Gettysburg, Pennsylvania; Lutheran Theological Seminary at Philadelphia, Philadelphia, Pennsylvania; Lutheran Theological Southern Seminary, Columbia, South Carolina; Pacific Lutheran Theological Seminary, Berkeley, California; Trinity Lutheran Seminary, Columbus, Ohio; Wartburg Theological Seminary, Dubuque, Iowa.

Colleges and Universities: Augsburg College, Minneapolis, Minnesota; Augustana College, Rock Island, Illinois; Augustana College, Sioux Falls, South Dakota; Bethany College, Lindsberg, Kansas; California Lutheran University, Thousand Oaks, California; Capital University, Columbus, Ohio; Carthage College, Kenosha, Wisconsin; Concordia College at Moorhead, Moorhead, Minnesota; Dana College, Blair, Nebraska; Gettysburg College, Gettysburg, Pennsylvania; Grand View College, Des Moines, Iowa; Gustavus Adolphus College, St. Peter, Minnesota; Lenoir-Rhyne College, Hickory, North Carolina; Luther College, Decorah, Iowa; Muhlenberg College, Allentown, Pennsylvania; Newbury College, Newbury, South Carolina; Pacific Lutheran University, Tacoma, Washington; Roanoke College, Salem, Virginia; St. Olaf College, Northfield, Minnesota; Susquehanna University, Selingrove, Pennsylvania; Texas Lutheran College, Seguin, Texas; Thiel College; Greenville, Pennsylvania; Upsala College, East Orange, New Jersey; Wagner College, Staten Island, New York; Waldorf College, Forest City, Iowa; Wartburg College, Waverly, Iowa; Wittenberg University, Springfield, Ohio.

Periodicals: *The Lutheran*, 8765 W. Higgins Rd., Chicago, IL 60631.

Sources: Johannes Knudsen, *The Formation of the Lutheran Church in America*. Philadelphia: Fortress Press, 1978; Fred W. Meuser, *The Formation of the American Lutheran Church*. Columbus, OH: The Wartburg Press, 1958. Todd W. Nichol, *All Those Lutherans*. Minneapolis, MN: Augsburg Publishing House, 1986. Herbert W. Chilstrom, *Foundations for the Future*. Minneapolis, MN: Publishing House of the Evangelical Lutheran Church in America, 1988.

★167★
EVANGELICAL LUTHERAN CHURCH IN CANADA
1512 St. James St.
Winnipeg, MB, Canada R3H 0L2

Lutheranism in Canada dates to the last half of the eighteenth century when German Lutherans began to migrate into Nova Scotia. Periodic migrations, especially from America in the nineteenth century, led to the formation of Canadian parishes attached to what became two of the three largest American Lutheran bodies, the American Lutheran Church and the Lutheran Church in America. The American Lutheran Church, formed in 1960 by a merger of several Lutheran bodies, began an immediate process of facilitating the Canadian congregations' autonomy. They became fully autonomous in 1967 as the Evangelical Lutheran Church of Canada. In 1986 that church merged with the three Canadian synods of the Lutheran Church in America to form the Evangelical Lutheran Church in Canada. This merger anticipated the 1988 merger of the American Lutheran Church, the Lutheran Church in America, and the Association of Evangelical Lutheran Churches to form the Evangelical Lutheran Church in America (1988).

The new Evangelical Lutheran Church in Canada retains a formal working relationship with the Evangelical Lutheran Church in America providing for the exchange of pastors and complete altar and pulpit fellowship. The church meets in convention every two years. Foreign work is supported in Liberia, Columbia, Uruguay, and Papua-New Guinea. The church is a member of both the Canadian Council of Churches and the World Council of Churches.

Membership: In 1986 the church reported 210,718 baptized members, 654 congregations, and 792 ordained ministers

Educational facilities: Lutheran Theological Seminary, Saskatoon, Saskatchewan; Waterloo Lutheran Seminary, Waterloo, Ontario; Camrose Lutheran College, Camrose, Alberta; Luther College, Regina, Saskatchewan; Luther Colligiate Bible Institute, Outlook, Saskatchewan.

Periodicals: *Canada Lutheran*, 1512 St. James St., Winnipeg, MB, R3H 0L2 Canada.

Sources: Carl R. Cronmiller, *A History of the Lutheran Church in Canada*. Toronto: Evangelical Lutheran Synod of Canada, 1961.

★168★
EVANGELICAL LUTHERAN SYNOD
% Rev. George Orvick, President
447 N. Division St.
Mankato, MN 56001

The Evangelical Lutheran Synod was formed at Lake Mills, Iowa, in 1918 by a group of 40 pastors and laymen (the conservative wing of Norwegian Lutherans) who declined to enter the merger of other Norwegian Lutherans deciding instead to establish an independent synod. The name Norwegian Synod of the American Evangelical Lutheran Church was adopted. The present name was assumed in 1957. In 1920 it was received into the conservative-oriented Lutheran Synodical Conference but withdrew along with the Wisconsin Evangelical Lutheran Synod in 1963. It rejects fellowship with all who deny the essence of Lutheran belief.

Doctrine is the same as the Lutheran consensus with a conservative interpretation (similar to the Wisconsin Synod) and the Evangelical Lutheran Synod has in the past used the Wisconsin and Missouri Synods' seminaries for training its ministers. It is congregational in polity. Resolutions passed by the synod are not binding until sent to the congregations for acceptance. The officers of the synod direct the work of common interest. Home missions are conducted in nine states. Foreign mission work is conducted in Lima, Peru.

Membership: In 1986, the Synod reported 20,025 members in 120 congregations being served by 97 ministers.

Educational facilities: Bethany Lutheran College, Mankato, Minnesota; Bethany Lutheran Theological Seminary, Mankato, Minnesota; Centro Cristiano Seminary, Lima, Peru.

Periodicals: *Lutheran Sentinel*, Bethany Lutheran College, 734 Marsh St., Mankato, MN 56001.

★169★
FEDERATION FOR AUTHENTIC LUTHERANISM
(Defunct)

The Federation for Authentic Lutheranism was formed in 1971 by members of the Lutheran Church-Missouri Synod. They had signaled their intention to withdraw prior to the 1971 meeting of the Missouri Synod if it did not stop fellowship relations with the liberal American Lutheran Church, withdraw from the Lutheran Council in the U.S.A., (which included both the Lutheran Church in America and the American Lutheran Church), and discipline "errorists" in the synod. (An attempt at the latter action has resulted in the recent controversy in the Missouri Synod.) Seven congregations formed the original federation. Eleven more joined within two years.

Theology was exteremely conservative and pulpit fellowship was immediately declared with the Wisconsin Evangelical Lutheran Synod and the Evangelical Lutheran Synod. Positions have been taken against women's suffrage, the ordination of women, the Boy Scouts, and military chaplaincies. The federation was congregational in polity and run by a board of directors (half lay and half clerical) elected by the entire federation.

In the late 1970s, after less than a decade of existence, the federation disbanded, and its congregations joined either the Wisconsin Evangelical Lutheran Synod or the Evnagelical Lutheran Synod. During its brief existence, it published a periodical, *Sola Scriptura*.

★170★
LATVIAN EVANGELICAL LUTHERAN CHURCH IN AMERICA
6551 W. Montrose
Chicago, IL 60634

The takeover of several European countries by Marxist-Communist governments after World War II placed minority Lutheran Churches in a precarious position. Nationals who had fled Communist rule, and refugees who had left during the war and felt unable to return, established a church-in-exile with headquarters in Germany. Latvian Lutherans in the United States organized in 1957 as the Federation of Latvian Evangelical Lutheran Churches in America. The churches reorganized in 1976 to become the Latvian Evangelical Lutheran Church in America. It is the North American affiliate of the Lutheran Church of Latvia in Exile.

The Latvian Lutheran Church follows Lutheran doctrine and affirms the three ancient creeds (Apostles, Nicean, and Athanasian) as well as the unaltered Augsburg Confession, Luther's Small and Large Catechisms, and the other parts of the Book of Concord.

The synod, presided over by the church's president, meets every three years.

Membership: In 1985, the church had 13,576 members in 59 congregations served by 41 ministers in the United States, and an additional 269 members, nine congregations, and six ministers in Canada.

Periodicals: *Cela Biedrs*, 6551 W. Montrose, Chicago, IL 60634.

Sources: *Lutheran Churches of the World*. Minneapolis: Augsburg Publishing House, 1957.

★171★

LUTHERAN CHURCH-MISSOURI SYNOD
International Center
1333 S. Kirkwood Rd.
St. Louis, MO 63122

Of the largest Lutheran bodies, the Lutheran Church-Missouri Synod, often called simply the Missouri Synod, is by far the most conservative. In 1839, a group of Saxon Lutherans, who were fleeing the rationalism which had captured the Lutheran Church in Germany, arrived in New Orleans, Louisiana. They eventually settled south of St. Louis, Missouri on a large tract of land in Perry County. They were led by the Rev. Martin Stephan, who had been elected bishop. Also among the group was Carl Ferdinand Wilhelm Walther, a young Lutheran minister. Soon after settling in Perry County, Stephan was banished when the colonists discovered he had misappropriated funds to support his opulent lifestyle.

After Stephan's banishment, Walther became the acknowledged leader. He fought what he felt were the theological errors of Stephan's preaching. Chief among these were the beliefs that Lutheran Church was the church, without which there was no salvation; that the ministry was a mediatorship between God and man, hence, ministers were entitled to obedience in all things, even matters not treated by God's Word; and that questions of doctrine were to be decided by the clergy alone. Walther helped found the small school in Altenburg, Missouri, which eventually became Concordia Seminary in St. Louis. In 1841, he went to St. Louis as pastor and in 1844 began to publish the *Lutheraner*, which, issue after issue, championed orthodox Lutheranism as opposed to rationalism (a reliance on reason instead of faith). The *Lutheraner* fought for the rights and responsibility of the congregation in the church. In 1847, the Missouri Synod was founded on the principle of the autonomy of the congregation. There were 14 congregations and 22 ministers.

The Synod had been joined by some Franconians in Michigan and Hanoverians in Indiana. Over the years they were joined by other small synods, including the Illinois Synod (1880) and the English Synod of Missouri (1911). In 1963, the National Evangelical Lutheran Church merged into the Missouri Synod. In 1971, the Synod of Evangelical Lutheran Churches joined the Missouri Synod as one of its districts.

Doctrinally, significant differences exist between the Missouri, Synod and the Evangelical Lutheran Church in America, the other larger, American, Lutheran body (i.e. concerning ordination of women). Polity is congregational. The nodical Convention meets triennially. There are 39 districts represented. The convention elects a president and oversees the vast institutional and missional program. There are four seminaries (including Concordia in St. Louis) and 11 in the United States and Canada. A number of hospitals and homes dot the nation. Mission work is engaged in with missionaries and partner churches in Australia, Belgium, Botswana, Brazil, Chile, Denmark, France, Germany, Ghana, Great Britain, Hong Kong, India, Japan, Korea, Lebanon, Liberia, the Middle East, Mexico, New Guinea, New Zealand, Nigeria, Paraguay, Philippines, Sierra Leone, Sri Lanka, Taiwan, Thailand, Togo, Uruguay, and Venezuela.

Membership: In 1986 the Missouri Synod reported 2,660,000 members in 6,200 congregations. There were 6,000 pastors and 10,500 teachers.

Educational facilities: Christ College, Irvine, California; Concordia College (with campuses at Ann Arbor, Michigan; Austin, Texas; Bronxville, New York; Mequon, Wisconsin; Portland, Oregon; River Forest, Illinois; St. Paul, Minnesota; Selma, Alabama; Seward, Nebraska; and Edmonton, Alberta, Canada); St. John's College, Winfield, Kansas; and St. Paul's College, Concordia, Missouri. SEMINARIES: Concordia Theological Seminary (with campuses at St. Louis, Missouri; Ft. Wayne, Indiana; St. Catharines, Ontario, Canada; and Edmonton, Alberta).

Periodicals: *The Lutheran Witness*, 1333 S. Kirkwood Rd., St. Louis, MO 63122; *Reporter*, 1333 S. Kirkwood Rd., St. Louis, MO 63122.

Remarks: During the 1960s, the Missouri Synod was racked with doctrinal controversy that fouce on differing views about how the Bible can be considered the Word of God. The conservatives believe the Bible to be the inerrant Work of God and interpret quite literally. The more liberal members consider the Bible to bear the Word of God, i.e., Jesus Christ, to the church, and, as such, to be properly the object of historical criticism.

In the end (and for the first time in the twentieth century), the conservative viewpoint prevailed, but only after a decade of discussion. As a result, 200 of the 6,100 congregations, representative of the liberal faction, left the Synod to form the Association of Evangelical Lutheran Churches, which in 1988 merged with the Evangelical Lutheran Church in America.

Sources: Carl S. Meyer, *A Brief Historical Sketch of the Lutheran Church-Missouri Synod*. St. Louis: Concordia Publishing House, 1938; A. Graebner, *Half a Century of True Lutheranism*. Chattanooga, TN: J. A. Fredrich, n.d.; W. Arndt, *Fundamental Christian Beliefs*. St. Louis: Concordia Publishing House, 1938; *The Lutheran Annual 1986*. St. Louis: Concordia Publishing Company (issued annually); *Handbook*. St. Louis: Lutheran Church-Missouri Synod (issued biennially).

★172★

LUTHERAN CHURCHES OF THE REFORMATION
Current address not obtained for this edition.

In 1964, several congregations in the Midwest (formerly a part of the Lutheran Church-Missouri Synod) joined to form the Lutheran Churches of the Reformation. These congregations had protested what they considered the growing theological liberalism of the Missouri Synod. They follow the doctrine and life of their parent body but take a conservative position on doctrinal questions.

Membership: Not reported.

★173★
NORWEGIAN SEAMAN'S CHURCH (MISSION)
1035 Beacon St.
San Pedro, CA 90731

The Norwegian Seaman's Mission was founded in 1864 in Bergen, Norway to provide mission centers in port cities around the world. Such centers offer a Christian witness and a homelike atmosphere for Norwegian sailors in foreign lands. In many cites the missions have also developed into a community and worship center for first generation Norwegians in foreign lands. Reaching a peak in the nineteenth century of 35 missions worldwide, some of the centers, such as the one in Philadelphia, have closed in recent years. A few, such as the one in San Pedro, California, have opened more recently (1941). The missions provide services in accordance with the practices of the Church of Norway, the state Lutheran church.

Membership: In 1985 there were 25 Norwegian Seaman's Mission churches worldwide. The seven in the United States are located in San Pedro, San Francisco, Houston, New Orleans, Miami, Baltimore, and New York City.

Sources: Judy Gabriel, "A Refuge for Scandinavian Seamen," in *Los Angeles Times* (December 22 1985).

★174★
THE PROTES'TANT CONFERENCE
728 N. 9th St.
Manitowoc, WI 54220

History: The roots of the Protes'tant Conference can be traced to the arrival of Professor J. Ph. Koehler at the theological school of the Wisconsin Evangelical Lutheran Church in 1900. Over the years, Koehler grew restive and eventually broke with what he considered the synod's constraining bounds of entrenched and ossified tradition. The synod thought of theology merely as the study of a set of intellectual propositions, while Koehler felt that the roots of the Gospel, repentance and faith, should be emphasized and used as the basis of church renewal in the synod, its congregations, and its members.

Koehler's emphases were unsettling to many in the synod. Opposition finally appeared in the 1920s from August Piper, a colleague on the seminary faculty and former ally of Koehler. The arguments, heretofore largely confined to the seminary, were given a major public airing in a paper by Pastor W. F. Beitz, "God's Message to Us in Galatians--The Just Shall Live by Faith." Supporting Koehler, Beitz charged that the synod was preoccupied

with formalism, institutionalism, and membership growth. He called for repentance and a life lived by faith.

Beitz's paper brought the powers of the synod into the controversy and in the ensuing months some 40 professors, teachers, and pastors were ousted from the synod, including Professor Koehler. Those who were put out formed the Protes'tant Conference in 1928. They asserted that the conference was an intergral element in the synod, even though the synod refused to recognize them as such. In ensuing years, other Protes'tant-minded pastors have been ousted by the Wisconsin Synod.

Beliefs: The doctrinal position of the conference coincides with that of the Wisconsin Synod, but it places special emphasis upon Luther's understanding of the priesthood of all believers as well as the concept of doctrines as truth in action rather than an abstraction.

Organization: The church is organized around the conference, which meets three times a year.

Membership: In 1988 the conference reported about 1,000 members in seven congregations served by eight pastors. Two of the congregations maintain parochial schools.

Periodicals: *Faith-Life*, Box 2141, LaCrosse, WI 54644.

Sources: *The Wauwatosa Gospel: Which Is It?* Marshfield, WI: The Protestant Conference Press, 1928; J. P. Koehler, *The History of the Wisconsin Synod*. St. Cloud, MN: Sentinel Press, 1980.

★175★
SYNOD OF EVANGELICAL LUTHERAN CHURCHES
(Defunct)

Lutherans from Czechoslovakia began to migrate to the United States in the 1870s and early congregations were formed at Streator, Illinois; Freeland, Pennsylvania; and Minneapolis, Minnesota. Attempts to organize began in the 1890s, and the Slovak Evangelical Lutheran Synod was finally established at Connellsville, Pennsylvania, in 1902. Theologically, it declared itself at one with the Lutheran Synodical Conference. The move into the Synodical conference prooved the first step toward full merger with the Missouri Synod, which was accomplished in 1971. Thus the Synod of Evangelical Lutheran Church ceased to exist as a separate denomination and became a district within the Missouri Synod.

★176★
WISCONSIN EVANGELICAL LUTHERAN SYNOD
2929 N. Mayfair Rd.
Milwaukee, WI 53222

The Wisconsin Evangelical Lutheran Synod (popularly called the Wisconsin Synod) was established as a result of calls for pastoral service form German immigrants to Wisconsin in the 1840s. Ministers answered the call, and in May 1950, the First German Evangelical Lutheran Synod of Wisconsin was organized under the direction of President John Muelhaeuser at Salem Evangelical Lutheran Church, Milwaukee (Granville), Wisconsin.

In the 1840s, a Michigan Synod had also been organized among the Wuerttembergers by Stephan Koehler and Christoph Eberhardt. A Minnesota Synod was organized by "Father" J. C. F. Heyer and others in 1860. The Wisconsin, Michigan, and Minnesota Synods became conservative theologically and staunch defenders of Lutheran doctrine against the "compromises" of the larger bodies. In 1892, after all three had joined the Lutheran Synodical Conference, they federated to form the Evangelical Lutheran Joint Synod of Wisconsin, Minnesota, and Michigan. A merger in 1917 led to the formation of the Evangelical Lutheran Joint Synod of Wisconsin and Other States. The present name was adopted in 1959.

Doctrinally, the Wisconsin Synod is like the rest of Lutheranism but takes a stance slightly more conservative than the Lutheran Church-Missouri Synod. It is especially opposed to merger without doctrinal unity on all points. It had been active in the Synodical Conference for almost a century but withdrew in 1963.

The Synod meets biennially. It is divided into 12 districts spread across the nation, though membership is concentrated in Wisconsin and the Midwest. There is a network of parochial schools, three synodical preparatory high schools, 19 area high schools, and two colleges and a seminary. The Northwestern Publishing House in Milwaukee publishes books, Sunday school literature, and religious materials. A vigorous mission program is supported both at home and abroad. Missions are supported in Arizona among both the Apaches and the Latin Americans. Latin Americans missions are also conducted in Mexico, Columbia, Puero Rico, and in stateside cities. Foreign work is carried on in Brazil Nigeria, Malawi, Zambia, Japan, Hong Kong, Taiwan, India, and Indonesia.

Membership: In 1987 the Wisconsin Synod reported 420,000 members in the United States (with an additional 25,000 outside America), in 1,190 congregations served 1,104 ministers.

Educational facilities: Northwestern College, Watertown, Wisconsin; Dr. Martin Luther College, New Ulm, Minnesota. Seminaries: Wisconsin Lutheran Seminary, Mequon, Wisconsin.

Periodicals: *The Northwestern Lutheran*, 2929 N. Mayfair Rd., Wauwatosa, WI 53222; *Wisconsin Lutheran Quarterly*, 11831 N. Seminary Dr., 65 W., Mequon, WI 53092.

Sources: *Continuing in Word.* Milwaukee, WI: Northwestern Publishing House, 1951); *This We Believe.* (24 page pamphlet) 1967.

Section 4

Reformed-Presbyterian Family

An historical essay on this family is provided beginning on page 21.

Reformed

★177★
CHRISTIAN REFORMED CHURCH IN NORTH AMERICA
2850 Kalamazoo Ave.,S.E.
Grand Rapids, MI 49560

The Christian Reformed Church began in the Netherlands in the 1830's. At that time, some members of the Reformed Church of the Netherlands rejected an attempt to bring the church under the control of the Dutch monarchy. Despite the objections of these churchmen, the church was brought under state control. This led in 1834 to the Succession (the formation of a church independent from the monarchy). Succession leaders were Hendrik DeCock, Henrik Scholte, and Albertus C. van Raalte. They saw themselves as defenders of the historical faith that was being lost because of the indifference of the main body of the Reformed Church of the Netherlands. Following persecution and the failure of the potato crop in 1846, the dissidents supporting the Succession made plans to immigrate.

In 1847 the settlers arrived in western Michigan and by 1848 had formed the Classis Holland. Having been aided by members of the Reformed Church in America with whom they shared the same faith, they affiliated with them in 1850, becoming a classis within the Reformed Church in America. Members of the Classis Holland had the understanding that they could leave the Reformed Church in America if the ecclesiastical connection should prove a threat to their interests. For most it never did. However, one church that belonged to the Classis Holland did leave the classis and the Reformed Church in America in 1857, and others followed, eventually forming the Christian Reformed Church. The background of the schism starts with Gysbert Haan. Within a few years of the 1850 affiliation, Haan began to suggest that the Reformed Church in America was not sound. In 1857 four documents of Succession were received by the classis, urging the classis to leave the Reformed Church in America. The documents charged the Reformed Church in America with open communion, the use of a large collection of hymns, and the neglect of catechism preaching. Further, the documents asserted that the Reformed Church in America believed the Succession in the Netherlands had been unjustified. The classis received but did not approve these documents. One church left the classis in January 1857 and was soon joined by others. In 1859 these congregations became known as the Dutch Reformed Church. Growth was slow at first, and came primarily from additional immigration from the Netherlands. Immigration and growth were particularly heavy in the closing decades of the nineteenth century. Through a series of name changes the church became the Christian Reformed Church in 1904 and has retained that name.

The doctrine is strict and based on the Belgic Confession, the Heidelberg Catechism and the Canons of the Synod of Dort. In 1906 the Conclusions of Utrecht were adopted which recognized that some questions were open for disagreement. Only the children of confessing members are baptized. The church is staunchly anti-lodge and is a major supporter of the National Christian Association. Worship is ordered and derived from the practice of the church in the Netherlands. The early hymnology was largely confined to the Psalms but an expanded hymnology has developed in the twentieth century. Catechistic instruction is stressed. Polity is presbyterial. The general synod is the highest body and is composed of two ministers and two members of each of the 30 classes. There is no intermediate or particular synod between the classis and general synod. Classes meet biannually or quarterly.

There is an active mission program. Home missions include an active Jewish evangelism program, the Reformed Bible Institute, the Back to God Hour, and American Indian Missions. Foreign work is active in Nigeria, Japan, Taiwan, Sri Lanka (Ceylon), Argentina, Brazil, Australia, the Philippines, Mexico, Korea, Indonesia, and Guam. There are also a number of hospitals and homes.

Membership: In 1985 the church reported 219,998 members, 650 congregations, and 1,077 ministers.

Educational facilities: Calvin College, Grand Rapids, MI; Calvin Theological Seminary, Grand Rapids, MI.

Periodicals: *The Banner*, 2850 Kalamazoo Avenue, S.E., Grand Rapids, MI 49560; *De Wachter*, 4850 Kalamazoo Avenue, S.E., Grand Rapids, MI 49560.

Sources: *One Hundred Years in the New World*. Grand Rapids: Centennial Committee of the Christian Reformed Church, 1957.

★178★
CHURCH OF THE GOLDEN RULE
Current address not obtained for this edition.

The Church of the Golden Rule continues the French Huguenot tradition of the Alsacian Protestants who look to Martin Bucer and the city of Strassburg as the source of their faith. A congregation of Alsacian immigrants was formed in 1939 at Hempstead, Long Island, New York, under Pastor Alfred E. Huss. He was authorized by Pastor Boegner of the Alsacian Churches. When Huss died, the congregation relocated in California. In 1971 there were four congregations with about 600 families, all in California, under the leadership of Dr. Pierre Duval. The Church of the Golden Rule is under the Unite Huguenotte Francaise.

Membership: Not Reported.

★179★
CHURCHES OF GOD, GENERAL CONFERENCE
700 E. Melrose Ave.
Box 926
Findlay, OH 45839

The Churches of God, General Conference was formed by John Winebrenner (1797-1860), a German Reformed pastor of four churches in and around Harrisburg, Pennsylvania. Winebrenner, though a reformer in many areas, never intended to form a new denomination. However, in attempting to reform what he perceived as the spiritual apathy in the Reformed Church, he and other Reformed pastors adopted some of the "new measures" which had become popular during the Second Great Awakening. They began to preach the importance of personal acceptance of Jesus Christ as savior; they introduced prayer meetings in the homes of those concerned about their salvation; they prayed for people by name in their services; they initiated altar calls.

The vestry of the Harrisburg congregation served by Winebrenner took exception to these new devices. Their concern was heightened by their pastor accepting invitations to preach in the local Methodist church and by his refusal to baptize the children of unbelieving parents.

He was locked out of the church building in 1823, though he continued to serve other Reformed congregations and remained a member of the synod for several years.

In 1825 a Harrisburg congregation of persons loyal to Winebrenner and others attracted by his preaching was formed. The General Conference dates its beginning from this event. The name Church of God was adopted after a search of the scripture showed it to be the New Testament name of the church. The name was considered to be inclusive of all true believers. (Winebrenner was one of several early nineteenth-century movements which attempted to return to the New Testament model of the church. It was the first of many to follow which adopted the name "Church of God" as an element in their self-reformation.)

The essential teachings of the New Testament Church were taken to be redemption and regeneration through belief in Jesus Christ, justification by faith and the free moral agency. Three "ordinances" instituted by Jesus were followed: believer's baptism by immersion, the observation of the Lord's Supper, and footwashing. A presbyterial polity was followed, with preachers ordained as "teaching elders," assisted by "ruling elders" and deacons in the local congregation. The first organization of a group of churches into an eldership was accomplished in 1830. For many years the group was known as the Churches of God in North America, General Eldership.

While pastors and elders still participate with each other in the sixteen regional annual business meetings, most are now called "conferences" rather than "elderships." The triennial meeting of ministerial, lay and youth delegates from local conferences and elderships is called the General Conference.

An administrative council functions between the triennial meetings of the general conference. There are seven commissions which implement programs. The Commission on Church Vocations relates to the conference's educational facilities. The Commission on World Mission oversees work abroad. The Commission on Education oversees Christian education, leadership development and youth and children's ministries. A Commission on Church Development and a Commission on Evangelism direct and promote outreach and church growth ministries. The Commission on National Ministries oversees ministries to American Indians and to the aging and family life, and coordinates ministries of national lay organizations of the church. The Commission on Stewardship directs stewardship education.

Membership: In 1987, the church reported 35,000 members, 353 congregations, and 390 ministers in the United States. There were an additional 5,000 members in missions in India, Haiti, and Bangladesh.

Educational facilities: Findlay College, Findlay, Ohio; Winebrenner Theological Seminary, Findlay, Ohio.

Periodicals: *The Church Advocate*, Box 926, Findlay, OH 45839; *The Missionary Signal*, Box 926, Findlay, OH 45839.

Sources: *We Believe*. Findlay, OH: Churches of God Publications, 1986; Richard Kern, *John Winebrenner, 19th Century Reformer*. Harrisburg, PA: Central Publishes House, 1974; S. G. Yahn, *History of the Churches of God in North America*. Harrisburg, PA: Central Publishing House, 1926.

★180★

FREE AND OLD CHRISTIAN REFORMED CHURCH OF CANADA AND AMERICA
℅ Jacob Tamminga
950 Ball Ave., N.E.
Grand Rapids, MI 49503

The Free and Old Christian Reformed Church of Canada and America was formed in 1926 as the Free Reformed Church. In 1947 the church members developed corresponding relations with the Christian Reformed Church in the Netherlands (Christelijke Gereformeerde Herken in Nederland) and in 1949 adopted their present name. A synod of Canadian churches was organized in 1950. A synod for the congregations in Canada and the U.S. met for the first time in 1961. Their doctrine and organization (adjusted to size) are similar to the parent body, the Christian Reformed Church. A *Psalter* contains the creeds, forms of worship and hymns.

Membership: In 1966 the church had 3 congregations in the United States (one each in Michigan, New Jersey and California) and eight congregations in Canada.

★181★

HUNGARIAN REFORMED CHURCH IN AMERICA
℅ Rt. Rev. Dr. Andrew Harsanyi
P.O. Box D
Hipatcong, NJ 07843

Hungarian Reformed congregations were established in the United States in the late nineteenth century and in 1904 the Hungarian Reformed Church in America was formed under the care of the Reformed Church in Hungary. Following World War I, however, there was a series of negotiations with the Reformed Church in the United States resulting in the 1924 Tiffin Agreement. This agreement, made at Tiffin, Ohio, joined the Hungarian Reformed Church in America to the Reformed Church in the United States. The merged body is now a part of the United Church of Christ. Three congregations of the Hungarian Reformed Church did not wish to accept the Tiffin Agreement. These congregations and four new ones united to form the Free Magyar Reformed Church in America, which in 1958 adopted the name Hungarian Reformed Church in America.

Doctrinally, the church follows the Second Helvetic Confession and the Heidelberg Catechism. The constitution includes elements of both the presbyterian and episcopal systems. There is a diocese headed by a bishop and a lay curator. The New York, Eastern, and Western Classes are headed by a dean and lay curator. The diocese meets annually, with a constitutional meeting every three years. The church is a member of the World Alliance of Reformed Churches (Presbyterian and Congregational), the National Council of Churches, and the World Council of Chruches.

Membership: In 1986 the Church reported 11,000 members, 30 congregations, and 42 ministers.

Periodicals: *Magyar Egyhaz* (Magyar Church), ℅ Very Rev. Statan M. Torok, 311 Kirkland Pl., Perth Amboy, NJ 08861.

★182★

NETHERLANDS REFORMED CONGREGATIONS
℅ Dr. J. R. Beeke
2115 Romence, N.E.
Grand Rapids, MI 49503

The Netherlands Reformed Congregations were formed in 1907 by the merger of two independent Dutch Reformed churches. The Churches of the Cross had originated in 1834 by churches that had broken with the Succession (represented in the United States by the Christian Reformed Church). The Ledeboerian Churches had been established under the leadership of a Rev. Ledeboer, who had left the state church (the Netherlands Reformed Church) at a later date. The merged church was originally under the leadership of the Rev. G. H. Kersten. Doctrinal standards of the church are the Belgic Confession, the Heidelberg Catechism, and the Canons of the Synod of Dort. Though small, the church has been active in publishing.

Membership: In 1985 the church reported 5,000 members in 16 congregations in the United States. There were an additional 3,300 members in 10 congregations in Canada and more than 100,000 members worldwide, primarily in the Netherlands. Foreign congregations were located in Australia, Indonesia, New Zealand, Nigeria, and South Africa.

Educational facilities: Netherlands Reformed Theological Seminary, Grand Rapids, Michigan.

Periodicals: *Banner of Truth*, 1053 Maplegrove, N.W., Grand Rapids, MI 49504; *Paul*, ℅ Timothy Christian School, Castleman Rd., Chilliwack, BC, Canada; *Insight Into*, 4732 East "C" Ave., Kalamazoo, MI 49009.

★183★
ORTHODOX REFORMED CHURCH
3836 30th St.
Grandville, MI 49418

In the late 1960s within the Protestant Reformed Churches, charges of sin against some members of the First Protestant Reformed Church of Grand Rapids resulted in the excommunication of some of its members. Feeling the excommunication to be unjust and to be a denial of their rights, members of the First Protestant Reformed Church of Grand Rapids organized the Orthodox Reformed Church (unaffiliated) in the fall of 1970. In doctrine and polity the church is like its parent body though it does not "subscribe to the church political policies of the Protestant Reformed Churches after the year 1965." Worship is simple and expresses a love of decency and order.

The leader of the Church until his death in 1984, the Rev. Gerald Vanden Berg, had previously been the stated clerk of the Protestant Reformed Church. He had been active in forming the Fellowship of Reformed Churches, an ecumenical group of independent reformed congregations. Vanden Berg was succeeded by the Rev. Peter J. Breen. The church supports missionary activity in India and Pakistan. The Orthodox Reformed Publishing Society, an independent organization, is informally associated with the church.

Membership: In 1988, the single congregation had 61 members.

Periodicals: *The Reformed Scope*, 3268 S. Chestnut, Grandville, MI 49418.

Sources: Gerald VandenBerg, *Why Orthodox Reformed?* Grandville, MI: The Orthodox Reformed Publishing Society, n.d.

★184★
PROTESTANT REFORMED CHURCHES IN AMERICA
15615 S. Park Ave.
South Holland, IL 60473

In 1924 there arose in the Christian Reformed Church what has come to be known as the Common Grace controversy. J. Vander Mey, a member of Eastern Avenue Christian Reformed Church of Grand Rapids, Michigan, filed a protest against his pastor and objected to five views the pastor had been preaching. According to Vander Mey, Rev. Herman Hoeskema 1) believed that the grace of God was at all times particular and that He is gracious to the elect only; 2) placed excessive emphasis on the doctrine of election; 3) denied the good in the natural man (science and social reform); 4) failed to sound the earnest invitation to salvation in his preaching; and 5) stated that we must hate those that hate God, hence there is no fellowship with the world in the battle for truth. The articles represent a significant disagreement within Calvinist theology.

Soon after Vander Mey's protest the Rev. J. K. Van Baalen filed a similar protest against Hoeksema and the Rev. H. Danhof. All of the protests were referred to the Classis Grand Rapids East and Classis Grand Rapids West. In the course of the discussion the question of the consistory's rights versus the classes' rights was also raised. The Classis Grand Rapids West referred the matter to the synod. The synod adopted "The Three Points," which put it on record in favor of a view that God did show His grace to all men apart from the grace to the elect and that an unregenerate man was capable of civic good. Danhof and Hoeksema were seen as holding views contrary to "The Three Points" and the Utrecht Conclusions, and they were admonished to conform their doctrine to the synod's position.

Tension continued and in 1925 four consistories--Coopersville, Eastern Avenue, Hope, and Kalamazoo--were deposed. In 1926 the deposed consistories formed the Protestant Reformed Church. For doctrinal standards, the church uses the same documents as the Christian Reformed Church, but the particular grace interpretation is accepted. Government is presbyterian, but with greater emphasis on the autonomy of the local congregation. The general synod meets annually.

Membership: In 1988 the Church reported 5,219 members, 27 churches, and 24 ministers. There are two congregations in Canada. Sister churches are located in Northern Ireland, Singapore, and New Zealand. There is a mission in Jamaica with seven congregations.

Educational facilities: Theological School of the Protestant Reformed Church, Grandville, MI 49418.

Periodicals: *The Standard Bearer*, Grand Rapids MI; *The Reformed Messenger*, 15615 South Park Ave., South Holland, IL.

Sources: Herman Hoeksema, *The Protestant Reformed Churches In America*. Grand Rapids, MI: The Author, 1947; Herman Hoeksema, *Why Protestant Reformed?* Grand Rapids, MI: The Sunday School of the First Protestant Reformed Church, 1949.

★185★
REFORMED CHURCH IN AMERICA
475 Riverside Dr.
New York, NY 10115

History. The first Dutch settlers in America, members of Reformed Church in the Netherlands, brought that church to this country. A minister, the Rev. Jonas Michaelius, arrived here in 1628 and organized the first congregation, now known as the Collegiate Church of the City of New York. Because of a shortage of ministers, some people began to advocate ministerial training in the colonies. Queens College (now Rutgers University) was founded and a theological seminary established there. The independence of the American church was achieved in 1770 when John Henry Livingston returned from his theological work at Utrecht with a plan of union. In 1792 a constitution was adopted, and in 1819 the church was incorporated as the Reformed Protestant Dutch Church. It took its present name, the Reformed Church in America, in 1867.

The church spread through New York and New Jersey during the colonial era. In the middle of the nineteenth century a new wave of Dutch immigrants arrived. They settled primarily in Michigan and Iowa and from there moved to other states, particularly South Dakota.

Beliefs. Doctrinally the church has remained very conservative and accepted as its standard doctrine the Belgic Confession, the Heidelberg Catechism, and the Canons of the Synod of Dort. Worship is outlined in the *Liturgy* and is supplemented by the church's hymnal, *Rejoice in the Lord*. The liturgies of the Lord's Supper, baptism, and ordination are obligatory; those for the Sunday service and marriage are not.

Organization. The polity is presbyterial. The highest authority is the General Synod, which meets annually in June. A 24-member executive committee functions between sessions. The General Synod is divided into 46 classes. These classes are distributed in six particular synods made up of lay and clerical members of each classis. The voting members of the classis are all the ministers and an elder from each church in the classis. The ruling body at the congregational level is the consistory, composed of the ministers and elected elders and deacons.

Education has always been given high priority by the Reformed Church, and a Board of Theological Education keeps oversight of its seminaries. The General Program Council oversees work among American Indians; social services; Southern Normal High School in Brewton, Alabama; and foreign work in Mexico, several African countries, Japan, Arabia, Kuwait, Oman, Taiwan, Hong Kong, and the Philippines. The church is a member of the National Council of Churches and the World Council of Churches.

Membership: In 1986 the Church reported 346,846 members, an additional 211,890 active communicants, 957 churches, and 1,676 ministers.

Educational facilities: Seminaries: Western Seminary, Holland, Michigan; New Brunswick Seminary, New Brunswick, New Jersey.

Hope College, Holland, Michigan; Northwestern College, Orange City, Iowa; Central College, Pella, Iowa.

Periodicals: *The Church Herald*, 6157 28th St., S.E., Grand Rapids, MI 49506.

★186★
REFORMED CHURCH IN THE UNITED STATES
% Rev. Vernon Polleme, President
3930 Masin Dr.
Lincoln, NE 68521

In 1934 the Reformed Church in the United States merged with the Evangelical Synod. (In 1961 that merged body joined the United Church of Christ.) One classis of the Reformed Church in the United States, the Eureka Classis in South Dakota, decided not to enter the 1934 merger. So the Eureka Classis adopted the name of its parent body, the Reformed Church in the United States, and stayed separate from all the other classes that joined the 1934 merger. The present Reformed Church in the United States continues the polity and doctrines (adherence to the Heidelberg Confession) of the former Reformed Church in the United States. The classis meets annually.

Membership: In 1985 the church reported 3,778 members, 34 congregations, and 34 ministers.

Periodicals: *The Reformed Herald*, Box 276, Eureka, SD 57437.

Presbyterian

★187★
ASSOCIATE REFORMED PRESBYTERIAN
  CHURCH (GENERAL SYNOD)
Associate Reformed Presbyterian Center
One Cleveland St.
Greenville, SC 29601

The Associate Reformed Presbyterian Church (General Synod) stems from the Associate Reformed Presbyterian Church. In 1822, the Synod of the Carolinas broke with the Associate Reformed Presbyterian Church. It eventually became part of the United Presbyterian Church of North America and then the Presbyterian Church (U.S.A.).

The story of the Synod of the Carolinas starts with the Seceder Church formed in Scotland in 1743 as a dissenting body from the established Church of Scotland. Seceders, in America called Associate Presbyterians, settled in South Carolina following the Revolutionary War. They were joined by a few Covenanter congregations, which along with the Seceders had protested Scotland's established church. The Covenanters took their name from the Solemn League and Covenant of 1643, the guiding document of Scotch Presbyterians. In 1790 some Seceders and Covenanters formed the Presbytery of the Carolinas and Georgia at Long Cane, South Carolina. Rev. Thomas Clark and John Boyse led in the formation of this presbytery, a unit within the Associate Reformed Presbyterian Church. The presbytery represented the southern segment of that church.

In 1822 the southern branch became independent of the Associate Reformed Prebyterian Church in the northern states and formed the Associate Reformed Presbyterian Church of the South. "Of the South" was dropped in 1858 when the northern group joined the United Presbyterian Church and "General Synod" added in 1935. The General Synod is the denomination's highest court; it is composed of all the teaching elders and at least one ruling elder from each congregation.

Doctrinally, the church holds to the Westminister Confession of Faith. In 1959, the presbyteries approved 15 changes in the confession, including the arrangement of existing material into new chapters on the kHoly Spirit and the gospel. Liturgically, the synod has been distinguished by its exclusive use of Psalmody, a practice that became optional in 1946. The church is organized on a presbyterial system. Foreign mission work is conducted in Mexico, Pakistan, Liberia, Tanzania, and the Middle East. The church also supports a college, a seminary, several retirement centers, and a summer assembly grounds, "Bonclarken," at Flat Rock, North Carolina.

Membership: In 1987 the Church reported 32,438 members, 182 churches, and 230 ministers.

Educational facilities: Erskine College, Due West, South Carolina; Erskine Theological Seminary, Due West, South Carolina.

Periodicals: *The Associate Reformed Presbyterian*, One Cleveland St., Greenville, SC 29601.

★188★
BIBLE PRESBYTERIAN CHURCH
Haddon and Cuthbert Blvd.S
Collinswood, NJ 08108

History. The Rev. Carl McIntire (b. 1906) had been a student at Princeton Theological Seminary when J. Gresham Machen left to found the independent Westminster Theological Seminary. McIntire graduated from Westminster in 1931 and became the pastor of the Presbyterian congregation in Atlantic City, New Jersey. In September 1933, he became pastor of the Presbyterian congregation in Collinswood, New Jersey. He was suspended from the Presbyterian Church in the U.S.A. along with Machen and left with him and others to establish what became the Orthodox Presbyterian Church. In 1937, after the death of Machen, the church divided on three points. The Orthodox Presbyterians refused to take a stand against intoxicating beverages, rebuffed attempts to make it distinctly premillinnial in its eschatology, and declined further support of the Independent Board of Presbyterian Foreign Missions in favor of a church-controlled board. (A premillinnial eschatology refers to

the belief that before the millennium--Christ's predicted thousand-year reign on earth with his saints--Christ will return to earth to fight the Battle of Armageddon and bind Satan.) In 1938, McIntire and his supporters formed the Bible Presbyterian Church.

At times, the personality of McIntire seemed to have been a more significant factor in the formation of the Bible Presbyterian Church than any of his three objections to the Orthodox Presbyterian Church. He has led a zealous crusade against modernism, communism, and pacifism, and called for what he termed the "twentieth century reformation" to root out apostasy and build true churches. Prime targets have been the National Council of Churches and its sister organization, the World Council of Churches. McIntire called all true Christians to separate themselves from the apostasy of members of these councils.

McIntire provided followers with a variety of alternative organizations to support. In 1937, along with others, he founded Faith Theological Seminary. Four years later he was active in organizing the American Council of Christian Churches (ACCC) to bring together separatist churches from across the country. Separatist churches refuse to deal with liberal churches or with conservative churches that cooperate with liberal churches in any way. Just before the Amsterdam meeting of the World Council of Churches in 1948, McIntire joined with others to organize the International Council of Christian Churches (ICCC). because of criticism by some outstanding conservative Presbyterian leaders, the ACCC and ICCC lost much support, and in 1956 were repudiated by some who had been close followers of McIntire. In that same year, a faction of the synod of the Bible Presbyterian Church terminated its support of Faith Theological Seminary, the Independent Board of Presbyterian Foreign Missions, the ACCC, and the ICCC. The seminary and board, though largely supported by Bible Presbyterians, were both separate corporations. The ICCC and ACCC were both interdenominational and had been criticized for some of their activities in the early 1950s such as the Bible balloon project to send religious literature behind the Iron Curtain by balloon. In reputuiating these organizations, some of the churches also reputiated McIntire, who had been instrumental in founding the organizations as well as the church. The Bible Presbyterian Church then split into two factions. The larger group, those objecting to McIntire and the organizations, soon changed its name to Reformed Presbyterian Church, Evangelical Synod. It is now a constituent part of the Presbyterian Church in America.

The smaller group, the supporters of McIntire, included the presbyteries of New Jersey (of which he was moderator), California, and Kentucky-Tennessee. They declared themselves independent and free of the 1956 synod. At a meeting in Collinswood they created the new synod of the Bible Presbyterian Church. They returned support to ACCC, ICCC, Faith Theological Seminary, the Independent Board for Presbyterian Foreign Missions. and the Independent Board for Presbyterian Home Missions. However, in 1969, McIntire was removed from the board of ACCC, and he then helped form the American Christian Action Council, now the National Council of Bible-Believing Churches in America.

Beliefs. Doctrinally, the Bible Presbyterian Church accepts the Westminster Confession of Faith and the Larger and Smaller Westminster Catechisms. They are premillennial, which means that they believe Christ will return before the millennium. Premillennialists also look for Christ to come unexpectedly in the near future to fight the Battle of Armegeddon and bind Satan, thus ushering in the millennium. The Bible Presbyterians have also take strong stands against intoxicating beverages, the new evangelicalism, the Revised Standard Version of the Bible, evolution, civil disobedience, and the United Nations.

Organization. The polity is presbyterial, but there is a strong assertion of congregational autonomy. The church supports the Friends of Israel Testimony to Christ; The Five Civilized Tribe Ministry in Oklahoma; Reformation Gospel Publications; The Twentieth Century Reformation Hour, a radio broadcast; The Christian Admiral Bible Conference; and the Cape Canaveral Bible Conference in Florida, all independent corporations. The church also supports the Bible Presbyterian Home in Delanco, Florida.

Membership: Not reported.

Educational facilities: Independent schools supported by the Bible Presbyterian Church are: Shelton College, Cape May, New Jersey and Cape Canaveral, Florida; and Faith Theological Seminary, Elkins Park, Pennsylvania.

Periodicals: Unofficial: *The Christian Beacon*, 756 Haddon Avenue, Collingswood, NJ 08108.

Sources: Margaret G. Harden, *Brief History of the Bible Presbyterian Church and Its Agencies.* N.p.: 1965; *The Constitution of the Bible Presbyterian Church.* Collinswood, NJ: Independent Board of Presbyterian Foreign Missions, 1959; *Carl McIntire's 50-Years, 1933-1983.* Collinswood, NJ: Bible Presbyterian Church, 1983; Carl McIntire, *Twentieth Century Reformation.* Collinswood, NJ: Christian Beacon Press, 1944; Carl McIntire, *Modern Tower of Babel.* Collinswood, NJ: Christian Beacon Press, 1949; Carl McIntire, *Servants of Apostasy.* Collinswood, NJ: Christian Beacon Press, 1955.

★189★
CUMBERLAND PRESBYTERIAN CHURCH
Cumberland Presbyterian Center
1978 Union Ave.
Memphis, TN 38104

Before the American Revolution, most of the colonies had state churches, some Congregational, many Episocpal (Anglican). All the colonists supposedly belonged to the state church established by their colony. Immediately after the American Revolution, when state churches no longer existed in America, only fifteen per cent of the new nation chose to belong to a church. The remaining eighty-five percent had no religious affiliation. Around the turn of the nineteenth century, this situation ushered in a great drive to "save the nation," a wave of revivalism usually called the Second Great Awakening. One revivalist was the Rev. James McGready, who worked in Kentucky. While preparing to be a Presbyterian minister, he had a mystical conversion experience and became a strong evangelist. He was licensed by the Redstone Presbytery of the Presbyterian Church and moved to Logan County, Kentucky, where he began to preach regeneration, faith, and repentance. Through his work, revivals flourished and by 1800 spread beyond McGready's congregations. The Great Awakening in Kentucky became ecumenical, including Presbyterians, Methodists, and Baptists. Among the new practices that developed were the group meeting and the anxious seat or mourner's bench. Those in attendance at the revivals exhibited signs of emotional excess, loud, spontaneous behavior, and what today would be called altered states of consciousness (such as trances).

The issue of using unordained, uneducated men to fill leadership posts in the growing church had risen. Some of these men were ordained by the Cumberland Presbytery, which had been formed in 1802 from the Transylvania Presbytery of the Presbyterian Church. Critics of the Great Awakening protested the ordination of uneducated ministers and also complained that ministers did not believe in the Westminster Confession. In 1805 the Kentucky Synod judged against the ordinations of the Cumberland Presbytery and decided to examine those irregularly licensed and ordained and to judge their fitness. The Cumberland Presbytery, however, refused to submit to the Kentucky Synod's judgment. In 1806 the Synod dissolved the Cumberland Presbytery, but McGready and the ministers continued to function while appeal was made to the General Assembly of the Presbyterian Church. The efforts for appeal went unresolved and finally in 1810, in Dickson, Tennessee, three ministers—Finis Ewing, Samuel King, and Samuel McAdow—constituted a new presbytery, again called the Cumberland Presbytery. In 1813, those still unable to find reconciliation with the Kentucky Synod formed two more presbyteries, Elk and Logan, and created the Cumberland Synod.

Growth was quick and the Cumberland Synod spread in every direction from its Tennessee and Kentucky base. By 1829, when the General Assembly of the Cumberland Presbyterian Church was organized, the church had reached into eight states.

Post-Civil War efforts at reunion came to fruition in 1906 when the main body of the Cumberland Presbyterian Church reunited with the Presbyterian Church in the United States of America, now an integral part of the Presbyterian Church (U.S.A.). From the Cumberland point o f view, though, the union was not altogether a happy one. The union carried by only a slight majority of 60 presbyteries to 51, and a large segment of the church refused to go into the united church. They reorganized themselves as the continuing Cumberland Presbyterian Church, and took that name.

The theology of Cumberland Presbyterianism is derived from the Westminster Confession and is described as the middle ground between Calvinism and Arminianism, a theology which defends free will and opposes the belief in strict predestination. The Cumberland Presbyterians deny the five points of Calvinism with the exception of the perseverance of the saints. (The other four points of Calvinism, which this church rejects, are the utter depravity of man, total predestination, limited atonement, and irresistible grace.) The Cumberland Presbyterians have a presbyterian polity. Their General Assembly meets annually.

After 1906 the women took complete control of Cumberland Presbyterian missions. In 1965, foreign and domestic missions were united under a single board. Foreign work is now supported in Colombia, Hong Kong, Liberian, and Japan. Domestic work includes a Chinese (American) Cemberland Presbyterian Church in California, a Choctaw Indian mission in Oklahoma, and new church developments, some of which are union congregations with the Presbyterian church (U.S.A.). The church participates in the ecumenical Christian education curriculum development. Frontier Press issues books and religious literature for its board of publication and education.

Membership: In 1987 the Church reported 84,579 members, 756 churches, and 724 ministers in the United States. There were an additional 6,124 members in missions in Colombia, Hong Kong, Japan, and Liberia.

Educational facilities: Bethel College, McKenzie, Tennessee; Memphis Theological Seminary, Memphis, Tennessee.

Periodicals: *The Missionary Messenger*, 1978 Union Avenue, Memphis, TN 38104.

Sources: Thomas J. Campbell, *Good News on the Frontier* Memphis: Frontier Press, 1965; E. K. Reagin, *We Believe So We Speak*. Memphis: Department of Publication, Cumberland Presbyterian Church, 1960; John H. Hughey, *Lights and Shadows of the C. P. Church*. Decatur, IL: The Author, 1906. *A People Called Cumberland Presbyterians*. Memphis, TN: Frontier Press, 1970; *Confession of Faith for Cumberland Presbyterians*. Memphis, TN; Frontier Press, 1984.

★190★
ORTHODOX PRESBYTERIAN CHURCH
7401 Old York Rd.
Philadelphia, PA 19126

In the early years of the twentieth century the Presbyterian Church in the United States of America became a major focus of the fundamentalist-moder nist controversy. Conservatives felt that liberals were leading the church into compromise with the world and away from the witness to the gospel. Conservatives traced liberalism to the Plan of Union of 1801 between Presbyterians and Congregationalists. The Conservatives said that plan aligned Presbyterians with Congregationalists infected with the "New School theology" of Samuel Hopkins. Late in the nineteenth century the issues of compromise with the world and lack of witness to the gospel were raised anew by the heresy trials of Professors Charles A. Briggs and Henry Preserved Smith. In 1903 doctrinal standards were revised to facilitate the merger with the Cumberland Presbyterian Church.

In reaction against liberal Baptist Harry Emerson Fosdick's preaching in First Presbyterian Church in New York City, a group of conservatives drew up a document presented to and passed by the 1923 General Assembly calling for the ministry to uphold the essentials of the faith, namely the five fundamentals-the infallibility of the Scriptures, the virgin birth of Christ, the substitutionary atonement, Christ's bodily resurrection, and Christ's miracles. Although the assembly passed the conservative document, many of the church leaders were liberals and held key positions on the boards and agencies of the church. In protest of the assembly's vote, they joined with the 1,300 ministers who signed the Auburn Affirmation. This signpost of liberal faith created a storm of controversy, and the two sides were locked in battle.

The publication of *Re-Thinking Missions* by W.E. Hocking in 1932 began the final stage of the church's liberal-conservative battle. Hocking asserted, among other controversial opinions, that missionaries should not take conversions as their only goal, but should provide social services and do medical missionary work in addition to preaching the gospel. J. Gresham Machen, a theology professor at Princeton Theological Seminary, opposed Hocking's suggestion. With other conservative Presbyterians, Machen charged in 1932 that the board of Foreign Missions approved, sent, and supported missionaries who did not teach that Christ is the exclusive, unique way of salvation. The church countered with a mandate comparing non-support of the church boards with refusal to take communion. The fundamentalists replied with charges against other boards, and they condemned participation in the Federal Council of Churches. Machen was tried and convicted of disturbing the peace of the church. Machen and his supporters then left the Presbyterian Church in the United States of America and formed the Orthodox Presbyterian Church.

Doctrine of the new church is the Westminster Confession of Faith and the Westminster Larger and Shorter Catechisms which are accepted literally and in light of the five fundamentals. Organization ion is like the United Presbyterian Church. A general assembly meets annually. Over the years support for the Independent Board for Presbyterian Foreign Missions was dropped and a denominational board created. Great Commissions Publications produces a complete line of church school materials in cooperation with the Presbyterian Church of America. The church participates in the Reformed Ecumenical Synod and the North American Presbyterian and Reformed Council.

Membership: In 1986 the church reported 18,983 members, 171 congregations, and 335 ministers.

Sources: John P. Galbraith, *Why the Orthodox Presbyterian Church?* Philadelphia, PA: Committee on Christian Education, The Orthodox Presbyterian Church, 1965; *The Standards of Government, Discipline and Worship of the Orthodox Presbyterian Church.* Philadelphia: Committee on Christian Education, the Orthodox Presbyterian Church, 1965; Gary G. Cohen, *Biblical Separation Defended.* Nutley, NJ: Presbyterian and Reformed Publishing Co., 1977.

★191★
PRESBYTERIAN CHURCH IN AMERICA
% Stated Clerk
1852 Century Plaza, Suite 202
Atlanta, GA 30345

History: During the 1960s tensions began to rise between liberals and conservatives within the Presbyterian Church in the United States. Among expressions of this rift was the conservatives' protest of denominational support of the National Council of Churches and involvement in social issues, possible union with the United Presbyterian Church in the U.S.A. (which would put the conservatives in an even smaller minority position and which eventually occurred in 1983), liberal theology in *The Layman's Bible* published by the church, the ordination of women, support of abortion on demand for socioeconomic reasons, and liberal churchmen in positions of authority in the denomination.

In 1972-73 several presbyteries were formed by some 260 congregations with a combined communicant membership of over 41,000 that had left the denomination. These presbyteries were the Warrior Presbytery in Alabama, the Westminster Presbytery in Virginia and East Tennessee, and the Vanguard Presbytery at large. In December 1973 delegates gathered at Briarwood Presbyterian Church in Birmingham, Alabama, and organized the National Presbyterian Church. Rev. Frank Barker, pastor of the Brairwood Church, hosted the gathering. In 1974 the church adopted its present name.

In 1982 the Reformed Presbyterian Church, Evangelical Synod, merged into the Presbyterian Church in America. The Reformed Presbyterian Church, Evangelical Synod, had been formed in 1965 by a merger of the Evangelical Presbyterian Church and the Reformed Presbyterian Church in North America, General Synod.

Evangelical Presbyterian Church was the name taken by the larger segment of the Bible Presbyterian Church following the split in that church in 1956. (See the discussion of the split i n the entry on the Bible Presbyterian Church.) The name for the larger group had been adopted in 1961 to avoid confusion with Dr. Carl McIntire's smaller group. At the time of the split, the synod, controlled by the larger group, had voted to establish an official periodical, the *Evangelical Presbyterian Reporter*; a synod-controlled college and seminary, Covenant College and Covenant Seminary in St. Louis; and its own mission board, World Presbyterian Missions. Immediate efforts were directed toward healing the rift with the Orthodox Presbyterian Church and opening correspondence with the Reformed Presbyterian Church in North America. In 1960 the constitution was amended to allow any view of eschatology, not just premillennialism.

The Reformed Presbyterian Church in North America, General Synod, was of the Covenanter tradition, the church which adhered to the Solemn League and Covenant of 1643 which spelled out the doctrine and practices of Scotch Presbyterians. The General Synod (as the church was often called) dated to 1833 when the Reformed Presbyterian Church split over the issue of participation in civic affairs. One group within the church took the name Reformed Presbyterian Church in North America, General Synod, and allowed its members to vote and hold office. The General Synod also adopted the practice of allowing hymns as well as psalms to be sung at services and allowed instrumental music to be used in worship. Those who did not allow members to vote or hold office, and opposed hymns and instrumental music, are known today as the Reformed Presbyterian Church of North America. In 1965 the Reformed Presbyterian Church in North America, General Synod, merged with the Evangelical Presbyterian Church. The merged body became known as the Reformed Presbyterian Church, Evangelical Synod.

Beliefs: The Presbyterian Church in America adheres to the traditional Presbyterian documents, the Westminster Confession of Faith, and both the Longer and Shorter Westminster Catechisms. It is very conservative in its theological approach, a major point of difference between it and the larger Presbyterian Church (U.S.A.).

Organization: The church is organized presbyterially. The General Assembly meets annually. The church conducts mission work in 13 countries around the world. The church is a member of the National Association of Evangelicals.

Membership: In 1986 the church reported 159,105 communicant members, 924 congregations and 1,722 clergy.

Educational facilities: Covenant College, Lookout, Georgia; Covenant Theological Seminary, St. Louis, Missouri. Other schools supported by the church and/or its constituent presbyteries include these: Birmingham Theological Seminary, Birmingham, Alabama; Chesapeake Theological Seminary; Atlanta School of Biblical Studies, Atlanta, Georgia; Greenville Theological Seminary, Greenville, South Carolina; Christ Community Seminary, Nashville, Tennessee.

Periodicals: *The PCA Messenger*, 1852 Century Plaza, Atlanta, GA 30345.

Sources: *The Book on Church Order of the Presbyterian Church in America*. Atlanta, GA: Committee on Christian Education and Publications, 1983; Frank J. Smith, *The History of the Presbyterian Church in America: The Continuing Church Movement*. Manasa, VA: Reformation Education Foundation, 1985; John Edwards Richards, *The Historical Birth of the Presbyterian Church in America*. Liberty Hill, SC: Liberty Hill Press, 1987; Donald J. MacNair, *Hallmarks of the Reformed Presbyterian Church, Evangelical Synod*. St. Louis, MO: Presbyterain Missions, n.d.

★192★

PRESBYTERIAN CHURCH IN CANADA
50 Wynford Dr.
Don Mills, ON, Canada M3C 1J7

The Presbyterian Church in Canada is the continuing Presbyterian body formed by those members of the Presbyterian Church in Canada who did not wish to participate in the 1925 merger with the Canadian Methodists and Congregationalists who produced the United Church of Canada (UCC). Approximately thirty percent of the group which had voted to merge reconstituted the continuing church. As such, the Presbyterian Church in Canada shares the heritage of Canadian Presbyterianism with the UCC. The Presbyterian Church in Canada had originally been constituted in 1875 by the Presbyterian Church of the Lower Provinces, the Synod of the Presbyterian Church of the Maritime Provinces, the Synod of Canada Presbyterian Church, and the Synod of the Presbyterian Church of Canada in Connection with the Church of Scotland.

Those Presbyterians who disapproved of the merger into the United Church of Canada feared loss of such Presbyterian distinctives as conservative theology, as represented in the Westminster Confession of Faith, and structure. Theology was being equally threatened by Methodism and a growing liberalism. Many also argued that most of the rewards to be gained from the union could be gained by a federated relationship.

Doctrinally, the church adheres to the Westminster Confession of Faith and both the Longer and Shorter Westminster Catechisms. In 1875 Article 23 of the Confession, concerning civil magistrates, had been explicitly deleted from the Confession accepted by the new church. This issue was resolved in 1955 by the adoption of a "Declaration of Faith Concerning Church and Nation." In 1962 the church also recognized several of the European Reformed confessions, specifically the Belgic, the Second Helvetic, and the Gallican Confessions, as parallel to the Westminster and the Heidelberg Catechisms and permitted their teachings by church elders.

Though more conservative than the United Church of Canada, the Presbyterian Church in Canada has remained a vital part of the larger Protestant ecumenical movement. It is a member of both the Canadian Council of Churches and the World Council of Churches. In 1966 it admitted women to the ordained ministry. It has foreign work in Guyana, India, Japan, Nigeria, and Taiwan.

Membership: In 1986 the church reported 1,028 congregations, 159,179 members, and 1,102 clergy.

Educational facilities: Ewart College, Toronto, Ontario; Knox College, Toronto, Ontario. Presbyterian College, Montreal, Quebec.

Sources: R.C. Reed, *History of the Presbyterian Churches of the World*. Philadelphia, PA: Westminister Press, 1912; Claris Edwin Silcox, *Church Union in Canada*. New York: Institute of Social and Religious Research, 1933.

★193★

PRESBYTERIAN CHURCH OF THE LOWER PROVINCES
(Defunct)

(The Presbyterian Church of the Lower Provinces no longer exists as a separate entity. It is now a constituent part of the United Church of Canada and the Presbyterian Church in Canada.) The Presbyterian Church of the Lower Provinces (1817-1875) grew out of the Seceders, a faction of Scottish Presbyterianism which emerged during the revivals that swept the Scottish church in the early 1700s. The Seceders were united in their attack upon the patronage system of the established church of Scotland and its lack of spiritual awareness. They divided into two factions, usually termed Burgher and anti-Burgher, which resulted from the demand of an oath as part of the requirement to hold office in Scotland; the anti-Burgher party refused the oath, claiming it legitimized the established church.

Members of both parties arrived in Canada in the late 1700s. Three members of the Burgher Synod, Daniel Cook, David Smith, and Hugh Graham, organized the Presbytery of Truro in 1786. Almost contemporaneously, James McGregor and two other anti-Burgher ministers began work which culminated in the formation of the Presbytery of Pictou in 1795. Attempts at reconciliation in the new setting eventually led to the merger of the two presbyteries, the creation of a third presbytery (Halifax), and the formation of the Synod of Nova Scotia in 1817.

In 1825 the Church of Scotland organized the Glasgow Colonial Society, which sent missionaries to Canada. Those which settled in Nova Scotia and other Eastern Provinces refused to join the Synod of Nova Scotia. In 1833 the Presbyterian Synod in Connection with the Church of Scotland was organized. This synod prospered until 1843 when the Church of Scotland went through a period of turmoil which led to a number of ministers resigning and forming the Free Church of Scotland. In Canada, the Presbyterian Synod sided with the Free Church faction in the homeland. In 1860 this Free Church Synod merged with the Synod of Nova Scotia to form the Presbyterian Synod of the Lower Provinces.

In the disruption of 1843, one faction of the Presbyterian Church in Connection with the Church of Scotland, the Presbytery of New Brunswick (which had grown to become the Synod of New Brunswick), remained loyal to the established Church of Scotland. It became independent of the Free Synod. Three of its members in New Brunswick then withdrew and formed The (Free) Presbyterian Synod of New Brunswick, which in 1866 became a part of the Presbyterian Synod of the Lower Provinces.

In 1875 the Presbyterian Church of the Lower Provinces merged with three other Presbyterian churches to form the Presbyterian Church in Canada. In 1925 most of that church merged with the Methodist Church, Canada and Congregational Union of Canada to form the United Church of Canada.

Sources: R.C. Reed, *History of the Presbyterian Churches of the World*. Philadelphia, PA: Westminster Press, 1912; Claris Edwin Silcox, *Church Union in Canada*. New York: Institute of Social and Religious Research, 1933.

★194★
PRESBYTERIAN CHURCH OF THE MARITIME
  PROVINCES
(Defunct)

(The Presbyterian Church of the Maritime Provinces no longer exists as a separate entity. It is now a constituent part of the United Church of Canada and the Presbyterian Church of Canada.) The Presbyterian Church of the Maritime Provinces (1868-1975) traces its history to the arrival in Canada of ministers of the Church of Scotland in the 1820s. In 1833 the Presbyterian Synod in Connection with the Church of Scotland was organized by a group of ministers, many of whom had been sent to Canada by the Glasgow Missionary Society. At the same time, a Presbytery of New Brunswick had been designated as one of the synod's constituent units. During the next

decade the Presbytery of New Brunswick had grown into the Synod of New Brunswick. In 1943 the Church of Scotland had been disrupted by a dispute involving government powers in the appointment of ministers. Those who disagreed with the court's decision in the controversy left the Church of Scotland and formed the Free Church of Scotland. In Canada, the Presbyterian Synod in Connection with the Church of Scotland sided with the Free Church and broke its relation with the established Church of Scotland. The Synod of New Brunswick, however, remained loyal to the established church and became independent. Some members of the new Free Synod wished to return to their connection with the established church, and in 1854 established the Synod of Nova Scotia and Prince Edward Island. These two groups merged in 1868 to form the Church of the Maritime Provinces.

In 1875, the Church of the Maritime Provinces united with three other Presbyterian churches to form the Presbyterian Church in Canada. In 1925 the majority of that church merged with the Methodist Church, Canada and Congregational Union of Canada to form the United Church of Canada.

Sources: R.C. Reed, *History of the Presbyterian Churches of the World*. Philadelphia, PA: Westminister Press, 1912; Claris Edwin Silcox, *Church Union in Canada*. New York: Institute of Social and Religious Research, 1933.

★195★
PRESBYTERIAN CHURCH (U.S.A.)
475 Riverside Dr.
New York, NY 10115

The Presbyterian Church (U.S.A.) was formed in 1983 by the union of the United Presbyterian Church in the United States of America and the Presbyterian Church in the United States, the two largest Presbyterian bodies in the United States. It continues the beliefs and practices of the two churches, which originally had split over the same issues that divided the United States at the time of the Civil War.

History. The United Presbyterian Church in the United States of America was formed in 1958 by a merger of the Presbyterian Church in the United States of America and the United Presbyterian Church of North America. The Presbyterian Church in the United States of America inherited the tradition of early Presbyterianism in the colonies and is in direct continuity with the first synod organized in 1706. In the 1700s the Presbyterians were split between the revivalism of the Methodist, George Whitefield, who had influenced William Tennent and his brother, Gilbert Tennent, and the more traditional, creedal Calvinism with its ordered worship. The Tennents were the founders of a seminary which later became Princeton University. A split developed in the church in 1741 which lasted until 1758.

The church supported the Revolution and afterward reorganized for western expansion. On the heels of the cooperative Plan of Union of 1801 with the Congregationalists and the Second Great Awakening, the Presbyterians moved West and in the forty years after the Revolution grew more than tenfold. The nineteenth century, an era of expansion westward, saw the development of an impressive educational system and large-scale schism over revivalism and slavery. Other schisms would grow out of the fundamentalist debates in the early twentieth century.

The United Presbyterian Church of North America was formed in 1858 by a merger of the Associate Presbyterian Church and the Associate Reformed Presbyterian Church. These two churches continued the Scottish Covenanter and secession movements. The Covenanters were Scotch Presbyterians who seceded from the Church of Scotland, which was Reformed in theology but episcopal in government. The Covenanters formed their independent secession into a church in 1733. The Covenant to which the new church adhered was the Solemn League and Covenant ratified in 1643; it spelled out the doctrine and practices of Scotch Presbyterians.

People who followed the Covenant of 1643 found their way to the American colonies during the seventeenth century. These early Covenanters formed "societies" for worship because they had no minister. The first pastor was the Rev. Alexander Craighead, a Presbyterian attracted to the Covenanters because of their passion for freedom. In 1751, John Cuthbertson landed and began long years of work on a large circuit of Covenanters. He was joined in 1773 by Matthew Linn and Alexander Dobbin and the three constituted the Reformed Presbyterian Church.

The Covenanters represented one branch of the Scottish secession movement; the Seceders represented another. The Seceders developed from the revival movements of the 1700s in Scotland which attacked the patronage system of the established church and its lack of spiritual awareness. The Seceder Church was not formed in Scotland until 1743, although Seceders began to arrive in the colonies in the 1730s. In 1742 a plea for a minister was issued by a congregation in Londonderry, Pennsylvania. The problem of providing leadership was compounded by the Scottish split into Burgher and anti-Burgher factions. The two parties resulted from the requirement of an oath to hold public office in Scotland. The anti-Burghers felt the oath legitimized episcopacy and they therefore objected to it; the Burghers saw nothing wrong with taking the oath. Most of the Americans were anti-Burghers. Two anti-Burgher ministers, Alexander Gellatly and Andrew Arnot, arrived and in 1753 organized the Associate Presbyterian Church.

In 1782 the Associate Presbyterian Church and the Reformed Presbyterian Church merged to form the Associate Reformed Presbyterian Church. A few members of both merging churches declined to enter the merger and continued to exist under the names of their respective churches before 1782. Then in 1822 the Associate Reformed Presbyterian Church split into northern and southern branches. The southern branch continues today as the Associate Reformed Presbyterian Church (General Synod). The northern branch continued to be called the Associate Reformed Presbyterian Church. In 1858 this northern branch merged with the majority of the continuing Seceders, called the Associate Presbyterian Church. The new church formed in 1858 took the name the United Presbyterian Church of North America. In 1958, the United Presbyterian Church of North America united with the Presbyterian Church in the United States of America to form the United Presbyterian Church in the United States of America.

The Presbyterian Church in the United States arose out of the same controversies which had split the Methodists and Baptists in the years prior to the Civil War. Presbyterians were able, as a whole, to remain in the same ecclesiastical body until War actually broke. The General Assembly of the Presbyterian Church in the United States of America, meeting in Philadelphia only days after the firing on Fort Sumter and devoid of most southern delegates, declared its loyalty to the United States. Presbyterians in the South claimed the Assembly had no such right to make such a political statement. One by one the Southern presbyteries withdrew, and in December 1861 they organized the Presbyterian Church in the Confederate States (later changed to the Presbyterian Church in the United States).

The war divided the north from the south and feeling created by the conflict did much to keep the churches apart. The two churches had little disagreement on either doctrine or church polity. The southern church tended to be more conservative in its doctrinal stance and adopted a more loosely organized structure. It had replaced the church boards created by the Presbyterian Church in the United States of America with executive committees, unincorporated and devoid of permanent funds.

Beliefs. In 1967 the United Presbyterian Church adopted a new confession of faith. The Confession was a very present-minded document though it begins with a statement of continuity with the Reformed Confessional tradition. It is focused on the reconciling work of Christ through the grace of God. A significant section deals with the mission of the church, particularly in society, and has a vague eschatology. The Confession was published along with the Apostles' and Nicene Creeds, five Reformed Confessions, and the Shorter Catechism in a *Book of Confessions. The Book of Common Worship* contains the liturgical resources.

Organization. The merger of 1983 left many of the important questions of merging geographically overlapping synods and presbyteries and national offices, boards and agencies to be resolved in the future meetings of the annual General Assembly. For the moment, both national offices and much of the individual programs have been retained in the united church. The structure will remain in flux for several years into the future.

Membership: In 1985, the church reported 3,048,000 members, 19,345 ministers, and 11,554 congregations. Partnership efforts in Christian mission exist with churches in 63 nations.

Educational facilities: Theological seminaries; Austin Presbyterian Theological Seminary, Austin, Texas; Columbia Theological Seminary, Decatur, Georgia; University of Dubuque Theological Seminary, Dubuque, Iowa; Johnson C. Smith Theological Seminary, Atlanta, Georgia; Louisville Presbyterian Theological Seminary, Louisville, Kentucky; McCormick Theological Seminary, Chicago, Illinois; Pittsburgh Theological Seminary, Pittsburgh, Pennsylvania; Presbyterian School of Christian Education, Richmond, Virginia; Princeton Theological Seminary, Princeton, New Jersey; San Francisco Theological Seminary, San Anselmo, California; Union Theological Seminary in Virginia, Richmond, Virginia.

Colleges and Universities: Agnes Scott College, Decatur, Georgia; Alma College , Alma Michigan; Arkansas College, Batesville, Arkansas; Austin College, Sherman, Texas; Barber-Scotia College, Concord, North Carolina; Beaver College, Glenside, Pennsylvania; Belhaven College, Jacskon, Mississippi; Blackburn College, Carlinville, Illinois; Bloomfield College, Bloomfield, New Jersey; Buena Vista College, Storm Lake, Iowa; Carroll College, Waukesha, Wisconsin; Centre College of Kentucky, Danville, Kentucky; Coe College, Cedar Rapids, Iowa; Davidson College, Davidson, North Carolina; Davis & Elkins College, Elkins, West Virginia; University of Dubuque, Dubuque, Iowa; Eckerd College, St. Petersburg, Florida; College of Ganado, Ganado, Arizona; Grove City College, Grove City, Pennsylvania; Hampden-Sydney College, Hampden Sydney, Virginia; Hanover College, Hanover, Indiana; Hastings College, Hastings, Nebraska; Hawaii Loa College, Kaneohe, Oahu, Hawaii; Huron College, Huron, South Dakota; College of Idaho, Caldwell, Idaho; Illinois College, Jacksonville, Illinois; Jamestown College, Jamestown, North Dakota; Johnson C. Smith University, Charlotte, North Carolina; King College, Bristol, Tennessee; Knoxville College, Knoxville, Tennessee; Lafayette College, Easton, Pennsylvania; Lake Forest College, Lake Forest, Illinois; Lee Junior College, Jackson, Kentucky; Lees-McCrae College, Banner Elk, North Carolina; Lewis & Clark College, Portland, Oregon; Lindenwood College, St. Charles, Missouri; Macalester College, St. Paul, Minnesota; Mary Baldwin College, Staunton, Virginia; Mary Holmes College, West Point, Mississippi; Maryville College, Maryville, Tennessee; Missouri Valley College, Marshall, Missouri; Monmouth College, Monmouth, Illinois; Montreat-Anderson College, Montreat, North Carolina; Muskingum College, New Concord, Ohio; Occidental College, Los Angeles, California; College of the Ozarks, Clarksville, Arkansas; Peace College, Raleigh, North Carolina; Pikeville College, Pikeville, Kentucky; Presbyterian College, Clinton, South

Carolina; Queens College, Charlotte, North Carolina; Rocky Mountain College, Billings, Montana; St. Andrew's Presbyterian College, Laurinburg, North Carolina; School of the Ozarks, Pt. Lookout, Missouri; Schreiner College, Kerrville, Texas; Sheldon Jackson College, Sitka, Alaska; Southwestern at Memphis, Memphis, Tennessee; Sterling College, Sterling, Kansas; Stillman College, Tuscaloosa, Alabama; Tarkio College, Tarkio, Missouri; Trinity University, San Antonio, Texas; Tusculum College, Greeneville, Tennessee; University of Tulsa, Tulsa, Oklahoma; Warren Wilson College, Swannanoa, North Carolina; Waynesburg, College, Waynesburg, Pennsylvania; Westminster College, Fulton, Missouri; Westminster College, New Wilmington, Pennsylvania; Westminster College, Salt Lake City, Utah; Whitworth College, Spokane, Washington; Wilson College, Chambersburg, Pennsylvania; College of Wooster, Wooster, Ohio.

Periodicals: *Presbyterian Survey*, 341 Ponce de Leon Avenue, N.E., Atlanta, Georgia.

Sources: *Minutes* of the 195th General Assembly, United Presbyterian Church in the United States of America, 123rd General Assembly, Presbyterian Church in the United States, 195th General Assembly, Presbyterian Church (U.S.A.). Atlanta: Office of the General Assembly, Presbyterian Church (U.S.A.), 1983; *Study Draft, A Plan for Union of the Presbyterian Church in the United States and the United Presbyterian Church in the United States of America*. New York: Stated Clerk of the Presbyterian Church in the United States, 1974; Wallace N. Jamison, *The United Presbyterian Story*. Pittsburgh: The Geneva Press, 1958; Park Hays Miller, *Why I Am A Presbyterian*. New York: Thomas Nelson & Sons, 1956.

★196★
REFORMED PRESBYTERIAN CHURCH OF NORTH AMERICA

% Louis D. Hutmire, Stated Clerk
7418 Penn Ave.
Pittsburgh, PA 15208

The eighteenth-century Reformed Presbyterian Church was the embodiment of the Covenanter tradition in North America, those adhering to the Scotch Presbyterians' Solemn League and Covenant of 1643. In 1782 the majority of the Covenanter tradition merged with the Seceder Church, originally formed in Scotland in 1743 as a group seceding from the established Church of Scotland. The 1782 merger of Covenanters and Seceders resulted in the Associate Reformed Presbyterian Church, which is now a constituent part of the Presbyterian Church (U.S.A.).

However, some Reformed Presbyterians (Covenanters) did not join the 1782 merger. They remained Reformed Presbyterians and in 1833 they split over the issue of participation in government, specifically, over whether members would vote and hold office. The New Lights, those who allowed such participation, formed the Reformed Presbyterian Church, General Synod, which merged with the Evangelical Presbyterian Church in 1965. The merged church, the Reformed Presbyterian Church, Evangelical Synod recently merged into the Presbyterian Church in America, discussed above. The Reformed Presbyterian Church of North America is the continuing old school body, the group opposed to the New Lights in the 1833 split. The church is working for a constitutional amendment which recognizes Christ as king of men and nations. Until such reform is accomplished, members refuse to vote or hold office.

The Westminster Confession of Faith is the standard of doctrine. Worship is centered on the reading and exposition of the Bible. Hymns are limited to Psalms and there is no instrumental accompaniment. Organization is presbyterian. The synod meets annually. Foreign missions are conducted in Syria, Cyprus, China, Japan, Australia, and Ethiopia.

Membership: In 1985, the church reported 5,146 members in 71 churches being served by 123 ministers.

Educational facilities: Geneva College, Beaver Falls, Pennsylvania; Reformed Presbyterian Theological Seminary, Pittsburgh, Pennsylvania.

Periodicals: *The Covenanter Witness*, 800 Wood Street, Pittsburgh, PA 15221.

Sources: *Adventures in Psalm Singing.* Pittsburgh: Christian Education Office, 1970.

★197★
SECOND CUMBERLAND PRESBYTERIAN CHURCH IN U. S.
226 Church St.
Huntsville, AL 35801

In the early years of the Cumberland Presbyterian Church, following a pattern of the Methodist Episcopal Church, South, ministers of the Presbyterian Church established a slave mission throughout the South. White ministers served segregated black congregations as well as segregated white congregations. By 1860 some 20,000 black members were on the church rolls. Among these was Edmond Weir, who was sent as a missionary to Liberia. After the Civil War, attempts were accelerated to train black ministers, thus providing blacks with an adequate ministry. Separate regional synods were established for black members. Between 1871 and 1874, synods in such states as Tennessee, Kentucky, and Texas organized. By 1874, following again a pattern set by the Methodists, these regional synods established their broader governing unit, the general assembly, and the Colored Cumberland Presbyterian Church became a church separate from the Cumberland Presbyterian Church. The parent church, though, continued moderate financial and educational support of the new church, which is now called the Second Cumberland Presbyterian Church in the U. S.

The church is similar to its parent body in doctrine and organization. The General Assembly meets regularly. There are 19 presbyteries and four synods.

Membership: Recent statistics have not been reported. In 1959 the Church reported 221 church, 30,000 members and 125 ministers. There was an affiliated Presbytery in Liberia.

Educational facilities: Educational opportunities and ministerial training are pursued through the schools of the Cumberland Presbyterian Church.

Periodicals: *The Cumberland Flag*, 226 Church Street, Huntsville, AL 35801.

Sources: Thomas H. Campbell, *Good News on the Frontier.* Memphis, TN: Frontier Press, 1965.

★198★
SYNOD OF THE CANADA PRESBYTERIAN CHURCH
(Defunct)

(The Synod of the Canada Presbyterian Church no longer exists as a separate entity. It is now a constituent part of the United Church of Canada and the Presbyterian Church of Canada.) The Synod of the Canada Presbyterian Church (1861-1875) can be traced to 1832 with the arrival of three missionaries into Western Canada as representatives of the independent United Associate Synod of Scotland, one of the factions of Scotish Presbyterianism not connected with the established Church of Scotland. The church offered the missionaries the opportunity to join one of the two existing synods (the Presbyterian Church in Connection with the Church of Scotland or the United Synod of Upper Canada). However, the missionaries turned down the offer upon discovering that these already existing synods were quite willing to accept government support for their work, a position directly opposing that of the United Associate Synod. Therefore, in 1834 the ministers formed the Missionary Presbytery of the Canadas. In 1843 the Presbytery split into three presbyteries and organized the Missionary Synod of Canada.

In 1843, twenty-six ministers of the Presbyterian Church in Connection with the Church of Scotland left the church to found the Synod of the Free Church of Canada. This was done in reaction to ministers in the Church of Scotland who, in protest of governmental influence in clerical matters, resigned from the established church to form the Free Church of Scotland. In 1861 the Synod of the Free Church of Canada and the Missionary Synod of Canada merged to become the Synod of the Canada Presbyterian Church.

In 1875 the Synod of the Canada Presbyterian Church merged with three other Presbyterian churches to form the Presbyterian Church in Canada. The majority of the Presbyterian Church in Canada merged with the Methodist Church, Canada and the Congregational Union of Canada, forming the United Church of Canada.

Sources: R.C. Reed, *History of the Presbyterian Churches of the World*. Philadelphia, PA: Westminister Press, 1912; Claris Edwin Silcox, *Church Union in Canada*. New York: Institute of Social and Religious Research, 1933.

★199★
SYNOD OF THE PRESBYTERIAN CHURCH IN CONNECTION WITH THE CHURCH OF SCOTLAND
(Defunct)

(The Synod of the Presbyterian Church in Connection with the Church of Scotland no longer exists as a separate entity. It is now a constituent part of the United Church of Canada and the Presbyterian Church of Canada.) The Synod of the Canada Presbyterian Church (1861-1875) began with the arrival of Presbyterians in the eighteenth century into that part of Canada which was termed the Western Provinces (presently Quebec and Ontario). As early as 1796, Rev, John Bethune organized a Presbyterian congregation in Montreal. However, it was not until 1818 that enough growth and development had occurred to organize a presbytery. In that year the Revs. Robert Easton, William Stuart, William Bell, and William Taylor organized the Presbytery of the Canadas. These ministers were associated with the Burgher faction of Scottish Presbyterians who had seceded from the established Church of Scotland. Within a few years the Presbytery reorganized and took a new name, the United Presbytery of Upper Canada, which grew into the United Synod of Upper Canada in 1831.

As the United Synod was taking shape, ministers associated with the established church formed the Presbyterian Church in Connection with the Church of Scotland. In 1840 these two groups merged to become the Synod of the Presbyterian Church in Connection with the Church of Scotland. In 1875 the Synod of the Presbyterian Church in Connection with the Church of Scotland merged with three other Presbyterian Churches to form the Presbyterian Church in Canada. The majority of the Presbyterian Church in Canada merged in 1925 with the Methodist Church, Canada and the Congregational Union of Canada to become the United Church of Canada.

Sources: R.C. Reed, *History of the Presbyterian Churches of the World*. Philadelphia: Westminister Press, 1912; Claris Edwin Silcox, *Church Union in Canada*. New York: Institute of Social and Religious Research, 1933.

★200★
UKRAINIAN EVANGELICAL ALLIANCE OF NORTH AMERICA
% Rev. Wladimir Borosky
690 Berkeley Ave.
Elmhurst, IL 60126

The Ukrainian Evangelical Alliance of North America was formed in the United States in 1922 by Ukrainian Protestants of several denominations. The purpose of the Alliance was to spread the gospel among Ukrainians in both North America and the Ukraine. The Alliance was thus a missionary organization, and was not meant to be a separate denomination. However, over time the Alliance established mission congregations and in that sense has become a separate denomination. The member congregations typically retain their Ukrainian culture and language and are located in large cities. Most of the Ukrainian Reformed congregations in North America have become members of the larger Presbyterian bodies but two congregations of post-war immigrants, one in Detroit and one in Toronto, carry on the independent tradition and are under the direct guidance of the Ukrainian Evangelical Alliance of North America.

In 1925, the Ukrainian Evangelical Alliance of North America, with the aid of Several Reformed and Presbyterian churches, organized a Ukrainian Reformed Church in what was at that time Polish territory in the Western Ukraine. This church was virtually destroyed by the Communist take-over in World War II.

The Alliance is interdenominational in scope and has passed a resolution declaring denominational missions obsolete and unrealistic in their approach to Ukrainian-Russian relations, especially in their neglect of the native language. The Alliance wishes to be invited to cooperate in all missionary efforts. It has as a major part of its mission, the publication of Ukrainian literature which it distributes in both North America and the Ukraine.

Membership: At last report there were only two congregations solely attached to the Alliance, though congregations consisting of Ukrainian-Russian immigrants of the Reformed faith can be found in several of the larger Presbyterian bodies.

Periodicals: *News Bulletin.*

★201★
UPPER CUMBERLAND PRESBYTERIAN CHURCH
% Roaring River Upper Cumberland Presbyterian Church
Gainesboro, TN 38562

The Upper Cumberland Presbyterian Church was formed in 1955 by Rev. H. C. Wakefield, Rev. W. M. Dycus, Lum Oliver, and laymen from Sanderson's, Russell Hill, Pleasant Grove and Poston's Cumberland Presbyterian Churches, all of the Cooksville Presbytery in Tennessee.

At the 1950 General Assembly of the Cumberland Presbyterian Church, the Board of Missions and Evangelism reported its application for membership in the Home Missions Council of the National Council of Churches. This application raised the issue of support of the "liberal" social activist theology imposed by the National Council of Churches, and strong opposition to the application developed within the church. In 1952 a Fellowship of Conservative Presbyterians was formed which included Rev. Wakefield and Rev. Dycus. In assembly in the following year, the Fellowship elected a moderator and a stated clerk, urged organization on a presbyterial level, and objected to the Revised Standard Version of the Bible newly issued by the National Council of Churches. Rev. Dycus and Rev. Wakefield were deposed from the ministry of the Cumberland Presbyterian Church. IN 1955 they formed the Carthage Presbytery of the Upper Cumberland Presbyterian Church at a session with the Russell Hill Congregation in Macon County, Tennessee. Thus the Upper Cumberland Presbyterians came into existence. At the first session Lum Oliver was ordained.

The Upper Cumberland Presbyterians adopted the Confession of Faith of the Cumberland Presbyterian Church, with the addition of questions on the virgin birth of Christ and his visible return to the church covenant. Ministers must use the King James Bible.

Membership: In 1970 there were 9 churches and 300 members in the Upper Cumberland Presbyterian Church.

★202★
WESTMINSTER BIBLICAL FELLOWSHIP
Current address not obtained for this edition.

Following the 1969 meeting in which Dr. Carl McIntire was removed from his responsibilities with the American Council of Christian Churches (ACCC), several former leaders of the McIntire-led Bible Presbyterian Church also withdrew support from him. These included J. Phillip Clark, former General Secretary of the Independent Board for Presbyterian Foreign Missions and pastor of Calvary Bible Presbyterian Church in Glendale, California. After the 1969 ACCC meeting, Clark announced the formation of the Westminster Biblical Felllowship in order to provide a vehicle for Bible Presbyterians to remain with the ACCC. Other Bible Presbyterian leaders-Richard E. Smitley, Jack Murray and Arthur Steele-joined Clark. The Westminster Biblical Fellowship continues the faith of the Bible Presbyterian Church in general, but it objects to the strong crusading stance of Carl McIntire.

Membership: Not reported.

Sources: Carl McIntire, *A Letter to Bible Presbyterians.* Collinwood, NJ: Bible Presbyterian Church, 1969.

Congregationalism

★203★
CONGREGATIONAL UNION OF CANADA
(Defunct)

(The Congregational Union of Canada no longer exists as a separate entity. It is now a constituent part of the United Church of Canada.) The Congregational Union of Canada was formed in 1906 by the merger of the Congregational Union of Nova Scotia and New Brunswick and the Congregational Union of Ontario and Quebec. Together they represented the Congregational Church tradition which entered Canada from the United States in the eighteenth century.

Congregational beginnings in Canada awaited the British take over of Nova Scotia in 1748. At the invitation of the government, shiploads of settlers arrived from New England to establish towns and begin farming. The first Congregational Church was organized in Chester in 1759; others followed, and two years later a second one was formed in Liverpool. Though never a large and growing movement, these churches passed a generation in peace until, in the 1780s, they were disturbed by the independent revivalistic efforts of Henry Alline, whose preachings led to a split in many congregations. The new congregations, though remaining officially Congregational during Alline's lifetime, eventually became the core of Canadian Baptists in the area. Concurrently, the Methodists began their period of growth under William Black, Jr.. The competition between the Baptists and Methodists, coupled with the difficulties of obtaining ministers after the American Revolution, effectively hampered the future growth of Congregationalism.

At the same time settlements were being established in Nova Scotia, New Englanders traveled to New Brunswick. The first Congregational Church emerged in 1766 at Maugerville. Newfoundland's first congregation came a decade later at St. John's.

Organization of the scattered congregations awaited events in England. In the 1830s the Congregational Union of England and Wales was formed, thus consolidating Congregational efforts in Britain. In 1834 fraternal delegates were sent to Canada. They reported their findings, which led to the formation of the Colonial Missionary Society in 1836. This society, whose purpose was to aid churches through the British Empire, assisted the work in Canada and facilitated the formation of the Congregational Union of Nova Scotia and New Brunswick in 1846.

Congregationalism in Quebec and Ontario grew out of two separate movements. In the years after the American Revolution, settlers from New England began to move Northward across the border into Canada. A church was founded at Stamstead as early as 1798. As other churches were founded, ministers were drawn from Vermont. In the

1840s, the Congregationalist-sponsored American Home Missionary Society initiated work in Canada and organized several predominantly black congregations among former slaves who had fled to freedom.

As early as 1801 the British Congregationalists sent a representative of the London Missionary Society to Quebec. Most of that work was lost to the Presbyterians, and the New England-based church were all that survived. British settlers organized a joint Congregational-Presbyterian Church in Elgin County, Ontario in 1819. It survived to become fully congregational, the first in that province.

As with the churches in the Maritime Provinces, those in Quebec and Ontario received a boost from the 1834 delegation from England. Unions were organized in each province, and in 1853 they merged into the Congregational Union of Ontario and Quebec.

In 1807 the Congregational Union of Canada received the Canadian Conference of the United Brethren in Christ into its membership. This German body had become predominantly English-speaking in the late nineteenth century. Rather than becoming another small independent sect after breaking with the American branch, they chose to unite with the congregationalists.

In 1925 the Congregational Union of Canada joined with the Methodist Church, Canada and the Presbyterian Church in Canada to form the United Church of Canada.

Sources: Albert E. Dunning, *Congregationalists in America*. New York: J. A. Hill & Co., 1894; Claris Edwin Silcox, *Church Union in Canada*. New York: Institute of Social and Religious Research, 1933.

★204★
CONSERVATIVE CONGREGATIONAL CHRISTIAN CONFERENCE
7582 Currell Blvd., Suite 108
St. Paul, MN 55125

The Conservative Congregational Christian Conference can be dated to 1935 when Rev. Hilmer B. Sandine, then pastor of First Congregational Church of Hancock, Minnesota, began the publication of the *Congregational Beacon*. Beginning as a monthly parish publication, the *Beacon* became the organ for communication among theologically conservative Congregationalists. Emphasis was placed on Biblical evangelism and evangelical Christianity. Growing concern about liberal theology and social activism within the Congregational and Christian Churches led in 1945 to the formation of the Conservative Congregational Christian Fellowship at Minneapolis. During the previous year a plan of union with the Evangelical and Reformed Church had been published. In 1948, during the lengthy process of the formation of the United Church of Christ, the Conservative Congregational

Christian Fellowship became the Conference, a separate body from the Congregational and Christian Churches.

Among Congregationalists, the Conference represents the most theologically conservative group. The Conference is committed to the five fundamentals: the infallibility of the Scriptures, the virgin birth of Christ, the substitutionary atonement, Christ's bodily resurrection, and Christ's miracles. The Conference also emphasizes the historical Puritan beliefs in the sovereignty of God, the sinfulness of man, redemption through Christ, the indwelling Holy Spirit, the sacraments, the life of love and service, and the future life. They restricted membership to those who profess regeneration. The Conservative Congregational Christian Conference is a member of the National Association of Evangelicals.

In polity the Conservative Congregational Christian Conference accepts the interpretation that true congregationalism is to be identified with the independent or separated Puritan tradition. The local church is the seat of power. It joins in fellowship with other churches for cooperative endeavors. Ecclesiastical bodies or officers have no right to interfere in local church affairs. There is an annual meeting of the Conference.

Membership: In 1987, the conference reported 29,429 members, 176 congregations, and 575 ministers in the United States, and 289 members, five congregations, and 15 ministers in Canada.

Periodicals: *Foresee*, 7582 Currell Blvd., St. Paul, MN 55125.

★205★
INTERNATIONAL COUNCIL OF COMMUNITY CHURCHES
% Rev. J. Ralph Shotwell, Executive Director
900 Ridge Rd., Suite LL 1
Homewood, IL 60430

The International Council of Community Churches was formally organized in 1946, but possesses a history dating from the early nineteenth century when nonsectarian community churches began to appear as an alternative to the formation of separate denominationally affiliated congregations. Such community churches were especially welcomed in communities too small to support more than one viable congregation. Over the years, such congregations have frequently retained a fiercely independent stance. To their number were added other independent congregations that had separated from denominational structures and adopted a nonsectarian stance.

In the wake of the ecumenical movement in the early twentieth century, the most visible symbol being the Federal Council of Churches of Christ formed in 1908, many congregations merged across denominational lines, some forming independent federated or union churches, dropping all denominational affiliation. During this period, some community churches began to see, in light of their years of existence apart from denominational boundaries, that they had a particular role vis-a-vis Christian unity.

A first attempt to build a network of community churches was known as the Community Church Workers of the United States. At a national conference of individuals serving community churches in Chicago in 1923, a committee formed to hold a second conference and outline plans for a national association. Organization occurred the next year and the Rev. Orvis F. Jordan of the Park Ridge (Ill.) Community Church was named as secretary. He later became the first president of the group. The organization continued for over a decade, but died in the 1930s due to lack of support.

A second organization of community churches was also begun in 1923 among predominantly black congregations. Representatives of five congregations gathered in Chicago, Illinois, in the fall of 1923 to form the National Council of the People's Community Churches (incorporated in 1933 as the Biennial Council of the People's Church of Christ and Community Centers of the United States and Elsewhere). The Rev. William D. Cook, pastor of Metropolitan Community Church in Chicago, served as the first president.

Unable to gain recognition from the Federal Council of Churches, the independent community churches began a second attempt at organization in the last days of World War II. The Rev. Roy A. Burkhart, pastor of First Community Church of Columbus, Ohio, led in the formation of the Ohio Association for Community Churches in 1945. The next year representatives from nineteen states and Canada met and formed the National Council of Community Churches.

Almost immediately, the black and white groups began to work toward a merger. The merger, accomplished in 1950, created the International Council of Community Churches with a charter membership of 160 churches. By 1957, the several foreign congregations had ceased their affiliation with the council and the word "International" was dropped. In 1969, the name was changed to National Council of Community Churches. In 1983, however, foreign congregations in Canada and Nigeria affiliated and in 1984 the original name was again assumed.

There is no doctrinal statement shared by the council or its member churches, though most churches share a liberal, ecumenical-minded, Protestant perspective. The council describes itself as committed to Christian unity and working "toward a fellowship as comprehensive as the spirit and teachings of Christ and as inclusive as the love of God."

The council is a loosely organized fellowship of free and autonomous congregations. The national and regional officers facilitate communication between congregations and serve member congregations in various functions, such as representing them at the Consultation on Church Union and coordinating the securing of chaplains in the armed services.

Membership: In 1988, the council reported 300 member congregations serving 250,000 members and 500 clergy ministers. In addition, the council serves more than 1,000 other congregations (membership unknown). The council allows dual membership, and approximately five percent of the congregations have a denominational affiliation.

Educational facilities: As a matter of policy, the council has no educational institutions or mission projects of its own. It endorses and encourages member churches to support individual schools and missions that meet a council standard of being "postdenominational" and of promoting Christian unity while meeting human need.

Periodicals: *The Christian Community*, 900 Ridge Rd., Suite LL1, Homewood, IL 60430; *The Pastor's Journal*, 900 Ridge Rd., Suite LL1, Homewood, Il 60430.

Sources: *National Council of Community Churches, Directory.* Homewood, IL: National Council of Community Churches, 1982; J. Ralph Shotwell, *Unity without Uniformity.* Homewood, IL: Community Church Press, 1984. J. Philip Smith, *Faith and Fellowship in the Community Church Movement: A Theological Perspective.* Homewood, IL: Community Church Press, 1986.

★206★
MIDWEST CONGREGATIONAL CHRISTIAN CHURCH
Current address not obtained for this edition.

The Midwest Congregational Christian Fellowship was formed in 1958 by former members of the Congregational and Christian Churches. During the years of negotiating the forming of the United Church of Christ, one center of dissatisfaction was in the Eastern Indiana Association. Theologically conservative members of the association were opposed to the church's theologically liberal leadership. They felt there was too much emphasis on social action. The first meetings were held in 1957 in which attempts were made to withdraw the entire Association. Having failed, laymen devised a plan by which individual congregations could withdraw. Thirty churches, primarily small rural congregations removed themselves from the rolls in 1958. These quickly organized as the Midwest Congregational Christian Fellowship (now Church).

The doctrinal statement of the church reflects the Puritan heritage, the Christian non-creedal bias, and the evangelical perspective of the members. The statement affirms belief in the Trinity, salvation, the ministry of the Holy Spirit, the resurrection, and the unity of believers. The polity is a loose congregationalism with emphasis on local ownership of property. The church meets quarterly, with one meeting designated the annual meeting. There is an eight-man committee which includes the moderator and officers who oversee the work of the church.

Membership: In 1970 the Church reported 33 churches, 23 ordained ministers and 26 licensed ministers. Only three churches had a membership exceeding 100.

★207★
NATIONAL ASSOCIATION OF CONGREGATIONAL CHRISTIAN CHURCHES
8473 S. Howell Ave.
Box 1620
Oak Creek, WI 53154

Almost as soon as the merger of the Congregational and Christian Churches and the Evangelical and Reformed Church was proposed, opposition arose among Congregationalists in the Midwest. (The merger occurred in 1948, and the new church took the name, the United Church of Christ.) Opposition came, primarily from members who felt that the proposed merger would replace congregational government with a presbyterial form. One of the first protest meetings was held in 1947 at First Congregational Church, Evanston, Illinois. Several committees began to publish anti-merger materials, including the Committee for the Continuation of Congregational Christian Churches headed by Malcom K. Burton. The National Association of Congregational Christian Churches was formed in 1955. Among the prominent leaders of the new organization was Harry Butman.

There is little theological difference between members of the United Church of Christ and those of the National Association. Association spokespersons have described the United Church of Christ as a means for expressing and perpetuating Neo-Orthodoxy, a theological perspective originating with German theologian Karl Barth, and lacking the evangelical theological goals of other groups that did not join the united church. However, the Association leaders also saw the United Church of Christ as basically presbyterial, not congregational in government. In contrast, the polity of the National Association emphasizes local autonomy and the fellowship of the local churches. The National Association meets annually. It is seen as purely a spiritual fellowship. While it does not make pronouncements for the member churches, it does undertake a mutually cooperative program. The missionary society oversees work in 14 countries including Bolivia, England, West Germany, Italy, Greece, Hong Kong, India, Taiwan, and the Philippines.

Membership: In 1985 the association reported 108,115 members, 464 congregations, and 826 ministers.

Educational facilities: Olivet College, Olivet, Michigan; Piedmont College, Georgia.

Periodicals: *The Congregationalist,* 8473 So. Howell Avenue, Box 1620, Oak Creek, WI 53154.

Sources: Manfred Waldemar Kohl, *Congregationalism in America.* Oak Creek WI; The Congregational Press, 1977; Harry R. Butman, *The Lord's Free People.* Wauwatosa, WI; Swannet Press, 1968; Malcolm K. Burton, *Destiny for Congregationalism.* Oklahoma City: Modern Publishers, 1953.

★208★
UNITED CHURCH OF CANADA
The United Church House
85 St. Clair Ave., E.
Toronto, ON, Canada M4T 1M8

The United Church of Canada (UCC) was formed in 1925 by the union of the Methodist Church, Canada, the Congregational Union of Canada, the Council of Local Union Churches, and the majority of the Presbyterian Church of Canada. In 1968 the Canada Conference of the Evangelical United Brethren joined the UCC. This church is the most impressive result of the various Christian church union attempts in North America during the nineteenth and twentieth centuries; more than 40 church bodies from two major church families (Reformed and Methodist) were united.

French Huguenots, escaping persecution following the revocation of the Edict of Nantes, brought the Reformed Faith to Canada. But even in the New World their growth and development were restricted. After the ceding of Nova Scotia to England in 1713, and particularly after the ceding of all Canada in 1763 by the Treaty of Paris, the influx of Presbyterians from Scotland and Ireland completely overwhelmed the small French contingent. The first ministers from Scotland were Daniel Cook, David Smith, and Hugh Graham, who organized the Presbytery of Truro in 1786. In 1795, this presbytery was joined by a second, the Presbytery of Pictou, which represented another faction of Scottish Presbyterianism. In 1817 these two groups, joined by a few ministers from the Established Church of Scotland, were able to come together and form the Synod of the Presbyterian Church of Nova Scotia.

Concurrently with the events that led to the formation of the Synod of Nova Scotia, Presbyterians were moving into central and western Canada. As in eastern Canada, they brought the many divisions of the Scottish church with them and established several presbyteries and then synods, the first being the Presbytery of the Canadas in 1818. The establishment of new synodical structures continued through the first half of the nineteenth century, in part due to the importing of schisms within the church in Scotland, the arrival of non-English-speaking (Dutch Reformed) immigrants, and the opening of new territories in the West. By mid-century the trend began to reverse, and in 1875 a series of mergers led to the union of most Presbyterians into the Presbyterian Church of Canada.

Methodism in Canada is traced to Laurence Coughlan, an Irish Methodist preacher who came to Newfoundland in 1765. At the time of his arrival, he had left Wesley's connection and applied for work with the Anglican Society for the Propagation of the Gospel. Though a Methodist in practice, he became an Anglican minister. Upon his return to England, many of the people he organized openly declared themselves Methodists. Meanwhile, Methodists were migrating from England to Nova Scotia; among them was William Black, Sr.. In 1779, a revival among them led to the conversion of William Black, Jr., then but 19 years old. He began to preach, visiting several nearby settlements, and in 1781 travelled the whole of Nova Scotia to organize Methodist classes. His work expanded greatly two years later as immigrants loyal to Great Britain flowed into Nova Scotia after the American Revolution. In 1784, Black journeyed to Baltimore, Maryland, for the meeting that organized the new Methodist Episcopal Church. The Canadian work that Black had developed was taken under their care. The Canadian work grew and developed as an integral part of the Methodist Episcopal Church until 1828 when it became separate and independent. Meanwhile, Methodists from Great Britain migrated into Canada, and like the Presbyterians from Scotland, brought with them the several divisons of British Methodism. Mergers in 1874 and 1884 resulted in the Methodist Church, Canada being formed.

Congregationalism in Canada originated with the acceptance of the offer made by the British government which promised free land to New Englanders who would relocate in Nova Scotia. In 1759, several hundred immigrants founded new towns and gathered churches; the first was at Chester, and in 1761 the church at Liverpool was formed. In 1760, a colony began at Mungerville, New Brunswick; the first church was organized six years later. The first church in Newfoundland dates to 1777. From these and additional congregations a Congregational Union of Nova Scotia and New Brunswick was organized in 1846. In 1801, the British Congregationalists sent a missionary to organize a church in Quebec. That beginning led to the formation of the Congregational Union of Ontario and Quebec, which merged with the older group in 1906. The newly formed Congregational Union of Canada received the Ontario Conference of the American-based United Brethren in Christ (now part of the United Methodist Church) in 1907.

The final partner in the 1925 merger, the General Council of Union Churches of Western Canada, was the child of the early proposed Plan of Union that led to the founding of The United Church of Canada. A draft proposal of a plan of union was issued in 1908. In November of that year, a new congregation appeared in Saskatchewan that accepted as the basis of its local organization the proposed plan. Others soon followed, and the Congregational and Presbyterian judicatories allowed ministers to participate in the ecumenical experiment. In 1912 the several local congregations formed the General Council to handle practical matters and press forward in implementing the Plan of Union.

The merger in 1925 had one major dissenting voice. Approximately 30 percent of the Presbyterians refused to enter the merger, and continued as the Presbyterian Church of Canada. In 1926, a number of the Canadian congregations of the Christian Church (Disciples of Christ) affiliated with the new church. In 1968, the Canadian Conference of the Evangelical United Brethren, following a favorable vote and anticipating the merger of its parent body into the United Methodist Church, became part of the United Church of Canada. In 1943 a two-decade process of negotiation with the Anglican Church of Canada was initiated. It was joined by the Christian Church (Disciples of Christ). The Plan of Union was adopted by the general commission representing the three churches in 1972, but three years later was rejected by the Anglican Church of Canada. The three bodies remain separate entities, though the UCC and the Anglican have several joint enterprises.

The union effected in 1925 originated with merger talks between Methodists and Presbyterians in 1899, joined three years later by the Congregationalists. In the proposed Basis of Union, written between 1904 and 1910, a new doctrinal statement was written, based in large part upon the statements of the Presbyterian Church in the U.S.A. (now a part of the Presbyterian Church (U.S.A.) and the Presbyterian Church in England). It assumes a common affirmation of the Protestant Faith and assumes a position between the classical Calvinistic and Arminian positions, leaving considerable latitude for disagreement on issues such as predestination, election, and God's free grace to all persons.

The church is governed by a General Council that meets biennially. The national church is further divided into conferences and presbyteries. Local churches are administered by an official board. The UCC has retained membership in the Alliance of Reformed Churches (Presbyterian and Congregational), the World Methodist Council, the Canadian Council of Churches, and the World Council of Churches.

Membership: In 1988 the United Church of Canada reported 4,192 churches, 2,185,498 members and adherents, and 4,010 ordained clergy.

Educational facilities: Coughlin College, St. John's Newfoundland; Dr. Jesse Saulteaux Resource Centre, Fort Qu'Appelle, Saskatchewan; Huntington University, Sudbury, Ontario; Vancouver School of Theology, Vancouver, British Columbia; Westminster College, London, Ontario.

Periodicals: *United Church Observer*, 85 St. Clair Ave., Toronto, ON 4MT 1M8

Sources: Claris Edwin Silcox, *Church Union in Canada*. New York: Institute of Social and Religious Research, 1933; John Webster Grant, *The Canadian Experience of Church Union*. Richmond, VA: John Knox Press, 1967.

★209★

UNITED CHURCH OF CHRIST
105 Madison Ave.
New York, NY 10016

The United Church of Christ (UCC) was formed in 1957 by the merger of the Congregational-Christian Churches and the Evangelical and Reformed Church. The two uniting bodies were themselves products of mergers in the early twentieth century, and any account of the modern UCC must begin with a consideration of the four bodies which are now constituent parts of it: The Congregational Churches, the Christian Church, the Reformed Church in the United States, and the Evangelical Synod of North America.

The Congregational Churches. Through the Congregational Churches, the United Church of Christ reaches back to the first decades of the British presence in North America. They were the fourth church to arrive in the colonies (behind the French Reformed Church, Roman Catholic Church, and the Church of England). Coming from England by way of Holland, the Pilgrims first arrived in the Massachusetts Bay Colony in 1620. The Pilgrims were Separatists, Reformed in theology but believing strongly in the autonomous local congregation. The Puritans arrived a decade later, and for the next century they directed the New England settlement. The Puritans were congregationalists in that they placed most of the ecclesiatical power in the hands of the congregation, but also aligned those congregations to the colonial governments. They hoped to create a theocratic system and were intolerant of competing churches and religious groups. The single Pilgrim congregation at Plymouth was tolerated and eventually was absorbed into the larger body of Congregationalists, though the congregation itself eventually was lost to Unitarianism. Congregationalism was the established church of the New England colonies (except Rhode Island) until the Revolution and remained established in Connecticut until 1818 and in Massachusetts until 1833.

The early Congregationalists were committed to education. They established Harvard University (1636) soon after their arrival, and several generations later as they spread through New England, they founded Yale (1701). These were but the first of a system of institutions of higher education that have made the Congregational Church a major intellectual force in American culture. In 1810 Congregationalists founded the American Board of Commissioners for Foreign Missions, which is not only looked upon as the parent of the nineteenth century missionary thrust in American Protestantism, but which succeeded in taking Congregationalism around the world—to the Sandwich Islands (Hawaii), China, India, Africa, and the Middle East.

During the early years of the nineteenth century, Congregationalists, just beginning to slip from their position as the largest church in the new land, led the crusades to build a Christian land. They initiated organizations and took leadership roles in various movements on behalf of the causes of peace, women, children, immigrants, and the poor, as well as the abolition of slavery. They created a number of social service centers, especially in the Northeast, where most of their strength was concentrated.

Through the early nineteenth century, Congregationalists had only formed statewide associations of churches, but the rapid spread of the the church in the nineteenth century brough the call for a national organization. In 1852 a national council met for the first time and was soon meeting regularly every three years. In 1913, at a meeting of the triennial council in Kansas City, a new Congregational "platform" was adopted which included a preamble, a confession of faith, a form of polity, and a stand on wider fellowships.

Congregationalists have been tied together by a series of doctrinal statements beginning with the Cambridge Platform in 1648 which had affirmed the Reformed theological heritage. The Confession of 1913 adopted at Kansas City declared the "steadfast allegiance of the churches composing this council to the faith which our fathers confessed." But at the same time, the statement, as a whole, reflected the nineteenth-century theological trend usually called Modernism. Some Congregational ministers and theological professors had become the major intellectual pioneers of modernist thought, which placed a great emphasis upon individualism and progress, while stressing God's presence in the world over and against his transcendence, Christ's humanity over and against his divinity, and social activism (the social gospel).

In 1931 the National Council of the Congregational Churches united with the Christian Church to form the General Council of Congregational-Christian Churches.

The Christian Church. The Christian Church which was to become part of the United Church of Christ (there were other groups with the same name which stemmed from similar influences) was the product of the revivals of the post-Revolutionary War period and of the new wave of democratic thinking. In 1792 James O'Kelly withdrew from the Methodist Episcopal Church and formed the Republican Methodist Church, rejecting the strict episcopal authority exercised by Bishop Francis Asbury. Methodist bishops have the power to appoint Methodist ministers to their congregations, and O'Kelly continually objected to Asbury's appointments of him. Two years after leaving the Methodists, O'Kelly and his followers also moved against sectarian labels and resolved to be known as "Christians" only. A similar movement arose among Baptists in New England, where Abner Jones had decided that sectarian names and human creeds should be abandoned and that piety alone should be the test of Christian fellowship. He organized such a "Christian" fellowship in 1800 and was soon joined by others.

In 1819 various churches calling themselves "Christian" held a general conference in Portsmouth, New Hampshire. In 1833 a general convention was organized which in effect formed the Christian Church. The following year the church established a Christian Book Association. Concern for education led to the founding of Elon College in North Carolina. From 1854 to 1890, as a result of the forces that led to the Civil War, and occasioned by the adoption of an anti-slavery resolution by the general convention, the southern branch of the church separated itself from the general convention.

The general convention adopted no doctrinal statement but followed the central affirmations of Reformed Protestantism stressing the authority of the Bible and salvation by grace through faith. Considerable variation was allowed on doctrinal matters, even on the sacramants. The Southern branch of the church tended to favor adult believers baptism (reflecting their Baptists heritage).

Reformed Church in the United States. German-speaking adherents of the Reformed Church came into the United States soon after the founding of Pennsylvania. By 1730 there were more than 15,000 people at least nominally members of the Reformed Church in Pennsylvania. By 1800 the number had grown to 40,000. They had come originally at William Penn's invitation, but were spurred by various negative conditions in their homeland.

Soon after their arrival, these German believers took steps to organize churches. Short of ministers, they often appointed the local school teacher to hold services. One such, John Philip Boehm, eventually sought ordination in 1725 and financial support from the Dutch Reformed Church (which had a strong following in New York). That church sent Michael Schlatter to consolidate the scattered congregations into a denominational mold. In 1747 the clergy of these congregations formed the Coetus of the Reformed Ministerium of the Congregations of Pennsylvania. In 1793 the German Reformed Church in Pennsylvania and adjacent states reorganized as a Synod, independent of the Reformed Church in Holland.

In the mid-1880s the German Reformed Church in the U.S. was torn by a major controversy between the Mercersburg and the Old Reformed movements. The former, stimilated by the leadership of John W. Nevin (1803-1886), Philip Schaff (1819-1893), and their associates at the Reformed Seminary that had been established at Mercersburg, Pennsylvania, sought to oppose the inroads being made by revivalism (especially that of Charles G. Finney) and sectarianism. The Mercersburg theologians favored an altar-centered liturgy with responses and chants, ritual forms for the traditional

church year, read prayers, and more formal garb for the ministers and choirs. They also stressed the authority of the synod over that of regional and congregational powers, and the minister's authority in matters of local church order. The opponents of the Mercersburg perspective stood for pulpit-centered worship, congregational autonomy, and the control of the churches' order of worship in the hands of lay consistories.

The educational emphasis in the church first emerged in the formation of the semnary at Mercersburg (later moved to Lancaster, Pennsylvania) and the formation of a number of colleges--Heidelberg, Catawba, Hood, Franklin and Marshal, Ursinius, and Cedar Crest. Following the movement of German immigration communities, the church spread from Pennsylvania into 21 states and three Canadian provinces.

Mission work began in 1838 with the formation of the Board of Foreign Missions. For 28 years this board united with the American Board of Commissioners of Foreign Missions and then began to send its own missionaries to China, India, Japan and the Middle East.

The Evangelical Synod of North America. In 1917 King Frederick William II (1797-1840) united the congregations in his realm, some of which had Lutheran and some of which had Reformed leanings into a single Evangelical Church, the Church of the Prussian Union. He enforced one form of worship and one church government. Pietism and a more conciliatory spirit were encouraged and a united front against the inroads of rationalism was created through the development of interconfessioanl Bible, missionary, and tract societies.

One of these societies, the Basel Missionary Society, sent 288 missionaries as pastors for America, beginning in 1833, in response to appeals from German-American immigrants in the Midwest. The first to arrive were Joseph A. Rieger (1811-1869) and George Wendelin Wall (1811-1867). In 1840 a group of German Evangelical ministers in the St. Louis, Missouri area met and formed Der Deutsche Evangelishe Kirchenverein des Westens (the German Evangelical Church Society of the West). In 1866 the word "Kirchenverein" was changed to "Synod." The society/synod made every effort to avoid rigid institutional organization and to eliminate the bureaucratic features usually associated with synodical bodies. Membership was to consist of ordained pastors, lay delegates, and advisory members. No effort was made at this time to enlist individual churches to the society, and it was explicitedly stated that "neither the external nor the internal affairs of local congregations could be made the business of the society."

Reflecting their dual Lutheran and Reformed heritage, catechetical instruction in these Evangelical churches typically used one of several catechisms that were being used in Germany, usually uniting elements of Luther's

Smaller Catechism with parts of the Heidelberg Catechism of the Reformed Church.

Contemporaneously with the formation of the Synod of the West, two other like synods were being formed. The United Synod of the Northwest served churches in northern Illinois and southern Michigan. The United Synod of the East stretched from New York to Ohio. As early as 1851, union talks were held between the three bodies. In 1872 they merged to form the German Evangelical Synod of North America (dropping the word "German" in 1927).

Like the Reformed Church in the U. S. and the Congregationalist Churches, the Evangelical Synod placed a strong emphasis upon education, particularly demanding an educated ministry. Eden Seminary was begun in 1850 and Elmhurst College in 1872. Parochial schools were attached to most congregations. The synod was also deeply involved in the revival of the deaconess movement in the last half of the nineteenth century. A deaconess hospital in St. Louis in 1853 spurred other healing efforts in the church and hospitals were established in Cleveland, Ohio; Evansville, Indiana; Detroit, Michigan; and Chicago, Illinois.

No other German church body, save the Moravians, developed as extensive a missionary effort as did the Evangelical Synod. It formed missions to the American Indian and sent foreign missionaries to India and Honduras. Domestic missions included the Seaman's Mission in Baltimore, Maryland; Caroline Mission in St. Louis; Back Bay Mission in Biloxi, Mississippi; and others in the Ozarks and on Madeline Island, Wisconsin.

The talks leading toward the 1934 merger of the Evangelical Synod and the Reformed Church began in 1929. The new Evangelical and Reformed Church (E&R Church) was in place only a short time before talks began with the newly formed General Council of the Congregational-Christian Churches.

The United Church of Christ. As early as 1941 the Committee on Church Relations of the E&R Church held informal conversations with the corresponding committee of the Congregational-Christian Churches. By 1944 a common procedure was agreed upon for dealing with a formal basis of union and a uniting general synod was planned for 1950. This, however, was postponed for nearly a decade due to legal challenges within the Congregational-Christian Churches. The formal beginning of the United Church of Christ was the Uniting General Synod in Cleveland in June 1957.

The United Church of Christ adopted a constitution in 1961 that provides for a General synod as its chief policymaking body. The synod is composed of ministerial and lay delegates from the conferences. The delegates elect an executive council which acts between meetings of the synod. Under the general synod are a variety of boards and agencies, the most important being the Board of Homeland Ministries, the Board of World Ministries, and the Pension Board of the United Church (all of which continue older organizations and are separately incorporated).

The polity of the church included elements of both congregational and presbyterial styles of government. Local churches are guaranteed the right to own their own property, call their own ministers, and withdraw unilaterally from the denomination. But the associations, in which clergy and denominations hold their denominational standing, can withdraw that standing on their own initiative. Conferences, the general synod, and instrumentalities can advise local churches and individual members, but their statements and decisions are not binding.

Geographically, the church is divided into 38 conferences (with an additional conference serving Hungarian-American congregations), and each conference is further divided into associations, each related to the other and the general synod in a covenantal fashion. Local churches are governed by local councils or consistories, variously composed of the pastor, a moderator or president, and other officers.

The statement of faith, adopted by the General Synod of the United Church of Christ in 1959, and rephrased in doxalogical form in 1981, is open to a variety of interpretations, but the Reformed theological background of most ministerial leadership is still evident.

The United Church of Christ has a reputation as one of the most socially liberal and active of American church bodies. At the national level, it has identified with numerous concerns related to peace and justice issues. It is also theologically liberal, continuing its modernist heritage, and maintains a wide variety of theological perspectives. It is broadly ecumenical, yet has developed a variety of specific official partnership commitments to the Christian Church (Disciples of Christ); the Evangelical Church Union (East and West Germany), the Pentecostal Church of Chile, the Presbyterian Church, Republic of Korea, and the United Church of Christ (Philippines). The UCC is a member of the National Council of Churches, the World Council of Churches, and the World Alliance of Reformed Churches (Presbyterian and Congregational).

Membership: In 1986 the church reported 1,676,000 members, 6,404 churches, and 10,071 clergy.

Educational facilities: *College and Universities*: Beloit College, Beloit, Wisconsin; Carleton, College, Northfield, Minnesota; Catawba College, Salisbury, North Carolina; Cedar Crest College, Allentown, Pennsylvania; Deaconess College of Nursing, St. Louis, Missouri; Defiance College, Defiance, Ohio; Dillard University, New Orleans, Louisiana; Doane College, Crete, Nebraska; Drury

College, Springfield, Missouri; Elmhurst College, Elmhurst, Illinois; Elon College, Elon College, North Carolina; Fisk University, Nashville, Tennessee; Franklin and Marshall College, Lancaster, Pennsylvania; Grinnel College, Grinnell, Iowa; Heidelberg College, Tiffin, Ohio; Hood College, Frederick, Maryland; Hawaii Loa College, Kenehoe, Hawaii; Huston-Tillotson College, Austin, Texas; Illinois College, Jacksonville, Illinois; Lakeland College, Sheboygan, Wisconsin; Lemoyne-Owen College, Memphis, Tennessee; Northland College, Ashland, Wisconsin; Olivet College, Olivet, Michigan; Pacific University, Forest Grove, Oregon; Ripon College, Ripon, Wisconsin; Rocky Mountain College, Billings, Montana; Talladega College, Talladega, Alabama; Tougaloo College, Tougaloo, Misissippi; Ursinius College, Collegeville, Pennsylvania; Westminister College, Salt Lake City, Utah.

Seminaries: Andover Newton Theological Seminary, Newton Center, Massachusetts; Bangor Theological Seminary, Bangor, Maine; Chicago Theological Seminary, Chicago, Illinois; Eden Theological Seminary, St. Louis, Missouri; Hartford Seminary, Hartford, Connecticut; Harvard University School of Divinity, Cambridge, Massachusetts; Howard University School of Divinity, Washington, District of Columbia; Interdenominational Theological Center, Atlanta, Georgia; Pacific School of Religion, Berkeley, California; Lancaster Theological Seminary, Lancaster, Pennsylvania; Seminario Evangelico de Puerto Rico, Hato Rey, Puerto Rico; United Theological Seminary of the Twin Cities, New Brighton, Minnesota; Union Theological Seminary, New York, New York; Yale Divinity School, New Haven, Connecticut.

Periodicals: *United Church News*, 105 Madison Ave., New York, NY 10016.

Sources: David Dunn et al., *A History of the Evangelical and Reformed Church*. Philadelphia, PA: Christian Education Press, 1961; Louis H. Gunneman, *The Shaping of the United Church of Christ*. New York: Thomas Nelson, 1962; Douglas Horton, *The United Church of Christ*. New York: Thomas Nelson, 1962; Marion L. Starkey, *The Congregational Way*. Garden City: NY: Doubleday, 1966.

Section 5

Pietist-Methodist Family

An historical essay on this family is provided beginning on page 27.

Scandinavian Pietism

★210★
**EVANGELICAL COVENANT CHURCH OF
   AMERICA**
5101 N. Francisco Ave.
Chicago, IL 60625

The Pietist movement in Sweden was opposed almost from the beginning by the Lutheran state church as being offensive to order and breeding ground for heresy. The movement had been constantly suppressed but periodically re-emerged. In the early nineteenth century a new revival was started by several non-Swedish agents. One of these, George Scott from England, was brought to Sweden to minister to English industrial workers in Stockholm and influenced Carl Olof Rosenius, a layman, Andrew Wilberg, a Lutheran priest, and Oscar Ahnfelt, a musician. Rosenius became editor of *Pietisten*, Scott's periodical. Rosenius also began to hold conventicles, meetings similar to the English religious societies of the early eighteenth century, and aided the development of a revived hymnody. Under Rosenius' leadership a national revival swept Sweden.

Members of the revival movement migrated to America in the mid-nineteenth century. The Swedes attempted to stay within the Augustana Synod of Lutherans in the Midwest and within other synods. After these attempts failed, the Swedes began to organize their own churches. Two synods were formed, the Swedish Lutheran Mission Synod in 1873 and the Swedish Lutheran Ansgarius Synod in 1884. In 1885 the two synods merged to form the Swedish Evangelical Mission Covenant Church of America. In 1937 the word "Swedish" was dropped; in 1957 the word "Mission" was dropped.

Doctrinally the church is essentially Lutheran, but no statement of faith has been officially adopted. A report on "Biblical Authority and Christian Freedom" presented in 1963 to the annual meeting of the church emphasized the double theme of the Bible as the Word of God and the only perfect rule for faith and practice, and of freedom within that authority. They accept as biblical truth the life and significance of Christ and a relationship with him by faith. They believe in the dedicated life and the unity of all Christians.

The church is organized on a congregational polity, which means that local churches operate autonomously and that congregations call their own ministers. The Covenant holds an annual meeting, and a Covenant Ministerium oversees ordination. There are 11 regional conferences. An Executive Committee of twenty members oversees activities during the year. A Council of Admnistrators includes the heads of the several boards. The Board of Benevolence oversees eight hospitals and homes. Foreign missions are conducted in Alaska, Zaire, Taiwan, Japan, Hong Kong, Indonesia, and Korea. Covenant Press is the publishing arm.

Membership: In 1985 the church reported 85,150 members, 566 congregations, and 912 ministers.

Educational facilities: North Park Theological Seminary, Chicago, Illinois; North Park College, Chicago, Illinois.

Periodicals: *Covenant Companion*, 5110 Francisco, Chicago, IL; *Covenant Home Altar*, Chicago, IL; *Covenant Quarterly*, 5110 Francisco, Chicago, IL.

Sources: Karl A. Olsson, *A Family of Faith*. Chicago: Covenant Press, 1975; *Covenant Memories*. Chicago: Covenant Book Concern, 1935; C. V. Bowman, *The Mission Covenant of America*. Chicago: The Covenant Book Concern, 1925; P. Matson, E. B. Larsson, and W. D. Thornbloom, eds., *Covenant Frontiers*. Chicago: Board of Mission, Evangelical Mission Covenant Church of America, 1941.

★211★
EVANGELICAL FREE CHURCH OF AMERICA
1551 E. 66th St.
Minneapolis, MN 55423

The Evangelical Free Church of America was formed in 1950 by the merger of two Scandinavian independent Pietistic churches which had grown out of nineteenth-century revivals: the Swedish Evangelical Free Church and the Norwegian-Danish Evangelical Free Church Association. The Swedish Evangelical Free Church came into existence in 1884. It was composed of congregations that did not want to enter the merger of Swedish synods that took place the following year, the merger forming the Swedish Evangelical Mission Covenant Church of America. These congregations had strong feelings about maintaining their own autonomy, and at the same time desired to sponsor missionary ministry overseas through an association of churches rather than the typical synodical structure. This association was established at a meeting in Boone, Iowa in 1884. An independent religious periodical, *Chicago-Bladet*, established by John Martenson, was a catalyst that brought together the 27 representatives at Boone.

The Norwegian-Danish Evangelical Free Church Association was formed by immigrants from Denmark and Norway who had been influenced by the pietistic revivals in their homeland. The ministry of Rev. Fredrick Franson of Bethlehem Church in Oslo led to the formation of the Mission Covenant Church of Norway, to which some of the immigrants had belonged. In 1889 a periodical *Evangelisten*, was launched in Chicago; and in 1891 the Western Evangelical Free Church Association was organized. Later that same year an Eastern Association of Churches was formed. A merger of the Eastern and Western groups was made in 1909, with the church taking the name of the Norwegian-Danish Evangelical Free Church Association.

The church formed in 1950, the Evangelical Free Church of America, adopted a Confession of Faith which stresses the essentials of the Reformation tradition, though the definite influence of evangelicalism is evident. The Bible is declared to be "the inspired Word of God, without error in the original writings." The second coming is seen as personal (meaning Jesus will come in person), premillennial (he will come before the millennium to bind Satan, and he will reign for a thousand years with his saints on earth), and imminent. Polity is congregational. There is an annual conference to oversee the cooperative endeavors of the church, including the credentialing ministers and a ministerial fellowship.

Mission work is carried on in Japan, Singapore, the Philippines, Malaysia, Zaire, Hong Kong, Brazil, Peru, Venezuela, Belgium, France, Austria, and Germany. The church has two children's homes in the United States, and six nursing home facilities. Overseas there are two hospitals, a children's home, a seminary, a bible institute, and other related institutions.

Membership: In 1987 the church reported 110,000 members, 968 churches, and 1,791 ministers in the United States; 5,600 members, 113 churches, and 113 ministers in Canada; and an additional 65,000 members in 14 foreign countries.

Educational facilities: Trinity Evangelical Divinity School, Deerfield, Illinois; Trinity College, Deerfield, Illinois; Trinity Western University, Langley, British Columbia, Canada.

Periodicals: *The Evangelical Beacon*, 1515 E. 66th Street, Minneapolis, MN 55423.

Sources: Arnold Theodore Olson, *Believers Only*. Minneapolis: Free Church Publications, 1964; W. Wilbert Norton, et al, *The Diamond Jubilee Story*. Minneapolis: Free Church Publications, 1959; Arnold Theodore Olson, *This We Believe*. Minneapolis: Free Church Press, 1961.

★212★
MORAVIAN CHURCH IN AMERICA
Northern Province
1021 Center St.
Box 1245
Bethlehem, PA 18016-1245

The Moravian Church in America dates to the arrival of Bishop August Gottlieb Spangenberg in Georgia in 1735. After the Georgia work was established, he traveled to Pennsylvania and began work there, setting the stage for the arrival of Bishop David Nitschmann and the settlements of Nazareth, Bethlehem, and Lititz. From these three centers a concentrated effort was made to bring into the Moravian Church the many groups which William Penn had brought to Pennsylvania: Quakers, Mennonites, and Brethren. The church spread as other Moravian settlements were established.

In 1753, Spangenberg began work in North Carolina, in a town first called Bethania. In 1771 Moravians founded Salem, now called Winston-Salem. The town is in what is now Forsyth County. Salem became the headquarters fo r the So uthern Province. In the 1850s, work was begun in Wisconsin among the German and Scandinavian immigrants.

No discussion of the Moravians would be complete without mentioning their missionary zeal. They were among the first of the modern churches to realize that the world would remain essentially un-Christian and that Christians would therefore always have to be missionaries. Before the Moravians, Christians believed Christianity eventually would become the dominant religion of the whole world. The Moravians saw that belief as unrealistic and, recognizing Christians as a minority, saw the implications for ministering to the non-Christians. They began work in the West Indies in 1732 and a main motive in coming to America was to preach to theIndians. The Moravians stand behind the whole nineteenth century Christian mission enterprise.

In order to make American Moravians self-supporting, a plan by Spangenberg called the "Economy" was established. It amounted to a communal system with Bishop Spangenberg and a board of directors as supervisors. All the church members placed their time, talents, and labor at the church's disposal. In return they were assured of a home, food, and clothing, as well as the fellowship of the church. By this means affluent agricultural and industrial centers were established, missionaries supported, and books printed and circulated. The missionaries itinerated throughout the colonies and abroad. The "Economy" lasted about two decades, although Moravians maintained closed communities in Pennsylvania and North Carolina into the nineteenth century. mid-nineteenth century.

Presently the church is organized into two provinces, northern and southern. Each province is governed by a provincial elders' conference which includes laypersons and clergy. Each local church has a council council of elders (who handle the spiritual) and trustees (who handle the temporal). Ministers are placed through the provincial governing board. Each decade there is a meeting of the Unity, that is, the representatives of all the provinces world-wide.

Doctrinally the Moravians follow the motto: "In essentials unity; in non-essentials liberty; in all things love." The Moravian Church holds to the essentials of Protestant doctrine, which they see to include the Bible as the source of Christian doctrine; the depravity of human nature; the love of God for humanity; the Trinity, and the divinity and humanity of Christ; reconciliation and justification; the work of the Holy Spirit; good works as the fruit of the Holy Spirit; the fellowship of believers; and the second coming of Jesus.

The Moravians are distinguished by certain practices developed to reflect Pietist concerns. The love feast, a simple shared meal became an expression of communal oneness. They use the church year and have developed a simplified liturgy. Infant baptism and holy communion (on certain designated feast days) are practiced. While most clerical vestments were abandoned, the surplice is still worn by ministers for communion. The Holy Week services, culminating in the Easter Sunrise Service, is the height of the Christian year. Christmas is celebrated in all Moravian churches with a decorative, many-pointed star and the Christmas putz, a decoration which pictures the Christmas story. Music, which was an important part of the Pietist renewal, was furthered among the Moravians by Zinzendorf and James Montgomery, both prolific hymn writers.

Congregations of the Moravian Church continue to be concentrated in Pennsylvania and North Carolina, though some are scattered around the country. The mission tradition is reflected in the fact three-fourth of the world's Moravians are in Africa or the Caribbean Basin. Both provinces have an active church history and archive program, one of the best among American church bodies.

The Moravian Church is a member of both the National Council of Churches and the World Council of Churches. Affiliated provinces in the Caribbean are affiliated with the Caribbean Conference of Churches.

Membership: In 1987, the Northern Province reported a membership of 34,205 and the Southern Province reported 21,722 for a total membership of 55,927. There were 178 a ctive ministers in 160 churches. Worldwide membership was 507,269.

Educational facilities: Moravian College and Theological Seminary, Bethlehem, Pennsylvania; Salem Academy and College, Winston-Salem, North Carolina; Linden Hall School for Girls, Lititz, Pennsylvania; Moravian Academy, Bethlehem, Pennsylvania.

Periodicals: *The North American Moravian*, Box 1245, Bethehem, PA 18016-1245.

Sources: J. Taylor Hamilton and Kenneth G. Hamilton, *A History of the Moravian Church--The Unitas Fratrum, 1722-1957*. Bethlehem, PA: Interprovincial Board of Christian Education/Moravian Church in America, 1957; George Neisser, *A History of the Beginnings of Moravian Work in America*, translated by William N. Schwarze and Samuel H. Gapp. Bethlehem, PA: The Archives of the Moravian Church, 1955; Allen W. Schattschneider, *Through Five Hundred Years*. Bethlehem, PA: Comenius Press, 1974; John S. Groenfeldt, *Becoming a Member of the Moravian Church*. Winston-Salem, NC: Comenius Press, 1954; Walser H. Allen, *Who Are the Moravians*. Bethlehem, PA: The Author, 1966. John R. Weinlick, *The Moravian Church through the Ages*. The Moravian Church in America, 1988.

★213★
UNITY OF THE BRETHREN
% Dr. Mark L. Labaj
4202 Ermine
Temple, TX 76501

While many of the Moravians fled to Saxony, following the persecutions in the eighteenth century, some remained behind in Moravia and Bohemia. In the mid-nineteenth century, some of these Brethren migrated to Texas. There, under the leadership of the Rev. A. Chumsky and H. Juren, they organized the Evangelical Union of Bohemian and Moravian Brethren in North America. A Mutual Aid Society was organized in 1905 and the Hus Memorial School, to train church school teachers, in 1914. In 1924 the Hus Memorial Home was founded in Temple, Texas.

An independent group, organized by A. Motycha joined the Evangelical Union 1919, and the name Evangelical Unity of Bohemian and Moravian Brethren in North America (later shortened to Unity of the Brethren) was adopted.

Doctrinally, the Unity uses the 1608 Moravian Catechism and the Confessions of the Luthern and Reformed Churches. It emphasizes the Protestant consensus of theological belief. It practices infant baptism and open communion with all Christians; it's ministers are seminary trained. Government is presbyterian, with power invested in a biennial synod of ministers and church delegates. The synod meets in July on the anniversary of Hus's death. Ministers are called by the congregations.

Membership: At last report in 1971, the Brethren had 27 churches and 3,249 members, a significant decrease from 1964 (32 churches and 6,142 members).

Periodicals: *Brethren Journal*, 5905 Carleen Drive, Austin, TX 78731.

United Methodism

★214★
UNITED METHODIST CHURCH
% Council on Ministries
601 W. Riverside Ave.
Dayton, OH 45406

In 1968 with the formation of the United Methodist Church, for the first time in over a century a majority of those Americans in John Wesley's lineage found themselves in one organization. The United Methodist Church is the successor to five of the larger formerly existing bodies in the Wesleyan tradition, namely, the Methodist Episcopal Church, Methodist Episcopal Church, South, United Brethren in Christ, Evangelical Association, and Methodist Protestant Church. (Three of these churches merged in 1939; the other two formed one church in 1946; then those new churches formed the United Methodist Church in 1968.)

History. Apart from the Methodist Episcopal Church, those formed earliest were the church of the United Brethren in Christ and the Evangelical Association. The United Brethren in Christ formed as a result of the work of Philip Otterbein, a German Pietist, with the help of Martin Boehm. Otterbein and Boehm began evangelistic work among the German immigrants in Pennsylvania. The growth of the work led in 1789 to a first meeting of preachers connected with the work. In 1800 these meetings became an annual affair and the ministers agreed that Otterbein and Boehm should superintend the work. They began to use the name United Brethren in Christ. Otterbein had been associated with Francis Asbury and the Methodists: he took part in the ordination of Asbury, the first bishop of the Methodist Episcopal Church.

A second German-speaking group developed through the work of Jacob Albright in Pennsylvania. A movement gathered around his preaching and in 1803 a conference of those acknowledging Albright as leader was held. This meeting was the beginning of what became the Evangelical Association.

The Evangelical Association suffered a schism in 1894 when the United Evangelical Church was formed. This schism was largely overcome by the 1922 merger that produced the Evangelical Church. In the 1930s, the United Brethren in Christ entered into merger negotiations with the Evangelical Church, and in 1946 a merger was effected which resulted in the formation of the Evangelical United Brethren.

Within the Methodist Episcopal Church agitation on lay rights and the appointment system (by which a bishop assigns a minister to his church) led to widespread protest, particularly in New England and the Western states. Several dissident periodicals were begun and leaders such as Asa Shinn, Dennis Dorsey, and Nicholas Snethen pressed for reform along more democratic lines. Following the 1828 General Conference, when it became obvious that the church was not going to move in the direction of reform, schism occurred.

Congregations using the name Associated Methodist Churches were formed. These in turn formed the Methodist Protestant Church two years later. A non-episcopal form of government termed "connectionalism" was worked out. Lay representation at conference (the legislative body) was given. The annual conference assumed the duty of stationing the ministers, a duty formerly left to the bishop.

A second schism of the Methodist Episcopal Church occurred in 1844, when the General Conference voted to divide itself and form two General Conferences of one church. This split, one of the most unusual in church history, was prompted by heated debates about slavery and the power of bishops. The result was two churches, the Methodist Episcopal Church (North) and the Methodist Episcopal Church, South, and a tremendous amount of animosity in those areas where both had congregations. A major issue, long blocking reunion, was the denial by many northern Methodists of the legitimacy of the General Conference action and the right of the Methodist Episcopal Church, South to share the tradition. (In general, until 1939 the Methodist Episcopal Church (North) continued to call itself the Methodist Episcopal Church, and that is how it will be referred to throughout this work.)

Continual attempts at reunion of the Methodist Protestant Church and the Methodist Episcopal Churches, North and South, were frustrated until the 1930s. Finally in 1939 a reunion did occur and The Methodist Church (1939-1968) was organized. It was this body that merged with the Evangelical United Brethren in 1968 to form the United Methodist Church.

Since the middle of the nineteenth century, Methodist women have served their congregations as unordained evangelists. When the Methodist Church was established in 1939, it was decided that women could be trained for the ministry and ordained, but that they could not become "members of conference," that is, ministers guaranteed an appointment to a congregation and thereby guaranteed a salary. In 1956 women were given full ministerial status. Ordained women thereafter could be "members of conference" and received annual appointments to churches.

Schism in Methodism has centered around two issues: centralized government and race. The protest of episcopal and clerical authority was the first issue to disturb the harmony of the Methodists. The first protest centered on the Rev. James O'Kelly, a prominent minister, who refused to accept Asbury's appointments. O'Kelly broke away in 1792 and formed the Republican Methodist Church, which eventually became part of the Christian Church. Other schisms, now defunct, based on protest of the centralized authority of the Methodist Episcopal Church, occurred in 1792 in Charleston, South Carolina, where William Hammett led a group in forming the Primitive Methodist Church, not to be confused with the presently existing church of the same name); in 1814 with the Reformed Methodist Church led by Pliny Brett of Vermont; and in 1820 in New York City where Samuel Stillwell and his nephew William Stillwell formed the Methodist Society.

During the twentieth century, Methodists became affiliated with the ecumenical movement. This movement, in tune with the reunionist tendencies of Methodism otherwise, became the occasion of schisms, protesting the growth of a "super" church or the loss of Methodist distinctives. In 1939 when the non-episcopal Methodist Protestant Church moved into the Methodist Episcopal Church, a number of congregations remained out of the reunion and formed new denominations.

Race has been the second point at issue among American Methodists. The first blacks joined the Methodist Episcopal Church during Wesley's lifetime; Methodism moved freely among blacks in the 1700s and early 1800s. In the decades prior to the Civil War, the church established a slave mission which brought many thousands of black people into the church. The Methodist Episcopal Church became the major tool for the education of blacks and the development of their organizational skills. The church's very success in evangelizing both slaves and free black people prior to the Civil War made it a victim of the same social upheavals which split the nation at various times. It should be noted that racial schisms have affected American religion whenever a large proportion of non-Caucasians have become part of a family group. Methodists join Baptists, Holiness churches, Pentecostals, and Buddhists in racial separations. Some Methodist churches are segregated; some are integrated. The United Methodist Church is integrated.

During the period 1880-1914, Methodism was rent by a number of schisms related to the Holiness Movement, a revivalistic movement centered on Wesley's doctrine of perfection. According to that doctrine, after a person is saved, he or she should go on to be perfected in love and receive the "second blessing," an experience certifying holiness. The growth of the holiness movement and of its child, the Pentecostal movement, resulted in two new family groups: the holiness churches, discussed in chapter seven, and the Pentecostal churches, discussed in chapter eight.

Beliefs. While affirming the central theological propositions of Western Christianity, Methodists have generally placed greater emphasis upon piety and religious experience than doctrine. While accepting the faith as defined in the Twenty-five Articles of Religion sent by John Wesley to the American church, it has done so in a spirit of freedom, accepting no statement of doctrine as final or free from error. Generally, Methodists accept four landmark documents as definitive of the Wesleyan tradition: the Twenty-five Articles, the early minutes of the British Wesleyan Conference, John Wesley's Sermons (in which he outlined his basic doctrinal stance), and Wesley's *Explanatory Notes on the New Testament.* There are two sacraments, baptism (form optional but usually by sprinkling) and holy communion. Communion is open to all Christians, and congregations vary widely on the number of communion services held (some quarterly, some monthly and a few weekly). To these are added the General Rules of the Methodist Church, an early definition of Methodist practice. During the twentieth century, the Social Creed, first adopted by the Methodist Episcopal Church and quadrennially revised, has become the major statement of Methodist policy in the political, economic, and social arenas.

Organization. The United Methodist Church is governed by the General Conference, a representative body of an equal number of lay and clerical members, which meets quadrennially. This body legislates for the entire church and its decisions are printed in *The Discipline,* the church's rulebook. It assigns tasks to the various boards and agencies es and sets policy within which every organization within the church operates. Between meetings, the Council on Ministries guides and coordinates the church nationally and internationally. The United Methodist Publishing House is a major publisher of religious literature through Abingdon Press.

Geographically, the church is divided into a number of annual conferences, to whom is assigned the tasks of implementing the church's program in a particular area through the numerous congregations. The annual conference has the responsibility, through the bishop and the district superintendents, of appointing all ministers to pastor churches or to various special tasks. Ministers join one annual conference and assume a covenant of reciprocal accountability. The annual conferences have broad freedom for developing their own program within the guideline of *The Discipline*. Annual conferences are organized locally along the same pattern of boards and agencies as established by the General Conference.

Within the United States, conferences are divided into five geographical jurisdictions. A jurisdictional conference meets quadrennially following General Conference. It is assigned the major task of electing new bishops for the jurisdiction. (Conferences outside the United States are organized into seven central conferences which meet for the election of bishops.) Following the jurisdictional conference, the bishops collectively assign each to a particular episcopal area, consisting of one or two annual conferences in the jurisdiction.

The work of the United Methodist Churchworldwide is delegated to the Board of Global Ministries. Missionary work is carried on in most countries of the world, though there has been an increasing tendency to grant foreign conferences (of which there were 31 as of 1983) an autocephalous status. In those areas, the Board of Global Ministries works cooperatively under the guidance of local leadership in establishing and staffing any work. Also under the Board of Global Ministries is the United Methodist Committee on Relief (UMCOR) which has gained international acclaim for its ability to respond to emergencies and natural disasters with relief assistance.

The United Methodist Church has been a leader in the ecumenical movement. It is a member of both the National Council of Churches and the World Council of Churches. It has signed a corcordat with the Methodist Church in the Caribbean and the Americas (directly represented in the United States by the United Wesleyan Methodist Church of America, a member of the Caribbean Conference of Churches.

Membership: In 1983 the Church reported 9,405,164 members, 38,181 churches, and 36,676 ministers.

Educational facilities: Theological seminaries: Boston School of Theology, Boston, Massachusetts; Candler School of Theology, Atlanta, Georgia; Drew University, the Theological School, Madison, New Jersey; Duke University, the Divinity School, Durham, North Carolina; Gammon Theological Seminary, Atlanta, Georgia; Garrett Evangelical Theological Seminary, Evanston, Illinois; Iliff School of Theology, Denver, Colorado; The Methodist Theological School of Ohio, Delaware, Ohio; Perkins School of Theology, Dallas, Texas; Saint Paul School of Theology, Kansas City, Missouri; School of Theology at Claremont, Claremont, California; United Theological Seminary, Dayton, Ohio; Wesley Theological Seminary, Washington, D.C. (Gammon Theological Seminary participates with three other schools in the Interdenominational Theological Center, the largest

facility for training black ministers in the United States.) Predominantly black colleges: Bennett College, Greensboro, North Carolina; Bethune-Cookman College, Daytona Beach, Florida; Claflin College, Orangeburg, South Carolina; Clark College, Atlanta, Georgia; Dillard University, New Orleans, Louisiana; Huston-Tillotson College, Austin, Texas; Meharry Medical College, Austin, Texas; Morristown College, Morristown, Tennessee; Paine College, Augusta, Georgia; Philander Smith College, Little Rock, Arkansas; Rust College, Holly Springs, Mississippi; Wiley College, Marshall, Texas. Colleges and Universities: Adrian College, Adrian, Michigan; Alaska Pacific University, Anchorage, Alaska; Albion College, Albion, Michigan no longer affiliated; Albright College, Reading, Pennsylvania; Alleghany College, Meadville, Pennsylvania; American University, Washington, District of Columiba; Baker University, Baldwin City, Kansas; Birmingham-Southern College, Birmingham, Alabama; Boston University, Boston, Massachusetts; Centenary College, Hackettstown, New Jersey; Centenary College of Louisiana, Shreveport, Louisiana; Central Methodist College, Fayette, Missouri; Columbia College, Columbia, South Carolina; Cornell College, Mount Vernon, Iowa; Dakota Wesleyan University, Mitchell, South Dakota; DePauw University, Greencastle, Indiana; Dickinson College, Carlisle, Pennsylvania; Drew University, Madison, New Jersey; Duke University, Durham, North Carolina; Emory and Henry College, Emory, Virginia; Emory University, Atlanta, Georgia; Ferrum College, Ferrum, Virginia; Florida Southern College, Lakeland, Floria; Greensboro College, Greensboro, North Carolina; Hamline University, St. Paul, Minnesota; Hawaii Loa College, Kaneohe, Hawaii; Hendrix College, Conway, Arkansas; High Point College, High Point, North Carolina; Huntington College, Montgomery, Alabama; Illinois Wesleyan University, Bloomington, Indiana; Iowa Wesleyan College, Mount Pleasant, Iowa; Kansas Wesleyan, Salina Kansas; Kendall College, Evanston, Illinois; Kentucky Wesleyan College, Owensboro, Kentucky; LaGrande College, LaGrande, Georgia; Lambuth College, Jackson, Tennessee; Lebanon Valley College, Annville, Pennsylvania; Lycoming College, Wiliamsport, Pennsylvania; MacMurray College, Jacksonville, Illinois; McKendree College, Lebanon, Illinois; McMurry College, Abilene, Texas; Methodist College, Fayetteville, North Carolina; Millsaps College, Jackson, Mississippi; Morningside College, Sioux City, Iowa; Mount Union College, Allaince, Ohio; Nebraska Wesleyan University, Lincoln, Nebraska; North Carolina Wesleyan College, Rocky Mount, North Carolina; North Central College, Naperville, Illinois; Ohio Northern University, Ada, Ohio; Ohio Wesleyan University, Delaware, Ohio; Oklahoma City University, Oklahoma City, Oklahoma; Otterbein College, Westerville, Ohio; Pheiffer College, Misenheimer, North Carolina; Randolph-Macon College, Ashland, Virginia; Randolph-Macon Women's College, Lynchburg, Virginia; Rocky Mountain College, Billings, Montana; Shenandoah College and Conservatory of Music; Winchester, Virginia; Simpson College, Indianola, Iowa; Southern Methodist University, Dallas Texas; Southwestern College, Winfield, Kansas;

Southwestern University, Georgetown, Texas; Syracuse University, Syracuse, New York; Tennessee Wesleyan College, Athens, Tennessee; Texas Wesleyan College, Fort Worth, Texas; Union College, Barbourville, Kentucky; University of Denver, Denver, Colorado; University of Evansville, Evansville, Indiana; University of Puget Sound, Tacoma, Washington; University of the Pacific, Stockton, California; Virginia Wesleyan College, Norfolk, Virginia; Wesley College, Dover, Deleware; Wesleyan College, Macon, Georgia; Westmar College, Le Mars, Iowa; Westminister College, Salt Lake City, Utah; West Virginia Wesleyan College, Buckhannon, West Virginia; Willamette University, Salem, Oregon; Woffor College, Spartansburg, South Carolina.

Periodicals: *The Circuit Rider*, United Methodist Publishing House, Box 801, Nashville, TN 37202.

Sources: Jack M. Tuell, *The Organization of the United Methodist Church*. Nashville: Abingdon, 1977; Nolan B. Harmon, *Understanding the United Methodist Church*. Nashville: Abingdon, 1977; Roy I Sano, *From Every Nation without Number*. Nashville: Abingdon, 1982; *The Structure of the United Methodist Church*. Evanston, IL: United Methodist Communications, 1983.

Non-Episcopal Methodism

★215★
APOSTOLIC METHODIST CHURCH
Current address not obtained for this edition.

The Apostolic Methodist Church was organized in 1932 in Loughman, Florida, by E. H. Crowson and a few others. In 1931, the Rev. Crowson, an elder in the Florida Conference of the Methodist Episcopal Church, South, had been located (deposed from the itinerant ministry) for "unacceptability." The new group published a *Discipline* in which they complained about episcopal authority and the departure of the Methodist Episcopal Church, South, from its standards of belief and holiness. The Apostolic Methodists believe in the premillennial return of Jesus, his return to earth to bind Satan before his one-thousand-year reign on earth with his saints. The church emphasizes holiness of a "second blessing" type: after being justified or saved, a person can proceed to be perfected in love and have that ratified by a personal religious experience called the "second blessing." In 1933 F. L. Crowson, the father of E. H. Crowson, was tried by the Florida Conference and suspended. He withdrew and joined his son's new group.

The church operates the Gospel Tract Club at Zephyr Hills, Florida.

Membership: At its peak in the 1960s, the church had only a few congregations and less than 100 members.

★216★
ASBURY BIBLE CHURCHES
% Rev. Jack Tondee
Box 1021
Dublin, GA 31021

The Asbury Bible Church parallels the John Wesley Fellowship in most ways, but is organizationally separate. Like the John Wesley Fellowship, the Asbury Bible Churches were organized in 1971 by former members of the Southern Methodist Church who withdrew when that church dropped its membership in the American Council of Christian Churches. They follow the same conservative interpretation of Wesleyan doctrine and loose congregational polity and draw on the Francis Asbury Society of Ministers for their pastors. The Churches are also members of the American Council of Christian Churches.

Membership: Not reported.

★217★
ASSOCIATION OF INDEPENDENT METHODISTS
Box 4274
Jackson, MS 39216

The Association of Independent Methodists (AIM) was organized in 1965 in Jackson, Mississippi, by former members of the Methodist Church (1939-1968) which, in 1968, merged into the United Methodist Church. The organization rejected the Methodist Church's episcopal polity, the doctrinal liberalism felt to exist in the ecumenial movement of which the Methodist Church was a major supporter, and the neo-evangelicalism in the Sunday school literature, clergy, and church supported colleges and seminaries.

Doctrinally, the church accepts the Twenty-five Articles of Religion of John Wesley common to all Methodists. However, a statement on sanctification and new articles on the duties of the Christian to the civil authority and the separation of church and state were added.

Polity is congregational. There is an annual meeting each summer. It elects the associations officers including a president, vice-president, secretary, treasurer, and executive director. They serve with other officers on an executive committee. The executive committee and representatives from each church constitute a board of directors which meets quarterly. The church supports missionaries from the World Gospel Mission of Marion, Indiana. It also supports the Methodist Bible Hour of Marietta, Georgia, an independent Methodist weekly radio ministry and Bible correspondence school. This mission reaches the Caribbean, and Central and South America.

Membership: From a beginning with five churches, the Association in 1987 reported more than 3,000 members in 33 congregations with 47 ministers licensed or ordained by the association. All of the congregations are located in Mississippi, Alabama, and Florida.

Educational facilities: Wesley Biblical Seminary, Jackson, Mississippi.

Periodicals: *The Independent Methodist Bulletin*, Box 4274, Jackson, MS 39216

Remarks: AIM was established in 1965 as the Methodist Church was beginning the process of eliminating the racially segregated Central Jurisdiction, and as the South was experiencing the height of the civil rights movement. In the original articles of religion of AIM an article was added supporting the social separation of the races as "neither anti-Christian nor discriminatory." More recently, that article has been deleted.

Sources: Ivan J. Howard, *What Independent Methodists Believe.* Jackson, MS: Association of Independent Methodists, n.d.; *Constitution of Churches Organized as Independent Methodist Churches by the Association of Independent Methodists.* [Jackson, MS: Association of Independent Methodists, n.d.

★218★
CHURCH OF DANIEL'S BAND
% Rev. Wesley James Haggard, President
Croll Rd.
Beaverton, MI 48612

The Church of Daniel's Band was formed in 1893 at Marine City, Michigan, as an effort to revive primitive Methodism and continue the class meeting, the regular meeting of small classes for discussion, exhortation, Bible study, prayer, confession, and forgiveness. The doctrine and polity are Methodist with a strong emphasis on evangelism, perfectionism, Christian fellowship, religious liberty, and abstinence from worldly excess. Several articles of faith have been added to the standard twenty-five emphasizing belief in the resurrection and judgment of the dead, divine healing, and the laying on of hands for the gift of the Holy Spirit.

Membership: In 1988 there were four churches, approximately 217 members, and eight ministers.

Sources: *The Doctrine and Discipline of the Church of Daniel's Band.* N.p.: 1981.

★219★
CONGREGATIONAL METHODIST CHURCH
Box 155
Florence, MS 39073

The Congregational Methodist Church was formed by a group of laymen led by local preachers who withdrew from the Georgia Conference of the Methodist Episcopal Church, South. The group met in the home of

Mickleberry Merritt on May 8, 1852, and organized. William Fambough was elected chairman. Rev. Hiram Phinazee was appointed to draw up a *Discipline*, which was approved and published soon afterward. Three main issues seemed to disturb those who withdrew: the itinerant system, as then practiced, which was plagued with large circuits and weekday preaching to empty pews; the Church's neglect of the local preachers who did most of the work with the congregations and received no credit; and the government of the Methodist Episcopal Church, South, which deprived laymen of a voice in church business.

On August 12, 1852, a conference was convened. Except for local church conferences, this was the first Methodist conference composed of more laymen than ministers and the first body of Methodists whose total representation was by election of the local congregations. By 1880, the church expanded to include conferences in six states and work in several surrounding ones, with a total membership of approximately 6,000.

The Congregational Methodist Church is conservative in its theology. Its members are premillennialists (they believe Christ will come to earth to bind Satan before the millennium, his reign for one thousand years with his saints on earth). They believe in a literal "heaven" and "hell" and use only the King James Version of the Bible. The addition of Articles of Religion on regeneration and on sanctification in 1941 became the occasion for a dissenting group to leave and form the First Congregational Methodist Church of the United States of America. In 1957, these two articles plus ones on tithing, eternal retribution, and the resurrection of the dead, were formally adopted by the Congregational Methodist Church.

The publishing board of the church oversees Messenger Press, which publishes the church's periodical and the church school literature. In 1953, Westminster College and Bible Institute at Tehuacana, Texas, was established; it later moved to Florence, Mississippi. A mission program in cooperation with World Gospel Mission has missionaries in Africa and South America and among American Indians. Though not a member, the Church cooperates with the Christian Holiness Association.

Membership: Not reported. In 1961 the Church had 14,879 members and 242 congregations organized in 10 conferences.

Educational facilities: Westminster College and Bible Institute, Florence, MS 39073.

Periodicals: *Congregational Methodist Messenger*, Box 555, Florence, MS 39073.

Sources: *Minutes of the General Conference of the Congregational Methodist Church, 1869-1945.* Tehuacana, TX: Westminister College Print Shop, 1960; S.C.

McDaniel, *The Origin and Early History of the Congregational Methodist Church.* Atlanta: Jas. P. Harrison, 1881.

★220★
CUMBERLAND METHODIST CHURCH
(Defunct)

The Cumberland Methodist Chruch withdrew from the Congregational Methodist Church in 1950 because of a disagreement on both polity and doctrine. It was organized at Laager, Grundy County, Tennessee, in the mountainous country near Chattanooga. Membership never reached beyond the several counties in southeastern Tennessee. Since its founder's death, no trace of the existence of the Cumberland Methodist Church has been found.

★221★
EVANGELICAL METHODIST CHURCH
3000 W. Kellogg
Wichita, KS 67213

The Evangelical Methodist Church was founded by former members of the Methodist Church led by Dr. J. H. Hamblen of Abilene, Texas. In 1945, Dr. Hamblen began serving an independent congregation in Abilene. Calls from other congregations led to the founding of the Evangelical Methodist Church at a Memphis, Tennessee, conference on May 9, 1946. The main cause of dissatisfaction was the "modernism" that had infiltrated the parent body.

At the first Annual Conference at Kansas City, Missouri, in 1946, Dr. Hamblen was elected the first general superintendent. E. B. Vargas brought the Mexican Evangelistic Mission into the new church as the first mission district. In subsequent sessions Lucian Smith and Ralph Vanderwood were elected to the office of general superinte ndent.

The church holds a conservative theological perspective and believes very strongly the Articles of Religion of the former Methodist Episcopal Church, South, to which it has added an article on "perfect love." In describing themselves, members say, "The Church is fundamental in belief, premillennial regarding the second coming, missionary in outlook, evangelistic in endeavor, cooperative in spirit, and Wesleyan in doctrine."

Organizationally the Church is congregational yet connectional. It is congregational in that each congregation owns its own property and calls its own pastor. It is connectional in that all member churches agree to abide by the *Discipline* of the Evangelical Methodist Church. The denomination, as a whole, is governed by the conference system. The General Conference, presided over by the General Superintendents, is the highest legislative body in the church. It meets every four years and oversees the several district conferences, and the local churches.

In cooperation with the World Gospel Mission and the OMS International, the church has sent more than sixty-five missionaries. The church is also affiliated with both the National Association of Evangelicals and the Christian Holiness Association.

Membership: Not reported. In 1985 the Church had 9,040 members and 126 churches.

Periodicals: *Evangelical Methodist Viewpoint*, 3000 W. Kellogg, Wichita, KS 67213.

★222★
EVANGELICAL METHODIST CHURCH OF AMERICA
Box 751
Kingsport, TN 37662

Largest of several fellowships of independent fundamentalist Methodist churches, the Evangelical Methodist Church of America was established in 1952 by dissenting members of the Evangelical Methodist Church. The issues that led to withdrawal centered around a longstanding doctrinal and organizational disagreement between Dr. J. H. Hamblen and Rev. W. W. Beckbill (d.1974). Rev. Beckbill and his followers did not accept the doctrine of holiness proposed by Dr. Hamblen. There was also conflict over membership in the National Association of Evangelicals.

The withdrawing body, led by Beckbill, established an organization similar to that of the parent body. Membership was established in the fundamentalist American Council of Christian Churches and International Council of Christian Churches, and close working relations were set up with the Southern Methodist Church, the Fundamental Methodist Church, and the Methodist Protestant Church which jointly sponsored Bible Methodist Missions and the International Fellowship of Bible Methodists. Following the withdrawal of the Southern Methodist Church from the American Council of Christian Churches, the Evangelical Methodist Church aligned itself with the Asbury Bible Churches and the Fellowship of Independent Methodists.

Missions are conducted in Jamaica, Argentina, Chile, and Paraguay.

Membership: Not reported.

Educational facilities: Maranath School of Theology, Hollidaysburg, Pennsylvania.

Periodicals: *The Evangelical Methodist.*

Sources: *Discipline.* Altoona, PA: Evangelical Methodist Church, 1962.

★223★
FELLOWSHIP OF FUNDAMENTAL BIBLE CHURCHES
Box 43
Glassboro, NJ 08028

The Fellowship of Fundamental Bible Churches, formerly the Bible Protestant Church, is the continuing Eastern Conference of the Methodist Protestant Church (1828-1939). In 1939, as a conference, it had refused to join the denomination's merger with the Methodist Episcopal Church and the Methodist Church (1939-1968). The conference withdrew and reorganized at Scullville, New Jersey. The fellowship was known as the Bible Protestant Church from 1940 until 1985, when it adopted its present name.

The church is conservative in its interpretation of the Wesleyan tradition. Its members believe in the verbal inspiration of the Bible, i.e., the inspiration of each word, and they also await the premillennial return of Jesus, i.e., his return to earth to bind Satan before his millennial (thousand year) reign on earth with his saints. Bible Protestants think Satan exists as a person, and they ascribe to the bodily resurrection of the dead and the eternal conscious punishment of the wicked. They separate themselves from people who do not share their same understanding of orthodox Christianity.

The polity is similar to that of the former Methodist Protestant Church with the exception that the general conference is no longer in existence. There is one annual conference in which authority is vested. Local congregations are autonomous but freely accept the fellowship's standards.

Conference grounds have been located at Port Jervis, New York. Bible Protestant Mission, Inc., has work in Japan, the Philippine Islands, Mexico, and at Seabrook Farm, Bridgeton, New Jersey. The church is a member of the American Council of Christian Churches.

Membership: In 1984 the church had 31 churches, 1,840 members, and 52 ministers.

Periodicals: *Bible Protestant Messenger*, Rd 1, Box 12, Port Jarvis, NY 12771

★224★
FILIPINO COMMUNITY CHURCHES
Current address not obtained for this edition.

The Filipino Community Churches of Hawaii began when the Rev. N. C. Dizon, a Methodist minister, went to Hawaii after World War I to establish a mission. In 1927 he withdrew from the Methodist church and formed the First Filipino Community Church at Honolulu. In 1957 a congregation was added at Wahiawa, and a congregation in Hilo is informally associated. Joseph H. Dizon became pastor of the headquarters church in Honolulu. Its membership consists almost entirely of Filipino-Americans.

Membership: Not reported.

★225★
FIRST CONGREGATIONAL METHODIST CHURCH OF THE U.S.A.
Decatur, MS 39327

The First Congregational Methodist Church of the U.S.A. was formed by members of the Congregational Methodist Church who withdrew from that body in 1941. Disagreement had arisen about the addition in 1933 of Articles of Religion on regeneration and sanctification and paragraphs on the duty of pastors' collecting superannuate funds (for retired ministers), ladies' work, youth work, trials of ministers charged with misconduct, and the prohibition of special sessions of the general conference called to reverse action of a regular session. Following eight years of conflict, Rev. J. A. Cook, then president of the General Conference, led a segment of the church to withdraw immediately after the 1941 General Conference, at which a two-thirds majority approved adding the articles and paragraphs in dispute.

The new body adopted the pre-1933 *Discipline* and followed essentially the polity and doctrine of the parent body.

Membership: Not reported. In 1954 the Church had 7,500 members in 100 congregations, all in the South.

★226★
FUNDAMENTAL METHODIST CHURCH
1034 N. Broadway
Springfield, MO 65802

The Fundamental Methodist Church was formed by former members of the Methodist Protestant Church who withdrew from the Methodist Church (1939-1968) following the union in 1939. The schism began with John's Chapel Church in Missouri on August 27, 1942, under the leadership of Rev. Roy Keith. Two years later, after having been joined by other congregations, they established an organization.

The church is both congregational and connectional in polity. It is congregational in that the local congregations associate with each other as free and autonomous bodies, and retain the power to hold property and call (appoint) pastors. They are connectional in that their General Conference is the highest legislative body in the church. It is composed of one lay delegate and one minister from each church.

The Fundamental Methodists are fundamentalists theologically. They are members of the American Council of Christian Churches, Bible Methodist Missions, and the International Fellowship of Bible Methodists. They cooperate with other independent fundamentalist Methodist groups in a variety of activities. They are also one of the few Methodist groups to retain the class meeting structure devised by John Wesley, the founder of Methodism. He divided the early societies (congregations) into classes of about twelve members and a class leader. The classes met weekly for mutual discussion, exhortation, prayer, confession and forgiveness, Bible study, and growing in grace. Each person tried to bring to the class a penny a week to help the poor. It is said that some early class leaders supplied the penny for the class member who could not afford to make the contribution.

Membership: Not reported. In 1975 there were 15 churches, 19 ministers, and 745 members. The church supports a mission in Matamoros, Mexico.

Periodicals: *The Evangelical Methodist*, Street, MD 21154 (with the Evangelical Methodist Church of America).

Sources: Roy Keith and Carol Willoughby, eds., *History and Discipline of the Faith and Practice*. Springfield, MO; The Fundamental Methodist Church, 1964.

★227★
JOHN WESLEY FELLOWSHIP AND THE FRANCIS ASBURY SOCIETY OF MINISTERS
Current address not obtained for this edition.

The John Wesley Fellowship and the Francis Asbury Society of Ministers are two structures formed by former ministers and members of the Southern Methodist Church in 1971 following the Southern Methodist Church's withdrawal from the ultra-fundamentalist American Council of Christian Churches. The John Wesley Fellowship is a loose fellowship of independent congregations, and the Francis Asbury Society of Ministers is an association of pastors. While officially two separate organizations, ministers of the Society serve churches of the Fellowship.

The Society has added to the twenty-five Articles of Religion (printed earlier in this chapter) statements on the Bible as the Word of God (an affirmation not specifically made in the original article on the sufficiency of Scripture), separation from apostasy, and the premillennial return of Jesus. *The Guidelines for Independent Methodist Churches*, published by Rev. Thomas L. Baird, serves unoffically as a discipline for the congregations. Beyond the Articles of Religion are seventeen statements which make a significant departure from Wesleyan emphases. The statement on the church defines the invisible church as all who are known of Christ, "Whether they have joined the visible church or not." The premillennial return of Christ, segregation of the races, and the impossibility of

back sliders to be reclaimed (based on Hebrew 6:4-6) are all affirmed. The church has only white members.

The Francis Asbury Society began publication of the *Francis Asbury Society Evangel* in 1971. Both the Society and Fellowship cooperate with Bible Methodist Missions organized by the Evangelical Methodist Church of America. Maranath School of Theology, also sponsored by the Evangelical Methodist Church of America, and Bob Jones University are recommended schools. The Society and Fellowship belong to the American Council of Christian Churches.

Membership: Not reported.

Periodicals: *Francis Asbury Society Bulletin*.

Sources: Thomas L. Baird, ed., *Guidelines for Independent Methodist Churches*. Colonial Heights, VA: The Author, 1971.

★228★
METHODIST PROTESTANT CHURCH
℅ Rev. F. E. Sellers
Monticello, MS 55362

The continuing Methodist Protestant Church was formed by ministers and members of the Mississippi Conference of the former Methodist Protestant Church who did not wish to join in the 1939 Methodist merger because of the liberalism of the newly formed church, The Methodist Church (1939-1968). They emphasize the Bible as the literal word of God, the indwelling of the Holy Spirit subsequent to regeneration (subsequent to being "born again"), and the premillennial return of Jesus Christ. All members of the church are white and believe that racial segregation best serves the interest of both blacks and whites. The church's motto is, "Earnestly contend for the faith which was once delivered to the saints."

The church has congregations in Mississippi, Alabama, Missouri, Louisiana, and Ohio, in three conferences. Mission work has been established in Korea and in two locations in British Honduras. A church camp is located at Collins, Mississippi. The Church is a member of the American Council of Christian Churches and the International Council of Christian Churches. It is not a member but cooperates with the Christian Holiness Association.

The government is a representative democracy modeled on the United States government. Equal representation is given laymen in all functions of the church. There are no bishops.

Membership: Not reported.

Educational facilities: Whitworth College, Brookhaven, MS.

★229★
NEW CONGREGATIONAL METHODIST CHURCH
% Bishop Joe E. Kelley
354 E. 9th St.
Jacksonville, FL 32206

Not a direct schism but related to the Congregational Methodist Church is the New Congregational Methodist Church. It was formed in 1881 by members of the Waresboro Mission and others involved in a rural church consolidation enforced by the Board of Domestic Missions of the Georgia Conference of the Methodist Episcopal Church, South. In protest of the consolidation, the group withdrew and formed the new body at Waycross, Georgia, using the constitution of the Congregational Methodist Church as a model. They adopted a loosely connectional system, rejecting particularly the system of annual conference assessments. They also baptized by immersion and allowed foot washing at communion.

An early period of growth was stopped by the death of several leaders and the withdrawal of a number of congregations who joined the Congregational Methodist Church. They have no connections with any ecumenical bodies.

Membership: Not reported. In 1967 there were 13 congregations (7 in Georgia and 6 in Florida).

★230★
PEOPLE'S METHODIST CHURCH
Current address not obtained for this edition.

The People's Methodist Church was formed in North Carolina by members of the Methodist Episcopal Church, South, who did not wish to join the Methodist merger of 1939. (That merger united the Methodist Episcopal Church, South, with the Methodist Episcopal Church and the Protestant Methodist Church.) The People's Methodist Church is conservative and stresses "the second blessing," an experience ratifying one's perfection in holiness.

Membership: Not reported.

Educational facilities: John Wesley Bible School, Greensboro, NC.

★231★
REFORMED NEW CONGREGATIONAL CHURCH
(Defunct)

The Reformed New Congregational Methodist Church was organized in 1916 by the Rev. J. A. Sander and the Rev. Earl Wilcoxen, a minister in the Congregational Methodist Church. A large following was built in southern Illinois and Indiana; however, no data has been located since 1936 when there were eight churches.

★232★
SOUTHERN METHODIST CHURCH
% Rev. W. Lynn Corbett
Box 132
Orangeburg, SC 29116-0132

The Southern Methodist Church was formed in 1934 by members of several congregations of the Methodist Episcopal Church, South, who did not wish to participate in the 1939 merger with the Methodist Episcopal Church. They felt that the Methodist Episcopal Church was apostate and full of heresy and infidelity and also that merger, forming The Methodist Church (1939-1968), would event uate in the racial integration of the annual conferences and churches. (That integration did occur.)

The withdrawing members, meeting in convocation at Columbia, South Carolina, set up plans to perpetuate what they considered to be the Methodist Episcopal Church, South. In attempting to retain local church property and the name "Methodist Episcopal Church, South," the group became the center of a series of landmark court decisions culminating in the mandate of Judge George Bell Timmerman on March 12, 1945. The group lost its case to the merged church, The Methodist Church. The bishops of The Methodist Church were legally established as representatives of the membership of the former Methodist Episcopal Church, South with control over property; and the name "Methodist Episcopal Church, South," was the property of its legal successor, The Methodist Church (now the United Methodist Church). The name Southern Methodist Church was then adopted by the withdrawing group.

The church adopted the Methodist Episcopal Articles of Religion printed earlier in this chapter. The church added statements of belief on prevenient grace (grace is shed abroad in the hearts of all), the witness of the Spirit, Christian perfection, and the evangelization of the world. It has also added statements on the creation account of Genesis, premillennialism, Satan and a lengthy statement on the continued segregation of the races. The church has only white members.

Departing from its episcopal heritage, the new body is congregational in polity. It has four annual conferences and a general conference, but it has dropped the office of district superintendent and replaced the bishop with a quadrennially elected president.

The Southern Methodist Church was a member of both the American Council of Christian Churches and International Council of Christian Churches but withdrew in 1971. Missions are supported in Cyprus, Italy, Mexico, Sri Lanka, Venezuela, and Zimbabwe.

Membership: In 1985, the church reported 150 congregations in four conferences covering territory from Virginia to Texas. There were 7,231 members and 94 ministers.

Educational facilities: Southern Methodist College, Orangeburg, SC.

Periodicals: *The Southern Methodist*, Foundry Press, Orangeburg, SC 29115.

Sources: *The Doctrines and Discipline of the Southern Methodist Church.* Orangeburg, SC: Foundry Press, 1970; Jerry Ballard, *To the Regions Beyond.* Orangeburg, SC: Board of Foreign Missions, the Southern Methodist Church, 1970.

Black Methodism

★233★
AFRICAN METHODIST EPISCOPAL CHURCH
500 8th Ave., S.
Nashville, TN 37203

A short time after the founding of the Methodist Episcopal Church in 1784, friction developed between the blacks and the whites of St. George's Church in Philadelphia. The situation was intensified by the erection of a gallery to which the blacks were relegated. The long-standing grievances came to a head on a Sunday morning in November 1787, when whites tried to pull several blacks from their knees at the altar rail. Richard Allen led the group of blacks out of the church, and they formed a church of their own.

Allen was a former slave whose master had been converted by Freeborn Garrettson (a Methodist preacher). His master allowed Allen to buy his freedom. As a freeman he became a prosperous businessman and a licensed Methodist preacher. After leaving St. George's, Allen purchased an abandoned blacksmith shop, and in 1744 Methodist Bishop Francis Asbury dedicated it as Bethel Church. In 1799 Allen was ordained a deacon, the first black so honored.

Differences continued between the leaders of Allen's Bethel Church and St. George's. The former wished to be independent but with a nominal relation to the Methodists. Finally, in 1816, the issues were settled in a court suit when Bethel was granted full independence.

In Baltimore, blacks at the two white churches formed an independent Colored Methodist Society after they had been put in galleries and not allowed to take communion until after the whites. In 1801 Daniel Coke arrived in Baltimore and took over the leadership of the Society. Through his work an independent Methodist Church, also named Bethel, was formed. A call was issued in 1816 for a national meeting of black Methodists for the purpose of forming an African Methodist Episcopal (AME) Church. The *Discipline*, Articles of Religion, and General Rules of the Methodist Episcopal Church were adopted, and Richard Allen was elected bishop. The AME Church remains close in doctrine, practice and polity to the United Methodist Church, the successor to the Methodist Episcopal Church, with whom it has engaged in some serious merger conversations.

Growth in the church throughout the North and Midwest was steady through 1865. After the Civil War a rapid expansion throughout the South occurred, and conferences were established across the territory of the former confederacy.

A missionary imperative was an e arly part of African Methodist concern, and in 1827 Scipio Bean was ordained as an elder and sent to Haiti. From that small beginning (and slow growth due to lack of funds), a twentieth-century mission program has emerged with stations in Africa, South America, and the West Indies. The primary work is with other people of African descent.

Publishing was seen as an integral part of the evangelistic, missionary and cultural life of the church from the beginning, and the items published by this church have had a major impact on the black community. The AME Book Concern was the first publishing house owned and operated by black people in America. *The Christian Recorder*, a newspaper begun as *The Christian Herald*, published continuously since 1841, is the oldest black periodical in the world; *The AME Review*, started in 1883, is the oldest magazine published by black people in the world. Education joined publishing as an early concern, and the first AME affiliated college, Wilberforce University, was established in 1856. Educational concerns have been carried to the mission field as well, and the church has established a number of schools from the primary grades through college for its African membership. West Africa Seminary was founded in Sierre Leone.

The church is governed episcopally. An international general conference meets quadrennially. The church is divided into 18 episcopal districts. Districts one through 13 oversee work in the United States, Canada, and Bermuda. The remaining districts oversee foreign work in 20 African countries, Jamaica, Haiti, the Dominican Republic, the Virgin Islands, the Windward Island, Guyana, and Surinam.

The church is a member of both the National Council of Churches and the World Council of Churches. Affiliated congregations in Barbados and the Caribbean are members of the Caribbean Conference of Churches.

Membership: In 1981 the church reported 2,210,000 members, 6,200 churches, and 6,550 ministers.

Educational facilities: Payne Theological Seminary, Wilberforce, Ohio; Wilberforce University, Wilberforce, Ohio; Allen University, Columbia, South Carolina; Paul Quinn College, Waco, Texas; Edward Waters College, Jacksonville, Florida; Morris Brown College, Atlanta Georgia; Kittrell College, Kittrell, North Carolina;

Shorter College, Little Rock, Arkansas; Campbell College, Jackson Mississippi; Payne University, Birmingham, Alabama; Western University, Quindaro, Kansas. In 1958 Turner Theological Seminary in Atlanta, Georgia joined three other schools to form the Interdenominational Theological Seminary, the largest complex for the education of black Christian ministers in the nation.

Periodicals: *A.M.E. Christian Recorder*, 500 8th Avenue South, Nashville, Tennessee 37203; *A.M.E. Review*, 468 Lincoln Drive, N.W., Atlanta, Georgia 30318; *The Voice of Missions*.

Sources: Andrew White, *Know Your Church Manual*. Nashville, TN: Division of Christian Education, African Methodist Episcopal Church, 1965; George A. Singleton, *The Romance of African Methodism*. New York: Exposition Press, 1952; Carol V. R. George, *Segregated Sabbaths*. New York: Oxford University Press, 1973; Richard Allen, *The Life Experience and Gospel Labors of the Rt. Rev. Richard Allen*. Nashville: Abindon Press, 1960; Joseph Gomez, *Polity of the African Methodist Episcopal Church*. Nashville: Division of Christian Education, African Methodist Episcopal Church, 1971; R. R. Wright, Jr., comp., *Encyclopedia of African Methodism*. Philadelphia, PA: The Book Concern of the AME Church, 1947; Howard D. Gregg, *History of the A M. E. Church*. Nashville, TN: A. M. E. Sunday School Union, 1980.

★234★

AFRICAN METHODIST EPISCOPAL ZION CHURCH
Box 23843
Charlotte, NC 28232

In the late 1790s a movement for independence among New York blacks was begun when a group petitioned Bishop Francis Asbury, the first bishop of the Methodist Episcopal Church, to let them hold separate meetings. They complained of not being allowed to preach or join the conference and itinerate. Asbury granted the request, and meetings were held immediately. In 1801 a charter was drawn up for the "African Methodist Episcopal Church (called Zion Church) of the City of New York." It was to be supplied with a minister from the white John's Street Church. Zion Church was thus assured of regular preaching and the sacraments.

In 1813 Zion Church split and Asbury Church was formed as a second black Methodist congregation. Both churches were being served by William Stillwell of John's Street Church in 1820, when Stillwell left the Methodist Episcopal Church with about 300 white members. Blacks, afraid of losing their property to the Methodist Episcopal Church, separated themselves from John's Street Church. They also voted not to join the African Methodist Episcopal Church. Several independent black churches in New Haven and Philadelphia petitioned them for

ministers. A *Discipline*, based upon the one of the Methodist Episcopal Church, was drawn up.

Several attempts at reconciliation were made, the most important being a petition to establish the several black congregations as an annual conference within the Methodist Episcopal Church. This request was refused, and the African Methodist Episcopal Zion (AMEZ) Church emerged. Ordination was accepted from William Stillwell, and in 1822 James Varick was elected the first superintendent.

Doctrinally, the AMEZ Church accepts the Twenty-five Articles of Religion common to Methodists and has an episcopal polity similar to the Methodist Episcopal Church. Church boards implement programs of the quadrennial General Conference. The Publishing House and Book Concern are located in the headquarters complex in Charlotte, North Carolina, and publish a complete line of church school material. The church is a member of both the National Council of Churches and the World Council of Churches.

Membership: In 1984 the church reported 1,202,229 members, 6,057 churches, and 6,275 ministers.

Educational facilities: Hood Theological Seminary, Salisbury, North Carolina; Livingston College, Salisbury, North Carolina; Clinton Junior College, Rock Hill, South Carolina; Lomax-Hannon Junior College, Greenville, Alabama.

Periodicals: *Star of Zion*, Box 31005, Charlotte, NC 28231; *Quarterly Review*, 1814 Tamarack St., N.W., Washington, DC 20012.

Sources: William J. Walls, *The African Methodist Episcopal Zion Church*. Charlotte, NC: The A.M.E. Zion Publishing House, 1974; David C. Bradley, *A History of the A.M.E. Zion Church*. Nashville: Parthenon Press, I, 1956. II, 1970.

★235★

AFRICAN UNION FIRST COLORED METHODIST PROTESTANT CHURCH
2611 N. Claymont St.
Wilmington, DE 19802

History. The origins of the African Union First Colored Methodist Protestant Church can be traced to 1813 and the formation of the Union Church of Africans, an event that present-day church leaders point to with pride. The Union Church of Africans was the first church in the United States to be originally organized by and afterward wholly under the care of black people.

The Union Church of Africans began in a series of disputes in the Asbury Methodist Episcopal Church, a congregation in Wilmington, Delaware. In 1905, black members under the leadership of Peter Spencer (1782-1843) and William Anderson (d. 1843) withdrew from what had been an integrated congregation, formed an all black congregation, Ezion Church, and erected a building. They cited as reasons for their departure the denial of religious privileges and lack of freedom in exercising their "spiritual gifts." The black members had been segregated in a balcony and made to take communion after white members.

While breaking with the local congregation, Ezion was still a part of the predominantly white Methodist Episcopal Church. However, in 1912, a conflict arose with the white minister who had been assigned to preach to both Wilmington's congregations. The conflict resulted in the minister's dismissing all of Ezion's trustees and class leaders. That action led to a court dispute that ended when the black members withdrew from the church. In 1913, they reorganized independently and elected Spencer and Anderson as their ministers. By 1837, there were 21 congregations.

In the generation after Spencer and Anderson, two events were most important. First, in 1850, a major schism occurred when a group arose in the Union Church that demanded the adoption of an episcopal polity. That group left to found the Union American Methodist Episcopal Church. The Union Church of Africans emerged from this struggle as the African Union Chruch. Then, after the Civil War, the church merged with the First Colored Methodist Protestant Church to form the present African Union First Colored Methodist Protestant Church.

The First Colored Methodist Protestant Church was formed about 1840 when members of the African Methodist Episcopal Chruch rejected episcopal leadership and reorganized along the principles of the Methodist Protestant Church, which included no episcopacy and lay representation of local preachers at the general conference. Since the Methodist Protestant Church was very similar to the African Union Church, they united in 1866.

Doctrine. The church accepts the commonly held articles of religion of United Methoidsm, but it has attached the Apostles Creed as the first article and deleted the article on "The Rulers of the United States." It has made a few changes in wording, for example, adding the words "and women" to the article on "The Church," which now reads, "The visible church is a congregation of faithful men and women."

Organization: The church is organized congregationally. Congregations are grouped into three districts: the Middle District, which includes New Jersey, Pennsylvania, New York, Delaware, and Canada; the Maryland District , which includes Maryland, the District of Columbia, Virginia, and all states south and southwest of Maryland; and the Southern and Western Missionary District, which includes all the southern and western states. A general conference meets quadrennially.

In 1966, the church moved to replace the titles of general president and general vice president, the two offices elected by the General Conference, with that of senior bishop and junior bishop. In 1971, the office of presiding elder of the combined districts of the church was created, and a second presiding elder was named in 1979.

There is no foreign mission work, and the home mission work is primarily the providence of the women.

Membership: In 1988, the church reported 6,500 members in 35 congregations served by 50 ministers. There was no membership reported in Canada.

Educational facilities: AU School of Religion, Wilmington, Delaware.

Sources: Lewis V. Baldwin, *"Invisible" Strands in African Methodism*. Metuchen, NJ: Scarecrow Press, 1983; Daniel James Russell, *History of the African Union Methodist Portestant Church*. Philadelphia: Union Star Book and Job Printing and Publishing House, 1920.

★236★
CHRISTIAN METHODIST EPISCOPAL CHURCH
564 Frank Ave.
Memphis, TN 38101

From 1844 until the end of the Civil War, slaves formed a large percentage of the membership of the Methodist Episcopal Church. In South Carolina they were in the majority. The proselytizing activity of both the African Methodist Episcopal Church and the African Methodist Episcopal Zion Church claimed many of these former slaves as soon as they were free; others remained with the Methodist Episcopal Church, South (MEC,S), the southern branch of the Methodist Episcopal Church which had split in 1844. Many white Methodists felt that given the blacks' new freedom, a new relationshp must follow. In 1870, following the wishes of their black members, the Methodist Episcopal Church, South helped them form a separate church named the Colored Methodist Episcopal Church (CME). In 1954 the church changed its name to the Christian Methodist Episcopal Church.

At the first General Conference nine annual conferences were designated, the *Discipline* of the MEC,S adopted with necessary changes, a publishing house established, and a periodical, *The Christian Index*, begun. Two MEC,S bishops ordained two colored Methodist Episcopal bishops. Throughout its history the Colored Methodist Episcopal Church has been aided financially in its program by the MEC,S and its successor bodies. Today, the church is very similiar to the United Methodist Church in belief and practice.

One of the keys to Colored Methodist Episcopal success was the 41-year episcopate of Isaac Lane. Besides traveling widely and bolstering the poverty-ridden church, he initiated the educational program by founding the CME High School, now (Lane College) in 1882. Education of former slaves and their children, a major enterprise of all Methodists, has been carried through the CME Church in the establishment of a number of schools across the South. Paine College, established MEC,S has been a traditional focus of CME and MEC,S. Growth and expansion beyond the 200,000 initial members was slowed by lack of funds. Movement northward followed the major migration of blacks into northern urban centers in the early twentieth century.

The CME Church is a member of both the National Council of Churches and the World Council of Churches.

Membership: In 1983, the church reported 718,922 members, 2,340 churches, and 2,650 ministers.

Educational facilities: Lane College, Jackson Tennessee; Paine College, Augusta, Georgia; Miles College, Birmingham, Alabama; Mississippi Industrial College, Holly Springs, Mississippi; Texas College, Tyler, Texas. In 1959 Phillips School of Theology moved from Jackson, Tennessee to Atlanta Georgia to become part of the Interdenominational Theological Center, a complex of four theological schools, the largest educational facility in the nation for the training of black Christian ministers.

Periodicals: *Christian Index*, Box 665, Memphis, TN 38101.

Sources: Othal Hawthorne Lakey, *The Rise of Colored Methodism*. Dallas, TX: Crescendo Book Publications, 1972; Joseph A. Johnson, Jr., *Basic Christian Methodist Beliefs*. Shreveport, LA: Fourth Episcopal District Press, 1978; Horace C. Savage, *Life and Times of Bishop Isaac Lane*. Nashville, TN: National Publication Company, 1958; Eula Wallace Harris and Naomi Ruth Patterson, *Christian Methodist Episcopal Church Through the Years*. Jackson, TN: Christian Methodist Episcopal Church Publishing House, 1965.

★237★
FREE CHRISTIAN ZION CHURCH OF CHRIST
1315 Hutchingson
Nashville, AR 71852

The Free Christian Zion Church of Christ was formed on July 10, 1905, at Redemption, Arkansas, by the Rev. E. D. Brown, a conference missionary of the African Methodist Episcopal Zion Church. He and ministers from other Methodist churches objected to what they considered a taxing of the churches for support of an ecclesiastical system and believed that the primary concern of the church should be the care of the poor and needy.

The doctrine is Wesleyan and the polity Methodist with several minor alterations. The bishop, who is called the chief pastor, presides over the work and appoints the

ministers and church officers. Pastors and deacons are the local church officers. There are district evangelists to care for the unevangelized communities.

Membership: In 1965 there were 16,000 members in 60 churches.

Periodicals: *Zion Trumphet*.

★238★
REFORMED METHODIST UNION EPISCOPAL CHURCH
% Rt. Rev. Leroy Gethers
1136 Brody Ave.
Charleston, SC 20407

The Reformed Methodist Union Episcopal Church was formed in 1885 by members of the African Methodist Episcopal Church who withdrew after a dispute concerning the election of ministerial delegates to the Annual Conference. The Rev. William E. Johnson was elected the first president. A strong sentiment approving of the non-episcopal nature of the new church was expressed. However, in 1896, steps were taken to alter the polity, and in 1919 after the death of the Rev. Johnson, E. Russell Middleton was elected bishop. He was consecrated by the Rt. Rev. Peter F. Stevens of the Reformed Episcopal Church. Following Middleton's death, a second bishop was elected and consecrated by the laying on of hands of seven elders of the church.

Doctrine was taken from the Methodist Episcopal Church. The polity has moved in the episcopal direction and was fully adopted in 1916. Class meetings and love feasts are also retained. Class meetings are regular gatherings of small groups for exhortation, discussion, confession and forgiveness, Bible study, and prayer. Love feasts are informal services centering on holy communion but also including a light meal, singing, and a talk by the officiating minister.

Membership: In 1983 the church reported 3,800 members, 18 churches, and 33 ministers.

Sources: *The Doctrines and Discipline*. Charleston, SC: Reformed Methodist Union Episcopal Church, 1972.

★239★
REFORMED ZION UNION APOSTOLIC CHURCH
% Deacon James C. Feggins
416 South Hill Ave.
South Hill, VA 23970

The Reformed Zion Union Apostolic Church was founded by a group from the African Methodist Episcopal Church interested in setting up a religious organization "to aid in bringing about Christian Union, whose fruit will be Holiness unto the Lord." Led by the Rev. James Howell, the group met at Boydton, Virginia, in April 1869, and organized the Zion Union Apostolic Church with the Rev. Howell as the president. Harmony and growth prevailed until 1874, when changes in polity led to the election of the Rev. Howell as bishop with life tenure. Dissatisfaction with this action nearly destroyed the organization, even though Bishop Howell resigned. In 1882 a re-organization was effected, the four-year presidential structure reinstituted, and the present name adopted.

The representative conference structure is maintained with the law-making power invested in the quadrennial General Conference. Over the years the four-year presidency has again been dropped in favor of life-tenure bishops. A Board of Publication has control over church literature and prints the church school material and the *Union Searchlight*, a periodical.

Membership: Not reported. In 1965 the church reported 1,832 members and 27 churches.

Periodicals: *Union Searchlight*.

Sources: *General Rules and Discipline of the Reformed Zion Union Apostolic Church*. Norfolk, VA: Creecy's Good-Will Printery, 1966.

German Methodism

★240★
CHURCH OF THE UNITED BRETHREN IN CHRIST
% Bishop C. Ray Miller
302 Lake St.
Huntington, IN 46750

The United Brethren in Christ grew out of the German pietism and revivalism of such preachers as Philip Otterbein (of the German Reformed Church) and Martin Boehm (of the Mennonite Church), both of whom had been affected by Methodism and eighteenth-century Evangelicalism and who became the first bishops of the United Brethren. Their evangelistic efforts led to the formation of a church in 1800. Its earliest concentration of membership was in Maryland, Virginia, and eastern Pennsylvania.

In 1841 the United Brethren adopted its first constitution. During the next four decades the church was disrupted by the debate over the issues of freemasonry and membership in secret societies and pro rata representation and lay representation at General Conference. The crisis came to a head when the General Conference of 1889 was asked to ratify a new constitution which liberalized the rule against belonging to a secret society, allowed for pro rata and lay representation at General Conference and altered the Church's Confession of Faith.

The majority ratified the new constitution. They continued to exist as the United Brethren in Christ until

1946 when they merged with the Evangelical Church to form the Evangelical United Brethren which in turn merged in 1968 with The Methodist Church (1939-1968) to form the United Methodist Church. The minority objected both to the changes and the method of ratification which they felt were illegal. Bishop Milton L. Wright (father of the Wright brothers) led the minority in conserving the original United Brethren in Christ along the lines of an allegiance to the original constitution. The minority group tried to claim property, but was unsuccessful. They opened a new publishing house which moved to Huntington , Indiana, in 1897. *The Christian Conservator*, a paper which had supported their cause since its founding in 1885, was adopted as the official newspaper of the church. (In 1954 *The Christian Conservator* was combined with several other periodicals to become the present periodical, *The United Brethren*.)

The continuing minority adhered to the original constitution. They believe in the Trinity and the deity, humanity, and atonement of Christ. Observance of strict scriptural living is required of all members, who are fobidden the use of alcoholic beverages membership in secret societies, and participation in aggressive nondefensive war. Baptism and the Lord's Supper are observed as ordinances of the church.

Local, annual, and general conferences are held; the general conference meets quadrennially and is composed of ministers, district superintendents (presiding elders), general church officials, bishops, and lay delegates. Both men and women are eligible for the ministry and are ordained only once as elders. Missionary societies administer work in evangelism and church aid in the United States and on foreign fields in Sierra Leone, Jamaica, Honduras, Nicaraugua, and Hong Kong. Elementary and secondary schools have been opened in Honduras and Sierra Leone. A Bible Institute is operated by the church in Honduras and a Bible college, affiliated jointly with the Missionary Church, Wesleyan Church, and European Baptist Church, is supported in Sierre Leone.

Since 1974, the United Brethren have developed a close relationship with the Primitive Methodist Church and the Evangelical Congregational Church, and they work together with them in a federation arrangement. They share support of missionaries, publish church school literature, and hold seminars and consultations. The church is a member of the National Association of Evangelicals. The Sandusky Conference of the United Brethren is a member of the Christian Holiness Association.

Membership: In 1988 the church reported 25,983 members in 255 churches in the United States. There were 10 churches in Canada. Worldwide membership was 35,696.

Educational facilities: Huntington College Graduate School of Christian Ministries, Huntington, IN; Huntington College, Huntington, IN.

Periodicals: *The United Brethren*, 302 Lake St., Huntington, IN 46750.

★241★
EVANGELICAL CONGREGATIONAL CHURCH
100 W. Park Ave.
Box 186
Myerstown, PA 17067

The history of this church goes back to the 1894 schism in the Evangelical Association, now a constituent part of the United Methodist Church. The schismatic church took the name of the United Evangelical Church, and reunited with the parent body in 1922, when the two formed the Evangelical Church. The many deep scars created by the 1894 schism, however, were not all healed before the 1922 reunion. Therefore, as efforts toward the 1922 reunion progressed, voices of dissent were raised in the United Evangelical Church, opposing merger. Some United Evangelical Church members were still bitter over the loss of their church buildings to the Evangelical Association in court battles. By the 1920s, congregations of the United Evangelical Church had built new churches, which they did not want to share with or give to those who had taken their buildings in the court cases. After merger was voted, a special session of the East Pennsylvania Conference was called and a motion to refrain from merger passed, and the Evangelical Congregational Church formed. an independent anti-merger periodical, *The United Evangelical*, was taken over as a church organ. Former Bishop W. F. Heil was elected bishop and editor of the church paper.

Doctrinally the Evangelical Congregational Church is Arminian-Wesleyan, against the theory of p redestination and for the theory of free will, the belief that grace is available to all and all can exercise free will to accept grace. The church upholds the Twenty-five Articles of Religion adopted in 1894 by the United Evangelical Church. The polity is episcopal, but the churches are autonomous and the bishops' powers are strictly limited. There are two Annual Conferences divided into districts. Bishops and district superintendents are elected quadrennially. Ministers are appointed to their charges. Boards and Divisions implement the program of the General Conference.

Missions are located in Colombia, Surinam, Spain, Kenya, Japan, India, Zaire, France, Indonesia, New Guinea, Turkey, Philippines, Mexico, Austria, Malaysia, Germany, Australia, and Liberia. In the United States there are missions to the Jews, Latin Americans, and the mountain people in Kentucky. A retirement village is located near the headquarters complex at Myerstown.

In 1974 the Evangelical Congregational Church entered a federation agreement with the Primitive Methodist Church and the Church of the United Brethren in Christ which led to joint support of missionaries, shared production of church school literature and mutually supported conferences and seminars. The church is a member of the National Association of Evangelicals.

Membership: In 1985 the church reported 159 churches and 281 ministers. There were 35,584 members in the United States and more than 100,000 members worldwide.

Educational facilities: Evangelical School of Theology, Myerstown, PA.

Periodicals: *The United Evangelical*, Church Center Press, 100 W. Park Avenue, Myerstown, PA 17067.

★242★
UNITED CHRISTIAN CHURCH
℅ Elder Henry C. Heagy, Moderator
Lebanon R.D. 4
Lebanon County, PA 17042

The United Christian Church was the second schism of the United Brethren in Christ. Formed also during a war, this time the Civil War, some members felt that the voluntary bearing of firearms was wrong. They had interpreted certain resolutions of the East Pennsylvania Conference as justifying military service. The withdrawing group, led by George W. Hoffman, also opposed infant baptism, secret societies, and human slavery. The withdrawing group also dissented from the position of the United Brethren on the issue of human depravity. A long debate, lasting several years in the Church of the United Brethren, was highlighted by that church's decision to support the doctrine of total depravity in 1853 and to reaffirm its support of the doctrine in 1857. In 1857 reaffirmation became additional cause for the withdrawal of the people who formed the United Christian Church. (The 1857 reaffirmation statement had been adopted by the United Brethren by only one vote.)

Organization of the United Christian Church was informal for more than a decade; then in January 1877, at a meeting in Campbelltown, Pennsylvania, a Confession of Faith was adopted. The name was chosen the following year and a Constitution and Discipline in 1894. The *Discipline* of the 1841 United Brethren in Christ was accepted; the last revision was in 1947. Footwashing is one of the ordinances recognized.

Activities of the church include an annual camp meeting, services in prison and at homes for the elderly, direct support of a mission in Jamaica, and, through the Brethren in Christ, support of missions in Japan. An annual conference has the power to legislate for this small church body. The Church is a member of the National Association of Evangelicals.

Membership: In 1988 the church reported 11 churches, 12 ministers, and approximately 430 members.

Sources: *Origin, Doctrine, Constitution and Discipline of the United Christian Church.* Myerstown, PA: Church Center Press, 1950; *This We Believe.* N.p.: United Christian Church, 1978.

British Methodism

★243★
THE METHODIST CHURCH, CANADA
(Defunct)

(The Methodist Church, Canada no longer exists as a separate entity. It is now a constituent part of the United Church of Canada.) The Methodist Church, Canada (1884-1925) was formed by the merger of the Methodist Church of Canada with three smaller Methodist bodies, two of which had been transported to Canada by representatives of the various divisions of British Methodism (the Primitive Methodist Connection of Canada and the Bible Christian Church), the third a product of a schism within Canadian Methodism in 1833 (the Methodist Episcopal Church of Canada (1833-1884)). The Methodist Church of Canada was formed in 1874 by the merger of several Methodist bodies, the result of American and British Methodists who had completed their efforts to unite.

Methodism in Canada had been taken under the guidance and leadership of the Methodist Episcopal Church as soon as that church emerged as a separate entity in 1784. Itinerants were initially sent to Nova Scotia, but in 1791 William Losse was sent to Kingston, Ontario by the New York Conference and work developed in the Western Provinces under the New York and later the Genesee (Western New York) Conferences. In 1828 this work became independent as the Methodist Episcopal Church in Canada (1828-1833). In 1833 a merger of the Methodist Episcopal Church in Canada (1828-1833) and the British Wesleyan Connection, then still directly tied to the British headquarters, was accomplished. A minority of those formerly associated with the Methodist Episcopal Church in Canada (1828-1833) rejected the merger and reorganized as the Methodist Episcopal Church in Canada (1833-1884). They wanted an independent Canadian church, free of control from England, and they wanted to keep the episcopal polity. (The British had not developed an episcopacy as had the American Methodists.)

An initial conference of the dissenting ministers was held in 1834 and a general conference the following year at which a bishop was selected and the new jurisdiction formally organized. Since most of the meeting halls and members had been lost in the merger, the new church began with almost nothing, but by 1837 reported over 3,500 members. By 1843 there were over 8,000 members, and the single conference was divided into two

conferences. A third conference was designated in 1875. The Primitive Methodist Church of Canada had roots similar to those of the Primitive Methodist Church in the United States, begun in the 1820s. It grew out of the Primitive Methodist Connection in England, a group of Methodists attached to revival and camp meetings and generally known for the emotional displays at their gatherings. In 1829, at about the same time the Primitive Methodist Church began work in New York and Pennsylvania, William Lawson and his family arrived in Toronto. Lawson had been a local preacher in the Wesleyan Methodist Connection, but had been expelled and joined the Primitive Methodists. In Toronto, Lawson organized a class and preached to a small gathering. In 1830 Rev. William Watkins was sent from England to assist in the work. He was replaced a year later by William Summersides, one of the original missionaries sent to America. The Primitive Methodists in Canada formed their conference in 1854. Lawson became the first secretary. The church grew slowly but steadily through the next generation, but welcomed the prospect of union with the rest of Canadian Methodism.

The Bible Christians began in England in the second decade of the nineteenth century out of the work of William O'Bryan, a Methodist local preacher, who continually found himself at odds with his superiors and was twice expelled from the Wesleyan Connection for his operating outside of the discipline of the church. He was an effective preacher, and raised a following in some areas of Cornwall and Devon not otherwise touched by Methodism. O'Bryan organized the first Bible Christian society in October 1815. The first quarterly conference in January 1816 reported 11 societies in the fellowship. At the first conference of the Connection in 1819 16 male and 14 female itinerant preachers were reported, with a following of 2000.

In 1831 the Connection sent two missionaries to Canada to work among Cornish immigrants: John Hicks Eynon to Upper Canada and Francis Metherall to Prince Edward Island. From these small beginnings, other missionaries came and the church grew rapidly. There were over 1000 members at the first district meeting in 1844. The church slowly became self-supporting and by the time the Canadian conference was organized in 1855, had freed itself from British support. From the time of the formation of the conference until the merger in 1884, the church more than doubled its membership.

Membership: At the time of their merger in 1884, the four uniting churches reported as follows: Methodist Church in Canada, 128,644 members; Methodist Episcopal Church in Canada, 25,671 members; Primitive Methodist Church, 8,090 members; Bible Christian Church, 7,398 members.

Sources: Rupert Davies, A. Raymond George, Gordon Rupp, eds., *A History of the Methodist Church in Great Britain.* London: Epworth Press, 1978. Vol. II; J. E. Sanderson, *Methodism in Canada.* Toronto: William

Briggs, 1910. 2 Vols.; *Centennial of Canadian Methodism*. Toronto: William Briggs, 1891; Claris Edwin Silcox, *Church Union in Canada*. New York: Institute of Social and Religious Research, 1933; Thomas Shaw, *The Bible Christians, 1815-1907*. London: Epworth Press, 1965.

★244★

METHODIST CHURCH IN CANADA
(Defunct)

(The Methodist Church in Canada no longer exists as a separate entity. It is now a constituent part of the United Church of Canada.) The Methodist Church in Canada was formed in 1874 by the merger of the Wesleyan Conference of Eastern British North America, the Conference of the Wesleyan Methodist Church in Canada, and the Methodist New Connexion Church in Canada.

The Wesleyan Conference of Eastern British North America continued the earliest Methodist work in Canada. In 1772 a group of Methodists from Yorkshire settled in Cumberland County, Nova Scotia, an area familiar with revivals. In the 1780s it became the site of one initiated by Congregationalist minister Henry Alline, which had split the older Congregational churches and produced a set of rival Separatist congregations. Among the Methodists, 19-year-old William Black, Jr. emerged as a preacher who began to travel through the county and then all of Nova Scotia, organizing small groups of believers. In 1784 he traveled to Maryland to attend the founding conference of the Methodist Episcopal Church and to ask their assistance in the work he had begun. The prospects for Methodism in the Maritime Provinces were enhanced by the migration of many American colonists still loyal to the British government. The first conference was held in 1786.

The work in Nova Scotia and New Brunswick came under the care of the New York Conference of the Methodist Episcopal Church, which appointed ministers throughout the 1790s. However, these ministers experienced open rebuke for their disloyalty to the British government, and the last departed in 1799. That same year Black traveled to England and appealed to the Wesleyan Connexion for ministers. Four returned with him in 1800, others followed. The work spread through the Maritime Provinces. In 1790 a mission in Bermuda was inspired by the efforts of John Stephenson. Until 1855 the work was under the direct supervision of the English Wesleyans and was administered by its London Missionary committee. In that year the work was organized into affiliated conferences and designated the Wesleyan Methodist Connexion of Eastern British America. The British Connexion, besides continuing financial support, retained the right of ratifying the election of the conference president and vetoing actions of the conference. This relationship (tied to the British but independent of efforts further west) remained until 1874.

The Wesleyan Methodist Church in Canada originated with the movement of Methodism into what is today Quebec and Ontario (designated Upper and Lower Canada in the late 1700s). Methodist work began in 1780 with the arrival of a British officer by the name of Tuffey in Quebec. Tuffey was also a Methodist preacher. Six years later Major George Neal, also a Methodist preacher, began preaching in the Niagara area. Their work was taken into an area of Canada organized by former American colonists still loyal to the British government. Among the immigrants were Paul Heck and his wife Barbara Heck, loyalists who had been instrumental in the founding of Methodism in New York prior to the Revolution. They formed a class in Augusta (Ontario) in 1788. The first itinerant, William Losee, arrived in 1790, and in 1791 he led in the organization of a number of classes.

A decade later the Canadian work had grown to become a separate district. In 1810, western New York was separated from the New York Conference and designated the Genesee Conference. The Canadian work was transferred to the Genesee Conference and was also divided into two districts, Upper and Lower Canada. The work was disrupted during the War of 1812, when the area became a battlefield. After the war, the work resumed. The New England Conference developed two charges across the border in Quebec. In 1824 the General Conference separated the Canadian work from the Genesee Conference, and created a new Canada Conference. By this time many of the ministers, including leading minister and presiding elder Henry Ryan, were firmly convinced that full independence of the Canadian Methodists was in order. They worked for that independence during the next four years and in 1828 the General Conference granted it: the Canadian Conference became the Methodist Episcopal Church in Canada. No bishop was ever elected to head the church, which existed only five years.

As the War of 1812 was drawing to a close, the British Methodists appointed a missionary to Canada. John B. Strong arrived in Quebec in 1814 to begin the growth of a rival to the American-based effort. Its growth was augmented by the movement of many Methodists with anti-American sentiments into the new jurisdiction. Competition between and duplication of efforts by the two conferences were somewhat lessened in 1820, when a division of territory was agreed upon. The Americans concentrated on Upper Canada, the British on Lower Canada. In 1833, five years after the Methodist Episcopal Church conference had become independent, a merger between the two finalized. The new Canadian Wesleyan Conference remained in close relationship with the British Methodists, and its polity (which had no bishop) was accepted. The union proved unsatisfactory to many; those committed to an episcopal polity withdrew and formed the Methodist Episcopal Church in Canada (1833-1884).

Of intense concern after the 1833 merger was the reception by the British Methodists of Canadian government funds which were to be used to underwrite Indian missions and to stop the political activities of the Canadian Methodists. The Canadian Methodists were, on the other hand, opponents of state aid to religion. The issues led to a break between the groups in the 1840s. As that break proceeded, some independent efforts developed in Quebec as the Eastern District Meeting. This independent effort merged with the reunited Wesleyans to form the Wesleyan Methodist Church in Canada in 1854. That church continued until 1874. The Methodist New Connexion emerged after the death of John Wesley (1703-1791) in a dispute over the status of Methodism as a dissenting movement. Under Wesley and his immediate successors, Methodists considered themselves Anglicans. They would not schedule meetings to conflict with parish worship, advised their members to have their babies baptized by the local Anglican priest, and encouraged members to receive their sacrament at the local Church of England. William Thom (1751-1811) and Alexander Kilham (1762-1798) disagreed and argued that Methodism should become a dissenting movement and offer the sacraments directly to its members. They also argued for a variety of lay rights in the choice of class leaders (then exclusively the perogative of the preachers) and representation at the annual conference. In 1797 they led in the formation of the Methodist New Connexion.

The Methodist New Connexion Church in Canada began in the 1820s after a wealthy layman, William Ridgeway, visited it and reported its needs to the British Connexion. A short time later a retired minister settled there and began to preach. In 1832 Joseph Clementson traveled to Toronto, only to return and report on the continued needs of the population. Finally, in 1837 John Addyman was sent to formally institute a mission. He was followed two years later by Henry O. Crofts. The work made an immediate advance by its encounter and subsequent merger in 1841 with a small group, the Canadian Wesleyan Methodist Church.

The Canadian Wesleyan Methodist Church was formed in 1829 by Rev. Henry Ryan (1775-1833). Ryan had been a presiding elder working in Canada in the Genesee Conference of the Methodist Episcopal Church. After the War of 1812, he was among the loudest voices appealing for independence for Canadian Methodism from American control. Impatient with the slow process, Ryan became a severe critic of the conference, so much so that after independence was declared in 1828, he led a schismatic movement of several hundred members to the formation of the Canadian Wesleyan Methodist Church. It had grown to approximately 2,000 members when it united with the New Connexion.

The merged church became known as the Canadian Wesleyan Methodist New Connexion, with a direct link to the New Connexion Missionary Society in England through a superintendent appointed by the British leaders. In 1843 the Connexion absorbed the small body of Methodist Protestants, a Canadian conference affiliated with the Methodist Protestant Church which had been

organized in 1836. At that time the Methodist Protestants had less than 600 members. In 1864 the Connexion changed its name to the Methodist New Connexion Church in Canada, the name it carried into the union of 1874.

In 1884, the Methodist Church of Canada merged with the Bible Christian Church, the Methodist Episcopal Church in Canada, and the Primitive Methodist Church in Canada to become the Methodist Church, Canada.

Sources: *Centennial of Canadian Methodism*. Toronto: William Briggs, 1891; J. E. Sanderson, *The First Century of Methodism in Canada*. Toronto: William Briggs, 1908. 2 Vols.; Rupert Davies, A. Raymond George, and Gordon Rupp, eds., *A History of the Methodist Church in Great Britain*. London: Epworth Press, 1978. Vol II; Claris Edwin Silcox, *Church Union in Canada*. New York: Institute of Social and Religious Research, 1933.

★245★
PRIMITIVE METHODIST CHURCH
40 E. Northampton St.
Wilkes-Barre, PA 18702

The Primitive Methodist Church is one of the two Methodist bodies in the United States which does not trace its history to the Methodist Episcopal Church, an American church, but to the British Wesleyan Methodist tradition. The Primitive Methodist Church grew from the work of two English ministers, the Revs. Hugh Bourne and William Clowes. They had been influenced by a somewhat eccentric American Methodist minister, Lorenzo Dow, who had gone to England and taken the idea and practice of camp meetings with him. Out of their evangelistic efforts and new church itself developed in England. Connecticut-born Dow became a successful preacher among various British schismatic groups: independent Protestants and schismatic Methodists. Dow's desire to promote American frontier camp meetings in England caused many to condemn him, but others accepted him warmly, particularly Broune and Cowles. At their request he held a camp meeting at Harriseahead, a gathering place for English Methodists of the Wesleyan Methodist Connection, Broune and Cowles were expelled from the Wesleyan Methodist Connection, and their expulsion led to the formation of the Primitive Methodist Church in 1811. The church accepted the polity of the Wesleyan Methodists and did not create bishops as did its American counterpart, but it did allow women into the ministry, an action unheard of in its day. By 1829, the call for ministers by Primitive Methodists who had migrated to the United States was heard. Four missionaries were sent--William Summersides, Thomas Morris, Ruth Watkins, and William Knowles. Growth was slow and confined to New York, New Jersey, Pennsylvania, and Connecticut. In 1840 the American group separated itself from its British parent but kept fraternal relations. Growth increased, particularly in the Pennsylvania coal fields. In 1842 a Primitive Methodist

Church was founded in Galena, Illinois, and became the base for a second conference in the Midwest. The two conferences existed in close relation but operated autonomously until 1889 when the General Conference was organized.

The Primitive Methodist Conference meets annually and is both the administrative and legislative body for the church. It has direct oversight of all the boards and committees. As of 1984, there were six districts: Eastern, Wyoming, Schuylkill, Pittsburgh, Western, and Florida. They provide administrative guidance along with the district and local church quarterly conference. The Conference is presided over by the president, who is elected to a four-year term. There is equal representation of clergy and laity at all levels of administration. There is one fulltime officer--the Executive Director, who is in charge of promotion of the denomination. Mission work is carried on in Spain and Guatemala.

The church is a member of the National Association of Evangelicals and though not a member cooperates with the Christian Holiness Association. In 1974 it entered into a federation agreement with the Evangelical Congregational Church and the Church of the United Brethren in Christ which had led to the mutual support of church conferences and seminars, missionary activities, and the production of church school material.

Membership: In 1984 there were 85 churches, 9,617 members, and 109 ministers.

Periodicals: *The Primitive Methodist Journal,* 4 Longmeadow Drive, R.D. 2, Straatsburg, NY 12580.

Sources: Julia Stewart Werner, *The Primitive Connection.* Madison: University of Wisconsin Press, 1984; *Primary Helps and Biblical Instruction for Primitive Methodists.* N.p.: (1958); Paul R. Wert, J. Allan Ranck, and William C. F. Hayes, *The Christian Way.* Dayton: The Otterbein Press, 1950.

★246★
UNITED WESLEYAN METHODIST CHURCH OF AMERICA
% Rev. David S. Bruno
270 W. 126th St.
New York, NY 10027

The United Wesleyan Methodist Church of America was formed in 1905 by Methodists who immigrated to the United States from the West Indies and wished to carry on the tradition of the Methodist Church in the Caribbean and the Americas, a Wesleyan church with historical ties to British Methodists. Their doctrine is Wesleyan, and their polity is like its West Indian counterpart (nonepiscopal). A general conference meets biennially. In 1976 the Methodist Church in the Caribbean and the Americas entered into a concordant with the United Methodist Church which aligned their work and led to a number of jointly sponsored projects in the Islands. The church is a member of both the World Council of Churches and the Caribbean Conference of Churches.

Membership: In 1978 there were 4 congregations, all in New York City. In 1982, the church in the West Indies reported 68,898 members.

Sources: Lisa Bessil-Watson, comp., *Handbook of the Churches in the Caribbean.* Bridgetown, Barbados: The Cedar Press, 1982.

Section 6

Holiness Family

An historical essay on this family is provided beginning on page 35.

Nineteenth Century Holiness

★247★

AMERICAN RESCUE WORKERS
% General Paul E. Martin, Commander-In-Chief
2827 Frankford Ave.
Philadelphia, PA 19134

The American Rescue Workers was formed in 1882 following a controversy between William Booth, founder of the Salvation Army, and Thomas E. Moore, who had been given the charter as head of the American branch of the Army. Moore felt that money raised in America should stay here and not be sent to England as Booth demanded. Booth disagreed, arguing that the work of the Army was worldwide, and no Salvationist should call any country his own. Moore and a number of the American officers withdrew from Booth and incorporated independently as the Salvation Army in America. In 1889 Moore left the American Salvation Army to become a Baptist minister and was succeeded by Col Richard Holz who almost immediately opened negotiations with Ballington Booth, William Booth's son who had been appointed head of those Salvationists in America still loyal to Booth. Before the year was over, an agreement was reached, and most of the officers returned to the parent organization. About 25 posts remained independent of the Booth organization and reorganized under Major Gratton. In 1896 they reincorporated as the American Salvation Army. Headquarters were established first in Mohawk and then in Saratoga Springs, New York. (It is of interest to note that in 1896, Ballington Booth left the Salvation Army to found the Volunteers of America.)

Gratton was succeeded as Commander-In-Chief by Staff Captain William Duffin, who remained in that post until 1948 and his death at the age of 86. During this period, the organization assumed its present name (1913) and later moved its headquarters to Philadelphia.

The American Rescue Workers are headed by their General and Commander-in-Chief. He is elected for a five-year term by the Grand Field Council. The Council also elects a Board of Managers who administer the ongoing affairs of the Workers. All properties are in the name of the national organization. Doctrinally, the American Rescue Workers are the same as the Salvation Army with the exception of practicing the sacraments of baptism and the Lord's Supper. They believe in equal rights for women, and in the organization's constitution the term "man" is understood to include women.

Membership: In 1984 the Workers reported 4,000 members in 45 centers, served by 200 ministers.

Periodicals: *The Rescue Herald*, 2827 Frankford Ave., Philadelphia, PA 19134.

Sources: *Ritual and Manual.* The American Rescue Workers, n.d.

★248★

ASSOCIATION OF FUNDAMENTAL MINISTERS AND CHURCHES
Current address not obtained for this edition.

The Association of Fundamental Ministers and Churches, Inc. was formed in 1931 by Reverend Fred Bruffett, Hallie Bruffett (his wife), Reverend Paul Bennett, Reverend George Fisher, and six other former ministers of the Church of God (Anderson, Indiana). Bennett had been disfellowshipped because of his fellowshipping with other churches. The Association believes that the new birth is the only necessity for fellowship.

Doctrine is like that of the Church of God (Anderson, Indiana). Healing is stressed and the ordinances are not emphasized. The Association meets annually and elects four officers to handle business affairs. There are 25 state conventions. Missions are conducted in Guatemala, Hong Kong, and Alaska.

Membership: Not reported.

Periodicals: *The Fundamental News.*

★249★
BIBLE FELLOWSHIP CHURCH
℅ Pastor W. B. Hottel
404 W. Main St.
Terre Hill, PA 17581

The Bible Fellowship Church was formed in 1947 by churches withdrawing from the Mennonite Brethren in Christ when the Brethren changed their name to the United Missionary Church and dropped all Mennonite connections. Members of the Bible Fellowship Church see themselves as continuing the tradition of the Mennonite Brethren in Christ and date their origin to 1883. Their doctrine follows that of the parent body. They abide by the Dort Confession of Faith (common to most Mennonites), but add statements on sanctification as a second work of grace received instantaneously (the uniquely "holiness" doctrine), divine healing, and the millennium. Baptism is by immersion.

All the churches of the Bible Fellowship Church are in Pennsylvania and are organized into two districts, each headed by a superintendent. There is an annual conference of the entire church. Polity is congregational. Mission work is supported in Colombia, Venezuela, Kenya, and Sweden. Recent statistics are not available.

Membership: Not reported. In 1966 there were 37 churches and 48 ministers.

★250★
BIBLE HOLINESS MOVEMENT
Box 223
Postal Station A
Vancouver, BC, Canada V6C 2M3

The Bible Holiness Movement, originally called the Bible Holiness Mission, was formed as a church in 1949. It grew out of the earlier work of William J. Wakefield. He and his wife had been Salvation Army officers. Upon their retirement as active officers, due to health, the Wakefields took charge of a city mission (an urban center for transients) in Vancouver, British Columbia. William Wakefield developed several doctrinal emphases distinct from those of the Salvation Army. For example, he believed the sacraments were real means of grace, not just symbolic ordinances. The Salvation Army does not practice the sacraments at all. The Wakefields directed the mission until Wakefield's death in 1947.

Wesley H. Wakefield succeeded his father, William, and formed the Bible Holiness Mission in 1949. The name changed to the Bible Holiness Movement in 1971. Wesley H. Wakefield continues to direct the church as its international leader.

Beliefs: The Bible Holiness Movement continues the traditional holiness theology passed to it from the Salvation Army. It affirms the authority of the Bible, the deity of Christ, and the necessity of a personal experience with Christ for the individual believer. For believers it also offers the hope of total sanctification and directs them to disciplined lives of love, evangelism, and social activism. Movement members are also exhorted to lives of simplicity and holiness, including total abstinence, and no affiliations with secret societies.

Organization: The movement is organized similarly to the Salvation Army. It is headed by its bishop-general, Wesley H. Wakefield. Members of both sexes and all races are admitted to all levels of ministerial leadership. Within its permanent structure there are committees on religious freedom and on racial equality.

From its Vancouver headquarters, the movement has an international outreach. Mission work began as a result of the circulation of movement material around the world. In some cases, people were converted as a result of reading literature, and in others, leaders of independent holiness churches overseas contacted the movement for affiliation. Currently, the church conducts work in Egypt, Ghana, Haiti, India, Kenya, Liberia, Malawi, Nigeria, the Philippines, South Korea, Uganda, and Zambia. Its ministry reaches 89 countries in 42 languages through literature, radio, and audio-cassettes. The movement belongs to the Christian Holiness Association, the Evangelical Fellowship of Canada, and the National Black Evangelical Association.

Membership: In 1988, the movement reported 418 members, 30 congregations, and 11 ministers in Canada and the United States. The two congregations in the United States are located in Phoenix, Arizona, and Kent, Washington. The international membership is 27,416.

Periodicals: *Truth on Fire*, Box 223, Postal Station A, Vancouver, BC, Canada V6C 2M3; *On the March*, Box 223, Postal Station A, Vancouver, BC, Canada V6C 2M3.

Sources: *Triumph with Christ.* Vancouver: The Bible Holiness Movement, 1984; Wesley H. Wakefield, *Bible Doctrine.*

★251★
THE CHRISTIAN AND MISSIONARY ALLIANCE
350 N. Highland Ave.
Nyack, NY 10960

The Christian and Missionary Alliance grew out of the work of the Reverend Albert Benjamin Simpson, a Presbyterian minister who was healed under the ministry of Episcopal minister Charles Cullis, who ran a summer campground at Old Orchard, Maine. Simpson left the Presbyterian Church and began an independent ministry that was both evangelistic and missionary in character. In 1887 two societies--the Christian Alliance for home work and the International Missionary Alliance for foreign missions--were begun by Simpson. In 1897 these two societies were united as The Christian and Missionary Alliance, the present name.

The Alliance tried to remain a mission agency and not become another denomination. However, congregations were established and institutions created, and the denominational character of the group was slowly accepted. Cooperation with other Christian bodies continues to be a major goal, however.

The organization is centered on the annual general council which enacts all legislation. The council, composed of delegates of the denomination's members, elects the board of managers and regulates the Alliance's affairs. As a polity there are no high-paid executives or officials. The use of un-Scriptural or undignified methods of money raising is avoided.

Simpson preached a simple doctrine, usually referred to as the four-fold gospel--Christ as Savior, Sanctifier, Sealer, and Coming King. The Christian and Missionary Alliance was among the first of the holiness churches to emphasize the role of spiritual healing in the Christian life. The mission thrust of the Christian and Missionary Alliance has carried its representatives all over the world. Current work is sustained in almost every area of the world and includes a variety of home missions.

Membership: In 1986 the Alliance reported 238,734 members, 1,785 churches, and 2,154 ordained ministers. There were 1,052,663 members worldwide in 53 countries. Work in Canada is coordinated from headquarters in Willowdale, Ontario.

Educational facilities: Nyack College and Alliance Theological Seminary, Nyack, New York; St. Paul Bible Institute, St. Paul, Minnesota; Simpson College and Simpson Graduate School, San Francisco, California; Toccoa Falls Bible College, Toccoa Falls, Georgia.

Periodicals: *Alliance Witness*, 350 N. Highland Ave., Nyack, NY 10960.

Sources: Albert B. Simpson, *The Four-fold Gospel*. Harrisburg, PA: Christian Publications, n.d.; Albert B. Simpson, *A Larger Christian Life*; Harrisburg, PA: Christian Publications, n.d.; *Manual*. New York: Christian and Missionary Alliance, 1965.

★252★
CHRISTIAN NATION CHURCH, U.S.A.
% Rev. Harvey Monjar, General Overseer
Box 142
South Lebanon, OH 45065

In 1892 eight young evangelists who called themselves "equality Evangelists" began to work in central Ohio. Their efforts met with success, and in 1895 the Christian Nation Church was incorporated at Marion, Ohio.

Doctrinally, the group is related to the Christian and Missionary Alliance, and preaches the four-fold gospel of its founder Albert Benjamin Simpson. It is very strict in forbidding worldly amusements, fashionable attire, Sabbath desecration, and divorce. Marriage with non-members is discouraged. Large families are encouraged as being divinely sanctioned.

The polity of the Christian Nation is congregational with district and annual conferences. The pastors' licenses are renewed annually. Camp meetings are an active part of the program.

Membership: In 1982 the Church reported 226 members, 5 churches and 18 ministers.

★253★
CHRIST'S SANCTIFIED HOLY CHURCH (LOUISIANA)
S. Cutting Ave. at E. Spencer St.
Jennings, LA 70546

In 1903 members of Christ's Sanctified Holy Church (South Carolina) came to West Lake, Louisiana, and proselytized a group of black people, who in 1904 organized the Colored Church South. Among the leaders were Dempsey Perkins, A. C. Mitchell, James Briller, Sr., and Leggie Pleasant. The church soon changed its name to Christ's Sanctified Holy Church Colored. Over the years the church members dropped the word "Colored" from their title and returned to using the same name as their parent body, Christ's Sanctified Holy Church. The parent body is white and has headquarters in South Carolina, whereas the church under discussion here is headquartered in Louisiana. Organization and doctrine are as in the parent body, except that the ministers in Christ's Sanctified Holy Church (Louisiana) are salaried.

Membership: Not reported. At last report (1957) there were 600 members in 30 churches.

★254★
CHRIST'S SANCTIFIED HOLY CHURCH (SOUTH CAROLINA)
Box 1376
CSHC Campgrounds and Home for the Aged
Perry, GA 31068

History. In the year 1887, Joseph Lynch, a member and class leader in the Methodist Episcopal Church, Chincoteague Island, Virginia, began to preach scriptural holiness, which at that time was in opposition to the direction being taken by the church. Following his conviction, he sought and obtained the experience of sanctification, the second blessing believed by holiness churches to make the believer perfect in love. Assisting him in his early labors was Sarah E. Collins. The resistance of the church to his preaching on this doctrine led Lynch and 58 members to withdraw from the church. In 1892, they established Christ's Sanctified Holy Church;

19 members operated as trustees and were designated Board No. 1. Succesors of Board No. 1 incorporated the church in Chatham County, Georgia, in 1932 . The trustee established auxiliary boards of extention (1938) and a general conference (1950) but reserved the corporate church affairs and management in the hands of Board No. 1.

Beliefs. Christ's Sanctified Holy Church is Trinitarian in its beliefs an centered upon the experience of sanctification. It recognizes one baptism of the Holy Spirt (Eph. 4:5) as sanctification, and hence does not practice water baptism. It also does not practice the Lord's Supper, believing that no act or ritual is necessary to establish a relationship between God and humans. The church is pacifist and believes that no person should take part in war. Clothing, demeanor, and decorum in worship is regulated. There are no paid ministers. Women share equal participation in all church functions.

Organization. Christ's Sanctified Holy Church has no individual membership nor a congregational form of internal governance. It is governed by a non-congregational trusteeship whereby the church corporation draws from various separate corporate church entities and associations of like religious faith who may gain recognition under prescribed religious qualifications. Congregations are entitled to representation on the governing boards and use of the church's physical facilities for religious worship. At Perry, Georgia, the church owns a campground, a place for internment, and a home for the aged.

Membership: In 1988, the church reported approximately 1,000 members, 17 congregations, and 17 ministers.

★255★
CHURCH OF GOD (ANDERSON, INDIANA)
Box 2420
Anderson, IN 46018

Daniel Warner, a minister of the General Eldership of the Churches of God in North America, now called the Church of God, General Council, was affected by the holiness movement. He became an ardent advocate of sanctification as a second work of grace. For that belief he was tried and expelled from the church. Warner argued that sanctification led to an identification of the invisible church with the visible church, the concrete embodiment of the spiritual body of Christ.

The new Church of God was organized in 1880 by Warner. Like its parent body, the Church of God has no creed, but it follows the holiness theological consensus. It believes in the inspiration of Scripture, the Trinity, the divinity of Jesus, the indwelling of the Holy Spirit, sin, repentance, and atonement in Christ. There is a distinctive eschatology. While the members look for the second coming of Christ, they hold that it has no connection with a millennial reign. The kingdom of God is here and now.

There will be a judgment day with reward for the righteous and punishment for the wicked.

Three ordinances, symbolic of acts of obedience and experience with Christ, are commonly practiced: baptism, the Lord's Supper, and footwashing. Baptism is by immersion. Footwashing is usually practiced on Maunday Thursday by separate groups of men and women. These symbolic acts are but highlights of a Christian life of stewardship and high moral and ethical conduct. Spiritual healing is practiced, as is tithing.

Warner's distinctive doctrine of the church led to a rejection of the presbyterial system. The church uses a congregational form of government as the form that allows only the authority of God to operate. No membership is held in a formal way: there is no formal initiation rite for members, and membership lists are not made. Beyond the local church there are state and regional associations, and each year a General Assembly is held in connection with the International Convention. Anderson, Indiana, is home to the church. Located there are its headquarters, college, theological school, and Warner Auditorium (site of the International Convention). There is an active outreach program conducted by the general church. The Christian Brotherhood Hour is heard over three hundred stations, including some Spanish-speaking stations. Missions are conducted in Kenya, Egypt, Lebanon, Greece, Switzerland, West Germany, Denmark, England and Ireland, India, Korea, Japan, and throughout Central and South America. Warner Press publishes many books, pamphlets and tracts, and most of the educational material used by the church. The church is a member of the National Association of Evangelicals, and many of its congregations are associated with the Christian Holiness Association.

Membership: No formal membership figures are kept, but an informal count is made periodically. In 1985 the church reported 185,593 members, 2,291 congregations, and 3,227 ministers. There are an additional 183,989 members worldwide.

Educational facilities: Anderson College, Anderson, IN; Warner Pacific College, Portland, OR; Gulf-Coast Bible College, Houston, TX.

Periodicals: *Vital Christianity*, % Warner Press, Box 2420, Anderson, IN 46018; *Leadership*, % Warner Press, Box 2420, Anderson, IN 46018; *Missions*, % Warner Press, Box 2420, Anderson, IN 46018.

Sources: Barry L. Callen, ed., *The First Century*. Anderson, IN: Warner Press, 1979. 2 vols.; Milburn H. Miller, *"Unto the Church of God"*. Anderson, IN: Warner Press, 1968; R. Eugene Sterner, *We Reach Our Hands in Fellowship*. Anderson, IN: Warner Press, 1960.

★256★
CHURCH OF GOD (GUTHRIE, OKLAHOMA)
% Faith Publishing House
7415 W. Monsur Ave.
Guthrie, OK 73044

The Church of God (Guthrie, Oklahoma) was formed by some ministers and laymen of the Church of God (Anderson, Indiana) who separated in 1910-/11 over what they felt had been compromises and changes in doctrine and practice, and drifting into worldliness. Among the new practices coming into the Church of God (Anderson, Indiana) were the segregation of the races and the wearing of neckties. In 1910 C. E. Orr began publishing *The Herald of Truth* in California, advocating the original position of Daniel S. Warner, founder of the Church of God (Anderson, Indiana). A movement supporting schism developed around Orr.

In doctrine and practice the Church of God (Guthrie, Oklahoma) is almost identical with the Church of God (Anderson, Indiana), but it is stricter in its practice of holiness and refusal to compromise with the world. Like the members of the parent body, the members of the Church of God (Guthrie, Oklahoma) believe in healing and reject the idea of a literal millennium.

In 1923 Fred Pruitt moved from New Mexico to Guthrie and began to print *Faith and Victory* which continues as the organ of the movement. Today from the Faith Publishing House, Lawrence D. Pruitt continues his father's work and also publishes many tracts and *The Beautiful Way*, a children's quarterly. A vigorous mission program is supported in the Philippines, Nigeria, Mexico, and India. A national camp meeting has been held each July since 1938. Lesser camp meetings are held across the United States and in Mexico and Canada.

Membership: Not reported.

Periodicals: *Faith and Victory*, % Faith Publishing House, 920 W. Monsur Avenue, Guthrie, OK 73044; *The Beautiful Way*, % Faith Publishing House, 920 W. Monsur Avenue, Guthrie, OK 73044.

Sources: Fred Pruitt, *Past, Present and Future of the Church*. Guthrie, OK: Faith Publishing House, n.d.; Daniel S. Warner, *The Church of God*. Guthrie, OK: Faith Publishing House, n.d.; S. O. Susag, *Personal Experiences*. Guthrie, OK: Faith Publishing House, 1976; S. L. Speck and H. M. Riggle, *Bible readings for Bible Students*. Guthrie, OK: Faith Publishing House, 1975.

★257★
CHURCH OF GOD (HOLINESS)
7415 Metcalf
Overland Park, KS 66204

History. The origin of the Church of God (Holiness) dates to the very beginning of the "come-out" crisis of the early 1880s, a movement whose leaders advocated coming out of the mainline Protestant churches in order to establish independent holiness congregations. The ideal of the one New Testament church, a divine institution headed by Christ, was opposed in their thinking to what they saw as denominational, man-made organizations. Thus local congregations organized in conformity to the New Testament ideal became the movement's immediate goal. The first independent congregations which were established served primarily those holiness people with no previous church (denominational) affiliation, but eventually included people leaving the older churches.

During the decades when holiness advocates had been welcome in the mainline denominations, holiness associations had formed. These were not churches, but simply groups loosely affiliated with the non-holiness churches. As the come-out movement intensified, these associations fell into disfavor among many holiness proponents. Among those most strongly affected by come-outism were members of the Southwestern Holiness Association covering the states of Kansas, Missouri and Iowa. By 1882 six ministers, leaders of the Association, had decided to withdraw from their parent denominational bodies as soon as it was convenient. A minister in the Methodist Episcopal Church, South, A. M. Kiergan, emerged as their leader and spearheaded the drive toward independent holiness congregations. The dominance of the come-outers in the Southwestern Holiness Association caused its dissolution in 1887 and the formation of a new church, the Independent Holiness People, the following year. In 1895 the name was changed to Church of God (known as Independent Holiness People). *The Good Way*, formerly serving the Southwestern Holiness Association, became the church newspaper.

Almost as soon as the church formed, two factions arose. One wanted complete local congregational sovereignty. The other said the elders should interpret doctrine and be spiritual rulers for the church, and should in turn be subject to a presbytery of elders. Kiergan and John P. Brooks, an early leader of the come-outers in Illinois, led the sovereignty faction. The crux of the issue was representation in the annual convention. In 1897 a "Declaration of Principles" was published by the sovereignty faction. The local sovereignty supporters wanted representation of the congregations at the annual meeting, and the others wanted the elders represented. Following the publication of the Declaration, the church split into the Independent Holiness People (sovereignty faction) and Unity Holiness People (elder faction). A reunion of the two factions was accomplished in 1922. The name of the reunited church is Church of God (Holiness). The new church merged with the Missionary Bands of the World, now a contituent part of the Wesleyan Church, but the merger fell through in 1938.

Beliefs. Four doctrines are central in the Church of God (Holiness)--the New Birth, Entire Sanctification, the one New Testament church, and the second coming followed by a literal millennium. The one New Testament church idea is a distinctive feature of the Church of God (Holiness). The doctrinal statement in the reunited church reads:

The New Testament Scriptures teach that there is one true Church, which is composed only of those who have savingly believed in the Lord Jesus Christ, and who willingly submit themselves to His divine order concerning the ministries of the Church through the instrumentalities of God--chosen elders and deacons, ordained in the Chruch by laying on of the hands of the presbytery. The attributes of the Church are unity, spirituality, visibility, and catholicity. (Matt. 16:18; Eph 4:4;Col. 1:18; I Tim. 3: 1-7; Titus 1:5).

The government of the Church of God (Holiness) is congregational, but a delegated annual convention has responsibility for the election of individuals to serve on the various boards of church-wide ministries. The board of publications oversees Herald and Banner Press, the churc's publishing house, which publishes the church magazine and a full line of church school materials, "The Way, Truth, & Life Series." The church has a worldwide missions program under the direction of the foreign Islands, England, Haiti, Jamaica, Mexico, and Nigeria. The home missions board is responsible for encouraging church extension ministries in the United States, including ethnic group ministries among native American Indians, Hispanic, Asian and Haitian immigrants, and blacks. Both the home and world mission programs are directed by an executive secretary who is appointed by their respective boards.

Membership: In 1988 the church reported 1,500 members and 120 congregations in the United States and a worldwide membership of 16,000.

Educational facilities: Kansas City College and Bible School, Overland Park, Kansas; Fort Scott Christian Heights, Fort Scott, Kansas; Holiness Bible School, Gravette, Arkansas; Kirksville Bible School, Kirksville, Missouri; Mount Zion Bible School, Ava, Missouri; Mountain State Christian School, Culloden, West Virginia; Overland Christian School, Overland Park, Kansas.

Periodicals: *The Church Herald and Holiness Banner*, Box 4060, Overland Park, KS 66204; *Regions Beyond*, Box 4711, Overland Park, Kansas 66204.

Sources: Clarence Eugene Cowen, *A History of the Church of God (Holiness)*. The Author, 1948; John P. Brooks, *The Divine Church*. El Dorado Springs, MO: Witt Printing Company, 1960.

★258★
CHURCH OF THE NAZARENE
6401 The Paseo
Kansas City, MO 64131

When the hostility of leaders in both the Methodist Episcopal Church and the Methodist Episcopal Church, South, the two denominations in which most holiness advocates were originally members, made the holiness people feel that a new church was their only option, small schisms began to occur. Independent congregations and holiness associations came into existence. By the turn of the century these smaller groups began to seek wider fellowship by way of mergers. The Church of the Nazarene is the product of a set of such mergers.

Phineas Bresee is looked upon as the founding father of the Church of the Nazarene. In 1895 Bresee, a former Methodist pastor, organized the First Church of the Nazarene, which superceded the Peniel Mission in Los Angeles, California, where he had been preaching for a year. Coincident with Bresee's efforts, the Association of Pentecostal Churches was formed in New York. In 1896 this group united with the Central Evangelical Association with member congregations primarily located in New England. In October, 1907, the Association of Pentecostal Churches and the First Church of the Nazarene merged to form the Pentecostal Church of the Nazarene. On October 13, 1908, the Holiness Church of Christ united with the Pentecostal Church of the Nazarene in their joint meeting at Pilot Point, Texas; they retained the name of the latter group. This date is accepted as the official beginning of the Church of the Nazarene. In 1915 the Pentecostal Church of Scotland united with the Pentecostal Church of the Nazarene.

In 1919 the word "Pentecostal" was dropped to avoid confusion with the "tongues" sects. Over the years other groups have united with the Church of the Nazarene, including the Laymen's Holiness Association (1922); the International Holiness Mission, an English group (1952); the Calvary Holiness Church, also English (1955); and the Gospel Workers Church of Canada (1958).

The Church of the Nazarene looks upon itself as firmly Wesleyan in doctrine and practice and keeps in essence the Articles of Religion and General Rules as sent to America by Methodist founder, John Wesley. The church has, however, added statements on the plenary inspiration of Scripture, regeneration, entire sanctification, divine healing, and eschatology and has changed completely Wesley's article on the church. The major emphasis is upon the entire sanctification subsequent to regeneration and the personal holiness of the believer.

Government in the groups which formed the Church of the Nazarene was of all types: congregational, representative, and episcopal. The final outcome was a representative government. The highest law-making body is the general assembly, composed equally of ministerial and lay delegates elected by the district assemblies. A general board, elected by the general assembly, has oversight of specialized general assembly concerns: evangelism, missions, publication, education, and ministerial benevolences. The general assembly, presided over by the general superintendents who are elected every four years, has final authority in all matters except changes in the constitution. Such changes must be voted upon by the district assemblies, as well as the general assembly. The district assembly orders the work of the district, having direct supervision over the local churches and ministers. The local church calls its pastor and conducts its own affairs in accordance with general asembly guidelines.

Missions began in what was to become the Church of the Nazarene as far back as 1897 when Mr. and Mrs. M. D. Wood, Miss Carrie Taylor, Miss Lillian Sprague, and Mr. F. P. Wiley sailed for India. The work has grown until, at present (1988), there are more than 85 countries with work under the direction of the Department of World Missions of the General Board.

Publishing began in the Church of the Nazarene in 1896 with the monthly *Nazarene Messenger*. Early in 1900, the Nazarene Publishing Company was founded to carry on the work of the growing denomination. After the 1908 mergers, plans were made to establish a centrally located Nazarene publishing house, which was done in 1911. The new publishing house—Beacon Hill Press in Kansas City, Missouri—is now the largest publisher of holiness literature in the world. The Church of the Nazarene is a member of the Christian Holiness Association and the National Association of Evangelicals.

Membership: In 1987 the church reported 5,232 churches in North America with 543,762 members in the United States and 10,260 members in Canada. There were 838,136 members worldwide.

Educational facilities: Nazarene Theological Seminary, Kansas City, Missouri; Southern Nazarene University, Bethany, Oklahoma; Eastern Nazarene College, Quincy, Massachusetts; Mid-America Nazarene College, Olathe, Kansas; Mount Vernon Nazarene College, Mt. Vernon, Ohio; Nazarene Bible College, Colorado Springs, Colorado; Northwest Nazarene College, Nampa, Idaho; Olivet Nazarene University, Kankakee, Illinois; Point Loma Nazarene College; San Diego, California; Trevecca Nazarene College, Nashville, Tennessee; Nazarene Indian Bible College, Albuquerque, New Mexico; Canadian Nazarene College, Winnipeg, Manitoba, Canada; British Isles Nazarene College, Manchester, England; Korea Nazarene Theological Seminary, Chonan City, Korea; Africa Nazarene Theological College, Forida, South Africa; Asia Pacific Nazarene Theological Seminary, Manila, Philippine Islands; Australasian Nazarene Bible College, Thronlands, Queensland, Australia; Luzon Nazarene Bible College, Baguio City, Philippine Islands; Caribbean Nazarene Theological Seminary, Port of Spain, Trinidad; European Nazarene Bible College, Schaffhausen, Switzerland; Indonesia Nazarene Bible College, Yogakarta, Indonesia; Japan Christian Junior College, Chiba Shi, Japan; Seminario e Instituto Biblico de Ingreja de Nazareno, Sao Paulo, Brazil; Seminario Nazareno de las Americas, San Jose, Costa Rica; Seminario Nazareno Mexicano, Mexico; Taowan Nazarene Theological Seminary, Taiwan, Republic of China; Visayan Nazarene Bible College, Cebu City, Philippine Islands.

Periodicals: *Herald of Holiness*, 6401 The Paseo, Kansas City, MO 64131; *World Mission*, 6401 The Paseo, Kansas City, MO 64131.

Sources: M. E. Redford, *The Rise of the Church of the Nazarene*. Kansas City, MO: Beacon Hill Press, 1948; Ross E, Price, *Nazarene Manifesto*. Kansas City, MO: Beacon Hill Press, 1968; E. A. Girvin, *Phineas F. Bresee: A Prince in Israel*. Kansas City, MO: Pentecostal Nazarene Publishing House, 1916; Timothy Smith, *Called Unto Holiness*. Kansas City, MO: Nazarene Publishing House, 1962; W. T. Purkiser, *Called Unto Holiness, II*. Kansas City, MO: Nazarene Publishing House, 1983; Donald P. Brickley, *Man of the Morning*. Kansas City, MO: Nazarene Publishing House, 1960.

★259★
CHURCHES OF GOD (INDEPENDENT HOLINESS PEOPLE)
1225 E. First St.
Fort Scott, KS 66701

In 1922 the Church of God (Independent Holiness People) and the Church of God (Unity Holiness People) united to become the Church of God (Holiness). However, some members of the Church of God (Independent Holiness People), those often referred to as the sovreignty faction and most committed to the strong sovreignty of the local congregation, did not join the merger. They reorganized and established headquarters at Ft. Scott, Kansas. The continuing church has no doctrinal differences with the Church of God (Holiness), only distinctive by its firm allegiance to a congregational government. The church has stanchly advocated a pacifist position and has annually at its conventions passed resolutions against Christian participation in war. Membership is concentrated in the Southwest. Missionary work is conducted in Japan and Mexico and among American Indians in South Dakota and Wyoming.

Membership: Not reported. In 1972, 15 churches were represented at the annual convention.

Periodicals: *The Church Advocate and Good Way*, 1225 E. First St., Fort Scott, KS 66701.

★260★
EMMANUEL ASSOCIATION
West Cucharas at 27th St.
Colorado Springs, CO 80904

The Emmanuel Association was formed in 1937 by Ralph G. Finch, a former general superintendent of Foreign Missions of the Pilgrim Holiness Church, now a constituent part of the Wesleyan Church. The Emmanuel Association was run by Finch until his death in 1949. Now, the Association is run by the general conference made up of all ordained and licensed ministers. It establishes all rules and elects the officers. Local churches function under the general conference. There is also a provision for affiliated membership for both ministers and congregations.

Doctrine is like that of the Pilgrim Holiness Church, but with a very rigid behavior code, the "Principles of Holy Living." Members are conscientious objectors, believing that war is murder. Foreign missionary work is carried on in Guatemala.

Membership: Not reported. In the 1970 there were 17 churches in the United States and Canada and an estimated membership of 400.

Educational facilities: People's Bible College, Colorado Springs, CO.

Periodicals: *Emmanuel Herald*, W. Cucharas at 27th, Colorado Springs, CO 80904.

Sources: *The Guidebook of the Emmanuel Association.* Colorado Springs, CO: Emmanuel Association, 1966; *Ralph Goodrich French, the Man and His Mission.* Colorado Springs, CO: Emmanuel Press, 1967.

★261★
EVANGELICAL CHRISTIAN CHURCH
(WESLEYAN)
Box 277
Birdsboro, PA 19508

The Evangelical Christian Church (Wesleyan) was formed as an evangelistic endeavor by three men and two women known as the Heavenly Recruits, who were doing street preaching and conducting tent revivals and camp meetings in the Philadelphia area. The need for pastoral care for the many converts became pressing. In 1889 resolutions were passed calling for a presiding elder. Several crises led to the call for a centralized polity, and in 1894 C. W. Ruth was elected president. The name was changed in 1889 from the Heavenly Recruit Association to the Holiness Christian Association and finally to Holiness Christian Church in 1897. Work in Indiana as a separate conference and home missions in the West were begun as a prelude to moving the headquarters to Indiana. As the church spread, Ruth encountered the groups then merging into the Pentecostal Church of the Nazarene (later called

the Church of the Nazarene) and in 1908 took most of the Holiness Christian Church into the Pentecostal Church of the Nazarene. Then in 1919 the Holiness Christian Church voted to merge with the International Apostolic Holiness Church, now a constituent part of the Wesleyan Church. Only a remnant of the original Heavenly Recruits Association in eastern Pennsylvania remained out of the merger, but it slowly began to rebuild and is today the Evangelican Christian Church (Wesleyan). A periodical was begun in 1937.

The church is headed by a general superintendent. The conference of churches meets annually. Mission work is supported in Jamaica and Nigeria. The church is a member of the Christian Holiness Association.

Membership: In 1988 the church reported 1,300 members, 31 churches, and 41 ministers in the United States. There were 2,800 members worldwide.

Periodicals: *The Christian Messenger*, Box 227, Birsboro, PA 19508.

Sources: *The Manual of the Evangelical Christian Church (Wesleyan).* [Birdsboro, PA:Evangelical Christian Church (Wesleyan), 1987.

★262★
FAITH MISSION CHURCH
1813 26th St.
Bedford, IN 47421

Faith Mission Church is a single, independent, holiness congregation that was formed as a center of the Pentecostal Bands, one of the original holiness associations, later renamed the Missionary Bands of the World. In 1958, the Missionary Bands merged into the Wesleyan Methodist Church (now a constituent part of the Wesleyan Church). Members of the congregation in Bedford, Indiana, which had been originally chartered in the early 1920s, rejected the merger and became independent. Under their pastor, the Rev. Ray Snow, the church adopted its present name in 1963. The church is currently pastored by Leonard Sankey.

Membership: Faith Mission Church is an independent congregation that had approximately 100 members in 1988.

★263★
FIRE-BAPTIZED HOLINESS CHURCH
(WESLEYAN)
600 College Ave.
Independence, KS 67301

The Fire Baptized Holiness Church (Wesleyan) was established in 1890 by holiness people in the Methodist Episcopal Church of southeastern Kansas. The original name, the Southeast Kansas Fire Baptized Holiness

Association, was changed in 1945. The church is organized in an episcopal mode taken from the Methodist Episcopal Church. A general assembly meets annually. The Wesleyan holiness doctrine is emphasized, and strong prohibitions exist against alcohol, tobacco, drugs, secret societies, television, immodest clothing, jewelry, and frivolous ammusements. Members regularly tithe. The church is opposed to war and members are conscientious objectors. The church is aggressively evangelistic. Missions are supported on Grenada, Windward Islands.

Membership: In 1988 the church reported 1,200 members, 50 churches and 92 ministers in the United States.

Educational facilities: Independence Bible School, Independence, Kansas; Troy Holiness School Troy, Missouri; Holiness School, Afton, Oklahoma; Brothers School Grenada.

Periodicals: *The Flaming Sword*, 10th & Country Club Road, Independence, KS 67301; *John Three Sixteen*, 10th Street & Country Club Road, Independence KS 67301.

★264★
FREE METHODIST CHURCH OF NORTH AMERICA
901 College
Winina Lake, IN 46590

History. The Free Methodist Church of North America was organized in 1860 in western New York by ministers and lay people who had formerly been members of the Genesee Conference of the Methodist Episcopal Church. The Rev. Benjamin Titus Roberts (1823-1893) was the leader of the group and was elected general superintendent (later termed bishop). He and other leaders of the conference, both laity and clergy, had been expelled from the church for "insubordination." After an appeal of the case had been denied by the Methodist General Conference in 1860, those excommunicated men and others met to form a new Methodist institution.

Roberts and others had been calling the Methodists to return to what they considered to be the primitive doctrines and lifestyle of Methodism. They especially emphasized the Wesleyan teaching of the entire sanctification of life by means of grace through faith. In their writings and preaching they condemned with vigor their less radical brothers for worldliness and their departure from Methodist doctrine and experience. Because of their strong opposition to secret societies, the leaders of Free Methodism incurred the ill-will of members of the conference who held membership in such lodges and fraternal orders. Also, Roberts and most of his followers were radical abolitionists in the years immediately prior to the Civil War, at a time when many within the Methodist Episcopal Church were hesitant in their condemnation of the practice of slavery. Also important, the early Free Methodists condemned the growing practice of selling pews in Methodist churches

and advocated free pews for all, an issue which in part gave them their name.

Beliefs. The Free Methodist Church had little doctrinal quarrel with the Methodist Episcopal Church and orginally adopted a modified form of the 25 Articles of Religion. It added an article on entire sanctification and made a few minor changes. However, in 1974, an entirely new and expanded set of articles of religion were adopted by the church. Not only do they cover some issues not touched on in the earlier articles (such as eschatology), they have appended a lengthy set of biblical references which detail the scriptural underpinnings for each statement. The new articles do not in any way deviate in essential content from the earlier set.

From its beginning, the Free Methodist Church has made Christian holiness a significant distinctive of its teaching. The church has interpreted the Bible and the writings of John Wesley to teach that all Christian may be inwardly cleansed from sinful rebellion against God's will. It believes that the sanctification of the affections and will may be experienced instantly, in a moment of faith, when the wholly committed Christian accepts the atonement of Jesus Christ and the fullness of the Holy Spirit for the cleansing of his/her motives and the perfection of his/her love toward God and other persons. According to the church, the sanctification of life is a process of growth and development in holiness through the empowering of the Holy Spirit in the life of the Christian. The Free Methodist Church has endeavored to follow the teachings of Wesley regarding the sanctification of life by forming both general and special rules to guide Christians in the way of holiness. All adult members of the church covenant to refrain from any use of tobacco and alcoholic beverages. They promise to give a tithe of their income to benevolent and Christian causes. They vow to keep themselves free from membership in secret societies, that their loyalties may not be divided. They disavow all racism and political and social discrimination against ethnic minorities. They promise to regard marriage and the family as sacred, and they avoid divorce except for the cause of adultery or desertion.

Organization. The government of the church is a modified episcopacy. From the beginning, when lay leaders and ministers met to form the new denomination, provision was made for equal representation of clergy and laity in all the councils of the church, both local and general. A general conference meets every four to five years to review and establish the polity and programs of the denomination and to elect the bishops. Annual conferences bring together the ministers and delegated representatives of the local congregations in 36 districts in the United States and Canada. Pastors are appointed by the annual conference, with the bishop serving as chairman of a ministerial appointments committee. All church property is held in trust for the denomination.

The church is a member of both the Christian Holiness Association and the National Association of Evangelicals.

Membership: In 1987, the church reported 73,455 members, 1015 congregations, and 1,766 ministers in the United States. There were 123 congregations and 211 ministers in Canada. Worldwide membership including missions in 26 countries was 234,326.

Educational facilities: Aldersgate College, Moose Jaw, Saskatachewan; Central College, McPherson, Kansas; Greenville College, Greenville, Illinois; Roberts Wesleyan College, Rochester, New York; Seattle Pacific University, Seattle, Washington; Spring Arbor College, Spring Arbor, Michigan. The church is affiliated with Asbury Theological Seminary, Wilmore Kentucky and Western Theological Seminary, Portland, Oregon. It cooperates with, but does not sponsor, Azusa Pacific University, Azusa, California.

Periodicals: *Life and Light Magazine*, 901 College, Winona Lake, IN 46590; *The Missionary Tidings*, 901 College, Winona Lake, IN 46590; *The Free Methodist Pastor*, 901 College, Winona Lake, In 46590.

Sources: Leslie R. Marston, *From Age to Age a Living Witness*. Winona Lake, IN: Life and Light Press, 1960; William T. Hogue, *History of the Free Methodist Church*. Chicago: Free Methodist Publishing House, 1918. 2 Vols.; J. Paul Taylor, *Holiness, the Finished Foundation*. Winona Lake, IN: Life and Light Press, 1963; B. T. Roberts, *Holiness Teachings*. Salem, OH: H. E. Schmul, 1964.

★265★
INDEPENDENT HOLINESS CHURCH
% Rev. R. E. Votary, Gen. Supt.
Sydenham, ON, Canada K0H 2T0

The Independent Holiness Church dates to the preaching activity of Ralph Cecil Horner (1854-1921). Horner, a member of the Montreal conference of the Methodist Church, Canada, refused to assume his pastoral appointments during the 1890s, preferring to engage in evangelistic activity. He was committed to a holiness perspective (an emphasis upon God's second work of grace which brings sanctification or perfect love to the believer) at a time when sanctification as a progressive process was becoming the dominant perspective in Methodism. In 1895 Horner was discharged from his ministerial duties and formed the Holiness Movement Church. In 1919 the church asked Horner to retire. Instead, he left the Holiness Movement Church and formed the Standard Church of America.

In 1959 the Holiness Movement Church merged into the Free Methodist Church. As the time of the merger approached, several congregations voiced their disapproval by breaking away and reconstituting themselves as the Independent Holiness Church. The doctrinal statement is similar to other holiness bodies, affirming belief in the

Trinity, salvation in Christ, and the possibility of entire sanctification for every believer. Members are expected to live a holy life and give evidence of this by refraining from the use of alcohol, tobacco, and drugs, fasting once a week, avoiding worldly entertainments, and dressing modestly. The church promotes tithing and daily scripture reading and is against games of chance and secret societies. Divorce is frowned upon and remarriage after a divorce is not allowed within the voting membership. The church is congregational in organization and has a general conference which meets every two years.

Membership: In 1987 the church had 13 congregations (12 in Canada and one in the United States), and approximately 250 members.

Periodicals: *Gospel Tidings*, Wellesley, ON N0B 2T0.

★266★
METROPOLITAN CHURCH ASSOCIATION
323 Broad St.
Lake Geneva, WI 53147

The Metropolitan Church Association was formed in 1894. It grew out of a holiness revival at the Metropolitan Methodist Episcopal Church in Chicago. It was first known as the Metropolitan Holiness Church and adopted its present name in 1899. Members had a reputation for emotional displays at worship and ascetic behavior patterns. Early in its life, it adopted a communal form of organization, a factor which slowed its growth in the long run.

Besides its early emphasis upon inner city missions, foreign missions were begun around the globe. The one in India has been most productive, and a school and hospital are supported there. Other missions are supported in Mexico and in Cape Town and Swaziland (South Africa). There is an annual camp meeting for revival and fellowship, held since 1971 at the Salvation Army's Camp Wonderland at Camp Lake, Wisconsin. Business is conducted by an annual general assembly.

Membership: Not reported. In the 1970s there were 15 churches and approximately 400 members.

Periodicals: *The Burning Bush*, 323 Broad St., Lake Geneva, WI 53147.

Sources: G. W. Henry, *Shouting: Geniune and Spurious*. Chicago: Metropolitan Church Association, 1903.

★267★
MISSIONARY CHRISTIAN AND SOUL WINNING FELLOWSHIP
350 E. Market St.
Long Beach, CA 90805

The Missionary Christian and Soul Winning Fellowship was formed in 1957 by Reverend Lee Shelley, a minister of the Christian and Missionary Alliance. It continues the evangelistic and missionary interests of the Christian and Missionary Alliance, but its doctrinal statement has deleted any reference to healing, a particular interest of CMA founder, A. B. Simpson.

A missionary program has work in nineteen countries. In the United States there is a single congregation (Christian in Action Chapel) at Long Beach, California. A school provides vocational training for Christian workers. Within the United States a Jewish ministry in Los Angeles led by Abe Schneider is supported, as is an Apache Indian Mission.

Membership: There is a single congregation in California.

★268★
MISSIONARY CHURCH
3901 S. Wayne Ave.
Fort Wayne, IN 46807

The Missionary Church was formed in 1969 by the merger of the United Missionary Church and the Missionary Church Association. The Missionary Church Association was formed in 1898 at Berne, Indiana, by a group headed by J. E. Ramseyer. It was similar to the Christian and Missionary Alliance in both faith and practice. The United Missionary Church dates to an evangelistic effort in Lehigh County, Pennsylvania, among the Mennonites. In 1858 a conference formed using the name Evangelical Mennonites. In 1869 a Canadian Mennonite minister professed conversion after some years in the ministry and instituted protracted meetings in his effort to spread the new experience of grace. He was censured, but his movement spread and in 1874 took the name Reformed Mennonites. The next year they were joined by a small body called the New Mennonites and took the name United Mennonites. The United Mennonites and the Evangelical Mennonites merged in 1879 to form the United Evangelical Mennonites. This body merged with a small splinter of the River Brethren called the Brethren in Christ in 1883 to become the Mennonite Brethren in Christ. The change of name in 1947 to United Missionary Church was a recognition of its having moved away from its Mennonite background. In 1969 it merged with the Missionary Church Association to form the Missionary Church.

The Missionary Church Association generally followed the four-fold gospel emphasis presenting Christ as savior, sanctifier, healer, and coming king. This presentation of the gospel derived from the teachings of Albert Benjamin

Simpson, founder of the Christian and Missionary Alliance. Without moving from the truths so held, the Missionary Church has adopted a more comprehensive presentation of its evangelical, conservative and holiness faith. Government is congregational. A general conference meets every two years to elect a president and other officers. The Board of Overseas Missions has work in Brazil, the Dominican Republic, Ecuador, France, Haiti, India, Jamaica, Mexico, Nigeria, and Sierre Leone.

Membership: In 1985 the church reported 26,734 members, 303 churches, and 513 ministers in the United States and 6,431 members, 92 churches, and 129 ministers in CanadaIn addition, there were 24,098 baptized members and 18,038 adherents overseas.

Educational facilities: Bethel College, Mishawaka, Indiana; Fort Wayne Bible College, Fort Wayne, Indiana; Emmanuel Bible College, Kitchner, Ontario; Mountain View Bible College, Didsbury, Alberta.

Periodicals: *Emphasis*, 3901 South Wayne Street, Fort Wayne, IN 46807; *Catalyst*, 3901 South Wayne Street, Fort Wayne, IN 46807.

Sources: Eileen Lageer, *Merging Streams*. Elkhart, IN: Bethel Publishing Company, 1979.

★269★
MISSIONARY METHODIST CHURCH OF AMERICA
Rte. 7
Morganton, NC 28655

The Missionary Methodist Church was formed in 1913 in Forest City, North Carolina, by Reverend H. C. Sisk and four other former members of the Wesleyan Methodist Church. (The Wesleyan Methodist Church subsequently merged with the Pilgrim Holiness Church to form the Wesleyan Church.) The Missionary Methodist Church was originally called the Holiness Methodist Church, but the name was changed upon learning of another group with the same name. The original disagreement that led to the founding of the church was over the number of rules and regulations of the Wesleyan Methodist Church. A two-paragraph Creed includes belief in sanctification, which burns out all inbred sin; living every day above sin; keeping the self unspotted from the world; a personal devil; a literal, burning hell; and the premillennial return of Christ. "There are," states the Creed, "no hard man-made rules to bind one down, you can have freedom in the Missionary Methodist Church...." In 1939 the Oriental Missionary Society was adopted as the missionary agency of the church.

Membership: In 1984 the Church reported 1,708 members, 12 congregations, and 32 ministers.

Sources: *Doctrine, Creed and Rules for the Government of the Missionary Methodist Church of America.* (Morganville, NC): 1969.

★270★
NEW TESTAMENT CHURCH OF GOD
Box 611
Mountain Home, AR 72653

The New Testament Church of God, Inc. was founded in 1942 by G. W. Pendleton and Martha Pendleton, his wife, both former members of the Church of God (Anderson, Indiana). They opposed the Church of God's cooperation and financial support of the National Council of Churches, but kept the doctrines of the parent body. The members hold camp meetings and state and regional conventions, publish gospel literature, and have regular radio broadcasts.

Membership: Not reported. Congregations are found across the United States, but no membership count has been made.

Periodicals: *Seventh Trumpet,* Box 611, Mountain Home, AR 72653.

★271★
PENIEL MISSIONS
(Defunct)

The first Peniel Mission was founded by T. P. Ferguson and his wife Manie Ferguson in Los Angeles in 1886. Ferguson had been influenced by the preaching of Charles G. Finney, an early nineteenth century holiness theologian and evangelist. In 1880 he experienced sanctification under some holiness evangelists. Given the success of the Los Angeles work, he established rescue missions in the urban areas of the West Coast in attempts to win the urban masses to Christ. The missions have been marked by intense evangelistic endeavor, spiritual guidance, and stress on sanctification and sinlessness. For a short time, Phineas Bresee, founder of the Church of the Nazarene, worked at the Los Angeles center. By 1900 work had spread north along the West Coast and in Alaska, Hawaii, and Egypt. In 1949 responsibility for the Egyptian mission was assumed by the National Holiness Missionary Society, currently known as the World Gospel Mission, located in Winona Lake, Indiana.

Membership: Not reported.

Periodicals: *Peniel Herald.*

★272★
SALVATION ARMY
799 Bloomfield Ave.
Verona, NJ 07044

The Salvation Army is an international religious and charitable movement organized and operated on a quasi-military model. Its juxtaposition of two strong motivations, love of God and a practical concern for the needs of humanity, results in a ministry dedicated to preaching the Christian gospel and disseminating its teaching while actively supplying basic human necessities. It offers personal counseling and a program of spiritual regeneration and physical rehabilitation. This dual focus, and the passion with which it is carried out, have served in the secular community to make the Salvation Army at once a target of popular satire and one of the most respected agencies delivering social services to the community at large.

History: In 1865 William Booth, an independent Methodist minister, began to preach in the slums at the East End of London, England. He organized the East London Christian Mission and began a magazine, the *East London Evangelist.* The mission met a genuine need; within a few years it had spawned 12 others and began to reach beyond London. The name was changed to Christian Mission in 1868. As activities increased over the next decade, Booth began to see the need for a more disciplined core of workers to carry out the demanding program, and he started to think in terms of a "Salvation Army." Step by step the name of the mission was changed, the magazine became the *Salvationist,* the uniform was adopted, and Booth was transformed into "the General." Within two years the Army had spread through England.

As the work of the organization progressed, Booth became aware of the physical needs of the poor among whom the Army had been preaching. His broad investigation of their situation was published in a volume, now a classic of socially concerned Christianity, *In Darkest England and the Way Out* (1890). He proposed a total program of assistance and rehabilitation. This book set the emphases followed by the Army to this day.

The Army was brought to America in 1880 when Commissioner George Scott Railton and seven female officers, known as the "Seven Hallelujah Lassies," arrived in New York City. The Army was brought to Canada two years later by Jack Addie, a convert from Scottish Presbyterianism, and Joseph Ludgate, who started an open-air mission in London, Ontario.

Beliefs: The Army's program of social service has made it famous and respected by many who are quite unaware of its existence as a holiness church body. The Salvation Army was founded as an evangelical organization, dedicated to bringing people into a right relationship with God through Christ. It emphasizes a balanced ministry of social and spiritual work. Its doctrinal basis is that of the Wesleyan-Arminian tradition. It also holds that it is the privilege of believers to be "wholly sanctified." Distinctive to Salvationists is their belief about the sacraments. Salvationists have looked upon the whole of life, the Gospel proclaimed, and the ministry in Christ's name as sacramental, both to the receiver and the giver. Hence, the traditional sacraments of baptism and communion have not been considered by the Army as a necessity to salvation and spiritual growth.

Organization: The Army is organized on a military model. The international leader of the Salvation Army holds the rank of general and operates out of the international headquarters in London, England. The highest ranking officer in the United States is a commissioner. One commissioner serves in the capacity of a national commander over the four territorial headquarters, each operated by a commissioner as a territorial commander. Officers (ministers) begin with the rank of cadet and two years of training at one of the four officers' training schools. Upon graduation, the officer is commissioned (ordained) as a lieutenant and begins to rise in rank.

The Army also is distinguished by its early opening of the ranks of the ordained ministry to females. Catherine Booth, William Booth's wife, had actually been preaching in London before her husband joined her and wrote one of the earliest tracts defending an ordained female ministry. The American work was largely initiated by females. Females have served prominently at every rank and, as of 1988, the Army is headed by General Eva Burrows.

The social program of the Army has become one of the most far-reaching of any church organization. It includes feeding, and housing the homeless, disaster relief, alcohol and drug rehabilitation, youth camps and programs, senior citizen camps and programs, hospital and prison visitation, support for unwed mothers, to mention only a sample. These pioneering efforts have provided a model for many other churches.

Membership: In 1986, the Army reported 432,893 members, 10,591 corps (churches), and 5,301 officers in the United States. There were 565 centers and churches and 1,990 ministers in Canada. Affiliated centers were located in 87 countries.

Educational facilities: Salvation Army Schools for Officer Training, Suffern, New York; Chicago, Illinois; Atlanta, Georgis; Palos Verdes Estates, California.

Periodicals: *The War Cry*, 799 Bloomfield Ave., Verona, NJ 07044; *Young Salvationist*, 799 Bloomfield Ave., Verona, NJ 07044; *The Musician*, 799 Bloomfield Ave., Verona, NJ 07044.

Sources: Edward H. McKinley, *Marching to Glory*. New York: Harper & Row, 1980; Sallie Chesham, *Born to Battle*. Chicago: Rand McNally & Company, 1965; Robert Sandall, *The History of the Salvation Army*. London: Thomas Nelson, 1947; Milton S. Agnew, *Manual of Salvationism*. New York: The Salvation Army, 1968; Bernard Watson, *A Hundred Years' War*. London: Hodder and Stoughton, 1964; Cyril Barnes, *God's Army*. Elgin, IL: David C. Cook, 1968; *The Sacraments, the Salvationist's Viewpoint*. London: Salvationist Publishing and Supplies, 1960; Samuel Logan Brengle, *The Way of Holiness*. London: Salvationist Publishing and Supplies, 1960.

★273★
STANDARD CHURCH OF AMERICA
Box 488
Brockville, ON, Canada K6V 5V7

Ralph C. Horner had been an evangelist in both the Methodist Church in Canada and the Wesleyan Methodist Church, now a constituent part of the Wesleyan Church, in the late nineteenth century, but left them to found his own organization, the Holiness Movement Church, in 1895. As its bishop, he ruled with all the authority of both a bishop and charismatic personality, and within five years there were 118 places of worship. Churches were planted across Canada, into New York, with foreign work in Ireland, Egypt, and China. Then in 1918 the aging bishop was asked to retire. Not satisfied with the request of the church, he, with his supporters, left and founded the Standard Church of America, incorporated at Watertown, New York, in 1919. (The Holiness Movement Church eventually merged with the Free Methodist Church, which accounts for that church's large membership in Egypt.)

Like the Holiness Movement Church, the Standard Church of America is Methodist in doctrine with a strong emphasis on holiness and evangelism. Polity is episcopal. Pastors are stationed by the annual conferences for four-year terms. There are four conferences: Western, Kingston, New York, and Egyptian. A Bible School and printing establishment are maintained adjacent to the headquarters. There is missionary work in China and Egypt.

Membership: Not reported.

Educational facilities: Brockville Bible College, Brockville, Ontario, Canada.

Periodicals: *Christian Standard*, Brockville, Ontario, Canada.

★274★
UNDENOMINATIONAL CHURCH OF THE LORD
Current address not obtained for this edition.

The Undenominational Church of the Lord was founded at Placentia, California in 1918 by Pastor Jesse N. Blakeley, a holiness minister. Previously, he had helped form the Pentecost Pilgrim Church at Pasadena (which merged into what became the Pilgrim Holiness Church, now a constituent part of the Wesleyan Church). Blakeley became pastor of the Independent Holiness Mission in Placentia following a revival in Santa Ana. He felt the Holy Spirit leading him south and discovered the pastorless congregation in Placentia praying for the Lord to send them the right person. The Independent Holiness Mission became the Undenominational Church of the Lord.

A second branch of the church was founded in 1920 in Anaheim and became the headquarters. In 1922 the Placentia church was consolidated with the Anaheim church. In 1930 Blakeley was succeeded by Elsie Heughan, and in 1941 the headquarters returned to Placentia.

Doctrine of the Undenominational Church of the Lord is holiness. Evangelism, especially by the printed word, is emphasized. Mission churches have been established in Nigeria, India, and Korea, all of which are not autonomous. Though there are fewer than 100 members in the United States, there are many thousands in the foreign fields.

Membership: At last report (1970s) there were 3 congregations: Placentia, California; Chillicothe, Ohio; and Sheridan, Oregon. There were less than 100 members.

Periodicals: *The Second Comforter*, Box 291, Placentia, CA 92677.

★275★
VOLUNTEERS OF AMERICA
3813 N. Causeway Blvd.
Metairie, LA 70002

The Volunteers of America was formed in 1896 by Ballington Booth and Maud Booth, the son and daughter-in-law of William Booth. While very much like the Salvation Army from which it sprang, it differs in several ways; it is more democratic, though keeping the quasi-military organization; it practices both baptism and the Lord's Supper; the early emphasis on sanctification and holiness has lessened in favor of a more general evangelical faith.

Membership: In 1984 the Volunteers reported 70 centers served by 290 ministers.

Periodicals: *The Gazette*, 3813 N. Causeway Blvd., Metairie, LA 70002.

★276★
WESLEYAN CHURCH
Box 50434
Indianpolis, IN 46250-0434

The Wesleyan Church was formed in 1968 by the merger of the Wesleyan Methodist Church and Pilgrim Holiness Church. In the merger two diverse streams of holiness tradition (one pre-Civil War and the other from the late nineteenth century) were brought together.

The Wesleyan Methodist church had been formed in 1843 by ministers and laymen who withdrew from the Methodist Church during the height of the slavery controversy. Reverends Orange Scott, LeRoy Sunderland (later to join the Unitarian Association), and L. C. Matlock were all abolitionists who continually fought the compromise on the slavery issue made by the Methodist Episcopal Church in the early nineteenth century. (A note on that compromise: the eighteenth-century Methodist Episcopal Church did not allow any of its members to have slaves. Over the years, the church reneged on that strong anti-slavery position and allowed slaveholders to membership in the church.) Along with slavery, the reformers also began to attack the abuses of the episcopacy and the failure to teach and practice various forms of piety. By 1843 tension had reached such a level that, feeling no redress of grievances was possible, the reformers withdrew and took twenty-two ministers and 6,000 members and formed the Wesleyan Methodist Church in America. In the first *Discipline*, their book of church order, statements were made against slavery, against the use of alcohol and tobacco, against secret societies, and for modesty in dress. The new structure provided for annual conferences with lay delegates and an elected president (instead of a bishop). There was also a General Conference.

The Pilgrim Holiness Church grew out of the holiness movement of the late nineteenth century. Martin Wells Knapp, a former minister in the Methodist Episcopal Church, and Rev. Seth Cook Rees organized the International Holiness Union and Prayer League in 1897 in Cincinnati, Ohio. The Union was to be a fellowship, not a church. It was established as a completely Wesleyan movement with emphases on holiness, healing the sick, the premillennial coming of Christ, and evangelization. From a small beginning, rapid growth ensued, augmented by mergers with several other holiness bodies. In 1900 foreign missionary work was begun. The growth of the Union led to a change of character, and the fellowship became a church. It underwent several name changes, and 1922 finally took the name of the Pilgrim Holiness Church. The other holiness groups that merged with the Union (later called the Pilgrim Holiness Church) were the following (with merger dates): Indiana Conference of the Holiness Christian Church (1919); Pilgrim Church of California (1922); Pentecostal Rescue Mission (1922); Pentecostal Brethren in Christ (1924); People's Mission Church (1925); and Holiness Church of California (1946).

The Wesleyan church has a modified episcopal government headed by the general superintendent. The general conference is the supreme governing body and elects the general superintendent to four-year term(s). A General Board of Administration operates between general conference sessions. The church is divided into districts. Headquarters of the Wesleyan Church are in Marion, Indiana. The Wesleyan Publishing House located there is responsible for a wide range of books, religious literature, and church school material. The Commission on World Mission oversees a vast foreign mission program, including the work of the Africa Evangelistic Mission, an independent work in South Africa which was received into the Pilgrim Holiness Church in 1962.

Membership: In 1987 the church reported 110,241 members, 1714 churches, and 2,996 ministers in the United States. There were 81 congregations and 149 ministers in Canada. There were 185,641 members worldwide in 19 countries.

Educational facilities: Bartlesville Wesleyan College, Bartlesville, Oklahoma; Central Wesleyan College, Central, South Carolina; Houghton College, Houghton, New York; Marion College, Marion, Indiana; United Wesleyan College, Allentown, Pennsylvania; Wesleyan Seminary Foundation, Indianapolis, Indiana; Bethany Bible College, Sussex, British Columbia. In addition to the schools listed, the church also approves the ministerial training programs at: Asbury Theological Seminary, Wilmore, Kentucky; Evangelical School of Theology, Pine Grove, Pennsylvania; Nazarene Theological Seminary, Overland Park, Kansas; Wesley Biblical Seminary, Jackson, Mississippi; and Western Evangelical Seminary, Portland, Oregon.

Periodicals: *The Wesleyan Advocate*, Box 2000, Marion, IN 46592; *Wesleyan World*, Box 2000, Marion, IN 46592.

Sources: Ira Ford McLeister and Roy S. Nicholson, *History of the Wesleyan Methodist Church*. Marion, IN: Wesley Press, 1959; Paul Westphal Thomas and Paul William Thomas, *The Days of Our Pilgrimage*. Marion, IN: , 1976; Martin Wells Knapp, *Holiness Triumphant or Pearls from Patmos*. Cincinnati: God's Bible School Book Room, n.d.

Twentieth Century Holiness

★277★
CALVARY HOLINESS CHURCH
3415-19 N. Second St.
Philadelphia, PA 19140

In 1963, the Brethren in Christ church experienced a split among members; some rejecting what they saw as liberalizing and diversifying trends in the church. Members in the Philadelphia, Pennsylvania, congregation under the leadership of William L. Rosenberry saw the church loosing its stand on separation from the world and practical holiness. This small congregation incorporated in 1964 as the Calvary Holiness Church. It was joined by members who left from Brethren in Christ congregations in Hanover and Millersberg, Pennsylvania, and Massillon, Ohio.

The church follows the general beliefs of the Brethern in Christ, differing primarily in the strictness with which its holds to the beliefs and practices. As with other Wesleyan holiness churches, it believes in the experience of entire santification as a second work of grace in the life of the believer. Members observe the ordinances of baptism in the name of the Trinity, the Lord's Supper, and the washing of the saints' feet. Women wear a veil during worship. The holy kiss (I Peter 5:14) is used as a form of greeting. Believers are admonished to live a life of separation from the follies, sinful practices, and methods of the world, most especially in following a spirit of nonresistance in all matters according to Christ's Sermon on the Mount. Members refrain from use of intoxicating substances, worldly amusements (including television), membership in lodges and secret societies, and activity that does not glorify God on the Lord's Day.

Members wear a version of the "plain people" garb which for men includes a suit of plain material, black or brown shoes, and conservative hats. No neckties or jewelry is allowed. Women wear conservative dresses with full-length sleeves. They may not wear shorts, slacks, socks, jewelry, lace, bows, or artificial means to bedeck the hair or face. During all waking hours they wear a "prayer and prophecy veil" in the shape of a bonnet of white (which is covered with a black bonnet for the out-of-doors).

The church follows a congregational polity. There is an executive council which handles matter of polity, doctrine, and standards at a general church level.

Membership: Not reported. In the early 1970s, there were only two congregations and 38 members, though the church reported a number of constitutency members and the monthly magazine had a circulation of 7,000.

Periodicals: *The Gospel Witness*, 3415-19 N. Second St., Philadelphia, PA 19140.

Remarks: This church should not be confused with the Calvary Holiness Church of England (1930-1955) which is now an integral part of the Church of the Nazarene.

★278★
CHRISTIAN PILGRIM CHURCH
Current address not obtained for this edition.

The Christian Pilgrim Church was formed in 1937 by a group of holiness people, including Reverends Fannie Alldaffer, C. W. Cripps, and Tracy Alldaffer. They gathered at Coldwater, Michigan, to build a holiness church that could function without "so much law and order or machinery in the church." Officers were elected for life or as long as they remained in agreement with the Bible and the church.

The doctrine is Trinitarian and holiness (i.e., in essential agreement with the other churches discussed in this chapter). Healing is stressed but speaking in tongues is considered contrary to the Word of God; Baptism by any mode is desired; tithing is insisted upon; secret societies are condemned; Christ's imminent premillennial second coming is expected.

There is a General Assembly which meets annually. The church is divided into districts. A general superintendent has general oversight of the work and is aided by two assistants. Congregations are found in the South and Midwest.

Membership: Not reported. In the mid-1970s, the Church had 15 congregations and approximately 250 members.

Periodicals: *The Christian Voice.*

★279★
CHURCH OF THE GOSPEL
Current address not obtained for this edition.

The Church of the Gospel was formed in 1911 in Pittsfield, Massachusetts, by the Reverend and Mrs. C. T. Pike and members of the Advent Christian Church. In 1912 the group incorporated as the Church of God but adopted its present name in 1930 to avoid confusion with other groups. Basic doctrinal perspective is drawn from the Wesleyan holiness tradition. The members practice baptism by immersion and believe in the imminent second coming. The church has distributed "Narrow Way" tracts by the thousands across the country.

Membership: Not reported. Never a large body, in the 1940s there were only four or five churches. In 1971 there was only a single congregation in Virginia and scattered remnants in New England.

★280★
CHURCHES OF CHRIST IN CHRISTIAN UNION
1427 Lancaster Pike
Circleville, OH 43113

As a result of a holiness dispute within the Christian Union (described elsewhere in this volume), those who held the holiness doctrine withdrew and in 1909 organized the Churches of Christ in Christian Union of Ohio at Washington Court House, Ohio. In 1952 the Reformed Methodist Church, an 1814 splinter from the Methodist Episcopal Church over episcopal polity, joined the Churches of Christ in Christian Union as the Northeastern District.

The Reformed Methodist Church was formed in 1814 in Readsborough, Vermont, by a group of Methodists led by Pliny Brett, a local preacher. At their first conference, February 4, 1814, they adopted the Methodist "Articles of Religion" and some democratic rules for church government. The government was essentially congregational with no sharp distinctions being made between ministers and laymen. While the Methodist system of representative conferences was kept, ministers were delegates only if elected, not ex-officio. The local church was the focus of power, having the right to ordain elders, select its own ministers, and do whatever else was necessary to carry on its work. Ministers, likewise, could pick their field of service.

Doctrine of the Churches of Christ in Christian Union is holiness in emphasis (i.e., similar to the other churches discussed in this chapter). It stresses healing and the second coming of Jesus. Polity is congregational. Spiritual officers are the pastor and the elders, and business affairs are conducted by a board of trustees. An annual general council is held. There is an active world-wide mission program.

Membership: In 1985 the churches reported 11,400 members, 260 congregations, and 373 ministers.

Educational facilities: Mount of Praise Bible School, Circleville, OH.

Periodicals: *Advocate*, 1426 Lancaster Pike, Circleville, OH 43113; *Missionary Tidings*, 1426 Lancaster Pike, Circleville, OH 43113.

★281★
EVANGELICAL CHURCH OF NORTH AMERICA
7525 S.E. Lake Rd., Suite 7
Milwaukie, OR 97267

The Evangelical Church of North America was formed in 1968 by members of the Evangelical United Brethren who did not wish to proceed into the merger with the The Methodist Church (1939-1968) that created the United Methodist Church, described in the preceding chapter. The schism in the Evangelical United Brethren involved 50 congregations in the church's Northwest Conference and 23 churches from the Montana Conference. For several decades the Northwest Conference had been a center of holiness theology with many of the pastors being trained in the Western Evangelical Seminary (established in 1945 and firmly holiness in its doctrine and emphases).

Almost as soon as the Evangelical Church of North America was formed, the Holiness Methodist Church, with headquarters in Minneapolis, voted to join the new church, and in 1969 it became the North Central Conference of the new church. The Holiness Methodist Church was a result of the "holiness" revival movement that swept the United States in general and Methodism in particular during the late 1800s. The Northwestern

Holiness Association was formed at Grand Forks, North Dakota, on March 24, 1909, as a fellowship of those following the holiness way. This informal association changed its name to the Holiness Methodist Church in 1920, recognizing that the association had become a denomination. In 1977 the small Wesleyan Covenant Church, with congregations in Detroit and in Brownsville, Texas, but an extensive Mexican Mission, merged into the Evangelical Church.

The doctrine of the Evangelical Church of North America follows the tradition of Methodism as developed within the Evangelical United Brethren. It includes a special emphasis on entire sanctification.

The Evangelical Church of North America has seven annual conferences--the Pacific, the Eastern, the Western, the East Central, the North Central, Southeastern and Canada. A council of superintendents consisting of the superintendents of the various conferences coordinates programs. The highest executive office, that of general superintendent, was created in 1976. Missions are primarily conducted through independent holiness mission agencies, but support is given to the Bolivian Mission of the former Holiness Methodist Church and the Mexican Mission of the former Wesleyan Covenant Church. The Church is a member of the National Association of Evangelicals and the Christian Holiness Association.

Membership: In 1988 the Church reported 13,154 members, 144 churches, and 193 ministers in the United States. There were 47 congregations and 59 ministers in Canada, members in Canada, Germany and Bolivia numbered 4,263.

Educational facilities: Wesley Biblical Seminary, Jackson, Mississippi; Western Evangelical Seminary, Portland, Oregon; Hillcrest Christian College, Medicine Hat, Alberta, Canada.

Periodicals: *The Overview*, 7525 S.E. Lake Rd., Suite 7, Milwaukie, OR 9 7222.

Sources: John M. Pike, *Preachers of Salvation.*

★282★
GOSPEL MISSION CORPS
Box 175
Hightstown, MD 08520

The Gospel Mission Corps was founded by Robert S. Tarton II, a graduate of the Pillar of Fire Bible Seminary of Zarephath, New Jersey. He began a mission at Hightstown, Maryland, which grew into the Gospel Mission Corps in 1962. Its doctrine is like that of the Pillar of Fire, and the ministers are nonsalaried.

Membership: Not reported. In 1972 there were seven churches, 175 members, and seven ministers.

Periodicals: *Gospel Missionary*, Box 175, Hightstown, MD 08520.

★283★
GRACE AND HOPE MISSION
4 S. Gay St.
Baltimore, MD 21202

The Grace and Hope Mission was founded in 1914 by Miss Mamie E. Caske and Miss Jennie E. Goranflo , who opened a gospel mission in Baltimore. The work grew so that by the late 1960s there were 12 centers, mostly in large cities. The doctrine is Wesleyan-Protestant with an emphasis on evangelism, holiness, and the hope of the second coming. The officers, all single females, wear a black uniform with red trimming and the Mission's emblem. There is an annual conference at which the assignments of officers for the coming year are made.

Membership: In 1988 the mission reported 12 centers. There is no formal membership, but approximately 800 people participate in the mission's activities.

★284★
HOLINESS CHURCH OF GOD, INC.
℅ Bishop B. McKinney
602 Elm St.
Graham, NC 27253

The Holiness Church of God, Inc., is a small body established in 1920 at Madison, North Carolina, and incorporated eight years later at Winston-Salem. It holds an annual general assembly. There is a president, bishop, vice bishop and general secretary. Overseers are appointed for five areas in the South and East.

Membership: Not reported. At last report (1968) the Church had 28 churches, 36 ministers, and 927 members.

★285★
HOLINESS GOSPEL CHURCH
Rte. 2, Box 13
Etters, PA 17319

The Holiness Gospel Church was founded in 1945 by former members of the Evangelical United Brethren and the Church in God. Its theology is Wesleyan holiness. The church sponsors camp meetings and conducts a radio ministry.

Membership: Not reported. In the 1970s there were 3 congregations and 180 members.

★286★
KENTUCKY MOUNTAIN HOLINESS ASSOCIATION
Star Rte. 1, Box 350
Jackson, KY 41339

The Kentucky Mountain Holiness Association was begun in 1925 by Lela G. McConnell, a deaconness in the Methodist Episcopal Church. Following her ordination in 1924 she began a vigorous ministry in the mountains of eastern Kentucky. She preached a Wesleyan-Protestant doctrine with a strong emphasis on sanctification. The Association maintains a high school and a three-year college level Bible Institute, a radio station, and a camp ground. J. Eldon Neidorf is the current association president.

Membership: In 1988 the Association reported 16 churches served by resident pastors with the exception of one church pastored by students.

Educational facilities: Kentucky Mountain Bible Institute, Jackson, KY.

Sources: Lela G. McConnell, *The Pauline Ministry in the Kentucky Mountains*. Jackson, KY: The Author, 1942.

★287★
LUMBER RIVER ANNUAL CONFERENCE OF THE HOLINESS METHODIST CHURCH
% Bishop C. N. Lowry
Rowland, NC 28383

The Lumber River Annual Conference of the Holiness Methodist Church was organized in 1900 by members of the Methodist Episcopal Church, South, at Union Chapel Church, Robeson County, North Carolina. The members of the Lumber River Annual Conference had an intense interest in the holiness movement with its stress on the second blessing, a religious experience certifying holiness. At the time, the holiness movement was criticized by many Methodists, so the holiness advocates among the Conference decided to form a new church. In addition to their interest in the holiness movement was their concern for home missions.

The Church follows Wesleyan-Protestant doctrine and has adopted an episcopal polity. Some features of nineteenth-century Methodism--attendance at class meetings (regular gatherings of small classes for mutual discussion, Bible study, confession and forgiveness, and prayer) and six months' probationary membership--are retained. The itinerant ministry has been dropped.

Membership: Not reported. In the early 1970s there were 7 churches and slightly over 500 members.

★288★
PILLAR OF FIRE
Zarephath, NJ 08890

The existence of the Pillar of Fire is due in part to the reluctance of the Methodist Episcopal Church to allow female ministers in its churches in the late nineteenth century. Alma White (1862-1946), a Methodist minister's wife, began to preach both in revivals and in her husband's pulpit. Her success led to notoriety and then to opposition from Methodist officials, so she began to organize her converts into independent missions modeled on the early Methodist societies within the the Church of England. After initially cooperating with the Metropolitan Church Association, she incorporated the missions in 1902 as the Pentecostal Union, which gradually emerged as a body separate from the association. The name Pillar of Fire was adopted in 1917.

The doctrine of the church is typically Wesleyan holiness, and it adopted a slightly modified form of the Methodist Twenty-five Articles of Religion early in the twentieth century. The church believes in healing, accepts premillinnialism, and advocates a strong stance against participation in war.

The church is organized episcopally and Alma White was its first bishop (among the first women in modern times to assume that role). Women can occupy all ministerial roles. As part of its commitment to women's rights, the church for many years published a periodical called *Women's Chains*.

The headquarters of the church are at Zarephath, New Jersey. The location of the original headquarters, Denver, Colorado, functions as a second major center of activity. At both locations there is a college, Bible seminary, prep school, radio station (KPOF in Denver and WAWZ in Zarepahth), and a branch of the Pillar of Fire Press. A third station, WAKW, and a school are located in Cincinnati, Ohio, and other schools are located in Jacksonville, Florida; Los Angeles, California; and London, England. There is also an active foreign mission program.

Following Alma White's death, her two sons Ray B. White (1892-1946) and Arthur K. White (1889-1981) inherited the leadership of the church. Arthur K. White became the new bishop and directed its activities for more than 30 years. Dr. Donald J. Wolfram is the present bishop and general superintendent.

Membership: Membership is not counted and is unknown. In 1988 there were 20 congregations in the United States and 56 in foreign countries, including Great Britain, India, Liberia, Malawi, Nigeria, the Philippines, Spain, and Yugoslavia.

Educational facilities: Belleview Junior College and Bible Seminary, Westminster, Colorado; Pillar of Fire Bible Seminary, Zarephath, New Jersey.

Periodicals: *Pillar of Fire*, Zarephath, NJ 08890; *Mission News Around the Globe Today*, 8354 Grove St., Westminster, CO 80030.

Remarks: Alma White was an advocate of a variety of controversial causes, including vegetarianism and women's rights. She was also an active supporter of the Ku Klux Klan in the 1920s. She wrote a book, *Guardians of Liberty*, defending them as God's agent in maintaining the social order, but the church disassociated itself from the Klan many years ago.

Sources: Alma White, *The Story of My Life*. Zarephath, NJ: Pillar of Fire, 1919-34. 6 Vols.; Alma White, *The New Testament Church*. Zarephath, NJ: Pillar of Fire, 1929; James McRobbie, *What the Bible Teaches*. Salem, OH: Schmul Publishing Co., 1983; Alma White *Why I Do Not Eat Meat*. Zarephath, NJ: Pillar of Fire, 1938; Alma White, *Hymns and Poems*. Zarephath, NJ: Pillar of Fire, 1946.

★289★
SANCTIFIED CHURCH OF CHRIST
2715 18th Ave.
Columbus, GA 31901

The Sanctified Church of Christ was formed in 1937 at Columbus, Georgia, by a group of former members of the Methodist Episcopal Church. The group was led by Brother E. K. Leary and Sister Jemima Bishop, and their purpose was to preserve the rich heritage of true scriptural holiness. Their doctrine was Wesleyan-Protestant with a distinct emphasis upon entire sanctification. Particular rules were made against secret oathbound societies, immodest dress such as shorts, jewelry, make-up, public and mixed bathing, women cutting their hair, television, and divorce. Members are conscientious objectors.

There is an annual conference that elects the general superintendent, secretary, treasurer, and the council of twelve members, which is the chief legislative body of the church . The council approves all candidates for the ministry.

Membership: Not reported. In the early 1970s there were 7 congregations spread across the deep south. There were approximately 1,000 members.

★290★
WESLEYAN TABERNACLE ASSOCIATION
626 Elliott Ave.
Cincinnati, OH 45215

The Wesleyan Tabernacle Association is a small holiness church. It was formed in 1936 for the purpose of promoting Christian love and fellowship among godly leaders of various undenominational bodies and to open a greater field of service for holiness evangelistic preachers and singers. The Association asserts belief in the Trinity, salvation and sanctification by God's free grace, divine healing, baptism and the Lord's Supper as ordinances, and the premillennial return of Christ. Polity is congregational. There is an annual Association Convention which elects officers to oversee publications, missions, and cooperative endeavors with like-minded groups. Women are freely admitted to the ministry. The Association supports a children's home and an extensive mission in Haiti.

Membership: Not reported. In the 1970s the Association had 26 congregations in the United States. It supports 173 ordained ministers, 53 licensed ministers, 10 song evangelists and 19 commissioned Christian workers, some of whom are under the direction of independent holiness mission agencies.

Periodicals: *The Evangel*.

Sources: *Yearbook*. N.p.: Wesleyan Tabernacle Association, 1965.

Black Holiness

★291★
ASSOCIATED CHURCHES OF CHRIST
(HOLINESS)
1302 E. Adams Blvd.
Los Angeles, CA 90011

On the West Coast the Church of Christ (Holiness) U.S.A. was formed in 1915 by Bishop William Washington and work was carried on independently of the work in the east and south by the church's founder, C. P. Jones. A few years later, Jones went to Los Angeles and held a revival meeting. At that time the two men worked out an agreement for cooperative endeavor. The agreement was in effect until 1946-47. Because of what the manual of the Associated Churches of Christ (Holiness) calls the "manipulating of some administrative problems in the upper circles of the Church," the West Coast churches withdrew from the Church of Christ (Holiness) U.S.A. They now continue under the original incorporation of Bishop Washington. Doctrine and polity are identical with the Church of Christ (Holiness) U.S.A.

Membership: Not reported. In the early 1970s there were 6 churches and 1 mission in the Associated Churches.

★292★
CHURCH OF CHRIST (HOLINESS) U.S.A.
329 E. Monument St.
Jackson, MS 39202

In 1894 C. P. Jones and Charles H. Mason formed the Church of God in Christ as a holiness body, following their exclusion from fellowship with black Baptists in Arkansas. Mason took most of the body into pentecostalism in 1907. Those who remained were reorganized by Jones as the Church of Christ (Holiness) U.S.A. Jones himself, residing in Jackson, Mississippi, became well known as a composer and publisher of holiness gospel songs. Doctrinally, the Church of Christ (Holiness) U.S.A. is very close to the Church of the Nazarene, with which it almost merged. It follows the Methodist Articles of Religion printed elsewhere in this volume, and stresses the second blessing of the Holy Spirit which imparts sanctification to the believer. Race issues prevented close relations betwe en the Church of Christ (Holiness) U.S.A. and predominantly white holiness churches.

The church is episcopal in structure with a senior bishop as the highest official. There are seven dioceses. A convention held every two years is the highest legislative authority. Missionary work is sponsored in Mexico. There is a publishing house in Los Angeles. Present leader of the church is Bishop M. R. Conic.

Membership: In 1984 the Church had over 10,000 members and 170 congregations.

Educational facilities: Christ Missionary and Industrial College, Jackson, MS; Boydton Institute, Boydton, VA.

Sources: Otho B. Cobbins, *History of the Church of Christ (Holiness) U.S.A., 1895-1965.* New York: 1966; C. P. Jones, *His Fulness.* Jackson, MS: 1901; C. P. Jones, *The Story of My Songs.* Los Angeles: n.d.

★293★
CHURCH OF GOD (SANCTIFIED CHURCH)
1037 Jefferson St.
Nashville, TN 37208

In the early years of the Church of Christ (Holiness) U.S.A., discussed elsewhere in this chapter, the church existed as an unincorporated entity called the "Church of God" or the "Holiness Church." It was only after the schism over Pentecostalism in 1907 that the church was incorporated and its present name was adopted. Before the incorporation, one of the ministers, Elder Charles W. Gray, established the church in Nashville, Tennessee, and the surrounding areas. When the Church of Christ (Holiness) U.S.A. incorporated, Gray continued his work independently as the Church of God (Sanctified Church). The doctrine was the same as that of the Church of Christ (Holiness) U.S.A., but the polity was congregational with local churches operating

autonomously and appointing their own ministers. The associated churches remained unincorporated. In 1927 there arose a move within the Church of God (Sanctified Church) to incorporate and to consolidate the work under a board of elders. Among those who constituted the newly incorporated church were Elders J. L. Rucker, R. A. Manter, R. L. Martin, M. S. Sowell, B. Smith, and G. A. Whitley. The move to incorporate led to further controversy and a schism. However, under the incorporation, the elders retained the rights to direct the church, and it continues as the Church of God (Sanctified Church). Elder Gray, founder of the church, withdrew to found the Original Church of God (or Sanctified Church).

The Church of God (Sanctified Church) is headed by a general overseer. The first was Elder Rucker. He has been suceeded by Elder Theopolis Dickerson McGhee (d.1965) and Elder Jesse E. Evans. Mission work is conducted in Jamaica.

Membership: Not reported.In the early 1970s the Church reported 60 congregations, approximately 5,000 members.

★294★
CHURCH OF UNIVERSAL TRIUMPH/THE DOMINION OF GOD
% Rev. James Shaffer
8317 LaSalle Blvd.
Detroit, MI 48206

Rivaling Sweet Daddy Grace and Father Divine as charismatic leaders in the black community was the Rev. James Francis Marion Jones, better known as Prophet Jones (1908-1971). Born in Birmingham, Alabama, the son of a railroad brakeman and a school teacher, he was raised in Triumph the Church and Kingdom of God in Christ. Even as a child, he preached (he did so regularly after his eleventh birthday). In 1938 he was sent to Detroit as a missionary and became successful quickly. Tension with headquarters arose before the year was out, however, when members began to shower Jones with expensive gifts. The headquarters claimed them. Rather than surrender his new affluence, Jones left the church and founded the Church of Universal Triumph/the Dominion of God.

The new church, modeled on the parent body, was built upon Jones' charisma. During the 1940s and 1950s he became known for his wealth. His possessions included a white mink coat, a 54-room French chateau which had been built in 1917 by a General Motors executive, five Cadillacs each with its own chauffeur, jewelry, perfumes, and wardrobe of almost 500 ensembles. Jones claimed to be in direct contact with God, who instructed him in the form of a breeze fanning his ear. Among his practices was dispensing solutions to personal problems after inviting individuals to mount his dais and whisper their problems in his ear. Most of Prophet Jones' wealth came from people grateful for Jones' healing ability. Followers were to be found in all the large northern cities. Jones was titled, "His Holiness the Rev. Dr. James F. Jones, D.D., Universal Dominion Ruler, Internationally known as Prophet Jones."

The Church, like the parent body, is very strict. Members are not allowed to smoke, drink, play games of any kind, use coffee or tea, fraternize with non-Dominionitetry, attend another church, or marry without the consent of the ruler of the church. Women must wear girdles and men health belts. The major theological tenet concerns the beginning of the millennium in 2,000 A.D. All alive at that time will become immortal and live in the heaven on earth.

The upward path of Prophet Jones came to an abrupt end in 1956 when a vice raid on his home led to his arrest and trial for gross indecency. He was acquited, but the damage had been done and his following declined from that time. During the year prior to his death in 1971, he commuted between Detroit and Chicago. Following his death, his assistant, the Rev. Lord James Schaffer became the Dominion Ruler. He was named by the Dominion Council and Board of Trustees. Some 20 ministers and 5,000 members attended the funeral of Prophet Jones in 1971.

Membership: Not reported.

★295★
CHURCHES OF GOD, HOLINESS
170 Ashby St., N.W.
Atlanta, GA 30314

The Churches of God, Holiness, were formed by Bishop King Hezekiah Burruss (d.1963), formerly of the Church of Christ (Holiness) U.S.A. Burruss began a church in Atlanta in 1914 that belonged to that organization, and by 1920, the Atlanta congregation was large enough that it hosted the national convention of the Church of Christ (Holiness) U.S.A. Shortly after that Atlanta meeting, however, Burruss formed his own church. Doctrine is like the doctrine of the parent body.

The highest authority is the national convention. There are also annual state conventions. Practically speaking the government developed during the period of strong leadership exercised the founding bishop. The bishop appoints the state overseers who assign all pastors. The present bishop is Titus Paul Burruss.

Membership: Not reported. In 1967 there were 42 churches, 16 ministers abd 25,600 members, mostly along the East Coast.

Periodicals: *The Bethlehem Star.*

★296★
GOSPEL SPREADING CHURCH
2030 Georgia Ave., N.W.
Washington, DC 20003

The Gospel Spreading Church, sometimes called Elder Michaux Church of God or the Radio Church of God, was founded by Lightfoot Solomon Michaux (1885-1968), a minister in the Church of God (Holiness). At one point he served as the church's secretary-treasurer. However, he came into conflict with C. P. Jones, founder of the Church of God (Holiness) and left to found an independent church in Hampton, Virginia in 1922, retaining the name he had previously used, the Gospel Spreading Tabernacle Association. In 1928 he moved to Washington, D. C. and established the Church of God and Gospel Spreading Association.

His early success continued in the nation's capital, and he had discovered the potential of radio while in Virginia. In 1929 he began broadcasting on WJSV. Shortly thereafter CBS bought the station and his show expanded through the system. By 1934 he was on over 50 stations nationwide, with an estimated audience of 25,000,000. His show was also carried internationally by shortwave. He was the first black person to receive such exposure. He mixed holiness themes with positive thinking. His magazine was entitled *Happy News.*

From his radio audience, congregations began to form in black communities, primarily in the East. However, by the beginning of World War II his radio ministry had declined and he was heard only a few stations, in those cities where congregations had formed. In 1964 he reorganized his followers as the Gospel Spreading Church, but most of the congregations continued to call themselves the Church of God.

Membership: Not reported.

Sources: Lilian Ashcraft Webb, *About My Father's Business.* Westport, CT: Greenwood Press, 1981; Pauline Lark, ed. *Sparks from the Anvil of Elder Micheaux.* Washington, DC: Happy News Publishing Company, 1950.

★297★
KODESH CHURCH OF EMMANUEL
% Dr. Kenneth O. Barber
932 Logan Road
Bethel Park, PA 15102

The Kodesh Church of Emmanuel is a black holiness sect that was formed by Reverend Frank Russell Killingsworth when he withdrew from the African Methodist Episcopal Church in 1929 along with 120 followers. In common with other holiness churches, this church emphasizes entire sanctification as a second definite work of grace conditioned upon a life of absolute consecration. The church forbids use of alcohol, tobacco and prideful dress;

membership in secret societies; and profaning the Sabbath. In 1934, a merger was effected with the Christian Tabernacle Union of Pittsburgh.

The church is governed by a quadrennial general assembly. Regional assembly assemblies annually. There is mission work in Liberia.

Membership: In 1980 there were five churches, 326 members, and 28 ministers.

★298★
MOUNT CALVARY HOLY CHURCH OF AMERICA
% Bishop Harold Williams
1214 Chowan St.
Durham, NC 27713

The Mt. Calvary Holy Church is a small black holiness church headquartered in Boston, Massachusetts, founded by Bishop Brumfield Johnson. Its doctrine is similar to that of the United Holy Church of America. Churches are located in North Carolina; Baltimore, Maryland; New York; Boston; and other cities on the east coast.

Membership: Not reported.

★299★
TRIUMPH THE CHURCH AND KINGDOM OF GOD IN CHRIST
Box 77056
Birmingham, AL 35228

Triumph the Church and Kingdom of God in Christ was founded by Elder E.D. Smith in 1902. The founding followed by five years a divine revelation given to Smith. According to the literature of the church, the 1902 organization of the church marked the time when the revelation was "speeded to earth." Finally, in 1904, the content of the revelation was announced. Headquarters for the church were established in Baton Rouge, Louisiana, then were moved to Birmingham, Alabama, and later to Atlanta, Georgia. The founder was in charge of the church until 1920, when he moved to Addis Ababa, Ethiopia.

The church follows the holiness beliefs common to holiness churches, but also believes in fire baptism, a spiritual experience of empowerment by the Holy Spirit. Fire baptism was first received by the Apostles in the upper room on Pentecost, when tongues of fire appeared above their heads (Acts 2). As practiced by the several nineteenth and twentieth century "fire- baptized" churches, fire baptism is similar to the pentecostal experience of the baptism of the Holy Spirit, except it is typically not accompanied by speaking in tongues. (See separate entry on the Fire-Baptized Holiness Church, Wesleyan.)

Triumph the Church and Kingdom of God in Christ holds a unique view of itself as a church in relation to Christendom, traditionally called the church militant. This view is reflected in the following passage from the church's catechism: *Question* Was there another Church in the earth before Triumph? *answer.* Yes. Church Militant; *Question* Is there any difference between the Triumph Church and Church Militant? *answer* Yes. Church Militant is a Church of warfare, and Triumph is a Church of Peace; *Question* What happened to Church Militant when Triumph was revealed? *answer* God turned it upside down and emptied His Spirit into Triumph; *Question* Is Triumph just a Church only? *answer* No. It has a Kingdom with it.

Polity is episcopal with bishops elected for life. Under the bishops is a hierarchy of state and local workers. Every four years the church holds an International Religious Congress.

Membership: Not reported. At last report (1972) there were 475 churches, 53,307 members, and 1,375 ministers.

Glenn Griffith Movement

★300★
ALLEGHENY WESLEYAN METHODIST CONNECTION
1827 Allen Dr.
Salem, OH 44460

The Allegheny Wesleyan Methodist Connection (Original Allegheny Conference) was formed in 1968 due to the merger of the Wesleyan Methodist Church of America (1843) with the Pilgrim Holiness Church to form the Wesleyan Church. Prominent among the leaders of the new connection were Reverends H. C. Van Wormer, T. A. Robertson, J. B. Markey, and F.E. Mansell. These men, along with a majority of the conference, opposed the merger on the grounds that they believed in a congregational form of church governance and in Wesleyan Methodist standards of behavior, which they believed were being abandoned in the new church. Legal technicalities forced them to add the words "Original Allegheny Conference" to their name. Allegheny was one of the original conferences formed by the Wesleyan Methodist Church when it broke away from the Methodist Episcopal Church in 1843.

The connection follows the traditional holiness doctrine of the former Wesleyan Methodist Church. It emphasizes the belief that the atonement in Christ provides both for the regeneration of sinners and the entire sanctification of believers.

The connection serves as an agency of the cooperative endeavor. There is a strong thrust in the foreign missions with work in Haiti and Peru. Domestic missions are conducted among the Indians of the Northwestern Unted States and Canada.

Membership: Not reported. In 1986 there were 126 churches and 2,302 members.

Educational facilities: Northwest Indian Bible School, Alberton, Montana; Allegheny Wesleyan College, Salem, Ohio.

Periodicals: *The Allegheny Wesleyan Methodist*, 1827 Allen Dr., Salem, OH 44460.

Sources: *Discipline of the Allegheny Wesleyan Methodist Connection*. Titusville, PA: 1986; H. C. Morrison, *Baptism with the Holy Ghost*. Salem, OH: The Alleghany Wesleyan Methodist Connection, 1978.

★301★
BIBLE HOLINESS CHURCH
Current address not obtained for this edition.

The Bible Holiness Church is a small group which separated from the Bible Methodist Connection of Tennessee. The members include a statement on healing among their beliefs, which otherwise are staunchly conservative and holiness in content.

Membership: Not reported. In 1968 there were 9 congregations and approximately 200 members in Tennessee and Virginia.

★302★
BIBLE METHODIST CONNECTION OF CHURCHES
% Rev. V.O. Agan
Box 523
Pell City, AL 35125

Bible Methodists in Alabama and southwestern Ohio organized in 1966 as the Bible Methodist Church and the Wesleyan Connection of Churches, respectively. In 1970 these two bodies merged to form the Bible Methodist Connection of Churches. The doctrine is conservative and holiness.

Membership: Not reported. In 1970 there were 27 churches in Alabama, 17 in Ohio, 794 members, 21 conference preachers and 48 elders.

Periodicals: *Bible Methodist*, Brent, AL.

★303★
BIBLE METHODIST CONNECTION OF TENNESSEE
% Rev. D.P. Denton
Evangelist of Truth
Box 22309
Knoxville, TN 37933

Protesting both the centralization of authority and the lack of holiness for years in the Wesleyan Methodist Church was D. P. Denton, editor of the *Evangelist of Truth*, an independent monthly out of Knoxvillle, Tennessee. On October 17, 1966, Denton led a meeting in Knoxville with represenatatives of the various factions opposed to the merger of the Wesleyan Methodist Church and the Pilgrim Holiness Church into the Wesleyan Church, a merger finally effected in 1967. At the Knoxville meeting, representatives opposed to merger decided to organize a new "connection," a new association of churches. The new group would continue the use of Wesleyan Methodist *Discipline* (a book of church order), with the exception that each church would be completely autonomous. The new connection would be formed as the merger was consummated. After the negotiations were completed and those who stayed out of the merger settled on the price of buying their property from the new Wesleyan Church, three new bodies emerged: the Bible Methodist Connection of Tennessee, the Bible Holiness Church, and the Bible Methodist Connection of Churches.

From the former Wesleyan Methodist Church, the members of the Tennessee Conference led by Denton became the Bible Methodist Connection of Tennessee. Denton was elected president. The former Conference paper, *Tennessee Tidings*, became the new church's organ. A campground outside of Knoxville serves the church. The *Evangelist of Truth* continues as an independent monthly.

Membership: Not reported. In 1970 there were 19 churches, 136 members, and 28 ministers.

Periodicals: *Tennessee Tidings*, Box 22309, Knoxville, TN 37933.

★304★
BIBLE MISSIONARY CHURCH
822 S. Simms
Denver, CO 80211

Following the successful revival led by Church of the Nazarene minister, Rev. Glenn Griffith near Nampa, Idaho, the group of conservative holiness people attracted to Griffith's message were organized into the Bible Missionary Union. Word of the action spread quickly and within ten months congregations of like minded people had been established in twenty states. Joining Griffith were J. E. Cook, Spencer Johnson, and H. B. Huffman. The first general conference of the church was held in Denver in 1956, at which the present name was selected.

Membership in the church has been augmented by the failure in 1956 of conservatives to have the Nazarene Council Assembly condemn television.

Like its parent, the Church of the Nazarene, doctrine is Wesleyan with an emphasis on holiness. Entire sanctification, as freedom from original sin and a state of entire devotion to God, is stressed. The future life, heaven and hell, and the premillennial return of Jesus are also central beliefs. The church is understood as "composed of all spiritually regenerated persons whose names are written in heaven." The general rules have also been expanded with the addition of much detail on points of behavior. The difference between the Bible Missionary Church and the parent body, the Church of the Nazarene, is primarily on strictness of personal holiness regulations. The Church has endorsed the King James Version of the Bible for use in its churches and has gone on record against modern versions of the Bible, especially the Revised Standard Version, the Living Bible, the New English Translation, the Readers' Digest Condensed Version, and the New International Version.

The Church is headed by two general moderators who preside over the general conference, the highest law making body for the church. Foreign mission work is supported in Guyana, Venezuela, St. Vincent (West Indies), Canada, Nigeria, Honduras, Japan, the Philippines, Papua New Guinea, Barbados, and Mexico; a home mission project is on the Navaho Reservation at Farmington, New Mexico. A children's home is operated in Beulah Heights, Kentucky.

Membership: Not reported. There are 14 district conferences overseeing churches across the United States.

Educational facilities: Bible Missionary Institute, Rock Island, IL.

Periodicals: *The Missionary Revivalist*, 822 S. Simms, Denver, CO 80211

Sources: *Manual*. Rock Island, IL: Bible Missionary Church, periodically revised; Mrs. Roy Keene, *"Love-Threads Reaching"*. (Rock Island, IL): Bible Missionary Church, 1979; J. E. Cook, *W. M. Tidwell (A Life that Counted)*. Ann Arbor, MI: Mallory Lithographing, Inc., n.d.

★305★
CHURCH OF THE BIBLE COVENANT
Rte. 8, Box 214
450 N. Fortville Pike
Greenfield, IN 46140

In 1966 four Indiana-based ministers of the Church of the Nazarene (Marvin Powers, Amos Hann, Donald Hicks, and Granville Rogers) formed a steering committee that led to the establishment of the Church of the Bible Covenant the following year at the John T. Hatfield

Campground near Cleveland, Indiana. The four invited their former district superintendent, Remiss Rehfeldt, to join them. On August 10, 1967, the new church elected Rehfeldt and Powers as general presiding officers. Those who gathered for that meeting then spread across the country under the leadership of twelve regional presiding officers to develop local congregations.

The Church's doctrine follows essentially that of the Wesleyan-Protestant tradition, with a strong emphasis on holiness and a high code of ethical standards. A general convention meets quadrennially, during which time elections are held and legislation considered. In 1982 Rehfeldt retired and was granted emeritus status. Donald Hicks was elected as new general presiding officer.

Membership: In 1984 the church reported 90 churches in the United States and 75 churches and preaching points overseas. Total membership was 2,000 but approximately 4,000 attended church school each Sunday.

Educational facilities: Covenant Foundation College, Greenfield, Indiana. The church maintains three Bible-training institutions overseas.

Periodicals: *The Covenanter*, New Castle, Indiana 47352.

Sources: *Articles*. Knightsville, IN: Church of the Bible Covenant, 1970.

★306★
EVANGELICAL WESLEYAN CHURCH
Current address not obtained for this edition.

The Evangelical Wesleyan Church was formed in 1963 by the merger of the Evangelical Wesleyan Church of North America and the Midwest Holiness Association, both churches composed of members who had left the Free Methodist Church. The Evangelical Wesleyan Church of North America was organized at a convention held near Centerville, Crawford County, Pennsylvania, with a dedication to restore old-time Free Methodism. (The members sought a stricter interpretatin of personal moral codes; e.g., they were concerned about women's hair styles, makeup, and the length of dresses.) The Midwest Holiness Association was formed in 1962 as a protest against worldliness and apostasy in the Free Methodist Church. The organizing convention of the Midwest Holiness Association was held in Ansley, Nebraska. The Evangelical Wesleyan Church is set against the compromise of old doctrines and standards of Free Methodism and follows its patterns.

Membership: Not reported. Membership is concentrated in Nebraska, Pennsylvania, and New York.

Educational facilities: Adirondack Bible College, Northville, New York; John Fletcher Bible College, Kearney, Nebraska.

Periodicals: *The Ernest Christian*.

★307★
GOD'S MISSIONARY CHURCH
% Rev. Paul Miller
Swengal, PA 17880

God's Missionary Church is one of the older conservative
holiness bodies. It was formed in 1935 as a result of a
dispute in the Pennsylvania and New Jersey District of
the Pilgrim Holiness Church.

It has become a conservtive body, very strict in discipline.
It is also opposed to participation in war, somewhat
reflective of the Quaker influence in the founding of the
Pilgrim Holiness Church. The church is congregational,
but headed by a general superintendent. There is
missionary work in Haiti and among Cuban refugees in
Florida. It cooperates with the Interdenominational
Holiness Convention.

Membership: Not reported. In 1971 there were 595
members, 532 of which resided in Pennsylvania.

Educational facilities: Penn View Bible Institute, Penns
Creek, PA.

Periodicals: *God's Missionary Standard*.

Sources: *Official Handbook and Discipline*. Watsontown,
PA: God's Missionary Church, 1971.

★308★
LOWER LIGHTS CHURCH
Ann Arbor, MI

The Lower Lights Church was formed in 1940 as a single
congregation (the Lower Light Mission) in Ann Arbor,
Michigan. It subsequently branched out to neighboring
communities and now cooperates with the
Interdenominational Holiness Convention.

Membership: Not reported. There are several
congregations in Michigan and Ohio with several hundred
members.

★309★
**NATIONAL ASSOCIATION OF HOLINESS
   CHURCHES**
351 S. Park Dr.
Griffith, IN 46319

The National Association of Holiness Churches was
formed in 1967. H. Robb French (1891-1985), a former
pastor in the Wesleyan Methodist Church and one of the
founders of the Interdenominational Holiness Convention,
was the chief moving force in its founding and early
development. He was the first general chairman, a post
held until his resignation in 1973. The association exists as

a loose confederation of independent ministers and
churches formed for purposes of promoting holiness and
providing fellowship. An annual camp meeting and
association general conference is held in June. Missionary
work is supported in Mexico, Brazil, and India.

Membership: In 1988, there were 17 congregations in the
association and 86 affiliated ministers. Many of the
ministers and churches affiliated with the association are
also affiliated with other conservative holiness church
bodies.

Periodicals: *The NAHC Bulletin*, % Rev. John Brewer,
818 Marshall St., Hagerstows, MD 21740.

★310★
PILGRIM HOLINESS CHURCH OF NEW YORK
32 Cadillac Ave.
Albany, NY 12205

The Pilgrim Holiness Church of New York traces its
history to the Pentecostal Rescue Mission organized in
1897 in Binghamton, New York. In 1922 that Mission
affiliated as an autonomous district with the International
Holiness Church which the following year took the name
Pilgrim Holiness Church. During the 1960s the Pilgrim
Holiness Church began a process of centralizing authority
in the national headquarters and preparing for merger
with the Wesleyan Methodist Church (a merger which
was completed in 1968 with the creation of the Wesleyan
Church). In 1963, asserting its autonomous status, the
New York Conference left the Pilgrim Holiness Church
and has continued as an independent organization.

The Church is very conservative in doctrine and strict in
practice, as are those churches which are affiliated with
the Interdenominational Holiness Convention. Missions
are directly supported in Brazil, Haiti, and Winnepeg,
Manitoba, Canada and other locations through various
missionary agencies. Churches are located in New York,
New Jersey, Ohio, Pennsylvania, Massachusetts, and
Canada.

Membership: In 1988 the Church reported 950 members,
54 churches, and 87 ministers in the United States and
275 members, 5 churches and 5 ministers in Canada.

Educational facilities: The Church has no school of its
own, but financially supports and recommends God's
Bible School, Cincinnati, Ohio; Hobe Sound Bible School,
Hobe Sound, Florida (sponsored by the National
Association of Holiness Churches); Alleghany Wesleyan
College, Salem, Ohio; and Penn View Bible Institute,
Penns Creek, Pennsylvania (sponsored by God's
Missionary Church).

Periodicals: *Pilgrim News*, 32 Cadillac Ave., Albany, NY
12205.

★311★
PILGRIM HOLINESS CHURCH OF THE MIDWEST

% Union Bible Seminary
434 S. Union St.
Westfield, IN 46074

The Pilgrim Holiness Church of the Midwest was formed in 1970. Three years earlier ten congregations affiliated with the Pilgrim Holiness Church had withdrawn to become the Midwest Conference of the Pilgrim Holiness Church of New York. But the ten congregations eventaully decided to remain independent, though they have stayed friendly with the New York group. They adopted their own *Discipline* (a book of church order). Mission work is through the Evangelical Faith Missions and Evangelical Bible Missions.

Membership: Not reported. In 1969 there were 13 churches and 246 members.

Educational facilities: Union Bible Seminary.

★312★
UNITED HOLINESS CHURCH OF NORTH AMERICA

Cedar Springs, MI 49319

The United Holiness Church of North America was formed in 1955 by conservatives within the Free Methodist Church at a camp meeting at Carson City, Michigan. Headquarters are at the Bible College at Cedar. It resembles its parent body, but is more strict in its standards of holiness. The Church cooperates with the Interdenominational Holiness Convention.

Membership: Not reported.

Educational facilities: Jordan College, Cedar Springs, MI.

Periodicals: *United Holiness Sentinel*, Cedar Springs, MI 49319.

★313★
VOICE OF THE NAZARENE ASSOCIATION OF CHURCHES

Current address not obtained for this edition.

One focus within the Church of the Nazarene of the post-World II conservative holiness movement was a magazine, *The Voice of the Nazarene*, published at Finleyville, Pennsylvania by W. L. King. Following the 1956 decision in the Church of the Nazarene in favor of television, some groups in the East against watching television associated with King. They formed the Voice of the Nazarene Association of Churches. It is a loosely congregational organization. The literature from the Finleyville headquarters has been characterized by its extreme conservatism, politically as well as religiously. It is strongly opposed to Communism, the National Council of Churches, and the Roman Catholic Church.

Membership: Not reported. In 1967 there were 8 members congregations (plus 18 cooperating congregations) and 31 Association evangelists.

Periodicals: *Universal Challenger*; *Voice of the Nazarene*.

★314★
WESLEYAN HOLINESS ASSOCIATION OF CHURCHES

108 Carter Avenue
Dayton, OH 45405

History: After only four years with the Bible Missionary Church, the Rev. Glenn Griffith left it in protest of its alleged compromise of receiving divorced persons into the membership and/or ministry. He and his supporters felt that there had been a drifting from the old Wesleyan revival fervor and standards. At an informal meeting of ministers and laypeople in August 1959, Griffith was chosen the general leader, and an initials general conference with an accompanying camp meeting was set for the next year at Colorado Springs, Colorado. At that meeting, Griffith was unanimously elected to the post of general moderator (now general superintendent) and the Wesleyan Holiness Association of Churches organized. Among its objectives were to emphasize the doctrine and experience of entire sanctification and to raise the standard of holiness in daily living.

Beliefs: The Association follows a six-article statement of doctrine with the basic affirmations of traditional Wesleyan Christianity. Article IV is concerned with God's plan of redemption and affirms free will, faith, repentance, and justification. It emphasizes sanctification as a second act of God in believers. The first act is said to be justification, where believers are made free of original sin, are brought into a state of entire "devotement" to God, and their obedience of love is perfected. Sanctification is followed by a continued growth in grace. There are two sacraments: baptism and the Lord's Supper. Baptism may be by sprinkling or pouring, but immersion is preferred. The Association believes in divine healing. it is opposed to drafting individuals into military service. The Association's general rules establish a strict code of personal conduct.

Organization: The Association is congregationally governed. Each church owns its own property and calls its ministers. Churches are grouped into five districts, each served by a district superintendent. A representative general conference meets biennially. It elects a general board consisting of the general superintendent, assistant general superintendent, general secretary, general treasurer, the district superintendents, and a lay delegate from each district. The Association's home missionary program includes work among American Indians in Arizona; its foreign missionaries can be found in Bolivia, the Dominican Republic, Guatemala, Haiti, Honduras, and New Guinea.

Membership: In 1988, the Association reported 40 congregations served by 100 ministers.

Periodicals: *Eleventh Hour Messenger*, 108 Carter Ave., Dayton, OH 45405.

Sources: *Declaration of Principles*. Dayton, OH: Wesleyan Holiness Association of Churches, 1981; Glenn Griffith, *I Sought for a Man*. Phoenix, AZ: The Author, n.d.

Section 7

Pentecostal Family

An historical essay on this family is provided beginning on page 41.

White Trinitarian Holiness Pentecostals

★315★
THE APOSTOLIC FAITH MISSION OF
PORTLAND, OREGON, INC.
6615 S.E. 52nd Ave.
Portland, OR 97206

Among those receiving the baptism of the Holy Spirit during the early Pentecostal revival meetings at the Pacific Apostolic Faith Movement's mission on Azusa Street in Los Angeles was Florence L. Crawford, a Methodist laywoman. At her baptism in the Spirit, she related that God "permitted me to speak in the Chinese tongue which was understood by a Christian Chinese who was present." She also experienced a healing of her eyes, which had been damaged by spinal meningitis. Crawford became an active worker, assisting mission leader W. J. Seymour. Her first ministries were along the West Coast where she worked as an itinerant home missionary. In Portland, Oregon, the people were so taken with her ministry that the pastor of a little independent church turned the pulpit over to her permanently. She immediately discontinued taking offerings at meetings and began to rely solely on tithes and freewill gifts. She also broke with Seymour, but continued to use the name Apostolic Faith, claiming as her heritage the work begun by Rev. Charles Parham and Seymour. She began to travel under her own sponsorship throughout the West and into the Midwest and Canada. In 1908, having brought the mailing list of the mission with her, she distributed the first issue of a new periodical, *The Apostolic Faith*. Portland was established as headquarters of the growing movement. In 1922, the large headquarters building, a landmark in downtown Portland, was erected and a large neon sign saying "Jesus the Light of the World," first erected in 1917, was transferred to the new structure.

Following Seymour's teachings, Crawford preached a holiness doctrine like that of the Church of God (Cleveland, Tennessee). Her followers practice a very strict moral code, keeping from worldliness and refraining from being "unequally yoked" in marriage with unbelievers. Footwashing as a third ordinance joins baptism and the Lord's Supper.

The church is governed by a board of five trustees headed by a general overseer. There is also a board of 24 elders. The polity is presbyterian and each local congregation is under the leadership and direction of the Portland headquarters. Loyce C. Carver is the current general overseer. Both home and foreign missions have emerged on a large scale, with work in 21 countries in Africa, Asia, and Europe. The largest mission field is in Nigeria, where there are approximately 20,000 members. Camp meetings remain a central feature of the program, and there are denominational campgrounds in Portland, Oregon; Murfrysboro, Illinois; and Century, Florida.

Membership: In 1987 the church reported approximately 4,000 members, in 40 congregations with 90 ministers in the United States and six congregations and ten ministers in Canada. There are approximately 50,000 members in foreign lands. Membership is very low; the church counts all who regularly attend as members.

Periodicals: *The Light of Hope*, 6615 S.E. 52nd Avenue, Portland, OR 97206.

Sources: *A Historical Account of the Apostolic Faith*. Portland, OR: Apostolic Faith Publishing House, 1965; *The Light of Life Brought Triumph*. Portland, OR: Apostolic Faith Publishing House, 1955; *Saved to Serve*. Portland, OR: Apostolic Faith Publishing House, 1967.

★316★
CAROLINA EVANGELISTIC ASSOCIATION
% Cannon Cathedral
Box 31773
Charlotte, NC 28231-1773

Dr. A. G. Garr was the first foreign missionary of the Church of God (Cleveland, Tennessee). He left the church in 1906, immediately after receiving the baptism of the

Holy Spirit. He continued to do foreign missionary work until 1912, when he returned to the United States and began to operate as an evangelist in the days when Pentecostals were still a small, scattered group. He was particularly active in the early years of the Angelus Temple, the Los Angeles center for the International Church of the Foursquare Gospel headed by Aimee Semple McPherson. In 1930, he went to Charlotte, North Carolina, to conduct a tent revival. After three months, those who had been saved, healed, and helped asked him to remain. Fifty-six years old then, he remained and built a tabernacle. An abandoned city auditorium was bought, remodeled, and named Garr Auditorium; it remains as the headquarters of the association. Dr. Garr died in 1944 and was succeeded by his wife and son as pastors.

The Carolina Evangelistic Association carries on an active program through Garr Auditorium and Faith Chapel, both in Charlotte. There are missionaries supported by the Association in numerous countries. A regular program of services is conducted in the county jail and the county home. The "Morning Thought for the Day Magazine" radio show is their radio ministry. Camp Lurecrest for youth is located at Lake Lure, North Carolina. The church is a member of the Pentecostal Fellowship of North America.

Membership: Not reported. Approximately 1,000 people regularly attend worship at Garr Auditorium.

★317★
CHURCH OF GOD (CLEVELAND, TENNESSEE)
Keith St. at 25th St., N.W.
Cleveland, TN 37311

Most of the Pentecostal churches which bear the name "Church of God" can be traced to a holiness revival in the mountains of northwest Georgia and eastern Tennessee. In 1884, R. G. Spurling, a Baptist minister in Monroe County, Tennessee, began to search the Scriptures for answers to the problems of modernism, formality, and spiritual dryness. An initial meeting of concerned people was held on August 19, 1886, at the Barney Creek Meeting House to organize a new movement that would preach primitive church holiness and provide for reform and revival of the churches. Christian Union was the name accepted by the first eight members enrolled that day. Spurling died within a few months and was succeeded in leadership by his son, R. G. Spurling, Jr.

After ten years of little growth, three laymen influenced by the Spurlings' work claimed a deep religious experience similar to that written about by John Wesley, the founder of Methodism, and as a result began to preach sanctification. (Wesley attended a service at Aldersgate Street in London in 1738 where he "felt his heart strangely warmed." He and his followers interpreted this as a work of God which again sanctified the person who had already experienced a justifying faith in Christ). The three laymen began to hold services at Camp Creek, in Cherokee County, North Carolina, among a group of unaffiliated Baptists. Spurling and the Christian Union moved their services to Camp Creek and united with the group in North Carolina. During the revival that followed this merger, spontaneous speaking in tongues occurred. After searching the Scriptures, the group recognized the phenomena as a Biblical occurrence and as a new outpouring of the Holy Spirit.

The Christian Union, as it grew, suffered from both persecution and fanaticism: as its unrestrained members spoke in tongues and held noisy services, various members of the local community complained. Some leaders of the Christian Union, responding to the criticism, decided to make the services more orderly. They devised a simple plan of government at a meeting in the home of W. F. Bryant. The group's name was changed to the Holiness Church. In 1896, during the revival, Ambrose J. Tomlinson (1865-1943), an Indiana Quaker and agent of the American Bible Society, came to the hill country to sell Bibles and religious literature. In 1903, he cast his lot with the group and became pastor of the Camp Creek Church. This event can be viewed as the real beginning of the Church of God movement. Having been influenced by the Church of God (Anderson, Indiana), Tomlinson persuaded the Holiness Church to accept the Biblical name the Church of God. He is also the probable source for the pacifist emphasis which permeates many Pentecostal churches. Tomlinson began a publishing enterprise and printed for distribution the doctrines of the new church. Headquarters were soon established in his home at Culbertson, Tennessee, and he emerged as the dominant leader. Tomlinson later settled in Cleveland, Tennessee, and eventually led a congregation there to unite with the Holiness Church. The church's period of expansion had begun.

With the establishment of further congregations, the members saw the necessity of an assembly for dealing with questions of mutual concern. The first assembly convened in 1906 at Camp Creek and decisions were made about footwashing--it was to be observed at least annually--and mid-week and family services--they were to be encouraged. At the 1907 assembly, the name was officially changed to the Church of God.

The 1908 assembly was attended by G. B. Cashwell, who was to introduce many holiness people to the baptism of the Holy Spirit and the experience of speaking in tongues which had occurred at the mission of the Pacific Apostolic Faith Movement on Azusa Street in Los Angeles. After the assembly, he preached a revival. Tomlinson received the baptism and spoke in tongues. The following year, in a gesture symbolic of the church's acceptance of the new truth preached by Cashwell and experienced by Tomlinson, he was selected general moderator of the young church, a position he held until 1922. In 1914, he was elected general overseer for life. Accelerated growth, with the exception of losses of schismatic bodies, has continued unabated.

Doctrinally, the Church of God believes in the baptism of the Holy Spirit as an experience subsequent to sanctification. Practices include baptism by immersion, the Lord's Supper, and footwashing. Members believe in holiness-of-life, which excludes the use of cosmetics, costly apparel, and shorts or slacks on women. They accept a premillennial second coming (the coming of Christ to bind Satan before Christ's thousand-year reign on earth with his saints).

Government of the Church of God is centralized. Authority is vested in the general assembly, which meets every two years and is chaired by the general overseer. A supreme council operates between general assemblies, and a general executive committee oversees the boards and agencies. State overseers have charge over the churches in their areas and appoint the pastors. Tithing is a central feature in finances. The height of centralization came in 1914 when the annual elections of the general overseer were discontinued and Tomlinson became overseer for life.

Tomlinson's authority was attacked in the 1920s. In 1922, a committee ordered to investigate the church's finances (which Tomlinson completely controlled) reported unfavorably, and Tomlinson was impeached and removed from office. The overseer's authority had been reduced earlier by the addition of two new offices to control functions previously controlled by Tomlinson (publishing and education). These were supplemented in 1922 by the new constitution, adopted despite Tomlinson's opposition.

The Church of God Publishing House produces a large selection of books, pamphlets and tracts, and a full line of church school material. Missions, both foreign and domestic, are widespread (in seventy-two countries) and supported by the tithe of members. The Church is a member of the National Association of Evangelicals.

Membership: In 1984 the church reported 505,775 members, 5,346 churches, and 9,638 ministers.

Educational facilities: Lee College, Cleveland, Tennessee; Northwest Bible and Music Academy, Minot, North Dakota; West Coast Bible School, Pasadena, California.

Periodicals: *Church of God Evangel*, Church of God Publishing House, 1080 Montgomery Avenue, Cleveland, TN 37311; *Lighted Pathway*, Church of God Publishing House, 1080 Montgomery Avenue, Cleveland, TN 37311.

Sources: Charles W. Conn, *Like a Mighty Army*. Cleveland, TN: Church of God Publishing House, 1955; Charles W. Conn, *Pillars of Pentecost*. Cleveland, TN: Pathway Press, 1956; James L. Slay, *This We Believe*. Cleveland, TN: Pathway Press, 1963; Ray H. Hughes, *Church of God Distinctives*. Cleveland, TN: Pathway Press, 1968; June Glover Marshall, *A Biographical Sketch of Richard G. Spurling, Jr.* Cleveland, TN: Pathway Press, 1974.

★318★
CHURCH OF GOD (JERUSALEM ACRES)
% Chief Bishop John A. Looper
Box 1207
1826 Dalton Pike (Jerusalem Acres)
Cleveland, TN 37364-1207

History. The Church of God (Jerusalem Acres) began in 1857 when Grady R. Kent initiated a reformation of the Church of God of Prophecy aimed at a reestablishment of its biblical order. Kent had been a pastor in the church since 1933. In 1943, he was placed in charge of the Church of God of Prophecy Marker Association begun by Ambrose J. Tomlinson, the church's founder, as an auxiliary to locate, mark, beautify, and maintain prominent places in the world connected with the Church of God of Prophecy. One place of particular interest was the Fields of the Wood--a mountainside Bible monument, based on Psalms 132:6 and Habakkuk 2:2-3, located on Burger Mountain in western North Carolina. The monument includes a replica of the Ten Commandments in seven-foot tall letters and an altar on the top of the mountain. The altar marks the spot where Tomlinson prayed, immediately prior to declaring the Church of God to be in existence. Kent also supervised the White Angel Fleet, pilots and airplanes used for public demonstrations of ministry at airports throughout the United States. Between 1948 and 1957, Kent objected to the Church of God of Prophecy replacing the general overseer with the general assembly as the highest authority in the church (which, in effect, repeated the history of the church and led to its formation in the early 1920s). Faced with having to recant his objection to the actions of the general assembly, as well as other controversial ideas he had developed, Kent resigned in 1957. With 300 supporters, many from South Carolina, Kent established a new Church of God, with himself as general overseer.

Beliefs. The Church believes in an experiential understanding of justification by faith, sanctification as a second work of grace, and the baptism of the Holy Spirit evidenced by speaking in tongues. It also believes in the restoration of both ministerial (Ephesians 4:11) and spiritual (I Corinthians 12) gifts to the Church.

In areas of worship and service, the church has developed a comprehensive program termed "New Testament Judaism," a term coined by Kent in 1962 on a visit to Israel. The church observes the biblical (Old Testament) calendar that includes the sabbath as a day of worship; Passover as a time for celebrating communion; Pentecost as a festival for spiritual renewal and dedication to the work of the church; and Tabernacles as a remembrance of the time of Christ's birth and a foreshadowing of his return. Various symbols generally associated with Judaism are used alongside of the cross. The church does not celebrate the holidays of Easter, Halloween, and Christmas.

Organization. The polity is theocratic, government by God through an annointed leader. There is a chief bishop who sits as the final authority (as contrasted to the total authority) in matters of both judicial and executive government. The church has no legislative body, but has a council of apostles and elders, the purpose of which is judicial--that is, to interpret the laws of God in the Bible, both Old and New Testaments, as they relate to the church. The primary officers in the council are the chief bishop, the 12 apostles, the seven men of wisdom, and the 70 elders.

Membership: In 1987, the church reported 10,000 members, 145 churches, and 255 ministers.

Periodicals: *The Vision Speaks*, Jerusalem Acres, Cleveland, TN 37364-1207; *Greater Light*, Jerusalem Acres, Cleveland, TN 37364-1207.

Sources: Grady R. Kent, *Treatise on the 1957 Reformation Stand.* Cleveland, TN: Church Publishing Company, the Church of God, n.d.; *Introduction to Apostles' Doctrine.* Cleveland, TN: Church Publishing Company, 1984; *Manual of Apostles Doctrine and Business Procedure.* Cleveland, TN: Church Publishing Company and Press.

★319★
CHURCH OF GOD OF PROPHECY
Bible Place
Cleveland, TN 37311

Alternate address: Canadian headquarters: 1st Line East. R. R. 2, Brampton, ON L6V 1A1.

History. The Church of God of Prophecy shared the early years of the Pentecostal-holiness movement in the southern United States with the Church of God (Cleveland). Ambrose J. Tomlinson (1865-1943) was one of the pioneers of that church and for many years served as its overseer. However, in 1921 he separated himself from that organization for a variey of reasons and reorganized his following as the Tomlinson Church of God (changed to the present name in 1952). Following A. J. Tomlinson's death, his son, Milton A. Tomlinson, succeeded him as leader of the organization. His tenure as general overseer continues to the present day.

Beliefs. The Church of God of Prophecy accepts the authority of the whole Bible as the Word of God and hence has no creed. However, it has summarized what it considers to be "Twenty-Nine Important Bible Truths" which show it to be in basic agreement with traditional trinitarian Christian beliefs. It places special emphasis on sanctification (holiness of the believer) and the doctrine of Spirit-baptism that includes speaking-in-tongues as initial evidence. Other prominent doctrinal commitments include: an eschatology that involves a premillennial return of the risen Jesus, which, according to the church, will be preceded by a series of events; a call for sanctity in the home that includes denial of multiple marriages; practice of baptism by immersion, the Lord's Supper and washing the saints' feet; total abstinence from intoxicating beverages and tobacco; a concern for modesty in all dimensions of life; and an appreciation for various gifts of the Holy Spirit with special attention to divine healing.

Organization. The church is headed by its general overseer. An annual general assembly meets at the church's world headquarters at Bible Place, in Cleveland, Tennessee. The assembly addresses the various doctrinal and business concerns as come before it, and all resolutions must receive unanimous consent of all male members in attendance to be adopted. These resolutions are then ratified by each local assembly. The general assembly concludes with the general overseer appointing all national and international leaders, who in turn are responsible for appointing the various leaders under their jurisdiction.

The church has developed a strong program of youth ministries, foreign and domestic missions, and various parochial educational ministries. One distinctive activity involves the church marking places of significance to the church. The most famous memorial site is the Field of the Woods, near Murphy, North Carolina, marking the site of the reappearance of the Church of God in 1903. The site has been developed into a biblical-theme park that includes the worlds largest cross, the Ten Commandments depicted in five-foot letters, and biblical markers that portray the message of Christ.

In 1916 the church developed the Assembly Ban Movement, a unique program which organizes cell groups of eight to twelve people and aims to foster religious commitment and growth. These groups resemble the classes organized in the nineteenth century by the early Methodists.

In 1933 the church adopted an official church flag which is on display in all church facilities.

Membership: In 1987 the church reported 74,588 members, 2,085 churches, and 123 missions in the United States. Outside of the United States there were 172,153 members, 3,048 churches, and 964 missions. In 1985 there were 2,091 members in 38 Canadian churches.

Educational facilities: Tomlinson College, Cleveland, Tennessee.

Periodicals: *White Wing Messenger*, Bible Place, Cleveland, TN 37311; *The Happy Harvester*, Bible Place, Cleveland, TN 37311.

Remarks: The problems which led to the withdrawal of A. J. Tomlinson from the Church of God (Cleveland, Tennessee) in 1922 are described quite differently by the two groups. According to Homer Tomlinson, one of A. J. Tomlinson's sons, the occassion of the schism was the desire of some church elders to organize a Golden Rule Supply Company to operate as a co-op for members, and to use the profits to support the church's mission program. Reportedly, the Rev. Joe S. Lewellyn and others campaigned against Tomlinson, which undermined his support and the confidence in his leadership. In any case, Tomlinson strongly objected to the church's reorganization in 1921 which substantially stripped many of the powers from the office of general overseer.

Sources: C. T. Davidson, *Upon This Rock*. Cleveland TN: White Wing Press, 1973-76. 3 Vols.; Lillie Duggar, *A. J. Tomlinson*. Cleveland, TN: White Wing Publishing House, 1964; James Stone, *The Church of God of Prophecy: History and Polity*. Cleveland, TN: White Wing Press, 1977; Raymond M. Pruitt, *Fundamentals of the Faith*. Cleveland, TN: White Wing Publishing House and Press, 1981.

★320★
CHURCH OF GOD OF THE APOSTOLIC FAITH
Current address not obtained for this edition.

The Church of God of the Apostolic Faith was organized in 1914 by four independent Pentecostal ministers who saw the need for some organization and church government. Not wishing to follow the plan of government adopted by the Assemblies of God, which had been formed that year in nearby Hot Springs, Arkansas, the Reverends James O. McKenzie, Edwin A. Buckles, Oscar H. Myers, and Joseph P. Rhoades held a meeting which led to the creation of the Church of God of the Apostolic Faith at Cross Roads Mission near Ozark, Arkansas. They adopted a presbyterial form of government based on Acts 15. The Church also had a doctrinal difference with the Assemblies of God, believing as did the Church of God (Cleveland, Tennessee) that one must seek sanctification before having the baptism of the Holy Spirit. Like the Church of God, healing, tithing, and nonparticipation in war are emphasized.

The general conference of the Church meets annually. It elects the general presbytery of seven ministers, including the general overseer and two assistants. The conference owns all the property and the presbytery controls the ministry. The church is currently divided into five districts. There is a mission in Mexico.

Membership: Not reported. In the mid-1970s there were approximately 1,400 members in 27 congregations.

Periodicals: *Church of God Herald*; *Christian Youth*.

★321★
CHURCH OF GOD OF THE MOUNTAIN ASSEMBLY
Florence Ave.
Jellico, TN 37762

The Church of God of the Mountain Assembly grew out of a holiness revival in 1895 in the South Union Association of the United Baptist Church. From 1895 until 1903, members and ministers who adopted the holiness belief in a second work of grace which imparts sanctification by the power of the Holy Spirit, remained within the United Baptist Church. However, in 1903, the Baptists decided to revoke the licenses of all ministers who were preaching sanctification according to the holiness movement. In 1906, these holiness ministers-- Reverends J. H. Parks, Steve Bryant, Tom Moses, and William O. Douglas--met at Jellico, Tennessee, with members of their several churches and organized the Church of God. The words "Mountain Assembly" were added in 1911 after the group heard of other Church of God groups. In 1906-07, the group learned of the baptism of the Holy Spirit as evidenced by speaking in tongues and accepted it as a fuller expression of their ideas. At the second assembly in 1907, S. N. Bryant was elected moderator, a post he held until 1938, except for two years.

The doctrine of the Church of God of the Mountain Assembly is similar to that of the Church of God (Cleveland, Tennessee). The Church is very conservative in its faith, and only the King James Version of the Bible is used. Present polity was adopted in 1914. The offices of general overseer, assistant overseer, and state overseer were established and filled. The overseers operate in a basically congregational system. The assembly meets annually. From its headquarters in Jellico, Tennessee the Church of God of the Mountain Assembly has spread throughout the South and into the Midwest as far as Ohio, Michigan, and Wisconsin.

Membership: Not reported. In 1977 the church reported 105 churches, 3,125 members, and 162 churches.

Periodicals: *Gospel Herald*, Jellico, TN 37762.

Sources: Luther Gibson, *History of the Church of God Mountain Assembly*. The Author, 1954.

★322★
CHURCH OF GOD OF THE ORIGINAL MOUNTAIN ASSEMBLY
Williamsburg, KY 40769

In 1939 Steve N. Bryant, longtime leader of the Church of God of the Mountain Assembly died. He was succeeded by A. J. Long, who led the Church in a reorganization in 1944. However, in 1946, Long was not reelected as moderator. That same year, with his supporters, he left and founded the Church of God of the Original Mountain

Assembly. Approximately one fourth of the membership (fifteen ministers, eight deacons, and approximately 300 people) established the new church on the original structure of the parent body. The church is headed by a general overseer and a council of twelve. The first meeting of the Church of God of the Original Mountain Assembly was held at Williamsburg, Kentucky. The doctrine of the parent body was adopted, from the covenant originally made when it was incorporated in 1917, but articles were added on the need for harmony between pastors and deacons (lay leaders), the subordinate role of women and opposition to snake handling.

Membership: Not reported. In 1967 there were 11 churches and 17 ministers.

★323★
CHURCH OF GOD OF THE UNION ASSEMBLY
Box 1323
Dalton, GA 30720

The Church of God of the Union Assembly is a small schism formed in 1920 from the Church of God of the Mountain Assembly. It began when the congregation in Center, Jackson County, Georgia withdrew. The immediate occasion for the split was the issue of tithing. The Union Assembly rejects the tithing system established in 1919 by the Mountain Assembly, believing it to be an Old Testament practice not taught by Jesus or his apostles. The group also believes the kingdom of God is a spiritual kingdom; that David's throne is established in heaven, not on earth; and that Christ's coming will be followed by the end of time, not the millennium (Christ's reign on earth for 1,000 years with his saints). The Union Assembly's present leader is Jesse Pratt, who has written a number of pamphlets disseminated through the church. Congregations have spread to seventeen states.

Membership: Not reported.

Periodicals: *Quarterly News*, Box 1323, Dalton, GA 30720.

★324★
CHURCH OF GOD, THE HOUSE OF PRAYER
% Rev. Charles Mackenin
Markleysburg, PA 15459

Harrison W. Poteat joined the Church of God (Cleveland, Tennessee) in its early years and was an overseer in the Northeast for more than twenty years. In 1933, he established churches on Prince Edward Island. In 1939, he broke with the Cleveland headquarters and founded the Church of God, the House of Prayer. Many of the churches which Poteat had established went with him. A suit was brought by the parent body, which was able to recover occupancy in many of the church properties, and the loss of the property cut deeply into Poteat's support. Some congregations withdrew from the Church of God,

the House of Prayer, and became independent. Doctrine follows that of the parent body.

Membership: Not reported. In 1967 the church reported 24 churches in the northeast and 2 in Canada, with a total membership of 1,200.

★325★
CHURCH OF GOD (WORLD HEADQUARTERS)
1270 Willow Brook, S.E., Apt. 2
Huntsville, AL 35802

A. J. Tomlinson, founder of the Church of God (Cleveland, Tennessee) and the Church of God of Prophecy died in 1943. Before his death, however, he designated his eldest son Homer Tomlinson, his successor as general overseer. However, the General Assembly set aside that appointment and selected the younger son, Milton A. Tomlinson as the new general overseer. Homer Tomlinson rejected their action, called his followers to a meeting in New York and reorganized the Church of God, generally distinguished from other similarly-named groups by the additional phrase, "World Headquarters." A struggle in court over control of the Church resulted in Milton and his followers being recognized as the legal successors. They were awarded all properties and trademarks. Homer continued as head of the group of loyal followers and rebuilt the Church which he led until his death in 1968. He was succeeded by Voy M. Bullen.

The doctrine, which follows closely that of the other Church of God bodies, is contained in the *Book of Doctrines/1903-1970*. The only doctrinal divergence in the entire Church of God movement occurs in the Church of God (World Headquarters). Its members replace the premillennialism of the other branches with a belief that the Church of God has the keys to bring the kingdom of God on earth, and that the kingdom will come by the setting up of the saints of God in the governments of the nations of the world now, here upon earth. Saints are encouraged to become responsible rulers and to preach the gospel of the kingdom. This doctrine was based upon the Bible as interpreted by A. J. Tomlinson, who gave Homer a commission to plant the church flag in every nation of the earth. Given that commission, Homer established the "World Headquarters" of the Church of God in Jerusalem.

After Bishop Homer's death in 1968, the American headquarters was moved from Queens, New York, to Huntsville, Alabama, a location more central to the congregations. The church's administrative offices are there. An annual assembly is held at Cape Girardeau, Missouri. A vigorous mission program, attributed in part to Homer's tireless traveling, has seen affiliated Churches of God established in England, Scotland, Panama, Nigeria, Barbados, Jamaica, Kenya, the Philippine Islands, the Virgin Islands, Canada, Egypt, Haiti, Greece, and Ghana. The Theocratic Party, as sociated with the

Church, runs candidates for both state and national offices in the United States.

Membership: Not reported. In 1973, there were 2,035 churches, 75,890 members and 2,737 ministers, wordwide.

Periodicals: *The Church of God*, 1270 Willow Brook, S.E., Apt. 2, Huntsville, AL 35802.

Sources: *Book of Doctrines, 1903-1970.* Huntsville, AL: Church of God Publishing House, 1970; Homer A. Tomlinson, *The Shout of a King.* Queens Village, NY: The Church of God, 1968.

★326★
CONGREGATIONAL HOLINESS CHURCH
3888 Fayetteville Hwy.
Griffin, GA 30223

In 1920 a controversy over divine healing arose in the Georgia Conference of the Pentecostal Holiness Church, now known as the International Pentecostal Holiness Church. One faction contended that the healing provisions in the atonement were sufficient, and that human aids (doctors) were unnecessary. While this faction admitted the therapeutic value of effective remedies, such remedies were not considered necessary for God to heal. The other faction, led by Rev. Watson Sorrow, insisted that God had placed medicine on earth for man's use. The group against doctors relied on the Biblical phrase about Christ's passion, "By his stripes you are healed."

The names of the Rev. Watson Sorrow and Hugh Bowling were dropped from the ministerial roll of the Pentecostal Holiness Church without their first being tried by the board of the Georgia annual conference of which they were members. A number of ministers withdrew with them, and together they organized the Congregational Holiness Church. They expressed differences with their parent body on the concentration of power in a few hands, so they attempted to democratize the church government. Consequently their polity is not episcopal, like that of the Pentecostal Holiness Church. Their polity is a moderate connectional system: local churches are grouped in associations which elect delegates to a general association with legislative powers. Pastors are called by vote of the congregation. Only men may be ordained. Mission work is going forth in Cuba, Costa Rica, Brazil, Mexico, Honduras, Guatemala, India, Nicaragua, and Spain.

Membership: In 1987 the Church reported 6,378 members, 170 churches, and 455 ministers.

Periodicals: *Gospel Messenger*, 3888 Fayetteville Hwy., Griffin, GA 30223.

Sources: B. L. Cox, *History and Doctrine of the Congregational Holiness Church.* Gainesville, GA: The

Author, 1959; B. L. Cox, *My Life Story.* Greenwood, SC: C. H. Publishing House, n.d.

★327★
DOOR OF FAITH CHURCH AND BIBLE SCHOOL
1161 Young St.
Honolulu, HI 96814

The Door of Faith Church and Bible School was founded by Mildred Johnson Brostek. Raised a Methodist, she experienced the baptism of the Holy Spirit in an Assemblies of God church in Florida. She later joined the Pentecostal Holiness Church (now known as the International Pentecostal Holiness Church), which licensed her to preach. She graduated from the Holmes Theological Seminary and soon thereafter went to the Hawaiian Islands where she had earlier felt a call from God to go as a missionary. In 1937, she began to hold evangelistic services on Molokai in the home of a native Hawaiian. The services prospered and in 1940, the Door of Faith Churches of Hawaii was chartered and the work soon spread to the other islands.

The church is headed by the Rev. Brostek who is the church's overseer. There is an annual conference. A daily radio ministry is broacast over two stations, one in Honolulu and one in Hilo, Hawaii.

Membership: Not reported. There are churches at a number of locations in Hawaii and a prosperous mission has developed in the Philippines, where a Bible college has been opened. There is one church in New York. In 1979, there were 40 churches and 3,000 members in Hawaii and missions work in Okinawa and Indonesia.

Educational facilities: Door of Faith Bible School, Honolulu, Hawaii.

Sources: Robert D. Donovan, *Her Door of Faith.* Honolulu, HI: Orovan Books, 1971.

★328★
EMMANUEL HOLINESS CHURCH
Box 818
Bladenboro, NC 28320

In 1953, controversy over standards of dress among the members of the Pentecostal Fire-Baptized Holiness Church led to a vote to divide the church. One issue which occasioned the split was the use of neckties, which the Pentecostal Fire-Baptized Holiness Church explicity forbids. Those who voted for the split elected Rev. L. O. Sellers chairman and formed the Emmanuel Holiness Church. It differs from its parent body only on minor points of dress, a more congregational form of government, and tithing which is required of members. A general assembly of all ministers and one delegate from each church has limited legislative powers.

Membership: Not reported. In 1967 there were 72 congregations and 118 ministers.

Periodicals: *Emmanuel Holiness Messenger.*

★329★
EVANGELISTIC CHURCH OF GOD
Current address not obtained for this edition.

The Evangelistic Church of God was incorporated at Denver, Colorado in 1949. It grew out of the work of Norman L. Chase, former minister of the Church of God (Cleveland, Tennessee) and of the (Original) Church of God. By 1955 the group claimed 774 members in twelve churches. The general assembly meets annually.

Membership: Not reported.

Periodicals: *The Church of God Final Warning*, Soddy, TN.

★330★
FIRST INTERDENOMINATIONAL CHRISTIAN ASSOCIATION
Calvary Temple Holiness Church
1061 Memorial Dr., S.E.
Atlanta, GA 30315

In 1946, the Rev. Watson Sorrow, who had been one of the founders of the Congregational Holiness Church, formed the First Interdenominational Christian Association, centered upon his own congregation, Calvary Temple in Atlanta. The Association is like the Congregational Holiness Church but less definite in doctrine. The parent body's statements on war, eschatology, and the forbidding of varying doctrinal beliefs among ministers were dropped. Retained were statements on healing, footwashing, and Pentecostalism. Several churches have joined Sorrow by adopting the congregational polity and policies of Calvary Temple.

Membership: Not reported. In the late 1960s, Calvary Temple had about 100 members.

★331★
FREE WILL BAPTIST CHURCH OF THE PENTECOSTAL FAITH
Current address not obtained for this edition.

The Free Will Baptist Church of the Pentecostal Faith was formed in the 1950s when some members of the South Carolina Pentecostal Free Will Baptist Church Conference decided not to participate in the reorganization that led to the formation of the Pentecostal Free Will Baptist Church. Those who abstained adopted a constitution and chose a new name. They are at one doctrinally with the other Pentecostal Free Will Baptists.

The polity is congregational. The annual conference is to approve teachings, methods and conduct, and to encourage fellowship and evangelism. A general board headed by the conference superintendent functions between conference meetings. The Foreign Missions Department oversees work in Costa Rica. Camp meetings are periodically sponsored.

Membership: Not reported. In 1967 there were 33 congregations and 39 ministers.

Sources: *Faith and Government of the Free Will Baptist Church of the Pentecostal Faith.* 1961.

★332★
FULL GOSPEL CHURCH ASSOCIATION
Box 265
Amarillo, TX 79105

The Full Gospel Church Association, Incorporated, was organized by the Rev. Dennis W. Thorn at Amarillo, Texas, in 1952 for the purpose of bringing together a number of small, independent Pentecostal churches and missions, most of them with fewer than 100 members in the South and Southwest.

Doctrinally, the Full Gospel Church is similar to the Church of God (Cleveland, Tennessee). It emphasizes healing, tithing, and a literal heaven and hell, and uses only the King James Version of the Bible. It practices footwashing. Bearing arms is a matter of individual judgment. It does forbid disloyalty, insubordination, and criticism of the Association by its individual members. One unique element is the requirement that each church have an "Altar of God" in its building as a condition of its recognition by the Association.

The Association is congregational in polity. A general convention meets regularly. The general board of directors meets quarterly; its executive directors are the supreme council of the Association. Mission workers were active in Mexico, the Philippines, and Africa.

Membership: Not reported. In 1967 there were 67 churches with a total combined membership of 2,010.

★333★
GENERAL CONFERENCE OF THE EVANGELICAL BAPTIST CHURCH
Kavetter Bldg.
3400 E. Ash St.
Goldsboro, NC 27530

The General Conference of the Evangelical Baptist Church was organized in 1935 as the Church of the Full Gospel, Inc. It is Pentecostal and holiness in emphasis, following a theology close to that of the Pentecostal Free Will Baptist Church. It stresses spiritual gifts, healing, and the pretribulation, premillennial return of Christ. Four ordinances are recognized--baptism by immersion, communion, the dedication of children, and tithing. The dedication of children is a form of christening that is distinct from baptism.

The polity is congregational. There is an annual conference which elects officers. In the local church, the pastor is the chief officer. He is elected by the congregation and has the power to appoint or nominate all church officers.

Membership: Not reported. In 1952 there were 31 churches, 2,200 members and 37 ministers.

Educational facilities: Evangelical Theological Seminary, Goldsboro, North Carolina; William Carter College, Goldsboro, North Carolina.

Periodicals: *Evangelical Baptist*, 2400 E. Ash Street, Goldsboro, NC 27530.

Sources: *Discipline of the General Conference of the Evangelical Baptist Church.*

★334★
HOLINESS BAPTIST ASSOCIATION
Current address not obtained for this edition.

The Holiness Baptist Association can be traced to 1893 when, because of their teaching on "sinless perfection," two congregations and several ministers were expelled from the Little River Baptist Association. The next year, together with two additional newly-organized churches, representatives met at the Pine City Church in Wilcox County, Georgia and formed the Association. The Association mixes the Wesleyan understanding of sanctification with traditional Missionary Baptist standards of faith and decorum. Tongues-speech, while permitted by the group, is not regarded as evidence of the baptism of the Holy Spirit. The Association operates a campground on the Alma Highway seven miles east of Douglas, Georgia. Association business is transacted there annually during camp meeting.

Membership: Not reported. In the mid-1970s there were 46 congregations (all in Georgia and Florida) and approximately 2,000 members.

★335★
HOLINESS CHURCH OF GOD
% Bishop B. McKinney
602 E. Elm St.
Graham, NC 27253

The Holiness Church of God was formed in 1920 by members from several holiness churches which had received the baptism of the Holy Spirit. Three years before, a revival, called the Big May Meeting, led by Elder James A. Foust had occurred in Madison, North Carolina. The entire membership of several congregations became Pentecostals, including the Kimberly Park Holiness Church in Winston-Salem. The church incorporated in 1928. Churches are found in New York, Virginia and West Virginia.

Membership: Not reported. In 1968 there were 28 congregations and 927 members.

★336★
INTERNATIONAL PENTECOSTAL CHURCH OF CHRIST
Box 439
2245 U.S. 42, S.W.
London, OH 43140

The International Pentecostal Church of Christ was formed in 1976 by a merger of the International Pentecostal Assemblies and the Pentecostal Church of Christ. The International Pentecostal Assemblies was formed in 1936 by the merger of the Association of Pentecostal Assemblies and the National and International Pentecostal Missionary Union. The former body was an outgrowth of a periodical, *The Bridegroom's Messenger*, which had been founded in 1907. The Association of Pentecostal Assemblies was founded in 1921 in Atlanta by Elizabeth A. Sexton, Hattie M. Barth, and Paul T. Barth. The National and International Pentecostal Missionary Union was founded in 1914 by Dr. Philip Wittich.

In 1908, evangelist, John Stroup of South Solon, Ohio, received the baptism of the Holy Spirit, signified by his speaking in tongues. In 1913, he began to travel through southeastern Ohio and the adjacent territory in Kentucky and West Virginia, organizing churches in that area. In 1917 at Advance (Flatwoods), Kentucky, a group of ministers met, organized the Pentecostal Church of Christ, and appointed Stroup bishop. In 1927, the Pentecostal Church of Christ was incorporated.

The doctrine of the merged church follows closely that of the Church of God (Cleveland, Tennessee). Members believe in healing, the premillennial return of Christ, a personal devil, Sunday as the Lord's rest day, and two ordinances--baptism and the Lord's Supper. Footwashing is optional for local assemblies and believers.

Organization of the small church is congregational with a bishop or general overseer elected every two years. Women are admitted to the ordained ministry. *The Bridegroom's Messenger* continues as the official periodical and is now the oldest continuously published Pentecostal publication. Missions are supported in Hong Kong, India, Uganda, Nigeria, Mexico and Brazil.

Membership: In 1985 the Church reported 3,500 members, 74 churches and 201 ministers.

Educational facilities: Beulah Heights Bible College, Atlanta, GA 30316.

Periodicals: *The Bridegroom's Messenger*. Route 3, Box 56, Elizabeth City, NC 27909; *The Pentecostal Leader*, Box 439, London, OH 43140.

★337★
INTERNATIONAL PENTECOSTAL HOLINESS CHURCH
7300 N.W. 39th Expressway
Bethany, OK 73008

In addition to those Pentecostal churches that derive from the Rev. Charles Parham and the Apostolic Church and the Topeka Bible School, which he founded, there is a Pentecostal group that begins with Benjamin Hardin Irwin. He was a Baptist who had received the experience of sanctification under the influence of the Iowa Holiness Association, a group made up mostly of Methodists. As a holiness minister, he began to delve into Methodist writings, in particular those of John Fletcher, the eighteenth-century Wesleyan divine. In Fletcher he found what he felt to be an experience for sanctified believers, described as a "baptism of burning love." Eventually Irwin claimed to have received this "baptism of fire" and he began to teach and preach about it. Also called "fire baptism," the experience was related to the Apostles' reception of the Holy Spirit in the form of tongues of fire on Pentecost, as recorded in the Acts of the Apostles. Irwin's preaching of a third experience beyond justification and sanctification (called the "second blessing" in the holiness churches) led to controversy. He and his followers were the objects of intense criticism.

The "third blessing" spread across the Midwest and South. In 1895, the Fire-Baptized Holiness Association was organized in Iowa. Other state and local organizations followed. Irwin exercised authority over each and appointed the presidents. From July 28 to August 8, 1898, a First General Convention was held at Anderson, South Carolina, and formal organization of the Fire-Baptized Holiness Association occurred. Among those in attendance was W. E. Fuller, who later founded the Fire-Baptized Holiness Church of God of the Americas. The 1898 convention adopted a *Discipline*, which provided for life tenure for the general overseer who was given wide-ranging authority and control over the work. The Association soon took the name of the Fire-Baptized Holiness Church. Within two years, involved in a personal scandal, Irwin left the church and turned it over to J. H. King, a former Methodist minister who had been assisting him in running the church.

Contemporaneous with the ministry of Irwin was that of A. B. Crumpler. Crumpler, a Methodist minister in North Carolina, had received the second-blessing sanctification experience (the "second blessing" was the basic distinguishing mark of the holiness movement). Crumpler received his sanctification experience through the ministry of the Rev. Beverly Carradine, a famous Southern Methodist holiness preacher. He became the leading exponent of the "second blessing" in North Carolina, and

in 1896, a great holiness movement began there. In 1899, Crumpler was tried for "immorality," withdrew from the Methodist Church, and the following year formed the Pentecostal Holiness Church at Fayetteville, North Carolina.

In 1906, the Rev. G. B. Cashwell, a Pentecostal Holiness minister, attended the Pentecostal revival services which were occurring on Azusa Street in Los Angeles, California, and received the baptism of the Holy Spirit evidenced by his speaking in tongues. Cashwell headed eastward to introduce the experience to his brothers and sisters. On New Years's Eve, 1906, he began a revival at Dunn, North Carolina, and introduced the experience to the Pentecostal Holiness Church. He also led J. H. King into the experience. Not without controversy, both the Pentecostal Holiness Church and the Fire-Baptized Holiness Church accepted the new experience in 1908. A merger under the name of the former occurred in 1911. It became the International Pentecostal Holiness Church in 1975.

The Pentecostal Holiness Church insists that the Pentecostal experience of the baptism of the Holy Spirit, signified by speaking in tongues, is valid only as a "third blessing." In other words, the Pentecostal experience can come only to those who have already been justified (accepted Jesus as their personal savior) and sanctified (received the "second blessing" which was the key experience of the holiness movement). By contrast, most Pentecostals believe the baptism of the Holy Spirit is available to any believer at any time, and brings with it power for a holy life. Most Pentecostals seek only "two experiences," while the Pentecostal Holiness Church seeks three.

The Pentecostal Holiness Church is a direct outgrowth of the holiness movement: that explains why it retains the "second blessing." The church also has a Methodist heritage, so it derives its doctrinal statement from the Methodist Articles of Religion. In line with its Methodist roots, the church is among the few Pentecostal bodies to allow baptism by methods other than immersion. Footwashing is optional.

The polity of the Pentecostal Holiness Church is episcopal. One bishop elected by the general conference and other officers form a general board of administration to administer the affairs of the denomination. Under the administrative board are various other boards and agencies. Property is owned by the general church. Among the boards are those on education, missions, and publication. The Board of Education oversees the work at the four colleges. The Foreign Mission Board, created in 1904, oversees missions in 32 countries. Foreign work in those countries has been set off as autonomous churches that remain aligned ideologically and filially: the Pentecostal Wesleyan Methodists of Brazil, the Pentecostal Methodist Church of Chile, and the Pentecostal Holiness Church of Canada (1971). A vigorous publishing program is pursued by the Advocate Press.

Membership: In 1986 the church reported 112,000 members, 1,460 congregations, and 3,000 ministers in the United States.

Educational facilities: Emmanuel College, Franklin Springs, Georgia; Southwestern College of Christian Ministries, Oklahoma City, Oklahoma; Holmes College of the Bible, Greenville, South Carolina; Pacific Coast Bible College, Sacramento, California; Berea Bible Institute, McAllen, Texas.

Periodicals: *The Advocate*, 7300 N.W. 39th Expressway, Bethany, OK 73008; *The Helping Hand*, 7300 N.W. 39th Expressway, Bethany, OK 73008.

Sources: A. D. Beacham, Jr., *A Brief History of the Pentecostal Church of God*. Franklin Springs, GA: Advocate Press, 1983; Joseph E. Campbell, *The Pentecostal Holiness Church, 1898-1948*. Franklin Springs, GA: Publishing House of the Pentecostal Holiness Church, 1951; Joseph H. King, *Yet Speaketh*. Franklin Springs, GA: Publishing House of the Pentecostal Holiness Church, 1949; Vinson Synan, *The Old Time Power*. Franklin Springs, GA: Advocate Press, 1973.

★338★
(ORIGINAL) CHURCH OF GOD
Box 3086
Chattanooga, TN 37404

The first schism in the Church of God (Cleveland, Tennessee) occurred in 1917, and was led by the Rev. Joseph L. Scott, a pastor in Chattanooga. Among the issues involved were local autonomy, the tithe (obligatory versus voluntary), and the reception of divorced persons into the church. After the schism a less centralized government was established in the newly formed church. Each congregation is autonomous and takes the name of its location; for example, "The Church of God at Chattanooga." Above the local church is a general office which serves as headquarters and publishing house, which publishes Sunday school literature and the church's two periodicals. A presbytery has oversight of the ministry. The official name of the church includes the word "Original" in parentheses.

There are five ordinances in the (Original) Church of God, Inc.- baptism by immersion, Biblical church government, footwashing, the Lord's Supper, and tithing. Previously divorced persons can be accepted by pastors as church members.

Membership: Not reported. In 1971 there were 70 churches (including one in Trinidad), 20,000 members and 124 ministers.

Periodicals: *The Messenger*, Box 3086, Chattanooga, TN 37404; *The Youth Messenger*, Box 3086, Chattanooga, TN 37404.

Sources: *Manual or Discipline of the (Original) Church of God*. Chattanooga, TN: General Office & Publishing House, 1966.

★339★
PENTECOSTAL FIRE-BAPTIZED HOLINESS CHURCH
Taccoa, GA 30577

The enforcement of discipline in the Pentecostal Holiness Church, now the International Pentecostal Holiness Church, led in 1918 to a schism by those who wanted stricter standards concerning dress, amusements, tobacco, and association between the sexes. In the Pentecostal Fire-Baptized Holiness Church, the schismatic church, women's dresses are to be at least mid-calf in length; women are not to bob or wave their hair, or wear jewelry, gold, or costly apparel. Men are not to wear neckties. Attending fairs, swimming pools, and theaters is forbidden. The strict group was joined by a few who never approved the 1911 merger of the Pentecostal Holiness Church and the Fire-Baptized Holiness Church. The pre-1911 name was adopted and the word "Pentecostal" added. The group also was joined in 1921 by the North Carolina Conference of the Pentecostal Free Will Baptist Church.

The church had 1,929 members in 85 churches in 1952. However, the next year more than half the members left to form the Emmanuel Holiness Church. That schism began a period of unabated decline.

The polity is connectional. A general convention meets biennially, with power to legislate. A seven-member board of missions, elected at the general convention, oversees work in Haiti and Mexico. A campgrounds and printing establishment are owned at Toccoa Falls, Georgia, where the church headquarters are located.

Membership: By 1981 the church had decreased to 298 members.

Periodicals: *Faith and Truth*, Nicholson, GA.

★340★
PENTECOSTAL FREE WILL BAPTIST CHURCH
Box 1568
Dunn, NC 28334

The Pentecostal Free Will Baptist Church was formed in a merger and reorganization of several Free Will Baptist Associations, mainly in North Carolina. Pentecostalism had entered the Free Will Baptist Church through the efforts of the ubiquitous G. B. Cashwell. In 1907 he conducted a revival in Dunn, North Carolina, and persuaded many members of the Cape Fear Conference of the Free Will Baptist Church of the truth of his position. The Conference accepted a Pentecostal doctrine, but remained within the national Free Will Baptist Association. In 1907, the Cape Fear Conference split into two geographic associations; the second body became the Wilmington Conference, and the first retained the original name. In 1911, a third association was formed in southeastern North Carolina as the New River Conference. The following year, the Cape Fear Conference split over the Pentecostal issue. Finally, in 1912 a South Carolina Conference was organized.

In 1943, a group of ministers and laymen of the four Pentecostal conferences: Cape Fear, Wilmington, New River, and South Carolina Conferences, met. They formed a general conference but the organization proved unsatisfactory. In 1959, it was decided to dissolve all the conference structures and organize under one charter and one name. Thus, in 1959, the Pentecostal Free Will Baptist Church was formed.

The doctrine is almost identical to that of the Church of God (Cleveland, Tennessee), and includes belief in three experiences of grace: baptism by immersion, footwashing, and premillennialism. It is this group's position that Benjamin Randall, the founder of the Free Will Baptist Church, taught sanctification as an instantaneous act of God.

The church is congregational in structure with a bi-annual conference. The general superintendent heads an executive board for implementing the program. There are four districts; the World Missions Board oversees missions in Costa Rica, Pueto Rico, Mexico, Venezuela, Nicaragua, the Philippines. Churches are primarily in North Carolina, with congregations in South Carolina, Virginia, Georgia, and Florida.

Membership: In 1988 the church reported 15,110 members and 137 churches.

Educational facilities: Heritage Bible College, Dunn, North Carolina.

Periodicals: *The Pentecostal Free-Will Baptist Messenger*, Box 1081, Dunn, NC 28334.

Sources: *Discipline of the Pentecostal Free Will Baptist Church.* 1962; Don Sauls, *The Ministerial Handbook of the Pentecostal Free Will Baptist Church.* N. P.: 1971; Herbert Carter, *The Spectacular Gifts, Prophecy, Tongues, Interpretations.* Dunn, NC: The Author, 1971; *Faith and Practices of the Pentecostal Free Will Baptist Church, Inc..* Franklin Springs, GA: Advocate Press, 1971.

★341★
ROMANIAN APOSTOLIC PENTECOSTAL
  CHURCH OF GOD
(Defunct)

The Romanian Apostolic Pentecostal Church of God had its origins in the influx of the Pentecostal awakening within the Romanian-American community in the early twentieth century. The first congregation was founded in Detroit, Michigan, in 1922. Eventually more than 40 congregations were part of a loose fellowship. However, in 1981, the majority of these congregations joined the Church of God (Cleveland, Tennessee) and five more have joined the Assemblies of God. Some remain independent. One congregation in California of about 50 members continues to use the name of the older fellowship.

The Church of God congregations work together as the Romanian Pentecostal Ministries and publish a periodical, *Propovaduitorul.* The Rev. Ioan J. Buia, pastor of the original Detroit congregation (now located in Dearborn Heights, Michigan), conducts a Romanian radio ministry, Maranatha, that is heard over one station in Michigan and one in Kitchner, Ontario. There is also a continuing annual convention of the Romanian Pentecostal congregations. In 1987, it met in Detroit and in 1988, in Portland, Oregon.

Sources: Ioan J. Buia, *Pine Pe Unde* (Bread on Waves). Detroit, Romanian Penetcostal Church of God, 1987; *Romanian Pentecostal Church of God, 1937-1987, Semicentinar.* Detroit, MI: Romanian Penetcostal Church of God, 1987.

White Trinitarian Pentecostals

★342★
AMERICAN INDIAN EVANGELICAL CHURCH
Box 25019
Minneapolis, MN 55440-6019

During the early twentieth century, conditions forced many American Indians into the cities. By 1945, 8,000 had settled in the Minneapolis/St. Paul metropolitan area. In that year a group of Indians organized the American Indian Mission. In 1956, the Mission became the American Indian Evangelical Church, and Iver C. Grover (a Chippewa) was elected president. He was joined by seven others. In 1959, a committee on ordination was appointed to facilitate the development of an Indian ordained ministry, and four men were ordained.

Doctrine is in line with fundamental evangelicalism. The doctrinal statement of the church begins with the Apostles' Creed and moves on to affirm the Trinity, the divinity of Jesus, and the conscious suffering of the wicked. Baptism by immersion and the Lord's Supper are practiced. The polity is congregational, but the pastor is viewed as the spiritual overseer of the congregation.

Membership: Not reported.

★343★
ANCHOR BAY EVANGELISTIC ASSOCIATION
Box 188
New Baltimore, MI 48047

Roy John Turner and his wife Blanche A. Turner became Pentecostals in 1916. Dr. Turner was a medical doctor and his wife a nurse, and they continued to function as medical professionals while leading prayer meetings. Following a revival campaign in 1918 by evangelist, Mrs. M. B. Woodworth-Etter, a church was formed in New Baltimore. In 1923, Dr. Turner was ordained and became pastor of the congregation. The old opera house in New Baltimore, Michigan, was purchased and remodeled as Bethel Temple. From 1938 to 1940, Turner served as an executive with the International Church of the Foursquare Gospel, the congregation in New Baltimore remained independent. Finally, in 1940, the Turners left the Foursquare Gospel and the Anchor Bay Evangelistic Association was formed and incorporated. After the Turners' deaths, they were succeeded by their daughter, Lucy Evelyn Turner.

The doctrine of the Anchor Bay Evangelistic Association is like that of the International Church of the Foursquare Gospel. Mission work is conducted in Belize, Turkey, the Philippines, South India, West Africa, Indonesia, and Mexico. The church is a member of the Pentecostal Fellowship of North America.

Membership: In the late 1960s there were 320 ministers and 115 churches worldwide.

Educational facilities: Anchor Bay Institute, New Baltimore, Michigan.

★344★
THE APOSTOLIC CHURCH
142 N. 17th St.
Philadelphia, PA 19103

Alternate address: California headquarters: 10841 Chapman Ave., Garden Grove, CA 92640; Canadian headquarters: 27 Castlefield Ave., Toronto, ON M4H 1G3.

The Apostolic Church grew out of the Apostolic Faith Church founded in England in 1908 by W. O. Hutchinson. The Apostolic Faith Church was one of the first Pentecostal bodies in England, and it had roots both in the Azusa Street revival in Los Angeles, and the Welsh Revival led by Evan Roberts that began in 1904. Distinctive of the Apostolic Faith Church was to give precedence to the Holy Spirit in everything, and an accompanying belief that one of the primary purposes for the exercise of spiritual gifts is to bring a revelation from God, through either prophecy or speaking-in-tongues and the interpretation. Prophecy could then be used in matters such as the selection of church officers and the making of various decisions. To some people, the practice produced only fanaticism and intolerable excesses. Thus the Rev. Daniel Powell Williams led a group of members out of the Apostolic Faith Church to found what in 1916 became the Apostolic Church. From its headquarters in Wales, within a decade it had circled the globe, especially in British colonial lands.

The church came to North America in 1924 when a church was founded in Canada. From that original congregation, churches have been formed in Pennsylvania and California, which operate as two separate districts. The Canadian churches support missions in Brazil, Barbados, and Jamaica, but the North American churches remain part of the worldwide church headquartered in Wales.

Membership: Not reported. In the 1970s, there were 700 members in 13 churches in Canada and 250 members in seven churches in the United States.

★345★
APOSTOLIC FAITH (KANSAS)
1009 Lincoln Ave.
Baxter Springs, KS 66713

In 1898, the Rev. Charles Parham (1873-1929) left the Methodist Episcopal Church and established a home for divine healing in Topeka, Kansas. That same year he began to publish a periodical, *Apostolic Faith*, and two years later opened Bethel Bible College. It was at Bethel that Agnes Ozman had the initial experience of speaking in tongues, an event from which the modern Penetecostal movement is dated. After Mrs. Ozman's experience and its acceptance by others, Parham began to spread the word of modern Pentecostalism in Kansas, Oklahoma, Missouri, and Texas. In 1905, he established a Bible school in Houston, Texas. Among those who attended was William J. Seymour, a black holiness preacher affiliated with the Church of God (Anderson, Indiana), who related the experience at Azusa Street, Los Angeles, California.

Parham is hardly mentioned in Pentecostal history after 1906. The split between he and the emerging leadership of the movement began toward the end of that year when he arrived in Los Angeles to observe firsthand the revival about which he had read. He did not like what he saw. He felt that the revival had taken on elements of fanaticism and was quick in his words of reproof. The disagreement led to his immediate split with Seymour and the leaders of the revival in southern California. Then early in 1907 he also resigned his role as "Projector of the Apostolic Faith Movement," as a means of opposing the spirit of leadership and the attempts to organize the movement.

Returning to the East and Midwest, he took up his ministry and continued to preach. However, he was soon faced with accusations of scandalous personal behavior which further ruined his reputation within the movement.

Though he remained active until his death, his efforts were cut off from the movement as a whole. Those who received his ministry were eventually consolidated in a very loose fellowship centered on Baxter Springs, Kansas. The Apostolic Faith was not incorporated until 1976. No membership records have ever been kept, but there is a directory of churches and ministers.

In 1950, Baxter Springs also became the permanent site chosen for the group's Bible college. Following Parham's direction, the college charges no tuition, but operates on a freewill offering plan. No salary is paid to the faculty, who are also supported by freewill offerings.

Beliefs of the Apostolic Faith are similar to those of the Assemblies of God, and include a strong emphasis on spiritual healing. Footwashing, baptism, and the Lord's Supper are observed as ordinances. No collections are taken, the ministry being supported by tithes. Organization is informal and congregational. The Apostolic Faith did not formally incorporate until 1976. There is a seven-person board of trustees which oversees the Bible college.

Membership: No membership records are kept by the Apostolic Faith. These are an estimated 10,000 adherents. In 1988 there were 100 churches and 118 ministers.

Educational facilities: Apostolic Faith Bible College, Baxter Springs, Kansas.

Periodicals: *Apostolic Faith Report*, Box 653, Baxter Springs, KS 66713.

Sources: Sarah E. Parham, *The Life of Charles F. Parham*. Joplin, MO: Hunter Printing Company, 1930; Charles F. Parham, *A Voice of One Crying in the Wilderness*. Baxter Springs, KS: Apostolic Faith Bible College, 1910; W. F. Carothers, *The Baptism with the Holy Ghost*. Zion City, IL: The Author, 1907.

★346★

ASSEMBLIES OF GOD, GENERAL COUCIL OF
1445 Boonville Ave.
Springfield, MO 65802

The December 20, 1913, issue of *Word and Witness*, an independent Pentecostal periodical published by editor E. N. Bell, issued a call for "A General Convention of Pentecostal Saints and Churches of God in Christ," to be held in Hot Springs, Arkansas, April 2-12, 1914. The purpose was to decide upon some doctrinal standards; a policy of cooperation; missionary, ministerial, educational, and publishing interests; and government religious requirements for business. Bell and J. Roswell Flower, editor of the *Christian Evangel*, quickly emerged as dominant figures in the meeting attended by more than 300 delegates from twenty states and several foreign countries. A loose organization was effected and the new church took the name of the Assemblies of God. The

General Council, representative of Pentecostal assemblies and churches, was formed. *The Word and Witness* was accepted as the official periodical and the *Christian Evangel* was combined with it.

During the next two years, the doctrinal position of the Assemblies of God was hammered out in heated debate on the "Jesus only" or "oneness" issue. Oneness Pentecostals believed that Jesus was "Jehovah rediscovered" and demanded rebaptism in Jesus' name, thus opposing baptism in the name of the Trinity. The assemblies adopted a strong statement on the Trinity as integral to the church's belief. The statement, finally adopted in 1916, also reflected the absence of "Holiness theology of the Holy Spirit," and recognized that the baptism of the Holy Spirit is by no means limited to the sanctified, nor is santification viewed as a distinct work of grace. The church's statement of fundamental truths includes belief in the Bible as the Word of God, the fall of man, salvation in Christ, baptism by immersion, divine healing, and the resurrection.

The organization of the Assemblies of God is congregational, but the General Council has centralized control over missionary, educational, ministerial, and publishing concerns. One of the first acts of the Hot Springs meeting was the appointment of a 12-person presbytery to oversee mission work. The Division of Foreign Missions was created in 1919, and the missionary effort has seen the spread of the Assemblies to 118 countries of the world. The Division of Home Missions oversees work among American Indians, Jews, the deaf, the blind, and in various ethnic groups. It also supervises military and institutional chaplains. The first publishing efforts of the Assemblies of God have grown into the Gospel Publishing House, one of the major publishers of Christian literature in the United States. There is also a vast Sunday school department and a radio department which produces the popular "Revivaltime" broadcast on radio.

Membership: In 1986, the council reported 2,135,104 members, 10,886 congregations, and 30,204 ordained ministers. There were 16,376,818 members worldwide.

Educational facilities: American Indian Bible College, Phoenix, Arizona; Assemblies of God Theological Seminary, Springfield, Missouri; Berean College of the Assemblies of God, Springfield, Missouri; Bethany Bible College, Santa Cruz, California; Central Bible College, Springfield, Missouri; Evangel College, Springfield, Missouri; Latin America Bible College, La Puente, California; North Central Bible College, Minneapolis, Minnesota; Northwest College of the Assemblies of God, Kirkland, Washington; Southeastern College of the Assemblies of God, Lakeland, Florida; Southern Arizona Bible College, Hereford, Arizona; Southern California College, Costa Mesa, California; Southwestern Assemblies of God College, Waxahachie, Texas; Trinity Bible Institute, Ellendale, North Dakota. Valley Forge Christian

College of the Assemblies of God, Phoenixville, Pennsylvania; Western Bible Institute, Phoenix, Arizona.

Periodicals: *Pentecostal Evangel*, Gospel Publishing House, 1445 Boonville Avenue, Springfield, MO 65802; *Assemblies of God Heritage*, Assemblies of God Archives, 1445 Boonville Avenue, Springfield, MO 65802.

Sources: William W. Menzies, *Annointed to Serve*. Springfield, MO: Gospel Publishing House, 1971; Carl Brumback, *Suddenly from Heaven*. Springfield, MO: Gospel Publishing House, 1961; Mario G. Hoover, *Origin and Structural Development of the Assemblies of God*. Southwest Missouri State College, M.A. Thesis, 1968; Noel Perkin and John Garlock, *Our World Witness*. Springfield, MO: Gospel Publishing House, 1963; G. Raymond Carlson, *Our Faith and Fellowship*. Springfield, MO: Gospel Publishing House, 1977.

★347★
ASSOCIATION OF VINEYARD CHURCHES
902 E. Yorba Linda Blvd.
Box 909
Placentia, CA 92670

The Association of Vineyard Churches was formed in 1986 but dates to an earlier Bible study group in Yorba Linda, California, formed in 1978 by John Wimber. The original group of approximately 150 affiliated with Calvary Chapel Church, a pentecostal church in Costa Mesa, California, which had developed a number of affiliates throughout the greater Los Angeles area. After a brief period of association, Wimber felt that his work, which included an emphasis upon the manifestation of the gifts of the Spirit to all age groups, was distinct from that of Calvary Chapel, which appealed primarily to young adults.

Closely approaching Wimber's perspective was the Vineyard Christian Fellowship, a congregation which had originated from a Bible study group formed by Kenn Gullikson in 1974. In 1982 Wimber changed his congregation's name to Vineyard Christian Fellowship of Yorba Linda. The following year he moved it to Anaheim, California and within a short time over 4,000 were attending Sunday services. Several other congregations merged with the two Vineyard fellowships, and Vineyard Ministries International was created to direct the outreach of the movement. Wimber became the object of much media attention, especially after his being asked to teach a course at Fuller Theological Seminary in Pasadena, California, concerning the gifts of the Spirit. In the wake of the publicity, the movement grew rapidly as both independent pastors and congregations, most in southern California, affiliated. However, the structure of Vineyard Ministries International proved inadequate to deal with the increased size and geographic spread of the movement. Very basically, the church needed a means to ordain pastors and credential churches and ministers. In 1986 leaders in the movement organized the association of

Vineyard Churches. Vineyard Ministries International continues as the facilitator of numerous programs and seminars centered upon church growth, Christian life, and gifts of the Spirit.

The churches affiliated with the association are similar in doctrine to Calvary Chapel, but have a distinct emphasis upon the ministry of the gifts of the Spirit and a strong program of church growth and evangelism. At the time of the association's formation, Wimber was appointed International Director and Sam Thompson was named its National Director. Initially, six Regional Pastoral Coordinators were named from among the ministers who were leading stable Vineyard congregations. It is their task to oversee and guide emerging fellowships and to foster a collegiate relationship between the churches in the association.

Membership: In 1987 the association reported approximately 50,000 members in 150 Vineyard congregations, including four in Canada. There are also two international congregations, in London, England, and in Johannesburg, South Africa.

Periodicals: *The Vineyard Newsletter*, Box 9590, Anaheim, CA 92805; *First Fruits*, Vineyard Ministries International, Box 65004, Anaheim, CA 92805.

Sources: John Wimber with Kevin Springer, *Power Evangelism*. *Praise Offerings*. Anaheim, CA: Vineyard Christian Fellowship, 1977; John Loftness, "A Sign for Our Times!," in *People of Destiny Magazine* 3, 4 (July/August 1985).

★348★
BETHEL TEMPLE
2033 Second Ave.
Seattle, WA 98121

The Bethel Temple was formed in 1914 as the first Pentecostal congregation in the state of Washington. Its doctrine is like that of the Assemblies of God. Loosely affiliated with the temple are eight congregations, seven in the state of Washington, and one in Alaska. There are also 10 congregations in Holland and missions are conducted in Japan and Indonesia. The Indonesian Pentecostal churches, the Gereja Pantekosta de Indonesia, look to Bethel Temple as their founder. A Bible school opened in 1952 was discontinued in 1987.

Membership: In 1987 there were approximately 300 members in eight congregations in the United States.

Periodicals: *Pentecostal Power*, 2033 Second Avenue, Seattle, WA 98121.

★349★

BIBLE CHURCH OF CHRIST
1358 Morris Ave.
Bronx, NY 10456

The Bible Church of Christ is a small Pentecostal body founded on March 1, 1961 by Bishop Roy Bryant, Sr. Its doctrine is like that of the Assemblies of God, emphasizing a belief in a trinitarian God and the authority of the Bible as the inspired Word of God. Members receive the baptism of the Holy Spirit and miracles of healing are frequently experienced. Congregations are reported in both Jamaica and Africa.

Membership: In 1986 the church reported 4,350 members, six churches, and 41 ministers. Congregations are located in New York, Delaware, and North Carolina.

Periodicals: *The Voice*, 1356 Morris Ave., Bronx, NY 10656.

★350★

CALIFORNIA EVANGELISTIC ASSOCIATION
Current address not obtained for this edition.

The California Evangelistic Association began in 1933 (incorporated, 1934) as the Colonial Tabernacle of Long Beach California. The tabernacle had been established by Oscar C. Harms, a former pastor in the Advent Christian Church. Additional assemblies became associated with it, and in 1939, it assumed its present name. It is in essential doctrinal agreement with the Assemblies of God, except that it is amillennial. Polity of the Association is congregational, with affiliated congregations remaining autonomous. Churches are found along the West Coast. The California Evangelistic Association supports missionaries in Italy, Zambia, Brazil, Colombia, and Mexico.

Membership: Not reported. In the 1970s there were 62 associated congregations and approximately 4,700 members.

Sources: *Constitution and By-Laws*. Long Beach, CA: California Evangelistic Association, 1939.

★351★

CALVARY CHAPEL CHURCH
Box 8000
Costa Mesa, CA 92626

In 1965 Chuck Smith, an independent Pentecostal minister, accepted the call to pastor a small independent congregation, Calvary, in Costa Mesa, California. The congregation had just begun to grow when "hippies" began to invade the beach front near Costa Mesa. His work among the hippies led to the development of a series of "houses" throughout the communities in greater Los Angeles where youthful converts could gather. Sunday services were held at the congregations' building in Costa Mesa, and the church became famous as a center of the "Jesus People Revival" that moved across the United States in the early 1970s. As membership grew in the Los Angeles area, other Calvary Chapels were established in different communities. As the fame of Calvary Chapel grew, individuals who had visited the church began congregations modeled upon it across America.

A very simple statement of belief has been developed which emphasizes the non-denominational character of Calvary Chapel. The church refuses to over-emphasize those doctrinal differences that have divided Christians in the past. Agape love is held up as the only true basis of Christian fellowship. The church is Pentecostal, in that the gifts of the Spirit are accepted and practiced. There is no emphasis placed upon speaking-in-tongues as the necessary sign of the baptism of the Holy Spirit. Emphasis is placed upon the Biblical teachings concerning the end time, a subject of many of Smith's books, and an accompanying expectation of seeing some of the predicted events in this generation.

Calvary Chapel has developed a variety of outreach ministries under the name "The Word for Today," which includes cassettes, video tape and literature production and distribution, radio shows, Spanish-language tape ministry, and Bible studies for home use.

Membership: Not reported.

Sources: Robert S. Ellwood, Jr., *One Way*. Englewood Cliffs, NJ: Prentice-Hall, 1973; Church Smith, *What the World Is Coming To*. Costa Mesa, CA: The World for Today, 1980; Church Smith, *Future Survival*. Costa Mesa, CA: The Word for Today, 1980; Church Smith, *The Final Curtain*. Costa Mesa, CA: The Word for Today, 1984; Church Smith, *Charisma vs. Charismania*. Eugene, OR: Harvest House Publishers, 1983.

★352★

CALVARY MINISTRIES, INC., INTERNATIONAL
1400 W. Washington Center Rd.
Fort Wayne, IN 46825

Calvary Ministries, Inc., International was founded in 1978 as an umbrella organization for those congregations and ministries which developed from the work of Calvary Temple, an independent Pentecostal church in Fort Wayne, Indiana. Calvary Temple was begun in 1950 by Dr. Paul E. Paino, a graduate of the Assemblies of God's Central Bible College in Springfield, Missouri. Under his leadership the church membership grew into the thousands, and in 1978 a new building complex was erected to house the expanding program.

In the late 1960s two men who wished to be ordained to the ministry began training with Paino. In 1971 seven more began work. These enrollments led to the formation of the Christian Training Center in 1972. Among the early graduates of the center were those ready to begin the pastoral ministry and start new congregations. In part, Calvary Ministries, Inc., International was created to facilitate their ordinations and the granting of proper credentials for their ministry. Calvary Ministries follows a congregational polity. The affiliated churches support a common mission program which has work in foreign countries and several U.S. states.

During the early years of the Jesus People Revival, the Temple sponsored a youth ministry originally located in a coffeehouse called "The Landing," later known as Adam's Apple. Adam's Apple soon became self-supporting but has retained a close fraternal tie to the Temple.

Calvary Ministries has a statement of faith almost identical to that of the Assemblies of God, out of which Dr. Paino came. It differs only in that it does not include the additional statements on ministry adopted by the Assemblies in 1969.

Membership: In the early 1980s there were 14 affiliated chapels located in Indiana and Ohio. Over 3,000 are affiliated with Calvary Temple. Foreign work is supported in Africa, Great Britain, Japan, Korea, Mexico, South Africa, and Spain.

Educational facilities: Christian Training Center, Fort Wayne, Indiana.

Periodicals: *The Communicator*, 1400 W. Washington Center Rd., Fort Wayne, IN 46825; *The Worker*, 1400 W. Washington Center Rd., Fort Wayne, IN 46825; *Juicy News*, 1400 W. Washington Center Rd., Fort Wayne, IN 46825.

★353★
CALVARY PENTECOSTAL CHURCH
% Rev. Leroy Holman
1775 Yew, N.E.
Olympia, WA 98506

The Calvary Pentecostal Church was formed in 1931 by a group of Pentecostal ministers in the northwestern United States who were dissatisfied by what they regarded as "a sad departure from the entire dependence on the power of God that had brought the Pentecostal revival." They formed a ministerial fellowship in Olympia, Washington, which was the following year named the Calvery Pentecostal Church. What was originally intended as an interdenominational fellowship became a denomination as churches began to affiliate.

The doctrine is like that of the Assemblies of God. Healing is emphasized. Adult baptism by immersion is practiced, but when parents request it, infants are dedicated to God (not baptized). The literal second coming is awaited. The church is governed in a loose presbyterial system headed by a presbyterial board and the general superintendent. A general meeting of all ministers and local church delegates is held annually. The local church is governed by the minister, elders, and deacons. The church supports a home for the aged in Seattle. Foreign work is done in Brazil and India.

Membership: Not reported. In the early 1970s there were 22 churches and approximately 8,000 members.

★354★
ELIM FELLOWSHIP
7245 College St.
Lima, NY 14485

In 1924, the Rev. and Mrs. Ivan Q. Spencer opened a pentecostal Bible institute in Endicott, New York, to train young men and women for full-time revival ministry. Graduates of the Elim Bible Institute formed the Elim Ministerial Fellowship in 1932, which eventually became the Elim Fellowship in 1972. In 1951, the school moved to Lima, New York, where it occupies the campus of the former Genesee Wesleyan Seminary, founded in the nineteenth century by the Methodist Church.

The doctrine of the Fellowship is similar to that of the Assemblies of God, with a strong emphasis upon the Holy Spirit-filled and sanctified life of the believer. Spencer was strongly affected by the Latter Rain revival which began in Canada in 1948. He and others brought the revival to the school, publicized it in the *Elim Herald*, and took a leadership role in spreading the renewed emphasis upon the gifts of the Spirit being poured out on God's people in the last days.

The fellowship is governed congregationally. An annual meeting is held each spring at Lima. Elim Fellowship-sponsored missionaries are currently at work around the world, on all continents. The founder's son, I. Carlton Spencer succeeded his father in the leadership of the fellowship, overseeing it from 1947 to 1985. Rev. Elmer A. Frink is the current general overseer. The Fellowship holds membership in the Pentecostal Fellowship of North America, the Network of Christian Ministries, and on the North American Renewal Service Committee.

Membership: In 1988, the fellowship reported 20,000 members, 200 congregations, and more than 300 ministers in the United States. There were 20 congregations in Canada and 5,500 congregations worldwide in 11 countries.

Educational facilities: Elim Bible Institute, Lima, New York; Lima Trade School, Lima, New York; Nairobi Pentecostal Bible College, Nairobi, Kenya; Instituto Biblico de Elim, Belen, Costa Rica.

Periodicals: *Elim Herald*, 7245 College, St., Lima, NY 14485; *The Elim Bell Tower*, Elim Bible Institute, 7245 College St., Lima, NY 14485; *Single Impact*, 7245 College St., Lima, NY 14485.

Sources: Marion Meloon, *Ivan Spencer, Willow in the Wind.* Plainfield, NJ: Logos International, 1974.

★355★

FELLOWSHIP OF CHRISTIAN ASSEMBLIES
Current address not obtained for this edition.

Formed in 1922 as the Independent Assemblies of God, the Fellowship of Christian Assemblies adopted its present name in 1973. The Assemblies was disrupted in 1948 by the adherence of many members and pastors to the Latter Rain movement, a revival movement which had begun in Canada and had placed a new emphasis upon the manifestation of the gifts of the Spirit, particularly prophecy and healing. Those opposed to the revival viewed it as possessed of fanatical elements. The group which eventually became the Fellowship of Christian Assemblies is that element of the Independent Assemblies that did not follow the Latter Rain.

Organization of the Fellowship is congregational and its basic principle is fellowship among autonomous churches. The pattern in mission work has also been to establish autonomous churches. National gatherings for counsel and fellowship are held and are planned by a committee working with the local churches. A secretary compiles and publishes a directory. Some of the churches have become members of the Fellowship Press Publishing Corporation; its main function is to publish the monthly periodical, *Conviction.* Mission work is supported in Africa, South America, Japan, and India.

Membership: Not reported. There are an estimated 10,000 members in the churches affiliated with the Fellowship.

Periodicals: *Conviction.*

★356★

FILIPINO ASSEMBLIES OF THE FIRST BORN
1229 Glenwood
Delano, CA 93215

The Filipino Assemblies of the First Born was founded at Stockton, California, by the Rev. Julian Barnabe, an immigrant to the United States. The organization took place at a convention which met June 26 to July 4, 1933. Headquarters were established in Fresno and moved to San Francisco in 1942 and to Delano, California, in 1943. Doctrine and practice are like those of the Assemblies of God; the group is primarily an ethnic church with preaching often done in the Filipino language.

Membership: Not reported. In 1969 there were 15 churches in California and 17 in Hawaii.

★357★

FREE GOSPEL CHURCH, INC.
% Rev. Chester H. Heath
Box 477
Export, PA 15632

The Free Gospel Church was founded in 1916 as the United Free Gospel and Missionary Society by two brothers, the Reverends Frank Casley and William Casley. It adopted its present name in 1958. An early emphasis upon missions led to initial efforts in Guatemala, though the work was lost to the Church of God (Cleveland, Tennessee). In doctrine, it is similar to the Assemblies of God. Missions are conducted in Sierra Leone, India, and the Philippines.

Membership: Not reported. In the early 1970s there were approximately 25 churches and 2,000 members.

Educational facilities: Free Gospel Institute, Export, Pennsylvania.

★358★

FULL GOSPEL EVANGELISTIC ASSOCIATION
5828 Chippewa Blvd.
Houston, TX 70086

In the late 1940s a controversy developed in the Apostolic Faith Church over issues of taking offerings in church, visiting churches not in fellowship, foreign mission work, and using doctors. Some who supported these activities formed the Ministerial and Missionary Alliance of the Original Trinity Apostolic Faith, Inc., for which they were disfellowshipped. In 1952, they formed the Full Gospel Evangelistic Association. Except for the points at issue, the doctrine is like that of the Apostolic Faith.

Headquarters, established at Kuty, Texas, were moved to Webb City, Missouri, in 1967. The Association supports missions in Mexico, Peru, Guatemala, and Taiwan. Annual camp meetings are held in Oklahoma and Texas.

Membership: Not reported. In the mid-1970s there were 30 congregations and approximately 4,000 members.

Educational facilities: Midwest Bible Institute, Houston, Texas.

Periodicals: *Full Gospel News,* 5828 Chipawa Blvd., Houston, TX 70086.

★359★

GENERAL ASSEMBLIES AND CHURCH OF THE FIRST BORN
Current address not obtained for this edition.

The General Assembly and Church of the First Born, formed in 1907, is a small Pentecostal body without church headquarters or paid clergy. It has about 30 congregations across the country. Congregations are concentrated in Oklahoma and California, with individual congregations at Montrose and Pleasant View, Colorado, and Indianapolis, Indiana. Members believe in the Trinity, deny original sin, believing that we will be punished only for our own sin, and assert that man can be saved by obedience to the laws and ordinances of the gospel. There are four ordinances--faith in Jesus Christ, repentence, baptism by immersion, and laying-on-of-hands for the gift of the Holy Spirit. The group makes use of all of the gifts of the Spirit and holds the Lord's Supper in conjunction with footwashing, but does not seek the help of doctors.

Elders oversee the local congregations, which are organized very informally. Some elders are ordained and serve as preachers. No membership rolls are kept. The Indianapolis church has published a hymnal. There is an annual campmeeting in Oklahoma each summer.

Membership: Not reported. In 1976 there were approximately 6,000 members.

Remarks: In 1976 the Church of the First Born was involved in a controversy following the death of a member's child after medical treatment was withheld. A district court in Oklahoma made a second child a ward of the court, ruling that the state had a right to intervene when religious beliefs might lead to harm of a minor.

★360★
INTERNATIONAL CHURCH OF THE FOURSQUARE GOSPEL
1100 Glendale Blvd.
Los Angeles, CA 90026

Alternate address: Canadian headquarters: Foursquare Gospel Church of Canada, 7895 Welsley Dr., Burnaby, BC V5E 3X4.

History. The International Church of the Foursquare Gospel was founded by Aimee Semple McPherson (1890-1944), the flamboyant and controversial pastor of Angelus Temple in Los Angeles, California. Aimee's mother, a member of the Salvation Army, had promised God to dedicate her daughter to the ministry. At the age of 17, the teenage Aimee was converted, baptized with the Holy Spirit, and soon married to evangelist Robert James Semple. In 1910, the couple travelled to China as missionaries, and while serving there, Robert Semple died of malaria, just one month before the birth of their daughter, Roberta. With her daughter, Aimee returned to the United States where she later married Harold S. McPherson and to them was born a son, Rolf Kennedy McPherson. Together the McPhersons began to conduct independent itinerant pentecostal evangelistic meetings. Following her divorce from McPherson, Aimee continued the ministry which had already begun. In 1917, she began a periodical, *Bridal Call*, which served her ministry for many years.

Unsupported and berated by other ministers who did not believe in women speaking from a pulpit, Aimee won success through her oratorical abilities, her charisma, her expounding the teaching of the Foursquare Gospel, and her use of unusual and heretofore untried methods which brought widespread publicity. During her early ministry, she spent much time with T. K. Leonard and William H. Durham, both early pentecostal leaders. In 1918, Aimee settled in Los Angeles and with the help of those who has responded to her her ministry, built and dedicated Angelus Temple in 1923. Throughout the remainder of her ministry, the temple became the focus of numerous spiritual extravaganzas, including religious drama, illustrated messages, and oratorios, which brought Sister Aimee, as she was affectionately called, a reputation for the unconventional. In 1926, Aimee disappeared for more than a month and upon her return, she said that she had been kidnapped. A major controversy developed, with critics claiming that she had disappeared of her own volition, yet no proof was substantiated to disprove her claim.

An evangelistic and training institute was opened even before the temple was dedicated and it began to educate leaders who went on to found numerous Foursquare churches. The creation of some 32 churches in southern California by 1921 spurred the formation of the Echo Park Evangelistic Association, and in 1927, the International Church of the Foursquare Gospel was incorporated. The church also built and began operation of KFSG, the third oldest radio station in Los Angeles. It currently operates 24 hours daily in southern California.

Work expanded to Canada; first to Vancouver and then eastward to Ontario. The Western Canada District was set off from the Northwest District in 1964. The Church of the Foursquare Gospel of Western Canada was established as a provincial society in 1976. A federal corporation was created in 1981 and the Foursquare Gospel Church of Canada emerged as a autonomous sister church.

Beliefs. The church has adopted a lengthy declaration of faith which affirms the authority of scripture and the traditional beliefs of protestant evangelical Christianity. There are two ordinances, baptism and the Lord's Supper. The baptism of the Holy Spirit is emphasized, but along with an equal emphasis upon the Spirit-filled life and the gifts and fruits of the Spirit. Tithing is acknowledged as the method ordained of God for the support of the ministry.

Organization. The organization of the church is vested in the president, a position held by Aimee until her death in 1944. She was succeeded by her son who held the post until his retirement in 1988. The third president is John R. Holland. A board of directors, which includes the president and other appointed or elected members, serves as the highest administrative body for the denomination's business affairs. A missionary cabinet and executive council advise the board of directors and the president.

Throughout the United States the church is divided into nine districts with each area overseen by a district supervisor.

Membership: In 1987, the church reported 187,277 members, 1,293 churches, and 3,044 ministers in the United States. The affiliated Foursquare Gospel Church of Canada reported 6,961 members, 125 churches, and 211 ministers. Worldwide membership in the church was approximately one million in 15,000 churches in 60 countries.

Educational facilities: L.I.F.E. (Lighthouse of International Foursquare Evangelism) Bible College, Los Angeles, California; Mt. Vernon Bible College, Mt. Vernon, Ohio. The Foursquare Gospel Church of Canada sponsors L.I.F.E. Bible College of Canada, Vancouver, British Columbia. There are also more than 40 Bible colleges and institutes in foreign mission fields around the world.

Periodicals: *The Foursquare World Advance Magazine*, 1100 Glendale Blvd., Los Angeles, CA 90026.

Sources: Raymond L. Cox, ed., *The Foursquare Gospel*. Los Angeles: Foursquare Publications, 1969; Aimee Semple McPherson, *The Story of My Life*. Waco, TX: Word Books, 1973; Lately Thomas, *The Vanishing Evangelist*. New York: Viking Press, 1959; Nancy Barr Mavity, *Sister Aimee*. Garden City, NY: Doubleday, 1931; Guy P. Duffield and Nathaniel M. Van Cleave, *Foundations of Pentecostal Theology*. Los Angeles: L.I.F.E. Bible College, 1983.

★361★
ITALIAN PENTECOSTAL CHURCH OF CANADA
6724 Fabre St.
Montreal, PQ, Canada H2G 2Z6

Italian Presbyterians were the first of the Italian-Canadians to receive the baptism of the Holy Spirit and experience speaking-in-tongues. Though some Italians in Chicago became Pentecostals as early as 1907 and began missionary work in the United States, the Canadian work had an entirely independent origin, beginning in 1913 in Hamilton, Ontario with the ministry of a Christian-Jewish missionary named Cohen. In 1914, two of the men who had received the baptism, Charles Pavia and Frank Rispoli, took the experience to Toronto, where they visited door-to-door in the Italian community. By 1920 the fervor spread to Montreal and other Italian-Canadian communities. Among the early leaders of the movement were Luigi Ippolito and Ferdinand Zaffuto.

Upon his return to the United States, evangelist Cohon informed the Italian Pentecostals in Chicago of the Canadian group, and a delegation visited the Hamilton and Toronto churches. The doctrine and practice of the Italian Pentecostal Church of Canada is similiar to that of the Pentecostal Assemblies of Canada, with whom they

share fraternal relations. A missionary program is supported in Australia, Argentina, Brazil, England, France, Germany, Italy, and Switzerland.

Membership: In 1987, the church reported 18 congregations and 21 ministers in canada. There were 5,000 members worldwide, of which approximately 3,500 were in Canada.

Educational facilities: Eastern Pentecostal Bible College, Peterborough, Ontario; Italian Bible Institute.

Periodicals: *Voce Evanglica* (Evangel Voice), 6724 Fabre St., Montreal, PQ H2G 2Z6.

Sources: Louis De Caro, *Our Heritage*. Sharon, PA: General Council, Christian Church of North America, 1977; Luigi Zucchi, *Origin and Brief History*. Montreal: Italian Pentecostal Church of Canada, 1987.

★362★
LAMB OF GOD CHURCH
612 Isenburg St.
Honolulu, HI 96817

The Lamb of God Church was founded in 1942 by Rev. Rose Soares. It is a small church with its several congregations all located on Oahu, Hawaii. The faith and practice are Pentecostal. The churches primarily serve native Hawaiians.

Membership: In 1988 there were three congregations and approximately 300 members.

Educational facilities: Lamb of God Bible School, Honolulu, Hawaii.

★363★
MT. ZION SANCTUARY
21 Dayton St.
Elizabeth, NJ 07202

The Mt. Zion Sanctuary was formed in 1882 by Mrs. Antoinette Jackson, a member of the Baptist Church. Rejecting the idea that she was suffering as an invalid for the glory of God, she sought healing by prayer and fasting, and was instantly cured on July 14, 1880. She became blessed with the gifts of the Spirit, particularly healing, and others who were blessed by her ministry gathered around her.

Mt. Zion Sanctuary members believe in the Trinity as God the Father, God the Son, and the Holy Spirit who is the executive power of God. Humans find deliverance from sin and sickness in the vicarious sacrifice of Jesus. Believers are sanctified as they obey the truth. Baptism by immersion is practiced and the sabbath is kept. The church is considered to be the society of born-again believers who live a holy life. Church members believe in

Christ's premillennial second coming, i.e., Christ will return to find Satan prior to His one-thousand-year reign on earth with His saints.

Mrs. Jackson was succeeded by Pastor Ithamar Quigley, who was healed under her ministrations.

Membership: In 1988 the sanctuary reported 100 members in two centers led by four ministers in the United States. Internationally, there were two churches in England, 10 in Nigeria, and 12 in Jamaica.

★364★
MUSIC SQUARE CHURCH
Box 398
Alma, AK 72921

History. Music Square Church (also known as the Holy Alamo Christian Church Consecrated) began in 1969 as a street ministry in Hollywood, California, by Susan Alamo (born Edith Opal Horn) (d. 1982), an independent Pentecostal minister, and Tony Alamo (born Bernie Lazar Hoffman), her husband, whom she had converted. They began a ministry in Hollywood in the mid-1960s and opened a church there in 1969 where their first converts gathered. The church was originally known as the Tony and Susan Alamo Christian Foundation, but in 1981 Music Square Church was incorporated and in 1982 superceded the foundation.

During its formative years, the church became known as one segment of the Jesus People movement, however, it remained separate organizationally. As much of the larger movement was incorporated into various Baptist and Pentecostal churches, it survived as an independent organization heavily committed to an evangelistic street ministry. In the early 1970s, the church became quite controversial and was heavily criticized because of the format its ministry had developed. Church members (associates of the foundation's ministry) generally worked the streets of Hollywood inviting potential converts to evening services at the church which had, by that time, been established at Saugus (a rural community approximately an hour's distance). The mostly young recruits were taken by bus to Saugus for an evangelistic meeting and meal. Many of those who did convert remained in Saugus to be taught the Bible and become lay ministers.

In 1976, as the Foundation grew, it purchased land at Alma and Dyer, Arkansas, where Susan Alamo grew up and where it transferred its headquarters. There it developed a community of several hundred foundation associates and established printing facilities, a school, and a large tabernacle. As part of its rehabilitation program it began to develop several businesses in which associates (many of whom were former drug addicts) could begin a process of reintegration into society. As the organization expanded further, churches (evangelistic centers) were opened in cities around the country (including Nashville,

Tennessee; Chicago, Illinois; Brooklyn, New York; Miami Beach, Florida.) Associated with the church in Nashville, a retail clothing store was opened.

Beliefs. Music Square Church is a Pentecostal church with doctrine similar to the Assemblies of God. It accepts the authority of the Bible (using only the King James Version) and places its emphasis upon the preaching of Jesus Christ as the son of the Living God who died for humanity. The church adheres to a strict moral code, and members condemn drugs, homosexuality, adultery, and abortions. Both Susan and Tony Alamo were Jewish and they developed a special interest in evangelism of Jews.

Organization. Music Square Church has developed as an ordered community of people dedicated to evangelism. Converts who wish to remain associated with the church (i.e., to receive its training and participate in its ministry) take a vow of poverty agreeing to turn over all their real property to the church. In return the church agrees to provide the necessities of life (housing, clothes, food, medical assistance), including the education of children through high school. The church is headed by a three-person board presided over by Tony Alamo, the church's pastor. Alamo and the board set the policy and direction for the ministry.

Approximately half of the associates of the church reside on church property near Alma. Others reside at the several church centers around the United States. The headquarters complex includes housing units for the associates, a Christian school for grades one through 12, a large community dining hall, and offices. Periodically associates are sent out on evangelistic tours around the United States, frequently using the established church centers as bases of operation. Services are held daily at each of the church centers and generally free meals are served.

The church publishes a variety of evangelistic tracts which are passed out in the street witnessing and are mailed around the country and to a number of foreign countries as requested. The church also distributes numerous tapes of sermons by former pastor Susan Alamo and present pastor Tony Alamo. Among those associated with the church are a number of talented musicians and the church had produced a set of records and tapes featuring Tony Alamo and other members. A national television ministry begun in the 1970s has been largely discontinued.

Membership: In 1988 the Church had approximately 400 members and six churches.

Remarks: The Alamo Christian Foundation and Music Square Church have been targets of controversy since the early 1970s, most growing out of attacks of the anti-cult movement. In the late 1970s, the U.S. Department of Labor filed suit against the church seeking wages for former members who had worked in the several businesses operated by the church. In the wake of negative rulings by the court most of the business were shut down and those remaining serve only the church (car repair and building materials). Also following the court's ruling in 1985, the Internal Revenue Service moved to deny tax-exempt status, in a case currently being ajudicated.

The church has raised an equally strong controversy by its opinions against the Roman Catholic Church, which church publications have labeled "Satan's church." The pope has been termed an "antichrist devil," and his possible role as a secret manipulator of the U. S. government condemned.

Sources: Robert S. Ellwood, Jr., *One Way*. Englewood Cliffs, NJ: Prentice-Hall, 1973; *We're Your Neighbor*. Alma, AK: The Holy Alamo Christian Church Consecrated, [1987].

★365★
OPEN BIBLE STANDARD CHURCHES, INC.
2020 Bell Ave.
Des Moines, IA 50315-1096

The Open Bible Standard Churches, Inc., was founded in 1935 by the merger of two evangelistic movements--the Open Bible Evangelistic Association and Bible Standard, Inc.. The former body had been founded by John R. Richey in Des Moines, Iowa, in 1932 and the latter in Eugene, Oregon, by Fred Hornshuh in 1919. At the time of the merger there were 210 ministers. Doctrine is like that of the Assemblies of God (discussed elsewhere in this volume) with a strong emphasis on healing, a literal heaven and hell, resurrection, tithing, and the belief that every Christian should identify with the visible church of Jesus Christ.

The polity is congregational. Congregations are grouped into districts and regions. A general conference meets biennially and includes all ministers an d a layman from each church. There are fourteen administrative departments. Missions are conducted in thirty countries around the world.

Membership: In 1987 the Church reported over 40,000 members in 300 congregations, 25 nonchartered cooperating churches, and 883 ministers. There were also 1,000 members in Canada and 26,000 members overseas.

Educational facilities: Eugene Bible College, Eugene, Oregon.

Periodicals: *Message of the Open Bible*, 2020 Bell Avenue, Des Moines, IA 50315; *The Overcomer*, 2020 Bell Avenue, Des Moines, IA 50315; *Outreach*, 2020 Bell Avenue, Des Moines, IA 50315.

Sources: Robert Bryant Mitchell, *Heritage & Horizons*. Des Moines, IA: Open Bible Publishers, 1982; *Policies and Principles*. Des Moines, IA: Open Bible Standard Churches, Inc., 1986.

★366★
PENTECOSTAL ASSEMBLIES OF CANADA
10 Overlea Blvd.
Toronto, ON, Canada M4H 1A5

Among the people drawn to Los Angeles by the news of the Pentecostal revival which had broken out at the little mission on Azusa Street in 1906 were several Canadians, most prominently R. E. McAlister. McAlister brought the revival to Ottawa. In addition, A. H. Argue encountered the first wave of the revival which swept Chicago, and he returned to Winnipeg with its message. In 1907 he began a magazine, *The Apostolic Messenger*, to spread the word. Within a few years Pentecostal assemblies had been established across Canada.

Organization proceeded slowly, though as early as 1909 a Pentecostal Missionary Union was formed. In 1917 ministers from the eastern part of Canada met at Montreal and formed the Pentecostal Assemblies of Canada. Two years later, ministers in the west formed the Western Canada District of the Assemblies of God, attached to the United States group headquartered in Springfield, Missouri. In 1921 the eastern group also affiliated with the Assemblies of God. In 1922 the government charter was finalized.

Soon after the affiliation with the American Pentecostals, the Canadians began to see that they were at a disadvantage and gradually they moved to separate themselves and assume the original name of the eastern organization. Headquarters were reestablished in Ottawa and later moved to Toronto. Several reasons for the organizational split (which implied no break in fraternal relations) are generally given. First, the Canadians placed less emphasis upon doctrine and were thus open to more latitude of belief. Second, there was a greater ethnic diversity, with one out of ten congregations not speaking English. Third, there was the influence of such Canadian voices as James Eustace Purdie, who argued for Canadian autonomy.

Doctrinally, the Canadian assemblies largely agree with the Assemblies of God. They advocate tithing, and have strict rules about divorce, especially among ministers. They are also fraternally related to the Pentecostal Assemblies of Newfoundland, with whom they share the same doctrinal statement.

Membership: In 1986 there were 1,036 churches, 178,743 members, and 1,377 ministers.

Educational facilities: Berea Bible Institute, Pierrefonds, Quebec; Canadian Pentecostal Correspondence College, Clayburn, British Columbia; Central Pentecostal College, Saskatoon, Saskatchewan; College Biblique Quebec: Formation Timothee, Charlesbourg Quest, Quebec;

Eastern Pentecostal Bible College, Peterborough, Ontario; Northwest Bible College, Edmonton, Alberta.

Periodicals: *The Pentecostal Testimony*, 10 Overlea Blvd., Toronto, ON M4H 1A5.

★367★
PENTECOSTAL ASSEMBLIES OF NEWFOUNDLAND
57 Thoburn Rd.
St. John's, NF, Canada A1B 3N4

Pentecostalism spread to Newfoundland in 1910 and on Easter Sunday, 1911, the first assembly, Bethesda Pentecostal Mission, opened at St. John's. The work was incorporated in 1925 as the Bethesda Pentecostal Assemblies, the name by which it was known until it assumed its present name in 1930. That same year, using a ship, *The Gospel Messenger*, the assemblies moved into towns in Laborador.

The assemblies are separate from the Pentecostal Assemblies of Canada, but maintain close fraternal ties and hold to the same doctrinal position.

Membership: In 1987 the assemblies reported 167 churches, 36,000 members, and 190 ministries.

Periodicals: *Good Tidings*, 57 Thoburn Rd., St. John's, NF A1B 3N4; *Reach*, 57 Thoburn Rd., St. John's, NF A1B 3N4.

★368★
PENTECOSTAL CHURCH OF GOD
4901 Pennsylvania
Joplin, MO 64802

History. The Pentecostal Church of God was formed in Chicago, Illinois, in 1919 by a group of pentecostal leaders. They chose the Rev. John C. Sinclair as their first moderator and Pentecostal Assemblies of America as their name. That name was changed to the Pentecostal Church of God of America in 1922. The words "of America" were dropped in 1979. The church enjoyed a steady growth over the years. It moved its headquarters to Ottumwa, Iowa in 1927. The following year the Pentecostal Young Peoples Association was organized. The expansion of the youth ministry was further manifested in the issuance of the first Sunday school material published by the church in 1937. Missionary support began as early as 1921, and was formalized in a church department in 1932.

Beliefs. church's beliefs follow the central affirmation of evangelical Pentecostal Christianity. It affirms the authority of scripture, the Trinity, the deity of Christ, and humanity's need of salvation in Christ. The ordinances of the Lord's Supper and baptism by immersion are practiced. The church affirms the baptism of the Holy Spirit received subsequent to the new birth (faith in Christ) which is evidenced by the initial sign of speaking-in-tongues. Foot washing is observed at the discretion of local congregations. Prayer for divine healing of bodily ills is a regular part of church life. The church is not pacifist, but supports conscientious objectors in their search for alternative service. Tithing is advocated.

Organization. The church is headed by the general superintendent, assisted by the general secretary-treasurer, director of world missions, director of Indian missions, director of christian education, president of the Penetcostal Young Peoples Association, and the president of the Penetcostal Ladies Auxiliary. The church is divided into districts headed by district superintendents, district presbyters, and district secretary-treasurers. The general convention meets biennially with district conventions meeting annually.

Membership: In 1986, the church reported 42,225 members, 1,114 congregations, and 2,895 ministers. There was a reported constitutency of 90,902 in the United States. There were 180,000 members worldwide in 26 countries.

Educational facilities: Messenger College, Joplin, Missouri. In the mission field, there are 15 resident Bible schools and 29 extension training centers.

Periodicals: *The Pentecostal Messenger*, Box 850, Joplin, MO 64802.

Sources: Elmer Louis Moon, *The Pentecostal Church*. New York: Carleton Press, 1966; Aaron M. Wilson, *Basic Bible Truth*. Joplin, MO: Messenger Press, 1988; *General Constitution and By-Laws*. Joplin, MO: Pentecostal Church of God, 1984.

★369★
PENTECOSTAL CHURCH OF ZION
% Zion College of Theology
Box 110
French Lick, IN 47432

As a youth in Kentucky, Luther S. Howard was converted by an independent Pentecostal minister and, in 1920, was ordained a minister of the Holy Bible Mission at Louisville. He served as a minister and then vice-president. Upon the death of its founder, Mrs. C. L. Pennington, the Mission was dissolved. Its ministers felt the need to continue their work and, in 1954, formed a new organization, the Pentecostal Church of Zion, Inc. Elder Howard was elected president and, in 1964, bishop. Since most of the work of the Holy Bible Mission was in Indiana, the new organization was headquartered at French Lick, Indiana.

The Pentecostal Church of Zion is like the Assemblies of God in most of its doctrine but differs from it on some points. The group keeps the ten commandments, including the Saturday Sabbath, and the Mosaic law concerning clean and unclean meats. (Cows and sheep are clean and may be eaten; pigs and other animals with cloven hooves may not be eaten because they are considered unclean). Most important, the group does not have a closed creed, but believes that members continue to grow in grace and knowledge. Anyone who feels that he has new light on the Word of God is invited to bring his ideas to the annual convention, where they can be discussed by the executive committee. By such a process, a decision was made in the 1960s to drop the Lord's Supper as an ordinance. The church now believes in the celebration of Passover by daily communion with the Holy Ghost.

Polity is episcopal. There is one bishop with life tenure and an assistant bishop elected for a three-year term. An annual meeting with lay delegates is held at the headquarters.

Membership: Not reported. In 1974 there were 5 congregations in Indiana and 1 in Oregon.

Educational facilities: Zion College of Theology, French Lick, Indiana.

Periodicals: *Zion's Echoes of Truth*, Box 110, French Lick, IN 47432.

★370★
PENTECOSTAL EVANGELICAL CHURCH
% Rev. Ernest Beroth
Box 4218
Spokane, WA 99202

The Pentecostal Evangelical Church was founded in 1936. Its first bishop, G. F. C. Fons, had been the moderator of the Pentecostal Church of God of America in the period directly preceeding the formation of the new body. Its doctrine is similar to that of the Pentecostal Church of God of America, and its polity is a mixture of congregationalism and episcopal forms. Each local church is autonomous. The general conference meets every two years and elects a general bishop (for a four-year term), a vice-president (for two years), and a district superintendent (as an assistant bishop). Missions are supported in the Philippines, Bolivia, India and Guyana.

Membership: Not reported.

Periodicals: *Gospel Tidings*, Box 4218, Spokane, WA 99202.

★371★
PENTECOSTAL EVANGELICAL CHURCH OF GOD, NATIONAL AND INTERNATIONAL
Riddle, OR 97469

The Pentecostal Evangelical Church of God, National and International was founded at Riddle, Oregon in 1960. It

holds to beliefs similar to those of the Assemblies of God. It ordains women to the ministry. A General Convocation meets annually.

Membership: Not reported. In 1967 there were 4 congregations and 14 ministers.

Periodicals: *Ingathering*, Riddle, OR ; *Golden Leaves*, Riddle, OR.

★372★
SEVENTH DAY PENTECOSTAL CHURCH OF THE LIVING GOD
1443 S. Euclid
Washington, DC 20009

The Seventh Day Pentecostal Church of the Living God was founded by Bishop Charles Gamble, a Pentecostal who had adopted some of the Old Testament practices including the seventh-day Sabbath. Gamble was a Roman Catholic and Baptist before becoming a Pentecostal. The church follows the Jesus-Only nonTrinitarian theology of the Apostolic churches.

Membership: Not reported. In the early 1970s there were 4 congregations with an estimated membership of less than 1,000.

★373★
UNITED FULL GOSPEL MINISTERS AND CHURCHES
Current address not obtained for this edition.

The United Full Gospel Ministers and Churches was incorporated May 16, 1951. Arthur H. Collins was the first chairman. Within a few years it had grown to include more than fifty clergy and a number of congregations. The church is governed by four executive officers, one of whom faces election at each annual meeting. The group has an affiliate in India--the Open Bible Church of God, founded by Willis M. Clay, who at one time also served as treasurer of the United Full Gospel Ministers and Churches.

Membership: Not reported.

★374★
UNITED FUNDAMENTALIST CHURCH
Current address not obtained for this edition.

The United Fundamentalist Church was organized in 1939 by the Rev. Leroy M. Kopp of Los Angeles. It was at one time a member of the National Association of Evangelicals and accepts the Association's doctrinal position. In addition, it is Pentecostal, and prophecy and healing are emphasized. Members are expected to believe that "The divine healing of the sick is not only to honor the prayer of faith (James 5:14, 15) but is to be a sign to confirm the word as it is preached at home and abroad

(Mark 16:15-20)." Signs are given until the end of this age, when they will no longer be needed.

The general officers of the United Fundamentalist Church, together with the territorial supervisors and state district superintendents, constitute a council which settles all doctrinal disputes. Zion Christian Mission is sponsored in Jerusalem. Proselyting other Christian denominations is not practiced. A radio ministry was begun in 1940 by Kopp and still continues. The Rev. E. Paul Kopp has succeeded his father as head of the group.

Membership: Not reported. In 1967 there were approximately 250 ministers and missionaries.

Deliverance Pentecostals

★375★
BRANHAM TABERNACLE AND RELATED ASSEMBLIES
% The William Branham Evangelistic Association and The Branham Tabernacle
Box 325
Jeffersonville, IN 47130

Alternate address: The Voice of God Recordings, Inc., Box 950, Jeffersonville, IN 47130

William Marrion Branham (1909-1965) was a Pentecostal prophet who, as a child, began to hear the voice of one he claimed to be an angel of the Lord. Healed as a young man in a Pentecostal Church, he became a preacher and his success led to the building of a tabernacle in his home town of Jeffersonville, Indiana. Another angelic visitation in 1946 launched his evangelical career as a seer with a healing ministry. He spoke of being called by God to pray for the sick, and the angel told him that he had been sent with a gift. He began to travel around the country leading revival services. He met Gordon Lindsey, a young Assemblies of God pastor in Oregon, who joined Branham and in 1948 began *The Voice of Healing*, to publicize Branham's work and bring supporters together. As Branham's tours and fame spread nationally and internationally, other ministers with a gift for healing associated themselves with him and *The Voice of Healing*. During the 1950s, Branham led the revival in healing that would project such people as Oral Roberts, Morris Cerullo, and A. A. Allen into the spotlight as leaders of their own organizations.

Around 1960, Branham became separated from the majority of the healing evangelists when he allowed divergent opinions which he had always held but rarely spoken about to become frequent topics in his sermons. He denounced denominationalism as the mark of the beast of the Book of Revelation. He openly denounced trinitarian doctrine, which led many to see him as an advocate of Jesus Only nontrinitarian theology. Jesus Only Pentecostals believe that Jesus is the name of the One

God, and that Father, Son, and Holy Spirit are not distinct persons in the Godhead. They baptize in the name of Jesus. Branham, while possibly sharing their ideas about the Godhead, taught that baptism was to be in the name of the "Lord Jesus Christ." Then in 1963, he began to emphasize the message of Malachi 4:5, that God had promised to send his prophet, Elijah. While never identifying himself as that messenger, he left the door open for his followers, many of whom came to believe that he was the one spoken about by Malachi. This issue alienated Branham from many of his former followers. His attempt to recover his former widespread support ended when he died in a car accident two years later.

Those who followed Branham's message, who believed him to be the one with the spirit of Elijah, began immediately to preserve and perpetuate his message. Copies of sermon tapes and transcripts of sermons were reproduced and circulated by Spoken Word Publications and The Voice of God Recordings, Inc., both of which were headquartered a few blocks from the tabernacle in Jeffersonville. Recently Spoken Word merged into The Voice of God, which now houses the most complete archive of Branham tapes and written material. The Voice of God regularly sends out copies of Branham's sermons which it is publishing one-by-one as a series of pamphlets under the general heading *The Spoken Word*. The Voice of God is headed by Joseph Branham.

The Rev. Billy Paul Branham now heads the William Branham Evangelistic Association and preaches at the tabernacle. Besides the Branham Tabernacle, there are a number of independent churches which follow the message initiated by Branham. There is no association, no bishops or overseers, only an informal fellowship. Many of these churches regularly order materials from The Voice of God and offer financial support of its work. Besides the following in the United States and Canada, support comes from Australia, New Zealand, and India.

Membership: Not reported. More than 100 pastors and churches regularly receive the materials circulated by Voice of God Recordings, Inc.

Periodicals: *The Witness,* Box 950, Jeffersonville, IN 47130; *Only Believe,* Believers International, Box 56270, Tucson, AZ 85703.

Sources: C. Douglas Weaver, *The Healer-Prophet, William Marrion Branham: A Study in the Prophetic in American Pentecostalism.* Macon, GA: Mercer University Press, 1987; David Edwin Harrell, Jr., *All Things Are Possible.* Bloomington, IN: University of Indiana Press, 1975; Gordon Lindsey, *William Branham, A Man Sent From God.* Jeffersonville, IN: William Branham, 1950; William Branham, *Footprints on the Sands of Time.* Jeffersonville, IN: Spoken Word Publications, n.d.; Terry Sproule, *A Prophet to the Gentiles.* Blaine, WA: Bible Believers, n.d.; William Marrion Branham, *Conduct, Order, Doctrine of* *the Church.* Jeffersonville, IN: Spoken Word Publications, 1974.

★376★
FIRST DELIVERANCE CHURCH OF ATLANTA
Current address not obtained for this edition.

The First Deliverance Church was founded in Atlanta in 1956 by the Reverends Lillian G. Fitch and William Fitch, two deliverance evangelists. The church teaches three experiences (justification, sanctification, and baptism of the Holy Spirit), emphasizes healing, and practices tithing. Fasts are an important feature of church life. Occasionally members hold a shut-in fast, when they stay at the church for three days over the weekend. Among distinctive practices is their kneeling in prayer upon entering the church. Congregations headed by licensed ministers are located in Georgia, Florida, Oklahoma, and California.

Membership: Not reported.

★377★
FULL GOSPEL FELLOWSHIP OF CHURCHES AND MINISTERS INTERNATIONAL
1545 W. Mockingbird Ln., Suite 1012
Dallas, TX 75235

In the early 1960s, Gordon Lindsay, founder of the Christ for the Nations Institute, in Dallas, Texas, and publisher of the The Voice of Healing magazine, called together a group of independent Pentecostal ministers. The ministers expressed a desire to give expression of the unity of the Body of Christ under the leadership of the Holy Spirit, a unity that would go beyond individuals, churches, or organizations. Thus the Full Gospel Fellowship of Churches and Ministers International was formed in 1962.

The fellowship has adopted a set of Suggested Articles of Faith that they offer to member churches. While assuming an essential doctrinal agreement among member churches and ministers, individual churches may choose to revise the articles. The articles affirm belief in the Bible as the inspired Word of God, the Trinity, the need of people for salvation, sanctification, the second coming and millenial reign of Christ, heaven, and hell. Baptism of the Holy Spirit with the initial evidence of speaking in tongues is strongly advocated.

The fellowship is an organized association of independent churches and is designed to perform only those services that churches cannot easily or conveniently provide for themselves. Individual churches, groups of churches, and organizations of churches may be recognized within the fellowship. Each church is free to carry out its own program and missionary work and to ordain and/or license ministers as it deems necessary. Those ministers recognized by the fellowship are subsequently issued a membership card and certificate of ministerial status. Annually, an international and several regional conventions are held to provide opportunities for fellowship and to support the objectives and goals of local and national ministries. The business meeting is held during the international meeting each July.

While the fellowship is not a governing body, it has been recognized by the Internal Revenue Service as an organization qualified to offer independent congregations tax-exempt status under its group exemption umbrella.

Membership: In 1988 the fellowship reported 800 clergy members and 423 congregation members in the United States. There were three clergy members from Canada and 47 clergy members from 15 countries worldwide.

Periodicals: *Fellowship Tidings*, Suite 1012, 1545 W. Mockingbird Lane, Dallas, TX 75235.

Remarks: Gordon Lindsay (1906-1973), whose efforts were so important in initiating the fellowship's organization, was a former pastor in the Assemblies of God, and, in the late 1940s, a close associate of evangelist William Marrion Branham. He served as president of the Voice of Healing Publishing Company and edited *The Voice of Healing*, a magazine thet publicized and coordinated the activities of many of the prominent healing evangelists of the 1950s. In 1949 he called together the first meeting of the evangelists and ministers who supported the healing emphases that had grown from Branham's original efforts. The last of these annual conventions was held in 1961, the year before the formation of the Full Gospel Fellowship of Churches and Ministers International. Lindsay's work has been carried on by his widow, Freda Lindsay, through Christ for the Nations and its affiliated activities.

Sources: Gordon Lindsay, *The Gordon Lindsay Story*. Dallas: The Voice of Healing Publishing Company, n.d. (1970?); Gordon Lindsay, *Bible Days Are Here Again*. Shreveport, LA: The Author, 1949; Freda (Mrs. Gordon) Lindsay, *My Diary Secrets*. Dallas: Christ for the Nations, 1976.

★378★
HALL DELIVERANCE FOUNDATION
Box 9910
Phoenix, AZ 85068

The Hall Deliverance Foundation was established in 1956 in San Diego, California, as the focus of the ministry of the Reverend Franklin Hall, an independent Pentecostal minister, who began his ministerial career in 1946 as a Methodist. Hall also founded and pastored the International Healing Cathedral in San Diego, California. During the years in the Pentecostal ministry prior to the organization of the foundation, Hall was closely connected with the evangelist Thelma Nickel.

Hall teaches what he terms "body-felt" salvation. It is his belief that salvation is for the body as well as the biblical text, "By his stripes you are healed" and also by his own obtaining of the full baptism of the Holy Ghost (or Spirit) and Fire, as mentioned in Matthew 3:11. According to Hall, this teaching was alluded to by Jesus in Acts 1:8. The Holy Ghost power coming upon the physical body keeps the body well and healed, just as long as the believer keeps that portion of the Holy Spirit called the "Fire" upon the physical body. The believer, therefore, has "body-felt" salvation, as there is no sickness. Those who participate in the body-felt salvation also participate in a miracle ministry finds its demonstration in a wide variety of healings and deliverance from natural disasters and dangerous situations. Also, the experience of the Holy Spirit when it comes upon the person is felt tangibly as a pleasant warmth to heal the body or to bring healing protection energy. This sensation is related to the fire portion of the Holy Spirit baptism (Acts 2:3), which Jesus urged his disciples to obtain (Acts 1:8). Hall also recommends prayer and fasting. The latter enables one to become a powerful conductor of divine and spiritual forces, according to Hall.

Hall continues to travel the United States from his base in Phoenix, Arizona. He distributes numerous pieces of literature and has recently begun a television ministry. Affiliated work takes place in Mexico, Canada, the Bahamas, Australia, New Zealand, Great Britain, West Germany, Finland, France, Sweden, the Philippines, Nigeria, Ghana, th e Ivory Coast , Ethiopia, Tanzania, Kenya, Malaya, South Africa, and India.

Membership: In 1984, The Foundation reported 60 associated churches, 60 ministers, and 3,200 members across the United States. There are approximately 150,000 members overseas.

Educational facilities: Glory Knowledge Bible School Phoenix, Arizona.

Periodicals: *Miracle Word*, Box 9910, Phoenix, AZ 85068; *The Healing Word News*, Box 9910, Phoenix, AZ 85068.

Sources: Franklin Hall, *The Body-Felt Salvation*. Phoenix: Hall Deliverance Foundation, 1968; Franklin Hall, *Our Divine Healing Obligation*. Phoenix: The Author, 1964; Thelma Nickel, *Our Rainbow of Promise*. Tulsa, OK: Vickers Printing Co., 1950; Franklin Hall, *Atomic Power with God*. San Diego, CA: The Author, 1946; Franklin Hall, *The Baptism of Fire*. San Diego, CA: The Author, 1960.

★379★
INTERNATIONAL CONVENTION OF FAITH CHURCHES AND MINISTERS
3840 S. 103 E. Avenue, #132
Tulsa, OK 74146-2445

The International Convention of Faith Churches and Ministers was founded in 1979 by Dr Doyle Harrison and a number of independent Pentecostal pastors and evangelists, some of whom head their own national and international ministries, and a few of whom had become very well known for their work on Christian television-- Kenneth Hagin, (Tulsa, Oklahoma), Kenneth Copeland (Fort Worth, Texas), Frederick K. C. Price (Los Angeles), Norvel Hayes (Cleveland, Tennessee), Jerry J. Savelle (Fort Worth, Texas) and John H. Osteen (Houston, Texas). Hagin is pastor of RHEMA Bible Church and heads Kenneth Hagin Ministries, Inc.. Copeland, assisted by Gloria Copeland, his wife, heads Kenneth Copeland Ministries and Publications. Price, a black minister, heads Ever Increasing Faith Ministries and pastors Crenshaw Christian Center. Savelle heads Jerry Savelle Ministries and founded the Overcoming Faith Churches of Kenya in Africa. Osteen heads the John Osteen World Satellite Network. Norvel Hayes, a successful businessman, is also an independent healing evangelist. Doyle Harrison pastors Faith Christian Fellowship International Church in Tulsa.

Not only does their work center upon healing, but they subscribe to the "faith confession" doctrine which holds that a child of faith can publically confess or claim something from God and be assured of getting it. The Convention admits both churches and individuals to membership. Many of the students trained at RHEMA Bible Training Center, started in 1974 by Hagin, have created new congregations partially drawing upon listeners of the television programs of the Convention founders. In 1975 Harrison, founded Harrison House, a book concern, which publishes many of the healing evangelists' materials.

Membership: In 1985 the Convention had over 800 ministers and churches on its rolls.

Educational facilities: RHEMA Bible Training Center, Tulsa, Oklahoma; Crenshaw Christian Center School of Ministry, Box 90000, Los Angeles, CA 90009.

Periodicals: *International Faith Report*, 3840 S. 103 E. Aveue, No. 132, Tulsa, OK 74146. Unofficial (periodicals issued by ministries associated with the Convention): *The Word of Faith*, Kenneth Hagin Ministries, Box 50126, Tulsa, OK 74150; *Ever Increasing Faith Messenger*, Crenshaw Christian Center, Box 90000, Los Angeles, CA 90009; *Believers Voice of Victory Magazine*, Kenneth Copeland Ministries, Box 2908, Fort Worth, TX 76113.

Remarks: Some of the leading ministers of the Convention (Hagin, Copeland, Price) are among a group of evangelists-teachers who have been attacked by other Pentecostal leaders for what has been termed "faith formula theology," that is a belief that by publically confessing (claiming) something from God, believers will be given it according to their faith.

Sources: Kenneth E. Hagin, *How You Can Be Led by the Spirit of God*. Tulsa, OK: Kenneth Hagin Ministries, 1978; Gloria Copeland, *God's Will for You*. Fort Worth: Kenneth Copeland Publications, 1972; Frederick K. C. Price, *How to Obtain Strong Faith*. Tulsa, OK: Harrison

House, 1980; John H. Osteen, *This Awakening Generation*. Humble, TX: The Author, 1964; Norvel Hayes, *7 Ways Jesus Heals*. Tulsa, OK: Harrison House, 1982.

★380★

INTERNATIONAL DELIVERANCE CHURCHES
Box 353
Dallas, TX 75221

Among the deliverance evangelists associated with William Marrion Branham was W. V. Grant. After several years as an active evangelist, he settled in Dallas because of health problems and became a prolific writer of deliverance literature. He became pastor of the Soul's Harbor Church in Dallas and the leading force in the International Deliverance Churches.

From the Dallas Center, annual conventions have been held each summer since 1962. During this period, classes are held for two weeks, and ministers are ordained. In recent years Grant has been joined by his son, W. V. Grant Jr.

Membership: Not reported.

Periodicals: *Dawn of a New Day*, Box 353, Dallas, TX 75221.

Sources: W. V. Grant, *The Grace of God in My Life*. Dallas: The Author, 1952; W. V. Grant, *Faith Cometh*. Dallas: The Author, n.d.; W. V. Grant, *The Truth About Faith Healers*. Dallas: Faith Clinic, n.d.

★381★

KATHRYN KUHLMAN FOUNDATION
(Defunct)

Kathryn Kuhlman emerged in the 1970s as the most famous and sought-after spiritual healer in the country. Born in Concordia, Missouri, and reared in the Methodist church, she could not preach for the Methodists because she was a woman, so she became a Baptist and was ordained by the Evangelical Church Alliance. While she pastored a church in Franklin, Pennsylvania, spontaneous healings began to occur. These were coincidental with some personal mystical/psychical experiences of Mrs. Kuhlman, experiences that included a trancelike state in which her consciousness left her body. From that time on, spectacular healing activity was characteristic of her services. She was reported to have cured such illnesses as muscular dystrophy, emphysema, terminal cancer, and blindness. In 1947, she moved to Pittsburgh where her work was later institutionalized as the Kathryn Kuhlman Foundation. She died in 1976.

Kuhlman was pastor of a congregation in Pittsburgh and once a month held Sunday morning services in Los Angeles. She was a popular speaker for the Full Gospel Businessmen's Fellowship International. In 1970, the Foundation was subsidized by approximately 21 churches in countries around the world. The Foundation operated a vigorous radio and television ministry, a food assistance program, and a college scholarship program.

Sources: Allen Spraggett, *Kathryn Kuhlman, The Woman Who Believes in Miracles*. New York: New American Library, 1970; Helen Kooiman Hosier, *Kathryn Kuhlman*. Old Tappan, NJ: Fleming H. Revell, 1971; Kathryn Kuhlman, *Nothing Is Impossible with God*. Englewood Cliffs, NJ: Prentice-Hall, 1974; Kathryn Kuhlman, *God Can Do It Again*. Englewood Cliffs, NJ: Prentice-Hall, 1969; Kathryn Kuhlman, *I Believe in Miracles*. Englewood Cliffs, NJ: Prentice- Hall, 1962.

★382★

LEROY JENKINS EVANGELISTIC ASSOCIATION
Current address not obtained for this edition.

Leroy Jenkins is a healer who has become known as "the man with the golden arm" for his healing work. When he was five years old, so the story goes, the Lord spoke to him in an audible voice. Four years later, God spoke to him again and he levitated and floated through the air. In an accident in 1960, his arm was almost cut off. He was healed instantly (after refusing amputation) in a meeting conducted by A. A. Allen in Atlanta. With Allen's encouragement, he began to preach and his evangelistic association was formed in 1960. Originally headquartered in Tampa, Florida, he moved to Delaware, Ohio, where a large tabernacle was build in the 1970s. In 1971, his radio ministry was being heard over 57 stations.

In 1977 Jenkins moved to Greenwood, South Carolina, and opened the Spirit of Truth Church. However, in April 1979 Jenkins was arrested and convicted on two counts of conspiracy to commit arson related to the burning of a state trooper's home in Ohio. Jenkins protested his innocence, but was sentenced to serve 12 years. He was paroled in June 1985 and has since resumed his ministry.

Membership: Not reported. The magazine of the Association is mailed to over 100,000 supporters.

Periodicals: *Revival of America*, Delaware, OH.

Sources: Leroy Jenkins, *How I Met the Master*. Delaware, OH: Leroy Jenkins Evangelistic Association, n.d. (1970?); Leroy Jenkins, *God Gave Me a Miracle Arm*. Delaware, OH: Leroy Jenkins Evangelistic Association, 1963; Leroy Jenkins, *How You Can Receive Your Healing*. Delaware, OH; Leroy Jenkins Evangelistic Association, 1966; James Randi, *The Faith Healers*, Buffalo, NY: Prometheus Books, 1987.

★383★
MIRACLE LIFE FELLOWSHIP INTERNATIONAL
11052 N. 24th Ave.
Phoenix, AZ 85029

Asa Alonzo Allen was born of a poor Arkansas family, saved in a Methodist revival, and later baptized with the Holy Spirit in a Pentecostal meeting. He joined the Assemblies of God and felt called to preach. In the early 1940s, he began to seek a ministry of signs and wonders, particularly healing. He had what amounted to a theological conversion when, during a prayer time, he formulated the thirteen requirements for a powerful ministry. He became convinced that he could do the works of Jesus, and do more than Jesus did; that he could be flawless and perfect (in the Biblical sense), and should believe all the promises. During World War II, his throat became, according to one throat specialist, "permanently ruined," but Allen was healed.

In 1951, he purchased a tent and began the crusade in earnest. Headquarters of A.A. Allen Revivals, Inc., were established in Dallas and *Miracle Magazine* was begun. From that time until his death, Allen was an immensely popular evangelist speaking both to integrated and predominantly black audiences. As early as 1960, he was holding fully integrated meetings in the South. In 1958, he was given 1,250 acres near Tombstone, Arizona, which were named Miracle Valley and which became the international headquarters. Allen died in 1970 and was succeeded by Don Stewart, who chose the new name for the organization: Miracle Revival Fellowship. Miracle Valley was created as a totally spiritual community. Allen founded a Bible school and publishing house, located adjacent to radio and television studios, the healing pool of Bethesda, and the headquarters. He also operated a telephone Dial-a-Miracle prayer service. The church seats 2,500. As a result of Allen's accomplishments and success, missionary churches were begun and independent ministers have become associated wtih him. Miracle Revival Fellowship, (now Miracle Life Fellowship International) at first a department of A.A. Allen Revivals, was established as a ministerial fellowship and licensing agency. After Allen's death, the Bible college was turned over to the Central Latin American District Council of the Assemblies of God and is now known as Southern Arizona Bible College. A. A. Allen Revivals became the Don Stewart Association.

Membership: In 1988, the fellowship of ministers had 350 clergy members in the United States and an additional 50 in other countries.

Periodicals: *Miracle Magazine*, Box 2960, Phoenix, AZ 85062-9984. Feed My People Magazine, 11052 N. 24th Ave., Phoenix, AZ 85029.

Sources: A. A. Allen, with Walter Wagner, *Born to Loose, Bound to Win*. Garden City, NY: Doubleday, 1970; A. A. Allen, *My Cross*. Miracle Valley, AZ: A. A. Allen

Revivals Inc., n.d.; Don Stewart with Walter Wagner, *The Man from Miracle Valley*. Long Beach, CA: The Great Horizons Company, 1971; Don Stewart, *Blessings from the Hand of God*. Miracle Valley, AZ: Don Stewart Evangelistic Association, 1971; Don Stewart, *How You Can Have Something Better Through God's Master Plan*. Phoenix, AZ: Don Stewart Evangelistic Association, 1975.

★384★
MIRACLE LIFE REVIVAL, INC.
Box 20707
Phoenix, AZ 85036

Independent Pentecostal evangelist Neal Frisby became known in the early 1960s for possessing a gift of prophecy. In 1967, he began regularly to release prophetic scrolls; by 1974, there were 60 and they were published in book form. In 1972, Capstone Cathedral, a large pyramid-shaped church was completed on the outskirts of Phoenix, Arizona. It serves as a publishing center and headquarters. The church also houses a television studio and produces films concerning worldwide events. In recent years, Frisby has released a number of pictures in which strange, "supernatural" lights are said to have appeared.

Membership: Not reported. Besides the congregation in Phoenix, there is a mailing list of "special partners" around the United States who regularly support the ministry.

Sources: Neal Frisby, *The Book of Revelation Scrolls*. Phoenix: The Author, n.d.; W. V. Grant, *Creative Miracles*. Dallas: Faith Clinic, n.d.

★385★
MITA MOVEMENT
Calle Duarte 235
Hata Rey, PR 60919

The Mita Movement is a Puerto Rican Pentecostal movement imported to the continental United States by the immigration of some of its members. It was founded in 1940 by Mrs. Juanita Garcia Peraga, who saw in her sudden healing after a long illness, a divine revelation and a sign that God had chosen her body to be the dwelling place of the Holy Spirit. The name Mita, which she adopted, was given in the revelation.

The Mita Movement was built upon the personality of Mita, who has been an instrument of physical healings and moral conversions. Her followers see her as a sanctified messenger of God, an equal of the Old Testament prophets. Among other things, she is thought able to affect the weather. Worship services are very spontaneous. The main gathering is on Saturday. Hymns that are used were written either by Mita in an inspired state or by several composers ordained for their work by the church.

At the headquarters in Hato Rey, there is a complex of buildings which includes a home for men, a hospice for women, two restaurants, a supermarket, and some shops. In nearby Arecibo is a home for the aged. The movement was brought to the United States after World War II and currently has churches in New York City; Jersey City, Passaic, and Paterson, New Jersey; Washington, D.C.; Philadelphia, and Chicago.

Membership: Not reported.

Apostolic Pentecostals

★386★
APOSTOLIC ASSEMBLIES OF CHRIST, INC.
Current address not obtained for this edition.

The Apostolic Assemblies of Christ was formed in 1970 by former members of the Pentecostal Churches of the Apostolic Faith led by Bishop G. N. Boone. During the term of presiding bishop Willie Lee, questions of his administrative abilities arose. In the midst of the controversy, he died. In the organizational disaray the church splintered, and one group formed around Bishop Boone and Virgil Oates, the vice-bishop. The new body is congregational in organization and continues in the doctrine of the parent body, since no doctrinal controversy accompanied the split.

Membership: In 1980 the Assemblies had approximately 3,500 members, 23 churches and 70 ministers.

★387★
APOSTOLIC CHURCH OF CHRIST
2044 Stadium Dr.
Winston-Salem, NC 27107

The Apostolic Church of Christ was founded in 1969 by Bishop Johnnie Draft and Elder Wallace Snow, both ministers in the Church of God (Apostolic). Draft, for many years an overseer in the church and pastor of St. Peter's Church, the denomination's headquarters congregation, expressed no criticism of the Church of God (Apostolic); rather, he stated that the Spirit of the Lord brought him to start his own organization. The church differs from its parent body in its development of a centralized church polity. Authority is vested in the executive board, which owns all the church property. Doctrine follows that of the Church of God (Apostolic).

Membership: In 1980 the Apostolic Church of Christ had 6 churches, 300 members, 15 ministers, and one bishop.

★388★
APOSTOLIC CHURCH OF CHRIST IN GOD
% Bethlehem Apostolic Church
1217 E. 15th St.
Winston-Salem, NC 27105

The Apostolic Church of Christ in God was formed by five elders of the Church of God (Apostolic): J. W. Audrey, J. C. Richardson, Jerome Jenkins, W. R. Bryant, and J. M. Williams. At the time of the split, the Church of God (Apostolic) was formally led by Thomas Cox, but, due to his ill health, Eli N. Neal was acting as presiding bishop. The dissenting elders were concerned with the authoritarian manner in which Neal conducted the affairs of the church as well as with some personal problems that Neal was experiencing. Originally, three churches left with the elders, who established headquarters in Winston-Salem, North Carolina. J. W. Audrey was elected the new presiding bishop.

The new church prospered and in 1952 Elder Richardson was elected as a second bishop. In 1956 Audrey resigned and Richardson became the new presiding bishop. Under his leadershp the Apostolic Church enjoyed its greatest success. He began The *Apostolic Gazette* (later the *Apostolic Journal*) which served the church for many years. He also instituted a program to assist ministers in getting an education. However, his efforts were frustrated by several schisms that cut into the church's growth, most prominently the 1971 schism led by former-bishop Audrey.

The church retained the doctrine and congregational polity of the Church of God (Apostolic).

Membership: In 1980 the church had 2,150 members in 13 congregations being served by five bishops and 25 ministers.

★389★
APOSTOLIC CHURCH OF JESUS
Current address not obtained for this edition.

The Apostolic Church of Jesus was founded by Antonio Sanches, who had been converted in an evangelistic meeting led by Mattie Crawford in Pueblo, Colorado in 1923, and his brother George Sanches. The Sanches brothers began to preach to the Spanish-speaking population of the city and in 1927 organized the first congregation of the Apostolic Church of Jesus. In subsequent years, congregations were established throughout the state and elsewhere and can now be found in Denver, Westminister, Fountain, Walsenbury, and Ft. Garland, Colorado; Palo Alto, California; San Luis, Trinidad; and Velarde, New Mexico. The group, presently under the leadership of Raymond P. Virgil, has a weekly radio ministry.

Membership: Not reported.

Periodicals: *Jesus Only News of the Apostolic Faith.*

★390★
APOSTOLIC CHURCH OF JESUS CHRIST
Current address not obtained for this edition.

The Apostolic Church of Jesus Christ is a second body that grew out of the Pentecostal Assemblies of the World after the death of Garfield Thomas Haywood (1880-1931), who founded the "oneness" work in Indianapolis, Indiana. The Church believes in the indispensability of baptism for salvation.

Membership: Not reported.

Periodicals: *The Voice of the Wilderness*, Indianapolis, IN.

★391★
APOSTOLIC FAITH (HAWAII)
1043 Middle St.
Honolulu, HI 96819

The Apostolic Faith Church, a local congregation in Honolulu, was founded by the Rev. Charles Lochbaum and his wife, Ada Lochbaum, who came to Honolulu in 1923. They began to hold services emphasizing the baptism of the Holy Spirit and divine healing. A tent was set up, services were held throughout the islands, and a building was erected in 1924. An aggressive evangelism program, which included street preaching and evangelizing the planatations, was begun. The first branch of the Apostolic Faith was set up in Kaimuki.

The Apostolic Faith preaches the kingdom of God message, emphasizing entrance into the kingdom by baptism (immersion) in Jesus' name, healing, and the imminent coming of Jesus. The Apostolic Church is a "Jesus only" group which preaches three experiences--justification, sanctification, and baptism of the Holy Spirit. Divorce and participation in secret societies are not condoned. Tithing and free will offerings are stressed; unlike many Pentecostal churches, this one sees conscientious objection as disloyalty to the established government.

The Apostolic Faith is run by a five-member board of trustees who succeeded Lochbaum in 1959. Branch churches in Hawaii were established in Kaimuki, Lahainia, Kuhului, Kanunakakai, and Hilo. A radio ministry was begun in 1969.

Membership: Not reported.

Periodicals: *Kingdom of God Crusader*, 1043 Middle Street, Honolulu, HI 96819.

Sources: *Kingdom of God Crusader*. Honolulu: Apostolic Faith Church of Honolulu, 1969.

★392★
APOSTOLIC FAITH MISSION CHURCH OF GOD
3344 Pearl Ave. N.
Birmingham, AL 36101

Among the people who visited the early Pentecostal revival which occurred in 1906-08 in Los Angeles was F. W. Williams (d.1932), a black man from the deep south. He received the Baptism of the Holy Spirit under the ministry of William J. Seymour and returned to Mississippi to establish an outpost of the Apostolic Faith Mission. Not having great success, he moved to Mobile, Alabama, where a revival occurred under his ministry. Among those converted was an entire congregation of the Primitive Baptist Church. The members gave him their building as the first meeting house for the new mission parish. The church was organized on July 10, 1906.

In 1915 Bishop Williams became one of the first to adopt the Oneness or non-Trinitarian theology which had been espoused through Pentecostal circles. He broke with Seymour and renamed his church the Apostolic Faith Mission Church of God. He incorporated the new church on October 9, 1915. The church continues to place a strong emphasis upon divine healing, allows women preachers, and practices footwashing with communion. Baptism is in the name of the "Lord Jesus Christ," and without the use of the name, the baptism is considered void. Intoxicants, especially tobacco, alcohol and drugs are forbidden. Members are admonished to marry only those who have been "saved." The church is headed by the Senior Bishop and a Cabinet of Executive Officers composed of the bishops, overseers and the general secretary.

Membership: In 1984 the church reported 17 congregations (most of which were in Alabama), 1,500 members, and 38 ministers.

★393★
APOSTOLIC GOSPEL CHURCH OF JESUS
CHRIST
Current address not obtained for this edition.

The Apostolic Gospel Church of Jesus Christ was founded in Bell Gardens, California, in 1963 by the Rev. Donald Abernathy. During the next five years, four other congregations, all in the Los Angeles area, were added and a new denomination emerged. In 1968, Abernathy reported a series of visions in which it was revealed to him that the entire West Coast of North America would be destroyed in an earthquake. He reported the vision to the other congregations, and one pastor, the Rev. Robert Theobold, reported a confirming vision. As a result, the five congregations decided to move East. Abernathy took his congregation to Atlanta. The church at Avenal went to Kennett, Missouri; the church at Porterville to Independence, Missouri; the church at Port Hueneme to Murfreesboro, Tennessee; and the Lompoc congregation to Georgia.

The church accepts "oneness" doctrines, identifying Jesus with the Father. It does not approve of the use of medicines, doctors, or hospitals--only divine healing. Footwashing is practiced. Members are pacifists. There is a strict code of dress that prohibits bathing suits, slacks, shorts, tightly fitting or straightcut skirts, dresses with hemlines shorter than halfway between the knee and ankle, jewelry, and short hair for women. Long hair, short sleeves, and tightly fitting pants are prohibited for men.

The church is ruled by bishops (or elders) and deacons, and includes in its structure apostles, prophets, evangelists, pastors, and teachers. The attempt is to build a perfect church to which Christ will return. The perfect church will manifest both the fruits and gifts of the Spirit.

Membership: There are five congregations.

★394★

APOSTOLIC OVERCOMING HOLY CHURCH OF GOD

% Bishop Jasper C. Roby
1120 N. 24th St.
Birmingham, AL 35234

History. The Apostolic Overcoming Church of God was founded by William Thomas Phillips (1893-1973), the son of a Methodist Episcopal Church minister. However, at a tentmeeting service in Birmingham, Alabama, Phillips was converted to the message of pentecost and holiness under the ministry of Frank W. Williams of the Faith Mission Church of God. Williams ordained Phillips in 1913, and three years later Phillips launched his career as an evangelist in Mobile, Alabama. In 1917, he was selected by the people who has responded to his ministry as the bishop of the Ethiopian Overcoming Holy Church of God. The new organization was incorporated in 1920. It adopted its present name in 1941 in realization that the church was for all people, not just Ethiopians, a popular designation for black people in the early twentieth century.

Beliefs. The AOH Church of God follows the Oneness theology. It believes in One God who subsists in the union of Father, Son, and Holy Spirit. The church, however, rejects any hint of tri-theism and believes that the One God bears the name of Jesus, a name that can express the fulness of the Godhead. Out of this belief, the church baptizes members in the name of Jesus. Baptism is by immersion and considered necessary for salvation.

The church teaches that God acts in the believer both to baptize in the Spirit (which will be signified by speaking-in-tongues) and progressively over a lifetime to sanctify (make holy). Besides baptism, there are two other ordinances--the Lord's supper and foot washing. The church also teaches divine healing and exhorts members to tithe.

Organization. Though headed by bishops, the AOH Church of God is basically congregational in polity with each church owning its own property and managing its own affairs. Churches are grouped into districts presided over by bishops and overseers. A General Assembly, to which all churches send representatives, convenes annually. It is led by the presiding bishop. After serving the church for 57 years, Bishop Phillips was succeeded by Bishop Jasper Roby, the present senior presiding bishop. He is assisted by five associate bishops. The church's periodicals are published by the church's publishing board. Missions are supported in Haiti and Africa.

Membership: In 1988, the church reported 12,000 members, approximately 200 churches, and 750 ministers.

Educational facilities: AOH Theological Seminary, Birmingham, Alabama.

Periodicals: *People's Mouthpiece,* 1120 N. 24th St., Birmingham. AL 35234; *Young Educator,* 1120 N. 24th St., Birmingham, AL 35234.

Sources: Juanita R. Arrington, *A Brief History of the Apostolic Overcoming Holy Church of God, Inc. and Its Founder.* Birmingham, AL: Forniss Printing Company, 1984; *Doctrine and Discipline.* Birmingham, AL: Apostolic Overcoming Holy Church of God, 1985.

★395★

ASSEMBLIES OF THE LORD JESUS CHRIST, INC.

Current address not obtained for this edition.

The Assemblies of the Lord Jesus Christ was formed in 1952 by the merger of three "Jesus only" groups which had sprung up around the country--the Assemblies of the Church of Jesus Christ, the Jesus Only Apostolic Church of God, and the Church of the Lord Jesus Christ. The Assemblies closely resembles the United Pentecostal Church in doctrine. The group preaches two experiences--justification and the baptism of the Spirit, emphasizes healing, washes feet, tithes, and forbids participation in secret societies. While holding respect for the civil government, members do not participate in war. Worldly amusements are forbidden, as are school gymnastics and clothes which immodestly expose the body.

The government is congregational in form. There is an annual general conference. A general board oversees the church during the year. The church is divided into state districts which are located in the South, Midwest, and Southwest. The Foreign Mission Committee oversees the mission program in Uruguay and Columbia.

Membership: Not reported. In 1971 there were approximately 350 churches.

Periodicals: *Apostolic Witness,* Memphis, TN.

★396★

ASSOCIATED BROTHERHOOD OF CHRISTIANS
Current address not obtained for this edition.

Described as an "association of churches and ministers working together for the up-building of the Church of the Lord Jesus Christ, and the Spread of the New Testament Gospel," the Associated Brotherhood of Christians is a "oneness" Pentecostal body. It was formed under the leadership of E. E. Partridge and H. A. Riley to facilitate fellowship among all "blood-bought" people, those who believe Christ atoned for sins through the blood he shed in the crucifixion. Formation of the Associated Brotherhood of Christians was necessary because other Pentecostal churches were refusing fellowship to the ministers who eventually formed this church. The other Pentecostal churches objected to the ministers' divergence from the churches' doctrines. The original meetings to consider forming the Associated Brotherhood of Christians were held in 1933, with the incorporation taking place during World War II. (This facilitated exemption from military duties for ministers.)

While attempting to facilitate wider fellowship, the group has a definite doctrinal perspective. The "oneness" Pentecostalism of this church is of the "two-experiences" variety, focusing on justification and the baptism of the Holy Spirit. Baptism in Jesus' name is the only ordinance; the church's statement of beliefs includes a specific article on why foot-washing is not practiced. The group accepts the so-called "Bread of life" message, or what is termed spiritual communion. The emphasis of the message is not on the literal eating of literal elements but on the proper discernment of the body of Christ in the church. The church is pacifist, and conscientious objection is recommended to members.

Polity is congregational. There is an annual conference. The association is headed by an official board of three members: a chairman, vice-chairman, and secretary-treasurer. State presbyters are appointed by the official board. Churches are located across the South and Midwest and along the Pacific Coast.

Membership: Not reported. In the early 1970s there were 40 congregations, approximately 2,000 members and 100 ministers.

Periodicals: *Our Herald*, Wilmington, CA.

★397★

BETHEL MINISTERIAL ASSOCIATION
4350 Lincoln Ave.
Evansville, IN 47715

The Bethel Ministerial Association is a fellowship of ministers founded in 1934 by theRev. Albert Franklin Varnell as an outgrowth of his desire to offer fellowship to ministers who held similar doctrinal views without the organizational pressures of that day on the local church.

Varnell began his ministry as a tent evangelist. In 1933, the church to which he belonged decided that all members should believe that speaking in tongues was the first evidence of the reception of the Holy Spirit. Varnell opposed this teaching. He believed that the new birth and the baptism of the Holy Spirit were the same and that the filling of the believer by the Spirit was a subsequent event which occurred when the born again believer yields to the Spirit. Varnell felt speaking-in-tongues was a supernatural manifestation of the Spirit among those who had been filled with the Spirit.

The association also teaches that God manifests in the flesh as Jesus. Jesus is the name of the One God. It denies the traditional doctrine of the Trinity (God as three persons) but affirms that the One God (Jesus) expresses Himself in the Trinity personalities of Father, Son, and Holy Spirit. It accepts the Bible as the Word of God. Water baptism is by immersion in the name of Jesus.

Organization. Bethel churches are independent and self-governing, and membership in the association is available to ministers only. The association has a publishing house in Evansville, Indiana. An aggressive missionary program supports over 50 missionaries around the world. The association also operates Circle J Ranch, a youth c amp facility in southern Indiana, and the Bethel Ministerial Academy, a ministerial training program.

Membership: In 1988, the association had 120 ministers, missionaries, evangelists, and administrators as members. There are approximately 35 associated churches in the United States and more than 120 churches in other lands.

Educational facilities: International Bible Institute, San Antonio, Texas.

Periodicals: *The Bethel Link*, 4350 Lincoln Ave., Evansville, IN 47715.

Sources: *It Does Make a Difference What You Believe!* Decatur, IL: Bethel Ministerial Association, Incorporated, n.d.

★398★

BIBLE WAY CHURCH OF OUR LORD JESUS CHRIST WORLD WIDE, INC.
1130 New Jersey Ave., N.W.
Washington, DC 20001

The Bible Way Church of Our Lord Jesus Christ World Wide, Inc., was formed in 1957 by former members of some seventy churches of the Church of Our Lord Jesus Christ of the Apostolic Faith. Smallwood E. Williams became the presiding bishop. The purpose of organizing the new body was to effect a less autocratic leadership than in the parent body. (Prior to that time, Bishop R. C. Lawson had refused to consecrate other bishops for his church.) Besides Bishop Williams, John S. Beane, McKinley Williams, Winfield A. Showell, and Joseph

Moore were also consecrated as bishops. A bishop of the Pentecostal Assemblies of the World officiated at the consecration service. Doctrine remains the same. A general conference meets annually. Williams has become best known for his work on social conditions within the black community in Washington, DC.

Membership: In 1988 the church reported approximately 250,000 members in 250 churches.

Periodicals: *The Bible Way News Voice*, 1130 New Jersey Avenue, Washington, DC.

Sources: Smallwood Edmond Williams, *This Is My Story*. Washington, DC: Wm. Willoughby Publishers, 1981; Smallwood E. Williams, *Significant Sermons*. Washington, DC: Bible Way Church Press, 1970; Smallwood Edmond Williams, *Significant Sermons*. Washington, DC: The Bible Way Church, 1970; *Official Directory, Rules and Regulations of the Bible Way Church of Our Lord Jesus Christ World Wide, Inc.*. Washington, DC: Bible Way Church of Our Lord Jesus Christ Worl Wide, Inc., 1973.

★399★
BIBLE WAY PENTECOSTAL APOSTOLIC CHURCH
Current address not obtained for this edition.

The Bible Way Pentecostal Apostolic Church was founded by Curtis P. Jones. Jones began as a pastor in North Carolina in the Church of God (Apostolic), but left that church to join the Church of Our Lord Jesus Christ of the Apostolic Faith under Robert Clarence Lawson. He became pastor of the St. Paul Apostolic Church in Henry County, Virginia. Jones left during the internal disruption within Bishop Lawson's church in 1957, but did not join with Smallwood E. Williams' Bible Way Church of Our Lord Jesus Christ. Rather, in 1960, with two other congregations in Virginia, he founded a new denomination. A fourth church was soon added.

Membership: In 1980 the Church had four congregations, all in Virginia.

★400★
CHURCH OF GOD (APOSTOLIC)
Saint Peter's Church of God (Apostolic)
125 Meadows St.
Beckley, WV 25801

The Church of God (Apostolic) was formed in 1877 by Elder Thomas J. Cox at Danville, Kentucky, as the Christian Faith Band. It was one of a number of independent holiness associations of the late nineteenth century. In 1915, it voted a name change, and in 1919 became the Church of God (Apostolic). In 1943, Cox was succeeded by M. Gravely and Eli N. Neal as co-presiding bishops. Headqaurters were moved to Beckley, West Virginia. Two years later Gravely divorced his wife and remarried. He was disfellowshipped from the church. In

1964 Neal was succeeded by Love Odom who died two years later and was succeeded by David E. Smith. These two bishops did much to put the national church in a firm financial condition. They were suceeded by the present general overseer, Ruben K. Hash.

It is a strict church, opposing worldliness and practicing footwashing with the monthly Lord's Supper. Baptism by immersion is in the name of Jesus. The church is headed by a board of bishops, one of whom is designated the general overseer who serves as the church's executive head. There is a general assembly annually.

Membership: In 1980 the church had 15,000 members, 43 congregations and approximately 75 ministers.

★401★
CHURCH OF OUR LORD JESUS CHRIST OF THE APOSTOLIC FAITH
2081 Seventh Ave.
New York, NY 10027

The Church of Our Lord Jesus Christ of the Apostolic Faith was founded in Columbus, Ohio, in 1919 by Robert Clarence Lawson (d. 1961), who as a pastor in the Pentecostal Assemblies of the World had founded churches in Texas and Missouri. At one point in his early life when he was ill he had been taken to the Apostolic Faith Assembly Church, a leading church of the Pentecostal Assemblies, and its pastor, Garfield Thomas Haywood. Healed, Lawson joined the Assemblies, and adopted their non-trinitarian theology. However, in 1913 he left Haywood's jurisdiction and, moving to New York City, founded Refuge Temple, the first congregation in his new independent church. Given Lawson's effective leadership, the organization grew quickly. Other congregations were established and a radio ministry , a periodical, a day nursery, and several businesses were initiated. In 1926 he opened a bible school to train pastors.

In the 1930s, Lawson began a series of trips to the West Indies which led to congregations being formed in Jamaica, Antigua, the Virgin Islands, and Trinidad. His lengthy tenure as bishop of the Church was a time of steady growth, broken only by two schisms by Sherrod C. Johnson, (Church of the Lord Jesus Christ of the Apostolic Faith, 1930) and Smallwood E. Williams, (Bible Way Church of Our Lord Jesus Christ, 1957). Lawson was succeeded by Hubert J. Spencer and by the present presiding apostle, William Bonner.

Doctrine is like the older Pentecostal Assemblies of the World. Footwashing is practiced and the baptism of the Holy Spirit is believed to be necessary for salvation. The church is headed by the presiding apostle, who is assisted by six regional apostles. There is an annual convocation. Affiliated churches can be found in the West Indies, Africa, England and Germany.

Membership: In 1988, the church reported 30,000 members in 500 churches.

Educational facilities: Church of Christ Bible Institute, New York, New York.

Periodicals: *The Contender for the Faith*, 2081 Seventh Avenue, New York, NY 10027.

Sources: Arthur M. Anderson, ed., *For the Defense of the Gospel*. New York: Church of Christ Pub. Co., 1972.

★402★
CHURCH OF THE LORD JESUS CHRIST OF THE APOSTOLIC FAITH (PHILADELPHIA)
22nd & Bainbridge Sts.
Philadelphia, PA 19146

The Church of the Lord Jesus Christ of the Apostolic Faith was founded in 1933 by Bishop Sherrod C. Johnson, formerly of the Church of Our Lord Jesus Christ of the Apostolic Faith. Johnson protested what he felt were too liberal regulations espoused by Bishop Robert Clarence Lawson in regard to the appearance of female members. Lawson allowed the wearing of jewelry and make-up. Johnson insisted upon female members wearing cotton stockings, calf-length dresses, unstraightened hair and head coverings. Johnson also opposed the observance of Lent, Easter and Christmas. Upon Bishop Johnson's death in 1961, he was succeeded by S. McDowell Shelton, the "Bishop, Apostle, and Overseer of the Church." This church has been most aggressive and has approached its parent body in members hip.

The doctrine is a typical "oneness" doctrine, though the church is known for its conservatism. It does demand that baptism must be in the name of the "Lord Jesus" or "Jesus Christ," but not just "Jesus." This exacting formula is to distinguish the Lord Jesus from Bar Jesus (Acts 13:6) and Jesus Justas (Col. 4:11), two other Biblical characters. The church members also believe one must be filled with the Holy Ghost in order to have the new birth. The church's conservatism is most manifest in its rigid behavior code. Prohibited are women preachers and teachers, remarriage after divorce, dressing like the world, and wearing costly apparel.

The church is episcopal. There is a national convention annually at the national headquarters in Philadelphia. Lay people have an unusually high participation level in the national church, holding most of the top administrative positions. There is an active radio ministry, "The Whole Truth," carried on 50 stations. Missions are conducted in Liberia, West Africa, England, Honduras, Jamaica, Haiti, Bahamas, Jordan, Portugal, and the Maldives.

Membership: In 1980 there were approximately 100 congregations.

Periodicals: *The Whole Truth*, 22nd and Bainbridge Streets, Philadelphia, PA 19146.

★403★
GLORIOUS CHURCH OF GOD IN CHRIST APOSTOLIC FAITH
Current address not obtained for this edition.

The Glorious Church of God in Christ Apostolic Faith was founded in 1921 by C. H. Stokes, its first presiding bishop. He was succeeded in 1928 by S. C. Bass who was to head the church for over a quarter of a century. However, in 1952, after the death of his first wife, Bass remarried a woman who was a divorcee. It had been taught for many years that marrying a divorced person was wrong. Bass' actions split the fifty-congregation church in half. Those who remained loyal to Bishop Bass retained the name, but the founding charter was retained by the other group, which took the name Original Glorious Church of God in Christ Apostolic Faith.

★404★
GOD'S HOUSE OF PRAYER FOR ALL NATIONS
Current address not obtained for this edition.

God's House of Prayer for All Nations, Inc., was founded in 1964 in Peoria, Illinois, by Bishop Tommie Lawrence, formerly of the Church of God in Christ. The doctrine is "oneness" Pentecostal, identifying Jesus with the Father, and the polity is strongly episcopal. Great stress is placed on healing as one of the signs of the spirit and there is much fellowship with the churches of the Miracle Revival Fellowship founded by the late A. A. Allen.

Membership: Not reported. There are several congregations, all in northern Illinois.

★405★
HIGHWAY CHRISTIAN CHURCH OF CHRIST
436 W St. N.W.
Washington, DC 20001

The Highway Christian Church of Christ was founded in 1929 by James Thomas Morris, formerly a minister with the Pentecostal Assemblies of the World. Relations between the two groups remained cordial, and in 1941 Bishop J. M. Turpin of the Assemblies consecrated Morris to the episcopal leadership of the Highway Church. Morris died in 1959 and was succeeded by his nephew, J. V. Lomax, formerly a member of the Church of Our Lord Jesus Christ of the Apostolic Faith.

The Highway Church has a reputation as one of the more conservative Pentecostal church bodies. Members are encouraged to wear only black (suits and skirts) and white (shirts and blouses), and to avoid bright colors as too ostentatious. The church will accept ordained women from other denominations, but will neither ordain females nor allow them to pastor congregations.

Membership: In 1980 there were 13 congregations and about 3,000 members.

★406★
INTERNATIONAL MINISTERIAL ASSOCIATION
Current address not obtained for this edition.

The International Ministerial Association, Inc. was formed in 1954 by W. E. Kidson and twenty other pastors formerly with the United Pentecostal Church. It practices baptism by immersion and foot-washing. Tithing is believed to be the financial plan of the church. A strong belief in the Second Coming is taught, and the group believes in a distinct judgment where believers only will be rewarded.

An annual international conference is the place for fellowship of the ministers, who hold credentials through the Association and the members of the autonomous congregations which accept the statement of faith. Herald Publishing House is located in Houston, Texas.

Membership: Not reported. In the early 1970s, there were 440 ministerial members and 117 affiliated congregations.

Periodicals: *The Herald of Truth.*

★407★
MOUNT HEBRON APOSTOLIC TEMPLE OF OUR LORD JESUS OF THE APOSTOLIC FAITH
Mount Hebron Apostolic Temple
27 Vineyard Ave.
Yonkers, NY 10703

The Mount Hebron Apostolic Temple of Our Lord Jesus of the Apostolic Faith was founded in 1963 by George H. Wiley III, pastor of the Yonkers, New York, congregation of the Apostolic Church of Christ in God. As his work progressed, Wiley came to feel that because of his accomplishments for the denomination he should be accorded the office of bishop. He had had particular success in the area of youth work, and his wife, Sister Lucille Wiley, served as president of the Department of Youth Work. However, the board of the Apostolic Church denied his request to become a bishop. He left with his supporters and became bishop of a new Apostolic denomination.

Wiley has placed great emphasis upon youth work and upon radio work, establishing an outreach in New York, one in North Carolina, and another in South Carolina. The temple continues the doctrine and polity of the Apostolic Church of Christ in God and has a cordial relationship with its parent organization.

Membership: In 1980 the temple reported 3,000 members in nine congregations being served by 15 ministers. There are two bishops.

★408★
NEW BETHEL CHURCH OF GOD IN CHRIST (PENTECOSTAL)
Current address not obtained for this edition.

In 1927, the Rev. A.D. Bradley was admonished by the board of bishops of the Church of God in Christ to refrain from preaching the "Jesus only" doctrine. (The Church of God in Christ was the oldest and among the largest of the predominantly-black trinitarian Pentecostal churches.) He refused, and with his wife and Lonnie Bates established the New Bethel Church of God in Christ (Pentecostal). Bradley became the church's presiding bishop. Doctrine is similar to other "Jesus only" groups. The three ordinances of baptism, the Lord's Supper, and foot-washing are observed. The group is pacifist but allows alternative noncombatant positions to be held by law-abiding church members. The group disapproves of secret societies and of school activities which conflict with a student's moral scruples.

The presiding bishop is the executive officer and presides over all meetings of the general body. A board of bishops acts as a judicatory body and a general assembly as the legislative body.

Membership: Not reported.

★409★
ORIGINAL GLORIOUS CHURCH OF GOD IN CHRIST APOSTOLIC FAITH
Current address not obtained for this edition.

The Glorious Church of God was founded in 1921. However, in 1952 its presiding bishop, S. C. Bass married a divorced woman. Approximately half of the fifty-congregation church rejected Bass and reorganized under the leadership of W. O. Howard and took the name Original Glorious Church of God in Christ Apostolic Faith. The term "Original" signified their claim to the history of the church, demonstrated by their retention of the founding charter. Howard was succeeded by Bishop I. W. Hamiter, under whose leadership the church has grown spectacularly and developed a mission program in Haiti, Jamaica and India. Hamiter has also led in the purchase of a convention center for the church's annual meeting in Columbus, Ohio.

Membership: In 1980 the Church had 55 congregations in the United States, 110 congregations overseas, 200 ministers and approximately 25,000 members worldwide.

★410★
PENTECOSTAL ASSEMBLIES OF THE WORLD
% James A. Johnson, Presiding Bishop
3939 Meadows Dr.
Indianapolis, IN 46205

Oldest of the Apostolic or "Jesus Only" Pentecostal churches, the Pentecostal Assemblies of the World began as a loosely-organized fellowship of trinitarian pentecostals in Los Angeles in 1906. J. J. Frazee (occasionally incorrectly reported as "Frazier") was elected the first general superintendent. Early membership developed along the West Coast and in the Midwest. From 1913 to 1916, the annual convention was held in Indianapolis, soon to become the center of the organization. Growth in the organization was spurred when it became the first group of pentecostals to accept the "Jesus Only" Apostolic theology, which identified Jesus as the Jehovah of the Old Testament and denied the Trinity. Many ministers from other pentecostal bodies joined the Assemblies when the group within which they held credentials rejected Apostolic teachings. In 1918, the General Assemblies of the Apostolic Assemblies, a recently formed Apostolic body, which included such outstanding early movement leaders as D. C. O. Opperman and H. A. Goss, merged into the PAW.

From its beginning the Pentecostal Assemblies of the World was fully integrated racially, though predominantly white in membership. In 1919, following the influx of so many ministers and members, especially the large newly-merged body, the Pentecostal Assemblies reorganized. Four of its twenty-one field superintendents were black, among whom were Garfield Thomas Haywood, (1880-1931) who would later become presiding bishop. In 1924, most of the white members withdrew to form the Pentecostal Ministerial Alliance, now an integral part of the United Pentecostal Church. The remaining members, not totally, but predominantly black, reorganized again, created the office of bishop, and elected Haywood to lead them. He remained presiding bishop until his death in 1931.

Shortly after Haywood's death, the Apostolic Churches of Jesus Christ, a name briefly assumed by the former Pentecostal Ministerial Alliance that was then in a phase of consolidatiing various Apostolic groups into a single organization, invited the Assemblies to consider merger. The merger attempt failed, but the Assemblies again lost individual congregations and members to the Apostolic Churches of Jesus Christ, and a large group who formed a new church, the Pentecostal Assemblies of Jesus Christ, as a prelude to the merger which failed. In the face of the new losses, a third reorganization had to occur in 1932. For several years, the church was led by a small group of bishops, enlarged to seven in 1935. Two years later, Samuel Grimes, a former missionary in Liberia, was elected presiding bishop, a post he retained until his death in 1967. Under his guidance, the Pentecostal Assemblies church experienced its greatest era of expansion. Contrary to most black Pentecostal bishops, Grimes did not also serve a parish, hence he was able to devote himself full-time to his episcopal duties.

Doctrine of the Assemblies is similar to that of the Assemblies of God except that it does not believe in the Trinity. Holiness is stressed and the group believes that for ultimate salvation, it is necessary to have a life wholly sanctified. Wine is used in the Lord's Supper. Healing is

stressed and foot-washing practiced. Members are pacifists, though they feel it is a duty to honor rules. There is a strict dress and behavior code. Divorce and remarriage are allowed under certain circumstances.

There is an annual general assembly which elects the bishops and the general secretary. It also designates the presiding bishop, who heads a board of bishops. The church is divided into 30 districts (dioceses) headed by a bishop. The Assemblies are designated joint members of each local board of trustees. A missionary board oversees missions in Nigeria, Jamaica, England, Ghana, and Egypt.

Membership: In 1980 the Assemblies had 450,000 members in 1,000 churches divided into 30 districts, each headed by a bishop.

Educational facilities: Aenon Bible School, Indianapolis, Indiana.

Periodicals: *Christian Outlook*, 3040 N. Illinois Street, Indianapolis, IN 46208.

Sources: Morris E. Golder, *History of the Pentecostal Assemblies of the World*. Indianapolis: The Author, 1973; Paul P. Dugas, comp., *The Life and Writings of Elder G. T. Haywood*. Portland, OR: Apostolic Book Publishers, 1968; Morris E. Golder, *The Life and Works of Bishop Garfield Thomas Haywood*. Indianapolis: the Author, 1977; James L. Tyson, *Before I Sleep*. Indianapolis: Pentecostal Publications, 1976.

★411★
PENTECOSTAL CHURCH OF GOD
9244 Delmar
Detroit, MI 48211

The Pentecostal Church of God (not to be confused with the Pentecostal Church of God of America headquartered at Joplin, Missouri) is a predominantly black Pentecostal body founded by Apostle Willie James Peterson (1921-1969). Peterson grew up in Florida, and though his family attended the Baptist church there, he was never baptized. The course of his life was interrupted in his early adult years by a dream in which he was in the presence of God and His angels. Peterson began a period of prayer, after which God called him to preach. He became an independent evangelist and had come to believe in the Apostolic or non-Trinitarian position. He began to preach that doctrine in 1955 in Meridian, Mississippi, and to raise up congregations across the South. At the time of his death, Peterson was succeeded by the four bishops of the church, William Duren, J. J. Sears, C. L. Rawls, and E. Rice.

It is the belief of the Pentecostal Church of God that Peterson was an apostle, anointed by God for his task through revelation. The essence of the revelation was an understanding of the Kingdom of God. Peterson taught that conversion meant turning away from worldliness (the kingdom of this world ruled by Satan) to godliness (the kingdom of Heaven). Peterson identified the Roman Catholic Church with Babylon, the Mother of Harlots, spoken of in Revelation 17:3-5. Satanic doctrine was taught in that church and in its daughter churches, Protestantism. To accept the gospel of the kingdom is to turn from the false teachings of the Babylonish churches to God's truths which include repentance as godly sorrow for one's sins; baptism by immersion in the name of Jesus Christ; a rejection of the unbiblical doctrine of the Trinity; an understanding of heaven as the realm of God and his angels and hell as a place of confinement; the nonobservance of holidays such as Christmas, Easter, and New Year's Day; nonparticipation in human government (which includes pacifism, not saluting the flag, and not voting); and holy matrimony performed by a holy minister.

Membership: Not reported.

Sources: Jennell Peterson Faison, *The Apostle W. J. Peterson.* Detroit, MI: The Pentecostal Church of God, 1980.

★412★
PENTECOSTAL CHURCHES OF APOSTOLIC FAITH
Current address not obtained for this edition.

The Pentecostal Churches of Apostolic Faith was formed in 1957 by former members of the Pentecostal Assemblies of the World under the leadership of Bishop Samuel N. Hancock. Hancock was one of the original men selected as a bishop of the Assemblies following its reorganization in 1925. In 1931 he was one of the leaders in the attempt to unite the Assemblies with the predominantly white Pentecostal Ministerial Alliance, and he helped form the Pentecostal Assemblies of Jesus Christ, a body whose polity was more acceptable to the Alliance. Within a few years, Hancock returned to the Assemblies as an elder and was elected as a bishop for the second time.

However, soon after Hancock's return, it was discovered that he had deviated on traditional Apostolic doctrine in that he taught that Jesus was only the son of God, not that he was God. His position forced the Assemblies to issue a clarifying statement of its position, but Hancock's teachings were tolerated. Hancock also felt that he should have become the presiding bishop. Disappointment at not being elected seems to have fueled the discontent felt throughout the 1950s. Hancock carried two other bishops into the new church formed in 1957, including Willie Lee, pastor of Christ Temple Church, the congregation pastored by Garfield Thomas Haywood, the first presiding bishop of the Assemblies. Lee succeeded Hancock as presiding bishop of the Churches upon the latter's death in 1963. The following year, a major schism occurred when the majority of the Churches rejected the doctrinal position held by Hancock and also taught by Lee. Elzie Young had the charter and claimed the support of the

Churches to become the new presiding bishop. The church returned to the traditional Apostolic theology.

The Pentecostal Churches of the Apostolic Faith are congregational in polity, and headed by a presiding bishop (Elzie Young) and a council of bishops. Under Young's leadership, the Churches have grown and stablized their original shaky financial condition. A mission program developed, and the Churches support missionaries in Haiti and Liberia, where they have built a school.

Membership: In 1980 the Churches had approximately 25,000 members, 115 churches and 380 ministers.

★413★
REDEEMED ASSEMBLY OF JESUS CHRIST, APOSTOLIC
% Bishop Douglas Williams
734 1st St., S.W.
Washington, DC 20024

The Redeemed Assembly of Jesus Christ, Apostolic was formed by James Frank Harris and Douglas Williams, two bishops of the Highway Christian Church who rejected the leadership of that church by Bishop J. V. Lomax. They complained of his control, bypassing other bishops and pastors and making decisons in conference with the elders of the congregation he headed in Washington, D.C. Tthe new church is headed by a presiding bishop, assistant presiding bishop, and an executive council consisting of the bishops and all the pastors. There was no doctrinal conflict in the split.

Membership: In 1980 the Church had six congregations, one in Richmond, Virginia, one in New York City, and four in the Washington, D.C. area.

★414★
SHILOH APOSTOLIC TEMPLE
1516 W. Master
Philadelphia, PA 19121

The Shiloh Apostolic Temple was founded in 1953 by Elder Robert O. Doub, Jr., of the Apostolic Church of Christ in God. In 1948 Doub had moved to Philadelphia to organize a new congregation for the Apostolic Church of Christ in God. He not only succeeded in building a stable congregation, Shiloh Apostolic Temple, but assisted other congregations throughout the state to organize. In light of his accomplishments, Doub felt that he should be made a bishop and so petitioned the church. He believed that the state overseer was taking all the credit Doub himself deserved. Doub's petition was denied. He left with but a single congregation in 1953 and incorporated separately in 1954.

The energetic work that characterized Doub's years in the Apostolic Church of Christ in God led Shiloh Apostolic Temple to outgrow its parent body. Doub began a periodical and purchased a camp, Shiloh Promised Land

Camp, in Montrose, Pennsylvania. He also took over foreign work in England and Trinidad. The doctrine, not at issue in the schism, remains that of the parent Church of God (Apostolic) from which the Apostolic Church of Christ in God came.

Membership: In 1980 the church had 4,500 members of which 500 were in the congregation in Philadelphia. The church reported 23 congregations, of which 8 were in England and 2 in Trinidad.

Periodicals: *Shiloh Gospel Wave*, 1516 West · Master, Philadelphia, Pennsylvania 19121.

★415★
TRUE VINE PENTECOSTAL CHURCHES OF JESUS
Current address not obtained for this edition.

Dr. Robert L. Hairston had been a pastor in several trinitarian Pentecostal groups and had been a co-founder with Willaim Monroe Johnson of the True Vine Pentecostal Holiness Church. However, in 1961 Hairston accepted the Apostolic "Jesus Only" teachings. He left the church he had founded and formed the True Vine Penetcostal Churches of Jesus. Also causal factors in the formation of the new denomination were differences between Hairston and Johnson over church polity and Hairston's marital situation. Hairston rejected the idea of local congregations being assessed to pay for the annual convocation of the church. Also, he had divorced his first wife and remarried, an action frowned upon in many Pentecostal circles.

The Church follows standard Apostolic teachings. Women are welcome in the ministry. Growth of the group was spurred in 1976 by the addition of several congregations headed by Bishop Thomas C. Williams.

Membership: In 1980 the Church reported 10 churches and missions, two bishops, 14 ministers and approximately 900 members.

★416★
UNITED CHURCH OF JESUS CHRIST (APOSTOLIC)
% Monroe Saunders, Presiding Bishop
5150 Baltimore National Pike
Baltimore, MD 21229

The United Church of Jesus Christ (Apostolic) dates to 1945 when Randolph Carr left the Pentecostal Assemblies of the World to found the Church of God in Christ (Apostolic). During the 1960s, Monroe Saunders, chief assistant to Carr, criticized him for contradicting in action his stated position on divorce and remarriage. Carr asked Saunders to leave the Church, and most of the group followed him. They reorganized as the United Church and elected Saunders the presiding bishop. Doctrine stresses

the authority of the Bible and the unity of the Godhead. There are three ordinances, including foot-washing.

The Church is headed by a presiding bishop, a vice-bishop, and three other bishops. As presiding bishop, Saunders, who completed his post-graduate education, has led the church in emphasizing an educated ministry, and with the development of The Center for a More Abundant Life, which provides a variety of social services to people living in Baltimore. Missions are supported in Mexico, Trinidad, Jamaica, and other West Indian Islands.

Membership: In 1985 the Church had 75 congregations, approximately 100,000 members and over 150 ministers in the United States. There were approximatly 50,000 additional members overseas.

Educational facilities: Institute of Biblical Studies, Baltimore, Maryland.

Sources: Monroe R. Saunders, Sr., *The Book of Church Order and Discipline of the United Church of Jesus Christ (Apostolic)*. Washington, DC: 1965.

★417★
UNITED CHURCHES OF JESUS, APOSTOLIC
Current address not obtained for this edition.

The United Churches of Jesus, Apostolic was formed by several bishops of the Apostle Church of Christ in God who rejected the leadership of presiding bishop J. C. Richardson Sr. Richardson had married a divorced woman. The church is headed by a general bishop, J. W. Ardrey (one of the founders of the Apostle Church) and a board of bishops. Doctrine is like the parent body.

Membership: In 1980 the United Churches had 2,000 members, 20 churches, 30 ministers and six bishops.

★418★
UNITED PENTECOSTAL CHURCH
8855 Dunn Rd.
Hazelwood, MO 63042

History: The United Pentecostal Church International was formed in 1945 by a merger of the Pentecostal Church, Inc. and the Pentecostal Assemblies of Jesus Christ. Both organizations dated to a 1924 schism of the Pentecostal Assemblies of the World. During the early 1920s, which ministers within the assemblies had become convinced that, due in part to various laws in the south about the mixing of blacks and whites, its interracial makeup was hindering the spread of its message. Members who left eventually formed three separate organizations.

Members who left the Pentecostal Assemblies of the World met in a separate hall before leaving the 1924 Chicago, Illinois, conference at which the split occurred to lay plans for a new organization. That organization was chartered the next year as the Pentecostal Ministerial Alliance. It continued to function under that name until 1932, when it became the Pentecostal Church, Inc.

Some who had pareticipated in the formation of the Pentecostal Ministerial Alliance were upset over the final organization as it provided only for the ministers and not for the members of the congregations. Meeting in Texas in October 1925, they formed Emmanuel's Church in Jesus Christ. A third group gathered in St. Louis and formed the Pentecostal Churches of Jesus Christ. In 1927, these two groups merged to become the Pentecostal Church of Jesus Christ.

In 1931, the Pentecostal Church of Jesus Christ voted to merge with the Pentecostal Assemblies of the World, the body from which it had originally derived. The newly merged interracial body was called the Pentecostal Assemblies of Jesus Christ. However, as the decade proceeded, racial tensions again arose. For example, many southerners who constituted a significant part of the group) were concerned that the church's conferences could never be in the South because of racial laws. Beginning around 1936, black ministers and predominantly black congregations began to resign and return to the Pentecostal Assemblies of the World, eventually leaving the Pentecostal Assemblies of Jesus Christ an all-white body. As such it entered the 1945 merger.

The oneness doctrine taught by the United Pentecostal was first articulated by a Canadian, R. E. McAleister, and the first assembly began in Toronto, Ontario in 1915. From that time to the present, there has been a Canadian presence in the bodies which constituted the United Pentecostal Church International. There are now United Pentecostal congregations across Canada and two Bible colleges.

Beliefs: According to the rather lengthy statement of faith issued by the church, its basic and fundamental doctrine is "repentance, Baptism in water by immersion in the name of the Lord Jesus Christ for the remission of sins, and the baptism of the Holy Ghost with the initial sign of speaking with other tongues as the Spirit gives utterance." The statement also affirms belief in the one true God who manifested in the flesh as Jesus Christ and, since Christ's ascension, as the Holy Spirit. The church practices footwashing and healing and follows a holiness code which includes disapproval of secret societies, mixed bathing, women cutting their hair, worldly amusements, home television sets, and immodest dress. While stongly affirming loyalty to the government, the church is against bearing arms or taking human life.

Organization: Government of the church is congregational. A general conference meets annually. A general superintendent, two assistants, and a secretary/treasurer are members of a general board consisting of superintendents, executive presbyters, and division heads.

A foreign missions division oversees missions around the world in about 100 countries. Under the name World Aflame Press, the Pentecostal Publishing House in Hazelwood, Missouri, publishes books, Sunday school material, and a wide variety of religious literature. The Church is divided into 51 districts that include churches in every state and all ten Canadian provinces. The church supports nine bible colleges, the Tupelo, Mississippi, Children's Mansion, the Lighthouse Ranch for Boys, and the Spirit of Freedom Ministries.

Membership: In 1988 the Church reported 400,000 members, 3,496 churches in the United States and Canand served by 7,064 ministers. There were 1,200,000 members worldwide.

Educational facilities: Apostolic Bible Institute, St. Paul, Minnesota; Apostolic Missionary Institue, Oshawa, Ontario; Christian Life College, Stockton, California; Gateway College of Evangelism, Florissant, Missouri; Indiana Bible College, Seymour, Indiana; Jackson College of Ministries, Jackson, Mississippi; Kent Christian College, Dover, Delaware; Texas Bible College, Houston, Texas; United Pentecostal Bible Institute, Fredericton, New Brunswick.

Periodicals: *The Pentecostal Herald*, 8855 Dunn Road, Hazelwood, MO 63042; *The Global Witness*, 8855 Dunn Road, Hazelwood, MO 63042.

Sources: Fred J. Foster, *Their Story: 20th Century Pentecostals*. Hazelwood, MO: World Aflame Press, 1981; Arthur L. Clanton, *United We Stand*. Hazelwood, MO; Pentecostal Publishing House, 1970; Andrew D. Urshan, *My Study of Modern Pentecostals*. Portland, OR: Apostolic Book Publishers, 1981.

★419★
UNITED WAY OF THE CROSS CHURCHES OF CHRIST OF THE APOSTOLIC FAITH
Current address not obtained for this edition.

The United Way of the Cross Churches of Christ of the Apostolic Faith was founded by Bishop Joseph H. Adams of the Way of the Cross Church of Christ and Elder Harrison J. Twyman of the Bible Way Church of Our Lord Jesus Christ World Wide, Inc. The new church was formed when the two founders, both pastors of congregations in North Carolina, discovered that God had given each a similar vision to form a new church. Also, Adams, a bishop in North Carolina for the Way of the Cross Church of Christ, had developed some concerns with the administrative procedures of the church. The church grew, in part, from the addition of pastors and their congregations who had previously left other Apostolic bodies.

Membership: In 1980 the United Way of the Cross Churches had 1,100 members in 14 churches. There were 30 ministers and four bishops.

★420★
WAY OF THE CROSS CHURCH OF CHRIST
332 4th St., N.E.
Washington, DC 20003

The Way of the Cross Church of Christ was founded in 1927 by Henry C. Brooks, an independent black Pentecostal minister. Brooks had founded a small congregation in Washington, D.C. which became part of the Church of Our Lord Jesus Christ of the Apostolic Faith founded by R.C. Lawson. At that time there was another small congregation under Bishop Lawson in Washington headed by Smallwood E. Williams, and Lawson wanted Brooks' congregation to join Williams'. Brooks rejected the plan, left Lawson's jurisdiction and founded a separate organization. A second congregation in Henderson, North Carolina became the first of several along the East Coast. Brooks pastored the mother church for forty years and built a membership of over 3,000.

The Way of the Cross Church is headed by by a presiding bishop. John L. Brooks, the son of the founder, succeeded to that post. He is assisted by twelve other bishops. Missions are supported in Ghana and Liberia.

Membership: In 1980 the Way of the Cross Church of Christ had 48 affiliated congregations and approximately 50,000 members.

★421★
YAHWEH'S TEMPLE
Box 652
Cleveland, TN 37311

Yahweh's Temple was founded in 1947 as the Church of Jesus and has through the decades of its existence sought the name that best expressed its central doctrinal concern of identifying Jesus with the God of the Old Testament. In 1953 the Church became The Jesus Church, and it adopted its present name in 1981. The Temple is headed by Samuel E. Officer, its bishop and moderator, a former member of the Church of God (Cleveland, Tennessee). The Temple follows the "oneness" doctrine generally, but has several points of difference from other bodies. From the Sacred Name Movement it has accepted the use of the Hebrew transliterations of the names of the Creator. It also keeps the Saturday Sabbath. It derives its name from a belief that Jesus is the "new and proper name of God, Christ, and the church." Specifically rejected are names such as "Church of God," "Pentecostal," and "Churches of Christ." The organization of the Temple is based upon an idea that all the members have a special place to work in a united body. From Ezekiel 10:10, a model of four wheels within wheels has been constructed. Each wheel consists of a hub of elders, spokes of helpers, a band for service, and the rim of membership. At the center is the international bishop, who exercises episcopal and theocratic authority. There are national and state bishops, and local deacons.

Membership: Not reported. In 1973 there were approximately 10,000 members.

Periodicals: *The Light of the World*, Box 652, Cleveland, TN 37311.

Black Trinitarian Pentecostals

★422★
AFRICAN UNIVERSAL CHURCH
Current address not obtained for this edition.

The African Universal Church was established in 1927 in Jacksonville, Florida, by Archbishop Clarence C. Addison. The movement which became the African Universal Church was founded in the Gold Coast, West Africa, by a number of tribal chiefs. Among the leaders was Laura Adanka Kauffey, a Christian and daughter-in-law of an African king. Unfortunately, Princess Kauffey was assassinated in 1928 in Miami.

The church is Pentecostal, but believes in four experiences: justification, sanctification, baptism of the Holy Ghost, and baptism with fire. The baptism of the Holy Ghost is for the sanctified. The baptism with fire is seen as a "definite Scriptural experience, obtainable by faith on the part of the Spirit-filled believer." The church also believes in healing and the Second Coming. The church does not baptize with water nor does it use wine in the Lord's Supper.

A subsidiary of the African Universal Church is the Commercial League Corporation formed in 1934. It operates as an insurance company for members and pastors. Its motto, printed on all church literature, is, "You need our protection; we need your cooperation; we protect our members financially as well as spiritually." The League has been an expression of black nationalism, which Addison constantly preached. He opposed both "civil rights" and integration, but believed in a black nation in Africa. His anti-integration position made him a popular speaker for conservative white groups such as the Congress of Christian States of America.

The polity of the church is episcopal. There is a general assembly which meets every four years. The church is divided into state districts headed by overseers. Parish mothers (deaconesses) are organized under a senior mother and district mothers.

Membership: Not reported. In 1970 there were fewer than 100 congregations.

★423★
ALPHA AND OMEGA PENTECOSTAL CHURCH OF GOD OF AMERICA, INC.
3023 Clifton Ave.
Baltimore, MD 21216

The Alpha and Omega Pentecostal Church of God of America, Inc., was formed in 1945 by the Rev. Magdalene Mabe Phillips, who withdrew from the United Holy Church of America and, with others, organized the Alpha and Omega Church of God Tabernacles, soon changed to the present name. Like the Church of God (Cleveland, Tennessee), the church's doctrine reserves the baptism of The Holy Spirit for the sanctified.

Membership: Not reported. In 1970 there were three congregations, six missions, and approximately 400 members, all in Baltimore.

★424★
CHURCH OF GOD IN CHRIST
272 S. Main St.
Memphis, TN 38103

The Church of God in Christ was established in 1894 in Jackson, Mississippi by Charles H. Mason, at that time an independent Baptist minister who four years previously had been affected by the holiness movement and sanctified. With a colleague, Elder C. P. Jones, he had founded the Church of Christ (Holiness) U.S.A.. He had as a child of twelve been healed suddenly of a sickness that almost killed him. In 1907, two events further changed his life. Elder Jones convinced him that he did not yet have the fullness of the Holy Spirit, for, if he did, he would have the power to heal the sick, cast out devils, and raise the dead. He also heard of the meetings at Azusa Street in Los Angeles, went there, was baptized in the Spirit and spoke in tongues.

In August, 1908, the new doctrine and experience was presented to the representatives of the Church of Christ (Holiness) U.S.A. convention in Jackson. At a meeting of those who accepted Pentecostalism, a General Assembly of the Church of God in Christ was organized. Mason was elected general overseer. (This brief history is at odds with the history presented in the item elsewhere in this *Encyclopedia* on the Church of Christ (Holiness) U.S.A.; the two churches involved tell two different stories.)

The Church of God in Christ was organized in an ascending hierarchy of overseer (pastor), state overseer, and general overseer. There are annual state convocations which decide on disputed matters and assign pastors, and a general convocation for matters of the general church.

Upon the death of Bishop Mason in 1961, a series of reorganizational steps began. Power reverted to the seven bishops who made up the executive commission. This group was extended to twelve in 1962 and O. T. Jones, Jr., was named "senior bishop." An immediate controversy began over the focus of power and a constitutional convention was scheduled. In 1967, a court in Memphis ruled that the powers of the senior bishop and executive board should remain intact until the constitutional convention in 1968. That year reorganization took place and power was invested in a quadrennial general assembly and a general board of twelve with a presiding bishop to conduct administration between meetings of the general assembly.

Doctrine is similar to that of the Pentecostal Holiness Church. The group believes in the Trinity, holiness, healing, and the premillennial return of Christ. Three ordinances are recognized: baptism by immersion, the Lord's Supper, and foot-washing.

Membership: In 1987 the church reported 3,000,000 members, 10,500 congregations and 31,896 ministers in the United States. There were 21 congregations and 33 ministers in Canada and an additional 700,000 members in 43 countries around the world.

Educational facilities: Charles H. Mason Theological Seminary, Atlanta, Georgia; In addition to the seminary in Atlanta (now part of the Interdenominational Theological Center), the church supports the C.H. Mason System of Bible Colleges which includes a number of schools attached to local congregations both in the United States and abroad.

Periodicals: *Whole Truth*, Box 329, Memphis, TN 38101; *The Voice of Missions*, Box 329, Memphis, TN 38101.201.

Sources: J. O. Patterson, German R. Ross, and Julia Mason Atkins, *History and Formative Years of the Church of God in Christ with Excerpts from the Life and Works of Its Founder--Bishop C. H. Mason*. Memphis, TN: Church of God in Christ Publishing House, 1969; W. A. Patterson, *From the Pen of W. A. Patterson*. Memphis, TN: Deakins Typesetting Service, 1970; Lucille J. Cornelius, *The Pioneer History of the Church of God in Christ*. The Author, 1975; Mary Esther Mason, *The History and Life Work of Elder C. H. Mason and His Co-Laborers*. Privately printed, n.d. 93 pp.

★425★
CHURCH OF GOD IN CHRIST, CONGREGATIONAL
1905 Bond Ave.
East St. Louis, IL 62201

The Church of God in Christ, Congregational, was formed in 1932 by Bishop J. Bowe of Hot Springs, Arkansas, who argued that the Church of God in Christ should be congregational, not episcopal, in its polity. Forced to withdraw, Bowe organized the Church of God in Christ, Congregational. In 1934, he was joined by George Slack. Slack had been disfellowshipped from the church because of his disagreement with the teaching that if a saint did not pay tithes, he was not saved. He was convinced that tithing was not a New Testament doctrine. He became the junior bishop under Bowe. In 1945, Bowe was wooed back into the Church of God in Christ, and Slack became senior bishop.

Doctrine is like that of the Church of God in Christ, but with disagreements on matters of polity and tithing. Members are conscientious objectors.

Membership: Not reported. In 1971 there were 33 churches in the United States, 4 in England, and 6 in Mexico.

Sources: George Slack, William Walker, and E. Jones, *Manual.* East St. Louis, IL: Church of God in Christ, Congregational, 1948.

★426★
CHURCH OF GOD IN CHRIST, INTERNATIONAL
% Rt. Rev. Carl E. Williams, Presiding Bishop
170 Adelphi St.
Brooklyn, NY 11025

In 1969, following its constitutional convention and reorganization, a major schism of the Church of God in Christ occurred when a group of fourteen bishops led by Bishop Illie L. Jefferson rejected the polity of the reorganized church, left it and formed the Church of God in Christ, International, at Kansas City. The issue was the centralized authority in the organization of the parent body. The new group quickly set up an entire denominational structure. The doctrine of the parent body remained intact.

Membership: In 1982 the Church reported 200,000 members, 300 congregations and 1,600 ministers.

Periodicals: *Message*, Hartford, CT; *Holiness Code*, Memphis, TN.

★427★
CHURCH OF THE LIVING GOD (CHRISTIAN WORKERS FOR FELLOWSHIP)
% Bishop W. E. Crumes
434 Forest Ave.
Cincinnati, OH 45229

The Church of the Living God (Christian Workers for Fellowship) was formed in 1889 by a former slave, the Rev. William Christian (1856-1928) of Wrightsville, Arkansas. Christian was an early associate of Charles H. Mason, also a Baptist minister who left the Baptist Church to form the Church of God in Christ. Christian claimed to have had a revelation that the Baptists were preaching a sectarian doctrine and he left them in order to preach the unadulterated truth. He created the office of "chief." Mrs. Ethel L. Christian succeeded her husband

after his death and was, in turn, succeeded by their son, John L. Christian. Mrs. Christian claimed that the original revelation came to both her husband and herself.

The doctrine is trinitarian and somewhat Pentecostal. The group rejects the idea of "tongues" as the initial evidence of the baptism of the Holy Spirit, although "tongues" are allowed. However, "tongues" must be recognizable languages, not "unintelligible utterance." Footwashing is a third ordinance. Salvation is gained by obeying the commandments to hear, understand, believe, repent, confess, be baptized, and participate in the Lord's Supper and in foot-washing.

The Church of the Living God also has a belief that Jesus Christ was of the black race because of the lineage of David and Abraham. David in Psalms 119:83 said he became like a bottle in the smoke (i.e., black). The church members also hold that Job (Job 30:30), Jeremiah (Jer. 8:21), and Moses' wife (Numbers 12:11) were black. These teachings were promulgated at a time when many Baptists were teaching that blacks were not human, but the offspring of a human father and female beast. The Church of the Living God countered with the assertion that the saints of the Bible were black.

The polity is episcopal and the church is modeled along the lines of a fraternal organization. Christian was very impressed with the Masons, and there are reportedly many points of doctrine known only to members of the organization. Tithing is stressed. Churches are called temples.

Membership: In 1985 the church reported 170 churches, 42,000 members, and 170 ministers.

Periodicals: *Fellowship Echoes*, St. Louis, MO; *The Gospel Truth*, 424 Forest Ave., Cincinnati, OH 45229.

★428★
CHURCH OF THE LIVING GOD, THE PILLAR AND GROUND OF THE TRUTH
4520 Hydes Ferry Pike
Box 5735
Nashville, TN 37208

The Church of the Living God, the Pillar and Ground of the Truth, Inc. traces its beginning to 1903 when Mary L. Tate (1871-1930), generally referred to as Mother or Saint Mary Magdalena, a black woman, began to preach first at Steel Springs, Tennessee, and Paducah, Kentucky, and then throughout the South. By 1908, when a number of holiness bands had been formed by people converted under her ministry, she was taken ill. Pronounced beyond cure, she was healed and given the baptism of the Holy Spirit and spoke in tongues. She called an assembly in Greenville, Alabama, during which the Church of the Living God was organized. She became the chief overseer. The church quickly spread to the surrounding states of Georgia, Florida, Tennessee, and Kentucky and by the end of the next decade had congregations across the eastern half of the United States.

In 1919, the first of two major schisms occurred. Led by the church in Philadelphia, Pennsylvania, some members left to found the House of God, Which Is the Church of the Living God, the Pillar and Ground of Truth. Then, in 1931, following Mother Tate's death, the church reorganized, and three persons were ordained to fill the office of chief overseer. The three chosen were Mother Tate's son F. E. Lewis, M. F. L. Keith (widow of Bishop W. C. Lewis), and B. L. McLeod. These three eventually became leaders of distinct church bodies. Lewis' following is the continuing Church of the Living God, the Pillar and Ground of the Truth, Inc. Keith's group became known as the House of God Which Is the Church of the Living God, the Pillar and Ground of Truth Without Controversy.

Bishop McLeod's organizationis known as the Church of the Living God, the Pillar, and Ground of Truth, Inc. affirms the central doctrines of traditional Christianity including the Trinity and salvation through Christ. It teaches that people are justifies and cleansed by faith in Christ and glorified and wholly sanctified by receiving of the Holy Ghost and Fire. Evidence of the reception of the Holy Ghost is speaking in tongues. The unknown tongue is a sign of God's victory over sin. There are three ordinances: baptism by immersion, the Lord's Supper, and foot washing.

Organization: The church is headed by a bishop, designated the chief overseer. After the death of Bishop F.E. Lewis in 1968, Bishop Helen M. Lewis, the present head of the church, became the chief overseer. She administers the affairs of the church with the assistance of the general assembly, which meets annually, a board of trustees, and the supreme executive council consisting of the other bishops and seven elders. The New and Living Way Publishing House is the church's publishing arm.

Membership: In 1988, the church reported approximately 2,000 members and approximately 100 ministers.

Periodicals: The True Report, 4520 Hydes Ferry Pike, Box 5735, Nashville, TN 37208.

Sources: *The Constitution, Government and General Decree Book.* Chattanooga, TN: The New and Living Way Publishing Co., n.d.; Helen M. Lewis and Meharry H. Lewis, *75th Anniversary Yearbook.* Nashville, TN: Church of the Living God, Pillar and Ground of Truth, 1978.

★429★
DELIVERANCE EVANGELISTIC CENTERS
505 Central Ave.
Newark, NJ 07107

The initial Deliverance Evangelistic Center was formed in Brooklyn, New York in the 1950s by Arturo Skinner (d.

1975). Skinner had been stopped from committing suicide by what he believed to be the voice of God which told him, "Arturo, if you but turn around, I'll save your soul, heal your body, and give you a deliverance ministry." He was twenty-eight years old at the time, and though he had a full gospel background, he had never heard of anything termed a "deliverance ministry." In a period of retreat following his encounter with God, Skinner fasted and had a number of visions and dreams. He also consecrated his life to the ministry to which he had been called. After the founding of the first center, others were founded and pastors ordained to care for them. Women have been accepted into the ordained ministry as both evangelists and pastors.

The statement of belief of the centers includes an affirmation in the authority of the Bible as inspired and infallible, the Trinity, Jesus Christ as redeemer, the Holy Spirit who empowers and baptizes believers, speaking-in-tongues as evidence of the baptism of the Holy Spirit, creation, the necessity of repentence, sanctification, and water baptism by immersion. Skinner was the church's first Apostle. He was succeeded by Ralph Nickels.

Membership: There are centers in Brooklyn and Poughkeepsie, New York; Philadelphia; Washington, D.C.; Orlando, Florida; and Asbury Park and Newark, New Jersey.

Periodicals: *Deliverance Voice*, 505 Central Ave., Newark, NJ 07107.

★430★
FIRE-BAPTIZED HOLINESS CHURCH OF GOD OF THE AMERICAS
Current address not obtained for this edition.

W. E. Fuller (1875-1958), the only black man in attendance at the 1898 organizing conference of the Fire-Baptized Holiness Church, became the leader of almost a thousand black people over the next decade. Feelings of discrimination led to their withdrawal and they organized the Colored Fire-Baptized Holiness Church at Anderson, South Carolina, on May 1, 1908. The white body gave them their accumulated assets and property at this time. Rev. Fuller was elected overseer and bishop. Doctrine is the same as in the International Pentecostal Holiness Church, the body that absorbed the Fire-Baptized Holiness Church.

Legislative and executive authority are vested in a general council that meets every four years and in the eleven-member executive council (composed of bishops, district elders, and pastors). Mission work is under one of the bishops.

Membership: Not reported. In 1968 the Church reported 53 churches and 9,088 members.

Periodicals: *True Witness.*

Sources: *Discipline*. Atlanta: The Board of Publication of the F. B. H. Church of God of the Americas, 1962.

★431★
FREE CHURCH OF GOD IN CHRIST
Current address not obtained for this edition.

The Free Church of God in Christ dates from 1915 when J. H. Morris, a former pastor in the National Baptist Convention of the U.S.A., Inc., and a group of members of his church experienced the baptism of the Holy Spirit and spoke in tongues. The group, mostly members of Morris' family, founded a Pentecostal group which they called the Church of God in Christ. They chose as their leader the founder's son, E. J. Morris, who believed he was "selected" for the role. In 1921, the group united with the larger body led by Bishop Charles H. Mason, which had the same name. The union lasted for only four years, and Morris' group adopted its present name when it again became independent in 1925. It has the same doctrine and polity as the Mason body. By the late 1940s the church had 20 congregations.

Membership: Not reported.

Remarks: No direct contact has been made with the Church since the 1940s and its present condition is unknown. It may be defunct.

★432★
HOUSE OF GOD WHICH IS THE CHURCH OF THE LIVING GOD, THE PILLAR AND GROUND OF TRUTH
Current address not obtained for this edition.

Not to be confused with the church of the same name which derives from the movement begun by Mary L. Tate known as the Church of the Living God, the Pillar and Ground of Truth, the church presently under discussion derives from the work begun by William Christian. In the early twentieth century, the Church of the Living God (Christian Workers for Fellowship), which Christian founded, was splintered on several occasions. In 1902, a group calling itself the Church of the Living God, Apostolic Church, withdrew and, six years later under the leadership of Rev. C. W. Harris, became the Church of the Living God, General Assembly. It united in 1924 with a second small splinter body. In 1925, a number of churches withdrew from the Church of the Living God (Christian Workers for Fellowship) under the leadership of Rev. E. J. Cain and called themselves the Church of the Living God, the Pillar and Ground of Truth. The Harris group joined the Cain group in 1926 and they later adopted the present name. The Church is one in doctrine with the Church of the Living God (Christian Workers for Fellowship). Polity is episcopal and there is an annual general assembly.

Membership: Not reported.

Remarks: The last independent source on this body is the 1936 *Census of Religious bodies*. Later sources often confuse it with the Philadelphia-based group of the same name. Its present location and strength is unknown.

★433★
HOUSE OF GOD, WHICH IS THE CHURCH OF THE LIVING GOD, THE PILLAR AND GROUND OF TRUTH, INC.
6107 Cobbs Creek Pkwy.
Philadelphia, PA 19143

In 1919 the Church of the Living God, the Pillar and Ground of Truth founded by Mary L. Tate, experienced a schism led by the congregation in Philadelphia. The new group, the House of God, the Church of the Living God, the Pillar and Ground of Truth continues the doctrine and episcopal polity of the parent body, but is administratively separate. The general assembly meets annually.

Membership: Not reported. In the early 1970 the Church reported 103 churches and 25,860 members.

Periodicals: *The Spirit of Truth Magazine*, 3943 Fairmont Street, Philadelphia, PA 19104.

★434★
HOUSE OF GOD WHICH IS THE CHURCH OF THE LIVING GOD, THE PILLAR AND GROUND OF TRUTH WITHOUT CONTROVERSY (KEITH DOMINION)
% Bishop J. W. Jenkins, Chief Overseer
Box 9113
Montgomery, AL 36108

In 1931, following the death of founder Bishop Mary L. Tate, the Church of the Living God, the Pillar and Ground of the Truth, Inc., appointed three chief overseers. Eventually, each became the head of a distinct segment of the church and then of an independent body called a dominion. One of the three chief overseers was M. F. L. Keith, widow of Bishop Tate's son, W. C. Lewis. Her dominion became known as the House of God Which is the Church of the Living God the Pillar and Ground of Truth Without Controversy (Keith Dominion).

The church is headed by a Chief Overseer (Bishop J. W. Jenkins succeeded Bishop Keith in that post) and a Supreme Executive Council.

Membership: Not reported.

★435★
HOUSE OF THE LORD
Current address not obtained for this edition.

The House of the Lord was founded in 1925 by Bishop W. H. Johnson, who established headquarters in Detroit.

The doctrine is Pentecostal but departs on several important points. A person who enters the church is born of water and seeks to be born of God by a process of sanctification. The Holy Ghost may be given and is evidenced by speaking in tongues. But sanctification is evidenced by conformity to a very rigid code which includes refraining from worldly amusements, whiskey, policy rackets (the "numbers game"), becoming bell hops, participating in war, swearing, secret organizations, tithing, and life insurance (except as required by an employer). A believer is not sanctified if he owns houses, lands, or goods. Water is used in the Lord's Supper. Members are not to marry anyone not baptized by the Holy Ghost.

The church is governed by a hierarchy of ministers, state overseers, and chief overseer. There is a common treasury at each local church from which the destitute are helped.

Membership: Not reported.

★436★

LATTER HOUSE OF THE LORD FOR ALL PEOPLE AND THE CHURCH OF THE MOUNTAIN, APOSTOLIC FAITH
Current address not obtained for this edition.

The Latter House of the Lord for All People and the Church of the Mountain, Apostolic Faith, was founded in 1936 by Bishop L. W. Williams, a former black Baptist preacher from Cincinnati. The founding followed an enlightenment experience and spiritual blessing realized in prayer. The doctrine is Calvinistic, but adjusted to accommodate Pentecostal beliefs. The Lord's Supper is observed, with water being used instead of wine. The Church members are conscientious objectors. The chief overseer is appointed for life.

Membership: Not reported. In 1947 there were approximately 4,000 members.

★437★

MOUNT SINAI HOLY CHURCH
Current address not obtained for this edition.

Ida Robinson grew up in Georgia, was converted at age seventeen, and joined the United Holy Church of America. She moved to Philadelphia where she became the pastor of the Mount Olive Holy Church. Following what she believed to be the command of the Holy Spirit to "Come out on Mount Sinai," she founded the Mount Sinai Holy Church in 1924. Women have played a prominent role in its leadership from the beginning.

The doctrine is Pentecostal, with sanctification a prerequisite for the baptism of the Holy Spirit. One must be converted before becoming a member. Bishop Robinson believed that God ordained four types of human beings: the elect or chosen of God, the compelled (those who could not help themselves from being saved), the "who so

ever will" who can be saved, and the damned (ordained for hell). Spiritual healing is stressed. Foot-washing is practiced. Behavior, particularly sexual, is rigidly codified and rules are strictly observed. Short dresses, neckties, and worldly amusements are frowned upon.

The Mt. Sinai Holy Church is episcopal in government. Bishop Robinson served as senior bishop and president until her death in 1946. She was succeeded by Bishop Elmira Jeffries, the original vice-president, who was, in turn, succeeded by Bishop Mary Jackson in 1964. Assisting the bishops is a board of presbyteries, composed of the elders of the churches. There are four administrative districts, each headed by a bishop. There is an annual conference of the entire church, and one is held in each district. Foreign missions in Cuba and Guinea are supported.

Membership: Not reported. In 1968 there were 92 churches, and approximately 2,000 members.

★438★

ORIGINAL UNITED HOLY CHURCH INTERNATIONAL
% Bishop H. W. Fields
Box 263
Durham, NC 27702

The Original United Holy Church International grew out of a struggle between two bishops of the United Holy Church of America. The conflict led to Bishop James Alexander Forbes and the Southern District being severed from the organization. Those put out of the church met and organized on June 29, 1977 at a meeting in Raleigh, North Carolina. The new body remains in essential doctrinal agreement and continues the polity of the United Holy Church

The Original United Holy Church is concentrated on the Atlantic coast from South Carolina to Connecticut, with congregations also found in Kentucky, Texas, and California. Bishop Forbes also serves as pastor of the Greater Forbes Temple of Hollis, New York. The church supports missionary work in Liberia. On January 24, 1979, in Wilmington, North Carolina, an agreement of affiliation between the Original United Holy Church and the International Pentecostal Holiness Church was signed, which envisions a close cooperative relationship between the two churches.

Membership: In 1985 the church had approximately 210 congregations and over 15,000 members.

Educational facilities: United Christian College, Goldsboro, North Carolina.

Periodicals: *Voice of the World.*

★439★
SOUGHT OUT CHURCH OF GOD IN CHRIST
Current address not obtained for this edition.

The Sought Out Church of God in Christ and Spiritual House of Prayer, Inc., was founded in 1947 by Mother Mozella Cook. Mother Cook was converted in a service led by her physical mother, an ecstatic person who was once hauled into court to be examined for lunacy because of her mystical states. Mother Cook's mother seemed to go into trances and was "absent from this world while she talked with God." Mother Cook moved to Pittsburgh and there became a member of the Church of God in Christ founded by Charles H. Mason, but left it to found her own church, which she formed in Brunswick, Georgia, after feeling a divine call.

Membership: Not reported. In 1949 the Church had four congregations and 60 members.

★440★
TRUE FELLOWSHIP PENTECOSTAL CHURCH OF GOD OF AMERICA
4238 Pimlico Rd.
Baltimore, MD 21215

The True Fellowship Pentecostal Church of God of America was formed in 1964 by the secession of the Rev. Charles E. Waters, Sr., a presiding elder in the Alpha and Omega Pentecostal Church of God of America, Inc.. Doctrine is like the Church of God in Christ, differing only in the acceptance of women into the ministry as pastors and elders. Bishop Waters and his wife operate a mission for those in need in Baltimore.

Membership: Not reported. In 1948 the church reported three congregations and about 120 members, all in Baltimore.

★441★
TRUE GRACE MEMORIAL HOUSE OF PRAYER
205 V St., N.W.
Washington, DC 20001

In 1960 after Bishop Marcelino Manoel de Graca (Sweet Daddy Grace) died, Walter McCoullough was elected bishop of the United House of Prayer for All People, but approximately six months later criticism was directed at him for his disposal of church monies without explanation to the other church leaders. The elders relieved him of his office and a lawsuit ordered a new election, at which time he was re-elected. Complaints continued that he was assuming false doctrines, such as claiming that he and only he was doing God's work or that he had power to save or condemn people. Shortly after the second election, he dismissed a number of the church leaders. Twelve dissenting members, with Thomas O. Johnson (d. 1970) as their pastor, formed the True Grace Memorial House of prayer in Washington, D.C. (Elder Johnson had been dismissed after 23 years of service as a pastor.) In 1962

the church members adopted a church covenant in which they agreed to assist one another in loving counsel, prayer, and aid in times of sickness and distress; to do all good to all, in part, by assisting them to come under the ministry of the church; to avoid causes of divisions, such as gossip; and to refrain from any activity that might bring disgrace on the cause of Christ. The present head of the church is Elder William G. Easton.

Membership: Not reported. In the 1970s there were eight congregations which could be found in Washington, D.C., Philadelphia, New York City, Baltimore, Savannah, Hollowood, Florida and in North Carolina.

★442★
UNITED HOLY CHURCH OF AMERICA
825 Fairoak Ave.
Chillum, MD 20783

The United Holy Church of America was formed as the outgrowth of a holiness revival conducted by the Rev. Isaac Cheshier at Method, North Carolina (near Raleigh), in 1886. In 1900, the group became known as the Holy Church of North Carolina (and as growth dictated, the Holy Church of North Carolina and Virginia). In the early twentieth century, the church became Pentecostal and adopted a theology like the Church of God (Cleveland, Tennessee). The present name was chosen in 1916.

Membership: Not reported. In 1970 there were approximately 50,000 members in 470 churches and over 400 ministers.

Periodicals: *The Holiness Union*, Silver Spring, MD.

★443★
UNITED HOUSE OF PRAYER FOR ALL PEOPLE
1721 1/2 7th St., N.W.
Washington, DC 20001

Sweet Daddy Grace, as Bishop Marcelino Manoel de Graca (1884-1960) was affectionately known by his followers, was born in 1884 on Brava, Cape Verde Islands, and was a former railroad cook who began preaching in 1925. He founded the United House of Prayer for All People, which in the 1930s and 1940s was one of the most famous religious groups in the black community.

In doctrine, the church resembles the holiness Pentecostal bodies. It teaches the three experiences-conversion, sanctification, and baptism with the Holy Spirit. There is a strict behavior code. What sets the House of Prayer apart is the role that Daddy Grace assumed in the group, i.e., that of a divine being. In an often repeated quote, he was heard to have admonished his worshippers:

Never mind about God. Salvation is by Grace only...Grace has given God a vacation, and since God in on His vacation, don't worry Him...If you sin against God, Grace can save you, but if you sin against Grace, God cannot save you.

Thus, while the House of Prayer derives from and continues to grow in relation to the Pentecostal framework, the framework was significantly changed by Grace's assumption of deific powers. Grace reigned supreme as an autocrat until his death. He appointed the ministers and all church officials. A line of Daddy Grace Products included soap, toothpaste, writing paper, face powder, shoe polish, and cookies. There is an annual convocation.

Grace died in 1960 and, after a period of court fights, Bishop Walter McCoullough was acknowledged as head of the church. He has assumed Grace's powers, if not his divine claims. Under his leadership, the church has assumed more traditional Pentecostal stance. In 1974, it launched a $1.5 million housing project in Washington, D.C.

Membership: Not reported. In 1974 Bishop McCollough claimed 4,000,000 members. There were four congregations in Washington, D.C., and others throughout the nation.

★444★
UNIVERSAL CHRISTIAN SPIRITUAL FAITH AND CHURCHES FOR ALL NATIONS
Current address not obtained for this edition.

The Universal Christian Spiritual Faith and Churches for All Nations was founded in 1952 by the merger of the National David Spiritual Temple of Christ Church Union (Inc.) U.S.A., St. Paul's Spiritual Church Convocation, and King David's Spiritual Temple of Truth Association. National David Spiritual Temple of Christ Church Union (Inc.) U.S.A. had been founded at Kansas City, Missouri, in 1932 by Dr. David William Short, a former Baptist minister. He became convinced that no man had the right or spiritual power "to make laws, rules or doctrines for the real church founded by Jesus Christ" and that the "denominational" churches had been founded in error and in disregard of the apostolic example. Bishop Short claimed that the temple was the true church, and hence dated to the first century.

The merged church differs from many Pentecostal churches in that it denies that only those who have spoken in tongues have received the Spirit. It does insist, however, that a full and complete baptism of the Holy Ghost is always accompanied by both the gift of "tongues" and other powers. The members of the church rely on the Holy Spirit for inspiration and direction. The church is organized according to I Corinthians 12:1-31 and Ephesians 4:11. It includes pastors, archbishops, elders, overseers, divine healers, deacons, and missionaries.

Bishop Short is the chief governing officer. In 1952, he became archbishop of the newly merged body. He is assisted by a national executive board which holds an annual assembly.

Membership: Not reported. In the mid-1960s there were reportedly 60 churches and 40,816 members.

Educational facilities: St. David Christian Spiritual Seminary.

Periodicals: *The Christian Spiritual Voice*.

Signs Pentecostals

★445★
CHURCH OF GOD WITH SIGNS FOLLOWING
Current address not obtained for this edition.

The Church of God with Signs Following is a name applied to an informally organized group of Pentecostal churches, ministers and itinerant evangelists popularly known as snake-handlers, who are distinguished by their practice of drinking poison (usually strychnine) and handling poisonous serpents during their worship services. Among those who handle snakes and drink poison, the actions are called "preaching the signs." The terms "signs" refers to Jesus' remarks in Mark 16: 17-18: "And these signs will accompany those who will believe: in my name they will cast out demons; they will speak in new tongues; they will pick up serpents; and if they drink any deadly thing, it will not hurt them; they will lay their hands on the sick, and they will recover." The practice, an object of curiosity scorned and ridiculed by outsiders, is a commonplace to believers.

The practice of snake-handling began with George Went Hensley, a minister with the Church of God (Cleveland, Tennessee) in the very early days of the spread of the Pentecostal message throughout the hills of Tennessee and North Carolina. Converted, Hensley erected a brush arbor at Owl Holler outside of Cleveland and began to preach. One day during a service in which he was preaching on Mark 16, some men turned over a box of rattlesnakes in front of Hensley. According to the story, he reached down, picked up the snakes and continued to preach.

Ambrose J. Tomlinson, then head of the Church of God, having become convinced that his ministry was a further proof of the pouring of power on the Church in the last days   invited Hensley to Cleveland to show church members what was occurring. By 1914 the practice had spread through the Church of God, though practiced by only a small percentage of members. Hensley settled in Grasshopper Valley, near Cleveland, and pastored a small congregation. A number of years later, after a member almost died from a bite, Hensley moved to Pine Mountain, Kentucky

Meanwhile, the Church of God was growing and in the 1920s, after Tomlinson's leaving the Church, the early support for the practice of snake-handling turned to strong opposition. In 1928 the Assembly of the Church of God denounced the practice, and it became the activity of a few independent churches, primarily scattered along the Appalachian Mountains. It was largely forgotten until the 1940s.

During the 1940s new advocates of snake-handling appeared. Raymond Hays and Tom Harden started the Dolly Pond Church of God with Signs Following in Grasshopper Valley not far from where Hensley had worked two decades earlier. Over the years since, that church has been the focus of the most intense controversy concerning the practice and become the most best known congregation of the signs people. In 1945 Lewis Ford died of a bite received at the Dolly Pond Church. His death led to the passing of a law against the practice by the state of Tennessee and the subsequent suppression of the group by authorities. Persecution against and demonstrations for the group led to the arrest of Hensley in Chattanooga (convicted of disturbing the peace in 1948) and the disruption of an interstate convention of believers in Durham, North Carolina in 1947. Following these events the group again withdrew from the public eye, and, except for the death of Hensley, bitten in a service in Florida in 1955, was forgotten for several decades.

Then in 1971 the group again was in the news when Buford Peck, a member of the Holiness Church of God in Jesus' Name, a second snake-handling church located not far from the Dolly Pond Church, was bitten. Though he did not die, he did loose his secular job. Over the next few years three persons in Tennessee and Georgia died, two, including Peck and Jimmie Ray Williams, his pastor, from strychnine poison taken during a service. Subsequent court battles, in part to test the law against the practice, led to a 1975 ban on snake-handling and the drinking of poison in public religious services by the Tennessee Supreme Court. Followers vowed to continue the practice.

Members of the snake-handling churches are Pentecostals who accept the basic theology by which people seek and receive the baptism of the Holy Spiirt, evidenced by speaking in tongues. The snake-handlers, however, go beyond the Pentecostals in their belief that snake-handling and the drinking of poison (and for some, the application of flames to the skin) are a sign of an individual's faith and possession by the Holy Spirit. It should be noted that the handling of snakes and the drinking of poison are done only while the believer is in an ecstatic (trance-like) state, referred to by members as being "in the Spirit." Scholars who have examined the movement have frequently questioned the low frequency of bites, given the number of occasions the snakes are handled and the generally loud atmosphere of the services.

The snake-handlers accept the rigid holiness code of the Pentecostal and holiness churches. Dress is plain, The Bible is consulted on all questions having to do with the nature of "worldly behavior." The kiss of peace is a prominent feature of gatherings. Worship is loud, spontaneous and several hours in length.

Congregations of signs people can be found from central Florida to West Virginia and as far west as Columbus, Ohio. Each church is independent (and a variety of names are used, mostly variations on the Church of God). They are tied together by evangelists who move from one congregation to the next. They produce no literature.

Membership: Observers of the snake handlers estimate between 50 to 100 congregations and as many as several thousand adherents.

Sources: Weston La Barre, *They Shall Take Up Serpents*. New York: Schocken Books, 1969; Robert K. Holliday, *Test of Faith*. Oak Hill, WV: The Fayette Tribune, 1966; Karen W. Carden and Robert W. Pelton, *The Persecuted Prophets*. New York: A. S. Barnes, 1976; J. B. Collins, *Tennessee Snake Handlers*. (Chattanooga): the Author, (1947).

★446★
ORIGINAL PENTECOSTAL CHURCH OF GOD
Current address not obtained for this edition.

Rarely recognized by observers of snake-handling groups, the Original Pentecostal Chruch of God represents a significant departure from the commonly accepted belief and practice of signs people. They do not believe in "tempting God" by bringing snakes into church services. However, should the occasion arise where the handling of a serpent provides a situation for a test and witness to one's faith, it is done. Members recount times in which they have encountered rattlesnakes or copperheads outside the church and have picked them up as they preached to those present.

The Original Church of God emerged from the Free Holiness people, the early Pentecostals, in rural Kentucky during the first decade of the twentieth century. Tom Perry and Tom Austin founded churches in rural Tennessee. Perry carried the Pentecostal message to Alabama and in 1910 converted P. W. Brown, then president of the Jackson County Baptist Association. Brown became the pastor of the Bierne Avenue Baptist Church in Huntsville, Alabama, one of the leading congregations of the Original Pentecostal Church. There is little formal organization nor are there "man-made rules." Congregations are scattered throughout the deep South.

Membership: Not reported.

Spanish-Speaking Pentecostals

CONCILIO OLAZABAL DE IGLESIAS LATINO AMERICANO
1925 E. First St.
Los Angeles, CA 90033

The revival on Azusa Street in Los Angeles which launched the Pentecostal movement soon spread and attracted some Spanish-speaking Christians. Most were affiliated with the Assemblies of God, formed in 1914. Among the early leaders was the Rev. Francisco Olazabal (1886-1937). Mexican-born Olazabal had become a Methodist minister and worked among the Methodists of southern California. In 1917, however, he received the baptism of the Holy Spirit in a prayer meeting in the home of George Montgomery and his wife Carrie Judd Montgomery. As a minister in the Christian and Missionary Alliance, George Montgomery had had a direct influence on Olazabal's conversion and entry into the ministry. By 1917 the Montgomerys had become Pentecostals. He left the Methodists and became an Assemblies pastor. He experienced great success in establishing new churches and recruiting pastors. Then in 1923 he led a movement out of the Assemblies, which he had come to feel had placed an insensitive Anglo in charge of the Spanish-speaking work. With his supporters he began independent work along the West Coast and the Mexican border. In 1931, he came to New York, after which he made visits to Mexico City and in 1934 to Puerto Rico. In 1936 he organized the Concilio Olazabal de Iglesias Latino Americano. In 1937, Rev. Olazabal died and was succeeded by Reverend Miguel Guillen. The present name was adopted after Olazabal's death as a means to honor his life work.

Rev. Olazabal had close contact with Ambrose J. Tomlinson and his son Homer Tomlinson then with the Church of God of Prophecy, and he noted Olazabal's natural affinity to Church of God doctrine rather than that of the Assemblies of God. Olazabal followed the emphasis upon the three experiences of justification, sanctification and the baptism of the Holy Spirit. The Assemblies position negated the necessity of sanctification prior to the baptism. The Council is also, like the Church of God, pacifist in orientation.

Membership: Not reported. In 1967 there were seven churches with 275 members with an additional four churches in Mexico.

Periodicals: *El Revelator Christiana*, Los Angeles, CA.

Sources: Homer A. Tomlinson, *Miracles of Healing in the Ministry of Rev. Francisco Olazabal*. Queens Village, NY: The Author, 1939; Victor DeLeon, *The Silent Pentecostals*. Taylor, SC: Faith Printing Company, 1979.

DAMASCUS CHRISTIAN CHURCH
℅ Rev. Enrique Melendez
170 Mt. Eden Parkway
Bronx, NY 10473

The Damascus Christian Church is a small Pentecostal body formed in 1939. It grew out of the work of Francisco Rosado and his wife Leoncai Rosado in New York City. By 1962 it had spread to New Jersey, with foreign affiliated congregations in Cuba and the Virgin Islands. The Church is headed by a bishop who is assisted by a council of officers and a mission committee.

Membership: Not reported. In 1962 the Church had 10 congregations and approximately 1,000 members.

DEFENDERS OF THE FAITH
Current address not obtained for this edition.

The Defenders of the Faith was formed in 1925 by an interdenominational group of pastors and laymen headed by Dr. Gerald B. Winrod, an independent Baptist preacher. Winrod gained a reputation in the 1930s not only for his fundamentalism but also for his support of right-wing political causes. The Defenders of the Faith became the instrument by which Winrod promoted his ideas, and during his lifetime it was a large organization. After Winrod's death in 1957, the group lost many members. However, in 1963, it began a three-year revival under Dr. G. H. Montgomery, who died suddenly in 1966. Since then, it grew slowly and steadily under Dr. Hunt Armstrong, its new leader.

Its main program consists of publishing a magazine, *The Defender*, and numerous pamphlets and tracts; administering six retirement homes in Kansas, Nebraska, and Arkansas; maintaining a school (opened in 1957) and headquarters in Kansas City and conducting a vigorous mission program.

The Defenders of the Faith was not intended to be a church-forming organization nor to be associated with Pentecostalism. In 1931, however, Gerald Winrod went to Puerto Rico to hold a series of missionary conferences. He met Juan Francisco Rodriguez-Rivera, a minister with the Christian and Missionary Alliance. Winrod decided to begin a missionary program and placed Rodriguez in charge. A center was opened in Arecibo, and *El Defensor Hispano* was begun as a Spanish edition of *The Defender*. Rodriguez's congregation became the first of the new movement. In 1932, Rodriguez accompanied Francisco Olazabal founder of the Concilio Olazabal de Iglesias Latino Americano on an evangelistic tour of Puerto Rico. The Defenders of the Faith received many members as a result of the crusade and emerged as a full-fledged Pentecostal denomination. A theological seminary was opened in 1945 in Rio Piedras. Members of the Defenders of the Faith migrated to New York in the late 1930s. In

1944, the Defenders' first church in New York was begun by J. A. Hernandez. From there the movement spread to other Spanish-speaking communities in the United States.

Doctrinally, the churches are not specifically Pentecostal; e.g., they do not insist that speaking in tongues is the sign of the baptism of the Holy Spirit. They are fundamentalist, believing in the Bible, the Trinity, salvation by faith, and the obligation of the church to preach the gospel, to carry on works of charity, and to operate institutions of mercy. Baptism is by immersion. Beyond the basic core of theological consensus, there is a high degree of freedom. Many congregations have become Pentecostal. Others are similar to Baptist churches. Premillennialism is accepted by most.

A central committee directs the work of the Defenders of the Faith. An annual assembly is held. Ties to the national office in Kansas City, which in 1965 discontinued all specific direction for the Spanish-speaking work, are very weak. It does continue support of missionaries and pastors. American congregations are located primarily in the New York City and Chicago metropolitan areas.

Membership: Not reported. In 1968 there were 14 churches and approximately 2,000 members in the United States, and 68 churches and 6,000 members in Puerto Rico.

Educational facilities: Defenders Seminary, Kansas City, Missouri.

Periodicals: *The Defender*, 928 Linwood Blvd., Kansas City, MO 64109.

★450★
LATIN-AMERICAN COUNCIL OF THE PENTECOSTAL CHURCH OF GOD OF NEW YORK
115 E. 125th St.
New York, NY 10035

The Latin-American Council of the Pentecostal Church of God of New York, Inc. (known also as the Concilio Latino-Americano de la Iglesia de Dios Pentecostal de New York, Incorporado) was formed in 1957 as an offshoot of the Latin American Council of the Pentecostal Church of God. (The latter is a Puerto Rican church without congregations in the U.S., and therefore not discussed in this encyclopedia.) Work in New York had begun in 1951 and the New York group became autonomous in 1956, though it remains loosely affiliated with the Puerto Rican parent body.

Doctrinally, it is like the Assemblies of God. Healing, tithing, and a literal heaven and hell are stressed. The matter of participation in war is left to the individual members. Secret societies are forbidden and no political activity is advised beyond voting. An unaccredited three-year school of theology with an average enrollment of 500

trains Christian workers. Mission activity is carried on in Central America and the Netherland Antilles, among other places.

Membership: Not reported. In 1967 there was an estimated 75 churches, most in the New York metropolitan area.

★451★
SOLDIERS OF THE CROSS OF CHRIST, EVANGELICAL INTERNATIONAL CHURCH
636 N.W. 2nd St.
Miami, FL 33128

The Soldiers of the Cross of Christ, Evangelical International Church was founded as the Gideon Mission in the early 1920s in Havana, Cuba. Its founder, affectionately known among his followers as "Daddy John," was Wisconsin-born Ernest William Sellers. He was assisted by three women--Sister Sarah, Mable G. Ferguson, and Muriel C. Atwood. Successful efforts led to the spread of the mission throughout Cuba. In 1939, the periodical *El Mensajero de los Postreros Dias* (*Last Day's Messenger*) was begun. Until 1947, Daddy John functioned as the bishop. But at the annual convention of that year, he was named apostle, and a three-man board of bishops was selected. In 1950, the church sent out its first missionaries, Arturo Rangel Sosa, to Panama, and Arnaldo Socarras to Mexico.

Prior to his death in 1953, Daddy John named Bishop Angel Maria Hernandez y Esperon as his successor. During Hernandez's eight years as an apostle, special attention was given to overseas missions, which were started in nine countries. Plans for starting a mission in the United States were also made.

After the death of Apostle Angel M. Hernandez, Bishop Arturo Rangel became the third apostle. He was in office during the Cuban revolution and the persecution of the church by the Castro government. The periodicals were cancelled and many churches were closed and/or destroyed. In 1966, the same year the American mission was opened, Apostle Rangel, one bishop, and one evangelist disappeared and have not been heard of since. The remaining members of the board took control of the church, and in 1969 moved its headquarters to Miami, Florida.

The Soldiers of the Cross Church is a sabbatarian pentecostal body. Members believe in keeping the Law of God (the Ten Commandments) and the dietary restrictions on unclean food (Genesis 7:2; Leviticus 11). They believe in baptism as the first step to salvation, the Lord's Supper as commemorating Christ's death (not his resurrection), and washing the feet as a sign of humility. They believe in the Second Coming of Jesus, and have a strong belief in the gifts of the Spirit, especially prophecy and revelation by means of dreams and visions. Ministers are not to be involved in politics.

After Apostle Rangel disappeared, Bishops Florentino Almeida and Samuel Mendiondo headed the church. They were designated archbishops in 1971. They revived *The Last Day's Messenger*. In the United States, because of the similarity of the church's name with that of the Gideons International, the Gideon Mission used the name Gilgal Evangelistic International Church. At the annual convention held in Jersey City, New Jersey in 1974, the church adopted its present name.

The church conducts work in twenty Latin American countries as well as Spain and Germany. Much of the work is in the Spanish language.

Membership: In 1984 the church reported 23 congregations, 75 ministers, 1,500 members in the United States, and 100,000 members worldwide.

Periodicals: *The Last Day's Messenger*, 636 N.W. 2nd St., Miami, FL 33128.

Latter Rain Pentecostals

★452★
BODY OF CHRIST MOVEMENT
% Foundational Teachings
Box 6598
Silver Spring, MD 20906

Along with the neo-Pentecostal movement of the 1960s, there deveoped what can be termed the Body of Christ movement, focused in the ministry of Charles P. Schmitt and Dorothy E. Schmitt of the Fellowship of Christian Believers in Grand Rapids, Minnesota. The basic idea is that God has moved among his people in each generation and has poured out his Spirit upon them in a vital manner. In the eighteenth century, this outpouring occurred through the Wesleyan revival, and in the early twentieth century, through the Pentecostal revival. In the late 1940s, the "Latter Rain" movement swept Canada. According to Schmitt, the outpouring on the present generation is the most momentous of all because this is the last generation and in it shall be manifest the full intent of God (I Cor. 4:1).

Initiation into the "mysteries" is through the baptism of the Holy Spirit. The central mystery of the church as the Body of Christ is that God is preparing a glorious church for himself. God is pouring out his Spirit in every denomination to bring forth the bride of Jesus Christ in this hour. The church as the Body of Christ is the very fullness of Jesus, who fills everything, everywhere with himself.

Doctrine, beyond the core of Pentecostal and Protestant affirmation, is not emphasized. The true basis of fellowship is in God and Jesus Christ. The Body of Christ Movement is organized on a family model, under the care of the responsible brethren (elders) and the ones possessed of spiritual gifts (I Cor. 12:11-14.)

The Body of Christ Movement originated in Grand Rapids, Minnesota. Fellowship Press was established and it has issued numerous pamphlets on a wide variety of topics. The Schmitts began a tape ministry and a home Bible study course, "Words of Truth and Life." From Grand Rapids, ministers were sent out to cities across the United States. Centers were rapidly established. In the early 1980s, the Schmitts moved their headquarters to the Washington, D. C. area where a strong following had developed. Camp Dominion in rural northern Minnesota is the scene of national gatherings during the summer.

Membership: In 1988 there were several hundred congregations and tens of thousands of people involved in the movement.

Periodicals: *Foundational Teachings*, Box 6598, Silver Spring, MD 20906.

★453★
BOLD BIBLE LIVING
International Headquarters
5774-132 A St.
Surrey, BC, Canada 98230

Alternate address: American headquarters: Box 2, Blaine, WA, 98230.

The Bold Living Society is the organization facilitating the worldwide ministry of evangelist/missionary Don Gossett. Gossett had been the editor of *Faith Digest*, the magazine of the T. L. Osborn Evangelistic Association. While editor, Gossett was also an evangelist who toured North America, holding evangelistic campaigns and working as a radio minister. During the 1950s, his desire to become a full-time radio evangelist grew, and in 1961 he moved to British Columbia and organized the Bold Living Society.

During the 1950s Crossett became a devoted student of the writings of the late E. W. Kenyon, an early radio evangelist on the West Coast, and founder of the New Covenant Baptist Church in Seattle. After his death, Kenyon's daughter continued to publish his books through the Kenyon Gospel Publishing Society in Fullerton, California. Gossett obtained a copy of Kenyon's *The Wonderful Name of Jesus* in 1952 and eventually obtained an entire set of his writings. Kenyon emphasized the power of the Word, the Bible, and the power of confessing that Word as a means of exercising faith and bringing God's promises into visible reality.

Gossett emerged in the 1970s as a major exponent of what has been termed the "positive confession" perspective, a popular emphasis within the larger Pentecostal community. He maintains the Bible is the Word of God, and that people need to affirm the Bible's truth. It is through the confession of the believers' lips that Jesus gives life and love. Gossett applies Biblical promises for physical healing and contends God will supply people's every need. Confession of negative states traps individuals in sickness and poverty.

Gossett's radio work began in Canada and reached out to the United States. In 1964 he began broadcasting from stations in Puerto Rico and Monte Carlo, and soon a second office was opened in Blaine, Washington. As the audience grew, he wrote and published *School of Praise*, a home Bible study course, and numerous books and booklets. Besides the two congregations in British Columbia which are affiliated with the society, Gossett has a world-wide ministry which takes him on evangelistic campaigns around the world; his radio show is aired in over 100 countries.

Membership: There are two congregations with an approximate membership of 100, both in British Columbia. There are affiliated churches in Barbados. In 1988 there were 4,000 partners who support the ministry scattered across the United States and 3,000 others in Canada and the West Indies.

Sources: E. W. Kenyon, *In His Presence*. Seattle, WA: Kenyon's Gospel Publishing Society, 1969; Don Gossett and E. W. Kenyon, *The Power of the Positive Confession of God's Word*. Cloverdale, BC: Don Gossett, 1981; Don Gossett, *What You Say Is What You Get*. Springdale, PA: Whitaker House, 1976; Don Gossett, *There's Dynamite in Praise*. Springdale, PA: Whitaker House, 1974; Don Gossett, *I'm Sold on Being Bold*. Springdale, PA: Whitaker House, 1979.

★454★
CHURCH OF THE LIVING WORD
Box 858
North Hollywood, CA 91603

The Church of the Living Word, often informally called "The Walk," was founded by John Robert Stevens (1919-1983), formerly a pastor with the International Church of the Foursquare Gospel. Because of Stevens' interest and involvement with the new Latter Rain Revival, the Church of the Foursquare Gospel defrocked him in 1949. A few months later he was admitted to the Assemblies of God. However, the Assemblies developed a growing dislike of the developing Latter Rain movement, and in 1951 also revoked Stevens' credentials. That year he opened an independent chapel in South Gate, California, the first congregation of the Church of the Living Word. The church gained strength quickly when a congregation of the Foursquare Gospel in Iowa, led by his father, affiliated with Stevens' new church.

The beliefs of the Latter Rain movement are similar to those of traditional Pentecostals, as represented by the Assemblies of God, differing more in emphasis than in doctrine. Those who became a part of the movement firmly believed that they were living at the end of time when God was giving new knowledge and gifts to restore the church to what it should be in the last days. Among the first things to be restored was the five-fold ministry of Ephesians 4:11; the church is headed by apostles, prophets, evangelists, pastors, and teachers, Stevens is considered to be an apostle and a prophet. Especially coming to the fore during the last days was the gift of prophecy (Acts 2). The Latter Rain and the Church of the Living Word have emphasized this role to bring forth the word of God in particular situations.

Through the Church of the Living Word, members believe God is rejecting Babylon and denominational Christianity, and restoring the Divine Order among his chosen last day remnant. Leadership will be exercised by his instruments. It is the duty of Christians to submit to that Order. As the Church of the Living Word moved into the New Divine Order, it developed a variety of ideas which have separated it from other Pentecostal groups. One such idea is termed "aggressive appropriation." Prayer, according to the church, is part of God's system of self-imposed limitation. God works through human beings who are consecrated to him, and who actively and aggressively appropriate God's promises and blessings. This appropriation will lead them above and beyond the Apostles and the Bible into the "greater works" mentioned in John 14:12.

The Church of the Living Word is organized as a fellowship of congregations tied together by their acceptance of the apostolic authority of John Robert Stevens and the ministering authority of those called to the five-fold ministry. A retreat center is located in Kalona, Iowa. Communication centers have been established in Panorama City, California and Des Moines, Iowa. An extensive tape ministry, consisting primarily of Stevens' sermons, functions through the church from four distribution centers in Virginia, Iowa, California, and Hawaii.

Membership: In the mid-1970s there were 75 congregations across the United States and an additional 14 congregations in Brazil, Canada, Germany, Ghana, Guam, Japan, Mexico, the Netherlands, the Philippine Islands, and South Africa.

Periodicals: *This Week*, Box 958, North Hollywood, CA 91603.

Remarks: As the Church of the Living Word has developed under the ministry of prophecy, many critics have complained that it strayed into occultic practices and doctrines which have denied basic Christian affirmations.

Sources: John Robert Stevens, *Living Prophecies*. North Hollywood, CA: Living Word Publications, 1974; *It Shall Be Called Shiloh*. North Hollywood, CA: Living Word Publications, 1975; John Robert Stevens, *The Lordship of Jesus Christ*. North Hollywood, CA: Living Word Publications, 1969; John Robert Stevens, *Baptized in Fire*.

North Hollywood, CA: Living Word Publications, 1977; John Robert Stevens, *Present Priorities*. North Hollywood, CA: Living Word Publications, 1968.

★455★
COMMUNITY CHAPEL AND BIBLE TRAINING CENTER
18635 8th Ave. S.
Seattle, WA 98148

Community Chapel and Bible Training Center grew out of the Charismatic movement of the late 1960s. Some individuals with a variety of denominational backgrounds began to meet in the home of Pentecostal minister Donald Lee Barnett for Bible study. The study led to the formation of a church in 1967. Meeting at first in members' homes, the group outgrew available facilities and in 1969 began construction of a church building. At about the same time a Bible college was begun. Within a decade the church facility, expanded to seat over a thousand, was inadequate, and in 1979 a new sanctuary with seating for 2,200 was completed. Enrollment in the Bible college grew to approximately 900. The center has a lengthy statement of faith which affirms belief in the authority and inerrancy of the Bible; God as Father and Creator; Jesus Christ as fully God and fully human; the Holy Spirit; the necessity of repentance; water baptism by immersion for the remission of sins; the Lord's Supper as a memorial feast; strict church order led by pastors, elders and deacons; tithing; divine healing for the body; the gifts of the Holy Spirit; and a premillennial eschatology. There is no clear affirmation of the Trinity. The center is led by the pastor, who has complete authority in spiritual matters. Administratively, the center is led by a four-member Board of Senior Elders. Over 125 people are on the paid staff of the center which includes the college, a Christian school (kindergartern through high school), a music program, recording studios, and a number of evangelical and social outreach ministries in the greater Seattle area. Members are encouraged to participate in one or more of the 150 active ministries. Community Chapel Publications has published a number of booklets by Barnett and a set of cassette tapes reflecting the center's music program.

Membership: In 1984 there were 2,800 members of the center in Seattle, and a number of affiliated congregations around the United States. Foreign work is conducted in Greece, the Philippines, Sweden, and Switzerland.

Periodicals: *Balance*, Community Chapel Publications, 18635 8th Ave. S., Seattle, WA 98148.

Remarks: During the early 1980s, Community Chapel faced a variety of widely-publicized charges from former members. These charges include accusations that Barnett asked members to shun the businesses of former members, that former longtime members suffered mental problems related to their association with the church and its understanding of demon possessions, and the disruption of

marriage relations due to the encouragement of close "spiritual connections" (which do not include any sexual liaison) between men and women apart from their spouses. The latter accusation is directly related to a church practice of dancing with one's spiritual connection during church services. Members of the center have staunchly defended the pastors and church leaders from such charges and from additional charges of leaders from other churches that the group is a "cult." Several lawsuits are currently under ajudication.

★456★
ENDTIME BODY-CHRISTIAN MINISTRIES, INC.
Miami, FL

The Endtime Body-Christian Ministries Inc. (a.k.a. the Body of Christ Movement and Maranatha Christian Ministries) was founded in the early 1960s by Sam Fife (d. 1979). A former Baptist minister, Fife became a Pentecostal after his involvement in the Latter Rain Movement, a Pentecostal revival movement which began in Canada in the late 1940s. Fife founded his organization in New Orleans, but soon moved to Miami where he had formerly worked as a contractor and singer. Fife's messages emphasized what he believed was the approaching end of the world. One sign of the end was the emergence of visions among Christians. In one vision, he was told that he would father a child who would be a great prophet. The woman designated as the mother was not his wife; however, with the consent of his wife and the church, he lived with her for a year, until he became convinced of the error of the vision.

Fife also called his members to prepare for the second coming of Christ by separating themselves from the world. They are in the process of preparing a perfected bride (i.e., church body) for Christ to find upon his return to earth. To accomplish this task, he organized a series of commuanl farms in the United States, Canada and Latin America. Many of the church members have sold their possessions and moved into these rural communities. The group also established a set of parochial schools for its children. The process of separation from the world led to the disruption of many families, especially where only one spouse was a strong member of the group. Also, the presence of single young adults in the group, often living at rather primitive (by middle class standards) levels, in the 1970s led to several deprogrammings and the focus of attention on the group by segments of the anti-cult movement.

Membership: Not reported. There were reported to be between 6,000 and 10,000 members at the time of Fife's death. Approximately 25 communal farms had been established.

★457★
GOSPEL HARVESTERS EVANGELISTIC ASSOCIATION (ATLANTA)
1521 Hurt Rd., S.W.
Marietta, GA 30060

The Gospel Harvesters Evangelistic Association was founded in 1961 in Atlanta, Georgia, by Earl P. Paulk, Jr. and Harry A. Mushegan, both former ministers in the Church of God (Cleveland, Tennessee). Mushegan is a cousin of Demos Shakarian, founder of the Full Gospel Businessmen's Fellowship International, while Paulk's father had been the General Overseer of the Church of God. Each man began a congregation in Atlanta. Gospel Harvester Tabernacle, founded by Paulk, moved to Decatur, an Atlanta suburb, and changed its name to Chapel Hill Harvester Church. The Gospel Harvester Chapel, begun by Mushegan, became Gospel Harvester Church, and in 1984 Gospel Harvester Church World Outreach Center, at the time of its move to suburban Marietta, Georgia. To traditional Pentecostal themes, inherited from the Church of God, the Gospel Harvesters have added an emphasis upon the message of the endtire Kingdom of God. According to Paulk, creation has been aiming at a time when God will raise up a spiritually mature generation who will be led by the Spirit of God speaking through his prophets. Given a clear direction from God, that generation, represented by the members of the Gospel Harvester Church and others of like spirit, will overcome many structures in society opposed to God's will.

Both congregations in the Gospel Harvesters Evangelistic Association have developed a variety of structures to make visible the kingdom. The churches support Alpha, a youth ministry; House of New Life, for unwed mothers (an alternative to abortion); a drug ministry; a ministry to the homosexual community; and the K-Center, a communications center.

The government of the Association is presbyterial, though the two senior pastors-founders have been designated bishops. They are members of the International Communion of Charismatic Churches, formerly the World Communion of Pentecostal Churches, that includes congregations in Brazil, Nigeria, and Jamaica. Bishop John L. Meares, pastor of the Evangel Temple in Washington, D.C. and head of the International Evangelical Church and Missionary Association, is also part of the Communion.

Membership: In 1984 there were two churches in the United States; the church in Marietta had 1,000 members, and the one in Decatur, 6,000.

Periodicals: *The Fire,* Gospel Harvester Church, 1710 DeFoor Avenue, NW, Atlanta, GA 30318; *Harvest Time,* Chapel Hill Harvester Church, 4650 Flat Shoals Road, Decatur, GA 30034

Remarks: In 1985 Bishop Paulk became the object of attack by popular (non-Pentecostal) evangelical writer, Dave Hunt. Hunt labeled Paulk one of a number of "seductive forces within the contemporary church." Paulk was included along with a number of popular pentecostal leaders including Oral Roberts, Kenneth Hagin, Kenneth Copeland and Fred Price. Hunt, one of several who have attacked Paulk's kingdom message, was quickly answered by Pentecostal leaders, who came to Paulk's defense.

Sources: Harry A, Mushegan, *Water Baptism.* Atlanta: Gospel Harvester World Outreach Center, n.d.; Earl Paulk, *Ultimate Kingdom.* Atlanta: K Dimensions Publications, 1984; Earl Paulk, *Satan Unmasked.* Atlanta: K Dimensions Publications, 1984.

★458★
INDEPENDENT ASSEMBLIES OF GOD, INTERNATIONAL
Current address not obtained for this edition.

Among the many independent Pentecostal churches that did not join the Assemblies of God in 1914, were congregations consisting primarily of Scandinavian immigrants, converts of the Scandinavian Pentecostal movement. Petrus Lewi Johanson of Stockholm and Thomas Ball Barrett of Oslo were the dominant figures in the Scandinavian Pentecostal movement. The Scandinavians were extreme congregationalists and believed that all discipline, even of ministers, should be vested in the local level.

In the United States, the extreme congregationalism worked for a while, but gradually loose federations began to develop. In 1918, a Scandinavian Assemblies of God in the United States, Canada and Other Lands was formed in the northwestern states. In St. Paul, Minnesota, in 1922, a fellowship of independent churches was formed. A third group, the Scandinavian Independent Assemblies of God, was formed around Pastor B. M. Johnson, who had founded the Lakeview Gospel Church in Chicago in 1911, and A. A. Holmgren, who published the *Scanningens Vittne,* a periodical for Scandinavian Pentecostals. In 1935, the latter group dissolved its corporation, and the three groups united to form the Independent Assemblies of God. They began to Americanize and to move beyond their ethnic exclusiveness.

In 1947-1948, there was a division in the Independent Assemblies of God over participation in the "Latter Rain" Movement, a revival that swept western Canada and which became known for extreme doctrine and practices in some phases. The words "Latter Rain" refer to the end of the world when God will pour out his Spirit upon all people. One group accepted the revival as the present movement of God, as God's deliverance promised in the Bible. This group, under the leadership of A. W. Rasmussen, became the Independent Assemblies of God, International. Missions are supported in seventeen countries around the world.

Membership: Not reported. In the mid-1970s there were approximately 300 congregations affiliated with the Assemblies.

Periodicals: *The Mantle.*

Sources: A. W. Rasmussen, *The Last Chapter.* Monroeville, PA: Whitaker House, 1973.

★459★
INTERNATIONAL EVANGELICAL CHURCH AND MISSIONARY ASSOCIATION
% Evangel Temple
610 Rhode Island Ave., N.E.
Washington, DC 20002

The International Evangelical Church and Missionary Association is a charismatic fellowship of churches formed in the early 1980s under the leadership of John Meares, pastor of Evangel Temple in Washington, D.C. Meares was raised in the Church of God (Cleveland, Tennessee), the nephew of the general overseer. After serving several Church of God congregations, Meares went to Washington, D.C., in 1955 to begin the Revival Center (soon renamed the National Evangelistic Center), a new Church of God outreach for the city. However, he soon encountered controversy within the Church of God because he had started an unlicensed ministry. This led to his disfellowshipping in May 1956. He continued his independent ministry, however, which emerged in new quarters as Evangel Temple in 1957. Membership of the integrated congregation was approximately two-thirds black.

In the early 1960s, Meares became aware of Bethesda Missionary Temple, one of the principle congregations of the Latter-Rain movement. From his observation of the life of the temple, he picked up a new emphasis on praise and the gift of prophecy which he introduced to Evangel Temple. This coincided with the heightened tensions of the civil rights movement which climaxed for Meares and the temple in the rioting that followed the assassination of Martin Luther King. Most of the white members withdrew, and Meares emerged in the early 1970s as the white pastor of a largely black church. Membership dropped to several hundred. The church slowly rebuilt, however, and in 1975 moved into new three million dollar facilities.

During his years in Washington, many independent Pentecostal pastors had begun to look to Meares for leadership and guidance. The International Evangelical Churches and Missionary Association emerged out of that relationship. In 1982, Bishops Benson Idahosa of Nigeria, Robert McAleister of Brazil, and Earl P. Paulk, Jr. of Atlanta, Georgia, all members of the International Communion of Charismatic Churches, consecrated Meares a bishop.

Over the years, Meares and Evangel Temple have become major voices in the Pentecostal community speaking to the issues of racism. Since 1984, Evangel Temple has become the site of an annual national Inner City Pastors' Conferences, attended primarily, but by no means exclusively, by black Pentecostal pastors from around the United States and Canada. More than 1,000 pastors attended the 1987 conference.

Membership: Not reported.

Sources: John Meares, *Bind Us Together.* Old Tappen, NJ: Chosen Books, 1987; Steve Haggerty, "A Spiritual Powerhouse," in *Charisma* 10, 10 (May 1985); John L. Meares, *The Inheritance of Christ in the Saints.* Washington, DC: Evangel Temple, 1984; *Evangel Temple's Thirtieth Anniversary.* Washington, DC: Evangel Temple, 1985.

★460★
LATTER-RAIN REVIVAL, INDEPENDENT CHURCHES OF THE
No central address.

Alternate address: Important centers: Faith Temple, 672 N. Trezevant, Memphis, TN 38112; Glad Tidings Temple, 3456 Fraser St., Vancouver, BC V5V 4C4; House of Prayer Church, Box 707, Springfield, MO 65801; Bethesda Missionary Temple, Box 4682, Detroit, MI 48234; Praise Tabernacle, Box 785, Richlands, NC 28574; Restoration Temple, 2633 Denver St., San Diego, CA 92110.

History. The Latter-Rain Movement emerged after World War II among Pentecostals who had come to believe that the Pentecostal Movement which had grown from the revival at Azusa Street in Los Angeles, California, earlier this century had reached a low ebb. The movement had divided into a number of warring factions, and worship had become dry and formalized. In February 1948, a spiritual revival brokeout at the Sharon Bible College, an independent Pentecostal school at North Battleford, Saskatchewan, headed by George Hawtin, a former minister with the Pentecostal Assemblies of Canada. The revival was characterized by the development of a number of doctrinal innovations and new practices, including the laying-on-of-hands for the reception of the baptism of the Holy Spirit, the five-fold ministry, a recognition of the importance of the Jewish feast of Pentecost and Tabernacles; a distrust of denominations and denominationalism; and the manifestation of the sons of God. There was also a renewed emphasis upon the gifts of prophecy and healing in contrast to the older Pentecostal churches where they had largely disappeared.

As the revival spread, ministers and leaders from the older churches came to Battleford to see what was occurring. Their news about the doctrinal emphases and the variant practices led to a break between the revival's leaders and promoters with the Pentecostal Assemblies of Canada and the Assemblies of God, the two largest

Pentecostal bodies in Canada and the United States respectively. Pastors and denominational officials who continued to participate in the revival and spread its doctrines were expelled from the Assemblies. Their break with the older Pentecostal bodies merely served to increase their dislike of denominational powers. Many of these became itinerate evangelists while others established independent congregations. These congregations rejected any formal denominational life. Many remained as simple small independent churches (frequently sharing a pastor with his secular job). Many of these new independent congregations, over subsequent decades, developed into a fellowship of associated congregations, and hence became, in effect, a new denomination. Included in this category would be the Body of Christ Movement, the Endtime Body-Christian Ministries, Inc., The Independent Assemblies of God, and the Church of the Living God. However, many congregations have remained free and independent through the last four decades. Together they form a distinct group of Pentecostal churches and will be the possible seedbed for new circles of fellowship. These congregations have developed an informal relationship through the sharing of publications, speakers, and various special events. Thus each church remains completely autonomous, keeping is own name and issuing its own literature, while relating to other congregations which grew out of the revival through support of locally promoted national conventions, camp meetings, shared publications, and missionary tours by prominent elders. Several hundred such independent congregations exist in North America, and form a circle of interlocking fellowship. A very few of the prominent centers are discussed below.

Major Beliefs. The Latter-Rain Movement accepted the basic beliefs of Pentecostalism. It did not so much reject any of the doctrines of the Assemblies of God and the Pentecostal Assemblies of Canada as it added to them and added in such a way as to create a new way of understanding the faith. Decisive for the movement was its understanding of history and of the present time being the final climax to history, i.e., the "latter days." Members of the movement view Christian history as a movement of disintergration and restoration. Following the apostolic era, the church began to fall away from the pristine nature of the original generations. That process gained ascendency through the Roman Catholic Church. However, beginning with Luther, God began a process of restoring the church. That process continued through John Wesley and the Methodists and more recently the Pentecostals. The Latter-Rain continues the Restoration process. The unique teachings and practices of the movement restore at least a remnant of the church to its destined state, the purity and holiness necessary for it to be the bride of Christ.

Most of the new ideas emerged during the original revival in North Battleford. Undergirding these new ideas as a whole was an interpretation of Isaiah 43: 18-19, which equated the "new things" mentioned in the verses with revelation yet to come. The new move of God included

the following: (1) the practice of laying-hands on people so that they could receive the baptism of the Holy Spirit and initiate the exercise of various gifts of the Spirit (I Corinthians 12:4-11). This practice contrasted sharply with the common practice in Pentecostalism to advise those seeking the baptism to tarry or wait upon God until it was given as God willed.

(2) The acceptance of the local church (as opposed to denominational structures) as the basic unit of church life. From Ephesians 4:11-12, the revival saw a divinely appointed church order in the five-fold ministry of apostles, prophets, missionaries (or evangelists), pastors, and teachers. The controversy surrounded the addition of apostles and prophets. The apostles were people who operated on a trans-local church context as divinely appointed leaders, as opposed to denominational executives. Prophets brought immediate inspired words of revelation to the congregation of believers. Almost from the beginning of the revival, the prophets spoke "directive prophecies," i.e., words understood as direct messages from God which offered particular advice and/or admonition to people and groups.

(3) The restoration of all nine gifts of the Spirit of I Corinthians 12. Through the Christian and Missionary Allaince, the gift of healing had been restored, and through the Pentecostal Movement, the gift of tongues. However, as the revival proceeded, all of the gifts, especially the gift of prophecy, began to operate.

(4) The modern fulfillment of the Jewish "feast of tabernacles." This teaching, ascribed to George Warnock, saw the three great feasts of Israel being fulfilled in the Church, the New Israel. The feast of Passover was fulfilled in Christ's death and resurrection. The feast of Pentecost was fulfilled in the creation of the Church and the giving of the Spirit. Yet to be fulfilled was the prayer of Jesus recorded in John 17:21 concerning the bringing together of the body of Christ free of spots and wrinkles.

(5) The idea of the manifested sons of God. Members of the movement believed that God would in the near future glorify individual people who would in turn be invested with authority to set creation free from its present state of bondage and decay. Those so prepared would be fit vessels as the bride of Christ.

Prominent Ministries. As is to be expected the Latter-Rain Movement spread first throughout Western Canada. Reg Layzell, pastor of Glad Tidings Temple in Vancouver, British Columbia, attended meetings at North Battleford in the summer of 1948, and in November invited Hawtin and others from Sharon to bring their message to his church. As a result, Glad Tiding Temple accepted the new truths and became a major center for dissiminating the message throughout the continent. Layzell authored several important books and developed a particular emphasis within the movement as a whole upon the praise of God as a special activity for believers. He was suceeded by B. Maureen Gaglardi as senior pastor.

The Bethesda Missionary Temple in Detroit, Michigan, was among the first congregations in the United States to join in the revival. When in November 1948, Hawtin and others from the school carried the Latter-Rain message to Glad Tiding Temple, Myrtle D. Beall, a pastor of the Assemblies of God, was present and became an enthusiastic supporter of the revival. Returning to Detroit, a revival brokeout in her church which attracted many future converts and leaders of the revival including Ivan Q. Spencer, head of the Elim Missionary Assemblies and Stanley Frodsham, prominent leader in the Assemblies of God. In 1949 Beall led in the construction of a larger church building which could seat 3,000 people. The new building was completed in time to encounter the first major attacks by the Assemblies of God on the Latter-Rain Movement and the church soon became independent. In 1951 Beall began the Latter Rain Evangel, which helped spread the Latter-Rain across the United States.

Today the Bethesda Missionary Temple is pastored by James Lee Beall who succeeded his mother as pastor. The church operates the Bethesda Christian Schools which provide education for first grade through high school. The church sponsors two annual festivals each spring and fall which bring many outstanding Pentecostal ministers to Detroit each year. Plans for a new sanctuary in Sterling Heights, a Detroit suburb, have been announced.

Among the oldest of Latter-Rain churches is Faith Temple in Memphis, Tennessee. The Rev. Paul N. Grubb and his wife, the Rev. Lula J. Grubb, were dropped from the ministerial list of the Assemblies of God in December 1949 (at the same time that Myrtle Buell was dropped, and they were possibly the first spokespersons for the revival in the south and has continued to head the church he founded almost forty years ago. He also established a bible school and sponsors an annual national convention each summer. He authored two influential books, *The End-Time Revival* and *Manifested Sonship*. Restoration Temple in San Diego, California, is pastored by Graham Truscott, and his wife, Pamela Truscott. Graham Truscott is from New Zealand, where he was raised a Methodist. He became a lay minister but while in college he heard about and then accepted the baptism of the Holy Spirit. He became a missionary to India in 1960. Upon his return to the United States he began Restoration Temple. Truscott is best known in the Latter-Rain circles as the author of *The Power of His Presence*, a lengthy treatment on the feast of tabernacles. The church distributes this book and others he has authored, as well as numerous cassette tapes on Latter-Rain or Restoration themes.

The House of Prayer Church was started in Springfield, Missouri, in the early 1960s by Bill Britton (1918-1986), a former Assemblies of God Minister. Following several years as a marine in World War II, Britton attended Central Bible College and in 1949 was ordained by the Assemblies. However, having become involved in the Latter-Rain revival, he left the Assemblies and denominationalism the following year. For the next decade he worked as an evangelist, during which time he speant one important semester as an instructor at the bible school operated by Faith Temple in Memphis. (Faith Temple was also an important early Latter-Rain congregation, led for many years by Paul Grubb.) While in Memphis, Britton developed his understanding of the "overcomers." He came to feel that the church would have to go through the times of tribulation in the last days, as opposed to many of his colleagues who believe that the church will be raptured out of the world before this last terrible time for the earth. Shortly after leaving the school, he also developed the idea of a plurality of leadership in the local church. He felt that the church should be headed by a group of elders who mutually submit to each other rather than by a single autocratic pastor. This idea was later instituted in his congregation.

Britton became a popular speaker and writer in Latter-Rain circles. Voice of the Overcomer, the literature ministry established even prior to the congregation, regularly distributes numerous tapes, books, and tracts. He also initiated a correspondence course, and Park Avenue Christian School, a Bible school for kindergarten through high school. Semiannual national conventions are held in March and October. The church supports missionaries in 10 countries. Since Britton's death, the family, particularly Britton's son Philip Britton, and the Voice of the Overcomer staff continued the evangelistic and pastoral work.

Praise Tabernacle in Richlands, North Carolina, was founded in 1978 by Kelley H. Varner (b. 1949), a close associate of the late Bill Britton. Varner is one of the best educated leaders in the Latter-Rain Movement having several graduate degrees and having been for seven years a former Bible school teacher. It was during the years he taught that he accepted the truth of the Restoration message and left his teaching position to become pastor of congregation. Varner has become one of the major advocates of the Latter-Rain emphases through his radio ministry and the broad distribution of numerous tapes (many of his radio show) and writings across the United States. He publishes an extensive catalog of tapes and books biannually.

Membership: There are several hundred congregations which have developed out of the Latter-Rain Movement in the United States and Canada, but no census of the membership has been attempted.

Educational facilities: Overcomer Training Center, Springfield, Missouri;

Periodicals: *Good News*, Praise Tabernacle, Box 785, Richlands, NC 28574; *Foibles, Fables and Facts*, Bethesda Missionary Temple, 7616 E. Nevada, Detroit, MI 48234.

Remarks: The Latter-Rain Movement was opposed almost from the beginning by the Assemblies of God and the Pentecostal Assemblies of Canada. In the 1980s, it has joined the list of groups attacked by the Christian counter-cult spokespersons and organizations. Of particular concern has been the doctrine of the manifested sons of God. Critics of the Latter-Rain have accused them of teaching that humans who enter into the sonship experience are considered essentially divine themselves, thus obscuring the distinction between creature and Creator, a vital part of orthodox Christian thought. Latter-Rain spokespersons deny any such attempt to assume the role of God, but state that sonship is an actual gaining of the image and likeness of Christ by members of the His church as stated in I Corinthians 15 :45-47.

Sources: Richard Michael Riss, *The Latter Rain Movement of 1948 and the Mid-Twentieth Century Evangelical Awakening*. Vancouver, BC: Regent College, M.C.St. thesis, 1979; Raymond G. Hoekstra, *The Latter Rain*. Portland, OR: Wings of Healing, n.d. [1950]; George R. Hawtin, *Pearls of Great Price*. Battleford, SK: The Author, n.d.; George H. Warnock, The Feast of Tabernacles . Springfield, MO: Bill Britton, n.d.; Myrtle Beall, *The Plumb Line*. Detroit, MI: The Latter Rain Evangel, 1951; Paul N. Grubb, *The End-Time Revival*. Memphis, TN: Voice of Faith Publishing House, n.d.; Graham Truscott, *The Power of His Presence*. San Diego, CA: Restoration Temple, 1969; K. H. Varner, *Prevail*. Little Rock, AR: Revival Press, 1982; Becky Britton Volz, *Prophet on Wheels*. Springfield, MO: Bill Britton, n.d., 10 Vols.; David Graham, *The Doctrine of Sonship, A Theological Investigation*. Springfield, MO: Bill Britton, n.d.

★461★
MARANATHA CHRISTIAN CHURCHES
Box 1799
Gainesville, FL 32602

History. Maranatha Christian Churches began in 1972 as a campus ministry. It founders were Bob Weiner, a former youth pastor for the Assemblies of God, and his wife, Rose Weiner. Bob Weiner had dropped out of Trinity College, the school of the Evangelical Free Church at Deerfield, Illinois, and joined the U.S. Air Force. However, a chance encounter with Albie Pearson, a former baseball player turned evangelist-pastor, led to his receiving the baptism of the Holy Spirit. Weiner finished his commitment to the Air Force and soon became involved with a coffeehouse ministry. With Bob Cording he formed Sound Mind, Inc. to evangelize youth, and in 1971 began to tour college campuses as an evangelist. He eventually settled at the Christian Life Center in Long Beach California. In 1972, he moved to Paducah, Kentucky, (where his wife's father was a minister in the United Methodist Church) and began a campus ministry at Murray State University.

As campus minister, Weiner sought to convert students and train them in the fundamentals of the Christian faith. While focusing on Murray State, he continued to travel as an evangelist and develop other ministries. By the end of the decade 30 Maranatha Campus Ministries had been established. As national ministries grew and members finished their college careers, Maranatha Campus Ministries became part of the larger work which was named Maranatha Christian Churches.

Beliefs. The doctrine and practice of Maranatha follow the common affirmations of Protestant Christianity and Penetcostalism, but have developed a few distinctives of practice. Weiner emphasizes a "scriptural pattern" for church organization based upon Ephesians 4:11, and attempts to build each center as a strong fellowship and training ground for practical discipleship. In previous years each center had a dorm in which converts could live while attending college, but that is no longer the case. General meetings of the fellowship are held weekly and most members also participate in small group fellowships. Prophecy is an important practice in Maranatha and is seen as ongoing confirmation of God's present activity in the church.

Organization. Maranatha's work is focused in campus ministry, and all the congregations are adjacent to a college or university. The Weiners have written a series of books published by Maranatha Publications, which are used as textbooks in the discipleship training work. Maranatha Leadership Training School, often featuring a variety of charismatic leaders not otherwise associated with Maranatha, offers more advanced training for people on a national basis.

There is also a world leadership conference every two years. In 1985, Maranatha began a satellite TV network show as a televised prayer meeting in which 60 churches, tied together for the broadcast, pray for specific requests phoned in by viewers.

Membership: In 1988, the churches reported 5,000 members, 150 churches (campus outreach locations), and 300 ministers in the United States. There was one Canadian center, work in 17 foreign countries, and 7,000 members worldwide.

Educational facilities: Maranatha Leadership Institute, Gainesville, Florida

Periodicals: *The Forerunner*, Box 1799, Gainesville, FL 32602

Remarks: During the early 1980s, Maranatha became the center of a variety of accusations centered around their intense program for training their new members. Many of these accusations proved unfounded and in other cases program adjustments made which have largely put the controversies in the past. Most importantly, a program of parent-student contact was broadly implemented thus reducing the problems which had arisen because of lack of knowledge by parents of Maranatha and the life shared by new members, most of whom are students.

Sources: Sherry Andrews, "Maranatha Ministries," in *Charisma* 7, 9 (May 1982); Bob Weiner and Rose Weiner, *Bible Studies for the Lovers of God*. Gainesville, FL: Maranatha Publications, 1980; Bob Weiner and Rose Weiner, *Bible Studies for the Life of Excellence*. Gainesville, FL: Maranatha Publications, 1981; Bob Weiner and Rose Weiner, *Bible Studies for a Firm Foundation*. Gaineville, FL: Maranatha Publications, 1980.

★462★
NEW COVENANT CHURCHES OF MARYLAND
804 Windsor Rd.
Arnold, MD 21012

The New Covenant Churches of Maryland is a fellowship of churches which emerged in the mid-1970s. The fellowship was originally centered upon the New Life Christian Center in Arnold, Maryland. Most notable among the leaders of New Life Christian Center is Robert Wright, a retired Naval officer and director of the center. He was instrumental in building the early association which, by 1977, included five congregations. He assumed the office of apostle (senior presbyter) for the affiliated churches and has engaged in a ministry of founding new churches and strengthening local churches who have joined the fellowship.

The New Covenant Church accepts the basic Pentecostal perspective, including the contemporary operation of the charismatic gifts (I Corinthians 12). Further, while accepting the main body of doctrine agreed upon by other trinitarian Pentecostal churches, the New Covenant Churches are among those groups which believe in restoring the fivefold ministry of apostle, prophet, pastor, evangelist, and teacher according to Ephesians 4:11, an emphasis which grew out of the Latter Rain Revival in the late 1940s.

The New Covenant Churches have been active in the development of Christian parochial schools. In 1983 these schools were removed from the Maryland Association of Christian Schools, the Maryland branch of the American Association of Christian Schools, an organization representing conservative evangelical church schools headed by fundamenatalist leaders. The schools were put out of the organization, a decision later accepted by the national organization, as a rejection of the Pentecostal doctrine of the supporting churches. In reaction, Wright has led in the formation of a National Federation of Church Schools.

Membership: In 1984, there were 24 congregations in the fellowship of churches.

Periodicals: *Koinonia*, 804 Windsor Rd., Arnold, MD 21012

Sources: Robert Wright, "Key Questions Concerning Apostles," in *People of Destiny Magazine* 2, 1 (January/February 1984).

★463★
PEOPLE OF DESTINY INTERNATIONAL
7881-B Beechcraft Ave.
Gaithersburg, MD 20879

Within the Charismatic Renewal Movement of the 1970s were many who received the baptism of the Holy Spirit and left the denomination in which they were raised for the independent Pentecostal movement represented by such organizations as the Full Gospel Business Mens Fellowship International. Larry Tomczak, a member of the Roman Catholic Church, received the baptism of the Holy Spirit in the early 1970s and became active within the Roman Catholic phase of the Charismatic Movement as a lay evangelist and author. As his participation in ecumenical aspects of the movement grew, Tomczak absorbed some ideas which had gained some accendancy from the Latter Rain Movement. Among those prominent ideas was that the Pentecostal Movement was not merely a renewal movement for the church, but had come as part of God's action to restore the fullness of correct Biblical church life in preparation for the last days. One facet of church life that was to be restored was the five-fold ministry mentioned in Ephesians 4:11--apostles, prophets, evangelists, pastors, and teachers. In this opinion, Tomczak was influenced by restorationists such as British apostle Arthur Wallis, author of *The Radical Christian* (1981), and Robert R. Wright, apostle of the New Covenant Church of Maryland.

In the early 1980s Tomczak, as leader of the independent Pentecostal church Covenant Life Church, located north of Washington, D.C. organized a group of pastors to carry through the restoration process by organizing as an apostolic team. The apostolic team was to be a group of men of proven ministry commissioned by a local church for the work of an apostle, establishing and offering oversight to new and old congregations in the process of transformation/restoration. He also founded People of Destiny International and *People of Destiny Magazine* as a "literary instrument" for the team.

It has been the opinion of the Apostolic Team led by Tomczak that most pentecostal churches have operated with only three-fifths of the "full-gospel," in that they have evangelists, pastors, and teachers, but neither prophets nor apostles, which, according to Ephesians 2:20, is the foundation of the church. Hence the team has concentrated upon the definition and establishment of their role in the churches which they have found or welcomed into their fellowship. Apostles are seen as builders, giving general oversight to the various church fellowships. Prophets are people who have a special gift from God to speak his word creatively and immediately to the church. It is in the exercise of the apostolic and prophetic offices that churches associate with People of

Destiny International. These differences have not excluded leaders of People of Destiny International, such as Tomczak and C.J. Mahaney, from being widely accepted in Charismatic ecumenical events.

Membership: In 1988, there were 17 churches related to the Apostolic Team led by Larry Tomczak.

Educational facilities: School of Ministry, Washington, D.C.; Cross-Cultural Training School, Pasadena, California.

Periodicals: *People of Destiny Magazine*, 7881-B Beechcraft Ave., Gaithersburg, MD, 20879; *People of Destiny Update*, 7881-B Beechcraft Ave., Gaithersburg, MD 20879.

Sources: Larry Tomczak, *Clap Your Hands*. Plainfield, NJ: Logos International, 1973; Larry Tomczak, *Divine Appointments*. Ann Arobr, MI: Servant Publications, 1986.

Other Pentecostals

★464★

ALPHA AND OMEGA CHRISTIAN CHURCH
96-171 Kamahamaha Hwy.
Pearl City, HI 96782

The Alpha and Omega Christian Church was formed in 1962 by Alezandro B. Faquaragon and other former members of the Pearl City Full Gospel Church. A congregation, primarily of Filipino nationals, was established in Pearl City. Four years later, a few members of the church returned to the Philippines and established a congregation at Dingras, Ilocos Norte. In 1968 a flood struck Pearl City and destroyed the meeting hall of the church. Many of the members withdrew after that event, though the church has survived and been rebuilt. The group is small, restricted to the Hawaiian Islands, and completely independent.

Membership: There are only two congregations, one in Hawaii and one in the Philippines.

Educational facilities: Alpha and Omega Bible School, Pearl City, Hawaii.

★465★

AMERICAN EVANGELISTIC ASSOCIATION
℅ World Evangelism
Box 660800
Dallas, TX 75266

The American Evangelistic Association was founded in 1954 in Baltimore, Maryland, by the Rev. John E. Douglas, its president, and seventeen other independent ministers. Many of these had been affected by the Latter Rain Movement which had begun in Canada in the late

1940s. It licenses independent pastors, mostly Pentecostals, but also some other conservtive evangelical ministers. Government is congregational, with congregations affiliating with the national headquarters. The Association is headed by a five-man executive committee. The Association was formed to promote doctrinal, ethical, and moral standards for independent ministers and churches, many of whom had come out of Pentecostal "denominations."

The American Evangelistic Association is missionary in outlook and oversees more than 1,000 workers outside of the United States, mostly in India, Korea, Hong Kong, and Haiti. Headquarters for the Association are in Baltimore, and for the missionary department, World Missionary Evangelism, in Dallas. Its periodical, *World Evangelism*, primarily an informational and promotional work for its many missions, circulates over a half-million copies The group sponsors the annual Christian Fellowship Convention.

Membership: Not reported. In 1968 there were a reported 2,057 ministers whose congregations had over 100,000 members.

Periodicals: *World Evangelism*, Box 660800, Dallas, TX 75266.

★466★

ASSOCIATION OF SEVENTH-DAY PENTECOSTAL ASSEMBLIES
℅ Elder Garver C. Gray, Chairman
4700 N.E. 119th St.
Vancouver, WA 98686

The Association of Seventh-Day Pentecostal Assemblies (incorporated in 1967) had existed as an informal fellowship of congregations and ministers since 1931. It is a very loose association headed by a chairman and a co-ordinating committee. The committee has a responsibility for joint vetures, but has no authority over local church programs or affairs. Doctrinally, the Association has taken a non-sectarian stance, affirming some minimal beliefs commonly held but leaving many questions open. No stance, for example is taken on the Trinity, though most ministers hold an non-Trinitarian position. Baptism is by immersion, but a variety of formulas are spoken. The Association believes in sanctification by the blood, Spirit and the Word, the baptism of the Holy Spirit, the Ten Commandments (each of equal worth) and the millennium. The association is congregationally organized. Each local church is autonomous and sets its own policy and mission. There is an annual association camp meeting. The association supports missions in Canada, Ghana, and Nigeria, and works in other countries through its congregations.

Membership: Not reported.

Periodicals: *The Hour of Preparation*, 4796 Lincoln Road, Blaine, WA 98230.

★467★
B'NAI SHALOM
Current address not obtained for this edition.

During the 1950s, Elder Reynolds Edward Dawkin, an elder in the Gospel Assemblies (Sowder), had several visions, among them one in which he was instructed to begin work in Palestine, looking toward the restoration of Israel and the end of the Gentile age which began in 1959. Following the death of William Sowders, founder of the Gospel Assemblies, the movement reorganized with a presbyterial form of government. Dawkins rejected that polity in favor of an apostolic order of the five-gifted ministry of Romans 13, the church led by pastor, teacher, evangelist, and prophets, and (over all) the apostle. Dawkins was accepted by his followers as an apostle and his revelations are highly revered.

Dawkins died in 1965 and was succeeded by Elder Richard Tate. He leads a core membership called "overcomers," members who have given three years in living wholly for the body of Christ or who give at least fifty-one percent of their time, money and life for the body. Membership has spread to Jamaica, the Netherlands, Hong Kong, India, Nigeria and Israel. The Peace Publishers and Company serves as the body's financial and publishing structure.

Membership: Not reported. In the early 1970s, there were 8 congregations in the United States and 11 outside, with a total membership of approximately 1,000.

Periodicals: *B'nai Shalom*, 6401 Eighth Place, Phoenix, AZ.

★468★
CHRIST FAITH MISSION
6026 Echo St.
Los Angeles, CA 90042

Christ Faith Mission continues the work begun in 1908 by Dr. Finis E. Yoakum, a Denver Methodist layman and medical doctor. In Los Angeles in 1895 following a near fatal accident, he was healed in a meeting of the Christian and Missionary Alliance, the holiness church founded by Albert Benjamin Simpson, which had been among the first modern churches to emphasize divine healing. As a result of his healing, he dedicated himself to the work of the Lord and began his efforts among the derelicts, outcasts and street people of the city. In 1908 he opened Old Pisgah Tabernacle in Los Angeles. He began to hold gospel services and to provide meals for the hungry. In 1909, he began to publish the *Pisgah Journal*.

Yoakum had a utopian spirit, and envisioned a series of communities that would embody the life of the early church. He opened Pisgah Home for the city's hungry and homeless; Pisgah Ark in the Arroyo Seco, for delinquent girls; and Pisgah Gardens in the San Fernando Valley for the sick. His most famous experiment was Pisgah Grande, a model Christian commune estalished near Santa Susana, California in 1914. The community attracted people from across the United States, including some who had formerly lived at Zion, Illinois, the community built by John Alexander Dowie, several decades earlier. Piscah Grande, already weakened by charges of financial mismanagement and unsanitary conditions, was thrown into further confusion by Yoakum's death in 1920. They eventually incorporated and took control of the Los Angeles property. They bought property in the San Bernadino Mountains and then moved to Pikesville, Tennessee.

In 1939 James Cheek, formerly the manager of Pisgah Grande, took control of the Pisgah Home property in Los Angeles and founded Christ Faith Mission, continuing the heritage of Yoakum's inner city work. He began a periodical. In 1972, the surving Pisgah group in Tennessee united their work with that of Cheek and merged their periodical into *The Herald of Hope*, which he published.

Under Cheek's leadership, the old Pisgah movement reborn as Christ Faith Mission has become a world-wide full gospel (Pentecostal) ministry. He continued the healing emphasis, and the present-day mission sends out prayer cloths to any sick person who requests them. The Mission operates the Christ Faith Mission Home near Saugus, California, and the Pisgah Home Camp Ground at Pikeville, Tennessee. A radio ministry is heard over stations in Los Angeles and Long Beach, California. Foreign language editions of *The Herald of Hope* are sent to mission stations in Korea, Mexico, India, Indonesia, and Jamaica.

Membership: Not reported. In 1984 several hundred attended the headquarters center in Los Angeles.

Periodicals: *The Herald of Hope*, Los Angeles, CA.

Sources: Paul Kagan, *New World Utopias*. Baltimore: Penguin Books, 1975.

★469★
CHURCH OF GOD BY FAITH
3220 Haines St.
Jacksonville, FL 32206

The Church of God by Faith was organized in 1919 by Elder John Bright and chartered in 1923 at Alachua, Florida. Its doctrine is like that of the Church of God (Cleveland, Tennessee) It believes in one Lord, one faith and one baptism, and in the Word of God as the communion of the body and blood of Christ. Members isolate willful sinners from the church. Polity is episcopal and officers consist of the bishop, general overseer, and executive secretary. A general assembly meets three times a year. Matthews-Scippio Academy (grades 1-12) was opened in 1963 in Ocala, Florida. Churches are located in Florida, Georgia, Alabama, South Carolina, Maryland, New Jersey, and New York.

Membership: In 1983, the church reported 4,500 members, 105 congregations, and 150 ministers.

Periodicals: *The Spiritual Guide*, 3220 Haines Street, Jacksonville, FL 32206.

★470★
CHURCH OF THE LITTLE CHILDREN
Current address not obtained for this edition.

The Church of the Little Children was formed in 1916 by John Quincy Adams (1890-1951) in Abbott, Texas, following his withdrawal from the Baptist ministry. In 1930, he transferred his headquarters to Gunn, Alberta. After his death, his widow succeeded him, remarried, and returned to the United States (Black Rock, Arkansas).

The church is "oneness" Pentecostal--denying the Trinity and identifying Jesus with the Father--and has picked up elements of doctrine from a number of traditions. The writings of Adams constitute the sole source of doctrinal teachings. The group practices foot-washing. Wine is used in communion. The Trinity, Sunday Sabbath, Christmas, Easter, shaving the male beard, wearing neckties, and using the names of the pagan deities for the days of the week are viewed as vestiges of pagan phallic worship. Conscientious objection is required and no alternative service allowed. Healing is emphasized and modern medicine is rejected. There is a major thrust toward acts of love for little children; members try to prevent any child from suffering want or hunger.

The church is headed by a superintendent. Organization is loose and informal. Congregations are located in Arkansas, Missouri, Nebraska, Montana, Wyoming, and Saskatchewan. Each congregation is quite small and meets in a home. Contact between congregations is by correspondence.

Membership: Not reported. In the early 1970s there were eight congregations and fewer than 100 members.

★471★
COLONIAL VILLAGE PENTECOSTAL CHURCH OF THE NAZARENE
Current address not obtained for this edition.

The Colonial Village Pentecostal Church of the Nazarene grew out of an independent congregation founded in 1968 by Bernard Gill, a former minister in the Church of the Nazarene. There followed an attempt to form the true church composed solely of "wholly sanctified holy people with the gifts of the Spirit operating among them," who then accepted as their goal and mission the reformation of the parent denomination.

Gill had begun to think of himself as "God's Prophet of the Latter Rain," and he received numerous revelations directly from God, as did one of the members, Mescal McIntosh. These were published in a periodical, the *Macedonian Call* in 1974. In the July 3rd issue, a resurrection was predicted. Two weeks later, Gill died. On August 11 a letter to readers of the *Macedonian Call* announced the belief of Gill's faithful followers that the prophecy obviously applied to their pastor, and that they were waiting in faith.

Membership: Not reported. No recent information has been received and the present status of the Church is unknown.

★472★
EVANGELICAL BIBLE CHURCH
2444 Washington Blvd.
Baltimore, MD 21230

The Evangelical Bible Church was founded by the Rev. Frederick B. Marine in 1947. The doctrine is similar to that of the Assemblies of God discussed earlier in this chapter, but great emphasis is placed on the three baptisms for New Testament believers--the baptism into Christ when a person is "born again," water baptism, and Spirit baptism. The church teaches that any doubtful practice that is not forbidden in the New Testament should be left to individual judgment. There are definite statements on meat, drinks, observing the Sabbath, and dressing for show. The church teaches conscientious objection and is against worldly organizations. A pretribulation, premillennial eschatology is taught.

The polity is congregational and there is an annual convention of both ministers and laity. Officers of the church include the general superintendent, the assistant general superintendent, and the general secretary. There are four orders of ministers-- novice, deacon, evangelist, and ordained elder. Foreign missions are conducted in the Philippines where the Church is known as the Evangelical Church of God.

Membership: Not reported. In 1960 there were four churches (three in Maryland and one in Pennsylvania) and 250 members.

★473★
FAITH ASSEMBLY
Wilmot, IN 46590

Faith Assembly was founded by Hobart E. Freeman (1920-1984), originally a minister with the Southern Baptist Convention. Among other things, Freeman began to criticize the Baptists for the celebration of Christmas and Easter, which he felt were Pagan holidays. In 1959 he entered Grace Theological Seminary at Winona Lake, Indiana, the seminary of the Fellowship of Grace Brethren Churches, which he joined. After receiving his doctorate in 1961, Freeman joined the faculty to teach

Old Testament. He became increasingly critical of the Brethren Church, especially on the issue of holidays, and in 1963 was dismissed from the seminary and excommunicated from the Fellowship of Grace Brethren Churches. Fellowship meetings held in Freeman's home became the Church at Winona Lake, Indiana. It soon moved to Claypool, Indiana. The initial beliefs of the church were similar to those of the Brethren, though they espoused a concept of closed worship.

In 1966, in Chicago, Freeman experienced the baptism of the Holy Spirit. He began to read the works of popular charismatic leaders such as Kenneth Hagin, Kenneth Copeland, and John Osteen, as well as those of the late E. W. Kenyon. He also met Mel Greide, who owned a large barn near North Webster, Indiana, which was converted into a church hall. From 1972 to 1978 Faith Assembly, as the church had been renamed, met at "Glory Barn." After a split with Greide, Freeman moved the assembly to Warsaw, Indiana until a facility could be built at Wilmot. During the 1970s, Freeman began to write many books and booklets which circulated through the larger charismatic movements and he frequently spoke at charismatic conventions. His books and tapes led to the formation of home groups around the Eastern half of the United States, with a concentration in the Midwest.

The beliefs of Faith Assembly are similiar to those of the Assemblies of God, differing more in emphases than in doctrine. Freeman taught what is popularly called "positive confession" or "Faith-formula theology." Freeman, like other faith-formula teachers, taught that when genuine faith is exercised by the believer and accompanied by a positive confession of that faith, anything is possible, especially physical healing. Unlike such faith-formula teachers as Kenneth Hagin or Kenneth Copeland, Freeman taught that medicine was Satanic and he forbade members from using the services of doctors. Assembly members remove seat belts from their cars and do not take immunization shots or use medicines. He also emphasized a rigid behavioral code which included personal separation from smoking, alcohol, drugs, and popular entertainment such as movies. Members do not borrow money. Young adults are counseled to not work at careers in law, medicine, insurance, or pharmacology. Abortion was also forbidden, and natural childbirth recommended.

Membership: There are approximately 2,000 members of the main church in Wilmot, Indiana and an estimated 15,000 in an unknown number of other congregation in 20 states. There are also members in Canada, Australia, Switzerland, and Germany.

Remarks: During the 1970s, family members of people associated with Faith Assembly congregations began to complain of its disturbing family relations. Several deprogrammings occurred. In 1983 a major controversy erupted around the Faith Assembly when charges were made that a number of people, many of them children,

had died of medically treatable ailments. In 1984 several parents were convicted of child neglect and reckless homicide, and Freeman was indicted on felony charges for responsibility in the death of an assembly member's child. He died before going to trial.

Sources: Hobart E. Freeman, *Positive Thinking & Confession*. Claypool, IN: Faith Publications, n.d.; Hobart E. Freeman, *Charismatic Body Ministry*. Claypool, IN: Faith Publications, n.d.; Hobart E. Freeman, *Deeper Life in the Spirit*. Warsaw, IN: Faith Publications, 1970; Hobart E. Freeman, *Angels of Light?*. Plainfield, NJ: Logos International, 1969; Rodney J. Crowell, *The Checkbook Bible: The Teachings of Hobart E. Freeman and Faith Assembly*. Maimisburg, OH: The Author, 1981.

★474★

FULL GOSPEL DEFENDERS CONFERENCE OF AMERICA

Current address not obtained for this edition.

The Full Gospel Defenders Conference of America is a small Pentecostal body with headquarters in Philadelphia. Its emphasis is on evangelism and Christ's authority as manifested by the miracles and signs.

Membership: Not reported.

★475★

FULL GOSPEL MINISTER ASSOCIATION
East Jordan, MI 49727

The Full Gospel Minister Association is a fellowship of Pentecostal ministers and churches believing in the infallibility of the Bible, the Trinity, the fall of man and his need for redemption in Christ, the necessity of holy living, and heaven and hell. Members are conscientious objectors to war. The group sees ministry as being two-fold: the evangelism of the world and the edifying of the body of Christ and the "confirming of the Word with Signs Following and evidence of the power of God." The Association meets annually and elects officers. It issues credentials for both churches and ministers.

Membership: Not reported.

★476★

GLAD TIDINGS MISSIONARY SOCIETY
3456 Fraser St.
Vancouver, BC, Canada

The Latter Rain Movement, a revival movement within the larger Pentecostal movement, began in 1948 in a bible school in North Battleford, Saskatchewan. Among the first places which leaders of the new movement were invited to speak was the Glad Tiding Temple in Vancouver, British, Columbia, where Reg Layzell pastored. Layzell became an enthusiastic supporter of the revival and the Temple became a major center from which the revival spread around the continent. The Glad Tidings Missionary Society began as an extension of the Glad Tidings Temple of Vancouver, British Columbia. Over the years, other congregations affected by the Latter Rain (in Canada and the state of Washington) became associated witht the Temple through it. It has become a primary religious body itself. Mission work is conducted in Africa, Taiwan, and the Arctic.

Membership: Not reported. In the 1970s there were eight churches, three in Washington and five in Canada.

★477★
GOSPEL ASSEMBLIES (JOLLY)
Current address not obtained for this edition.

In 1952, Elder Tom M. Jolly became pastor of the Gospel Assemblies (Sowders) congregation in St. Louis, succeeding Dudley Frazier. In 1965, Jolly led supporters to separate from the older, larger Gospel Assemblies group. Under his leadership there has been a marked tendency to centralized congregations in or near major urban areas, followed by the centralization of funds in preparation for the purchase of land upon which the congregations can settle away from the evil influences of contemporary cities. Twice yearly, members gather for pastoral conferences, fellowship meetings and youth rallies. Doctrine follows that of the parent body. The number of congregations (originally twelve) had more than doubled in the first five years.

Membership: Not reported. In 1970 there were approximately 30 congregations and 4,000 members.

★478★
GOSPEL ASSEMBLIES (SOWDERS/GOODWIN)
Gospel Assembly Church
7135 Meredith Dr.
Des Moines, IA 50322

History. William Sowders (1879-1952) was one of the early Pentecostal leaders in the Midwest. He was brought into the movement through the labors of Bob Shelton who had established work in Olmstead, Illinois. In 1912, Sowders, a former Methodist, was converted and received the baptism of the Holy Spirit on a gospel boat which Shelton was operating on the Ohio River. In 1914, Sowders began preaching at various locations, finally settling in Evansville, Indiana, in 1921.

In 1923, Sowders conducted his first camp meeting at Elco, Illinois. Here he began to introduce the distinctive teachings that were to separate him from the main body of Pentecostals and lead to the emergence of what became known as the Gospel of the Kingdom movement or the Gospel Assembly Churches movement. Sowders developed his ideas in the context of the debates between the trinitarian Pentecostals and the Apostolic or Oneness Pentcostals, whose ideas denying the traditional doctrine of the Trinity had been spread through the Midwest by

Thomas Garfield Haywood, founder of the Pentecostal Assemblies of the World. Sowders proposed a middle position and suggested that there were two persons in the Godhead, God the Father, a Spirit being, and Jesus the Son, a Heavenly Creature. The Holy Ghost was not a person, it was the essence or Spirit of God which filled all space. Since the Son possessed the same name as the Father, God's name was Jesus. Jesus was the name given to the family of God in Heaven and in earth. Baptism was, therefore, in the name of the Father, Son and Holy Spirit, i.e., Jesus. He also emphasized that the formula for baptism was not as important as the action, that baptism become an action done in Jesus' name and for his sake.

In 1927, Sowders relocated in Louisville, Kentucky, where he lived for the rest of his life. In 1935, he purchased a 350-acre tract near Shepherdsville, Kentucky, which became the Gospel of the Kingdom Campground, a place for camp meetings and annual ministerial gatherings. Estimates vary, but as many as 200 ministers and 25,000 members in 31 states were associated with the movement at the time of Sowders' death in 1952.

Following his death there were attempts by several ministers to assume leadership and several schisms emerged. The movement continued, however, as a loose fellowship of ministers who pastored independent gospel assemblies. Among these men was Lloyd L. Goodwin, a young minister at the time of Sowders passing, whose parents had been among the early converts of Sowders' ministry. In 1963, Goodwin moved to Des Moines, Iowa, to pastor the Gospel Assembly Church, a congregation of less than 30 members. Over the next decade he built it into a large stable congregation. In the late 1960s, due to his missionary activities, new congregations were started in Minneapolis, Minnesota, and Salem, Oregon. In the early 1970s, Goodwin began to encounter tension with the larger fellowship of Gospel of the Kingdom ministers who rejected some of the ideas which Goodwin believed had been revealed to him by God through his study of the scriptures. The break with the fellowship came in 1972.

After the break with the larger fellowship, a new movement began to grow around Goodwin beginning with those few ministers and congregations who sided with him. In 1973, he outlined a six-point program to his congregation in Des Moines. It included the development of the local assembly, the presevation of Goodwin's work in print and sound media, and the sending of ministers to found other assemblies both in the United States and abroad. In 1974, the Gospel Assembly Christian Academy, a Christian elementary school, was opened. The following year foreign work was initiated in Toronto, Canada, and Poona, India. A book and tape ministry was launched in 1977. Goodwin has written a number of substantial volumes which detail his distinct Bible teachings, especially on eschatological matters. A radio ministry begun on one station in 1981 had grown by 1987 to 17 stations that reached most of the eastern half of the United States and the West Indies.

Beliefs. Apart from the distinctive ideas about the Godhead first articulated by Sowders, the Gospel Assemblies have a lengthy statement of faith which affirms many of the tradition evangelical Christian beliefs in the authority of the Bible, creation, the fall of humanity, the vicarious substitutionary atonement of Christ, water baptism, and the imminent second coming. It is the belief of the movement that Christ will come while some who are alive today are still living. The ordinace of holy communion is also recognized and observed.

Organization. The Gospel Assemblies is described as a fellowship of ministers and saints around the world, where no church is organized above the local level, and yet where each assembly is in fellowship with all, and all acknowledge and are part of each in the fellowship. The churches recognize five offices in the church. First, apostles establish the work throughout the body of Christ. According to the Gospel Assemblies, "There is not another office in the ministry as authoritative as that of the apostle. The apostle stands next to Christ." Goodwin is such an apostle. Second, the prophet exhorts, edifies, and comforts. Third, the evangelists preach the news of salvation. Fourth, the pastors shepherd the saints. Fifth, the teachers instruct the church in doctrine. The five offices are not appointed, but recognized as possessed by some. A single individual may hold several of these offices. Appointed to handle the affairs of the local church are deacons and elders (or bishops). There are regular conventions of the churches around the country, the main convention being held at Des Moines each May.

Membership: Not reported. In 1970, there were 90 congregations and approximately 10,000 members. Gospel assemblies in fellowship with the Gospel Assembly Church in Des Moines can now be found across the United States (including Hawaii), Canada, and a number of foreign countries.

Periodicals: *The Gospel of Peace*, 7135 Meredith Dr., Des Moines, IA 50322.

Sources: *The Former Days.* Des Moines, IA: Gospel Assembly Church, n.d.; *Gospel Assembly, Twenty-Five Years, 1963-1988.* Des Moines, IA: Gospel Assembly Church, 1988; Lloyd L. Goodwin, *Prophecy Concerning the Church.* Des Moines, IA: Gospel Assembly Church, 1977. 2 Vols.; Lloyd L. Goodwin, *Prophecy Concerning the Resurrection.* Des Moines, IA: Gospel Assembly Church, 1976; Lloyd L. Goodwin, *Prophecy Concerning the Second Coming.* Des Moines, IA: Gospel Assembly Church, 1979; *Ministers' Address Directory.* Norfolk, VA: Gospel Assembly Ministers' Fund, 1970.

★479★
GOSPEL HARVESTERS EVANGELISTIC ASSOCIATION (BUFFALO)
Current address not obtained for this edition.

A second Pentecostal body, identical in name to the church headquartered in Atlanta and completely separate in organization, is the Gospel Harvesters Evangelistic Association in Buffalo, New York, founded in 1962 by Rose Pezzino. No information on doctrine or polity is available. Foreign work has been started in Manila and India.

Membership: Not reported. There are two congregations, one in Buffalo and one in Toronto. There are individual believers in the South. In the mid-1970s, there were an estimated 2,000 adherents.

★480★
GRACE GOSPEL EVANGELISTIC ASSOCIATION INTERNATIONAL INC.
(Defunct)

The Grace Gospel Evangelistic Association International, Inc. was formed in the mid-1930s by Pentecostals of a Calvinist (predestinarian) theological background who rejected the Arminian (free will) theology of the main body of Pentecostals. The association was organized congregationally. By the early 1970s the association had approximately 70 ministers and missionaries, and foreign congregations could be found in Canada, Jamaica, Colombia, Formosa, Japan, and India. A periodical, *Grace Evangel*, was published. In the late 1980s, however, the association was disbanded and many of the formerly affiliated congregations merged into other pentecostal groups or became independent churches.

★481★
INTERNATIONAL CHRISTIAN CHURCHES
2322-22 Kanealii Ave.
Honolulu, HI 96813

The International Christian Churches, founded in 1943 by Rev. Franco Manuel, is a Pentecostal group formed by former members of the Disciples of Christ Church in Hawaii. Members consider themselves "Disciples by Confession and Pentecostal by Persuasion." They accept the Pentecostal doctrines and place emphasis on the life in the Spirit.

In Honolulu, where there is" a single congregation consisting mainly of Filippino-Americans. There are, however, an additional seven churches in the Philipines. The church functions on the loose congregational polity typical of the Disciples of Christ.

Membership: Not reported. In the 1970s there was one congregation with several hundred members.

★482★

INTERNATIONAL EVANGELISM CRUSADES
14617 Victory Blvd.
Van Nuys, CA 91411

The International Evangelism Crusades was founded in 1959 by Dr. Frank E. Stranges, its president, and Revs. Natale Stranges, Bernice Stranges, and Warren MacKall. Dr. Stranges has become well-known as president of the National Investigations Committee on Unidentified Flying Objects and for his claims that he has contacted space people. The International Evangelism Crusades was formed as a ministerial fellowship to hold credentials for independent Pentecostal ministers. As a denomination, it is loosely oranized as an association of ministers and congregations and unhampered by a dictating central headquarters.

The doctrine of the organization is similar to the Assemblies of God. A Canon of Ethics is stressed, the breaking of which constitutes grounds for expulsion from the fellowship.

Membership: In 1984 the International Evangelism Crusades reported forty congregations and 125 ministers in the United States and a worldwide membership of 350,000. Associated foreign congregations can be found in 57 countries.

Educational facilities: The International Evangelism Crusades formed the International Theological Seminary, in Van Nuys, California. Three seminaries serve the congregations in Asia: Heavenly People Theological Seminary, Hong Kong; International Christian Seminary of South Korea; and International Theological Seminary of Indonesia.

Periodicals: *IEC Newsletter*, 14617 Victory Boulevard, Van Nuys, CA 91411.

Sources: Frank N. Stranges, *Like Father-Like Son*. Palo Alto, CA: International Evangelism Crusades, 1961; Frank E, Stranges, *My Friend from Beyond Earth*. Van Nuys, I. E. C. Inc, 1960; Frank E. Stranges, *The UFO Conspiracy*. Van Nuys, CA: I.E.C. Publishing Co., 1985.

★483★

INTEGRITY COMMUNICATIONS (AND RELATED MINISTRIES)
Box Z
Mobile, AL 36616

In the midst of chaos in the emerging pentecostal/charismatic movement of the early 1970s, a group of experienced pastor/leaders stepped forward with a proposed solution. They suggested that submission, discipline, and respect for law and order were needed, and that the movement stood under a divine mandate to develop a program for discipleship and the development of Christian maturity along Biblical principles. They

suggested that the New Testament norm was that each believer become directly accountable for others as a shepherd or spiritual guide that would demonstrate the Christian life. This concept became popularly known as discipling/shepherding.

Leading proponents of the discipling/shepherding concept were Charles Simpson, a former minister with the Southern Baptist Convention, Bob Mumford, former Dean of Elim Bible Institute, Ern Baxter, formerly a colleague of healer William Branham, Derek Prince, an independent leader of a radio ministry, John Poole, pastor of a church in Philadelphia, and Don Basham, a former minister with the Christian Church (Disciples of Christ). In 1970 these six men made a personal covenant with each other and began the task of making disciples who could, in turn, become shepherds engaged in making disciples. In their many travels they established local presbyteries of elders who became leaders of congregations related to the six ministers. These elders then fulfilled roles as apostlic leaders for those congregations. (The relationship between the local congregational elders and the leaders in Fort Lauderdale has been referred to as a "translocal" relationship.) Simpson, Mumford, Baxter, Prince, and Basham then founded Good News Church in Fort Lauderdale, Florida and began Christian Growth Ministries. A magazine, *New Wine*, disseminated their teachings. Numerous books and tapes were produced which dealt with various aspects of church life and Christian growth. While working together, some of the original group also developed independent ministries under different names, such as Bob Mumford's Life Changers.

In 1975 the issues raised by the group became a matter of intense controversy within the larger charismatic community, and major steps were taken to resolve the differences. Critics were concerned over the abuse of authority which occurred in the shepherding relationship; shepherds interfered in the personal affairs of those whom they were leading. In the more extreme cases, anti-cultists attempted deprogrammings of people in congregations which were organized around the shepherding principles. Several meetings between the leaders of Christian Growth Ministries and other Charismatic movements resulted in the resolution of the many misunderstandings which had grown out of rumors and unverified accusations. Differences on the shepherding principle remained, however.

In 1978 Christian Growth Ministries and *New Wine* were moved to Mobile, Alabama. At that time, Derek Prince, who had served as chairman of the board, stepped down in favor of Simpson. Simpson initiated a new congregation, Gulf Coast Covenant Church, and Christian Growth Ministries became Integrity Communications. Leaving the Fort Lauderdale work in local hands, Basham, Mumford, and Baxter joined Simpson in Mobile. Prince remained in Fort Lauderdale as head of his own Derek Prince Ministries. As early as January 1975, following a visit by Simpson to Costa Rica, a Spanish-speaking congregation was established and elders were appointed. Christian Growth Ministries immediately initiated *Vino Nuevo*, the Spanish edition of *New Wine*. By 1980 it was being sent to believers in fifteen countries.

In 1984 Derek Prince announced his withdrawal from Integrity Communications. Among his reasons, he cited his disagreement with the opinion that every Christian should have a personal human pastor, and the practice of one pastor overseeing another translocally.

It has been the stated goal of the leaders of Integrity Communications not to allow the congregations asociated with it, or the elders who derive authority from them, to develop into a "denomination." However, those churches and congregations have formed a distinct grouping within the larger Pentecostal community. In 1986, the four remaining leaders of Integrity Communications decided to decentralize their ministries as a means of stopping a trend toward "denominationalism." With this decision, Baxter moved to San Diego, Mumford to San Rafael, California, and Basham to Cleveland. *New Wine* was discontinued and replaced with *Christian Conquest*, edited by Simpson, who has remained in Mobile, Alabama. The group continues to meet periodically.

Membership: In 1986, *New Wine* had a circulation of 55,000, though its audience went far beyond the members of the church.

Periodicals: *Christian Conquest*, Box Z, Mobile, AL 36616.

Sources: *Vintage Years*. Mobile, AL: New Wine Magazine, 1980; Charles Simpson, *A New Way to Live*. Greensburg, PA: Manna Christian Outreach, 1975; Don Basham, *Ministering the Baptism of the Holy Spirit*. Monroeville, PA: Whitaker Books, 1971; Don Basham, *A Handbook on Holy Spirit Baptism*. Monroeville, PA: Whitaker Books, 1969; Bob Mumford, *Take Another Look at Guidance*. Plainfield, NJ: Logos International, 1971.

★484★
LIGHTHOUSE GOSPEL FELLOWSHIP
Current address not obtained for this edition.

The Lighthouse Gospel Fellowship is a Pentecostal church founded in 1958 by Drs. H. A. Chaney and Themla Chaney of Tulsa, Oklahoma. There are a set of beliefs held in common by ministers and members. The fellowship is trinitarian. It believes in the virgin birth, the bodily resurrection of Jesus, baptism of the Holy Spirit evidenced by speaking in tongues, the laying on of hands for the confirmation of ministry and imparting of the gifts of the Spirit. However, the group also conceives of itself as nonsectarian and hence home to a variety of views on less essential beliefs.

Membership: Not reported.In the 1970s there were approximately 100 congregations and 1,000 members.

★485★
JESUS PEOPLE CHURCH
2924 Rahn Way
St. Paul, MN 55122-2329

The Jesus People Church grew out of a "discipleship ministry" led by Dennis Worre, Roger Vann, and four other young men who created a Christian home in order to become better established in the Christian life. Worre and Vann led weekly Bible study meetings for what became formally known as Disciple Homes, when a girl's home was added a year later. As the ministry grew, a church building was purchased for Sunday services and, with fifty charter members, Jesus People Church begun. The church grew steadily through the 1970s and by the early 1980s two Sunday services were required to hold the congregation. Over 7,000 received the monthly bulletin, and a number of smaller churches began in the St. Paul-Minneapolis area.

The Jesus People Church is Pentecostal in belief. Its statement of faith affirms belief in the Bible as infallible and authoritative, the Trinity, the Deity of Christ, healing from the redemptive work of Christ on the cross, the present-day reality of the baptism of the Holy Spirit as recorded in Acts 2, and the resurrection.

The Jesus People Church has created a variety of outreach programs. Worre, a former actor, organized the Academy of Christian Theatre Sciences which puts on periodic professional drama for the public. Jesus People Institute is a lay educational program conducted through the week. A radio show, "Today's Walk in the Spirit," is heard over several area stations. The church owns a retreat center, Shepherd's Inn, located ninety miles north of Minneapolis, and operates Hesed and Fishnet, ministries to high school and junior high students. Foreign missionaries are supported in Canada, Germany, Haiti, Mexico, the Philippines, South Africa, and Thailand. There is also a missionary in Hawaii, and a domestic mission among Cambodian refugees.

Membership: In 1984 the church reported 550 members in Minneapolis, served by six ministers.

Educational facilities: Jesus People Institute, Minneapolis, Minnesota.

Periodicals: *Come to Life*, 2924 Rahn Way, St. Paul, MN 55122.

Remarks: The Jesus People Church suffered a major setback in 1983 when Dennis Worre admitted to several indiscretions with women. Worre was asked to step aside from his leadership role, though he soon returned to active duty as senior pastor. The indiscretions did not include adultery.

★486★

THE NEVERDIES
Current address not obtained for this edition.

Known locally in the communities of West Virginia as the Church of the Living Gospel or the Church of the Everlasting Gospel, the Neverdies are Pentecostals who believe in immortality not only of the soul but also of the body. The soul, they believe, returns to earth in a series of reincarnations until it succeeds in living a perfect life. At that point, the body can live forever. The origin of the group has been lost, but among the first teachers was Ted Oiler, born in 1906, who in 1973 was still traveling a circuit through the mountains of Virginia and North Carolina. The congregations are rather loosely knit, held together by their acceptance of what is a rather unusual doctrine for the mountain area. Among the leaders is Rev. Henry Holstine of Charleston, West Virginia.

Membership: Not reported.

★487★

LIBERTY FELLOWSHIP OF CHURCHES AND
MINISTERS
2732 Old Rocky Ridge Rd.
Birmingham, AL 35216

The Liberty Fellowship of Churches and Ministers was organized in 1975 in Pensacola, Florida by Ken Sumrall and twenty other ministers. Sumrall, a former pastor in the Southern Baptist Convention, received the baptism of the Holy Spirit in February 1964. The following month he organized Liberty Baptist Church (later Liberty Church) as a congregation for Spirit-filled Baptists. At first the work grew slowly, but membership increased markedly in 1966, the year the college began adjacent to the church. In 1972 land was purchased on the edge of Pensacola, and a building complex was constructed. During the 1970s, other independent charismatic pastors who saw the need of oversight for themselves and their congregations began searching for a proper structure. In that search, they were influenced by other Pentecostal leaders who had been influenced by the Latter-Rain Movement. Such leaders as Bill Britton of Overcomers Fellowship in Springfield, Missouri, believed the church was properly led by a five-flood ministry of apostles, evangelists, prophets, pastors, and teachers (Ephesians 4:11-12).

The fellowship's doctrine is close to that of the Assemblies of God, including belief in the triune God, salvation through Christ, two ordinances (baptism and the Lord's Supper), divine healing, the present-day operation of the gifts of the Holy Spirit (I Corinthians 12), and the baptism of the Holy Spirit as an immediate possibility for the believer.

The fellowship is governed by a presbytery headed by the president. The first president, Sumrall, is considered the apostle of the fellowship. He will serve in that capacity until he dies or retires. The presbytery ordains and appoints pastors to local churches and within its membership the entire five-fold ministry is represented. Local congregational affairs are administered by elders and deacons elected by the congregation and confirmed by the presbytery.

Membership: Congregations within the fellowship are scattered throughout the South.

Educational facilities: Liberty Christian College, Pensacola, Florida.

Sources: Ken Sumrall, *New Wine Bottles*. Pensacola, FL: Liberty Creative Press, 1976; Ken Sumrall, *Practical Church Government: Organized Flexibility*. Pensacola, FL: The Author, 1982.

★488★

UNITED CHRISTIAN CHURCH AND
MINISTERIAL ASSOCIATION
Box 700
Cleveland, TN 37311

The United Christian Ministerial Association was founded in 1956 by the the Rev. H. Richard Hall as an association of independent Pentecostal ministers. The local church in Cleveland, Tennessee, was formed in 1972 at which time the name of the organization was changed to United Christian Church and Ministerial Association. Doctrinally the church is described as fundamental and pentecostal.

The association is headed by Hall and a board of directors. Ministerial training is offered for resident students through the United Christian Academy and for nonresident students though a correspondence institute. The association offers exhorter and ordination licenses to all charismatics who feel called to preach in any one of 16 categories including apostles, bishops, pastors, teachers, missionaries, and ministering through the various gifts of the Spirit as outlined in I Corinthians 12. There is an annual minister's convention in Cleveland during which one day is set aside for the ordination of ministers and one for graduation for students of the United Christian Academy.

Membership: In 1988, the association reported more than 12,000 licensed and ordained ministers and 83 affiliated congregations.

Educational facilities: United Christian Academy, Cleveland, Tennessee; United Christian Bible Correspondance Institute, Cleveland, Tennessee;

Periodicals: *Shield of Faith*, Box 700, Cleveland, TN 37311.

Sources: Patsy Sims, *Can Somebody Shout Amen!* New York: St. Martin's Press, 1988.

★489★
UNITED EVANGELICAL CHURCHES
Current address not obtained for this edition.

The United Evangelical Church was formed in 1960, one of the first structural responses to the neo-Pentecostal revival. It is made up especially of those ministers and laymen from mainline churches who, since their baptism with the Holy Spirit, have not felt free to remain in their mainline churches. As a fellowship, they hope to avoid some of the evils of institutionalism, namely, the excessive control of man that prevents control by the living Spirit of God. Because of its origin, the church continues to be open to charismatics who choose to remain in their own churches.

The tenets of faith of the United Evangelical Church profess belief in the Bible as the Word of God, the Trinity, the virgin birth and resurrection of Christ, the inability of man to save himself, salvation in Christ, regeneration by the Holy Spirit, the present ministry of the Holy Spirit which empowers Christians and manifests itself in gifts and ministries, and the judgment of Christ.

The church is governed by an executive council and there is a conference of the church every two years. Churches are divided into three regions-Western, Central, and Eastern. Churches (in 1970) were found in twenty-four states. Foreign work was located in India, Korea, Formosa, Hong Kong, Singapore, Japan, Ghana, Kenya, Jamaica, Guatemala, El Salvador, Colombia, Mexico, Costa Rica, Honduras, and Iran.

Membership: Not reported.

★490★
UNIVERSAL CHURCH, THE MYSTICAL BODY OF CHRIST
Current address not obtained for this edition.

The Universal Church, the Mystical Body of Christ, is an interracial Pentecostal group which emerged in the 1970s. It is distinguished by its belief that in order to serve God freely, members must come out of a corrupt government, society, and churches of this land, and establish a separate government on another continent where a theocratic system can be constructed. Only then, can perfection exist in society. Members call upon all Christians to join them. They believe that these are the end-times and that God is calling together his 144,000 mentioned in Revelation.

The church has a strict moral code and disapproves of short dresses for women, long hair for men, and women preachers and elders. Women cover their heads during worship. The group fasts, uses wine and unleavened bread at the Lord's Supper, and believes in baptism for the remission of sins, divine healing, speaking in tongues, and the unity of the church. The Universal Church is headed by Bishop R. O. Frazier. Members do not think of themselves as another denomination, but as the one true body of Christ.

Membership: Not reported.

Periodicals: *The Light of Life Herald*, Box 874, Saginaw, MI 48605.

★491★
UNIVERSAL WORLD CHURCH
123 N. Lake St.
Los Angeles, CA 90026

The Universal World Church was formed in 1952 by former Assemblies of God minister Dr. O. L. Jaggers, its president. It differs from other Pentecostal bodies primarily in organization and its doctrine of the sacrament. Under Jaggers are twenty-four elders who form the governing executive body. Their role is taken from Exodus and from Revelations 4:4, 10; 5:6-8. The elders' custom of wearing robes and golden crowns is based on these texts. There are 144 bishops, one for each state of the United States and the rest for the various countries of the world. Elders and bishops must be graduates of the University of the World Church.

One is received into the church by baptism following repentance and faith in Jesus Christ as personal Lord and savior. The reception is the first process of new birth and new creation. Following the new birth, one may receive the genuine baptism with the Holy Spirit of resurrection power and fire, a baptism called the second process. After the second process, one is allowed to partake of the third, the transubstantiation communion which is offered once every three months. At that time twenty-four elders, by faith in Christ and the power of God, perform the miracle of changing bread and wine into the sacred body and blood of the Lord Jesus Christ. This act is done before the golden altar of the church in Los Angeles.

The World Church has come under considerable attack for its flamboyance, which some feel smacks more of showmanship than religion. In spite of these attacks, however, the church has grown. There were 11,315 members of the mother church in 1969. There were approximately 800 congregations in the United States and around the world. The 3,170 ministers are organized into the World Fellowship of the World Church. The World Church schools operate on the elementary and high school levels, and the university on the college level. All ministers are university graduates.

Membership: Not reported. In 1969, the Church reported 11,315 members in the mother church in Los Angeles. There were 800 congregations in the United States and the world, with 3,170 ministers organized into a World Fellowship of the World Church. These figures have been questioned by many who claim that the movement consists merely of the single congregation in Los Angeles.

Educational facilities: University of the World Church, Los Angeles, California.

Section 8

European Free-Church Family

An historical essay on this family is provided beginning on page 49.

German Mennonites

★492★
BRETHREN IN CHRIST
% Dr. R. Donald Shafer
Box 245
Upland, CA 91786

The Brethren in Christ derive from the informally organized River Brethren who formed in the intense religious atmosphere of Lancaster County, Pennsylvania, in the 1770s. The Brethren, mennonites influenced by the Dunker tradition, accepted triune immersion. The first immersions were by Jacob Engel and Peter Witmer for each other. The original group of fourteen met in the upper room of Engel's home at Lobata, Pennsylvania, and had a love feast. The Anabaptist practice of a beard without moustache was continued.

At a later meeting, organization was effected and Jacob Engel was elected bishop. Triune immersion was a central feature. Doctrine was drawn from the Anabaptist-Brethren consensus, but with a strong emphasis on evangelism. The consensus remained until the mid-nineteenth centu ry when three groups emerged from the original one because of doctrinal and accommodationist differences. The three groups were the Brethren in Christ, the Old Order (or Yorker) River Brethren, and the United Zion Church.

The Brethren in Christ was the last of the three groups to organize, but represented the largest wing of the River Brethren. The name was adopted in 1863 although the church was not incorporated until 1904. The church through its continued evangelistic thrust, has spread across the United States and Canada.

The Brethren in Christ is congregationally organized, but six regional conferences and a General Conference serve to carry out churchwide programs. A Board for World Missions overseas missions in India, Japan, Nicaragua, Zimbabwe, Zambia, Cuba, Great Britian, Columbia and Ven ezuela. Evangel Press, Nappanee, Indiana, is the church's publishing house. Two retirement centers, Messiah Village, in Mechanicsburg, Pennsylvania and Upland Manor, in Upland, California are supported by the Church. The Brethren are members of the National Association of Evangelicals and the Christian Holiness Association, and the Mennonite Central Committee.

Membership: In 1987 the Brethren reported 15,535 members in the United States and 2,689 in Canada, 400 congregations and 435 ministers.

Educational facilities: Messiah College, Grantham, Pennsylvania; Niagara Christian College, Fort Erie, Ontario.

Periodicals: *Evangelical Visitor*, Nappanee, IN 46550.

Sources: Carlton O. Wittlinger, *Quest for Piety and Obedience*. Nappanee, IN: Evangel Press, 1978; *Manual of Doctrine and Government*. Nappanee, IN: Evangel Press, 1968; *Manual for Christian Youth*. Nappanee, IN: Evangel Press, 1959; Paul Hostetler, ed., *Perfect Love and War*. Nappanee, IN: Evangel Press, 1974.

★493★
CHURCH OF GOD IN CHRIST, MENNONITE
420 N. Wedel
Moundridge, KS 67107

John Holdeman, a member of the Mennonite Church, had, at the age of 21, an intense religious experience which changed his life. He felt that he had been called to preach and, following his baptism, began a period of serious study of the Bible and of the writings of Menno Simons. As a result of his studies, he came to believe that his church had departed from the true way. Holdeman emerged as a young rebellious prophet and visionary. His self-assertion at such an age (his early 20s) and his visions caused controversy.

He began to hold meetings at his home, and spread his concerns through the writing and publishing of his major books. He felt that the Mennonite Church had grown worldly and departed from the true faith; it did not rigidly screen candidates for baptism to insure that they had been born again; the avoidance of the excommunicated was neglected, and members took part in political elections. He also objected to choosing ministers by lot, especially since he had been called to the ministry through his visions. He also felt it was wrong to receive money on loans. While he found much agreement with his observations, few would join him in reformative action.

Growth of his church was slow until the late 1870s when he encountered the German-speaking immigrants who had just arrived from Russia. In 1878 the first church was built, and the first conversion of many people to his church occurred in the Lone Tree Community of McPherson County, Kansas. Holdeman became the first minister to successfully introduce revivalism into a Mennonite framework . Revivals accounted for much of the rapid growth of his movement in the late nineteenth century, especially in the immigrant communities in Kansas and Manitoba. A slow and steady growth period followed through the early twentieth century, followed by a rapid expansion in both North America and abroad after World War II. The greatest concentration of members is in Kansas and Manitoba.

The Church follows the Anabaptist-Mennonite doctrinal concensus with strong emphasis upon repentance and the new birth, a valid believer's baptism, separation from the world, excommunication of unfaithful members, a humble way of life, nonresistance, plain and modest dress, the wearing of the beard for men and devotional covering for women.

The Church is headed by a delegated General Conference which meets when the need arises. It is composed of all ministers and deacons (all unsalaried) and lay people. Its decisions are binding on the congregations. It oversees Gospel Publishers, the publishing arm of the church, and three mission boards. There are congregations in 21 states, 5 Canadian provinces, Brazil, Belize, the Dominican Republic, Guatemala, Haiti, India, Mexico, Nigeria, and the Philippines. Most North American congregations have an elementary parochial school attached to them. The Church supports one hospital, eight nursing homes, four children's homes, and one outpatient home for American Indians.

Membership: In 1987 the church reported 9,233 members in the United States and 3,120 in Canada. There were a total of 13,732 members worldwide in 100 congregations and 105 mission stations.

Periodicals: *Messenger of Truth*, 420 N. Wedel, Moundridge, KS 67107; *Christian Mission Voice*, 420 N. Wedel, Moundridge, KS 67107.

Sources: Clarence Hiebert, *The Holdeman People*. South Pasadena, CA: William Carey Library, 1973.

★494★
CONGREGATIONAL BIBLE CHURCH
% Congregational Bible Church
Marietta, PA 17547

The Congregational Bible Church was formed in 1951 at Marietta, Pennsylvania, as the Congregational Mennonite Church. The name was changed in 1969. The original members of the churdh were from six congregations of the Mennonite Church. The statement of faith is at one with Mennonite belief, but includes a statement on anointing the sick and emphasizes separation from the world. The group has an aggressive evangelistic ministry. The church is organized with a congregational government as a fellowship of like-minded churches. The bishop or pastor is the chief officer.

Membership: Not reported.

★495★
CONSERVATIVE MENNONITE FELLOWSHIP (NON-CONFERENCE)
Box 36
Hartville, OH 44632

The Conservative Mennonite Fellowship (nonconference) was the result of a protest movement in the main branches of the Mennonite Church in the mid-1950s. The conservatives were concerned that Mennonites were conforming to the world (e.g., women were neglecting to cover their hair or were letting it fall down to their shoulders instead of being tied into a knot), that Mennonites were not resisting the military (e.g., the young men were joining the Army as noncombatants instead of staying out of the Army), and that Mennonites were becoming involved in civil affairs (e.g., they were voting or holding office or becoming policemen). The conservatives were also concerned about the growing acceptance of neo-orthodox theology in Mennonite circles. The Fellowship was formed in 1956. It added to the prior disciplinary standards (the Apostles' Creed, the Dordrecht Confession and the Schleitheim Confession) the Christian Fundamentals, which emphasize strict discipline and separation from the world. These were adopted at a fellowship meeting in 1964.

Membership: Not reported. In 1967 there were 23 congregations with 980 members and an additional 50 cooperating congregations with 2,400 members.

★496★
MENNONITE CHURCH
528 E. Madison St.
Lombard, IL 60148

The largest of the Mennonite bodies is the Mennonite Church. It is the oldest and was for many years the only

Mennonite body. Most other U.S. Mennonite groups derive from it. Organization within the church was slow since each congregation tended to be autonomous. In 1727, a conference of Pennsylvania congregations was called to consider, among other things, an English translation of the Confession of Dordrecht. Other conferences were called in particular regions to deal with controversy. Formal conferences began to emerge in the nineteenth century. At present, a biennial General Assembly meets as an advisory body for the entire church. District conferences counsel and provide resources at a local level.

Developing autonomously, but cooperating with the conferences, have been various service and mission agencies. The Mennonite Board of Missions now supervises a program that includes North American volunteer ministries (that engage more than 80 volunteers), media ministries, and church development. Overseas ministries engage 114 workers in 22 countries. Herald Press is the publishing arm of the church and operates under the Publication Board. The Board of Education oversees the several colleges and seminaries. Other services are provided by the Board of Congregational Ministries and the Mennonite Mutual Aid Board. A General Board coordinates and oversees the five program boards.

While still holding to Anabaptist separatist practices—pacifism, a disciplined membership, believers' baptism—the church has endeavored to minister to urban society. It carries on a vast mission program with congregations on every continent. In the United States, home mission work is conducted among American Indians, Jews, the Spanish-speaking, Asian refugees, and the deaf.

Membership: In 1985 the Church reported 91,167 members, 989 churches and 2,399 ministers.

Educational facilities: Goshen Biblical Seminary, Elkhart, Indiana; Eastern Mennonite Seminary, Harrisonburg, Virginia; Eastern Mennonite College, Harrisonburg, Virginia; Goshen College, Goshen, Indiana; Rosedale Bible Institute, Irwin, Ohio; Hesston College, Hesston, Kansas; Conrad Grebel College, Waterloo, Ontario.

Periodicals: *Gospel Herald*, Scottdale, PA 15683; *Mennonite Historical Bulletin*, Goshen, IN 46526; *Mennonite Quarterly Review*, Goshen, IN 46526.

Sources: J. C. Wenger, *The Mennonite Church in America*. Scottdale, PA: Herald Press, 1966. *An Invitation to Faith*. Scottdale, PA: Herald Press, 1957; James E. Horsch, ed., *Mennonite Yearbook*. Scottdale, PA: Mennonite Publishing House, issued biennially.

★497★
OLD ORDER (OR YORKER) RIVER BRETHREN
Current address not obtained for this edition.

The Old Order (or Yorker) River Brethren separated in 1843 from their parent church, the River Brethren (now known as the Brethren in Christ), protesting what they saw as laxity in matters of nonconformity to the world and non-resistance to the military. The group was led by Bishop Jacob Strickler, Jr., of York County, Pennsylvania (hence the nickname). It was joined in the 1850s by a Franklin County group headed by Bishop Christian Hoover, who had been expelled for being "too orthodox."

The Old Order River Brethren remain the smallest of the River Brethren groups, having only four congregations, all in southeastern Pennsylvania. Three small independent congregations have split off at various times in disputes over modes of transportation. All worship is conducted in home, not in churches. The Old Order River Brethren are also agriculturists.

Membership: Not reported. In 1963 there were 4 congregations and 340 members.

Sources: Laban T. Brechbill, *Doctrine, Old Order River Brethren*. The Author, 1967.

★498★
OLD ORDER (REIDENBACH) MENNONITES
% Henry W. Riehl
Rte. 1
Columbiana, OH 44408

During World War II, the issue of the draft was of great concern to the Old Order Mennonites. There was a consensus that all the draft-age youths should be conscientious objectors. However, among the Old Order (Wenger) Mennonites there developed a group who felt that prison, not alternative service (medical work, etc.) should be the only course in reaction to the draft. This group further insisted that those youths who accepted alternative service should be excommunicated.

This group was not supported by the majority of the Wengerites. Thirty-five members of the group began to build a separate meeting house near Reidenbach's store in Lancaster County (hence the name). They remain the most conservative of the Pennsylvania Mennonites. They still use candles instead of coal oil for lighting. Rubber tires on carriages are prohibited. They are the only Pennsylvania group which currently opposes the use of school buses.

Among the Reidenbach Mennonites there are a number of specific regulations to keep them separate from the world. Farm equipment is restricted; for example, manure spreaders are not allowed. Children go only to the one-room school and not beyond the elementary grades. The group has only one congregation.

305

Membership: Not reported. There is only one congregation, in Lancaster County, Pennsylvania.

★499★
OLD ORDER (WENGER) MENNONITES
% Henry W. Riehl
Rte. 1
Columbiana, OH 44408

Among the Old Order (Wisler) Mennonites of Southeastern Pennsylvania, several schisms have developed over the continuing issue of accommodation to change. In the 1930s, the use of the automobile on a limited basis was advocated by Bishop Moses Horning. Bishop Joseph Wenger rejected the idea, believing automobiles should not be used for either occupational transportation or coming to worship. Wenger's group became the more conservative wing of the Old Order Mennonites. The group holds no evening services and uses only German in the pulpit. Jail, rather than alternative service, is advocated for boys of draft age.

Membership: Not reported. There are an estimated 1,000 members in southeastern Pennsylvania.

★500★
OLD ORDER (WISLER) MENNONITE CHURCH
% Bishop Henry W. Riehl
Rte. 1
Columbiana, OH 44408

In the 1860s the Yellow Creek congregation of the Mennonite Church, located near Elkhart, Indiana, found itself caught between two vocal leaders. Daniel Brenneman demanded a progressive policy and the adoption of such innovations as English preaching, Sunday schools, protracted meetings, and four-part singing. He was opposed by Jacob Wisler, who opposed all innovations and deviations. Wisler began to place under the ban anyone deviating from the past. Wisler's arbitrary manner of enforcing his ideas resulted in a church trial and he was removed from his office. He then took his followers and formed a new congregation in 1870.

During the following decades, other churches of like perspective were founded and then these united with Wisler's group. A group in neighboring Medina County, Ohio, was the first. A Canadian group headed by Bishop Abraham Martin from Woolwich Township, Waterloo County, Ontario, who opposed speaking in English, sunday schools, evening meetings , "falling"-top buggies, and other modernisms, formed a separate church and later allied itself with the Wislerites. In 1901 followers of Bishop Jonas Martin and Gabriel D. Heatwole formed a church; that church later joined the Wislerites. Bishop Jonas Martin had been the leader of the Mennonite Church in Lancaster County, Pennsylvania, until controversy arose about installing a new pulpit in the church. Martin opposed the new pulpit because he was

against innovations, and with a third of the congregation he left the Mennonite Church. A separate group of Mennonites in Rockingham county, Virginia, led by Gabriel D. Heatwole, joined Martin's group and then this church joined the Wislerites.

As a group, the Old Order Mennonites remain among the most conservative in dress, forms of worship, and social customs. They are very close to the Amish in their thinking, but meet in church buildings instead of homes and do not wear beards.

Membership: Not reported. In 1972 they reported 38 congregations, 8,000 members and 101 ministers.

★501★
REFORMED MENNONITE CHURCH
% Bishop Earl Basinger
1036 Lincoln Heights Ave.
Ephiata, PA 17522

The oldest splinter from the Mennonite Church that still survives dates from 1812. It grew out of a previously existing separatist congregation headed by Francis Herr, who had been expelled from the church for irregularities in a horse trade. After Herr's death, his son John Herr, never a religious man, took up his father's faith, became convicted of sin, was baptized, and soon rose to a position of leadership. He was then chosen bishop. John Herr and his associates immediately began to issue a set of pamphlets charging the Mennonite Church with being worldly and corrupt. They complained of laxity in enforcing discipline and separation from the world. Based on Herr's ideas, the Reformed Mennonite Church was created.

In relation to the Mennonite Church, the Reformed Mennonites emphasize the exclusive claims of their particular faith, practices and community. All who are not Reformed Mennonites are considered to be of the world. The Reformed Mennonites practice the ban and avoidance rigidly. They dress plainly and tend to live in plain surroundings. Membership is located primarily in southeastern Pennsylvania.

Membership: Not reported. In 1988 there were 12 churches, 21 clergy and approximately 500 members in the United States and several hundred in Canada.

Sources: *Christianity Defined.* Lancaster, PA: Reformed Mennonite Church, 1958; John F. Funk, *The Mennonite Church and Her Accusers.* Elkhart, IN: Mennonite Publishing Company, 1878; *The Reformed Mennonites, Who They Are and What They Believe.* Lancaster, PA: Reformed Mennonite Church, n.d. Robert Bear, *Delivered Unto Satan.* Carlisle, PA: the Author, 1974;

★502★

STAUFFER MENNONITE CHURCH

% Bishop Jacob S. Stauffer
Rte. 3
Ephrata, PA 17522

Jacob Stauffer, a minister in the Mennonite Church at Groffdale, Pennsylvania, was the leader of a group in a progressive-conservative split. The issue was the ban, which Stauffer and colleague Joseph Wenger of the Old Order (Wenger) Mennonites believed should be applied more strictly. About forty members withdrew from the Mennonite Church, demanding that when the ban was used there should be no communion between the church and the offender.

The Stauffers have continued in their conservative ways. They are part of the horse and buggy culture but, unlike the Amish, are cleanshaven and will ride trains on long trips. They prefer the one-room school and refrain from politics (even voting). Though never large, and hurt by one major schism, the group has grown steadily by maintaining a rather high birth rate.

Membership: Not reported. There are three congregations (Lancaster County, Pennsylvania; Snyder County, Pennsylvania and St. Mary's County, Maryland) and approximately 750 members.

★503★

UNITED ZION CHURCH

% Bishop Alvin H. Eberly
Rte. 2
Denver, PA 17517

The United Zion's Children originated in 1855 following the expulsion of Bishop Matthias Brinser from the River Brethren (i.e., the Brethren in Christ) for building and holding services in a meetinghouse. Other than the use of church buildings, there were no doctrinal differences. An annual conference is held but the government is congregational. The United Zion's Children was strengthened within a few years by some churches formed by Henry Grumbein and Jacob Pfautz. These groups accepted Brinser because of a revelation, but remain a separate unit within the church. They constitute one of three districts which send representatives to the annual conference. Mission work is supported through the Brethren in Christ. One home for the aged is maintained.

During the twentieth century several attempts have been made to improve the relationship between the United Zion Church and the Brethren in Christ, and even to look toward a future reunion. In 1967 the Brethren in Christ passed a resolution asking for the forgiveness of the United Zion Church for the action of the Church's council in 1855 and the continued lack of humility on their part which has kept the two groups apart. The next year the United Zion Church issued a formal statement offering complete forgiveness. These resolutions became the basis for cooperative action on the mission field and in higher education. A member of United Zion Church currently sits on the board of Brethren in Christ-founded Messiah College.

Membership: In 1983 there were 13 churches, 929 members, and 20 ministers.

Educational facilities: Messiah College, Grantham, PA.

Periodicals: *Zion's Herald.*

Sources: Carlton O. Wittlinger, *Quest for Piety and Obedience.* Nappanee, IN: Evangel Press, 1978.

★504★

WEAVER MENNONITES

Current address not obtained for this edition.

The one schism affecting the Stauffer Mennonite Church was occasioned by the issue of the strictness of the ban. In 1916, the son of aged Bishop Aaron Sensenig married outside the faith. The girl was received into the Stauffer Mennonite Church but later returned to her earlier heritage. The church was split over the strictness of the ban to be applied to the girl. The lenient group, led by Sensenig and John A. Weaver, left and began a new congregation and constructed a meeting house near New Holland, Pennsylvania.

Membership: Not reported. There is one congregation of approximately 60 members.

★505★

WEAVERLAND CONFERENCE OLD ORDER (HORNING OR BLACK BUMPER) MENNONITES

Current address not obtained for this edition.

Bishop Moses Horning (1870-1955) established a liberal wing of the Old Order (Wisler) Mennonites. His followers use automobiles, but only for necessary purposes. The car must be black and without "frivolous" trim. Most of the members cover the chrome with black paint to avoid further ostentation.

Membership: Not reported. There are five congregations, all located in southeastern Pennsylvania, and approximately 1,700 members.

Russian Mennonites

★506★
CONSERVATIVE MENNONITE CHURCH OF ONTARIO
Current address not obtained for this edition.

Among the Mennonite population of Canada in the early twentieth century, three tendencies arose. Some Mennonites, most of whom had migrated from Europe, sought means of accommodating the new situation of living in Canada. Others resisted any form of accommodation. Many, however, took a "middle-of-the-road" position, accommodating where necessary, and only in ways that did not threaten the faith. This latter group was generally called the Old Mennonites. In Ontario, the Old Mennonites were of Swiss and southern German origin. During the 1950s part of the Old Mennonite faction, some of whom were members of the General Conference Mennonite Church, decried the departure of fellow members and leaders from traditional standards of faith and practice. They disapproved of liberal views on biblical inspiration and moral latitude. Bishops Moses H. Roth and Curtis C. Cressman became the spokespersons of the traditionalist position. They and the ministers and congregations which followed them were expelled in 1959, whereupon they formed the Conservative Mennonite Church of Ontario.

In 1952 the Conference adopted a Constitution and a Faith and Practice which affirmed the Dordrecht Confession of 1632 and the "Christian Fundamentals," which were adopted by the General Conference in 1921. Much of the attention of the Conference was directed to a definition of the believers' stance in relation to secular society which has been spelled out in a seies of prohibitions. Members are prohibited from participation in war (including any type of military service), politics (including voting and jury duty), and membership in worldly organizations (such as secret societies, life insurance societies, etc.). Members refrain from strong drink, tobacco, worldly amusements (such as movies and organized sports), television, jewelry (such as wedding bands and gold watches), and remarriage after divorce. Members may use radios, but may not listen to programs which are not conducive to holiness. All are called to simple modest dress, which for women includes uncut hair and veiled heads. Churches do not use instrumental music, nor do they allow floral displays at weddings or funerals.

Membership: In the 1970s there were 8 congregations with less than 300 members.

★507★
FELLOWSHIP OF EVANGELICAL BIBLE CHURCHES
5800 S. 14th St.
Omaha, NE 68107

The Fellowship of Evangelical Bible Churches grew out of a merger in 1889 of two conservative Mennonite groups that had been founded by Elders Isaac Peters and Aaron Walls respectively. Isaac Peters (1826-1911) had migrated from Russia in 1874, settled in Henderson, Nebraska, and joined the Bethesda Mennonite Church. As an elder he began to voice some of the ideas that had previously led to a break with the church in Russia. He was a vigorous proponent of evangelism and all the means to accomplish that task, including lively preaching, indoctrination of the youth, prayer meetings, and Bible study. He saw a separated life as a sign of regeneration. He also opposed baptism by immersion and the doctrine of the millennium. With a minority of the Henderson congregation, he withdrew in 1880 and formed the Ebenezer congregation.

Aaron Wall (1834-1905) had migrated from Russia in 1875 and settled near Mountain Lake, Minnesota. After his election in 1876 as elder of the Bergfelder Church, he stressed the need for regeneration and the new life in Christ to an extent that he and his followers felt compelled to leave the Bergfelder Church. In 1889 he founded an independent congregation. In October of that year, he led in the union of the congregation with that led by Peters and the resulting formation of the United Mennonite Brethren of North America. The name was soon changed to Defenseless Mennonite Brethren of Christ in North America. In 1937 the name was changed to Evangelical Mennonite Brethren Conference. At the annual conference in 1987 the present name was adopted.

Born in an evangelical awakening, the fellowship gave early emphasis to church schools and world missions. From early congregations in Nebraska, Minnesota, and South Dakota, the church spread throughout the Midwest and Canada. Missions are currently supported in Europe, Africa, India, Southeast Asia, Japan, Taiwan, and South America. The church is a member of the National Association of Evangelicals.

Membership: In 1987 the fellowship reported 14 congregations, 2,114 members and 44 ministers in the United States. Worldwide membership is 4,498. There are 22 congregations in Canada and South America.

Periodicals: *Gospel Tiding*, 5800 S. 14th St., Omaha, NE 68107.

★508★
EVANGELICAL MENNONITE CONFERENCE (KLEINE GEMEINDE)
Box 1268
440 Main St.
Steinbach, MB, Canada R0A 2A0

The Evangelical Mennonite Conference (EMC) came about as a result of a renewal movement among a small group of Mennonites in Southern Russia in 1812. Their leader was Klaas Reimer, a Mennonite minister. Reimer had become lax in discipline and that it condoned such practices as card playing, smoking, and drinking. He also felt that the church had also become too closely aligned with the Russian government as evidenced by its contributions to the war against Napoleon. Around 1812 Reimer and several others began to hold separate worship services. By 1814 the Reimer group had separated entirely from the main body of Mennonites. They became known as the Kleine Gemeinde (small fellowship).

Increasing pressure on the group from the Russian government in such matters as military conscription finally led to a migration in 1874-75 of the entire membership to North America. A total of 158 families settled in Manitoba, Canada, while 36 settled near Jansen, Nebraska. The Nebraska group eventually was lost to the conference.

The name Evangelical Mennonite Conference was chosen in 1952 to replace the earlier designation. The group saw itself as evangelical, i.e., standing for the true gospel message of Jesus Christ; Mennonite in that it holds to the traditional characteristics of Mennonite faith; and as a conference that works together to carry out its ministry.

The conference membership is now spread over five Canadian provinces. To facilitate fellowship, growth, and administration, the congregations have been grouped into eight regions. A Bible college in Manitoba educates many of the church's ministers, missionaries, and volunteer lay workers. The church had developed a strong missionary program that had, as of June 1987, some 150 workers in 23 countries under the guidance of the board of missions and several approved independent faith missions. In Mexico, Nicaragua, and Paraguay, the conference churches have organized as nationally directed conferences.

Membership: In 1988 the church reported 5,720 members, 47 churches, and 120 ministers in Canada. Missions are supported in Mexico, Nicaragua, Paraguay, and Germany.

Educational facilities: Steinbach Bible College, Steinbach, Manitoba, Canada.

Periodicals: *The Messenger*, Box 1268, Steinbach, Manitoba, Canada R0A 2A0.

Remarks: The members of the Kleine Gemeinde that settled in Nebraska were gradually, over a period of several decades, lost to other Mennonite bodies, primarily the Evangelical Mennonite Brethren Conference. The last congregation, which had moved to Kansas, dissolved in 1944.

Sources: *The Golden Years, The Mennonite Kleine Gemeinde in Russia (1812-1849)*. Steinbach, MN: D. F. P. Publications, 1985.

★509★
EVANGELICAL MENNONITE MISSION CONFERENCE
Box 126
Winnipeg, MB, Canada R3C 2G1

In 1936-37, I. P. Friesen, a member of the General Conference Mennonite Church Missions Committee, led evangelistic services among the Sommerfeld Mennonites in Manitoba, Canada. The Summerfeld Mennonites were a conservative ethnic faction within the larger body of Dutch and North German immigrants who had moved to Canada from Russia. Accompanying the spiritual awakening, especially among the younger members and ministers, was a demand for such innovations as Sunday schools, choir practices, and evening services. As a result of several meetings called to discuss the issues, approximately 1,200 baptized members and 1,600 unbaptized left to found the Rudnerweider Mennonite Church, named for the Manitoban village in which the schism occurred. The group explored the possibility of merger with other groups, but in the end remained independent.

There were few doctrinal points of disagreement and the Rudnerweider Mennonite Church continued the beliefs and practices of the older group. The Dordrecht Confession is accepted as the doctrinal standard. After the schism, the new faction instituted the practice of using unfermented grape juice in the communion service. The church allows ministers to preach their own sermons taken from a biblical text rather than read sermons of previous generations. The church has been known for its evangelical and missionary endeavors. Missions have been established in Belize, Bolivia, and Mexico, and missionaries are supported in Brazil, Ecuador, Germany, Japan, Java, St. Lucia, and Trinidad.

Membership: In the 1970s there were 26 churches and a membership of approximately 2,400.

Sources: Frank H. Epp, *Mennonites in Canada, 1920-1940*. Toronto: Macmillan of Canada, 1982.

★510★
GENERAL CONFERENCE MENNONITE CHURCH
722 Main St.
Newton, KS 67114

History. John H. Oberholtzer was an educated young minister in the Franconia District (located in Pennsylvania) of the Mennonite Church. Oberholtzer being of a progressive nature, encountered trouble soon after entering the ministry by protesting the plain, collarless coat worn by most ministers. He felt that the coat was an arbitrary requirement from outside the Mennonite creed. He next asked for the Conference of the Franconia District to adopt a written constitution so proceedings could be conducted more systematically. The result of Oberholtzer's agitation was a parting of the ways. He withdrew in 1847 from the Franconia District at the same conference which proceeded to expel him. With sixteen ministers and several congregations, he led in the organization of a new conference. A major thrust of Oberholtzer's movement was the union of all Mennonite congregations. New practices were initiated, including a more liberal view of the ban, open communication, intermarriage with persons of other denominations and, within a short time, a salaried clergy. Oberholtzer proved a zealous advocate and founded the first Mennonite paper in America, the *Religioeser Botschafter* (later *Das Christliche Volksblat*).

Meanwhile, other liberal leaders were emerging and bringing into existence new churches. Daniel Hoch, a minister to several Mennonite churches in Ontario, had joined hands with an Ohio congregation led by Rev. Ephraim Hunsberger to form, in 1855, the Conference Council of the Mennonite Communities of Canada-West and Ohio. In Lee County , Iowa, two congregations found themselves in isolation, banded together, and called for united efforts in evangelism among members who had settled at some distance from the main body in the East. At a meeting in 1860 in Iowa, representatives of some of the above groups met. Oberholtzer was chosen chairman and the General Conference Mennonite Church was organized. Their vision was the union of all Mennonite congregations in the United States and Canada. Its basis was to be a liberal enforcement of the ban and understanding of heresy. What, in effect, happened was the coming together of a number of liberal elements.

Beliefs. The doctrine of the General Conference is in accord with the other Mennonite bodies with two exceptions: John 13:4-15 is not interpreted as a command to institute footwashing as an ordinance, and I Corinthians 11:4-15 is not understood so as to make obligatory the covering of female heads.

Organization. Polity is congregational. The General Conference meets triennially. A Commission on Education oversees the production of Church school materials and Faith and Life Press and Mennonite Press. The Commission on Home Ministries oversees both Spanish-language ministries and American Indian ministries. The Commission on Overseas Missions sponsors work in Bolivia, Botswana, Brazil, Burkina Faso, China, Colombia, France, Germany, Hong Kong, India, Japan, Lesotho, Mexico, Nepal, Paraguay, Taiwan, Transkei (South Africa), Uruguay, and Zaire. Canadian Members have organized as the Conference of Mennonites in Canada. The South American Conference includes chruches in Brazil, Paraguay and Uruguay.

Membership: In 1986, the church reported 35,170 members, 155 congregations, and 225 ministers in the United States. Worldwide there were 56,017 members.

Educational facilities: Associated Mennonite Biblical Seminaries, Elkhart, Indiana; Bethel College, North Newton, Kansas; Bluffton College, Bluffton, Ohio.

Periodicals: *The Mennonite*, 722 Main Street, Newton, KS 67114; *Der Bote*, 722 Main Street, Newton, KS 67114; *Being in Touch*, Box 347, Newton, KS 67114-0347.

Sources: Samuel Floyd Pannabecker, *Open Doors, A History of the General Conference Mennonite Church.* Newton, KS: Faith and Life Press, 1975; Edmund G. Kaufman, *General Conference Mennonite Pioneers.* North Newton, KS: Bethel College, 1973; H. P. Krehbiel, *The History of the General Conference of the Mennonite Church of North America.* Newton, KS: the Author, I, 1889. II, 1938; James H. Waltner, *This We Believe.* Newton, KS: Faith and Life Press, 1968; *Constitution and Charter of the General Conference Mennonite Church.* (Newton, KS): 1984; Burton G. Yost, *Finding Faith and Fellowship.* Newton, KS: Faith and Life Press, 1963.

★511★
MENNONITE BRETHREN CHURCH OF NORTH AMERICA (BRUEDERGEMEINDE)
Hillsboro, KS 67063

In the mid-1800s, Pastor Edward Wuest, a fiery evangelical preacher, toured the German colonies in Russia. His message was the free grace of God and the need for a definite religious experience. His influence led a number of Mennonites to become dissatisfied with the formality of their church meeting. They also felt themselves too pure to participate in the communion with others and demanded a separate sacramental service. When the elders refused their request, they began to hold secret sacramental meetings. When they were discovered, opposition was intense and they withdrew, and on January 6, 1860, wrote a statement of protest. After bitter controversy, the government accepted their separate existence and they took the name Mennoniten Bruedergemeinde (Mennonite Brethren). They were one in doctrine with other Mennonites, but did emphasize religious experience. Among the Russian Mennonites they introduced footwashing (with the Lord's Supper) and baptism by immersion (backwards), the latter a unique practice among Mennonites. The Bruedergemeinde members began to arrive with the first immigrants in America. In 1879, Elder Abraham Schellenberg arrived and began to tour the settlements and organize strong congregations. By 1898, the group was supporting a German Department at McPherson College and in 1908, founded Tabor College in Hillsboro, Kansas. A vigorous mission program was established.

As the Brudergemeinde was developing, Jacob Wiebe, a member of the Kleine Gemeinde, now the Evangelical Mennonite Conference, in the Crimea, organized in 1869 the Crimean Brethren, similar in nature to the Bruedergemeinde. The Crimean Brethren came to America in 1874 and settled in Kansas. They were similar to the Mennonite Brethren but had a few differences. They prohibited excessive worldliness, buying of land, and attendance at public amusements. They took Biblical positions against life insurance, voting, and oaths. Marriage with non-members was forbidden. In 1960, the Mennonite Brethren Church absorbed the Krimmer Mennonite Brethren Church (as the Crimean Brethren became known).

The Church is a member of the National Association of Evangelicals.

Membership: Not reported. In 1975 the Church had 120 churches, 16,155 members, and 131 ministers.

Periodicals: *The Christian Leader*, Hillsboro, KS 60763.

Sources: John H. Lorenz, *The Mennonite Brethren Church*. Hillsboro, KS: Mennonite Brethren Publishing House, 1950; *Fundamentals of Faith*. Hillsboro, KS: Mennonite Brethren Publishing House, 1963.

Amish

★512★
BEACHY AMISH MENNONITE CHURCHES
9650 Iams Rd.
Plain City, OH 43064

A split in the Pennsylvania Amish was occasioned by the refusal of Bishop Moses Beachy to pronounce the ban and avoidance on some former Old Order Amish who left to join a Conservative Mennonite congregation in Maryland. The conservative element withdrew fellowship with the bishop, who then, with his supporters, separated and formed a new association. The Beachy Amish have become more accommodating to modern culture. Churches have been built, and in recent years, the automobile has been allowed, as are tractors and electricity. Missionary-aid work for needy people has become a project in contrast to the strictly separatist Old Order group.

Membership: In 1985 the Beachy Amish reported 5,862 members, 79 congregations, and 278 ministers.

Periodicals: *Calvary Messenger*.

★513★
**CONFERENCE OF THE EVANGELICAL
MENNONITE CHURCH**
1420 Kerrway Court
Fort Wayne, IN 46805

Around 1865, Henry Egli (also spelled Henry Egly), an Amish minister in Adams County, Indiana, began to emphasize the necessity of a conversion experience for all members. Because of the inherited nature of the Amish culture, few members could profess such an experience. Egli also complained of their "too liberal dress." An Amish since 1853, he had come to feel that the Amish had degenerated into a mere organization, and with his followers he withdrew, forming a new group on the basis of a fellowship of born-again believers, baptized after their confession of faith. On the strength of his evangelistic preaching, his movement grew and became known as the Defenseless Mennonites. Under Egli, the group was ultrastrict in dress and rebaptized all who came into the movement who could not confess a true conversion experience. It also introduced immersion as an optional mode of baptism. (Mennonites generally baptized by pouring.) That teaching led to some tension, as in 1896 the church expelled a minister for teachig that immersion was the only true form of baptism. That minister, J. A. Ramseyer, and his followers formed the Missionary Church Association (now part of the Missionary Church). Over the years, both the strictness and the distinctiveness of the group Egli began have lessened. The present name was adopted in 1948.

Beliefs: The church draws its beliefs form the Mennonite-Amish tradition. It accepts the Dordrecht Confession of Faith and places special emphasis upon the church as a living spiritual entity and a fellowship of regenerate beings. Though never consummating a merger, the church has always been open to ecumenical efforts with like-minded denominations. In 1944, it joined the National Association of Evangelicals. Missionary work is supported in Botswana, Burkina Faso, the Dominican Republic, Lesotho, Transkai, Venezuela, and Zaire. There is an annual meeting of the conference each August.

Membership: In 1988 the Church reported 3,841 members, 24 churches, and 62 ministers.

Periodicals: *EMC Today*, 1420 Kerrway Court, Fort Wayne, IN 46805.

Sources: Stan Nussbaum, *A History of the Evangelical Mennonite Church*. The Author, 1980.

★514★

CONSERVATIVE MENNONITE CONFERENCE

% Ivan J. Miller
Grantsville, MD 21536

After the establishment of the Old Order Amish Mennonite Church, more liberal Amish gradually began to separate from the church. Some of these congregations became associated and, in 1910, met at Pigeon, Michigan, for a first general conference. These congregations took the name Conservative Mennonite Conference. They introduced innovations to the Amish community such as the use of meeting houses, Sunday schools, protracted meetings, and English language services. Conservative Mennonites are located primarily in the Midwest, but congregations are located as far away as Florida, Arizona, and Delaware.

Membership: Not reported.

★515★

OLD ORDER AMISH MENNONITE CHURCH

Pathway Publishers
Rte. 4
Aylmer, ON, Canada N5H 2R3

The Old Order Amish are in practice the continuation of the original Amish who settled in America. They are strictly conservative and may be identified by their horse-and-buggy culture. The men must grow beards but moustaches are forbidden. The plain dark blue, gray, brown, or black suit for men and bonnet and apron for women are uniforms. Buttons are used on men's shirts and pants, but none are allowed on suit coats, vests, or coats. Marriage with non-Amish is forbidden.

The Amish society is an agricultural community in which church life and worldly life are not separated. Symbolic of their life are the Amish barn raisings in which the congregation gathers to build a member's barn, usually in several days. Worship is held in the homes of the members every other Sunday on a rotating basis. During the three-hour service, the congregation is divided according to sex and ma rital status.

Schooling beyond the "3R's" is frowned upon within the church, and prior to a Supreme Court ruling in 1972 trouble with various state governments (such as Pennsylvania) became a major cause of immigration westward to more lenient states (such as Missouri). Ministers are chosen by lot from a nominiated few. Since this is not a missionary church, new members generally come into the community from the children of members. In the last generation there have been converts, some highly educated, and recent studies have shown that approximately eight percent of the present membership is made up of descendents of such converts.

Membership: Not reported. In 1988 there were approximately 24,000 members in the United States and 900 in Canada.

Periodicals: *The Dairy*, 3981 E. Newport Rd., Gordonville, PA 17529; *Blackboard Bulletin*, Route 4, Box 266, La Grange, IN 46761; *Family Life*, Route 4, Box 266, La Grange, IN 46761; *Die Botschaft*, 200 Hazel St., Lancaster, PA 17601; *The Budget*, 134 N Factory St., Sugarcreek, OH 44681.

Sources: John A. Hoestetler, *Amish Society*. Baltimore: Johns Hopkins University Press, 1968; William I. Schreiber, *Our Amish Neighbors*. Chicago: University of Chicago Press, 1962; Clyde Browning, *Amish in Illinois*. The Author, 1971; Charles S. Rice and Rollin C. Steinmetz, *The Amish Year*. New Brunswick, NJ: Rutgers University Press, 1956; *Amish Life in a Changing World*. York, PA: York Graphic Services Incorporated, 1978.

Brethren

★516★

ASSOCIATION OF FUNDAMENTAL GOSPEL CHURCHES

9189 Grubb Court
Canton, OH 44721

The Association of Fundamental Gospel Churches was formed in 1954 by the coming together of three independent Brethren congregations: Calvary Chapel of Hartsville, Ohio; Webster Mills Free Brethren Church of McConnellsburg, Pennsylvania; and Little Country Chapel of Myersburg, Maryland. Prime leader in the new association was G. Henry Besse (d.1962), a former member of the Reformed Church who had in 1937 become a minister among the Dunkard Brethren. He withdrew from their fellowship in 1953 complaining about their strictures agains wearing neckties, wristwatches and jewelry and their demands that women always wear the prayer veil or cap. Former members of the Church of the Brethren were also opposed to that Church's participation in the National Council of Churches.

In general, members of the Association follow Brethren doctrine and practice. They reject as unbiblical participation in war, but allow members to accept noncombatant military service. They do not allow the taking of oaths, suing at law (including for reason of divorce), or wearing ornamental adornment. They do not practice the kiss of peace.

The association meets annually to elect officers and conduct business. Ministers are chosen from among the congregation's members. They are not required to have advanced education. G. Henry Besse was succeeded by his two sons, Lynn Besse and Clair Besse, both of whom have pastored Calvary Chapel.

Membership: In 1980 there were an estimated 150 members in three congregations.

★517★
BIBLE BRETHREN
Current address not obtained for this edition.

The Bible Brethren was formed in 1948 by a small group who withdrew from the Lower Cumberland (Cumberland County, Pennsylvania) congregation of the Church of the Brethren. Clair H. Alspaugh (1903-1969), a farmer and painter who had been called to the ministry in the congregation in 1942, led the group that assumed a traditional Brethren posture. Alspaugh protested the Church of the Brethren's association with the Federal Council of Churches (now the National Council of Churches and the failure of the Brethren to endorse doctrinal preaching as inspired by the Holy Spirit.

The original group constructed a church building following simple nineteenth-century Brethren patterns (with a long preachers' desk and straight-back pews) at Carlisle Springs, Pennsylvania. A second congregation was formed at Campbelltown, Pennsylvania. It was strengthened by the addition of a group under Paul Beidler which had withdrawn from the Dunkard Brethren, but was lost when Biedler led the entire congregation away in 1974 to form Christ's Ambassadors. A third congregation of Bible Brethren formed in 1954 at Locust Grove Chapel, near Abbotstown, York County, Pennsylvania.

Membership: In 1979 there were approximately 100 members of the Bible Brethren in two congregations.

Sources: Elmer Q. Gleim, *Change and Challenge: A History of the Church of the Brethren in the Southern District of Pennsylvania*. Harrisburg, PA: Southern District Conference History Committee, 1973.

★518★
BRETHREN CHURCH (ASHLAND, OHIO)
524 College Ave.
Ashland, OH 44805

Agitation among the Brethren began in the late nineteenth century against what some considered outmoded practices. The lack of educational opportunities, an unlearned clergy, and the plain dress were main objections. The crisis came to a head with the expulsion in 1882 of Henry R. Holsinger of Berlin, Pennsylvania. Holsinger had objected to the authority of the annual meeting over the local congregation. Others left with him and formed what was called the Progressive Dunkers (named Dunkers in reference to baptism).

The Progressive Dunkers are like the Church of the Brethren in most respects, with the exceptions of having been the first to move toward an educated and salaried ministry, modern dress, and missions. While generally conservative in theology, and expecting a high degree of doctrinal consensus among its ministers, the Church has refused to adopt a statement of faith (though it does have a doctrinal statement) on the grounds that the New Testament is its creed. During the 1930s, a group supportive of a dispensational fundamentalist doctrinal position left the Church to found the National Fellowship of Brethren Churches, now the Fellowship of Grace Brethren. The Church practices baptism by triune immersion, a communion service usually in the evening which includes footwashing, and the laying on of hands for ordination, confirmation and/or healing. Elders (ordained ministers) lead the church in spiritual affairs. Deacons, who may be or either sex, handle local church affairs.

The church follows a congregational polity and an annual conference conducts common business. Missionary activity is supported in Argentina, Columbia, India, Malaysia and Mexico. The Brethren Publishing Company produces church school materials and other literature. Two retirement homes (Ashland, Ohio; and Flora, Indiana) are supported. The Church is a member of the National Association of Evangelicals.

Membership: In 1988 the church reported 14,965 members in 125 churches.

Educational facilities: Ashland Theological Seminary, Ashland, Ohio; Ashland College, Ashland, Ohio.

Periodicals: *The Brethren Evangelist*, 524 College Avenue, Ashland, OH 44805.

Sources: The Task Force on Brethren History and Doctrine, *The Brethren: Growth in Life and Thought*. Ashland, OH: Board of Christian Education, the Brethren Church, 1975.

★519★
CHRIST'S AMBASSADORS
Current address not obtained for this edition.

Christ's Ambassadors traces its origin to a dispute in 1968 within the Dunkard Brethren congregation at Lititz, Pennsylvania. Leaders in the congregation protested an unauthorized prayer meeting conducted by some of the members under the leadership of Paul Beidler. Beidler led the members in withdrawing and forming an independent congregation. The small group affiliated with the Bible Brethren congregation at Campbelltown, Pennsylvania, in 1970. However, four years later Beidler led the entire congregation to withdraw from the Bible Brethren and formed Christ's Ambassadors. The group follows traditional Dunkard Brethren practice and beliefs, but places great emphasis upon the freedom of expression in worship.

Membership: In 1980 Christ's Ambassadors had approximately fifty members meeting in two congregations, one at Cocalico and one at Myerstown, Pennsylvania.

CHRIST'S ASSEMBLY
Current address not obtained for this edition.

Krefeld, Germany, in the lower Rhine Valley, was one place that dissenting Pietists found relative safety and toleration during the eighteenth century, and several groups, including the one which would later become the Church of the Brethren upon its arrival in America, had members among the Krefeld residents. In 1737 two Danes, Soren Bolle and Simon Bolle, visited Krefeld and joined the Brethren. They soon returned to Copenhagen and began to preach and gather a following. While they had been baptized by the Brethren, they had been influenced as well by other Pietist Groups, most notably the Community of True Inspiration (which later migrated to America and formed the colonies at Amana, Iowa). The movement under the Bolles, Christ's Assembly, spread through Sweden, Norway, and Germany.

During the 1950s Johannes Thalitzer, pastor of Christ's Assembly in Copenhagen, learned of the continued existence of the Brethren in America through his encounter with some remnants of the recently disbanded Danish Mission of the Church of the Brethren. He initiated contact with several Brethren Groups, especially the Old German Baptist Brethren, who sponsored a visit by Thalitzer to the United States in 1959. In subsequent visits he became acquainted with all of the larger Brethren factions, but felt each was deficient in belief and/or practice. In 1967 he organized a branch of Christ's Assembly at a love feast with nine Brethren (from several Brethren groups) at Eaton, Ohio.

Christ's Assembly largely follows Brethren practice, but like the Community of True Inspiration places great emphasis upon the revealed guidance of an apostolic leadership. In more recent years it has been further influenced by the Pentecostal (Charismatic) Movement which has swept through most major denominations.

As Christ's Assembly grew it included members from four states and all the major Brethren branches. A second congregation was formed in the 1970s in Berne, Indiana.

Membership: Christ's Assembly has two congregations and an estimated 100 members.

Sources: F. W. Benedict and William F. Rushby, "Christ's Assembly: A Unique Brethren Movement" in *Brethren Life and Thought*, vol.18 (1973), pp. 33-42.

CHURCH OF THE BRETHREN
1451 Dundee Ave.
Elgin, IL 60120

The Church of the Brethren developed out of the wave of radical Pietism in early eighteenth century Germany. Hearing William Penn's invitation to come to the American colonies, most of the Brethren immigrated; those who remained were absorbed into the Mennonite movement. Their first American congregation was instituted in Germantown, Pennsylvania, on Christmas Day 1723. Important leaders of the first generation included Alexander Mack, Sr. (1679-1735), the first recognized minister; Christopher Sauer II (1721-1784), a noted colonial printer; Alexander Mack, Jr. (1712-1803); and Peter Becker (1687-1758). Until the early twentieth century, Brethren were commonly known as "Dunkers" (or Tunker), after their manner of thrice-fold immersion baptism. The formal name, German Baptist Brethren, used during most of the nineteenth century, was changed to the current designation on the anniversary of the church's bicentennial in 1908.

In colonial Pennsylvania, the Brethren shared with the Mennonites a German cultural background and Anabaptist theology, and with the Friends (Quakers) a commitment to peace and simplicity. All of these groups sought a separation from secular influences, wore distinctive plain dress, and opposed slavery. Brethren practiced strong church discipline (although not the ban), selected leaders who were not salaried or expected to obtain theological education, and refrained from voting, taking oaths, or entering lawsuits. One of the most distinctive features of Brethren worship has been their observance of the love feast, a communion service that includes foot washing, a love meal, and the taking of unleavened bread and wine/grape juice.

As one of the historic peace churches, Brethren were opposed to military service in the American Revolution and the Civil War. This resulted in limited persecution, including fines and imprisonment. The program of alternative service has been available to conscientious objectors in World War II and later conflicts.

Although the early Brethren were open to urban life, most preferred an agricultural setting and followed the farming frontier across the continent. Congregations were established in Kentucky and Ohio during the 1790s, Missouri and Illinois during the 1810s, and California and Oregon during the 1850s. Brethren settlement of the West at the turn of the century was greatly aided through colonization programs of the transcontinental railroads. The small movement of Brethren into Canada was aided by the Canadian Pacific Railroad, encouraging immigration in the early twentieth century. Between 1903 and 1922 as many as twelve congregations, mostly in Alberta and Saskatchewan, were founded. By 1968 only two of these congregtaions remained and they became part of the United Church of Canada.

The Brethren began to meet in a yearly meeting for worship and business during the 1740s, although no minutes were recorded until the 1780s. By the 1840s a delegated conference of lay representatives and ministers had become the highest authority in the church. Following the Civil War, the church took an active interest in missionary work (foreign and domestic), publishing, and education. Foreign mission efforts began in Denmark in the 1890s. Fields were also opened in India, China, Nigeria, and Equador. The Brethren Press, founded in 1897, produced a supply of books, periodicals, church school materials, and other literature. Numerous educational institutions were founded, six of which evolved into fully accredited independent liberal arts colleges and a university. The church also supported a theological seminary.

Tensions within the denomination in the late nineteenth century produced a painful three-way division. In addition to the original group, an "old order" movement that opposed innovation and venerated the tradition of earlier Brethren organized the Old German Baptist Brethren in 1881. A "progressive" faction organized the Brethren Church (Ashland, Ohio) in 1883.

The twentieth century has seen rapid change in Brethren life. Following an important decision on dress at the annual conference of 1911, the distinctive dress of the church has virtually disappeared. The free, plural ministry was transformed into salaried, professional pastoral leadership. Women became eligible for ordination in 1957. Efforts at evangelism and new church development have produced a more inclusive membership that includes several black, hispanic, and Korean congregations.

The extensive world mission program began a process of dramatic change in 1955, resulting in the creation of indigenous and independent religious bodies. The Ecuadorian congregations joined the United Evangelical Church of Ecuador in 1965; the India mission program merged into the Church of North India in 1970; and the Nigerian churches became the independent Brethren Church of Nigeria in 1973. The mission program in China folded when western missionaries were sent home in 1950.

Perhaps Brethren have been best known around the world for their efforts in relief and rehabilitation work in Europe following World War II. Brethren service projects later stretched into India and China and fostered ecumenical organizations such as Heifer Project International, founded by layman Dan West; Christian Rural Overseas Program (CROP), and International Christian Youth Exchange (ICYE). The denomination also organized and administers SEERV (Salves Exchange for Refugee Rehabilitation Vocations), the largest marketing program of its type for third world handicrafts.

Since 1946 a general board of 25 members elected by the annual conference employs a program and administrative staff in the areas of parish ministries, world ministries and disaster response, publishing, and stewardship. The general offices and Brethren Press are located in Elgin, Illinois; a service center is operated in New Windsor, Maryland. The church is a founding member of both the World Council of Churches and the National Council of Churches. The Brethren Church of Nigeria is also a member of the World Council.

Membership: In 1986 the Brethren reported 159,184 members, 1,045 congregations, and 1,196 ordained ministers in the United States and Puerto Rico.

Educational facilities: Bethany Theological Seminary, Oak Brook. Illinois; Bridgewater College, Bridgewater, Virginia; Elizabethtown College, Elizabethtown, Pennsylvania; Juniata College, Huntingdon, Pennsylvania; Manchester College, North Manchester, Indiana; McPherson College, McPherson, Kansas; University of La Verne, La Verne, California.

Periodicals: *Messenger*, 1451 Dundee Ave., Elgin, IL 60120; *Brethren Life and Thought*, Bethany Theological Seminary, Butterfield and Meyer Rds., Oak Brook, IL 60521.

Sources: Donald F. Durnbaugh, ed., *The Brethren Encyclopedia*. Philadelphia, PA: The Brethren Encyclopedia Inc., 1983. 3 Vols.; Roger E. Sappington, ed., *The Brethren in the New Nation*. Elgin, IL: Brethren Press, 1976; Floyd E. Mallot, *Studies in Brethren History*. Elgin, IL: Brethren Publishing House, 1954; *Manual of Brotherhood Organization and Polity*. Elgin, IL: Church of the Brethren, General Offices, 1965; *Book of Worship, The Church of the Brethren*. Elgin, IL: Brethren Press, 1964.

★522★
CONSERVATIVE GERMAN BAPTIST BRETHREN
Current address not obtained for this edition.

The Conservative German Baptist Brethren is a small Brethren body body which dates to the 1931 withdrawl of a group under the leadership of Clayton F. Weaver and Ervin J. Keeny from the Dunkard Brethren Church in Pennsylvania. In 1946 Loring I. Moss, a prominent exponent of the conservative element of the Brethren Movement and one of the organizers of the Dunkard Brethren Church, withdrew and formed the Primitive Dunkard Brethren. Noting the similar concern to keep stricter Brethren standards, Moss led his new group into the Conservative German Baptist Brethren, though personally, he later withdrew and joined the Old Brethren.

Membership: In 1980 the Conservative German Baptist Brethren had two congregations, one at New Madison, Ohio, with ten members and one at Shrewsbury, Pennsylvania, with twenty-five members.

★523★
DUNKARD BRETHREN CHURCH
% Dale E. Jamison, Chairman
Board of Trustees
Quinter, KS 67752

The Dunkard Brethren Church grew out of a conservative movement within the Church of the Brethren which protested what it saw as a worldly drift and a lowering of standards in the church. The movement formed around *The Bible Monitor*, a periodical begun in 1922 by B. E. Kesler, a minister who had joined the Church of the Brethren in the first decade of the twentieth century. He was one of seven people chosen to write the report on dress standards adopted by the church in 1911. However, in the ensuing decade he saw the dress standards being increasingly ignored. Men began to wear ties and women were adopting fashionable clothes and modern hair styles. Kesler also protested the acceptance of lodge and secret society membership, divorce and remarriage, and a salaried educated ministry (which was pushing aside the traditional lay eldership).

The emergence of the *Bible Monitor* movement led to much tension within the Church of the Brethren. In 1923 Kesler was refused a seat at the annual conference. That same year he met with supporters at Denton, Maryland, to further organize efforts to reform the church. Subsequent meetings were held in different locations over the next few years. However, by 1926 it became evident that the church would not accept the movement's perspective, and at a meeting at Plevna, Indiana, the Dunkard Brethren Church was organized.

The Dunkard Brethren Church follows traditional Brethren beliefs and practices, and until recently has rebaptized members who joined from less stict branches of the church. The Dunkard Brethren adopted and enforces the dress standards accepted by the Church of the Brethren in 1911. Modesty and simplicity (though not uniformity) of dress is required. No gold or other jewelry is worn. Women keep their hair long and simply styled. They generally wear a white cap. Men cut their hair short. Divorce and remarriage are not allowed. Life insurance is discouraged. No musical instruments are used in worship.

The church has three orders of ministry. Elders marry, bury, and administer the ordinances; ministers preach and assist the elders in their sacramental role; deacons attend to temporal matters. All are laymen elected by their local congregations. The standing committee, composed of all the elders of the church, has general oversight of the church. Together with the ministers and elders elect ed by the local churches as delegates, they form the general conference, the highest legislative body in the church. Its decisions are final on all matters brought before it. The church is organized into four districts which meet annually.

The Dunkard Brethren Church also supports the Torreon Navajo Mission in New Mexico.

Membership: In 1980 the Dunkard Brethren reported 1,035 members in twenty-six congregations.

Periodicals: *The Bible Monitor*, % Editor, 1138 E. 12th St., Beaumont, CA 92223.

Sources: *Dunkard Brethren Church Manual*. Dunkard Brethren Church, 1971. *Dunkard Brethren Church Polity*. 1980; *Minutes of the General Conference of the Dunkard Brethren Church from 1927 to 1975*. Wauseon, OH: Glanz Lithographing Company, 1976.

★524★
EMMANUEL'S FELLOWSHIP
Current address not obtained for this edition.

Emmanuel's Fellowship was formed in 1966 by members of the Old Order River Brethren, under the leadership of Paul Goodling of Greencastle, Pennsylvania. Goodling rejected the Brethren's insistence on baptism by immersion and their allowing members to accept social security benefits. The Fellowship baptizes by pouring, as the candidate stands in water. There are very strict dress requirements.

Membership: Not reported. In 1967 there was one congregation of 15 members.

★525★
FELLOWSHIP OF GRACE BRETHREN CHURCHES
Winona Lake, IN 46590

The movement which led to the founding of the Fellowship of Grace Brethren Churches developed within the Brethren Church (Ashland, Ohio) during the 1930s. Conservatives within the Church voiced concern over liberal tendencies within the church and more particularly at the church-supported school, Ashland College. Led by ministers such as Alva J. McClain, the National Ministerial Association drew up and adopted the "Message of the Brethren Ministry," a statement of the Brethren position. The entire church refused to adopt the statement on the grounds that it seemed to be a substitute for their adherence to the New Testament as their only creed.

Conservatives scored a second victory in 1930 when a graduate school of theology opened at Ashland under McClain's leadership. However, in 1937, both McClain, then dean of the school, and Professor Herman A. Hoyt were dismissed. Their supporters organized Grace Theological Seminary as a new institution for ministerial training, which set the stage for a confrontation at the 1939 General Conference of the Church. After the exclusion of some of the new seminary's supporters, all walked out and formed the National Fellowship of Brethren Churches, which in 1976 assumed its present name.

The new church adopted the 1921 "Message of the Brethren Ministry" as its doctrinal position. That document was replaced in 1969 by a revised and expanded "Statement of Faith." The new statement affirms the conservative evangelical theology of the original document but adds a lengthy statement on various eschatological issues such as the premillennial return of Christ, eternal punishment for nonbelievers and a belief in a personal Satan. The church practices baptism by triune immersion and a threefold communion that includes footwashing, a meal, and partaking of the elements of bread and the cup.

The Fellowship adopted a congregational polity. The Conference of the Fellowship meets annually and oversees the several schools and a vigorous mission program. The Foreign Mission Society operates in Argentina, Brazil, Africa, France, Germany, Hawaii, Mexico, and Puerto Rico. The National Council of Churches is stanchly opposed.

Membership: In 1985 the fellowship reported 41,767 members, 312 congregations, and 519 ministers.

Educational facilities: Grace Theological Seminary, Winona Lake, Indiana; Grace College, Winina Lake, Indiana.

Periodicals: *Brethren Missionary Herald*, Winona Lake, IN 46590.

Sources: Louis S. Baumann, *The Faith*. Winona Lake, IN: Brethren Missionary Helard Co., 1960; Herman A. Hoyt, *Then Would My Servants Fight*. Winona Lake, IN: Brethren Missionary Herald Company, 1956; Alva J. McClain, *Daniel's Prophecy of the Seventy Weeks*. Grand Rapids, Zondervan Publications, n.d.

★526★
FUNDAMENTAL BRETHREN CHURCH
Current address not available for this edition.

The Fundamental Brethren Church was formed in 1962 by former members of four congregations of the Church of the Brethren in Mitchell County, North Carolina, under the leadership of Calvin Barnett. The doctrinally conservative group adopted the "Message of the Brethren Ministry," a statement written by some ministers in the Brethren Church (Ashland, Ohio) in the 1920s as their doctrinal standard. Among the issues involved in their leaving the Church of the Brethren, its participation in the National Council of Churches and use of the Revised Standard Version of the Bible were prominent. The group added to its doctrinal statement that the King James Version of the Bible is authoritative. It also adopted a fundamental premillennial dispensational theological

stance. By 1967, there were four congregations with 200 members.

Membership: In the 1970s there were 3 congregations of less than 200 members.

★527★
INDEPENDENT BRETHREN CHURCH
Current address not obtained for this edition.

The Independent Brethren Church was formed in 1972. On February 12 of that year, the Upper Marsh Creek congregation at Gettysburg, Pennsylvania, of the Church of the Brethren withdrew and became an independent body. Later that year, members from the Antietam congregation left and established the independent Blue Rock congregation near Waynesboro, Pennsylvania. These two congregations united as the Independent Brethren Church. They are conservative in their following of Brethren belief and practice. They have kept the plain dress and oppose any affiliation with the National Council of Churches.

Membership: In 1980 the Independent Brethren Church had approximately 85 members in two congregations.

★528★
OLD BRETHREN CHURCH
Current address not obtained for this edition.

The Old Brethren Church, generally termed simply the Old Brethren, is a name taken by two congregations which split from the Old German Baptist Brethren in 1913 (Deer Creek congregation in Carroll County, Indiana) and in 1915 (Salida congregation in Stanislaus County, California). Though widely separated geographically, the two congregations banded together and in 1915 published *The Old Brethren's Reasons*, a twenty-four page pamphlet outlining their position. The Old Brethren dissented from the Old German Baptist Brethren's refusal to make annual meeting decisions uniformly applicable and from their allowing divergences of practice and discipline among the different congregations. Also, the Old Brethren called for greater strictness in plain dress and called for houses and carriages shorn of any frills which would gratify the lust of the eye.

In particular, the Old Brethren denounced the automobile and the telephone. Use of either caused a believer to be hooked into the world and inevitably led to church members being yoked together with unbelievers. In practice, over the years, the Old Brethren have been forced to change and have come to closely resemble the group from which they originally withdrew. Even prior to World War II, they began to make accommodation to the automobile.

Members of the Old Brethren meet annually at Pentecost, but keep legislation to a minimum. They allow the congregations to retain as much authority as possible.

Beginning with two congregations, the Old Brethren Church has experienced growth in spite of a schism in 1930 t hat led to the formation of the Old Brethren German Baptist Church. A third meeting house was built in the 1970s.

Membership: In 1980 the Old Brethren had approximately 130 members and three congregations (Salida, California; Deer Creek, Indiana; Gettysburg, Ohio). Individual members could be found in Tennessee, Mississippi, and Brazil (where a group of Old German Baptist Brethren had settled in 1969).

Periodicals: *The Pilgrim*, 19201 Cherokee Road, Tuolumne, California 95379.

★529★
OLD BRETHREN GERMAN BAPTIST CHURCH
Current address not obtained for this edition.

The Old Brethren German Baptist Church originated among the most conversative members of the Old Brethren Church and the Old Order German Baptist Brethren Church. Around 1930 members of the Old Brethren Deer Creek congregation near Camden, Indiana, began to fellowship with the Old Order Brethren in the Covington, Ohio, area. However, by 1935 the traditionalist Old Brethren found themselves unable to continue their affiliations with the Ohio Brethren. They continued as an independent congregation until they made contact with a few Old Order Brethren near Bradford, Ohio, who met in the home of Solomon Lavy. In 1939 the two groups merged and adopted the name Old Brethren German Baptist Church. They were joined in 1953 by a group of Old Order Brethren from Arcanum, Ohio.

The Old Brethren is the most conservative of all Brethren groups. They use neither automobiles, tractors, electricity, or telephones. Their only accommodation to modern mechanization is that they do permit occasional use of stationary gasoline engines and will hire nonmembers for specific tasks requiring machinery. Members follow a strict personal code of nonconformity to the world. Homes and buggies are plainly furnished and simply painted. No gold or jewelry is worn. Farmers do not raise or habitually use tobacco. Members do not vote or purchase life insurance.

Membership: Among the smallest of Brethren groups, the Old Brethren, in 1980, reported 45 members in three congregations: Camden and Goshen, Indiana and Arcanum, Ohio.

★530★
OLD GERMAN BAPTIST BRETHREN
% Elder Clement Skiles
Rte. 1, Box 140
Bringhurst, IN 46913

The Old German Baptist Brethren represents the conservative wing in the Brethren movement. This group withdrew in 1881, the year before Henry R. Holsinger, a leader of what became known as the Progressive Brethren (now the Brethren Church (Ashland, Ohio)) was expelled from the Church of the Brethren.] The group was protesting innovative tendencies and was opposed to Sunday schools, missions, higher education, and church societies and auxiliaries. It has lessened its opposition to higher education among members and now sponsors parochial schools. No missions are supported, and children attend the regular services of the church instead of having a church school.

The Old German Baptist Brethren retain plain garb and are committed to non-participation in war, government, secret societies, and worldly amusements. They do not object to participation in government (i.e., voting) by members whose conscience allows it. They remain conservative on oaths, lawsuits, non-salaried ministry, and veiled heads for women at worship.

Membership: In 1988 the Brethren reported 5,277 members in 52 churches served by 236 ministers.

Periodicals: *The Vindicator*, 1876 Beamsville Union City Rd., Union City, OH 45390.

Sources: H. M. Fisher, et al., *Doctrinal Treatise*. Covington, OH: The Little Printing Company, 1954.

★531★
OLD ORDER GERMAN BAPTIST CHURCH
Current address not obtained for this edition.

As the Old German Baptist Brethren continued to deal with questions of accommodating to a fast-moving society in the early twentieth century, a group of members withdrew in 1921 because of the departure of the Old German Baptist Brethren from the established order and old paths. The petitioners, as they were informally called, could be found throughout the brethren, but were concentrated in the congregations at Covington and Arcanum, Ohio.

Staunchly set against most modern conveniences, the Old Order German Baptists have over the year been forced to accommodate. Automobiles are forbidden, but tractors are now allowed for farm work. Members do not use electricity or telephones. Increasingly, younger members have been forced to leave the farm and seek employment in nonfarm occupations.

Membership: In 1980 the church had less than 100 members and three congregations, all in Ohio (Gettysburg, Covington, and Arcanum).

Quakers (Friends)

★532★

ALASKA YEARLY MEETING
% Walter E. Outwater
Box 687
Kotzebue, AK 99752

As early as 1897 Quaker missionaries from the California Yearly Meeting, an independent programmed meeting of Friends, began work among the Eskimo people in Alaska. In 1970 the work had grown to the point that it was organized as a yearly meeting affiliated with the California Meeting, which maintained a Bible Training School. A goal of turning the work of the Meeting entirely over to its Eskimo constituency was completed in 1982 when the last of the missionaries were withdrawn and the Alaska Yearly meeting became fully independent. The California Meeting has joined the Friends United Meeting.

Membership: In 1981 there were 11 congregations and 2,860 members.

Educational facilities: Bible Training School.

★533★

CENTRAL YEARLY MEETING OF FRIENDS
% Ollie McCune, Supt.
Route 1, Box 226
Alexandria, IN 46001

The Central Yearly Meeting of Friends was formed in 1926 by several meetings in eastern Indiana who were protesting the liberalism of the Five Years Meeting. Doctrinally, the Central Yearly Meeting of Friends is evangelical and very conservative in matters of personal holiness. Worship is programmed. Churches of this small body are found in Indiana, Arkansas and Michigan. Missionary work is sponsored in Bolivia.

Membership: In 1981 the Meeting reported 11 congregations (monthly meetings) organized into 3 quarterly (district) meetings and 446 members.

Educational facilities: Union Bible Seminary, Westfield, IN.

Periodicals: *Friends Evangel*, Box 215, Westfield, IN 46074.

★534★

EVANGELICAL FRIENDS CHURCH, EASTERN DIVISION
1201 30th St., N.W.
Canton, OH 44709

Prior to 1971 known as the Ohio Yearly Meeting of Friends, the Evangelical Friends Church is that branch of the Friends most influenced by the holiness movement (discussed in chapter seven). The Evangelical Friends have a programmed worship service with a minister who preaches. Formed in 1813, the Ohio Yearly Meeting of Friends supported the Gurneyites, followers of Joseph John Gurney, a promoter of beliefs in the final authority of the Bible, atonement, justification, and sanctification. After the Civil War, the Ohio Yearly Meeting became open to the holiness movement through the activities of such workers as David B. Updegraff, Dougan Clark, Walter Malone and Emma Malone. The latter founded the Cleveland Bible Insititute (now the Malone College) in 1892, and it now serves an interdenominational holiness constituency. Worship is programmed.

The Evangelical Friends Church, never a member of the Five Years Meeting, has become a haven of conservative congregations who have withdrawn from the Friends United Meeting in both the United States and Canada. Mission work is sustained in Taiwan and India. The Church participates in the Evangelical Friends Alliance.

Membership: In 1981 there were 8,612 members in 86 churches.

Educational facilities: Malone College, Canton, OH.

Periodicals: *The Facing Bench*, 1201 30th Street N.W., Canton, OH 44709.

Sources: Charles E. DeVol, *Focus on Friends*. Canton, OH: The Missionary Board of the Evangelical Friends Church–Eastern Division, 1982; *Faith and Practice, the Book of Discipline*. Canton, OH: Evangelical Friends Church–Eastern Region, 1981.

★535★

FRIENDS GENERAL CONFERENCE
1520-B Race St.
Philadelphia, PA 19102

The Friends General Conference is an association of otherwise autonomous yearly meetings in the United States and Canada, most of which emphasize the authority of the direct leading of the Inner Light, are open to theological diversity and the enrichment it can bring, and follow an unprogrammed pattern of worship. In general the yearly meetings which make up the conference continue the tradition most associated with Elias Hicks (1748-1830).

History. Elias Hicks appeared among the American Quakers in the 1820s. He was an eloquent preacher, but as his ideas developed, his emphasis upon asceticism, rationalism, and subjectivism irritated many of the Quaker faithful. Hick's followers assigned a most significant role to the Inner Light, even to the extent of considering all outward forms useless and possibly harmful. Worship should be unprogrammed, not planned ahead of time. Hicks also attacked the divinity of Christ and expounded an exemplary theory of Christ's saving work. He was strong in his condemnation of amusements and other activities for self-gratification.

Controversy over Hick's views became public in 1823 at the Philadelphia Yearly Meeting, where complaints were lodged by some more "orthodox" members. Four years of tension ensued in which many non-theological factors (sociological differences and personal feelings, among others) led to further polarization of the pro-Hicks and anti-Hicks factions. In 1827 the pro-Hicks faction made what was termed a "quiet retreat" from the controversy. They called a conference and organized a separate yearly meeting. Separations followed in New York, Ohio, and across the East and Midwest. Seven yearly meeting were soon established.

In 1868 a Sunday school conference began efforts to coordinate and communicate among the various Hicksite yearly meetings, and in 1900 the General Conference emerged to aid in their common witness. Originally, four coordinating organizations merged to form the conference, including the First-Day School Conference and the Friends Union for Philathropic Labor (organized in 1882). The conference is for fellowship and service only, and has no legislative authority over the participating yearly meetings.

Organization. The conference held biennial conferences until 1968, ever since that time it has held an annual "FGC Gathering of Friends." At constituent yearly meetings, members are appointed to a central committee and to an executive committee which are responsible for the direction and administration of the conference's year-round program.

The program in carried out by six standing committees: advancement and outreach, Christian and interfaith relations, long range conference planning, ministry and nurture, publications and communication, and religious education. The Friends Meeting House Fund, Inc., which holds funds for meetings in need of buying, building or remodeling buildings, operates with a separate board of directors appointed by the central committee. The *Friends Journal*, though not an official conference publication, is managed by a board partially appointed by the central committe and is closely identified with it.

Included in the conference are the Baltimore, Canadian, Illinois, Lake Erie, New England, New York, Northern, Ohio Valley, Philadelphia, South Central, and Southeastern Yearly Meetings; the Southern Appalachian Yearly Meeting and Association, Piedmont Friends Fellowship (NC), Central Alaska Friends Conference, and number of monthly meetings.

Membership: In 1988 the conference reported approximately 32,000 affiliated Qaukers in 490 meetings and worship groups. Approximately 26,000 housefolds receive *The FGC Quarterly*.

Periodicals: *The FGC Quarterly*, 1520-B Race St., Philadelphia, PA 19102; unofficial: *Friends Journal*, 1501 Cherry St., Philadelphia, PA 19102.

Sources: Robert W. Doherty, *The Hicksite Separation*. New Brunswick, NJ: Rutgers University Press, 1967; Rufus M. Jones, *The Latter Periods of Quakerism*. Westport, CT: Greenwood Press, 1970. 2 Vols.; Margaret Hope Bacon, *Mothers of Feminism*. San Francisco: Harper & Row, 1986; Elsie Boulding, *My Part in the Quaker Adventure*. Philadelphia: Religious Education Committee, Friends General Conference, 1858; Jane P. Rushmore, *Testimonies and Practice of the Society of Friends*. Philadelphia: Friends General Conference, 1945.

★536★
FRIENDS UNITED MEETING
101 Quaker Hill Dr.
Richmond, IN 47374

The largest of all the Quaker bodies, the Five Years Meeting of Friends was formed in 1902 as a loose coordinating agency by twelve yearly meetings. By the addition of programs and agencies, a full denominational structure has developed. There are now fourteen yearly meetings in what became in 1965 the Friends United Meeting.

The Friends United Meeting represents the continuation of the "orthodox" Friends who had survived the Hicksite (Friends General Conference) and Wilburite (Religious Society of Friends (Conservative)) schisms, but who had existed throughout the nineteenth century as independent, geographical yearly meetings. Most worship is programmed. Ecumenical efforts began in the 1880s and a series of conferences every five years led to the formation of the Five Years Meeting.

The statement of faith of the Meeting, based upon the teachings of Jesus as "we understand them," includes beliefs in 1) true religion as a personal encounter with God rather than ritual and ceremony; 2) individual worth before God; 3) worship as an act of seeking; 4) essential Christian vitures of moral purity, integrity, honesty, simplicity, and humility; 5) Christian love and goodness; 6) concern for the suffering and unfortunate; and 7) continuing revelation through the Holy Spirit.

Organization. The work of the Meeting is carried out through its General Board and three commissions. The

World Ministries Commission oversees missions in Cuba, Jamaica West Bank in Israel, Kenya, Uganda, Tanzania, and the United States. The Meeting Ministries Commission serves the needs of the local congregations promoting spiritual development and christian education programs. The Communications Commission oversees the publication of the denominational magazine and the production of the literature needed to inform the constituency. There are 18 annual meetings: Baltimore, Canadian, Cuba, East Africa, East Africa (South), Elgon, Indiana, Jamaica, Iowa, Nairobi (Kenya), Nebraska, New England, New York, North Carolina, South West, Southeastern, Western, and Wilmington. It is a member of both the World Council of Churches and the National Council of Churches.

Membership: In 1987 the Meeting had approximately 58,000 members in the United States and Canada with an additional 140,000 members in Africa, Cuba, Jamaica, Mexico, and Israel.

Educational facilities: Earlham College, Richmond, Indiana; Earlham School of Religion, Richmond, Indiana; Guilford College, Greensboro, North Carolina; Whittier College, Whittier, California; William Penn College, Oskaloosa, Iowa.

Periodicals: *Quaker Life*, 101 Quaker Hill Dr., Richmond, IN 47374.

Sources: Francis B. Hall, "Friends United Meeting" in Francis B. Hall, ed., *Friends in the Americas*. Philadelphia: Friends World Committee, Section of the Americas, 1976.

★537★
INTERMOUNTAIN YEARLY MEETING
℅ Ms. Anne White
624 Pearl St., No. 302
Boulder, CO 80302

In the early 1970s, the Pacific Yearly Meeting devised a plan to divide its widely scattered membership into more geographically workable units. Members in Arizona and New Mexico joined with otherwise independent friends in Arizona, New Mexico, and Colorado, as well as Colorado Friends who had withdrawn from the Missouri Valley Yearly Meeting, to form the Intermountain Yearly Meeting. The group had its first annual session in 1975. Most congregations are unprogrammed. The Mexico City congregation affiliated with the Pacific Yearly Meeting also participates in the Intermountain fellowship.

Membership: In 1981 the Meeting reported 655 members in 15 monthly meetings and 10 worship groups.

★538★
IOWA YEARLY MEETING OF FRIENDS
℅ Stephen Main, Gen. Supt.
Box 703
Oskaloosa, IA 52577

The Iowa Yearly Meeting of Friends was established in 1877 by Conservative Friends who separated from the Iowa Yearly Meeting now a part of the Friends United Meeting. It keeps unprogrammed meetings for worship. Scattergood School, a coeducational college-preparatory high school, is operated at West Branch, Iowa.

Membership: In 1982 there were 709 members in 11 monthly meetings.

Sources: Francis B. Hall. ed. *Friends in the Americas*. Philadelphia, PA: Friends World Committee 1976.

★539★
LAKE ERIE YEARLY MEETING
℅ Richard W. Taylor, Clerk
492 Miller St.
Kent, OH 44240

The Lake Erie Yearly Meeting began in 1939 as the Association of Friends Meetings. In 1963 it became a yearly meeting and assumed its present structure in 1969. Congregations are located in Pennsylvania and Ohio with one in Ann Arbor, Michigan. Most meetings are in urban areas or college towns. Worship is unprogrammed. While independent, it has undertaken ecumenical efforts with a wide variety of Friends' groups. It carries on work in Korea with the Ohio Yearly Meeting of the Conservative Friends.

Membership: In 1981 the Meeting had 1,061 members in 23 congregations and worship groups.

Periodicals: *The Lake Erie Bulletin*, 572 Briar Cliff Rd., Pittsburgh, PA 15221.

★540★
MID-AMERICA YEARLY MEETING
2018 Maple
Wichita, KS 67213

The movement westward brought Friends into the South Central states in the early 1800s. The Kansas Yearly Meeting was formed in 1872 and includes churches in Texas, Oklahoma, Colorado, and Missouri. The doctrine is one with other Friends and a pastoral ministry is supported. Worship is programmed. From 1900 to 1937, the Kansas Meeting was in the Five Years Meeting, but withdrew as conservative evangelical elements became dominant in the Kansas Meeting. In 1934, an African mission in the Congo (now Zaire) was established. Camp Quaker Haven at Arkansas City, Kansas, serves the youth. In 1957, the Kansas Meeting joined the Evangelical Friends Alliance.

Membership: In 1988 the Meeting reported 7,600 members, 73 congregations, and 80 ministers.

Educational facilities: Friends Bible College and Academy, Haviland, Kansas; Friends University, Wichita, Kansas.

Periodicals: *Scope*, 2018 Maple, Wichita, KS 67213; *Evangelical Friend*, Box 232, Newberg, OR 97132.

Sources: Ralph E. Choate, *Dust of His Feet*. The Author, 1965; *Discipline*. Kansas Yearly Meeting of Friends, 1966; Paul W. Barnett, *Educating for Peace*. Board of Publications, Kansas Yearly Meeting of Friends, n.d.

★541★
MISSOURI VALLEY FRIENDS CONFERENCE
% John Griffith
5745 Charlotte
Kansas City, MO 64110

The Missouri Valley Friends Conference was formed in 1955 as an association of unprogrammed Quaker meetings in the Midwest which were not affiliated with any other established yearly meeting. The conference meets annually. Over the years some of the local groups have affiliated with the yearly meetings and discontinued participation in the conference. At the same time, new unaffiliated meetings have joined the conference, so attendance has remained fairly constant.

Membership: In 1988 the conference reported approximately 150 members in six congregations.

★542★
NORTH CAROLINA YEARLY MEETING OF FRIENDS (CONSERVATIVE)
% Louise B. Wilson, Clerk
113 Pinewood Rd.
Virginia Beach, VA 23451

The North Carolina Yearly Meeting of Friends (Conservative) is the result of a separation among Friends in North Carolina at the beginning of the century. At that time there was a move to form what would become the Five Years Meeting (now known as the Friends United Meeting). As part of the developments, a new book of discipline was adopted. The Cedar Grove Monthly Meeting opposed the new trends it saw emerging and placed special emphasis on the retention of the unprogrammed meetings for worship. In 1904 they formed a separate yearly meeting and over the years other monthly meetings have been added. They have found fellowship with the other conservative Friends in the Ohio and Iowa Yearly Meetings, and periodically gather with them for fellowship.

Membership: In 1982 there were 375 members in seven monthly meetings.

★543★
NORTH PACIFIC YEARLY MEETING OF THE RELIGIOUS SOCIETY OF FRIENDS
% University Friends Center
4001 9th Ave., N.E.
Seattle, WA 98105

In the early 1970s the Pacific Yearly Meeting, which had congregations spread over a cumbersome distance, divided into several yearly meeetings. In 1972 members in Oregon and Washington became the North Pacific Yearly Meeting and held the first session in 1973. Since its formation groups have been added in Idaho and Montana. The meeting keeps close ties with the parent body with whom it jointly supports a periodical. It also participates in the Pacific Yearly Meeting's Friend-in-the-Orient Program. The meeting is governed in a non-hierarchical fashion. A steering committee provides continuity and a clerk convenes its gatherings, records its minutes, and represents it to to others.

Membership: In 1988 the Meeting reported 11 monthly meetings, four quarterly preparative meetings, and 18 worship groups gathered in the quarterly meetings.

Periodicals: *Friends Bulletin*, 2160 Luke St., San Francisco, CA 94121.

Sources: *Faith and Practice*. Corvallis, OR: North Pacific Yearly Meeting of the Religious Society of Friends, 1986.

★544★
OHIO YEARLY MEETING OF THE SOCIETY OF FRIENDS
61830 Sandy Ridge Rd.
Barnesville, OH 43712

History. The Ohio Yearly Meeting of the Religious Society of Friends was established in 1813 and originally included most of the Friends west of the Alleghany Mountains. The meeting was also one of those most affected by the the conflict in the 1840s between English Quaker Joseph John Gurney and John Wilbur. Gurney had absorbed much from the British Methodists, and Wilbur saw Methodist doctrine replacing the traditional Quaker reliance on the Inner Light. Beginning in 1845, Wilbur's supporters began to separate from the main body of Quakers and are generally known as Conservative Friends. The Ohio Yearly Meeting aligned itself with the Conservative cause.

Beliefs. The Ohio Yearly Meeting places great emphasis upon providing a form of worship which is simple, pure, and spiritual. They advocate the unprogramed meetings in which believers wait in silence for the movement of the Spirit. The yearly meeting has taken a strong stand in opposition to capital punishment, the taking of oaths, participation in war, racial discrimination, and the use of intoxicants.

Organization. The yearly meeting, composed of representatives of the monthly meetings, provides general oversight of the society. Each monthly meeting appoints two members of each gender to act as overseers to have responsibility for pastoral care of members and spiritual oversight of the meeting for worship; two elders to have oversight of the ministry; and ministers as are called.

The yearly meeting is a member of the Friends World Committee for Consultation. Fellowship is kept with the other two remaining Conservative Yearly meetings--North Carolina and Iowa--and there are periodic gatherings of members from the three groups. There is no direct missional program, but a number of service projects are supported through the American Friends Service Committee.

Membership: In 1987 the meeting reported 692 members in 10 monthly meetings.

Periodicals: *Ohio Conservative Friends Review*, Rte 1, Box 147, Salem, WV 26426.

★545★
NORTHWEST YEARLY MEETING OF FRIENDS CHURCH
Box 190
Newberg, OR 97132

Quaker settlers in the northwest first gathered in the fertile Willamette Valley in Oregon in the late nineteenth century. These early settlers were from Iowa and associated with the Iowa Yearly Meeting. In 1893 they were officially established as an independent yearly meeting by the Iowa Yearly Meeting with the name Oregon Yearly Meeting of Friends. Because churches were also in Oregon, Washington, and Idaho, the name was changed to Northwest Yearly Meeting of Friends. From 1902 to 1936, the Oregon Yearly Meeting was a part of the Five Years Meeting, but has in more recent years affiliated with the Evangelical Friends Alliance.

The doctrine of the Northwest Yearly Meeting (NWYM) is biblically based with a central message of the Lordship of Jesus Christ. The emphasis of salvation through the Lord coupled with a strong sense of social commitment have been the two dominant themes of the meeting.

NWYM operates four camping facilities, Friendsview Manor (a retirement home), Barclay Press (a printing company), George Fox College (a four-year liberal arts school), and several elementary and high schools. Missionary work is carried out in cooperation with the Evangelical Friends Alliance. A joint mission program is supported in Mexico, Rwanda, Burundi, Taiwan, Peru, and Bolivia.

Membership: In 1987 NWYM reported 7,898 members, 56 churches, nine extension churches, and five mission points.

Educational facilities: George Fox College, Newberg, Oregon.

Periodicals: *Evangelical Friend*, Box 190, Newberg, OR 97132.

Sources: *This Story of the Friends in the Northwest.* Newberg, OR: Barclay Press, n.d.

★546★
PACIFIC YEARLY MEETING OF FRIENDS
% Stratton Jaquette
258 Cherry Ave.
Los Altos, CA 94022

Quakers began to establish congregations on the West Coast in the 1880s. In 1931, with impetus from Howard H. Brinton and Mary Brinton, a meeting was called which led to the formation of the loosely organized Pacific Coast Association of Friends. In 1947, the Pacific Year Meeting was established within the Association. Over the next decade it grew to include forty congregations as far apart as Mexico City, Honolulu and Canada. Is a result, a committee recommended the division of the meeting into three meetings which led to the establishment of the North Pacific Yearly Meeting (1972) and the Intermountian Yearly Meeting (1973). Though each is independent, there are close familial ties and they jointly publish a periodical.

Its worship is unprogrammed. Membership though concentrated in California includes congregations in Mexico City and Honolulu. Interest in Asia led to the establishment of a Friends-in-the-Orient Program which annually sends a several members to different Asian locations for a year. The Committee publishes *Windows: East and West* to keep interested Friends informed of developments along the Pacific rim.

Membership: In 1981 the Meeting reported 1,452 members in 35 congregations.

Periodicals: *Friends Bulletin.*

Sources: *Faith and Practice.* San Francisco: Pacific Yearly Meeting of the Religious Society of Friends, 1973; Howard H. Brinton, *Guide to Quaker Practice.* Wallingford, PA: Pendle Hill Publications, 1955.

★547★
★547★
ROCKY MOUNTAIN YEARLY MEETING
Box 9629
Colorado Springs, CO 80932

The Rocky Mountain Yearly Meeting was established in 1957 by separation from the Nebraska Yearly Meeting and did not continue the latter's affiliation with the Friends United Meeting. Worship is programmed. Mission work is carried on among the Navajo Indians at the Rough Rock Friends Mission near Chinle, Arizona. Ouaker Ridge Camp is maintained north of Woodland Park, Colorado.

Membership: In 1987 the Meeting reported 1,394 members in 23 congregations located in Colorado, New Mexico, Nebraska, and South Dakota. These include five Navajo churches in the Rough Rock area.

Periodicals: *The Traveling Minute*, Box 9629, Colorado Springs, CO 80932; *Evangelical Friend*, Box 190, Newberg, OR 97132.

Sources: *Faith and Practice of the Rocky Mountain Yearly Meeting of Friends Church*. Pueblo, CO: Riverside Printing Co., 1978; 25th Anniversary Committee, *Friends Ministering Together*. Pueblo, CO: Riverside Printing Co., 1982.

★548★
THE ROGERENES
(Defunct)

The Rogerenes were a small religious group which began as Baptists but were strongly influenced by members of the Society of Friends. They were orginally led by John Rogers (1648?-1721). James Rogers, John's father, had settled in New London, Connecticut, in 1656 and soon became one of the wealthiest men in the colony. Then in 1674 John and his wife Elizabeth withdrew from the Congregational Church and joined the Seventh-Day Baptist Church at Newport, Connecticut. Soon afterward, Elizabeth's father pursuaded her to leave her husband and return home, a separation that became permanent. But other members of the family joined him, and they began a Baptist congregation in New London. John Rogers became the pastor. He actively attacked the state-supported Congregational Church, especially its support of infant baptism and the forced payment of church taxes. As Rogers ideas became more radical, the congregation also broke its ties to the Baptists in Newport around 1677. One of the radicalizing influences was the visits in 1675 between John and members of the congregation and William Edmundson, a Quaker from Ireland visiting America. Out of these discussions, the Rogerenes, as they were soon to be known, dropped the sabbatarian beliefs. But though they worshipped on Sunday, they felt that all days were alike. Rogers especially attacked idolatry which for him included many of the practices of the Congregational Church, such as a salaried ministry and the use of elaborate titles of respect. The group adopted plain clothes, refused to use oaths, and opposed war and violence. John Rogers became a shoemaker as a means of demonstrating the belief that ministers should make their own living. They also opposed contemporary medical practice, replacing it with clean living, good nursing, homemade remedies, and prayer. The group continued to disagree with the Quakers on the issue of sacraments. They baptized new members and celebrated the Lord's Supper annually.

Almost from the beginning the group was persecuted and John Rogers seems to have spent as much as one-third of his life in jail for his religious beliefs. It should be noted that the group did little to decrease the tension with the state church. Members refused to pay church taxes. They would travel on Sunday to attend meetings in defiance of state regulations. They periodically staged demonstrations against idolatrous practices. For example, they would attend the Congregational services and bring work with them. They would interupt and contradict the minister. Gordon Saltonstall, the Congregational minister in New London and later governor of Connecticut, led the persecution until his death in 1724. A final period of intense persecution occurred in the mid-1760s.

John Rogers was succeeded in leadership of the group by his son John Rogers Jr. (d.1853) and he by John Walterhouse, John Bolles, Samuel Whipple, and Jonathan Whipple (1794-1877). Bolles was an early abolitionist who had freed his slaves in the 1720s. In 1735 a group of Rogerenes moved to Morris County, New Jersey, and established a colony. Three years later they moved to Monmouth County, New Jersey, near present-day Ocean City. The settlement died out by the end of the century. During the 1740s, land was purchased near Groton and Mystic, Connecticut, and over a generation the group migrated eastward. Its prosperity in spite of difficulties during the Revolution and the War of 1812 is shown by the erection of a new large meetinghouse in 1815 and an even larger one in the post-Civil War era.

The twentieth century saw the decline of the church. Some families had moved west before the turn of the century, and others drifted to other churches. By the 1940s only a small group was left in Mystic and a smaller group in California. A generation later, while some descendents of former Rogerene families still identified themselves with the group, it seems to have ceased to exist as a church body.

Sources: Ellen Starr Brinton, "The Rogerenes," in *The New England Quarterly*, 16 (March 1943) 3-19; Corliss Fitz Randolph, "The Rogerenes," in *Seventh Day Baptists in Europe and America* (Plainfield, NJ: Seventh Day Baptist General Conference, 1910.

★549★
SOUTHEASTERN YEARLY MEETING
% Gene E. Beardsley
Route 2, Box 108F
Gainesville, FL 32606

The Southeastern Yearly Meeting is a small body established in 1962 and is composed mostly of Friends who migrated south to Florida. They support a retreat and study center near Orlando, Florida. In 1967, there were ten congregations, one of which was in Georgia, with a membership of 389. Membership is from various Friends' traditions.

Membership: In 1981 the Meeting reported 445 members and 22 congregations and worship groups.

Periodicals: *SEYM Newsletter*, 1375 Talbot Ave., Jacksonville, FL 32205.

★550★
SOUTHERN APPALACHIAN YEARLY MEETING
AND ASSOCIATION
% Thomas Lynn, Clerk
902 State Lick Road
Berea, KY 40403

The Southern Appalachian Yearly Meeting and Association of Friends was formed in 1970 at Crossville, Tennessee. It was established by congregations in Alabama, Tennessee, Georgia, Kentucky, West Virginia, South Carolina, and North Carolina, some of which had been associated together as early as 1940 in the South Central Friends Conference (and later in the Southern Appalachian Association of Friends). Congregations are unprogrammed, and there are no paid ministers. Annual meetings, held in May, center on silent worship, a search together on a chosen theme, and social concerns. While existing for some years as an independent Meeting, the Southern Appalachian Association has recently become a constituent part of the Friends General Conference.

Membership: See Friends General Conference (separate entry).

Periodicals: *Southern Applachaian Friend*, Box 1, Micaville, NC 28755.

Other European Free Traditions

★551★
APOSTOLIC CHRISTIAN CHURCH (NAZAREAN)
Apostolic Christian Church Foundation
Box 151
Tremont, IL 61568

The Apostolic Christian Church (Nazarean) traces its history to the movement begun by Samuel Heinrich Froelich (1803-1857), a Swiss clergyman who led a revival in the late 1820s. In 1830, he was deprived of a pulpit by the Swiss state church for preaching the "Gospel of reconciliation in its original purity." The movement, called "Nazarean" on the Continent, spread throughout Europe and was persecuted. Many immigrants flocked to America and congregations were established: Froehlich himself came in 1850 and began immediately to organize his followers as the Apostolic Christian Churches of America. Around 1906/1907 some members of the Apostolic Churches withdrew over several points of doctrine. They adopted the designation "Nazarean," the popular name by which the group is known on the Continent.

Members of the church believe in Christ, are baptized in the name of the Father, Son and Holy Spirit, and form a covenant with God to live a sanctified life and to seek to become rich in good works. They reject the priesthood, infant baptism and transubstantiation, and refuse to be bound with oaths or to participate in war. The church consists only of baptized believers, but affiliated with it are "Friends of Truth," those being converted. Apart from refusing to bear arms and kill in the country's wars, the church is completely law-abiding.

The church is congregationally governed. Elders serve the local church with powers to baptize, lay on hands, administer the Lord's Supper and conduct worship. The Apostolic Catholic Church Foundation is a service organization. It recently moved from Akron, Ohio to its present location.

Membership: In 1985, the church reported 2,799 members, 48 congregations, and 178 ministers.

Periodicals: *Newsletter*, Box 151, Tremont, IL 61568.

★552★
APOSTOLIC CHRISTIAN CHURCHES OF
AMERICA
3420 N. Sheridan Rd.
Peoria, IL 61604

The Apostolic Christian Churches of America began in the protest of a new catechism introduced in 1830 by the Reformed Church in Switzerland. Samual Heinrich Froehlich (1803-1857), a Reformed minister, rejected the new catechism as too rationalistic and in the resulting controversy was dismissed. Rebaptized by Mennonites, he organized the Community of Evangelical Baptists. The nonresistance stance (including refusal to bear arms) adopted by the Community led to considerable tension with the government and occasioned the migration of many members beginning in the 1840s.

The first congregation in America began among members of the Old Order Amish Mennonites of Lewis County, New York. They requested leadership from Froehlich, and he sent an elder, Benedict Weyeneth to found a congregation at Croghan. He ordained Joseph Virkler to the ministry and returned to Switzerland. He soon returned to the United States and established a second congregation in Woodford County, Illinois. Froehlich visited the churches in 1850. Growth came slowly, primarily from German-speaking immigrants to the Midwest.

Following Froehlich, the Church draws upon the Reformation concensus of the Reformed and Mennonite churches. It preaches the salvation of souls, the change of heart through regeneration, a life of godliness guided and directed by the Holy Spirit, and a striving for entire sanctification. Members are non-combatants, but loyal to the laws of the United States. A mission in Japan is supported.

Membership: In 1986, the church reported 16,916 members, 80 congregations, and 347 ministers.

Periodicals: *The Silver Lining*, Graybill, IN.

Sources: *Footsteps to Zion, A History of the Apostolic Christian Church of America*; S. H. Froehlich, *The Mystery of Godliness and the Mystery of Ungodliness.* Apostolic Christian Church, n.d.; S. H. Froehlich, *Individual Letters and Meditations.* Syracuse, NY: Apostolic Christian Publishing Co., 1926.

★553★
CHRISTIAN APOSTOLIC CHURCH (FOREST, ILLINOIS)
Forrest, IL 61741

The Christian Apostolic Church grew out of unrest within the German Apostolic Christian Church during the 1950s. Elder Peter Schaffer, Sr., one of the founders of the German Apostolic Christian Church, protested the attempts of church leaders in Europe to direct the life of the American congregations. Beginning with members in Illinois and Oregon, he organized congregations in Forest and Morton, Illinois; Silverton, Oregon; and Sabetha, Kansas in 1955. Doctrine and practice of the parent body were continued.

Membership: In 1988 the church reported four congregations with several hundred members.

★554★
CHRISTIAN APOSTOLIC CHURCH (SABETHA, KANSAS)
Sabetha, KS 66534

The Christian Apostolic Church was founded in the early 1960s when members of the German Apostolic Christian Church in Illinois and Kansas withdrew under the leadership of William Edelman. The members were protesting several points of "interpretation of the statues and customs" of the Church.

Membership: Not reported. There are three congregations.

★555★
CHRISTIAN COMMUNITY AND BROTHERHOOD OF REFORMED DOUKBOHORS (SONS OF FREEDOM)
Site 8, Comp. 42
Cresent Valley, BC, Canada V0G 1HO

The Christian Community and Brotherhood of Reformed Doukbohors, better known as the Sons of Freedom, emerged within the larger Doukhobor community in Canada in the early twentieth century. They were the ardent supporters of Peter Verigin (d. 1924) who was the leader of the Doukhobors at the time of their migration to Canada in 1899. Verigin was left behind in prison, but was released in 1902 and rejoined the community. The Sons of Freedom were that element of the group most loyal to Verigin and most opposed to the Canadian government's varied attempts to integrate the Doukhobors into the larger social context. They particularly opposed the establishment of public schools and the government imposing secular education on Doukhobor children.

For many years they existed as an integral part of the Doukhobor community. They supported the leadership of Peter Christiakov Verigin who succeeded the elder Verigin in 1924. During his tenure in office the number of the Sons of Freedom greatly expanded, and by the early 1930s, there were more than 1,000. The actual break with the larger community came in 1933, occasioned by a letter from P. C. Verigin, at the time in prison, asking all Doukhobors to refrain from paying any dues to the directors of the Christian Community of Universal Brotherhood (CCUB). They followed Verigin's orders, and the CCUB expelled them from the larger body. The break was healed for a short while during World War II when the Sons of Freedom were invited into the Union of Doukhobors of Canada. Formed in 1945, the Union soon fell apart, and the Sons of Freedom emerged as a fully independent group.

The Sons of Freedom were particularly critical of John Verigin who succeeded to the leadership of the larger group of the Union of Spiritual Communities of Christ (Orthodox Doukhobors of Canada) after the death of P. C. Verigin in 1937. His plans to accomodate government pressure were denounced as a distortion of Doukhobor faith. They were especially resistant to any introduction of public schools which they felt would simply educate people into an acceptance of war and the exploitation of working class people, and lead to the distruction of families and communities.

In 1950 Stephan Sorokin, an immigrant from Russia and former member of the Russian Orthodox Church, came to the Doukobors to claim a leadership role. After fleeing from Russia, he wandered from many years and successively joined the Plymouth Brethren, the Lutherans, the Baptists, and the Seventh-day Adventist Church. He came to Canada in 1949 and lived among the members of the Society of Independent Doukhobors in Saskatchewan, learning the ways of the community, particularly their songs. He also learned of the story of Peter Christtiakov Verigin, the leader who died in 1939. It would have been the place of his son, Peter Verigin II to assume the role as spiritual leader of the Doukhobors, but it was assumed that he was in a Russian prison camp. Though it was later learned that he had died in prison in 1942, many in the community awaited the arrival of the "lost" son of Peter Christiakov Verigin.

Sorokin arrived among the Doukhobor settlements in April 1950. He was introduced among the Sons of Freedom by one of their prominent leaders, John Lebedoff, who departed three months later to begin serving a two year prison term. Under Lebedoff's period of influence, there was heightened violence and tension between the Sons of Freedom and the state. However, the majority of the Sons of Freedom accepted Sorokin as the lost spiritual leader and reorganized themselves as the Christian Community and Brotherhood of Reformed Doukhobors.

Over the years of their existence, the Sons of Freedom had gained a reputation for more extreme forms of civil disobedience in their attempts to prevent the loss of Doukhobor ideals by accomodation to the government, and the late 1940s and early 1950s were years of heightened anti-government protests. The Sons of Freedom were accused of bombings and arson (of new school buildings), and periodically underscored their displeasure with demonstrations in the nude. When tried and convicted of actions associated with their protests, many of the group served prison terms. However, under the leadership of Sorokin, the group began restraining from participation in such activities, which lessened the overall tension level between the Doukhobor community, its neighbors, and the Canadian government.

Membership: Not reported. There are several thousand Sons of Freedom primarily at Kerstova and Gilpin, British Columbia. In 1982 they were reported to have a congregation of 2,250 members near Krestova.

Sources: George Woodcock and Ivan Avakumovic, *The Doukhobors.* Toronto: Oxford University Press, 1968; Florence E. Lebidoff, *The Truth about the Doukhobors.* Cresent Valley, BC: The Author, 1948; *A Public Indictment of J. J. Verigin.* Krestova, BC: Christian Community of Reformed Doukhobors, (Sons of Freedom), 1954.

★556★
GERMAN APOSTOLIC CHRISTIAN CHURCH
Current address not obtained for this edition.

The German Apostolic Christian Church is the result of a schism in the Apostolic Christian Churches of America. During the 1930s the pressure to discard the German

language in worship, pressure which had greatly intensified since World War I, led the majority of the church to begin to use English. A group led by Elder Martin Steidinger protested that the loss of German would be accompanied by a loss of piety and lead to the influx of worldliness. With the encouragement of some European church leaders, he led members in the founding of the German Apostolic Christian Churches with initial congregations in Sabetha, Kansas, Silverton and Portland, Oregon and several locations in Illinois. Support came primarily from first generation immigrants. Doctrine and practice are like that of the parent body.

Membership: Not reported. There are an estimated 500 members.

★557★
MOLOKAN SPIRITUAL CHRISTIANS
(POSTOJANNYE)
841 Carolina St.
San Francisco, CA 94107

The Postojannye are those Molokan Spiritual Christian who reject the practice of enthusiastic jumping during worship services which characterize their Pryguny Molokans. The split in the Molokan community into the Postojannye (the Steadfast) and the Jumpers occurred in the mid-nineteenth century in Russia. The Postojannye also reject the authority of the charismatic- prophetic leaders who arose at that same time, such as Maksim Gavrilovic Rudometkin. Otherwise the beliefs and practices of the Postojannye and Pryguny are similiar.

The first Postojannye came to the United States in 1905. They tried to work in the sugar field of Hawaii, but in 1906, shortly after the earthquake, moved to San Francisco and settled on Potrero Hill.

Membership: Not reported. There were an estimated 2,000 Postojannye Molokans in the mid 1970s. They live in San Francisco, the greater Bay area and in Woodburn, Oregon.

Sources: Ethel Dunn and Stephen P. Dunn, "Religion and Ethnicity: The Case of the American Molokans" in *Ethnicity* vol. 4, no. 4, (December 1977) pp. 370-79.

★558★
MOLOKAN SPIRITUAL CHRISTIANS (PRYGUNY)
% Paul I. Samarin
944 Orme St.
Los Angeles, CA 99923

Among numerous free evangelical groups which derived from the Russian Orthodox Church, only a few have come to the United States. Among these few are the Molokans, founded by Simeon Uklein (b.1733). He was a son-in-law of a leader of the Doukhobors, a mystical Russian group which is now found in western Canada. Forsaking mysticism, Uklein returned to the Russian

Orthodox Church, and began to preach a Bible-oriented faith. He claimed that the church fathers had diluted the true faith with pagan philosophy. The true church, which existed visibly until their time, disappeared and survived only in scattered and persecuted communities. Uklein taught a form of unitarianism and gnosticism. Both the Son and the Holy Spirit were seen as subordinate to the Father; Christ was clothed in angelic, not human, flesh. Uklein tended to be anti-ritualistic and denied the sacraments and rites. Baptism means hearing the word of God and living accordingly; confession is repentance from sin; and the anointing of the sick is prayer. A ritual was constructed from Scripture and hymns. Molokans drink milk during Lent (from which the name Molokans or Milk Drinkers is derived), a practice forbidden in the Russian Orthodox Church. Uklein also adopted some of the Mosaic dietary law.

In the 1830s a great revival, an outpouring of the Holy Spirit, began in the Molokan community. It led to much enthusiastic religious expression, especially the jumping about of worshippers and the appearance of a number of charismatic prophetic leaders, the most popular one being Maksim Gavrilovic Rudometkin (d.1877). The acceptance of these new emphases which grew out of the revival split the Molokans into the Postoiannye (the Steadfast) who reject the practice of jumping and the teachings of Rudometkin and the Pryguny (jumpers). The urge to migrate to America began among the Molokans after the introduction of universal military service by the Russian government in 1878, but came to a head with their refusal to bear arms during the Russo-Japanese War. Over 2,000 left, primarily between 1904 and 1914 (when Russia stopped legal immigration) and settled in California. After World War I, some 500 more who had originally settled in the Middle East were allowed into the United States.

The Pryguny Molokons, the largest group to migrate to the United States, settled in Los Angeles from which they have moved into surrounding suburbs and communities. Various studies of the community found an estimated 3,500 (1912), 5,000 (late 1920s), and then 15,000 (1970). Churches can be found in Kerman, Porterville, Sheridan, Shafter, Delano, Elmira, and San Marcos, California. There is also a group in Glendale, Arizona and a small group in Baja California.

Membership: Not reported. There are an estimated 15,000 to 20,000 Prygun Molokons as of the mid-1980s.

Sources: Paul I. Samarin, comp., *The Russian Molokan Directory*. Los Angeles: the Author,(issued annually); Willard Burgess Moore, *Molokan Oral Tradition*. Berkeley: University of California Press, 1973; Stephen P. Dunn and Ethel Dunn, *The Molokan Heritage Collection. I, Reprints of Articles and Translations*. Berkeley: Highgate Road Social Science Research Station, 1983.

★559★
SCHWENKFELDER CHURCH IN AMERICA
Pennsburg, PA 18073

A surviving group of the followers of Caspar Schwenckfeld (1489-1561) left Silesia in 1734 because of persecution and came to America. In 1782 they organized the Schwenkfelder Church. The present general conference is a voluntary association of five churches, all in southeastern Pennsylvania. It meets semi-annually.

The Schwenkfelders follow the spiritual-mystical lead of their founder. Schwenckfeld, at one time a wealthy German nobleman, came to believe that all externals, though to be used, are of the perishable material world, and he sought to discover the spiritual imperishable reality behind them. He found them in the inner word, the church of those redeemed and called, the invisible spiritual sacrament, faith, and liberty--all emphasized by contemporary Schwenkfelders. Baptism is for adult believers only, but communion is open to all. No distinctive dress is worn. Both public office and military service is allowed (a practice which separates them from many of the Pennsylvania German groups).

Membership: In 1988 there were 5 churches, 2,700 members and 13 ministers.

Periodicals: *The Schwenkfeldian*, 1 Seminary Street, Pennsburg, PA 18073.

Sources: Howard Wiegner Kriebel, *The Schwenkfelders in Pennsylvania*. Lancaster, PA: Pennsylvania-German Society, 1904; Peter C. Erb, *Schwenckfeld in His Reformation Setting*. Valley Forge, PA: Judson Press, 1978; Selina Gerhard Schultz, *A Course of Study in the Life and Teachings of Caspar Schwenckfeld von Ossig (1489-1561) and the History of the Schwenkfelder Religious Movement (1518-1964)*. Pennsburg, PA: The Board of Publication of the Schwenkfelder Church, 1964.

★560★
SMITH VENNER
% Lothar Dreger
470 Ediron Ave.
Winnipeg, MB, Canada R2G 0M4

The Smith Venner, more popularly known as the "friends" of Johann Oskar Smith (b. 1871), is a loosely-organized Norwegian group which emphasizes piety and living the Christian life as opposed to the emphasis placed on doctrine by the Norwegian state church. Smith Venner spread as Norwegians migrated to other countries around the world. In the 1970s, some 3,500 where reported to have attended the annual meetings, representing some 20 nations. Membership in the United States is centered in the Northwest, with additional members spread across the western half of Canada. During the 1970s, the group was served by two periodicals, *Skjulte Skatter* (in Norwegian) and *The Way* (in English), but published in Salem,

Oregon. In 1979 *The Way* was superceded by *Hidden Treasures*.

Membership: Not reported.

Periodicals: *Hidden Treasures*, %Lothar Dreger, 470 Winnipeg, MB R2G 0M4.

★561★
SOCIETY OF INDEPENDENT DOUKHOBORS
Current address not obtained for this edition.

The Doukhobors migrated to Canada from Russia beginning in 1899. There, a communal organization, the Christian Community of Universal Brotherhood, was implemented. A number of members of the community, people who otherwise accepted Doukhobor belief, soon rejected the communal lifestyle. In addition, these individuals came to reject the special role of the community's spiritual leader, Peter Verigin, though they continued to live on the edge of the community and interact with its members.

The issue of the Independents, as they had come to be called, came into sharp focus as World War I began. Verigin, angered by their dissent, cut them off from the protection provided by the National Service Act of 1917. In 1918 the Independents organized the Society of Independent Doukhobors. Following the death of Peter Verigin, the society was briefly reconciled to the leadership of Verigin's son, Peter Christiakov Verigin, and cooperated in the formation of the Society of Named Doukhobors. In 1937, as the communal structures were dissolving, the Independents denounced Verigin and broke relations with his organization. During World War II, the Independents briefly joined in with the Union of Spiritual Communities of Christ, the successor to the Society of Named Doukhobors, and the Sons of Freedom (a third faction) to form the short-lived Union of Doukhobors of Canada. It fell apart when the Union of Spiritual Communities of Christ withdrew. The Independents expelled the Sons of Freedom. Since that time the Independents have existed separately. Not bound by communal economic restraints, they have spread across western Canada as far east as Manitoba.

Membership: In the mid-1970s the society had 23 affiliated centers in British Columbia, Alberta, and Saskatchewan, and one center in Manitoba.

★562★
SONS OF FREEDOM (DOUKHOBORS)
Krestova, BC, Canada

Soon after the arrival of the Doukhobors in Canada from Russia, Peter Verigin's leadership was protested. Some felt he was compromising the teachings of his letters, which had guided the group during his exile in Siberia. They marched through the early settlements in Saskatchewan, preaching the renunciation of the world and calling

themselves "Svobodniki," literally "Freedomites," but generally referred to as "Sons of Freedom." To call the members of the community to the simple life and to dramatize their own God-given Adamic nature, they marched naked. They were eventually arrested and some sent to an asylum. Through the next few decades, though often disapproving of its actions, they remained a part of the larger Doukhobor community.

In 1923 a public school in the community was burned to the ground shortly after opening. The Sons of Freedom have been blamed for that burning and the many others that have occurred over the years. The school burnings represented a new motif in the protests which had previously been directed at other community members. They began protesting outside forces, government regulations that were against the Law of God.

The Sons of Freedom initially accepted the new leadership of Peter Christiakov Verigin III, who succeeded his father as spiritual leader of the Doukhobors in 1924. But as he proceeded with the reorganization of the communal life and dealt with the governmental demands of the province, the Sons of Freedom began to voice their dissent. In 1928 they issued an open letter denouncing, among other things, the acceptance of public schools (which had been forced upon the community) and the payment of taxes.

The Sons of Freedom gained support during the 1930s as the communal corporation disintegrated and as the main body of community members formed the Society of Named Doukhobors. The Sons of Freedom were excluded from the larger body when they did not pay their annual dues. The apparent break was healed for a short time during World War II, when the Sons of Freedom were invited into the Union of Doukobors of Canada. Formed in 1945, the Union soon fell apart and the Sons of Freedom emerged as a fully independent group. The succeeding decades have been a time of the rise and fall of leaders, periodic protests by the Sons of Freedom (including fires, bombings, and nude demonstrations), and periods of relative calm.

In 1950 the Sons of Freedom experienced a schism when Stephan Sorokin appeared among them. A former member of the Russian Orthodox Church, Sorokin appeared as a leader capable of reuniting the loosely organized group. His main rival was John Lebedoff, who in July 1950 began a prison term. Subsequently, many of the Sons of Freedom accepted Sorokin and left to found the Christian Community and Brotherhood of Reformed Doukhobors. When Lebedoff returned in 1952, he was unable to become the sole leader of the remaining Sons of Freedom. They have remained loosely and informally organized. They have also remained in a high degree of tension with both the government of British Columbia and the surrounding non-Doukhobor society (tension ably demonstrated by the 1965 polemic against the Sons of Freedom by Simma Holt, *Terror in the Name of God*.

Membership: There are three centers in British Columbia, one at Agassiz, Gilpin, and Krestova, and several hundred adherents.

Sources: Simma Holt, *Terror in the Name of God.* New York: Crown Publishers, 1965; George Woodcock & Ivan Avakumovic, *The Doukhobors.* Toronto: Oxford University Press, 1968.

★563★
UNION OF SPIRITUAL COMMUNITIES OF CHRIST (ORTHODOX DOUKHOBORS IN CANADA)
% USCC Central Office
Box 760
Grand Forks, BC, Canada V0H 1H0

The Union of Spiritual Communities of Christ is the oldest and largest of several Doukhobor, or "Spirit Wrestler," groups in western Canada. The Doukhobors originated out of the great schism in the Russian Orthodox Church which began in the reforms of Patriarch Nikon. Nikon assumed control of the church in 1652. Over the years a number of sectarian groups appeared, including the Khlysty, or People of God, who originated in the early eighteenth century and perpetuated a mystical doctrine of the inner guiding light and the dwelling of God in the human soul. The Khlysty developed some extreme doctrines, especially those surrounding the claims to godhood by several early leaders. In the mystical life of the Doukhobors there was no place for water baptism, only spirit baptism. They seemed to have originated from the Khlysty, though they drew strongly from the Unorthodox Unitarian Protestantism that had also penetrated Russia from Poland.

The exact origins of the Doukhobors as a separate "sect" is a matter of controversy. But by 1730, when Sylvan Kolesnikoff formed a community of followers in the village of Nikolai, Ekaterinoslav, the Doukhobors had been established. Kolesnokoff was succeeded by Ilarion Pobirokhin as the new leader of the group. During his tenure, which ended in his exile in Siberia, Ambrosia, the Russian Orthodox bishop of Ekaterinoslav, gave the group its name, Doukhobors. Ambrosia intended "Doukhobor" to be a derisive term, implying the group's defiance of the Spirit of God in the Russian Church; the group interpreted the term as denoting their wrestling against spiritual pride and lust by the Spirit of God.

The next century saw the Doukhobors experiencing alternate periods of persecution and toleration. After Pobirokhin's exile, Sabellius Kapustin assumed leadership. In 1802, with the blessing of Czar Alexander I, Kapustin organized the Doukhobors in Molochnyne Valley, where they had been exiled in isolation from the Orthodox. He established a communal system, the memory of which periodically reappears in the larger Doukhobor community.

In 1886 Peter Verigin (d. 1924) became the leader. He was opposed by a minority group led by Alesha Zubkov, who created a schism in the community. Zubkov was also able to have Verigin arrested and exiled to Siberia. From Siberia, however, Verigin was able to stay in contact with the group and continued to exercise leadership. He also learned of Leo Tolstoy, through whom he led the group to accept pacifism and to deny the state's right to register birth and marriage. Communal ownership of property was reasserted. With Tolstoy's financial assistance and the aid of American and British Quakers, the Verigin group migrated to Canada, the first Doukhobor arriving in January 1899. They settled in Saskatchewan, and in 1902 the Russian government released Verigin so he could also migrate. He led the group until 1924 when his son, Peter Christiakov Verigin, succeeded him.

Even as plans began to be made for the migration, the Doukhobors reorganized as a communal group, named the Christian Community of Universal Brotherhood (C.C.U.B.). In Saskatchewan the Christian Community was almost immediately reestablished. But in 1907, when the group members refused to acknowledge the Oath of Allegiance, as required by the Homestead Act, the government took back the land upon which they had settled. A new settlement in British Columbia was begun.

Under Verigin's son, in 1928, the C.C.U.B. was reorganized as the Society of Named Doukhobors. In 1934 a Declaration outlining Doukhobor belief and practice was published. The decade proved a financial disaster for the communally organized C.C.U.B. Beset by schism of its more activist members and a slow recovery from the Depression, the C.C.U.B. went bankrupt in 1940. The land was taken over by the government, who payed the debts and became its "trustee." it was also at this time that the Union of Spiritual Communities of Christ superceded the Society of Named Doukhobors.

Peter Christiakov Verigin died in 1937; his son was in Russia in prison. In his absence John Verigin, a nephew, became the group's leader, but never assumed the role of "spiritual leader," the position of his uncle. Under his leadership, a plan for reclaiming the land was pursued, and most was returned to the group in 1963.

The Union of Spiritual Communities of Christ was able to retain the loyalty of the majority of Doukhobors, though challenged by several factions in the 1930s. The Union has no creed, but its beliefs find expression in the Doukhobor Psalms and the Declaration of 1934. In the Psalms, God is seen as an eternal spiritual being, the creator. God frequently chooses to speak through the mouths of men, historically the Doukhobor leaders. Christ was the savior of whom God spoke most perfectly. Within the human self God places a divine spark, and it is the believer's duty to recognize and nurture it. Believers best approach God through worship and by following the inward law of God. The spiritual knowledge attained from this inward divinity is the sustaining force in times of persecution. The

Declaration identifies the Doukhobors as of "the Law of God and Faith of Jesus." They advocate pacifism and refuse to vote, but consider themselves law-abiding in all matters not contrary to the Law of God and Faith of Jesus. They strive toward a communal life. They have taken an activist stance in the peace movement, and have frequently come into conflict with the govenment by defending their beliefs against what they consider government interference.

Membership: In the mid-1970s the Union had 36 community branches, all within a seventy-mile radius of Grand Forks, British Columbia.

Periodicals: *Iskra*, Grand Forks, BC V0H 1H0

Remarks: The U.S.C.C. is to be distinguished from the most activist and often violent wing of the Doukhobor movement, the Sons of Freedom, which became quite controversial in the early 1960s for their public demonstrations against Canadian-government policy.

Sources: F. M. Mealing, *Doukhobor Life*. Castlegar, BC: Cotinneh Books, 1975; George Woodcock and Ivan Avakumovic, *The Doukhobors*. Toronto: Oxford University Press, 1968; Koozma J. Tarasoff, *A Pictorial History of the Doukhobors*. Saskatoon, SK: Modern Press, 1969; Aylmer Maude, *A Peculiar People*. New York: Funk & Wagnalls, 1904.

Indexes

Educational Institutions Index

An alphabetical listing of post-secondary educational institutions sponsored and/or supported by religious organizations described in the directory sections of the *Encyclopedia*. Numbers cited in this index refer to entries in the directory sections (Part 2 of each volume), not to page numbers. Directory entries 1–563 will be found in Volume I; 564–1089 in Volume II; 1090–1588 in Volume III.

Periodicals Index

An alphabetical listing of periodicals and newsletters regularly issued by the religious organizations outlined in the directory sections. Numbers noted in this index refer to entries in the directory sections (Part 2 of each volume), not to page numbers. Directory entries 1–563 will be found in Volume I; 564–1089 in Volume II; 1090–1588 in Volume III. (This index does not cover source material listed at the end of each of the essays, nor publications listed under the heading "Sources" within each directory sections entry.)

Geographic Index

The United States appears first, with entries arranged alphabetically by state and subarranged by city. Canadian entries are listed next, with entries arranged alphabetically by province and subarranged by city. Entries include organization name and address, followed by the directory entry number in parentheses. Directory entries 1–563 will be found in Volume I; 564–1089 in Volume II; 1090–1588 in Volume III.

UNITED STATES

Alabama

APOSTOLIC FAITH MISSION CHURCH OF GOD (392)
3344 Pearl Ave. N.
Birmingham, AL 36101

APOSTOLIC OVERCOMING HOLY CHURCH OF GOD (394)
% Bishop Jasper C. Roby
1120 N. 24th St.
Birmingham, AL 35234

LIBERTY FELLOWSHIP OF CHURCHES AND MINISTERS (487)
2732 Old Rocky Ridge Rd.
Birmingham, AL 35216

TRIUMPH THE CHURCH AND KINGDOM OF GOD IN CHRIST (299)
Box 77056
Birmingham, AL 35228

UNIVERSAL CHURCH OF SCIENTIFIC TRUTH (923)
1250 Indiana St.
Birmingham, AL 35224

CHURCH OF GOD (WORLD HEADQUARTERS) (325)
1270 Willow Brook, S.E., Apt. 2
Huntsville, AL 35802

SECOND CUMBERLAND PRESBYTERIAN CHURCH IN U. S. (197)
226 Church St.
Huntsville, AL 35801

INTEGRITY COMMUNICATIONS (AND RELATED MINISTRIES) (483)
Box Z
Mobile, AL 36616

HOUSE OF GOD WHICH IS THE CHURCH OF THE LIVING GOD, THE PILLAR AND GROUND OF TRUTH WITHOUT CONTROVERSY (KEITH DOMINION) (434)
% Bishop J. W. Jenkins, Chief Overseer
Box 9113
Montgomery, AL 36108

BIBLE METHODIST CONNECTION OF CHURCHES (302)
% Rev. V.O. Agan
Box 523
Pell City, AL 35125

ASSEMBLY OF YAHVAH (723)
Box 89
Winfield, AL 35594

Alaska

MUSIC SQUARE CHURCH (364)
Box 398
Alma, AK 72921

HARMONY BUDDHIST MISSION (1535)
% Rev, Frank Newton
Clarksville, AK 92830

CHRISTIAN IDENTITY CHURCH (746)
Box 1779
Harrison, AK 72601

ALASKA YEARLY MEETING (532)
% Walter E. Outwater
Box 687
Kotzebue, AK 99752

Arizona

UNITED ORDER EFFORT (813)
% Leroy Johnson
Colorado City, AZ 86021

OASIS FELLOWSHIP (1170)
Box O
Florence, AZ 85232

SONS AHMAN ISRAEL (812)
% SAI Acres
Fredonia, AZ 86022

OLD EPISCOPAL CHURCH (69)
% Rt. Rev. Jack C. Adam
Box 2424
Mesa, AZ 85204

BEREAN BIBLE FELLOWSHIP (659)
52nd & E. Virginia Sts.
Phoenix, AZ 85008

BETHANY BIBLE CHURCH AND RELATED
INDEPENDENT BIBLE CHURCHES OF THE
PHOENIX, ARIZONA, AREA (644)
6060 N. Seventh Ave.
Phoenix, AZ 85013

CHURCH OF ESSENTIAL SCIENCE (934)
% Rev. Brian Seabrook
Box 31129
Phoenix, AZ 85046

HALL DELIVERANCE FOUNDATION (378)
Box 9910
Phoenix, AZ 85068

MIRACLE LIFE FELLOWSHIP INTERNATIONAL
(383)
11052 N. 24th Ave.
Phoenix, AZ 85029

MIRACLE LIFE REVIVAL, INC. (384)
Box 20707
Phoenix, AZ 85036

NATIONAL COLORED SPIRITUALIST ASSOCIATION
OF CHURCHES (954)
% Rev. Nellie Mae Taylor
1245 West Watkins Rd.
Phoenix, AZ 85007

THEOCENTRIC FOUNDATION (1085)
3341 E. Cambridge Ave.
Phoenix, AZ 85008

UNIVERSITY OF LIFE CHURCH (979)
% Rev. Richard Ireland
5600 Sixth St.
Phoenix, AZ 85040

HOHM (1372)
% Anthony Zuccarello, President
Box 25839
Prescott Valley, AZ 86312

AQUARIAN EDUCATIONAL GROUP (1118)
Box 267
Sedona, AZ 86336

RUBY FOCUS OF MAGNIFICENT CONSUMMATION
(1156)
P.O. Drawer 1188
Sedona, AZ 86336

UNIVERSARIUN FOUNDATION (1024)
Box 890
Taylor, AZ 85939

INFINITE WAY (877)
Box 215
Youngtown, AZ 85363

Arkansas

CHRISTIAN RESEARCH, INC. (747)
Box 385
Eureka Springs, AR 72632

THE REGISTRY (679)
Box 279
Leslie, AR 72645

BAPTIST MISSIONARY ASSOCIATION OF AMERICA
(569)
716 Main St.
Little Rock, AR 72201

ORTHODOX CHURCH OF AMERICA (126)
% Most Rev. David Baxter
502 East Childress
Morrilton, AR 72110

NEW TESTAMENT CHURCH OF GOD (270)
Box 611
Mountain Home, AR 72653

FREE CHRISTIAN ZION CHURCH OF CHRIST (237)
1315 Hutchingson
Nashville, AR 71852

NEW LIFE FELLOWSHIP (729)
Box 75
Natural Dam, AR 72948

SOVEREIGN GRACE BAPTIST CHURCHES (591)
Calvary Grace Baptist Church
Box 7464
Pine Bluff, AR 71611-7464

SHILOH TRUST (853)
% Rev. James Janisch
Sulfur Springs, AR 72763

AMERICAN BAPTIST ASSOCIATION (564)
4605 N. State Line Ave.
Texarkana, AR 75501

California

VEDANTIC CENTER (1417)
3528 N. Triunfo Canyon Rd.
Agoura, CA 91301

HOME OF TRUTH (901)
1300 Grand St.
Alameda, CA 94501

ASSOCIATES FOR SCRIPTURAL KNOWLEDGE (686)
Box 7777
Alhambra, CA 91802-7777

THE (LOCAL) CHURCH (669)
% Living Stream Ministry
1853 West Ball Rd.
Anaheim, CA 92804

ESOTERIC FRATERNITY (845)
Box 37
Applegate, CA 95703

THE SYNANON CHURCH (873)
50300 Highway 245
Box 42
Badger, CA 93603

THE GEORGIAN CHURCH (1226)
1908 Verde St.
Bakersfield, CA 93304

LECTORIUM ROSICRUCIANUM (1094)
Western North American headquarters
Box 9246
Bakersfield, CA 93389

BESHARA SCHOOL OF INTENSIVE ESOTERIC
  EDUCATION (1310)
2448 Prospect St.
Berkeley, CA 94704

CHURCH OF DIVINE MAN (1041)
% Berkeley Psychic Institute
2436 Haste St.
Berkeley, CA 94704

COVENANT OF THE GODDESS (1215)
Box 1226
Berkeley, CA 94704

PRANA YOGA ASHRAM (1392)
International Headquarters
% Swami Sivalingam
488 Spruce St.
Berkeley, CA 94708

RIGPA FELLOWSHIP (1523)
Box 7866
Berkeley, CA 94707

VEDANTIC CULTURAL SOCIETY (1418)
2324 Stuart St.
Berkeley, CA 94705

DEVA FOUNDATION (1362)
336 S. Doheny Drive, 7
Beverly Hills, CA 90211

INDEPENDENT CHURCH OF ANTIOCH (1134)
% The New Church Center
350 Santa Cruz St.
Boulder Creek, CA 95006

TAUNGPUPU KABA-AYE DHAMMA CENTER (1460)
18335 Big Basin Way
Boulder Creek, CA 95006

VAJRAPANI INSTITUTE FOR WISDOM CULTURE
  (1527)
Box I
Boulder Creek, CA 95006

MISSIONARY DISPENSARY BIBLE RESEARCH (728)
Box 5296
Buena Park, CA 90622

CHURCH OF THE ETERNAL SOURCE (1212)
Box 7091
Burbank, CA 91510-7091

WORLD COMMUNITY SERVICE (1421)
1021 E. Magnolia Blvd.
Burbank, CA 91501

THE COLONY (843)
Burnt Ranch, CA 95527

HINDU TEMPLE SOCIETY OF SOUTHERN
  CALIFORNIA (1432)
1600 Las Virgenes Canyon Rd.
Calabasas, CA 91302

PRE-NICENE CHURCH (DE PALATINE) (1145)
% Most Rev.Seiji Yamauchi
23301 Mobile St.
Canoga Park, CA 91307-3322

CONCORDANT PUBLISHING CONCERN (662)
15570 W. Knochaven Drive
Canyon Country, CA 91351

TWENTIETH CENTURY CHURCH OF GOD (702)
Box 4010
Carlsbad, CA 92008

SUBUD (1321)
% Chairman Locksin Thompson
4 Pilot Rd.
Carmel, CA 93924

AMERICAN INDEPENDENT ORTHODOX CHURCH
  (BRIDGES) (85)
516 W. Caldwell
Compton, CA 90220

BROTHERHOOD OF PEACE AND TRANQUILITY
  (778)
Box 2142
Costa Mesa, CA 92626

CALVARY CHAPEL CHURCH (351)
Box 8000
Costa Mesa, CA 92626

NOOHRA FOUNDATION (908)
% Dr. Rocco A. Errico
720 Paularino Ave.
Costa Mesa, CA 92626

FRATERNITAS L. V. X. OCCULTA (1185)
Box 5094
Covina, CA 91723

HOLY APOSTOLIC-CATHOLIC CHURCH OF THE
  EAST (CHALDEAN-SYRIAN) (146)
% Metropolitan Mikhael
190 Palisades Dr.
Daly City, CA 94015

ORTHODOX CATHOLIC SYNOD OF THE SYRO-
  CHALDEAN RITE (150)
% Most Rev. Bashir Ahmed
100 Los Banos Ave.
Daly City, CA 94014

CATHOLIC APOSTOLIC CHURCH AT DAVIS (142)
% Gates of Praise Center
921 W. 8th St.
Davis, CA 95616

FILIPINO ASSEMBLIES OF THE FIRST BORN (356)
1229 Glenwood
Delano, CA 93215

JOHANNINE CATHOLIC CHURCH (1136)
% Archbishop J. Julian Gillman
Box 227
Dulzura, CA 92107

MEXICAN NATIONAL CATHOLIC CHURCH (26)
% Rt. Rev. Emile F. Rodriguez-Fairfield
4011 E. Brooklyn Ave.
East Los Angeles, CA 90022

UNARIUS-SCIENCE OF LIFE (1022)
143 S. Magnolia
El Cajon, CA 92022

PROSPEROS (1320)
% Inner Space Center
Box 5505
El Monte, CA 91734

MAZDAZNAN MOVEMENT (1335)
1701 Aryana Dr.
Encinitas, CA 92024

ALL-ONE-FAITH-IN-ONE-GOD STATE (1580)
% Dr. E. H. Bonner
Box 28
Escondido, CA 92025

CHRISTWARD MINISTRY (1165)
Route 5, Box 206
Escondido, CA 92025

NICHIREN SHOSHU TEMPLE (1470)
7576 Etiwanda Ave.
Etiwanda, CA 91739

SACRED SOCIETY OF THE ETH, INC. (1157)
Box 3
Forks of Salmon, CA 96031

SEICHO-NO-IE (916)
North American Missionary Headquarters
14527 S. Vermont Ave.
Gardena, CA 90247

UNITED SPIRITUALIST CHURCH (972)
813 W. 165th Place
Gardena, CA 90247

ANN REE COLTON FOUNDATION OF NISCIENCE
  (1162)
336 W. Colorado
Glendale, CA 91209

APOSTOLIC EPISCOPAL CHURCH (7)
% Mt. Rev. Paul Schultz
Box 6
Glendale, CA 91209

PERFECT LIBERTY KYODAN (1586)
700 S. Adams St.
Glendale, CA 91205

TEMPLE OF THE PEOPLE (1112)
Box 7095
Halcyon, CA 93420

AUM NAMO BHAGAVATE VASUDEVAYA
  FOUNDATION (1352)
Box 73
Harbor City, CA 90710-0073

AETHERIUS SOCIETY (1012)
6202 Afton Place
Hollywood, CA 90028

DUANE PEDERSON MINISTRIES (1562)
Box 1949
Hollywood, CA

INTERNATIONAL BABAJI KRIYA YOGA SANGAM
  (1377)
595 W. Bedford Rd.
Imperial City, CA 92251

INSTITUTE OF MENTALPHYSICS (1068)
59700 - 29 Palms Hwy.
Joshua Tree, CA 92252

WHITE STAR (1025)
Box 307
Joshua Tree, CA 92252

CHURCH OF COSMIC ORIGIN AND SCHOOL OF
  THOUGHT (1166)
Box 257
June Lake, CA 93529

EWAM CHODEN (1513)
254 Cambridge St.
Kensington, CA 94707

ANANDA ASHRAMA AND VEDANTA CENTRE
  (1348)
Box 8555
La Crescenta, CA 91214

AMERICAN CATHOLIC CHURCH (1126)
% Most Rev. Simon Eugene Talarczyk
430 Park Ave.
Laguna Beach, CA 92651

OLD CATHOLIC EPISCOPAL CHURCH (1141)
% Most Rev. John Charles Maier
489 Jasmine Street
Laguna Beach, CA 92651

TEACHING OF THE INNER CHRIST, INC. (1084)
% Inner Christ Administrative Center, Inc.
3150 Main St.
Lemon Grove, CA 92045

MISSIONARY CHRISTIAN AND SOUL WINNING
  FELLOWSHIP (267)
350 E. Market St.
Long Beach, CA 90805

MORNINGLAND-CHURCH OF THE ASCENDED
  CHRIST (1153)
2600 E. 7th St.
Long Beach, CA 90804

TRIDENTINE OLD ROMAN COMMUNITY
  CATHOLIC CHURCH (JONES) (55)
% Most Rev. Charles T. Sutter
1956 Gardena Ave..
Long Beach, CA 90813

PACIFIC YEARLY MEETING OF FRIENDS (546)
% Stratton Jaquette
258 Cherry Ave.
Los Altos, CA 94022

UNITED LIBERTARIAN FELLOWSHIP (775)
% Will Barkley, President
1220 Larnel Place
Los Altos, CA 94022

AGASHA TEMPLE OF WISDOM (929)
460 Western Ave.
Los Angeles, CA 90004

AMERICAN PRELATURE (5)
% Most Rev. Derek Lang
2103 S. Portland St.
Los Angeles, CA 90007

ASSOCIATED CHURCHES OF CHRIST (HOLINESS)
(291)
1302 E. Adams Blvd.
Los Angeles, CA 90011

BUILDERS OF THE ADYTUM (1182)
5105 N. Figueroa
Los Angeles, CA 90042

BYZANTINE CATHOLIC CHURCH (100)
% Most Rev. Mark I. Miller
Box 3682
Los Angeles, CA 90078

CALIFORNIA BOSATSUKAI (1478)
5632 Green Oak Dr.
Los Angeles, CA 90068

CENTER OF BEING (1357)
3272 Purdue Ave.
Los Angeles, CA 90066

CHIROTHESIAN CHURCH OF FAITH (1038)
1757 N. Normandie
Los Angeles, CA 90027

CHRIST FAITH MISSION (468)
6026 Echo St.
Los Angeles, CA 90042

CHURCH OF LIGHT (1103)
Box 76862
Los Angeles, CA 90076

CHURCH OF SCIENTOLOGY (1044)
% Flag Service Org(anization)
Box 23751
Los Angeles, CA 33650-3751

CHURCH OF WORLD MESSIANITY (1538)
3068 San Marino St.
Los Angeles, CA 90006

CONCILIO OLAZABAL DE IGLESIAS LATINO
AMERICANO (447)
1925 E. First St.
Los Angeles, CA 90033

ECCLESIA GNOSTICA (1129)
% Most Rev. Stephan Hoeller
4516 Hollywood Blvd.
Los Angeles, CA 90027

ESTONIAN ORTHODOX CHURCH IN EXILE (103)
% Rev. Sergius Samon
5332 Fountain Ave.
Los Angeles, CA 90029

THE GNOSTIC ASSOCIATION OF CULTURAL AND
ANTHROPOLOGICAL STUDIES (1104)
Box 291488
Los Angeles, CA 90029

HIGASHI HONGWANJI BUDDHIST CHURCH (1466)
505 E. Third St.
Los Angeles, CA 90013

INDEPENDENT FUNDAMENTALIST BIBLE
CHURCHES (651)
% Dr. M. H. McReynolds, Jr.
205 N. Union Ave.
Los Angeles, CA 90026

INTERNATIONAL BUDDHIST MEDITATION
CENTER (1455)
928 S. New Hampshire
Los Angeles, CA 90006

INTERNATIONAL CHURCH OF THE FOURSQUARE
GOSPEL (360)
1100 Glendale Blvd.
Los Angeles, CA 90026

KANZEONJI ZEN BUDDHIST TEMPLE (1482)
944 Terrace 49
Los Angeles, CA 90042

KONKO KYO (1543)
% Rev. Alfred Y. Tsyyuki
2924 E. 1st St.
Los Angeles, CA 90033

KOREAN BUDDHIST CHOGYE ORDER (1506)
% Kwan Um Sa Temple
4265 W. Third St.
Los Angeles, CA 90020

LAO BUDDHIST SANGHA OF THE U.S.A. (1456)
938 N. Hobart Blvd.
Los Angeles, CA 90029

METROPOLITAN COMMUNITY CHURCHES,
UNIVERSAL FELLOWSHIP OF (1577)
5300 Santa Monica Blvd., 304
Los Angeles, CA 90029

MOLOKAN SPIRITUAL CHRISTIANS (PRYGUNY)
(558)
% Paul I. Samarin
944 Orme St.
Los Angeles, CA 99923

MOVEMENT OF SPIRITUAL INNER AWARENESS,
CHURCH OF THE (1447)
3500 W. Adams Blvd.
Los Angeles, CA 90018

ORIENTAL MISSIONARY SOCIETY HOLINESS
CHURCH OF NORTH AMERICA (655)
3660 S. Gramercy Pl.
Los Angeles, CA 90018

PHILOSOPHICAL RESEARCH SOCIETY (1107)
3910 Los Feliz Blvd.
Los Angeles, CA 90027

RAMA SEMINARS (1394)
1015 Gayley Ave.
Suite 1116
Los Angeles, CA 90024

REIYUKAI AMERICA (1472)
2741 Sunset Blvd.
Los Angeles, CA 90026

RINZAI-JI, INC. (1485)
2245 W. 25th St.
Los Angeles, CA 90018

RISSHO KOSEI KAI (1473)
% Rev. Kazuhiko K. Nagamoto
118 N. Mott
Los Angeles, CA 90033

SELF-REALIZATION FELLOWSHIP (1400)
3880 San Rafael Ave.
Los Angeles, CA 90065

SHRINE OF THE ETERNAL BREATH OF TAO (1503)
117 Stonehave Way
Los Angeles, CA 90049

SOCIETY OF CHRIST, INC. (965)
% Bishop Dan Boughan
3061 Harrington St.
Los Angeles, CA 90006

SOTO MISSION (1486)
Zenshuji Soto Mission
123 S. Hewitt St.
Los Angeles, CA 90012

SUPERET LIGHT DOCTRINE CHURCH (969)
2516 W. Third St.
Los Angeles, CA 90057

TENRIKYO (1548)
Tenrikyo Mission Headquarters in America
2727 E. First St.
Los Angeles, CA 90033

THUBTEN DARGYE LING (1524)
2658 La Cienga Ave.
Los Angeles, CA 90034

TRUTH CENTER, A UNIVERSAL FELLOWSHIP (919)
6940 Oporto Dr.
Los Angeles, CA 90068

UNITED CHURCH OF RELIGIOUS SCIENCE (921)
3251 W. 6th St.
Box 75127
Los Angeles, CA 90075

UNITED LODGE OF THEOSOPHISTS (1116)
245 W. 33rd St.
Los Angeles, CA 90007

UNIVERSAL WHITE BROTHERHOOD (1176)
Prosveta U. S. A.
Box 49614
Los Angeles, CA 90049

UNIVERSAL WORLD CHURCH (491)
123 N. Lake St.
Los Angeles, CA 90026

UNIVERSE SOCIETY CHURCH (1023)
Box 38132
Los Angeles, CA 90038

VIET NAM BUDDHISTS (1462)
Congregation of Vietnamese Buddhists in the U.S.

863 S. Berendo
Los Angeles, CA 90005

ZEN CENTER OF LOS ANGELES (1488)
923 S. Normandie Ave.
Los Angeles, CA 90006

CHURCH OF REVELATION (HAWAII) (937)
21475 Summit Rd.
Los Gatos, CA 95030

SCHOOL OF NATURAL SCIENCE (1003)
25355 Spanish Ranch Rd.
Los Gatos, CA 95030

ELAN VITAL (1445)
Box 6130
Malibu, CA 90264

ARCANA WORKSHOPS (1119)
Box 605
Manhattan Beach, CA 90266

THE DIVINE SCIENCE OF LIGHT AND SOUND (1443)
2554 Lincoln Blvd.
Box 620
Marina del Rey, CA 90291

MINISTRY OF CHRIST CHURCH (752)
4241 Usona Rd.
Mariposa, CA 95338

NEW, REFORMED, ORTHODOX ORDER OF THE GOLDEN DAWN (1233)
% Rowan Fairgrove
Box 360607
Milpitas, CA 95035

UNIVERSAL LIFE CHURCH (791)
601 Third St.
Modesto, CA 95351

MILLENNIAL CHURCH OF JESUS CHRIST (810)
% Leo Peter Evoniuk LeBaron
177 Webster St.
Monterey, CA 93940

ASCENDED MASTER TEACHING FOUNDATION (1147)
Box 466
Mount Shasta, CA 96067

ASSOCIATION OF SANANDA AND SANAT KUMARA (1013)
Box 35
Mount Shasta, CA 96067

CHURCH OF ANTIOCH (1128)
% Most Rev. Herman Adrian Spruit
Box 1015
Mountian View, CA 94042

ORDER OF BUDDHIST CONTEMPATIVES (1484)
Box 199
3612 Summit Dr.
Mt. Shasta, CA 96067-0199

ORDER OF THELEMA (1190)
% The Magic Bookstore
2306 Highland Ave.
National City, CA 92050

ANANDA (1347)
14618 Tyler Foote Rd.
Nevada City, CA 95959

INSTITUTE FOR THE DEVELOPMENT OF THE HARMONIOUS HUMAN BEING (1316)
Box 370
Nevada City, CA 95959

RADHA SOAMI SATSANG BEAS (1449)
% Roland G. de Vries
10901 Mill Springs Dr.
Nevada City, CA 95959

AHMADIYYA ANJUMAN ISHAAT ISLAM, LAHORE, INC (1324)
36911 Walnut St.
Newark, CA 94560

CHURCH OF THE LIVING WORD (454)
Box 858
North Hollywood, CA 91603

TARA CENTER (1124)
Box 6001
North Hollywood, CA 91603

THAI-AMERICAN BUDDHIST ASSOCIATION (1461)
Wat Thai of Los Angeles
12909 Cantara St.
North Hollywood, CA 91506

INNER LIGHT FOUNDATION (1065)
Box 761
Novato, CA 94948

DIANIC WICCA (1220)
% Susan B. Anthony Coven No. 1
Box 11363
Oakland, CA 94611

DIOCESE OF CHRIST THE KING (65)
% Rt. Rev. Robert S. Morse
St. Peter's Pro-Cathedral
6013 Lawton
Oakland, CA 94618

TEMPLE OF COSMIC RELIGION (1410)
174 Santa Clara Ave.
Oakland, CA 94610

TEMPLE OF THE GODDESS WITHIN (1247)
2441 Cordova St.
Oakland, CA 94602

ROSICRUCIAN FELLOWSHIP (1097)
2222 Mission Ave.
Box 713
Oceanside, CA 92054

ECUMENICAL MINISTRY OF THE UNITY OF ALL RELIGIONS (1167)
107 N. Ventura St.
Ojai, CA 93023

KRISHNAMURTI FOUNDATION OF AMERICA (1383)
Box 1560
Ojai, CA 93023-0216

LIFE ACTION FOUNDATION (1298)
Box 263
Ojai, CA 93023

MEDITATION GROUPS, INC. (1121)
Box 566
Ojai, CA 93023

REFORMED DRUIDS OF NORTH AMERICA (1241)
% Live Oak Grove
616 Minor Rd.
Orinda, CA 94563.

GEORGE OHSAWA MACROBIOTIC FOUNDATION (1500)
1511 Robinson St.
Oroville, CA 95965

WORLD PLAN EXECUTIVE COUNCIL (1422)
17310 Sunset Blvd.
Pacific Palisades, CA 90272

ANGLICAN EPISCOPAL CHURCH OF NORTH AMERICA (62)
% Most Rev. Walter Hollis Adams
789 Allen Ct.
Palo Alto, CA 94303

ECCLESIA GNOSTICA MYSTERIUM (1130)
% Most Rev. Rosa Miller
3437 Alma, 23
Palo Alto, CA 94306

FOUNDATION FOR BIBLICAL RESEARCH (697)
Box 499
Pasadena, CA 91102

INTERNATIONAL ALLIANCE OF CHURCHES OF THE TRUTH (905)
690 E. Orange Grove Blvd.
Pasadena, CA 91104

TEMPLE OF TRUTH (1199)
Box 93124
Pasadena, CA 91109

THEOSOPHICAL SOCIETY (1114)
Post Office Bin C
Pasadena, CA 91109

WORLD INSIGHT INTERNATIONAL (704)
Box 35
Pasadena, CA 91102

WORLDWIDE CHURCH OF GOD (705)
300 W. Green St.
Pasadena, CA 91129

BLUE MOUNTAIN CENTER OF MEDITATION (1355)
Box 477
Petaluma, CA 94953

CHINMAYA MISSION (WEST) (1359)
% Sandeepany West
Box 9
Piercy, CA 95467

ASSOCIATION OF VINEYARD CHURCHES (347)
902 E. Yorba Linda Blvd.
Box 909
Placentia, CA 92670

AJAPA YOGA FOUNDATION (1344)
% Shri Janardan Ajapa Yoga Ashram
Box 1731
Placerville, CA 95667

HAIDAKHAN SAMAJ (1368)
% Paul Gessler
104 Blue Jay
Placerville, CA 95667

LEMURIAN FELLOWSHIP (1105)
Box 397
Ramona, CA 92065

CHURCH OF GENERAL PSIONICS (1043)
204 N. Catalina
Redondo Beach, CA 90277

THE ORIGINAL NEO-KLEPTONIA NEO-AMERICAN
  CHURCH (1031)
Box 11
Mandalit Elk Ridge
Redway, CA 95560

NEW ORDER OF GLASTONBURY (1139)
Box 324
Rialto, CA 92376

NORTH AMERICAN OLD ROMAN CATHOLIC
  CHURCH-UTRECHT SUCCESSION (29)
% Rt. Rev. E. R. Verostek
3519 Roosevelt Ave.
Richmond, CA 94805

CHRIST MINISTRY FOUNDATION (1039)
% The Seivertsons
2411 Roland Rd.
Sacramento, CA 95821

NEW WICCAN CHURCH (1234)
Box 162046
Sacramento, CA 95816

EDTA HA THOMA (1131)
% Mar Petros
578 Green No. 5-20
San Bruno, CA 94066

AMERICAN ASSOCIATION FOR THE
  ADVANCEMENT OF ATHEISM (757)
Box 2832
San Diego, CA 92112

FIRST CHRISTIANS' ESSENE CHURCH (1057)
2536 Collier Ave.
San Diego, CA 92116

INNER CIRCLE KETHRA E'DA FOUNDATION, INC.
  (992)
Box 1722
San Diego, CA 92112

INTERNATIONAL SOCIETY FOR KRISHNA
  CONSCIOUSNESS (1378)
% ISCKON International Ministry of Public Affairs
1030 Grand Ave.
San Diego, CA 92109

LOVE PROJECT (1072)
Box 7601
San Diego, CA 92107

NEW PSYCHIANA (1077)
% Psychiana Study Group
4069 Stephens St.
San Diego, CA 92103

RELIGIOUS SCIENCE INTERNATIONAL (913)
3230 5th Ave.
San Diego, CA 92103

SEAX-WICA (1244)
Box 99324
San Diego, CA 92109

ANCIENT TRIDENTINE CATHOLIC CHURCH (6)
Box 26414
San Francisco, CA 94126

BUDDHA'S UNIVERSAL CHURCH (1492)
702 Washington St.
San Francisco, CA 94108

BUDDHIST CHURCHES OF AMERICA (1464)
1710 Octavia St.
San Francisco, CA 94109

CATHOLIC APOSTOLIC CHURCH IN AMERICA
  (101)
% Mt. Rev. Jerome Joachim
600 Fell St., Suite 400
San Francisco, CA 94102

CHAPORI-LING FOUNDATION SANGHA (1511)
% Dr. Norbu Lompas Chen
766 8th Ave.
San Francisco, CA 94118

CHURCH FOR THE FELLOWSHIP OF ALL PEOPLE
  (1556)
2041 Larkin St.
San Francisco, CA 94109

CHURCH OF SATAN (1258)
Box 210082
San Francisco, CA 94121

COMMUNITY OF THE LOVE OF CHRIST
  (EVANGELICAL CATHOLIC) (1574)
% Most Rev. Mikhail Francis Itkin
Priory of St. Thomas of India
1546 Hayes St.
San Francisco, CA 94117

FOUNDATION OF REVELATION (1366)
59 Scott St.
San Francisco, CA 94117

GAY AND LESBIAN ATHEISTS (1576)
Box 14142
San Francisco, CA 94114

GURDJIEFF FOUNDATION (1313)
Box 549
San Francisco, CA 94101

KERISTA COMMUNE (864)
543 Frederick St.
San Francisco, CA 94117

MOLOKAN SPIRITUAL CHRISTIANS
  (POSTOJANNYE) (557)
841 Carolina St.
San Francisco, CA 94107

ORDO LUX KETHRI (1192)
584 Castro St.
San Francisco, CA 94114

ORTHODOX EPISCOPAL CHURCH OF GOD (1578)
Box 1528
San Francisco, CA 94101

SHINNYO-EN (1476)
1400 Jefferson St.
San Francisco, CA 94123

SM CHURCH (1245)
% Robin Stewart, Priestess
Box 1407
San Francisco, CA 94101

STILLPOINT INSTITUTE (1459)
2740 Greenwich, 416
San Francisco, CA 94123

SUFI ISLAMIA RUHANIAT SOCIETY (1322)
410 Precita Ave.
San Francisco, CA 94110

TEMPLE OF SET (1263)
Box 29271
San Francisco, CA 94129

ZEN CENTER OF SAN FRANCISCO (1490)
300 Page St.
San Francisco, CA 94102

ANCIENT AND MYSTICAL ORDER OF THE ROSAE
    CRUCIS (1090)
San Jose, CA 95191

CHRISTIAN ASSEMBLY (889)
72 N. 5th St.
San Jose, CA 95112

CHRISTIAN PROPHETS OF JEHOVAH (710)
Box 8302
San Jose, CA 95555

SRI CHAITANYA SARASWAT MANDAL (1358)
% Guardian of Devotion Press
62 S. 13th St.
San Jose, CA 95112

UNITED CHRISTIAN SCIENTISTS (881)
Box 8048
San Jose, CA 95155

BADARIKASHRAMA (1354)
15602 Maubert Ave.
San Leandro, CA 94578

CHURCH OF THE TRINITY (INVISIBLE MINISTRY)
    (895)
% A. Stuart Otto
Box 37
San Marcos, CA 92069

ETHERIAN RELIGIOUS SOCIETY OF UNIVERSAL
    BROTHERHOOD (1055)
Box 446
San Marcos, CA 92069

GEDATSU CHURCH OF AMERICA (1465)
353 San Antonio Ave.
San Mateo, CA 94401

SATYANANDA ASHRAMS, U.S.A. (1399)
1157 Ramblewood Way
San Mateo, CA 94403

NORWEGIAN SEAMAN'S CHURCH (MISSION) (173)
1035 Beacon St.
San Pedro, CA 90731

FREE DAIST COMMUNION (1367)
% Harry Dent
750 Adrian Way
San Rafael, CA 94903

HALLOWED GROUNDS FELLOWSHIP OF
    SPIRITUAL HEALING AND PRAYER (945)
% Rev. George Daisley
629 San Ysidro Rd.
Santa Barbara, CA 93108

JOY FOUNDATION, INC. (1152)
2821 De la Vina
Santa Barbara, CA 93105

UNIVERSAL CHURCH OF THE MASTER (974)
National Headquarters
501 Washington St.
Santa Clara, CA 95050

AVADHUT ASHRAM (1353)
Box 8080
Santa Cruz, CA 95061

BIBLICAL CHURCH OF GOD (687)
Box 1234
Santa Cruz, CA 95061

FEDERATION OF ST. THOMAS CHRISTIAN
    CHURCHES (1132)
% Archdeacon Joseph Eaton, S.T.M.
Mission St., No. B
Santa Cruz, CA 95060

HOLY GRAIL FOUNDATION (946)
% Rev. Leona Richards
1344 Pacific Ave., Suite 100
Santa Cruz, CA 95060

SRI RAMA FOUNDATION (1407)
Box 2550
Santa Cruz, CA 95063

CHURCH OF EDUCTIVISM (1042)
3003 Santa Monica Blvd.
Santa Monica, CA 90404

NEW AGE BIBLE AND PHILOSOPHY CENTER
    (1095)
1139 Lincoln Blvd.
Santa Monica, CA 90403

OLD CATHOLIC CHURCH IN NORTH AMERICA
    (CATHOLICATE OF THE WEST) (31)
% Rev. Dr. Charles V. Hearn
2210 Wilshire Blvd., Suite 582
Santa Monica, CA 90403

TAYU FELLOWSHIP (1579)
Box 11554
Santa Rosa, CA 95406

ATHEISTS UNITED (763)
Suite 211
14542 Ventura Blvd.
Sherman Oaks, CA 91403

UNIVERSAL INDUSTRIAL CHURCH OF THE NEW
    WORLD COMFORTER (874)
1868 Princeton Ave.
Stockton, CA 95204

DHARMA REALM BUDDHIST ASSOCIATION (1497)
City of Ten Thousand Buddhas
Talmage, CA 95481-0217

MAHIKARI OF AMERICA (1544)
Los Angeles Dojo
6470 Foothill Blvd.
Tujunga, CA 91042

CHURCH OF ALL WORLDS (1208)
Box 1542
Ukiah, CA 95482

ASTARA (1100)
800 W. Arrow Hwy.
Box 5003
Upland, CA 91785

BRETHREN IN CHRIST (492)
% Dr. R. Donald Shafer
Box 245
Upland, CA 91786

INTERNATIONAL EVANGELISM CRUSADES (482)
14617 Victory Blvd.
Van Nuys, CA 91411

S. A. I. FOUNDATION (1396)
14849 Lull St.
Van Nuys, CA 91405

DIVINE WORD FOUNDATION (986)
26648 San Felipe Rd.
Warner Springs, CA 92086

Colorado

ASSEMBLY OF YHWHHOHUA (724)
% David K. Johnson
50006 Olson Rd.
Boone, CO 81025

CHURCH OF TZADDI (939)
Box 13729
Boulder, CO 80308-3729

INTERMOUNTAIN YEARLY MEETING (537)
% Ms. Anne White
624 Pearl St., No.302
Boulder, CO 80302

MOKSHA FOUNDATION (1388)
745 31st St.
Boulder, CO 80303

TRUTH CONSCIOUSNESS (1414)
% Sacred Mountain Ashram
10668 Gold Hill Rd.
Boulder, CO 80302-9763

VAJRADHATU (1526)
1345 Spruce St.
Boulder, CO 80302

EMMANUEL ASSOCIATION (260)
West Cucharas at 27th St.
Colorado Springs, CO 80904

ROCKY MOUNTAIN YEARLY MEETING (547)
Box 9629
Colorado Springs, CO 80932

TRADITIONAL CATHOLICS OF AMERICA (51)
Box 6827
Colorado Springs, CO 80934

AMERICAN ORTHODOX CATHOLIC CHURCH
  (IRENE) (87)
% Most Rev. Milton A. Pritts
851 Leyden St.
Denver, CO 80220

ANANDA MARGA YOGA SOCIETY (1349)
854 Pearl St.
Denver, CO 80203

BIBLE MISSIONARY CHURCH (304)
822 S. Simms
Denver, CO 80211

CATHOLIC LIFE CHURCH (11)
% Most Rev. A. L. Mark Harding
1955 Arapahoe St., Suite 1603
Denver, CO 80202

COLORADO REFORM BAPTIST CHURCH (608)
% Bishop William T. Conklin
Box 12514
Denver, CO 80212

DIVINE SCIENCE FEDERATION INTERNATIONAL
  (898)
1819 E. 14th Ave.
Denver, CO 80218

GENERAL CONFERENCE OF THE CHURCH OF
  GOD (SEVENTH DAY) (699)
General Conference Offices
Box 33677
Denver, CO 80233

HOUSE OF PRAYER FOR ALL PEOPLE (751)
Box 837
Denver, CO 80201

UNIVERSALIA (1010)
Box 6243
Denver, CO 80206

EMISSARIES OF DIVINE LIGHT (1053)
5569 N. Country Rd. 29
Loveland, CO 80537

LAW OF LIFE ACTIVITY (1148)
8575 S. Crow Cutoff
Rye Star Rte.
Pueblo, CO 81004

BROTHERHOOD OF THE WHITE TEMPLE (1101)
Sedalia, CO 80135

CHURCH OF SEVEN ARROWS (1211)
4385 Hoyt St., Apt. 201
Wheatridge, CO 80033

Connecticut

CHRISTIAN MILLENNIAL FELLOWSHIP (709)
307 White St.
Hartford, CT 06106

COMMUNITY OF CATHOLIC CHURCHES (14)
% Most Rev. Thomas Sargent
3 Columbia St.
Hartford, CT 06106

UNIVERSAL LIFE-THE INNER RELIGION (1008)
Box 3579
New Haven, CT 06525

LIFE STUDY FELLOWSHIP FOUNDATION, INC.
  (906)
Noroton, CT 06820

KUNDALINI RESEARCH FOUNDATION (1384)
Box 2248
Noroton Heights, CT 06820

AUTOCEPHALOUS SYRO-CHALDEAN CHURCH OF NORTH AMERICA (95)
% Most Rev. Bertram S. Schlossberg (Mar Uzziah)
9 Ellington Ave.
Rockville, CT 06066

INDEPENDENT OLD ROMAN CATHOLIC HUNGARIAN ORTHODOX CHURCH OF AMERICA (23)
% Most Rev. Archbishop Edward C. Payne, Catholicos-Metropolitan
Box 261
Weatherfield, CT 06109

DHYANYOGA CENTERS (1364)
Woodbury Yoga Center
122 West Side Rd.
Woodbury, CT 06798

Delaware

AFRICAN UNION FIRST COLORED METHODIST PROTESTANT CHURCH (235)
2611 N. Claymont St.
Wilmington, DE 19802

District of Columbia

AHMADIYYA MOVEMENT IN ISLAM (1325)
2141 Leroy Place, N.W.
Washington, DC 20008

BIBLE WAY CHURCH OF OUR LORD JESUS CHRIST WORLD WIDE, INC. (398)
1130 New Jersey Ave., N.W.
Washington, DC 20001

CHURCH OF THE SAVIOR (842)
2025 Massachusetts Avenue, N.W.
Washington, DC 20036

DRIKUNG DHARMA CENTERS (1512)
% Drikung Kyabgon
3454 Macomb St., N.W.
Washington, DC 20008

FOUNDATION CHURCH OF DIVINE TRUTH (990)
Box 66003
Washington, DC 20035-6003

GOSPEL SPREADING CHURCH (296)
2030 Georgia Ave., N.W.
Washington, DC 20003

HANAFI MADH-HAB CENTER, ISLAM FAITH (1329)
7700 16th St.
Washington, DC 10012

HIGHWAY CHRISTIAN CHURCH OF CHRIST (405)
436 W St.,N.W.
Washington, DC 20001

INNER PEACE MOVEMENT (1066)
Box 4897
Washington, DC 20008

INTERNATIONAL EVANGELICAL CHURCH AND MISSIONARY ASSOCIATION (459)
% Evangel Temple
610 Rhode Island Ave., N.E.
Washington, DC 20002

MORAL RE-ARMAMENT (1583)
1707 H St., N.W., 900
Washington, DC 20006

NATIONAL SPIRITUAL SCIENCE CENTER (958)
5605 16th St., N.W.
Washington, DC 20011

PROGRESSIVE NATIONAL BAPTIST CONVENTION, INC. (606)
601 50th St., N.E.
Washington, DC 20019

REDEEMED ASSEMBLY OF JESUS CHRIST, APOSTOLIC (413)
% Bishop Douglas Williams
734 1st St., S.W.
Washington, DC 20024

ROMAN CATHOLIC CHURCH (1)
National Conference of Catholic Bishops
1312 Massachusetts Ave., N.W.
Washington, DC 20005

SELF-REVELATION CHURCH OF ABSOLUTE MONISM (1401)
4748 Western Ave., N.W.
Washington, DC 20016

SEVENTH-DAY ADVENTIST CHURCH (680)
6840 Eastern Avenue, N.W.
Washington, DC 20012

SEVENTH DAY PENTECOSTAL CHURCH OF THE LIVING GOD (372)
1443 S. Euclid
Washington, DC 20009

SUNNI MUSLIMS (1307)
% Islamic Center
2551 Massachusetts Ave., N.W.
Washington, DC 20008

TRUE GRACE MEMORIAL HOUSE OF PRAYER (441)
205 V St., N.W.
Washington, DC 20001

UNITED HOUSE OF PRAYER FOR ALL PEOPLE (443)
1721 1/2 7th St., N.W.
Washington, DC 20001

WAY OF THE CROSS CHURCH OF CHRIST (420)
332 4th St., N.E.
Washington, DC 20003

Florida

REX HUMBARD MINISTRY (657)
Box 3063
Boca Raton, FL 33431

NATIONAL SPIRITUALIST ASSOCIATION OF
CHURCHES (959)
Box 128
Casadega, FL 32706

MARK-AGE (1018)
Box 290368
Fort Lauderdale, FL 33329

LAODICEAN HOME MISSIONARY MOVEMENT (714)
Rte. 38
9021 Temple Rd., W.
Fort Myers, FL 33912

CHURCHES OF CHRIST (NON-INSTRUMENTAL,
RESTORING) (625)
Crossroads Church of Christ
2720 S. W. 2nd Ave.
Gainesville, FL 32607

MARANATHA CHRISTIAN CHURCHES (461)
Box 1799
Gainesville, FL 32602

SOUTHEASTERN YEARLY MEETING (549)
% Gene E. Beardsley
Route 2, Box 108F
Gainesville, FL 32606

THE AFRO-AMERICAN SOCIAL RESEARCH
ASSOCIATION (1032)
Box 2150
Jacksonville, FL 32203

CHURCH OF GOD BY FAITH (469)
3220 Haines St.
Jacksonville, FL 32206

LIBERAL CATHOLIC CHURCH INTERNATIONAL
(1137)
1736 Holly Oaks Ravine Dr.
Jacksonville, FL 32225

NEW CONGREGATIONAL METHODIST CHURCH
(229)
% Bishop Joe E. Kelley
354 E. 9th St.
Jacksonville, FL 32206

UNIVERSAL RELIGION OF AMERICA (977)
% Christ Universal Church
295 N. Tropical Trail
Merritt Island, FL 32952

ENDTIME BODY-CHRISTIAN MINISTRIES, INC.
(456)
Miami, FL

HEBREW ISRAELITES (1288)
2766 N.W. 62nd St.
Miami, FL 33147

NATION OF YAHWEH (HEBREW ISRAELITES)
(1290)
% Temple of Love
2766 N. W. 62nd Street
Miami, FL 33147

ROOSEVELT SPIRITUAL MEMORIAL BENEVOLENT
ASSOCIATION (963)
% Rev. Nellie M. Pickens
Box 68-313
Miami, FL 33138

SOLDIERS OF THE CROSS OF CHRIST,
EVANGELICAL INTERNATIONAL CHURCH (451)
636 N.W. 2nd St.
Miami, FL 33128

YOGA RESEARCH FOUNDATION (1425)
6111 S.W. 74th Ave.
Miami, FL 33143

LIGHT OF SIVANANDA-VALENTINA, ASHRAM OF
(1385)
3475 Royal Palm Ave.
Miami Beach, FL 33140

EPIPHANY BIBLE STUDENTS ASSOCIATION (712)
Box 97
Mount Dora, FL 32757

UNITED EPISCOPAL CHURCH OF AMERICA (76)
% Rt. Rev. Charles E. Morley
Box 18223
Pensacola, FL 32523

AMERICAN EVANGELICAL CHRISTIAN CHURCHES
(639)
Waterfront Dr.
Pineland, FL 33945

OLD ROMAN CATHOLIC CHURCH (SHELLEY/
HUMPHREYS) (36)
% Most Rev. John J. Humphreys
5501 62nd Ave.
Pinellas Park, FL 33565

LOTUS ASHRAM (952)
% Rev. Noel Street
264 Mainsail
Port St. Lucie, FL 33452

EASTERN ORTHODOX CATHOLIC CHURCH IN
AMERICA (102)
% Most Rev. Dismas Markle
321 S. Magnolia Ave.
Sanford, FL 32771

CHURCH OF METAPHYSICAL CHRISTIANITY (935)
2717 Browning St.
Sarasota, FL 33577

UNIVERSAL HARMONY FOUNDATION (976)
% Rev. Helene Gerling
5903 Seminole Blvd.
Seminole, FL 33542

CHURCH OF THE HUMANITARIAN GOD (768)
% Ron Libert
Box 13236
St. Petersburg, FL 33733

NATIONAL SPIRITUAL AID ASSOCIATION (956)
5239 40th St., N.
St. Petersburg, FL 33714

NATIONAL PRIMITIVE BAPTIST CONVENTION OF
THE U.S.A. (598)
Box 2355
Tallahassee, FL 32301

THE CATHOLIC CHURCH OF THE ANTIOCHEAN
RITE (1127)
% Most Rev. Roberto C. Toca, Bishop Primate
Box 8473
Tampa, FL 33674-8473

CHURCHES OF CHRIST (NON-INSTRUMENTAL, CONSERVATIVE) (627)
% Florida College
119 Glen Arven Ave.
Tampa, FL 33617

KORESHAN UNITY (850)
% Claude J. Rahn
2012 28th Avenue
Vero Beach, FL 32960

CHURCH OF THE NEW SONG (1581)
% World Faith Exchange
Box 3472
West Palm Beach, FL 33402

Georgia

CYMRY WICCA (1216)
Box 4196
Athens, GA 30605

ANGLICAN CHURCH OF NORTH AMERICA (61)
% Rt. Rev. Robert T. Shepherd
Chapel of St. Augustine of Canterbury
1906 Forest Green Dr., N.E.
Atlanta, GA 30329

CHURCHES OF GOD, HOLINESS (295)
170 Ashby St., N.W.
Atlanta, GA 30314

FIRST INTERDENOMINATIONAL CHRISTIAN ASSOCIATION (330)
Calvary Temple Holiness Church
1061 Memorial Dr., S.E.
Atlanta, GA 30315

PRESBYTERIAN CHURCH IN AMERICA (191)
% Stated Clerk
1852 Century Plaza, Suite 202
Atlanta, GA 30345

SANCTIFIED CHURCH OF CHRIST (289)
2715 18th Ave.
Columbus, GA 31901

CHURCH OF GOD OF THE UNION ASSEMBLY (323)
Box 1323
Dalton, GA 30720

ASBURY BIBLE CHURCHES (216)
% Rev. Jack Tondee
Box 1021
Dublin, GA 31021

CONGREGATIONAL HOLINESS CHURCH (326)
3888 Fayetteville Hwy.
Griffin, GA 30223

PRIMITIVE BAPTISTS-PROGRESSIVE (601)
% Banner Bookstore
Box 4
Jesup, GA 31545

CHURCH OF THE CHRISTIAN SPIRITUAL ALLIANCE (1361)
Lake Rabun Road
Box 7
Lakemont, GA 30552

GOSPEL HARVESTERS EVANGELISTIC ASSOCIATION (ATLANTA) (457)
1521 Hurt Rd., S.W.
Marietta, GA 30060

CHRIST'S SANCTIFIED HOLY CHURCH (SOUTH CAROLINA) (254)
Box 1376
CSHC Campgrounds and Home for the Aged
Perry, GA 31068

PENTECOSTAL FIRE-BAPTIZED HOLINESS CHURCH (339)
Taccoa, GA 30577

Hawaii

SHINREIKYO (1545)
% Mr. Kameo Kiyota
310C Uulani St.
Hilo, HI 96720

APOSTOLIC FAITH (HAWAII) (391)
1043 Middle St.
Honolulu, HI 96819

BODAIJI MISSION (1463)
1251 Elm
Honolulu, HI 96814

CELTIC EVANGELICAL CHURCH (64)
% Rt. Rev. Wayne W. Gau
1666 St. Louis Dr.
Honolulu, HI 96816

CHINESE BUDDHIST ASSOCIATION (1495)
42 Kawananake Place
Honolulu, HI 96817

CHOWADO HENJO KYO (1532)
% Rev. Reisai Fugita
1757 Algaroba St.
Honolulu, HI 96814

CHURCH OF THE LIVING GOD (1559)
632 Mokauea
Honolulu, HI 96819

DIAMOND SANGHA (1480)
Koko An
2119 Kaloa Way
Honolulu, HI 96822

DOOR OF FAITH CHURCH AND BIBLE SCHOOL (327)
1161 Young St.
Honolulu, HI 96814

HAWAII CHINESE BUDDHIST SOCIETY (1501)
1614 Nuuanu Ave.
Honolulu, HI 96817

HONKYOKU SHINTO (1539)
Honkyoku-Daijingu Temple
61 Puiwa Rd.
Honolulu, HI 96817

HOOMANA NAAUOA O HAWAII (1568)
910 Cooke St.
Honolulu, HI 96813

INARI SHINTO (1540)
Hawaii Inari Taisha
2132 S. King St.
Honolulu, HI 96817

INTERNATIONAL CHRISTIAN CHURCHES (481)
2322-22 Kanealii Ave.
Honolulu, HI 96813

JINGA SHINTO (1541)
Hawaii Ichizuchi Jinga
2020 S. King St.
Honolulu, HI 96817

JINSHA SHINTO (1542)
Kotohira Jinsha Temple
1045 Kama Lane
Honolulu, HI 96817

JODO MISSION (1467)
1429 Kakiki St.
Honolulu, HI 96822

KA HALE HOANO HOU O KE AKUA (1569)
1760 Nalani
Honolulu, HI 96819

KEALAOKAMALAMALAMA (1570)
1207 Prospect
Honolulu, HI 96822

KWAN YIN TEMPLE (1502)
170 N. Vineyard St.
Honolulu, HI 96817

LAMB OF GOD CHURCH (362)
612 Isenburg St.
Honolulu, HI 96817

NICHIREN MISSION (1469)
3058 Pali Hwy.
Honolulu, HI 96817

PALOLO KWANNON TEMPLE (TENDAI SECT)
  (1471)
3326 Paalea St.
Honolulu, HI 96816

PHILIPPINE INDEPENDENT CHURCH (70)
% St. Andrew's Episcopal Cathedral
Queen Emma Sq.
Honolulu, HI 96813

SHINGON MISSION (1474)
915 Sheridan St.
Honolulu, HI 96810

SHINSHU KYOKAI MISSION (1475)
Bentenshu Hawaii Kyokai
3871 Old Pali Rd.
Honolulu, HI 86817

TAISHAKYO SHINTO (1547)
215 N. Kukui St.
Honolulu, HI 96817

TENSHO-KOTAI-JINGU-KYO (1549)
Hawaii Dojo
888 N. King St.
Honolulu, HI 96817

TODAIJI HAWAII BEKKAKU HONZAN (1477)
% Bishop Tatsusho Hirai
2426 Luakini St.
Honolulu, HI 96814

SAIVA SIDDHANTA CHURCH (1397)
Box 10
Kapaa, HI 96746

NECHUNG DRAYANG LING (1521)
Box 250
Pahala, HI 96777

ALPHA AND OMEGA CHRISTIAN CHURCH (464)
96-171 Kamahamaha Hwy.
Pearl City, HI 96782

Idaho

SEVENTH DAY CHURCH OF GOD (701)
Box 804
Caldwell, ID 83606-0804

CHURCH OF JESUS CHRIST CHRISTIAN, ARYAN
  NATIONS (749)
Box 362
Hayden Lake, ID 83835

RAINBOW FAMILY OF LIVING LIGHT (868)
Route 1, Box 6
McCall, ID 83638

GENERAL COUNCIL OF THE CHURCHES OF GOD
  (700)
1827 W. 3rd St.
Meridian, ID 83642-1653

Illinois

PLYMOUTH BRETHREN (EXCLUSIVE: THE
  TUNBRIDGE WELL BRETHREN) (637)
No central headquarters. For Information:
% Bible Truth Publishers
59 Industrial Dr.
Addison, IL 60101

BAPTIST GENERAL CONFERENCE (607)
2002 S. Arlington Heights Rd.
Arlington Heights, IL 60005

CHURCH OF CHRISTIAN LIBERTY (645)
502 W. Euclid Ave.
Arlington Heights, IL 60004

UKRAINIAN EVANGELICAL BAPTIST
  CONVENTION (592)
% Olexa R. Barbuiziuk
6751 Riverside Dr.
Berwyn, IL 60402

AFRICAN ORTHODOX CHURCH OF THE WEST (79)
% Most Rev. G. Duncan Hinkson
St. Augustine's African Orthodox Church
5831 S. Indiana St.
Chicago, IL 60637

AMERICAN MUSLIM MISSION (1326)
Masjid Hon. Elijah Muhammad
7351 S. Stony Brook Ave.
Chicago, IL 60649

BEREAN BIBLE FELLOWSHIP (CHICAGO) (660)
7609 W. Belmont
Chicago, IL 60635

COSMIC CIRCLE OF FELLOWSHIP (1015)
% Edna Valverde
4857 N. Melvina Ave.
Chicago, IL 60630

ECUMENICAL INSTITUTE (844)
4750 N. Sheridan Rd.
Chicago, IL 60640

EVANGELICAL COVENANT CHURCH OF AMERICA
(210)
5101 N. Francisco Ave.
Chicago, IL 60625

EVANGELICAL LUTHERAN CHURCH IN AMERICA
(1988) (166)
8765 W. Higgins Rd.
Chicago, IL 60631

EVANGELICAL MINISTERS AND CHURCHES,
INTERNATIONAL, INC. (646)
105 Madison
Chicago, IL 60602

JESUS PEOPLE USA (862)
4707 N. Malden
Chicago, IL 60640

KOREAN BUDDHIST BO MOON ORDER (1505)
% Rev. Bup Choon
Bul Sim Sa Temple
5011 N. Damen
Chicago, IL 60625

LATVIAN EVANGELICAL LUTHERAN CHURCH IN
AMERICA (170)
6551 W. Montrose
Chicago, IL 60634

MONASTERY OF THE SEVEN RAYS (1187)
Box 1554
Chicago, IL 60690-1554

MOODY CHURCH (653)
1630 N. Clark
Chicago, IL 60614

NARAYANANANDA UNIVERSAL YOGA TRUST
(1389)
N.U. Yoga Ashram
2937 N. Southport Ave.
Chicago, IL 60657

THE NATION OF ISLAM (FARRAKHAN) (1333)
Box 20083
Chicago, IL 60620

NORTH AMERICAN OLD ROMAN CATHOLIC
CHURCH (SCHWEIKERT) (28)
4200 N. Kedvale
Chicago, IL 60641

OLD ROMAN CATHOLIC CHURCH (ENGLISH
RITE) AND THE ROMAN CATHOLIC CHURCH
OF THE ULTRAJECTINE TRADITION (38)
% Most Rev. Robert Lane
4416 N. Malden
Chicago, IL 60640

SABAEAN RELIGIOUS ORDER OF AMEN (1243)
% El Sabarum
3221 N. Sheffield
Chicago, IL 60657

TEMPLE OF KRIYA YOGA (1411)
2414 N. Kedzie
Chicago, IL 60647

TEMPLE OF THE PAGAN WAY (1248)
Box 60151
Chicago, IL 60660

TEMPLE OF UNIVERSAL LAW (971)
5030 N. Drake
Chicago, IL 60625

THEE ORTHODOX OLD ROMAN CATHOLIC
CHURCH (50)
Box 49314
Chicago, IL 60649

TRADITIONAL ROMAN CATHOLIC CHURCH IN
THE AMERICAS (53)
% Most Rev. John D. Fesi
Friary Press
Box 470
Chicago, IL 60690

UNIVERSAL FOUNDATION FOR BETTER LIVING
(924)
11901 Ashland Ave.
Chicago, IL 60643

URANTIA BROTHERHOOD (1088)
533 Diversey Pkwy.
Chicago, IL 60014

CHRISTIAN BELIEVERS CONFERENCE (707)
% Berean Bible Students Church
5930 W. 29th St.
Cicero, IL 60650

CHURCH OF SAINT JOSEPH (13)
2307 S. Laramie
Cicero, IL 60650

INDEPENDENT SPIRITUALIST ASSOCIATION OF
THE UNITED STATES OF AMERICA (948)
% Rev. Harry M. Hilborn
5130 W. 25th St.
Cicero, IL 60650

PLYMOUTH BRETHREN (EXCLUSIVE: REUNITED
BRETHREN) (636)
No central headquarters. For information
Grace and Truth
210 Chestnut St.
Danville, IL 61832

CHURCH OF GOD IN CHRIST, CONGREGATIONAL
(425)
1905 Bond Ave.
East St. Louis, IL 62201

CHURCH OF THE BRETHREN (521)
1451 Dundee Ave.
Elgin, IL 60120

UKRAINIAN EVANGELICAL ALLIANCE OF
NORTH AMERICA (200)
% Rev. Wladimir Borosky
690 Berkeley Ave.
Elmhurst, IL 60126

REBA PLACE CHURCH AND ASSOCIATED
COMMUNITIES (869)
727 Reba Place
Evanston, IL 60602

LIBERAL CATHOLIC CHURCH, PROVINCE OF THE
UNITED STATES (1138)
% Rt. Rev. Lawrence J. Smith
9740 S. Avers
Evergreen Park, IL 60642

CHRISTIAN CONSERVATIVE CHURCHES OF
AMERICA (745)
Box 575
Flora, IL 62839

CHRISTIAN APOSTOLIC CHURCH (FOREST,
ILLINOIS) (553)
Forrest, IL 61741

FREE SERBIAN ORTHODOX CHURCH—DIOCESE
FOR THE U.S.A. AND CANADA (105)
% Metropolitan Iriney *Kovachevich*
Box 371
Grayslake, IL 60030

INTERNATIONAL COUNCIL OF COMMUNITY
CHURCHES (205)
% Rev. J. Ralph Shotwell, Executive Director
900 Ridge Rd., Suite LL 1
Homewood, IL 60430

HINDU TEMPLE OF GREATER CHICAGO (1430)
% Ramalayam Hindu Temple
Box 99
Lemont, IL 60439

SERBIAN EASTERN ORTHODOX CHURCH FOR
THE U.S.A. AND CANADA (132)
% Rt. Rev. Bishop Firmilian
St. Sava Monastery
Box 519
Libertyville, IL 60048

MENNONITE CHURCH (496)
528 E. Madison St.
Lombard, IL 60148

ZEN BUDDHIST TEMPLE OF CHICAGO (1487)
865 Bittersweet Dr.
Northbrook, IL 60062-3701

NORTH AMERICAN BAPTIST CONFERENCE (583)
1 S. 210 Summit Ave.
Oakbrook Terrace, IL 60181

CHURCH OF GOD GENERAL CONFERENCE
(ABRAHAMIC FAITH) (673)
131 N. Third St.
Box 100
Oregon, IL 61061

APOSTOLIC CHRISTIAN CHURCHES OF AMERICA
(552)
3420 N. Sheridan Rd.
Peoria, IL 61604

NEW TESTAMENT ASSOCIATION OF
INDEPENDENT BAPTIST CHURCHES (582)
1079 Westview Dr.
Rochelle, IL 61068

SALEM ACRES (871)
R.R.1, Box 175A
Rock City, IL 61070

I AM RELIGIOUS ACTIVITY (1151)
Saint Germain Foundation
1120 Stonehedge Dr.
Schaumberg, IL 60194

GENERAL ASSOCIATION OF REGULAR BAPTIST
CHURCHES (577)
1300 N. Meacham Rd.
Schaumburg, IL 60195

APOSTOLIC CATHOLIC ASSYRIAN CHURCH OF
THE EAST, NORTH AMERICAN DIOCESE (141)
% His Grace, Mar Aprim Khamis, Bishop of the North
American Diocese
744 N. Klidare
Skokie, IL 60076

PROTESTANT REFORMED CHURCHES IN
AMERICA (184)
15615 S. Park Ave.
South Holland, IL 60473

CONCORDIA LUTHERAN CONFERENCE (164)
Central Ave. at 171st Place
Tingley Park, IL 60477

APOSTOLIC CHRISTIAN CHURCH (NAZAREAN)
(551)
Apostolic Christian Church Foundation
Box 151
Tremont, IL 61568

CONSERVATIVE BAPTIST ASSOCIATION (573)
Box 66
Wheaton, IL 60189

PLYMOUTH BRETHREN (OPEN OR CHRISTIAN
BRETHREN) (638)
Interest Ministries
218 W. Willow
Wheaton, IL 60187

THE THEOSOPHICAL SOCIETY IN AMERICA (1115)
Box 270
Wheaton, IL 60189

BAHA'I FAITH (1338)
% National Spiritual Assembly of the Baha'is of the U.S.
536 Sheridan Rd.
Wilmette, IL 60091

CHRISTIAN CATHOLIC CHURCH (1553)
Dowie Memorial Dr.
Zion, IL 60099

Indiana

CENTRAL YEARLY MEETING OF FRIENDS (533)
% Ollie McCune, Supt.
Route 1, Box 226
Alexandria, IN 46001

CHURCH OF GOD (ANDERSON, INDIANA) (255)
Box 2420
Anderson, IN 46018

UNIVERSAL SPIRITUALIST ASSOCIATION (978)
% Maple Grove
5848 Pendleton Ave.
Anderson, IN 46013

FAITH MISSION CHURCH (262)
1813 26th St.
Bedford, IN 47421

ZOROASTRIAN ASSOCIATIONS IN NORTH
AMERICA (1337)
% Center for Zoroastrian Research
3270 E. Robinson Rd.
Bloomington, IN 47401-9301

OLD GERMAN BAPTIST BRETHREN (530)
% Elder Clement Skiles
Rte. 1, Box 140
Bringhurst, IN 46913

BETHEL MINISTERIAL ASSOCIATION (397)
4350 Lincoln Ave.
Evansville, IN 47715

CALVARY MINISTRIES, INC., INTERNATIONAL
(352)
1400 W. Washington Center Rd.
Fort Wayne, IN 46825

CONFERENCE OF THE EVANGELICAL
MENNONITE CHURCH (513)
1420 Kerrway Court
Fort Wayne, IN 46805

MISSIONARY CHURCH (268)
3901 S. Wayne Ave.
Fort Wayne, IN 46807

PENTECOSTAL CHURCH OF ZION (369)
% Zion College of Theology
Box 110
French Lick, IN 47432

MACEDONIAN ORTHODOX CHURCH (119)
% Rev. Spiro Tanaskaki
51st & Virginia Sts.
Gary, IN 46409

APOSTOLIC CATHOLIC CHURCH OF THE
AMERICAS (92)
% Most Rev. Gordon I. DaCosta
408 S. 10th St.
Gas City, IN 46933

CHURCH OF THE BIBLE COVENANT (305)
Rte. 8, Box 214
450 N. Fortville Pike
Greenfield, IN 46140

NATIONAL ASSOCIATION OF HOLINESS
CHURCHES (309)
351 S. Park Dr.
Griffith, IN 46319

CHURCH OF THE UNITED BRETHREN IN CHRIST
(240)
% Bishop C. Ray Miller
302 Lake St.
Huntington, IN 46750

CHRISTIAN CHURCH (DISCIPLES OF CHRIST) (618)
222 S. Downey Ave.
Box 1986
Indianapolis, IN 46206

CHRISTIAN ISRAELITE CHURCH (733)
1204 N. Rural St.
Indianapolis, IN 46201

ORTHODOX CATHOLIC CHURCH OF AMERICA
(123)
% Most Rev. Alfred Lankenau
Box 1222
Indianapolis, IN 45206

PENTECOSTAL ASSEMBLIES OF THE WORLD (410)
% James A. Johnson, Presiding Bishop
3939 Meadows Dr.
Indianapolis, IN 46205

WESLEYAN CHURCH (276)
Box 50434
Indianpolis, IN 46250-0434

BRANHAM TABERNACLE AND RELATED
ASSEMBLIES (375)
% The William Branham Evangelistic Association
and The Branham Tabernacle
Box 325
Jeffersonville, IN 47130

TRUTH FOR TODAY BIBLE FELLOWSHIP (666)
Box 6358
Lafayette, IN 47903

SOULCRAFT (1109)
Box 192
Noblesville, IN 46060

FRIENDS UNITED MEETING (536)
101 Quaker Hill Dr.
Richmond, IN 47374

PILGRIM HOLINESS CHURCH OF THE MIDWEST
(311)
% Union Bible Seminary
434 S. Union St.
Westfield, IN 46074

FAITH ASSEMBLY (473)
Wilmot, IN 46590

FREE METHODIST CHURCH OF NORTH AMERICA
(264)
901 College
Winina Lake, IN 46590

FELLOWSHIP OF GRACE BRETHREN CHURCHES
(525)
Winona Lake, IN 46590

Iowa

THE NUDIST CHRISTIAN CHURCH OF THE BLESSED VIRGIN JESUS (1585)
Box 1316
Welch Ave. Station
Ames, IA 50010

GOSPEL ASSEMBLIES (SOWDERS/GOODWIN) (478)
Gospel Assembly Church
7135 Meredith Dr.
Des Moines, IA 50322

OPEN BIBLE STANDARD CHURCHES, INC. (365)
2020 Bell Ave.
Des Moines, IA 50315-1096

AMANA CHURCH SOCIETY (CHURCH OF TRUE INSPIRATION) (840)
% Charles L. Selzer, President
Homestead, IA 52236

IOWA YEARLY MEETING OF FRIENDS (538)
% Stephen Main, Gen. Supt.
Box 703
Oskaloosa, IA 52577

ANGLICAN CATHOLIC CHURCH (60)
% The Most Rev. Louis W. Falk
4807 Aspen Dr.
West Des Moines, IA 50265

Kansas

APOSTOLIC FAITH (KANSAS) (345)
1009 Lincoln Ave.
Baxter Springs, KS 66713

CHURCHES OF GOD (INDEPENDENT HOLINESS PEOPLE) (259)
1225 E. First St.
Fort Scott, KS 66701

MENNONITE BRETHREN CHURCH OF NORTH AMERICA (BRUEDERGEMEINDE) (511)
Hillsboro, KS 67063

FIRE-BAPTIZED HOLINESS CHURCH (WESLEYAN) (263)
600 College Ave.
Independence, KS 67301

CHURCH OF GOD IN CHRIST, MENNONITE (493)
420 N. Wedel
Moundridge, KS 67107

GENERAL CONFERENCE MENNONITE CHURCH (510)
722 Main St.
Newton, KS 67114

CHURCH OF GOD (HOLINESS) (257)
7415 Metcalf
Overland Park, KS 66204

DUNKARD BRETHREN CHURCH (523)
% Dale E. Jamison, Chairman
Board of Trustees
Quinter, KS 67752

CHRISTIAN APOSTOLIC CHURCH (SABETHA, KANSAS) (554)
Sabetha, KS 66534

FOUNTAIN OF LIFE FELLOWSHIP (698)
Valley Center, KS 67147

EVANGELICAL METHODIST CHURCH (221)
3000 W. Kellogg
Wichita, KS 67213

MID-AMERICA YEARLY MEETING (540)
2018 Maple
Wichita, KS 67213

Kentucky

SOUTHERN APPALACHIAN YEARLY MEETING AND ASSOCIATION (550)
% Thomas Lynn, Clerk
902 State Lick Road
Berea, KY 40403

KENTUCKY MOUNTAIN HOLINESS ASSOCIATION (286)
Star Rte. 1, Box 350
Jackson, KY 41339

SEPARATE BAPTISTS IN CHRIST (587)
% Rev. Roger Popplewell, Moderator
Rte. 5
Russell Springs, KY 42642

CHURCH OF GOD OF THE ORIGINAL MOUNTAIN ASSEMBLY (322)
Williamsburg, KY 40769

Louisiana

CHURCH OF MERCAVAH (1045)
Box 66703
Baton Rouge, LA 70896

NATIONAL BAPTIST CONVENTION OF THE U.S.A., INC. (604)
% Dr. T. G. Jemison, President
915 Spain St.
Baton Rouge, LA 70802

CHRIST'S SANCTIFIED HOLY CHURCH (LOUISIANA) (253)
S. Cutting Ave. at E. Spencer St.
Jennings, LA 70546

NEW CHRISTIAN CRUSADE CHURCH (754)
Box 426
Metairie, LA 70004

VOLUNTEERS OF AMERICA (275)
3813 N. Causeway Blvd.
Metairie, LA 70002

RELIGIOUS ORDER OF WITCHCRAFT (1256)
% Witchcraft Shop
521 St. Philip
New Orleans, LA 70116

CONGREGATIONAL CHURCH OF PRACTICAL
THEOLOGY (1049)
31916 Pat's Lane
Springfield, LA 70462

Maine

UNITED SOCIETY OF BELIEVERS IN CHRIST'S
SECOND APPEARING (855)
Sabbathday Lake, ME 04274

Maryland

NEW COVENANT CHURCHES OF MARYLAND (462)
804 Windsor Rd.
Arnold, MD 21012

ALPHA AND OMEGA PENTECOSTAL CHURCH OF
GOD OF AMERICA, INC. (423)
3023 Clifton Ave.
Baltimore, MD 21216

EVANGELICAL BIBLE CHURCH (472)
2444 Washington Blvd.
Baltimore, MD 21230

EVANGELICAL CATHOLIC COMMUNION (18)
% Most Rev. Marlin Paul Bausum Ballard
Box 8484
Baltimore, MD 21234

GRACE AND HOPE MISSION (283)
4 S. Gay St.
Baltimore, MD 21202

METROPOLITAN SPIRITUAL CHURCHES OF
CHRIST, INC. (953)
% Dr. I. Logan Kearse
4329 Park Heights Ave.
Baltimore, MD 21215

MOORISH SCIENCE TEMPLE OF AMERICA (1330)
762 W. Baltimore St.
Baltimore, MD 21201

MOORISH SCIENCE TEMPLE, PROPHET ALI
REINCARNATED, FOUNDER (1331)
2119 Aiken St.
Baltimore, MD 21218

SAVITRIA (1083)
2405 Ruscombe
Baltimore, MD 21209

TRUE FELLOWSHIP PENTECOSTAL CHURCH OF
GOD OF AMERICA (440)
4238 Pimlico Rd.
Baltimore, MD 21215

UNITED CHURCH OF JESUS CHRIST (APOSTOLIC)
(416)
% Monroe Saunders, Presiding Bishop
5150 Baltimore National Pike
Baltimore, MD 21229

WITNESS AND TESTIMONY LITERATURE TRUST
AND RELATED CENTERS (671)
Testimony Book Ministry
Box 34241
Bethesda, MD 20817

SCRIPTURE RESEARCH ASSOCIATION (730)
14410 S. Springfield Rd.
Brandywine, MD 20613

UNITED HOLY CHURCH OF AMERICA (442)
825 Fairoak Ave.
Chillum, MD 20783

PEOPLE OF DESTINY INTERNATIONAL (463)
7881-B Beechcraft Ave.
Gaithersburg, MD 20879

AMERICAN ZEN COLLEGE (1504)
16815 Germantown Road (Route 18)
Germantown, MD 20767

CONSERVATIVE MENNONITE CONFERENCE (514)
% Ivan J. Miller
Grantsville, MD 21536

GOSPEL MISSION CORPS (282)
Box 175
Hightstown, MD 08520

FIVEFOLD PATH (1365)
Box 710
Randallstown, MD 21133

UNION OF MESSIANIC JEWISH CONGREGATIONS
(658)
% Rev. David C. Juster
Beth Messiah Congregation
2208 Rockland Ave.
Rockville, MD 20851

BODY OF CHRIST MOVEMENT (452)
% Foundational Teachings
Box 6598
Silver Spring, MD 20906

Massachusetts

INSIGHT MEDITATION SOCIETY (1454)
Pleasant St.
Barre, MA 01005

CHURCH OF CHRIST, SCIENTIST (875)
Christian Science Center
Boston, MA 02115

UNITARIAN UNIVERSALIST ASSOCIATION (774)
25 Beacon St.
Boston, MA 02108

UNITED CHURCH AND SCIENCE OF LIVING
INSTITUTE (920)
% Rev. Frederick Eikerenkotter II
Box 1000
Boston, MA 02103

NEW AGE TEACHINGS (997)
Box 346
Brookfield, MA 01506

BOSTONER HASIDISM (1272)
% New England Chasidic Center
1710 Beacon St.
Brookline, MA 02146

EAST WEST FOUNDATION (1498)
17 Station St.
Brookline, MA 02147

SOCIETY OF JOHREI (1546)
Box 1321
Brookline, MA 02146

TALNOYE (TALNER) HASIDISM (1283)
Talner Beth David
64 Corey Rd.
Brookline, MA 02146

AFRICAN ORTHODOX CHURCH (78)
% Rt. Rev. James A. Ford
137 Allston St.
Cambridge, MA 02139

CAMBRIDGE BUDDHIST ASSOCIATION (1479)
75 Sparks St.
Cambridge, MA 02138

NITYANANDA INSTITUTE, INC. (1390)
6 Linnaean St.
Cambridge, MA 02138

THE TRUTH (1588)
Box 1023
Cambridge, MA 02238

MAHASIDDHA NYINGMAPA CENTER (1519)
Box 87
Charlemont, MA 01339

ALBANIAN ORTHODOX DIOCESE OF AMERICA
(81)
% The Rev. Ik. Ilia Katra, Vicar General
54 Burroughs St.
Jamaica Plain, MA 02130

NATIONAL SPIRITUAL ALLIANCE OF THE U.S.A.
(957)
RFD 1
Lake Pleasant, MA 01347

KRIPALU CENTER FOR YOGA AND HEALTH
(1381)
Box 973
Lenox, MA 01240

OLD CATHOLIC CHURCH-UTRECHT SUCCESSION
(33)
% Most Rev. Roy G. Bauer
21 Aaron St.
Melrose, MA 02176

ANGLO-SAXON FEDERATION OF AMERICA (742)
Box 177
Merrimac, MA 01860

ALBANIAN ORTHODOX ARCHDIOCESE IN
AMERICA (80)
270 Cabot St.
Newton, MA 02160

GENERAL CONVENTION OF THE NEW
JERUSALEM IN THE UNITED STATES OF
AMERICA (927)
48 Sargent St.
Newton, MA 02158

NEW ENGLAND EVANGELICAL BAPTIST
FELLOWSHIP (581)
% Dr. John Viall
40 Bridge St.
Newton, MA 02158

SLAVES OF THE IMMACULATE HEART OF MARY
(47)
Box 22
Still River, MA 01467

RENAISSANCE CHURCH OF BEAUTY (870)
Box 112
Turner's Falls, MA 01376

Michigan

LOWER LIGHTS CHURCH (308)
Ann Arbor, MI

CHURCH OF DANIEL'S BAND (218)
% Rev. Wesley James Haggard, President
Croll Rd.
Beaverton, MI 48612

ISRAELITE HOUSE OF DAVID (734)
Box 1967
Benton Harbor, MI 49022

ISRAELITE HOUSE OF DAVID AS REORGANIZED
BY MARY PURNELL (735)
Box 187
Benton Harbor, MI 49022

UNITED HOLINESS CHURCH OF NORTH AMERICA
(312)
Cedar Springs, MI 49319

CHURCH OF CHRIST IMMANUEL (820)
1308 Davison Rd.
Davison, MI 48423

AMENDED CHRISTADELPHIANS (617)
% Christadelphian Book Supply
14651 Livonia
Detroit, MI 48154

CHURCH OF UNIVERSAL TRIUMPH/THE
DOMINION OF GOD (294)
% Rev. James Shaffer
8317 LaSalle Blvd.
Detroit, MI 48206

NATION OF ISLAM (JOHN MUHAMMAD) (1334)
14880 Wyoming
Detroit, MI 48238

NATIONAL BAPTIST EVANGELICAL LIFE AND
SOUL SAVING ASSEMBLY OF THE U.S.A. (605)
441-61 Monroe Ave.
Detroit, MI 48226

PAN AFRICAN ORTHODOX CHRISTIAN CHURCH (1292)
13535 Livernois
Detroit, MI 48238

PENTECOSTAL CHURCH OF GOD (411)
9244 Delmar
Detroit, MI 48211

ROMANIAN ORTHODOX CHURCH IN AMERICA (127)
% His Eminence The Most Rev. Archbishop Victorin (Ursache)
19959 Riopelle
Detroit, MI 48203

SHI'A MUSLIMS (1306)
% Islamic Center of Detroit
15571 Joy Rd.
Detroit, MI 48228

CHURCH OF NATURE (766)
Box 407
Dryden, MI 48428

FULL GOSPEL MINISTER ASSOCIATION (475)
East Jordan, MI 49727

SOCIETY FOR HUMANISTIC JUDAISM (1302)
28611 W. Twelve Mile Rd.
Farmington Hills, MI 48018

CHRISTIAN REFORMED CHURCH IN NORTH AMERICA (177)
2850 Kalamazoo Ave.,S.E.
Grand Rapids, MI 49560

FREE AND OLD CHRISTIAN REFORMED CHURCH OF CANADA AND AMERICA (180)
% Jacob Tamminga
950 Ball Ave., N.E.
Grand Rapids, MI 49503

GRACE GOSPEL FELLOWSHIP (663)
1011 Aldon St., S.W.
Grand Rapids, MI 49509

NETHERLANDS REFORMED CONGREGATIONS (182)
% Dr. J. R. Beeke
2115 Romence, N.E.
Grand Rapids, MI 49503

ROBIN'S RETURN (1002)
1008 Lamberton St., N.E.
Grand Rapids, MI 49505

INDEPENDENT FUNDAMENTAL CHURCHES OF AMERICA (650)
Box 810
Grandville, MI 49468

ORTHODOX REFORMED CHURCH (183)
3836 30th St.
Grandville, MI 49418

ASSEMBLIES OF YAHWEH (EATON RAPIDS, MICHIGAN) (722)
Box 102
Holt, MI 48842

ROMANIAN ORTHODOX EPISCOPATE OF AMERICA (128)
% Rt. Rev. Nathaniel, Bishop
2522 Grey Tower Rd.
Jackson, MI 49201

ANCHOR BAY EVANGELISTIC ASSOCIATION (343)
Box 188
New Baltimore, MI 48047

FULL SALVATION UNION (1566)
Northville, MI 48167

CHURCH OF ETERNAL LIFE AND LIBERTY (765)
Box 622
Southfield, MI 48037

BHARATIYA TEMPLE (1429)
6850 Adams Rd.
Troy, MI 48098

OLD ROMAN CATHOLIC CHURCH IN NORTH AMERICA (34)
% Most Rev. Francis P. Facione
3827 Old Creek Rd.
Troy, MI 48084

MARIAVITE OLD CATHOLIC CHURCH, PROVINCE OF NORTH AMERICA (25)
% His Eminence, Most Rev. Robert R. J. M. Zaborowski
2803 10th St.
Wyandotte, MI 48192

COPTIC FELLOWSHIP OF AMERICA (1050)
1735 Pinnacle, S.W.
Wyoming, MI 48509

Minnesota

CHURCH OF THE LUTHERAN BRETHREN OF AMERICA (162)
1007 Westside Dr.
Box 655
Fergus Falls, MN 56537

EVANGELICAL LUTHERAN CHURCH IN AMERICA (165)
% Truman Larson
Rte. 1
Jackson, MN 56143

EVANGELICAL LUTHERAN SYNOD (168)
% Rev. George Orvick, President
447 N. Division St.
Mankato, MN 56001

AMERICAN INDIAN EVANGELICAL CHURCH (342)
Box 25019
Minneapolis, MN 55440-6019

ASSOCIATION OF FREE LUTHERAN CONGREGATIONS (161)
3110 E. Medicine Lake Blvd.
Minneapolis, MN 55441

BROTHERS OF THE EARTH (1206)
% Church of the Earth
Box 13158
Dinkytown Station
Minneapolis, MN 55414

CHURCH OF THE LUTHERAN CONFESSION (163)
460 75th Ave., N.E.
Minneapolis, MN 55432

ECKANKAR (1444)
Box 27300
Minneapolis, MN 55427

EVANGELICAL FREE CHURCH OF AMERICA (211)
1551 E. 66th St.
Minneapolis, MN 55423

MINNESOTA BAPTIST ASSOCIATION (580)
% Dr. Richard L. Paige, Jr., Executive Secretary
5000 Golden Valley Rd.
Minneapolis, MN 55422

MINNESOTA ZEN MEDITATION CENTER (1483)
3343 Calhoun Pkwy.
Minneapolis, MN 55408

PLYMOUTH BRETHREN (EXCLUSIVE: AMES
BRETHREN) (633)
% Christian Literature, Inc.
Box 23082
Minneapolis, MN 55423

APOSTOLIC LUTHERAN CHURCH OF AMERICA
(155)
% Rev. George Wilson, President
New York Mills, MN 56567

AURUM SOLIS (1179)
% The Administrator General
Box 43383-OSV
St. Paul, MN 55164

CONSERVATIVE CONGREGATIONAL CHRISTIAN
CONFERENCE (204)
7582 Currell Blvd., Suite 108
St. Paul, MN 55125

JESUS PEOPLE CHURCH (485)
2924 Rahn Way
St. Paul, MN 55122-2329

Mississippi

FIRST CONGREGATIONAL METHODIST CHURCH
OF THE U.S.A. (225)
Decatur, MS 39327

CONGREGATIONAL METHODIST CHURCH (219)
Box 155
Florence, MS 39073

ASSOCIATION OF INDEPENDENT METHODISTS
(217)
Box 4274
Jackson, MS 39216

CHURCH OF CHRIST (HOLINESS) U.S.A. (292)
329 E. Monument St.
Jackson, MS 39202

METHODIST PROTESTANT CHURCH (228)
% Rev. F. E. Sellers
Monticello, MS 55362

Missouri

CHURCH OF GOD EVANGELISTIC ASSOCIATION
(689)
11824 Beaverton
Bridgeton, MO 63044

HUNA RESEARCH ASSOCIATES (1064)
126 Camillia Drive
Cape Girardeau, MO 63701

CHRISTIAN UNION (1555)
106 W. Broadway
Excelsior Springs, MO 64024

DAVIDIAN SEVENTH-DAY ADVENTISTS
ASSOCIATION (676)
Bashan Hill
Exeter, MO 65647

DAWN OF TRUTH (1051)
% Shepherdsfield
R.R. 4, Box 399
Fulton, MO 65251

UNITED PENTECOSTAL CHURCH (418)
8855 Dunn Rd.
Hazelwood, MO 63042

CHRIST CATHOLIC CHURCH (PRUTER) (12)
% Most Rev. Karl Pruter
Box 98
Highlandville, MO 65669

CENTER BRANCH OF THE LORD'S REMNANT
(814)
709 W. Maple
Independence, MO 64050

CHURCH OF CHRIST (BIBLE AND BOOK OF
MORMON TEACHING) (815)
1515 S. Harvard
Independence, MO 64052

CHURCH OF CHRIST (FETTING/BRONSON) (816)
1138 East Gudgell
Independence, MO 64055

CHURCH OF CHRIST, NONDENOMINATIONAL
BIBLE ASSEMBLY (821)
1515 S. Harvard
Independence, MO 64052

CHURCH OF CHRIST (TEMPLE LOT) (818)
Temple Lot
Independence, MO 65051

THE CHURCH OF CHRIST 'WITH THE ELIJAH
MESSAGE,' ESTABLISHED ANEW IN 1929 (822)
608 Lacy Road
Independence, MO 64050

CHURCH OF JESUS CHRIST (CUTLERITE) (831)
819 S. Cottage St.
Independence, MO 64050

CHURCHES OF CHRIST IN ZION (827)
18713 E. 30th Terrace
Independence, MO 64057

REORGANIZED CHURCH OF JESUS CHRIST OF LATTER DAY SAINTS (828)
The Auditorium
Box 1059
Independence, MO 64051

RESTORATION BRANCHES MOVEMENT (829)
No central address. For information contact:
Price Publishing Company
207 W. Southside Blvd.
Independence, MO 64055

RESTORED CHURCH OF JESUS CHRIST (WALTON) (838)
Box 1651
Independence, MO 64055

TRUE CHURCH OF JESUS CHRIST RESTORED (839)
1533 E. Mechanic
Independence, MO 64050

CHURCH OF JESUS CHRIST (ZION'S BRANCH) (826)
108 S. Pleasnat
Indpendence, MO

PENTECOSTAL CHURCH OF GOD (368)
4901 Pennsylvania
Joplin, MO 64802

CHURCH OF JESUS CHRIST (TONEY) (825)
Box 35656
Kansas City, MO 64134

CHURCH OF THE NAZARENE (258)
6401 The Paseo
Kansas City, MO 64131

MISSOURI VALLEY FRIENDS CONFERENCE (541)
% John Griffith
5745 Charlotte
Kansas City, MO 64110

CHURCH OF CHRIST (RESTORED) (817)
% Mr. Uel Sisk
609 C Lilac Place, John Knox Village
Lee's Summit, MO 64063

ZION'S ORDER, INC. (801)
Route 2, Box 104-7
Mansfield, MO 65704

GENERAL ASSOCIATION OF GENERAL BAPTISTS (609)
100 Stinson Dr.
Poplar Bluff, MO 63901

YAHWEH'S ASSEMBLY IN MESSIAH (732)
Rte. 1, Box 364
Rocheport, MO 65279

CHURCH OF CHRIST AT HALLEY'S BLUFF (819)
Schell City, MO 64783

CHURCH OF ISRAEL (748)
Box 62 B3
Schell City, MO 64783

ASSEMBLIES OF GOD, GENERAL COUCIL OF (346)
1445 Boonville Ave.
Springfield, MO 65802

BAPTIST BIBLE FELLOWSHIP (568)
Box 191
Springfield, MO 65801

CHURCHES OF CHRIST (NON-INSTRUMENTAL, NON-CLASS, ONE CUP) (623)
% *Old Paths Advocate*
Box 10811
Springfield, MO 65808

FUNDAMENTAL METHODIST CHURCH (226)
1034 N. Broadway
Springfield, MO 65802

AMERICAN RATIONALIST FEDERATION (761)
2001 St. Clair Ave.
St. Louis, MO 63144

LUTHERAN CHURCH-MISSOURI SYNOD (171)
International Center
1333 S. Kirkwood Rd.
St. Louis, MO 63122

UNIVERSAL GREAT BROTHERHOOD (1174)
Administrative Council of the U. S. A.
Box 9154
St. Louis, MO 63117

UNITY SCHOOL OF CHRISTIANITY (922)
Unity Village, MO 64065

Montana

CHURCH UNIVERSAL AND TRIUMPHANT (1150)
Box A
Livingston, MT 59047

HUTTERIAN BRETHREN-DARIUSLUET (846)
% Rev. Elias Walter
Surprise Creek Colony
Stanford, MT 59479

HUTTERIAN BRETHREN-LEHRELEUT (847)
% Rev. Joseph Kleinsasser
Milford Colony
Wolf Creek, MT 59648

Nebraska

REFORMED CHURCH IN THE UNITED STATES (186)
% Rev. Vernon Polleme, President
3930 Masin Dr.
Lincoln, NE 68521

BEREAN FUNDAMENTAL CHURCHES (643)
Box 549
North Platte, NE 69101

FELLOWSHIP OF EVANGELICAL BIBLE CHURCHES (507)
5800 S. 14th St.
Omaha, NE 68107

FUTURE FOUNDATION (1060)
Box 26
Steinauer, NE 68441

Nevada

CHURCH OF REVELATION (CALIFORNIA) (936)
517 E. Park Paseo
Las Vegas, NV 89104

FOUNDATION FAITH OF GOD (1058)
Faith Center
3055 S. Bronco
Las Vegas, NV 89102

INSTITUTE OF COSMIC WISDOM (1067)
3528 Franciscan Lane
Las Vegas, NV 89121

**ORTHODOX BAHA'I FAITH UNDER THE
   REGENCY (1341)**
% National House of Justice of the U.S. and Canada
Box 1424
Las Vegas, NV 87701

PANSOPHIC INSTITUTE (1522)
Box 2422
Reno, NV 89505

New Hampshire

SANT BANI ASHRAM (1450)
Franklin, NH 03235

**OUR LADY OF ENCHANTMENT, CHURCH OF THE
   OLD RELIGION (1237)**
Box 1366
Nashua, NH 03061

New Jersey

BIBLE PRESBYTERIAN CHURCH (188)
Haddon and Cuthbert Blvd.S
Collinswood, NJ 08108

DAWN BIBLE STUDENTS ASSOCIATION (711)
199 Railroad Ave.
East Rutherford, NJ 07073

MT. ZION SANCTUARY (363)
21 Dayton St.
Elizabeth, NJ 07202

**ANTIOCHIAN ORTHODOX CHRISTIAN
   ARCHDIOCESE OF NORTH AMERICA (91)**
% Metropolitan Philip, Primate
358 Mountain Rd.
Englewood, NJ 07631

**FELLOWSHIP OF FUNDAMENTAL BIBLE
   CHURCHES (223)**
Box 43
Glassboro, NJ 08028

**HUNGARIAN REFORMED CHURCH IN AMERICA
   (181)**
% Rt. Rev. Dr. Andrew Harsanyi
P.O. Box D
Hipatcong, NJ 07843

COPTIC ORTHODOX CHURCH (143)
% Archpriest Fr. Gabriel Abdelsayed
427 West Side Ave.
Jersey City, NJ 07304

**SYRIAN ORTHODOX CHURCH OF ANTIOCH
   (ARCHDIOCESES OF THE UNITED STATES AND
   CANADA) (JACOBITE) (152)**
% Archbishop MarAthanasius Y. Samuel, Primate
49 Kipp Ave.
Lodi, NJ 07644

AMERICAN VEGAN SOCIETY (1346)
501 Old Harding Hwy.
Malaga, NJ 08328

DELIVERANCE EVANGELISTIC CENTERS (429)
505 Central Ave.
Newark, NJ 07107

PHILANTHROPIC ASSEMBLY (717)
709 74th St.
North Bergen, NJ 07047

**SHANTI YOGI INSTITUTE AND YOGA RETREAT
   (1402)**
943 Central Ave.
Ocean City, NJ 08226

RESTORED ISRAEL OF YAHWEH (737)
% Mrs. Nancy Micsko
649 2nd St.
Somers Point, NJ 08244

**UKRAINIAN ORTHODOX CHURCH OF THE U.S.A.
   (135)**
Box 495
South Bound Brook, NJ 08880

BYELORUSSIAN ORTHODOX CHURCH (99)
190 Turnpike Rd.
South River, NJ 08882

SALVATION ARMY (272)
799 Bloomfield Ave.
Verona, NJ 07044

**OLD ORTHODOX CATHOLIC PATRIARCHATE OF
   AMERICA (120)**
66 N. Brookfield St.
Vineland, NJ 08360

UNITED HINDU TEMPLE OF NEW JERSEY (1436)
% Dr. Raj P. Misra
1 CeCamp Court
W. Caldwell, NJ 07006

TIBETAN BUDDHIST LEARNING CENTER (1525)
R.D. 1, Box 306 A
Washington, NJ 07882-9767

PILLAR OF FIRE (288)
Zarephath, NJ 08890

New Mexico

WORLD UNDERSTANDING (1026)
Box 614
Alamagordo, NM 88311

QUIMBY CENTER (1082)
Box 453
Alamogordo, NM 88310

SEMJASE SILVER STAR CENTER (1019)
Box 797
Alamogordo, NM 88311

CHURCH OF JESUS CHRIST OF LATTER-DAY
SAINTS (STRANGITE) (833)
% Vernon Swift
Box 522
Artesia, NM 88210

T.O.M. RELIGIOUS FOUNDATION (970)
Box 52
Chimayo, NM 87522

CITY OF THE SUN FOUNDATION (1149)
Box 370
Columbus, NM 88029

NEW AGE CHURCH OF TRUTH (1075)
Star Route 2
Box CLC
Deming, NM 88030

ORTHODOX BAHA'I FAITH, MOTHER BAHA'I
COUNCIL OF THE UNITED STATES (1340)
3111 Futura
Roswell, NM 88201

LAMA FOUNDATION (865)
Box 44
San Cristobal, NM 877564

SIKH DHARMA (1442)
% Chancellor to the Siri Singh Sahib
M.S.S. Guru Terath Singh Khalsa
Box 845
Santa Cruz, NM 87567

HANUMAN FOUNDATION (1369)
Box 478
Santa Fe, NM 87501

THIRD CIVILIZATION (1550)
Box 1836
Sante Fe, NM 87501

New York

PILGRIM HOLINESS CHURCH OF NEW YORK (310)
32 Cadillac Ave.
Albany, NY 12205

AMERICAN HUMANIST ASSOCIATION (760)
7 Harwood Dr.
Box 146
Amherst, NY 14226-0146

OUR LADY OF THE ROSES, MARY HELP OF
MOTHERS SHRINE (41)
Box 52
Bayside, NY 11361

GRAIL MOVEMENT OF AMERICA (991)
2081 Partridge Lane
Binghamton, NY 13903

AUSAR AUSET SOCIETY (1091)
% Oracle of Thoth, Inc.
Box 281
Bronx, NY 10462

BIBLE CHURCH OF CHRIST (349)
1358 Morris Ave.
Bronx, NY 10456

DAMASCUS CHRISTIAN CHURCH (448)
% Rev. Enrique Melendez
170 Mt. Eden Parkway
Bronx, NY 10473

ECLESIA CATOLICA CRISTIANA (942)
2112 Grand Ave.
Bronx, NY 10453

ETHIOPIAN ORTHODOX CHURCH IN THE UNITED
STATES OF AMERICA (144)
% His Eminence Abuna Yeshaq, Archbishop
Holy Trinity Ethiopian Orthodox Church
140-142 W. 176th St.
Bronx, NY 10453

ANSAARU ALLAH COMMUNITY (1327)
716 Bushwick Ave.
Brooklyn, NY 11221

BLUZHEVER HASIDISM (1270)
Belzer Bet Midrash
662 Eastern Pkwy.
Brooklyn, NY 11213

BOBOV HASIDISM (1271)
% Rabbi Solomon Halberstamm
Yeshiva Bnai Zion
4909 15th St.
Brooklyn, NY 11219

BRATSLAV HASIDISM (1273)
% Rabbi Leo Rosenfeld
864 44th St.
Brooklyn, NY 11219

CHERNOBYL HASIDISM (1274)
% Rabbi Israel Jacob Twersky
1520 49th St.
Brooklyn, NY 11232

CHURCH OF GOD IN CHRIST, INTERNATIONAL
(426)
% Rt. Rev. Carl E. Williams, Presiding Bishop
170 Adelphi St.
Brooklyn, NY 11025

CONFRATERNITY OF CHRISTIAN DOCTRINE,
SAINT PIUS X (15)
% Most Rev. Msgr. Hector Gonzales
10 Stagg St.
Brooklyn, NY 11206

ETHIOPIAN ORTHODOX COPTIC CHURCH,
DIOCESE OF NORTH AND SOUTH AMERICA
(145)
1255 Bedford Ave.
Brooklyn, NY 11216

JEHOVAH'S WITNESSES (713)
25 Columbia Heights
Brooklyn, NY 11201

LUBAVITCH HASIDISM (1277)
770 Eastern Pkwy.
Brooklyn, NY 11213

NOVOMINSK HASIDISM (1279)
% Rabbi Nahum M. Perlow
1569 47th St.
Brooklyn, NY 11220

SATMAR HASIDISM (1280)
% Congregation Y L D'Satmar
152 Rodney
Brooklyn, NY 11220

SIGHET HASIDISM (1281)
152 Hewes St.
Brooklyn, NY 11211

STOLIN HASIDISM (1282)
Stolin Bet Midrash
1818 54th St.
Brooklyn, NY 11211

TRIDENTINE CATHOLIC CHURCH (54)
% Archbishop Leonard J. Curreri, Primate
Sacred Heart of Jesus Chapel
1740 W. Seventh St.
Brooklyn, NY 11223

UNITED OLD ROMAN CATHOLIC CHURCH
(WHITEHEAD) (56)
% Most Rev. Armand C. Whitehead
527 82nd St.
Brooklyn, NY 11209

UNIVERSAL SHRINE OF DIVINE GUIDANCE (137)
% Most Rev. Mark A. G. Karras
30 Malta St.
Brooklyn, NY 11207

MALANKARA ORTHODOX (SYRIAN) CHURCH
(149)
% His Grace Dr. Thomas Makarios
Episcopal Diocesan House
1114 Delaware Ave.
Buffalo, NY 14209

TRUE CHURCH OF CHRIST, INTERNATIONAL
(1086)
Box 2, Station G
Buffalo, NY 14213

SERVANT CATHOLIC CHURCH (46)
% Most Rev. Robert E. Burns
50 Coventry Lane
Central Islip, NY 11722

TIOGA RIVER CHRISTIAN CONFERENCE (630)
% Rev. Calvin Duvall
R.D. 1, Box 134
Cherry Valley, NY 13320

YOGI GUPTA ASSOCIATION (1427)
94-15 51st Ave.
Elmhurst, NY 11373

HINDU TEMPLE SOCIETY OF NORTH AMERICA
(1431)
45-57 Brown St.
Flushing, NY 11355

SWAMINARAYAN MISSION AND FELLOWSHIP
(1435)
43-38 Bowne St.
Flushing, NY 11355

ARUNCHALA ASHRAMA (1350)
72-63 Yellowstone Blvd.
Forest Hills, NY 11375

LONGCHEN NYINGTHIG BUDDHIST SOCIETY
(1518)
Box 302
Harris, NY 12742

AUROBINDO, DISCIPLES OF SRI (1351)
% Sri Aurobindo Association
Box 372
High Falls, NY 12440

MIRACLE EXPERIENCES, INC. (907)
Box 158
Islip Terrace, NY 11752

REMEY SOCIETY (1342)
80-46 234 St.
Jamaica, NY 11427-2116

SRI CHINMOY CENTRES (1360)
Box 32433
Jamaica, NY 11431

UKRAINIAN ORTHODOX CHURCH IN AMERICA
(ECUMENICAL PATRIARCHATE) (136)
St. Andrew's Ukrainian Orthodox Diocese
90-34 139th St.
Jamaica, NY 11435

KIRPAL LIGHT SATSANG (1446)
Merwin Lake Rd.
Kinderhook, NY 12106

NEW AGE CHURCH OF THE CHRIST (1154)
Box 333
Kings Park, NY 11754

HOLY ORTHODOX CHURCH IN AMERICA (117)
10 E. Chestnut
Kingston, NY 12401

SOCIETAS ROSICRUCIANA IN AMERICA (1098)
10 E. Chestnut
Kingston, NY 12401

SUFI ORDER (1323)
Sufi Order Secretariat
Box 574
Lebanon Springs, NY 12114

ELIM FELLOWSHIP (354)
7245 College St.
Lima, NY 14485

EMBASSY OF THE GHEEZ-AMERICANS (1052)
Mt. Helion Sanctuary
Rock Valley Rd., Box 53
Long Eddy, NY 12760

AMERICAN ORTHODOX CATHOLIC CHURCH -
WESTERN RITE MISSION, DIOCESE OF NEW
YORK (4)
% Most Rev. Joseph J. Raffaele
318 Expressway Dr., S.
Medford, NY 11763

INTERCOSMIC CENTER OF SPIRITUAL
  AWARENESS (1376)
% Ananda Ashram
R.D. 3, Box 141
Monroe, NY 10950

CONGREGATION OF NEW SQUARE (SKVER
  CHASIDISM) (1275)
North Main St.
New Square, NY 10977

AGNI YOGA SOCIETY (1160)
319 W. 107th St.
New York, NY 10025

AMERICAN BUDDHIST MOVEMENT (1529)
301 W. 45th St.
New York, NY 10036

AMERICAN ETHICAL UNION (759)
2 W. 64th St.
New York, NY 10023

ANTHROPOSOPHICAL SOCIETY (1163)
Rudolf Steiner Information Center
211 Madison Ave.
New York, NY 10016

ARCANE SCHOOL (1120)
113 University Place, 11th Floor
Box 722, Cooper Station
New York, NY 10276

ARICA INSTITUTE (1308)
150 Fifth Ave.
New York, NY 10011

ARMENIAN APOSTOLIC CHURCH OF AMERICA
  (139)
% Archbishop Mesrob Ashjian
138 E. 39th St.
New York, NY 10016

ARMENIAN CHURCH OF AMERICA (140)
% His Eminence Torkom Manoogian, Primate
630 Second Ave.
New York, NY 10016

ASSOCIATION OF OCCIDENTAL ORTHODOX
  PARISHES (93)
% Father Stephen Empson
57 Saint Marks Place
New York, NY 10003

AUTOCEPHOLOUS SLAVONIC ORTHODOX
  CATHOLIC CHURCH (IN EXILE) (94)
2237 Hunter Ave.
New York, NY 10475

BRAHMA KUMARIS WORLD SPIRITUAL
  UNIVERSITY (1356)
% N.G.O. Offices
Church Centre
777 UN Plaza
New York, NY 10017

BUDDHIST ASSOCIATION OF THE UNITED STATES
  (1494)
3070 Albany Cresent
New York, NY 10463

BUDDHIST FELLOWSHIP OF NEW YORK (1530)
331 Riverside Dr.
New York, NY 10025

BULGARIAN EASTERN ORTHODOX CHURCH
  (DIOCESE OF NORTH AND SOUTH AMERICA
  AND AUSTRALIA) (96)
Metropolitan Joseph
550 A, W. 50th St.
New York, NY 10019

CHURCH OF BIBLE UNDERSTANDING (1557)
Box 841
Radio City Station
New York, NY 10019-0841

CHURCH OF OUR LORD JESUS CHRIST OF THE
  APOSTOLIC FAITH (401)
2081 Seventh Ave.
New York, NY 10027

COMMANDMENT KEEPERS CONGREGATION OF
  THE LIVING GOD (1287)
1 W. 123rd St.
New York, NY 10027

CONGREGATION KEHILLATH YAAKOV (KEHILAT
  JACOB) (1296)
390 Fort Washington Ave.
New York, NY 10033

CONSERVATIVE JUDAISM (1266)
United Synagogue of America
155 Fifth Ave.
New York, NY 10010

EARTHSTAR TEMPLE (1222)
35 W. 19th St.
New York, NY 10011

EASTERN STATES BUDDHIST ASSOCIATION OF
  AMERICA (1499)
64 Mott St.
New York, NY 10013

ECUMENICAL ORTHODOX CATHOLIC CHURCH-
  AUTOCEPHALOUS (17)
% Most Rev. Francis J. Ryan, Primate-Apostolos
  WesternRite
Box 637, Grand Central Station
New York, NY 10017

EUCHARISTIC CATHOLIC CHURCH (1575)
% Bishop Robert Clement
348 W. 144 St.
New York, NY 10011

FIRST ZEN INSTITUTE OF AMERICA (1481)
113 E. 30th St.
New York, NY 10016

GARDNERIAN WICCA (1225)
% Lady Rhiannon
Box 6896, FDR Station
New York, NY 10150

GENERAL ASSEMBLY OF SPIRITUALISTS (944)
% Rev. Rose Ann Erickson
Ansonia Hotel
2107 Broadway
New York, NY 10023

GREEK ORTHODOX ARCHDIOCESE OF NORTH
   AND SOUTH AMERICA (107)
% His Eminence Archbishop Iakovos
8-10 E. 79th St.
New York, NY 10021

HOLY SPIRIT ASSOCIATION FOR THE
   UNIFICATION OF WORLD CHRISTIANITY (1063)
4 W. 43rd St.
New York, NY 10036

INDEPENDENT ASSOCIATED SPIRITUALISTS (947)
% Rev. Marion Owens
124 W. 72nd St.
New York, NY 10023

INDO-AMERICAN YOGA-VEDANTA SOCIETY (1374)
330 West 58th St., Apt. 11-J
New York, NY 10019

INTERNATIONAL METAPHYSICAL ASSOCIATION
   (878)
20 E. 68th St.
New York, NY 10021

JETSUN SAKYA CENTER (1515)
623 W. 129th St.
New York, NY 10027

KHANIQAHI-NIMATULLAHI (1318)
306 W. 11th St.
New York, NY 10014

LATIN-AMERICAN COUNCIL OF THE
   PENTECOSTAL CHURCH OF GOD OF NEW
   YORK (450)
115 E. 125th St.
New York, NY 10035

LITTLE SYNAGOGUE (1299)
155 E. 22nd St.
New York, NY 10010

ORDO TEMPLI ORIENTIS (1194)
International headquarters
JAF Box 7666
New York, NY 10116

ORTHODOX CATHOLIC CHURCH IN AMERICA
   (VERRA) (122)
% Most Rev. Michael Edward Verra
238 Mott St.
New York, NY 10012

ORTHODOX JUDAISM (1269)
% Rabbinical Council of America
275 Seventh Ave.
New York, NY 10001

PRESBYTERIAN CHURCH (U.S.A.) (195)
475 Riverside Dr.
New York, NY 10115

PROTESTANT EPISCOPAL CHURCH IN THE U.S.A.
   (71)
815 Second Ave.
New York, NY 10017

REFORM JUDAISM (1268)
Union of American Hebrew Congregations
838 Fifth Ave.
New York, NY 10021

REFORMED CHURCH IN AMERICA (185)
475 Riverside Dr.
New York, NY 10115

RUSSIAN ORTHODOX CHURCH OUTSIDE OF
   RUSSIA (130)
% His Eminence Vitaly, Metropolitan
75 E. 93rd St.
New York, NY 10028

RUSSIAN ORTHODOX CHURCH IN THE U.S.A.,
   PATRIARCHIAL PARISHES OF THE (129)
St. Nicholas Patriarchal Cathedral
15 E. 97th St.
New York, NY 10029

SCHOOL FOR ESOTERIC STUDIES (1122)
40 E. 49th St., Suite 1903
New York, NY 10017

SEVENTH DAY CHRISTIAN CONFERENCE (682)
246 W. 138th St.
New York, NY 10030

SHA'AREI ORAH (1301)
15-A 73 St.
New York, NY 10023

SPIRITUAL SCIENCE MOTHER CHURCH (967)
% Spiritualist Science Center of New York
274 Madison Ave.
New York, NY 10016

SRI LANKAN SANGHA COUNCIL OF NORTH
   AMERICA (1458)
No central address, for information contact:
American-Sri Lanka Buddhist Association, Inc.
84-32 126th St., Kew Gardens
New York, NY 11415

SYRIAN ORTHODOX CHURCH OF MALABAR (153)
% Dr. K. M. Simon
Union Theological Seminary
Broadway and 120th St.
New York, NY 10027

UNIFICATION ASSOCIATION OF CHRISTIAN
   SABBATH KEEPERS (683)
255 W. 131st St.
New York, NY 10027

UNITED CHURCH OF CHRIST (209)
105 Madison Ave.
New York, NY 10016

UNITED ISRAEL WORLD UNION (1305)
1123 Broadway
New York, NY 10010

UNITED WESLEYAN METHODIST CHURCH OF
   AMERICA (246)
% Rev. David S. Bruno
270 W. 126th St.
New York, NY 10027

VEDANTA SOCIETY (1416)
34 W. 71st St.
New York, NY 10023

WITCHES INTERNATIONAL CRAFT ASSOCIATES
   (1251)
153 W. 80th St.
New York, NY 10024

YESHE NYINGPO (1528)
19 W. 16th St.
New York, NY 10011

ZEN STUDIES SOCIETY (1491)
223 E. 67th St.
New York, NY 10021

THE CHRISTIAN AND MISSIONARY ALLIANCE
   (251)
350 N. Highland Ave.
Nyack, NY 10960

AMERICAN MISSION FOR OPENING CHURCHES
   (640)
6419 E. Lake Rd.
Olcott, NY 14126

AMERICAN WORLD PATRIARCHS (90)
% Most Rev. Emigidius J. Ryzy
19 Aqueduct St.
Ossining, NY 10562

SOCIETY OF ST. PIUS V (48)
8 Pond Place
Oyster Bay Cove, NY 11771

SOCIETY OF JEWISH SCIENCE (1303)
88 Sunnyside Blvd.
Plainview, NY 11803

SIKH COUNCIL OF NORTH AMERICA (1441)
95-30 118th St.
Richmond Hill, NY 11419

HUTTERIAN BRETHREN OF NEW YORK, INC.
   (849)
P.O. Woodcrest
Rte. 213
Rifton, NY 12471

LATIN-RITE CATHOLIC CHURCH (24)
Box 16194
Rochester, NY 14616

MEGIDDO MISSION (1571)
478 Thurston Rd.
Rochester, NY 14619

ZEN CENTER OF ROCHESTER (1489)
Seven Arnold Park
Rochester, NY 14607

PROCESS CHURCH OF THE FINAL JUDGMENT
   (1081)
Box 621
Round Lake, NY 12151-0621

PEOPLE'S CHRISTIAN CHURCH (678)
402 Melrose St.
Schenectady, NY 12306

AMERICAN ORTHODOX CATHOLIC CHURCH
   (PROPHETA) (88)
% Mt. Rev. Dom Lorenzo, O.S.B.
Holy Trinity Monastery
Box 323
Shirley, NY 11967

SIDDHA YOGA DHAM ASSOCIATES (1403)
Box 600
South Fallsburg, NY 12779

MA YOGA SHAKTI INTERNATIONAL MISSION
   (1386)
114-23 Lefferts Blvd.
South Ozone, NY 11420

JERRAHI ORDER OF AMERICA (1317)
864 S. Main St.
Spring Valley, NY 10977

NORTH AMERICAN OLD ROMAN CATHOLIC
   CHURCH (ROGERS) (27)
% Most Rev. Archbishop James H. Rogers
118-09 Farmers Blvd.
St. Albans, NY 11412

INTERNATIONAL NAHAVIR JAIN MISSION (1438)
Acharya Sushil Jain Ashram
722 Tomkins Ave.
Staten Island, NY 10305

GREEK ARCHDIOCESE OF VASILOUPOLIS (106)
44-02 48th Ave.
Sunnyside/Woodside, NY 11377

ORTHODOX CHURCH IN AMERICA (125)
% Most Blessed Theodosius, Archbishop of Washington,
   Metropolitan of All America and Canada
Very Rev. Daniel Hubiak, Chancellor
Box 675
Syosset, NY 11791

ECUMENICAL CATHOLIC DIOCESE OF AMERICA
   (16)
151 Regent Place
W. Hemstead, NY 11552

KAGYU DHARMA (1516)
127 Sheafe Rd.
Wappinger Falls, NY 12590

INSTITUTE FOR RELIGIOUS DEVELOPMENT (1315)
Chardavogne Rd.
Warwick, NY 19990

KARMA TRIYANA DHARMACHAKRA (1517)
352 Meads Mountain Rd.
Woodstock, NY 12498

MOUNT HEBRON APOSTOLIC TEMPLE OF OUR
   LORD JESUS OF THE APOSTOLIC FAITH (407)
Mount Hebron Apostolic Temple
27 Vineyard Ave.
Yonkers, NY 10703

North Carolina

ORIGINAL FREE WILL BAPTISTS, NORTH
   CAROLINA STATE CONVENTION (612)
Box 39
Ayden, NC 28513

EMMANUEL HOLINESS CHURCH (328)
Box 818
Bladenboro, NC 28320

ADVENT CHRISTIAN CHURCH (672)
Box 23152
Charlotte, NC 28212

AFRICAN METHODIST EPISCOPAL ZION CHURCH
(234)
Box 23843
Charlotte, NC 28232

CAROLINA EVANGELISTIC ASSOCIATION (316)
% Cannon Cathedral
Box 31773
Charlotte, NC 28231-1773

THE PATH OF LIGHT (1155)
3427 Denson Pl.
Charlotte, NC 28215

PENTECOSTAL FREE WILL BAPTIST CHURCH (340)
Box 1568
Dunn, NC 28334

MOUNT CALVARY HOLY CHURCH OF AMERICA
(298)
% Bishop Harold Williams
1214 Chowan St.
Durham, NC 27713

ORIGINAL UNITED HOLY CHURCH
INTERNATIONAL (438)
% Bishop H. W. Fields
Box 263
Durham, NC 27702

BLACK PRIMITIVE BAPTISTS (596)
% Primitive Baptist Library
Rte. 2
Elon College, NC 27244

CHRISTIAN SPIRIT CENTER (932)
Box 114
Elon College, NC 27244

PRIMITIVE BAPTISTS-ABSOLUTE
PREDESTINARIANS (599)
% Primitive Baptist Library
Rte. 2
Elon College, NC 27244

PRIMITIVE BAPTISTS-MODERATES (600)
% Primitive Baptist Library
Rte. 2
Elon College, NC 27244

GENERAL CONFERENCE OF THE EVANGELICAL
BAPTIST CHURCH (333)
Kavetter Bldg.
3400 E. Ash St.
Goldsboro, NC 27530

HOLINESS CHURCH OF GOD (335)
% Bishop B. McKinney
602 E. Elm St.
Graham, NC 27253

HOLINESS CHURCH OF GOD, INC. (284)
% Bishop B. McKinney
602 Elm St.
Graham, NC 27253

SHILOH TRUE LIGHT CHURCH OF CHRIST (738)
% Elder James Rommie Purser
Rt. 1, Box 426
Indian Trail, NC 28079

CHURCH OF GOD, BODY OF CHRIST (688)
Rte. 1
Mocksville, NC 27028

MISSIONARY METHODIST CHURCH OF AMERICA
(269)
Rte. 7
Morganton, NC 28655

CHURCH AND SCHOOL OF WICCA (1207)
Box 1502
New Bern, NC 28560

CHURCH OF THE CREATOR (767)
Box 400
Otto, NC 28763

LUMBER RIVER ANNUAL CONFERENCE OF THE
HOLINESS METHODIST CHURCH (287)
% Bishop C. N. Lowry
Rowland, NC 28383

ANGLICAN ORTHODOX CHURCH (63)
% Most Rev. James Parker Dees
323 E. Walnut St.
Box 128
Statesville, NC 28677

CHRISTIAN UNITY BAPTIST ASSOCIATION (572)
% Elder Thomas T. Reynolds
Thomasville, NC 27360

NEW BEGINNINGS (753)
Box 228
Waynesville, NC 28786

APOSTOLIC CHURCH OF CHRIST (387)
2044 Stadium Dr.
Winston-Salem, NC 27107

APOSTOLIC CHURCH OF CHRIST IN GOD (388)
% Bethlehem Apostolic Church
1217 E. 15th St.
Winston-Salem, NC 27105

Ohio

ORTHODOX CATHOLIC CHURCH OF NORTH AND
SOUTH AMERICA (124)
Box 1213
Akron, OH 44309

BRETHREN CHURCH (ASHLAND, OHIO) (518)
524 College Ave.
Ashland, OH 44805

OHIO YEARLY MEETING OF THE SOCIETY OF
FRIENDS (544)
61830 Sandy Ridge Rd.
Barnesville, OH 43712

ASSOCIATION OF FUNDAMENTAL GOSPEL
CHURCHES (516)
9189 Grubb Court
Canton, OH 44721

EVANGELICAL FRIENDS CHURCH, EASTERN
DIVISION (534)
1201 30th St., N.W.
Canton, OH 44709

CHRISTIAN CHURCHES AND CHURCHES OF
CHRIST (619)
No central address, for information:
North American Christian Convention
3533 Epley Rd
Cincinnati, OH 45239

CHURCH OF THE LIVING GOD (CHRISTIAN
WORKERS FOR FELLOWSHIP) (427)
% Bishop W. E. Crumes
434 Forest Ave.
Cincinnati, OH 45229

WESLEYAN TABERNACLE ASSOCIATION (290)
626 Elliott Ave.
Cincinnati, OH 45215

CHURCHES OF CHRIST IN CHRISTIAN UNION
(280)
1427 Lancaster Pike
Circleville, OH 43113

CHURCH OF GOD (JESUS CHRIST THE HEAD)
(691)
% Pastor M. L. Bartholomew
Box 02026
Cleveland, OH 44102

CHURCH OF GOD (O'BEIRN) (692)
Box 81224
Cleveland, OH 44181

CHURCH OF GOD AND SAINTS OF CHRIST (1286)
% Biship James R. Grant
10703 Wade Park Ave.
Cleveland, OH 44106

OLD ORDER (REIDENBACH) MENNONITES (498)
% Henry W. Riehl
Rte. 1
Columbiana, OH 44408

OLD ORDER (WENGER) MENNONITES (499)
% Henry W. Riehl
Rte. 1
Columbiana, OH 44408

OLD ORDER (WISLER) MENNONITE CHURCH (500)
% Bishop Henry W. Riehl
Rte. 1
Columbiana, OH 44408

HOLY CATHOLIC CHURCH, ANGLICAN RITE
JURISDICTION OF THE AMERICAS (68)
% Most. Rev. G. Wayne Craig, Archbishop
Box 14352
Columbus, OH 43214

UNITED METHODIST CHURCH (214)
% Council on Ministries
601 W. Riverside Ave.
Dayton, OH 45406

WESLEYAN HOLINESS ASSOCIATION OF
CHURCHES (314)
108 Carter Avenue
Dayton, OH 45405

CHURCHES OF GOD, GENERAL CONFERENCE
(179)
700 E. Melrose Ave.
Box 926
Findlay, OH 45839

CONSERVATIVE MENNONITE FELLOWSHIP (NON-
CONFERENCE) (495)
Box 36
Hartville, OH 44632

LAKE ERIE YEARLY MEETING (539)
% Richard W. Taylor, Clerk
492 Miller St.
Kent, OH 44240

INTERNATIONAL PENTECOSTAL CHURCH OF
CHRIST (336)
Box 439
2245 U.S. 42, S.W.
London, OH 43140

OHIO BIBLE FELLOWSHIP (654)
% Rev. John Ashbrook
5733 Hopkins Rd.
Mentor, OH 44060

THE WAY INTERNATIONAL (667)
Box 328
New Knoxville, OH 45871

SCHOOL OF LIGHT AND REALIZATION (SOLAR)
(1123)
Box 2276
North Canton, OH 44720

BULGARIAN EASTERN ORTHODOX CHURCH,
DIOCESE OF NORTH AND SOUTH AMERICA (97)
519 Brynhaven Dr.
Oregon, OH

BEACHY AMISH MENNONITE CHURCHES (512)
9650 Iams Rd.
Plain City, OH 43064

ALLEGHENY WESLEYAN METHODIST
CONNECTION (300)
1827 Allen Dr.
Salem, OH 44460

CHRISTIAN NATION CHURCH, U.S.A. (252)
% Rev. Harvey Monjar, General Overseer
Box 142
South Lebanon, OH 45065

LIGHT OF THE UNIVERSE (994)
161 N. Sandusky Rd.
Tiffin, OH 44883

Oklahoma

INTERNATIONAL PENTECOSTAL HOLINESS
CHURCH (337)
7300 N.W. 39th Expressway
Bethany, OK 73008

UNITED SEVENTH-DAY BRETHREN (703)
% Myrtle Ortiz
Box 225
Enid, OK 73701

CHURCH OF GOD (GUTHRIE, OKLAHOMA) (256)
% Faith Publishing House
7415 W. Monsur Ave.
Guthrie, OK 73044

BIBLE CHURCHES (CLASSICS EXPOSITOR) (661)
% Dr. C. E. McLain
1429 N.W. 100th St.
Oklahoma City, OK 73114

GNOSTIC ORTHODOX CHURCH (1133)
% Abbot-Bishop George Burke
3500 Coltrane Rd.
Oklahoma City, OK 73121

OLD HOLY CATHOLIC CHURCH, PROVINCE OF
   NORTH AMERICA (1142)
% Most Rev. Alvin Lee Baker
Box 60235
Oklahoma City, OK 73146

FOLLOWERS OF CHRIST (1564)
% Elder Marion Morris
Ringwood, OK 73768

CHURCH OF THE CHRISTIAN CRUSADE (1558)
Box 977
Tulsa, OK 74102

INTERNATIONAL CONVENTION OF FAITH
   CHURCHES AND MINISTERS (379)
3840 S. 103 E. Avenue, 132
Tulsa, OK 74146-2445

Oregon

SOLAR LIGHT CENTER (1020)
7700 Avenue of the Sun
Central Point, OR 97501

CHURCH OF GOD, THE ETERNAL (695)
Box 755
Eugene, OR 97440

FOUNDATION OF HUMAN UNDERSTANDING
   (1059)
Box 811
Grants Pass, OR 97526

RAJNEESH FOLLOWERS OF BHAGWAN (1440)
% Swami Anand Vibhaven
13041 S.W. Knaus Rd.
Lake Oswego, OR 97034

EVANGELICAL CHURCH OF NORTH AMERICA
   (281)
7525 S.E. Lake Rd., Suite 7
Milwaukie, OR 97267

NORTHWEST YEARLY MEETING OF FRIENDS
   CHURCH (545)
Box 190
Newberg, OR 97132

THE APOSTOLIC FAITH MISSION OF PORTLAND,
   OREGON, INC. (315)
6615 S.E. 52nd Ave.
Portland, OR 97206

LAST DAY MESSENGER ASSEMBLIES (664)
Box 17406
Portland, OR 97217

PENTECOSTAL EVANGELICAL CHURCH OF GOD,
   NATIONAL AND INTERNATIONAL (371)
Riddle, OR 97469

CHURCH OF THE NEW COVENANT IN CHRIST
   (809)
Box 3910
Salem, OR 97302

MU FARM (866)
Yoncalla, OR 97499

Pennsylvania

WESTERN ORTHODOX CHURCH IN AMERICA (138)
% Most Rev. C. David Luther
1529 Pleasant Valley Blvd.
Altoona, PA 16602

ASSEMBLIES OF YAHWEH (721)
Bethel, PA 19507

KODESH CHURCH OF EMMANUEL (297)
% Dr. Kenneth O. Barber
932 Logan Road
Bethel Park, PA 15102

MORAVIAN CHURCH IN AMERICA (212)
Northern Province
1021 Center St.
Box 1245
Bethlehem, PA 18016-1245

EVANGELICAL CHRISTIAN CHURCH (WESLEYAN)
   (261)
Box 277
Birdsboro, PA 19508

GENERAL CHURCH OF THE NEW JERUSALEM
   (926)
% Rt. Rev. L. B. King, Executive Bishop
Bryn Athyn, PA 19009

LORD'S NEW CHURCH WHICH IS NOVA
   HIEROSOLYMA (928)
% Rev. Philip Odhner
Box 4
Bryn Athyn, PA 19009

LAYMAN'S HOME MISSIONARY MOVEMENT (715)
Chester Springs, PA 19425

UNITED ZION CHURCH (503)
% Bishop Alvin H. Eberly
Rte. 2
Denver, PA 17517

AMERICAN MEDITATION SOCIETY (1345)
Box 314
Dresher, PA 19025

REFORMED MENNONITE CHURCH (501)
% Bishop Earl Basinger
1036 Lincoln Heights Ave.
Ephiata, PA 17522

STAUFFER MENNONITE CHURCH (502)
% Bishop Jacob S. Stauffer
Rte. 3
Ephrata, PA 17522

HOLINESS GOSPEL CHURCH (285)
Rte. 2, Box 13
Etters, PA 17319

FREE GOSPEL CHURCH, INC. (357)
% Rev. Chester H. Heath
Box 477
Export, PA 15632

THE PEACE MISSION MOVEMENT (851)
% The Woodmont Estate
1622 Spring Mill Road
Gladwyne, PA 19035

UNIVERSAL PEACE MISSION MOVEMENT (856)
% The Woodmont Estate
1622 Spring Mill Rd.
Gladwyne, PA 19035

HIMALAYAN INTERNATIONAL INSTITUTE OF
  YOGA SCIENCE & PHILOSOPHY (1370)
RD 1
Honesdale, PA 18431

AMERICAN CARPATHO-RUSSIAN ORTHODOX
  GREEK CATHOLIC CHURCH (82)
% Rt. Rev. Nicolas Smisko
312 Garfield St.
Johnstown, PA 15906

UNITED CHRISTIAN CHURCH (242)
% Elder Henry C. Heagy, Moderator
Lebanon R.D. 4
Lebanon County, PA 17042

CONGREGATIONAL BIBLE CHURCH (494)
% Congregational Bible Church
Marietta, PA 17547

CHURCH OF GOD, THE HOUSE OF PRAYER (324)
% Rev. Charles Mackenin
Markleysburg, PA 15459

CHURCH OF JESUS CHRIST (BICKERTONITE) (830)
Sixth & Lincoln Sts.
Monogahela, PA 15603

EVANGELICAL CONGREGATIONAL CHURCH (241)
100 W. Park Ave.
Box 186
Myerstown, PA 17067

SEVENTH DAY BAPTISTS (GERMAN) (616)
R.D. 1, Box 158
New Enterprise, PA 16664

SCHWENKFELDER CHURCH IN AMERICA (559)
Pennsburg, PA 18073

AMERICAN RESCUE WORKERS (247)
% General Paul E. Martin, Commander-In-Chief
2827 Frankford Ave.
Philadelphia, PA 19134

THE APOSTOLIC CHURCH (344)
142 N. 17th St.
Philadelphia, PA 19103

AQUARIAN RESEARCH FOUNDATION (858)
5620 Morton St.
Philadelphia, PA 19144

BAWA MUHAIYADDEEN FELLOWSHIP (1309)
5820 Overbrook Ave.
Philadelphia, PA 19131

CALVARY HOLINESS CHURCH (277)
3415-19 N. Second St.
Philadelphia, PA 19140

CHURCH OF THE LORD JESUS CHRIST OF THE
  APOSTOLIC FAITH (PHILADELPHIA) (402)
22nd & Bainbridge Sts.
Philadelphia, PA 19146

FRIENDS GENERAL CONFERENCE (535)
1520-B Race St.
Philadelphia, PA 19102

HOLY EASTERN ORTHODOX CHURCH OF THE
  UNITED STATES (113)
% Most Rev. Trevor W. Moore
1611 Wallace St.
Philadelphia, PA 19130

HOUSE OF GOD, WHICH IS THE CHURCH OF THE
  LIVING GOD, THE PILLAR AND GROUND OF
  TRUTH, INC. (433)
6107 Cobbs Creek Pkwy.
Philadelphia, PA 19143

INTERNATIONAL SOCIETY OF DIVINE LOVE (1380)
234 W. Upsal St.
Philadelphia, PA 19119

ORTHODOX PRESBYTERIAN CHURCH (190)
7401 Old York Rd.
Philadelphia, PA 19126

P'NAI OR RELIGIOUS FELLOWSHIP (1300)
6723 Emlen St.
Philadelphia, PA 19119

REFORMED EPISCOPAL CHURCH (73)
4225 Chestnut St.
Philadelphia, PA 19104

RUSSIAN/UKRAINIAN EVANGELICAL BAPTIST
  UNION OF THE U.S.A., INC. (586)
Roosevelt Blvd. & 7th St.
Philadelphia, PA 19120

SHILOH APOSTOLIC TEMPLE (414)
1516 W. Master
Philadelphia, PA 19121

SWAMI KUVALAYANANDA YOGA FOUNDATION
  (1408)
527 South St.
Philadelphia, PA 19147

ASSOCIATED GOSPEL CHURCHES (641)
1919 Beach St.
Pittsburgh, PA 15221

THE CHURCH OF HOLY LIGHT (781)
Box 4478
Pittsburgh, PA 15205

**REFORMED PRESBYTERIAN CHURCH OF NORTH
  AMERICA (196)**
% Louis D. Hutmire, Stated Clerk
7418 Penn Ave.
Pittsburgh, PA 15208

SRI VENKATESWARA TEMPLE (1437)
South McCully Rd.
Penn Hills
P.O. Box 17289
Pittsburgh, PA 15235

FRATERNITAS ROSAE CRUCIS (1092)
Beverly Hall
Quakertown, PA 18951

CALVARY GRACE CHURCHES OF FAITH (780)
Box 333
Rillton, PA 19140

POLISH NATIONAL CATHOLIC CHURCH (44)
% Mt. Rev. John F. Swantek
1002 Pittston Ave.
Scranton, PA 18505

HOLY SHANKARACHARYA ORDER (1373)
RD 3, Box 400
Stroudsburg, PA 18360

GOD'S MISSIONARY CHURCH (307)
% Rev. Paul Miller
Swengal, PA 17880

BIBLE FELLOWSHIP CHURCH (249)
% Pastor W. B. Hottel
404 W. Main St.
Terre Hill, PA 17581

**ASSOCIATION OF EVANGELICALS FOR ITALIAN
  MISSIONS (566)**
314 Richfield Rd.
Upper Darby, PA 19082

**UNITED EPISCOPAL CHURCH OF NORTH
  AMERICA (77)**
% Most Rev. C. Dale D. Doren
2293 Country Club Dr.
Upper St. Clair, PA 15241

**AMERICAN BAPTIST CHURCHES IN THE U.S.A.
  (565)**
Valley Forge, PA 19481

PRIMITIVE METHODIST CHURCH (245)
40 E. Northampton St.
Wilkes-Barre, PA 18702

**INTERNATIONAL CHURCH OF AGELESS WISDOM
  (949)**
Box 502
Wyalusing, PA 18853

**FEDERATION OF RECONSTRUCTIONIST
  CONGREGATIONS AND HAVUROT (1267)**
Church Rd & Greenwood Ave.
Wyncote, PA 19095.

Puerto Rico

MITA MOVEMENT (385)
Calle Duarte 235
Hata Rey, PR 60919

Rhode Island

KWAN UM ZEN SCHOOL (1507)
K. B. C. Hong Poep Won
RFD No. 5
528 Pound Rd.
Cumberland, RI 02864

CHURCH OF PAN (1210)
114 Johnson Rd.
Foster, RI 02825

GENERAL SIX-PRINCIPLE BAPTISTS (610)
Rhode Island Conference
350 Davisville Rd.
North Kingston, RI 02852

CAMBODIAN BUDDHISM (1452)
% Ven. Maha Ghosananda
Khmer Buddhist Society of New England
178 Hanover St.
Providence, RI 02907

South Carolina

**REFORMED METHODIST UNION EPISCOPAL
  CHURCH (238)**
% Rt. Rev. Leroy Gethers
1136 Brody Ave.
Charleston, SC 20407

**ASSOCIATE REFORMED PRESBYTERIAN CHURCH
  (GENERAL SYNOD) (187)**
Associate Reformed Presbyterian Center
One Cleveland St.
Greenville, SC 29601

SOUTH CAROLINA BAPTIST FELLOWSHIP (588)
% Rev. John R. Waters
Faith Baptist Church
1600 Greenwood Rd.
Laurens, SC 29360

SOUTHWIDE BAPTIST FELLOWSHIP (590)
% Rev. John R. Waters
Faith Baptist Church
1607 Greenwood Rd.
Laurens, SC 39360

MEHER BABA, LOVERS OF (1336)
% Meher Spiritual Center
10200 Hwy. 17 No.
Myrtle Beach, SC 29577

SOUTHERN METHODIST CHURCH (232)
% Rev. W. Lynn Corbett
Box 132
Orangeburg, SC 29116-0132

**GENERAL ASSOCIATION OF DAVIDIAN SEVENTH-
  DAY ADVENTISTS (677)**
Route 1, Box 384
Salem, SC 29676

AFRICAN THEOLOGICAL ARCHMINISTRY (1252)
% Oyotunji African Yoruba Village
Box 51
Sheldon, SC 29941

South Dakota

HUTTERIAN BRETHREN-SCHMIEDELEUT (848)
% Rev. David D. Decker
Tachetter Colony
Olivet, SD 57052

Tennessee

HOLY ORTHODOX CHURCH, AMERICAN
  JURISDICTION (115)
% Most Rev. W. Francis Forbes
Box 400
138 Overby Dr.
Antioch, TN 37013

PEOPLE OF THE LIVING GOD (852)
Hwy.56
Beersheba Springs, TN 37305

OPEN WAY (1171)
Box 217
Celina, TN 38551

(ORIGINAL) CHURCH OF GOD (338)
Box 3086
Chattanooga, TN 37404

CHURCH OF GOD (CLEVELAND, TENNESSEE) (317)
Keith St. at 25th St., N.W.
Cleveland, TN 37311

CHURCH OF GOD (JERUSALEM ACRES) (318)
% Chief Bishop John A. Looper
Box 1207
1826 Dalton Pike (Jerusalem Acres)
Cleveland, TN 37364-1207

CHURCH OF GOD OF PROPHECY (319)
Bible Place
Cleveland, TN 37311

UNITED CHRISTIAN CHURCH AND MINISTERIAL
  ASSOCIATION (488)
Box 700
Cleveland, TN 37311

YAHWEH'S TEMPLE (421)
Box 652
Cleveland, TN 37311

UPPER CUMBERLAND PRESBYTERIAN CHURCH
  (201)
% Roaring River Upper Cumberland Presbyterian Church
Gainesboro, TN 38562

ASSEMBLIES OF THE CALLED OUT ONES OF YAH
  (719)
231 Cedar St.
Jackson, TN 38301

CHURCH OF GOD OF THE MOUNTAIN ASSEMBLY
  (321)
Florence Ave.
Jellico, TN 37762

EVANGELICAL METHODIST CHURCH OF
  AMERICA (222)
Box 751
Kingsport, TN 37662

BIBLE METHODIST CONNECTION OF TENNESSEE
  (303)
% Rev. D.P. Denton
Evangelist of Truth
Box 22309
Knoxville, TN 37933

FIRST CHURCH OF VOODOO (1255)
Box 2381
Knoxville, TN 37917

CHRISTIAN CONGREGATION (620)
% Rev. Ora Wilbert Eads, General Supt.
804 W. Hemlock St.
La Follette, TN 37766

CHRISTIAN METHODIST EPISCOPAL CHURCH (236)
564 Frank Ave.
Memphis, TN 38101

CHURCH OF GOD IN CHRIST (424)
272 S. Main St.
Memphis, TN 38103

CUMBERLAND PRESBYTERIAN CHURCH (189)
Cumberland Presbyterian Center
1978 Union Ave.
Memphis, TN 38104

UNITED EPISCOPAL CHURCH (1945) ANGLICAN/
  CELTIC (75)
Office of the Chancery
526 North Maple
Murfreesboro, TN 37130

AFRICAN METHODIST EPISCOPAL CHURCH (233)
500 8th Ave., S.
Nashville, TN 37203

CHURCH OF GOD (SANCTIFIED CHURCH) (293)
1037 Jefferson St.
Nashville, TN 37208

CHURCH OF THE LIVING GOD, THE PILLAR AND
  GROUND OF THE TRUTH (428)
4520 Hydes Ferry Pike
Box 5735
Nashville, TN 37208

DISCIPLES OF FAITH (897)
Box 50322
Nashville, TN 37205

NATIONAL ASSOCIATION OF FREE WILL
  BAPTISTS (611)
Box 1088
Nashville, TN 37202

NATIONAL BAPTIST CONVENTION OF AMERICA
  (603)
% National Baptist Publishing Board
7145 Centennial Blvd.
Nashville, TN 37209

SOCIETY ORDO TEMPLI ORIENTIS IN AMERICA
(1198)
Box 90018
Nashville, TN 37209

SOUTHERN BAPTIST CONVENTION (589)
% Executive Committee
460 James Robertson Pkwy.
Nashville, TN 37219

SOUTHERN EPISCOPAL CHURCH (74)
% Most Rev. B. H. Webster
2315 Valley Brook Rd.
Nashville, TN 37215

THE FARM (861)
156-C Drakes Ln.
Summertown, TN 38483

DUCK RIVER (AND KINDRED) ASSOCIATION OF
BAPTISTS (574)
Duck River Association
% Elder A. B. Ray, Moderator
500 Regan St.
Tullahoma, TN 37388

Texas

HOUSE OF YAHWEH (ABILENE, TEXAS) (726)
Box 242
Abilene, TX 79604

FULL GOSPEL CHURCH ASSOCIATION (332)
Box 265
Amarillo, TX 79105

WORLD BAPTIST FELLOWSHIP (595)
3001 W. Division
Arlington, TX 76012

AMERICAN ATHEISTS, INC. (758)
% Jon G. Murray
Box 2117
Austin, TX 78767

CHURCHES OF CHRIST (NON-INSTRUMENTAL)
(621)
% Firm Foundation
Box 610
Austin, TX 78767

OLD CATHOLIC CHURCH IN AMERICA
(BROTHERS) (30)
% Metropolitan Hilarion
1905 S. Third St.
Austin, TX 78704

PLANETARY LIGHT ASSOCIATION (1080)
Box 180786
Austin, TX 78718

HINDU TEMPLE SOCIETY OF TEXAS (1433)
4533 Larch Lane
Bellaire, TX 77401

AMERICAN GNOSTIC CHURCH (1178)
Box 1219
Corpus Christi, TX 78403

AMERICAN EVANGELISTIC ASSOCIATION (465)
% World Evangelism
Box 660800
Dallas, TX 75266

FULL GOSPEL FELLOWSHIP OF CHURCHES AND
MINISTERS INTERNATIONAL (377)
1545 W. Mockingbird Ln., Suite 1012
Dallas, TX 75235

HOLY ORTHODOX CATHOLIC CHURCH (114)
% Most Rev. Paul G. Russell
5831 Tremont
Dallas, TX 75214

INTERNATIONAL DELIVERANCE CHURCHES (380)
Box 353
Dallas, TX 75221

TODAY CHURCH (918)
13531 N. Central Expwy., Bldg. 2100, Suite 2133
Box 832366
Dallas, TX 75243

WISDOM INSTITUTE OF SPIRITUAL EDUCATION
(925)
1236 S. Marlborough
Dallas, TX 75208

WORD FOUNDATION (1117)
Box 18235
Dallas, TX 75218

CHURCHES OF CHRIST (NON-INSTRUMENTAL,
ECUMENICAL) (622)
% Restoration Review
1201 Windsor Dr.
Denton, TX 76201

SOCIETY OF ST. PIUS X (49)
Box 1307
Dickinson, TX 77539

ESP LABORATORY (1223)
Box 216
219 S. Ridge Dr.
Edgewood, TX 75117

CHURCH OF THE FIRST BORN OF THE FULLNESS
OF TIMES (806)
5854 Mira Serana
El Paso, TX 79912

CHRIST TRUTH LEAGUE (888)
2400 Canton Dr.
Fort Worth, TX 76112

STELLE GROUP (1110)
405 Mayfield Ave.
Garland, TX 75041

CHURCHES OF CHRIST (NON-INSTRUMENTAL,
NON-SUNDAY SCHOOL) (626)
% Gospel Tidings
500 E. Henry
Hamilton, TX 76531

BERACHAH CHURCH (642)
5139 W. Alabama
Houston, TX 77056

FULL GOSPEL EVANGELISTIC ASSOCIATION (358)
5828 Chippewa Blvd.
Houston, TX 70086

INDEPENDENT BIBLE CHURCH MOVEMENT (648)
% Church Multiplication, Inc.
Box 79203
Houston, TX 77279

TIMELY MESSENGER FELLOWSHIP (665)
% R. B. Shiflet
Box 473
Mineral Wells, TX 76067

CHURCHES OF CHRIST (PENTECOSTAL) (628)
Conference on Spiritual Renewal
Box 457
Missouri City, TX 77459

CHURCH OF THE WHITE EAGLE LODGE (982)
% Rev. Jean Le Fevre
St. John's Retreat Center
Box 930
Montgomery, TX 77356

HOUSE OF YAHWEH (ODESSA, TEXAS) (727)
% Jacob Hawkins
Box 4938
Odessa, TX 79760

DEVATMA SHAKTI SOCIETY (1363)
Rte. 1, Box 150 C-2
Paige, TX 78659

SRI MEENAKSHI TEMPLE SOCIETY OF HOUSTON
(1434)
Rt. 5, Box 5725
Pearland, TX 77584

MAYAN ORDER (1106)
Box 2710
San Antonio, TX 78299

UNITY OF THE BRETHREN (213)
% Dr. Mark L. Labaj
4202 Ermine
Temple, TX 76501

OMNIUNE CHURCH (788)
309 Breckenridge
Texarkana, TX 75501

CHURCH OF GOD, INTERNATIONAL (690)
Box 2525
Tyler, TX 75710

BRANCH SDA'S (675)
Box 4098
Waco, TX 76705

Utah

CONFEDERATE NATIONS OF ISRAEL (807)
% Alexander Joseph, Presiding King
Long Haul, Box 151
Big Water, UT 84741

APOSTOLIC UNITED BRETHREN (802)
3139 W. 14700 S., A
Bluffsdale, UT 84065

AARONIC ORDER (793)
Box 7095
Murray, UT 84107

THE BUILDERS (859)
Box 2278
Salt Lake City, UT 84110

CHURCH OF JESUS CHRIST OF LATTER-DAY
SAINTS (795)
50 E. North Temple
Salt Lake City, UT 84150

SUMMUM (1587)
707 Genesee Ave.
Salt Lake City, UT 84104

UNIVERSAL ASSOCIATION OF FAITHISTS (1007)
% Universal Faithists of Kosmon
Box 664
Salt Lake City, UT 84110-0664

Vermont

NORTHEAST KINGDOM COMMUNITY (867)
Box 443
Island Pond, VT 05846

Virginia

SAWAN KIRPAL RUHANI MISSION (1451)
8605 Villge Way, No. C
Alexandria, VA 22309-1605

WORLD COMMUNITY (1420)
Route 4, Box 265
Bedford, VA 24523

INTEGRAL YOGA INTERNATIONAL (1375)
% Satchidananda-Yogavilles
Rte. 1, Box 172
Buckingham, VA 23921

AMERICAN EPISCOPAL CHURCH (59)
155 Riverbend Dr., 4
Charlottesville, VA 22901

FRIENDS OF BUDDHISM-WASHINGTON D.C. (1534)
% Dr. Kurt Leidecker
306 Caroline St.
Fredericksburg, VA 22401

INTERNATIONAL GENERAL ASSEMBLY OF
SPIRITUALISTS (950)
1809 E. Bayview Blvd.
Norfolk, VA 23503

UNAMENDED CHRISTADELPHIANS (631)
No central address. For further information:
% Lawrence Dodl
5104 Cavedo Lane
Richmond, VA 23231

SEVENTH-DAY ADVENTIST CHURCH, REFORM
MOVEMENT (681)
Box 7239
Roanoke, VA 24019

REFORMED ZION UNION APOSTOLIC CHURCH (239)
% Deacon James C. Feggins
416 South Hill Ave.
South Hill, VA 23970

FELLOWSHIP OF THE INNER LIGHT (988)
Rte. 1, Box 141
Timberville, VA 22853

ASSOCIATION FOR RESEARCH AND
  ENLIGHTENMENT (1034)
Box 595
Virginia Beach, VA 23451

NORTH CAROLINA YEARLY MEETING OF
  FRIENDS (CONSERVATIVE) (542)
% Louise B. Wilson, Clerk
113 Pinewood Rd.
Virginia Beach, VA 23451

Washington

RAJ-YOGA MATH AND RETREAT (1393)
Box 547
Deming, WA 98244

LORIAN ASSOCIATION (1071)
Box 663
Issaquah, WA 98067

CALVARY PENTECOSTAL CHURCH (353)
% Rev. Leroy Holman
1775 Yew, N.E.
Olympia, WA 98506

COSMIC AWARENESS COMMUNICATIONS (985)
Box 115
Olympia, WA 98507

REMNANT OF ISRAEL (756)
11303 E. 7th
Opportunity, WA 99206

CALVARY FELLOWSHIP, INC. (744)
Box 128
Rainier, WA 98576

VENUSIAN CHURCH (1250)
23301 Remond-Fall City Hwy.
Redmond, WA 98053

ADVENTURES IN ENLIGHTENMENT, A
  FOUNDATION (882)
Box 528
Rochester, WA 98579

AMERICAN FELLOWSHIP CHURCH (777)
Box 4693-G
Rolling Bay, WA 98061

ASSOCIATED CHURCHES, INC. (685)
Box 4455
Rolling Bay, WA 98061

DHIRAVAMSA FOUNDATION (1453)
1660 Wold Rd.
Friday Harbor
San Juan, WA 98250

AQUARIAN FOUNDATION (931)
% Rev. Keith Milton Rhinehart
315 - 15th Ave. E.
Seattle, WA 98112

AQUARIAN TABERNACLE CHURCH (1203)
Box 85507
Seattle, WA 98145

BETHEL TEMPLE (348)
2033 Second Ave.
Seattle, WA 98121

CHURCH OF ARMAGEDDON (860)
617 W. McGraw St.
Seattle, WA 98119

COMMUNITY CHAPEL AND BIBLE TRAINING
  CENTER (455)
18635 8th Ave. S.
Seattle, WA 98148

MONASTERY OF TIBETAN BUDDHISM (1520)
5042 18th Ave.,N.E.
Seattle, WA 98105

NORTH PACIFIC YEARLY MEETING OF THE
  RELIGIOUS SOCIETY OF FRIENDS (543)
% University Friends Center
4001 9th Ave., N.E.
Seattle, WA 98105

PENTECOSTAL EVANGELICAL CHURCH (370)
% Rev. Ernest Beroth
Box 4218
Spokane, WA 99202

SABIAN ASSEMBLY (1108)
% Sabian Publishing Society
Box 7
Stanwood, WA 98292

AMICA TEMPLE OF RADIANCE (1161)
763 S. 53rd St.
Tacoma, WA 98408

ASSOCIATION OF SEVENTH-DAY PENTECOSTAL
  ASSEMBLIES (466)
% Elder Garver C. Gray, Chairman
4700 N.E. 119th St.
Vancouver, WA 98686

ORTHODOX CHURCH OF THE EAST (151)
% Archbishop John Marion Stanley
Rte. 4, Box 322
Vashon, WA 98070

West Virginia

CHURCH OF GOD (APOSTOLIC) (400)
Saint Peter's Church of God (Apostolic)
125 Meadows St.
Beckley, WV 25801

CLAYMONT SOCIETY FOR CONTINUOUS
  EDUCATION (1312)
Box 112
Charlestown, WV 25414

INTERNATIONAL SOCIETY FOR KRISHNA
CONSCIOUSNESS OF WEST VIRGINIA (1379)
R.D. 1, Box 318
Moundsville, WV 26041

CHURCH OF GOD (SEVENTH DAY, SALEM, WEST
VIRGINIA) (694)
79 Water St.
Salem, WV 26426

PRIMITIVE ADVENT CHRISTIAN CHURCH (674)
% Donald Young
1640 Clay Ave.
South Charleston, WV 25312

Wisconsin

CHURCH OF JESUS CHRIST OF LATTER DAY
SAINTS (STRANGITE, DREW) (832)
35315 Chestnut
Burlington, WI 53105

CHURCH OF JESUS CHRIST (STRANGITE, DREW)
(834)
35315 Chestnut
Burlington, WI 53105

SEVENTH DAY BAPTIST GENERAL CONFERENCE
USA AND CANADA LTD. (615)
Seventh Day Baptist Center
3120 Kennedy Rd., P.O. Box 1678
Janesville, WI 53547

METROPOLITAN CHURCH ASSOCIATION (266)
323 Broad St.
Lake Geneva, WI 53147

FREEDOM FROM RELIGION FOUNDATION (770)
Box 750
Madison, WI 53701

THE PROTES'TANT CONFERENCE (174)
728 N. 9th St.
Manitowoc, WI 54220

ORTHODOX CATHOLIC CHURCH IN AMERICA
(121)
% Most Rev. Walter X. Brown
2450 N. 50th St.
Milwaukee, WI 53210

PASTORAL BIBLE INSTITUTE (716)
4454 S. 14th St., Suite 2
Milwaukee, WI 53221-0539

WISCONSIN EVANGELICAL LUTHERAN SYNOD
(176)
2929 N. Mayfair Rd.
Milwaukee, WI 53222

CHURCH OF CIRCLE WICCA (1209)
% Circle Sanctuary
Box 219
Mt. Horeb, WI 53572

FOR MY GOD AND MY COUNTRY (20)
Necedah, WI 54646

NATIONAL ASSOCIATION OF CONGREGATIONAL
CHRISTIAN CHURCHES (207)
8473 S. Howell Ave.
Box 1620
Oak Creek, WI 53154

GANDEN TEKCHEN LING (1514)
Deer Park
4548 Schneider Dr.
Oregon, WI 53575

DISCIPLES OF THE LORD JESUS CHRIST (1561)
% Rama Behera
Shawano, WI 54166

CANADA

Alberta

CANADIAN BAPTIST CONFERENCE (570)
% Rev. Allen E. Schmidt, Director of Missions
Box, 7, Site 4, R. R. 1
Cochrane, AB, Canada T0L 0W0

British Columbia

CHRISTIAN COMMUNITY AND BROTHERHOOD OF
REFORMED DOUKBOHORS (SONS OF FREEDOM)
(555)
Site 8, Comp. 42
Cresent Valley, BC, Canada V0G 1HO

UNION OF SPIRITUAL COMMUNITIES OF CHRIST
(ORTHODOX DOUKHOBORS IN CANADA) (563)
% USCC Central Office
Box 760
Grand Forks, BC, Canada V0H 1H0

YASODHARA ASHRAM SOCIETY (1423)
Box 9
Kootenay Bay, BC, Canada V0B 1X0

SONS OF FREEDOM (DOUKHOBORS) (562)
Krestova, BC, Canada

BOLD BIBLE LIVING (453)
International Headquarters
5774-132 A St.
Surrey, BC, Canada 98230

BIBLE HOLINESS MOVEMENT (250)
Box 223
Postal Station A
Vancouver, BC, Canada V6C 2M3

GLAD TIDINGS MISSIONARY SOCIETY (476)
3456 Fraser St.
Vancouver, BC, Canada

KABALARIAN PHILOSOPHY (1070)
908 W. 7th St.
Vancouver, BC, Canada V5Z 1C3

OLD CATHOLIC CHURCH OF BRITISH COLUMBIA
AND SOCIETY (1140)
715 E. 51st Ave.
Vancouver, BC, Canada V5X 1E2

Manitoba

EVANGELICAL MENNONITE CONFERENCE
(KLEINE GEMEINDE) (508)
Box 1268
440 Main St.
Steinbach, MB, Canada R0A 2A0

EVANGELICAL LUTHERAN CHURCH IN CANADA
(167)
1512 St. James St.
Winnipeg, MB, Canada R3H 0L2

EVANGELICAL MENNONITE MISSION
CONFERENCE (509)
Box 126
Winnipeg, MB, Canada R3C 2G1

SMITH VENNER (560)
% Lothar Dreger
470 Ediron Ave.
Winnipeg, MB, Canada R2G 0M4

UKRAINIAN GREEK-ORTHODOX CHURCH OF
CANADA (134)
9 St. John's Ave.
Winnipeg, MB, Canada R2W 1G8

Newfoundland

PENTECOSTAL ASSEMBLIES OF NEWFOUNDLAND
(367)
57 Thoburn Rd.
St. John's, NF, Canada A1B 3N4

Ontario

OLD ORDER AMISH MENNONITE CHURCH (515)
Pathway Publishers
Rte. 4
Aylmer, ON, Canada N5H 2R3

STANDARD CHURCH OF AMERICA (273)
Box 488
Brockville, ON, Canada K6V 5V7

PRESBYTERIAN CHURCH IN CANADA (192)
50 Wynford Dr.
Don Mills, ON, Canada M3C 1J7

OLD CATHOLIC CHURCH OF CANADA (32)
216 Tragina Ave., N.
Hamilton, ON, Canada L8H 5E1

CANADIAN BAPTIST FEDERATION (571)
7185 Millcreek Drive
Mississauga, ON, Canada L5N 5R4

CHURCH OF JESUS CHRIST RESTORED (824)
Box 551
Owen Sound, ON, Canada N4K 5R1

INDEPENDENT HOLINESS CHURCH (265)
% Rev. R. E. Votary, Gen. Supt.
Sydenham, ON, Canada K0H 2T0

ANCIENT BRITISH CHURCH IN NORTH AMERICA
(THE AUTOCEPHALOUS GLASTONBURY RITE IN
DIASPORA) (1573)
9-47 Marion St.
Toronto, ON, Canada M6R 1E6

ASSOCIATION OF REGULAR BAPTIST CHURCHES
(CANADA) (567)
130 Gerrard St., E.
Toronto, ON, Canada M5A 3T4

BRITISH-ISRAEL-WORLD FEDERATION (CANADA)
(743)
313 Sherbourne St.
Toronto, ON, Canada M5A 2S3

BYELORUSSIAN AUTOCEPHALIC ORTHODOX
CHURCH IN THE U.S.A. (98)
% Archbishop Mikalay, Primate
Church of St. Cyril of Turau
524 St. Clarens Ave.
Toronto, ON, Canada

OLD ROMAN CHURCH IN CANADA (40)
% Most Rev. Fredricke P. Dunleavy
1065 Woodbine Ave.
Toronto, ON, Canada M4C 4C5

PENTECOSTAL ASSEMBLIES OF CANADA (366)
10 Overlea Blvd.
Toronto, ON, Canada M4H 1A5

PEOPLES CHURCH (656)
374 Sheppard Ave. E.
Toronto, ON, Canada M2N 3B6

UNITED CHURCH OF CANADA (208)
The United Church House
85 St. Clair Ave., E.
Toronto, ON, Canada M4T 1M8

ZEN LOTUS SOCIETY (1508)
86 Vaughan Rd.
Toronto, Canada, ON, Canada M6C 2M1

FELLOWSHIP OF EVANGELICAL BAPTIST
CHURCHES IN CANADA (575)
74 Sheppard Ave. W.
Willowdale, ON, Canada M2N 1M3

Quebec

CATHOLIC CHARISMATIC CHURCH OF CANADA
(8)
La Cite de Marie
11,141 Rte. 148, R.R. 1
Ste. Scholastique
Mirabel, PQ, Canada J0N 1S0

ITALIAN PENTECOSTAL CHURCH OF CANADA
(361)
6724 Fabre St.
Montreal, PQ, Canada H2G 2Z6

CATHOLIC CHURCH OF THE APOSTLES OF THE
 LATTER TIMES (10)
Monastery of the Apostles
Box 308
St. Jovite, PQ, Canada J0T 2H0

SIVANANDA YOGA VEDANTA CENTERS (1404)
673 8th Ave.
Val Morin, PQ, Canada J0T 2R0

FOREIGN

Australia

TEMPLE SOCIETY (854)
% Dr. Richard Hoffman
152 Tucker
Bentleigh, Australia

Denmark

MARTINUS INSTITUTE OF SPIRITUAL SCIENCE
 (995)
Mariendalsvej 94-96
2000
Copenhagen F, Denmark

England

PLYMOUTH BRETHREN (EXCLUSIVE: RAVEN-
 TAYLOR BRETHREN) (635)
% Stow Hill Bible and Tract Depot
5 Fife Rd.
Kingston-on-Thames, England

ORDO ADEPTORUM INVISIBLUM (1191)
% Gerry Ahrens
18 Crampton House
Patmore St.
London, England

UNIVERSAL LINK (1009)
1, St. Georges Square
St. Annes, Lancashire, England

Israel

WORKERS TOGETHER WITH ELOHIM (731)
Box 14411
Jerusalem, Israel

CHURCH OF GOD (JERUSALEM) (725)
Box 10184
Jerusalem 91101, Israel

Netherlands

THEOSOPHICAL SOCIETY (HARTLEY) (1113)
% Blavatskyhius
de Ruyterstratt 74
2518 A V Gravenhage 070231776, Netherlands

Philippines

AMERICAN ORTHODOX CHURCH (89)
% Archbishop Aftimios Harold J. Donovan, Exarch
San Antonio, Los Vanos
Laguna 3732, Philippines

South Africa

SCHOOL OF TRUTH (915)
% Dr. Nicol Campbell
Box 5582
Johannesburg, South Africa

Personal Name Index

An alphabetical listing of persons mentioned in the introductory essays, essay chapters, and directory sections of the *Encyclopedia*. Because of the difference between the essays and directory sections, citations referring to pages in the introductory essays and essay chapters are designated with a volume number and "p." and are separated from the directory references by a semicolon. Directory entries 1–563 will be found in Volume 1; 564–1089 in Volume II; 1090–1588 in Volume III.

A-Lan 1026
Abads (Dr.) II p.25
Abbenhouse, Dorothy 1115
Abbey, W. H. 1569
Abbinga, Herman P. 7
Abd-ru-shin 991
Abdel-Messiah, Marcos 143
Abdelsayed, Gabriel 143
Abdu'l-Baha III p.32, p.33; 1338, 1340, 1343
Abdul-Jabbar, Kareem 1329
Abdurrahman, Shaikh 1321
Abell, Theodore Curtis 760
Abernathy, Donald 393
Abgar (Ruler of Oshroene) I p.11
Abhayananda, Swami 1406
Abhedananda (Swami) III p.38; 1348
Abraham III p.24
Abraham, David 1567
Achad, Frater 1183, 1191
Acharya (Pundit) III p.38; 1412
Acker, Richard C. 75, 76
Adam III p.29
Adam, Jack C. 69
Adams, A. P. II p.24
Adams, A. P. 751
Adams, Barry 868
Adams, John Quincy 470
Adams, Joseph II p.51
Adams, Joseph H. 419
Adams, Ruth 1089
Adams, Walter Hollis 62
Adamski, George II p.64; 1011, 1014
Adaros, Premel El 1413
Addai I p.11
Addie, Jack 272
Addison, Clarence C. 422
Addyman, John 244
Adler, Cyrus 1266
Adler, Felix 759
Adler, Margot 1220
Aetherius of Venus, Master 1012
Afton, Anita 997, 1009
Agan, V. O. 302
Agapoa, Tony 947
Agasthiya 1377
Agathangelos of Prinkipo 133
Agnes, Sister 843

Aguinaldo, Emilio 70
Agyeman, Jaramogi Abebe 1292
Ahmad, Hazrat Mirza Ghulam 1325
Ahmad, Mirza Ghulam Hazrat 1324
Ahmed, Bashir 150
Ahnfelt, Oscar 210
Ahrens, Gelrry 1191
Aihara, Herman 1500
Aiken, John W. 1027
Aiken, Louisa 1027
Aitken, Anne 1480
Aitken, Robert 1480
Aivanhov, Omraam Michael 1134, 1176
Ajari 1468
Ajiki, Henry 1538
Akana, Akaiko 1570
Akana, Francis K. 1570
Akana, Jr., Francis K. 1570
Akhenaten 1212
Akizaki, Takeo 1540
Akizaki, Yoshio 1540
Al-Adawiya, Rabi'a III p.31
Al-Ghazali III p.31
Al-Habib, Muhammed Ibn 1314
Al-Jerrahi, Muzaffer Ozak 1317
al-Yafi-i, Abdullah 1318
'Ala-ud-din, Halveti Sheikh Ali 1317
Alamo, Susan 364
Alamo, Tony 364
Alan, Jim 1209
Alban (Saint) III p.7
Albright, Jacob 214
Alexander (Dr.) III p.17
Alexander, Agnes Baldwin 1338
Alexander, Archbishop 103
Alexander I (Czar) 563
Alexander II (Czar) I p.54, III p.26
Alexander, Mar 115
Alexander VI (Pope) p.xxiv
Alexandros, Archbishop 107
Alexis (Patriarch) I p.10
Alexis, Bishop 109
Aleyin, Frater 1193
Ali III p.29
Ali, Duse Mohammed III p.30
Ali, Haj III p.30
Ali, Maulawi Muhammad 1324
Ali, Noble Drew 1326, 1330, 1331

Ali 2d, Noble Drew 1331
Ali 3d, Noble Drew 1331
Ali, R. German 1330
Alioto, Thadeus B. J. 6
Alisauskas, Jr., Joseph W. 124
Alldaffer, Fannie 278
Alldaffer, Tracy 278
Allen, A. A. I p.46; 375, 382, 383, 404
Allen, Ethan II p.31
Allen, J. H. II p.26
Allen, James 895
Allen, Richard p.xxxvi, I p.31; 233
Allen, Stuart 659, 666
Alline, Henry p.lii, I p.24, p.32, II p.4; 203, 244, 571
Allingham, Cedric II p.64
Allred, Owen 802
Allred, Rulon C. 802, 806, 808, 809, 813
Almeida, Florentino 451
Alper, Frank 939
Alpert, Richard II p.63; 865, 1369
Alspaugh, Clair H. 517
Altenbach, Conrad 24
Altisi, Jackie 1021
Alvarez of Ceylon I p.4
Alvarez, Julius 150
Amar Joyti, Swami 1414
Amenhotep IV 1022, 1090
Amman, Jacob I p.53
Amos, Clifford 1261
Amritananda, Swami 1399
Ananda III p.44
Ananda Yogi, Gururaj 1345
Anandakapila, Swami 1399
Anandamayi, Sri Sri 1133
Anandamurti, Shrii 1349, 1388, 1424
Anderson, Carl II p.64
Anderson, David p.lviii
Anderson, Lester B. 871
Anderson, William 235
Anderson, Wing 1007
Andreae, Valentin III p.2
Andrew, J. J. II p.10
Andrew, James O. p.xxxvi
Andrew, W. Martin 1574
Andrews, E. A. 1566
Andrews, James F. 1566
Andrews, Timothy I p.1

393

Flowers, Amanda 948
Fludd, Robert III p.2
Fonda, Jane 1422
Fons, G. F. C. 370
Forbes, James Alexander 438
Forbes, W. Francis 115
Forbes, William Francis 115, 123
Ford, Arnold Josiah III p.27; 1287
Ford, Arthur 950, 1063
Ford, Ismael 1131
Ford, Lewis I p.46; 445
Ford, Patricia duMont 46
Forest, Julia 958
Forfreedom, Ann 1247
Forgostein, Carolyn 1112
Forgostein, Harold 1112
Forrest, Julia O. 967
Fort, Charles II p.64
Fosdick, Harry Emerson 190
Foster, Charles II p.36
Foster, Harry 671
Foster, Jane 1183
Foster, Mrs. Thomas III p.50
Foster, Nelson 1480
Foster, Randolph S. I p.36, p.37
Foster, Robert II p.36
Foulds, Sam E. 909
Fourier, Charles II p.42
Foust, James A. 335
Fox, Arthur H. 790
Fox, Diane 790
Fox, Earl G. 986
Fox, Emmet 895, 898, 905
Fox, George I p.52, p.55
Fox, Kate II p.61
Fox, Margaretta II p.61
Fox, Selena 1209
Fox, Stephen S. 1581
Foxe, John I p.51
France, Jesse 901
Francesca, Aleuti 1020
Francis of Assisi 1
Francis, Brother 1009
Francis, Marianne 1020
Francis (St., of Assisi) II p.41
Franck, Sebastian I p.51
Francke, August Hermann I p.27
Frangquist, David 1241
Franke, Elmer E. 678
Franklin, Ben 621
Franklin, Benjamin p.xxxi
Franson, Frederick 211
Fraser, James 1241
Frazee, J. J. 410
Frazier, Dudley 477
Frazier, Henry D. 1043
Frazier, R. O. 490
Frederick I II p.21
Frederick II I p.21
Frederick William II, King 209
Fredriksen, Norman C. 966
Freeman, Carole 987
Freeman, Hobart E. 473
Freeman, William T. 669
Freer, Gedaliah 1273
Freking, F. W. 20
Frelinghuysen, Theodore J. p.xxix

French, H. Robb 309
Freud, Sigmund III p.23
Freytag, F. L. Alexander 717
Friede, Johannes 986
Friedlander, Ira II p.65
Friedman, Daniel 1302
Friesen, I. P. 509
Frink, Elmer A. 354
Fris, Howard 37, 38, 89
Frisby, Neal I p.46; 384
Fritz, Daniel 1134
Frobisher, Martin I p.1
Frodsham, Stanley I p.47; 460
Froelich, Samuel Heinrich 551
Fromke, DeVern 671
Frost, Gavin 1207
Frost, Yvonne 1207
Frothingham, Octavius Brooks II p.32
Frumentius (Bishop) I p.13
Fry, Daniel 1026
Fry, Russell G. 62
Fuge, Albert J. 67
Fujita, Reisai 1532
Fujuhana, Kyodo 1467
Fuller, Andrew 565
Fuller, Henriette 571
Fuller, Richard II p.5
Fuller, W. E. 337, 430
Fullerton, Alexander III p.6; 1115
Fung, Paul F. 1492
Funk, Christian I p.52
Ga, Macario V. 68
Gaard, Conrad II p.26
Gaebelein, Arno E. II p.15
Gaglardi, B. Maureen 460
Gaines, James A. 95
Gale, William Potter 752
Galen II p.60
Galerius 1
Galphin, John II p.7
Gamble, Charles 372
Gandhi, Mahatma 1346
Gandhi, Nemi Chand 1398
Gandhi, Virchand A. III p.40
Gangadhar Tirth Maharaj, Swami 1363
Gangopadhyay, Kali Kishore 1363
Ganneau III p.14
Gantt, Dwyatt 628
Gardner, Gerald B. II p.16, p.18; 1220, 1225, 1233
Gardner, Jack E. 1077
Gardunio, Paul L. 810
Garman, W. O. H. 641
Garr, A. G. 316
Garrett, Leroy 622
Garrettson, Freeborn 233
Garrique, Florence 1121
Garvey, Marcus III p.27, p.30; 78, 1029, 1287, 1293, 1330
Gasan, Jito III p.47
Gaskin, Ina May 861
Gaskin, Stephen 861
Gasquoine, Earl P. 53
Gasteiner, Lovie Webb 1171
Gates, Walter L. 816
Gattell, Benoni B. 1117
Gau, Wayne W. 64

Gaudio, Luciano 112
Gautama, Siddhartha III p.43
Gawr, Rhuddlwm 1216
Gay, Ben F. 785
Gay, Columbia I p.46
Gay, John p.li
Gay, Marvin 722
Gaylor, Anne Laurie 770
Gaylor, Anne Nicol 770
Gayman, Daniel 819
Gayman, Duane 819
Geddes, Francis 1556
Gelberman, Joseph H. 1299
Gelesnoff, Vladimir M. 662
Gellatly, Alexander 195
Gentzel, Charles Boyd 1018
George, David II p.7
George, James H. 59
George, Robin 1378
Georgius, Mar 6, 7, 35, 57, 95, 117
Gerling, Helene 976
Gerling, J. Bertram 976
Germain, Bishop 93
Germain, Bishop of Paris, Saint 93
Germain, Saint III p.7; 1146, 1156
Germanos, Metropolitan 91, 134
Germer, Karl Johannes III p.15; 1194, 1195, 1198
Geshe Rinpoche, Tomo 1510
Gessler, Paul 1368
Gestefeld, Ursula II p.51
Gethers, Leroy 238
Ghosananda, Maha 1452
Ghose, Sri Aurobindo 1351
Gibson, John Paul 990
Gilbert, Humphrey I p.1
Gilbert, Nathaniel I p.31
Gilbert, Violet 1016
Gilead, Foster 126
Gill, Bernard 471
Gillespie, James B. 64
Gillman, J. Julian 1136
Gillman, Rita Anne 1136
Gilquist, Peter 91
Girandola, Anthony 36
Giri, Nirmalananda 1133
Gladkov, Peter 858
Glanvill, Joseph II p.58, p.60
Glas, John II p.8
Glassman, Bernard Tetsugen 1488
Gleason, Matt 1089
Glendenning, Maurice Lerrie 793
Glenn, Laura 1348
Glover, Goodwife II p.58
Gnosticus 1224
Goddard, Dwight III p.50
Goenka, S. N. 1454
Goerz, David I p.54
Gold, E. J. 1316
Goldsmith, Joel II p.52
Goldsmith, Joel S. 875, 877
Goldstein, Joseph 1454
Goldwater, Barry 1558
Gomez, Clemente Dominguez 21
Gonyo, Elrick 4
Gonzales, Hector 15
Gonzales, Roberto T. 26

Heatwole, Gabriel D.   500
Heck, Barbara   244
Heck, Paul   244
Hedrick, Granville   818
Hegg, Verner   1163
Heideman, A. L.   159
Heideman, Arthur Leopold   I p.18; 157
Heideman, Paul A.   157, 159
Heidenreich, Alfred   1163
Heil, W. F.   241
Heindel, Augusta Foss   1097
Heindel, Max   1095, 1097
Heinemann, Barbara   840
Heinlein, Robert   1208, 1260
Heline, Corinne S.   1095, 1152
Heline, Theodore   1095
Heller, Arnold Krumm   1104
Heller, Patrick A.   765
Hellman, Sylvia   1423
Helwys, Thomas   II p.2
Hembree, Maud   1571
Hendrickson, Andrew   796
Hennadij, Archbishop   94, 135
Henninges, H. C.   707
Henry IV (King)   I p.23
Henry VIII (King)   I p.2, p.5
Hensley, Becky   1581
Hensley, George Went   I p.46; 445
Hensley, Kirby J.   791
Henzsel, Johanna   986
Hepker, George H.   1040
Herberg, Will   p.xliii
Herford, Ulric Vernon   6, 18, 95, 150, 1574
Herjulfson, Bjarni   I p.1
Herman, Father   125
Herman, Mordecai   III p.27
Hermes   1222
Hernandez y Esperon, Angel Maria   451
Hernandez, J. A.   449
Herodotus   II p.57
Herr, Francis   501
Herr, John   501
Herremon (Prince)   II p.26
Herrigel, Wilhelm   1343
Herzl, Theodore   III p.25
Herzog, Bishop   44
Herzog, Eduard   I p.3
Hesketh, Harrison Roy   937
Heughan, Elsie   274
Heyer, 'Father' J. C. F.   176
Hibbert, Joseph   1293
Hickerson, John   851, 856
Hickey, L. D.   833
Hicks, Donald   305
Hicks, Donald Ned   649
Hicks, Elias   535
Hieronimus, Robert   1083
Higbee, C. L.   II p.36
Higbee, Francis   II p.37
Higgins, Jerry   950
Higgins, John   13
Higgins, Melvin   1411
Higgins, Minnie   1103
Higginson, Thomas Wentworth   II p.32
Higuchi, Kiyoko   1538
Hilborn, Harry M.   948

Hillebrand, Wilhelm   III p.50
Hills, George   p.lix
Hillshafer, Linda   1211
Hillyer, Nelson D.   40
Himes, Joshua   II p.22
Hindmarsh, Robert   II p.59
Hinds, Robert   1293
Hine, Edward   743
Hinkins, John-Roger   1447
Hinkle, George M.   II p.36
Hinkson, G. Duncan   78, 79
Hinton, Daniel C.   2, 43, 1126
Hippolytus   II p.20
Hirai, Kaeko   1477
Hirai, K. R.   III p.50
Hirai, Ryuki   III p.49
Hirai, Tatsusho   1477
Hirano, Toshio   655
Hirayama, Bunjiro   1543
Hirsh, R. H.   716
Hisamatsu, Shinichi   1479
Hitchcock, William Mellon   II p.63
Hobson, Elizabeth   II p.60
Hoch, Daniel   510
Hochweber, Wilhelm   1163
Hocking, W. E.   190
Hockley, Fred   III p.14
Hodges, Edward Lewis   1102
Hodgson, William B.   III p.30
Hodson, Richard   III p.5
Hodur, Francis   44
Hoefle, Emily   712
Hoefle, John J.   712, 714
Hoeller, Stephan A.   1129, 1130, 1142
Hoeskema, Herman   184
Hoffman, Bernie Lazar   364
Hoffman, George W.   242
Hoffmann, Christopher   854
Hofmann, Albert   II p.63
Hofmann, Melchior   I p.49,   II p.21
Hohman, John   III p.23
Hoiles, C. Douglas   775
Holbrook, John Lee   I p.46
Holdeman, John   493
Holland, John R.   360
Holley, James Theodore   68
Holloway, Gilbert N.   1075
Holloway, June   1075
Holman, Leroy   353
Holmes, Ernest S.   II p.53; 894, 898, 900, 905, 913, 916, 921
Holmes, Fenwicke   916, 921
Holmgren, A. A.   458
Holsinger, Henry R.   518, 530
Holstine, Henry   486
Holt, Herrick   I p.46
Holt, Simma   562
Holz, Richard   247
Holzer, Hans   1229
Homer, Gladys A.   943
Honen   III p.46, p.51
Honey, C. A.   1011
Hong, Frederick   1492
Hoo-Kna-Ka   1003
Hooker, Thomas   I p.26
Hoosier, Harry   p.xxxvi,   I p.31
Hoover, Christian   497

Hopkins, Charles Henry   886
Hopkins, Emma Curtis   II p.47, p.51, p.52, p.53; 875, 888, 898, 901, 905, 921, 922
Hopkins, Jane Hanford   886
Hopkins, Samuel   190
Hopwood, Freeman   757
Horioka, Chimyo   1479
Horn, Edith Opal   364
Horner, Ralph Cecil   p.lxiii; 265, 273
Horning, Moses   499, 505
Hornshuh, Fred   365
Horoshij, Michael   134
Horowitz, David   1304, 1305
Horowitz, Levi   1272
Horowitz, Meier   1272
Horowitz, Pinchas D.   1272
Horwitz, Jacob Isaac   1278
Hoskins, I. F.   716
Hoton   II p.36
Hottel, W. B.   249
Houdin, Michel   p.lii
Houdini, Harry   II p.61
Hough, Joseph Damian   39, 53
Houser, Alvin E.   629
Houser, Dwain   64
Houteff, Victor T.   675, 676, 677
Howard, D. H.   784
Howard, Luther S.   369
Howard, W. O.   409
Howe, Julia Ward   p.88
Howell, James   239
Howell, Leonard   1293
Howgill, Francis   p.55
Hoyt, Herman A.   525
Hua, Hsuan   1497
Huba, Ihor   118
Hubbard, L. Ron   III p.15; 1042, 1044, 1444
Hubbard, Mary Sue   1044
Hubiak, Daniel   125
Hubmaier, Balthasar   I p.50
Hudler, James   765
Hudson, Henry   p.xxvii
Huff, Paul   p.liv
Huffer, Elizabeth Louise   1152
Huffer, Richard   1152
Huffman, H. B.   304
Hugh, John   1161
Hugh, Paola   1161
Hughes, Charles Franklin   1552
Hughes, Frank Ellsworth   1139
Hughes, Thomas I. C.   683
Hui-K'o   III p.46
Hui-Neng   III p.46
Humbard, Rex   657
Humble, Floyd   972
Humphreys, John J.   26, 36
Hung-Jen   III p.46
Hunsberger, Ephraim   510
Hunt, Dave   457
Hunt, Ernest   III p.50
Hunt, P. G.   I p.46
Hunt, Robert   p.xxvi,   I p.5
Hunt, Roland   1161
Hunter, Edwin Wallace   6, 27
Hunter, Neva Dell   1082
Huntley, Clyde M.   741

Judge, William Quan 1112, 1114, 1115, 1116, 1117
Judson, Adoniram II p.5; 565
Judson, Ann 565
Juren, H. 213
Juster, David C. 658
Jyotir Maya Nanda, Swami 1425
Kagahi, Soryu III p.48
Kahl, Gordon II p.27
Kahlil, Phez 1320
Kai, Ku 1474
Kaichen, Troy A. 62
Kailashananda, Swami 1427
Kaiser, Elsworth Thomas 736
Kalupahana, David J. 1458
Kamala, Srimata 1401
Kaminski, Stephen 43, 44, 120
Kamp, Beata 1089
Kanski, Francis 1126
Kaplan, Mordecai M. 1267
Kapleau, Philip 1489
Kappeler, Max II p.52; 878
Kapustin, Sabellius I p.57; 563
Karahissaridis, Paul Eftymios 133
Karahissaridis, Socrates Ermis 133
Kardec, Allan 942
Kardec, Allen 932
Karish, Bella 989
Karmapa, Gyalwa 1517
Karoli Baba, Neem 1369
Karras, Mark 137
Karsleigh, Daisy 1024
Karsleigh, Zelrun 1024
Karthar Rinpoche, Khenpo 1517
Kary, Hans 1418
Kashta 1224
Katagiri, Dainin 1483
Katashima, Kokichi 1543
Katoda, Tetsuei 1474
Katra, Ik. Ilia 81
Kauffey, Laura Adanka 422
Kaufman, Ishi III p.27
Kauikeaouli 1064
Kawahara, Senyei III p.49
Kawasaki, Kazoe 1539
Kawasaki, Masasato 1539
Kawate, Bunjiro 1543
Kaythawa, U 1460
Kazi, Sonam 1518
Kearse, I. Logan 953
Keck, Jr., Herman 779
Kedrovsky, Nicolas 129
Kedrowsky, John I p.10, p.11; 129
Kedrowsky, Nicholas I p.10, p.11
Keeny, Ervin J. 552
Kees, Amy Merritt 939
Keith, M. F. L. 428, 434
Keith, Roy 226
Keith, W. Holman 1231
Keizer, Lewis S. 1131, 1132, 1134
Keller, Charles W. 7
Keller, Karl III p.15
Keller, Kelly 901
Keller, Kenneth 1020
Kelley, Joe E. 229
Kellog, J. 652
Kelly, Aiden 1215

Kelly, Clarence 48, 49
Kelly, Ted D. 75
Kelly, William II p.13; 636
Kelpius III p.2
Kelsh, Louis 813
Kember, Jane 1044
Kenelly, John 37, 89
Kenn, Charlie 1064
Kennaugh, Robert Q. 68
Kennedy, John F. 1018, 1582
Kennedy, Richard II p.49
Kennett Roshi, Jiyu 1484
Kenny, Saint 1078
Kent, Grady R. 318
Kenworthy, Lionel 887
Keopuolani, Queen 1064
Kerekes, Richard H. 790
Kerry, Lady 1232
Kerry, Reginald G. II p.52
Kersten, G. H. 182
Keshavadas, Sant 1410, 1429
Kesler, B. E. 523
Kessler, Gerard J. 4
Keyhoe, Donald II p.64
Khaalis, Hammas Abdul 1329
Khan, Hazrat III p.31
Khan, Hazrat Inayat 1322, 1323, 1336, 1409
Khan, Vilayat 855, 865, 1319, 1322, 1323
Khanna, J. 1449
Khanna, T. S. 1451
Khapa, Tsong 1522
Khashoggi, Adnan 1398
Khedemel, Frater 1199
Kheiralla, Ibrahim III p.32
Kheirella, Ibrahim 1338
Khomeini, Ayatollah 1306, 1307
Khul, Djwhal III p.6
Khyentse Rinpoche, H. E. Dingo 1520
Khyentse Rinpoche, H. E. Dzongsar 1520
Kidd, James 979
Kidson, W. E. 406
Kieninger, Richard 1110
Kiergan, A. M. 257
Kierkegaard, Soren 844
Kilgore, Marl 801, 834
Kilgore, Merl 832
Kilham, Alexander 244
Killingsworth, Frank Russell 297
Kilpatrick, R. L. 622
Kim, Paik Moon 1063
Kim, Young Oon 1063
Kimball, Edward A. II p.52
Kimball, Robert S. 1048
Kimball, Spencer W. 795
King, Elizabeth Delvine 1036
King, Eugene K. 1341
King, Francis III p.14
King, Franzo 79
King, George 1012
King, Godfre Ray III p.7
King, Godfre-Ray 1156
King, J. H. 337
King, L. B. 926
King, Lotus 1156
King, Martin Luther 606, 1560
King, Reginald B. (Rex) 1341

King, Ruth L. 1341
King, Samuel 189
King, Stanley M. 824
King, Theodore Q. 1341
King, Thomas 1341
King, W. L. 313
King, Walter Eugene 1252
Kingham, Emma 962
Kingham, John 962
Kinghorn, Michael 1219
Kingold, Charles 1179
Kingston, Merlin 808
Kinley, Henry Clifford 1168
Kino, Eusebio p.xxv
Kirby, Jay Davis 1133, 1141
Kiril, Bishop 119
Kirkland, R. Lee 650
Kitamura, Kiyokazu 1549
Kiyoto, Kameo 1545
Klassen, Ben 767
Kleinsasser, Joseph 847
Klemp, Harold 1444
Klep, Art II p.63
Kleppinger, Thomas J. 62
Kleps, Arthur 1031
Klimowicz, Joseph I p.11; 120
Knapp, Martin Wells 276
Kneitel, Judy 1225
Kneitel, Tom 1225
Knight, Gareth 1184
Knight, J. Z. II p.62
Knight, John I p.1
Knight, W. S. M. 95
Knoch, Adolph Ernst 662
Knoch, A. E. II p.14
Knoche, Grace F. 1114
Knorr, Nathan H. 713
Knowles, Brian 704
Knowles, William 245
Knox, John I p.23
Ko Bang 1507
Kobo Daishi 1532
Koch, Gerka 747
Koehler, J. Ph. 174
Koehler, Stephan 176
Koho Zenji, Chisan 1484
Kok, D. J. P. 1113
Kolesnikoff, John 593
Kolesnikoff, Sylvan 563
K'on-dkon-mch'og rgyal-po 1513
Kongpo, Gedatsu 1465
Konko, Setsutane 1543
Koot Hoomi 1156
Kopp, E. Paul 374
Kopp, Leroy S. 374
Korenchan, Brother John 843
Kornfield, Jack 1454
Korteniemi, Solomon I p.18
Kosen, Imokita III p.47, p.49
Koshi, Shuntetsu 1491
Koshiway, Jonathan 1030
Koskela, John 158
Koski, Marnie 977
Kotani, Kimi 1472
Kovalevsky, Evgraph 93
Kowalski, John I p.4
Kowalski, John Michael 25

Kozlowska, Feliksa Magdalena   25
Kozlowska, Maria Franciska   45
Kozlowski, Anthony   44
Krajenski, G.   25
Kratzer, Glenn A.   II p.52
Kraut, Ogden   807
Krauth, Charles P.   p.xxxv
Krewson, John W.   714
Kripalvanandji, Swami   1381, 1402
Krishna, Gopi   1384
Krishna Venta   857
Krishnahara   1087
Krishnamurti, Jiddu   II p.5, p.39; 1097,
   1124, 1163, 1175, 1383, 1419
Krishnananda, Rishi   II p.39; 1391
Kristof, Civet   133
Kriyananda, Goswami   1411
Kriyananda, Swami   1347, 1411
Krolhodc, Bodhin   1489
Kroll, Maria   53
Kroneberg, Hans B.   85
Kuang, Stephen   669
Kubo, Kakutaro   1472
Kubose, Gyomay   1466
Kueshana, Eklal   1110
Kuhlman, Kathryn   I p.46; 381
Kumar, Muni Sushul   1438
Kumarji, Muni Sushil   III p.40
Kumoto, Paul K.   916
Kunga, Lama   1513
Kunz, Dora   1115
Kupihea, Margaret   1064
Kurtz, Paul   760
Kushi, Michio   1498
Kuvalayanandaji, Swami   1408
Kuzuhara, Sadaichi   655
Kyabgon, Drikung   1512
Kyrillos VI, Pope   143
Kyritsis, Theodore   108
Labaj, Dr. Mark L.   213
Ladner, Johanne   986
LaDue, Francis A.   1112
Lady Rhiannon   1225
Laestadius, Lars Levi   I p.18
Laird, Margaret   II p.52; 879
Laisney, Francois   49
Lake, John D.   I p.45
Lalibela (King)   I p.13
Lalitananda, Swami   1425
Lambert, W. Noel   I p.4
Lamboune, Arthur E.   659
Lamech   II p.8
Lammers, Arthur   1034
Lamsa, George M.   667, 908
Landas Berghes, Duc de   23, 27, 30
Landbeck, Christoph Friedrich   986
Lane, David Christopher   1444
Lane, Isaac   236
Lane, Robert   38
Lang, Derek   5
Lang, Ruth H.   739
Langford, Jack   668
Langlois, Kongo   1487
Lankenau, Alfred Louis   84, 121, 123
Lanting, Ronald E.   1259
Lao-Tzu   III p.45; 1496
LaPlante, Gerard   1140

Lapointe, Lafond   68
Lapp, William Arnold   1361
Laqu, Kadar   1014
Larkin, Clarence   II p.11, p.13
Larson, Christian D.   921
LaSalle, Robert   p.xxv
Lashley, James F. A.   122, 131
LaVal, Francois de Montmorency   p.li
Laveau, John   III p.17
Laveau, Marie   III p.17
LaVey, Anton   III p.19; 1258, 1259, 1260,
   1265
LaVoison   III p.16
Lavy, Solomon   529
Law, William   II p.36
Law, Wilson   II p.36
Lawrence, D. H.   660
Lawrence, Joshua   II p.6
Lawrence, Reginald   933
Lawrence, Tommie   404
Lawson, Robert Clarence   398, 399, 401,
   402, 420
Layne, Meade   992
Layzell, Reg   460, 476
Le Fevre, Jean   982
Le Galyon, Carolyn Barbour   894
Lea, H. C.   I p.3
Leadbeater, Charles W.   III p.5; 1124,
   1138
Leary, E. K.   289
Leary, Timothy   II p.63; 1031, 1369,
   1406
LeBaron, Alma Dayer   806
LeBaron, Jr., Alma   806
LeBaron, Benjamin F.   806
LeBaron, Ervil   802, 806, 808, 810
LeBaron, Floren   806
LeBaron, Joel   805, 806, 808
LeBaron, Leo Peter Evoniuk   810
LeBaron, Norman   807
LeBaron, Owen   806
LeBaron, Ross Wesley   805, 806
LeBaron, Verlan M.   806
Lebedoff, John   555, 562
Ledbetter, Hoy   622
Lee, Ann   855
Lee, Carl Q.   1553
Lee, Gloria   II p.64; 1018, 1021
Lee, Harold B.   795
Lee, Jesse   596
Lee, Robert E.   II p.31
Lee, Willie   386, 412
Lee, Witness   669, 671
Leek, Sybil   III p.18; 1225
Leeser, Isaac   1268, 1269
Lefberne, Mar Antoine   7
Lefebvre (Bishop)   I p.5
Lefebvre, Marcel   24, 48, 49
Lehman, John E.   869
Leibrecht, Walter   844
Leifeste, Harriette   965
Leighton, Edward M.   940
Lein-Quan, Thiet-Dieu   1455
Lekh Raj, Dada   1356
Leland, Charles B.   1251
Lennox, Ruth Scoles   1159
Lenz, Frederick   1394

Leo Christopher (Skelton)   100
Leonard, Gladys Osborne   II p.61
Leonard, T. K.   360
Leontios of Chile, Archbishop   110
Leskinen, Andrew   158
Lessing, Kitty   1227
Letellier, Andre   8
Letellier, J.   8
Leutzinger, Rudy   829
Lever, Marshall   983
Lever, Quinta   983
LeVesque, Doris C.   1025
Levi, Eliphas   III p.12, p.14
Levine, Stephen   1369
Levington, William   II p.60
Levy, Clifton Harby   1303
Lewellyn, Joe S.   319
Lewis, F. E.   428
Lewis, H. Spencer   1090
Lewis, Helen M.   428
Lewis, Joseph   771
Lewis, Samuel L.   865, 1322, 1323
Lewis, Sol   949
Lewis, W. C.   428, 434
Lewis (Wolford), Janet Stine   936
Lichtenstein, Morris   1303
Lichtenstein, Tehilla   1303
Liholiho   1064
Lilly, William   III p.2
Lincoln, Abraham   857
Lindsay, Freda   377
Lindsay, Gordon   I p.46; 377
Lindsey, Gordon   375
Lindsey, Holden   1018
Lindsey, Theophilus   II p.30
Lindstrom, Paul   645
Lines, Gregory   43, 1126, 1128
Lingen, Gary   1206
Linn, Matthew   195
Lipa, Mark I.   81
Lipscomb, David   621
Lisle, George   II p.7
Litch, Josiah   II p.22
Litchtenberger, Bishop Arthur   35
Little, R. J.   636
Little, Robert Wentworth   III p.2; 1099
Littlewood, W. E.   67
Littlewood, William Elliott   19, 62
Livingston, John   799
Livingston, John Henry   185
Lloyd, Frederick E. J.   I p.4; 2, 43, 84,
   123, 1126, 1128
Lloyd, Robert J.   617
Lloyd, Sherman Russell   800
Lochbaum, Ada   391
Lochbaum, Charles   391
Lochen Rinpoche, Jetsun   1518
Lodo, Lama   1516
Lodroe, Jamyang Khyentse Choekyi
   1523
Lomax, J. V.   405, 413
Long, A. J.   322
Long, Aaron   I p.46
Long, E. E.   819
Long, James A.   1113, 1114
Long, Max Freedom   1064
Long, S. E.   666

405

Morton, John p.lx II p.4
Morusca, Policarp 127, 128
Mory, C. A. 636
Morya, El 1018
Moses III p.23, p.24, p.29
Moses, Alfred Geiger 1303
Moses, Tom 321
Moshier, Bud 918
Moshier, Carmen 918
Moss, Harold 1212
Moss, Loring I. 522
Mote, James O. 60
Mother Boats 1240
Mott, Francis J. 876
Mott, Lucretia II p.30
Motta, Marcelo Ramos 1194, 1198
Moulton, Ebenezer II p.4; 571
Mountain, Jacob p.liii
Moyle, Olin 1305
Mozoomdar, Protap Chunder III p.38
Mozumdar, A. K. III p.39
Mozumdar, A. K. 784
Mudge, James I p.37
Muelhaeuser, John 176
Mueller, George 583
Muhaiyaddeen M. R. Guru Bawa,
    Shaikh 1309
Muhammad Al Madhi, As Sayyid Abdur
    Rahman 1327
Muhammad, Clara 1326
Muhammad, Elijah 1326, 1329, 1332,
    1333, 1334
Muhammad, Emmanuel Abdullah 1332
Muhammad, John 1334
Muhammad Rahmaan Al Madhi, As Sayyid
    Al Haadi Abdur 1327
Muhammad, Siyyad Ali III p.32
Muhammad, Wallace D. 1326, 1332
Muhammad, Wallace Fard 1326, 1330,
    1332
Muhammad, Warith Deen 1326
Muhammed III p.29, p.31
Muhammed Ahmed Ibn Abdullah 1327
Muhammed, Mirza Ali 1338
Muhlenberg, Henry Melchior p.xxx,
    I p.17
Mukerji, A.P. (Swami) III p.39
Mukerji, A. P. 1413
Mukerji, Surendranath 1382
Muktananda, Swami 1367, 1390
Mulholland, John F. III p.45
Mulvin, Jerry 1443
Mumford, Bob 483
Mumford, John 1399
Mumford, Robert 753
Mumford, Stephen II p.8; 705
Munari, Franco 24
Muncaster, David A. 787
Munck, Jens I p.17
Munindra, Anagarika 1454
Munnik, Gerret 147
Munnik, Gerrit 1138
Muntzer, Thomas I p.49, p.50, II p.20,
    p.21
Murano, Senchu 1469
Muriel Isis 1169
Murphy, Bridey 1059

Murphy, Joseph 898
Murphy, Ural R. 1361
Murray, Jack 202
Murray, John II p.30
Murray, Jon G. 758
Murray, Margaret III p.16; 1233, 1262
Murray, W. John 898, 905
Murray, William J. 758
Murro, Jonathan 1162
Muschell, Helen 1089
Musey, George J. 24
Mushegan, Harry A. 457
Musiel, Ruth 946
Musser, Joseph White II p.38; 802, 806,
    809, 813
Myers, Harvey 1449
Myers, John 671
Myers, Mary L. 1155, 1171
Myers, Michael 1228
Myers, Oscar H. 320
Myers, Peter 1347
Myman, Martin 1046
Myneta, Mary 1158
Myoko, Naganuma 1473
Na, Eachta Eacha 811
Nachman of Bratslav 1273
Nada, Lady 1018, 1156
Nagamoto, Kazuhiko K. 1473
Nagaraj, Kriya Babaji 1377
Nagasaki, Toyokichi III p.49
Nagatomi, Masatoshi 1479
Nagayama, Baron Taketoshi 1472
Nagorka, Diane S. 958
Nagorka, Henry J. 958
Nahum ben Zevi, Menahem 1274
Nakagawa, Soen 1478, 1479, 1489, 1491
Nakayama, Miki 1548
Nanak, Guru III p.39; 1442, 1449, 1451
Nanda, Gulzarilal 1398
Napier, Mari Mae 1177
Narayan Tirth Dev Maharaj, Swami 1363
Narayanananda Maharaj, Swami 1389
Narayaniah III p.5
Narshinhran, Purushottan 1345
Nast, William I p.37
Natalino, Umile 112
Natalli, Ramon 992
Neal, Eli N. 388, 400
Neal, George 244
Nechung Rinpoche 1521
Nee, Watchman 669, 671
Neidorf, J. Eldon 286
Nelson, Buck II p.64
Nelson, Herman F. 68
Nelson, Norman 1241
Nephi, Angel 839
Nerren, Thomas B. 816, 819
Neruda, Milton J. 1214, 1239
Nesnick, Mary 1201
Nestorius I p.1, p.11
Neth, Joseph Edward 61, 1137
Nevada Slim 1069
Nevin, John W. 209
Nevin, John Williamson I p.25
New, John Fair 1584
New, N. N. 1584
Newbrough, John B. II p.61

Newbrough, John Ballou 1007
Newcomb, Vesta 850
Newell, Chris 1236
Newell, Simon 1236
Newhouse, Flower A. 1165
Newman, Hugh George de Willmott I p.3,
    p.4; 6, 7, 9, 18, 35, 57, 59, 95, 151,
    949, 1145, 1574
Newman, John Henry 71
Newmark, George Augustus 6
Newton, Benjamin W. II p.14
Newton, Frank 1535
Newton, Isaac 1090
Ni, Master 1503
Nichiko 1470
Nichiren III p.46; 1469, 1470, 1472
Nichols, L. T. 1571
Nichols, William Albert 115, 117
Nicholson, Harold Percival 57
Nickel, Thelma 378
Nicolas, Bishop 125
Nicoll, Maurice 1313
Niebuhr, H. Richard I p.25; 844
Niebuhr, Reinhold I p.25
Nikon (Patriarch) I p.56, p.57; 563
Ni'matullah, Nur ad-din M. 1318
Nimbarkiacharya III p.36
Niranjannan Saraswati, Swami 1399
Nisbet, James p.lviii
Nishida, Mugaku 1472
Nitschman, David I p.28, 29
Nitschmann, David 212
Nityananda, Bhagwan 1403
Nityananda, Swami 1390, 1403
Nityananda, Tantracharya 1388
Niwano, Nikkyo 1473
Noah III p.29
Noble, Abel II p.8
Noble, Kerry 750
Nobunaga, Oda III p.146
Noebel, David 1558
Nolan, David James 881
Noli, Fan Stylin I p.11; 80, 81, 120
Nome, Sage Bhagavan 1353
Noonan, Allen II p.45
Noonan, Allen Michael 874
Norman, Ernest L. 1022
Norman, Ruth II p.65; 1022
Norris, J. Frank 568, 595
Norton, Joseph 571
Nosereddine III p.30
Noth, Samdech Prah Sangha Raja
    Chuon 1452
Novack, Michael 1238
Novak, Penny 1238
Nowell, Claude Rex 1587
Noyes, John Humphrey II p.44
Nurbakhsh, Javad 1318
Nurse, Gladstone St. Claire 78
Nurse, Goodwife III p.17
Nyah 1029
Nybladh, Carl A. 78
Nyima, Choskyi 1522
Nyland, Wilhem A. 1315
Oates, Virgil 386
Oba Efuntola Oseijeman Adelabu Adefunmi
    I, King 1252

Phillips, J. B. 660
Phillips, Magdalene Mabe 423
Phillips, Osborne 1144, 1179
Phillips, William Thomas 394
Phinazee, Hiram 219
Phoenix 1225
Phoenix, Lord 1237
Photios, Bishop 108, 109
Phylos the Tibetan 1001, 1105
Pickens, Nellie M. 963
Piepkorn, Arthur C. I p.5; 35
Pierce, Theodore M. 1146
Pieres, Carl H. 967
Pierre, Lawrence F. 86, 88, 142
Pierson, Arthur T. II p.14
Pierson, Nicolas 571
Pigott, F. W. 1137
Pike, C. T. 279
Pike, Diane K. 1072
Pike, James A. 1072
Pillai, K. C. 59
Pinachio, Bishop 131
Pinkerton, L. L. 621
Piper, Alta II p.61
Piper, August 174
Pitashriji 1356
Pitcairn, Theodore 928
Pius V, Pope 15
Pius XII, Pope 15, 49, 101
Piyananda, Pandita Mahathera
    Dickwela 1458
Plache, Richard 704
Plato 1103
Platon, Archbishop 125
Platon, Metropolitan I p.10; 80, 130
Plauen-Brankovic, M. H. Speierer-Ruess
    von 146
Pleasant, Leggie 253
Plockhoy, Cornelius Pieter I p.52,
    II p.41
Plummer, George Winslow 117, 1098
Plummer, Howard Z. 1286
Plummer, William H. 1286
Plunkett, Mary II p.51
Pobirokhin, Ilarion 563
Pojo III p.45
Poland, Jefferson 1240
Polikarp, Metropolitan 98
Poling, Charles S. 645
Poliwailehua, J. H. 1568
Polleme, Vernon 186
Poole, Elijah 1326
Poole, John 483
Popp, Nathaniel 128
Popplewell, Roger 587
Portal, Fernand 7
Porter, James L. 698
Poteat, Harrison W. 324
Potter, Charles Francis 760
Potter, Edwin 972
Powell, Adam Clayton II p.7
Powell, Ronald 1145
Powers, Marvin 305
Poyen, Charles II p.58, p.60
Prabhupada, A. C. Bhaktivedanta
    Swami 1358, 1378, 1379
Prajapita Brahma, Sri 1356

Prakashanand Saraswati, Swami H. D.
    1380
Prakashmani, Dadi 1356
Pramukh Swami, Shree 1435
Pratap, Vijayendra 1408
Pratt, Jesse 323
Prazsky, Andrew 94
Preiman, Bishop 97
Prem Ananda, Baba 1357
Prem Paramahansa Mahaprabho,
    Swami 1352
Premananda, Swami 1401, 1444, 1482
Presmont, John 864
Preus, J. A. O. 166
Price, Fred 457
Price, Frederick K. C. 379
Price, Iru 1510
Price, Richard 829
Pride, Hinton 75
Pridmore, James 723
Priebe, H. H. (Tissa) 1537
Priestley, Joseph II p.31
Prince, Charles H. I p.46
Prince, Derek 483, 753
Printz, Thomas 1154
Pritchard, Alfred 902
Pritts, Milton A. 87
Probert, Irene 992
Probert, Mark 992
Prochniewski, R. M. J. 43, 52
Prophet, Elizabeth Clare 1150, 1177
Prophet, Mark L. 1150
Propheta, Walter A. I p.11; 69, 86, 87,
    88, 90, 126, 133, 142, 145, 151
Provencher, Joseph Norbert Abbe p.lvii
Provoost, Samuel p.xxxii, I p.6; 71
Pruitt, Fred 256
Pruitt, Lawrence D. 256
Pruter, Karl I p.5; 12, 40, 75, 120, 146,
    1574
Pryse, James Morgan 1129
Puckett, John L. 620
Pugh, Liebie 1005, 1009
Puharich, Andrija II p.62
Purcell, Robert II p.62
Purdie, James Eustace 366
Purnananda Paramahansa, Guru 1344
Purnell, Benjamin 734, 735, 751
Purnell, Mary 735
Purser, James Rommie 738, 741
Purvis, Eldon 753
Pyman, Frederick Littler 19, 62
Pyorre, Juho I p.18
Pyrahmos 1175
Pythagoras 1103
Pythia II p.57
Quigley, Ithamar 363
Quimby, Phineas Parkhurst II p.47, p.48,
    p.49, p.50; 875, 876, 1082
Quinn, C. F. 92
Quinn, John R. 72
Quinn, John Raphael 1576
Quinn, Richard Earl 1012
Ra Un Nefer Amen 1091
Raamah, Ingra 912
Raatamaa, Juhani I p.18
Raattamaa, Juhani 156

Rabinowicz, Isaac Jacob 1278
Rabinowicz, Jacob Isaac 1278
Rabinowicz, Joshua Hershal 1278
Rabinowicz, Nathan David 1278
Rabinowicz, Yechiel Joshua 1278
Rachevsky, Zina 1527
Radar, Paul 653
Rader, Paul I p.45
Radha Appu 1536
Rado, Christoforus 106
Raffaele, Joseph J. 4
Rahman, Tasibur Uddein 1329
Rahmea 1175
Rahn, Claude J. 850
Rahula, Walpola 1458
Rai, Iqhaljeet 1448
Railton, George Scott 272
Rainier of Monaco, Prince 1398
Rajneesh, Bhagwan Shree 1440
Rakshasi 1103
Raleigh, Robert 39, 1126, 1128
Ram Dass, Baba 865, 1403
Ram, Rai Salig 1449
Rama, Master 1394
Rama, Swami 1370
Ramacharacka (Swami) III p.38
Ramaiah, S. A. A. 1377
Ramakrishna (Sri) III p.36, p.38
Ramakrishna, Sri 1416
Ramanuja III p.36
Ramanuja, Sri 1435
Ramm, Ronald R. 7
Ramseyer, J. E. 268
Ramseyer, J. A. 513
Rand, Howard B. 742
Randall, Benjamin 340
Randall, John Herman 760
Randolph, P. B. 1092
Randolph, Pascal Beverly III p.3, p.15
Rangel, Arturo 451
Rapp, George II p.43
Rasheed, Hakeem Abdul 890
Rasmussen, A. W. 458
Ratcleife, Agnes 1205
Rathbun, Beulah A. 1210
Rauf, Muhammad Abdul 1307
Rauschenbusch, August 583
Rauschenbush, Walter 565
Raven, F. E. 635, 636
Ravi Das, Guru 1449
Rawls, C. L. 411
Rawson, R. L. 876
Raymond, Ralph F. 987, 1009
Redpath, Alan 653
Reed, Daniel 1379
Reed, Elizabeth A. 1382
Reed, Violet B. 1164
Rees, Seth Cook 276
Reese, Curtis W. 760
Regardie, Israel 1181, 1184, 1256
Rehfeldt, Remiss 305
Reilly, Jr., Thomas 1029
Reimer, Klaas 508
Reinhardt, Prof. 1223
Reinkens, Joseph Hubert I p.3
Reiss, George 722
Remey, Charles Mason 1340, 1341, 1342

Vredenbregh, Joseph L. 1132
Vredenburgh, Joseph L. 1132
Vrionis, Pangratios 106
Vruyneel, Anthony 50
Wadia, B. P. 1116
Wadle, Lowell Paul 1126, 1128, 1139
Wagner, Belle M. 1103
Wagner, Henry 1103
Wai, Chuen 1501
Wains 1018
Waite, A. E. III p.12, p.15; 1103
Wakefield, H. C. 201
Wakefield, Wesley H. 250
Wakefield, William J. 250
Waldner, Michael 848
Waldo, Peter II p.24
Waldo, Samuel I p.17
Waldrop, Donald L. 1068
Walker, George 670
Walker, Helen V. 914
Walker, Kenneth 1210
Walker, Thane 1320
Walker, William J. 756
Wall, George Wendelin 209
Wallace, Austin D. 978
Wallace, Charlotte P. 1366
Wallis, Arthur 463
Walls, Aaron 507
Walsh, John T. 672
Walter, Darius 846
Walter, Elias 846
Walter, William W. II p.52
Walterhouse, John 548
Walters, J. Donald 1347
Walthall, Jethro I p.42
Walther, Carol Ferdinand Wilhelm I p.17; 171
Walton, Eugene O. 838
Wangchen, Kyungtrul Pema 1518
Wangchug, Trichen Ngawang Thoptok 1520
Wangpo, Jugme Losel 1523
Wangyal, Geshe 1525
Wannarat, Phra 1461
Ward, Anthony 49
Ward, Henry Dana II p.22
Ward, Robert 591
Wardall, Ray Marshall 1137, 1138
Warfield, Benjamin I p.25
Warkentin, Bernard I p.54
Warner, Daniel S. I p.37; 255, 256
Warner, James K. 754
Warnock, George 460
Warren, Fred Anthony 985
Warren, Judi D. 905
Warren, Sterling 1021
Warrington, A. P. 1115
Washington, George p.xxxi, II p.30; 1130
Washington, William 291
Wasson, David II p.32
Wasyly, Metropolitan 134
Watanabe, Ryugen 1482
Waterman, Robert D. 1082
Waters, Charles E. 440
Waters, Frank 1211
Waters, John R. 588, 590

Waterstraat, Wilhelm 19
Watkins, Joseph L. 666
Watkins, Ruth 245
Watson, John p.lxi
Watson, Wingfield 832, 833
Watters, Warren 1134
Watterson, Peter F. 60
Weaver, Clayton F. 522
Weaver, John A. 504
Webb, Muhammed Alexander Russell III p.30
Webber, David 661
Webster, B. H. 74
Wedgwood, James Ingall 1138
Weekly, H. F. 1449
Weeks, Eugene B. 922
Weiner, Bob 461
Weiner, Rose 461
Weir, Edmond 197
Weir, Irving 670
Weishaupt, Adam III p.2; 1180
Weiss, Jann 1080
Weiss, John II p.32
Welch, Charles II p.13, p.16; 659, 663, 666
Welch, Holmes 1479
Wells, Alice 1011
Wells, Erma 905
Wendell, Jonas II p.23
Wendland, John 15
Wenger, Joseph 499, 502
Weor, Samael Aun 1104
Weschcke, Carl 1179, 1202, 1224
Weschcke, Sandra 1224
Wesley, John p.xxix, p.xxx, I p.23, p.28, p.29, p.32, p.35, p.36, p.55, II p.58, p.59, p.60; 214, 226, 258, 317
West, Dan 521
West, John p.lviii
West, Wayne 1259
Westcott, Dr. Wynn 1099
Westcott, Wynn III p.14
Weyand, Christian 1086
Weymouth, George I p.1
Wharton, Edward 1236
Wheeler, Frederick 680
Wheeler, Kenneth 1001
Whipple, Jonathan 548
Whipple, Leander II p.51
Whipple, Samuel 548
Whitaker, Alexander p.xxvi, p. xxvii, I p.5, p.24
White, Alice 1170
White, Alma 288
White, Anne 1199
White, Arthur K. 288
White, Charles Edward I p.36
White, Ellen G. 676, 679, 680, 699, 736, 751
White, Garry A. 1057
White, George 1170
White, James 680, 734
White, Jr., L. J. 1558
White, Kathleen J. 775
White, L. S. II p.24
White, Ms. Anne 537
White, Nelson H. 1199

White, Ray B. 288
White, Ruth 1343
White Star, Jackie 1021
White, William p.xxxii, I p.6; 71
White, William C. 775
Whitefield, George p.xxix, II p.30; 195, 584
Whitehead, Armand C. 33, 56
Whiting, Chauncey 831
Whiting, Earl 831
Whiting, Erle 831
Whiting, Isaac 831
Whiting, Julian 831
Whitley, G. A. 293
Whitman, R. Manley 1405
Whitman, Rev. 674
Whitmer, David II p.36
Whitted, John B. II p.63
Whitten, Ivah Bergh 1161
Whitten, Lawrence A. 772
Whitty, Michael 1182
Whorf, Ray 1121
Widmann, Johannes 986
Widmar, Siegfried 806
Wiebe, Jacob 511
Wieck, John 681
Wiersbe, Warren 653
Wierwille, Donald E. 667
Wierwille, Victor Paul 667
Wigglesworth, Smith I p.45
Wilberg, Andrew 210
Wilbur, John 544
Wilcox, Hal 1023
Wilcoxen, Earl 231
Wiley, F. P. 258
Wiley III, George H. 407
Wiley, Lucille 407
Wilkerson, Clark 891, 1067
Wilkerson, David 1563
Wilkes, Henry p.liv
Wilkie, Herbert F. 2
Wilkins, Charles H. II p.38
Willard, Frances I p.37
William of Orange I p.23
Williamowicz, Peter M. 120
Williams, B. M. 5
Williams, Carl E. 426
Williams, Daniel Powell 344
Williams, Douglas 413
Williams, Frank W. 392, 394
Williams, George 796, 797
Williams, George M. 1470
Williams, Harold 298
Williams, J. M. 388
Williams, Jimmie Ray 445
Williams, L. W. 436
Williams, Leonard E. 712
Williams, McKinley 398
Williams, Richard I p.46
Williams, Robert L. 30, 1133
Williams, Roger p.xxviii, II p.3, p.7; 608, 610
Williams, Smallwood E. 398, 399, 401, 420
Williams, Thomas C. 415
Williams, Thomas W. 823
Williamson, A. E. 707

Williamson, Bernese 892
Williamson, George p.xxxi, II p.64
Williamson, George Hunt 147, 1013, 1014
Williamson, Richard 49
Willoughby, Frederick Samuel I p.4
Wilson, Rev. George 155
Wilson, John II p.25, p.26; 743
Wilson, Joseph 1238
Wilson, Louise B. 542
Wilson, Robert Anton 1180, 1221
Wimber, John 347
Wine, Sherwin T. 1302
Winebrenner, John 179, 673
Winegar, Jack 838
Winkler, E. Arthur 1049
Winrod, Gerald B. 449
Wipf, Jacob 847
Wise, Isaac 1268
Wise, John 1559
Wisler, Jacob 500
Witmer, Peter 492
Witowski, Stanislaus 1098
Wittek, Gabriele 1008
Wittgenstein, Ludwig III p.23
Wittich, Philip 336
Wojtyla, Cardinal 25
Wolcott, Louis Eugene 1333
Woldymyr I, Patriarch 88, 151
Wolfall I p.1
Wolff, Joseph II p.21
Wolfram, Donald J. 288
Wolsey, William F. 57
Wood, J. A. I p.37
Wood, M. D. 258
Woodford, A. F. A. III p.14
Woodmen, W. R. 1099
Woodruff, Wilford II p.38; 795
Woods, Richard III p.11
Woodward, Orlando J. 63, 75
Woodworth, W. N. 711
Woodworth-Etter, Mrs. M. B. 343
Woolley, John W. II p.38
Woolley, Legrand 813
Woolley, Lorin C. II p.38; 802, 811, 813
Woolman, John I p.55
Worcester, David E. 1004
Workman, Benjamin p.lvi
Workman, George p.lxi
Worre, Dennis 485
Wovoka p.xxxvii

Wren, William 131
Wright, Allen 837
Wright IV, Gridley Lorimer 872
Wright, J. D. 716
Wright, James 1398
Wright, Milton L. 240
Wright, Robert 462
Wright, Robert R. 463
Wroe, John 733, 734
Wuest, Edward 511
Wulf, Elizabeth Clare 1150
Wurmbrand, Richard 645
Wuytiers, Cornelius I p.3
Wyatt, Evelyn I p.46
Wycliff, John II p.24
Wylie, Ann 1115
Xavier, Francis III p.46
Yaganathan, Jnaniguru 1397
Yahiro, George 655
Yahweh ben Yahweh 1290
Yahya, Mirza 1338
Yamada Ko'un Roshi 1480
Yamamoto, Kodo 1474
Yamauchi, Seiji 1145
Yano, Hatsu 655
Yasodhara, Samma 1493
Yasutani, Hakuun 1478, 1480, 1488, 1491
Yeang, C. H. 1156
Yeats, Kent Michael 750
Yeats, William Butler II p.11
Yeshaq, Abuna 144
Yin, Tsu 1501
Ying, Leong Dick 1502
Ying, Mrs. James 1499
Yoakum, Finis E. 468
Yogananda, Paramahansa III p.39; 859,
    866, 904, 949, 997, 1002, 1347, 1361,
    1368, 1400, 1401, 1411, 1423
Yoganandaji Maharaj, Shri 1363
Yogashakti Sarawati, Ma 1386
Yogaswami, Siva 1397
Yogeswar Ji Maharaj, Sri 1374
Yogiji, Shri Singh Sahib Bhai Harbhajan
    Singh Khalsa III p.40
Yojan, Tsuruta 916
Yokhannan, Mar 95, 151
Yolanda 1018
Yonchev, Kyrill 97
Yoneyama, Hanako 655
York, Dick 1565

Yosif Emmanuel II Thomas, Maran Mar 7
Younan, Rafael 143
Young, Bicknell II p.52
Young, Brigham II p.37, p.38; 795, 798,
    802, 828, 830, 831, 833
Young, Donald 674
Young, Edward 993
Young, Elzie 412
Young, George Paxton p.lxi
Young, Sai 1378
Young, William Henry 773
Yu, Dora 669
Yujiri, Hogen 1474
Yukawe, Kazue 1473
Yukteswar, Sri 1400
Yun, Hsu 1497
Zaborowski, Robert R. J. M. 4, 25
Zaddik, Twersky III p.26
Zaffuto, Ferdinand 361
Zaharakis, Michael G. 1131, 1132
Zain, C. C. 1103
Zalman, Schneur 1277
Zamora, Adolfo 24
Zan-Thu 1018
Zarathustra III p.32
Zareh I 139
Zedikiah (King) II p.26
Zeiger, Robert S. 8, 92, 116
Zell, Morning Glory 1208
Zell, Tim III p.19; 1208
Zenor, Richard 929
Zevi, Shabbetai III p.26
Zielonka, Joseph 30, 45, 120
Zimmer, Hermann 1343
Zinzendorf p.xxix, I p.28
Zitko, Howard John 1083
Zitting, Charles 813
Znepolski, Joseph 96
Zollinger, Walter J. 1138
Zopa Rinpoche, Lama Thubten 1527
Zoroaster III p.32; 1339
Zotikos, Mar 1573
Zotique, Jonathan V. 1573
Zubkov, Alesha 563
Zuccarello, Anthony 1372
Zuk, Joseph 102, 135
Zurawetzky, Peter A., I p.11; 12, 23,
    90, 92, 113, 137
Zurndorfer, Frederich W. 787
Zwingli, Ulrich I p.21, p.22, p.50

Subject Index

Provides access to the material in the introductory essays, essay chapters, and directory sections through a selected list of subject terms. Because of the difference between the essays and directory sections, citations referring to pages in the introductory essays and essays chapters are designated with a volume number and "p." and are separated from the directory sections citations with a semicolon. Directory entries 1–563 will be found in Volume I; 564–1089 in Volume II; 1090–1588 in Volume III.

Abolitionism p.liii, II p.5, p.23; 209, 276, 548

Abortion 12, 20, 41, 53, 60, 95, 121, 191, 364, 457, 473, 620, 748, 1029, 1558

Acupuncture 1362, 1503

Agnosticism 770, 773

Ahimsa III p.36, p.40; 861, 872, 1346, 1404, 1438

Akashic records 988, 1016, 1169

Alchemy III p.12; 1100, 1108, 1182, 1185, 1189, 1192

Alcoholic beverages 188, 240, 263, 264, 265, 276, 277, 297, 392, 435, 473, 509, 530, 699, 723, 736, 738, 768, 851, 856, 859, 870, 873, 892, 926, 1097, 1098, 1372, 1442, 1552, 1553, 1584

Altar fellowship 166

American Indians 12, 74, 189, 811, 831, 1030, 1211

Americanism 44, 856

Americanization I p.2, p.10; 30, 120, 556

Ancestor worship 1472, 1477

Angels II p.64, III p.29, p.32; 375, 647, 797, 812, 833, 839, 946, 961, 984, 1007, 1009, 1013, 1015, 1152, 1155, 1162, 1165, 1187, 1287

Animal sacrifice 1181, 1205, 1243

Annihilationism II p.15, p.16; 617, 631, 663

Anti-Catholicism II p.22; 1, 472

Anti-cult movement 456, 795

Anti-Semitism II p.26; 642, 746, 749, 754, 757, 767, 1109, 1333

Anointing 494, 558, 614, 616

Apocalypticism II p.19; 1081, 1110

Apostasy I p.1; 24, 227, 803, 824

Apostolic succession 87, 564, 1128, 1139

Apparitions of the Virgin Mary I p.13; 10, 21, 41

Apparitions of the Virgin Mary—Fatima II p.64; 1, 13, 20, 981

Apparitions of the Virgin Mary—Guadalupe 1

Apparitions of the Virgin Mary—La Salett 10

Apparitions of the Virgin Mary—Lipa 20

Apparitions of the Virgin Mary—Lourdes 1

Apparitions of the Virgin Mary—Necedah 20

Aquarian age 931, 964, 987, 1018, 1035, 1082, 1083

Arianism 1

Armageddon 713, 734, 1571

Arminianism I p.23, p.30, II p.2, p.3, p.4, p.7; 189, 480, 571, 584, 585, 607, 608, 609, 610, 613, 614, 615, 639

Ascended masters III p.3, p.6, p.7; 931, 937, 1013, 1014, 1021, 1023, 1024, 1025, 1033, 1146, 1147, 1148, 1149, 1150, 1151, 1152, 1153, 1154, 1156, 1157, 1158, 1162, 1164, 1167, 1177

Ashrams III p.36

Ashtar command 1016, 1025

Assumption (of the Virgin Mary) 25, 33

Astral travel II p.57; 1044, 1192, 1443, 1444

Astrology I p.50, II p.47, p.57, III p.12, p.18; 863, 887, 1047, 1060, 1096, 1097, 1103, 1108, 1152, 1167, 1174, 1184, 1185, 1202, 1223, 1243, 1256, 1361, 1411, 1579

Atheism II p.32, III p.40; 757, 758, 762, 763, 767, 769, 770, 771, 773, 776, 1302

Atlantis III p.3, p.7, p.12; 942, 970, 980, 988, 1101

Atonement II p.24; 1022

Atonement—General 574

Aura 893, 969, 1041, 1082, 1169, 1447

Automatic writing 990, 1007, 1014, 1018

Avasthology 1167

Avatar III p.5, p.36

Ayurvedic medicine 1362

Ban I p.51, p.52, p.53; 53, 361, 463, 501, 512, 521

Baptism I p.15, III p.39; 1, 46, 185, 607, 608, 610, 631, 650, 655, 697, 751, 797, 883, 927, 982, 1108, 1150, 1258, 1442, 1564

Baptism—Alien 451, 564

Baptism—Backwards 511

Baptism—Believers I p.50, II p.8, p.9; 209, 493, 496, 551, 559, 597, 841, 848

Baptism—By immersion I p.45, II p.6, p.9, p.23, p.37; 229, 249, 255, 279, 319, 333, 338, 340, 342, 346, 353, 359, 363, 368, 391, 400, 406, 411, 424, 429, 449, 455, 466, 507, 511, 513, 567, 584, 587, 597, 619, 638, 641, 644, 649, 654, 678, 680, 682, 688, 719, 722, 723, 724, 736, 821, 828, 838, 852, 860, 862, 871, 1286

Baptism—By pouring I p.13, p.51; 524

Baptism—By sprinkling 214, 738

Baptism—Infant I p.27; 212, 213, 242, 548, 551

Baptism—In the name of Jesus only 240, 478, 487, 839, 841

Baptism—Of the dead 815, 818, 837

Baptism—Of the Holy Spirit p.xl, I p.41, p.43, p.44, p.46, p.56; 151, 254, 318, 319, 349, 351, 368, 397, 460, 473, 478, 485, 487, 502, 504, 667, 698, 719, 723, 724, 729, 736, 744, 852, 862, 867, 871, 1069, 1086

Baptism—Rebaptizing I p.50, p.52, p.54, II p.2, p.9; 317, 674, 796, 816, 838

Baptism—Three baptisms 155, 472

Baptism—Triune immersion I p.51, p.54; 492, 518, 521, 525, 616, 1553

Bible I p.15; 210, 349, 738

Bible—Infallibility of II p.15; 429, 475, 485, 567, 649, 746, 748, 862, 1072

Bible—Interpretation of 166, 1073, 1175

Bible—Literal interpretation p.xxxviii

Bible—Verbal inspiration II p.14, p.15; 166, 223, 568, 589, 664

Bible—Versions—American Revised 662

Bible—Versions—Concordant 662

Bible—Versions—Douay-Rheims 41

Bible—Versions—Inspired (Joseph Smith's) 820, 829, 838

Bible—Versions—King James Version (KJV) 62, 76, 201, 219, 321, 332, 364, 579, 662, 728, 1564

Bible—Versions—New World Translation 526, 713

Bible—Versions—Peshitta 146, 667, 908

Bible—Versions—Revised Standard Version (RSV) 87, 188, 201, 590, 662, 792

Bible—Versions—Rotherham 728

Bible—Versions—Sacred Name versions 728, 730

Bible—Versions—True Complete Bible 1086

1022, 1034, 1036, 1038, 1039, 1040, 1041, 1047, 1048, 1053, 1055, 1058, 1060, 1062, 1069, 1075, 1077, 1079, 1082, 1223, 1230, 1253, 1254, 1287, 1376, 1423, 1482, 1503, 1532, 1545, 1549, 1566, 1582
Healing—Divine I p.42; 218, 248, 250, 258, 267, 276, 278, 280, 288, 290, 319, 320, 326, 330, 332, 333, 336, 345, 346, 355, 365, 368, 374, 375, 376, 377, 378, 379, 380, 381, 382, 383, 384, 385, 391, 392, 393, 394, 395, 401, 404, 410, 418, 422, 424, 428, 437, 444, 450, 453, 455, 468, 470, 487, 649, 688, 722, 734, 871, 875, 1054, 1544, 1553, 1584
Healing—Magnetic II p.58
Healing—Mental II p.47, p.54; 875, 894, 921, 1303
Healing—Miracle 349
Healing—Sacramental 46
Healing—Spiritual II p.49, p.57; 117, 251, 255, 256, 713, 895, 923, 935, 939, 941, 942, 950, 952, 955, 959, 965, 967, 969, 972, 976, 979, 1046, 1074, 1133, 1146, 1169, 1170, 1177, 1319, 1323, 1522, 1538, 1548
Healing—Tibetan 1511
Hell, Doctrine of II p.23, p.29; 44, 332, 365, 411, 450, 475, 640, 649, 684, 797, 821, 1571
Henotheism 1072
Heresy I p.2, p.11; 46, 636, 638, 642, 1092
Heresy—Arianism 667
Heresy—Gnosticism 1, 558, 635
Heresy—Monophysism I p.12, p.13
Heresy—Monthanism II p.20; 1, 564
Heresy—Nestorianism I p.11
Heresy—Unitarianism 558, 673, 713, 1182
Hermetics 939, 1085, 1100, 1192
Hierarchy, spiritual 1092, 1097, 1100, 1101, 1103, 1108, 1110, 1112, 1118, 1120, 1121, 1122, 1124, 1143, 1146, 1149, 1151, 1154, 1156, 1157, 1158, 1160, 1161, 1164, 1166, 1169, 1176, 1177
Hoax III p.20; 20, 1019, 1572
Holiness 214, 215, 222, 230, 258, 265, 273, 274, 278, 281, 283, 296, 317, 424, 428, 442, 506, 534, 1563
Holistic health 1053, 1323, 1361, 1402, 1411, 1420, 1447, 1526
Holy water 1, 189
Homeopathic medicine 1362
Homosexuality I p.3; 14, 60, 71, 85, 87, 95, 114, 116, 123, 150, 364, 457, 750, 791, 1029, 1136, 1140, 1142, 1181, 1201, 1206, 1207, 1239, 1243, 1245, 1573, 1574, 1575, 1576, 1577, 1578, 1579
House churches 14
Humanism 760, 770
Huna 1040, 1064, 1067, 1559
Hypnotism II p.47; 1003, 1026, 1043, 1045, 1049, 1059, 1064, 1067, 1069, 1074, 1086, 1251, 1362

I Ching 1223, 1496
Immaculate Conception (of the Virgin Mary) 1, 25, 32, 33, 811
Immortality (of the soul) 486, 617, 672, 680, 703, 738, 951, 958, 983, 990, 1003, 1043, 1073, 1078, 1338, 1571
Immortality (of the body) 486, 733, 901, 922, 1102, 1584
Immortality, conditional 672
Indra's net 1477
Infallibility 1, 5, 30, 33, 40
Initiation III p.2, p.6, p.17
Intentional community 1110, 1112, 1114, 1149
Interdict 544
Intoxicants 20, 188, 277, 612, 680
'Jesus Only' (See also Non-Trinitarian theology) p.lxiii, I p.44, p.45
Jewish evangelism p.xxi, II p.21; 177, 267, 346, 364, 496, 725, 731
Jumping 557, 558
Kaballah (Qabala) III p.12, p.14, p.26; 812, 978, 1091, 1101, 1108, 1142, 1168, 1182, 1183, 1184, 1185, 1186, 1192, 1193, 1195, 1199, 1235, 1248, 1256, 1277, 1284, 1287, 1300, 1308
Kibbutz 727
Kirtans III p.37; 1354
Kiss of Peace 445, 516
Koan III p.46; 1480
Kriyas 1393
Kundalini III p.38; 1041, 1104, 1362, 1363, 1364, 1371, 1376, 1377, 1384, 1390, 1393, 1403, 1415, 1421, 1442, 1443, 1536
Latihan 1321
Latter Rain Revival p.lxiii, I p.46, p.47; 354, 355, 454, 458, 462, 463, 487
Laying-on-of-hands p.lxiii, II p.37; 6, 10, 155, 218, 359, 460, 484, 518, 551, 578, 610, 838, 883, 1046, 1321, 1564
Leipzig Interim of 1548 19
Lemuria III p.3; 866, 980, 1007, 1014, 1022, 1101, 1105
Levitation II p.61; 1394, 1422
Liberalism 228
Libertarianism 765, 766, 770, 775
Life insurance 156, 435, 511, 523, 529
Liturgical year 1, 212
Liturgy—Mar Addai and Mar Mari I p.11; 22, 44, 95
Liturgy—St. Basil 83, 100
Liturgy—St. Germain 89
Liturgy—St. John Chrysostom 100, 111, 117
Liturgy in English 32, 40
Love feast I p.28, p.30, p.54; 212, 238, 492, 520, 521, 841
Macrobiotics III p.11; 1498, 1500, 1503
Magic(k) p.xxiii, III p.47, p.51; 884, 978, 1064, 1179, 1180, 1181, 1182, 1183, 1184, 1186, 1187, 1188, 1189, 1190, 1191, 1192, 1193, 1194, 1195, 1196, 1197, 1198, 1199, 1202, 1207, 1209, 1222, 1223, 1224, 1226, 1229, 1230, 1233, 1241, 1248, 1256, 1258, 1259, 1284, 1513

Mail, ordination by 777, 778, 779, 780, 781, 782, 783, 784, 785, 786, 787, 788, 789, 790, 791, 792, 990, 1474
Manichaeism 1232
Manisis 1092
Mantras 992, 1023, 1036, 1062, 1150, 1322, 1323, 1345, 1356, 1368, 1371, 1378, 1382, 1393, 1415, 1422, 1423, 1426, 1474
Marriage 1, 46
Marriage—With nonmembers 252
Martial arts 1052, 1372, 1388, 1439, 1493, 1496, 1503
Massage 1362
Meditation II p.65, III p.2, p.6, p.36, p.37, p.40, p.43; 859, 865, 868, 883, 898, 903, 916, 919, 939, 981, 982, 983, 988, 992, 994, 997, 1008, 1018, 1041, 1045, 1050, 1055, 1059, 1061, 1062, 1065, 1068, 1074, 1083, 1089, 1098, 1108, 1121, 1122, 1125, 1148, 1163, 1165, 1167, 1170, 1174, 1177, 1184, 1185, 1209, 1299, 1300, 1308, 1323, 1339, 1345, 1347, 1349, 1352, 1354, 1355, 1356, 1360, 1361, 1362, 1363, 1364, 1369, 1370, 1372, 1385, 1388, 1390, 1393, 1403, 1405, 1406, 1407, 1410, 1411, 1413, 1414, 1415, 1419, 1422, 1424, 1426, 1439, 1440, 1444, 1453, 1454, 1455, 1459, 1460, 1461, 1463, 1465, 1474, 1479, 1480, 1481, 1482, 1483, 1484, 1485, 1489, 1490, 1491, 1496, 1497, 1503, 1504, 1507, 1508, 1510, 1512, 1513, 1514, 1516, 1519, 1520, 1522, 1523, 1526, 1529, 1533, 1534, 1536, 1587
Mediumship II p.57, p.60, p.61; 733, 931, 978, 1023, 1080, 1400
Mermaids 1208
Mentalvivology 884
Midwifery 861
Military chaplains 169
Millennium II p.21, p.24, p.41; 257, 294, 466, 507, 649, 680, 799, 986
Miracles 20, 41, 907, 974, 1396, 1582
Missions—Africa 162, 185, 219, 233, 242, 332, 343, 349, 352, 355, 378, 394, 401, 402, 476, 507, 525, 536, 603, 604, 623, 624, 637, 663, 685, 700, 723, 915, 1090, 1104, 1155, 1522
Missions—American Indian p.xxiii, p.xxv, I p.29, p.32; 176, 212, 219, 244, 259, 267, 346, 496, 510, 1553
Missions—Antigua 326, 401, 683
Missions—Arabia 185
Missions—Argentina 93, 177, 222, 361, 518, 525, 592, 594, 607, 1121, 1280, 1416
Missions—Australia 91, 96, 98, 101, 135, 171, 177, 182, 196, 241, 361, 375, 378, 473, 586, 594, 617, 623, 642, 681, 685, 690, 700, 705, 711, 716, 733, 756, 760, 767, 828, 851, 856, 868, 921, 926, 1044, 1064, 1104, 1114, 1128, 1148, 1150, 1155, 1162, 1173, 1310, 1315, 1345, 1358, 1367, 1368, 1375, 1389, 1399,

Religious Organizations and Institutions Index

An all-inclusive alphabetical listing of the religious organizations and groups discussed in the *Encyclopedia*. Index citations refer to the introductory essays, essay chapters, and directory sections. Because of the difference between the essays and directory sections, citations referring to pages in the introductory essays and essay chapters are designated with a volume number and ''p.'' and are separated from the directory sections citations with a semicolon. A boldface number indicates the organization's main entry in the directory sections. Directory entries 1–563 will be found in Volume I; 564–1089 in Volume II; 1090–1588 in Volume III.